Principles of Property Law

Principles of Property Law offers a critical and contextual analysis of fundamental property law concepts and principles, providing students with the necessary tools to enable them to make sense of English land law rules in the context of real world applications.

This new book adopts a contextual approach, placing the core elements of a qualifying law degree property and land law course in the context of general property principles and practices as they have developed in the UK and other jurisdictions in response to a changing societal relationship with a range of tangible and intangible things. Also drawing on concepts of property developed by political and legal theorists, economists and environmentalists, *Principles of Property Law* gives students a clear understanding of how property law works, why it matters and how the theory connects with the real world.

Suitable for undergraduate law students studying property and land law in England, Wales and Northern Ireland, as well as postgraduate students seeking an accessible analysis of property law as part of a course in law, land administration, environmental law or development studies.

Alison Clarke is a property lawyer who started out as a solicitor in private practice specialising in commercial land transactions, but has spent most of her career teaching property law principles, mainly at the Faculty of Law in the University of Southampton and at the Faculty of Laws at University College London, but also at law schools in Germany, France, China and Japan. She teaches and writes on property law from a comparative perspective, with special interests in communal, collective and co-operative resource use, plural property rights systems and indigenous land rights, and the role of property law in regulating our relationships with the natural and built environment. For many years, she has also co-edited one of the leading practitioner textbooks on land transactions in England and Wales. She is currently Emeritus Professor of Law in the School of Law at the University of Surrey.

The Law in Context Series

Editors: William Twining (University College London),
Maksymilian Del Mar (Queen Mary, University of London) and
Bronwen Morgan (University of New South Wales).

Since 1970 the Law in Context series has been at the forefront of the movement to broaden the study of law. It has been a vehicle for the publication of innovative scholarly books that treat law and legal phenomena critically in their social, political and economic contexts from a variety of perspectives. The series particularly aims to publish scholarly legal writing that brings fresh perspectives to bear on new and existing areas of law taught in universities. A contextual approach involves treating legal subjects broadly, using materials from other social sciences, and from any other discipline that helps to explain the operation in practice of the subject under discussion. It is hoped that this orientation is at once more stimulating and more realistic than the bare exposition of legal rules. The series includes original books that have a different emphasis from traditional legal textbooks, while maintaining the same high standards of scholarship. They are written primarily for undergraduate and graduate students of law and of other disciplines, but will also appeal to a wider readership. In the past, most books in the series have focused on English law, but recent publications include books on European law, globalisation, transnational legal processes, and comparative law.

Books in the Series
Acosta: *The National versus the Foreigner in South America*
Ali: *Modern Challenges to Islamic Law*
Alyagon Darr: *Plausible Crime Stories: The Legal History of Sexual Offences in Mandate Palestine*
Anderson, Schum & Twining: *Analysis of Evidence*
Ashworth: *Sentencing and Criminal Justice*
Barton & Douglas: *Law and Parenthood*
Beecher-Monas: *Evaluating Scientific Evidence: An Interdisciplinary Framework for Intellectual Due Process*
Bell: *French Legal Cultures*
Bercusson: *European Labour Law*
Birkinshaw: *European Public Law*
Birkinshaw: *Freedom of Information: The Law, the Practice and the Ideal*
Broderick & Ferri: *International and European Disability Law and Policy: Text, Cases and Materials*
Brownsword & Goodwin: *Law and the Technologies of the Twenty-First Century: Text and Materials*
Cane & Goudkamp: *Atiyah's Accidents, Compensation and the Law*
Clarke: *Principles of Property Law*
Clarke & Kohler: *Property Law: Commentary and Materials*
Collins: *The Law of Contract*
Collins, Ewing & McColgan: *Labour Law*
Cowan: *Housing Law and Policy*

International Journal of Law in Context: A Global Forum for Interdisciplinary Legal Studies

The *International Journal of Law in Context* is the companion journal to the Law in Context book series and provides a forum for interdisciplinary legal studies and offers intellectual space for ground-breaking critical research. It publishes contextual work about law and its relationship with other disciplines including but not limited to science, literature, humanities, philosophy, sociology, psychology, ethics, history and geography. More information about the journal and how to submit an article can be found at http://journals.cambridge.org/ijc

Principles of Property Law

ALISON CLARKE

University of Surrey

CAMBRIDGE
UNIVERSITY PRESS

University Printing House, Cambridge CB2 8BS, United Kingdom

One Liberty Plaza, 20th Floor, New York, NY 10006, USA

477 Williamstown Road, Port Melbourne, VIC 3207, Australia

314–321, 3rd Floor, Plot 3, Splendor Forum, Jasola District Centre, New Delhi – 110025, India

79 Anson Road, #06–04/06, Singapore 079906

Cambridge University Press is part of the University of Cambridge.

It furthers the University's mission by disseminating knowledge in the pursuit of
education, learning, and research at the highest international levels of excellence.

www.cambridge.org
Information on this title: www.cambridge.org/9781107090538
DOI: 10.1017/9781316106891

First published 2020

Printed in the United Kingdom by TJ International Ltd, Padstow Cornwall 2020

A catalogue record for this publication is available from the British Library.

Library of Congress Cataloging-in-Publication Data
Names: Clarke, Alison Clarissa, 1950– author.
Title: Principles of property law / Alison Clarke, University of Surrey.
Description: Cambridge, United Kingdom ; New York, NY, USA : Cambridge University Press, 2020. |
Series: Law in context | Includes bibliographical references and index.
Identifiers: LCCN 2019051268 (print) | LCCN 2019051269 (ebook) | ISBN 9781107090538 (hardback) |
    ISBN 9781107462564 (paperback) | ISBN 9781316106891 (epub)
Subjects: LCSH: Property–England. | Property–Philosophy.
Classification: LCC KD810 .C53 2020 (print) | LCC KD810 (ebook) | DDC 346.4204–dc23
LC record available at https://lccn.loc.gov/2019051268
LC ebook record available at https://lccn.loc.gov/2019051269

ISBN 978-1-107-09053-8 Hardback
ISBN 978-1-107-46256-4 Paperback

Additional resources for this publication at www.cambridge.org/clarkeproplaw.

Contents

Preface

This book is about the legal relationships we – as individuals, as groups and as communities – have with the land we inhabit and with some of the other resources we utilise (or perhaps value for something other than their utility). Property law emerges, in characteristic ways, in all societies to regulate these relationships. The underlying objectives of this book are to explore why it does so, and how the nature and content of the law are shaped by the social, economic and political conditions out of which the law emerges, and in which it develops. The idea is to bring readers to the point where they can (and feel inclined to) question assumptions and arguments about what the institution of property is, what it is for, what it can achieve and whether it does in practice achieve what we want it to achieve. In particular, the book invites readers to take a critical view of the property rights system as it operates in England and Wales today, focussing on the way it operates in relation to land, taking 'land' in its broadest sense, encompassing not only the surface of the earth and things growing in or built on it or lying beneath it, but also the physical spaces we live, work and socialise in and move through, the ecosystems we depend on and the landscapes we value.

Current orthodoxy is that, if we want to understand what property law is, we have to let go of this idea that property is about a lineal relationship we have with a thing. On this orthodox view, what it is 'really' about is the relationships that individuals (human and corporate) *have with each other* in respect of things, and the core relationships are relationships of exclusion and power: property is about one person's right to exclude others from a tangible or intangible thing and consequently to dictate the terms on which others may use it. This book challenges the orthodox view by bringing in three crucial elements of property law which the orthodox view tends to miss or obscure, and which are particularly relevant to property interests in land.

The first crucial element is that, to the extent that property is indeed about social relationships between people, it is also about relationships of inclusion and co-operation, as well as relationships of exclusion and power. If we really want to know how property works, we need also to take into account the ways in which people share resources (as families, communities, neighbours, or common interest groups where each member's use of the resource affects the ways in which it can be used by the others), and we need to look at the legal rules we have developed to regulate these kinds of shared resource use.

The second, and related, element is that the orthodox property analysis under-states the rich variety of property interests and property interest-holdings that the law has developed, particularly in relation to land. On the orthodox view, the single private owner is the paradigm holder of property interests. The focus is on the single human being who has a monopoly of the legal rights and powers over his bicycle, or his piece of land or whatever else he owns. However, whilst some resources are indeed wholly owned by a single private human individual, this is more likely to be true of bicycles than it is of land. The reality is that this kind of absolute ownership is just one of many different kinds of property interest that property law recognises in things, and that all of these different kinds of property interest (including absolute ownership) can be held not just by a private human individual but also by a wide range of other entities (co-owners, trustees, commercial corporations, public and private organisations carrying out public or charitable functions, and unincorporated groups and communities of all kinds). If we assume that property law revolves around the paradigm of the single human absolute owner, we misunderstand how it operates in the real world. So, this book aims to map out the range of property interests recognised in our property rights system, and the kinds of entity that can hold them, contrasting them with the range recognised in other jurisdictions, and seeing how they differ depending on whether we are talking about property interests in land as opposed to, say, in broadcast frequencies or human bodies and human bodily products.

The third correction to the orthodox view of property law is to question the assumption that property law is *only* about the relationships people have between themselves in respect of things. It is also, to an important extent, about the direct relationship humans and human enterprises have with our natural environment, and again this is most obviously true when we look at property interests in land. Scientific advances have enabled us to understand the direct impact that our actions have on our environment, and to appreciate that we have responsibilities towards the resources we control, utilise or inadvertently affect. The idea that property law might have a role in enforcing those responsibilities is beginning to be accepted in our legal culture and in property rights systems similar to ours, and, as we aim to show, it has always been central to property rights systems in other cultures. So, whilst we certainly do not claim to cover even the most basic principles of environmental law, we do aim to open up the question of the proper role of property law in regulating our relationship with our physical environment.

So, although the book focusses on land law in England and Wales, it takes a broader view than other texts. It looks at our system by reference to underlying common law property principles, and also invites readers to look beyond our own jurisdiction to explore how things are done in other kinds of legal system. It makes no claims to provide any kind of systematic comparative study: the idea is to alert readers to interesting comparisons and contrasts they may want to pursue for themselves. The book also introduces and utilises concepts of property developed by economists, philosophers and legal theorists, and by scholars from other disciplines. The aim is to provide undergraduate property law students – the primary audience for the book – and scholars from other jurisdictions and other disciplines, with the tools that will enable them to make sense of what are often thought of as boring and mystifying English land law rules, and to see how they fit into the bigger picture.

In building up this more wide-ranging picture of property, the book aims to cover all the topics generally taught in a Qualifying Law Degree property law course in England and Wales, although – inevitably – not always at the length or in the detail that some will want. As a teaching book, it is aimed at teachers (and students) who choose to cover a few topics in depth in the limited time allowed in the curriculum for property, rather than take a quick gallop through everything.

With that in mind, each chapter is, as far as possible, self-standing, and starts with an introduction designed to give an overview of the chapter and explain how it connects with the others. Each chapter then ends with some general questions and lists of recommended materials to read. Most of this recommended reading consists of extracts from cases and other materials, and some of these extracts can be found on the book's website, www.cambridge.org/clarkeproplaw, alongside suggested topics for further research. The reading is listed roughly in the order it appears in the text. Generally, the law is up-to-date to May 2019, although it has been possible to include some later material.

The book would not have been possible without the generous help and encouragement of colleagues, family and friends, and the intellectual stimulation provided by them and by generations of students. Out of the many colleagues whose ideas about property and property law have helped to shape mine, I must record specific thanks to three great friends and collaborators: Christine Godt, who first introduced me to the glories of comparative property law in general and German property law in particular, and whose friendship, company and hospitality I have enjoyed ever since; Julian Farrand, who knows more about property law than I shall ever know, and whose knowledge and understanding have informed and entertained me over the many happy years we have spent as friends and co-writers; and Rosalind Malcolm, my great ally and friend at the University of Surrey, for stimulating my interests in the political dimensions of property, and for introducing me to the world of environmental law and encouraging me to explore where and how property law fits in. The other colleague and friend whose help I must acknowledge is William Twining, a colleague at University College London for many years, whose help and encouragement in embarking on the book – and, even more, in finishing it – have been invaluable: the book would not have been written without him. I also want to record my thanks to the people at Cambridge University Press who have continued to provide outstandingly patient and persistent support and encouragement throughout the over-long period it has taken me to produce the manuscript. Finally, I have to thank Leo, to whom the book is dedicated, whose patience in waiting for me to finish the book proved to be inexhaustible – but only just.

Acknowledgements

Public sector information quoted here is reproduced under Open Government Licence v3.0 www.nationalarchives.gov.uk/doc/open-government-licence/version/3/.

Extracts from Helena R. Howe, 'Making Wild Law Work – The Role of 'Connection with Nature' and Education in Developing an Ecocentric Property Law' (2017) 29 *Journal of Environmental Law* 1, 19–45 are reproduced with the kind permission of the author and of Oxford University Press.

Table of Cases

The references in the Table of Cases are to the numbered paragraphs in which the case is cited in the book, not to page numbers.

Great Britain

European Court of Human Rights

Australia

Canada

United States of America

Germany

South Africa

1

What Property Is and Why It Matters

PART I INTRODUCTION

1.1 What Property Is

Property is about the rights we have in things – all kinds of tangible and intangible things, from land and cars to poems and broadcast frequencies. More specifically, property is about the rights we have in things which we can enforce against other people and against the state.

There is, of course, much more to be said about it than that. What do we mean by 'rights' in this context? Who has them in which things and how do they get them? And why would a society adopt a system which gives people enforceable rights in things anyway – what is the point of property? Even if we as a society decide we do want a system of property rights, on what basis do we decide who is to have those rights, and what are the implications of giving rights in some things to some people and not to others?

We explore these questions in this chapter and the following chapters. In this chapter we make a start in Part II *The Classic Analysis of Property* by looking at the traditional common law analysis of what property is and why it matters. This classic analysis takes property to mean private ownership held by autonomous individuals (which matches what many non-lawyers take it to mean) and it focusses on the benefits that this kind of property provides for the private individual. We outline these benefits at the end of Part II.

However, as we argue in Part III *Broadening the Analysis*, the property world presented by this classic analysis forms only part of a broader property picture. It is certainly true that our legal system does recognise simple private ownership of the kind assumed in the classic analysis, and that most of us do indeed have this kind of ownership of some things. However, our legal system, like most others, also recognises and enforces other types of property interest as well. These arise out of a broad range of other more complex relationships that people have amongst themselves with respect to things, not only in their capacities as individuals, but also as families, communities and members of the public. If we look more closely at these complex relationships that we and others have, and at the wide diversity of tangible and intangible things to which they relate, we see that property law covers a much broader field than that suggested by the traditional classic analysis. In the real world, simple private ownership lies along a spectrum of different kinds of property interest which the law recognises, each of which comprises a different set of reciprocal rights, freedoms, powers, duties and liabilities relating to the thing in question. Also, unsurprisingly given the many different forms that 'things' take, the kinds of property interest that may be appropriate for one kind of thing (houses, perhaps) may not be appropriate for another (perhaps human body parts or databases). In particular, some kinds of thing (land is the best example) are capable of being used by different people at the same time in different ways, and it is commonplace to have multiple property interest holders, each holding different property interests in such a thing at the same time. And, as we see below, it would be a mistake to assume that property is just about autonomous individuals and their private resources. It is also about the rights and interests that people have in what they think of as family or group resources, and rights and interests held by communities and the public, and also rights and interests held by commercial non-human legal entities such as companies. We need to take this wider range of stakeholders into account when we consider what property is, why we need it and the benefits that property can bring.

Our objective in Part III of this chapter is to map out this broader picture, laying the framework for the following chapters where we look at all these questions in detail. To help make sense of what follows in the rest of the book, we end this chapter with Part IV *Distinctions, Relationships and Definitions* which aims to clarify some of the ideas and the terminology we come across in later chapters. In Part IV we look at the different ways in which the term 'property' is used,[1] and we introduce the distinctions W. N. Hohfeld draws between different kinds of entitlements and obligations and their opposites and correlatives.[2] These distinctions help to clarify the distinctions we make in this and later chapters between different kinds of property interest. We also consider the different ways in which property can be said to involve relationships between people in respect of things,[3] and consider what distinguishes a property right or interest in a thing from other rights and interests in things.[4] Our last terminological clarification is to point out that whereas some property commentators argue or assume that 'property' exists independently of 'property law', others take property to have no independent existence but to be simply the product of law. We consider this distinction and the implications of it in para. 1.27, and then in para. 1.28 we end this chapter with a working definition of property to take us through the rest of the book.

PART II THE CLASSIC ANALYSIS OF PROPERTY

1.2 Property and Exclusion

The classic view of property is that it is all about rights to exclude others. If a house is my property, neither you nor anyone else can prevent me using it, or put obstacles in

---

[1] Paras. 1.19–1.22.   [2] Para. 1.23.   [3] Para. 1.25.   [4] Para. 1.26.

the way of me using it, or enter it or damage it without my permission. 'Anyone else' here includes not just other private individuals but also the state. If the house is my property, even the state cannot invade or interfere with it or with my use of it unless the law permits it to do so in the specific circumstances.

Of course, if the house next door to my house is your house, our positions are reversed in relation to your house. You will be the person who has the right to exclude me and everyone else from your house, and I will be one of the people who is forbidden from entering it or interfering with it or with your use of it. In other words, property creates reciprocal relationships between people in respect of things. The protection that property confers on the property holder necessarily involves restricting the rights of everyone else.

If, as this classic account has it, this is what property is, why do we need it? What are the benefits of this kind of exclusionary property?

1.3 Why We Need Property

Assume we live in a society like ours, where individuals live in houses with their families. Assume also that we have a legal system which is very like the one we actually have in this country now, except that we have a rule that no-one can have property rights in houses (or in anything else). In other words, in this system, no-one has rights in houses which are enforceable against other people. If no-one has any rights enforceable against anyone else in respect of any house, it follows that I am free to live in any house I want: if neither you nor anyone else has a right to stop me or to object to me living in the house I select, it must be the case that I can live there or not as I choose. The snag is that whilst I am free to live in that house, so too are you, and so too is everyone else. And because I have no *right* in respect of that house I cannot object if, after I move into the house, you then decide you want to live there and throw me out (assuming you can do that without infringing any of the non-property rights I *do* have – for example, my right not to be physically assaulted). Similarly, since I have no rights in any house, I am not entitled to stop you wantonly destroying all the houses, leaving me and everyone else homeless. My freedom consists only in being free from any legal constraints which might prevent me from living in any house that happens to be there and that I happen to choose.

The inconveniences of this non-property arrangement are obvious. If there are more than enough houses to go round and we are peaceable co-operative people who know our neighbours, we might sort out between ourselves who lives in which house without coming to blows about it. We could agree between ourselves who should be allocated which house, and also agree that none of us will interfere with anyone else's occupation of their allocated house. However, various factors might make it difficult to maintain the consensus. Outsiders may come in who do not know or care about our arrangement, and they may ignore it, taking over whichever house they want. Even if there is no attack or disruption from outsiders, circumstances may change so that the present allocation of houses is not so convenient for some of us, forcing us to renegotiate the deal or face the breakdown of our co-operative arrangement. Meanwhile, since none of us individually has secure rights in any one house, but we all have a collective self-interest in ensuring that the houses are properly maintained and repaired, we will have to come to some agreement about how these matters are to be arranged, and at whose cost.

All this so far assumes no scarcity. If, however, there is a shortage of houses – fewer houses than people who want to live in them – these problems will become more acute. It will be more difficult for us to arrange between ourselves how to share the houses out. Any arrangement will either leave some of us worse off than others (some of us may end up with no house) or result in equal misery for all (perhaps we could ration the time anyone is allowed to live in a house, so that we each have to accept homelessness for three months a year). Faced with these alternatives, and given the inherent difficulties in getting everyone to agree to anything anyway, it seems more likely that we will fail to reach agreement, and perhaps not even try. The strongest will take what they want and can defend, leaving the weakest with nowhere to live. Those in houses will be obliged to spend time, money and effort defending them, and their lives will be disrupted whenever someone else attempts to evict them. They will also find it difficult to sell their houses, because they have nothing of value that they can give to a buyer: even after the buyer has paid over the money, anyone – even the seller – is free to evict the buyer at any time and take the house for herself. And, of course, it is very doubtful that houses would exist at all in any significant numbers if we did not recognise property in houses. Why would you want to build a house in the first place if it could be snatched away from you at any time?

1.4 The Benefits Property Brings

Many property theorists would accept this narrative, and would argue that, if we want a peaceful, just and prosperous society which respects the freedom and dignity of all individuals, we must be able to call on the legal system to defend things like the houses we live in against arbitrary state interference and against interference from other citizens. In other words, we must have a property law system. The security that this will provide, so the classic argument goes, will provide us with many benefits. It will encourage us to spend time and ingenuity in improving our things and making them more productive, and in inventing or creating new things. Once the state guarantees protection of all rights in things, whoever holds them, the rights themselves will acquire an independent value. We will be able to find people prepared to buy our rights and we will feel sufficiently confident to buy other people's rights for ourselves. This enables us to develop a market economy which generates capital, and also steers the rights into the hands of those best able to exploit them, so ensuring that things are put to their most efficient use.

This immediate prosperity and efficiency is not the only benefit we will gain from a property law system, so this argument goes. If we recognise property rights in things it will provide us with even more significant benefits on a human level. It will guarantee us a secure private sphere in which we can flourish, safe from interference by the government and by outsiders. This guarantees our freedom and independence as autonomous individuals. It will also ensure respect and protection for the way in which our lives become bound up with the things we use and value. And it will enable us to secure the prosperity of our family because it gives us rights in things which we can pass on to future generations, and this in turn will encourage us to take a long-term view of the value of things, and will strengthen family ties.

PART III BROADENING THE ANALYSIS

1.5 Questioning the Classic Analysis

However, this classic analysis of what property is, why we need it and how it benefits us, requires closer scrutiny. It assumes that property means absolute private owner-ship held by a single private autonomous individual for her own benefit, whereas in most legal systems, as we see in para. 1.10, there are many different kinds of property interest, and they may be held not only by private individuals (human and corpor-ate) but also by groups of individuals, by communities, by the public and by the state. What is more, each of these groups may hold their property interests in a variety of different capacities. In addition, the classic analysis assumes a very particular kind of thing – a house. Are the effects of property, and the benefits it brings, the same for all kinds of property interest, and whatever the nature of the thing, or is property (in whatever form) suitable only for some kinds of thing? We look more closely at these and other questions in the rest of this part of the chapter.

1.6 What Kind of Things?

We have already noted that every legal system recognises property rights in some things but not in others, and in Chapter 6 *New Property Interests and the Numerus Clausus* and Chapter 7 *Objects of Property Interests* we see how this works out in our jurisdiction. At this stage, however, it is worth taking a preliminary look at the factors which influence decisions about whether or not to make a particular thing the subject of property rights, and thinking about how far this matches up with the classic analysis of why we need property.

(a) Natural Things and Products of Human Endeavour

Houses are products of human endeavour, and there are obvious arguments for saying that we need to have exclusionary private property rights in them, on the lines suggested in the classic analysis. There is the practical argument that this kind of property provides an incentive for people to build houses, and also the moral argument that those who have invested their labour in creating something ought to acquire rights in it. However, it is not so obvious that the incentive or reward should take the form of outright private ownership, as opposed to more limited property interests, nor is it obvious that the property interest should always go to an individual. If, for example, the thing in question was the product of communal endeavour (perhaps a house built by all the adult members of a family, or a local meeting house built by members of the community) the relevant group or community would seem to have a stronger practical and moral claim than any one of its individual members.

Similar considerations arise if the individual human endeavour involves improving natural things or utilising materials, expertise or experience of others. Again, there may be a case for giving the individual *some* property interest in the end product, but perpetual absolute ownership seems too much if all we are aiming to do is incentivise her and give her a just return for her endeavours. We look at all of this in more detail in Chapter 2 *Conceptions and Justifications*.

In any event, none of these arguments are of much relevance when we think about propertising wholly natural things, for example oceans, wild animals, oil and other mineral resources whilst still underground, undeveloped land, or human bodies. As we see in Chapter 7 *Objects of Property Interests*, some of these can be privately owned in some legal systems, some are state owned in some legal systems, and some are regarded as incapable of being owned. Also, many legal systems recognise property interests short of ownership in some of these things. In particular, they might recognise private, communal or public property rights to exploit (as opposed to own) natural resources, for example rights to hunt wild animals or catch fish, or abstract oil or water from natural sources. The reasons why a legal system might choose one of these options rather than another are going to differ depending on the nature of the natural thing (consider the differences between owning an ocean or exploiting oil, for example, and owning or exploiting a human body or a human body part). Choices will also be influenced by local cultural, political and economic considerations, and these may change over time. Some cultures have moral or religious objections to ownership of things like human bodies or land. Some states regard natural resources as part of their national heritage, to be kept under the control of the state so that they can be preserved for the nation and for future generations. Others see them as resources in which the public or local communities have inalienable rights. Yet others regard them as valuable assets which ought to be commercially exploited so as to increase the overall wealth of the nation.

(b) Intangible Things

Houses are tangible things, and the idea of exclusionary ownership makes some sense when applied to bounded tangible things. But what about intangible things? Some intangible things, like songs or internet domain names or credit balances in bank accounts or rights to catch a quota of cod in the North Sea, are created by humans; others, for example broadcasting frequencies or the flow of water in a river, arise naturally but can be utilised by humans. Do we need property for all these things as well, and if so is it the same kind of property as the kind of property the classic account advocates for houses, and is it necessary or desirable for the same kinds of reasons? Again, it is instructive that different legal systems come to different conclusions about this. So, for example, common law property systems like ours generally have no difficulty in recognising rights in intangible things, and categorising some of these rights as property rights, although they will not necessarily all choose to propertise the same intangible things. However, the position is different in some civil law systems. Their systems might recognise very similar legally enforce-able rights in some intangible things (most systems now, for example, recognise legally enforceable rights in broadcast frequencies), but they would categorise them as personal rights only. In these systems, rights in intangible things cannot be property rights.

(c) Scarcity, Rivalrousness and Excludability

In addition to the distinctions between natural things and products of human endeavour, and between tangible and intangible things, there are other distinctions between things that make a difference. We have already noted the question of scarcity: is it true that the need for property arises if and only if a thing is scarce? Most people would now accept that the reality is more complex. Even if houses are plentiful, I might still want the law to give me secure rights in the particular house I have chosen – perhaps I have spent time and money improving it, or I particularly like the view, or I have become emotionally attached to it, or I want to avoid the disruption of being evicted from this house and having to move into another house. So, a case can be made for property in non-scarce things as well as scarce things, although as we noted in para. 1.3 additional reasons come into play when the things becomes scarce.

In addition, we probably need to take into account *rivalrousness* and *excludability* as well as scarcity. Houses are both rivalrous and excludable. Things are rivalrous if use by one person diminishes the total supply of such things available for others. Houses are rivalrous in that if I have the exclusive right to live in a particular house, and the supply of houses is finite, that is one less house available for you to live in. Songs, on the other hand, and television reception and the internet, are non-rivalrous: your freedom and opportunity to sing a particular song or pick up a television signal, or look something up on the internet are in no way diminished or affected by the fact that someone next door did the same thing yesterday, or is doing the same thing at the same time as you. On the classic analysis property is necessary for rivalrous things, because use of rivalrous things is competitive. However, the same does not apply to non-rivalrous things: they are inexhaustible. So, if we are to propertise them (and as we see later, we often do), we will need some other kind of justification. We come back to this point in Chapter 2 *Conceptions and Justifications*.

Excludability is more straightforward. Houses are excludable things in that it is relatively easy to exclude outsiders from them. We describe a thing as non-excludable if it is impossible, or disproportionately difficult or expensive, to exclude outsiders. Light from lighthouses (when lighthouses were used in order to provide such a thing) and national security provided by national armed forces are non-excludable: if you provide them at all, it is difficult to see how you can do so without making the same benefit available to everyone who happens to be within reach of them. Because of this, private ownership is not appropriate for non-excludable things according to the classic analysis. The argument is that it is not in the rational self-interest of anyone to own a thing from which others can take a benefit without having to pay for it. But again, this may be simplistic. Not all private owners are self-interested individuals who act only for their own personal benefit. In the real world, some private owners are philanthropic, either because they want to be or because they are required to be. So, for example, it would be entirely appropriate for a private institution to own its own lighthouses if it was a charitable institution whose purpose was to provide lighthouses in the public interest. Similarly, it may be in the collective interests of a group of self-interested individuals that they should own a non-excludable thing: to take the lighthouse example again, a group of ship owners might want to club together to build and run lighthouses for their own benefit, and may not mind too much that others will also incidentally take advantage of the light. And we know that whilst some commercial providers of internet resources choose to use pay-walls in order to make their resources excludable, others find it commercially viable to sacrifice excludability and provide their resources free to the user.

We look at all these questions in more detail in Chapter 2 *Conceptions and Justifications* (where we come back to the lighthouse and internet examples) and in Chapter 7 *Objects of Property Interests* where we look more closely at the things we do propertise in this jurisdiction and at our categorisations of propertised things.

1.7 Bundling Things

There is another complicating factor to take into account when we are considering which things are propertised and why. This is that different property law systems 'bundle' things in different ways. Again, land provides the best example. In most western legal systems, including ours, ownership of 'land' means ownership of the surface of the land and the three dimensional space above and below the surface, and of everything directly and indirectly attached to the ground (including buildings, trees, growing crops and some sub-surface minerals).[5] Other legal systems disaggregate what we think of as 'land' and recognise separate ownership of different elements of it.

(a) Land and Buildings

The most significant difference between legal systems in this respect is that some recognise separate ownership of buildings whereas others (including ours) do not. In our system, if you own land then you are taken to own the structures built on it as well. It is technically possible to separate the ownership of land from the ownership of the structures attached to the land but there are formidable legal obstacles and in practice it is rarely done. This means that when we talk about owning a house, what we really mean is ownership of the land on which the house is built. In other words, in our system a house is never a 'thing' which is capable of ownership in its own

---

[5] This is subject to some qualifications in most systems. In ours, as we see in Chapter 7 *Objects of Property Interests*, the position is a bit more complicated in two respects. The first is that technological changes have forced us to re-think how far up into the sky and down into the earth property interests can realistically go. The second is that some things on or under the surface of the land, such as water, are unowned in most circumstances, and others, such as oil, gas and minerals, may be separately owned.

right (or at least not whilst it is attached to the land), and the 'thing' that is land necessarily includes any house built on it, as long as it remains attached to the land.

(b) Dividing up the Three Dimensional Space

However, we can and do split up ownership of the three dimensional space which constitutes land in our system, making each spatial section into a separate 'thing' for property purposes. We have separate ownership of horizontal slices of sub-surface land quite often, for example when the land is a highway. We can do the same with horizontal slices of the airspace above the surface of land, although in practice (for reasons we consider in Chapter 13 *Non-Possessory Land Use Rights*) we are more likely to keep the whole of the surface and air space in the ownership of a single owner, who then grants long leases of the horizontal spatial sections to separate lessees. This sounds more mysterious than it is. This is the property interests structure we use routinely for blocks of flats, or commercial buildings split up into units for separate occupation as offices or shops. There will be a single owner of the land on which the building is built, who (for the reasons already explained) will also own the building itself. That single owner will then grant a lease of each flat or commercial unit to a separate person. As we see in Chapter 17 *Leases*, the leases will be very long in the case of residential flats (99 and 999 year leases are common), but usually much shorter for commercial units (anything between two and 25 years is quite common). What each lessee actually gets is a lease of the airspace occupied by her unit and of the physical structure of the unit, with ancillary rights over the rest of the building. This means that if the building collapses before the end of the lease, each lessee still has her lease of what is now an empty slice of airspace (worth having, if the owner now wants to build into that space).

We look at all this in detail in Chapter 7 *Objects of Property Interests*, but for present purposes the point is that, when we talk about property, we need to be careful that we identify correctly the 'thing' in which we can and do have property rights.

1.8 What Kind of Benefits Can We Expect from Property?

When we outlined in para. 1.4 the beneficial effects of a property law system, our focus was on benefits to individual humans. Do we need to look more broadly than that?

(a) Environmental Benefits

It should be obvious that if we propertise things, we generally give the holders of property interests in them rights, freedoms and powers to use them in ways which can have an effect on our physical environment. It makes sense, then, to take these potential environmental effects into account when we decide whether and how to propertise anything. We said in para. 1.4 that property – there meaning private ownership – provides us with incentives to improve things and make them more productive: what about when we want to conserve them, or to regulate their use so as to reverse climate change or reduce carbon emissions, for example? This question comes up again at various points in later chapters, particularly in Chapter 9 *Multiple Property Rights Systems*, where we look at the property rights systems evolved by indigenous peoples in Australia and Canada. As we see there, one of the many interesting differences between their property rights systems and the colonial property rights systems which were introduced into their countries is that the indigenous systems were less good at producing personal wealth for their peoples, but were generally more successful in conserving their natural resources and using them sustainably. The comparison can therefore give us useful insights into the environmental effects of different property rights systems.

(b) Benefits to Humans

In para. 1.4 we also took a rather narrow view of what constitutes a benefit to humans. In the classic property analysis the human benefits emphasised are those most relevant to humans as autonomous individuals. But what about benefits to humans as social beings? Does property in its various forms promote (or undermine) other values, such as sociability, co-operation, community cohesiveness, civic responsibility, community, ethnic or national identity, or the development or preservation of cultural heritage? We follow these questions up in Chapter 2 *Conceptions and Justifications*.

(c) Property and Commodification

The development of a market economy was another thing we listed in para. 1.4 as a benefit which would accrue from propertising things. Does that mean that property is appropriate only for societies which want to have western-style market economies, or that we should only propertise things that we want to buy and sell? Are there other kinds of property systems which do not require or even allow property rights to be bought and sold? And are there some kinds of things that, even in a predominantly market economy, should be treated as property but not commodified? If we are talking about property in houses in this country and at this time, few people doubt that we ought to recognise property in houses; nevertheless it is controversial how far we should rely solely on markets to distribute and maintain the standard of our scarce housing resources. In the case of other things, for example human body parts, the consensus against commodification is much stronger – few people want to see kidneys taken from live donors being sold to the highest bidder. But, as we see in Chapter 7 *Objects of Property Interests*, property does not necessarily mean commodification, and there are compelling reasons for recognising some kind of property interest in at least some kinds of body part in at least some circumstances.

1.9 Allocation and Distribution

It will be noted that the classic account of the benefits of property we set out in para. 1.4 does not even attempt to solve the basic scarcity problem. According to that account, if we propertise things we will be more productive, innovative and prosperous and more fulfilled as autonomous individuals – but we will still have fewer houses than there are people who want to live in them. We could argue that we can use our new prosperity to build more houses, but it is not obvious why a market economy would produce that particular result. This raises allocation and distribution problems which we consider in Chapter 3 *Allocation of Property Rights*. The allocation problem is this. When we first propertise scarce things, how do we decide whose property they should become? Should they be allocated to the person who created them? Or to the first person to take possession of them, or to improve them? Or should they go to the people who need them most, or would make the best use of them? And after they have been propertised, should we leave it to the market to distribute them, so that they can get passed on only by inheritance, sale or gift?

It is important to appreciate that the subsequent distribution of resources will be affected by the duration of the rights initially allocated when the resource was first propertised. In the account of property given in para. 1.4 many of the benefits described assume that property rights are necessarily indefinite in duration, lasting for so long as the thing itself continues to exist, and by necessary implication also transmissible, passing through the hands of successive holders through sale or inheritance in the way we explain in para. 1.26(b). Do the rights we allocate initially have to be like this? If so, it has important implications, especially if the thing itself is virtually indestructible. Land again provides our best example. Land is scarce, and in general it is fixed in quantity. It is not as immutable as once thought, but nevertheless, with trivial exceptions and leaving aside the possibilities of environmental disasters, no new land can be created and the land that exists now will continue to exist for as long as humans exist. To give the first allocatees of land perpetual transmissible rights therefore seems to give them and their descendants a startlingly large advantage, gained at the expense of two categories of people. The first disadvantaged category is the class of people who, before the first allocation, were free to use the land but are now prohibited from doing so. The second is all those born after the last piece of land has been allocated, who will never have the chance of receiving this amazing windfall.

Nevertheless, although we do limit property rights in some things to fixed durations (patents and copyrights, for example), perpetual rights are the norm in the case of land in this jurisdiction (and in some but not all others). This makes it all the more important to consider the next question, which is, what about the people who end up with no initial allocation of a particular thing? How are they to acquire these things? Can they do so only by 'just transfer' (a phrase we come across again in Chapter 3 *Allocation of Property Rights*), in other words by purchase, inheritance or gift from one of the original allocatees or their descendants, or are there other possibilities? At first sight, 'just transfer' seems merely to reinforce the advantage gained by the first allocatees and their descendants (although, as we see in Chapter 3, not everyone would agree). Are there property law systems which provide more effective mechanisms for re-distribution of scarce resources? In fact our jurisdiction, like many others, does provide some mechanisms by which people can acquire property rights by means other than purchase, inheritance and gift. These are outlined in Chapter 3 and considered in more detail in Chapter 12 *Adverse Posses-sion of Land* and Chapter 14 *Acquiring Interests Informally.* Nevertheless, we can note here that they apply only in strictly limited circumstances, and have only a marginal effect on distribution.

1.10 What Kinds of Property Interest?

As we noted in para. 1.5, one of the problems with the classic analysis of property is that it wrongly assumes that 'property' is synonymous with 'private ownership'. We have already pointed out in the preceding paragraphs that this is an untenably narrow view. If we think of 'property' as a set of enforceable rights we have in things as against others and as against the state, 'ownership' is the name of one particular set of these rights. We also recognise other sets of these rights, some comprising some but not all of the rights in the ownership set, others comprising quite different rights, and yet others comprising a mix of the two. If we call all of these sets of property rights 'property interests', we can say that ownership is a property interest, but it is only one of a spectrum or range of different property interests. Again, this is not as mysterious as it might at first appear. We are all familiar with the notion that, if I own my house (in the sense described in para. 1.7), I can let it to a friend for, say, five years by granting her a lease, and mortgage it to the bank by granting the bank a mortgage, and give my next-door neighbour a right of way over the front drive. Leases, mortgages and rights of way are all property interests (as is ownership) and in our example they are all property interests in the same land on which the house is built. We all know that my ownership of the land gives me a certain set of rights in it, my friend's lease gives her a different set, and these are different again from the set of rights which make up the bank's mortgage and the neighbour's right of way.

Most if not all legal systems recognise a spectrum or range of different property interests. In most systems something akin to private ownership is one of the property interests in that range, but even within these systems the meaning and importance of private ownership varies from jurisdiction to jurisdiction. Since the range of different kinds of property interest mirrors the diverse ways in which people interact with each other in relation to things, we would expect to find a common set of property interests recognised in all culturally similar societies. To some extent this is what happens, as we see in Chapter 6 *New Property Interests and the Numerus Clausus*, and also when we look in detail at specific property interests in land recognised in this jurisdiction in Chapter 5 *Ownership and Other Property Interests*, Chapter 13 *Non-Possessory Land Use Rights* and Chapter 17 *Leases.* However, we should be wary of the notion that there is a universally applicable template of property interests, even in a universal resource such as land. The reality is that different types of property interest evolve in different cultures and in different physical environments. As already noted in para. 1.8, we come back to these differences in Chapter 9 *Multiple Property Rights Systems*, where we contrast the patterns of land use evolved by indigenous peoples in Australia and Canada with those evolved by the common law and exported to Australia and Canada by the colonial powers.

1.11 Implications of the Property–Ownership Confusion

Although most modern property commentators would probably agree that the classic analysis takes too narrow a view when it treats 'property' as synonymous with 'private ownership', in practice the two terms are often used as if they do mean the same thing, especially by some property theorists. We see several examples of this in the materials we consider in Chapter 2 *Conceptions and Justifications* and in Chapter 3 *Allocation of Property Rights*. The terminology is unfortunate because it reinforces a misconception that, as a matter of universal principle, nothing short of private ownership can ever count as 'property' and that all relationships relating to things which fall short of private ownership are necessarily inferior to it and must be subordinated to it. As we see in Chapter 4 *Property and Human Rights* and in Chapter 9 *Multiple Property Rights Systems*, this misconception has had serious consequences for people who utilise their resources in a way that does not conform to the standard western 'ownership' model.

1.12 Ownership and the Fragmentation of Ownership Metaphor

In Chapter 5 *Ownership and Other Property Interests* we look more closely at the concept of private ownership and its place in English land law, but for present purposes we can think of it as 'absolute dominion' over a thing, meaning perpetual exclusive rights to use, manage and control it and to exclude all others from it. As we have already noted, other property interests recognised in our system and in other jurisdictions give fewer and/or different rights over the thing and, whilst they may be perpetual, they may also be for a limited duration. One way of looking at this overall picture is to say that the constituent rights which make up absolute dominion ownership can be split up between different rights holders, both quantitatively and temporally. As we see in Chapter 5 and in Chapter 6 *New Property Interests and the Numerus Clausus*, sometimes this can be a helpful way of looking at the range of property interests which are recognised in our law in relation to land, because land can most easily fulfil different functions for different people simultaneously.

So, going back to the ownership–lease–mortgage–right of way example in para. 1.10, one way of looking at it is as a process of splitting up the constituent elements of private ownership to form three new sub-interests, leaving a hollowed-out form of ownership in the original owner's hands. In that example I started out with private ownership of the land on which the house is built. When I granted the five year lease to my friend, I gave her the right to possession of the land, including the house, for those five years, leaving me with a present right to retake possession at the end of the five years. So, during those five years, she has the right to exclude me from the land. When I then mortgaged my property interest (which by that stage was ownership subject to the lease) to the bank, I granted to the bank the right to sell my property interest (ownership subject to my friend's lease) if I failed to keep up with the mortgage payments. If I had meanwhile (i.e. before granting the lease and the mortgage) granted the right of way to my neighbour, I would, in effect, have split up the right to exclude everyone from my land (which I had by virtue of my ownership) so that I no longer had a right to exclude my neighbour from using my front drive, and he correspondingly acquired a right to exclude me from doing anything on my front drive that interfered with his right of way.[6] Viewed in this way, I have carved the lease, the mortgage and the right of way out of my ownership interest, creating three new property interests and ending up with the elements of my original ownership distributed amongst the four of us.

1.13 Limitations of the Fragmentation Metaphor

However, the fragmentation of ownership metaphor is only a metaphor and it has its limits. It gives a central role to ownership which is not always appropriate, especially when we are considering land.

(a) Fragmentation Leads to Proliferation of Reciprocal Rights, Duties, etc.

The most serious objection to the fragmentation metaphor appears from our ownership–lease–mortgage–right of way example, where the metaphor initially appeared so attractive. The point is that whenever an owner of a thing (or the holder of any other property interest in it) grants someone else another property interest in it, both grantor and grantee acquire new and very specific rights, powers, duties and liabilities as against each other. Consider, for example, repair and maintenance of land. A sole absolute private owner of land owes some duties to neighbours and to public authorities not to allow the land and buildings on it to get into such a poor state that they cause or threaten harm to neighbouring land or to the public or the environment. However, such an owner has no other duties or liabilities to anyone to keep them in good repair and condition, nor of course does anyone owe him any such duties or liabilities. All this changes when the owner enters into an ongoing property relationship with someone else about the land, for example by granting a lease, mortgage or even a right of way over it. It will almost certainly be a term of each of those relationships that one party or the other has rights, freedoms or powers to carry out repairs to the land or buildings they would not otherwise have had, and/or duties or liabilities to the other in respect of the condition of the land or buildings. So, even where it is helpful to think of ownership being fragmented, it is important to bear in mind that fragmentation involves not only the re-distribution of pre-existing entitlements and obligations, but also the creation of new rights, freedoms, powers, duties and liabilities.

---

[6] If I had granted the right of way after granting the lease and the mortgage, it would not have affected either the lease or the mortgage (in other words, my neighbour would not have been able to exercise the right of way without my tenant friend's consent during her lease, and if the mortgagee had wanted to sell my ownership, it would have been subject to the lease but not subject to the right of way). All this follows from our rules about enforceability and priority of property interests, which we look at in Chapter 15 *Enforceability and Priority of Property Interests: General Principles* and Chapter 16 *Registration*.

(b) Ownership May Be the Least Important Interest in a Piece of Land

In this jurisdiction, with minor exceptions, every piece of land is owned by someone.[7] However, as we have already seen, the ownership interest in a piece of land is often subject to other property rights which are so extensive that the residual ownership is virtually worthless. Consider, as an extreme example, the 999 year leases we noted in para. 1.7. During the lease, ownership continues to exist, but it would be grotesque to regard the 999 year lease as a subordinate interest carved out of the ownership interest, since most of the characteristics we would associate with ownership are found in the 999 year lease bundle, not in the ownership bundle.

(c) Proprietary Use Rights Can Make Ownership Rights Unexercisable

More importantly for present purposes, ownership of land may be subject to other property interests which are not particularly extensive in themselves, but which make it unlawful for the owner to exercise many of its ownership rights, freedoms or powers. In these cases it becomes impossible to identify the constituent elements of ownership in anyone's hands.

This is what happens when land which is privately owned becomes registered as common land or as a town or village green under the Commons Registration Act 1985 or Commons Act 2006. As we see in Chapter 13 *Non-Possessory Land Use Rights*, the effect of registration is that user groups or local communities acquire property rights over the land: these are rights to communally graze animals or harvest natural produce on the land, or rights to use the land for recreational purposes. The private owner of the land remains private owner, but there are virtually no ownership rights, freedoms or powers she can exercise over the land. These have not been transferred to the user groups or local communities, but because the owner is subject to their rights (in other words, must do nothing that interferes with them) she cannot exercise all her ownership rights.

Public parks provide an example of a different kind. A public park is usually owned by the local authority or some other private or public body. Generally, the public has a right to use the park for recreational purposes and the park owner is under a legally enforceable obligation not to use it for any purposes other than as a park. Consequently, the owner's rights in relation to the land are very limited. Unless and until the public park status is removed, the only thing the owner can do is to regulate the exercise of the public recreational rights, and there is not much scope for other people to have other kinds of property interest in the land either. So, a public park is usually land in which the public has a limited use right, the landowner's ownership 'bundle' of rights contains only rights to control and regulate the public use rights, and no-one else has any other property rights over it at all. In other words, most of the things that a single private owner can do on or with her own land

---

[7] When we talk about land ownership here (and in the rest of the chapter) we mean 'freehold' ownership, rather than the vestigial interest which the Crown has in all land in England and Wales: we explain the difference in para. 1.18 below.

cannot be done at all by anyone on land which is a public park. In this situation, as in the case of privately owned land which is common land or a town or village green, it is simply wrong to describe the ingredients of private ownership as being split between different property interest holders.

Both of these are extreme examples, but we will come across many others which are less extreme in later chapters.

(d) Regulatory Property Rights

There are other groups of property rights where the concept of fragmentation of ownership is equally unhelpful. In Chapter 6 *New Property Interests and the Numerus Clausus* we look at regulatory property rights. These are licenses or permits issued by states or other bodies, for example to emit a certain amount of carbon, or to abstract water from a river, or to use a broadcast frequency or an airport slot. As we see in Chapter 6, there is now a general consensus that at least some of these rights are property rights. However, whilst it might make sense to talk about ownership of these rights, we have to appreciate that the rights the 'owner' has depend entirely on the terms of the licence or permit and may bear no resemblance to conventional ownership rights. Also, although these property rights often amount to a licence to exploit a specific resource in a particular way, it makes no sense at all to talk about them as rights which have somehow become split off from ownership of that resource. In fact, as we have already noted, the resource is often unowned and the permit or licence may be the only property interest which is recognised in it.

(e) Jurisdictions not Centred on Private Ownership

Finally and for obvious reasons, the fragmentation of ownership metaphor is also not at all helpful when looking at property interests recognised in jurisdictions which do not give private ownership the central role it has in our jurisdiction. For example, some modern jurisdictions, including Russia, China and Nigeria, do not recognise private ownership of land at all, but they do recognise private use rights to land which in some respects perform similar functions to the functions private ownership performs in, say, civil law jurisdictions. If we were trying to compare their property law systems to ours, we would be seriously misled if we started from the premise that the property interests they recognise are made up of the ingredients of ownership as we understand it, only divided up in different ways. In other words, we cannot assume that in all jurisdictions, if we take the aggregate of all property interests enforceable in respect of any given piece of land at any one time, we will find all (and only) the constituents of private ownership as we know it, only split up in different ways.

1.14 Viable Alternatives to Propertisation

Another problem with the classic analysis is that it assumes that the things that property can do can *only* be done by property: on the classic analysis, if things are not propertised no-one can have secure use or control of them. However, the reality is that, even in similar legal, political and social cultures, the ends achieved by propertising things can often be achieved equally well by other legal institutions. So, whilst some jurisdictions might choose to achieve those ends by propertising a thing, others will choose to do so by personal or contractual rights or by public regulation. Leases provide a good illustration, as we see in Chapter 17 *Leases*. Leases of land are commonly used for residential and commercial premises in this jurisdiction and in many civil law countries in Europe, in order to provide secure rights to accommodation for a limited period. But whereas leases are property interests in England and Wales, they are not property interests in most European civil law systems. In those jurisdictions landlord and tenant are bound to each other only by contract, and the enforceability of the tenant's interest against third parties and the outside world depends on statutory rights. There are interesting reasons why common law and civil law systems have developed in different ways in this respect, but the end *effect* appears to be remarkably similar in both types of system: in both systems tenants are generally able to prevent outsiders from interfering with their rights in the land during the lease term.

A similar situation appears to be developing in relation to property in human bodies and human body parts. Because of developments in medical techniques, particularly in reproductive medicine and in organ, tissue and DNA transplants, body parts detached from human bodies are now of high value throughout the world. The general consensus globally is that the law ought to develop rules which will safeguard human autonomy and dignity whilst also enabling us to make the best use of this new technology. One way of doing this might be to propertise human body parts, and in this jurisdiction we have already done so to a limited extent, as we see in Chapter 7 *Objects of Property Interests*. However, there is no consensus that this is the only, or even the best, means of achieving the same ends, and as we see in Chapter 7 other jurisdictions may well adopt different means.

1.15 Private Property, Communal Property, Public Property and State Property

We have already noted that the classic analysis of property we described in Part II of the chapter assumes a certain kind of property interest holder, namely an autonomous private individual holding property interests for her own benefit. It will be apparent from the previous paragraphs that this too presents only part of a more complex picture. It has shortcomings even as a description of those who hold private property interests, because it assumes that all holders of private property interests are autonomous individuals motivated by self-interest who are free to do whatever they want with their property: this misses the point that private individuals can, and do, also hold property interests on behalf of others or for strictly limited purposes. We come back to this point in para. 1.16.

Another problem, however, is that the classic account of property fails to take into account that property interest holders may not be private individuals at all, but may instead be communities, or the public, or even the state itself. This is probably true of all jurisdictions, although some do not categorise public or state rights in things as property but as public law and in others the mix between private, communal, public and state property varies considerably between jurisdictions.

We look at private, communal, public and state holders of property interests in detail in Chapter 8 *Property Interest Holders*. Here, however, we outline the main differences between the categories because the distinction becomes important in Chapter 2 *Conceptions and Justifications*. When we consider the functions and effects of property, as we do in Chapter 2, it makes a difference whether we are talking about private property (and if so, of what kind), communal property, public property or state property.

1.16 Private Property

We can categorise as private property any property interest which is held by a private individual. In the classic account of property the individual private property interest holder is usually taken to be a human person, and every property rights holder is taken to be a self-sufficient being, responsible only for her own flourishing as an autonomous person. None of these assumptions is necessarily correct.

(a) Human and Non-Human Holders of Private Property Interests

The terms 'individual' and 'person' are ambiguous in law. Sometimes they are used to refer only to human beings, but more often they refer to both human and non-human legal entities. As far as property law is concerned, any legal entity can hold a private property interest: it may be a human, but it may also be a corporate person or any other kind of artificial legal person. Non-human legal entities encompass a wide range of very different organisations – anything from a small family business to a global commercial enterprise, a charitable organisation, or a body carrying out private, non-charitable but not-for-profit activities.

For our purposes, a property interest is private property if it is held by a human person or by any artificial (i.e. non-human) legal entity *which is not a public authority*. There is no fixed legal definition of 'public authority', but here we take it to mean a body which is 'governmental' by nature (so it would include, for example, a government department, a local authority, the police and the armed forces) or if its functions include 'functions of a public nature' (for example, a commercial organisation running a prison).[8]

As we see in the following chapters, most property theory (and most property law) assumes that we can and should treat all private legal entities in the same way when considering private property holdings (even, as we see in Chapter 4 *Property and*

---

[8] This adopts the definition of public authority given in s. 6 of the Human Rights Act 1986, on the basis that a body which is a public authority for human rights purposes is not entitled to human rights protection as against the state – in other words, in this respect its property interests are not enforceable against the state: see *Aston Cantlow* v. *Wallbank* [2003] UKHL 3, Lord Nicholls at paras. 7–8 and see further para. 4.21, Chapter 4 *Property and Human Rights*.

Human Rights, when considering property and human rights). We need to examine whether this is always appropriate: arguments founded on human dignity and the psychological bonds that people develop with their things are not exactly compelling when applied to corporate persons, for example.

(b) Self-interest

When an individual (a human person or private non-human legal entity) holds a property interest it does not necessarily hold it for its own benefit, nor is it necessarily free to do whatever it wants with the property interest. When we think about private property, we tend to think about property interests held by private individuals who are free to use them (or not use them) to pursue their own selfish best interests, or their own private inclinations. Private property in that form certainly does exist in our jurisdiction and it is probably the most prevalent form of property holding by human individuals. However, even human individuals can, and quite often do, hold property interests on trust for other people, or for charitable or (sometimes) non-charitable purposes,[9] rather than for their own benefit. Private corporate individuals are in a slightly different position. Most private commercial corporate individuals hold their property interests for their own benefit, but it is important to appreciate that in our jurisdiction they *must* act to promote the commercial success of the company for the benefit of their members (i.e. shareholders) – they are not free to do otherwise, as a human individual is.[10] Also, there are many forms of private corporation which impose even greater limits on what the corporation may do with its property interests. Within this jurisdiction there are, for example, asset-locked incorporated associations whose main purpose is to preserve and manage a particular asset or resource, and who are not allowed to transfer their property interests in it. There are also not-for-profit associations which may not distribute profits made from their property interests to their members or to anyone else, and all kinds of other private association which are required to use their property interests for specified purposes only, which may or may not benefit the association itself. We look at all these forms of private property holding in Part II of Chapter 8 *Property Interest Holders*.

(c) Autonomy, Self-sufficiency and Family Property

Even if we focus only on human persons, it is a mistake to assume that we are all self-sufficient autonomous beings at all times and for all purposes. The reality is that most humans utilise their personal resources, and sometimes their business resources, in family groups. Some legal systems take account of this interdependency of family members by recognising forms of family property. To a surprisingly great extent, we do not do so in this jurisdiction, as we see in Part IV of Chapter 8.

---

[9] See Chapter 5 *Ownership and Other Property Interests*, Part V 'Trusts'.

[10] Section 172 of the Companies Act 2006, setting out the general statutory duties of a company director: companies can act only by their directors.

Nevertheless, even in this jurisdiction, there may be strong social and moral constraints on human individuals to use their property interests for the benefit of the family as a whole or for other family members, rather than for their own individual benefit. This should make us wary of, for example, economic theories of property which assume we are all guided by individual self-interest when making decisions about property.

1.17 Communal Property

By communal property we mean property interests that are held by communities rather than by individuals. The resources in which communities have property interests are sometimes also referred to as 'communal property' or as 'common property', or 'commons' or 'common pool resources'. This terminology is used even when individuals, the public and/or the state also have property interests in the same resource. So, for example, in this jurisdiction land is 'common land' if a group of people have communal rights to graze animals on the land, even though the land may be owned by a private individual or by the local authority (a private or state property interest), and even though the public has rights of access over it (a public property interest).[11]

(a) 'Communities' and Communal Property

For these purposes, a community is a group of people defined by reference to a shared characteristic. The characteristic may have something to do with locality (perhaps they all inhabit a defined geographic area) or with a common interest (they may be a group of local farmers who all graze sheep on the same pastureland, or different people who all use the same stretch of water for different purpose and who form a group in order to co-ordinate their use and management of the water in their collective self-interest). Equally, they might be a communal living community, either sharing communal parts of a residential development because they chose to buy or rent flats or houses in that development, or electing to live together communally for reasons of ideology, convenience or tradition.

We are interested in these communities in so far as they make collective use of a thing (any kind of thing, although we are interested primarily in land, buildings or other resources such as water) so that every member of the community is entitled to use it in common with every other member, and to the exclusion of non-members. The exclusion of non-members or outsiders is important, even if it is not rigorously enforced, because it is this that separates community use from public use.

The 'use' that members of the community make of the thing in common with each other might be so extensive that it amounts to the use that an owner would make of it, or it might be a more limited use (perhaps using it in a particular way, or for a particular purpose or extracting a particular benefit from it). Also, every

---

[11] See Chapter 8 *Property Interest Holders*, Parts V and VI and Chapter 13 *Non-Possessory Land Use Rights*, Part V. Common parts of residential developments sometimes fall into a similar category.

member might make the same use of the thing in common with all the others, or they might all be making different uses of it at the same time.

These communal uses amount to communal property interests when they are enforceable by the state against outsiders and against the state. It is important to appreciate that in most jurisdictions, including ours, a community can acquire a communal property interest not only when such an interest is expressly granted or transferred to it: it can also, in some circumstances, acquire it by long use or custom. In other words, when a collective use of a resource by a community has become established over a period of time, the state may (or must) recognise and enforce that collective use as a communal property interest. We have more to say on this in Chapter 9 *Multiple Property Rights Systems*, when we look at indigenous property rights in Australia and Canada, and also in Chapter 12 *Adverse Possession of Land* and Chapter 13 *Non-Possessory Land Use Rights*, when we consider how property interests in general can be acquired by long use.

(b) The Community as an Entity

A community as such is not a legal entity, but in many jurisdictions, including ours, it can nevertheless hold property interests in its own right in some circumstances. This goes without saying in the case of the indigenous groups in Australia and Canada which we look at in Chapter 9 *Multiple Property Rights Systems*, but it also happens in this country. So, for example, when land is registered as a town or village green under the Commons Act 2006 a community consisting of the inhabitants of a specified local area have the right to use it for 'lawful sports and pastimes'.[12] As we see in Chapter 2 *Conceptions and Justifications*, even this kind of community, which consists of a fluctuating body of individuals, is capable of devising and enforcing its own rules to regulate its own use of the shared resource. However, it is not so easy for it, or any other kind of community which is not a legal entity, to deal with outsiders. For this and other reasons some communities incorporate themselves so that the community becomes a legal person. The community's property interests are then held by a private corporate individual, and so, as far as the outside world is concerned, they become private property interests. These property interests therefore sit somewhere on the borderline between private and communal property interests: probably the best description is that they are private property from the outside but communal property on the inside.[13]

(c) Distinguishing 'Communal', 'Open Access' and 'Public'

The term 'communal property' is sometimes also used to refer to 'open access' resources, as we see in Part III of Chapter 2 *Conceptions and Justifications*. This is an unfortunate source of confusion. The term 'open access' resource is best reserved for

---

[12] See further Chapter 13 *Non-Possessory Land Use Rights*, Part VI.

[13] The description was first suggested by Carol M. Rose, 'The several future of property: Of cyberspace and folk talks, emission trades and ecosystems' (1988) 83 *Minnesota Law Review* 129 at p. 144.

something that everyone is *free* to use – in other words, it is an unpropertised thing. This is different from something that everyone is *entitled* to use, which, as we see in the next paragraph, is best described as public property. And, of course, it is different again from something which a *community* is *entitled* to use to the exclusion of outsiders, which, as we have just seen, is properly called 'communal property'.

1.18 Public Property and State Property

(a) Public Property

By public property we mean property interests that are held by the public, so that every member of the public has a *right* to exercise the property interest in common with every other citizen, and this right is enforceable against every other citizen (i.e. no member of the public may interfere with the exercise of the right by any other member of the public) and against the state (i.e. the state cannot extinguish or interfere with the exercise of public property interests any more easily than it can do so with private or communal property interests). The best examples in this jurisdiction are public rights of way, and public rights of access over uncultivated land under the Countryside and Rights of Way Act 2000. We come across some of these in later chapters. Like communal property interests, public property interests may exist over privately owned or state owned land.

(b) Distinguishing Public, 'Open Access' and State Property

From the citizens' perspective there is a real difference between public property, no-property (i.e. the open access property referred to in the previous paragraph) and state property. If things in a state are open access, that is, not propertised at all, every citizen is free to use them; if things are state owned, all citizens are prohibited from making any use of them without permission of some sort from the state; if things are subject to a public property interest, every citizen has a right to use them in the authorised way.

(c) State Property

In this book we categorise as state property all property interests held by a public authority, as defined in para. 1.16(a). In other words a property interest is state property if it is held by a government department or any other body which is 'governmental' by nature, such as a local authority or the armed services, and it is also state property if held by a body whose functions include 'functions of a public nature' (a hybrid public authority), in so far as it holds the property interest as part of its public functions, as opposed to its private functions.

We look at this in detail in Chapter 8 *Property Interest Holders*, but here we should just note that the Crown is in a special position in relation to land ownership. In England and Wales, all land is said to be 'owned' by the Crown but it is a hollow, vestigial form of ownership: in our property law system we long ago carved out of

Crown 'ownership' of land a type of private ownership interest which is unique to the common law (generally called 'freehold' or 'fee simple' ownership). In nearly all respects freehold ownership of land is indistinguishable from classic private ownership, and the underlying Crown 'ownership' has almost no real-world content or consequences. We come back to this in Chapter 5 *Ownership and Other Property Interests* where we look at land ownership in England and Wales in detail.

When either a state body or a private individual 'owns' land, the property interest it holds is freehold ownership. When held by the state, freehold ownership closely resembles classic private ownership, and the interests carved out of it in favour of private citizens might range from mere temporary use permissions to secure long-term property interests.

PART IV PROPERTY TERMINOLOGY AND PROPERTY CONCEPTS

1.19 The Three Functions of the Term 'Property'

It will be apparent from what we have said so far that the word 'property' is used in a number of different ways. The potential ambiguity in the word is sometimes perceived as a problem but there is no reason why it should be. Broadly, in this book we use 'property' to mean any one of three things: either the institution of property, or the tangible or intangible thing which is the object of property interests, or property interests themselves. We need to say a bit more about each of these.

1.20 The Institution of Property

In property literature the term 'property' is often used to refer to the set of rules adopted and enforced by a state which regulate the use and control of resources over which the state has sovereignty, by conferring property interests in those things on its citizens (individually or collectively or as members of the public) or on itself. The term may also be used in some contexts to refer to an informal set of rules evolved by a community within the state, which regulate the use and control of resources under the community's control and which the community itself and its members regard as binding.

In this book we tend to use the term 'property system' or 'property rights system' instead of 'property' when we are referring to property as an institution, particularly when we are trying to make the point that every state has its own idiosyncratic property system, reflecting its own physical environment and economic conditions, and its own cultural, social, moral and political preferences.

1.21 Property as Things

'Property' is of course routinely used to refer to the thing in which we have property rights and interests. Some property writers disapprove of this usage (common amongst non-lawyers). It can obscure the crucial fact that what a property system confers on people, and what it protects against interference by others, is not things but property interests in (or to) things. If the only kind of property right in or to a thing was ownership, this would not much matter: everyone would understand that 'my car' or 'my cat' is simply shorthand for 'my ownership of that car' or 'my ownership of that cat', and everyone would know that the rights, duties, liabilities, etc. which comprise car ownership are essentially the same as those comprising cat ownership. However, as we have already noted, we recognise different kinds of property interest in different things. If I offer to sell you my car or my cat I almost certainly do mean I am offering to sell you my ownership of the car or the cat, because as a matter of fact in this country the property interest people have in their cars and their cats is overwhelmingly likely to be ownership.[14] If on the other hand I offer to sell you my house, my flat, or my carbon emission allowance, what I am probably offering to sell you is my fee simple ownership of the land on which the house is built, as we saw in para. 1.7, my lease of the airspace containing the flat (also para. 1.7), and the tradeable EUA units I hold which entitle the holder to emit a certain amount of carbon (Chapter 6 *New Property Interests and the Numerus Clausus*). So, if we talk about selling the thing as if the thing itself was property, we are omitting vitally important information about the set of entitlements and obligations etc. that you will acquire over the thing if you buy it.

However, it is doubtful whether anyone is actually deceived or confused, and it has to be said that lawyers quite often adopt this usage, and it even crops up in legislation.[15]

1.22 Property as Rights or Interests in Things

The third way in which 'property' is used is as an adjective. That is to say, it is used to describe or qualify the kind of right or interest we have in a thing, or the kind of relationship we have with others in respect of a thing. We use 'property' in this way because not all rights and interests we have in things are property rights or interests, and not all relationships we have with others in respect of a thing are property relationships – some are property, others are not. In para. 1.26 we consider what differentiates property rights, interests and relationships in respect of things from those which are non-proprietary, but first we need to say something more about rights, interests and relationships.

1.23 Rights and Freedoms: Hohfeld's Analysis

Throughout this chapter we have been distinguishing between *rights* to use things like houses and *freedoms* to do so, noting that everyone is free to use things which

---

[14] Leasing or other hiring arrangements are alternatives for cars, but they do not generally give the lessee/hirer rights that can be sold to third parties.

[15] See, for example, s. 436 of the Insolvency Act 1986, which defines 'property' as including 'money, goods, things in action, land and every description of property wherever situated and also obligations and every description of interest, whether present or future or vested or contingent, arising out of, or incidental to, property'. The first four listed are things, and the definition then goes on to list interests in things.

are not subject to property rights. This distinction between rights and freedoms in relation to things is fundamental to an understanding of property. In particular it brings out the essential truth that the immediate effect of propertising a thing is to destroy the freedom that everyone previously had to use that thing (within the limits of the general law), because granting a property right in a thing to one person necessarily involves imposing a correlative duty on everyone else not to interfere with that person's right in the thing.

(a) Hohfeld's Distinctions Between Different Legal Entitlements

This distinction between rights and freedoms, and the recognition that conferring a right on one person necessarily involves the imposition of a duty on another, derive from W. N. Hohfeld's highly influential analysis of legal entitlements, first published in 1913.[16] Hohfeld pointed out that we tend to talk loosely about rights and duties as if all kinds of legal relationships between people are reducible to simple rights and duties. The reality, he argued, is that we can distinguish at least four different kinds of entitlement and each of them has an opposite and a correlative. His argument is that if we want to understand complex legal relationships we must distinguish between these different kinds of entitlement and their various opposites and correlatives. The best way of doing this, he said, is to pair them so that we can see the opposite, and the correlative, of each kind of entitlement. His four entitlements are rights, privileges (which are what we call 'freedoms' in this book), powers and immunities; the four opposites/correlatives to them are duties, no-rights, liabilities and disabilities. He pairs each entitlement with its opposite and correlative in the following way:

Hohfeld's table of opposites and correlatives

Opposites		Correlatives	
Right	No-right	Right	Duty
Privilege	Duty	Privilege	No-right
Power	Disability	Power	Liability
Immunity	Liability	Immunity	Disability

Hohfeld was not talking specifically about property law relationships (although he uses some property law examples) but the distinctions he makes are fundamental to any analysis of property relationships in the common law world, even if his terminology is not always respected. For these reasons it is worth spending some time understanding the basic distinctions, especially those in the first two lines of the above table.

---

[16] Wesley Newcomb Hohfeld, 'Fundamental legal conceptions as applied in judicial reasoning' (1913) 23 *Yale Law Journal* 16.

(b) Hohfeld's Rights, No-Rights, Duties and Privileges

One way of explaining Hohfeld's analysis in property law terms is to consider the example of a right of way I have over a path on your land. This is a property interest which gives me a *right* to walk along the path in common with you. The opposite of my *right* to walk along the path is a *no-right*: were it not for this property interest I have in the land you own, I would have a *no-right* to walk along your path ('no-right' has not proved to be a popular label). In other words, when you granted me the right of way, my *no-right* was converted into a *right*. The correlative to my *right* to walk along your path, on the other hand, is the corresponding *duty* it imposes on you not to prevent or obstruct me in walking along it: in a sense, the contents of my right and your duty are the same, viewed from different perspectives (mine and yours). According to Hohfeld, an ingredient of your ownership of your land is a *privilege* (or *freedom*) for you to walk anywhere you like on your own land (including on the path, since you did not give me an exclusive right to use it). I have the opposite of such a *privilege/freedom* in relation to all your land (except the path); in other words I have a *duty* not to walk anywhere on your land except the path. The correlative of your *privilege* to walk anywhere on your land is my *no-right* that you should not do so. There are, of course, other ways of putting this. We could say that one ingredient of your ownership is a *right* to exclude me from your land: you have that *right* in respect of all parts of your land apart from the path, and in relation to the path you have a *no-right* to exclude me. Your *right* to exclude me from everywhere else entails a correlative *duty* on me not to enter your land other than on the path.

The application of the model to this kind of property relationship is not perfect. For example, we all agree that if you own the land you can walk wherever you want on it, except to the extent that you have granted other people *rights* which impose *duties* on you not to do so. However, it is not clear why we should call that entitlement, which is something you have by virtue of your ownership, a *privilege* (i.e. a freedom) rather than a *right*. In particular, given that we share the entitlement to walk along the path, it seems odd to say that my entitlement, arising out of my right of way, is a *right*, whereas yours, arising out of your ownership, is only a *privilege*.

Nevertheless, the fault seems to lie in Hohfeld's application of the model to the entitlements of owners, rather than in the model itself. The important point is that the model clarifies that both privileges (i.e. freedoms) to use resources and rights to do so are 'entitlements' to use them, but they are very different in effect.

(c) Hohfeld's Powers, Immunities, Disabilities and Liabilities

Hohfeld's other entitlements (powers and immunities) and their opposites and correlatives (disabilities and liabilities) also make useful distinctions for property lawyers, although in more specialised contexts.

Broadly, in a property context a *power* is an entitlement to alter legal relationships in respect of a thing and a *disability* is a no-power. Examples of *powers* that I have as an owner are that I can abandon my ownership (although it is not an easy thing to do in English law), or I can sell it (so transferring ownership from me to the buyer) or sub-divide it (for example by granting you a five year lease). Such powers are quite straightforward and easy to recognise.

Other powers are more esoteric. Some non-ownership property interests include a power to remove the ownership interest held by the owner and transfer it to someone else. It may seem surprising that any property interest holder should have such a power, and indeed these powers are exceptions to the general property principle that you cannot transfer what you do not have (the *nemo dat* principle we consider in Chapter 15 *Enforceability and Priority of Property Interests: General Principles*). It makes more sense, however, when we realise that this is the principal power that a mortgagee holds. If you mortgage your house to the bank and default on the mortgage payments, the bank mortgagee's remedy is to exercise this power by selling *your* property interest in your house to a third party purchaser, and use the sale proceeds to pay off what you owe under the mortgage. The bank mortgagee's power of sale is properly called a *power*, in the Hohfeldian sense, because it enables the bank to transfer the full ownership which you hold (and not just the mortgage interest the bank holds) to the purchaser. To complete the Hohfeldian analysis of the situation, this means that by granting the mortgage to the bank, you acquired a *liability* which is correlative to the mortgagee's *power* to sell: your liability to have your ownership transferred to a purchaser without your consent if you default on the mortgage payments. As we can see from Hohfeld's table, the opposite of a *liability* is an *immunity*, and this is what you will regain if and when you pay off all the mortgage payments without defaulting: from then on you are immune from your bank mortgagee's *power* to sell off your ownership of the property.

1.24 Rights Compared to Interests

The terms 'property right' and 'property interest' are sometimes used interchange-ably, and often so in this book. However, sometimes we need to distinguish between a right which is an ingredient of a property interest and the interest itself. In those circumstances, when we use the term 'property right' we mean a proprietary right or power (in the Hohfeldian sense) to do something specific to, or in relation to, a thing, whereas when we use the term 'property interest' we mean the sum total of *all* the Hohfeldian entitlements and their correlatives and opposites (i.e. rights, powers, privileges, duties, liabilities and immunities) that the interest holder has in respect of that thing. Hence we would say that ownership is one kind of property interest which we recognise in land, involving a number of different rights, duties, etc. in respect of the land, and that a lease is another kind of property interest in land, which involves a different set of rights, duties, etc.

1.25 Property as Relationships

Most modern property theorists prefer to think of property not as an institution, nor as things, nor as rights or interests in things, but as relationships between people in respect of things. At one level this makes sense, because, as Hohfeld helps us to understand, all entitlements in respect of things entail consequences for other people. However, we also need to understand that there are at least three different ways in which property can be said to be a 'relationship' between people.

(a) Relationships Arising out of Hohfeld's Entitlements and Correlatives

In Hohfeld's analysis every property entitlement (i.e. right, power, privilege or immunity) necessarily gives rise to a relationship between two people because one person's entitlement always gives rise to a correlative effect on someone else. So, my ownership right in my pen, conferring on me a right to exclude you from the pen, simultaneously confers on you and the rest of the world the duty not to interfere with my right. This means that by buying the pen I enter into property relationships with every other person in the world in respect of the pen.

However, mostly these Hohfeldian relationships are of no significance, particularly when viewed from the perspective of everyone else but me. My pen has been in someone's private ownership ever since it was manufactured. You have always had a duty not to interfere with that pen. The only consequence of my purchase from the previous owner is that the duty you once owed to the previous owner you now owe to me. To say that, when I bought the pen, a right–duty relationship arose between you (who perhaps live in Northumberland and are unaware of the existence of me or the pen) and me (living in London with the pen) has an air of unreality about it.

Nevertheless, the relationship will become more significant if the thing was unpropertised before I acquired ownership of it, or (to a lesser extent) if you owned it before I acquired my interest. In both cases, my acquisition gives rise to a significant change in the relationship between you and me in respect of the thing. Before I catch a fish in the sea, no-one has property rights in it, but you and I (in common with the rest of the world) had the freedom (or Hohfeldian privilege) to catch it. Of course, since neither of us had a *right* in respect of the fish before I caught it, neither of us could complain if the other caught it first, or scared it away or poisoned it. Nevertheless, it was a genuinely valuable potential source of food for both of us before I caught it, and each of us was free to capture that value. Now, however, the positions of both of us as against the other have changed dramatically. This is a truly significant change in the relationship we have between ourselves with respect to that fish, and we will be saying more about it in Chapter 3 *Allocation of Property Rights.*

Similarly, you and I might have a meaningful change in our relationship in respect of a thing if it was once yours but then becomes mine. If I become owner of your house, for example, our rights–duties relationship in respect of the house is reversed. If the change of ownership was a voluntary sale and purchase agreed between the two of us, the change in our relationship is unremarkable. However, it becomes problematic if the change was not voluntary: perhaps you were forced to flee from your home when your country was invaded by my government, and I became owner under the new government's resettlement scheme. This is a problem of restitution for the dispossessed and we come across it again in later chapters where we consider how, if at all, it can be resolved: see in particular Chapter 3 *Allocation of Property Rights*, Chapter 4 *Property and Human Rights* and Chapter 9 *Multiple Property Rights Systems*.

(b) Shared Resource Relationships

We have already noted that in a property rights system like ours it often happens that resources – things – are shared between people who have different property interests subsisting in them simultaneously. Very real, and often quite complex, continuing relationships routinely arise between these resource sharers. This happens most often in relation to land, but it also happens to some extent in relation to other things.

Sometimes the terms of these resource-sharing relationships are laid down by law, sometimes they are agreed by contract, and sometimes they are informal rules or norms of behaviour which have evolved over time between those particular people in those particular circumstances. Quite often, the relationship is governed by a combination of all three. Whatever the source of the terms of the relationship, the people involved will have to deal in some way or another with the management of the shared resource, balancing the interests of those with short-term and long-term entitlements and providing mechanisms for deciding and enforcing rules about exactly who is entitled to do (or responsible for doing) exactly what and when. To return to an example we used earlier, consider what happens if I am the owner of land on which I build a block of flats, and I grant leases of each flat to a different lessee. In practice, those leases are likely to be very long (999 years is common, since the objective is to make the lease of each flat approximate to ownership). Some of these lessees will have taken their lease because they want to live in the flat. Others will have taken it as an investment, and they will want to sub-let their flats to short-term sub-tenants. Whether living there or sub-letting, most of those holding long leases will have mortgaged their leases to lenders. So, in that one piece of land there will be a complex of different property interests held by different people for different purposes. Some of them will involve direct sharing of resources (consider, for example, lifts, stairs, entrance halls, structural parts of the building, common services such as broadband cables, water pipes, electric cables and the ground surrounding the building). However, even to the extent that the property interest confers exclusive use rights (rights for individual lessees or sublessees to occupy their own flat, for example), the Hohfeldian correlatives are of significant effect because the flats are physically interdependent and because of the continuing relationships that the parties have as neighbours.

These complex leasehold arrangements are very common in this country, as we see in Chapter 17 *Leases*. Functionally similar (although legally different) arrangements exist in most legal systems wherever commercial or residential units in a single development are under the same management but intended for separate occupation. All involve continuing relationships between people in respect of the shared space and shared resources, and the relationships are of real significance. The same applies to less complex resource sharing, such as (to take another example we used earlier) the resource sharing that arises when you grant me a right of way over the path on your land: thereafter we will have a significant continuing relationship between us which will govern our shared use of the path.[17] Similarly, significant resource sharing relationships exist when property interests are co-owned, as we see in Part III of Chapter 8 *Property Interest Holders*, and whenever property interests are held by communities or by the public: in all cases expressed or implicit rules have to develop to regulate the sharing relationship.

Nevertheless, whilst resource sharing is ubiquitous in relation to land and other natural resources (water is another good example), we should remember that it is unusual in relation to other things, such as pens. If we are to say, as some property theorists do, that property is *always* (or generally) a relationship between people in respect of things, we therefore need to look for some other kind of relationship.

(c) Property as social obligation

For progressive property theorists and others, the relationship is provided by social obligations which property owners owe towards others simply by virtue of their property holding. This idea that property imposes duties and obligations towards others, or to society as a whole, as well as conferring rights, is familiar in other jurisdictions. As we see in Chapter 4 *Property and Human Rights*, it is articulated in some human rights instruments and in the Constitutions of some states. For example, the 1969 American Convention of Human Rights (the regional human rights instrument for nations in the American continent, though not ratified by the USA or Canada) provides in art. 32.2 that all convention rights 'are limited by the demands of the general welfare'.[18] More explicitly, art. 14(2) of the *Grundgesetz* of the Federal Republic of Germany provides:

> (2) Property entails obligations. Its use shall also serve the public good.

We consider the implications of this provision later in Chapter 4 *Property and Human Rights*,[19] and in Chapter 2 *Conceptions and Justifications* we look at the property theories which place obligation and social responsibility at the heart of the concept of property and treat it as integral to its justification. For present purposes, however, we should note that there are alternative property theories (also considered in Chapter 2) which do not conceptualise property in this way. We should also consider, when we look at how property law works in this country in later chapters, whether it is descriptively accurate to say that the law in England and Wales regards property as entailing obligations as well as entitlements.

1.26 Distinguishing Property Rights and Interests from Non-Property Rights and Interests

By now it will be apparent that our legal system recognises many kinds of rights, interests and relationships between people in respect of things which are *not*

---

[17] We consider the terms of the relationship in Chapter 13 *Non-Possessory Land Use Rights*, Part II.
[18] See para. 4.11(b), Chapter 4 *Property and Human Rights*.   [19] Para. 4.14.

property rights, interests or relationships. What are the differences between those which *are* proprietary and those which are not?

(a) Enforceability

The most important difference is that property rights and interests are different in effect from non-property rights and interests, in that property rights and interests are enforceable against everyone, including the state, whereas non-property rights and interests generally are enforceable bilaterally only.

So, if you grant me a right which is not a property right (for example, a right to stay in your hotel for a week next month on payment of £100 a night) I can enforce it against you in contract law but I cannot enforce it against else. So, if you sell the hotel to a purchaser before the end of the month and the purchaser refuses to honour my booking, I can sue you in breach of contract but I cannot sue the purchaser.[20] If, however, you granted me a property interest (perhaps an option to purchase your hotel) and then you sell to a purchaser, my interest will be enforceable against her.[21] In other words, your purchaser simply steps into your shoes: I have the same entitlements (and am subject to the same duties and liabilities, etc.) as against her as I had against you.

The only anomalous category is the non-proprietary rights we have in our own bodies under the law of persons (for example, rights not be physically assaulted, or enslaved or falsely imprisoned). These rights are indeed enforceable against everyone under the law of tort: propertising them would not have the effect of increasing the range of enforceability, although, as we see in Chapter 7 *Objects of Property Interests*, it might well have other effects.

(b) Alienability and Transmissibility

Many, but not all, property interests are both alienable and transmissible. A right or interest is *alienable* if the holder of it has the power to dispose of it, either by selling, donating or surrendering it to someone during her life-time or by leaving it to someone by will when he dies. It is *transmissible* if it is not personal to the original holder, in the sense that it continues to exist in the same form and extent whoever happens to become the holder of the right, whether the right has changed hands by alienation (in one of the ways just described) or has automatically vested in someone because the previous holder died without making a will, or went bankrupt so that all his property automatically went to his trustee in bankruptcy to be sold for his creditors. Consider, for example, my right to the income from a trust fund during my life-time (which is a property interest). It is *alienable*, in that I have the power to sell it (but not to leave it by will, for obvious reasons). It is transmissible in that, if

---

[20] Unless perhaps she has some liability in tort to me, if her conduct amounted to a procurement of your breach of contract.
[21] Subject to the rules about enforceability and priority we look at in Chapter 15 *Enforceability and Priority of Property Interests* and Chapter 16 *Registration*.

I sell it, or if I go bankrupt and it vests in my trustee in bankruptcy, the right that my purchaser or trustee in bankruptcy acquires is identical to the right I held: it is a right to the income until the day I die (not until the current holder dies). My life measures the length of the interest, but it does not make the interest personal to me.

It is sometimes said that it is a necessary characteristic of a property interest that it is alienable, but this is not correct, at least in the law of England and Wales. In our law alienability is neither necessary nor sufficient for an interest in a thing to be a property interest. In other words, some property interests in things are not alienable, and some non-proprietary rights in things are alienable.

This makes sense because alienability is important primarily for marketable rights and interests. A right or interest in a thing cannot operate as a commodity unless the present rights holder can transfer her rights to someone else in exchange for value. But we see in later chapters many examples of property interests that are not intended to be, or are not capable of being, traded.[22] For these kinds of property interest, alienability is unnecessary and often positively undesirable.

(c) Rights to accretions, income and substitutions

It is a general, although not universal, characteristic of ownership and of some other property interests, that if you hold such an interest in a thing, you will also be entitled to the income benefits from the thing (if you own an apple tree, you will also own the apples) and entitled to all capital it generates (such as bonus shares issued to existing shareholders, or prizes won on lottery tickets you own). In addition, if someone sells or exchanges the thing on your behalf, or wrongly misappropriates it, your property rights in the thing may automatically transfer to the proceeds of sale or the exchange product (or, in the case of a wrongful misappropriation, you can elect whether to retain your rights in the thing and enforce them against whoever holds it now, or to have your rights transfer to the exchange product). We look at this characteristic again in Chapter 5 *Ownership and Other Property Interests* and we also come across it in other chapters, particularly where we are considering the operation of interests under trusts.

(d) Insolvency

One of the effects of categorising my interest in a thing as a property interest rather than a personal interest is that I will be in a much better position if you, who hold another interest in the same thing, become insolvent and go bankrupt. So, for example, if you are the freehold owner of farmland worth £1 million and you owe me £900,000 and you go bankrupt before you repay me, I will be much better off if

---

[22] For example communal and public property interests, and private property interests that are personal to the holder, such as the statutory right a tenant of business premises may have to renew the tenancy (see Chapter 17 *Leases* para. 17.2), or the 'home rights' a spouse or civil partner has under s. 30 of the Family Law Act 1996 to occupy what is or was the matrimonial/civil partnership home (Chapter 6 *New Property Interests and the Numerus Clausus*, Part III).

have a mortgage over your interest in the farmland to secure repayment of the debt than I would be if I simply had a contractual right to repayment. Similarly, if you are the freehold owner of a theatre and you have granted me an exclusive right to put on plays at your theatre for the next 10 years, I will be much better off if the arrangement gives me a 10 year lease of the theatre than I would be if it gave me just a personal right against you.

The reason is that if you go bankrupt, all your property interests automatically vest in an official (a trustee in bankruptcy) whose function is to sell all your property and divide the proceeds between all your creditors, rateably in proportion to how much you owe them. The same applies if you are a company and go into insolvent liquidation. In either case, since you are by definition insolvent (i.e. the total value of your property is less than the total amount of your debts), each of your creditors will receive only a proportion of what they are owed (usually a very small proportion).

So, if we take the farmland example, if I do not have a mortgage interest over it, your freehold interest (worth £1 million) will be taken by the trustee in bankruptcy and sold, and the sale proceeds divided between your creditors. I will be one of your creditors – you owe me £900,000 – but I will get only my proportionate share of the proceeds of sale of all your assets, and that is bound to be less than £900,000. If, on the other hand, I had a mortgage over your interest in the farmland to secure repayment of the £900,000, you have already carved my mortgage interest out of your freehold interest, so that the only property interest that can go to the trustee in bankruptcy is the freehold interest subject to the mortgage (worth in total £100,000). I, of course, still hold my mortgage interest unaffected by your bankruptcy (your trustee in bankruptcy gets only your property interests, not mine), so all I have to do is sell the farmland for £1 million[23] and take £900,000 out of that to repay the debt, paying the balance of £100,000 over to your trustee in bankruptcy. So, whilst all your other creditors get back only a portion of what they are owed when you go bankrupt, I get back 100 per cent. Which is why the bank is more likely to lend you £1 million if you mortgage your property to it to secure repayment of the loan than if you just promise to repay the money.

The theatre example produces a similar result. If our agreement that I can put plays on in your theatre is enforceable between us only in contract, your trustee in bankruptcy will get your freehold interest in the theatre to sell for the creditors, and because I have no property interest in it she can sell it free from my right to put on plays there. This will give me a claim against you for damages for breach of contract, but this will rank as just a debt you owe me, and so I will get back just a proportion of the damages. If, however, our agreement amounted to a 10 year lease of the theatre to me, the only property interest the trustee in bankruptcy has to sell is your freehold interest in the theatre subject to my lease. In other words, my lease of the theatre remains unaffected by your bankruptcy, except that I now have a new landlord.

---

[23] As mortgagee, I have the power to transfer your ownership of the farmland to a purchaser, free from my mortgage, as noted in para. 1.23(c).

(e) Human Rights Protection

However, in most jurisdictions the most important consequence of categorising an interest in a thing as a property interest is that it then becomes protectable either as a human right or as a constitutional right (sometimes both). Generally this means that the state is not entitled to interfere with the property interest except in the public interest and on payment of just compensation. We look at the extent of this protection generally and at how it works in this jurisdiction in Chapter 4 *Property and Human Rights*.

(f) Formal Categorisation: The *Numerus Clausus*

This leaves the question of how we can tell whether any given interest in respect of a thing is or is not a property interest. The first step in answering that question is straightforward. Some rights are property rights because the law has formally categorised them as such. Some states do this on an *ad hoc* basis, and see no particular problem in recognising new types of property interest, or recognising property interests in new kinds of thing. Other states, however, have a fixed (and short) list of recognised types of property interest (a *numerus clausus*) and, in theory at least, will not add new types of property interest to the list. Our property law system lies somewhere between those two extremes. As we see in Chapter 6 *New Property Interests and the Numerus Clausus* we do have a fixed (although unwritten) list of recognised property interests, but we are quite relaxed about admitting new types of interest on to the list, and equally relaxed about recognising property rights in things that have so far not been propertised. Sometime this is done by legislation, but most often it is left to the courts to decide. We consider the factors the courts take into account in coming to these decisions in Chapter 6 and in Chapter 7 *Objects of Property Interests*.

1.27 Property and Property Law

This brings us to a final question which is superficially terminological – does 'property' mean the same as 'property law' – but which masks a big philosophical question, beyond the scope of this book but difficult to avoid. The big philosophical question is whether property can be said to exist independently of property law, and it will be obvious from the following chapters that this is a question on which there are differing views.

(a) Property as an Institution Existing Independently of Law

On one view, property as an institution has an existence and legitimacy outside law, so that property law's function is not to create property, but merely to recognise or give expression to it. If that is its function, it follows that the law is deficient only in so far as it does not accurately give legal effect to these independently legitimate rules and principles. We come across a number of views of this kind in Chapter 2

Conceptions and Justifications and in Chapter 3 *Allocation of Property Rights.* As we see from these chapters, even within this group there are significant differences of opinion as to the source of this independently legitimate property. There are those who regard property as a natural right which we have because it is bestowed on us by God or by some other kind of transcendent being. Others, however, regard a right to property as something that is innate in us, a natural (as opposed to legal) right we have by virtue of being human. The function of property law, on this view, is to ensure respect and protection for this innate right of all humans. Yet others regard property as an institution that naturally evolves in all functioning societies as people work out how to organise their resource use collectively for their mutual benefit. Property law's function here is to track and enforce these naturally evolving rules, and is wrong only in so far as it does not do so.

(b) Property as the Product of Law

Others, however, disagree with these views and regard property as simply the product of law. On this view the governing bodies within a state lay down rules regulating the relationships between citizens in respect of things, and property as an institution is the sum of those regulatory provisions. So, taking this view, property is what property law says it is. As Jeremy Bentham puts it:

> Property and law are born together, and die together. Before laws were made there was not property; take away laws and property ceases.[24]

This view of the relationship between property and property law is perhaps the closest to the view we take in the rest of this book, as will be apparent from the working definition we give in the next paragraph. The essential point for our purposes is, however, that this view does not commit us to saying that property law is always right. We can still say that a property law rule is wrong and ought to be changed. We can say that it is wrong because it is unjust, or inefficient, or unworkable because it does not reflect the way people in reality interact with their resources, or inconsistent with principles underpinning other property law rules, or because it promotes and reinforces inequality, or on any one of many other legitimate grounds. What we cannot say is that a property law rule is wrong because it does not accurately reflect 'true' property principles.

1.28 Property: A Working Definition

We are now in a position to provide a working definition of property, focussing here on property as interests in things as opposed to the thing itself or the institution of property:

---

[24] Jeremy Bentham, 'Of Property', *Principles of the Civil Code, in Theory of Legislation: Translated from the French of Etienne Dumont, by R. Hildreth (1871)* (New York: Cornell University Library, 2009) Part I Ch. VIII at p. 113.

> Property consists of a set of all or any of the following – rights, freedoms, powers, immunities, duties or liabilities – which are legally enforceable in relation to a tangible or intangible thing, against others generally and against the state, so that the property holder – who may be any legal entity, or a community, or the public or the state itself – is entitled to rely on the law to prevent all others and (where appropriate) the state from interfering with or infringing her interest in the thing or any of its constituent elements.

This working definition is more complex than the short description at the beginning of the chapter, but probably more useful.

RECOMMENDED READING

This chapter is designed to be read as a self-standing introduction to property law for those who know nothing at all about it. However, since it involves mapping out what is to be discussed in detail in the rest of the book, some parts of it will be hard-going on a first introductory reading, and – like most introductions – it might usefully be read again at a much later stage. The following materials are not essential introductory reading (although they should help clarify some of the obscurities) but they will add a lot to a later re-reading of the chapter.

Felix Cohen, 'Dialogue on private property' (1954) 9 *Rutgers Law Review* 357 at pp. 357–374.

Laura S. Underkuffler *The Idea of Property: Its Meaning and Power* (Oxford: Oxford University Press, 2003) pp. 11–17.

Wesley Newcomb Hohfeld, 'Fundamental legal conceptions as applied in judicial reasoning' (1913) 23 *Yale Law Journal* 16 at pp. 28–37 and (in less detail) pp. 44–47, 53–55 and 58–59.

Kit Barker, 'Private law, analytical philosophy and the modern value of Wesley Newcomb Hohfeld: A centennial appraisal' (2018) 38 *Oxford Journal of Legal Studies* 585 at pp. 585–593.

Franz von Benda-Beckmann, Keebet von Benda-Beckmann and Melanie G. Wiber, 'The properties of property', in Franz von Benda-Beckmann et al., *Changing Properties of Property* (New York and Oxford: Berghahn Books, 2007).

Questions

(1)   On the basis of what you know from this chapter, list property interests you have. In the case of each interest, identify:
  (i) the thing in which you have the interest;
 (ii) the kind of property interest it is;
(iii) the capacity in which you hold the interest (on your own behalf as a private individual, or jointly or in common with someone else, or in your capacity as a member of a community, or as a member of the public, or in some other capacity?); and
(iv) whether anyone else also has property interest(s) in the same things, and if so, what they are.

(2)   List things that are important to you but in which, as far as you know, you have no property interest. They may be tangible or intangible: perhaps the place you live, places you go, services or facilities you use, tangible objects and natural resources which you use or which provide you with some benefit – or any other kind of thing. In the case of each of these things, do you have:

  (i) a freedom to enjoy it in the way you do; or

 (ii) a personal permission from someone; or

(iii) a contractual right; or

(iv) some other kind of legally enforceable right?

Does anyone else have property interests in any of these things? If so, what are they?

(3)   On the basis of Questions 1 and 2, how important is property to you?

2

Conceptions and Justifications

PART I INTRODUCTION

2.1 Why Property?

In a world without property, everyone would be free to use whatever resources they wanted. Property removes resources from this free-use pool by assigning exclusive rights in propertised resources to selected people and groups of people. This is good for those who acquire these exclusive rights, but their gain is everyone else's loss: those of us who were free to use those resources for ourselves are now prohibited from doing so. Hence Proudhon's comment that 'property is theft',[1] and the anonymous nineteenth century English rhyme about the enclosure of common land:

> The law locks up the man or woman
> Who steals the goose from off the common
> But leaves the greater villain loose
> Who steals the common from the goose[2]

How do we justify this diminution in our freedom to use whatever resources we want, whenever we want? What is it that convinces us that it is in our interests to remove resources from the free-use pool by propertising them, even though it means each of us has to give up the universal freedom to use all things in exchange for a hope of being allocated exclusive rights in some few things? In Chapter 1 we suggested some possible answers.[3] In this chapter we examine these supposed benefits of propertisation more closely, and look more broadly at how the institution of property has been justified by property theorists.

---

[1] Pierre-Joseph Proudhon, *What is Property?* Donald R. Kelley and Bonnie G. Smith, eds. and trans. (Cambridge: Cambridge University Press, 1994).

[2] *The Oxford Dictionary of Quotations* (6th edn, Oxford: Oxford University Press, 2004) attributes the rhyme (in a slightly different form) to an anonymous contributor in *The Tickler Magazine*, 1 February 1821. This version appears in Edward Potts Cheyney, *An Introduction to the Industrial and Social History of England* (1920) p. 188.

[3] Paras 1.4 and 1.8.

2.2 Three Fundamental Questions

(a) Why Should There be any Property Rights at all?

Our starting question in this chapter – why should there be any property rights at all – is what Lawrence Becker calls *the problem of general justification* of property rights. However, he points out that there are two other related issues which are difficult to isolate from the problem of general justification. He calls these related issues *the problem of particular justification* and *the problem of specific justification*.[4]

(b) Particular Justification – Who Should Have Property Rights?

Becker's problem of particular justification is this. We have just said that when we propertise things, we each give up our universal freedom to use them, and what we each acquire in exchange is a 'hope' of being allocated exclusive rights in some few things. But surely our willingness to agree to propertisation depends on the principles which will be applied to decide *who* is to get exclusive rights in which things? There is a wide range of principles to choose from, as we see in Chapter 3. We could, for example, adopt a first come, first served principle, so that the first person to take control of a thing in the free-use pool has exclusive rights to it. In addition (or perhaps instead) we could have a principle that whoever makes a thing, or expends labour on it, should thereby acquire exclusive rights in it. Alternatively, we might decide that the state should take on the role of allocating exclusive rights in things to people, in accordance with a democratically agreed set of principles of distribution. The principles of distribution might be based on, for example, fairness, or equality, or need or efficiency. Becker's point is that we need to be able to justify not only the general decision to allow exclusive property rights in things, but also the decisions we then make about the particular principles we are going to apply to determine who gets these exclusive property rights and in which things.

(c) Specific Justification: What Kind of Property Rights and What Things?

This brings us to what Becker calls the problem of specific justification:

> Given that there should be property rights of some kind, what kind(s) should there be? What sorts of things should be owned, and in what ways?

In other words, our enquiry into why we should have property at all and, if we should, the principles to apply in deciding who gets what, is complicated by two factors. The first is that, as we saw in Chapter 1 *What Property Is and Why It Matters*, property rights and interests come in many different forms.[5] Whilst some property theorists talk as if the only alternative to no property is absolute private

---

[4] Lawrence C. Becker, 'The moral basis of property rights' in J. Roland Pennock and John W. Chapman (eds.), *Property: Nomos 22* (New York: New York University Press, 1980) p. 187, at pp. 187–188.
[5] Paras 1.10–1.18.

ownership, most legal systems (our own included) recognise many different kinds of property interest, of which absolute private ownership is just one kind.

Different Kinds of Property Interest

Absolute private ownership of a thing gives a private individual the perpetual right to exclude everyone else in the world (including the state) from the thing, leaving her free to do whatever she wants with it.[6] As we see in Chapter 5 *Ownership and Other Property Interests*, other kinds of property interest may give a different set of rights, freedoms, powers, duties or liabilities in relation to the thing. These other kinds of property interest may be limited in duration rather than perpetual, lasting perhaps only for a fixed period of time, or only for the holder's lifetime. They may give the interest holder only limited rights in relation to the thing (for example, just a right to make use of it in a particular way, or a right to control who uses it). They may require the holder to maintain the thing and manage it in the interests of others rather than in their own interests (consider, for example, the rights and obligations held by a trustee, or by a private charitable organisation such as the National Trust or the Canal and River Trust, over the things they control). Also, as we see in Chapter 8 *Property Interest Holders*, some of these different kinds of property interest may be held by a group of people in common rather than by a single private individual, or they may be held by the public at large, or by the state. All of these different property interests involve exclusion of others and/or the state to some extent, but to a lesser degree or in a different way from the exclusion inherent in absolute private ownership.

Combinations of Different Kinds of Property Interests

The problem of specific justification – what kinds of property interest do we want – is further complicated by the fact that the best solution may involve a combination of different kinds of property interest. In most societies any number of different people and groups may hold different kinds of property interest in the same thing at the same time. So, whilst it does happen quite often that there is a single private absolute owner of a thing, with no-one else having any other property interest in it (in most societies you are probably the only person in the world to have a property interest in your own toothbrush, and that property interest is likely to be absolute private ownership), we are just as likely to encounter more complex resource-sharing webs of property interests.

   For example, in our jurisdiction land containing a reservoir may be owned by an absolute private owner and she may be the only person in the world to have any property interests in the land and in the water.[7] If that is the case, she has the perpetual right to exclude everyone from the land and from the water in the

---

[6] Provided it does not infringe the legal rights of others or contravene general laws relating to, for example, environmental regulation or public health and safety.

[7] In English law she owns the water itself only if the reservoir is 'discrete', i.e. cut off from all other inland waters. The general principle is that no-one owns water unless (and only for so long as) it is 'captured', for example, in a bottle or tanker or some other kind of container. Once the water escapes, no-one owns it.

reservoir. However, she may grant rights to abstract a limited amount of water from the reservoir to each of the neighbouring farmers, she may allow all local inhabitants to fish in the reservoir, and may give her next-door neighbour a right to use a path running across her land. Any of these rights may be perpetual or for a limited period of time. It is equally possible in our law for the land and the reservoir to be owned jointly by the neighbouring farmers (or by any other legal entity), and for them to regulate such things as rights to fish or to abstract water or to gain access over the land by agreement between themselves and/or by granting rights to outsiders. Again, any of these rights may be perpetual or limited in time. In any event, whoever owns the land and whoever holds other property interests in it, no-one is entitled to abstract more than twenty cubic metres of water a day from the reservoir without an abstraction licence issued by the Environment Agency in accordance with the Water Resources Act 1991. These state abstraction licences are themselves property interests.[8]

All the players in these examples hold property interests of one kind or another in the land and/or the water. Becker's point is simply that whilst we may or may not decide that it is justifiable to allow absolute private ownership of land or of water in a reservoir, different considerations arise in relation to different kinds of property interests. So, for example, if we think propertising water is a good thing but we do not think it should be privately owned, there are several viable alternatives we could consider. We might perhaps opt for state ownership, with fishing rights held by the local community and individual abstraction rights held by local farmers. Alternatively we might consider joint or communal ownership of the water by the local farmers as a group, or ownership by a local stakeholder group consisting of representatives of local farmers, anglers, industrial and domestic water users and environmental activists. In both kinds of group – the farmers group and the stakeholder group – each member of the group might be bound by an agreement they have negotiated between themselves as to how the water should be managed in their separate and collective interests. Whoever owns the water might then be subject to state regulation of, for example, the total amount of water that may be abstracted, and the steps that must be taken to maintain drinking water quality and avert environmental damage or flooding.

Different Kinds of Things

The second complicating factor leads on from that. Things also come in many different forms, as we noted in Chapter 1 *What Property Is and Why It Matters*,[9] and forms of property interest that are justifiable for water, for example, may not be justifiable for other things. Consider the differences between, say, water, wild animals, human bodies, student residences, forests, cars and railways. Some of these kinds of thing might be best left unpropertised, so that everyone is free to use them. Others might be best privately owned by individuals who are given the power to

[8] See para. 6.12 of Chapter 6 *New Property Interests and the Numerus Clausus* on 'regulatory licenses' as property interests.
[9] Paras 1.6–1.7.

exclude everyone in the world from them. Others again might be best made subject to some other kind of property interest, or to a combination of different kinds of property interest, so that various different people have different rights to use or control them, either together or at different times, or in different ways.

2.3 Analytical Approaches

So, when we ask the question 'Why should we have property at all?' we should not expect a simple answer. It is likely to depend on how property is to be allocated (the problem of particular justification), and on what kind of property interests we have in mind and what kinds of things we are talking about (the problem of specific justification).

We need to bear these qualifications in mind when considering the theoretical analyses outlined in this and the following chapter. Historically civil law and common law property theorists have not paid much attention to the problem of specific justification, and their arguments for the general justification of property have proceeded on the basis that property means private ownership, in accordance with the classic analysis of property we outlined in Part II of Chapter 1 *What Property Is and Why It Matters*.

In the common law world this self-limiting approach was not seriously challenged until two strands of argument developed in the second half of the twentieth century. The first came from economists and environmentalists who, whilst still taking property to mean private ownership, pointed out that different kinds of thing might demand different property regimes. The second emerged out of Elinor Ostrom's fundamental reassessment of the historic and contemporary significance of communal property.[10] These two developments enable us to scrutinise traditional justificatory theories more closely, as we see in Part III of this chapter.

In the rest of this chapter we consider some traditional and more modern approaches to the questions of general and specific justification – why do we have property at all, and what kind of a property rights system should it be? We move on to the overlapping question of allocation in Chapter 3 *Allocation of Property Rights*.

In Part II of this chapter we look at John Locke's labour-desert justification for private property, which has dominated common law property theory for the last two centuries. Locke's argument is most obviously about wealth maximisation (without property, so the argument goes, we would neglect or squander the natural resources of the planet and fail to invent or develop new things or new ideas) but it is also about individualism (progress and prosperity come from individual human enterprise, not from the state).

In Part III we link Locke's argument with the economic arguments about property and wealth maximisation which emerged with the development of the economic analysis of property law in the second half of the twentieth century. These economic arguments no longer have the ascendancy they once had, but nevertheless they

---

[10] Elinor Ostrom, *Governing the Commons: The Evolution of Institutions for Collective Action* (Cambridge: Cambridge University Press, 1990); see further paras 2.15–2.17 below.

remain influential in common law market economies. We end Part III by looking at Elinor Ostrom's response to these arguments and at other modern critiques of the economic analysis model.

In Part IV we return to traditional justifications of property by looking briefly at two continental philosophers, Kant and Hegel, and their theories of property. Their ideas about property are interesting for our purposes because historically they have been particularly influential in civil law jurisdictions, and because they form the basis of (relatively) new ideas about property and social welfare which are now developing in common law jurisdictions. Kant and Hegel (and the modern neo-Kantians and neo-Hegelians) are concerned not so much with wealth maximisation as with human flourishing: the basic argument is that property is necessary for us to function as free and independent human beings.

Finally in Part V we outline recent developments in US property rights theory which take us in a different direction. In contemporary US property rights theory the focus of attention has shifted from the question of how we justify the institution of property to the question of what property is. Property theorists engaged in this debate are not directly concerned with the question of why we have property at all, nor really in what kinds of property interest we should have, or how property rights should be allocated. Their concern instead is with identifying the essential nature of property, so as to provide society with guidance as to the proper function of property – what it does, and what it is proper for it to do. In Part V we look at two of the dominant opposing schools of thought involved. On the one hand, there is a group of scholars, sometimes called 'information theorists', whose argument, founded on law and economics principles, is that the right to exclude others from things forms the core of property. On that basis, so the argument goes, property's overriding concern is to provide standardised signals to tell all the world to keep off things owned by others. On the other hand, there is a rather more disparate group, the 'progressive property' theorists, who argue that, in resolving property conflicts and in designing property institutions, 'we must look to the underlying human values that property serves and the social relationships it shapes and reflects'.[11]

PART II LOCKE AND PRIVATE PROPERTY

2.4 Locke's Labour-Desert Justification for Private Property

The main part of John Locke's property argument is to be found in Chapter V 'Of Property' in his second *Treatise of Government* published in 1690. He confronts head-on the question we asked at the beginning of this chapter: what is the justification for removing a resource from the common-use pool, depriving us all of our freedom to use it, and instead making it the exclusive property of a private individual? His answer is that it can only ever be justifiable if that individual has

---

[11] Gregory S. Alexander, Eduardo M. Peñalver, Joseph William Singer and Laura S. Underkuffler, 'A statement of progressive property' (2009) 94 *Cornell Law Review* 743.

exerted his labour[12] on the resource, and even then only if two conditions (his provisos) are satisfied. The first proviso, usually called the 'spoilation proviso', is that an individual is justified in taking only 'as much as anyone can make use of to any advantage of life before it spoils ... Whatever is beyond this is more than his share, and belongs to others' (para. 31). The second, the 'sufficiency proviso', is that taking the resource out of the common pool is justified only 'where there is enough, and as good left in common for others' (para. 27).[13]

2.5 Why Should Mixing Your Labour With Something Make It Yours?

(a) Self-ownership

Leaving these provisos aside for a moment – and as we see later, it is not at all clear how far they go – Locke offers two lines of reasoning in answer to the obvious question of *why* mixing your labour with something should make it yours. The first, which he first outlines in para. 27, proceeds as follows. Although everything else in the world is the common heritage of us all, we each have what Locke calls a 'property' in our own 'person', in the sense that no-one else but us has any right in it. It follows, he says, that the labour of our body and the work of our hands are properly ours. When we remove something out of the common pool and mix our labour with it, we join something of ours to it, and thereby make it our property:

> It being by [the labourer] removed from the common state Nature placed it in, it hath by this labour something annexed to it that excludes the common right of other men. For this 'labour' unquestionably being the property of the labourer, no man but he can have a right to what that is once joined to.

This must be right, Locke argues,[14] because we all accept that if someone gathers apples from under apple trees growing in the wild and takes them home and then cooks and eats them, at some point in that process the apples become his:

> I ask, then, when did they begin to become his? when he digested? or when he ate? or when he boiled? or when he brought them home? or when he picked them up?

You might think, as Jeremy Waldron suggests, that the obvious answer would be that the apples became his when his use of them became 'necessarily incompatible with others' common rights',[15] which would seem to be when he ate them. Up to that point he might have been gathering the fruit for the community and preparing it to be eaten by them all communally, but once he put them in his mouth he unequivocally appropriated them for himself to the exclusion of everyone else. However, this was not how Locke saw it. For him it was obvious that the apples

---

[12] Locke does not expressly rule out the possibility that the appropriator might be a woman, but it is clear she could not be a woman who was a wife, child, servant or slave: Barbara Arneil, 'Women as wives, servants and slaves' (2001) 34 *Canadian Journal of Political Science* 29, and see also Margaret Davies, *Property: Meanings, Histories and Theories* (Oxford: Routledge-Cavendish, 2007) pp. 86–96.

[13] See further para. 2.7 below.   [14] Locke para. 28.

[15] Jeremy Waldron, *The Right to Private Property* (Oxford: Clarendon Press, 1988) p. 172.

became the property of the apple gatherer as soon as he gathered them, because that was the point at which he 'mixed' his labour with them:

> ... it is plain, if the first gathering made them not his, nothing else could. That labour put a distinction between them and [the] common. That added something to them more than Nature, the common mother of all, had done, and so they became his private right.[16]

So, by mixing your labour with something, you make a difference to it. But why should that make it yours, bearing in mind that this means that you thereby become entitled to perpetual exclusive use and control of it, to the permanent disadvantage of all the rest of us, who were formerly free to use it? No-one asked you to expend the labour, as both Rousseau and Proudhon took trouble to point out, and we may have preferred you not to have done so:

> 'The rich,' exclaims Jean Jacques [Rousseau], 'have the arrogance to say, 'I built this wall; I earned this land by my labor.' Who set you the tasks? we may reply, and by what right do you demand payment from us for labour which we did not impose upon you?'[17]

And there is another obvious objection, pointed out by Robert Nozick:[18]

> Why isn't mixing what I own with what I don't own a way of losing what I own rather than a way of gaining what I don't? If I own a can of tomato juice and spill it in the sea so that its molecules (made radioactive, so I can check this) mingle evenly throughout the sea, do I thereby come to own the sea, or have I foolishly dissipated my tomato juice?

This is a serious objection, because neither Locke nor anyone else has ever suggested that if I, unasked by you, mix my labour with something that is *already your property*, I gain some entitlement to it. Locke is quite clear that appropriating something which has already become the property of someone else is wrong, however much labour you expend on it, and this is reflected in most legal systems. I simply lose my labour if I expend it on something of yours, and generally you do not even have to account to me for any increase in the value of your asset attributable to my improvements.[19] So Locke has to explain why the position is different when I laboured, unasked, on something that was the common property of us all.

(b) Locke's Labour Theory of Value

Locke's answer lies in his second line of reasoning, which expounds what Waldron calls a labour theory of value.[20] This is first suggested by Locke in para. 28, following on from the passage quoted above:

---

[16] Locke para. 28.

[17] Pierre-Joseph Proudhon, *What is Property? An Inquiry Into the Principle of Right and of Government* (first published 1876) p. 84.

[18] Robert Nozick, *Anarchy, State, and Utopia* (Oxford: Basil Blackwell, 1974) pp. 174–175.

[19] Peter Watts, 'Unrequested improvements to land' (2006) 122 *Law Quarterly Review* 553.

[20] Waldron, *The Right to Private Property*, fn. 15 above, pp. 191–194.

it is the taking any part of what is common, and removing it out of the state Nature leaves it in, which begins the property, *without which the common is of no use.*[21]

Locke's point is that without labour (in the form of human endeavour), land and other natural resources are worth very little. It is the addition of labour that makes them productive, and that gives them value. He explains in paras 40–43:

> 40. Nor is it so strange as, perhaps, before consideration, it may appear, that the property of labour should be able to overbalance the community of land, for it is labour indeed that puts the difference of value on everything; and let any one consider what the difference is between an acre of land planted with tobacco or sugar, sown with wheat or barley, and the same land lying in common without any husbandry upon it, and he will find that the improvement of labour makes the far greater part of the value. I think it will be but a very modest computation to say, that of the products of the earth useful to the life of man, nine-tenths[22] are the effects of labour.

He takes it as self-evident that this increased productiveness of natural resources is to the benefit of us all, not just to the benefit of the appropriator who gets to keep for himself the thing he has made more productive. He invites us to compare the conditions in England with those in America, which to European eyes at that time appeared to be rich in undeveloped natural resources and ripe for colonisation. The American nations, he says,

> are rich in land and poor in all the comforts of life … furnished as liberally as any other people with the materials of plenty – i.e. a fruitful soil, apt to produce in abundance what might serve for food, raiment, and delight; yet, for want of improving it by labour, have not one hundredth part of the conveniencies [sic] we enjoy, and a king of a large and fruitful territory there feeds, lodges, and is clad worse than a day labourer in England.[23]

We may doubt this conclusion, both as a statement of historical fact and as evidence of a universal principle that an increase in the wealth of private individuals necessarily benefits society as a whole. However, Locke's point is a general one: the material wealth of the eighteenth century European nations to which he and his readers belonged was, as he saw it, founded on the freedom of individual citizens to take for themselves resources which had been available for all, not just by appropriating them but by also labouring on them.

(c) Desert and Incentive

It is worth scrutinising more closely this link between labour and private property. Implicit in Locke's argument are some obvious moral and pragmatic justifications for awarding exclusive private ownership to the first person who laboured on a thing. In particular, there is a moral argument that the appropriator *deserves* the entitlement as a reward or payment for his labour, which, even if unsolicited, has

---

[21] Italics added.   [22] Later on in the same paragraph he changes this to 'ninety-nine hundredths'.
[23] Locke para. 41.

resulted in greater prosperity for us all. But there is also a pragmatic argument based on incentive, which has proved to be highly influential and which we come across again when we look at the economic arguments in Part III of this chapter. The argument is that people need to be confident that they will gain exclusive rights over a thing before they will be willing to mix their labour with it in the first place. Why would you work, unless you can keep the product of your labour? It is in the interests of us all that things are made productive, the argument goes, but in a free society things can only be made productive by individuals choosing to work on them, and people will not put labour into something which will remain freely available to all. They will do so only if they are able to appropriate the thing for their own private benefit. In the rest of this chapter we come across several challenges to this assumption. Elinor Ostrom points out that in certain situations people do voluntarily co-operate with each other to manage resources for their collective benefit, rather than striving individually to increase their own wealth, and there is ample evidence that this can provide more effective management of a resource than would have been achieved through putting it in the hands of an individual with exclusive control over it.[24] The incentive argument is also challenged at a different level and for different reasons by the progressive property theorists we look at later[25] and by environmentalists. For both groups the problem is that those who have unconstrained exclusive rights to exploit natural resources for their own private benefit are unlikely to take sufficient account of the effect of their actions on others and on the environment.

2.6 Practical Difficulties

However, before we look at these challenges we need to address some obvious practical difficulties with Locke's basic argument which have been raised by commentators.

(a) What Do We Mean by Labour?

First, we need to give some thought to what is going to count as 'labour' in Locke's account. Does it cover *every* action we perform in relation to a thing, regardless of why we performed it, no matter whether it actually improved the thing, and irrespective of whether the 'labour' is proportionate to the reward? Waldron uses an example of a ham sandwich dropped in a vat of wet cement which illustrates some of these difficulties,[26] and as we have already seen Robert Nozick sees similar

---

[24] Para. 2.16(c) below.   [25] Para. 2.26 below.

[26] Jeremy Waldron, 'Two worries about mixing one's labour' (1983) 33 *The Philosophical Quarterly* 37 at p. 43: 'Suppose there is a vat of wet cement lying about which belongs to nobody in particular, and I drop my ham sandwich into it. Before I can retrieve the sandwich, the cement hardens into a concrete block. (Or, better still: as in Locke's case, the cement is lying about and I intend to drop my sandwich into it, not wanting to retrieve it.) Can I now claim the concrete block in order to protect my entitlement to the sandwich? Can I object, when someone takes the block out of my control, that he is violating my entitlement to the sandwich? Surely that would be regarded as some sort of joke.' The

difficulties with labour which consists of tipping a can of tomato juice into the sea.[27] As Nozick goes on to say:

> Ignore the fact that labouring on something may make it less valuable (spraying pink enamel paint on a piece of driftwood that you have found). Why should one's entitlement extend to the whole object rather than just to the *added value* one's labor has produced?[28]

Locke himself provided no direct answers to these questions, but it has been plausibly argued that we can get round most of the difficulties by interpreting 'labour' here as confined to 'appropriative' or 'productive' labour. 'Appropriative' labour would be any action performed on a thing *with the intention* of appropriating it to the labourer, which deals with some of the difficulties. More of them could be removed by adopting Eric Claeys's argument, that Locke's analysis can be limited to 'productive' labour, by which Claeys seems to mean any activity which is intended to, and could, contribute towards the labourer's prosperity.[29] Hanoch Dagan goes even further, and suggests that, whatever Locke himself said or meant, the intuitive appeal that most people find in his theory assumes or demands that:

> Laborers deserve rewards if and only if they engage in the right kind of activity: useful and purposeful, rather than destructive, inconsequential, or simply inadvertent. They can make a claim to be rewarded if and only if they have added value. (A modified version may also allow such claims for unlucky good faith attempts to add value.) And, finally, the deserved reward must be proportional to the added value they indeed generated.[30]

However, the problem with all these suggested limitations on Locke's labour requirement is that, to a greater or lesser extent, they would require a state bureaucracy to assess and certify in every case whether claimants had exerted the right kind and amount of labour, and (in Dagan's articulation) what kind of property interest they should appropriately be awarded. This robs Locke's theory of what many see as its principle attraction, namely that it provides a bottom-up and largely self-executing allocation of property rather than top-down allocation by the state. We return to this point in para. 2.9.

(b) What Kinds of Thing?

The other practical difficulty is more easily resolved. Another example given by Nozick raises the question of whether it really is the case that I can make *any kind of*

---

point Waldron is making with this example is that the ham sandwich, like labour 'mixed' with an object, is effectively lost in the 'mixing' process.

[27] Para. 2.5(a) above.   [28] Nozick, *Anarchy, State, and Utopia*, fn. 18 above, pp. 174–175.

[29] Eric Claeys, 'Productive use in acquisition, accession, and labour theory' in James Penner and Henry E. Smith (eds.), *Philosophical Foundations of Property Law* (Oxford: Oxford University Press, 2013) p. 13, at pp. 23–24.

[30] Hanoch Dagan, *Property: Values and Institutions* (Oxford: Oxford University Press, 2011) p. 82.

thing mine, just by mixing my labour in it. Nozick gives the example of a private astronaut landing on Mars and clearing a place on it:

> has he mixed his labor with (so that he comes to own) the whole planet, the whole uninhabited universe, or just a particular plot?'[31]

As Claeys points out, examples like this do not just raise questions of exactly *how much* you get by labouring on part of a bigger thing, and whether it is disproportionately large compared to the extent of your labour. There is the additional worry that it seems to allow the labourer to appropriate Mars, or the universe, or (in Nozick's tomato juice example) the whole of the sea as his own private property. Claeys's short and effective answer to this supposed difficulty is that Locke's theory can only ever apply to things which are appropriate for private ownership. As we see in Part III, there is some disagreement about which things fall within this category, but no-one has ever suggested that it should include Mars, the universe or the sea.

2.7 Locke's Limitations – The Provisos

More important than any of these suggested limitations, are Locke's provisos. These are the limitations which he himself set to people's freedom, by labouring, to take natural resources formerly available to all for their own exclusive benefit. Locke was anxious to rebut any suggestion that appropriators were free to take *as much* as they could labour on:

> 31. It will, perhaps, be objected to this, that if gathering the acorns or other fruits of the earth etc. makes a right to them, then any one may engross as much as he will. To which I answer, Not so. The same law of Nature that does by this means give us property, does also bound that property too.

(a) The Spoilation Proviso

His first limitation was that resources were given to us all (whether by nature or, as he sometimes puts it, by God) 'to enjoy'. It follows, therefore, that it is not justifiable to appropriate (even by labour) more than one can make use of, even if there is no shortage and plenty is left for everyone else:

> As much as anyone can make use of to any advantage of life before it spoils, so much he may by his labour fix a property in. Whatever is beyond this is more than his share, and belongs to others. Nothing was made by God for man to spoil or destroy.[32]

Locke makes it clear that this is (only) a moral prohibition against waste of natural resources. It has nothing to do with fairness to others: in Locke's view there is no justification for taking more than you can use even if no-one is deprived because there is plenty left for everyone else. It is not necessary for us to believe that the

---

[31] Nozick, *Anarchy, State, and Utopia*, fn. 18 above, p. 174.   [32] Para. 31, and see also paras 37–38.

environment was provided by God (or by any other transcendental being) to agree with Locke that waste of natural resources is morally objectionable,[33] but we should be aware that this limitation does not go very far. Locke sees no objection to an appropriator taking more than he needs for his own purposes provided that he puts the surplus to use, for example by giving it away, or by bartering it or even, it appears, by selling it:

> 46 ... If he gave away a part to anybody else, so that it perished not uselessly in his possession, these he also made use of. And if he also bartered away plums that would have rotted in a week for nuts that would last good for his eating a whole year, he did no injury; he wasted not the common stock; destroyed no part of the portion of goods that belonged to others ... Again, if he would give his nuts for a piece of metal, pleased with its colour, or exchange his sheep for shells, or wool for a sparkling pebble or a diamond, and keep those by him all his life, he invaded not the right of others; he might heap up as much of these durable things as he pleased; the exceeding of the bounds of his just property not lying in the largeness of his possession, but the perishing of anything uselessly in it.

> 47. And thus came in the use of money; some lasting thing that men might keep without spoiling ...

> 48. And as different degrees of industry were apt to give men possessions in different proportions, so this invention of money gave them the opportunity to continue and enlarge them.

In other words, the waste proviso has nothing to do with equality of distribution either: the appropriator is free to amass vast wealth by appropriation, and then by barter and sale, provided only that he laboured to appropriate and that he let nothing that he appropriated waste or spoil.

(b) The Sufficiency Proviso

If the problem with the spoilation proviso is that it is so much narrower than it first appears, the problem with the sufficiency proviso is that it is not at all clear what the limitation is. When Locke says that an appropriation from the common is justifiable only if there is 'enough, and as good left in common for others', does he mean that the appropriation must leave 'enough and as good' for everyone else to continue to use in common as before, in other words that everyone else's opportunity to use that kind of thing in common is not diminished? Or does he mean that the appropriation must leave enough for everyone else to appropriate for themselves, in other words it must not lessen the opportunity of others to appropriate that kind of thing? Or does he mean that no-one else should be made worse off in general by the appropriation?

---

[33] Although Nozick, writing in 1974 at a time when there was perhaps less environmental awareness, remarked that if an appropriation from the common left 'enough and as good' for everyone else 'is there any motivation for Locke's further condition of non-waste?' (*Anarchy, State, and Utopia*, fn. 18 above, pp. 175–176).

If he means the first or the second – an appropriation must not worsen anyone else's freedom to use that kind of thing or freedom to appropriate that kind of thing – the proviso seems to leave too little room for justifiable appropriations. At best it allows appropriation for your own benefit only if and when the thing you mix your labour with is not scarce (not much help if you think property only becomes necessary when a resource is scarce); at worst, as Robert Nozick has argued, it can be construed as ruling out all appropriations.[34]

If, on the other hand, the proviso means only that appropriations from the common are justifiable if no-one is thereby made worse off in general, the proviso seems to rule out few, if any, appropriations. After all, Locke insists that when we appropriate from the common by mixing our labour with a thing, everyone benefits in a general kind of way. So, we may even, like Eric Claeys, end up with the conclusion that the sufficiency proviso is *always* satisfied, one way or another, in a society like ours.[35] As Claeys sees it, the sufficiency proviso does not rule out appropriations from the common which leave nothing left in the common for others to appropriate, because, he argues, the opportunity to purchase goods in market exchanges replaces (i.e. is 'as good as') the opportunity to appropriate from the common. Further, so he argues, no-one is made worse off by an appropriation from the common if everyone else is still left with an opportunity to earn a reasonable income sufficient for life's purposes (perhaps by being employed by the enriched appropriator, who, as we have just seen, is entitled to sell the surplus of what he has appropriated, and so now has money to employ others to labour on his behalf). And even if there are no sufficient job opportunities offering appropriate wages, Claeys argues that everyone else is still no worse off if they can rely on state welfare (paid for by taxing the appropriators). Writing in 2015, Claeys was content to assume that these requirements are satisfied by the English and American political systems 'tolerably well'.[36]

However, whilst it is not at all clear exactly what Locke meant by saying that an appropriation is legitimate only if it leaves 'as much and as good' for others, it is certainly clear that he did intend it as a significant limitation, even if we are not quite sure when it would come into operation.

2.8 A Third Limitation – The Principle of Charity

This brings us to a third limitation on people's freedom, by labouring, to take for their own exclusive benefit natural resources formerly available to all. This is, however, a different kind of limitation. It does not set up a limit on what, or how much, the first labourer can acquire. Instead, it requires an appropriator to give up some of what he has acquired to any person in 'extreme want'. This stems from

---

[34] For the reason Nozick explained in *Anarchy State and Utopia*, fn. 18 above, at p. 176.

[35] Eric Claeys, 'Productive use' in Penner and Smith (eds.) (fn. 29 above) at p. 27. Stephen Buckle comes to a similar conclusion in *Natural Law and the Theory of Property: Grotius to Hume* (Oxford: Clarendon Press, 1991) pp. 156–159. For criticisms see G. A. Cohen *Self-ownership, Freedom and Equality* (Cambridge: Cambridge University Press, 1995) p. 188.

[36] Claeys, 'Productive use', fn. 29 above, p. 27.

Locke's basic principle that resources were given to people in common 'for the preservation of mankind', giving every person a natural right to the means of subsistence. Locke's clearest expression of this principle, and the obligation he says it imposes on property owners, is not in Chapter V of the Second Treatise where Locke develops his main property argument, but in para. 42 of the First Treatise:

> 42 ... God ... has given no one of his children such a property in his peculiar portion of the things of this world but that he has given his needy brother a right in the surplusage of his goods, so that it cannot justly be denied him when his pressing wants call for it ... for as justice gives very man a title to the product of his honest industry and the fair acquisitions of his ancestors descended to him, so 'charity' gives every man a title to so much of another's plenty as will keep him from extreme want, where he has no means to subsist otherwise.

So, this is not just a personal obligation on private property owners to give to the poor. According to Locke, those in 'extreme want' are *entitled* to have their basic needs satisfied, and entitled to have them satisfied out of the 'surplusage' of appropriated resources. However, the entitlement is only for those who have 'no means to subsist otherwise', and Locke makes it clear elsewhere that those who can earn their living by hiring out their labour to others are not in this position: the principle of charity applies only to those unable to work.[37]

2.9 The Political Appeal of Locke's Theory

As Waldron pointed out in 2015,[38] Locke's account of the justification of private property is a 'bottom-up' theory.[39] In other words, it views property not as the creation of law, nor as something bestowed on people by God (whether directly or via a sovereign with divine right), but as something 'generated and sustained by individuals through their labour and exchange'.[40] As such, property has a legitimacy outside the law, and the only function of the legal system is 'to recognise and accommodate the existence of property rights that were already well established and to facilitate their circulation'.[41] As Locke put it elsewhere in the Second Treatise:

> 123. If man in the state of Nature be so free as has been said, if he be absolute lord of his own possessions, equal to the greatest and subject to nobody, why will he part with his freedom ... and subject himself to the dominion and control of any other power?

---

[37] Gopal Sreenivasan, *The Limits of Lockean Rights in Property* (Oxford and New York: Oxford University Press, 1995) pp. 44–47 and 102–104; see also Waldron, *The Right to Private Property*, fn. 15 above, p. 139.

[38] Jeremy Waldron, '"To bestow stability upon possession": Hume's alternative to Locke' in Penner and Smith (eds.) (fn. 29 above) p. 1 at pp. 1–2.

[39] Richard Epstein, *Design for Liberty: Private Property, Public Administration, and the Rule of Law* (Cambridge, MA: Harvard University Press, 2011), p. 99.

[40] Waldron, 'To bestow stability on possession', fn. 38 above, p. 1.

[41] Waldron, 'To bestow stability on possession', fn. 38 above, p. 2. In other words, Locke's view falls somewhere within the category we noted in para. 1.27(a) of Chapter 1 *What Property Is and Why It Matters*.

> To which it is obvious to answer, that though in the state of Nature he has such a right, yet the enjoyment of it is very uncertain and constantly exposed to the invasion of others . . . . it is not without reason that he seeks out and is willing to join in society with others who are already united, or have a mind to unite for the mutual preservation of their lives, liberties and estates, which I will call by the general name – property.
>
> 124. The great and chief end, therefore, of men uniting into commonwealths, and putting themselves under government, is the preservation of their property . . .

This, he adds, is a significant limitation on the legitimate exercise of power by governments which, if exceeded, justifies popular rebellion and revolution:

> 221 ... the legislative acts against the trust reposed in them [by the people] when they endeavour to invade the property of the subject, and to make themselves, or any part of the community, masters or arbitrary disposers of the lives, liberties, or fortunes of the people.
>
> 222. The reason why men enter into society is the preservation of their property . . . whenever the legislators endeavour to take away the property of the people [other than to limit the power and moderate the dominion of every part and member of the society for the protection of others], or to reduce them to slavery under arbitrary power, they put themselves into a state of war with the people , who are thereupon absolved from any further obedience . . . .

All of this helps to explain why Locke's justification for property has been found so attractive in common law countries. As Waldron goes on to say:

> [Locke's theory of justification is] an attractive theory, to a certain sort of mentality. What sort of mentality? Well, liberal, certainly, on account of its individualism and the orderly rights structure that it generates. Capitalist, obviously, on account of its consecration of industry and markets and its acceptance of the resultant inequality. And, above all, the Lockean account appeals to an anti-statist mentality – or, rather, not anti-statist in any anarchist sense (though there have been Lockeans of that stripe as well), but to any political sensibility that is suspicious of state action, any political sensibility that wishes to regard property rights as a prior constraint on government, relegating the state to the status of service-apparatus: the state doesn't invent property, it exists in order to sustain it.

Locke's acceptance of inequality is worth emphasising. As far as Locke is concerned, it does not matter that, for example, by labouring on a thing an appropriator will be disproportionately rewarded if the value of the thing is not increased by his labour. Nor does it matter that no-one can become a property-owner unless fortunate enough to have had the opportunity to be the first to labour on something available to all, or to be the descendant of such a person, or to be rich enough to buy resources from a first-labourer, or from someone who can trace her title back to a first-labourer. These are prices worth paying, for Locke, because they allow property to be acquired and allocated not by bureaucratic state machinery, calibrating what is a just reward or a fair allocation, but by individual endeavour and the invisible hand of the market. We return to this point in Part IV of Chapter 3 *Allocation of Property Rights*.

PART III PROPERTY, ECONOMICS AND SOCIETY

2.10 Relationship Between Property and Economics

Since economics and property law are both concerned with 'allocating entitlements to scarce resources among competing uses and users',[42] it is not surprising that scholars have attempted to analyse and justify property using basic principles of economics. Economic analyses of property law go back at least as far as the time of Adam Smith[43] and Karl Marx,[44] but the analyses we focus on here developed within the law and economics and institutional economics movements which emerged from the 1950s onwards in the USA.

As far as property law is concerned, the main contribution of these modern economic analyses has been in two areas. The first is the one we are considering in this chapter – what justifies the institution of property. The second concerns the resolution of conflicts between neighbours: for example, between me and the noisy family who live next door, or between a developer who wants to build a tall tower on her land, and her neighbour who complains that the tower will spoil his view and overshadow his garden. We look at this second area in Chapter 10 *Limitations on Property*.

In this part of the chapter we look at classic accounts of why we need (private) property provided by Garrett Hardin and Harold Demsetz, drawing on economic principles, and at some criticisms of their accounts, in particular the alternative analysis put forward by Elinor Ostrom. She provides a much richer picture of the role of property in resource management, and of the ways in which communities evolve systems for the collective management of their resources. She is not directly concerned with our central question in this chapter, of why have property at all. Her interest is in institutional arrangements for resource management, and she is not too concerned as to how they should be analysed in property terms. However, her analysis has profound implications for the kinds of property interest we should recognise in order to make the best use of resources – in other words, for Becker's problem of specific justification.

Before looking at these three accounts, we first need to say something about some of the economic concepts utilised in their arguments and the basic economic principles either assumed or challenged in them.

2.11 Basic Economic Concepts and Principles

(a) Rational Maximisation of Self-Interest

It is a basic assumption of earlier economic analyses of property law that people are rational maximisers of their own self-interest. As we will see, both Demsetz and

---

[42] Daniel H. Cole and Peter Z. Grossman, *Principles of Law & Economics* (2nd edn, New York: Wolters Kluwer, 2011) p. 53.

[43] Adam Smith, *An Inquiry into the Nature and Causes of the Wealth of Nations* (first published 1776, this edition Oxford: Oxford University Press, 1993), usually referred to as *The Wealth of Nations*.

[44] Karl Marx, *Communist Manifesto* (first published 1848) Chapter II: 'Proletarians and communists', and see also C. B. Macpherson (ed.) *Property: Mainstream and Critical Positions* (Toronto: University of Toronto Press, 1978) Chapter 5.

Hardin make this assumption, although it is later challenged by Ostrom (amongst others), drawing on behavioural economics.

What is being assumed here is that people make rational decisions, based on information available to them, so as to maximise their own utility, wealth or happiness. This is not the same as assuming that people are selfish, as Cole and Grossman explain:

> [the assumption that people are rational maximisers of their own self-interest] reflects two standard assumptions of economic theory: (1) that individuals look after their self-interest and (2) that they rationally respond to price signals [e.g. the price at which they could buy or sell something, relative to its value to them and to the price or value of alternative preferences] and to other incentives in the marketplace to garner as much utility, wealth, or happiness as possible. These assumptions often engender confusion, so it is important to be clear about what they mean and do not mean. Some critics of economic theory abhor the supposition that people are invariably selfish and greedy. But that is *not* what these assumptions maintain. They merely posit that people attempt to satisfy, to the maximum extent possible under the circumstances, whatever desires or preferences they have in life. To assume that Mother Theresa maximised her preferences to improve the lot of those less fortunate in life is emphatically *not* to assert that she was a greedy and egocentric individual; yet her behaviour was entirely consistent with economic theory.[45]

It is also important to appreciate that the assumption involves assuming that people do take positive action and respond to incentives. So, if someone discovers that she could buy for £30 a book that would be worth £35 to her, and she has £30, and it would maximise her utility or happiness to spend that £30 on the book rather than to do something else with it (such as spend it on something else or put it towards her savings), she will buy the book: she will not just sit back, not bothering to do anything.

(b) Markets and the 'Invisible Hand of the Market'

From this last proposition, that is, that people positively respond to incentives, Richard Posner derives what he describes as a basic economic principle, and which is one of the foundational principles of free market capitalism. This is that:

> resources tend to gravitate towards their most valuable uses if voluntary exchange – a market – is permitted .... By a process of voluntary exchange, resources are shifted to those uses in which the value to consumers, as measured by their willingness to pay, is highest. When resources are being used where their value is highest, we may say that they are being employed efficiently.[46]

In other words, to adopt the metaphor made famous by Adam Smith in *The Wealth of Nations*,[47] the market operates as an 'invisible hand'. This invisible hand of the

---

[45] Cole and Grossman, *Law & Economics*, fn. 42 above, at p. 8, and see also Richard A. Posner, *Economic Analysis of Law* (3rd edn Boston and Toronto: Little, Brown and Company, 1986) pp. 3–4.
[46] Posner, *Economic Analysis of Law* p. 9.   [47] Adam Smith, *Wealth of Nations* Book IV, fn. 43 above.

market ensures that when buyers and sellers are able to trade freely, even though each will pursue only her own interests, the cumulative effect of these voluntary exchanges is that we end up with what is, from the perspective of society as a whole, the most efficient allocation of resources (very much more efficient than anything that can be achieved by government regulation). This, so the argument goes, is because each voluntary exchange in a free market results in the resource moving to someone who values it more because he can see a better (more wealth-enhancing?) use for it.[48]

This has obvious political implications, but it also has important implications for the kind of property rights systems we might want to adopt. Generally, only private property interests can be bought and sold in markets. If free markets produce the most efficient use of resources, do we then have to assume that, if we want to ensure the most efficient use of resources, they must all be privately owned? We return to this question later.

For the present, however, we should note that it is generally accepted in modern economic theory that in the real world, markets never are perfect. A number of factors can prevent a voluntary exchange taking place at all, or make the exchange produce inefficient outcomes, so that the market does not operate effectively. For our purposes, the most important of these factors are those relating to the nature of the resource itself (markets are said not to work for 'public goods'), and the factors that economists refer to as transaction costs (which include the strategic behaviour of free-riders and hold-outs), and externalities.[49]

(c) Public Goods, Rivalrousness and Excludability

Even the most staunch free market economist does not believe that markets work for all kinds of resources. There are some resources – 'public goods' – which, so the argument goes, have to be supplied by governments because they provide benefits, or even essentials, to the public, but no individual person (or, at least, no rational maximiser of his own self-interest) is interested in owning them or providing them. A 'public good' is said to have two characteristics: it is non-rivalrous (which, as we saw in para. 1.6(c) of Chapter 1 *What Property Is and Why It Matters*, means that use by one person does not reduce the amount available to others), and it is 'non-excludable' (it is impossible, or at least disproportionately difficult or expensive, to exclude people from it). Lighthouses were traditionally put forward as a classic example of public goods.[50] Lighthouses were built in order to shine lights to guide ships in the sea. Light from a lighthouse is non-rivalrous: if I use it to guide me into a harbour it does not reduce the amount of light available to anyone else. It is also non-excludable: if you build and operate a lighthouse you will not be able to charge ship owners or any else for use of the light, so it is argued. This is because the light

---

[48] Ibid. Ch ii pp. 291–292.
[49] For a good overview, see Cole and Grossman, *Law & Economics*, fn. 42 above, pp. 16–21
[50] John Stuart Mill uses the example in *Principles of Political Economy* Book V Ch. XI, s. 15 (first published 1848, published London: Penguin, 1970, p. 342). He may not have been the first to do so.

will shine on everyone, whether they have paid for it or not, and it is simply too difficult or too expensive to exclude non-payers from the sight of it. So, no-one is going to want to build lighthouses.

There are a number of difficulties with this analysis. The first is that we are not even sure whether, historically, it was true even of lighthouses, never mind of anything else. In the 1970s Ronald Coase, probably the most influential figure in the law and economics movement in the twentieth century, decided to test the classic example and investigate who had in fact built and financed lighthouses in the past. He discovered that it was not true that they had invariably been provided out of public funds: he was able to find several historic examples of what he said were privately owned and financed lighthouses in England.[51] While some scholars have disputed this, arguing that Coase overlooked significant elements of government subsidy in the examples he considered,[52] it seems clear that the classic economic assumptions about public goods are oversimplifications. One complication is that, as Cole and Grossman point out, whether a resource qualifies as a public good may change over time:

> Something that is deemed a public good today (such as the atmosphere) may become efficiently privatisable at some point in the future, when the problems of nonexcludability and [non-rivalrousness] are resolved. Economists have explained, for example, that the innovation of barbed wire in the 1870s greatly reduced the cost of enclosing land, thereby facilitating settlement and privatisation of public lands in the Western United States. So, what counts as a public good may change.[53]

Perhaps more importantly, the internet has now taught us that there are many ways in which individuals can amass vast private wealth supplying non-excludable and non-rivalrous services to the public, for which the consumers of the service pay nothing and governments provide no subsidy. So, we know that in some circumstances private owners are very good at producing or regulating goods that come within the classic definition of public goods. This raises the question of whether perhaps the reverse is also true: perhaps private ownership is not always the best way of producing or regulating some non-public goods? We come back to this in para. 2.12 below.

(d) Transaction Costs

It is nearly always costly for people to enter into a transaction about resources, or to come to some other kind of an agreement about resources with each other. The cost, which may take the form of money, or time or labour or anything else, may be so

---

[51] Ronald Coase, 'The lighthouse in economics' (1974) 17 *Journal of Law and Economics* 357.

[52] E. Bertrand, 'The Coasean analysis of lighthouse financing: Myths and realities' (2006) 30 *Cambridge Journal of Economics* 389 and W. Barnett and W. Block, 'Coase and Van Zandt on lighthouses' (2007) 35 *Public Finance Review* 710.

[53] Cole and Grossman, *Law & Economics*, fn. 42 above, pp. 20–21. The barbed wire example comes from Terry L. Anderson and Peter J. Hill, 'The evolution of property rights: A study of the American West' (1975) 18 *Journal of Law and Economics* 163.

high that it prevents the transaction taking place or the agreement being made at all. These costs include the costs of obtaining information – all parties need to have full information about the resource itself, about the other parties, about the likely effect of the transaction on themselves and on the other parties and its likely value to themselves and to the others. In everyday transactions like buying or selling an ordinary house or flat it is quite easy (although not cheap) to find out all this information: market prices are readily available, skilled professionals can be hired, and there are standardised procedures for finding out about the physical state of the house and the property interest that the seller has to sell. In other situations, however, it is not so easy. Consider, for example, what you would need to find out, and how you would do it, if you wanted to buy (or sell) a derelict disused cinema, or you wanted to come to some agreement with your noisy neighbour about what should be done to your house and/or to theirs (and by whom and at whose cost) to ensure that you are no longer disturbed by the noise. In addition to the costs of obtaining the information, there will also be the costs of bargaining, negotiating and coming to an agreement about the terms of the transaction or agreement, followed by the costs of formalising it. And if the transaction or agreement involves an ongoing relationship between the parties, there will be the costs of monitoring its performance, deciding how to react to any breaches by other parties, and then taking any necessary enforcement action.

(e) Free-Riders and Hold-Outs

Transactions costs can be particularly high when groups of people are involved in agreements or transactions about resources. This is partly because of the obvious costs the members of the group will incur in co-ordinating their activities (arranging and attending meetings between themselves, for example, or pooling information and coming to a joint decision). However, economists point out that they face an additional transaction costs problem, which is the danger that some of those involved will engage in what economists call 'strategic behaviour'. There are two kinds of strategist to fear here: the free-rider and the hold-out. The argument is that the existence, or even the threat, of free-riders and hold-outs may make it impossible for any agreement about resources to be reached, and even if agreement is reached, it will probably be inefficient.

A free-rider is someone who refuses to share the costs and obligations involved in taking the action, knowing that the others can't or won't be able to exclude him from the benefits they will all get if the action is taken. So, if a group of ship owners decided to pool their resources to build a new lighthouse because they knew it would decrease the number of shipping accidents in that area, to the benefit of them all, the free-rider would be the ship owner who refused to pay his share, knowing that the light from the lighthouse will guide his ships as well as everyone else's, whether he pays his share or not. If there are too many free-riders, the others may not be able to afford to build the lighthouse; and even one free-rider might be enough to make the others unwilling to go ahead with the project, and will certainly increase the costs borne by each of those who participate if they do go ahead. A more up-to-date example might be a group of neighbours who want to campaign against the noise made by a nearby motor racing track. The free-rider is the neighbour who does mind about the noise but declines to take part in the campaigning activities, knowing that if the campaign succeeds she will benefit whether she has helped out or not.

A hold-out, on the other hand, is someone whose co-operation is essential for an action to go ahead, and who, realising that, holds out for a better deal than she would otherwise have accepted, knowing that the action cannot go ahead without her. Cole and Grossman give the example of a film company wanting to shoot a period film in a street, and offering to pay households $100 each to take down their satellite dishes for a week, a price that, in the film company's experience, most people are happy to accept. The hold-out is the householder who, realising this, refuses to take down her satellite dish unless she is paid $200,[54] knowing that one satellite dish visible in the street will be enough to ruin the film. Another example might be a group of neighbours who each have a right to use a communal garden. The grass has just been re-seeded and it will be spoilt if anyone walks on it for the next few weeks. The hold-out is the neighbour who refuses to stop walking on the grass unless the others pay him not to exercise his right to do so.

(f) Externalities

Most of the actions we take in relation to resources (and other things) have external effects which are not felt by us. They may be good effects or bad effects. *Externalities* are the good effects of our actions which bring us no benefits, and the bad effects of our actions which impose no costs (financial or otherwise) on us. If I grow flowers in my garden it may give great pleasure to my neighbour who enjoys looking at them through his window, and real misery to another neighbour who suffers badly from hay fever. If I am a rational maximiser of my own self-interest, I will not take into account either of the effects on my neighbours when I decide to grow the flowers (unless of course they are in some way brought home to me, for example by a law making me liable in tort for exacerbating my neighbour's hay fever). Whether any effect is, or is wholly, an externality does of course depend on the circumstances, and it is not always straightforward. My flowers might also attract birds and bees into the garden, which would be good for the environment, helping to sustain these species. Whether I take this into account when deciding whether to grow the flowers, and how much weight I give to it, depends on whether, how much, and for what reasons, I value their presence in my garden: I may be totally indifferent to them, or may quite enjoy watching them, or feel morally obliged to help to sustain them, or want them to come into the garden to eat the slugs and pollinate the flowers, making it easier for me to look after the garden.

Externalities are regarded by economists as inefficient. Generally speaking, resources will be put to their most efficient use (and the environment will suffer the least) if we bear all the consequences of our actions – or, as economists put it, if

---

[54] See Cole and Grossman, *Law & Economics*, fn. 42 above, pp. 22–23.

all the externalities are internalised.[55] It is difficult to think of any real world examples of relations with resources which produce no externalities (i.e. in which all externalities are internalised), but, as we shall see, law and economics advocates of private property systems take the view that one of the advantages of private property is that it provides the best means of internalising externalities.

(g) Prisoner's Dilemma

The 'prisoner's dilemma' is an example used by economists (and others) to demonstrate 'how strategies designed to maximise individually best outcomes may result in socially worst outcomes'.[56] It is relevant for our purposes because it is often used to explain how transaction costs (specifically, the costs of collective action) prevent individuals in a group acting in their collective self-interest. The example is this. A and B are two prisoners each facing a one year prison sentence for a minor offence which the police can prove they committed. The police suspect, but cannot prove, that they also committed a more serious offence. If they were convicted of the more serious offence they would each get three years. The police separate A and B so they cannot communicate with each other, and make the same offer to each of them: if you confess to the more serious offence and testify against the other you will get probation and the other will get five years. The best outcome for A and B combined would be if neither of them confessed (each would then get one year). But since neither of them knows what the other will do, it is in the best self-interest of each to confess (consider why). So, both will confess and each will get three years. We come back to this in para. 2.13, when we look at arguments by economists that communities are by their nature unable to regulate their shared resources efficiently.

2.12 Garret Hardin: 'The Tragedy of the Commons'

One of the most significant events in the study of property and economics in the twentieth century was the publication in 1968 of Garret Hardin's essay 'The Tragedy of the Commons'.[57] Hardin was not in fact an economist (or a lawyer). He was a socio-biologist and his main concern in 'The Tragedy of the Commons' was population control, not why we should have property in resources. Nevertheless, his graphic account of what happens when too many people are chasing too few resources has traditionally been used by free market economists in support of their arguments justifying private property. This in turn has led others to question

---

[55] The classic exponent of this view was Arthur Pigou, in *The Economics of Welfare* (first published in 1920, published by New York: Routledge, 2002), although his argument was that this should be done by government intervention, taxing or fining those who produced harmful externalities and providing subsidies for activities producing socially beneficial externalities. For the view that private (as opposed to communal) property is the most efficient means of internalising externalities see Harold Demsetz, 'Towards a theory of property rights' (1967) 57*American Economic Review* 347.

[56] Cole and Grossman, *Law & Economics*, fn. 42 above, p. 23, and see pp. 23–26 and 119–121 for a fuller account.

[57] Garrett Hardin, 'The tragedy of the commons' (1968) 162 *Science* 1243.

whether Hardin's account is necessarily a true account of what happens in the real world, and to develop more complex theoretical analyses of what property is, and the different ways in which it does and could shape our interactions with scarce resources.

(a) Hardin's Argument

Harding's argument in 'The Tragedy of the Commons' was that once a resource becomes scarce, it will inevitably become overexploited to the point of destruction if it is left 'open to all'. The principal example he used to illustrate his thesis was a pasture ground used by herdsmen to graze their cattle. He argued that each herdsman would want to keep as many cattle as possible on the pasture land, and that such an arrangement could work for centuries whilst 'tribal wars, poaching, and disease' kept the numbers below the carrying capacity of the pasture.[58] However, once full capacity is reached 'the inherent logic of the commons remorselessly generates tragedy'.[59] Each herdsman, as a rational being, will seek to maximise his gain, Hardin argues. Accordingly, he will calculate that, whilst he will be able to keep the whole of the profit to be made from raising and selling each extra animal he grazes on the pasture, he will have to bear only a fraction of the cost of the damage caused to the pasture by having to carry an additional animal. This is because the total cost will be shared with all the other herdsmen. In other words, a large proportion of the damage that will be caused if he increases the number of animals he grazes on the pasture will be an externality to him, whereas the benefit of doing so will be wholly internalised – he will be able to keep it all for himself. Each of the herdsmen comes to the same conclusion and, acting in their own rational self-interest, they each increase the number of cattle they graze on the pasture until it is irreversibly exhausted. Hardin famously concludes:

> Therein is the tragedy. Each man is locked into a system that compels him to increase his herd without limit – in a world that is limited. Ruin is the destination towards which all men rush, each pursuing his own best interest in a society that believes in the freedom of the commons. Freedom in a commons brings ruin to all.[60]

He argued that the same phenomenon threatens areas of outstanding natural beauty such as Yosemite Valley (there comes a point where there are so many visitors that their number destroys the qualities they came to enjoy) and inexorably leads rivers to be destroyed by pollution.[61] Hardin's conclusion was that the root of the problem lies in uncontrolled population growth (what he describes as the 'intolerable ... freedom to breed') and that the only real answer is compulsory birth control. As far as he was concerned, the resource examples he gave (the herdsmen, national park and river pollution examples) were analogous: the real problem was 'the commons',

---

[58] Ibid. p. 1244.
[59] By 'tragedy' he does not mean just any 'tragic' (in the sense of disastrous) event: he means a disastrous event that must inevitably happen if we follow a certain course of action.
[60] Hardin, 'The tragedy of the commons', fn. 57 above, p. 1244.   [61] Ibid. p. 1245.

by which he meant a resource which 'allowed freedom of access to all'. His answer was that freedom of access must be restricted. In the case of uncontrolled population growth, the only way of achieving that was, he argued, state imposed compulsory birth control. In the case of resources, they had to be either owned by the state, which would then have to regulate access, or they would have to be privately owned, because private ownership, by definition, prevents free access.[62]

(b) 'Commons' or 'No-Property'?

As far as resources are concerned, there are two fundamental criticisms that can be made of Hardin's argument, even if one accepts the basic economic principles he assumes (and as we see below, not everyone does). The first is that although Hardin uses the term 'the commons', what he is describing is not a 'commons' as we understand it, because he postulates that everyone is free to use the resource as they like. As we saw in para. 1.17 of Chapter 1 *What Property Is and Why It Matters*, a 'commons', in the generally accepted sense of the word, means a resource which is communally held, in other words it is owned, used or controlled by a limited group of people, with power (in law or in fact) to prevent access by outsiders. If everyone is free to use a resource as they like, then the resource is not propertised at all – no property regime of any kind applies to it. Most people would agree that the 'tragedy' described by Hardin can indeed threaten unpropertised resources which have become scarce. This is because there are no institutions for devising and enforcing a system for regulating use: by definition, unpropertised resources are subject to no property law system. However, such institutions can easily be supplied, and the tragedy averted, by the imposition of *any* property law regime, provided the property rules within that regime regulate the use of the resource effectively. This can be done by introducing a regime of private, communal, public or state property interests, or a regime that utilises a combination of all or some of them. The challenge, as Elinor Ostrom recognised, is to establish the kind of property regime best suited to the governance of that particular resource. We return to this point in paras 2.13 and 2.14, but meanwhile we can say that what Hardin describes is the 'tragedy' of a no-property world, not the tragedy of 'the commons'.

(c) Inevitability of Destruction?

The second difficulty with Hardin's analysis is that he does not sufficiently explain why destruction of the resource is inevitable, given the basic economic principles he assumes, nor does he fully explore the other potential problems that economics tells us can arise when everyone is free to use a scarce resource. We need to turn to Harold Demsetz's seminal article, 'Towards a Theory of Property Rights'[63] for a fuller and more persuasive account of what is essentially the same argument.

---

[62] Ibid. p. 1248.   [63] Demsetz, 'Towards a theory of property rights', fn. 55 above.

2.13 Harold Demsetz: 'Towards a Theory of Property Rights'

Hardin uses the word 'tragedy' to describe an inevitable outcome, and his argument is that destruction of the resource is inevitable because it is in each herdsman's rational self-interest to add another animal to graze on the pasture. But why is that so? Hardin's explanation (that each individual's gain exceeds that individual's share of the loss) is not of itself sufficient. Rational self-interest takes long-term as well as short-term gains and losses into account (even if not necessarily giving equal weight to each). Going back to Hardin's pasture example, suppose that at present five herders are each grazing 10 cattle on the pasture and at that level of grazing each animal gets just about enough to eat and the pasture still regenerates itself each year. Each herder must surely know that, if no more animals are added, the pasture will provide her with sufficient feed for her 10 cattle every year for the foreseeable future. She must also realise that if she adds another animal, there is a danger that the other herders will do the same, and so the pasture will be exhausted within, say, two years. So, if she decides not to add another animal, she will have enough feed for 10 cattle for an unlimited number of years into the foreseeable future; if she decides to add another animal, she will have instead just two years' worth of feed for 11 cattle. So why does she nevertheless add the 11th animal?

(a) Why Does the Herder Discount Long-Term Effects of Over-Use?

Hardin fails to provide an explanation, but Demsetz does.[64] The herder adds another animal even when she knows it will over-tax the pasture because she fears that, whether she does so or not, the other herders will add other animals for themselves. If they do that, the pasture will be exhausted within two years even if she does not add another animal herself. Since there is no way she can stop them (because each is either entitled or free to do whatever they want on the pasture) and cannot know in advance whether or when it will happen, it is rational for her to add the extra animal herself now. There is no point in her trying to mitigate the damage either, argues Demsetz, perhaps by adding fertiliser to the pasture so that it can support the additional animals. This is because, if she does that, she will bear all the cost of the improvement whereas the benefit of it will be spread between all five herders: the costs of the improvement would all be internalised to her, whereas most of the benefit would be an externality. So, once the pasture reaches that critical stage, she has only two real choices. She can continue to graze just 10 cattle, knowing that the pasture will probably be exhausted in two years because the others will probably increase their grazing whatever she does. Or she can increase the number of animals she grazes to 11, knowing that this will destroy the pasture in two years, but also knowing that for two years she will be able to feed 11 animals instead of 10 for the same outlay. Being a rational maximiser of her own self-interest, she will choose the second of these.

---

[64] Ibid. pp. 354–357.

(b) Why Don't the Herders Co-operate?

But if our herder sees all of this, so too must all the other herders. Why don't they get together and come to some agreement about sustainable use of the pasture, whether by rationing the number of animals each of them can graze on it, or by pooling resources to improve it so that it will take more animals, or by both? Demsetz's answer is that they will inevitably be deterred from doing so by transaction costs. He invites us to consider land that is 'communally owned'. According to Demsetz, this means that each member of the community has a right to do whatever he wants with it (every person 'has the right to hunt, till, or mine the land'). Like Hardin, he points out that, because of the externalities problem, the result will be that everyone 'will tend to overhunt and overwork the land because some of the costs of his doing so are borne by others [and so the] stock of game and the richness of the soil will be diminished too quickly'. He then goes on to say, at pp. 344–345, that transaction costs will prevent the community from getting together to regulate their use of the land:

> It is conceivable that those who own these rights, i.e., every member of the community, can agree to curtail the rate at which they work the lands if negotiating and policing costs are zero. Each can agree to abridge his rights. It is obvious that the costs of reaching such an agreement will not be zero. What is not obvious is just how large these costs may be.
>
> Negotiating costs will be large because it is difficult for many persons to reach a mutually satisfactory agreement, especially when each hold-out has the right to work the land as fast as he pleases. But, even if an agreement among all can be reached, we must yet take account of the costs of policing the agreement, and these may be large, also.

In other words, so the argument goes, the members of the community are in the kind of prisoner's dilemma we noted in para. 2.11(g): they are aware that by acting together they could, individually and as a group, gain more than by acting separately, but they are prevented by transaction costs and free-rider and hold-out problems from co-operating.

(c) Demsetz's 'Commons'

Before considering the substance of this argument, we should first note something odd about Demsetz's example. Unlike Hardin, Demsetz seems to be referring to communal property rather than to no-property (each member of the community has a *right* to use the land; it is not the case that everyone is just *free* to use it). However, this is not a kind of communal property that would ever exist in the real world, because it appears to give every member an unfettered right to do *whatever they want with the land* ('the right to hunt, till or mine the land'), regardless of how this affects the similar right held by every other member. This is a misunderstanding of the rights that members of a community have in a communally used resource. As we pointed out in para. 1.17 of Chapter 1 *What Property Is and Why It Matters*, each member of the community does indeed have a right to use the communal resource, but only in common with every other member of the community, who each has a like right. If we each had a right to do whatever we wanted with the land, we would, as Hohfeld pointed out, each also have a duty not to interfere with the exercise of everyone else's right to do whatever they wanted with the land. This leads to a stalemate: no-one can do anything on the land without infringing the rights of the others. The only way of breaking the stalemate is for everyone to agree *how* to exercise their individual rights in common with each other. So, if the land is communally owned and it is used in any way at all by anyone, it must be by virtue of some kind of agreement or social convention between the members of the community that it should be used in that way. The same applies here as it does to the exercise of public rights. We each have a right, in common with everyone else, to sit on a bench in a public park, but we cannot all sit on the same bench at the same time. Social conventions arise by consensus, telling us when it is acceptable to exercise our right to sit on the bench. So, Demsetz's model of communal property, where everyone has a *right* to do whatever they want on the land, cannot but be self-regulated to some degree, whether by express or tacit agreement within the community.

2.14 Elinor Ostrom: 'Governing the Commons'

In *Governing the Commons*,[65] first published in 1990, Elinor Ostrom's response to the economic analyses developed by Hardin and Demsetz was, essentially, to ask two questions. First, if they were correct, we would expect communal property to be rare and to be associated with poorly managed resources of deteriorating quality. But this is not the case. There are many well-documented examples from all over the world of long-lasting robust self-governing communal property institutions. How can we account for these?

Her second question was, if the 'Tragedy of the Commons' is not the inevitable outcome when resources are communally used or controlled, how do we identify which communal property institutions 'work' and which are likely to fail?

2.15 Ostrom's Analysis of Successful Communal Property Institutions

As Ostrom pointed out, evidence has been available for a long time of enduring communal property regimes which do not appear to be suffering the tragedy of the commons. In the mid-1980s Ostrom was able to bring together data collected by scholars from multiple disciplines who had, between them, studied at least 1000 cases of communal resource use involving different kinds of resources in many parts of the world. She was instrumental in setting up an international database of these and later communal property studies, and analysis of this data produced at least preliminary answers to both of Ostrom's questions. First, it was apparent that subsisting robust self-governing communal property institutions were not isolated anomalies.

---

[65] Ostrom, *Governing the Commons*, fn. 10 above.

Although communal resource users like Hardin's herdsmen did sometimes fail to develop workable resource-use rules, they also sometimes succeeded. The economists' argument that failure was inevitable was, therefore, simply untenable, at least in so far as it was said to apply to communal resource use as opposed to genuinely free-access resource use (i.e. where the resource was not propertised at all).

2.16 Ostrom's Critique of the *Tragedy of the Commons* Analysis

Given that communal property does seem to work in practice, at least in relation to some kinds of resource in some circumstances, there must be something wrong with the 'Tragedy of the Commons' thesis developed by Hardin and Demsetz. Ostrom argued that the basic problem was oversimplification. Mid-twentieth scholars like Hardin and Demsetz, she argued:

> posited two optimal organisational forms [private property and centralised government ownership], two types of goods [private goods and public goods], and one model of the individual [the rational maximiser of his own self-interest].[66]

As she pointed out, reality is more complex in all three respects.

(a) Oversimplification of Organisational Forms

We saw that for Hardin, the only choice of property regimes to avert the tragedy of the commons was private ownership or state ownership. We have already noted that this fails to take into account communal property as a viable alternative organisational form for resource governance. However, even if we add in communal property as a third possibility, we are still oversimplifying the picture. The complex reality, as we saw in paras 1.15–1.18 of Chapter 1 *What Property Is and Why It Matters*, is that these three forms each themselves come in a range of different forms, so that what we have is a spectrum of forms of property interest rather than three distinct types. And, to add to the complexity, management of any particular resource often involves a combination of these different forms of property interest. If we take Hardin's herders as an example, in real life there are likely to be at least three different forms of property interest involved. Each herder is the private owner of the cattle she grazes, and this is likely to be either simple absolute private ownership, or perhaps private ownership shared between her and members of her family. However, each herder also holds a property interest in the pastureland – the right that she has to graze her cattle on the pastureland in common with each of the other herders who have a like right. This is a hybrid private–communal right: she holds the right individually, but it is exercisable by her only in common with others. Then there is the pastureland itself. In most jurisdictions it will be owned by someone, but this 'ownership' will be different from the 'ownership' that the herders have in their cattle, because it is subject to the herders' grazing rights. So, the pasture owner will

---

[66] Elinor Ostrom, 'Beyond markets and states: Polycentric governance of complex economic systems' (2010) 100 *American Economic Review* 641, at p. 663.

have few of the benefits of simple private ownership. Also, the precise rights and obligations that the pasture owner may have as against the holders of the grazing rights, and the way in which the pastureland and the grazing are managed, will to a large extent depend on who the pasture owner is. It may be the herders themselves who co-own the pasture, or it may be owned by a private individual, or the state, or any other kind of public or private institution (perhaps a local authority, a local farmers' cooperative, or the National Trust or other conservation body, or a global commercial agricultural enterprise). This is very far from the kind of simple absolute private ownership or monolithic state control envisaged by Hardin.

For Ostrom and others, sceptical about the utility of the categorisations of property rights that lawyers tend to adopt, the important point is to distinguish between rights of access to a resource, rights of withdrawal,[67] rights of management,[68] rights of exclusion[69] and rights of alienation.[70] As we can see from our herders example, these rights might be split between different individuals or communities or institutions in a variety of different ways, and there are various ways in which these diverse rights might be combined to manage the resource. The resulting combinations might operate hierarchically or co-operatively or by a mix of both, and, depending on the social and ecological context, some combinations will work well, others will just about manage, and yet others will fail. As Ostrom said, reviewing studies of forest governance:

> We found that it is possible for local users of a forest to self-organize and develop their own set of rules for managing a forest. Some groups try and fail while others succeed. Others start a system that collapses over time . . . Further, we found some government forests that operate well and are able to sustain forest conditions in good shape over time. We found some private forests that work well and also some co-managed forests. In other words, it is not the general type of forest governance that makes a difference but rather how a particular governance arrangement fits the local ecology, how the specific rules are developed and adapted over time, and whether users consider the system to be legitimate and equitable.[71]

In particular, active participation of local users of the resource in its management seemed to be a key element, and so too did willingness of government 'to work with local and regional officials, nongovernment organisations, and local groups of citizens'.[72] So again, it is by no means correct to say that the management of such resources involves a stark choice between private ownership and state ownership.

---

[67] Usually taken to mean rights to withdraw benefits from it (the grass taken from the pasture when the cattle eat it); but 'withdrawal' can be extended to cover also other effects on the resource, such as the negative and positive effects the cattle have on the pastureland by trampling it and fertilising it.

[68] Rights to decide on, implement and police, the rules regulating the resource.

[69] Rights to decide who should have access to the resource and to the various benefits it provides.

[70] Rights or powers to, for example, sell, mortgage or sublet the resource itself or products of it or rights in it (bearing in mind that, in real-life property systems as opposed to the oversimplified economic model, not all property rights are alienable).

[71] Elinor Ostrom, 'A long polycentric journey' (2010) 13 *Annual Review of Political Science* 1, at pp. 16–17. The point is made in more detail and by reference to specific case studies carried out by Ostrom and others, in Ostrom, 'Beyond markets and states', fn. 66 above, at p. 658.

[72] Ostrom, 'Beyond markets and states' p. 664.

(b) Oversimplified Categorisation of Resources

As we have seen, the simple economic view distinguishes between 'private goods' and 'public goods'. It also sees private ownership as the natural form of property for private goods (because they are both excludable and rivalrous), and state ownership as the inevitable form of property for public goods (because it is too difficult or too expensive to exclude non-payers from them, and because they are non-rivalrous).

Doubting the Private Goods/Public Goods Dichotomy

This reduction of all different kinds of things into two apparently simple and distinct categories is consistent with the traditional economist's accompanying view of the institutional world. It too is seen as divided into two sharply distinct sectors: on the one hand, there are private property exchanges which take place in a market setting, and on the other, there is government-owned property organised by a public hierarchy.

But, as Ostrom pointed out, in the complex real world both distinctions break down – there are more than two kinds of goods, and the institutions involved in their management are much more varied and fluid. Rivalry of consumption is not an absolute, nor is excludability (some goods are more rivalrous than others and some have a greater degree of excludability than others), and so distinctions between different categories of goods are not absolute either. What is more, even if we look at things only in terms of excludability and rivalrousness, there are at least two additional categories of goods which can usefully be distinguished. These are what are sometimes called 'club goods', and 'common pool resources'.[73]

'Club Goods'

'Club goods' include things like theatres, concert halls, orchestras, sports clubs, private gyms and other private members' clubs. It is generally quite easy to exclude non-payers from benefits provided by these goods, and what they provide tends to be not very rivalrous. Club goods certainly can be provided by private commercial enterprises. However, because they tend to be regarded as primarily providing benefits for their members and/or for local or common interest communities, they are often self-generated, provided and managed by their members or by their communities, or by not-for profit or local government institutions heavily reliant on participation by their members and communities. With some notable exceptions (West End theatres and private gyms come to mind), in this country they tend not to be provided by the market economy, nor by top-down state hierarchies. They are more usually to be found in a different world, dominated by collective, community or local interests.

Common Pool Resources

The main focus of interest for Ostrom and others is, however, 'common pool resources'.[74] 'Common pool resources' include natural resources as well as resources

---

[73] Ibid. pp. 644–645.

[74] Ostrom *Governing the Commons*, fn. 10 above, pp. 32–33 explains the problems with common pool resources.

produced by human endeavour, including groundwater basins, rivers, lakes, irrigation systems, fisheries, forests and communal grazing pastures. Like public goods, common pool resources tend to be non-excludable, in that it is difficult or expensive to exclude people from taking benefits from the resource. Unlike public goods, however, they tend to be rivalrous: when one person takes a benefit from the resource, it diminishes or otherwise affects what is available for others. In other words, the key factor is that common pool resources face the dangers of over-use explained by Hardin and Demsetz, with all the problems associated with externalities, free-riders, hold-outs and other transactions costs. They face these dangers because there are multiple people with access to the resource, and the extraction of a benefit from the resource by any of them affects the availability of benefits to the others. The issues are therefore different from those that arise with pure public goods or pure private goods. In particular, there is a collective element in the use of the resource (everyone's use impinges on everyone else's to a much greater extent than in a pure public good), and this provides a strong incentive for the users to generate a collective solution to their collective action problem. So, this is an obvious arena for communal property interests, particularly within the complex mixed state-public-communal-private property systems we have already described.

(c) Defective Models of Human Behaviour

Demsetz's argument that communities are unable to get together to regulate their own use of resources which are threatened with overuse, is based on the rational choice model of human behaviour we noted in para. 2.11(a) above. In other words, it assumes that individuals always make rational decisions, based on the information available to them, so as to maximise their own utility, wealth or happiness. Most economists now accept that this is a misleadingly oversimplified model, and over the last few decades behavioural economics has produced a vast literature seeking to identify, by theoretical, experimental and empirical studies, 'prevalent and systematic deviations' from the standard rational choice model.[75] In other words, as Thomas Ulen puts it, if we study how people actually behave in any given situation, we can make generalisations about how they are likely to behave in the future, but the model will be much more complex than Demsetz and others assumed:

> the experimental results fail to confirm the predictions of [rational choice theory]. Just as importantly, the experimental findings do not show that human behaviour is chaotic or unpredictable. Quite to the contrary, the behavioural experiments find that human choice behaviour is predictable: Most humans behave in similar ways in similar circumstances; those ways, however, are not those predicted by rational choice theory. It follows that using rational choice theory to predict some behaviour may lead to mispredictions . . . people do not typically make decisions that enhance their welfare as much as they might.[76]

---

[75] Eyal Zamir and Doron Teichman, 'Introduction' in Eyal Zamir and Doron Teichman (eds.), *The Oxford Handbook of Behavioural Economics and the Law* (Oxford: Oxford University Press, 2014) p. 1.
[76] Thomas Ulen, 'The importance of behavioural law' in Zamir and Teichman (eds.), *Oxford Handbook of Behavioural Law and Economics* pp. 95–96.

As already noted, empirical evidence has established that, faced with a threatened tragedy of the commons, resource users can and do co-operate to evolve rules to regulate their resource use in some circumstances. In other words, they do not behave as either Hardin's model or the prisoners' dilemma model predicts. The behavioural analyses which seek to explain why this is the case, are beyond the scope of this book.[77] However, there are three key factors we can isolate here. The first is that, unlike in a prisoner's dilemma, communal resource users have the opportunity for repeated face-to-face communication.[78] This is hugely significant, not only because it means they can discuss the situation and decide between themselves what to do about it, but also because that process appears to build up trust, increasing everyone's willingness to rely on each other's promises and act reciprocally. The second factor is that, because they know their own social and environmental situation better than anyone else does, the rules they evolve to regulate their communal resource use are more likely to succeed than any that would be devised by outsiders. Also, because these rules are self-generated, they are more likely to be acceptable to all the participants. The third factor is that these rules appear to acquire moral force amongst the participants: they are deterred from breaking the rules by the fear of being found out and incurring the disapproval of others, and they feel morally outraged by infringements by others.[79] This factor appears strong enough to outweigh material benefit: individuals will forgo a material benefit for themselves not only in order to avoid censure from the others, but also in order to punish other defaulters.[80]

2.17 Ostrom's Design Principles

Whilst Hardin and Demsetz were confident in their predictions that scarce resources would be depleted unless privately owned or owned by the state, Ostrom was more circumspect about predicting when communal property institutions could avert the tragedy of the commons. She did not believe that it was possible to draw up a blueprint or template for successful communal resource use, if only because, as her research confirmed, the rules and systems that local communities evolve to govern the resources they use in common are dictated by local conditions, and therefore are

---

[77] For a brief overview see Cole and Grossman, *Law & Economics*, fn. 42 above, pp. 81–84. A full account can be found in Elinor Ostrom, 'Coping with tragedies of the commons' (1999) *Annual Review of Political Science* 493 at pp. 496 and 500–508 available at www.annualreviews.org/doi/pdf/10.1146/annurev.polisci.2.1.493.

[78] See Cole and Grossman, *Law & Economics*, fn. 42 above, pp. 119–121 explaining that, for this reason and others, members of a community trying to regulate a resource they all use are not in a prisoner's dilemma; they provide a fuller version of their argument in 'Institutions matter! Why the herder problem is not a prisoner's dilemma' (2008) available at http://ssrn.com/abstract=1114541 at pp. 3–5.

[79] Ostrom notes that students taking part in laboratory experiments simulating 'tragedy of the commons' situations 'were indignant about evidence of [broken promises by other participants] and expressed their anger openly . . . [and] those who broke their promise tended to revert to the promised level after hearing the verbal tongue-lashing of their colleagues' ('Coping with tragedies of the commons', fn. 77 above, at p. 505).

[80] Ibid.

highly idiosyncratic. However, in *Governing the Commons* in 1990 she did produce what she described as 'design principles illustrated by long-enduring common pool resource institutions'.[81]

These 'design principles' formulated the characteristics that seemed to enable communal property groups to self-manage their collective resources effectively. They have proved to be remarkably robust. Tested against the results of later case studies of communal resource use in different countries, the design principles seem to be broadly accurate: on the whole, successful communal property institutions conform to the design principles and the ones that failed did not.[82] Consequently, they are now widely used as a standard by those advising communities how to regulate their own resources.[83]

These design principles, re-formulated by Ostrom and others in 2014 in (relatively) non-technical language, are as follows:

(1) *Clearly defined boundaries.* The identity of the group and the boundaries of the shared resource are clearly delineated.

(2) *Proportional equivalence between benefits and costs.* Members of the group must negotiate a system that rewards members for their contributions. High status or other disproportionate benefits must be earned. Unfair inequality poisons collective efforts.

(3) *Collective-choice arrangements.* Group members must be able to create at least some of their own rules and make their own decisions by consensus. People hate being told what to do but will work hard for group goals that they have agreed upon.

(4) *Monitoring.* Managing a commons is inherently vulnerable to free-riding and active exploitation. Unless these undermining strategies can be detected at relatively low cost by norm-abiding members of the group, the tragedy of the commons will occur.

(5) *Graduated sanctions.* Transgressions need not require heavy-handed punishment, at least initially. Often gossip or a gentle reminder is sufficient, but more severe forms of punishment must also be waiting in the wings for use when necessary.

(6) *Conflict resolution mechanisms.* It must be possible to resolve conflicts quickly and in ways that are perceived as fair by members of the group.

(7) *Minimal recognition of rights to organise.* Groups must have the authority to conduct their own affairs. Externally imposed rules are unlikely to be adapted to local circumstances and violate principle 3.

---

[81] Ostrom, *Governing the Commons*, fn. 10 above, pp. 89–102.

[82] A re-evaluation exercise carried out in 2010 in the light of further research recommended only minor modifications: M. Cox, G. Arnold, and S. Villamayor-Tomas 'A review of design principles for community-based natural resource management' (2010) 15 *Ecology and Society* 38, www.ecologyandsociety.org/vol15/iss4/art38.

[83] See, for example, the contemporary advice given to farmers in England and Wales who want to set up communal Water Abstraction Groups: Bill Leathes et al. 'The emergence and evolution of Water Abstractors Groups in Eastern England' (2007) 35 *UK Irrigation* 7, available at www.ukia.org/journal of the association.

(8) [*Nested enterprises*] For groups that are part of larger social systems, there must be appropriate coordination among relevant groups. Every sphere of activity has an optimal scale. Large scale governance requires finding the optimal scale for each sphere of activity and appropriately coordinating the activities, a concept called polycentric governance. A related concept is subsidiarity, which assigns governance tasks by default to the lowest jurisdiction, unless this is explicitly determined to be ineffective.[84]

In other words, it seems from Ostrom's 'design principles' that communal property regimes work best when they are self-governing and genuinely collective, when they manage their resource use for themselves according to idiosyncratic rules they have evolved for themselves, and when their activities are co-ordinated with those of other organisations interested in the same resource. We return to these points when we look at specific communal property interests later on in the book, particularly when considering indigenous land rights in Australia and Canada in Chapter 9 *Multiple Property Rights Systems* and communal property interests in land currently recognised in English law in Chapter 13 *Non-Possessory Land Use Rights*.

2.18 Property and Society

If we turn back to our underlying concern in this chapter – why we recognise the institution of property at all – the analyses we have looked at in this part of the chapter seem to suggest that property is simply something that develops, from the bottom-up, as we organise ourselves into a society. It can develop in different forms, depending on the kind of society that emerges and on the economic and geophysical context. Some analysts, like Demsetz, have argued that the emergence of property follows a common pattern, with property rights developing as resources become scarce, first in an intermediate primitive form (communal property) which then in its turn inevitably gives way to private property as modern market economies emerge. On this view, surviving communal property regimes are either relics from the past, preserved out of sentiment,[85] or primitive property forms surviving because the society in which they operate is not yet sufficiently developed.[86] As societies progress, so the argument goes, they move towards private property because it

---

[84] David Sloan Wilson, Elinor Ostrom and Michael E. Cox, 'Generalizing the core design principles for the efficacy of groups' (2013) *Journal of Economic Behavior & Organization* pp. S21–S32.

[85] This seems to have been the prevailing view when the future of common land was being debated in post-war England and Wales: see Alison Clarke, 'Property law: Re-establishing diversity' in M. D. A. Freeman and A. D. E Lewis (eds.), *Current Legal Problems 1997, vol. 50: Law and Opinion at the End of the Twentieth Century* (Oxford: Oxford University Press, 1997) p. 119 at pp. 123–137, and see further Parts IV and V of Chapter 13 *Non-Possessory Land Use Rights*.

[86] Until comparatively recently this was assumed to be the case in developing countries, to be remedied by 'formalisation' (otherwise known as privatisation) of customary and indigenous communal property rights: D. W. Bromley, 'Formalising property relations in the developing world: The wrong prescription for the wrong malady' (2008) 26 *Land Use Policy* 20 and Daniel Fitzpatrick, 'Evolution and chaos in property rights systems: The Third World tragedy of contested access' (2006) 115 *Yale Law Journal* 996.

promotes individual autonomy and ensures the most efficient use and development of resources.

However, this evolutionary theory of property is now largely discredited.[87] It is historically inaccurate in respect of at least some countries and some resources,[88] and it fails to account for the longstanding communal property regimes identified by Ostrom or for the emergence of new commons in established market economies such as Scotland, which we consider in Chapter 8 *Property Interest Holders*.[89] So, whilst there is some consensus that property and society develop together as the inevitable result of people having to interact over their use of resources, it is by no means obvious what kind of property rights regime will develop in any given situation, and how it will happen.[90]

2.19 Property, Economics and Values

As we have seen in this part of the chapter, when traditional economists talk about property they are predominantly concerned with economic values and efficiency, although analysts such as Hardin and Demsetz also tend to equate efficiency with environmental sustainability. Environmental concerns also emerge strongly in the work of Ostrom and others, and it is an implicit assumption in the many case studies and analyses of communal property regimes that 'success' of collective resource can be measured at least in part by reference to environmental sustainability.[91]

However, as we suggested in para. 1.8 of Chapter 1 *What Property Is and Why It Matters*, we might also want to consider the social, moral, cultural and political causes and effects of any particular property rights regime. This is the central issue in contemporary US property scholarship, where it is usually formulated as a question of what values property should serve. We look more closely at the US scholarship on this question in Part V of the chapter, but first in Part IV we look at the notion, equally distant from economic values, that property is in some way centrally implicated in our humanity.

---

[87] Barry C. Field, 'The evolution of property rights' (1989) 42 *Kyklos* 319. See also more generally Stuart Banner, 'Transitions between property regimes' (2002) 31 *Journal of Legal Studies* 359 and Saul Levmore 'Two stories about the evolution of property rights' (2002) 31 *Journal of Legal Studies* 421.

[88] Water is a good example: Carol M. Rose, 'Energy and efficiency in the realignment of common law water rights' (1990) 19 *Journal of Legal Studies* 261; see also Joshua Getzler, *A History of Water Rights at Common Law* (Oxford: Oxford University Press, 2004) and James Salzman, 'Thirst: A short history of drinking water' (2006) 18 *Yale University Journal of Law and the Humanities* 94.

[89] Matthew Hoffmann, 'Why community ownership? Understanding land reform in Scotland' (2013) 31 *Land Use Policy* 289. For other examples of emerging new commons see Ting Xu and Alison Clarke (eds.), *Legal Strategies for the Development and Protection of Communal Property*, Proceedings of the British Academy, vol. 216 (Oxford: Oxford University Press, 2018).

[90] Katrina Wyman points out the difficulty and importance of the 'how' question in 'From fur to fish: Reconsidering the evolution of private property' (2005) 80 *New York University Law Review* 117.

[91] See for example Takeshi Murota and Ken Takeshita (eds.), *Local Commons and Democratic Environmental Governance* (Tokyo: United Nations University Press, 2013).

PART IV PROPERTY, FREEDOM AND AUTONOMY

2.20 Property as Essential for Human Flourishing

The analyses we looked at in Part III were centred on the idea that property is an institution that enables people to make better use of resources. In this part, where we look at Kant and Hegel and their influences, the central idea is instead that property is an essential feature of humanity. Again, the assumption is that property means private property, but the argument is that, in some way, property is an essential prerequisite for living as a fulfilled, free and independent human being. So, the answer to the general question – why do we recognise property at all? – is not, because it enables us to make the best use of the resources available to us, but because it enables us to lead fulfilled lives as human beings.

2.21 Immanuel Kant

(a) Context of Kant's Right to Property

Kant's property argument is not self-standing. It is part of a systematic exposition on individual rights which he developed in his major treatise on legal and political philosophy, the *Doctrine of Right*,[92] published in Konigsberg in 1797. Kant's central argument in the *Doctrine of Right* is that every individual has an innate 'right to freedom', by which he means a right to be 'independent of the will of others', and that this 'right to freedom' is something we all have by virtue of being human. As a consequence of our right to freedom, Kant argues, we also each have other rights: a right to bodily integrity (i.e. exclusive rights over our own person), a right to property, a right to enter into contracts with each other, and rights 'to persons' (this last one concerning essentially domestic relationships). So, we each have a right to property *because* we have an innate 'right to freedom'.

The important point about all of these rights is that they have to co-exist with everyone else's like rights. It is crucial to Kant's argument that this co-existence can be achieved only by us all agreeing to live in a civil society which will monitor and enforce our rights against each other, and the same applies in relation to the territorial rights of states as against each other. So, Kant's property argument in the *Doctrine of Right* is a political as well as a philosophical argument and it operates not only on an individual level: its broader purpose is the avoidance of conflict at a national and international level. As Byrd and Hrushka put it:

> Kant devotes the largest single part of his *Doctrine of Right* to showing how individual ownership rights are possible. If Kant can establish ownership rights for the individual, he can establish not only the basis of public law but, simultaneously, the basis of international law, or what should be called private law among states. By mutually

---

[92] Immanuel Kant, *The Doctrine of Right, Part I of the Metaphysics of Morals in Practical Philosophy*, trans and ed. Mary Gregor (Cambridge: Cambridge University Press, 1996).

recognizing acquisition and ownership, be it acquisition of individual property rights or acquisition of a state's territorial rights, we can avoid constant conflict and strive toward the single goal of the *Doctrine of Right*, namely perpetual peace.[93]

Kant's political argument in the *Doctrine of Right* goes further. His 'right to freedom' not only sets the parameters of our interactions with each other (in relation to things, as well as in other respects), and justifies state coercion, it also imposes limitations on the legitimate powers of the state.[94] No-one's 'right to freedom' can justifiably be restricted by the state (or anyone else) except 'for the sake of freedom itself',[95] in other words, except where necessary to preserve her own freedom or the freedom of others. It cannot justifiably be restricted or constrained for any other reason, such as in the interests of the state, or in the public interest.

All this becomes clearer as we look more closely at what is involved in Kant's 'right to freedom' and at why, according to Kant, it necessarily requires a right to property.

(b) The 'Right to Freedom'

Kant is very precise about the scope of his 'right to freedom'. It is the right to be free to set and pursue ends or purposes for ourselves, in the sense that no-one else has the right to decide what purposes we may pursue. In Kant's own words, it is 'independence from being constrained by another's choice'.[96] It is essentially a negative right, variously described as a right 'to move around freely without being coerced by others ... a negative right [relating to] freedom or *independence* from someone else',[97] or a right 'each person ... [has] to be his or her own master ... [and not] subordinated to the choice of any *other* particular person'.[98] As Ripstein says, the right to freedom means that 'nobody else gets to tell you what purposes to pursue'.[99] So, Kant's 'freedom' or 'independence' can be seen as a kind of personal sovereignty to which we are each entitled by virtue of being human.

However, it is important to appreciate the limits that Kant sees in this personal sovereignty. It is a freedom from interference by others with our choice of ends or

---

[93] B. Sharon Byrd and Joachim Hruschka, 'The natural law duty to recognize private property ownership: Kant's theory of property in his *Doctrine of Right*' (2006) 56 *University of Toronto Law Journal* 217 at pp. 218–219.

[94] This last element is best illustrated by Arthur Ripstein in *Force and Freedom: Kant's Legal and Political Philosophy* (Cambridge, MA: Harvard University Press, 2009) at pp. 221–222, where he points out the Kantian principles underpinning the decision of the German Constitutional Court decision *Bundersverfassungsgericht* (BverfG), I BvR 357/05 vom 15.2.2006 that 'the constitution could [not] authorise the minister of the interior to order a hijacked airliner to be shot down [because] it was in danger of being used as a missile against a populated area'.

[95] Kant, *Doctrine of Right*, fn. 92 above, 6.237.

[96] Ibid 6.237. Kant explains that 'choice' means here the ability to decide what purpose to pursue: ibid. 6.214.

[97] Byrd and Hruschka, 'The natural law duty', fn. 93 above, p. 219.

[98] Ripstein, *Force and Freedom*, fn. 94 above, p. 4. Italics in the original. Ripstein goes on to say at p. 5: 'Kant's full explanation of what it is for each person to be his or her own master rather than the servant of another will take up most of this book.'

[99] Ibid p. 34.

purposes, not a freedom to *achieve* our ends/purposes unhindered by others or by lack of resources: my independence is not violated if you 'pursue purposes of your own, and in so doing render things I had hoped to use unavailable'.[100] So, for example, if you occupy the space I hoped to stand in, or detain the person I had arranged to meet, you do not violate my right to freedom. All you have done is 'change the world in which [I] act'.[101]

(c) How the Right to Property Derives From the Right to Freedom

Although Kant's right to freedom is a negative right – a right to be free from interference by others – it can only be realised, according to Kant, if we have certain positive rights against each other. These positive rights include an innate right to bodily integrity, and also a right to hold property and a right to enter into contracts with each other. We need a right to bodily integrity and a right to hold property because we need to use our bodies and external objects in order to set and pursue our own ends or purposes. So, we cannot realise our right to freedom unless we are free from constraint in using our bodies and whatever external objects we choose. My right to bodily integrity will entitle me to constrain any interference by you with my person, and also with any external object that is within my physical grasp (because if you interfere with an object in my physical grasp, you necessarily also interfere with my bodily integrity). This is enough to give me a right to the space I occupy and in the external objects under my control (Kant gives the examples of the ground I lie on and the apple I hold), *but only for so long as I occupy that space or control that object*. I will not be able fully to utilise the space or the object as a means to set and pursue my own ends or purposes unless I can also constrain you from interfering with them when I am no longer in physical control of them. To constrain you from interfering with space I no longer occupy or an object which is outside my physical control, I need a right of property, that is, some way of making it 'mine' even when it is outside my physical control. In Kant's scheme of things, I make an object mine by bringing it under my control, with the intention of excluding all others from it, and by publicly signalling that it is mine.[102] Once I have done that, it remains mine even after it leaves my physical control. The right to enter into contracts with each other then becomes necessary so that, as and when we want, we can selectively authorise violations of these rights by others. This would, for example, allow me to employ you (which necessarily involves you being required to further my ends and purposes rather than your own), or to use, or buy from you, things that have become yours.

Like the innate right to freedom itself, the right to bodily integrity and the right to hold property are necessarily subject to the like rights which are held by others, as we have already noted. This means that I cannot make an external object mine if it

---

[100] Ibid p. 33. He elaborates this at pp. 33–39.   [101] Ibid p. 39.
[102] Kant, *Doctrine of Right*, fn. 92 above, 6:258. Compare these requirements with what is required in most legal systems to establish possession: see Chapter 11 *Possession and Title*.

already belongs to you: if I try to do so without your authorisation, I violate your right to hold property. If I want it, or want to use it, I must exercise my right to enter into a contract with you to authorise me to have it or use it.

(d) Reconciling Individual Freedoms: Property and the State

Under Kant's scheme, neither the right to hold property nor the right to enter into contracts can be fully realised except through a public legal institution that can act coercively, because it is only through such an institution that the rights to freedom that all individuals have can be reconciled. Without a coercive state, individuals would (at best) voluntarily agree to respect the 'property rights' of others, which would make the 'property' holders dependent on the will of others in their use of external objects, which means being subject to their choice, and so not free. Kant's argument is that I can only be free from your choice as to whether to respect my rights (and you can only be free from my choice as to whether to respect your rights) if my rights and your rights are enforceable by an agent who is independent of both of us. This necessarily involves the two of us recognising the authority of the state to enforce the rights of the other against us. It is not just that the formation of a state is *likely* to bring about the realisation of the right to freedom, or even that consenting to join the state is a 'prudent sacrifice[s] for individuals to make if they are concerned to secure their freedom'.[103] The point is that 'The consistent exercise of the right to freedom by a plurality of persons cannot be conceived apart from a public legal order'.[104] Therefore, every person is *obliged* to consent to enter into such a coercive state, because this is the only way of fulfilling her 'duty of rightful honour', in other words the duty she owes herself to be her own master, independent of the will of others.[105]

So, for Kant, there can be no property rights without a state, but the state comes into being only by omnilateral authorisation (which everyone is obliged to give) and its only function is to protect each individual's innate right to freedom, including their property holdings, so far as this can be done consistently with protecting everyone else's like rights.

Because none of us can be free unless we all live under the authority of a state which enforces our rights against others and their rights against us, it is justifiable to coerce each of us to accept the authority of the state whether we want to or not. So, although it may seem paradoxical, this apparent restraint on our freedom (i.e. being forced to live under a state) is necessary in order for each of us to be free. This does not mean that these rights (the right to bodily integrity, the right to property, the right to enter into contracts, etc.) are conferred by the state. We have these rights by virtue of being human, not as a result of a decision of the state (or a decree of a transcendental being). However, they become 'real' and logically coherent only when we live under a state.

---

[103] Ripstein, *Force and Freedom*, fn. 94 above, p. 9.   [104] Ibid.   [105] Ibid p. 37.

2.22 Georg Wilhelm Friedrich Hegel

Hegel's discussion of private property in *The Philosophy of Right*,[106] published in 1821, is famously difficult, and, to do it justice, it would have to be explained by reference to his philosophy as a whole, which is way beyond the scope of this book. However, for our purposes it is important because current debates about property often take Hegel's discussion of private property as a starting point. So, it is useful to have some idea of what it is that Hegel says, or at least of how other commentators interpret what he says.[107]

(a) Hegel's View of Property and Human Development

The first point to make is that Hegel is not seeking to justify property in the way that, for example, Locke did: this is not an argument about why we should recognise property, and if we do, what kind of property system we ought to have. It is much more a thesis on how property affects human development. As Alexander and Peñalver see it, what Hegel provides is an 'insight into how private property contributes to self-identification and self-development', and this, they say, is perhaps what constitutes 'Hegel's greatest contribution to property theory'.[108]

Like Kant, Hegel sees property as fundamentally about freedom but, as Blackburn points out,[109] Hegel's view of freedom is different from Kant's:

> The cornerstone of Hegel's system, or world view, is the notion of freedom, conceived not as simple licence to fulfil preferences but as the rare condition of living self-consciously and in a fully rationally organised community or state …

For Hegel, property was fundamental to freedom in this special sense. In Blackburn's words, the Hegelian view was that 'only in a framework of property rights is individual freedom possible'.[110]

(b) What Property-Owning Gives Us

In general terms, Hegel's argument is that property-owning is necessary for the ethical development of an individual – necessary for the individual to be free – because this development of the self cannot take place without some kind of transition from the inner subjective world of the individual to the external objective

---

[106] G. W. F. Hegel *Grundlinien der Philosophie des Recht*, published as *The Philosophy of Right*, translated with notes by T. M. Knox (Oxford: Oxford University Press, 1967).

[107] This account largely follows Waldron, *The Right to Private Property*, fn. 15 above. For criticisms of his account see Alain Pottage, 'Property: Re-appropriating Hegel' (a review article on Jeremy Waldron, *The Right to Private Property*) (1990) 53 *MLR* 259.

[108] Gregory Alexander and Eduardo Peñalver, *An Introduction to Property Theory* (Cambridge: Cambridge University Press, 2012) p. 68.

[109] Simon Blackburn, *Oxford Dictionary of Philosophy* (Oxford and New York: Oxford University Press, 1994) p. 168.

[110] Ibid. pp. 306–307 (in the entry on 'property').

world.[111] Private property is the means by which we make this transition, because it involves us embodying our will in external objects. As Waldron puts it:

> Property owning is said [by Hegel] to be important to the human individual since it is only through owning and controlling property that he can embody his will in external objects and begin to transcend the subjectivity of his immediate existence. In working on an object, using it, and having control over it, an individual confers on his will a stability and maturity that would not otherwise be possible ... unless he can establish himself as an owner, an individual's development in other areas of ethical life will be seriously at risk.[112]

For these purposes, so it seems, only private property will do: Hegel rejects the idea that communal property could contribute towards the ethical development of the individual members of the community in the same kind of way, and does not explore the possibility that it might contribute towards the self-identity of the community itself.[113]

Haochen Sun attempts to be a bit more specific about how this embodiment process is supposed to enable us to develop ethically:

> To be a person, one must, as Hegel points out, posit oneself in a way that is different from others. The determinations of interpersonal differences largely stem from the ways in which each person makes a multitude of varied choices to satisfy their own natural drives, desires, and inclinations. According to Hegel, having an external sphere of freedom is indispensable for actualizing the personal choice-making process ... This is because an external sphere provides the space within which one is left free to choose the individualized ways to satisfy his natural drives, desires, and inclinations. In doing so, one gradually develops his own distinctive contents and form of individuality ... Hegel thinks that a person can achieve the assertion of the self-consciousness of being free by going through a judgment-making process for himself as to whether and how he should place his individual will in a particular thing ... All these forms of taking possession of things are carried out by a person for himself as he sees fit. He decides to do it simply for his own purposes based upon his desires, preferences, and inclinations. In doing so, he makes a judgment for himself by deciding whether he should put his will in a thing and thereby take possession of it. The more judgments of this kind he makes for himself, the more he knows about his own free will as manifested by taking possession of things. Hence the judgment-making process of this type is the most direct self-assertion and self-positing of one's consciousness of being a free person.[114]

---

[111] Waldron, *The Right to Private Property*, fn. 15 above, p. 355.

[112] Waldron *The Right to Private Property*, fn. 15 above, at pp. 377–378. Waldron's immediate concern in this passage is with the difficult question of how, if this is correct, it can ever be justifiable for some people to have no property.

[113] Ibid pp. 373–374.

[114] Haochen Sun 'Designing journeys to the social world: Hegel's theory of property and his noble dreams revisited' (2010) 6 *Cosmos and History: The Journal of Natural and Social Philosophy*; University of Hong Kong Faculty of Law Research Paper No. 2011/010. Available at SSRN: http://ssrn.com/abstract=1942053 or http://dx.doi.org/10.2139/ssrn.1942053 at pp. 37–38.

The process is then reinforced by the external object mirroring the individual's will (which it now embodies) back to the individual, reinforcing the individual's self-understanding of himself as a free being.[115]

(c) How We Embody Our Will

Exactly what Hegel means by embodiment of our will is mysterious, but it is at least tolerably clear *how* we do it. We do it by taking possession of the external object in question, which for Hegel means doing one of three things. First, we can do it by taking intentional physical control of the object,[116] but this achieves only a temporary embodiment of our will, which lasts only for so long as we keep the object in our control. If we want to achieve a permanent embodiment of our will we must do one of two things. We must bring about some physical change in the object, by doing something like the labouring required by Locke for the acquisition of ownership. Alternatively, we must mark it as our own, for example by labelling or registering it, or by doing something like fencing-off a piece of land.

(d) Mutual Recognition

It is significant that these two ways of achieving a permanent embodiment of our will in an object each result in the object becoming 'affected in some way that can only be explained by reference to the workings of an active will'.[117] This is important for Hegel because in his scheme of things the embodiment of our will in a particular object must be capable of recognition by others in society. As Sun sees it, this is essential for Hegel because:

> Without this kind of recognition, personal freedom is, in fact, not realizable in the social world. Since property constitutes a person's external sphere of personal freedom, the recognition of his control over property from others is the way in which he is recognized and respected as a free person. In reciprocity, he recognizes others' control over their properties and thereby recognizes and respects others as persons as well.[118]

In other words, recognition is necessary for our self-development in two ways. We need others to recognise that we have taken control of some external object to make it ours, because by recognising our rights, they recognise and respect us as free persons. Our awareness of this external recognition and respect is part of our self-development, confirming to us our place as a person in the social world. But it goes further than this. We too must recognise the property rights of others, not for the practical reason that mutual recognition avoids civil conflict, but because joining the world of mutual recognition is also part of our self-development as a person: it is an

---

[115] Ibid.

[116] Which matches the common law notion of possession of tangible things, as we see in Chapter 11 *Possession and Title.*

[117] Waldron, *The Right to Private Property*, fn. 15 above, pp. 364–365.

[118] Sun, 'Designing journeys to the social world', fn. 114 above, pp. 40–41.

'indispensable step' towards full actualisation of our individual freedom. As Waldron says:

> To define oneself as a person is ... to realise that one's place in a network of other persons is itself constitutive of one's personality, and that one could not be a person except in a world of persons.[119]

This is very different from the way Locke and Kant see the need for mutual recognition of property rights. For both Locke and Kant it is what makes a coercive state necessary: only a coercive state can ensure that every person's property rights are enforceable against every other person. Although Hegel does have things to say about the relationship between property rights and the existence of a state,[120] his point about mutual recognition is that it is a step in the progress towards individual freedom.

2.23 Hegel's Influence on Contemporary Property Theory

We can see at least three strands of development from Hegel's ideas in contemporary property theory. One of them is the idea we have already noted, as voiced by Alexander and Peñalver and derived from both Kant and Hegel, that property contributes to our self-identification and self-development as human individuals. This has been picked up and developed by the progressive property theorists, as we see in Part V of this chapter.

The second and third strands derive from Hegel's idea of a moral or psychological bond between a person and their property. In one of these strands, Hegel's insight into the moral aspects of this bond has prompted an exploration of the fluidity of the relationship between the holder of property rights and the object of those rights. We look at this again in Chapter 8 *Property Interest Holders*, where we consider the blurring of the distinction between the two, and at how some 'things' can move from being the object that is owned to being the entity which owns.

The third strand is most closely associated with Margaret Jane Radin's seminal article, 'Property and Personhood'.[121] Using Hegel as a springboard, Radin takes the idea of investing our will in an object as a basis for a theory of property and personhood. In Radin's analysis, it is something like the investment of our will in an object which explains the particularly strong psychological bond we develop with some of the things that we regard as our own (things like wedding rings and homes). Her interest is in seeing how far this special bond can and should be reflected by law. In Chapter 7 *Objects of Property Interests* we look more closely at what Radin says about property and personhood, and also at what others have said about the fluidity of the value of things to humans.[122]

---

[119] Waldron, *The Right to Private Property* , fn. 15 above, p. 376.

[120] Sun, 'Designing journeys to the social world', fn. 114 above, pp. 51–58, and see also Alan Ryan, *Property and Political Theory* (Oxford: Basil Blackwell, 1984) pp. 118–141.

[121] Margaret Jane Radin, 'Property and personhood' (1982) 34 *Stanford Law Review* 957.

[122] Chapter 7 *Objects of Property Interests* para. 7.10.

PART V PROPERTY, EXCLUSION AND VALUES

2.24 Information Theory and Progressive Property

As we noted in para. 2.3, in contemporary US property rights theory the focus of attention has shifted from the question of how we justify the institution of property to the question of what property 'really' is. The quest is to identity the 'core', or essential nature, of property, and on this issue there are two dominant opposing views. One is put forward by scholars sometimes referred to as 'information theorists', who look at property from an economic perspective, building on the economic analysts we looked at in Part III of the chapter. The other is shared by a looser group of scholars who describe themselves as part of a 'progressive property' school, and they adopt a social perspective.

For the information theorists, the core of property is the right to exclude others from things. Exclusion is central to the idea of property, they say, because the essential defining characteristic of a property right (as opposed to a contract right, or a personal right) is that it is enforceable against the whole world. On that basis, they argue, the overriding function of property law is to provide clearly defined and standardised property rights so that everybody knows exactly who has what rights in which things, and from which things they are excluded. The progressive property theorists, on the other hand, regard exclusion as of peripheral importance. The essence of property, as they see it, is that it serves human values, and shapes and reflects social relationships.[123] Their argument is that it is these aspects of property which should be the predominant influence on us when we have to resolve property conflicts and design and operate property institutions.

We look more closely at these two opposing views on what property is 'really' all about in the following paragraphs. However, before doing so it is worth noting here that the starting point for both is a western capitalist system centred on private property, very much on the US model, and the argument is as to the essential nature of property *within that kind of system*. It is equally important that both sides claim to be providing both a descriptive and a prescriptive account of that system. In other words, each side argues that their account correctly identifies the true nature of property within their system, but each also argues that judges and legislators faced with the task of interpreting and developing property law and policy should act so as to reinforce rather than subvert what each urges is property's essential nature.

2.25 Information Theory

The main proponents of information theory are Thomas W. Merrill and Henry E. Smith.[124] Their argument centres on the *numerus clausus* principle, which, as we

---

[123] See further para. 2.26.

[124] They have both (together and separately) written extensively about information theory and related ideas. Their classic argument is best set out in Thomas W. Merrill and Henry E. Smith, 'Optimal standardization in the law of property: The numerus clausus principle' (2000) 110 *Yale Law Journal* 1. Their argument is developed (and in some respects qualified) in later articles.

noted in para. 1.26(f) of Chapter 1 *What Property Is and Why It Matters*, is observed to a greater or lesser extent in most civil and common law countries. According to this principle (which we look at again in Chapter 6 *New Property Interests and the Numerus Clausus*) only a limited range of property interests (a *'numerus clausus'*) should be recognised in any property rights system, and the characteristics of each type of interest should be clearly defined and fixed by law.

The Merrill and Smith argument is that property institutions must be geared to accommodate what they see as the core characteristic of property interests in things, which, as we have already noted, is that property rights, unlike contract rights or personal rights, 'stick' to the thing when it is bought and sold, and they are enforceable against the whole world. Given this characteristic, Merrill and Smith argue, property's primary function is to reduce the information-processing costs of potential purchasers of property rights (i.e. their costs in finding out precisely what they are buying) and of potential tortfeasors (i.e. their costs in finding out about the property rights with which they must not interfere). This is where the *numerus clausus* principle comes in. Merrill and Smith argue that the way we reduce these information-processing costs is by standardising property interests (so that everyone knows what the characteristics of each of them are) and by limiting the number of standard types allowed. In other words, we adopt a strict *numerus clausus* principle, which limits the range of allowable property interests recognised by the state to a small number of well-defined types. They go on to argue that there is an 'optimal standardization' of property rights, with 'the appropriate number of alternative forms being determined by a trade-off between the utility of having more forms and the confusion that more forms would engender'.[125]

We should note the assumptions underlying this argument. It is assumed that economic efficiency is the primary criterion we should use in evaluating property laws and property institutions, and in formulating property policies. Also, it is assumed that the primary objectives of property law are to facilitate market transactions in propertised things, and to protect private property owners. Information-processing costs are transaction costs, and as we saw in para. 2.11 above, it is a basic principle of law and economics that reducing transaction costs increases the efficiency of property markets and the efficient resolution of property conflicts between neighbours.

As we see in the following paragraph, these assumptions about the overriding need to facilitate markets and protect private owners are very different from the assumptions underlying progressive property theory.

2.26 Progressive Property

'Progressive property' is the label that a group of US property scholars have adopted as an umbrella term to refer to what they see as the common principles underpinning their individual approaches to property. In 2009 four of them – Gregory

---

[125] Henry Hansmann and Reinier Kraakman, 'Property, contract and verification: the numerus clausus problem and the divisibility of rights' (2002) 31 *Journal of Legal Studies* 373 at p. 374.

Alexander, Eduardo Peñalver, Joseph Singer and Laura Underkuffler – published a short 'Statement of Progressive Property' which sets out these common principles.[126]

The Statement needs to be read in full, but here we can summarise the ground it covers. The first of the principles is that, because of the inevitable impact of one person's property rights on others, the 'common conception of property as protection of individual control over valued resources . . . is inadequate as the sole basis for resolving property conflicts or for designing property institutions. For those tasks, we must look to the underlying human values that property serves and the social relationships it shapes and reflects'. The second principle is that these values are 'plural and incommensurable', and paragraph 2 of the Statement goes into detail about what these values are. The third principle is that even though these values are incommensurable, inevitable choices about property entitlements can and should be made rationally, by 'reasoned deliberation'. The last two principles, which are both wide-ranging and self-explanatory are:

> 4. Property confers power. It allocates scarce resources that are necessary for human life, development, and dignity. Because of the equal value of each human being, property laws should promote the ability of each person to obtain the material resources necessary for full social and political participation.

> 5. Property enables and shapes community life. Property law can render relationships within communities either exploitative and humiliating or liberating and ennobling. Property law should establish the framework for a kind of social life appropriate to a free and democratic society.[127]

The implications of these principles become clearer when we look at the approaches to property adopted by the authors of the Statement. Gregory Alexander's focus is on what he calls the 'social obligation norm', which he argues is latent in American property law and needs to be recognised and developed. The principle underlying the social obligation norm, which we come across again in later chapters, is that property owners, as social beings, owe obligations to the community 'to participate in and support the social networks and structures that enable us to develop' the human capabilities of us all, and to foster human flourishing.[128] This imposes limitations on property owners' freedom of action, and also justifies, or even requires, the subordination of the interests of property owners in appropriate cases.

Like Alexander, Eduardo Peñalver starts with a critique of the law and economics approach to property law and land-use decisions, emphasising both the simplistic nature of the assumption that owners will always maximise the long-term value of their land, and law and economics' avoidance of moral questions.[129] He advocates instead a virtue-based conception of property, arguing that property law can and should foster 'virtues'. Drawing on Aristotelian virtue ethics, he describes 'virtues' as

---

[126] Gregory S. Alexander, Eduardo M. Peñalver, Joseph William Singer and Laura S. Underkuffler, 'A statement of progressive property' (2009) 94 *Cornell Law Review* 743.

[127] Ibid. p. 744.

[128] Gregory S. Alexander, 'The social-obligation norm in American property law' (2009) 94 *Cornell Law Review* 745 at p. 770.

[129] Eduardo Peñalver, 'Land virtues' (2009) 94 *Cornell Law Review* 821.

'acquired, stable dispositions to engage in certain characteristic modes of behaviour that are conducive to human flourishing'.[130]

Joseph Singer echoes Alexander and Peñalver in pointing out the shortcomings of economic analysis of property law:

> In thinking about property and property law, we cannot confine ourselves to the techniques of economic theory or cost-benefit analysis. Rather, we must look to basic moral and political theory for the normative frameworks that economic theory lacks.[131]

However, the approach he adopts focusses on 'understanding the role that property and property law play in a free and democratic society that treats each person with equal concern and respect'.[132] In this democratic model, he argues, property law concerns

> not just relations between persons and things but *relations among persons* with respect to valued resources ... . Every legal right should be understood not merely by reference to the powers and rights it gives the owner but by reference to the impacts of the exercise of those powers on others and the shape and character of the social relationships engendered by those rights and powers.

This has a number of implications for Singer, just two of which we will pick out here. First, he explains that in his democratic model, where each person is to be treated with equal concern and respect, property law must exercise a supervisory role not only over the forms of allowable relationships arising between property owners and others (some relationships, such as those based on or incorporating slavery, feudalism or discrimination, are simply illegitimate) but also over the qualitative character of otherwise legitimate relationships:

> For example, the libertarian and efficiency schools consider voluntary deals to be mutually beneficial, welfare-promoting arrangements. When a bank offers to lend money to help someone buy a home, for example, these schools assume that the bank is offering the potential borrower a free choice; accepting the offer shows that both parties are better off with the deal than without it, and the resulting contract is therefore necessarily legitimate. But this conclusion is too facile. Whether the relationship is legitimate depends on a moral judgment that the relationship is acceptable in a free and democratic society .... . There are some things you should not ask of others; there are some demands that cannot justly be made in a free and democratic society. When a mortgage lender offers onerous terms to someone who is desperate to become a home owner and get a share in the American Dream, that lender is not merely giving that person a choice; she is offering to establish an exploitative relationship while misleading the buyer/borrower into thinking that the terms are acceptable. The fact that the buyer/borrower accepts such terms of recruitment does not mean that they are therefore legitimate.[133]

---

[130] Ibid. p. 870.
[131] Joseph Singer, 'Democratic estates: Property law in a free and democratic society' (2009) 94 *Cornell Law Review* 1009 at p. 1053.
[132] Ibid. p. 1047.   [133] Ibid. pp. 1047–1048.

In other words, as Singer says in a later passage, the democratic model 'recognizes that market relationships are legitimate only if they comply with minimum-standards regulations that ensure that individuals treat each other with common decency'.[134]

The second of the implications of Singer's democratic approach that we need to note here is that he sees it as imposing on property owners a 'duty of attentiveness' to the externalities of their actions:

> We are not free to ignore the effects of our actions on others; to the contrary, the common law requires us to pay attention to the immediate and not-so-immediate consequences of our actions, otherwise known as externalities. Those externalities may be of various kinds; we are not only concerned with the fair market value of property but the character of the neighbourhood in which property is situated. As Professor Peñalver argues, gentrification may increase property values in the neighborhood yet still be resisted by owners who fear a loss of their way of life.[135]

Singer makes it clear that this goes beyond observing formal property rules about, say, interfering with property rights of neighbours by trespassing on their land or polluting their land. In those ways, but also in a broader sense, we as property owners 'have obligations to avoid actions that harm the legitimate interests of others, if possible'.[136]

2.27 What Property Does and What It Should Do

As we noted in para. 2.24, and as will now be apparent, the frame of reference for both information theory and progressive property is a property rights system centred on private property which operates within a US-style Western democratic capitalist state. It will also be apparent that, whilst neither information theory nor progressive property challenges the fundamental nature or structure of this property system that they inhabit, they do have radically different views on what property does and what it should do within that system.

As Jane Baron explains, these differences arise because information theorists are interested in how property works, and their starting position is that, in their society, it *does* work. Progressive property theory, on the other hand, is interested in the outcomes of property, in other words in the ways in which property shapes or reflects society and social relationships:

> For information theorists, what is most interesting and important about property is how it works, practically speaking. In rem rights, operating through standardized forms, provide at low cost simple signals that effectively protect owners' rights by signaling to nonowners their duty to keep off. For progressive theorists, what is most interesting and important about property is the outcomes it produces. Property is at least capable of fostering human flourishing, virtue, freedom, and democracy and should be judged by the success with which it actually fosters these qualities. Of course, it is important not to overdraw the contrast ... information theorists value in rem rights because, in their view, such rights promote freedom; in the space from which nonowners are excluded, owners pursue self-chosen ends. Information theorists

---

[134] Ibid. p. 1052.   [135] Ibid. pp. 1048–1049.   [136] Ibid.

focus on *how* the system functions to create that space, whereas progressive theorists focus directly on the system's *results.*[137]

So, information theory gives property a much smaller role than that assigned to it by progressive property. For information theorists the overriding function of property is to enable their society to work efficiently. This, in their view, provides the space within which freedom and democracy will flourish. For progressive property theorists, on the other hand, it is property itself which reflects and determines the extent to which their society fosters human flourishing, virtue, freedom and democracy. As Baron points out, these two approaches are not compatible. Adopting the metaphors that have emerged in this debate – that for information theorists property is a machine, whereas for progressive property theorists it is a conversation – she says:

> Information theorists employ the metaphor of property as a machine – a machine which has long served to produce more or less on its own good-enough social ordering and which, with some restrained engineering, will continue to produce such ordering. This metaphor is inconsistent with the progressives' metaphorical view of property as a conversation. The conversation metaphor expresses the progressive theorists' view that we need to *question* whether the system in fact is good enough, that we need to debate – openly and continually – the quality of the human relationships that property produces, and that we must commit to redefine property rules that fail to fulfill the values for which the property system should stand … . Information theorists are mainly interested in the mechanics of the property system, in how it works logistically. Progressive theorists are mainly interested in the outcomes the property system produces: in what social relations it constructs … The rich discussions of plural values that progressive theorists regard as necessary to ensure that property reflects democracy, promotes freedom, and advances human flourishing will not send the simple signals that are, in the eyes of information theorists, central to the functioning of the property system. The standardization and formality that makes the property system 'go,' informationally speaking, are inconsistent with the range of conversations that progressive theorists believe should be taking place …[138]

We come back to these differences in later chapters.

RECOMMENDED READING

There is a lot of reading here – too much for one week. You could concentrate your reading on only one or two of the parts of the chapter if your time is very limited.

John Locke, 'Of property', *Second Treatise of Government* (1690).
Jeremy Waldron, *The Right to Private Property* (Oxford: Clarendon Press, 1988) (concentrate on Locke and Hegel, and on justifications for property generally, especially in Chs. 1, 2, 6 and 10).
Robert Nozick, *Anarchy, State, and Utopia* (Oxford: Basil Blackwell, 1974) pp. 174–182.

---

[137] Jane B. Baron, 'The contested commitments of property' (2009–2010) 61 *Hastings Law Journal* 917 at p. 932.
[138] Ibid. p. 920.

Margaret Davies, *Meanings, Histories, Theories* (Oxford: Routledge-Cavendish, 2007) pp. 86–96, Ch. 4.

Lisa Austin, 'Person, place or thing – property and the structuring of social relations' (2010) 60 *University of Toronto Law Journal* 445 (pp. 445–449 are most relevant for this chapter; the rest will be relevant for topics we look at in later chapters).

Daniel H. Cole and Peter Z. Grossman, *Principles of Law & Economics* (2nd edn, New York: Wolters Kluwer, 2011) (Chs. 1, 3 and 5 as background; Ch. 4 in more detail).

Garrett Hardin, 'The tragedy of the commons' (1968) 162 *Science* 1243.

Harold Demsetz, 'Towards a theory of property rights' (1967) 57 *American Economic Review* 347 (you can omit pp. 357–359).

Elinor Ostrom 'Beyond markets and states: Polycentric governance of complex economic systems' (2010) 100 *American Economic Review* 641, at pp. 641–645, 648–654 and 663–665 (you can skip tables and methodology if you don't find them helpful).

Daniel H. Cole and Elinor Ostrom, 'The variety of property systems and rights in natural resources' Indiana University School of Public and Environmental Affairs Research Paper No. 2010-08-01 (available at http://ssrn.com/abstract=1656418) at pp. 1–4 and 23–30 (you can skip some of the detail in the case studies if you want).

Gregory S. Alexander and Eduardo M. Peñalver, *An Introduction to Property Theory* (Cambridge: Cambridge University Press, 2012): Chs. 2–4 on Locke, Hegel and Kant respectively.

Gregory S. Alexander, Eduardo M. Peñalver, Joseph William Singer and Laura S. Underkuffler, 'A statement of progressive property' (2009) 94 *Cornell Law Review* 743.

Jane B. Baron, 'The contested commitments of property' (2009–2010) 61 *Hastings Law Journal* 917 at pp. 917–934, on progressive property v. information theory.

Questions

(1) Discuss the modern relevance of Locke's justification for private property. Do you think that the criticisms of it which are noted in this chapter and in the materials you have read are justified?

(2) If Locke had read Elinor Ostrom's accounts of successful communal resource use, would he agree that communities who labour on things collectively should acquire communal ownership of them?

(3) Has the Tragedy of the Commons been refuted, or do you think it still has something useful to tell us?

(4) How does Kant's view of property differ from Locke's?

(5) How does Hegel's view of property differ from Locke's?

(6) If we accept Hegel's argument that owning property is necessary for ethical development, does it mean that a civilised society must ensure that everyone has property? (You might want to come back to this question again after reading Chapter 3 *Allocation of Property Rights*.)

(7) What are the essential differences between Merrill and Smith's information theory and progressive property? Which model best describes property law in England and Wales (come back to this question at the end of the course).

3

Allocation of Property Rights

PART I INTRODUCTION

3.1 Alternatives to Lockean Allocation to First Labourers

In this chapter we are interested in Becker's problem of the particular justification for property – what principles should we apply in deciding who should have property in which things? We start by looking at it in relation to original acquisition: in other words, what principles should dictate the allocation of property rights in things that have so far been unpropertised? We saw in Chapter 2 that for Locke this question was inseparable from the question of why *anyone* should be entitled to take unpropertised things for themselves out of the common pool. His argument – that those who expend labour on things held in common should thereby become entitled to private ownership of them – justifies both why anyone should have private property and who should have it. In Part II of this chapter we look at other bases for allocating scarce things that are either new, or newly available, or for some other reason not yet propertised. They are all grounded in observable current practice. In other words, here we are examining some of the principles that societies have in fact developed for allocating first property rights in things. As we will see, Lockean principles are certainly evident here, but they are by no means the only operative principles.

In Part II of the chapter we examine three other bases for allocation of first property rights. The first – the obvious rival to Locke's principle of allocating to the first labourer – is the very familiar principle of allocation to the first taker or first occupier: the principle of first come, first served. This has strong intuitive attractions for most people, and, as we will see, it is routinely used in all kinds of different situations across different kinds of society, although it has some obvious (and less obvious) shortcomings.

We also look at two other situations where we tend to apply rather more complex allocation rules. The first is where a person creates or invents a new tangible or intangible thing. At first sight this looks like an archetypal Lockean situation, and, assuming the creator or inventor is acting on her own behalf rather than as agent or employee for someone else, we might expect a legal system to allocate property rights in the thing to her. In our legal system we do indeed do this, by applying intellectual property rules. However, the protection of creations and inventions by intellectual property law is very different from the protection provided by general property law in respect of other kinds of thing. It is certainly not at all like the absolute private ownership that Locke would award to a person who laboured on a pre-existing unpropertised thing. We consider how and why in para. 3.4.

The other situation we look at, in para. 3.5, is where, for one reason or another, the state decides to take charge of allocation of a particular new resource itself, and not just sit back and wait for a first labourer or first occupier to come along. This may be because of the strategic importance of the thing, its significance for human or environmental wellbeing, or perhaps its potential for generating wealth. One method of state allocation involves the state keeping full ownership, management and distribution of the new resource in its own hands. This is what happened in many countries when commercial air travel first became possible, for example: states ran their own state-owned commercial airlines (and indeed some still do). Another method – the one we are interested in here – is for the state to grant private individuals exclusive licences to exploit the new resource, usually in specified ways. Typically these licences will be granted for a fixed (perhaps renewable) duration, and the way in which the licence is operated by the licensee will be monitored and regulated by the government or by a government-appointed regulator. This basis for allocation of new resources is not new, but it is increasingly used by governments in free market economies. We look at this phenomenon in para. 3.5.

In practice, however original acquisition tells us only part of the story about how property interests are distributed in any society. It has been argued that original acquisition should form the basis of all property holdings, so that the only way of acquiring a lawful title now to any property interest should by acquiring it by transfer (by sale, gift, etc.) or inheritance from the person who acquired it by original acquisition, or from a person whose title similarly derived from the original acquirer. In other words, no-one should be entitled to a property interest now, unless their title goes back to a legitimate first acquirer, via a chain of legitimate transfers. In Part III *From Original Acquisition to Current Distribution* we look at Robert Nozick's argument that if we apply this principle we will have a just distribution of property in society ('justice in holdings'[1]) which ought not to be disturbed by the state. We examine his notion of justice in holdings and consider arguments for recognising the legitimacy of claims to property made on alternative bases. We also look at another bottom-up account of property, Hume's account of the emergence of property by convention, which arguably provides a better starting point for deciding how property should be allocated in a modern society than that provided either by Locke or by Nozick.

Finally in Part IV we look again at the question we first raised in Chapter 1, in para. 1.9. If property is good because it generates wealth and is essential for human flourishing, how can we justify a situation where there are people without property? There are essentially two issues here. If we are to apply Nozick's principle of 'justice in holdings' systematically, we are likely to end up with some people who are

---

[1] Robert Nozick, *Anarchy, State, and Utopia* (Oxford: Basil Blackwell, 1974) pp. 150–152.

impoverished *because* they have been denied access to the benefits of property. These are the people who were not lucky enough to be an original acquirer or a person who acquired property through a succession of lawful transfers or inheritances, nor lucky enough to have inherited access to the windfalls of wealth generated by original acquisition of property. These people seem to be the losers under a property rights system, because they have gained nothing from it yet they have lost the freedom to use all resources that they would have had if there had been no property system. Does this impose some obligation on property owners to compensate these people disadvantaged by the property system, on the basis that property owners' historical gains under the property system have been made at their expense? This question is given added impetus by growing concerns about entrenched inequality in western market economies organised around private property ownership.

There are, of course, other reasons why some people end up with no property, and perhaps the important point is not so much *why* they got into this situation as what should now be done about it. So, the second issue we look at in Part IV is this: if, for whatever reason, there are people without access to resources which are essential to their well-being, should they be entitled to make a claim on these resources which overrides property rights?

PART II ORIGINAL ACQUISITION: ALLOCATING PROPERTY IN UNPROPERTISED THINGS

3.2 First Takers, First Occupancy and the First Come, First Served Principle

The principle that is probably most commonly applied in practice in allocating scarce resources is the principle of first come, first served. It is a feature of several different property allocation systems, both bottom-up systems and top-down systems. A bottom-up allocation system is one where you acquire property rights in an unpropertised thing on your own initiative. For example, in a Lockean system you would do this by exerting your labour on the thing; in a first taking or first occupancy system (the system we are primarily interested in here) you do it by taking control of the thing for yourself.[2] The important point is that in these two bottom-up systems (unlike the other bottom-up systems we note in Part III) you acquire the property rights in the thing only by being the *first* person to have expended labour on it or taken control of it: subsequent labourers and controllers get nothing.

A top-down allocation system, on the other hand, is one where a government or other public or private body has a limited supply of a certain thing and it has to decide how it should be allocated. There are all kind of ways they can do this

---

[2] In this jurisdiction 'taking control' for the purposes of the first occupancy rule involves taking possession of the thing, i.e. taking physical control with the intention of keeping it for yourself. We look at this in more detail in Chapter 11 *Possession and Title.* In other jurisdictions there may be additional requirements, such as publicity, and we have already seen in Chapter 2 that both Kant and Hegel would require more than mere intentional physical control.

(including the licensing systems we consider in para. 3.5), but a common way is by applying the first come, first served principle, in other words by allocating the things to people who apply for them, in the order in which they apply. When this top-down allocation system is in operation, if we want what is on offer and we rule out violence, trickery and corruption, we have to queue for it.

We are focusing here on the bottom-up system of allocation to the first person to take control of something (still used in our law to acquire titles to goods and chattels by adverse possession and finding, as we see in Chapter 11, and also for acquiring ownership of wildlife by fishing, foraging and catching wild animals[3]) and the top-down system of allocation by queue (routinely used here and across the world to allocate tickets to events, to buy meals and drinks in restaurants, bars and cafes, to get seats on buses, trains and planes and in many other situations).

(a) Advantages of the First Come, First Served Principle

There are good reasons why we tend to use the first come, first served principle in these kinds of situation. People seem to feel intuitively that it is a fair and just allocation principle, and to disapprove of attempts to get round it – people don't like queue-jumpers. In fact, as several commentators have pointed out, it is an ordering system that people often adopt spontaneously amongst themselves, even when there are no formal rules or sanctions requiring or enforcing it, and even when (as is usually the case in a queue) they are 'a randomly assembled group of strangers'.[4] One of the reasons may be that it is a remarkably easy system for participants to run. The rules are easy to understand and surprisingly universal (although with interesting cultural variations[5]) and it is easy for participants to see who is next entitled – it is usually obvious who the first taker is, because she is the person who is in physical control, and in queuing cases the queue itself shows the order in which people arrived. Also, there is the feeling that the first in time rule is egalitarian and non-discriminatory. It offers all of us an equal opportunity to acquire the desired thing, and whether or not we succeed in acquiring it will not depend on our race, or our age, gender or wealth, or on anything else about us: the only relevant factor is the time we took control, or the time we arrived and the length of time we waited.

---

[3] But only, of course, where people are free to carry out these activities. In this country, for example, although catching fish and wild animals is regulated by private licences, fishing is prohibited without a state licence in many inland waters and wild animals captured on private land without a licence usually belong to the landowner rather than the captor. For foraging, see Jennifer Lee and Supriya Garikipati, 'Negotiating the non-negotiable: British foraging law in theory and practice' (2011) *Journal of Environmental Law* 415, and compare Anna Sténs and Camilla Sandström, 'Divergent interests and ideas around property rights: The case of berry harvesting in Sweden' (2013) 33 *Forest Policy and Economics* 56.

[4] Kevin Gray, 'Property in a queue', in Gregory S. Alexander and Eduardo M. Peñalver (eds.), *Property and Community* (Oxford: Oxford University Press, 2010) p. 165 at p. 167. See also Katharine G. Young, 'Rights and queues: On distributive contests in the modern state' (2016) 55 *Columbia Journal of Transnational Law* 65 and the texts she cites at p. 76.

[5] Young, 'Rights and queues', fn. 4 above, pp. 76–78, although Gray, 'Property in a queue', fn. 4 above, pp. 177–179, suggests that it is primarily an Anglo-Saxon phenomenon.

In both situations being ahead of others is perceived as conferring a moral entitlement. In the case of queues, as Young points out,[6] allocation goes first to those who have not only arrived earliest but also spent longest waiting. Getting there early has its own virtue: if you got there earlier in time, it probably means that you planned further ahead and took more trouble to get there early than someone who arrived later. And the longer you have waited, the greater your desert: waiting is taken to be an unpleasant activity[7] and by waiting in a queue for your turn you have demonstrated orderliness, patience, respect for the rights of others, and a willingness and ability to co-operate with strangers. So it is 'only fair' that you should get priority in allocation.

Some of that also applies in the first taking and first occupancy cases, but there are also other hardships and virtues to be taken into account. First takers and first occupiers demonstrate enterprise, hard work and autonomy, but in addition, in the capture cases in particular, there can also be an added Lockean moral claim, because capture tends to involve rather more labour than queuing. The classic capture cases all involve conflicts between hunters, where the first hunter on the scene has put a lot of time and effort into organising the hunt, locating the prey and trying to catch it, when the second hunter comes along and snatches it away before the first hunter has managed to take full control of it.[8]

However, it is not just that the first in time deserve their priority because they have worked for it and behaved virtuously. In addition there is the idea that first in time allocation is a good in itself, promoting civil society. It inculcates values that are good for society – not only the virtuous kinds of behaviour noted above but also social cohesion and co-operation, respect for social order, and respect for the rights of others and for common values. And it allows everyone to see that virtue is rewarded: first takers, first occupiers and queuers are seen to get prioritised access to resources.

The first in time principle has other practical advantages, at least partly attributable to the fact that people approve of it and obey it voluntarily. From the state's perspective, it is notably easy and cheap to operate administratively. As a bottom-up rule, the first taker and first occupancy rule is self-executing: you acquire property in the thing you take simply by taking it into your physical control. All the work is yours: the state has to do nothing except passively recognise the status quo. The queuing rule is top-down, in that there has to be someone to distribute the things people are queuing for, but even here the cost and effort involved is small. The

---

[6] Young, 'Rights and queues', fn. 4 above, p. 69.
[7] Gray, 'Property in a queue', fn. 4 above, pp. 171–172.
[8] The classic account of the arguments can be found in a celebrated US case about hunting foxes, *Pierson v. Post* (1805) 3 Cai R 175, where the majority held that, because the first hunters had not yet taken full control of the fox, the fox belonged to the interloper; the minority argued strongly that it should belong to the first hunters because of the hard work they had put into the hunt (everyone assumed that it would be socially desirable to encourage people to kill as many foxes as possible). The economic arguments for and against the decision of the majority are discussed by Dhammika Dharmapala and Rohan Pitchford, 'An economic analysis of "Riding to Hounds": Pierson v. Post revisited' (2002) 18 *Journal of Law, Economics, and Organization* 39, abstract available at https://doi.org/10.1093/jleo/18.1.39.

institution in charge has to do nothing more than work out the time order in which applications are made, and usually the queue system will do that for them anyway. It does not have to consider the comparative merits or qualifications or deserts of each applicant, or formulate or apply principles of allocation. Enforcement and policing is similarly relatively easy and cheap. People *do* approve of the rules, obey them voluntarily and apply social sanctions against those who attempt to subvert them, leaving little for the state or anyone else to do.

(b) Limits of the First Come, First Served Principle

We can put against these advantages some quite formidable disadvantages. The very fact that allocation does not take into account the personal qualities or personal circumstances of potential beneficiaries severely limits its scope. If we take the 'capture' cases first, the first person to take control of a resource is not necessarily the person best qualified (by knowledge, experience, expertise or personal characteristics) to make the 'best' use of it, whether we measure 'best' by reference to economic efficiency or by social or environmental good. Nor is she necessarily the person who needs it most or most deserves it, or 'ought' to have it judging by any other criteria. Also, there is the additional problem that if we award property to the first person to take control of a previously unpropertised thing, there is a real danger of over-taking (if in doubt, take more than you think you will need, to be on the safe side) and premature taking (catch the fish when they are not yet fully grown, because if you wait, someone else may get there first). This is not only potentially inefficient, viewed from an economic perspective, but it also has serious consequences for the conservation of natural resources.[9] Unsurprisingly, then, even when first taker rules do apply to the propertisation of environmentally sensitive natural resources, local communities often evolve their own self-regulating rules governing the quantities that each person can take, and when and how taking is permitted, as we saw in Chapter 2 *Conceptions and Justifications*. And if local communities fail to evolve or police effective rules and the sustainability of the resource is threatened, state regulation to impose similar limitations becomes necessary. So, for resources like water, fish and other wildlife, for example, even when the base rule for allocation remains the first taker rule, local, national and international regulation may well limit how much can be taken, when and how, and often even by whom.[10]

Some of these factors also limit the fairness and usefulness of the queue as an allocation device. The person ahead in the queue is not necessarily the person who will make the best use of the resource, nor the person who needs or deserves it most, and queuing begins to look less efficient if you factor in the opportunity costs of the queuers (i.e. the value of whatever else they could have been doing with the time and

---

[9] See David D. Haddock, 'First possession versus optimal timing: Limiting the dissipation of economic value' (1986) 64 *Washington University Law Quarterly* 775 for the economic arguments supporting our intuitive feelings about over-taking and premature taking.

[10] See, for example, the highly complex fishing quota system governing fishing in international waters described in *UK Association of Fish Producer Organisations* v. *Secretary of State for Environment, Food and Rural Affairs* [2013] EWHC 1959.

energy they expended on queuing).[11] For these reasons it can be argued that allocation purely by queue is appropriate only for recreational goods and services such as tickets for entertainment, arts or sports events, or for the orderly distribution of services – scarce and non-scarce – like seats on a bus or meals in a cafeteria.

And indeed allocation *solely* on a first come, first served principle is quite rare, even in queuing cases, and even where the queue is for something like tickets to attend an event. Many arts venues sell 'friends membership' (often several tiers of membership at different prices) which entitles members to priority in ticket allocation. This has two advantages, from the venue's point of view: the venue creates additional revenue for itself by selling priority (a point we return to later), and it goes some way towards ensuring that scarce tickets go first to loyal supporters. Football clubs use similar systems, as well as season-ticket sales and loyalty points giving priority tickets to regular attendees, and are also required to offer an allocation of tickets to away clubs, to ensure that away fans can also attend the match.[12] These and other venues, increasingly concerned about ticket touts and ticket touting websites, may also take steps like limiting the number of tickets each applicant can buy, or requiring queuing in person, or verification of credentials, in an attempt to ensure that tickets go directly to those who genuinely intend to attend the event rather than those who intend to sell the ticket on.

These kinds of modification to the basic queue are even more common outside the recreational context, where the queue is for essential goods or services and there has to be some way of giving priority to applicants who need them most, or most urgently. In situations like this it is very common for institutions to have a base principle of first in time allocation, but to move people up (and therefore also down) in the queue to accommodate applicants in special need. Queues for hospital treatment and for social housing operate on this kind of system in this country.[13]

3.3 Other Problems With First in Time Allocation

There are three other problems worth noting which limit the usefulness of the first in time principle of allocation. The first applies to allocations by queue and the other two to the 'capture' cases.

(a) Virtual Queues

Most of the theoretical literature on the virtues of the queue, and on the social values it inculcates and the personal qualities and endeavours it rewards, assumes a physical, visible queue, where queuers must attend and wait personally and can see others doing the same thing. It has always been questionable how far these beneficial effects of queues and queueing arise where the operation of the queue is

[11] For a fuller explanation of opportunity costs see Daniel H. Cole and Peter Z. Grossman, *Principles of Law & Economics* (2nd edn, New York: Wolters Kluwer, 2011) pp. 4–5.

[12] www.premierleague.com/tickets and see also www.efl.com/global/section5.aspx

[13] See Young, 'Rights and queues', fn. 4 above.

not visible to the queuers (as, for example, in a queue for hospital treatment or social housing), and so waiting for your turn does not involve a prolonged period of close proximity with your fellow queuers, leaving little scope for social interaction between all of you. In situations such as these, there is no community of queuers, only bilateral relationships between the allocating institution and each person in the queue, and each queuer must take it on trust that the queue is operating fairly. This objection becomes all the more important because physical queues are becoming increasingly rare in many of the situations where they were once routinely used in their simplest form: in the allocation of tickets to entertainments and events, physical queues are now almost wholly replaced by virtual electronic queues. If the non-physical queue is now the norm, we perhaps need a radical re-think about the benefits of queues as a resource allocation device.

(b) Problems of Proof and the Windfall Effect

When the first in time principle is used in the 'capture' cases – in other words, where a person acquires property in a previously unpropertised thing by taking control of it – there is a different problem, although one that is shared with allocation according to Lockean principles. In both cases, the first acquirer seems to get too much. By being the first person to take control of something or the first person to exert labour on it, you become owner of it without having had to pay anyone for it, and this ownership is perpetual, continuing long after your death for so long as the thing itself continues to exist. If the thing in question is part of the physical fabric of the earth this seems an extraordinary windfall for you and even more so for your descendants, who inherit either this perpetual ownership of part of the earth or the wealth you acquired during your lifetime by selling it to someone else. This is a problem we have already noted and we return to it again later on in this chapter, but there is a particular practical effect of the perpetual ownership reward given to first takers and first labourers which we should note here. This is that, because ownership arises out of a single physical event that took place at a fixed point in time, it becomes increasingly difficult to prove as time elapses.[14] We come back to this particular point in Part III of this chapter.

(c) Control, Exclusion and Possession

We have already said that, in this jurisdiction, where the first taker or first occupancy rule applies, you acquire property in a previously unpropertised thing by being the first person to take possession of it, in other words you have to take physical control of it on your own behalf and for your own benefit, with the intention of excluding others. This makes sense in a jurisdiction such as ours where possession and private ownership are closely linked, so that we can say that by taking possession of a thing

---

[14] Jeremy Waldron, "'To bestow stability upon Possession': Hume's alternative to Locke' in James Penner and Henry E. Smith (eds.), *Philosophical Foundations of Property Law* (Oxford: Oxford University Press, 2013) p. 1, at p. 5.

you are treating it as if it was yours.[15] However, in many societies people do not take 'possession' of the land and resources they use and regard as their own, in a way that we would recognise as possession. Our common law concept of possession involves exclusion of all others from a physical space or physical object. This is not appropriate for resource use patterns which involve, for example, pastoralism,[16] or sharing the use of (and responsibility) for natural resources between the inhabitants of an area so that different groups are entitled to make specific use of them at different times and for different purposes, in accordance with rules agreed between themselves. This pattern of resource use is common amongst many of the indigenous peoples of Australia, Canada, and other parts of the world, as we see in Chapter 9 *Multiple Property Rights Systems.* If we import into their legal systems our notion of acquiring property in unpropertised things by taking possession of them, it would mean that none of those people would be regarded as having acquired property interests in 'their' land and other resources, no matter how long-established their patterns of resource use were. This is certainly how early colonial settlers of those territories saw it – they regarded land occupied by indigenous people as unpropertised,[17] in other words as available for first taking by European settlers.[18] As we see in Chapter 9, it is only recently that national courts in Australia and Canada have come to appreciate that, if the first in time rule is to operate effectively in relation to land and other resources used and occupied by the indigenous peoples in their countries, 'first taking' and 'first occupancy' must not be defined in terms of western notions of possession. In Canada, for example, the Supreme Court in *Tsilhqot'in Nation* v. *British Columbia* in 2014[19] rejected the notion of exclusionary control as a basis for first occupancy in favour of a test based on 'communication' to outsiders, as Yaëll Emerich notes:

> The Supreme Court of Canada, as it attempts to establish a new form of possession for the purposes of Aboriginal title that is not tied to common law notions, has made the communicative role even more explicit. In order to ground a claim of Aboriginal title, 'the Aboriginal group in question must show that it has historically acted in a way that would *communicate to third parties* that it held the land for its own purposes'.[20]

3.4 Creators and Inventors

As we said in para. 3.1, at first sight it may seem uncontroversial that a legal system should award property in newly created and invented things to the creator or

---

[15] See further Chapter 11 *Possession and Title.*

[16] 'Pastoral' means the same as 'nomadic', i.e. moving from place to place rather than settling in a fixed place: 'nomadic' is regarded as a perjorative term in some countries.

[17] The technical term commonly used in this kind of context is 'terra nullius' (land belonging to no-one): see further Chapter 9 *Multiple Property Rights Systems.*

[18] As we saw in Chapter 2 *Conceptions and Justifications*, this was John Locke's view.

[19] *Tsilhqot'in Nation* v. *British Columbia* [2014] 2 SCR 256. See further Chapter 9.

[20] Yaëll Emerich, 'Possession' in Michele Graziadei and Lionel Smith (eds.), *Comparative Property Law: Global Perspectives* (Cheltenham and Northampton MA: Edward Elgar Publishing, 2017) p. 171 at p. 180. The passage he quotes from *Tsilqot'in* is at para. 38 of the Supreme Court of Canada's judgment (emphasis added by Emerich).

inventor, assuming she acted on her own behalf rather than as an employee or agent for someone else. This seems an obvious application of Lockean principles: the thing itself is the product of her labour, and so she deserves reward even more than the person who mixed his labour with a pre-existing thing, for all the reasons Locke gave. Indeed, Locke's arguments about incentive seems even more compelling, and so too do arguments about personhood and justice. And the case of the creator and the inventor is made even stronger by the fact that she took nothing out of the common pool of resources when she created or invented the thing: she took nothing away that others were formerly free to use.

(a) Intellectual Property Rights

Interestingly, however, although in our legal system we do sometimes award full exclusionary ownership of an unpropertised thing to a person who has mixed their labour with it, we do not do the same in true cases of creation or invention – in other words, where the creator or inventor conjures up a new thing using only their own intellectual efforts. The products of creation and invention that the law protects are intangible things – ideas, inventions, signs, designs, information, etc. – which have become embodied in physical form, and the law protects them (the intangible things, not their physical form) by intellectual property law. Lionel Bently and Brad Sherman illustrate the distinction between the physical form and the intangible thing embodied in it by giving the example of a letter sent to a recipient: the recipient becomes absolute owner of the physical letter, but the writer retains intellectual property rights in its contents.[21]

It is beyond the scope of this book to look at the different kinds of protection that intellectual property law gives to different kinds of creation and invention, but broadly it is provided by specialist property rights systems such as copyrights, patents, trade marks and registered design rights.[22] The rights that creators and inventors have under these specialist property rights systems vary widely from system to system (so, for example, the rights of the holder of the copyright in a novel are different from those of someone holding a patent in a new method of strengthening glass). However, none of them bears much resemblance to the full private ownership that Locke saw as the proper reward for first labourers and first takers. In particular, intellectual property rights tend to be neither perpetual nor wholly exclusionary. This has nothing to do with the fact that the things protected by

---

[21] Lionel Bently and Brad Sherman, *Intellectual Property Law* (4th edn, Oxford: Oxford University Press, 2014) p. 3.

[22] For reasons which are interesting but also beyond the scope of this book, the categorisation of these specialist rights systems as property rights systems is controversial: see Helena R. Howe and Jonathan Griffiths (eds.), *Concepts of Property in Intellectual Property Law* (Cambridge: Cambridge University Press, 2013); Hanoch Dagan, *Property: Values and Institutions* (Oxford: Oxford University Press, 2011) pp. 77–80 and 83–84; and Adam Mossoff, 'Trademark as a property right' (2017) George Mason Law & Economics Research Paper No. 17-15, available at: https://ssrn.com/abstract=2941763. However, much of the criticism of 'propertisation' of intellectual property wrongly assumes that property must mean absolute private ownership.

intellectual property law are intangible: our legal system has no difficulty with the idea that you can be the absolute private owner of, for example, money, or shares in a company, or the other intangible things we look at in Chapter 7 *Objects of Property Interests*.

(b) Special Features of Intellectual Property

Broadly, intellectual property rights are different because the intangible things that intellectual property protects have three features which make them special for present purposes, and not appropriate for simple private ownership.

The first is that they are non-rivalrous, in the sense we explained in Chapter 2 *Conceptions and Justifications* para. 2.11(c). In other words, use of the intangible thing by one person does not lessen anyone else's opportunity to use it: if you sing a song I wrote, it does not limit my own opportunity to go on singing it and to allow others to sing it. This is significant because, as we saw in Chapter 2 *Conceptions and Justifications* para. 2.11(c), it is not always appropriate to protect non-rivalrous things by private ownership.

The second special feature of the things protected by intellectual property law is that the moral claim of creators and inventors to property rights in their creation or invention is not quite the same as that of someone who has improved a previously unpropertised tangible thing by labouring on it. On the one hand, whilst the creator or inventor takes nothing away from the common pool of resources that were formerly freely available to all, she does owe a great deal to those who have gone before (most creations and inventions develop ideas embodied in earlier creations and inventions by others), so her moral claim to absolute ownership of her creation or invention is different from, but not necessarily stronger than, that of a Lockean labourer. On the other hand, she has an additional moral claim not appropriate for most Lockean labourers, which is a claim to have her work attributed to her even after she no longer has any other rights in it, in other words to have public recognition of her 'authorship'. After arguing that Lockean labourers ought only to be rewarded proportionately to the increase in value generated by their labour,[23] Hanoch Dagan makes both these points about the creator's moral claims:

> Creative activity always engages, invokes, and is inspired by – and thus vitally dependent upon – a cultural heritage: a range of pre-existing cultural raw materials, and a set of established methods, practices and techniques. Therefore, the requirements of added value and proportionality imply that [creators and inventors] are unlikely to deserve this entire value ... .
>
> Because authors' reward should not take a proprietary form that allows them to extract the entire market value of their intellectual products, labor theory does not require that authors enjoy an indefeasible right to exclude. In particular, labor theory is compatible with – although it does not necessarily require – an intellectual property regime that curtails in some cases the right to deny access, and limits copyright holders' material claims to some portion of the market value of their intellectual

---

[23] See Chapter 2 *Conceptions and Justifications* para. 2.6(a).

products, while insisting upon proper attribution as a necessary form of public praise and gratitude. (The requirement of attribution is not only important from the standpoint of desert; it is of course also a vital entailment of personhood theory.)[24]

However, the third and most important point is that there are different, and competing, policy considerations here. This is evident from the many interest groups currently engaged in fierce and polarised arguments, some arguing strongly that the protection provided by intellectual property law is inadequate and ought now to be increased, and others arguing equally strongly that it is excessive and ought to be diminished. As Bently and Sherman point out, this makes intellectual property law highly politicised, with debates about policy objectives tending to be caricatured as battles between 'good' and 'evil':

> On the one hand, there are groups who represent existing (or putative) right holders, which have tended to argue that the existing laws provide inadequate protection – that, for example, the threshold for patent protection for genetically modified biological material is set too high, that copyright and patent protection need to be explicitly extended to cover multimedia works and software, that trade mark owners are not sufficiently protected against cyber squatters who acquire related domain names, and so on. At the other extreme, there are a range of groups who oppose stronger intellectual property protection – whether they be representatives of the developing world, consumers and users of intellectual property (such as home tapers, digital samplers, appropriation artists, 'netizens', and librarians), defenders of free speech, classical liberal economic theorists, competition lawyers, post-modern theorists, ecologists, or religious groups.[25]

This makes the justifications for allocating intellectual property rights to creators and inventors complex, and quite far removed from those put forward to justify allocating property rights in other kinds of things to Lockean labourers or first takers.

3.5 Allocation by National or Supra-National Licensing

There are good reasons why a state might want to take charge of the allocation of newly created, or newly important, unpropertised things. If the development or conservation of a thing is a matter of national or public importance, the state has a responsibility to ensure that whoever ends up operating or controlling the thing will use it in ways that bring the maximum return and benefit to the state and to the public, and cause the least harm to the state, its citizens and the environment. Also, if there are to be multiple users of the thing, the state has the responsibility of ensuring that their activities are co-ordinated.

---

[24] Dagan, *Property: Values and Institutions* pp. 82–83. For 'personhood theory' see Margaret Jane Radin, 'Property and personhood' (1982) 34 *Stanford Law Review* 957 and Chapter 7 *Objects of Property Interests* para. 7.10.

[25] Bently and Sherman, *Intellectual Property Law* p. 4, and see also Lawrence C. Becker, 'Deserving to own intellectual property' (1992) 68 *Chicago – Kent Law Review* 69.

An obvious way of doing all this is for the state, or some supra-national body, to take charge of allocation itself rather than leaving it to chance or the market. This may or may not mean that the state takes full ownership and management of the thing for itself. We are interested here in the situations where it does not, but instead allocates licences to private individuals or bodies, giving them rights to operate the thing for their own private profit. The state, however, retains overall control by imposing conditions in the licence on the way the licensee is permitted to exploit the resource, and by requiring licensees to act in accordance with regulations imposed by a special purpose government regulatory authority which is set up to protect and promote the public interest in the exploitation of the resource.

Since the state is in charge of the allocation process and dictates the terms of the licences, it can ensure that licensees have the necessary knowledge and expertise, so it is not left to the market to arrange for management of the thing to be in competent hands. For the same reasons, the state should also be able to ensure that the licensee acts in the public interest and in accordance with approved environmental standards. How far this is compatible, in principle and in practice, with licensees also operating their licenses for private profit, is controversial.

However, for present purposes the important point is that this kind of government licence allocation system not only allows the government to regulate the exploitation of the newly propertised thing, it also makes allocatees pay for their allocation. This does not happen when resources are allocated by any of the other methods we have looked at in this chapter – allocating property to the first labourer, or on the first in time principle, or to creators and inventors.[26] Since an allocation of a previously unpropertised thing gives allocatees potentially lucrative monopoly rights in resources which were formerly open to all and can be seen as part of our human heritage (whether natural resources like water or the radio spectrum, or products of collective human ingenuity and endeavour, like the internet or transport infrastructure), it seems reasonable to require them to give something back to the common pool by way of exchange.

Rights to use the radio spectrum provide a good example of the way the regulatory licence system works in this jurisdiction. The radio spectrum is a natural resource consisting of a set of radio frequencies. It is used for a variety of commercial and public interest purposes, including radio and television broadcasting, mobile phone communication, civil aviation, the military, navigation systems, scientific research, surveillance, emergency services, meteorology and many other public services. It is a scarce resource (demand greatly exceeds supply), and use is rivalrous in the sense explained in Chapter 2 *Conceptions and Justifications* para. 2.11(c) ('two individuals cannot use the same frequency at the same time in the same place without cancelling out or interfering with both transmissions'[27]). Although there are those who

---

[26] Queuers are in a slightly different position, in that often there is a charge for whatever it is they are queuing for, and they may even have to 'buy' priority in the queue by e.g. joining 'members' clubs that offer priority booking, as we saw in para. 3.2(b).

[27] Marguerita Colangelo, *Creating Property Rights: Law and Regulation of Secondary Trading in the European Union* (Leiden and Boston: Martinus Nijhoff Publishers, 2012) p. 68.

advocate allocation of frequencies by the first taker principle,[28] at present at least it is done by international, regional and state authorities. At the international level the radio spectrum is allocated between states by the International Telecommunication Union, a United Nations body,[29] and the UK allocation is allocated to users in this country by Ofcom, the government regulatory body.[30] Ofcom awards licences to use specific frequency bands in the spectrum to successful bidders at an auction,[31] and the licences dictate how the allocation can be used and the fees payable by the licensee for its use. Since Ofcom also has powers to reorganise allocations to make space available for new entrants,[32] and the capacity of the spectrum is constantly being increased by technological advances,[33] there is an ongoing process of allocating frequencies. So, for example, Ofcom is in the process of auctioning additional parts of the spectrum for extra 4G high-speed mobile broadband services, made available by the Ministry of Defence as part of a wider Government initiative to free up public sector spectrum for civil uses,[34] and in April 2018 it held the first round of auctions selling off parts of the 5G spectrum, raising more than £1,350 million.[35]

Rights to abstract water from inland waterways, rights to catch fish in national and international waters, rights to use airport landing slots, and many other kinds of resource rights are all allocated by similar government licensing schemes. We consider their status as property rights in Chapter 6 *New Property Interests and the Numerus Clausus* para. 6.12.

PART III FROM ORIGINAL ACQUISITION TO PRESENT DISTRIBUTION

3.6 Nozick's Principle of Justice in Holdings

In para. 3.1 we referred to Robert Nozick's proposition that the state ought not to disturb the distribution of resources that comes about by applying the principles of 'justice in original acquisition' and 'justice in transfer'.[36] So, if originally the first ever title to a property interest in a thing was acquired legitimately, and it has since been passed on by a series of lawful transfers (by sale, or gift or inheritance, or by any of

---

[28] Richard A. Epstein, 'Possession and licences: The FCC, weak spectrum rights, and the LightSquared debacle' in Yun-chien Chang (ed.), *Law and Economics of Possession* (Cambridge: Cambridge University Press, 2015) pp. 237–265.

[29] www.ofcom.org.uk/about-ofcom/international/spectrum/itu.

[30] www.ofcom.org.uk/spectrum/spectrum-management; there is also extensive regulation at European level: see www.ofcom.org.uk/about-ofcom/international/spectrum/cept.

[31] S. 8 of the Wireless Telegraphy Act 2006. Competence and capacity of bidders is also taken into account.

[32] By 'clearance and co-existence' measures.   [33] www.ofcom.org.uk/spectrum/spectrum-management

[34] Following on after an earlier round of auctions for this re-released 4G spectrum: see Ofcom press release, 'Ofcom announces details of 2016 spectrum auction', 26 October 2015 www.ofcom.org.uk/about-ofcom/latest/media/media-releases/2015/2016-spectrum-auction: 'The auction is designed to be fair and transparent, enabling the spectrum to be awarded to those who can put it to the most efficient use in the best interests of consumers'.

[35] https://5g.co.uk/guides/5g-uk-auction/. We come back to this example in Chapter 7 *Objects of Property Interests* para. 7(6)(a), where we look at the nature of intangible property.

[36] Nozick, Anarchy, State, and Utopia, fn. 1 above, pp. 150–152.

the processes we note in para. 16.30 of Chapter 16 *Registration*[37]) it is not justifiable for the state to interfere with the title of the current property interest holder. This is how Nozick puts it:

> If the world were wholly just, the following inductive definition would exhaustively cover the subject of justice in holdings.
>
> 1. A person who acquires a holding in accordance with the principle of justice in acquisition is entitled to that holding.
> 2. A person who acquires a holding in accordance with the principle of justice in transfer, from someone else entitled to the holding, is entitled to the holding.
> 3. No one is entitled to a holding except by repeated applications of 1. and 2.[38]

This principle is part of Nozick's broader neo-liberal argument for a minimal state:

> a minimal state, limited to the narrow functions of protection against force, theft, fraud, enforcement of contracts, and so on, is justified; . . . any more extensive state will violate persons' rights not to be forced to do certain things, and is unjustified.[39]

So, as far as property is concerned, Nozick's point is that it is unjustifiable for a state to attempt to *redistribute* property acquired in accordance with his principles of justice in original acquisition and justice in transfer (except perhaps to rectify violations of these principles),[40] whether by taxation or by what US scholars would call 'takings' of property and we call compulsory purchase in the public interest.

However, we are not concerned here with Nozick's broader argument for a minimal state, and we look only briefly (in Part IV) at arguments challenging his view that the state should never interfere with property interests justly acquired and justly transferred. Our interest here is with two questions raised by this idea of justice in holdings. The first is whether it is a viable basis for assessing the legitimacy of our present distribution of property. The second is whether we can and should assess the legitimacy of current claims to property on some other basis. In other words, are there any other bases on which we can say that a person's claim to property is legitimate, even if she cannot prove that she can trace her title back to a legitimate original acquisition through an unbroken chain of just transfers – and even if we have positive evidence that this is *not* the way her property interest reached her?

3.7 Legitimacy of Property Holdings

The first point to make is that in practice, with some very limited exceptions, we do not test legitimacy of property holdings by seeing whether their original acquisition

---

[37] That is, transfers by operation of law, for example when an individual dies or goes bankrupt, or a company is dissolved or liquidated. For formal transfers, see Chapter 14 *Acquiring Interests Informally* paras. 14.1-14.2.

[38] Nozick, *Anarchy, State, and Utopia*, fn. 1 above, p. 151.

[39] Ibid. p. ix. Nozick expands his minimal state argument in Part I of the book.

[40] In other words, where property interests were acquired by fraud, theft, forcible taking or other illegitimate means: ibid. pp. 152–153, where Nozick acknowledges the difficulties in unpicking these violations and rectifying injustice in holdings. See further para. 3.8 below.

was legitimate and that title then passed to the current holder via a chain of just transfers. It is instructive to consider why this is so.

(a) Provenance

As we see in Chapter 11 *Possession and Title*, a rare exception is provided by cultural objects and some other valuable and unique goods, where we do indeed require sellers to prove 'provenance' to potential buyers, in other words to prove a chain of legitimate transfers by which the object moved from the original owner and came into their hands. You would not be regarded as the legitimate owner of, say, the *Mona Lisa* or a Henry Moore sculpture unless you could prove this. However, we rarely do the same for other goods. Our rules on acquiring a good title to goods are quite complex but generally people in physical possession of goods are taken to be the legitimate owners unless there is anything to suggest the contrary, and it is even possible to acquire legitimate ownership of something by buying it from a thief.[41]

In the case of land, until property interests started to become registrable at the beginning of the twentieth century, title to interests in land did in theory depend on provenance, but (for obvious reasons) it was never necessary to go back to original acquisition, at least in the case of ownership interests. The periods over which titles to ownership had to be traced back were progressively shortened so that now, even when it is necessary, the period can be as short as 15 years. And now that most land is covered by land registration, legitimacy of property holdings in land is generally now acquired by registration in the Land Register,[42] as it is in most common law and civil law jurisdictions.[43]

(b) Acquisitions Based on Long Use or Conduct

Also, we (and many other jurisdictions) allow property interests to be acquired and transferred by several processes which do not come within Nozick's descriptions of just original acquisition and just transfers. These include acquiring titles to land and to goods by taking possession of them (lawfully or unlawfully: see Chapter 11 *Possession and Title* and Chapter 12 *Adverse Possession of Land*), acquiring other property interests by long use (Chapter 13 *Non-possessory Land Use Rights*) and acquiring interests by doctrines such as estoppel and constructive trust, which allow the courts to award property interests on the basis of justice or fairness (Chapter 14 *Acquiring Interests Informally*). These nearly all involve violations of pre-existing property rights, but for reasons we look at in later chapters, we do not regard them as 'unjust'.

---

[41] Chapter 15 *Enforceability and Priority of Property Interests* para. 15.6(b).

[42] This does not totally remove the need to prove provenance, because anyone who wants to register a property interest at a registry still has to prove *to the Registry* that she is entitled to be registered.

[43] The USA is a notable exception: many states still rely in principle on the kind of attenuated proof of provenance rules described in this paragraph. However, their significance is minimal because of title insurance, by which insurance companies guarantee titles: see further Thomas W. Merrill and Henry E. Smith, *Oxford Introductions to US Law: Property* (Oxford: Oxford University Press, 2010) pp. 166–171.

(c) Acquisitions by Dispossession

However, the most important point is that most property holdings in this country, and probably in every country in the world, do not satisfy the justice in holdings principle, especially in relation to land holdings. The problem is that it can *only* be satisfied by people whose property rights descend from an entitlement which was established without dispossessing anyone else, and there must be very few people in the world in that category. Most countries in the world have had waves of revolutions, civil wars and tribal wars, invasions and persecution of religious or ethnic minorities, all involving mass land dispossessions, even without taking account of more isolated cases where the strong and powerful have taken land from the weak. As David Haddock points out,

> Mightiest possession explains more that has happened and more that has become law than does first possession.[44]

(d) The Insuperable Problem of Proof

Even more tellingly, if there are people whose land titles have indeed descended directly and legitimately from an original acquisition that did not involve the dispossession of someone else, how are they supposed to prove it? Jeremy Waldron points out the obvious problem:

> [Nozick's principle of justice in holdings] is tremendously demanding of information. It is, as he calls it, a historical conception: one justifies [the present property holder's] property in [the land] now, not by the truth of any factual proposition dated in the present, but by a succession of factual propositions dating back into the more and more distant past, back all the way into the dawn of time when a human first confronted [the land], hopefully under [conditions necessary to give rise to Lockean first taking or first occupancy]. The morality of this is not particularly edifying: is first occupancy's petulant claim, 'I was here first' really a good way of rebutting present claims of need? And quite apart from the morality, establishing who was where when is awfully difficult, as the modern indigenous rights industry reveals. Who did what first, and under what conditions things were subsequently done to them – all this has to be untangled at a historical (and indeed pre-historical) level, if any theory of the Nozickian form is to be applied to legitimize indigenous holdings. This may be simple, say, for New Zealand, with only one wave of relatively recent indigenous settlement (though even there it is not at all simple as the Waitangi Tribunal has found); but try thinking about it for India. Or Kosovo.[45]

(e) Querying 'Justice in Holdings'

So, for one reason or another, the distribution of property in this country bears no resemblance to the one we would have had if it had resulted from 'just acquisition' and 'just transfers', particularly in the case of land and other natural resources. Few of those who hold titles to land now, acquired them through an unbroken chain of

[44] Haddock, 'First possession versus optimal timing', fn. 9 above, p. 792.
[45] Waldron, '"To bestow stability upon possession"', fn. 14 above, p. 1 and p. 5.

just transfers going back to a just original acquisition, and even if they did, it is highly unlikely that they could prove it. In other words, Nozick's theory of distribution does not justify him in concluding that, *in the world as it is*, states should not disturb the present distribution of property. This has led Fennell and McAdams to suggest that Nozick's theory would be more useful if rephrased in an inverted form:

> Suppose we accept Nozick's idea that the justice of a distribution depends on its history, but reject the claim that our particular history gives people morally justifiable entitlements over the specific holdings that they currently have. The principle of rectification would [then] ... flip the advice about the state's role in addressing distribution. Instead of 'if all past holdings and transfers were just (or have been fully rectified where not just), then the current distribution is just,' the proper lesson is 'because not all past holdings and transfers were just (and the injustices have not been fully rectified), the current distribution is not just'.[46]

So, you could say that Nozick's argument provides good reasons why the state *ought* to interfere with the current distribution of property holdings in land, not reasons why it should not. At least, they would be good reasons if we accepted Nozick's notion of what amounts to 'justice in holdings', which many do not.

3.8 Force or Last Occupancy

Both Haddock[47] and Waldron have pointed out that a more plausible way of assessing the legitimacy of present property holdings might be by reference to last or prior occupancy rather than a series of just transfers deriving from legitimate original acquisition:[48]

> one view about the origin of property presents it as a matter largely of the successful use of force. The powerful and the cunning grab things, both from nature and from others who may already have the things in their possession, and the powerful and the cunning manage to hold on to the things they have grabbed and use their power, politically, to persuade the whole society to throw its force behind their depredations. This is a theory of occupancy, if you like, but it is not a theory of first occupancy; it is more like a theory of last occupancy. The group most recently in possession of land or resources at the time that a powerful state is established gets consecrated as the legal owner of that land, whether it was the first occupant or not.
>
> Informationally, this is a much less demanding theory; no need for any inquiry going back, as Locke's and Pufendorf's accounts have to go back, to the dawn of time.
>
> Morally, it is much less demanding also; in fact many would say it is morally bankrupt .... [49]

---

[46] Lee Anne Fennell and Richard H. McAdams, 'Inversion aversio' (2019) 86 *University of Chicago Law Review* 797 at pp. 801–802.
[47] Haddock, 'First possession versus optimal timing', fn. 9 above, p. 792.
[48] Waldron also disagrees with Nozick's basic proposition, that the state ought not to interfere with legitimate property holdings: see further Part IV below.
[49] Waldron, 'To bestow stability upon possession', fn. 14 above, pp. 5–6.

In other words, this is arguably a more realistic way of assessing the legitimacy of current property holdings because it is rooted in historical fact, it makes it easier for claimants to prove their entitlement, and it recognises the status quo.

3.9 Legitimising Customary Use and Control

Moreover, focussing attention on the present user and controller need not be as morally bankrupt as Waldron suggests. For example, if the established inhabitants of an area are invaded by strangers, they surely have moral standing to complain, without having to prove that they are the descendants of the first ever inhabitants of that land? We come back to this argument when we look at the claims of indigenous peoples in Chapter 9 *Multiple Property Rights Systems.* In later chapters we also look at the many other pragmatic and moral reasons why the claims of the present possessor or user are often recognised by the law, particularly if their possession and use is long-standing, and even if their possession and use violated pre-existing legal titles. Most jurisdictions, including ours, recognise squatter's titles at least to some extent, and allow possessors and customary users of resources to acquire unchallengeable property interests after a period of time, yet all of these processes violate pre-existing property rights.[50] Indeed, these methods of acquiring property interests are often the only ones available for communities and the public to acquire property interests, as we see in Chapter 13 *Non-Possessory Land Use Rights.* So, in relation to interests in land at least, it is often both realistic and morally justifiable to assess the legitimacy of current distributions of property holdings by reference to established patterns of resource use.

3.10 David Hume's Convention-Based Account for Property

The test for legitimacy suggested in the previous paragraph comes close to David Hume's account of property in *A Treatise of Human Nature.*[51] Waldron sees Hume's account as lying between 'theories which have a Nozickean shape and theories of force or last occupancy',[52] and having advantages over both.

As Waldron points out, Hume starts with an account of the instability of a world without property which is very similar to that put forward by other property theorists:

> There are different species of goods, which we are possess'd of; the internal satisfaction of our minds, the external advantages of our body, and the enjoyment of such possessions as we have acquir'd by our industry and good fortune. We are perfectly secure in the enjoyment of the first. The second may be ravish'd from us, but can be of

---

[50] See Chapter 11 *Possession and Title*, Chapter 12 *Adverse Possession of Land* and Chapter 13 *Non-Possessory Land Use Rights.*

[51] David Hume, *A Treatise of Human Nature* (first published in 1739–1740, see new annotated edition, David Fate Norton and Mary J, Norton (eds.), *David Hume: A Treatise of Nature* (Oxford: Oxford University Press, 2000) Book III, Part II, Section II.

[52] Waldron, 'To bestow stability upon possession', fn. 14 above, p. 6.

no advantage to him who deprives us of them. The last only are both expos'd to the violence of others, and may be transferr'd without suffering any loss or alteration; while at the same time, there is not a sufficient quantity of them to supply every one's desires and necessities. As the improvement, therefore, of these goods is the chief advantage of society, so the instability of their possession, along with their scarcity, is the chief impediment.[53]

However, in Hume's account there may come a point where fighting over possessions reaches a stalemate. At this point a stable equilibrium may emerge, as each possessor comes to realise that 'it will be for my interest to leave another in his possession of his goods, provided he will act in the same manner with regard to mine'. Once this realisation is articulated and communicated between possessors, a convention of reciprocal non-interference emerges. Property law's function is then merely to recognise and enforce this convention of respect for the de facto distribution of resources which has become a status quo.

So, in Hume's account, the legitimacy of property holdings does not rest on first labouring or on first taking, nor does it depend on force or last occupancy. It depends on who, after a history of strife over possessions, ended up in possession of what, at the point where equilibrium emerges. Moreover, Hume is not claiming that the resulting distribution of property is just, only that everyone is better off accepting it rather than continuing to fight over who should own what. As Waldron points out, Hume's account does not require us to accept that original acquirers had a moral entitlement to what they took, as Locke, Nozick and first occupancy theorists would have it, nor does it try to persuade us that the distribution of property resulting from it is just, as Nozick's account does. On the other hand, it is not wholly amoral:

> It resembles [the force/last occupancy theory] in certain respects – in particular, in its frank recognition of the likelihood of inequality and its complete lack of interest in first occupancy or first anything. But it does present a moral profile. Everyone is better off by the convention, on the Humean account, even given the lop-sided distributions that are likely to be characteristics of any natural equilibrium. Everyone is better off – that's the justification – which is different from the powerful just using their power to entrench a given distribution that they favour ...
>
> As bottom-up theories of property go, the Humean story has one advantage over the Lockean story: it is much more realistic. It is not in denial about the elements of conflict and depredation at the origins of property. It recognizes modern property as something that emerges out of an era of conflict rather than something that presents itself to us with an impeccable pedigree. . . .
>
> In particular it probably generates a different sense of the relation between the property rights that emerge in this way, and the activities of state and law. Hume, like Locke, believes that property can get under way without the help of law. But he is not sure that it can get very far on its own ... [Hume] hints, in several places, that his convention account ... cannot really explain or characterize the emergence of complex forms of property appropriate for large societies. That may require genuine top-down

---

[53] Hume, *Treatise of Human Nature* (fn. 51 above), Book III, Part II, Section 2.

creativity. Hume's theory, as I have explained, perhaps generates foundations for such a theory of property. But it cannot explain everything that is built on those foundations, and it is unlikely to generate a sense of strong entitlement whereby foundational claims of property can be used as points of resistance to more creative forms of state action.[54]

Waldron makes it clear that, as he sees it, this is an advantage that Hume's account has over that of others, not a disadvantage.

PART IV PROPERTY AND THE PROPERTYLESS

3.11 Property and Inequality

As we said in para. 3.1, our central and unavoidable problem is that, if property is good because it generates wealth and is essential for human flourishing, how can we justify a situation where some people have property but others do not? The problem is particularly acute if we have to admit that property by its nature enriches the few at the expense of the many, and so must inevitably cause inequality. So, there are two questions we have to ask. The first is whether property inequality is indeed the inevitable consequence of property. The second is whether, because of the advantages property brings (wealth generation, human flourishing, etc.), property owners are under an obligation to provide for the needs of the propertyless.

3.12 Why Should Property Give Rise to Inequality?

The classic argument (which we have already considered in Chapter 2 *Conceptions and Justification*) is that those who acquire property rights by original acquisition, whether by labouring on things or simply by taking control over them, acquire enduring exclusive rights to resources which had previously been freely available to everyone. This of itself leads to an initial inequality in the distribution of scarce resources, for all the reasons we looked at in Chapter 2. And, so the argument goes, the inequality can only be made worse if thereafter, the only way anyone else can acquire property rights in those resources is by buying or inheriting them from the original acquirer. As we saw in Part III, some theorists such as Nozick do not see a problem with this, or at least they believe that it is better to accept it rather than to allow the state to intervene to readjust the balance. Others, however, are not so happy with such an outcome, and there are those who see private property as inextricably linked to growing inequality in societies such as ours and in the United States. So, for example, Ezra Rosser[55] describes the problem of inequality as 'the property crisis of our time':

> the problems plaguing the current economic structure – inequitable opportunities, wage and wealth stagnation or decline, persistent multigenerational poverty, and lack of economic mobility – raise the possibility that property law serves a sliver of the population well, but does not serve society well.

---

[54] Waldron, 'To bestow stability upon possession', fn. 14 above, pp. 7–12.
[55] Ezra Rosser, 'De-stabilising property' (2015–2016) 48 *Connecticut Law Review* 397.

3.13 Property and Exclusionary Spaces

A potentially severe inequality created by property arises because one of the resources property annexes is physical space: property divides physical space up into exclusionary spaces, potentially leaving nowhere for the propertyless to be, except at the sufferance of others. As Waldron points out, this restricts the freedom of those without property, not just in the obvious sense of restricting their freedom of movement, but also by restricting their freedom to do anything else:

> Everything that is done has to be done somewhere. No one is free to perform an action unless there is somewhere he is free to perform it. Since we are embodied beings, we always have a location.[56]

The problem, as he sees it, is that in modern states all space is either privately owned (houses, restaurants, hotels, shops, etc.) and so usable by outsiders only on the say-so of someone else, or it is public access space (streets, parks, subways, etc.) to which the public has free access, but there are restrictions on the activities that can be performed there. It follows that, if you are not a private owner of space, or cannot get legally enforceable rights to do what you want in someone else's privately owned space, you are not free to do the things prohibited in public access space, because there is nowhere you are free to do them. But this means that people without a private place – the homeless – are not free to perform 'elementary human activities', because they are all activities that are prohibited in public access space:

> [the homeless have] no place to perform elementary human activities like urinating, washing, sleeping, cooking, eating, and standing around. Legislators voted for by people who own private places in which they can do all these things are increasingly deciding to make public places available only for activities other than these primal human tasks. The streets and subways, they say, are for commuting from home to office. They are not for sleeping; sleeping is something one does at home. The parks are for recreations like walking and informal ball-games, things for which one's own yard is a little too confined. Parks are not for cooking or urinating; again, these are things one does at home. Since the public and the private are complementary, the activities performed in public are to be the complement of those appropriately performed in private. This complementarity works fine for those who have the benefit of both sorts of places. However, it is disastrous for those who must live their whole lives on [public] land.[57]

One way of looking at it is to say that the problem is over-regulation of public space. Another is to say that property has consequences for those who do not have it.

3.14 Re-thinking the Property Model

However, not everyone accepts that inequality is an inevitable consequence of property. It can be argued that if we changed the way we allocate property, and

---

[56] Jeremy Waldron, 'Homelessness and the issue of freedom' (1991–1992) 39 *UCLA Law Review* 295 at p. 296.

[57] Ibid. p. 301, and see also Jeremy Waldron, 'Community and property – for those who have neither' (2008) 10 *Theoretical Inquiries in Law* 161.

look beyond the absolute private ownership model of property, it is possible to achieve a more egalitarian distribution of property so that everyone has enough to meet her needs. One way of doing it is to have state or community owned resources where members have property rights to use and control its resources in common with each other, and we look at some examples of that kind of property model in later chapters.

However, it might also be possible to achieve a more egalitarian distribution using a different kind of private property regime. Michael Otsuka, for example, argues for a more robust interpretation of Locke's sufficiency proviso, which would confine legitimate original acquisition to cases where it leaves 'enough so that everyone else can acquire *an equally good share* of unowned worldly resources'.[58] This leads to an initially egalitarian distribution of resources, and, so he says, this can be preserved by reading Locke's sufficiency proviso 'intergenerationally':

> the members of each generation are required to ensure that, at their deaths, resources that are at least as valuable as those they have acquired lapse back into a state of non-ownership. Since, moreover, individuals possess only lifetime lcaseholds on worldly resources, they have nothing more than lifetime leaseholds on whatever worldly resources they improve. Any worldly object they improve through their labour lapses into a state of non-ownership upon their death and hence is not bequeathable.[59]

The idea that private property does not have to mean perpetual inheritable property holdings is important, and there are moral and political arguments for saying that scarce resources should periodically go back to the unpropertised pot. Lee-Anne Fennell makes the argument at an economic level in relation to land ownership. She argues that, in urban areas at least, perpetual land ownership (which in the USA and in England and Wales takes the form of the fee simple'[60]) is obsolete:

> Property is a mechanism for delivering access to resources. The fee simple embodies a particular way of packaging and characterizing that access, one that resonates with a thing-based property paradigm. It purports to grant a 'chunk of the world' – a unique piece of the earth's surface and atmosphere – indefinitely to the party designated as owner. This formulation provided a useful shorthand for pairing inputs and outcomes in the mostly agrarian society in which the fee simple developed. Over time, however, it has become an anachronistic fiction that misses most of how urban property creates value .... . Granting a perpetual monopoly on a piece of physical space, as the fee simple does, [was once] an unbeatable strategy. But conditions have changed.
>
> We now live in a deeply interdependent society that is overwhelmingly urban. Over eighty percent of the U.S. population lives in urban areas. Spatial externalities are no

---

[58] Michael Otsuka, 'Appropriating Lockean appropriation on behalf of equality' in James Penner and Michael Otsuka (eds.), *Property Theory: Legal and Political Perspectives* (Cambridge: Cambridge University Press, 2018) 121 at p. 123 (emphasis added).

[59] Ibid. p. 126. Jeremy Waldron, *The Right to Private Property* (Oxford: Clarendon Press, 1988) also points out, at p. 243, that Locke's labour theory of acquisition appears to establish only personal entitlements, and that Locke would need to go further to justify not only original acquisition but also why on death the entitlement does not revert back to the common or to God.

[60] The fee simple, sometimes referred to as the 'freehold' is the common law equivalent of land ownership: see further Chapter 5 *Ownership and Other Property Interests* Part III.

longer confined to problems of wandering cattle or wafting factory smoke; rather, the relative position and aggregate configuration of urban space represents the primary way in which real property delivers and forfeits value. Spatially rooted estates of endless duration deal poorly with the problem of optimizing urban land use because they scatter everlasting vetoes among individual landowners over the most critical source of value in a metropolitan environment – the patterns in which land uses and land users are assembled in space. These patterns have become too important to ignore, but optimizing them over time requires a capacity for large-scale revision that the atomistic fee simple cannot provide.[61]

She explores various alternatives to perpetual length, including ownership rights which continue until the happening of a particular event, specified in advance, such as the government (or someone else) requiring the land for a specified re-development. She envisages that both the initial terminable interest and the right to end it on the happening of the specified event, could be private tradeable property interests, so the resource would not always go back into the unpropertised pot when the event happens. Nevertheless, it is clearly a mechanism that could also be used to ensure that resources automatically fall back into state ownership for redistribution on given events, if that was what we wanted to achieve.

3.15 Property Owners' Duty to Recompense the Propertyless

An alternative approach is that those who acquire property by original acquisition should be entitled to keep it, but must compensate those who are thereby deprived of the innate rights they had in it when it was part of the common heritage.

(a) Thomas Paine's Compensation Payments Scheme

Thomas Paine argued that this could be done by, in effect, requiring property owners to pay into a common fund a periodic 'rent', representing the value of the uncultivated resources they acquired, on the basis that they are entitled only to the proportion of the value of the resources which is attributable to the improvements they have made to them:

> the earth, in its natural uncultivated state was, and ever would have continued to be, the common property of the human race. In that state every man would have been born to property. He would have been a joint life proprietor with the rest in the property of the soil, and in all its natural productions, vegetable and animal.
>
> But the earth in its natural state, as before said, is capable of supporting but a small number of inhabitants compared with what it is capable of doing in a cultivated state. And as it is impossible to separate the improvement made by cultivation from the earth itself, upon which that improvement is made, the idea of landed property arose from that inseparable connection; but it is nevertheless true, that it is the value of the improvement only, and not the earth itself, that is individual property. Every

---

[61] Lee Anne Fennell, 'Fee simple obsolete' (2016) 91 *New York University Law Review* 1457, at pp. 1458–1561.

proprietor, therefore, of cultivated land, owes to the community a groundrent for the land which he holds.[62]

He proposed that this 'rent' should be a payment made into the common fund out of property passing on death, calculated by reference to the percentage of the value of the property which was attributable to the property in its unimproved state. The advantage of this would be that 'the fault can be made to reform itself by successive generations; and without diminishing or deranging the property of any of the present possessors'.[63]

This central fund would then be used to make fixed annual payments to every man and woman – £15 a year for those between the ages of 21 and 49, and £10 a year to those aged 50 and over – representing his or her share in this 'natural inheritance'.[64] Whilst his concern was over what he called 'the hard case of all those who have been thrown out of their natural inheritance by the introduction of the system of landed property', he nevertheless proposed that everyone should get the payments:

> It is proposed that the payments, as already stated, be made to every person, rich or poor. It is best to make it so, to prevent invidious distinctions. It is also right it should be so, because it is in lieu of the natural inheritance, which, as a right, belongs to every man,[65] over and above the property he may have created, or inherited from those who did. Such persons as do not choose to receive it can throw it into the common fund.[66]

The attraction of Paine's scheme (as he himself pointed out) is that it recognises the moral right of 'the hard cases' to receive payment for what has been taken away from them, whilst at the same time recognising and protecting the right of a property owner 'to the part [of his property] which is his'.[67]

(b) Locke's Principle of Charity

Others have argued for less generous recompense for losing one's 'natural inheritance' in the unpropertised Earth. As we saw in Chapter 2 *Conceptions and Justifications* para. 2.8, under Locke's 'principle of charity' those in 'extreme want' would be entitled to have their basic needs satisfied by appropriators, but only out of the 'surplusage' of appropriated resources. And even then, the entitlement would go only to those who have 'no means to subsist otherwise', and that would not include those who could earn their living by hiring out their labour to others.

---

[62] Thomas Paine, *Agrarian Justice* (first published 1797, digital edition published 1999, available at www .grundskyld.dk) p. 8. He proposed that, for convenience, this 'rent' should be a payment payable into the common fund whenever property passed on death, calculated by reference to the percentage of the value of the property which was attributable to the property in its unimproved state.

[63] Ibid. p.10.   [64] Ibid.

[65] It is clear from what Paine says on p. 10 that the payments would not go just to men but to women as well.

[66] Paine, *Agrarian Justice*, fn. 62 above, p. 12.   [67] Ibid. p. 9.

(c) Kant's Public Duty to Support the Poor Out of Taxation

Kant's notion of what is due to those without property is no more generous than Locke's. Weinrib argues that it is a necessary implication of Kant's argument justifying property which we looked at in Chapter 2 *Conceptions and Justifications* para. 2.21, that there is a public duty to support the poor by satisfying their basic needs, and this support must come from taxation.

In Kant's analysis, the innate right to hold property can only be fully realised by everyone agreeing to the formation of a coercive state. The problem is, as Weinrib says, that once the state comes into existence to enforce property rights, the accumulation of external things becomes possible:

> My range of rightful possibilities is now confined to what might be left over from others' efforts at accumulation. The possibility of amassing land makes it conceivable that, given the finitude of the earth's surface, all the land may be appropriated by others, leaving me literally with no place to exist except by leave of someone else. Moreover, it may turn out that I must now seek the food that is to sustain me from my neighbors. My continued existence may become dependent on the goodwill or sufferance of others, to whom I might then have to subordinate myself, making myself into a means for their ends ...[68]

Thus, the very institutions that enabled the right to freedom for some (the property holders), disabled it for others. This, so Weinreb argues, gives rise to a public duty to support the poor by satisfying their basic needs, because without such support they will be dependent on the will of others. The support must come from the state (and hence must be paid for by taxation) because this is the only way of making the poor immune from dependence on others (which is necessary for their right to freedom). Hence, the only way of ensuring that *no-one's* subsistence is dependent on the actions of others, is for everyone to join a coercive state (which enforces property protection formerly dependent on the will of others, and so ensures the right to freedom of property owners) and for that state to satisfy the basic needs of those who have been shut off from access to the resources necessary for their subsistence *by the state's protection and enforcement of property rights.*

3.16 Resource Rights Transcending Property Rights

Finally, we should notice here that the only other way of guaranteeing rights of access to resources for the propertyless is to give them rights to resources which transcend property rights. One way of doing that is by recognising and enforcing human rights to resources, as we see in Chapter 4 *Property and Human Rights*. As we see there, these rights can take a variety of forms, but the most promising for the propertyless are a right to *hold* property (i.e. a right to be a property rights holder), a

---

[68] Ernest J. Weinrib 'Poverty and property on Kant's system' (2003) 78 *Notre Dame Law Review* 795 at pp. 815–816, and see also pp. 816–818. Arthur Ripstein's interpretation of Kant on this point (essentially the same as Weinrib's) is summarised in *Force and Freedom: Kant's Legal and Political Philosophy* (Cambridge, MA and London: Harvard University Press, 2009) pp. 25–26.

right to respect for one's private life and home (which might protect you against eviction by whoever owns your home, if you yourself have no property right to remain there), and a right to be provided with resources of a particular kind (for example, a human right to water, or to sanitation, or to a reasonable standard of living). We see in the next chapter how far human rights such as these can and do in practice redress the balance in favour of the propertyless.

RECOMMENDED READING

Kevin Gray, 'Property in a queue' in Gregory S. Alexander and Eduardo M. Peñalver (eds.), *Property and Community* (Oxford: Oxford University Press, 2010).

Katharine G. Young, 'Rights and queues: On distributive contests in the modern state' (2016) 55 *Columbia Journal of Transnational Law* 65, especially pp. 67–69 and 75–82.

David D. Haddock, 'First possession versus optimal timing: Limiting the dissipation of economic value' (1986) 64 *Washington University Law Quarterly* 775 especially pp. 775–786 (the rest is interesting, but difficult for non-economists).

Marguerita Colangelo, *Creating Property Rights: Law and Regulation of Secondary Trading in the European Union* (Leiden and Boston, MA: Martinus Nijhoff Publishers, 2012) Chs. 1 and 3 (for those interested in knowing more about spectrum rights).

Robert Nozick, *Anarchy, State, and Utopia* (Oxford: Basil Blackwell, 1974), pp. 75–82.

Jeremy Waldron, 'Homelessness and the issue of freedom' (1991–1992) 39 *UCLA Law Review* 295.

Jeremy Waldron, 'Community and property – for those who have neither', (2008) 10 *Theoretical Inquiries in Law* 161.

Questions

(1) In *Property in a Queue*, Gray at p. 189 observes that 'queuing behaviour bears the imprint of elementary property forms. Embedded in the mores of the queue are rudimentary perceptions of ownership, self-ownership, and personhood. In the queue are found the coded traces of proprietary order and, perhaps more importantly, some clue as to the origins of that order'. Explain what aspects of queues and queuing behaviour provide these insights. To what extent is the same true of electronic queuing?

(2) Discuss the drawbacks of first possession and first taking principles. In what ways/ circumstances might allocation by national or supra-national licensing be better?

(3) Explain Nozick's principle of justice in holdings. Consider the criticisms made of his argument. How convincing are they?

(4) Explain what Waldron means when he says that it might be better to assess the legitimacy of present property holdings by reference to last or prior occupancy rather than first occupancy. Do you agree?

(5) Is it true that inequality is an inevitable consequence of property?

4

Property and Human Rights

PART I INTRODUCTION

4.1 Human Rights and Fundamental Universal Values

When we look at property and human rights we have to step outside the national frame, even if we are concerned only with the effect of human rights on property interests in England and Wales. At a mechanistic level, this is because human rights law affecting property rights in England and Wales largely derives from international and regional instruments. One of the consequences of this is that questions about the interpretation and application of the human rights law we apply in our own national courts and tribunals are litigated not only here but also in international and regional courts and tribunals and in those of other nation states. So, inevitably we have to look beyond national legislation and cases decided by our national courts.

More importantly, unless we agree with Jeremy Bentham that human rights are 'Nonsense Upon Stilts' and declarations of human rights are fundamentally misconceived,[1] we have to accept that human rights are by nature supra-national, universal standards by which domestic law is to be measured and judged. On most views, although human rights are articulated in legal instruments, these are articulations of fundamental universal values which have an objective existence independent of any given legal system.

However, there is no general consensus about either the derivation or the content of these fundamental values. John Tasioulas argues that there is a coherent notion of 'human rights', namely that they are universal moral rights, conceptually and historically 'continuous with what were once known as "natural rights"'.[2] We can identify these universal moral rights, he argues, by using natural reason. In other words, he says, they are not the product of 'the artificial reason of some institution, such as law, the conventionally accepted reasons upheld by some culture or

---

[1] Jeremy Bentham, 'Nonsense upon stilts' in Philip Schofield, Catherine Pease-Watkin and Cyprian Blamires (eds.), *Rights, Representation and Reform: Nonsense upon Stilts and Other Writings on the French Revolution*, in *The Collected Works of Jeremy Bentham* (Oxford: Clarendon Press, 2003), prompted by the appearance in 1795 of the French Declaration of Rights and Duties of Man and the Citizen.

[2] John Tasioulas, 'Human rights, legitimacy, and international law' (2013) 58 *The American Journal of Jurisprudence* 1 at pp. 2–3. His argument is outlined at pp. 1–13.

tradition, or the deliverances of divine revelation'.[3] Other commentators, however, have expressed doubts about whether moral rights or 'natural law' can provide a coherent basis for analysis, whether we are considering the nature and content of the human rights we actually recognise in our modern law, or the kind of rights which we think ought to be respected as human rights. After tracing the historical connection between natural law, natural rights, human rights and the Enlightenment, James Griffin concludes that we are now at a point in history where 'the term "human rights" is nearly criterionless'.[4] He nevertheless proceeds to argue for an alternative account of human rights based on personhood and practicalities.[5] This would enable us to identify which rights ought to be human rights, he argues, and this is a question we need to keep in mind in the rest of this chapter. For present purposes, however, the important point is that his account equally transcends any national or international legal order, and the same applies to the account based on fundamental democratic rights and freedoms often articulated in our domestic courts, for example by Lady Hale in *R (oao Countryside Alliance* v. *Attorney General* [2007] UKHL 52.[6] Considering the basis of the human rights protected by the UK Human Rights Act 1998 Lady Hale said:

> 114 ... the purpose of such human rights instruments is to place some limits upon what a democratically elected Parliament may do: to protect the rights and freedoms of individuals and minorities against the will of those who are taken to represent the majority. Democracy is the will of the people, but the people may not will to invade those rights and freedoms which are fundamental to democracy itself.

4.2 Human Rights and Property Rights

The distinctive feature of human rights is that they are rights that citizens have as against the state. Because of this, the relationship between human rights and property rights is not straightforward. When we talk in general terms about human rights to property, it is important to appreciate that this encompasses two quite different kinds of human right. The first is a human right *to the protection of property*, in other words a human right that I have, as against the state, that the property rights I have will not be taken away from me, by the state or by anyone else. This is the human right to property which appears in most human rights instruments, including our Human Rights Act 1998,[7] and it can be described as a human right to property for the 'property-haves'. However, there are also human rights *to* property in the literal sense: human rights that the state will provide me with, or

---

[3] Ibid.   [4] James Griffin, *On Human Rights* (Oxford, Oxford University Press, 2008) at p. 14.
[5] 'Personhood initially generates the rights; practicalities give them, where needed, a sufficiently shape': ibid. at p. 192.
[6] *R (oao Countryside Alliance)* v. *Attorney General* [2007] UKHL 52, the fox hunting case we consider in para 4.29(b).
[7] The Human Rights Act 1998, which we look at in Part IV of this chapter, incorporates into British law the rights set out in the European Convention on Human Rights (ECHR).

ensure that I can obtain, property rights to a thing that I want or need. We can describe these as human rights *to have* property, in other words human rights to property for the property-have-nots. Human rights of this kind can be found in some human rights instruments, often in the form of a right to a specific resource (perhaps water, or clean air, or adequate sanitation, or a home). In Part II of this chapter we look more closely at the differences between these two kinds of human right to property, both in nature and in effect. We also consider why these very different demands we make on the state – protection of our pre-existing property rights, and guaranteed provision of access to certain resources – should be regarded as human rights, and the implications of giving them that status.

In the rest of the chapter we look at how these different kinds of human rights to property are manifested in modern law. In Part III we look at some of the principal international and regional human rights instruments currently in force, and also at the constitutional rights to property which are contained in some national constitutions (although arguably not in ours), specifically the constitutions of Germany, the USA and South Africa. Against this background, we then look in Parts IV–VI at the nature and operation of the human rights in the European Convention on Human Rights (ECHR), set out in the Human Rights Act 1998, which most directly affect property rights in the UK. In Part IV we outline the way human rights relating to property are protected under the Human Rights Act 1998. We then look at the two principal provisions of the ECHR relating to property: the right to property in article 1 of Protocol 1 to the ECHR, sometimes referred to as A1P1 (Part V of this chapter) and the right to respect for home in article 8 of the ECHR itself (Part VI).

PART II RELATIONSHIP BETWEEN PROPERTY AND HUMAN RIGHTS

4.3 Human Rights to the Protection of Property and Human Rights to Have Property

We have already seen in para. 4.2 that we need to distinguish between the human right to have our pre-existing property rights protected by the state, and the very different human rights that we have called human rights *to, or to have* property: in other words the human right that the state should recognise us as having, or guarantee that we will have, property interests in specified resources in specified circumstances. In the following paragraphs we have more to say about each of these.

4.4 Human Rights to the Protection of Property

We need to consider quite carefully what it means to say that there is a human right to protection of property. Most formal declarations of human rights include such a human right, as we see in Parts III and IV of this chapter. However, it is important to recognise its inherent limitations.

At first sight a human right to the protection of one's pre-existing property rights does not seem to offer very much. As we saw in Chapter 1 *What Property Is and*

Why It Matters, a state cannot be said to recognise the institution of 'property' *at all* unless it has a system of rules which gives citizens rights in relation to things which are enforceable against the state itself, and also against other citizens. A state can be said to recognise the institution of property if and only if it provides and enforces criminal laws by which the state will restrain and punish any interference with the property rights of its citizens (laws of theft, criminal damage, etc.), and laws and procedures which enable every citizen to take action in a civil court to restrain any threatened interference with its property rights by the state or by other private citizens. In other words, a statement that every person has a human right to the protection of property seems to be saying no more than that every person has a human right that the state of which it is a citizen will recognise, respect and enforce the institution of property.

However, the human right gives citizens two important controls over the power of the state. Firstly, the human right to the protection of property limits the power of the state to pass laws that diminish or remove pre-existing property rights, or laws that permit other citizens to disregard them. Secondly, it puts a positive obligation on the state to have and to enforce laws and procedures that enable property owners to defend their property rights against actions of the state and actions of other citizens.

Nevertheless, these limitations and obligations imposed on the state are not absolute. For a state to function at all, it must have some control over resources such as physical space, water, air, minerals, transport, etc., and this requires powers to override private property interests at least to some extent. So, inevitably the human right to the protection of property has to be limited so as to allow the state to confiscate or regulate property rights when it is in the public interest to do so. However, most human rights instruments allow the state to do this only on payment of compensation, so far as this is necessary to recompense private citizens for giving up their private rights for the public good. We see how all this works out in the UK under the Human Rights Act 1998 in Part V of this chapter.

4.5 Human Rights to, or to Have, Property

We can identify at least four different kinds of human right *to, or to have* property.

(a) Human Right to be a Property Owner

The first is a human right to be a property owner. This appears as a fundamental human right in art. 17.1 of the principal international human rights instrument, the Universal Declaration of Human Rights 1948, which we look at in para. 4.10 below ('everyone has the right to own property alone as well as in association with others'). In one sense this can be seen as a right not to be discriminated against: a law which prohibited women, or slaves, or certain ethnic groups from holding property, or some kinds of property right, would be in violation of this kind of human right to property. In addition or alternatively, it can be seen as an expression of the view that the right to own property is an 'essential aspect of humanity or human dignity', as

Frankie McCarthy puts it.[8] She quotes two delegates to the Consultative Assembly of the Council of Europe expressing a similar view when considering what form the human right to property should take in what was to become the European Convention on Human Rights. Eamon de Valera, then leader of the Irish Republican Party Fianna Fáil, said: 'I believe that it is a fundamental right necessary for the full development of the human being that he should have the right to own property', and the French delegate Bastid described property as 'an extension of the man [*sic*]' and added 'I do not know if there is any right more ancient or more firmly established than the right to own property'.[9] Nevertheless, this kind of human right to property – the right to be a property-owner – has not found its way into the European Convention on Human Rights (incorporated into UK law by the Human Rights Act 1998), or at least not explicitly: see para. 4.24 below, and compare the German Constitutional Court's interpretation of art. 14(1) of the German Basic Law which we look at in para. 4.14 below.

(b) Human Right to a Specified Resource

The second kind of human right *to, or to have* property is a right to a specified resource. An example is the human right to water recognised by UN Resolution 64/292 2010,[10] which 'entitles everyone to sufficient, safe, acceptable, physically accessible and affordable water for personal and domestic uses'.[11] This kind of human right *to* property imposes on the state a straightforward requirement to ensure that all citizens have the minimum access to a specified resource that they need in order to survive (or perhaps to flourish). However, it will be noted that here 'property' is being used as a noun, simply to describe the thing in which people have rights, rather than as an adjective describing the nature of the rights themselves.[12] In practice, this kind of human right to property can be realised by the state in ways which do not involve giving everyone a *property right* in the resource in question. So, for example, the UK might satisfy the human right to water of UK citizens by requiring private water suppliers to supply every person with water, and to do so on reasonable contractual terms, and by restricting the right of suppliers to cut off the supply to customers unable to pay. We consider in more detail how this can work in relation to water in para. 4.17 below.

---

[8] Frankie McCarthy, 'Property as a human right: Another casualty of the "War on Terror"?' in Nicholas Hopkins (ed.), *Modern Studies in Property Law*, vol. 7 (Oxford and Portland, OR: Hart Publishing, 2013) p. 243 at p. 262.

[9] Council of Europe, Directorate of Human Rights, *Collected Edition of the 'Travaux Préparatoires' on the European Convention on Human Rights* (The Hague, Martinus Nijhoff, 1975) at vol. 2, p. 104 and vol. 6, p. 120.

[10] Resolution on Human Right to Water and Sanitation (UN General Assembly Resolution A/64/292, 28 July 2010), available on https://undocs.org/en/A/RES/64/292.

[11] Para. 2 of General Comment No 15 (2002) E/C.12/2002/11, 20 January 2003, which describes the normative content of the right: see para. 4.17 below.

[12] See Chapter 1 *What Property Is and Why It Matters* paras. 1.21 and 1.22.

(c) Human Right to Restitution of Property

The third and fourth kinds of human right *to, or to have* property do, however, require the state to confer property rights on property have-nots. The third is a right to restitution of property for the dispossessed. This kind of human right to property does not appear in the European Convention on Human Rights, despite continuing problems in some countries in providing restitution for displaced persons whose property rights were unjustly confiscated in the past. As we see in para. 4.28(a) below, the European Court of Human Rights (ECtHR) has declined to interpret the ECHR so as to cover property rights extinguished by wrongful expropriation or dispossession. A human right to restitution of property does, however, appear as a constitutional right in some national constitutions, for example in s. 25(7) of the post-apartheid Constitution of South Africa, as we see in para. 4.16 below.

(d) Human Right to Legal Recognition of Customary Resource Use

The fourth kind of human right to property is a human right that, whenever there is a customary relationship between people and the resources they utilise, the state categorises that relationship as a property relationship, respecting it as such and according it the same level of protection as it gives to formally created property rights. In other words, this human right to property requires the state to treat norms of resource use which people develop between themselves as legally enforceable property rights. This reflects at least three modern property doctrines.

Acquisition of Property Rights by Possession or by Long Use

First, a human right to property of this kind reflects the principle recognised in most modern states (England and Wales included), that proprietary land use rights, and sometimes even ownership of land and goods, can be acquired by long-term use by private individuals, communities and the public. We look at the way this operates in England and Wales, and the rationales put forward, in Chapter 12 *Adverse possession of land*, where we consider the institution of adverse possession (which extinguishes the rights of owners of land and goods who have failed to take action to remove long-term possessors, leaving the possessors as undisputed owners) and more briefly in Chapter 13 *Non-Possessory Land Use Rights*, where we look at some aspects of custom and prescription as they operate in England and Wales, allowing the acquisition of proprietary non-possessory land use rights by long use.

Recognition of Indigenous Land Rights

It sometimes happens that a particular group within a state has a customary pattern of resource use which does not fit into the template of property rights recognised under that state's legal system. In a situation like that, this kind of human right to property requires the state to adapt its template so as to accommodate that kind of resource use and recognise it as proprietary. This reflects the principle which has become accepted relatively recently across the world, that the customary patterns of resource use of indigenous peoples must be recognised by the nation state as proprietary resource use systems, and given equal protection under national law. We look at the way this has happened in post-colonial states such as Canada and Australia in Chapter 9 *Multiple Property Rights Systems*, where we also see how the general principle has become accepted as an international human right for all indigenous peoples. This was formally confirmed by the United Nations Declaration on the Rights of Indigenous Peoples 2007, as we see in Part V of Chapter 9.

Protection for Customary Land Rights of Disadvantaged or Minority Groups and for Culturally, Historically or Environmentally Significant Land Usages

Historically, the problem of 'invisible' land usages, not recognised within a state's property rights system, has not been confined to the resource usages of indigenous peoples within the state. There may be other vulnerable or disadvantaged people within society whose resource usages remain outside the property rights system. A human right to property which requires legal recognition of customary resource use might, for example, seek to articulate and protect women's traditional relationships with the resources they use within a particular culture, which have never been reflected in formal law, or to preserve the cultural identity of any particular group, whether indigenous or not, or to reverse the effect of past racially discriminatory laws and policies which have effectively de-propertised some individuals or groups (see for example s. 25(6) of the Constitution of South Africa noted in para. 4.16 below). Similarly, there may be long-standing customary usages that deserve legal recognition for cultural, historical or environmental reasons or simply because they reflect the reality of resource usage. Jérémie Gilbert gives the example of pastoral resource use. He argues that pastoral (nomadic) land use ought to be accepted as a legitimate pattern of resource use, and that the best way of achieving this is to recognise an international human right for communities to pursue a nomadic way of life, in other words to have this pattern of resource use respected and recognised as proprietary in the same way and to the same extent as private property land rights.[13]

4.6 Distributive Effect of Human Rights to Property

All of this leads to the question of how far human rights are distributive, in the sense of imposing restrictions on or upsetting the way in which a state chooses to allocate property rights between its citizens. A human right to the protection of property – the human right to property for the property-haves – is not in itself concerned with the distribution of property within a state. A state with a wholly inequitable distribution of property rights, in which some citizens are arbitrarily denied property rights, or have no opportunity to acquire property rights in even the most basic resources they require in order to survive and flourish, would nevertheless be human-rights compliant if the only human right relating to property was the human right to protection of property. The human right to the protection of property says

---

[13] Jérémie Gilbert, 'Nomadic territories: A human rights approach to nomadic peoples' land rights' (2007) 7 *Human Rights Law Review* 681.

only that once a state has decided how to allocate property rights within the state, it must respect and protect the rights so allocated.

The human rights *to* property of the kinds we considered in para. 4.5 above are, on the other hand, nearly always distributive, in the sense that they require the state to allocate property rights in a particular way. They are also often *redistributive*, in other words requiring the state to take property rights away from one person and give them to another, or to readjust the priority or hierarchy between one property right and another. In the case of interests in land, one person's human right *to* property almost invariably comes into conflict with another person's human right to protection of property. It is rare for a state to be able to fulfil one person's distributive human right to property in land or other natural resources without confiscating or interfering with another person's human right to protection of their pre-existing property rights: in most legal systems land and other natural resources are always owned by someone.

4.7 Is Human Rights Protection Confined to Private Property Rights?

In principle, the human right to protection of property appears equally applicable to communal property rights and to public property rights as it is to private property rights. If a state recognises communal and public property rights as well as private property rights, there seems no reason why it should have a greater or lesser freedom to disregard one category than it has to disregard another, nor why it should have more or less responsibility for protecting one category against interference by other citizens than it has for protecting another category.

As far as human rights *to* property are concerned, it is important to appreciate that in order to survive and flourish, cultural communities generally have as much need for human rights to property as do individuals. However, there is a problem that if we recognise all communities as holding human rights to property, in some kinds of community this will be incompatible with guaranteeing individual human rights to property for each of their members: not all communities are egalitarian. This raises questions about the balance between individualism and collectivism, and the extent to which traditional communities should be required to conform to international human rights standards, which we come to in Chapter 9 *Multiple property systems.*[14]

4.8 Who Has Human Rights in Relation to Property? Humans, Artificial Legal Persons, Communities and Public Authorities

A related but different question is whether property human rights can only be held by individual humans, or whether they can also be held by communities, or by the public, or by artificial legal persons such as commercial companies or public authorities.

---

[14] Paras. 9.19 and 9.25.

If the basis for human rights is moral rights or personhood it is not difficult to see why they should extend to individuals collectively as a community (although arguably not to all kinds of community) or as members of the public, as well as in their personal capacity.

However, it is more difficult to see the basis on which a corporate entity can claim human rights, other than as economic rights, and it is perhaps surprising that most human rights instruments do not distinguish between artificial and human persons, and that this has only recently been seriously contested.[15] In a particularly difficult case, *Société Colas Est* v. *France* [2002] ECHR 421, the ECtHR decided that a government raid on the offices of a commercial company is capable of being a violation of the company's right to respect for its home under art. 8 of the European Convention of Human Rights. We come back to this case in para. 4.36, and as we note there, it is difficult to reconcile this with any conceivable notion of 'home', even leaving aside any difficulties with the concept of human rights for commercial enterprises.

The idea of public authorities having human rights is equally difficult, although for different reasons. Since, as we see in para. 4.21, a core public authority is in effect an arm of the state, and so too is a hybrid public authority when carrying out public functions, it makes no sense to say that it has a human right to protection against interference by the state. More seriously, it seems wrong in principle that such a body should be entitled to human rights protection against interference with its property rights by private citizens. The core purpose of human rights is to protect humans against oppression by the state. This leaves no room for a human right that protects the property of the state against interference by humans. The House of Lords made these points in *Aston Cantlow Parish Council* v. *Wallbank* [2004] 1 AC 546, taking the view that a core public authority is incapable of holding human rights under the ECHR, whereas a hybrid public authority may in some circumstances do so.[16] Nevertheless, as Emma Lees points out,[17] in *Olympic Delivery Authority* v. *Persons Unknown* [2012] EWHC 1012 it was assumed by the High Court that the Olympic Delivery Authority (ODA), a public body set up to prepare the site and facilities for the 2012 London Olympic Games, did have such protection against a group of humans protesting against its activities. The protesters were occupying land giving access to the Olympic site over which the ODA had a non-proprietary license, and the judge accepted that by obstructing access to the Olympic site, the protesters were interfering with the ODA's human right to peaceful enjoyment of its 'possessions' under article 1 of Protocol 1 (A1P1) of the ECHR. Even more surprisingly, the court proceeded on the basis that the public body's supposed human right under

---

[15] Anna Grear, 'Challenging corporate 'humanity': Legal disembodiment, embodiment and human rights' (2007) 7 *Human Rights Law Review* 511; A. Scolnicov, 'Lifelike and lifeless in law: Do corporations have human rights?' (2013) *University of Cambridge Legal Studies Research Paper No. 13*; Marius Emberland, *Human Rights and Companies: Exploring the Structure of ECHR Protection* (Oxford University Press: Oxford, 2006).

[16] See e.g. Lord Nicholls in *Aston Cantlow Parish Council* v. *Wallbank* [2004] 1 AC 546 at paras. 8 and 11.

[17] Emma Lees, 'Actions for possession in the context of political protest: The role of Article 1 Protocol 1 and horizontal effect' [2013] *Conveyancer* 211 at pp. 214–216.

A1P1 had to be balanced against the protesters' human rights under arts. 10 and 11 of the ECHR (freedom of expression and freedom of assembly) – and concluded that in this case the interests of the state took precedence over the interests of the humans.

PART III INTERNATIONAL, REGIONAL AND CONSTITUTIONAL HUMAN RIGHTS RELATING TO PROPERTY

4.9 International, Regional and Constitutional Human Rights Instruments

Human rights relating to property largely derive from formal instruments, some passed by international bodies such as the United Nations and its specialised agencies like the International Labour Organisation, others produced by regional bodies such as the European Union, the Organisation of American States and the African Union. They can also be found in the constitutions of national states.

The principal general international instrument is the Universal Declaration of Human Rights 1948. It can be seen as the product of the human rights movement that developed internationally after the end of the second world war, and largely in response to it. International instruments relating to specified groups of people or specified resources developed later.

The origins and rationales of regional and national constitutional property rights are more various, reflecting local social, cultural and political conditions and, in the case of constitutional property rights and guarantees, heavily influenced by the particular circumstances surrounding the making of the constitution in that particular state.

4.10 Universal Declaration of Human Rights 1948

John Tasioulas has described the Universal Declaration of Human Rights 1948 as the 'key manifesto' of the modern human rights movement.[18] The underlying rationale of the Declaration appears from the emphasis on human dignity and individual equality and freedom in the opening of the Preamble:

> Whereas recognition of the inherent dignity and of the equal and inalienable rights of all members of the human family is the foundation of freedom, justice and peace in the world,
>
> Whereas disregard and contempt for human rights have resulted in barbarous acts which have outraged the conscience of mankind, and the advent of a world in which human beings shall enjoy freedom of speech and belief and freedom from fear and want has been proclaimed as the highest aspiration of the common people,
>
> Whereas it is essential, if man is not to be compelled to have recourse, as a last resort, to rebellion against tyranny and oppression, that human rights should be protected by the rule of law . . .

---

[18] Tasioulas, 'Human rights, legitimacy, and international law', fn. 2 above, p. 2.

Whereas the peoples of the United Nations have in the Charter reaffirmed their faith in fundamental human rights, in the dignity and worth of the human person and in the equal rights of men and women and have determined to promote social progress and better standards of life in larger freedom . . .

The Declaration was given legal force by the International Covenant on Economic, Social and Cultural Rights and the International Covenant on Civil and Political Rights, which were both adopted by the General Assembly of the United Nations in 1966 and ratified by the UK in 1976. The provisions directly relating to property are, however, in the Declaration itself.

(a) Article 17: Right to Hold Property and Protection from Arbitrary Deprivation

The core provision is art. 17, which, as we noted in para. 4.5(a), encompasses both a human right to be a property owner, and also a right to protection of property rights from 'arbitrary' deprivation, reflecting the Declaration's rationale as a reaction against the abuse of state power by authoritarian states:

Article 17

1. Everyone has the right to own property alone as well as in association with others.
2. No one shall be arbitrarily deprived of his property.

Consistently with this rationale, there is no reference in art. 17 to compensation: the focus is on improper deprivation of property by the state, not on deprivation in the public interest which might be justified if adequate compensation is paid.

(b) Article 12: Protection from Arbitrary Interference with Home

Two other provisions have an indirect bearing on property rights. Art. 12 includes a right to protection from arbitrary interference with one's home. The reference to 'arbitrary interference', the fact that the right appears within a general right to protection of private life and personal dignity, and the immediate post-second world war context, all confirm that the initial concern was with state violation of private life rather than to give special protection for people facing eviction from their home by landlords, mortgagees and creditors: we come back to this point in paras. 4.37 and 4.42 when we look at the right to respect for home under the European Convention on Human Rights.

(c) Article 24: Right to Adequate Standard of Living

The other indirectly relevant provision is art. 24. As elaborated by the International Covenant on Economic, Social and Cultural Rights and other international instruments such as UN Resolution 64/292 2010 on the Human Right to Water and Sanitation 2010 (para. 4.17 below), it has formed the basis for the development of what James Griffin has described as one of the three 'highest level' human rights, namely the right to welfare.[19] It encompasses a human right to property of the kind we note in para. 4.5(b) above, in this case a right to have access to the minimum level of resources necessary to survive and flourish as a human person:

> Article 24
>
> 1. Everyone has the right to a standard of living adequate for the health and well-being of himself and of his family, including food, clothing, housing and medical care and necessary social services, and the right to security in the event of unemployment, sickness, disability, widowhood, old age or other lack of livelihood in circumstances beyond his control.

As we saw in para. 4.5(b), property is tangential to this kind of human right: access to resources need not be by way of property rights, although it may well involve regulation of the property rights of others.

4.11 Regional General Human Rights Instruments

There are three principal regional human rights instruments, of which the European Convention on Human Rights – incorporated into UK law by the UK Human Rights Act 1998 – is one. The other two are the human rights declarations of the Association of American States and the African Charter on Human and Peoples' Rights. They all have property provisions resembling those in the Universal Declaration of Human Rights, but there are interesting differences.

(a) European Convention on Human Rights

The European Convention on Human Rights (ECHR) was signed in 1950 by member states of the Council of Europe, which include the UK and all other member states of the EU, but also include some non-EU states. The Council of Europe itself is separate from the EU, although it is a condition of membership of the EU that all member states must also be members of the Council of Europe and ratify the ECHR. Non-EU members of the Council of Europe include Russia, Bosnia & Herzegovina, Serbia and Montenegro. The ECHR is applied directly by the national courts of each Council of Europe country and by the European Court of Human Rights (ECtHR) in Strasbourg.

The UK Human Rights Act 1998 incorporates the provisions of the ECHR into British law. The convention rights themselves are set out in Schedule 1 of the 1998 Act. The rights directly affecting property are article 1 Protocol 1 to the Convention (right to peaceful enjoyment of possessions) and article 8 of the Convention itself (right to respect for private and family life, home and correspondence). We consider these two provisions in Part V and in Part VI of this chapter.

The ECHR must be distinguished from the Charter of Fundamental Rights of the European Union, which also sets out human rights enforceable in the UK but is concerned only with the acts of institutions and bodies of the EU and the acts of

---

[19] Griffin, *On Human Rights*, fn. 4 above, p. 186.

member states in so far as they are implementing EU law (art. 51). The right to respect for home is essentially the same in both the Charter and the ECHR, but there are other rights in the Charter relating to property which, cumulatively, are more extensive and more detailed than A1P1 of the ECHR. Specifically, art. 17 includes a human right to own property as well as a right to protection of property, and it is expressly provided that deprivation of possessions is prohibited unless in the public interest and 'subject to fair compensation being paid in good time for their loss'.

(b) Instruments of the Inter-American Commission on Human Rights

The Organisation of American States established the Inter-American Commission on Human Rights, which in turn proclaimed the American Declaration of the Rights and Duties of Man in 1948, some months before the Universal Declaration of Human Rights 1948. Thirty-five countries of the Americas are members of the Organisation of American States, including most Latin American countries and the USA and Canada.

The social and cultural ethos of the 1948 American Declaration, as it appears from its preamble and the range of substantive provisions, is very different from that of the 1948 Universal Declaration of Human Rights. Unlike the Universal Declaration of Human Rights, the emphasis is on the duties of individuals as well as their rights. There are also references to duties to promote spiritual and cultural development, as well as duties to respect moral values:

> Preamble
> All men are born free and equal, in dignity and in rights, and, being endowed by nature with reason and conscience, they should conduct themselves as brothers one to another.
>
> The fulfillment of duty by each individual is a prerequisite to the rights of all. Rights and duties are interrelated in every social and political activity of man. While rights exalt individual liberty, duties express the dignity of that liberty.
>
> Duties of a juridical nature presuppose others of a moral nature which support them in principle and constitute their basis.
>
> Inasmuch as spiritual development is the supreme end of human existence and the highest expression thereof, it is the duty of man to serve that end with all his strength and resources.
>
> Since culture is the highest social and historical expression of that spiritual development, it is the duty of man to preserve, practice and foster culture by every means within his power.
>
> And, since moral conduct constitutes the noblest flowering of culture, it is the duty of every man always to hold it in high respect.

Unusually amongst human rights instruments, the 1948 American Declaration did not include a right to the protection of property. It did, however, include a right to the inviolability of home (art. IX) which was separate from and independent of the right to protection against abusive attacks on honour, reputation and family and private life (art. V). In other words, 'home' was regarded as having an independent value, not necessarily valued only as an integral part of private life.

The 1948 American Declaration also had, in art. XXIII, a right *to* property which fully matched James Griffin's precepts for a welfare right:[20]

Article XXIII
    Every person has a right to own such private property as meets the essential needs of decent living and helps to maintain the dignity of the individual and of the home.

However, the 1948 Declaration has been superseded by the 1969 American Convention on Human Rights (also proclaimed by the Organisation of American States), sometimes called the Pact of San José. The 1969 Convention bears a much closer resemblance to the 1948 Universal Declaration of Human Rights, both in expressed ethos (the emphasis is on personal liberty, individual freedoms and social justice) and in substance (the many duties in the 1948 Declaration are replaced by a single 'responsibility' in art. 32.1 to family, community and mankind and a declaration in general terms in art. 32.2 that the rights of each person 'are limited by the rights of others, by the security of all, and by the just demands of the general welfare, in a democratic society').

As far as property related rights are concerned, the resemblance is even closer. In the 1969 Convention there is no longer a 'welfare right' to property and the right to protection against arbitrary interference with home is incorporated into a right to 'privacy' (art. 11). However, unlike art. 17 of the UDHR, the principal right to property provision in the 1969 Convention (art. 21) does not include a right to own property, only a right to protection of property subject to payment of compensation. Neither the USA nor Canada has ratified the 1969 Convention.[21]

(c) African Charter on Human and Peoples' Rights

The African Charter on Human and Peoples' Rights, known as the Banjul Charter, was approved by the Organisation of African Unity (now replaced by the African Union) in 1981 and came into effect in 1986. The Charter has been ratified by most countries in Africa. Its distinctive features are that it articulates fundamental rights not just of individuals but also of 'peoples',[22] and that the rights of humans and peoples to be free from the effects of colonialism, neo-colonialism, apartheid and slavery appear as central and fundamental underlying principles. Like the old 1948 American Declaration of the Rights and Duties of Man, the charter includes wide-ranging individual duties as well as rights (arts 27–28). The principal protection of property provision for individuals, art. 14, states only that 'The right to property shall be guaranteed' but does go on to provide that any 'encroachment' must be in the public and community interest and in accordance with law (but no mention of compensation).

---

[20] Para. 4.10(c) above.
[21] For Canada's position, and the continuing relevance of the 1948 Declaration, see Bernard Duhaime, 'Canada and the inter-America human rights system: Time to become a full player' (2011–2012) 67 *International Journal* 639.
[22] See further para. 4.8 above.

However, 'peoples' have rights under the Charter which come close to positive rights for peoples to 'their' wealth and natural resources such as land.[23]

4.12 Constitutional Property Rights: Germany, the USA and South Africa

In addition, most states also include in their constitution fundamental rights in relation to property which are, in function and effect, equivalent to formally designated human rights. Here we take three contrasting jurisdictions: Germany, a civil law jurisdiction which is also bound by the European Convention on Human Rights; the USA, which is largely common law; and South Africa, which is a mixed jurisdiction whose 1996 Constitution has been heavily influenced by its apartheid past.

4.13 German Constitutional Protection of the Home

The German Constitution (the Basic Law for the Federal Republic of Germany, the *Grundgesetz*) includes two property related provisions. The first, in art. 13, makes 'the home . . . inviolable'. The second, which we look at in para. 4.14, is art. 14, which guarantees property.

'Home' is protected by a stand-alone provision in art. 13: unlike art. 8 of the European Convention on Human Rights which we look at in Part VI of the chapter, art. 13 does not protect the home as part of an overall right of protection for private and family life. Nevertheless, it is firmly anchored in a context of protection against intrusion and surveillance by the state: art. 13(1) provides that 'the home is inviolable' and then the other six paragraphs of art. 13 impose detailed limitations on searches and surveillance by state bodies. Perhaps because of this, 'home' has consistently been interpreted by the German courts as including business premises. We come back to this point in paras. 4.35 and 4.36 below.

4.14 German Constitutional Guarantee of Property

Article 14 of the *Grundgesetz* sets out a guarantee of property in art. 14(1), and also makes provision in art. 14(3) for expropriation of property 'for the public good' on payment of compensation at a level which draws 'an equitable balance between the public interest and the interests of those affected.' In between those two principles, and governing both of them, is art. 14(2) which sets out the fundamental constitutional principle that 'property entails obligations' and that 'its use shall also serve the public good'. We consider the scope of art. 14(2) specifically in para. 4.15(b) below, but here we need to assess the overall effect of art. 14 as a whole, which is not immediately apparent on a first reading. The precise wording is as follows:

Article 14 Property – Inheritance – Expropriation

(1) Property and the right of inheritance shall be guaranteed. Their content and limits shall be defined by the laws.

---

[23] See arts. 21 and 22.

(2) Property entails obligations. Its use shall also serve the public good.

(3) Expropriation shall only be permissible for the public good. It may only be ordered by or pursuant to a law that determines the nature and extent of compensation. Such compensation shall be determined by establishing an equitable balance between the public interest and the interests of those affected ...

As Tom Allen explains, art. 14 has to be read in the light of the German Federal Constitutional Court's understanding that 'the overarching purpose of ... protecting fundamental rights in the Basic Law is the protection of personal liberty and autonomy'.[24] This helps to explain what the Constitutional Court says about the purpose of art. 14 in the leading case, the *Hamburg Flood Control Case*:[25]

> Article 14(1) of the Basic Law guarantees property both as a legal institution and as a concrete right held by the individual owner. To hold property is an elementary constitutional right which must be seen in close context with the protection of personal liberty. Within the general system of constitutional rights, its function is to secure its holder a sphere of liberty in the economic field and thereby enable him to lead a self-governing life ....
>
> [T]he property guarantee under Article 14(2) must be seen in relationship to the personhood of the owner – i.e., to the realm of freedom within which persons engage in self-defining, responsible activity. The property right is not primarily a material but rather a personal guarantee.

Because it adopts this approach to art. 14, the Federal Constitutional Court has declined to interpret 'property' in art. 14 as limited to, or meaning the same as, 'property' in the civil law, despite the provision in art. 14(1) that the 'content and limits' of property 'shall be defined by the laws'. In other words, the 'property' protected by art. 14 is an autonomous legal institution. The same applies to 'property' and 'possessions' in the ECHR, as we see in para. 4.27 below, but the position is rather different in relation to the German constitution. This is because the German court relates the autonomous meaning of art. 14 property to the overarching purpose of the Basic Law (protection of personal liberty and autonomy), rather than to general conceptions of property and possessions. As Tom Allen points out,[26] in some cases this means that the Federal Constitutional Court will recognise purely public law rights such as pension rights created under social welfare schemes as 'property' for the purposes of art. 14. In other cases it might involve refusing to accept a private property right as art. 14 'property'. Allen gives as an example the Federal Constitutional Court's decision that the right that the civil court found that a quarry owner had under the BGB to abstract groundwater under its land so that it could extract gravel, was not 'property' within art. 14 and so the state refusal to grant him a licence to abstract the water was not caught by art. 14. As Allen concludes:

---

[24] Tom Allen, 'The autonomous meaning of "possessions" under the ECHR' in Elizabeth Cooke (ed.), *Modern Studies in Property Law vol. 2* (Oxford and Portland, OR: Hart Publishing, 2003) p. 57 at p. 71.

[25] 24 BVerfGE 367 (trans. by Donald Kommers, *The Constitutional Jurisprudence of the Federal Republic of Germany* (2nd edn, Durham and London: Duke University Press, 1997) at pp. 251–252).

[26] Allen, 'The autonomous meaning of "possessions"', fn. 24 above, at pp. 71–73.

Article 14 property is not based simply on private law ... While it overlaps with private law property, in difficult cases its extent is determined by the need to protect personal autonomy. The 'realm of freedom within which persons engage in self-defining, responsible activity' includes the 'protection of economic existence', because economic measures can restrict the individual's capacity to engage in the 'self-defining, responsible activity' necessary to develop the personality. In constitutional terms, this interest is best described as property, and the justification for measures that interfere with this interest must be justified according to the principles of Article 14.[27]

4.15 Comparison Between German and US Constitutional Property Provisions

(a) Scope of 'Property'

However, whilst both the German Constitution and the European Convention on Human Rights give 'property' an autonomous meaning, so that it is not confined to what domestic law defines as 'property', the same is not true of US constitutional property rights. The only provisions in the US Constitution which relate to property are the 'due process' clause and the 'takings' clause, in the Fifth and Fourteenth Amendments to the United States Constitution. The 'due process' clause provides that 'No person shall ... be deprived of life, liberty, or property, without due process of law'. The 'takings' clause adds, 'nor shall private property be taken for public use, without just compensation'. The American courts now interpret both the Due Process Clause and the Takings Clause as strictly confined to protection of rights which are recognised in US law as private property rights. This makes the US property protection considerably narrower in scope than those in the German constitution or in the ECHR.[28] It is also narrower than the German constitutional protection of property in that art. 14(1) of the German constitution guarantees property as a fundamental right, which the US constitution does not.

(b) Limitations on Property

However, the US constitution has no equivalent of Germany's fundamental constitutional principle in art. 14(2) that property entails obligations and its use shall also serve the public good. Nevertheless, as US progressive property theorists have pointed out, the equivalent limitation on property can be found in the progressive property movement's conception of property. As we saw in Chapter 2 *Conceptions and justifications* para. 2.26, progressive property sees property owners as having, in Joseph Singer's words, 'obligations to avoid actions that harm the legitimate interests

---

[27] Ibid. p. 73.
[28] Thomas Merrill, 'The landscape of constitutional property' (2000) 86 *Virginia Law Review* 885, at pp. 885–889.

of others, if possible'[29] or, as Gregory Alexander puts it, 'property owners, as social beings, owe obligations to the community "to participate in and support the social networks and structures that enable us to develop" the human capabilities of us all, and to foster human flourishing'.[30] So, art. 14(2) can be seen as enshrining in German law the principle that the progressive property theorists argue is anyway implicit in the US conception of property. For this reason Alexander suggests that 'politically progressive [US] legal scholars should not categorically oppose extending strong constitutional protection to property. As the German example illustrates, property as a fundamental right need not have anti-redistributive consequences and may in fact advance a progressive vision'.[31]

4.16 South African Constitution

The Constitution of the Republic of South Africa was adopted in 1996 after the end of apartheid, and the property provisions in the Bill of Rights (Chapter 2 of the Constitution) are dominated by the state's recognition of the need to reverse the effects of South Africa's racially discriminatory past. This is immediately apparent from the wording of section 25, the main property provision. It includes a right not to be deprived of pre-existing property rights except in accordance with law and on payment of compensation and for a public purpose or in the 'public interest': subsections (1) – (3). However, this protection of pre-existing property rights is expressly made subject to two qualifications: subsection (4) provides that 'public interest' in subsection (2) includes 'the nation's commitment to land reform, and to reforms to bring about equitable access to all South Africa's natural resources', and subsection (8) states that no provision in s. 25 'may impede the state from taking legislative and other measures to achieve land, water and related reform, in order to redress the results of past racial discrimination . . .'.[32] In addition s. 25 also provides rights on the lines of the human rights *to* property considered in para. 4.5 above: there is a right to specified resources, in the form of a right of every citizen to gain access to land on an equitable basis (s. 25(5)); a right to restitution for the dispossessed, in the form of a right for persons or communities who were dispossessed by past racially discriminatory laws and practices to restitution of their property or equitable redress (s. 25(7)); and in subsections (6) and (9), a right resembling the right to legal recognition of customary resource use, namely a right for persons or communities 'whose tenure of land is legally insecure as a result of past racially discriminatory laws or practices' either to tenure which *is* legally secure or to 'comparable redress'.

---

[29] Joseph Singer, 'Democratic estates: Property law in a free and democratic society' (2009) 94 *Cornell Law Review* 1009 at pp. 1048–1049.

[30] Gregory S. Alexander, 'The social-obligation norm in American property law' (2009) 94 *Cornell Law Review* 745 at p. 770.

[31] Gregory S. Alexander, 'Property as a fundamental constitutional right? The German example' (2003) 88 *Cornell Law Review* 733 at p. 741.

[32] Provided that any limitations on s. 25 rights must be 'reasonable and justifiable in an open and democratic society based on human dignity, equality and freedom': s. 25(8) and s. 36(1).

The most significant right *to* resources, however, comes in section 26, which, under the heading of 'Housing', provides not just a positive right to 'adequate housing', but also a right of protection from eviction from one's home, which goes far beyond the right to respect for home we have seen in other human rights or constitutional rights instruments:

26. Housing

(1) Everyone has the right to have access to adequate housing.
(2) The state must take reasonable legislative and other measures, within its available resources, to achieve the progressive realisation of this right.
(3) No one may be evicted from their home, or have their home demolished, without an order of court made after considering all the relevant circumstances. No legislation may permit arbitrary evictions.

The constitutional court of South Africa has interpreted both s. 25 and s. 26, and the legislation intended to implement them, so as to significantly shift the balance between property haves and property have-nots. As far as the right to adequate housing in s. 26(1) and (2) is concerned, the Constitutional Court has set out in detail the action national, state and local governments can be expected to take to realise the right.[33] In property terms, however, the most radical provision has turned out to be s. 26(3), as elaborated by the Prevention of Illegal Eviction from and Unlawful Occupation of Land Act, 19 of 1998 ('PIE'), which is the primary legislation governing the eviction of unlawful occupiers. PIE includes provisions intended to 'regulate the eviction of unlawful occupiers from land in a fair manner, while recognising the right of land owners to apply to a court for an eviction order in appropriate circumstances'[34] Broadly, all evictions of unlawful occupiers require a court order, and by s. 4(6) a court may not grant an eviction order unless 'it is of opinion that it is just and equitable to do so, after considering all the relevant circumstances, including the rights and needs of the elderly, children, disabled persons and households headed by women'. In addition, if the unlawful occupier has been in occupation for more than six months, the court must also take into account 'whether land has been made available or can reasonably be made available by a municipality or other organ of state or another land owner for the relocation of the unlawful occupier'. The Constitutional Court has interpreted s. 26(3) of the Constitution and PIE as having the combined effect of requiring local housing authorities to be made parties to all applications for an eviction order which might result in someone being made homeless, whether the eviction order is sought by a public body or a private landowner. The local authority must then investigate and

---

[33] *Government of the Republic of South Africa* v. *Grootboom* (2001) (1) SA 46 (CC). The case concerned facilities on a sportsground which was temporarily housing 263 households who had moved there, having nowhere else to go following their unlawful eviction from an illegal settlement on private land. In addition to setting out in general terms actions required by the authorities to deal with such cases, where households were homeless and living in intolerable conditions, the court made an order specifying in detail the water and sanitation facilities and weather-proofing materials that it required the requisite authorities to provide on the site in this particular case to make the conditions 'adequate'.
[34] See the preamble to PIE.

present a report to the court, in effect explaining how in this case it will discharge its duties to provide housing for the occupant under s. 26(3).

The breadth of this jurisdiction can be contrasted with the strictly limited jurisdiction that the UK courts have under the Human Rights Act 1998 to refuse an eviction order sought by a public or private landowner against an occupier who has never had, or who no longer has, any legal right to remain in occupation: see paras. 4.41 and 4.42 below.

4.17 International Human Rights to Specific Resources: The Human Right to Water

In addition to the Universal Declaration on Human Rights 1948, which is a general international human rights instrument, there are other international human rights instruments which relate to specified resources. The human right to water recognised by UN Resolution 64/292 2010[35] encompasses such a right. It 'entitles everyone to sufficient, safe, acceptable, physically accessible and affordable water for personal and domestic uses'. This includes 'freedoms', which are essentially human rights to the protection of pre-existing water rights, consisting of 'the right to maintain access to existing water supplies necessary for the right to water, and the right to be free from interference, such as the right to be free from arbitrary disconnections or contamination of water supplies'. However, the distinctive feature of the human right to water is the 'entitlements'. These are positive distributive rights: 'the right to a system of water supply and management that provides equality of opportunity for people to enjoy the right to water'. In other words, States are obliged not only to respect and protect pre-existing access to water but also to fulfil the right by providing access to water where no adequate access exists.

What the United Nations expects States to do in order to comply with these obligations is set out in considerable detail in General Comment No. 15 (2002) E/C.12/2002/11, 20 January 2003, which, it is now accepted, settles the normative content of the rights declared in UN Resolution 64/292 (2010). It is clear from General Comment 15 that even the obligation to respect and protect pre-existing rights to water goes much further than protection of pre-existing property rights. For example, it includes not only an obligation to refrain from interfering directly or indirectly with the enjoyment of rights of water, but also an obligation to refrain from 'arbitrarily interfering with customary or traditional arrangements for water allocation' (para. 21). This brings it close to the kind of human right to property noted in para. 4.5(d) above, that is, a human right to legal recognition of customary resource use. The steps States are expected to take to comply with their obligation to 'fulfil' the right to water – in other words to implement the human right to have an

---

[35] As noted in para. 4.10(c) above, it is derived from the human right to an adequate standard of living, enshrined in art. 25 of the Universal Declaration of Human Rights, as elaborated in art. 11 of the International Covenant on Economic, Social and Cultural Rights (ICESCR): for the history of the 2010 Resolution and its subsequent recognition see further www.ohchr.org/Documents/Publications/FactSheet35en.pdf.

adequate supply of water – are notably specific and wide-ranging, and distinctions are drawn between steps that ought to be taken immediately and goals that can be attained progressively. In other words, General Comment 15 gives us some idea how a human right to be provided with a resource can be implemented in practical terms.

4.18 International Human Rights to Property for Specific Categories of People: UN Declaration on the Rights of Indigenous Peoples

There are also international human rights instruments which relate to the property rights of specified categories of people, such as women, children, or indigenous peoples. These include the United Nations Declaration on the Rights of Indigenous Peoples 2007,[36] which we look at in Part V of Chapter 9 *Multiple Property Rights Systems: Recognition of Indigenous Land Rights*. For present purposes the distinctive feature of the 2007 Declaration is that it deals with the rights of 'peoples' to their property, rather than with property rights that may be held by their individual members.

PART IV   PROPERTY AND HUMAN RIGHTS IN THE UK UNDER THE EUROPEAN CONVENTION ON HUMAN RIGHTS

4.19 Human Rights and Property Under the European Convention on Human Rights

The human rights protected under the European Convention on Human Rights (ECHR) include two which directly or indirectly affect property rights in England and Wales. These are the right to 'peaceful enjoyment' of 'possessions', which is set out in article 1 of the First Protocol to the Convention (A1P1), and the right to respect for private and family life, home and correspondence, set out in article 8 of the Convention (art. 8). We look in detail at A1P1 in Part V, and at art. 8 in Part VI. There are no equivalents in the ECHR of the provisions in the Universal Declaration of Human Rights 1948 which guarantee the right to own property (art. 17(1)) and the right to an adequate standard of living (art. 24).[37]

4.20 Effect of Violation of A1P1 and Article 8 Rights

The Human Rights Act 1998 makes provision for what is to happen if it is claimed that there has been a violation of a right guaranteed by the ECHR. Lady Hale sums up the effect of these provisions in *R (oao Countryside Alliance)* v. *Attorney General* [2007] UKHL 52:

> 113. The Human Rights Act 1998 has for the first time ... given us all rights against the state. Public authorities and officials must not act incompatibly with our

---

[36] United Nations Declaration on the Rights of Indigenous Peoples, GA Res 61/295, adopted by the General Assembly on 13 September 2007, UN Doc A/RES/47/1 (2007).

[37] para. 4.10(c) above.

Convention rights: s 6(1). If Parliament makes laws which might be incompatible with our Convention rights, the courts and others applying those laws must, so far as possible, read and give effect to them in a way which is compatible with the Convention rights: s 3(1). If Parliament makes a law which cannot be read compatibly with the Convention rights, the courts and others must still give effect to it, but the higher courts may declare that it is incompatible ... s 4. Such declarations have proved powerful incentives to Government and Parliament to put the matter right; for if the court is right, the United Kingdom is in breach of its international obligations in maintaining such a law on the statute book.

4.21 Public Authorities

The Human Rights Act 1998 gives us rights to complain only about something done, or something which should have been done, *by the state*, not by another private citizen or by a private entity. This is enshrined in the 1998 Act by s. 6(1), which makes it 'unlawful *for a public authority* to act in a way which is incompatible with a Convention right'.[38]

(a) What is a Public Authority?

'Public authority' is not defined, except by s. 6(3), which says that it includes 'a court or tribunal' (s. 6(3)(a)) and 'any person *certain of whose functions are functions of a public nature*', but only in relation to an act which is not of a private nature (s. 6(3)(b) and s. 6(5)).

In *Aston Cantlow and Wilmcote Parish Council* v. *Wallbank* [2004] 1 AC 546 the House of Lords took this to mean that, for the purposes of s. 6(1), there are two kinds of 'public authority': 'core' public authorities and what are usually referred to as 'hybrid' public authorities. According to Lord Nicholls, a 'core' public authority is a body 'whose nature is governmental in a broad sense of that expression'.[39] He gave as obvious examples government departments, local authorities, the police and the armed forces and said that:

> Behind the instinctive classification of these organisations as bodies whose nature is governmental lie factors such as the possession of special powers, democratic accountability, public funding in whole or in part, an obligation to act only in the public interest, and a statutory constitution.[40]

Applying this test, the courts generally have had no great difficulty in deciding whether a body is a core public authority, in other words, whether *its nature is governmental.*

---

[38] By s. 6(6) 'an act' includes a failure to act.
[39] *Aston Cantlow and Wilmcote Parish Council* v. *Wallbank* [2004] 1 AC 546 para. 7.
[40] Ibid., citing the 'valuable article' by Dawn Oliver, 'The Frontiers of the State: Public Authorities and Public Functions under the Human Rights Act' [2000] *Public Law* 476.

(b) Hybrid Public Authorities

The question which initially appears more complex is whether and when a body is a hybrid public authority. According to s. 6, as we have just seen, any non-governmental body will be a hybrid public authority body if *some* of its 'functions are of a public nature', but only in relation to acts which are 'not of a private nature'.

So, it depends what we mean by 'public functions' and 'private acts'. Lord Nicholls said in *Aston Cantlow* that the contrast between 'public' and 'private' which is being drawn here is 'essentially ... between functions of a governmental nature and functions, or acts, which are not of that nature'. However, he stressed that 'this is no more than a useful guide. The phrase used in the Act is public function, not government function'.[41] He also said that there was no simple test or determining factor for ascertaining whether a function is a public function:

> What, then, is the touchstone to be used in deciding whether a function is public for this purpose? Clearly there is no single test of universal application. There cannot be, given the diverse nature of governmental functions and the variety of means by which these functions are discharged today. Factors to be taken into account include the extent to which in carrying out the relevant function the body is publicly funded, or is exercising statutory powers, or is taking the place of central government or local authorities, or is providing a public service.[42]

This is less complicated than might at first seem. In practice, once the court has decided that a body is not a core public authority, it need look only at the act (or omission) which is claimed to violate a Convention right. If that act was a public act (i.e. one performed in carrying out a public function) then the body responsible for it is a hybrid public authority whatever its other functions are, and so the claim can proceed. If, however, it was a private act (performed in carrying out a private function) then the body is not a hybrid public authority *for these purposes*, even if it does have other functions which are public functions.

(c) Application of the Test in *Aston Cantlow*

The decision in *Aston Cantlow* itself provides a good illustration of how this works. The body in question was a Parochial Church Council (PCC), a local administrative body which is part of the administrative structure of the Church of England. Aston Cantlow PCC had served notice on the defendants requiring them, as owners of land which was once glebe land (broadly, land which had a historical connection with a local church) to pay more than £90,000 towards the costs of repairing the chancel of the local church. The defendants claimed that this was a violation of their human rights under the ECHR. The PCC argued that it was not a public authority for the purposes of s. 6 of the Human Rights Act 1998 and therefore the defendants had no

---

[41] *Aston Cantlow* v. *Wallbank*, fn. 39 above, para. 10, and see also Lord Hope at para. 49: 'The phrase "public functions" in this context is ... closely linked to the functions and powers, whether centralised or distributed, of government.'

[42] Ibid. para. 12, per Lord Nicholls.

claim against them. The House of Lords agreed. It said that although the Church of England is the established church in England it is not itself a core public authority because it is an organisation which is not governmental in nature:[43] it governs a religious organisation but is not part of the government of the state. The same is true of a PCC. It is part of the administration of a religious organisation and all its functions are to do with the administration of the Church of England. Although the Church of England does have some public functions in relation to births, marriages and deaths and maintaining public registers, a PCC is not responsible for any of those functions. The important point, however, was that its responsibilities include the maintenance of the fabric of the Church of England's churches, and in carrying out that function it did have statutory powers to serve notices like the one it served on the defendants. However, those notices cannot be served on the public at large or on any particular section of the public: the liability for chancel repairs lies only on certain private landowners, and it arises only as a consequence of their ownership of land which was historically tied to that specific liability. On that basis, the House of Lords decided, the service of the notices was a private act (a step in the enforcement of a private land obligation or debt), and therefore the PCC was not a hybrid public authority for these purposes, and so the defendants' human rights claim could not proceed.

(d) Outsourced Government Functions

This approach has been followed in subsequent cases, although it has to be said that in later cases it has caused more difficulties, particularly where services formerly provided by national or local authorities have been outsourced to private commercial organisations run at a profit. In a particularly controversial case, *YL v. Birmingham CC* [2007] UKHL 27, the House of Lords held by a majority that a commercially run private care home was not a public authority, and so residents could not bring complaints against it of violations of human rights. The argument for the residents was that the care home's function of providing them with accommodation and care was a function of a public nature because they were placed there and partially funded by the local authority carrying out its statutory duty 'to arrange care and accommodation' for those who needed it because of age, illness or disability. The argument was rejected by a majority in the House of Lords, who took the view that the care home was not exercising functions of a public nature, but private contractual functions provided on a commercial basis under a contractual agreement between itself and the local authority. The decision attracted considerable adverse attention, and its effect was quickly reversed by s. 145 of the Health and Social Care Act 2008, which provides that establishments such as care homes are, for the purposes of s. 6(3)(b) of the Human Rights Act 1998, taken to be exercising public functions.

---

[43] Also, it is not a legal entity in itself, so cannot be an 'authority'.

(e) Extension of Human Rights Liability to Private Sector Providers of Key Services?

Another controversial effect of confining liability for human rights violations to public authorities is that this discriminates against those people who have to rely on the private sector for provision of a particular service which is provided to others by core or hybrid public authorities. The area which currently causes most concern is housing, and we come back to the problem as it arises in that context in para. 4.42.

(f) Courts as Public Authorities

Finally, as we saw in (a) above, s. 6 specifically states that a court or tribunal is a public authority. This leads to the argument that when a private person claims that another private person has interfered with her right to peaceful enjoyment of her possessions or to respect for her home, the court hearing her complaint acts as a public authority when it decides whether or not her complaint is justified. This means, so the argument goes, that it is for the court to ensure that its decision is compatible with the human rights of both private parties. If either party feels that the decision is not compatible with its human rights, they can bring an action against the UK government under s. 6(1) of the Human Rights Act 1998. The Supreme Court recently considered this argument in *McDonald* v. *McDonald* [2016] UKSC 28, the housing possession case we look at in para. 4.42. It accepted in principle that a decision made by a court or tribunal in a dispute between private parties is caught by s. 6(1). However, it did not accept that this meant that the court hearing the private dispute had to deal with it in the same way as it is required to deal with a complaint by a private person against a public authority under the 1998 Act. We come back to this point as well in para. 4.42.

4.22 Decisions of the ECtHR

One other provision of the 1998 Act is relevant here. This is s. 2, which makes it clear that decisions of the ECtHR are not strictly binding on UK courts, but must be 'taken into account'. Over the last few years, divergence between decisions of the House of Lords and decisions of the ECtHR has been a particular problem in relation to the scope of art. 8 in housing possession proceedings, as we see in Part VI of this chapter. Bringing the UK Supreme Court back into line with ECtHR decisions on at least one of these problematic issues, Lord Neuberger in *Manchester City Council* v. *Pinnock* [2010] UKSC 45 stated the following principles to be followed in the future:

> 48. This Court is not bound to follow every decision of the ECtHR. Not only would it be impractical to do so: it would sometimes be inappropriate, as it would destroy the ability of the Court to engage in the constructive dialogue with the ECtHR which is of value to the development of Convention law (see e g *R* v. *Horncastle* [2009] UKSC 14). Of course, we should usually follow a clear and constant line of decisions by the ECtHR: *R (Ullah)* v. *Special Adjudicator* [2004] UKHL 26. But we are not actually bound to do so or (in theory, at least) to follow a decision of the Grand Chamber. As

Lord Mance pointed out in *Doherty* v. *Birmingham* [2009] 1 AC 367, para. 126, s. 2 of the HRA requires our courts to 'take into account' ECtHR decisions, not necessarily to follow them. Where, however, there is a clear and constant line of decisions whose effect is not inconsistent with some fundamental substantive or procedural aspect of our law, and whose reasoning does not appear to overlook or misunderstand some argument or point of principle, we consider that it would be wrong for this Court not to follow that line.

He concluded that there was such a 'clear and constant line of decisions' of the ECtHR on the issue in question (the court's jurisdiction in possession proceedings), and that therefore the Supreme Court should follow that line and not follow the relevant House of Lords decisions: see further in para. 4.41 below.[44]

4.23 Conflicting Human Rights

There are many opportunities for human rights protected under the ECHR to come into conflict with each other. In all property relationships between parties who are not core public authorities,[45] each party has a property interest covered by A1P1. Similarly, in all cases which involve a threat to someone's home coming from someone other than a public authority, there will usually be at least one other party with a property interest covered by A1P1. Also, property human rights may clash with other kinds of human rights.

Two general principles emerge from the cases dealing with conflicts of these kinds. The first is that it is at least arguable that some human rights rank higher than others, as we see in para. 4.32 below. The second is the Supreme Court's conclusion in *McDonald* v. *McDonald* [2016] UKSC 28 that in housing possession cases the courts do not have jurisdiction to question the balance that UK legislation has drawn between the competing interests of private landlords (i.e. protection of their A1P1 rights) and residential tenants (protection of their art. 8 rights). We look at this issue again in para. 4.41 below in the specific context of eviction proceedings in residential cases. Here, however, it is worth noting that the Supreme Court suggested that the same principle might apply to all cases where there is contractual relationship between the parties which is regulated to some extent by statute:[46]

Of course, there are many cases where the court can be required to balance conflicting Convention rights of two parties, e.g. where a person is seeking to rely on her article 8 rights to restrain a newspaper from publishing an article which breaches her privacy, and where the newspaper relies on article 10. But such disputes arise not from contractual arrangements made between two private parties, but from tortious or

---

[44] The principle was subsequently accepted by the Supreme Court in *McDonald* v. *McDonald* [2016] UKSC 28, deciding, however, that in that case there was no 'clear and authoritative guidance' from the ECtHR contrary to the view it took of the court's role in art. 8 cases where a tenant was complaining of eviction by a private sector landlord or mortgagee: see para. 4.42 below.

[45] See para. 4.21 above. Core public authorities are not entitled to human rights protection, although hybrid public authorities may be: *Aston Cantlow* v. *Wallbank*.

[46] As we see in later chapters where we focus on different kinds of property relationships, this applies to nearly all of them.

quasi-tortious relationships, where the legislature has expressly, impliedly or through inaction, left it to the courts to carry out the balancing exercise. It is in sharp contrast to the present type of case where the parties are in a contractual relationship in respect of which the legislature has prescribed how their respective Convention rights are to be respected.[47]

In other words, it seems that if statute regulates a property relationship between private parties, the court hearing a dispute is not entitled to question the way in which Parliament has directed that the dispute should be settled, unless it is being asked to consider whether the statutory provisions themselves are incompatible with human rights under the 1998 Act.[48]

PART V   PROTECTION OF PROPERTY BY ARTICLE 1 PROTOCOL 1 OF THE EUROPEAN CONVENTION ON HUMAN RIGHTS

4.24 Article 1 Protocol 1

Article 1 of the First Protocol to the European Convention on Human Rights (A1P1) provides that:

> Protection of property
> Article 1
> Every natural or legal person is entitled to the peaceful enjoyment of his possessions. No one shall be deprived of his possessions except in the public interest and subject to the conditions provided for by law and by the general principles of international law.
>   The preceding provisions shall not, however, in any way impair the right of a State to enforce such laws as it deems necessary to control the use of property in accordance with the general interest or to secure the payment of taxes or other contributions or penalties.

On a literal reading, this right to the peaceful enjoyment of possessions appears, on the face of it, to be a relatively narrow and rather unsatisfactory formulation of a human right to the protection of property. Unlike art. 17 of the Universal Declaration on Human Rights it does not include a right for every person to hold property, only a guarantee of pre-existing property rights. This may suggest at first sight that property is regarded more as an economic interest to be protected against others and against the state, rather than as an essential aspect of personhood and human dignity: there is no acknowledgement of the duties or responsibilities associated with property, as there is in art. 14 of the German Constitution,[49] and no equivalent of the right to welfare in art. 24 of the Universal Declaration of Human Rights.[50] Moreover, if we were to take the rationale as indeed only the protection of economic interests, the protection against the State does not appear to be very strong: on a literal reading there is no requirement for payment of compensation in the event of deprivation or control of use of property by the state, and it appears up to the State

---

[47] *McDonald* v. *McDonald*, fn. 44 above, para. 46.
[48] In which case it must make a declaration of incompatibility under s. 4: para. 4.20 above.
[49] para. 4.14 above.   [50] para. 4.10(c) above.

to decide whether any particular law is 'necessary' to control the use of property 'in accordance with the general interest'.

4.25 Nature and Origins

However, a literal reading of A1P1 is misleading, and as we see in the following paragraphs the courts have taken a broader view of both its rationale[51] and its effect.[52] This discrepancy between a literal reading of A1P1 and the interpretation adopted by the courts is perhaps explained by the origins of the provision. Although it was generally agreed that there should be a property provision in the Convention at the time when it was being drafted, there were fundamental differences of opinion between national delegates both as to its rationale and its content. At one point a provision equivalent to art. 17 of the Universal Declaration of Human Rights was included in the draft Convention, but it was hotly contested at many levels and on many disparate grounds. Eventually, in order to produce a draft that the parties were prepared to ratify, it was agreed that the property provision should be dropped altogether from the final draft, to be agreed later. As a result there was no property provision at all in the Convention when it was first ratified, and the provision as it now appears was a compromise added by the First Protocol two years later.[53]

4.26 Interpretation of Article 1 Protocol 1

However, the important point for present purposes is that neither the UK courts nor the ECtHR have felt constrained to adopt a literal interpretation of A1P1.

In 2008 in *JA Pye (Oxford) Ltd* v. *United Kingdom* (2008) 46 EHRR 44 the Grand Chamber of the ECtHR summed up what is now the generally accepted interpretation of A1P1.[54] This is that the three sentences in A1P1 have to be read as laying down three rules or principles. The first sentence sets out the fundamental principle that everyone is entitled to the peaceful enjoyment of their possessions (rule 1), with the second and third articulating two ways in which the state might interfere with the peaceful enjoyment of someone's possession (by *depriving* them of it or by *controlling their use* of it), and setting out the conditions under which the State is entitled to interfere with someone's peaceful enjoyment of their possessions in that particular way. So, the State is not entitled to *deprive* someone of their possessions 'except in the public interest and subject to the conditions provided for by law and by the general principles of international law' (rule 2), and it may not *control the use of* someone's possessions except by 'such laws as it deems necessary to control the

---

[51] See for example *Centro Europa* v. *Italy* [2012] ECHR 974 and the hunting cases in para. 4.29(b).

[52] para. 4.26 below.

[53] For a full account see Tom Allen, *Property and the Human Rights Act 1998* (Oxford: Hart Publishing, 2005) pp. 7–38.

[54] *JA Pye (Oxford) Ltd* v. *United Kingdom* (2008) 46 EHRR 44 at paras. 52–55, confirming the approach adopted by the ECtHR in *Sporrong and Lönnroth* v. *Sweden* (1983) 5 EHRR 35 para. 61.

use of property in accordance with the general interest' (rule 3).[55] However, the ECtHR said, the three rules are connected, in that rule 2 and rule 3 are concerned only with particular instances of interference with the right to peaceful enjoyment of property 'and should therefore be construed in the light of the general principle enunciated in the first rule'.[56]

One consequence of this is that an interference which does not amount to either a deprivation of a possession or a control over its use may still be treated as a violation of the overall principle in rule 1.[57] Another is that the courts are disinclined to draw sharp distinctions between rule 2 and rule 3. In particular, despite the differences in wording between rule 2 and rule 3, the process followed by the courts in deciding whether an interference is justified is essentially the same, whether the interference comes within rule 2 or rule 3, or within the overarching principle in rule 1.

Broadly, this process is as follows. The court must ask first whether there has been an 'interference' (whether by deprivation or control of use or otherwise) with a 'possession;' secondly, it must consider whether the interference complied with the principle of lawfulness (i.e. the public authority acted within the law, and observed due process requirements); and thirdly, if it was lawful in that sense, the court must decide whether it pursued a legitimate aim by means that were reasonably proportionate to the aim sought to be achieved. This third question requires the court to decide whether a fair balance has been struck between the demands of the general interest of the community and the requirements for the protection of the individual's fundamental rights, allowing the state an appropriate 'margin of appreciation'.

We look at these various elements in the following paragraphs.

4.27 'Possessions'

The initial question for the court is whether the right said to have been interfered with by the state is a 'possession'. This is not always an easy question. Despite the heading of A1P1 ('protection of *property*'), the overarching first sentence (rule 1) provides a right to the peaceful enjoyment of '*possessions*' (a term that has no legal significance in English law). 'Possessions' appears again in the rule 2 in the second sentence ('no person shall be deprived of his *possessions* . . .'), but it is replaced by the word 'property' in rule 3 in the third sentence ('. . . such laws as it deems necessary to control the use of *property*'). There are similar difficulties in the wording of the official French text: the equivalent terms are neither explicable in themselves, nor are they exact translations of the terms in the English text.[58]

---

[55] *JA Pye (Oxford) Ltd* v. *United Kingdom* para. 52.   [56] Ibid.   [57] See para. 4.29(c) below.

[58] The French text has 'propriété' in the heading where the English has 'property', but then has 'biens' in both rule 1 (where the English word is 'possessions') and in rule 3 (where the English is 'property'). As pointed out by Sir Gerald Fitzmaurice, giving a dissenting opinion in one of the first decisions of the ECtHR on the meaning of 'possessions' *Marckx* v. *Belgium* Series A No 31 (1979) 2 EHRR 33, 'biens' is best translated into English by 'assets', not by 'possessions' (which has no satisfactory French equivalent) nor by 'property', and anyway the closest French translation for 'assets' is 'avoirs', not 'biens'.

After considerable confusion (apparent in judgments of the English courts, the ECtHR and in academic commentaries) it is now settled that in A1P1 'possessions' means the same as 'property', but that both terms have an autonomous meaning. In other words, 'property' does not mean the same as it means under the domestic laws of any state. This is understandable enough, given that all states have different rules about what counts as 'property', and it is perhaps helpful if all states accept a uniform rule about what counts as property for the purposes of A1P1. But if 'possessions' means 'property', but not 'property' as defined in the law of any given domestic legal system, what *does* it mean?

4.28 The Autonomous Meaning of 'Possessions'

Neither the ECtHR nor the domestic courts suggest that the test for whether something is a 'possession' within A1P1 can be found by appealing to a universal natural law meaning of 'property'. Instead, the courts seem to be content to allow a definition to emerge pragmatically on a case by case basis.

(a) 'Possessions' and Property Interests

So, it is now established that 'possessions' includes but is not confined to owner-ship,[59] and it probably includes all interests that are categorised as property in the legal system under consideration (at least, there do not appear to be any cases where an interest which under the relevant domestic law was a property interest was found not to be a 'possession').

It does also include some interests that are not property interests in the national legal system under consideration, for example the Olympic Delivery Authority's non-proprietary licence in *Olympic Delivery Authority* v. *Persons Unknown* [2012] EWHC 1012 which we consider in para. 4.8 and in (c) below. However, it does not include past assets. For example, land rights extinguished by past wrongful expropriations have been held not to be 'possessions', and therefore dispossessed communities claiming restitution of land rights no longer recognised in domestic law do not have 'possessions' protected by A1P1.[60] Consistently with this, only pre-existing rights, such as the goodwill of a business, can be 'possessions': assets that the claimant hopes to receive in the future, such as the income the business expects to earn in the future, are not possessions. An enforceable *right* to obtain a property interest in the future is a possession, however, and so too is a legitimate expectation of obtaining one.[61] Also, some licences and permissions to carry out a particular activity (for example, to sell tobacco or alcohol),[62] are possessions, and so too are

---

[59] *Gasus Dosier und Fordertechnik GmbH* v. *The Netherlands* (1995) 20 EHRR 403, in relation to the interest of a seller under a retention of title clause (a kind of security interest).

[60] Allen, *Property and the Human Rights Act 1998*, fn. 53 above, pp. 57–64.

[61] *Centro Europa 7 Srl* v. *Italy* (2012) 32 BHRC 417.

[62] *Tre Traktörer AB* v. *Sweden* (1989) 13 EHRR 309.

most of the 'regulatory property' interests we consider in Chapter 6 *New Property Interests and the Numerus Clausus* para. 6.12.

Most of these distinctions are familiar to us from the criteria we use in the common law to distinguish property interests from non-property interests. For example, as we see in Chapter 5 *Ownership and other property interests* para. 5.22 (a) common law also distinguishes between a present right to future enjoyment (which is capable of being a property right) and a mere hope or expectation of future enjoyment (which is not), and between the present and future assets of a business. However, when we are considering A1P1 the autonomous meaning doctrine applies to these distinctions as well as to the words 'possessions' and 'property'. In other words, when we want to establish whether an asset or interest is a possession within A1P1, we cannot rely on the English law meaning of concepts such as 'legitimate expectation' or 'goodwill': their meaning is determined by the jurisprudence of the ECtHR. Lord Dyson made this point in the Court of Appeal in *Department for Energy and Climate Change* v. *Breyer Group PLC* [2015] EWCA Civ 408 where the issue was whether a Government proposal to cut financial incentives previously provided for solar energy installations interfered with the possessions of companies involved in the installation of such systems. It was agreed for the purposes of the appeal that the proposal had had 'an immediate and serious adverse impact' on the claimants' businesses, but it was contested how much of the loss was attributable to the goodwill of the businesses (which could be a possession) and how much was attributable to future assets (which could not). Lord Dyson said at para. 45:

> Goodwill is the present value of what has been built up [by past work]. It is to be distinguished from the value of a future income steam. From an accountants' point of view this distinction may make little practical sense. But it is the distinction that has been clearly drawn by the ECtHR for the purposes of A1P1 . . .

(b) Monetary Value and Marketability

None of this is of much help in trying to identify a general test for establishing whether an asset or interest is a 'possession'. However, in relation to regulatory property interests at least, a clear test does seem to have emerged. This is that an interest is a 'possession' if it has monetary value and is marketable. Cranston J. summed up the UK position in *UK Association of Fish Producer Organisations* v. *Secretary of State for Environment Food and Rural Affairs* [2013] EWHC 1959, which concerned a Government decision to reallocate unused fishing quota from the large fishing vessel sector of the British fishing fleet to the small fishing vessel sector, which would be able to make use of the extra quota. The government did this by re-allocating the 'fixed quota allocation units' by reference to which the total fishing quota issued by the Government in each year was distributed. The organisations of large vessels argued that this would be an interference with their possessions within A1P1. Cranston J agreed. He concluded from the authorities that such interests are 'possessions' if they 'have a monetary value and can be marketed for

consideration'.[63] On this basis, he decided, fixed quota allocation units were possessions because as a matter of fact they were traded even though there was no formal
system for doing so.[64]

(c) Limits of the Monetary Value and Marketability Test

However, this test of monetary value and marketability cannot apply to all kinds of
interest. Some interests may be of monetary value to the holder, but they may be
personal to the rights holder and so not marketable. So, for example, in *Olympic
Delivery Authority* v. *Persons Unknown,* [2012] EWHC 1012 noted above, the
Olympic Delivery Authority was assumed to be entitled to call on A1P1 to remove
protesters from land giving access to the site to be used for the London Olympic
Games, even though the ODA had only a non-proprietary licence over the site. Its
non-proprietary licence was assumed to be a 'possession', yet presumably the licence
was personal to the ODA and not marketable.

    Similarly, as also noted above, legitimate expectations of acquiring a property
interest have been found to be possessions, even though by their nature expectations
will usually be personal to their holder, and so not transferable. For example, in
Centro Europa7 SRL v. *Italy* [2012] ECHR 974 the Grand Chamber of the ECtHR
found that the claimant's legitimate expectation of obtaining an allocation of
broadcasting frequencies was a possession within A1P1. It is clear from the facts
of the case that whilst broadcasting frequencies were tradeable in Italy, the claimant's
legitimate expectation of being allocated a frequency was not something it could
have transferred to anyone else. It had already been granted a licence for nationwide
terrestrial television broadcasting but it could not actually operate its television
network unless and until it was allocated a broadcasting frequency. Its complaint
was that the Government had delayed doing this for five years, and that this
constituted an interference with its legitimate expectation of acquiring the access
to and use of broadcasting frequencies which would have allowed its exercise of
freedom of expression and the pursuit of an economic activity. The Grand Chamber
found that the Government's delay in dealing with the claimant's request was an
unlawful interference with the claimant's legitimate expectations, on the basis that a
'legitimate expectation' means a right to have its request (in this case for frequencies)
dealt with by the Government in a manner consistent with the criteria laid down by
domestic law.

    This decision is also important because of the view the Grand Chamber took of
the rationale of A1P1. It accepted that acquisition of the broadcasting frequency was
of value to the claimant not only because it would enable it to pursue an economic

---

[63] Applying the test suggested by Kenneth Parker J in *R (Nicholds)* v. *Security Industry Authority* [2006]
EWHC 1792 (who decided that on this basis licences to act as door supervisors at clubs and other
venues were not possessions) and subsequently approved by the Court of Appeal in *R (Malik)*
v. *Waltham Forest NHS Primary Care Trust* [2007] EWCA Civ 265 and by Lord Bingham in the House
of Lords in *R (Countryside Alliance)* v. *Attorney General* [2008] 1 AC 719, para. 22.

[64] However, he went on to decide that the proposed removal of unused units was not an interference
covered by A1P1, and therefore there was no violation of rights under A1P1: para. 4.29(a) below.

activity but also because it enabled it to exercise its rights of freedom of expression. If the exercise of a right to freedom of expression is a legitimate criterion for an interest to be treated as a possession, then it follows that even monetary value is not an essential attribute for a 'possession'.

4.29 Interference with Possessions

We have already seen that a claimant's right to peaceful enjoyment of her possessions is only infringed if there has been an interference with those possessions. A1P1 distinguishes between an interference that consists of a deprivation of the possession and one that consists of a control of its use, and as we saw in para. 4.26, an interference that falls into neither category can still amount to a violation of the principle in rule 1.

(a) Has There Been an Interference?

However, the first question to consider is whether there has been any interference at all. In *R (oao Malik)* v. *Waltham Forest NHS Trust* [2007] EWCA Civ 265 the Court of Appeal said that something would be an 'interference' with the claimant's possession if it had 'material economic consequences' for him. On that basis it held Dr Malik's suspension from the official list of those entitled to practice within the NHS was not an interference with his possessions. A right to practice within the NHS was not a possession anyway, the court said, because it gave him only an expectation of future income, not a right to it,[65] but even if it had been, suspension from the list would not have been an interference with that possession, because Dr Malik had not shown that the suspension would have material economic consequences for him.[66]

This 'material economic consequences' test was adopted by Cranston J In *UK Association of Fish Producer Organisations* v. *Secretary of State for Environment Food and Rural Affairs* [2013] EWHC 1959. He concluded that there had been no interference with the possessions of the claimant (the fixed fishing quota allocation units described in para. 4.28(b) above) if, as advocated by the ECtHR in *Sporrong and Lönnroth* v. *Sweden* (1982) 5 EHRR 35 para. 63, you 'look behind appearances and investigate the realities of the situation'. The proposed government action was a re-allocation of unused units to the small fishing vessel sector and, he said, the large fishing vessel organisations had failed to show that this would have 'material economic consequences' for them:

> 116 ... the realities are that the quota affected by the [Government's] decision has been consistently unused. Producer organisations and their members have no proprietary interest in the fishing stock itself and fixed quota allocation units, as explained earlier, give no rights to any specific amount of fishing stock in advance of the annual

[65] para. 4.28(b) above.
[66] *R (oao Malik)* v. *Waltham Forest NHS Trust* [2007] EWCA Civ 265 at paras. 50 and 77.

Ministerial decisions on quota. It is inherent in their character that for any one year the quota held by a producer organisation on behalf of its members might be substantially reduced from previous years, even to zero, depending on the decision of the [EU, which decides on quota to be distributed to national governments]. There is no evidence [that the producer organisations would suffer] the material economic consequences Rix LJ referred to in *Malik* indicative of any interference with possessions [if they lost part of their fixed quota allocation units] ... [although the claimants had produced projected figures suggesting otherwise] the methodology is opaque. Quite apart from that it is a puzzle that if the fixed allocation quota units [were indeed worth the valuation figure], they were not exploited. The economic reality is that for a variety of reasons it was not worthwhile for the fishermen entitled to these units to exploit the fishing stock they represented ... The reality is that fishermen have taken a business decision not to exploit part of their quota. That unused quota has now been reallocated to others, who it is expected will place a higher economic value upon it.

(b) Limits of the 'Material Economic Consequences' Test

However, as we saw in para. 4.28(c), something can be a 'possession' for the purposes A1P1 even if it has no monetary value. It would make no sense to say that enjoyment of a possession of that kind is violated only by an action that has 'material economic consequences'. Also, even if the possession in question does have monetary value, peaceful enjoyment of it may be injured by something which has no effect on that monetary value. This is evident from a group of cases on hunting. *Herrmann v. Germany* (2013) 56 EHRR 7 concerned a complaint by Herrmann, a German landowner, that the German Federal Hunting Act made it impossible for him to prohibit hunting on his land. The Act set up a scheme to regulate hunting in Germany, which required all landowners in a designated area to form a hunting association to manage hunting in that area on behalf of its members, either allocating hunting rights to members, or leasing them to outsiders, distributing the profits to the members. Herrmann was opposed to hunting on ethical grounds and wanted to terminate his membership of the hunting association because he found it morally repugnant to be associated with hunting and because he wanted to stop his land being used for hunting. The German Constitutional Court had already decided that his compulsory membership did not violate his Constitutional right to property under art. 14 of the Constitution (para. 4.14 above). He therefore applied to the ECtHR, complaining that his compulsory membership violated his Convention rights, including his right to peaceful enjoyment of land under A1P1, by imposing on him an obligation to tolerate the exercise of hunting rights on land. In *Chassagnou v. France* (2000) 29 EHRR 615 (Grand Chamber) and *Schneider v. Luxembourg* (2113/04) July 10, 2007 the ECtHR had already found that similar schemes in France and Luxembourg violated A1P1 rights, and in consequence of those decisions France and Luxembourg had already changed their hunting laws, and so too had some other EU states. As the Grand Chamber said in *Chassagnou*:

> 74. The Court notes that, although the applicants have not been deprived of their right to use their property, to lease it or to sell it, the compulsory transfer of the hunting rights over their land [to the hunting association] ... prevents them from making use

of the right to hunt, which is directly linked to the right of property, as they see fit. In the present case the applicants do not wish to hunt on their land and object to the fact that others may come onto their land to hunt. However, although opposed to hunting on ethical grounds, they are obliged to tolerate the presence of armed men and gun dogs on their land every year. This restriction on the free exercise of the right of use undoubtedly constitutes an interference with the applicants' enjoyment of their rights as the owners of property. Accordingly, the second paragraph of A1P1 is applicable . . . .[67]

In *Herrmann* the Grand Chamber, by a majority, came to the same conclusion in respect of the German Federal Hunting Act, confirming that the requirement to tolerate hunting on his land constituted an interference with Herrmann's possessions *because he found hunting morally repugnant*: the question of whether it affected the monetary value of the land was irrelevant.[68]

The issue also came up in the House of Lords in the English hunting case, *R (oao Countryside Alliance)* v. *Attorney-General* [2007] UKHL 52. This time, however, the claimants were pro-hunting rather than anti-hunting and their complaint was that the UK Hunting Act 2004, which banned the hunting of wild mammals with dogs and hare coursing, violated their Convention rights, including their rights to peaceful enjoyment of their possessions under A1P1. The claimants were not all landowners: some were people who made their living out of hunting, who could indeed argue that the hunting ban was an interference with their possessions in that it had 'material economic consequences' for them. However, Lord Bingham in the House of Lords made no attempt to distinguish between the claimants in this way:

> . . . it seems to me indisputable that certain of the claimants have suffered a loss of control over their possessions: there are, for instance, on the largely unchallenged evidence, landowners who cannot hunt over their own land or permit others to do so, those who cannot use their horses and hounds to hunt, the farrier who cannot use his equipment to shoe horses to be used for hunting, owners of businesses which have lost their marketable goodwill, a shareholder whose shares have lost their value, and so on.[69]

In other words, for some claimants the complaint was that the Act made their possessions (their hunting packs, or their businesses or their shares in a business) less valuable, but for others the complaint was that it prevented them from using their land in the way they wanted to use it. The House of Lords accepted that for all claimants the only issue was whether the effect on their possessions was significant.[70]

(c) Distinction Between Deprivation, Control of Use and Other Interferences

As noted in para. 4.26, in more recent cases the courts have not drawn sharp distinctions between deprivations, controls of use and other interferences with the

---

[67] *Chassagnou* v. *France* (2000) 29 EHRR 615.
[68] *Herrmann* v. *Germany* (2013) 56 EHRR 7 at para. 71.
[69] *R (oao Countryside Alliance)* v. *Attorney-General* [2007] UKHL 52 para. 20.
[70] The House of Lords held it was, although it decided that in the circumstances the interference was justified: para. 4.31(a) below.

peaceful enjoyment of possession. As Lord Reed said in *AXA General Insurance Ltd v. The Lord Advocate* [2011] UKSC 46:[71]

> Assessment of whether there has been a violation of A1P1 thus involves consideration of whether a 'possession' exists, whether there has been an interference with the possession, and, if so, the nature of the interference: whether, in particular, it constitutes a deprivation of the possession falling within the second rule, or a control on use falling within the third rule, or falls within the more general principle enunciated in the first rule. Given that the second and third rules are only particular instances of interference with the right guaranteed by the first rule, however, the importance of classification should not be exaggerated. Although, where an interference is categorised as falling under the second or third rule, the Strasbourg court will usually consider the question of justification under reference to the language of those specific provisions of A1P1, the test is in substance the same, however the interference has been classified . . .

Similarly, in *R (on the application of Mott)* v. *Environment Agency* [2018] UKSC 10, which we look at in more detail below, Lord Carnwath reviewed the ECtHR decisions on the issue and concluded that they show 'that the distinction between expropriation and control is neither clear-cut, nor crucial to the analysis'. In particular, the courts will not agonise over the question of whether a severe control of use which seriously diminishes the value of the claimant's possessions is 'really' a deprivation or some other kind of interference. Rather, the severity of the interference and its effect on the claimant are factors to be taken into account when the court has to decide whether, in the circumstances, the interference was lawful and pursued a legitimate aim by means that were reasonably proportionate to the aim sought to be achieved.

The same applies to compensation. At one time the courts took the view that compensation was generally required for a deprivation of possessions, but not for a control of use, unless the circumstances were exceptional.[72] However, it became apparent that this did not mean that compensation was automatic for a deprivation. As the ECtHR said in *Sporrong and Lönnroth*:

> A taking of property under [rule 2] without payment of an amount reasonably related to its value will normally constitute a disproportionate interference that cannot be justified under Article 1. The provision does not, however, guarantee a right to full compensation in all circumstances, since legitimate objectives of 'public interest' may call for less than reimbursement of the full market value . . .[73]

Similarly, Lord Carnwath observed in *Mott* that A1P1 gives no 'general expectation of compensation' for the adverse effects of necessary environmental controls.[74]

Conversely, in now seems clear that the courts do not have to find that a control of use is 'exceptional' before deciding that it is disproportionate without the payment of

---

[71] *AXA General Insurance Ltd* v. *The Lord Advocate* [2011] UKSC 46 at para. 108.
[72] Lord Neuberger in *R (Trailer and Marina (Leven) Ltd)* v. *Secretary of State for the Environment, Food and Rural Affairs* [2004] EWCA Civ 1580.
[73] *Sporrong and Lönnroth* v. *Sweden*, fn. 54 above, para. 54.
[74] *R (on the application of Mott)* v. *Environment Agency* [2018] UKSC 10 at para. 37.

compensation. It is probably now more accurate to say that the availability of compensation is a factor that is relevant (although not necessarily conclusive) in deciding whether an interference is proportionate, and that this applies whether the interference is categorised as a deprivation, a control of use or another kind of interference falling within the overarching principle in rule 1. This is apparent from the Supreme Court decision in *Mott*,[75] where a long-standing lessee of salmon fishing rights in the Severn Estuary complained that the way in which the Environment Agency proposed to limit his annual catch was, in the absence of compensation, a disproportionate interference with his A1P1 right to peaceful enjoyment of his fishing rights. The context was that the lessee, Mott, operated a traditional form of salmon fishing in that area, as did some others. However, whilst most of the others operated their fisheries as a hobby, taking a relatively small catch each year, Mott operated his on a commercial basis, relying on it for his livelihood. All operators of fisheries of this type in this area required an annual licence from the Environment Agency to exercise their fishing rights, and for the last few years Government policy had been to reduce salmon fishing in that area because of adverse environmental effects it was thought to be having on rivers feeding into the estuary. In 2012 the Environment Agency acquired new statutory powers, and it announced that in future years it was going to limit the catch each licensee was entitled to take under its licence to the average catch of the least productive of that group of salmon fisheries. This would have had little or no effect on the fisheries operated as hobbies, but would have had a massive effect on Mott's catch, cutting its value by at least 95 per cent and making his fishery uneconomic. The Supreme Court held that, in the absence of payment of compensation this was disproportionate (for the reasons we look at in para. 4.31(c) below), whether the interference was categorised as a deprivation or a control of use. They noted that the trial judge had thought that the interference was closer to a deprivation than to a change of use, but had not felt able, nor found it necessary, to decide which it was, and they confirmed his conclusion that:

> the effect is that even if the Agency could properly have imposed the total catch limit that it did, the size of that limit and the way in which it was apportioned would still have meant that the claimant has been required to shoulder an excessive and disproportionate burden, such that a breach of A1P1 could only be prevented by payment of compensation.[76]

Another type of interference which does not fit easily into either the 'deprivation' or the 'control of use' category is threatened action by a public authority which is later abandoned, but which meanwhile blights the value of the complainant's possessions. This was the kind of interference found in *Sporrong and Lönnroth* v. *Sweden* (1982) 5 EHRR 35, where properties had been officially earmarked for expropriation, and construction had been prohibited for several years before it was finally decided not to proceed with the expropriations. The Court of Appeal in England and Wales came to the same conclusion in the solar energy installation case noted in para. 4.28

---

[75] Ibid.   [76] Ibid. paras. 24 and 25.

(a) above, *Department for Energy and Climate Change* v. *Breyer Group PLC* [2015] EWCA Civ 408. It found that a Government Proposal to alter a scheme which, if implemented, would have harmed the claimants' businesses, was itself an interference with their possessions. This was because, so Lord Dyson said, the Proposal itself '*as a matter of fact* . . . did in a real and practical sense interfere with the claimants' business' even though it had no legal effect.[77] In coming to this conclusion Lord Dyson was not deterred by the argument that such a principle would make life difficult for governments and public authorities who wanted to consult on proposals for reform:

> 73 I accept that the Government and public authorities consult on proposals from time to time where the mere fact of consulting can affect the value of individuals' land and businesses. Proposals for the development of land are an obvious example. I see no difficulty in characterising such proposals as interferences with A1P1 rights. It will almost always be possible for the authority in question to justify the interference as being 'in the public interest and subject to the conditions provided for by law' . . .

Nevertheless, in this particular case Lord Dyson concluded that the interference was not justified, and that the government must compensate the claimants for the loss it caused: see further para. 4.31(c).

4.30 Was the Interference Justified?

Whether the interference is a deprivation or a control of use, or otherwise violates the overarching principle in rule 1 of A1P1, the question of whether it was justified depends first on whether it was lawful. It will be unlawful if the public authority did not act in accordance with domestic law, or failed to act with procedural fairness. If it was unlawful, the interference is an unjustified breach of the claimant's A1P1 rights.[78]

If, however, the court finds that the interference was in accordance with the law, then the interference is justified for the purposes of A1P1 if it was proportionate. As we have seen in the preceding paragraphs interference is proportionate if it pursued a legitimate aim by means that were reasonably proportionate to the aim sought to be achieved, striking a fair balance between the demands of the general interest of the community and the requirements for the protection of the individual's fundamental rights, allowing the state an appropriate 'margin of appreciation'.

4.31 Proportionality, Fair Balance and the Margin of Appreciation

The primary question of proportionality, involving consideration of whether a fair balance has been struck, and the question of how far the public authority's margin of

---

[77] *Department for Energy and Climate Change* v. *Breyer Group PLC* [2015] EWCA Civ 408 para. 72.

[78] It will also be challengeable under domestic administrative law, by judicial review. For the relationship between administrative law and human rights law challenges see Ian Loveland, 'Twenty years later – assessing the significance of the Human Rights Act 1998 to residential possession proceedings' (2017) *Conveyancer* 174.

appreciation extends, are all highly fact-sensitive. This makes it quite difficult to draw out general principles from the cases. However, the following general points can be made.

(a) Questioning the Decisions of a Democratically Elected Government

The starting point is always that it is for a democratically elected legislature to decide on matters of social, economic and political policy and national security. Nevertheless, the courts take the view that A1P1 entitles and requires them to look very closely, at a factual level, into the objectives the legislature was seeking to achieve, the factors the legislature took into account in adopting a particular policy, and whether the chosen policy and the means chosen for implementing it were justifiable. In reality this can add up to a high level of scrutiny of state action. The House of Lords' decision in *R (Countryside Alliance)* v. *Attorney General* [2007] UKHL 52, the English hunting case noted in para. 4.29(b) above, provides a good example. Whilst the House of Lords acknowledged that it was not for them to say whether the ban on hunting introduced by the Hunting Act 2004 was or was not in the public interest, Lord Hope in particular looked very closely at the arguments for and against hunting in order to determine whether it was open to Parliament to decide that a hunting ban was in the public interest, and whether the particular ban that was enacted was proportionate.[79] In other words, the House of Lords was willing to accept the state's decision on proportionality, but only if it fell within what the court considered to be a legitimate range of responses.

(b) Margin of Appreciation

However, the level of scrutiny the courts will give to the public authority's decisions on policy and on implementation of policy, depends very much on how broad a margin of appreciation the court is prepared to give to a public authority, with regard to both choosing the means of enforcement of its aim, and deciding whether the consequences of enforcement are justified in the general interest for the purpose of achieving the object of the law in question. It is clear from the cases that the margin of appreciation varies depending on the nature of the policy being pursued by the public authority. So, for example, the courts have always given national authorities a particularly wide margin of appreciation in formation and implementation of environmental controls, as the Supreme Court noted in *R (on the application of Mott)* v. *Environment Agency*, the salmon fishery case we looked at in para. 4.29(c).

(c) Impact on the Claimant

Ascertaining the precise impact of the state's action on this particular claimant's enjoyment of her possessions is clearly central to the proportionality or fair balance

---

[79] *R (Countryside Alliance)* v. *Attorney General* [2007] UKHL 52 paras. 75–78.

exercise – the whole point is whether this particular interference with this particular claimant's enjoyment of her possessions is justified in the common or public interest. If the public authority had decided in advance that its interference with the claimant's possessions was justified in the public interest, then the courts are unlikely to question its decision provided that the decision was within a legitimate range of decisions it could have reached. However, this applies only if the public authority can show that it did indeed give proper consideration to the likely impact on this particular claimant (or on others in a similar position). So, in *Mott*, the salmon fishery case, the Supreme Court held that the new licensing scheme violated the claimant's A1P1 rights because the method chosen for allocating the new licences meant that 'by far the greatest impact fell on him, as opposed to others whose use may have been only for leisure purposes' *and* because on the evidence the Environment Agency had 'given no consideration to the particular impact on his livelihood'.

So, both the anticipated and the actual impact of the interference on the claimant is a relevant factor in assessing proportionality. However, this is not at all the same thing as saying that the claimant must have been treated fairly. An interference with the claimant's enjoyment of its possessions may be found to be justified even if the end result is that a blameless claimant suffers uncompensated loss. In other words, individuals may be required to accept some suffering (or at least financial loss) in the public interest.[80] This was explicitly acknowledged by the House of Lords in *Wilson* v. *First County Trust Ltd* [2003] UKHL 40, which concerned a consumer who had pawned her car to a pawnbroker to secure a loan. Although the loan agreement made it clear exactly how much by way of interest the consumer would have to pay on the loan, it did not do so in the way then required by the Consumer Credit Act 1974. Under s. 127(3) of the 1974 Act the consequence of this failure was that the agreement was unenforceable, which meant that the consumer kept all the money the pawnbrokers had lent her[81] and the pawnbroker had to repay her the interest she had paid and give her back her car. The pawnbroker argued that this was disproportionate, and therefore a violation of its right to peaceful enjoyment of its possessions under A1P1. The House of Lords concluded that A1P1 did not apply because the Human Rights Act 1998 was not in force at the relevant time, but said that even if it had applied, the pawnbroker's argument would have failed. The members of the court gave different reasons for coming to this conclusion but Lord Nicholls said that given the social context (that money lending transactions as a class give rise to social problems of a kind and a severity that justified Parliament in deciding that this kind of sanction was appropriate), a fair balance had been drawn between the pawnbroker's fundamental right to the peaceful enjoyment of its possessions and the public interest:

---

[80] Provided, however, that the interference was 'rational in its incidence' – i.e. provided that this particular claimant was not unfairly or irrationally picked out for special treatment, as Bank Mellat was held to have been in *Bank Mellat* v. *HM Treasury (No 2)* [2013] UKSC 39: see para. 4.32 below.

[81] In fact, by the time the case reached court she had already repaid the loan with interest. The pawnbroker therefore had to pay her back everything she had paid them (i.e. loan plus interest) and give her back the car.

71 . . . Undoubtedly, as illustrated by the facts of the present case, section 127(3) may be drastic, even harsh, in its adverse consequences for a lender. . . [Nevertheless] the court will accept that a sanction imposed on a particular property owner is proportionate even if, as in the actual case the court is considering, it is disproportionate to any wrongdoing of the property owner (who in this case appears to have been blameless) and disproportionate to any harm caused to the other party (in this case, the miswording in the agreement could not have misled the consumer or caused her any other harm, and of course, as a result of the order she enjoyed the windfall of keeping both the money and the car). The government does not even have to establish that imposing the unmerited loss on the claimant is the *only* way of dealing with the social problem the sanction was intended to meet. The only relevant issue for the court is whether the sanction fell within a range of justifiable ways of dealing with the social problem.

However, it remains a question of balance between the interests of the individual and the general interest, and this may mean that even if the interference with the individual's possessions is justified, compensation ought to have been provided. The solar energy case considered in para. 4.28(a) and para. 4.29(c) above, *Department for Energy and Climate Change* v. *Breyer Group PLC* [2015] EWCA Civ 408, provides a good example. Although the Court of Appeal found that a 'Proposal' put forward by the government to cut incentives for solar energy installations was lawful and in pursuit of a legitimate aim, it concluded that it was an unjustifiable interference with the possessions of installation companies. The Proposal did not strike a fair balance between the interests of the public and those of the claimants, the Court of Appeal said, because it was unfair and disproportionate not to include in the Proposal compensation for loss likely to be caused to the claimants, given that their loss was estimated at between £1 million and £2 million and the estimated savings to the Government from implementing the Proposal were £1.6 billion.[82]

4.32 Protection of Property: A Second Order Human Right?

In deciding whether the harm to the individual is justified in the public interest, it appears to be accepted by the courts that some human rights are more important than others, and that the right to freedom from interference with possessions is a second order human right, weighing less heavily than other fundamental human rights. This was the view expressed by Lord Sumption in *Bank Mellat* v. *HM Treasury (No 2)* [2013] UKSC 39. The issue in that case was whether an Order made under the Counter-Terrorism Act 2008 which interfered with Bank Mellat's A1P1 rights (by excluding it from financial markets) was justified given that the Order was made as part of the UK's programme of sanctions again Iran, with the objective of putting pressure on Iran to halt its plans to develop nuclear weapons. Lord Sumption said that the balancing exercise required in that case was not the same as that which had been required in an earlier House of Lords case, *A* v. *Secretary of State for the Home Department* [2005] 2 AC 68, where the House of Lords had had to consider whether a measure permitting the detention of non-

---

[82] *Department for Energy and Climate Change v. Breyer Group PLC* [2015] EWCA Civ 408 at para. 96.

nationals who could not be deported but whose presence in the UK was considered by the Home Secretary to be a risk, was justified by the then current terrorist threat. The House of Lords held that it was not: even though national security was an area in which the executive had to be given a wide margin of judgment, this measure was not a proportionate response to the terrorist threat which provoked it and so it violated the detainees' convention rights. The difference between the two cases, Lord Sumption said, was that the human rights in question in the two cases were of a different quality:

> 26 ... The suppression of terrorism and the prevention of nuclear proliferation are comparable public interests, but the individual right to liberty engaged in *A* v. *Secretary of State for the Home Department* can fairly be regarded as the most fundamental of all human rights other than the right to life and limb. The right to the peaceful enjoyment of business assets protected by article 1 of the First Protocol, is not in the same category of human values ...

He nevertheless concluded, with the majority of the Supreme Court, that in the case before them the Order violated the Bank Mellat's A1P1 rights because, by singling Bank Mellat out for special treatment, it was 'irrational in its incidence and disproportionate to any contribution which it could rationally be expected to make to its objective'.

PART VI RIGHT TO RESPECT FOR HOME UNDER ARTICLE 8 OF THE EUROPEAN CONVENTION ON HUMAN RIGHTS

4.33 Right to Respect for Home Under Article 8: Property or Privacy?

The right to respect for one's home is included in article 8 of the Convention, encompassed within the right to respect for private and family life:

> Right to respect for private and family life
>   Article 8

1. Everyone has the right to respect for his private and family life, his home and his correspondence.
2. There shall be no interference by a public authority with the exercise of this right except such as is in accordance with the law and is necessary in a democratic society in the interests of national security, public safety or the economic well-being of the country, for the prevention of disorder or crime, for the protection of health or morals, or for the protection of the rights and freedoms of others.

As we saw in Part III of this chapter, most human rights instruments include a human right to be protected against interference with or violation of one's home. In most cases, this appears as part of a general human right to protection from interference with private life, family, home, correspondence and sometimes also reputation and honour. The context, then, of a human right to respect for one's home is the need to provide protection against the kind of invasions that occur in totalitarian states (arbitrary police searches, overt and covert surveillance and interception of communications, etc.) or other invasions of privacy. This is very apparent in, for example, art. 13 of the German Constitution, as we saw in para. 4.13 above.

At one time it might have been arguable that the effect of linking protection of home with protection of personal life in this way in art. 8 of the ECHR is to elevate the right to respect for home into the category of 'first order' human rights, carrying more weight than A1P1 rights (at any rate, A1P1 rights protecting commercial interests), in the way suggested in para. 4.23 above. Some sense of this appeared in the judgment of the ECtHR in *Connors* v. *United Kingdom* (2004) 40 EHRR 189. The case concerned eviction of a family of gypsies from a local authority site for travellers. The court emphasised that whereas when considering housing under A1P1 (i.e. as a matter of property rights) national legislatures have a wide margin of appreciation in deciding what is in the general interest, the margin is much narrower in a housing case considered under art. 8, 'which concerns rights of central importance to the individual's identity, self-determination, physical and moral integrity, maintenance of relationships with others and a settled and secure place in the community'.[83]

However, it now appears that, far from being a higher-order human right than an A1P1 right, the right to respect for one's home under art. 8 will almost invariably be defeated by an A1P1 claim unless the claimant also has a property interest in her home or at least a contractual or personal right to remain in it. Specifically, if a landowner or mortgagee lender seeks possession of a claimant's home, and the claimant has no legal defence in domestic law against the possession action, the claimant will be evicted in all but exceptional cases. We come back to this in para. 4.41.

4.34 What is a 'Home'?

(a) 'Sufficient and Continuous Links'

The classic judicial statement of what amounts to a 'home' for the purposes of art. 8 was given by the ECtHR in *Paulić* v. *Croatia* [2009] ECHR 1614 para. 33:

> 'Home' is an autonomous concept which does not depend on classification under domestic law. Whether or not a particular premises constitutes a 'home' which attracts the protection of article 8(1) will depend on the factual circumstances, namely, the existence of sufficient and continuous links with a specific place.

This factual 'sufficient and continuous links' test is now fully accepted.[84] However, it leaves open the question of the kind of links that are required. In considering housing rights Antoine Buyse[85] has distinguished three different conceptions of home which are helpful here: security, privacy and attachment:

---

[83] *Connors* v. *United Kingdom* (2004) 40 EHRR 189 at para. 82.
[84] Lord Hope in the Supreme Court in *London Borough of Hounslow* v. *Powell* [2011] UKSC 8 para. 33.
[85] Antoine Buyse, 'Strings attached: The Concept of "home" in the case law of the ECtHR' [2006] 3 *European Human Rights Law Review* 294.

... security ... lies at the core of housing rights: the protection a house can provide against physical hardship and insecurity. This is the traditional notion of housing as a shelter, a secure place which offers protection against weather and cold, against intrusions from nature and from fellow human beings...

[Privacy refers] to the relationships (and the boundaries thereof) that an inhabitant of a dwelling has with society at large. A house in this sense provides a private sphere where one can live as one likes, free from outside interference. This idea of a private sphere arose from the liberal concept of freedom at the end of the 18th century and throughout the 19th: every individual was to be able to lead an autonomous life. Such a life entailed a division between the private and the public. The idea materialised in legal provisions on the protection of the family, correspondence and the home, often much earlier than laws on the respect for private life in general. The notion of the home thus became not only the symbolic space for privacy, but also the material one: within the four walls of one's own house one was not to be disturbed by society, be it the state or other individuals ... Intrusions into one's house were more and more equated to intrusions into one's privacy. As such the home has been characterised as the 'headquarters of private life', the '*letzte Bastion der Privatsphäre*' and a '*rempart de l'intimité*'.

The third category is that of attachment. From this perspective a house is more than a useful protective shield. It contains the idea that one develops a bond with a certain place over time ...[86]

So, when we consider whether a person has 'sufficient and continuous' links with a place to justify calling that place 'home', we might mean links of security, that is, is this the place that functions as shelter for the person against the natural environment and the intrusion of others? Additionally or alternatively, we might mean links of privacy (is this place within and integral to the person's private sphere, the sphere within which every person should be free to do as she likes, free from outside interference?) and/or links of attachment (is this the place with which the person has developed a psychological attachment, so that it has become part of what Margaret Radin would call her 'personhood'?[87]).

(b) Voluntary and Involuntary Absences

These distinctions are helpful when considering whether a place can still be your home even if you have been absent from it for a long time, perhaps for several years. After several years' absence, it can hardly be providing you with shelter and physical security: it may have done so before you left, and you may be hoping that it will do so again when you return, but it is not doing so now. It may, however, still be within your private sphere, particularly if you intend to return: you may still keep papers or furniture there, or conduct your affairs from there whenever you visit. Equally, your

---

[86] Ibid. pp. 294–295. We come back to this complex idea of 'home' in Chapter 7 *Objects of Property Interests* para. 7.11.

[87] Margaret Radin, 'Property and personhood' (1982) 34 *Stanford Law Review* 957. We consider Radin's theory of property and personhood in Chapter 2 *Conceptions and Justifications* para. 2.23 and Chapter 7 *Objects of Property Interests* para. 7.10.

psychological attachment to your home will not necessarily have been lessened by absence, particularly if your absence has been involuntary, for example if you were forced to flee from your home and have not been allowed to return, or you are in prison or in hospital. The attitude of the courts to absences has in general followed these lines, without necessarily articulating these different conceptions of home. So, in *Gillow* v. *United Kingdom* (1989) 11 EHRR 335, which we look at again in para. 4.40, a house which a couple had built for themselves and their family in Guernsey was found by the court to be their home, even though the couple had left after two years and for the next 18 years had let the house out whilst they worked abroad on temporary contracts with various development agencies. By the time they returned on their retirement, intending to take up residence again, they were required by law to apply for a licence to live in the house. Their application for a licence was refused. The court found that the refusal was a violation of their art. 8 right to respect for their home. The house was the couple's 'home' despite their long absence, the court said, because when they first arrived in Guernsey they had sold their former home in Lancashire and moved from there to the new house in Guernsey with their family and furniture; they had lived there for two years, and whilst they were away they kept their furniture in the house and always intended to return; they had had no other home elsewhere in the UK whilst they were away; and by the time they applied for the licence they had already returned to the house and were starting repairs to enable them to live there.

Voluntary absence cases like *Gillow*, where the claimants always intended to return and it was up to them whether and when they did so, are very different from dispossession cases. Where a claimant has been dispossessed there are two possible violations of the claimant's right to respect for home. The first is the initial dispossession; the second is the refusal to allow her to return, which is a separate and continuing violation of her rights. Where the complaint is about the initial dispossession, the relevant question is whether the place was the claimant's home *at the time of the dispossession*: it is irrelevant whether subsequently it ceased to be her home at some time during the period when she was prevented from returning. If, however, the complaint is about the continuing violation during the years when she was prevented from returning, it should become relevant whether the length of absence has resulted in the place ceasing to be her home. However, the courts do not always make this distinction: see for example *Demades* v. *Turkey* [2003] ECHR 416 noted in (c) below, and also *Zavou* v. *Turkey* [2009] ECHR 1323 and the other cases cited there. In both cases the claimants were Greek Cypriots who had fled from their homes in northern Cyprus following the Turkish occupation in 1974. The court found that the actions of the Government of Turkey resulted in them being unable to return, and that this constituted a continuing violation of their rights to respect for their home. In both cases the court found that the houses in question were the homes of the claimants, but by looking only at the situation as at the date when they fled. No consideration was given to the question of whether there came a point during the following 20–30 years when the claimants could no longer be said to still have the necessary 'continuous and sufficient links' with the house. These two cases can, however, be compared to *Demopoulos* v. *Turkey* [2010] ECHR 30, also concerning claims of Greek Cypriots arising out of the 1974 occupation of northern Cyprus. One of the claimants was aged two when she and her family were forced to leave their family apartment in northern Cyprus. The apartment was owned by her father and she was entitled to inherit at least a share in it on his death, but she herself had never had a property interest in it. The issue was whether she was entitled to compensation for a violation of her art. 8 right to respect for her home. The court accepted that, nearly 36 years later, she 'retained continuous and strong links with the apartment which throughout her life has been held out to be the lost and irreplaceable family home of her childhood'. Nevertheless, the court concluded that it was not her home for the purposes of art. 8. In this kind of case, the court said, the claimant needs to be able to show that her links with the place remain '*concrete* and *persisting*' notwithstanding prolonged absence: continuous and persisting psychological or emotional attachment is not sufficient.[88]

(c) Multiple Homes

It is clear from the absence cases that the courts see no difficulty in a person having 'sufficient and continuous' (or even 'concrete and persisting') links with more than one place at the same time. The ECtHR dealt with the issue directly in *Demades* v. *Turkey* [2003] ECHR 416 noted in (b) above, where it concluded that the claimant's house in northern Cyprus was his 'home' for the purposes of art. 8 at the time when he and his family were forced to flee, even though at that time he regarded it as his second home (used regularly by him and his family for weekends, holidays, etc. and to entertain business associates and visiting dignitaries). The court said that in such cases 'it may not always be possible to draw precise distinctions, since a person may divide his time between two houses or form strong emotional ties with a second house, treating it as his home . . .'.[89] In this case, therefore, the second home appeared to conform to all three of Buyse's conceptions of home noted in (a) above: together with the claimant's primary home in Nicosia, the second home provided shelter and security and was an integral part of the family's private sphere, and the claimant and his family had the necessary psychological attachment to it as much as to the Nicosia house.

(d) Trespassers

It has long been accepted that a place may be a person's home even if she has no property right in it and no other legally enforceable right to be there. The same applies whether she entered as a trespasser or whether she initially had some authorisation to be there which subsequently expired or was terminated. This has been confirmed by the courts many times, for example Lord Bingham at para. 37 in

---

[88] For the present legal and political position on Greek Cypriot claims to violations of their rights under the ECHR arising out of the 1974 occupation see the rest of the judgment in *Demopoulos* v. *Turkey* [2010] ECHR 306 and Elena Proukaki, 'The right of displaced persons to property and to return home after Demopoulos' [2014] 14 *Human Rights Law Review* 701.

[89] *Demades* v. *Turkey* [2003] ECHR 416 at para. 62.

Leeds City Council v. *Price*, heard in the House of Lords with *Kay* v. *Lambeth London Borough Council* [2006] UKHL 10 (*Leeds* concerned gypsies who had moved their caravans onto a recreation ground owned by the local authority without its consent and remained there as trespassers); *Malik* v. *Fassenfelt* [2013] EWCA Civ 798 noted in (e) below; and *Yordanova* v. *Bulgaria* [2012] ECHR 758 para. 103 (illegal Roma settlement in Bulgaria found to be the home of the Roma people living there).

(e) Protest Camps

When trespassers are occupying land for a political protest it is a question of fact whether the protest camp has become the home of the protesters. If it has, then any attempt by the landowner to remove the protesters or to interfere with their activities on the site interferes with their right to respect for their home under art. 8. However, as we see in para. 4.41, the chances are that the court will find that it is nevertheless proportionate to order immediate possession to the landowner, whatever the nature of the protest and even if (as in *Malik* v. *Fassenfelt* [2015] EWCA Civ 793, as we see in para. 4. 41(d)) the protesters have carried out considerable improvements to the land and made themselves a valued part of the local community.

In any event, the protesters may not even be able to satisfy the court that the protest camp has become their home. In *Manchester Ship Canal* v. *Persons Unknown* [2014] EWHC 645, Pelling J found that neither of the two defendants to a possession action by the landowner had made out an arguable case that they had established their home in an anti-fracking protest camp established on the relevant land. Neither could establish the existence of 'sufficient and continuous links' with the land. One stayed overnight in the camp occasionally but usually returned home at night, so the link was neither sufficient nor continuous. The other had lived in the camp for about five months, first in a tent then in a caravan provided by a sympathiser. He had been renting a flat elsewhere but that was due to be sold very soon and he would then have nowhere else to go. In both cases, said Pelling J, the crucial fact undermining the existence of anything other than a temporary link was the fact that they were all intending to vacate the camp when the investigatory drilling ended and the oil company vacated the drilling site within the next month (para. 48). But in the case of the second defendant Pelling J also said 'Residing on the land for the more efficient conduct of the protest does not constitute a sufficient connection with the land for these purposes. It is not now and never has been his intention to remain on the land on an indefinite or permanent basis' (para. 51).

However, it is by no means clear that temporary housing can never be a person's home. Temporary housing for someone who has nowhere else to go fully conforms to the conception of home as shelter and security noted in (a) above.[90] It is therefore

---

[90] The point was conceded and so not argued in *R (oao ZH and CN)* v. *Newham and Lewisham* [2014] UKSC 62, where the issue was whether a local housing authority had to obtain a court order before evicting a person from temporary accommodation provided under its duty to house homeless people under the Housing Act 1996. The housing authority conceded that art. 8 was engaged, so conceding that the temporary accommodation was the home of the people it sought to evict.

doubtful whether this factor alone would have justified the decision in *Manchester Ship Canal.*

4.35 Extension of 'Home' to Private Workplace

It has always been accepted that art. 8 extends beyond interference with the place used as a person's private residence to cover also interference with the place used by her as her private workplace. On the basis that, for many people, the sphere of private life extends beyond home, this makes some sense. On any reading of art. 8, it must include interference with our private life wherever it is conducted. However, this in not quite how the courts see it. Instead of saying that interference with our workplace *may* involve an interference with our private life and so amount to a violation of our art. 8 rights, the line taken by the courts seems to be that 'home' in art. 8 *includes* our workplace, and therefore any interference with our workplace is as much a violation of our art. 8 rights as it would be if it was an interference with the place where we live. This line can be traced back to the classic statement of the principle in the ECtHR decision in *Niemietz* v. *Germany* (1993) 16 EHRR 97, where the claimant was a lawyer and it was decided that his art. 8 rights had been violated when the German police searched his office to obtain information about a third party who was under police investigation. In that case the ECtHR said that 'to interpret the words "private life" and "home" as including certain professional or business activities or premises would be consonant with the essential object and purpose of Article 8, namely to protect the individual against arbitrary interference by the public authorities'.[91] It also pointed out that in the French text of art. 8, the word used is 'domicile', which, the court said, 'has a broader connotation than the word "home" and may extend, for example, to a professional person's office'.[92]

4.36 Extension of Home to Company's Business Premises

The justifications given for extending 'home' to include a human individual's workplace come nowhere close to explaining why the principle established in *Niemietz* should be extended to cover the business premises of a company. Nevertheless, this extension was made by the ECtHR in *Société Colas Est* v. *France* [2002] ECHR 421, where it held that art. 8 encompassed a right for a company to respect for its business premises. The complaint was that during the course of a French government investigation into collusive practices by roadworks contractors, inspectors carried out raids on 56 companies (including the three who brought this complaint under art. 8) and seized thousands of documents. The claimant companies argued that these actions were violations of their rights under art. 8 to respect for their homes. The ECtHR agreed with them. It was accepted by the French government that 'home' in art. 8 did include the business premises of companies, but the court did go on to consider whether this assumption was correct. It

---

[91] *Niemietz* v. *Germany* (1993) 16 EHRR 97 para. 32.   [92] Ibid. para. 30.

concluded that it was, but gave no real reason for coming to this conclusion. The Court noted the point that 'domicile' in the French text is more apt to cover business premises than is 'home', but then said nothing more than that 'the time has come' to extend the *Niemietz* principle to companies:

> As regards the rights secured to companies by the Convention, it should be pointed out that the court has already recognised a company's right under art. 41 to compensation for non-pecuniary damage sustained as a result of a violation of art. 6.1 [right to a fair trial] (*Comingersoll* v. *Portugal* [2000] ECHR 160). Building on its dynamic interpretation of the Convention, the Court considers that the time has come to hold that in certain circumstances the rights guaranteed by art. 8 of the Convention may be construed as including the right to respect for a company's registered office, branches or other business premises . . .[93]

This is difficult to reconcile with any conception of home or private life, however broad. It is true that companies, like all entities, require security against arbitrary state interference, but what a company requires is very different from the physical shelter or physical space that a living human person requires. Similarly, companies do not have private spheres or private lives. For commercial reasons they require confidentiality for some of their affairs, but that is not the same thing as the respect for privacy necessary to maintain human dignity. Companies also have duties of accountability, accounting and audit which limit their freedom to keep their affairs private. And of course they simply do not have emotional or psychological attachments to place in the same way as humans. For all these reasons, the extension of art. 8 rights to companies is puzzling.[94]

4.37 What Violates the Right to 'Respect' for Home?

(a) Breaches of Privacy

Any interference with the claimant's home or its use prima facie violates the right to respect for home under art. 8. The earliest cases (and arguably the ones the drafters of the Convention had centrally in mind) were intrusions by a public body into the private sphere, whether by surveillance, by entering and searching premises, going through or seizing or intercepting records or other documents, or by physically invading or interfering with the premises or their contents in some other way.

(b) Use Restrictions

Restrictions on the occupier's use of the premises or on her activities in them may also come within art. 8, but this may depend on the nature of the restriction and the nature of the space protected. An interference with an occupier's use of her home by, for example, banning smoking there, might amount to a violation if the home is the

---

[93] *Société Colas Est* v. *France* [2002] ECHR 421 at para. 41.
[94] See para. 4.8 above for the general question of whether companies can properly be said to have human rights, other than to protect their economic interests.

occupier's own private home, but not if the home is a high security psychiatric hospital: *R. (oao G)* v. *Nottinghamshire Healthcare NHS Trust* [2009] EWCA Civ 795, where it was held that policy and legislation banning smoking at Rampton high security psychiatric hospital were not in breach of art. 8.

(c) Nuisance and Pollution

Similarly, environmental pollution adversely affecting the quality of the applicant's private life and the scope for enjoying the amenities of her home may amount to an interference with her right to respect for her private life and home. So, for example, in *Djemyuk* v. *Ukraine* [2014] ECHR 894 the ECtHR decided on this basis that there was a breach of the claimant's art. 8 rights when the local council continued to use a cemetery which the council had built too close to the claimant's village and which threatened to pollute the village water supply. Again, in *Hardy and Maile* v. *the United Kingdom* [2012] ECHR 261 the Court recognised that the potential risks to the environment caused by the construction and operation of two liquefied natural gas terminals established a sufficiently close link with the claimant's private live and home for the purposes of art. 8, so that they amounted to an interference with his right to respect for his private life and home.

In these cases the interference with the claimants' right to respect for their home arose directly out of state action or inaction in dealing with an environmental problem for which it was directly responsible. However, where the interference arises out of activities by private industry which are regulated by the state, the state will be responsible for the interference under art. 8 in so far as it arose out of a failure by the state to regulate the industry properly. So, for example, in *Hatton* v. *UK* (2003) 37 EHRR 28 it was found that the UK government was responsible under art. 8 for the noise suffered at night by people living near privately owned Heathrow Airport (although as we see in para. 4.40 below it was found that the interference was proportionate) because the government is responsible for regulating the number of night flights and the level of permitted noise.

(d) Eviction

As the ECtHR has frequently pointed out, loss of one's home is the most extreme form of interference with the right to respect for the home.[95] In UK law it is unlawful for anyone to recover possession of premises occupied as a dwelling without first obtaining a court order for possession, except in certain specified circumstances.[96] It

---

[95] For example, *McCann* v. *the United Kingdom*, no. 19009/04, 13 May 2008 para. 50 and *Kay* v. *United Kingdom* (2012) 54 EHRR 30 at para. 68.

[96] S. 3 of the Prevention of Eviction Act 1977 as amended. The exceptions include possession of mortgaged property sought by mortgagee lenders in some circumstances (*Ropaigealach* v. *Barclays Bank plc* [2000] 1 QB 263, CA) and also possession sought by a local authority to recover possession of premises provided as interim accommodation for someone whilst the authority investigates whether they have a duty to house her as a homeless person under s. 188(1) of the Housing Act 1996: *R (oao CN)* v. *Lewisham LBC* [2014] UKSC 62.

should go without saying, then, that whenever a public authority seeks possession from a residential occupier, art. 8 is engaged (in other words, the public authority is interfering with the occupier's right to respect for her home). This is self-evidently true if the occupier has an arguable defence against the eviction, but in principle it must also be true even if the public authority is absolutely entitled under domestic law to evict the occupier, for example because the occupier is a trespasser, or a former tenant whose tenancy has expired, or is in occupation under an agreement which the public authority is now entitled to terminate. The interference may be justifiable under art. 8, but it is nevertheless an interference that has to be justified. This is the position that the ECtHR has consistently maintained over a long period. As it said in *Kay* v. *United Kingdom* (2012) 54 EHRR 30:

> Any person at risk of an interference of this magnitude [with the right to respect for home] should in principle be able to have the proportionality of the measure deter-mined by an independent tribunal in light of the relevant principles under Article 8 of the Convention, notwithstanding that, under domestic law, his right to occupation has come to an end.[97]

However, the courts in England and Wales have been much slower in accepting the point, and it was only after considerable confusion and disagreement in the House of Lords that the Supreme Court finally decided in *Manchester City Council* v. *Pinnock* [2010] UKSC 45 and *Hounslow London Borough Council* v. *Powell* [2011] UKSC 8 that art. 8 is engaged whenever a public authority seeks possession of a person's home. In practical terms this means that even if under domestic law a court has no jurisdiction to refuse to grant the public authority an immediate possession order, the individual has a right to require the court to consider whether it is proportionate under art. 8 to make such an order.

The only question at issue is therefore now, not *whether* a claim for possession against a residential occupier by a public authority *is* an interference with her home under art. 8.1, but whether the interference is justified under the terms of art. 8.2. As we see in para. 4.41 below, this will rarely require the court to give the question of justification much scrutiny, and it will even more rarely prevent or even postpone the eviction of people from their homes when they have no rights under domestic law to remain, but it is something.

4.38 Is the Interference Justified?

So, the position now is that, whatever the nature of the interference by a public authority with a person's right to respect for private life and home, once the interference is established, it is for the court to decide whether it was justified. Specifically, this requires the court to be satisfied that the interference was 'in accordance with the law' and was 'necessary in a democratic society' (art. 8(2)).

According to Lord Neuberger in *Manchester City Council* v. *Pinnock* [2010] UKSC 45 this means that the interference is justified if it was 'a proportionate means

---

[97] *Kay* v. *United Kingdom*, fn. 95 above, at para. 68.

of achieving a legitimate aim'.[98] Encapsulated within that, there appear to be at least three elements for the court to scrutinise. It must first consider whether the aim of the policy or practice which interfered with the claimant's art. 8 right, and the way in which it was implemented, were lawful (i.e. complied with domestic law requirements and with human rights requirements such as for procedural fairness). Secondly, it must consider whether the aim was legitimate, in the sense of being 'necessary in a democratic society'. Finally, it must consider whether the interference with the applicant's rights was proportionate to the public authority's aim.

The last two raise issues of the appropriate margin of appreciation to be given to the public authority, and the proportionality of the interference, essentially the same issues as those that arise in an A1P1 case.

4.39 Margin of Appreciation and Proportionality

As in A1P1 cases, the difficulty the court faces is in deciding how far it can and should go in scrutinising policies, procedures and decisions lawfully made and implemented by a democratically elected national body. The way in which the court approaches this difficulty in relation to art. 8 depends very much on the type of interference. In cases of interference which falls short of eviction their approach is essentially the same as in A1P1 cases, as we see in para. 4.40 below. However, in residential possession cases the courts in England and Wales have shown much greater reluctance to interfere, at least in cases involving housing provided by public authorities. We look at these cases in para. 4.41.

4.40 Proportionality Where Interference Falls Short of Eviction

Leaving aside these eviction cases for the moment, the ECtHR decision in *Hatton v. UK* (2013) 37 EHRR 28 demonstrates the level of scrutiny the courts give in assessing proportionality in art. 8 cases where the interference falls short of eviction. This was a case about complaints by local residents that aircraft noise at night from Heathrow airport violated their art. 8 rights. Heathrow was (and is) privately owned, but the complaints were against the government, which is responsible for regulating the number of night flights and the level of permitted noise.

In cases such as this, the court said, public authorities had to be given a wide margin of appreciation. Nevertheless, that left two aspects of the enquiry into proportionality which the court could and should carry out:

> First, the Court may assess the substantive merits of the government's decision, to ensure that it is compatible with Article 8. Secondly, it may scrutinise the decision-making process to ensure that due weight has been accorded to the interests of the individual . . . In relation to the substantive aspect, the Court has held that the State must be allowed a wide margin of appreciation. In *Powell and Rayner v. United Kingdom* [1990] ECHR 2 [where the complaint had been of daytime aircraft noise

---

[98] *Manchester City Council* v. *Pinnock* [2010] UKSC 45 at para. 52.

from Heathrow] for example, it asserted that it was 'certainly not for the Commission or the Court to substitute for the assessment of the national authorities any other assessment of what might be the best policy in this difficult social and technical sphere', namely the regulation of excessive aircraft noise and the means of redress to be provided to the individual within the domestic legal system.[99]

On that basis the court looked in detail at the factual context in which the government formulated and implemented the relevant policy, assessing the factors they should have taken into account and considering how far they did so. So, the court scrutinised not only the 1993 Scheme for regulating night flights at Heathrow which was at the centre of the residents' complaints, but also its rationale as stated in a 1993 Consultation Paper, and the evidence the government relied on in deciding on the policy and details of the Scheme, including a 1992 sleep study. It accepted that the implementation of the 1993 Scheme had adversely affected the 'the quality of the [residents'] private life and the scope for their enjoying the amenities of their respective homes', and therefore adversely affected their art. 8 rights. Nevertheless, the court held that the government was justified in going ahead and implementing the Scheme, because taking into account the margin of appreciation which had to be allowed to it, the government had struck a fair balance between the competing interests of the individuals affected by the night noise and the community as a whole. In particular it was entitled to take the interests of the community as a whole as encompassing the economic interests of the operators of airlines and other enterprises as well as their clients, and also 'and above all' the economic interests of the country as a whole.

Similar attention to detail can be seen in other cases involving interference falling short of dispossession. So for example, in the *Gillow* v. *UK* case we looked at in para. 4.34(b) above, the ECtHR said that the economic well-being of Guernsey had to be balanced against the applicants' right to respect for their home. In considering whether the balance drawn was fair, and court concluded that it was within Guernsey's margin of appreciation to require the Gillows to apply for a licence before they could resume residence (because of acute housing shortages for local people in Guernsey) but a violation of the Gillows' art. 8 right for Guernsey then to refuse to grant them the licence, because Guernsey had given 'insufficient weight' to the applicants' particular circumstances.[100]

4.41 Proportionality in Eviction Cases

The policy of the UK courts in eviction cases is very different, at least in cases involving housing provided by public authorities. These cases are difficult because on the one hand the interference in question – eviction – is regarded as the most extreme of all interferences with the right to respect for home; on the other hand, in seeking possession the public authority is implementing the state's decisions as to how it should manage public sector housing in the public interest.

---

[99] *Hatton* v. *UK* [2013] 37 EHRR 28 at para. 100.   [100] *Gillow* v. *United Kingdom* [1989] 11 EHRR 335.

(a) Possession Decisions Made by Public Authority Landlords

There are two important points to make about the context here. The first is that a high volume of housing possession cases are heard in county courts every year, the hearings are usually very short, and in most cases the defendant has no legal grounds in domestic law to oppose an order of possession. In other words, if she ever had any legally enforceable property, contract or personal rights to remain in possession, they have now come to an end.

The second contextual matter is that there is a bewildering array of legislative schemes which govern the terms on which tenants and others occupy social housing in England.[101] Most of these schemes regulate the circumstances in which the public authority can evict the occupier, and also regulate the way in which it must be done. In some schemes this involves obtaining a possession order from a court which has a discretion under the scheme to decide whether, in view of the particular circumstances of the case, a possession order ought to be made. In others, however, although the landlord must obtain a possession order, the court has no jurisdiction to refuse or delay it. These schemes are, of course the product of deliberate government policy.

(b) Pre-*Pinnock*

For some years the House of Lords took the view that, because of these two factors, a court hearing a possession application in such cases was not required or entitled by art. 8 to look into the proportionality of making a possession order. The argument was that Parliament had, in effect, already carried out the proportionality exercise by legislating that, in specified circumstances, the landlord should or should not be entitled to possession, and the courts should or should not have discretion to delay or refuse it. Given that, it was not for the courts 'to second-guess housing allocation decisions entrusted by Parliament to local housing authorities'.[102] Also, so it was argued, it was not realistic or sensible to expect busy county courts to go through a time-consuming proportionality exercise every time it heard an application for possession, especially since it would rarely make a difference to the outcome.

However, the ECtHR has always taken a different view, and finally, after a great deal of uncertainty, the Supreme Court conceded in *Manchester CC* v. *Pinnock* [2010] UKSC 45 and *Hounslow LBC* v. *Powell* [2011] UKSC 8 that the UK courts must adopt the principles established in the ECtHR.

---

[101] Since Welsh devolution, housing law regimes in Wales have been different from those that apply in England: see Martin Partington, 'Wales' housing law (r)evolution: An overview: Parts 1 and 2' (2016) *Journal of Housing Law* 33 and 45.

[102] *Manchester City Council* v. *Pinnock* [2010] UKSC 45 at para. 45(a).

(c) Possession Proceedings by Public Authority Landlords after *Pinnock*

Specifically, in *Pinnock* Lord Neuberger (giving the judgment of the court) reviewed the decisions of the ECtHR and concluded that in any claim by a public authority for possession of residential premises, the court has to satisfy itself that any person at risk of eviction has the opportunity of having 'the proportionality of the measure determined by an independent tribunal in the light of the relevant principles under Article 8 of the Convention, notwithstanding that, under domestic law, his right of occupation has come to an end'.[103]

In other words, the Supreme Court has now accepted that in any eviction by a public authority of a person from his home, art. 8 does apply and the court hearing the possession application must give the occupier the opportunity to raise the question of the proportionality of the eviction. However, the Supreme Court went on to minimise the likelihood that the proportionality of an eviction order under art. 8 would ever be scrutinised in practice in such cases.

First, Lord Neuberger said that in 'virtually every case' where a residential occupier had no contractual or statutory rights to remain in occupation, so that the local authority landlord is entitled to possession as a matter of domestic law, 'there will be a very strong case for saying that making an order for possession would be proportionate'.[104]

Secondly, he said that, unless the public authority had special reasons for seeking possession in any particular case, it should be taken 'as a given' that its twin aims were to vindicate its ownership rights, and to 'comply with its duties in relation to the distribution and management of its housing stock, including, for example the fair allocation of its housing, the redevelopment of the site, the refurbishment of sub-standard accommodation, the need to move people who are in accommodation that now exceeds their needs, and the need to move vulnerable people into sheltered or warden-assisted housing'.[105] In other words, if those were its aims, they would not need to be explained or justified in court every time. It is only if the public authority landlord wants to rely on 'particularly strong or unusual' reasons for wanting possession that it needs to plead the reasons and produce evidence in support.[106]

Finally, 'as a general rule', in cases where the court has no jurisdiction in domestic law to refuse or delay possession, art. 8 *'need only be considered by the court if it is expressly raised by or on behalf of the residential occupier'*, and *'initially it should be considered summarily and only allowed to proceed if the court is satisfied that, were the facts alleged to be made out, it could affect the order the court might make'.*[107]

In *Hounslow London Borough Council* v. *Powell* [2011] UKSC 8, the same principles were applied to local authority tenancies governed by a different statutory

---

[103] Lord Neuberger in *Manchester City Council* v. *Pinnock* (ibid.) at para. 45 approving what was said in *McCann* v. *United Kingdom* [2008] 47 EHRR 913, para. 50, and see also *Hounslow London Borough Council* v. *Powell* [2011] UKSC 8 at paras. 78–79.

[104] Lord Neuberger in *Pinnock*, fn. 102 above, at para. 54.   [105] Ibid. para. 52.

[106] Ibid. para. 53, where Lord Neuberger also suggested that the public authority landlord 'should, in the absence of cogent evidence to the contrary, be assumed to be acting in accordance with its duties'.

[107] Ibid. para. 61, emphasis added.

housing regime and to accommodation provided under a local authority's duties towards the homeless. In these cases, the Supreme Court said, the court would only have to consider the proportionality issue if it had been raised by the occupier 'and it has crossed the high threshold of being seriously arguable'. Otherwise, the court could dispose of it summarily.[108]

(d) Possession Proceedings by Other Public Authorities

However, it now seems clear that these limiting principles do not apply where a public authority seeking possession of residential premises is doing so in a different capacity, that is, not as landlord of social housing. So, for example in *Jones* v. *Canal & River Trust* [2017] EWCA Civ 135 the Court of Appeal held that the county court had been wrong to assume that they applied where the Canal & River Trust ("CRT") sought a declaration that it was entitled to remove Mr Jones' houseboat from its moorings on a canal owned and managed by CRT. The houseboat was moored under the terms of a licence granted by CRT, and CRT argued that Jones had breached the terms of the licence, so entitling CRT to remove the boat. Jones argued that the houseboat was his home and so this would be in breach of his art. 8 rights. The Court of Appeal held that the principles established by *Pinnock* did not apply because CRT was not Jones's landlord providing him with social housing, and that therefore the county court should have considered whether CRT's interference with Jones' art. 8 right to respect for his private life and home was proportionate.

The ECtHR came to a similar conclusion in *Yordanova* v. *Bulgaria* [2012] ECHR 758 on very different facts. The case concerned an illegal Roma settlement in Bulgaria, built without authorisation or licence on municipal land. The ECtHR decided that the municipal authority's decision to evict the occupiers was a violation of their art. 8 rights even though the eviction order was in accordance with domestic law and pursued legitimate aims. It gave detailed scrutiny to the way in which the authority had tackled the problem of the illegal settlement against a background of harassment and discrimination against Roma people and concluded that in those circumstances the eviction was not 'necessary in a democratic society' as the decision-making procedure 'did not offer safeguards against disproportionate interference' with the applicants' right to respect for their home (para. 114).

It is also worth noting here Lord Justice Ward's minority judgment in *Malik* v. *Fassenfeld* [2013] EWCA Civ 798, which concerned a protest group called 'Grow Heathrow', which had taken over derelict privately owned land, formerly contaminated with spillage of car oils and fuels and used for fly-tipping. They had cleared the land, restored it as a market garden centre with a range of glass houses which in time became their homes. The landowner now sought possession, and the protest group argued that it would not be proportionate under art. 8 for a possession order to be made. Ward LJ argued convincingly that the common law rule that a court could not refuse or postpone the operation of a possession order against a trespasser was

---

[108] *Hounslow London Borough Council* v. *Powell* [2011] UKSC 8 para. 33.

incompatible with art. 8, and that the court ought to be permitted and required to consider whether immediate possession (as opposed to possession delayed for a time or until some event) was proportionate given the particular facts of the case. However, the other members of the Court of Appeal declined to consider the issue because the landowner was not a public authority (see para. 4.42 below), so for the present it remains open.

The point in all these cases is that, even if the residential occupier has no right under domestic law to resist a possession order, if the public authority seeking possession is *not* a housing authority, the proportionality exercise necessarily involves weighing considerations that are different from those relevant in the housing authority cases. In particular, the aims of the public authority in seeking possession cannot be assumed, nor can it be assumed that they are legitimate and proportionate: this is for the court to investigate under art. 8.

Finally, it should be appreciated that an occupier of social housing may have other defences against immediate eviction even if she has no property right to remain in possession as against the housing authority. In *Akerman-Livingstone* v. *Astor Communities Ltd* [2015] UKSC 15 an occupier of social housing argued that his eviction would amount to disability discrimination under s. 15 of the Equality Act 2010 as well as a violation of his art. 8 rights. When such an allegation is made against a landlord the onus is on the landlord to prove that any unfavourable treatment was 'a proportionate means of achieving a legitimate aim' (s. 15 of the 2010 Act). The Supreme Court held that the factors to be weighed in this proportionality exercise were quite different from those raised in a proportionality exercise carried out under art. 8, and that therefore it could not be carried out in the summary way now authorised for an art. 8 application.

4.42 Horizontal Effect: Application of Art. 8 as Against Private Landowners, Landlords and Mortgagees

The principal argument made by Ward LJ in *Malik* v. *Fassenfeld* [2013] EWCA Civ 798 noted above was that art. 8 ought to apply where private persons interfere with the right to respect for private life or home, not just where the interference is by a public authority. This is a hotly contested issue in this jurisdiction. A significant proportion of people rent their homes from private landlords rather than from social landlords, and those who own their homes are similarly at risk from possession proceedings brought by their mortgagees, who may be public bodies but are more likely to be private institutions. There are obvious difficulties in justifying different treatment for those whose home is provided or financed by a public body and those who are (not necessarily by choice) in the private sector. On the other hand, extending human rights protection into a private dispute between private persons is equally problematic, especially where, as in art. 8, the protection was originally designed to prevent state intrusion into private lives. Similar arguments apply where a landowner who is not a housing authority seeks possession from a person who entered as a trespasser. The essential issue is how to balance the competing claims of 'home' and 'property': the question of whether the property owner is a public body or a private person is usually irrelevant.

Although the ECtHR seems to be moving towards acceptance of the position that art. 8 does extend to interference by private persons, and there were signs that the UK courts might do the same,[109] this has now been ruled out by the Supreme Court in *McDonald* v. *McDonald* [2016] UKSC 28. In that case a private mortgagee company sought possession of a house the mortgagors had bought in their own names but for their daughter, who suffered from a severe mental disorder which made her particularly vulnerable to changes in her environment. The parents rented the house to her. They paid the mortgage payments regularly for a few years but then their business failed and they fell into arrears. The mortgagee lender decided to enforce the mortgage, which meant they had to obtain possession from the daughter. Because of the default under the mortgage the mortgagee lender was entitled to terminate her tenancy as if it was the landlord, and it did this by serving a statutory notice to quit on her and then bringing these proceedings for possession against her. Under the statutory provisions that governed her tenancy, the court was required to make a possession order against the daughter in those circumstances. However, she argued that the court was required by art. 8 to consider the proportionality of making the order. There was medical evidence that it would be very difficult for her to find alternative accommodation because of her mental health history, and that even if she did, the stress and upheaval of trying to move would very likely have a significantly detrimental effect on her mental health. In view of that, she argued, the court should have found that it was disproportionate for the mortgagee lender to take possession and should instead have either refused to make the order or delayed its operation. The Supreme Court disagreed, on the basis that the mortgagee lender was not a public authority.

The daughter's argument was one which had been made many times before. It was that although the mortgagee lender was not a public authority, the court asked to make the possession order was, because courts are specifically included in the definition of 'public authority' in s. 6(3)(a) of the Human Rights Act 1998.[110] It followed, so the argument goes, that no judge could make an order for possession of someone's home without first considering whether it was proportionate to do so. It was acknowledged that if it did so, the proportionality issue would not have been exactly the same as it would have been if the mortgagee lender had been a public authority, because the court would have had to take into account the fact that to refuse or delay possession would infringe the mortgagee lender's A1P1 rights, and balance those rights against the daughter's art. 8 rights. Nevertheless, so the daughter argued, the balance would still have come down in her favour.

Lord Neuberger and Lady Hale, giving the single opinion in the Supreme Court, with the other justices agreeing, rejected the argument. Their view was that although 'it may well be' that art. 8 is engaged when a judge makes an order for possession of a tenant's home on an application by a private landlord, art. 8 'could not justify a

---

[109] See for example HHJ Pelling in the protest camp case *Manchester Ship Canal* v. *Persons Unknown* [2014] EWHC 645, noted in para. 4.34(e) above.

[110] para. 4.21 above.

different order from that which is mandated by the contractual relationship between the parties, at least where, as here, there are legislative provisions which the democratically elected legislature has decided properly balance the competing interests of private sector landlords and residential tenants'.[111] In other words, a court does not have to (and may not) decide whether it is proportionate to grant a possession order to a private landlord (or anyone else) if the question of whether or not it is entitled to possession in those circumstances is governed by the contract between the parties and by the statutory provisions which regulate that contract.

The reasoning of the court has attracted a great deal of criticism,[112] not least because of the difficulty in accepting that proportionality does not have to be considered when art. 8 applies, given that art. 8 specifically states that proportionality *does* have to be considered in those circumstances.[113] However, it has effectively closed off this particular route towards allowing residential tenants and mortgagor borrowers to challenge possession orders under art. 8, when facing eviction by a private landlord or mortgagee lender.

RECOMMENDED READING

Frankie McCarthy, 'Property as a human right: Another casualty of the 'war on terror'?' in Nicholas Hopkins (ed.), *Modern Studies in Property Law*, vol. 7, p. 243, pp. 260–262.

Ian Loveland, 'Twenty years later – Assessing the significance of the Human Rights Act 1998 to residential possession proceedings' (2017) *Conveyancer* 174 (a detailed examination of the issue).

Société Colas Est v. *France* [2002] ECHR 421, paras. 28–34 and 40–42 (on meaning of 'home').

JA Pye (Oxford) Ltd v. *United Kingdom* (2008) 46 EHRR 44 (the decision of the Grand Chamber of the ECtHR: paras. 52–85 are most relevant to the issues noted in this chapter). We come back to this case again in Chapter 12 *Adverse possession of land*, when we look at the later House of Lords decision on the same facts; it would be useful to re-read this Grand Chamber decision then.

UK Association of Fish Producer Organisations v. *Secretary of State for Environment Food and Rural Affairs* [2013] EWHC 1959 paras. 1–55 (in outline only, to find out what a 'fixed fishing quota allocation unit' is), and then paras. 108–119 in detail.

Centro Europa7 SRL v. *Italy* [2012] ECHR 974 paras. 1–10 (in outline only, to establish the facts) and paras. 163–189 (on article 1 Protocol 1).

Herrmann v. *Germany* (2013) 56 EHRR 7 paras. 40–94, and also paras. 01–28 from separate opinions of Judge Pinto de Albuqyuerque and paras. 011-1 to 011-15 from dissenting opinions of Björgvinnson et al. (on the fox-hunting cases).

R (on the application of Mott) v. *Environment Agency* [2018] UKSC 10 (article 1 Protocol 1).

Manchester City Council v. *Pinnock* [2010] UKSC 45 paras. 21–54.

Malik v. *Fassenfeld* [2013] EWCA Civ 798.

---

[111] *McDonald* v. *McDonald* [2016] UKSC 28 para. 40.
[112] See e.g. Loveland, 'Twenty years later', fn. 78 above.
[113] See Emma Lees, 'Article 8, proportionality and horizontal effect' (2017) 133 *Law Quarterly Review* 31. The argument is also essentially the same as the one rejected by the ECtHR in relation to the earlier House of Lords decisions on proportionality we noted in para. 4.41, and which the Supreme Court had to abandon in *Manchester City Council* v. *Pinnock*, fn. 102 above.

Questions

(1)   Explain the difference between a human right to the protection of property and a human right to have property. To what extent are either or both of them found in (a) the Universal Declaration of Human Rights 1948 and (b) the Europe Convention on Human Rights?

(2)   Is human rights protection confined to private property rights held by human individuals? Should it be?

(3)   What is a 'public authority' for the purposes of the ECHR? Why does it matter whether a body is a public authority?

(4)   What does 'possessions' mean in article 1 Protocol 1 ECHR? What is the relationship between 'possessions' and 'property'? What is the relevance of monetary value?

(5)   Explain what it means to say that an interference with possessions is 'proportionate'. What factors does the court take into account in assessing proportionality?

(6)   Discuss the difficulties in the concept of 'home' developed in relation to art. 8 ECHR.

(7)   When is an interference by a public authority with a person's right to respect for private life and home justifiable?

(8)   If a public authority seeks possession from a residential occupier who has no right to possession as against the public authority, does the court have to consider the proportionality of the proposed eviction?

5

Ownership and Other Property Interests

PART I INTRODUCTION

5.1 Property Interests, Objects of Property Interests and Property Interest Holders

In Chapter 1 *What Property Is and Why It Matters* we pointed out that, in three respects, the classic analysis of property presents an oversimplified picture. The first oversimplification is that it equates property with private ownership: it assumes private ownership is the only, or at least the paradigm, kind of property interest, failing to recognise that private ownership is a point in a spectrum of different kinds of property interest. In this chapter and the next, Chapter 6 *New Property Interests and the Numerus Clausus*, we look more closely at that particular oversimplification. We examine the range of property interests recognised in this jurisdiction and see how private ownership fits within this range. We also compare our pattern of property interests with the patterns found in other jurisdictions.

We consider the second oversimplification – that the classic analysis of property does not sufficiently distinguish between the different kinds of thing in which property interests can be recognised – in Chapter 7 *Objects of Property Interests*. The third oversimplification in the classic analysis is that it assumes that the holder of property interests is always a self-interested autonomous human being. It fails to recognise the wide variety of legal and social entities that can hold property interests, and the different capacities in which they can hold them. We look at this in Chapter 8 *Property Interest Holders*.

5.2 Private Ownership and Other Property Interests

In this chapter we outline the range of property interests recognised in this jurisdiction, starting in Part II with a closer look at the concept of private ownership. In particular, we want to find out more precisely what we mean when we say that someone is the 'owner' of something, whether it means the same in the civil law as it means in the common law, and whether it is a necessary feature of all property rights systems.

As we see in Part II, in our jurisdiction private ownership means very much the same as it means in civil law jurisdictions if we are talking about ownership of things other than land. The same is essentially true of private ownership of land, although at a technical level it appears very different. This is because land ownership in England and Wales is still defined in feudal and medieval terms – we use a different technical language when we talk about ownership of land – and also because, when land is privately owned in England and Wales, the Crown retains a vestigial interest in it. However, these are differences in appearance rather than differences in substance. As we see in Part III of this chapter the Crown's vestigial interest in land has no remaining economic, social or political significance, and gives the Crown no 'rights' in the land whilst it is privately owned. So, even though it continues to exist, it does not prevent private ownership of land in England and Wales from being virtually indistinguishable in practice and in substance from private ownership of land in civil law countries.

5.3 Special Features of the Property Rights System in England and Wales

The aim of this chapter is to build up a picture of the framework of property interests recognised in England and Wales in our modern law, and in order to do that we need to bring in two additional technical features of our system. We share these two features with other common law property rights systems, but both are completely alien to civil law systems. Because of these two features, common law property rights systems operate in a different way from civil law property systems, and this time the differences are of substance, and of real practical importance.

(a) Legal Property Interests and Equitable Property Interests

The first uniquely common law technical feature is that in our system we categorise all property interests in all things as either '*legal*' *property interests* or '*equitable*' *property interests*. This gives us a two-tier property rights system, with interests in the top tier (legal property interests) being fully enforceable against everyone in the world, and those in the second tier – equitable property interests – having a more limited range of enforceability. The basic idea is that equitable property interests should not be enforceable against purchasers in market transactions, although they are enforceable against everyone else.[1] This distinction between legal property interests and equitable property interests applies to all things, not just land. It is fundamental to our system, although most non-lawyers are totally unaware of its existence. We look at it in more detail in Part IV of this chapter.

(b) The Trust

The other distinctive feature of common law systems is *the trust*, which we look at in Part V of this chapter. The trust is a device by which we split the powers and duties

---

[1] The precise rules about enforceability of legal and equitable property interests (which we outline in Part IV of this chapter) are more complex (and more dysfunctional) than this suggests. We look at them in detail in Chapter 15 *Enforceability and Priority of Property Interests: General Principles* and Chapter 16 *Registration*.

to manage a property interest from the right to the benefit of the property interest, vesting the management powers and duties in one person (the trustee) and the right to the benefit in another (the beneficiary). So, for example, if you hold the legal ownership of a car on trust for me, you as trustee will be responsible for its insurance, maintenance, etc., and for deciding how it is used and by whom (you may decide, for example, that it would benefit me, as beneficiary, more if the car was hired out rather than driven by me), and whether and when it should be traded in for another car or for something else altogether. In all these decisions, however, you as trustee are under a duty to act in my best interests. You must account to me for all income or other profits you get from the car, and if you do sell or exchange it, you will hold the sale proceeds or the thing you exchange for the car for my benefit in exactly the same way as you held the car.

The distinctive feature of the trust in the common law is that both the trustee and the beneficiary simultaneously hold property interests in the assets which are held on trust. In the car example, you as trustee are the legal owner of the car and I, as beneficiary under the trust, have an equitable property interest in the car. We look more closely at what that property interest is, and how it works when there is more than one beneficiary, in Part V.

A trust can be deliberately created by any property interest holder over any kind of property interest, but trusts can also be imposed by the courts in circumstances we outline in para 5.25 below. Also, in some circumstances (for example, whenever a property interest in land is co-owned) a trust arises automatically by operation of law. The combined effect of all this is that, in practice, trusts are pervasive throughout our property rights system.

5.4 Overview of Property Interests in Land in England and Wales

We end the chapter by outlining in Part VI the framework of property interests in land we recognise in England and Wales in our modern law. The aim of Part VI is to show how private ownership of land fits into the overall picture, and how it relates to the other kinds of property interest in land we recognise. We go on to look at some of these other kinds of property interest in more detail in later chapters.

By way of background to all of that, however, there are two other introductory matters which need to be noted here in Part I of this chapter. The first is about the historical background of our modern property rights system, and we deal with this in para. 5.5, although inevitably there is more to be said about historical origins in Parts II–V. The second is about the parallels we draw later on in the chapter between our system and the property rights systems in other jurisdictions. We have some general points to make about that in para. 5.6.

5.5 Historical Background

The property rights system in England and Wales we describe in Parts III–VI is a product of piecemeal historical developments spanning a period of nearly a thousand years. Over that period there have been no seismic changes to the system. As a result there is no overall design (as there is in codified property systems such as the French and German systems[2]) and, as we see in Parts III–V, some of the elements of our system are relics of historical institutions whose original functions and purposes have long since disappeared or become subverted.

Over this long period there have of course also been some statutory reforms affecting some parts of the system. For our purposes the most important of these occurred at the end of the nineteenth century and the beginning of the twentieth century.

(a) Sale of Goods

The first of these, the Sale of Goods Act 1893, codified and rationalised centuries of common law rules about buying and selling goods. It did not deal directly with the nature or form of property interests in goods, only with the rules governing how they could be bought and sold. It was a major milestone in the industrialisation of manufacturing processes and the mass production and marketing of goods and we have retained the basic principles it laid down, although they have been extensively modified and refined by the courts and by Parliament in response to changes in market conditions. The current provisions are now contained in the Sale of Goods Act 1979. The 1979 Act repealed and replaced the 1893 Act, codifying the 1893 provisions and the statutory amendments and that had been made to them. There have since been many other statutory amendments and additions, including provisions increasing consumer protection in transactions for the supply of goods, digital products and services by traders to consumers. Most of these can now be found in the Consumer Rights Act 2015.

(b) Property Interests in Land and the 1925 Property Legislation

The major statutory reforms affecting land took the form of seven Acts of Parliament passed in 1922–1925, usually referred to as the *1925 property legislation*. Unlike the Sales of Goods Acts, these Acts did affect the nature and form of property interests – primarily property interests in land – as well as the ways in which they can be transferred and inherited. However, as we see in the rest of the book, whilst the 1925 property legislation certainty made major changes to our property law system, it did so largely by simplifying, adapting and reorganising long-established principles and rules, rather than by introducing fundamentally different principles. So, sometimes we still need to go back before 1925 to understand our modern system.

As we see in Parts III–VI, the most important rationalisations made by the 1925 legislation related to the forms of land ownership, the nature of mortgages and charges over land, the range of property interests recognised in land, and the introduction of a national land registration system. There was also a radical

---

[2] See para. 5.12 below.

reorganisation of equitable property interests, and what has turned out to be a huge increase in the scope of the trust. This last change occurred because the 1925 legislation imposed a trust whenever any property interest in land is co-owned,[3] and co-ownership of land (relatively rare in 1925) is now very common.

The 1925 property legislation was the culmination of more than a century of contentious arguments about land law reform between lawyers (sometimes representing their own professional interests, sometimes those of wealthy landowning clients), politicians, social reformers and other interested parties, with major disagreements over the kinds of reform that were necessary, why they were needed and how they were to be achieved. Some scholars have seen the 1925 legislation that resulted from these disputes as marking a victory of conservative-minded protectionist lawyers over liberal law-reform Benthamites, and the triumph of market liberalism, favouring commodification of land over social reform of land tenure and the preservation of use rights.[4] However, these historical analyses are contentious, and other have argued that the evidence reveals a more complex picture.[5] It is probably true to say that the resulting legislation did not represent a clear victory for any of the warring factions. It was also something of a fudge, in that many of those responsible for the final drafting were heavily involved in the debate, and determined that the final legislation should reflect their own views, whatever anyone else wanted.[6] This should not surprise us, given the political upheavals of the time: in the critical period between 1921 and 1925, as Juanita Roche points out,[7] we had 'three general elections and five Governments [including the first ever Labour Government] under Liberal, Labour and Conservative Prime Ministers'. So, we should not expect to see simple clear objectives behind the legislation.

Nevertheless, the overall *effect* of the 1925 property legislation was to simplify land law so that it became easier to buy and sell land and to enter into other commercial

---

[3] See Part III of Chapter 8 *Property Interest Holders.* A trust is also imposed whenever two or more people have successive property interests in land, but this situation is now less common than it was in 1925.

[4] The classic ground-breaking analysis on these lines is Avner Offer, *Property and Politics 1870–1914: Landownership, Law, Ideology and Urban Development* (Cambridge: Cambridge University Press, 1981). The pro- and anti-marketisation arguments are best put in Kevin Gray and Susan Francis Gray, *Elements of Land Law* (5th edn, Oxford: Oxford University Press, 2009) at paras. 1.7.3–1.7.5.

[5] J Stuart Anderson, *Lawyers and the Making of the English Land Law 1832–1940* (Oxford: Oxford University Press, 1992). For illuminating examinations of the scope and importance of the works by Anderson and Offer (fn. 4 above) see Joshua Getzler 'Review of J Stuart Anderson, *Lawyers and the Making of the English Land Law*' (1993) 109 *Law Quarterly Review* 684 and A. W. B. Simpson, 'Review of J Stuart Anderson, *Lawyers and the Making of the English Land Law*' (1993) 56 *Modern Law Review* 608. See also Juanita Roche, 'Historiography and the Law of Property Act 1925: The return of Frankenstein' (2018) *Cambridge Law Journal* 600 for a fascinating historical account, arguing that the end result in 1925 was a rejection of, rather than a victory for, market-liberal attempts to extend doctrines such as overreaching (which we look at in Chapters 15 *Enforceability and Priority of Property Interests* and Chapter 16 *Registration*) so as to increase the marketability of land.

[6] Anderson notes that the drafting committee, led by Benjamin Cherry, was outraged when its 1920 Bill (an earlier draft) was rejected, but nevertheless 'smuggled back' into the draft of what became the Law of Property Act 1925 'the gist of what had been rejected in 1920': J. Stuart Anderson, 'The 1925 property legislation: Setting contexts' in Susan Bright and John Dewar (eds.), *Land Law Themes and Perspectives* (Oxford: Oxford University Press, 1998) p. 107 at p. 122.

[7] Roche, 'Historiography and the Law of Property Act 1925', fn. 5 above, at p. 614.

transactions affecting it, such as leasing it or mortgaging it. This put an increased emphasis on land as a commodity, and on the importance of improving the efficiency of land markets, rather than improving the security of those with use rights in the land. As we see later in the chapter, it involved, amongst other things, a simplification of ownership-type interests in land and a decrease in the range of property interests in any given piece of land that could affect anyone entering into a market transaction with the landowner. The effect was to give a stronger guarantee to market participants that if they acquired an interest in land on commercial terms, the interest would be free from any adverse property interest which was not reasonably discoverable.

The 1925 property legislation consisted of:

Law of Property Act 1922

The LPA 1922 abolished some of the remnants of the long obsolete feudal system of land tenure introduced into England in 1066, and made some other preliminary changes to land law rules which were later consolidated in the Law of Property Act 1925. It was repealed by the LPA 1925.

Law of Property 1925

This was (and still is) the most important of the 1925 Acts, reorganising and simplifying our basic land law rules and principles. Some of its provisions also apply to property interests in other things. Most of it is still in force, although some parts of it have since been amended. As we see later on in this chapter and in the rest of the book, it lays down the basic structure of our modern land law system. Although its object and effect was to simplify the law, the drafting is neither clear nor self-explanatory, and even today the courts are having to puzzle over the meaning of the sections setting out the most basic principles.[8]

Land Registration Act 1925

Registration of private property interests in land was first introduced in England and Wales by the Land Registry Act 1862, but our current registration system was established by the Land Registration Act 1925.[9] It was modified and replaced by the Land Registration Act 2002, which is the current statute governing the registration of private property interests in England and Wales. The 2002 Act was intended to make fundamental changes to land registration,[10] but it turned out to be less revolutionary than intended, and the courts still have to refer back to the 1925 Act quite frequently. We look at the current registration system in detail in Chapter 16 *Registration*.

---

[8] See for example *Baker* v. *Craggs* [2018] EWCA Civ 1126 (noted in Chapter 15 *Enforceability and Priority of Property Interests* para. 15.16) where the Court of Appeal reached a controversial decision on the meaning of ss. 1 and 2 of the Law of Property Act 1925, reversing the decision of the trial judge who had adopted a different construction.

[9] Chapter 16 *Registration* para. 16.5 and para. 16.15.

[10] The joint Law Commission and Land Registry Report whose recommendations were implemented by the LRA 2002 (Law Com No 271, 2001) was entitled *Land Registration for the Twentieth-first Century: A Conveyancing Revolution*.

Land Charges Act 1925

As we see in Chapter 16, the land registration system introduced by the Land Registration Act 1925 was brought into operation across different regions in England and Wales by stages, and even after it had spread across the whole of the two countries, an individual plot of land did not have to be brought into the system until it had changed hands. The process of bringing all land into the land registration system has therefore been slow – probably slower than Parliament envisaged in 1925 – and it is still not yet complete: as at the time of writing, 14.6 per cent of land in England and Wales is still unregistered.[11] However, it was always known that it would take some time, and so in the Land Charges Act 1925 Parliament introduced an interim system for unregistered land (i.e. land not yet brought into the system governed by the Land Registration Acts 1925-2002). The interim system required registration of a limited range of property interests in land[12] in a different kind of register (the Land Charges Register). The Land Charges Act 1925 was modified and replaced by the Land Charges Act 1972, which still applies to the last remaining stretches of unregistered land. People who live in areas where there is quite a lot of unregistered land left still need to know about unregistered land and the Land Charges Act 1972, but we do not cover it in this book.

Administration of Estates Act 1925

The rules about how property is to be distributed when someone dies intestate (i.e. without leaving a will directing who is to inherit their property interests) were simplified and rationalised by the Administration of Estates Act 1925. These rules apply to all kinds of property interest, not just property interests in land. They were amended by the Intestates' Estates Act 1952, which gave increased rights to spouses, and these rights were extended to civil partners by the Civil Partnership Act 2004 and to same sex spouses by the Marriage (Same Sex Couples) Act 2014.

Trustee Act 1925

The Trustee Act 1925 consolidated earlier legislation governing the powers, duties and liabilities of trustees. Parts of it were updated and replaced by the Trustee Act 2000, and, as far as land is concerned, significant changes were made by the Trusts of Land and Appointment of Trustees Act 1996, which introduced the new regime for trusts of land which we outline in Part V of this chapter.

Settled Land Act 1925

For several centuries most landed estates in England and Wales were held under a special kind of trust, a Settled Land Act settlement, which initially was devised by lawyers as a way of keeping the land of wealthy families in the family from generation to generation. Statutory reforms in the nineteenth century made this

---

[11] See Chapter 16 *Registration* para. 16.5 and para. 16. 15.

[12] Now listed in s. 2 of the Land Charges Act 1972. The most important are some types of mortgage and charge, some of the non-possessory land use rights we look at in Part VI of this chapter, and estate contracts, options to purchase and rights of pre-emption (as to which see paras. 5.22(a) below):

kind of settlement (once commonly called a 'strict' settlement) progressively more flexible, in particular by giving greater powers for the current head of the family (the 'tenant for life') and his (occasionally her) trustees to mortgage the land and sell off parts of it. This process culminated in the Settled Land Act 1925, which, in line with the general objective of encouraging market transactions, made it easier for land to be taken out of the settlement and gave the tenant for life greater autonomy in deciding what should be done with the land. The 1925 Act also simplified the statutory rules governing these settlements, but they remain highly complex. This and taxation disadvantages made Settled Land Act settlements increasingly unpopular and they were prospectively abolished by the Trusts of Land and Appointment of Trustees Act 1996: from 1996 all new trusts of land must take the form of the trust of land created by the 1996 Act, and since then it has been impossible to create a new Settled Land Act settlement. There were not many left in existence even in 1996, but the SLA 1925 continues to apply to the very few that still survive now.[13]

5.6 Parallels with Property Rights Systems in Other Jurisdictions

(a) Differences Between Different Legal Families

When we compare the property interests we recognise in England and Wales with those recognised in other jurisdictions, it is helpful to think of legal systems as grouped into legal 'families'. Legal systems belonging to the same legal 'family' (in the sense that they share a common origin, or their development has been shaped by a common ideology, such as feudalism or communism or free-market capitalism) tend to have broadly similar property rights systems. So, for example, property rights systems in common law jurisdictions have certain shared characteristics which differ in some respects from those shared by Continental European civil law jurisdictions, and which are different again from those shared by, for example, Nordic countries, Islamic law jurisdictions, or the socialist or post-socialist law systems of twenty-first century former communist states.

(b) Mixed Property Rights Systems

Categorising property rights systems into families in this way has its limitations. Some systems have mixed origins: Scotland's property law is a mixture of common law and civil law, and so too is the property law which developed in South Africa in colonial times, and which now (stripped of its apartheid accretions), still forms one strand in South Africa's present highly complex property law, interwoven with

---

[13] Elizabeth Cooke, 'What to do with an unbarrable entail?' (1994) *The Conveyancer* 492 commenting on *Hambro* v. *Duke of Marlborough* [1994] Ch 158, concerning the Settled Land Act settlement under which the Dukes of Marlborough had held Blenheim Palace (now a UNESCO World Heritage Site) ever since it was built in 1705. The 1994 litigation concerned ultimately unsuccessful attempts by the then Duke to ensure that, when he died, the estate would not pass on to his estranged son. See also A. W. B. Simpson *A History of The Land Law* (2nd edn, Oxford: Clarendon Press, 1986) pp. 208–209, 235–240 and 283–286.

indigenous property law systems and subsequent statutory reforms designed to reverse the effects of apartheid.

(c) Differences Within the Same Legal Family

Also, property law systems within the same legal family may differ from each other in quite significant respects, perhaps because of different political or cultural values or imperatives (some may be more influenced than others by socialist or by free market principles, some may give primacy to collectivism rather than individualism, others may have to adapt their systems to deal with developments such as rapid industrialisation, rural to urban migration, tourism, immigration or imminent climate change problems).

Another reason why property law systems within the same family may now be different from each other is that what were once close 'family' ties may have loosened over time, with systems which had a common origin developing in divergent directions. This is something we have to watch out for when we compare common law jurisdictions. English common law was exported to many different parts of the world by colonialism, but each colony adopted English property law as it stood at the date when the colony was settled,[14] which varied from colony to colony. Thereafter, colonial common law property rights systems were sometimes modified to track modifications subsequently made by UK legislation to English domestic property law, but often they were not, and increasingly each colony's property rights system developed on from there in its own way.[15] To take a specific example, the trust was firmly established in English law by 1700, and so was part of the English common law exported to Australia and to the United States of America, and it still remains a part of Australian and US common law,[16] and in more or less recognisable forms. However, the major changes made to land law in England and Wales by the 1925 property legislation which we noted in para. 5.5, were not replicated wholesale in Australia – although some states later adopted some of the changes – and they were not replicated at all in any of the states of the USA.[17] So, for example, the rule we adopted in 1925 that a trust must be imposed whenever a property interest in land is co-owned or divided into time slices[18] does not apply anywhere in the US or in Australia. Their co-ownership law is therefore very different from ours.

None of this makes comparisons with other property rights systems any less useful, as long as we appreciate that parallels and differences are rarely precise.

---

[14] Often with modifications to suit local conditions, as we see in Chapter 9 *Multiple Property Rights Systems*.

[15] To add to the complications, in former colonies which became federated states, such as Australia and the United States of America, property law is predominantly state law rather than federal law, and so differs from state to state.

[16] All states in the USA recognise the trust apart from Louisiana, which is a civil law jurisdiction.

[17] Brendan Edgeworth et al. (eds.), *Sackville and Neave: Australian Property Law* (8th edn, Chatswood, NSW: Nexis-Lexis Butterworths, 2008).

[18] para. 5.5 above and Part V of this chapter, and see also Part III of Chapter 8 *Property Interest Holders*, where we look at co-ownership in detail.

PART II WHAT IS 'OWNERSHIP'?

5.7 Blackstone's 'Sole and Despotic Dominion'

The most influential model of private ownership in the common law world over most of the last two and half centuries derives from a sweeping statement about 'the right of property' made by Sir William Blackstone in his *Commentaries on the Laws of England* in 1766.[19] This comes right at the beginning of Blackstone's discourse on 'property in general', where Blackstone describes 'the right of property' as:

> that sole and despotic dominion which one man claims and exercises over the external things of the world, in total exclusion of the right of any other individual in the universe.

It becomes clear in the rest of what Blackstone says that here he is equating 'property' with private ownership, in much the same way as John Locke did in his analysis of property we considered in Part II of Chapter 2 *Conceptions and Justifications*. Like Locke, Blackstone was not interested in analysing or delineating the concept of private ownership (or property generally) in any more detail. His concern was to explain its origin and justification (which he does in much the same way as Locke does).

5.8 Limitations of the 'Sole and Despotic Dominion' Model

Nevertheless, the 'sole and despotic dominion' label has stuck, as a good way of describing an absolutist model of private ownership, where, as Jane Baron puts it, 'nearly limitless rights [are] consolidated in a single owner, who can exclude all others'.[20] This absolutist model of private ownership is undeniably useful for ownership of simple physical things like books or bicycles. However, it is less useful for more complex things, and hardly ever appropriate as a model for land ownership, for at least three reasons.

(a) Shared and Subsidiary Interests

The first is that, in the case of land, it is actually quite unusual for a single human being to have sole and unrestricted rights over a defined geographic area. This is partly because, as we see in Chapter 8 *Property Interest Holders*, owners, like other property interest holders, come in a variety of different forms, including co-owners, trustees, and incorporated groups. In all these cases 'the owner' comprises two or more human persons, who may or may not be operating through a separate corporate entity, each having rights and obligations as against each other in relation

---

[19] William Blackstone, *Commentaries on the Laws of England*, Vol. 2 (first published 1766; reprinted Chicago and London: Chicago University Press, 1979), Book II, Ch. 1.

[20] Jane Baron, 'Rescuing the bundle-of-rights metaphor in property law' (2013–2014) 82 *University of Cincinnati Law Review* 57, at p. 58.

to the thing. In such cases there never is one person who has either 'sole' or 'despotic' dominion over anything: each person's rights are constrained by the rights of the others. Also, as we have already seen, private owners, whatever their form, can and frequently do grant subsidiary interests to others. So, to pick up again the example we used in para. 1.10 in Chapter 1 *What Property Is and Why It Matters*, if I am the private owner of my house, I can, for example, let it to a friend for five years by granting her a lease, and mortgage it to the bank by granting the bank a mortgage, and give my next-door neighbour a right of way over the front drive. We would still regard me as the owner, but now my friend, the bank and my neighbour also have property interests in my house, constraining my ownership rights and freedoms, and complicating the question of who can exclude whom, and from what and when.

(b) Other Constraints on Ownership

In all modern societies (and certainly our own) there are always restrictions on what a private owner can do with the thing she owns, even if she is the sole owner and no one else has a property interest in it. In the case of land, these restrictions are substantial. So, for example, planning control restricts her right to build what she wants on her land (and her right to demolish or alter buildings already there) and her freedom to change the use of the land; her neighbours can prevent activities on her land which adversely affect their land, and all kinds of regulatory bodies dictate whether, when and how she can abstract anything from her land or deposit anything on or into it. We look at these restrictions in Chapter 10 *Limitations on Property*, but for present purposes the point is that even a single absolute owner of land can hardly be said to have 'dominion' over it, still less 'despotic dominion'.[21]

(c) Ownership as a Complex Set of Relationships

The third limitation is that the sole and despotic absolutist model presents private ownership as a simple relationship between a person and a thing. This can be seriously misleading: other people are always brought into the picture. This is obviously so when any of the factors we have just noted in (a) and (b) above are present, but less obviously even when none of them is. Here we need to return to W. N. Hohfeld's analysis of property entitlements[22] which we introduced in Chapter 1 *What Property Is and Why It Matters*.[23] As Hohfeld pointed out, every property entitlement held by anyone necessarily gives rise to a corresponding correlative in someone else. So, even if I am the sole absolute owner of my land, my right (in the Hohfeldian sense) to exclude everyone in the world from the land necessarily puts you and the rest of the world under a duty (owed to me) not to enter the land or

---

[21] Blackstone himself would have agreed, although public constraints were less extensive in his day: see Gregory Alexander, 'The social-obligation norm in American property law' (2009) 94 *Cornell Law Review* 745 at p. 754.

[22] Wesley Newcomb Hohfeld, 'Fundamental legal conceptions as applied in judicial reasoning' (1913) 23 *Yale Law Journal* 16.

[23] paras. 1.23–1.25(a).

interfere with my rights and liberties in it. In other words, my ownership necessarily involves a relationship between me and you, and between me and everyone else in the world. This is as true for simple things like books and bicycles as it is for land. As we explained in para. 1.25(a), in simple situations these relationships are mostly of no great significance (except to me). But as soon as we bring in any of the factors in (a) and (b) above, the relationships proliferate and become more significant. For example, if I am not the sole human owner of the land but, say, a co-owner or a trustee or a community body of the kind we look at in Chapter 8 *Property Interest Holders*, there will be a complex web of entitlements and their correlatives as between all the humans and institutional bodies involved (i.e. the co-owners, the trustees as between themselves and as between each of them and each beneficiary, and as between the members and managers of the community body and any enforcement agencies involved). Similarly, if I as sole absolute owner grant you even the simplest property right over my land, such as a right to drive across my driveway to get to your house next door, I enter into a complex relationship with you. Using Hohfeld's terminology, the no-right to go on to the driveway you previously had is now converted into a right to drive along it to get to your house, giving rise to a duty on my part not to interfere with your exercise of that right, and changing my privilege to do whatever I want with the driveway into a privilege to do whatever I want with it that does not interfere with your right. And distributed between us, there will probably also be a mix of ancillary rights, powers and their correlative duties etc., which will deal with such matters as repair of the drive, parking on it and keeping gates locked or unlocked.

So, viewed in this way, even simple private 'ownership' is mostly not monolithic, but rather is 'a complex set of legal relations in which individuals [are] interdependent'.[24]

5.9 The Exclusionary Ownership Model and the 'Bundle of Sticks' Model

It is possible to acknowledge all these qualifications but still see absolute private ownership as forming the core of a liberal free-market property rights system. For many of those who take this view, the key factor in ownership is the right to exclude, which makes some sense if you cling to the Blackstonian 'sole and absolute dominion' model.[25] Current US property theory is sometimes said to be polarised between this exclusionary model of ownership and the 'fragmentation' or 'bundle of sticks' model we noted in paras. 1.12–1.13 of Chapter 1 *What Property Is and Why It*

---

[24] Gregory S. Alexander, *Commodity & Propriety: Competing Visions of Property in American Legal Thought, 1776–1970* (Chicago & London: *University of Chicago Press*, 1997) p. 323.

[25] For a more nuanced (and more helpful) account of the argument that the right to exclude is the core of a property rights system, see Henry E. Smith, 'The thing about exclusion' (2014) 3 *Brigham-Kanner Property Rights Conference Journal* pp. 95–124. Earlier, in 'Exclusion versus Governance: Two Strategies for Delineating Property Rights' (2002) 31 *Journal of Legal Studies* S453, Smith puts forward his argument that property rights in general 'fall on a spectrum between the poles of exclusion and governance' (at p. S454).

Matters.[26] In the 'bundle of sticks'[27] model, ownership is essentially a bundle of rights, powers, duties and liabilities etc., which can be – and in our system usually are – fragmented between different rights holders, so that at any one time any given thing can be the subject of complementary and reciprocal, or even conflicting, property rights and interests held simultaneously by different people. On this view, absolute ownership does exist, but equally it can be unpacked into its constituent parts. As we said in para. 1.12 of Chapter 1, this can be a helpful way of looking at the ways in which common law private property rights and interests fit together. More often, however, it can be seriously misleading, for all the reasons we looked at in para. 1.13: it ignores the fact that rights and duties proliferate and change form when owners grant subsidiary property interests, and sometimes disappear altogether (consider the public parks example in para. 1.13); it assumes that ownership retains its central role even after 'lesser' interests have been split off, which is often not true (consider the owner of land who grants a lessee a 999 year lease); and it does not work at all for some kinds of property interest (the example we gave in para. 1.13 was regulatory property rights), or for property rights systems which are not centred on private ownership (for example the indigenous property systems in Australia and Canada we look at in Chapter 9 *Multiple Property Rights Systems*).

5.10 Honoré's 'Liberal Concept' of Ownership

In his classic analysis of ownership published in 1961,[28] A. H. Honoré attempted something different. His aim was to give an account of the standard 'incidents' (or characteristics) of ownership. He argued that issues about the proper role of ownership in a property rights system, and the legitimacy of restrictions on ownership rights, can only be understood if we have a clear idea of what ownership *is*. He starts with a provisional definition of ownership as 'the greatest possible interest in a thing which a mature system of law recognises'.[29] He argues from there that if we look at the most extensive property interest recognised in the property rights system of each 'mature' legal system, we will find that 'certain important legal incidents are found, which are common to different systems'. We know this, he argues, because

---

[26] See for example Baron, 'Rescuing the bundle-of-rights metaphor', who provides a richer picture of the diversity of current US property theory, and places the views outlined here in the context of the theoretical approaches noted in Chapter 2 *Conceptions and Justifications*, Part V. For other views see e.g. Anna di Robilant, 'Property: A bundle of sticks or a tree' (2013) 66 *Vanderbilt Law Review* 86 and Jerry L. Anderson, 'Britain's right to roam: Redefining the landowner's bundle of sticks' (2006) 19 *Georgetown International Environmental Law Review* 375, each putting forward alternative models or metaphors.

[27] Sometimes referred to as a bundle of 'rights' rather than 'sticks', but 'sticks' is better because it allows the things in the bundle to include not only rights, but also the full Hohfeldian range of liberties, powers and immunities, and duties, liabilities and disabilities.

[28] A. M. Honoré, 'Ownership' in A. G. Guest, *Oxford Essays in Jurisprudence* (First Series) (Oxford: Clarendon Press, 1961) p. 107.

[29] Ibid. p. 108.

[I]f it were not so, 'He owns that umbrella', said in a purely English context, would mean something different from 'He owns that umbrella', proffered as a translation of 'Ce parapluie est à lui'. Yet, as we know, they mean the same. There is indeed, a substantial similarity in the position of one who 'owns' an umbrella in England, France, Russia, China, and any other modern country one may care to mention. Everywhere the 'owner' can, in the simple uncomplicated case, in which no other person has an interest in the thing, use it, stop others using it, lend it, sell it or leave it by will. Nowhere may he use it to poke his neighbour in the ribs or to knock over his vase. Ownership, *dominium*, *propriété*, *Eigentum* and similar words stand not merely for the greatest interest in things in particular systems but for a type of interest with common features transcending particular systems.[30]

Before explaining what these 'common features' are, Honoré is careful to clarify the limitations of what he is claiming. These limitations are important for us as well:

(a) The 'Liberal Concept of Ownership'

Honoré is talking specifically about ownership, which he distinguishes from other kinds of property interest.[31] Further, he is concerned only with the 'liberal' concept of 'full individual ownership'.[32] He equates this with 'personal' ownership and contrasts it with 'government' or 'collective' ownership (which he describes as a 'different though related' institution).[33] So, by ownership he means only private ownership.

(b) Fragmented Ownership

Similarly, Honoré confines his attention to 'simple' private ownership, in other words to cases where ownership is held by a sole private owner, and is not fragmented between different property interest holders, or at least not to any great extent.[34] He accepts that there are complicated cases where ownership is split up in such a way that it is difficult to assess who, if anyone, can properly be called 'the owner' (he gives the example of the owner granting a 2000 year lease), but he sees these as peripheral. What he is talking about is the paradigm case: as he points out, we need to analyse the incidents present in the 'ordinary, uncomplicated case' in order to be able to assess what he sees as the peripheral cases.[35]

(c) Extent of Ownership Within the System

Honoré also points out that not all mature legal systems attach equal importance to simple private ownership of the kind he analyses, giving as an example the limited use of this form of ownership at that time in what was then the Soviet Union.[36] In addition, he says, in nearly all legal systems there will be some things which cannot be owned at all, or in which the greatest possible interest which is recognised is too

---

[30] Ibid.   [31] Ibid. pp. 124–126.   [32] Ibid. p. 107.   [33] Ibid. p. 109.
[34] Ibid. pp. 110–112 and see also 124–126.   [35] Ibid. p. 111.   [36] Ibid. p. 109.

far from the simple private ownership paradigm to count as ownership. He gives as examples land in England in the early middle ages, and flick knives and Colorado beetles (the last two would have meant more to contemporary readers in 1961 than they do now). Also, he accepts that things incapable of ownership may well be different in different 'mature' systems.[37] We see a good example of this phenomenon in Part V of Chapter 7 *Objects of Property Interests* when we look at property interests in human bodies and human body parts.

(d) Incidents are Characteristic, Not Necessary Ingredients

Finally, Honoré makes it clear that his analysis is descriptive only – his primary concern is to see whether, and if so to what extent, legal systems do, as a matter of fact, recognise a common concept of private ownership. Consistently with that, he asserts that none of his listed standard incidents is individually necessary in every case.[38] Obviously, he points out, there may be cases where the property interest in question has so few of the standard incidents that we would hesitate to call it ownership, or would regard it as 'a modified version of ownership, either of a primitive or sophisticated sort'.[39] But that does not mean that no property interest counts as 'ownership' in his terms unless all the standard incidents of ownership are present.

5.11 Honoré's 'Standard Incidents' of Ownership

Honoré lists 11 'standard incidents'. His full account of them is essential reading, because he has important and not immediately obvious things to say about each of them. To summarise, though, the incidents are:

(1) *The right to possess*, by which Honoré means the right 'to have exclusive physical control of a thing'.[40]
(2) *The right to use*, taking 'use' in the narrow sense of 'personal use and enjoyment'.[41]
(3) *The right to manage*, meaning 'the right to decide how and by whom the thing owned shall be used'.[42]
(4) *The right to the income*, with 'income' here covering three kinds of income: 'the surrogate of use' (in other words 'a benefit derived from forgoing personal use

---

[37] Ibid. pp. 109–110.
[38] Ibid. p. 113. It has to be said, though, that some of Honoré's later remarks do seem to suggest that he regarded some incidents as more necessary than others. So, for example, he describes the right to possession as 'the foundation on which the whole superstructure of ownership rests' and says that 'unless a legal system provides some rules and procedures' to enforce rights to be put into and remain in exclusive physical control of a thing, 'it cannot be said to protect ownership' (p. 113).
[39] Ibid. p. 112.
[40] Ibid. p. 113. See para. 5.34 below for the more precise definition of possession currently accepted in the law of England and Wales.
[41] Ibid. p. 116.   [42] Ibid. p. 116.

of a thing and allowing others to use it'); reward for exploiting the thing; and the 'brute product of a thing, made by nature or by other persons'.[43]

(5) *The right to the capital*, which Honoré takes to mean the power to 'alienate the thing'[44] and the liberty to 'consume, waste or destroy the whole or part of it'.[45]

(6) *The right to security.* By this Honoré means a freedom from expropriation, either by the state (except on payment of compensation and, although Honoré does not explicitly say so, for strictly limited purposes) or by anyone else.[46]

(7) *The incident of transmissibility.* It is not easy to distinguish Honoré's 'transmissibility' from the 'alienability' he describes as forming part of the *right to capital*. As we saw in Chapter 1 *What Property Is and Why It Matters*,[47] when we talk about a property interest being 'transmissible' we usually mean that the property interest can pass unchanged through the hands of successive holders, either consensually when the current holder sells or gives it away, or automatically by operation of law when the current holder dies without having made a will or goes bankrupt.[48] So, transmissibility tells us something about the nature of the interest. 'Alienability', on the other hand, tells us something about the powers of the property interest holder: a property interest is alienable if the current holder of it has *the power* to transfer or bequeath it. The two usually coincide, but not always. So, for example, we would say that the freehold interest in land which is currently vested in a local authority as a public park is transmissible, in that it was once held by someone else before it was vested in the local authority, and will be passed on to someone else if, say, the local authority is disbanded. However, for as long as the freehold interest is held by the local authority as a public park, it is inalienable, because the local authority has no power to alienate it.[49] It is not immediately obvious that when Honoré talks about the *incident of transmissibility* he means what we mean by 'transmissibility', but he clearly does see it as something that is different from alienability.

(8) *The incidence of absence of term.* This relates to the duration of the interest. Honoré explains that a property interest may be *determinate* (fixed in duration to a specified length, such as a 99 year lease, or a life interest), or *determinable* (terminable on the happening of a future event which may never happen, such as a monthly tenancy which continues indefinitely until terminated by either

---

[43] Ibid. p. 117.

[44] It is not clear what Honoré means by power to alienate *a thing* (i.e. to dispose of it by a transfer or by will). When we talk about a person disposing of 'a thing', in legal terms we mean disposing of a *property interest in a thing*. Honoré, however, says an owner characteristically has both a power to dispose of the thing *and* power to dispose of her property interest in it (see ibid. p. 118), which is puzzling (as is his apparent confusion between alienability and transmissibility: see further below).

[45] Ibid. pp. 118–119.

[46] Ibid. pp. 119–120: Honoré's right to security has to be read subject to his 10th incident, *liability to execution*: see below.

[47] para. 1.26(b).   [48] See para. 1.26(b).

[49] More precisely, it has strictly limited powers set out in the statutory provisions governing that particular park.

party giving notice to quit to the other[50]) or *indeterminate* (perpetual in duration). It is a characteristic of ownership that it is indeterminate, or perpetual in duration, according to Honoré.

(9) *The prohibition of harmful use.* This means what it says: the fact that I am owner of a thing does not mean I can use it in a way that harms others. It is not clear why Honoré regards this as an incident of ownership rather than as a general law qualification of *the right to use*. It is true that ownership does not characteristically give you immunity from liability in tort or criminal law for harming others by your use of the land. But perhaps what Honoré means is that, if there was a legal system in which what would otherwise be ownership gave the 'owner' immunity from liability for such harm, that 'ownership' would not accord with his liberal conception of ownership.[51] In other words, he would regard that legal system as one which did not recognise the concept of ownership.

(10) *Liability to execution.* What Honoré means here is that it is a characteristic of ownership that the owner is liable to have her ownership taken away from her, either by a creditor if she fails to obey a court order to repay a debt, or if she goes bankrupt. We could say that this is just an exception to Honoré's *right to security*: Honoré's point, however, is that if there was no such exception to the right of security, the owner's interest in the thing would not amount to the liberal concept of ownership, because the 'owner' would be unable to participate in a market economy (because no-one would give her credit).[52]

(11) *Residuary character.* The idea of residuary character is quite difficult. What Honoré means is that if you, as owner, granted a subsidiary right to someone else (perhaps you, the freehold owner of land, granted a 99 year lease of it to a tenant) your ownership is always there in the background as a still subsisting property interest, so that the rights your granted to the tenant will always automatically spring back to you whenever the lease ends – even if it ends prematurely. There will never be a vacuum. And, however many subsidiary interests you may have granted, and however many sub-interests your subsidiary interest holders may have granted, your interest is still in existence somewhere there in the background and, ultimately, when all these interests and sub-interests are extinguished, everything falls back to you: ultimately you (or, rather, whoever then currently holds your ownership interest) will become, once again, absolute private owner.

5.12 Civil Law Ownership and Common Law Ownership

(A) A Common Concept of Ownership ...?

When considering Honoré's analysis of ownership, it is worth knowing that he was pre-eminently a Roman law specialist. So, he was at least as familiar with the civil

---

[50] We look at this example in more detail in Chapter 17 *Leases*, Part II.
[51] Because it would transform 'ownership' into 'a destructive force': Honoré, 'Ownership', fn. 28 above, p. 123.
[52] Ibid. p. 123.

law concept of private ownership as he was with common law ownership, and he clearly intended that his standard incidents should be taken to be characteristic of both. The definitions of ownership which appear in the French Civil Code and the German Civil Code (on which many other codes have been based, in Europe and internationally) seem to confirm this. They both reflect Roman law property principles which were reintroduced throughout Europe following the French Revolution and the abolition of feudalism. Unsurprisingly, therefore, their definitions of 'ownership' follow the Roman law notion of *dominium* as 'the exclusive, perpetual and sovereign right over a thing'.[53]

In the French Civil Code[54] ownership is defined in the following way:

> **Art. 544** Ownership [propriété] is the right to enjoy and dispose of things in the most absolute manner, provided they are not used in a way prohibited by statutes or regulations.

> **Art. 546** Ownership of a thing, either movable or immovable, gives a right to everything it produces and to what is accessorily united to it, either naturally or artificially . . . .

The equivalent provision in the German Civil Code, the *Bürgerliches Gesetzbuch* (BGB),[55] is s. 903:

> **903 Powers of the owner**
> The owner of a thing may, to the extent that a statute or third-party rights do not conflict with this, deal with the thing at his discretion and exclude others from every influence . . .[56]

So, to this extent we can say that when we talk about simple private ownership in the common law world, we mean much the same as a civil lawyer would mean.[57]

(b) ... Or Fundamentally Different Concepts?

However, despite these similarities, some argue that civil lawyers and common lawyers have fundamentally different concepts of ownership. The argument is that

---

[53] Sabina Praduroux, 'Objects of property rights: Old and new', in Michele Graziadei and Lionel Smith (eds.), *Comparative Property Law: Global Perspectives* (Cheltenham and Northampton MA: Edward Elgar Publishing, 2017) p. 51 at p. 52, and see also pp. 52–53 for a useful summary of the nature of 'ownership' in France, Germany and England and Wales.

[54] The French Code is the Code Civil, which came into force in 1804. It is divided into five Books: most of the property provisions are in Book 2 *Of Things and the Various Modifications of Ownership* (*Des biens et des différentes modifications de la propriété*). There have been extensive amendments to the Code since 1804, most significantly in relation to co-ownership and security interests (Sjef van Erp and Bram Akkermans (eds.) *Cases, Materials and Text on Property Law* (Oxford and Portland, OR: Hart Publishing, 2012) pp. 32–33).

[55] The BGB came into force in 1900 and has been much amended since then, although not significantly in relation to private property law (van Erp and Akkermans, *Property Law* pp. 34–35). Most of the property provisions are in Book 3 *The Law of Property*, but there are also some in Book 1 *The General Part*.

[56] S. 903 goes on to make special provision for ownership of animals, which we look at in Chapter 7 *Objects of Property Interests*.

[57] This does not mean that civil law systems all look at ownership in the same kind of way: see van Erp and Akkermans, *Property Law*, fn. 54 above, pp. 212–218.

whereas civil lawyers see ownership as unitary and absolute, common lawyers do not. This is easier to understand if we take separately the ideas of 'unitary' ownership and 'absolute' ownership.

Unitary Ownership

When civil lawyers talk about ownership as 'unitary', they mean that ownership cannot be split into two or more property interests each held by a different person.[58] This does not mean that other people cannot hold *other kinds of property interest* in the thing you own. So, for example, if you are the owner of land in France, Germany or Scotland others may have, for example, a right of way over your land or a mortgage or charge over it, in just the same way as they might over land you own in England. However, in France, Germany and Scotland these property interests are seen as separate, subordinate property interests which operate as burdens on the ownership interest.[59] Ownership itself remains undivided. This is said to be in stark contrast with common law ownership, which, so it is said, does allow ownership to be split between different rights holders by allowing fragmentation of ownership.

This argument is unsatisfactory in a number of ways. First, it is true that some common law property theorists do indeed see ownership as a bundle of rights or sticks which can be fragmented, with the fragmented parts (leases, mortgages, easements, etc.) forming separate property interests held by different people. However, as we pointed out in paras. 1.12–1.13 of Chapter 1 *What Property Is and Why It Matters*, the 'bundle of sticks'/fragmentation metaphor is just that – a metaphor – and not a particularly illuminating one. As we said in Chapter 1 and at the beginning of this chapter, it is more helpful to regard private ownership as just one kind of property interest found on a spectrum of different kinds of property interest (including, but not limited to, interests such as leases, mortgages, easements, etc.) rather than as the central feature of our property rights system from which all these other property interests are derived. This common law view of private ownership – as one of a number of different kinds of property interest – is not incompatible with the civil law idea of unitary ownership. In any event, even if it was true that the common law sees all other property interests as fragments of ownership, whereas the civil law sees them as subordinate interests which operate as burdens on ownership, it is difficult to see what practical significance that might conceivably have.[60]

A more serious argument is that the civil law idea of unitary ownership is fundamentally incompatible with the common law recognition of equitable interests

[58] This does not rule out co-ownership: in civil and common law systems co-ownership involves sharing a single interest, not dividing the interest up into separate parts held by different people. We come back to this point in Chapter 8 *Property Interest Holders* Part III.

[59] Roman law categorises them as *iure in re aliena* – rights in someone else's thing.

[60] See George L. Gretton and Andrew J. M. Steven, *Property, Trusts and Succession* (3rd edn, Haywards Heath, UK: Bloomsbury Professional, 2017) para. 3.2, reaching the same conclusion, and also noting the significant differences between French- and German-based civil law systems in this respect. On this latter point see also Michele Graziadei 'The structure of property ownership' in Graziadei and Smith (eds) p. 82; compare van Erp and Akkermans, *Property Law*, fn 54 above, pp. 224–226 and Murray Raff, *Private Property and Environmental Responsibility: A Comparative Study of German Real Property Law* (The Hague, London and New York: Kluwer Law International, 2003) p. 188.

(because this allows the common law to recognise both a legal owner and an equitable owner of the same thing at the same time) and also with its recognition of the trust (because the trust allows ownership of the trust property to be split between trustee and beneficiary). However, both the legal/equitable distinction and the trust represent a fundamental structural difference between our property rights system and civil law property rights systems. They are embedded within, and pervasive throughout, our modern property rights system and they apply to all kinds of property interests: neither is special to ownership. So, if we accept that the common law and the civil law have fundamentally different concepts of ownership *because* the common law recognises equitable as well as legal ownership and allows ownership to be held on trust, it must mean that, for the same reason, we have fundamentally different concepts of, for example, land burdens such as easements/servitudes and security interests such as charges. No-one has ever suggested that this is so.

Relativity of Title

Another major difference in our concepts of ownership is said to be that whereas civil law systems regard ownership as absolute – either you are owner or you are not – the common law does not, because it regards all titles to ownership as relative. It is this that leads some common law commentators to the rather startling conclusion that English law does not recognise the concept of ownership at all[61] – a conclusion that would have surprised Blackstone. However, this confuses 'ownership' with '*entitlement* to ownership'. We look at this in detail in Chapter 11 *Possession and Title*, but broadly in the common law 'title' means entitlement to a property interest.[62] Entitlement to ownership of a thing is complex because the common law recognises the concept of relativity of title to ownership: it is possible for more than one person to have title to ownership of the same thing at the same time, but those titles will not be of equal strength. This makes more sense when you appreciate that in our system there are two ways of obtaining title to ownership of a thing. One is by buying (or being given) the title of the absolute (i.e. undisputed) owner. The other is by taking possession of a thing without the consent of the absolute owner. An absolute owner has a title to ownership which is enforceable against everyone in the whole world (hence 'absolute'). So, if you are the absolute owner of your land or book and you sell or give your absolute ownership to me, I become absolute owner. If, however, I take possession of your land or book without your consent, you remain absolute owner – you have the absolute title – but I obtain a possessory title to ownership of your land or book. So now there are two simultaneous titles to the same land or the same book. However, mine is weaker than yours: yours is enforceable against everyone including me (i.e. you have a right

---

[61] For the classic argument, see Anthony Hargreaves, 'Terminology and title in ejectment' (1940) 56 *Law Quarterly Review* 376, which Honoré considers and rebuts (convincingly) in 'Ownership' (fn. 28 above) at pp. 136–141. The argument resurfaces briefly in Van Erp and Akkermans, *Property Law*, fn 54 above, pp. 306–307 (in relation to land), pp. 346–348 (goods) and p. 362.

[62] Chapter 11 *Possession and Title* para. 11.2.

to get the land or book back from me), whereas mine is enforceable against everyone *except* you (I have the right to get the land or book back from anyone who now tries to take it from me, *unless that person is you*).[63] The matter goes one step further. If I have a possessory title and I remain in possession for a sufficiently long period and you, as absolute owner, take no action to get your land or book back from me, then you will lose your right to do so. Your title will then be extinguished, and my possessory title will become an absolute title: at that point I become absolute owner.[64] However, for present purposes the important point is that most civil law systems have functionally equivalent doctrines which allow long term possessors to oust strangers and even oust absolute owners in certain circumstances,[65] but they do not conceptualise them as involving relativity of title. So, it is true that this idea of relativity of title is both central to our property rights system and alien to civil law property systems.[66] However, it is all (and only) about rival claims to ownership, that is, *who* is entitled to ownership at any one time and as against whom, not *what it is* that they are entitled to. So, it seems more accurate to say that we share the same concept of ownership, but recognise different processes for acquiring and losing it.[67]

5.13 Beyond the Common Law/Civil Law World

We should recall Honoré's warning that the importance of private ownership varies widely between jurisdictions, and outside the common law and civil law world it may be of only peripheral importance in the property rights system, not central to the whole system.[68] So, in some jurisdictions private ownership may be limited to what we sometimes call personal effects (perhaps your clothes, jewellery, household goods, etc.) or crops you grow or the place where you live, whereas in others even public goods such as rivers and canals or prisons are routinely privately owned.

   A separate factor to be noted here, however, is that the characteristics of what looks like private ownership in any given society (and what may be thought of as private ownership in that society) may vary depending on the nature of the society. So, for example, in economies not based on free market principles, your rights to sell or mortgage the things you own, or to bequeath them to whoever you want when you die, may be severely restricted or even non-existent. Similarly, in societies where the property rights system is essentially collectivist rather than individualistic, your ownership of your personal effects or your home may be dependent on your status within your family or your community. This may be particularly significant for women, who may be unable to acquire ownership of things other than by virtue of

---

[63] See further Chapter 11 *Possession and Title* para. 11.3(b). Honoré's discussion of unititular and multititular systems is helpful here, providing a more nuanced analysis of the distinctions between civil law and common law systems on this point: see Honoré 'Ownership', fn. 28 above, at pp. 136–141.

[64] This is the law of adverse possession, which we look at in Chapter 11 *Possession and Title* para. 11.3(c) and Chapter 12 *Adverse Possession of Land*. It is modified in England and Wales once the absolute title has been registered in the land register, as we see in Chapter 12.

[65] Chapter 12 *Adverse Possession of Land* para. 12.2.

[66] Honoré, 'Ownership', fn. 28 above, pp. 134–141.

[67] This is, essentially, Honoré's conclusion: ibid. pp. 136–141.   [68] para. 5.10(c) above.

their status as, for example, daughter, sister, wife, mother, aunt, widow or ex-wife, and who may retain ownership only for so long as they retain that status. In this kind of situation, their incidents of ownership will not necessarily match Honoré's incidents, but they may think of themselves as, and be regarded by the rest of their society as, private owners of 'their' things as against the rest of their society, in much the same way as we think of ourselves as private owners of 'our' things as against the rest of our society. We come back to this point in Chapter 9 *Multiple Property Rights Systems*.

PART III LAND OWNERSHIP IN ENGLAND AND WALES

5.14 Evolution of Land Ownership in England and Wales

As we noted in Chapter 1 *What Property Is and Why It Matters*,[69] ownership of land in England and Wales is technically different from ownership of anything else. This is because, as we noted in para. 5.5, our modern law of land ownership is the product of nearly a thousand years of incremental development by the courts, with only occasional interventions by Parliament. As a result, it still retains relics of its feudal origins and post-feudal legal, social and economic developments.

Two of these relics are relevant here. The first is that the Crown retains a notional interest in all land in England and Wales. It is sometimes said that this interest that the Crown has in all land in England and Wales is 'ownership', but this is not correct and never has been.[70] It is the last remnant of the feudal lordship which William I asserted over all land in the country when he conquered England in 1066. This 'lordship' put him at the top of the feudal structure of land tenures which he imposed throughout the country in 1066. Although that structure has long since collapsed and most of the incidents of the Crown's lordship have disappeared, the Crown's interest continues to exist in a vestigial form. Its only current function is to act as the residuary interest in all land. In other words, if the freehold ownership interest in a piece of land is extinguished, the land 'escheats', meaning that it falls back under Crown control. This does not mean that the Crown takes the land for its own benefit, or acquires any other beneficial incidents of ownership. The court has various powers to re-vest the extinguished freehold interest in someone else, or alternatively a new freehold may be granted by the Crown. Otherwise, however, the land remains in a kind of limbo. We see how all this works in para. 5.18, but it is worth noting here that most other national property rights systems have procedures to deal with land which, for one reason or another, has become ownerless. The only difference is that in this jurisdiction the procedures are ancient, complex and arcane and dealt with by the Crown, whereas in most modern states the procedures will have been purpose-built and made the responsibility of the state or a public body.[71]

The second historical relic is that private ownership of land is still defined in terms of the feudal tenures created in 1066 and the medieval doctrine of estates which grew

---

[69] para. 1.18(c).   [70] Simpson, *A History of the Land Law*, fn. 13 above, p. 1 and p. 47.
[71] See, for example, arts. 539 and 713 of the French Code Civile, and §928 of the German BGB.

up around them. So, the interest we mean when we talk about ownership of land in England and Wales is, technically, *a holding of land for freehold tenure, for an estate which is in fee simple, absolute and in possession* (usually referred to as 'freehold' or 'fee simple' ownership, or as the freehold or fee simple estate). We explain the technical terms in para. 5.16, but for present purposes the point is that this freehold ownership is indistinguishable in effect from civil law private ownership, or from English law ownership of pens and bicycles.[72]

These two anachronistic technicalities survive because we have never formally abolished feudalism. This puts us in a very different position from European countries such as France and Germany, who codified their systems of property law precisely because they wanted to introduce a new order, eliminating the social constructs surviving from feudalism and post-feudal hierarchies.[73] We have not done anything like that since 1066: at no point since then have we scrapped our pre-existing land law system and started all over again. Instead, we have just adapted what we had, to fit changing social, economic and political conditions. As we noted in para. 5.5, significant changes were made by the 1925 property legislation, but they were mainly confined to eliminating some of the pieces of the jigsaw and re-arranging the others, as we see in para. 5.16. In 2005 the Law Commission of England and Wales announced that its next three year law reform programme would include a project 'to consider the several residual but significant feudal elements that remain part of the [land] law of England and Wales'.[74] However, the project was deferred, and then apparently abandoned, on the basis that other reform projects would bring 'greater public benefit'.[75] So, it seems we have to live with these obscure and unnecessary technicalities, at least for the foreseeable future. Scotland has been more fortunate: all surviving elements of feudal law were removed from Scotland's land law in 2004 by the Abolition of Feudal Tenure etc. (Scotland) Act 2000, following recommendations of the Scottish Law Commission in 1999.[76]

5.15 Origins of the Crown's Interest in Land

It helps to understand the present nature and role of the Crown's interest in land if we appreciate that the feudal system imposed by William I in 1066 when he invaded England (accompanied by, as A. W. B. Simpson puts it, his 'band of military adventurers'[77]) was essentially a system for organising society, built around a hierarchy of tenures under which land holdings were dependent on the provision of services. Specifically, the means by which William I took and retained control over the country was by parcelling out all land amongst his key supporters, on terms that

---

[72] para. 5.12 above.

[73] Feudalism was eliminated from French property law by the Code Civile and from German property law by the *Bürgerliches Gesetzbuch* (BGB): see para. 5.12 above.

[74] Law Commission, 9th Programme of Law Reform.   [75] 10th and 11th Programme.

[76] Scottish Law Commission, *Report on Abolition of the Feudal System* (1999) Scot law Com No 168. For a brief but helpful explanation see Gretton and Steven, *Property, Trusts and Succession*, fn. 60 above, pp. 2–3 and Appendix pp. 497–504.

[77] Simpson, *A History of the Land Law*, fn. 13 above, p. 3.

they would hold their part of the country in exchange for providing him with armies, or money or other services which allowed the King to retain control of the country and maintain his court. Those who held land in this way, that is, those who held land directly from the Crown, were called tenants in chief, they were required to swear loyalty to the Crown, and their holdings ('fees') were dependent on them continuing to provide the agreed services.[78] The words 'tenure' and tenant' in this context have nothing to do with leases: the law of leases developed outside the feudal system, and landlords and tenants under a lease have always been in a completely different position from lords and tenants under the feudal system.

The terms on which feudal tenants held their fee (their 'tenure') depended on the kind of services required, and there were different kinds of tenure, each denoting a different kind of service. However, initially these tenants in chief were just the top rung of a pyramid of tenures and sub-tenures. Each tenant in chief could, and did, grant sub-holdings of parts of 'their' land to others, in exchange for and dependent upon services to be provided to them by these sub-grantees. The tenant in chief remained vassal of the Crown, responsible to the Crown for the services required by his tenure, but he was now himself lord of, and entitled to agreed services from, his vassals under the tenures of the fees they held from him. This process was called subinfeudation, and these sub-holders were entitled to subinfeudate in their turn, that is, to parcel out all or parts of their subholdings to a rung below, becoming lords of those to whom they subinfeudated – their vassals – and entitled to whatever services they required from their vassals under the tenures of the fees they granted to them. This process could continue down the line, ending up will a bottom rung of feudal tenants who actually occupied the land ('tenants in demesne'). So, tenants in chief (and those on the intermediate rungs in the pyramid) would not only be lords of those to whom they had subinfeudated parts of their land. They would also be tenants in demesne of the bits of land they retained for their own use. The vast majority of tenants in demesne, however, would have been the peasants who actually occupied and worked their land, and were lords of nobody.

The essential point about the relationship of tenure between feudal lord and tenant at each rung in the pyramid is that it was a personal relationship between superior and inferior which, as Simpson points out, was 'marked by reciprocal duties of protection and service'. The feudal tenant's rights to enjoyment of the land were dependent on faithful performance of the services, and the tenant was entitled to the protection, and subject to the jurisdiction, of the lord's court, which 'resembled a modern military tribunal in that it was concerned as much with discipline as with justice'.[79] The lord was entitled to homage and service from the tenant, and if that was given, the lord was bound to respect the tenants' rights and to provide him with protection. Initially at least, the relationship of tenure between them was 'very much a personal affair, which came to an end when either of them died',[80] and if the tenant's heir was allowed to succeed to the tenant's fee when the tenant died, it

---

[78] Simpson says that there were probably about 1500 tenants in chief by 1086, most of them from William I's Norman retinue (*A History of the Land Law*, fn. 13 above, p. 4).

[79] Simpson, *A History of the Land Law*, fn. 13 above, p. 2.   [80] Ibid. p. 49.

would be by way of a re-grant on payment of a fee. So, neither lord nor tenant had anything that resembled a modern private property right. In particular, if we leave aside land which the Crown occupied for itself – the 'royal demesne' – the Crown was never regarded as 'owner' of the land of which it was paramount lord, and neither was anyone else, because all others held only a fee under a relationship of tenure with their immediate lord.[81]

5.16 Modern Freehold Ownership: What It Is and How It Evolved

However, over time the interests of tenants in demesne (i.e. those actually occupying the land they held from their immediate lord) became more and more like modern private ownership. First, 'tenure' became virtually meaningless because the number of different kinds of tenure declined and the incidents of tenure (i.e. the services required) became less and less important and eventually disappeared altogether. Secondly, fees held by the last surviving kind of tenure – freehold tenure – became alienable, inheritable and perpetual. This was through the doctrine of estates. We need to say a bit more about each of these processes.

(a) Tenure

At quite an early stage the feudal pyramid collapsed because intermediate fees – that is, the interests of those in between the Crown as paramount lord and the tenant in demesne – gradually disappeared.[82] Once that process had been completed, all tenants in demesne ended up as the immediate feudal tenants of the Crown. By the time that had happened, nearly all incidents of the relationship of feudal tenure had also disappeared. The reciprocal personal obligations of services and protection evolved into a more impersonal relationship whereby the feudal tenant was required to pay money to continue to hold the land rather than provide services. This was reflected by a rationalisation of the different kinds of tenure, and the Tenures Abolition Act 1660 converted nearly all tenures into one kind – freehold tenure – which required no payments to the lord and no services. By 1922 there were only two kinds of tenure left – copyhold and freehold – and the LPA 1922 abolished copyhold tenure, so leaving freehold tenure as the only kind of tenure that can now exist. So, as a result of the 1925 legislation, there is now only one lord – the Crown – and whilst all land can only be held of the Crown by tenure, there is only one kind of tenure left – freehold tenure, and it involves no obligations whatsoever owed by the tenant to the Crown.

---

[81] Ibid. pp. 1 and 47.

[82] There was a natural process of attrition, because fees were liable to be forfeited, either to the immediate lord or to the Crown, for a variety of reasons including personal disloyalty or misconduct, failure to provide services faithfully, or by the tenant dying without a re-grant to heirs. These intermediate fees could not be replaced because subinfeudation was prohibited by the statute Quia Emptores in 1290. Also, many intermediate fees simply dropped out of the picture as services were replaced by money payments, which progressively decreased in value and so were no longer worth collecting: Simpson, *A History of the Land Law*, fn. 13 above, pp. 6–24.

(b) Estates

Meanwhile, the fee by which a tenant in demesne held land of the Crown was no longer linked to the life of the tenant, that is, automatically ending when the tenant died. Instead, it became possible for the tenant to alienate it, or leave it by will to his heirs. So, the fee became, in effect, perpetual in duration. However, lawyers began to develop devices for splitting these fees up into time slices, each slice comprising a separate property interest called an *estate*. An undivided fee – that is, one which was not divided up into time slices, and so could last perpetually, with the current fee holder entitled to sell it or leave it by will to whoever he wanted, and on whatever terms – came to be called a *fee simple estate*. Anyone who held a fee simple estate could, however, then divide it up into time slices by, for example, leaving it by his will to his daughter for her lifetime only, (in which case she would acquire a *life estate*) and directing that thereafter it should go to her husband if he survived her (so the husband has a life estate too), and thereafter to their eldest child (who would end up with the entire fee simple once both parents had died). Alternatively, the holder of the fee simple estate could direct that the fee should go to, for example, his eldest son for life and thereafter from eldest son to eldest son for successive generations, and if any current holder of the fee died without a son, the fee would go to the descendants of the original holder's brother for successive generations. In this kind of arrangement, the fee that each holder held for their lifetime was called a *fee tail*. Another possibility was that the holder of the fee simple could transfer or bequeath it to, say, his cousin to hold only until the happening of a certain event (for example, only for so long as the land was used as a school), or only if and when a certain event happened (for example, only if the cousin married before the age of 30). The cousin's fee would be a *conditional (or contingent) fee*, and it would necessarily give rise to an alternative fee to take effect if the condition was not (or not yet) satisfied. So, in the first half of the last example, someone (perhaps the cousin's brother) would hold a fee in the school land which would take effect in the future if and when the land stopped being used as a school (a conditional or contingent fee simple), and, in the second half of the example, someone else (assume again the cousin's brother) would hold a fee simple which was to take effect immediately but would be liable to be terminated if and when the cousin married before the age of 30.

All of this made land law immensely complex, because every fee (whether it was a life estate, or a fee tail, or a conditional or contingent fee) became a property interest as soon as the person entitled to it was sufficiently ascertained. Broadly, it became a property interest as soon as the designated holder became identifiable and reached the age of 21, even if at that point their fee had not yet come into effect, or might never do so, or was liable to be terminated by some future event.[83] So, at any one time there could be any number of time-limited property interests existing at the

---

[83] This is an over-simplification of what was (and still is) a complex rule governing the point at which a future interest 'vests', i.e. becomes a property interest: see further Stuart Bridge, Elizabeth Cooke and Martin Dixon *Megarry & Wade: The Law of Real Property* (9th edn, London: Sweet & Maxwell, 2018) paras. 8.001–8.007.

same time in the same land, only one of which would confer a present right to *present enjoyment* of the land[84] (in technical terms, the interest is then *in possession*) whilst others would give a present right to *future enjoyment* of the land (the interest is then said to be *in remainder* or *in reversion*). This often meant that at any one time there was no single person with the power to make long term decisions about the land, and, unless all the interest holders were able and willing to co-operate, it could be impossible to sell the fee simple or mortgage it to raise capital.

The point of all this was of course to allow fee simple holders to dictate what was to happen to 'their' land in the future, and there are obvious reasons why a fee simple holder might want to do this. However, for many people, particularly those who value the autonomy of the individual, it is morally and socially objectionable for a land owner to continue to control the land after she has disposed of her interest in it, and it is also thought by many to be incompatible with the notion of private ownership of land.[85] It has also long been argued by free market economists (and others) that it leads to inefficient land use and land distribution: the land is tied to uses dictated by past generations, and kept in the hands of people selected by criteria irrelevant to their abilities to make the best use of the land, instead of being channelled by the market into the hands of those most likely to maximise its utility.

In other words, the doctrine of estates threatened to impose severe restraints on the continuing process of commodifying land, and over the centuries both the courts and Parliament made attempts at curbing its worst excesses.[86] If anything, this made the law even more complex, as lawyers acting for landed families tried to find ways of getting round the new constraints to keep land in the family.

In most common law countries the doctrine of estates has never been abolished, and in some of these it remains important. So, for example, in the USA estates are still an integral part of the structure of land law, and an understanding of the estates system is regarded as essential.[87]

We are more fortunate. The 1925 legislation did not abolish the notion of estates, but instead it provided that property interests in land for anything less than a fee simple estate[88] cannot be legal property interests. Instead, they can only exist as equitable property interests under a trust.[89] So, after 1925 you can still divide *the benefit of* your fee simple estate into time slices, but you cannot time-slice the fee simple itself. What you have to do is declare that you hold your fee simple on trust

---

[84] If that interest was co-owned, it could itself be further sub-divided horizontally, by being co-owned by two or more people. The same applies to any future interests.

[85] The argument (best put in Gray and Gray, *Elements of Land Law* paras. 3.1.28–3.1.39) is that freedom to alienate to whoever you choose and on any terms you choose is an essential pre-requisite of private ownership, but that, paradoxically, this nevertheless makes it necessary for every private owner's freedom of alienation to be restricted so far as necessary to preserve the freedom of alienation of her successor.

[86] Including the rule against perpetuities, still in operation in England and Wales today (now governed by the Perpetuities and Accumulations Act 2009) but not covered in this book.

[87] See Thomas W. Merrill and Henry E. Smith, *Property* (Oxford: Oxford University Press, 2010) pp. 95–113 and J. W. Singer *Property* (4th edn, New York: Wolters Kluwer, 2014) pp. 302–347.

[88] Or a leasehold estate: leases were outside the system of estates described here.

[89] S. 1(1)–(3) of the Law of Property Act 1925.

(or transfer it to trustee to hold on trust) on terms that reflect the time slices you want to create. So, for example, if I now want to split my fee simple between my daughter and her husband and their child, as in our earlier example, I now must declare that I hold it on trust (or transfer it to someone else to hold on trust) for my daughter for her life, then to her husband for his life if he survives her, then to their eldest child absolutely. My daughter, her husband and their child will still acquire immediate property interests,[90] but now they will be equitable property interests under a trust. This makes a dramatic difference, because the trust will be a *trust of land* under what is now the Trusts of Land and Appointment of Trustees Act 1996, and in that kind of trust the trustees are free to sell or mortgage the fee simple, and if they do so the interests of the beneficiaries (my daughter, son-in-law and grandson) are transferred from the fee simple interest in the land into the sale or mortgage proceeds. This means that, in most cases, the interests of those with time-sliced fees are now, in effect, only interests in the wealth represented by the fee simple interest, and they do not interfere with its marketability.

It also means that the doctrine of estates is of almost no significance in modern English land law, except in the now comparatively rare cases where land is held in trust for successive generations of wealthy families.

(c) Modern Land Ownership

So, as far as modern land ownership is concerned, the story of estates parallels the story of tenures. At one time, land could be held of the Crown by any one of a number of different tenures, each carrying different obligations to an immediate lord, but now there is only one – freehold tenure – and it carries no obligations to the immediate lord, who is now always the Crown. Similarly, at one time land could be held of the Crown by a succession of different people, each of whom held a different time-slice of the fee (i.e. a different estate). Now, however, there are only two possible estates for legal property interests in land. One is the lease, which is and has always been outside the traditional 'estates' system, as we see in (d) below. The other is the fee simple estate (which is perpetual in duration) which is absolute (i.e. not conditional on some condition being satisfied or the happening or non-happening of an event) and in possession (i.e. the right to enjoyment of the land is immediate, rather than in the future).

If we put all these together, we get to our modern technical definition of *land ownership*, as *a holding of land by freehold tenure, for an estate which is in fee simple, absolute and in possession*. Just about any of the constituent technical terms can be picked out as a shorthand term for the whole: so, 'the freehold', 'the fee simple', 'freehold ownership', 'fee simple ownership', 'freehold estate' and 'fee simple estate' are all routinely used as shorthand for our version of private ownership of land.

---

[90] Subject to the rules about ascertainability mentioned in fn. 83 above.

(d) Leases, Freehold Ownership and Terminology

Neither the doctrine of tenure nor the doctrine of estates ever applied to leases, which developed completely outside the feudal system, emerging first as contractual interests and then evolving into sui generis property interests in land.[91] A lease is, essentially, a grant of possession of land for an ascertainable duration (usually a fixed period of years, or for successive weekly, monthly or yearly periods until terminated by a notice to quit). Any freehold owner can grant a lease of all or part of her land, and any tenant under a lease can grant a sublease of all or part of the land let to him.

Confusingly, modern leases use quite a lot of terminology which mirrors terminology used in feudal land holdings and in the doctrine of estates, but which means something different when used in relation to leases. As we have already noted, the relationship between a landlord and a tenant under a lease is not at all like the relationship of a feudal lord and tenant, and the rights and obligations of a tenant under a lease in relation to the leased land are very different are from those of a tenant under a feudal land holding. Similarly, although the property interest of a tenant under a lease is of limited duration, and so in one sense is a time-slice carved out of perpetual ownership, it was not an 'estate' within the traditional pre-1925 doctrine of estates.

However – and most confusingly of all – it is *now* an estate in land. This was one of the rationalisations made by the 1925 property legislation. Section 1(1) of the Law of Property Act 1925 defines 'legal estate in land' as including both legal freehold ownership of land *and* a legal lease of land.[92] This usage is now common, especially in statutes. So, freehold ownership of land is often referred to as 'the freehold estate' in the land, and a legal lease of land as a 'leasehold estate' in the land.

5.17 Nature and Function of the Crown's Interest in Land

Although it is inaccurate to say that the Crown 'owns' all land in England and Wales, there are some bits of the land that the Crown actually uses, occupies or manages for itself, either in the monarch's personal capacity or as sovereign, and it would be true to say that the Crown does indeed own this land, in much the same way that I own my pen or my bicycle. It includes parts of the foreshore, royal parks, royal residences and other personal estates, and some government department land.[93] This land is sometimes called royal demesne land, and there are no freehold owners of any of it.[94]

---

[91] Simpson, *A History of the Land Law*, fn. 13 above, pp. 247–256.

[92] S. 1(1): the technical terms are 'an estate in fee simple absolute in possession' and 'a term of years absolute', and s. 1(1) states that they are the *only* estates in land which can be legal: s. 1(1) (a), and s. 1(1)(b). S. 1(4) seems to say that legal easements, legal mortgages and a few other property interests in land which are now rarely encountered (e.g. rent charges and rights of entry) are also included in the definition of 'legal estate', but no-one is quite sure what s. 1(4) means: see Roche, 'Historiography and the Law of Property Act 1925', fn. 5 above.

[93] See generally Law Commission, *Land Registration for the Twenty-first Century: A Conveyancing Revolution* (2001) Law Com No 271, paras. 2.32–2.37 and 11.1–11.38.

[94] With a few possible exceptions, as to which see ibid. para. 11.9. Land held by the Royal Duchies of Cornwall and Lancaster is governed by separate and even more arcane and obscure regimes, which we do not cover in this book.

If we leave aside this royal demesne land, which the Crown does indeed own, we are left with two other categories of land. As we saw in para. 5.16, most of the rest of the land in England and Wales is held of the Crown by someone else, by freehold ownership, and the Crown's only interest in this land is a residuary interest which will come into effect only if, as occasionally happens, the freehold ownership interest comes to an end. This brings us to the only other category, which is land where the freehold ownership interest *has* come to an end. When this happens, the land is said to 'escheat' to the Crown. It is not regarded as owned by the Crown: rather, it is regarded, and treated, as ownerless land. We look at the Crown's role in relation to this kind of land in the next paragraph.

5.18 Ownerless Land

There are three routes by which land can become ownerless and escheat to the Crown. It is important to appreciate that escheat is an ancient doctrine, another relic of our feudal history, and that although there are some recent statutory provisions governing the routes to escheat, the law relating to escheat itself is ancient, obscure and uncertain. It was certainly not designed to deal with the problem of land that has become unowned.[95] It is also important to appreciate that about 500 freehold titles escheat every year, and that nearly all of them relate to land which has become a liability to its owner and to everyone else. Most often, this will be because the land is contaminated land containing environmental hazards,[96] or because buildings on it have become derelict so that it constitutes a danger to the public, and there are statutory restriction on demolition by a private owner because of the architectural or cultural value of the buildings.[97]

Escheat used to be the process by which the Crown forfeited feudal tenurial holdings, usually for treason or some other misdemeanour or failure. Now, however, it almost always occurs only when the Crown, or a trustee in bankruptcy, liquidator or other bankruptcy official *disclaims* a freehold ownership interest which it holds. Disclaimer is the process by which a property interest is extinguished by an official act. The Crown and any of the officials named above can disclaim any kind of

---

[95] Compare the provisions of the French Code Civile and the German BGB dealing with situations where, for example, an owner has died without leaving a will and without heirs, or has abandoned property: Van Erp and Akkermans *Property Law*, fn 54 above, pp. 950–955.

[96] See e.g. *Re Celtic Extraction Ltd (in liquidation)* [2001] Ch 275, CA, concerning a landfill site.

[97] See e.g. *Hunt* v. *Withinshaw* [2015] EWHC 3072 concerning Victoria Pier in Colwyn Bay, a derelict Grade II listed building, beyond repair and subject to a charge in favour of the local authority to recover costs of emergency repairs. For the long history of attempts to save the pier, see www .colwynvictoriapier.co.uk. Using the bankruptcy procedure noted in (c) below, the freehold interest was finally vested in the local authority. They eventually demolished the pier in June 2018, although there are plans to re-use some of the original metalwork and art deco decorations in a replacement, when the money can be found. See also *Hackney LBC* v. *Crown Estate Commissioners* (1996) 72 P & CR 233 (another derelict Grade II listed building, this time a house in Stoke Newington, charged to the local authority to recover money spent on pest control and under a Dangerous Structure Notice) and *Fenland DC* v. *Sheppard* [2011] EWHC 2829 (derelict former shop-site in Cambridgeshire, charged to the local authority to recover £72,000 spent to make the site safe).

property interest they hold in the circumstances we look at below.[98] However, it is only if the property interest disclaimed is freehold ownership that the land escheats to the Crown. This can happen in any of the following circumstances.

(a) Death of the Freehold Owner Intestate Without Traceable Heirs

When someone dies intestate owning a freehold estate, and no heirs come forward to claim her property, the freehold interest does not terminate automatically. Instead it is transferred to the Crown, as bona vacantia (lost property). The Crown advertises bona vacantia property to see if anyone wants to claim an interest in it. If nothing comes of that, then it will sell the freehold interest, passing the sale proceeds to the Treasury. If, however, the freehold interest is worthless or of negative value, the Crown will *disclaim* it. The freehold interest then ends, and the land escheats to the Crown. The land then enters the limbo state we refer to in (c) below.

(b) Dissolution of a Corporate Freehold Owner

Corporate bodies die by being formally dissolved by the relevant public authority. It happens when a company has been liquidated (either voluntarily, or because it is insolvent) or it has been struck off the register of companies for failure to comply with obligations or standards imposed by the Companies Acts. In all those circumstances there are procedures for selling all property interests held by the company before it is dissolved and dividing up the sale proceeds between the company's shareholders (if the company is solvent) or its creditors (if it is insolvent). However, if a property interest held by the company is overlooked and the company still holds it when it is dissolved, that property interest is automatically transferred to the Crown as bona vacantia (ownerless property), because the interest holder has ceased to exist. If the property interest is freehold ownership the Crown is then in an odd position, holding its vestigial interest in the land but also holding (in its different capacity as official holder of all bona vacantia property) the freehold ownership. A number of different possibilities then arise. If the freehold ownership is worth anything, the Crown will sell it at market value. If not, it will disclaim it, which will extinguish the freehold ownership, so that the Crown will now hold only its vestigial interest in the land. The usual outcome of that will be that the land will remain in a state of limbo (the Crown will not take possession of it, owes no liabilities in respect of it to anyone, takes no responsibility for it and takes no steps to defend its title) unless and until the Crown finds someone willing to buy a new freehold interest.[99]

---

[98] Disclaimer is now largely governed by statute. Its effects are peculiar because, whilst disclaimer extinguishes the disclaimed interest, it does not extinguish subsidiary property interests which are dependent on it: they continue in existence *as if* the disclaimed interest still existed. For the mental gymnastics required to come to terms with this conceptually awkward doctrine, and work out what it actually means in practical terms, see *Hindcastle Ltd* v. *Barbara Attenborough Associates Ltd* [1997] AC 70 and Julian Farrand and Alison Clarke (eds.), *Emmet & Farrand on Title* (London: Sweet & Maxwell, looseleaf updated to 30 April 2019) paras. 26.227–26.236.

[99] See *Emmet & Farrand*, fn. 98 above, para. 11.154 and the cases noted there.

(c) Disclaimer on Bankruptcy or Liquidation

If an individual goes bankrupt the main function of the bankruptcy official (the trustee in bankruptcy) is to sell all the bankrupt's property and divide the proceeds between the bankrupt's creditors, pro rata according to the amounts they are owed.[100] Problems arise when a property interest held by the bankrupt is worthless, or is a positive liability. For example, the bankrupt may be freehold owner of contaminated land, liable as landowner for remediation costs far exceeding the value of the land,[101] or of a derelict building, liable to reimburse public authorities who have had to spend money on emergency repairs.[102] When this happens (and it happens surprisingly often) the trustee in bankruptcy is entitled to 'disclaim' the property interest, provided it is 'unsaleable or not readily saleable or is such that it may give rise to a liability to pay money or perform any other onerous act'.[103] The disclaimed interest then ceases to exist, and, if it is the freehold ownership of the land, the land automatically escheats to the Crown, or, rather enters the limbo state described in (b) above.[104] Any 'interested person' may then apply to the court, which has a discretion to vest or re-vest the freehold ownership in them.[105] But if no-one applies, the land stays in the limbo state until someone wants to buy a new freehold interest.[106]

PART IV LEGAL PROPERTY INTERESTS AND EQUITABLE PROPERTY INTERESTS

5.19 Difference Between Legal Property Interests and Equitable Property Interests

At this point we need to return to the distinction between legal and equitable property interests we outlined in para. 5.3. As we explained in para. 5.3, this two-tier categorisation of property interests is unique to the common law and is embedded within, and pervasive throughout, the modern property rights systems of England and Wales. As we explained in para. 5.3, the important point is that although both legal property interests and equitable property interests are properly regarded as property interests, it is only legal property interests that fully satisfy the 'property' criterion of being enforceable against everyone else in the world. Equitable property interests have a more limited range of enforceability: they are enforceable against everyone else *except* a privileged class of people, consisting broadly of those

---

[100] The same applied when a company goes into insolvent liquidation (the corporate equivalent of bankruptcy), but to keep things simple we assume here that the insolvent debtor is an individual and that the insolvency procedure is bankruptcy rather than liquidation.

[101] As in *Re Celtic Extraction Ltd (in liquidation)* [2001] Ch 275, CA.

[102] See the cases cited in fn. 97 above.   [103] S. 178(3)(b) IA 1986.

[104] *Scmlla Properties* v. *Gesso Properties (BVI) Ltd* [1995] BCC 713 Ch D at 803.

[105] In all the cases noted in fn. 97, for example, the trustee in bankruptcy disclaimed the freehold interest and it was re-vested in the local authority.

[106] See The Crown Estate, *Escheat – A Brief Guidance Note by the Crown Estate*, www.thecrownestate.co.uk/en-gb/resources/faqs. The Crown Estate is the Government department which administers this aspect of the Crown's affairs.

who acquire property interests in the same resource in good faith through a market transaction. So, for example, if I own a car and I lease it to you for five years by granting you a legal lease of it, your lease will be enforceable against anyone to whom I may give, sell or mortgage the car within the five year term of the lease, even if they knew nothing at all about your lease. If, on the other hand, I held my car on trust for you, so that I was the legal owner of the car but you held the beneficial interest in it, your beneficial interest in the car (an equitable property interest) is much less secure. It will be enforceable against anyone who takes a gift of the car from me (for, example, if I give it to my sister), and against anyone who buys it from me or takes a mortgage of it when they knew or ought to have known about your interest. If, however, I manage to sell or mortgage the car to an unsuspecting purchaser or lender, pretending I am the absolute owner, your equitable interest will not be enforceable against them: it will be extinguished as a property interest in the car.[107]

The precise rules about the enforceability of equitable interests are quite complicated, and in some cases different rules apply to different kinds of equitable interest. Also, the rules tend to be modified when property interests are covered by a registration system, as is the case with property interests in land in England and Wales. We look at these precise rules in Chapter 15 *Enforceability and Priority of Property Interests: General Principles* and (in so far as they apply to land) in Chapter 16 *Registration*. However, the general principle underlying all these rules remains the same: equitable property interests are inferior to legal property interests because they are more vulnerable to outsiders than legal property interests are, in that equitable property interests are not enforceable against a privileged class of outsiders. This is the only significant difference between legal and equitable property interests in our modern law. In all other respects an equitable property interest is as good as a legal property interest.

However, this difference in the range of enforceability can be important, and so we often need to know whether any given property interest is legal or equitable. We look at the rules governing this question in paras. 5.21–5.23. However, these rules make more sense if you know something about how and why equitable property interests emerged in our property rights system in the first place, and how they evolved from there. We look at this historical background in the next paragraph.

5.20 Historical Background

From about the middle of the fifteenth century until the late nineteenth century we had two parallel systems of national courts.[108] The first was a system of Common Law Courts developed out of the King's court, and they applied the principles and rules of law laid down by Parliament as well as those that they themselves developed

---

[107] If, as in this example, your equitable interest is a beneficial interest under a trust (as opposed to any other kind of equitable property interest) you will automatically get instead the equivalent equitable property interest in the money I acquired by selling or mortgaging the car, as we see in Part V below. However, since I am a fraudster, you will be lucky if you ever recover any money from me.

[108] There were also various local courts, such as manorial courts, which belonged to neither system.

when deciding cases using the doctrine of precedent. Legal property interests were those that the Common Law Courts recognised and enforced, applying these common law principles and rules. By the middle of the fifteenth century these common law rules had become formalistic and inflexible, often producing absurd and/or unfair results. It became customary for people who were aggrieved by these decisions of the Common Law Courts to appeal to the King for justice, and these appeals were dealt with by the Lord Chancellor, regarded as the keeper of the Crown's conscience. The Lord Chancellor did not have power to reverse decisions of the common law courts but he did have power to mitigate what he saw as injustices resulting from the decisions of the common law courts, applying rules and principles which he developed and which became known as rules and principles of equity. By 1588 this jurisdiction of the Lord Chancellor was formalised into a separate Court of Chancery, presided over by the Lord Chancellor and specially appointed deputies, which applied and developed the rules and principles of equity and not common law rules and principles.

So, for 300 years all citizens were subject to two separate sets of rules and principles of law, each administered by a separate system of courts, each of which had jurisdiction over all civil disputes. This sounds like a recipe for chaos, but basically it worked (just about) because the two separate Court systems managed to develop a protocol for coexistence. This was that the Chancery courts (sometimes called the Courts of Equity) would not reverse decisions of the Common Law Courts or contradict common law rules or principles, but would only mitigate their effect. The Chancery courts did this by developing their own remedies which they would award to litigants to reverse the effect of what the Chancery courts regarded (applying the equitable principles they developed) as the unfair or unjust consequences of applying common law rules and principles.

The clearest example of how this was done is provided by the trust. The common law had strict rules which determined who was the legal holder of any given legal property interest, and the person entitled to hold the property interest according to those rules was the legal holder of that property interest for all legal purposes. This was the case even if he had acquired the legal property interest by mistake, or fraud, or in other circumstances in which it would be unjust for him to be allowed to keep if for himself. The Chancery courts could not deny that he was the legal holder of that property interest, but they could and did intervene by requiring him to hold it for the benefit of the person who, according to their equitable principles and rules, was entitled to it. So, whilst the common law courts would protect and enforce the property interest on behalf of the person who, according to their legal rules, was entitled to hold it – the legal title holder – the Chancery courts would acknowledge that the legal title holder held the legal title but would recognise the person they regarded as entitled to the benefit of the interest as the equitable holder of the property interest. The equitable holding of the property interest gave the holder rights (which the Chancery court would enforce against the legal title holder) to require the legal title holder to use the property interest solely for the benefit of the equitable title holder. So, the legal property interest was recognised and enforced by the Common Law Courts, but they had no jurisdiction to interfere with an equitable order made by the Chancery court requiring the holder of the legal property interest to use it only for the benefit of the person who the Chancery courts declared to be the holder of the equitable property interest.

Eventually, the Common Law Courts and the Chancery courts were amalgamated by the Judicature Acts 1875, and from then on the combined courts were required to apply both common law and equitable rules and principles.

5.21 How Can You Tell Whether a Property Interest is Legal or Equitable?

In our modern law some kinds of property interest can only be equitable. It is a short list, and we identify them in para. 5.22. Others will be either legal or equitable, depending on the way in which they are created. Specifically, if we leave aside the kinds of property interest that are exclusively equitable, all other kinds of property interest are legal in some circumstances but only equitable in others. We consider what those circumstances are in para. 5.23.

5.22 Property Interests Which Can Only Be Equitable

Most types of property interests which are exclusively equitable were developed by the Courts of Equity (the Chancery courts) before the two systems of courts were amalgamated by the Judicature Acts 1875. Others, however, are property interests which could have been legal property interests before 1925 but were demoted to equitable status by the Law of Property Act 1925, as part of the 1925 legislation's scheme for simplifying market transactions in land which we noted in para. 5.5(b) above. The rest are new forms of equitable property interest developed by the courts after the Judicature Acts, that is, after the two systems of Common law and Equity courts were amalgamated.

(a) Estate Contracts, Options and Rights of Pre-emption

Estate Contracts
The estate contract comes within the first of these categories. An estate contract is a contractually enforceable right to acquire a property interest in something at a future date. The contractual right takes effect as a property interest in the thing, immediately and in its own right. This property interest, the estate contract, is not the same as the property interest in the thing which will be transferred or granted by the seller to the buyer when the contact is carried out. It is an interim property interest which, if all goes well and the sale is duly completed, will last until the contractually promised property interest is transferred/granted to the buyer. So, if you and I enter into a contract that, on an agreed date in the future, I will sell you my property interest in something (perhaps my freehold interest in my farm), you automatically acquire an equitable property interest called an estate contract in the farm *as soon as we both become bound by the contract*. It will be replaced by the freehold interest in the farm when I transfer that to you. An estate contract qualifies as a property interest because, if I fail to transfer the freehold interest to you but

instead transfer it to, say, my cousin, he will be bound by it just as I was: he will be required to sell you the freehold interest in the farm on the same terms as those agreed between you and me.

The evolution of the estate contract demonstrates the way Equity worked, devising ways of getting round rules of the Common law courts which operated unjustly. The particular problem Equity saw itself as tackling here was that the only remedy that the Common law courts could offer someone who had contracted to buy land, if the seller refused to go ahead and transfer the land as agreed, was damages for breach of contract. This, in Equity's eyes, was an inadequate remedy for someone who had lost a legally enforceable right to acquire a particular piece of land. So, Equity devised a new kind of remedy for breach of a contract to sell land: an order of 'specific performance'. On application by the aggrieved purchaser, it would order the defaulting seller to transfer the land to the intended purchaser on the agreed terms (i.e. to 'perform' the contract), and if the defaulting purchaser had meanwhile sold it to someone else, Equity would make the same order against the transferee. So, from the moment the sale contract became binding, the contractual purchaser acquired a right to specific performance of the contractual right, and it was this right which attached to the land, in the sense that it was enforceable by Equity against anyone who subsequently acquired an interest in the land.[109]

We come on to a further elaboration of this in para. 5.23(c) below, when we look at what happens when the contractual date for me to transfer the freehold property interest to you has passed, and you have already performed your part of the bargain (paid me the money) or can show that you are ready and willing to do so, but I have not yet transferred the freehold interest to you. As we see in para. 5.23(c), at that point you acquire the equitable freehold property interest in my farm, whilst I still retain my legal freehold property interest.

Although the estate contract has been recognised as a property interest for a long time,[110] there is still some confusion over the rights and powers you have in relation to the land if you have an estate contract, and over the extent to which the seller owes you obligations to look after the land pending completion of the sale. This was evident in the Supreme Court decision in *Scott v. Southern Pacific Mortgages Ltd* [2014] UKSC 52, which we look at in Chapter 16 *Registration* para. 16.27(a), where the Supreme Court held that a fraudster who had an estate contract in land did not have the power to grant an estoppel interest in the land[111] to the victim of the fraud. The decision has been much criticised, as we see in para. 16.27(a), and in its 2018 Report *Updating the Land Registration Act 2002* the Law Commission described it as 'in tension with our view of the status of estate contracts as equitable interests in

---

[109] Unless that person could show they were a good faith purchaser of an interest in the land who had no notice of the contractual purchaser's right: as we saw in para. 5.19, the basic rule (which is itself modified by registration rules in the case of land) is that equitable property interests are never enforceable against good faith purchasers without notice.

[110] See Lord Walker in *Jerome* v. *Kelly* [2004] UKHL 25 at paras. 30–32, and the cases he cites there.

[111] An equitable property interest of the type noted in (e) below.

land'.[112] However, the Law Commission concluded that the point was outside the scope of that particular law reform project, and so said nothing more about it.

Options to Purchase and Rights of Pre-emption

Options to purchase and rights of pre-emption are variations of the estate contract. They are both equitable property interests as well.

In an option to purchase, the contract gives the buyer the *right* to buy on agreed terms, on an agreed date or the happening of a certain event, but imposes no *obligation* on him to buy. So, if I grant you an option to purchase my freehold interest in my field, you have a right to buy it on the agreed terms if you want to, but I cannot require you to do so. In a right of pre-emption, the buyer is also given a right to buy on the agreed terms, but it is exercisable *only if the seller decides to sell*. So, if I grant you a right of pre-emption over my freehold interest in my field, all I am granting you is a right that, before selling my freehold interest in the field to someone else, I must first offer to sell it to you.

Like an estate contract, an option to purchase has long been established as a property interest:[113] in both cases, the buyer has a contractual right to acquire an interest in land, which equity will enforce by granting an order of specific performance.

However, a right of pre-emption is different. The buyer's right to buy is conditional on the seller wanting to sell, so in some ways it is closer to a hope of acquiring a property interest in land rather than a right to do so. Nevertheless, we can now assume that it is a property interest when it affects registered land because the Land Registration Act 2002 expressly provides in s. 115 that, in relation to registered land, a right of pre-emption 'has effect from the date of creation as an interest capable of binding successors in title'. However, 'right of pre-emption' is not defined in the Act and earlier court decisions had distinguished different kinds of agreement which have all at times been referred to as 'rights of pre-emption', although giving the grantee different kinds of right. For example, some grants may specify the price at which the seller must sell to the buyer if he decides to sell, whereas others give the buyer the right to buy at the price which the seller is proposing to sell to a third party (in which case it is more properly called a right of first refusal). Presumably, all of these arrangements are now covered by s.115 and therefore are equitable property interests capable of being enforced against third parties. The effect of rights of pre-emption outside the land registration system does, however, depend on finer distinctions. In *Pritchard* v. *Briggs*[114] the Court of Appeal had decided by a majority that a right of pre-emption was not a property interest (because the question of whether the buyer would ever get the land was too dependent on the will of the seller), even though it was assumed in the 1925 property legislation that it was.[115]

---

[112] Law Commission Report, *Updating the Land Registration Act 2002* (2018) Law Com No 380, at fn. 5 to para. 6.7.

[113] *London & South Western Railway* v. *Gomm* (1881) 20 Ch D 562.

[114] *Pritchard* v. *Briggs* [1980] 1 Ch 338.

[115] It was – and still is – registrable as a land charge under the interim register of commercial equitable property interests set up by the Land Charges Act 1925 (which still applies to land which is not yet

The Court of Appeal later came to the opposite conclusion in *Dear v. Reeves*,[116] distinguishing *Pritchard* v. *Briggs* and deciding that a right of pre-emption *was* 'property' for the purposes of insolvency legislation.[117] Similarly, the Court of Appeal had also concluded in *Bircham & Co (Nominees No.2) Ltd* v. *Worrell Holdings Ltd* [2001] EWCA Civ 775 that a right of pre-emption *becomes* a property interest as soon as the vendor offers to sell to the buyer, provided the seller has no right to withdraw the offer (because at that point it is converted into an option to purchase), or otherwise when the buyer accepts the offer (because at that point it becomes an estate contract). These subtleties continue to be relevant for rights of pre-emption affecting land which is not yet within the land registration system,[118] and for rights of pre-emption granted over things other than land.

(b) The Interest of a Beneficiary Under a Trust

As we see in Part V below, in some circumstances the person who holds a property interest can be required to hold it on trust for (i.e. for the benefit of) someone else. It is a peculiarity of our law of trusts that both the trustee (the nominal holder of the property interest) and the beneficiary each hold a distinct property interest in the thing in question. The trustee's property interest may be either legal or equitable (in other words, the property interest he holds on trust may be either a legal property interest in the thing or an equitable property interest in it) but the beneficiary's property interest is always and necessarily an equitable property interest. We look at the nature of this kind of equitable interest in Part V below.

(c) The Restrictive Covenant

A restrictive covenant is a property interest held by a landowner which entitles the landowner to restrict the use of specified neighbouring land in a specified way, for example by preventing it from being used for anything other than residential purposes, or by prohibiting any building on the neighbouring land. It has always been possible for neighbouring landowners to enter into an enforceable contract whereby one of them promises to restrict her use of her land (the burdened land) in a specified way so as to benefit her neighbour's land (the benefitted land). By the middle of the nineteenth century the Courts of Equity developed a doctrine which, in effect, attached the benefit of that kind of contractual promise to the benefitted land and similarly attached the burden of it to the burdened land. This meant that successive owners of any part of the benefitted land were always entitled to enforce the use-restriction promise against whoever at that time was owner of the burdened land, even if she was not the original owner. This elevated what had originally been a

---

covered by our central land registration system: para. 5.5 above), with the result that it is enforceable against the whole world if registered.

[116] *Dear* v. *Reeves* [2001] EWCA Civ 277.

[117] See Chapter 6 *New Property Interests and the Numerus Clausus* para. 6.4(d).

[118] See para. 5.5(b) above.

contract right into a new kind of property interest – a restrictive covenant – but because it had been invented by the Courts of Equity (rather than by statute or the development of common law doctrines) it can only ever be an equitable interest. As we see in Chapter 13 *Non-Possessory Land Use Rights* where we look more closely at restrictive covenants, current proposals to reform the law of land obligations would change that, and make it possible for a new kind of use-restriction obligation entered into by one neighbour for the benefit of another to give rise to a legal property interest. Meanwhile, however, restrictive covenants are always and necessarily equitable property interests.

(d) The Mortgagor's Equity of Redemption

One of Equity's first endeavours was to provide protection for people who mortgaged their land to moneylenders. This was partly to prevent moneylenders from imposing extortionate financial terms on the mortgagor (the borrower), but also because early forms of mortgage (the property interest granted by the mortgagor owner to the mortgagee lender) gave the mortgagee lender disproportionately broad rights in, and powers over, the mortgaged land. Another way of putting it, if you want to adopt the 'bundle of sticks' metaphor for ownership, is that a mortgage granted by an owner transferred too many of the sticks in the owner's bundle of rights and powers into the mortgage bundle of rights etc. which was now held by the mortgagee lender. In fact, in the most common form of mortgage of both land and goods up until 1925, the mortgagor (the borrower, and the owner of the land or goods) transferred ownership itself to the mortgagee lender as soon as the money was lent, in exchange for a promise by the mortgagee lender to transfer it back if and when the mortgagor borrower repaid the loan together with all due interest etc. This meant that, until the loan was paid off in full, the mortgagee lender held the ownership interest in the mortgaged land or goods and the 'real' owner – the mortgagor borrower – had no property interest whatsoever.

Equity intervened to redress the imbalance by developing a new kind of property interest to be held by the mortgagor borrower for so long as the mortgage existed. This new property interest conferred on a mortgagor by Equity is called the 'equity of redemption' and, again, it is always and necessarily an equitable interest because developed by the courts of Equity.

Broadly, the equity of redemption gives the mortgagor borrower rights to prevent the mortgagee lender from exercising any of its rights in or powers over the property except so far as is necessary to protect or enforce the mortgage, and preserves the mortgagor borrower's right to get the property back on repaying everything due.

This kind of mortgage (sometimes called a property-transfer mortgage)where ownership of the mortgaged property is transferred to the mortgagee lender at the outset and the mortgagor borrower holds the equity of redemption instead until the loan is repaid, is still used for goods. It was abolished as a method of mortgaging interests in land by the Law of Property Act 1925 and replaced by the modern 'charge by way of legal mortgage'.

Under the charge by way of legal mortgage the mortgagor borrower retains her interest in the land (usually the legal freehold or long leasehold interest) and the mortgagee lender acquires a new kind of mortgage interest, called a 'charge by way of legal mortgage'. Confusingly, however, although the mortgagor now keeps her legal freehold or leasehold property interest under this new arrangement, she also still has, as a separate equitable property interest, this 'equity of redemption'. So, in our modern law, the property interest of a mortgagor borrower in the land she has mortgaged consists of the following elements. She has her legal freehold or leasehold property interest, which is, however, now subject to the mortgagee lender's legal property interest – the charge by way of legal mortgage – which gives the mortgagee lender extensive rights and powers over the mortgaged land until the loan is repaid. However, these legal rights and powers over the land which the mortgagee lender has, are in their turn subject to the mortgagor owner's additional equitable property interest – the equity of redemption – which *prevents the mortgagee from using its legal rights and powers except when it needs to use them to protect or enforce its property interest* (i.e. the mortgage). We come back to the nature of the modern legal mortgage of land in para. 5.37 below.

(e) The equitable charge

Partly because of the unsatisfactory nature of the mortgage, which was a common law creation, Equity devised a new kind of a security interest – the equitable charge – which gives a lender less extensive, but more appropriate, rights and powers over a borrower's property interest. A charge can be deliberately granted by a property interest holder over his property interest, or it can be imposed on it by law. Like a mortgage, it is granted by the property interest holder (or imposed on him by law) over his property interest, and it is granted to the lender (or to someone else owed an obligation by the property interest holder) solely in order to secure repayment of the debt or performance of the obligation. In other words, the charge (like a mortgage) automatically ends when the chargor pays up the money or performs the obligation. Unlike in a mortgage, however, the *only* rights and powers given to a chargee lender under a charge are 'rights of recourse' to the security. In other words, the chargee only has rights to apply to the court for the borrower's property interest to be sold if and when the borrower defaults, and to have the money she is owed repaid out of the proceeds. When a charge is deliberately granted by a borrower, it can only be equitable.

In addition, some statutes allow certain classes of debtor to apply to the court to have 'charging orders' imposed on the property interests of people who owe the debtor money or are under a statutory obligation to carry out works etc. The precise effect (and enforceability) of the charges imposed by these charging orders depends on the provisions of the statute governing that kind of charging order.

(f) Equities

Finally, there is a class of miscellaneous equitable property interests, sometimes called 'equities' or 'mere equities'. The most important of these are rights to have a property transaction set aside because, for example, it was procured by fraud, or misrepresentation or undue influence, the right to have a deed rectified on the grounds of mistake, and rights arising out of an estoppel (broadly, the right of someone who has relied on a mistaken belief that she has, or will acquire, a property interest, to be given that property interest or some other form of relief). These 'equities' are all close to the borderline between property interests and personal rights, but it is now established that these 'mere equities' and estoppel rights are property rights, in that they 'attach' to the land to which they relate, so that they are capable of being enforced against anyone who subsequently acquires a property interest in the land.[119] We come across most of them at various points in later chapters, but for present purposes the important point is that they undoubtedly are equitable and not legal property interests.

5.23 Property Interests Which Can be Either Legal or Equitable

(a) Property Interests Arising by Implication, Prescription or Adverse Possession

If we leave aside property interests which can only be equitable, all other kinds of property interest can be either legal or equitable, usually depending on how the interest arose. The first rule is that any property interest whatsoever that arises by implication, prescription or adverse possession (or by any other principles allowing property interests to arise by long use rather than by a deliberate grant) is always legal and never equitable. This is because these methods of acquiring property interests all developed in the common law courts, and they were never affected by equity. The rule is particularly important for freehold interests in land and owner-ship of goods acquired by adverse possession (Chapter 12 *Adverse Possession of Land*) and for many of the non-possessory land use rights we look at in Chapter 13 *Non-Possessory Land Use Rights*, such as easements, profits, rights of common and town and village green rights, which often (in some cases always) arise by implica-tion or long use rather than by deliberate grant.

(b) The Role of Formalities

As far as deliberate transfer or grant of a property interest is concerned, the basic rule in our system, as in most property systems, is that you cannot create or transfer a property interest without going through specified formalities, just as you cannot marry someone without going through a formal marriage ceremony. We look more closely at what these formalities are and why we have them in Chapter 14 *Acquiring Interests Informally*, but for the moment we are interested in what happens when a transferor or grantor does not comply with them. If I hold the legal freehold interest in a piece of land, for example, and I want to transfer it to you, we have to go

---

[119] This is confirmed by s. 116 of the Land Registration Act 2002 as far as they affect registered land, and see also *Mortgage Express* v. *Lambert* [2016] EWCA Civ 555 where Lewison LJ reviews the scope and effect of mere equities at paras. 16–18 and 23–24.

through a two-stage procedure. First, we must sign, in front of a witness, a formal written document called a deed,[120] in which I declare I transfer the freehold to you, and then you must apply to the land registry to have the transfer of the freehold interest into your name recorded in the Land Register. The point we are interested in here is that you do not acquire the legal freehold interest until the end of this process – that is, until you are registered as the holder of it in the Land Register.[121] However, you acquire the *equitable* freehold interest in the land at an earlier date. This will be, at the latest, at the point when we have completed the transfer deed and I have handed it over to you, but it may be earlier, under the principle we look at in (c) below. From that point up until the point when you are registered on the land register as holder of the legal freehold ownership, I hold the legal freehold interest and simultaneously you hold the equitable freehold interest.

It works in the same way, although with a slightly different result, if I am granting you a new property interest rather than transferring my property interest to you. So, for example, if I hold the legal freehold interest in a piece of land and I want to grant you a 99 year legal lease of it, again we must complete a deed stating that I grant you the lease and setting out the terms of the lease. I then hand the deed over to you and you send it to the land registry[122] to have it registered in your name. You do not acquire the *legal* lease unless and until the lease is registered in your name at the land registry, but you will acquire the equitable version of it (i.e. an equitable lease on exactly the same terms as the legal lease we agreed you have) at an earlier point: at the latest when we complete the deed and I transfer it over to you, or earlier under the same principle that applies on a transfer.

(c) Incomplete Formalities and the Rule in *Walsh* v. *Lonsdale*

When I transfer my property interest to you or grant you a new property interest, the transfer or grant is usually preceded by a binding contract between us whereby I agree to transfer/grant the interest to you at a later date and you agree to acquire it then on agreed terms. We saw in para. 5.22(a) that as soon as this contract becomes contractually binding, you acquire an estate contract in the land (or an option to purchase or right of pre-emption) which is a property interest in its own right (an equitable property interest). However, as we noted there, the situation changes when the contractually agreed date for the transfer/grant has passed and you are ready and

---

[120] A deed is a written document that describes itself as a deed, states what the transaction is, and is signed by the parties to the deed and also by a person declaring they witnessed the signatures of the parties to the deed: s. 1 of the Law of Property (Miscellaneous Provisions) Act 1989.

[121] As a separate point, as we see below, registration of you as owner of the legal freehold ownership will make you the owner of it even if it was transferred to you by mistake or as a result of your fraud (e.g. if you tricked me into naming you as the transferee in the transfer deed, when I had intended to transfer it to your sister who actually paid me the purchase price). We come back to this point in para. 5.23(e) below and again in Chapter 16 *Registration* paras. 16.16 and 16.17.

[122] To be precise, in long leases there are two deeds in identical terms – the Lease deed and the Counterpart Lease deed. I keep the Counterpart deed signed by you and you take the Lease deed and send it to the land registry.

willing to carry out your part of the bargain, but I am refusing to complete the necessary formalities.

From that point, as we said in para. 5.22(a), you have a right that equity will immediately grant you an order of specific performance, ordering me to complete the formalities immediately, whenever you ask for it. Equity has a long-standing maxim, or general principle, that, in appropriate circumstances, it will 'treat as done that which ought to be done'. Applying that maxim to these circumstances, Equity reasoned that, since you are now entitled to demand the freehold ownership in the farm at any time (to go back to the example we used in para. 5.22(a)), you should be treated by Equity *as if you already had it.* In other words, from the moment when the contractual date for me to transfer over the freehold interest has passed and you are ready to pay over the money, although *I* am still the legal freehold owner, Equity treats *you* as the 'real' owner of the freehold. So, the freehold property interest has been split into two: from that moment on, I hold the legal freehold property interest, and you hold the equitable property interest.

This equitable rule was established by the Court of Appeal in *Walsh* v. *Lonsdale*,[123] after the amalgamation of the Common law and Equity courts. This was a case of a grant of a new interest rather than a transfer of an existing interest. A mill owner entered into a contract with a prospective tenant by which the mill owner agreed to grant the prospective tenant a lease of a weaving shed for seven years at a rent payable annually in advance. The lease was never granted but the prospective tenant nevertheless moved in and started paying the agreed rent, except that he paid it quarterly in arrears rather than annually in advance. This continued for about three years but then the landlord and tenant fell out. It was common ground that the tenant had a lease, but the issue was what the terms of that lease were. There is an old common law rule (still part of our law) that if a landowner allows someone into possession and accepts rent from them without formally granting them a lease, a legal periodic lease arises by implication of law, the period (i.e. weekly, monthly or annually) and the rent payable under this implied legal periodic lease depending on the frequency with which the rent is actually paid, how much is paid, and how it is paid (i.e. in advance or in arrears).[124] So, if the Court of Appeal in *Walsh* v. *Lonsdale* had adopted that old common law rule, the tenant would have had a *legal yearly lease* at a rent paid annually *in arrears*, but (in accordance with the established rules about terminating periodic leases) the landlord would have been entitled to evict him at the end of any year by giving him notice to quit. However, the court held that that common law rule had to give way to an equitable principle that failure to complete the formalities necessary to grant a legal property interest does not make the new interest invalid. Instead, the lease takes effect as the equitable equivalent as soon as the intended grantee has performed his part of the bargain (or is ready and willing to do so). This is because at that point the grantee becomes entitled to go to equity and demand immediate specific perform- ance of the grantor's obligation to grant him the promised legal property interest, so

---

[123] *Walsh* v. *Lonsdale* (1882) 21 Ch D 9.   [124] See Chapter 17 *Leases* paras. 17.10–17.12.

the Court of Appeal said, and equity will treat as done that which ought to be done. In the case of a lease, the court said, the intended tenant reaches that point if (as in the *Walsh* v. *Lonsdale* case itself) he takes possession and starts to pay rent. Therefore, from that point the tenant had *an equitable lease on the same terms as those in the legal lease he had been promised.* This meant, so the court decided, that the tenant was required to pay the rent annually in advance (but he was also entitled to remain for the rest of the seven year term).

(d) Imposition of a Constructive Trust Relationship

If we go back to the situation where the formalities for a transfer (as opposed to a grant) have not been completed, there is another way of looking at the resulting relationship between the vendor and the purchaser. Instead of saying that the property interest to be transferred has been split into a legal version and an equitable version (the vendor retaining the legal property interest and the purchaser acquiring its equitable equivalent), we can say that equity has imposed a constructive trust on the vendor[125] (sometimes called a 'vendor–purchaser constructive trust'), requiring the vendor to hold the legal property interest on trust for the purchaser. Looked at in this way, we would say that although the vendor continues to hold the legal property interest, the purchaser now holds the entire beneficial interest – in other words, equity requires the vendor to hold the legal interest solely for the benefit of the purchaser.

However, these are essentially two different ways of saying the same thing – either we can say that the purchaser holds the equitable version of the property interest she was promised, or we can say that she holds the beneficial interest under a trust of the legal property interest she was promised. In either case she holds an equitable property interest, and in the vendor–purchaser situation they are identical, and create the same relationship between vendor and purchaser. It has to be said that there is quite a lot of disagreement amongst commentators as to precisely what that relationship is.[126] However, for the present at least, we can put those arguments aside.

(e) The Wrong Person Acquires a Legal Property Interest

The same applies when a legal property interest has ended up in the wrong hands. Suppose I trick you into transferring the freehold ownership of your land into my name (perhaps by persuading you that this will enable me to safeguard your interests whilst you are studying abroad for a few years). The immediate effect of that transfer, in our system, is that I will acquire the legal freehold ownership of the land, but, because I tricked you, you will have a personal right to get it back from me. The same

---

[125] para. 5.25(c) below.
[126] Lord Walker analyses the distinction in *Jerome* v. *Kelly*, fn. 110 above. For a persuasive explanation and analysis of the arguments see P. G. Turner, 'Understanding the constructive trust between vendor and purchaser' (2012) 128 *LQR* 582.

applies in most civil law jurisdictions. However, our system differs from civil law systems in that, at the point when I, the fraudster, acquire the legal freehold interest in your house, you (the victim) simultaneously acquire not only a personal right to get the legal ownership back, but also the equitable freehold interest in the house. In our example, where I acquired your legal property interest fraudulently, we can also adopt the constructive trust analysis and say that I hold the legal freehold interest on trust for you at the outset, and the equitable property interest you acquire is the beneficial interest under that trust.[127] In other words, from the outset I am under a duty (enforceable by you) not only to transfer the legal freehold interest ownership back to you, but also to exercise my legal ownership rights, powers and liberties solely for your benefit until I give you back the legal ownership.[128] Civil law systems can achieve the same end result – that is, can make me give legal ownership back to you, and account to you for any gains I made out of it – but they do so without giving you an interim property interest.

(f) Criteria for Categorising a Right as a Legal Property Interest Are Not All Satisfied

Finally, the Law of Property Act 1925 provide that some kinds of property interest can only be legal property interests if they satisfy specified criteria, and that if they fail to do so they take effect as equitable interests. These are mainly property interests which could have been legal before 1925 but were demoted to equitable status by the 1925 property legislation. The best example is freehold interests in land. After 1925 a freehold interest in land can only be legal if it is absolute and in possession.[129] So, if, for example, I transfer to you the freehold interest in my house 'for you to hold for so long as you continue to live there', you acquire only an equitable freehold interest (because it is conditional, not absolute).[130]

PART V TRUSTS

5.24 What a Trust Is

A full account of trusts law is outside the scope of this book, but trusts are part of the fabric of our property rights system and we need to know the basic principles. Broadly, a trust is a device by which we split the powers and duties to manage a

---

[127] This is sometimes called a bare trust – I acquire just the bare legal title, and you have the entire beneficial interest, which is, in effect the equitable freehold interest.

[128] It would be different if your legal freehold interest had been transferred to me by mistake. You would still (depending on the kind of mistake) have an equitable freehold property interest in the land until I transferred the legal property interest back to you, but I would not necessarily hold the legal interest on trust for you in the meantime (or at least, not unless and until I realised the mistake but failed to transfer the legal interest back to you).

[129] para. 5.16(c) above.

[130] Surprisingly, this would give rise to a quite complicated property rights set-up, and most lawyers would strongly advise me not to do it.

property interest from the right to the benefit of the property interest, vesting the management powers and duties in one person (the trustee) and the right to all benefits in another (the beneficiary). Any kind of property interest (legal or equitable) in any kind of thing can be held on trust. As we noted in para. 5.3(b), the most distinctive feature of a common law trust is that trustee and beneficiary each have separate property interests.

The trusts we are concerned with here are private trusts, that is, private law mechanisms whereby private individuals (human or corporate) hold property interests for the benefit of other private individuals, with duties to manage the property for the benefit of the beneficiaries. These duties are enforceable only by those beneficiaries, and they can do so only by applying to the court to order the trustees to carry out their duties (or appoint new trustees). No other public authority has any right or responsibility to enforce the duties the trustees owe to the beneficiaries, nor even to monitor the trustees' activities. We do recognise public trusts in this jurisdiction but they are quite different. Under a public trust, property is vested in trustees either for a charitable purpose (as opposed to for the benefit of specific people) or for a specific statutory purpose. Charitable trusts are supervised by the Charity Commission, which also has sole responsibility for enforcing the duties of the trustees under the trust. In the case of public statutory purposes, a special-purpose public authority is given those functions by the relevant statute.

Civil law systems have institutions that are functionally similar to private common law trusts, but in the civil law equivalents of the private trust, the beneficiaries have only personal rights against the trustee. They do not hold property interests in the trust assets. We come back to this point in para. 5.32.

5.25 How a Private Trust Arises

(a) Expressly Created Trusts

A private trust can be deliberately created by the holder of a property interest. So for example, if I own shares in UK Oil plc, and I want to retain the benefit of the shares but put them in the name of an offshore company (for any one of a variety of reasons), I can transfer the shares to the offshore company expressly stating that it must hold the shares on trust for me. The offshore company is then the legal owner of the shares, holding them on trust for me, the beneficiary under the trust. Alternatively, if I want to retain control of the shares but transfer the benefit of them to you, I can declare that I hold them on trust for you, leaving me as legal property owner of the shares but now under a duty to hold them solely for your benefit. Or perhaps I might want you to have the benefit of the shares but think it would be better for your mother to have control over them, in which case I can transfer them to her to hold on trust for you.

A trust that is deliberately created in one of these ways is sometimes called an 'express trust', but it is important to appreciate that this tells us only about the way the trust came into existence: it does not tell us anything else about it.

(b) Trusts Automatically Imposed by Operation of Law

Not all trusts are deliberately created. There are statutory provisions which provide that a trust is automatically imposed in certain specified circumstances. The most important are when a legal estate or interest in land is stated to be transferred or granted to a minor[131] or to two or more people concurrently.[132] The purported transfer or grant to a minor takes effect as a declaration of trust made by the transferor/grantor in favour of the minor.[133] So, if I attempt to transfer my legal fee simple interest in my farm to you when you are under 18, the transfer will be ineffective to transfer the legal fee simple from me to you, but it will result in me holding the legal fee simple on trust for you as beneficiary. The transfer or grant of a property interest in land to two or more people does pass the legal interest to them (or if there are more than four of them, to the first four named) but on terms that they hold it on trust for all of them.[134] So, if you and four other friends are granted a lease of a house, the effect will be that the first four named of you hold the legal lease jointly as trustees, to hold on trust for all five of you.

(c) Resulting and Constructive Trusts

In addition a trust can also be imposed on a property interest holder by operation of equitable principles of resulting trust or constructive trust. We see how this works in Part III of Chapter 14 *Acquiring Interests Informally*. Broadly, the position is that a resulting trust will be imposed on a legal owner in favour of someone who has paid all or part of the purchase price of the property, with the intention of acquiring an interest in it. A constructive trust, on the other hand, will be imposed in situations where the courts have decided that it would be unconscionable for the legal owner to keep the beneficial interest to herself. Again, it is important to keep in mind that resulting trusts and constructive trusts are not particular kinds of trust: the 'resulting' or 'constructive' label tells us only how the trust came into existence.

5.26 Characteristics of a Private Trust

(a) What Can be Held on Trust?

Any property interest whatsoever, in any kind of thing, whether tangible or intangible, can be held on trust. It is even possible for equitable property interests to be held on trust. So, if I hold an option to purchase land, I can hold it on trust for you, and equally if I am a beneficiary under a trust of land or money or anything else, I can hold my beneficial interest under the trust on a sub-trust for you.

---

[131] Someone under the age of 18.
[132] S. 1(6) and ss. 34–38 of the LPA 1925 as amended by Sch. 1 of the Trusts of Land and Appointment of Trustees Act 1997.
[133] S. 19 of the LPA 1925 as amended.   [134] S. 34(2) of the LPA 1925 as amended.

(b) The Beneficiaries

Any legal entity can be a beneficiary. Beneficiaries must be legal persons. It is not possible to have a private trust for the benefit of a purpose, as opposed to a legal person, mainly because, as already noted, private trusts are enforceable only by the beneficiaries.[135]

There can be any number of beneficiaries, and there are no restrictions on the ways in which the beneficial interest under the trust may be split between them. For example, it may be split horizontally and with the beneficiaries sharing either jointly, or in equal or unequal but as yet undivided shares. In addition or as well, the beneficial interest may be split vertically into time slices, as, for example, where I hold my legal freehold interest in land on trust for my daughter for her lifetime and when she dies for her adult children in equal shares. When the beneficial interest is split into time slices, the current beneficiary (my daughter in our example) has a present property interest in the asset now held on trust which entitles her to the present benefit of it. The other beneficiaries (in our example, her adult children), each acquires a property interest as soon as the conditions necessary for them to qualify as a beneficiary are satisfied (in our example, as soon as they reach the age of 18). From then on until their mother dies, each of these beneficiaries has a present property interest which gives them a present, enforceable right to benefit in the future (i.e. as soon as their mother dies). When their mother does die, their present right to future benefit are of course converted into present rights to present benefit.

The identity of the beneficiaries must be certain, but only in the sense that it must be possible for the trustees to identify a future beneficiary when the time comes for that beneficiary to acquire a property interest under the trust.

A person may be both a beneficiary under a trust and also a trustee of the trust, but, as we see in (c) below, it is not possible for a sole trustee to hold anything on trust solely for themselves.

(c) The Trustees

Any legal entity can be a trustee. There is no limit on the number of trustees unless the trust is of an interest in land, in which case the maximum number is four. Trustees hold the trust property jointly, and so must act jointly, which means that decisions must be unanimous. A trustee is under a duty to manage the trust property and is personally liable for any breach of trust. She is not entitled to take any benefit from the property interest she holds on trust, she must take on quite time-consuming duties and responsibilities, and she has quite wide discretionary powers. In other words, a trustee is someone who is carrying out a service. So, if you want to set up a trust, you would want to pick as a trustee someone you can trust, and any person you pick is unlikely to agree to take on the job unless either they are a

---

[135] For the possibility of now appointing 'protectors' of a trust, reference must be made to specialised trusts texts.

professional trustee who will charge you a fee for the work, or a friend or family member who is willing to do it as a favour or out of friendship or family obligation.

As already noted, any person can be both beneficiary and trustee under the same trust. However, a person cannot be both the sole trustee and sole beneficiary – the trust collapses, because it makes no sense to say that a person owes a duty to herself to manage the trust property for her own benefit. However, it is not only possible, but also quite common, for two trustees to hold on trust for themselves: this is how many couples own their family home. This works because each of the beneficiaries can sue a trustee who is not herself.

(d) The Settlor

The settlor, who is the person who created the trust, has no further role to play and no interest in the management of the trust or in the trust assets once the trust has been set up, unless the deed setting up the trust says otherwise. In particular, the settlor has no powers to monitor the trustees' activities or enforce their duties or complain about a breach of trust. However, there is nothing (apart from tax disadvantages) to stop the settlor from requiring in the trust deed that the trustees must obtain his consent before taking various actions. Alternatively, the settlor could retain some kind of control by making himself a trustee and/or a beneficiary under the trust. For obvious reasons, all of this applies only to express trusts.

5.27 Terms of the Trust

The rights and remedies of beneficiaries and the powers, duties, liabilities and discretions of trustees depend first on trust legislation, which sets out some mandatory and some default terms of the trust. In the case of a trust of land (i.e. any trust where the trust property is or includes an interest in land) the most important legislation is the Trusts of Land and Appointment of Trustees Act 1996. It contains mandatory provisions about, for example, when and how trustees may delegate their powers and functions. Default provisions of the 1996 Act include a duty imposed on trustees to consult adult beneficiaries and give effect to the wishes of the majority in value of them, so far as practicable, unless express terms of the trust provide otherwise. If the trust is not an express trust, all these statutory provisions will apply to the trust. If, however, the trust was expressly created, the deed setting up the trust will contain additional terms of the trust, which may modify the statutory terms so far as the statute allows that. In other words, express terms of the trust cannot exclude or modify mandatory provisions imposed by statute, but they can exclude or modify statutory default terms. General fiduciary principles also apply to all private trusts, however created.

5.28 Control Over the Actions of the Trustees

Management of the trust property by the trustees is on the lines of benevolent dictatorship. The trustees must act in the best interests of the beneficiaries, but (unless the trust deed or statutory provisions say otherwise) they are under no duty to act in accordance with their wishes or even consult them. If a beneficiary feels aggrieved by any action (or inaction) of the trustees there are two options. If the beneficiary thinks the trustees are in breach of any of their duties under the trust she can apply to the court, which has a wide discretion to order the trustees to remedy the breach. Alternatively, all the beneficiaries acting together can, if they are all adults and together they represent 100 per cent of the beneficial interest, apply to the court to end the trust and transfer the trust property to the beneficiaries in agreed shares.[136] The beneficiaries are entitled to do this at any time and regardless of whether they have any complaints about the trustees, and even if it contradicts the wishes or intentions of the settlor expressed in the trust deed.[137] This is because equity regards the beneficiaries as the collective equitable owners of the trust property.

5.29 Nature of the Beneficiary's Interest

This is a vexed question. The interest of a beneficiary in property held on trust for her is clearly a property interest by the criteria adopted in this book (it is an interest which is transmissible,[138] and capable of enforcement against third parties), and its status as a property interest has been re-affirmed by the Supreme Court in *Akers v. Samba Financial Group* [2017] UKSC 6. Nevertheless, many commentators disagree, arguing that the beneficial interest under a trust is more properly regarded as either consisting only of personal rights enforceable against the trustee, or of 'rights against the trustees' rights'.[139] This is not the place to go into these arguments, but they do perhaps help to explain why some lawyers (and sometimes the courts) argue against expansion of the circumstances in which the rights of beneficiaries are enforceable against third parties. We look at this issue in some detail in Part III of Chapter 15 *Enforceability and Priority of Property Interests*.

5.30 Enforceability of Beneficial Interests Under a Trust Against Third Parties

We said in our working definition of property in Chapter 1 that an interest is a property interest if it is enforceable against third parties generally, as well as against

---

[136] This is known as the rule in *Saunders* v. *Vautier* 41 ER 482; (1841) Cr & Ph 240.

[137] Or in the will of the settlor, if, as sometimes happens, the trust is set up by the settlor's will rather than by a deed he made during his lifetime.

[138] All transmissible interests are property interests (transmissible meaning here an interest that is not personal to the holder, in that it can pass automatically from one person to another, for example on death, rather than an interest which is personal to the holder, even though it can in some circumstances be transferred to someone else be), although not all property interests are transmissible (e.g. property rights you have by virtue of your status, such as the rights in your family home under Part IV of the Family Law Act 1996: Chapter 6 *New Property Interests and the Numerus Clausus* para. 6.11).

[139] For an excellent short summary of the differing views, see Michael Bridge et al., *The Law of Personal Property* (2nd edn, London: Sweet & Maxwell, 2018) para. 14.002; see also, amongst the vast literature, Jesse Wall, 'The functional-formal impasse in (trust) property' (2017) *International Journal of Law in Context* 437; Richard Nolan, 'Dispositions and equitable property' (2017) *Law Quarterly Review* 357 (on *Akers*); and Lionel Smith, 'Scottish trusts in the common law' (2013) *Edinburgh Law Review* 283.

the state. We look at the rules about enforceability and priority of beneficial interests under a trust in Chapters 15 *Enforceability and Priority of Property Interest* and 16 *Registration* but here we should draw attention to two limitations on enforceability which are particularly important.

(a) Narrower Range of Enforceability

The first limitation is the one we have already noted as shared by all equitable property interests. This is that they are not enforceable against the whole world, but only against a limited class of third parties. We summarised the relevant rules in para. 5.19 above; full accounts are in Chapter 15 and Chapter 16.

(b) Overreaching

The second limitation, however, applies only to beneficial interests under trusts.[140] This is the doctrine of overreaching, which we look at in detail in Chapter 15 *Enforceability and Priority of Property Interests* and Chapter 16 *Registration*. As we see in Part III of Chapter 15, overreaching is an antiquated doctrine modified in 1925, which now operates in circumstances very different from those envisaged in 1925. The basic principle is that, since the trustees have a duty to manage the wealth represented by the current trust assets, they must be free to sell and mortgage the trust assets and replace them with new ones as they think appropriate. This means that they must be free to sell and mortgage current trust assets free from the property interests of the beneficiaries, otherwise third parties would not be willing to buy or take mortgages over trust assets. Overreaching is a mechanism that allows this to happen. The rule is that when trustees sell or mortgage a trust asset, the equitable interests of the beneficiaries in that asset under the trust are 'overreached', meaning that they automatically shift from the trust asset to the proceeds of sale (or the mortgage loan, in the case of a mortgage), which the trustees now hold as a new asset of the trust in place of the one that has been sold or mortgaged. Under current law, this overreaching process happens automatically on any sale, mortgage or other disposition, provided that the money acquired by the sale/mortgage is paid to at least two trustees.[141] This made sense when most trusts were settlements of family wealth, and the whole idea was that the trustees should have the power to decide how the wealth should be invested and be under a duty to keep the investments under review to achieve the maximum benefit for the beneficiaries. Also of course, it made trust land more freely marketable, because the trustees were able to assure buyers and lenders that they need not concern themselves with the interests of the beneficiaries. And provided the exchange money was paid to at least two of the trustees, to hold on the same trusts, the beneficiaries were not disadvantaged, because they were not much concerned whether their interests were held in land or in money, because they were generally interested only in the monetary value of their trust interests.

---

[140] With a few exceptions that we can ignore for the present.
[141] Or to a 'trust corporation', which is rare.

However, the problem is that the trusts landscape has changed dramatically since 1925, and overreaching has not been adapted to fit current circumstances. The vast proportion of trusts are now trusts of family homes or other domestic property, and many of them are not deliberately created but arise automatically because they are co-owned or because a constructive trust is imposed by equity on the legal title holder requiring them to hold the legal title on trust for other beneficiaries living in and/or contributing towards the costs of the property. Often the people involved do not even realise that the legal owners are trustees, and in nearly all cases the beneficiaries expect to be consulted about, and have some say in, decisions about whether and when the property should be sold. Also, the old two-trustee rule[142] is hopeless as a safeguard against the modern professional land frauds involving trusts we come across in Chapter 15 *Enforceability and Priority of Property Interests* and Chapter 16 *Registration*. So, overreaching causes real problems in the modern law, as we see in Part III of Chapter 15, and also in Chapter 16.

5.31 Relationship Between Trusts and Equitable Property Interests

All interests under a trust are equitable property interests. But not all equitable property interests give rise to a trust. So, for example, if I grant you a long lease of my house and you fail to register it at the land registry, you will acquire only an equitable lease,[143] but neither I nor anyone else holds anything on trust for you. Similarly, if you acquire a restrictive covenant over my land, or an equity by estoppel over it,[144] I do not hold anything on trust for you.

5.32 Trusts in Civil Law Jurisdictions

Many property rights systems outside the common law world have property holding devices which are functionally similar to the common law trust, in that they require the apparent owner of a property interest to exercise her ownership functions only for the benefit of someone else. Examples include the Scottish trust, the German *Treuhand* and the French *fiducie*. However, in these and other similar institutions the beneficiary has to rely on contractual or personal rights to enforce the apparent owner's obligations: he, the beneficiary, does not have a property interest in the trust assets. The distinctive feature of the common law trust, as we have seen, is that the beneficiary *does* have a property interest in the trust assets. In the civil law trust or

---

[142] Based on the optimistic assumption that, whilst there is always the possibility that a settlor setting up a trust might choose as trustee one person who turned out to be dishonest, he would be very unlucky if two of them were.

[143] para. 5.23(c) above.

[144] para. 5.22 (c) and (e). A trust may, however, arise in relation to some of the other equities referred to in para. 5.22(f), e.g. if you have a right to have a transfer of your freehold interest into my name set aside on grounds of fraud or undue influence, I hold it on constructive trust for you as soon as I become aware of my duty to give it back to you.

equivalent, the 'trustee' is the full owner of the trust property, consistently with the civil law notion of unitary ownership which cannot be split into separate interests. However, typically the trustee owns the trust property in a different capacity from the capacity in which she owns her own property: the trust property she owns is ring-fenced, so that it is not available to her creditors.[145] In civil law terms, the trustee owns both her own assets and the trust assets, but they form different 'patrimonies'. Gretton and Reid explain what this means in relation to the Scottish trust:

> [A] patrimony is the totality of a person's assets and liabilities. The general principle is: one person, one patrimony. But in a trust, the trustee has two patrimonies. There is the ordinary, or general, patrimony. And there is the special patrimony of the trust. Each has its own assets and liabilities. A patrimony is like a suitcase, with two compartments, one for assets and the other for liabilities. A trustee has two suitcases. If an asset is sold, the asset leaves the suitcase but the price replaces it. The same happens in reverse if an asset is purchased. Again, if an asset generates income (for example rent from land, or dividends from shares, or interest from a loan) the income forms part of the same patrimony. The trustee is under a duty of segregation, to ensure that the two patrimonies remain distinct, so that there can never be any question to which patrimony an asset belongs. If, as commonly happens, there are two or more trustees, they hold the suitcase together . . .[146]

Similar analyses can be used to explain the French *fiducie* and the German *Treuhand*,[147] but whilst the Scottish trust strongly resembles the common law trust in other respects, the *fiducie* and the *Treuhand* are very different (and also significantly different from each other). Probably the most important difference for our purposes is that in the common law trust the settlor drops out of the picture as soon as he creates the trust, as we saw in para. 5.26(d): the effect of the creation of the trust is that the settlor makes an outright and irrevocable transfer of all his rights and interests in the trust property to the trustee.[148] This does not happen in either the *fiducie* or the *treuhand*, which are both revocable in certain circumstances, and where the settlor equivalent (the *constituent* or the *Treugeber*) retains significant rights and powers.[149]

---

[145] In Honoré's terms, the civil law trustee's ownership of the trust property lacks the characteristic of 'liability for execution' we noted in para. 5.11 above.

[146] Gretton and Steven, *Property, Trusts and Succession*, fn. 60 above, p. 362. On the following page all of this is set out in a set of diagrams which are not to be missed. See also Smith, 'Scottish trusts in the common law', fn. 139 above, at p. 285.

[147] Lionel Smith (ed.), *Re-imagining the Trust: Trusts in Civil Law* (2012); van Erp and Akkermans, *Property Law*, fn 54 above, esp. para. 6.4 (the Treuhand in Germany) and pp. 571–580, esp. pp. 573–574 (the more recently established *fiducie* in France). The common law trust, the *Treuhand* and the *fiducie* are compared in detail in van Erp and Akkermans, Ch. 6. There is a good comparative overview on pp. 611–615.

[148] If he declares himself as trustee, the transfer is, in effect, of the trust assets from himself in his personal capacity to himself as trustee – i.e. he loses, irrevocably, the beneficial interest in the trust assets, which is now held instead by the beneficiary.

[149] Van Erp and Akkermans, *Property Law*, fn 54 above, pp. 611–615.

PART VI FRAMEWORK OF PROPERTY INTERESTS IN LAND IN ENGLAND AND WALES

5.33 Property Interest Holders

We end this chapter by giving a brief taxonomy of property interests in land which are recognised in the law of England and Wales.

The first point to make is that there are some property interests in land in English and Welsh law which have to be held by a legal entity (i.e. an adult human person, or an artificial legal person such as a corporate body). These include the freehold and leasehold interests in land which are the equivalent of 'ownership' interests in our system. This means that neither a community (i.e. a group of people defined by reference to one or more shared characteristics, such as locality and/or shared resource use[150]) nor the public can hold these property interests *directly*. This can give a misleading impression that all land in England and Wales which is not owned by the state is privately owned. However, it is important to appreciate that legal entities holding ownership-type interests in England and Wales are not necessarily private owners. Communities can (and do) hold ownership-type property interests indirectly. This is done by having the legal title to the property interest put in the name of a legal entity owned and controlled by the community – usually a corporate body, but sometimes trustees. This kind of property holding by communities is therefore more properly categorised as communal property rather than private property. Similarly, legal entities holding property interests such as freehold and leasehold interests in land may be required to hold them for the benefit of the public, or for specified public purposes, and not for their own benefit. Again, it would be misleading to regard these interests as private rather than public property interests. We look at these questions in more detail in Chapter 8 *Property Interest Holders*.

In addition, there are other kinds of property interest in land which *can* be held directly by communities, and others which can be held directly by the public. Some (although not all) of them are of ancient origin, although they are now mostly regulated by statute. We see how all this works in Chapter 8, but here, where we are concerned just with sketching out the framework of property interests in land in England and Wales, we merely identify which property interests can only be held by a legal entity, which can be held directly by a community, and which can be held directly by the public.

5.34 Possessory Interests

When we look at the taxonomy of property interests in land in England and Wales, our starting point is the distinction between property interests which give a right to possession of the land and those which do not. We look at possessory property interests in this paragraph, and at non-possessory property interests in paras. 5.35 to 5.39.

---

[150] See further Part V of Chapter 8 *Property Interest Holders*.

Possession is a technical term, meaning intentional physical control of land or of a tangible thing.[151] As far as land is concerned, the only possessory interests in English law are freehold ownership and leases.[152] As already noted, freehold ownership and leases can only be held by legal entities. They cannot be held directly by communities or by the public.

(a) Freehold Ownership

As we have already seen, a freehold owner of land has a right to take and remain in physical control of the land, to the exclusion of all others, for a perpetual duration. The freehold owner is free to transfer his interest to anyone else, both during his lifetime and also by will when he dies. As we saw in Part III of this chapter, in this respect and in all other material respects freehold ownership is the same as civil law ownership of land. It is also, for all practical purposes, the same as private ownership of things other than land in English law.

(b) Leases

A lease is, by definition, a grant of a right to possession of land for a limited duration. Leases are also called tenancies. There is now no longer any difference between a lease and a tenancy, so either term can be used. In practice, we tend to use the term 'lease' when we are talking about a long lease and 'tenancy' for shorter leases. If the lease is a long lease, we often refer to the lessee as 'the leaseholder' or 'the leasehold owner'.

Leases are also alienable, although the right to alienate is often restricted by the lease terms imposed by the landlord when the lease is granted.

However, the duration of a lease has to be limited. If it is a legal lease it must be either for a fixed period, or for a periodic term (weekly, monthly, yearly, etc.).[153] Short leases are very common, but so too are leases for a very long duration. In particular, for reasons we look at in Chapter 17 *Leases*, it is common for long residential leases of flats (and sometimes houses) to be for 99 or even 999 years. In these cases the lessee is likely to think of herself as, and be generally regarded as, the owner of the flat (hence the use of the term 'leasehold owner'). There are, however, significant legal differences between a freehold owner and a leasehold owner, as we see in Chapter 17 *Leases*.

---

[151] We look more closely at what this means, and at the significance of possession in our property system, in Chapter 11 *Possession and Title* and Chapter 12 *Adverse Possession of Land*.

[152] Technically, legal mortgagees of land are also entitled to possession of the land, but that is only because in English law a legal mortgagee of land (who holds a legal property interest in the land called a 'charge by way of legal mortgage') is given by statute all the protection, powers and remedies it would have had if it had a long lease of the property: see s. 87 of the Law of Property Act 1925. In practice mortgagees of land rarely take possession of the land unless they have to do so in order to enforce their security, and usually there is a term in the mortgage, enforceable by the owner, prohibiting them from doing so in any other circumstances.

[153] There are other kinds of tenancy – tenancies at will and tenancies at sufferance – which are also legal, but they are comparatively rare and we can postpone dealing with them until we get to Chapter 17.

(c) Relationship Between Freehold Ownership and Lease

As we saw in Part III of this chapter, nearly all land in England and Wales has a freehold owner. The only exceptions are the comparatively few pieces of land which are held by the Crown for its own purposes,[154] and the even fewer ones which the Crown holds as a repository because the freehold ownership interest has ended and has not yet been replaced by a new one.[155]

A lease comes into existence when a freehold owner grants her right to possession of the land to someone else for a limited duration. When the lease ends (for whatever reason) the right to possession automatically reverts back to the freehold owner. We look at leases in detail in Chapter 17, but for present purposes the point is that any freehold owner can grant a lease of all or part of her land, and any lessee can then grant a sublease to someone else of all or part of that land. The sublease must be for a shorter duration than the lease, because it is carved out of the lease. The sublessee can then in his turn grant his right to possession to a sub-underlessee, and so on *ad infinitum*. In other words, a hierarchy of leases can exist in the same land at the same time, and the lessee at the bottom of the hierarchy is the person entitled to possession of the land for as long as her lease lasts.

(d) Possessory Interests and Use

If you have a right to possession of the land, you are allowed to use it in any way you want (or even not use it at all) *except* in so far as the use is restricted by specific limitations. Freehold owners are subject only to the limitations we look at in Chapter 10 *Limitations on Property*. These include public law restrictions imposed by, for example, planning or environmental law, and private law restrictions enforceable by neighbours, for example through the law of private nuisance or because they have restrictive covenants over your land. Lessees are subject to the same limitations, and also to any additional ones, enforceable by their landlord, which the landlord has imposed as a term of the lease. These will usually include a restriction on the use which the lessee may make of the land (for example, restricting it to use as a dwelling house, or a shop).

Holders of non-possessory property interests in land, on the other hand, either have only specific, limited rights to use the land, or no use rights at all.

(e) Relationship Between Possessory and Non-Possessory Interests

Because all land is held by a freehold owner, non-possessory interests in land will necessarily be exercisable over land which has a freehold owner and possibly also a lessee. The same applies in civil law systems, and it is worth noting that in civil law systems (including Scotland) non-possessory interests in land are often referred to as *iura in re aliena* – that is, rights in a thing belonging to someone else.[156]

---

[154] That is, royal demesne land: para. 5.15 above.
[155] This is land which has escheated to the Crown: para. 5.18 above.
[156] In the civil law leases (if they are recognised as property interests at all) are also regarded as *iure in re aliena*, for obvious reasons.

5.35 Non-Possessory Land Use Rights as Property Interests

Our first category of non-possessory property interests is made up of non-possessory land use rights. We look at these interests in detail in Chapter 13 *Non-Possessory Land Use Rights*. They are property interests which allow the interest holder either (i) to do something specific on someone else's land (such as walk across it), or (ii) to take some natural produce from the land (perhaps pick apples from apple trees on someone else's land), or (iii) to restrict the use of someone else's land in some other way (for example by restricting the kind of building they can erect on their land, or the kind of use they can make of their land).

Some kinds of non-possessory land use property interests can be held only by legal entities, others can only be held directly by communities, and others directly by the public.

(a) Individual Non-Possessory Land Use Property Interests: Easements, Profits and Restrictive Covenants

These property interests are, broadly, the equivalent of civil law *servitudes*. In the law of England and Wales non-possessory land use property interests are occasionally referred to as servitudes too, but this can mislead us into underestimating the differences between the two systems.

It is important to appreciate that in English and Welsh law, with a few exceptions, a non-possessory land use right held by an individual over someone else's land can only be a property interest if the rights holder owns a separate piece of neighbouring land, and if the right is *appurtenant* to that neighbouring land. We look at the meaning and significance of *appurtenance* in Chapter 13 *Non-Possessory Land Use Rights*, but for present purposes we can take it to mean that the right to use someone else's land (the *servient tenement* – i.e. the burdened land) must benefit neighbouring land belonging to the right-holder (the *dominant tenement*, or benefitted land). So, for example, if you and I are the freehold owners of two adjoining houses, and you grant me a right of way across the drive on your land, the right of way will only be a property interest (an 'easement') if it benefits my land in some way. The benefit might perhaps be that the right of way gives me a more convenient way to get from my garage to the public road outside our respective houses, or that it gives me a short cut from my house to a lane running alongside the back of your garden. Assuming the right of way does benefit my land in that kind of way, it becomes a property interest. What this means is that the benefit of the right of way becomes attached to my land (the dominant or benefitted land) and the burden of it becomes attached to your land (the servient or burdened land), so that *any* person who at any time is the freehold owner of my land can enforce the right against whoever at that time is the freehold owner of your land.[157]

---

[157] The same applies as against and as between leasehold owners.

Easements

A right held by a freehold or leasehold owner of land to do something specific on someone else's land is called an *easement.* The categories of easement are quite tightly controlled by the courts, as we see in Chapter 13,[158] and they must always be appurtenant to benefitted land owned by the right holder. Most easements are positive, in that they allow the owner of the dominant land to go on to the burdened land and do something on it. A right of way is the paradigm example. However, there are a few anomalous negative easements. These easements are negative in that they restrict what the burdened owner can do with the burdened land. The right to light is a good example of a negative easement: in English and Welsh law if I have a right to light over your land, it means only that I can prevent you from doing something on your land which would obstruct the natural light reaching any windows in the buildings on my land.[159]

Profits

A *profit* is a right to take a specified kind of natural produce (for example, gravel or hay) from someone else's land. The full technical term is *profit à prendre.* The paradigm profit is a right to graze animals on someone else's land: if I have a right to graze ten sheep on your field, it means I have the right to put my ten sheep on your field so that they can take the grass or other vegetation from your land by eating it.

A profit can give the profit holder the exclusive right to take that particular kind of produce from the burdened land. That kind of profit is a simple private property interest held by an individual.[160] Alternatively, two or more different people can be given rights to take that kind of produce from the burdened land in common with each other. The right is then called a *right of common,* and the community of rights holders together hold a communal property interest in the burdened land, as we see in (b) below. There are also a few public property rights to take produce from a particular source: see (c) below.

Most, but not all, profits held by an individual have to be appurtenant to benefitted land owned by the right-holder.

Restrictive Covenants

As we saw in para. 5.22(c), a restrictive covenant is a promise made by a freehold owner to a neighbouring freehold owner *not to do* something on the covenantor's land.[161] Again, it is enforceable as a restrictive covenant only if it benefits the covenantee's land. In other words, the right to enforce a restrictive covenant over someone else's land can only be a property interest if it is appurtenant to benefitted land owned by the right holder. A restrictive covenant must be restrictive, in the sense that it prohibits the covenantor from doing something: it must not require the

---

[158] Chapter 13 *Non-Possessory Land Use Rights* paras. 13.8–13.10.   [159] para. 13.11.
[160] We call that kind of profit an *exclusive* profit, but historically it was called a *sole* or *several* profit.
[161] In this respect it is the same as a negative easement, which is one of the many illogicalities in our categorisation of particular use rights in English and Welsh law: we come back to this point in Chapter 13 *Non-Possessory Land Use Rights.*

covenantor to do something positive. Positive covenants are not property interests in the law of England and Wales.

Statutory Use Rights

There are also a few anomalous statutory rights to make a particular use of someone else's land or to occupy someone else's land which are recognised as property interests. They include *wayleaves*, which are rights for utility companies (providers of services such as water, electricity, telecommunications, etc.) to install, maintain, repair, replace and use their infrastructure on private land.[162] They also include the *home rights* under Part IV of the Family Law Act 1996, which we look at in Chapter 6 *New Property Interests and the Numerus Clausus* (the rights of spouses and civil partners to occupy premises owned by the other spouse/civil partner and which have been or were intended to be the couple's matrimonial/civil partnership home). Many statutory use rights are by their nature personal to the holder of the interest, and therefore are not alienable. Nevertheless, they are enforceable against everyone who acquires any property interest in the land and therefore are categorisable as property interests.

(b) Communal Non-Possessory Land Use Rights

Some non-possessory land use rights can be held by a community as such (i.e. the property interest is held directly by a group of people in a defined community, each with a right to use the resource in common with each other) rather than by a legal entity which represents them. The distinctive feature of these communal use rights is the rules regulating their communal use. Sometimes they are imposed, policed and enforced by an outside body (for example, the owner of the land over which the use rights are exercisable). In other cases the community is self-regulating, in other words the members of the community devise or evolve, and also police and enforce, their own regulatory rules for themselves. In yet others, there is a mix of outside regulation and self-regulation. Communal use rights of this nature include *rights of common, town and village green rights* and the rights of tenants to use common spaces in *multi-tenanted developments*. We outline these use rights here, and then look at them in more detail in later chapters.

Rights of Common and Common Land

As already noted in (a) above, when two or more people have rights to take a particular kind of produce from the same burdened land in common with each other, the rights are called *rights of common,* and the land over which they are exercisable is called *common land*. Communal grazing rights are the most well-known examples of rights of common, and (like most other jurisdictions in the world) we have recognised them as property rights in this jurisdiction for centuries. In the present law, these communally exercisable rights of common are often self-

---

[162] For an interesting account see Norman Hutchinson and Jeremy Rowan-Robinson, 'Utility wayleaves: Time for reform' (2001) *Journal of Planning & Environment Law* 1247.

regulating, with or without input from the landowner, but they also exist within a statutory framework, now provided by the Commons Act 2006. Because of their agricultural and environmental importance, other public authorities are also involved in their regulation. In addition, the public has rights of access over all common land under the Countryside and Rights of Way Act 2000. We look at rights of common and common land in Part V of Chapter 13 *Non-Possessory Land Use Rights*.

Town and Village Green Rights

The inhabitants of a locality have the right to make recreational use of any land which is registered as a town or village green. Any land can become a town or village green if the local inhabitants can prove that they have used it for lawful sports and pastimes as of right for at least 20 years. The land does not have to be green, or in a town or village – greens are often derelict post-industrial land or left-over spaces in residential or commercial estates. Once the land is registered as a green the local inhabitants can go on using it for any sports and pastimes so far as compatible with the landowner going on using it as she was using it before registration: see further Part VI of Chapter 13 *Non-Possessory Land Use Rights*. Like rights of common, town and village green rights have been recognised in England for centuries but they were put on a statutory footing by the Commons Registration Act 1965 and are now regulated mainly by the Commons Act 2006. There have been many political objections to the increased re-assertion of town and village green rights in modern times, and in recent years the statutory provisions have been (and are still being) hotly contested in the courts, as we see in Part VI of Chapter 13.

Rights of Tenants etc. to Use Common Spaces in Multi-tenanted Developments and Condominiums

When developers build structures designed for multiple occupiers, with the intention that each occupier will have exclusive use of her own unit but will have rights to use common space in the development in common with all the other occupiers, the property rights structure usually adopted in England and Wales is that of landlord and tenant. The way it works is that the freehold interest of the whole of the land (including the buildings on it) will be held by a legal entity, who will grant a lease of each unit to each occupier. The leases may be short term or periodic leases, or very long leases, typically 99 or 999 years in some kinds of residential development. The common landlord may be a commercial organisation, and it usually will be if the units are shops, or other commercial units. If the units are residential, the landlord may be a commercial organisation, but it may also be a social landlord or a corporate entity owned and controlled by all the tenants (in which case we have communal freehold ownership held via a bespoke corporate entity, of the kind noted in para. 5.33 above). We look at these kinds of leasehold structures in Chapter 17 *Leases*, where we also consider why it is that we use them in this jurisdiction when most other common law and civil law jurisdictions use condominiums instead. For present purposes, however, the important point is the communal use rights held by the tenants. Sometimes the tenants' communal use of these spaces is regulated by the landlord, or by a management company employed by the landlord. In other cases it is regulated by the tenants themselves, either informally or by more formalised rules that the tenants have evolved or devised for themselves. And in yet other cases, there will be a mix of landlord regulation and self-regulation. We look at these tenants' communal use rights, and at the equivalent rights held by condominium owners, in paras. 8.15 and 8.23 of Chapter 8 *Property Interest Holders* and in Part III of Chapter 17 *Leases*.

(c) Public Non-Possessory Land Use Rights

The law in England and Wales recognises a wide range of public non-possessory land use rights. They are different from other public rights to use space in a particular way, such as rights of assembly, in that they attach to specific areas of land. This is what makes them classifiable as property rights: they are enforceable rights over a specific piece of land which remain attached to the land, in the sense that they are enforceable against anyone who subsequently acquires an interest in the land. Here we do no more than list the most well-known ones. They include public rights of way over defined routes on privately or publicly owned land, and over public highways; public fishing rights in waters of various categories; public navigation rights over navigable waters; rights of access to the coastline under Marine and Coastal Access Act 2009; public foreshore rights (although there is some dispute over their scope and status, as we see in para. 7.23 of Chapter 7 *Objects of Property Rights* and paras. 8.29 and 8.31 of Chapter 8 *Property Interest Holders*); the public 'right to roam' under the Countryside and Rights of Way Act 2000, which gives the public the right to enter and remain on any 'access' land for the purposes of outdoor recreation; and public recreational rights over various different kinds of public open space, under a wide variety of statutes.

5.36 Regulatory Licences

These are also non-possessory land use rights, but they are unusual in that they are granted by a public body or regulatory authority, and they licence the grantee to use a specific resource in a specific way. The essential feature of these rights – usually referred to as regulatory licences – is that they are granted as part of a regulatory scheme which makes it illegal for anyone to use that resource at all, or in that way, except in accordance with the terms of a licence which they have been granted by the regulatory authority. There are some ancient examples of such regulatory licences, such as rights to hold fairs and markets. However, this category of property interest has been revived in modern times and is now of considerable commercial and environmental importance, for the reasons we considered in Chapter 3 *Allocation of Property Rights* para. 3.5. Modern examples include Water Abstraction Licences, fishing licences, spectrum licences and petroleum exploration licences. We look at some of them in Chapter 6 *New Property Interests and the Numerus Clausus* para. 6.12.

5.37 Security Interests

In this jurisdiction we recognise a number of different kinds of security interest, including mortgages, charges, liens and pledges (sometimes called pawns). All of these are property interests. Mortgages, charges and equitable liens can be granted or imposed over any property interest in land. Pledges/pawns probably cannot: typically they are made by transferring possession of goods (usually personal belongings or household goods) to a lender to secure repayment of a short-term loan.

(a) Essential Features of a Security Interest

The essence of any proprietary security interest is that it is a subsidiary property interest which is granted by a property interest holder over her own property interest to another person, *for the purpose of securing repayment of money (or performance of some other obligation) which she owes to the other person.* The essential feature is that the security interest over the grantor's property interest automatically ends as soon as the money is repaid (or the secured obligation is performed), and if the grantor does not repay etc at the agreed time, the security interest holder can have the secured property seized and sold and use the proceeds of sale to pay off the debt in priority to all other debts owed by that debtor. So, for example, a mortgage (which is a particular kind of property interest which is typically granted by the freehold or leasehold owner of land, or the owner of any other thing) is a property interest granted by the owner over her ownership interest to someone (typically a bank) who has lent her money. The mortgage is a subsidiary property interest 'carved out of' her ownership interest, in much the same way as a lease is 'carved out of' a freehold or leasehold ownership interest. However, unlike a lease, which has a fixed or determinate length, a mortgage interest continues until the owner repays the money owed, or (if she fails to repay at the due time) until the bank exercises its rights and powers under the mortgage to sell her ownership interest and take what it is owed out of the proceeds of sale.

(b) Mortgages

We are not covering mortgages in any detail in this book, and this is intended to provide only a brief outline of the nature of modern mortgages of land and how they fit into the general structure of property interests in land in England and Wales.

As we saw in para. 5.22(d) above, the modern form of mortgage used to mortgage legal freehold and leasehold interests in land in England and Wales is a '*charge by way of legal mortgage*', nearly always abbreviated to 'legal mortgage'. The charge by way of legal mortgage was created by the Law of Property Act 1925 to remedy some of the inherent defects in the property transfer mortgage we described in para. 5.22 (d), which can no longer be used for mortgaging interests in land after 1925. Unfortunately, in order to understand the nature of the charge by way of legal mortgage, we need to know about an interim form of mortgage for mortgaging freehold and leasehold interests in land which was also introduced by the Law of Property Act 1925, to be used as an optional alternative to the charge by way of legal mortgage. This interim form was a *mortgage by demise*, which gave the mortgagee lender a 3,000 year lease of the mortgagor borrower's freehold interest (or if granted over a mortgagor borrower's leasehold interest, a sub-lease just shorter that the mortgagor's lease). This long lease automatically ended when the secured debt or obligation was paid or performed. The idea was that under the mortgage by demise, the mortgagor borrower remained the legal owner, even though the mortgagee lender was given a substantial property interest which gave it extensive rights over the mortgaged property until the debt was paid, and highly effective rights to manage or sell it if the mortgagor borrower defaulted.

The mortgage by demise never really caught on, and it is now obsolete and can no longer be used at all for mortgaging freeholds and leaseholds which are registered at the land registry. But, sadly, we cannot forget about it because the surviving form of land mortgage, the charge by way of legal mortgage, is defined in the Law of Property Act 1925 solely in terms of the mortgage by demise: by s. 87 the mortgagee under a charge by way of legal mortgage has 'the same protection, powers and remedies' as it would have had if it had a mortgage by demise. These rights, powers and remedies have since been modified to some extent by statute, and they can also be modified (but again, only to some extent) by the contractual terms of the mortgage. Also, we have to remember that, even under a modern mortgage, the mortgagor borrower still has the equity of redemption we described in para. 5.22(d) of this chapter. Nevertheless, under a modern legal mortgage of a freehold or leasehold interest in land, the mortgagee lender has extensive rights and powers over the mortgaged property. It can take possession of it, manage it by appointing a receiver, sell it and in some circumstances even grant leases of it, so far as required to protect or enforce the security. For precise details reference should be made to mortgage textbooks.

(c) Charges, charging orders and liens

We looked briefly at charges (and charging orders, which take effect as charges) in para. 5.22(e). Liens relevant to property interests in land include rights that solicitors and others have to retain possession of title deeds or documents to secure payment of fees charged for acting for the property interest holder in relation to the property; and rights for some creditors in some specific circumstances (most notably unpaid sellers of land who have transferred their title but not yet been paid in full) to have the property sold and their debts paid off in priority to all other debts. In other words, the primary remedy of a person holding a charge, a charging order or a lien over a property interest in land is to apply to the court to have the property interest sold, and to have the debt repaid out of the sale proceeds in priority to all other debts owed by the debtor whose property interest has been sold.

5.38 Proprietary Rights to Acquire Property Interests

These are the equitable property interests we noted in para. 5.22(a), that is, contractual rights to acquire property interests, which themselves have proprietary effect: Estate contracts, options to purchase or renew, rights of pre-emption.

5.39 'Equities': Mere Equities and Equities by Estoppel

These are the equitable property interests we noted in para. 5.22(f) under the heading 'equities', that is, rights to set aside a land transaction or a deed on the grounds of misrepresentation, undue influence or fraud, rights to set aside an unconscionable bargain, rights to rectify deeds, and estoppel rights. It is now established that these 'mere equities' and estoppel rights are property rights, in that they 'attach' to the land to which they relate, so that they are capable of being enforced against anyone who subsequently acquires a property interest in the land.[163]

What these property rights have in common is that they are property rights in land which arise out of some kind of misconduct or unconscionable behaviour by a pre-existing holder of property interests in the land, or are otherwise imposed on the pre-existing property interest holder so as to do justice to the claimant. Rights like these exist in most property rights systems but in civil law systems they are generally treated as purely personal claims against the pre-existing property interest holder, rather than (as in our system) property rights attaching to the land in their own right.

5.40 Trusts

To complete the framework we should recall from Part V of this chapter that in English and Welsh law any property interest in land held by an individual can be held by that individual on trust for one or more beneficiaries. If it is, the legal property interest is held by the individual as trustee, and the beneficiary or beneficiaries hold appropriate equitable property interests in the land.

RECOMMENDED READING

This chapter takes a detailed look at ownership in Parts II and III, and the following readings should help to fill that out. The rest of the chapter concentrates on providing an overview of the property interests and property principles applicable to land in England and Wales which we look at in later chapters. This overview is intended to provide a framework to support later chapters, and it needs no additional reading at this stage. We have, however, added at the end of the list of readings here some additional references for those who want to take a closer look at the historical background and at comparisons with Scotland.

Margaret Davies, *Property: Meanings, Histories, Theories*, (Abingdon: Routledge-Cavendish, 2007) pp. 57–71.

Jane Baron, 'Rescuing the bundle-of-rights metaphor in property law' (2013–2014) 82 *University of Cincinnati Law Review* 57 pp. 58–89 and 100.

A. M. Honoré, 'Ownership' in A. G. Guest, *Oxford Essays in Jurisprudence* (First Series) (Oxford: Clarendon Press, 1961) p. 107 at pp. 107–128.

James Penner 'The "Bundle of Rights" picture of property' (1996) 43 *UCLA Law Review* 711.

---

[163] This is confirmed by s. 116 of the Land Registration Act 2002 as far as they affect registered land, and see also *Mortgage Express* v. *Lambert* [2016] EWCA Civ 555 paras. 16–18 and 23–24.

Sjef van Erp and Bram Akkermans (eds.), *Cases, Materials and Text on Property Law* (Oxford and Portland, OR: Hart Publishing, 2012) pp. 32–35 and Chapter 3, concentrating on rights in immovables and on differences in concepts of ownership in different jurisdictions.

A. W. B. Simpson, *A History of the Land Law* (2nd edn, Oxford: Clarendon Press, 1986) Chapter I (on early history of land law) and Chapter XI (on beginnings of nineteenth century reforms).

Joshua Getzler 'Review of J Stuart Anderson, *Lawyers and the Making of the English Land Law*' (1993) 109 *Law Quarterly Review* 684.

A. W. B. Simpson, 'Review of J Stuart Anderson, *Lawyers and the Making of the English Land Law*' (1993) 56 *Modern Law Review* 608.

J. Stuart Anderson, 'The 1925 property legislation: Setting contexts' in Susan Bright and John Dewar (eds.), *Land Law Themes and Perspectives* (Oxford: Oxford University Press, 1998) p. 107 at p. 122.

George L. Gretton and Andrew J. M. Steven, *Property, Trusts and Succession* (3rd edn, Haywards Heath, UK: Bloomsbury Professional, 2017) pp. 13–14, 17–18, 23–27, 362–364 and 497–504 (Scotland).

Questions

(1) (a) Consider the following models:
  (i) Blackstone's model of private ownership
  (ii) the exclusionary model of property
  (iii) the bundle of sticks model of property
  (iv) Honoré's 'liberal' conception of ownership

Describe the main features of each and how they differ from each other.

(b) Which of the models is the most help in understanding *land ownership* in England and Wales? (You might want to come back to this part of the question at the end of the course.)

(2) Does 'ownership' mean the same in the civil law as it means in the common law?

(3) Is 'ownership' a necessary feature of all property rights systems?

(4) Is it accurate to describe the Crown as owner of all land in England and Wales?

(5) Explain the difference between legal property interests and equitable property interests in English law. Why is it significant?

Are there any equitable property interests in land you think we should abolish, leaving those who have equitable interests in land in the present law to rely only on personal rights and remedies? (This part of the question will need to be reconsidered at the end of the course.)

6

New Property Interests and the
Numerus Clausus

PART I INTRODUCTION

6.1 Recognition of New Kinds of Property Interest

Property is a necessarily fluid concept. There is a continuous process by which societal and technological changes alter our relationships with things, or bring new things into existence. As a result, the law often has to consider whether to recognise 'new' kinds of property interest, or whether a new kind of thing or a so far un-propertised thing should be propertised in some way. In this chapter we look at the first of these questions – how we decide whether to recognise new *types* of property interest and new variations on recognised types. We look at the second question – how we decide whether to propertise a new kind of thing or a so far un-propertised thing – in Chapter 7 *Objects of Property Interests*.

6.2 The *Numerus Clausus* of Property Interests

In Chapter 5 *Ownership and Other Property Interests* we looked at the range of different kinds of property interest we recognise in this jurisdiction. Some of these kinds of property interest are common to most jurisdictions. Others are characteristic of all jurisdictions within a legal family. For example, private ownership of land and rights to take security over private property are found in all common law and civil law jurisdictions. Similarly, territories with similar geophysical features tend to share similar kinds of property right which would not be found in other jurisdictions. So, for example, traditional Jewish and Islamic water law systems have often recognised the 'right of thirst' – a right not known to English law – which gives an outsider a right to take drinking water for himself from a water source in which local people have water rights, after local people have taken their own drinking water but before they may take water for their animals or crops.[1]

So, as a matter of observable fact, there seems to be a certain standardisation of types of property interest in most legal systems. At one level this is not particularly surprising. We would expect different legal systems to develop types of property

---

[1] See James Salzman, 'Thirst: A short history of drinking water' (2006) 18 *Yale Journal of Law and the Humanities* 94 at pp. 98–101 for its origins in various different countries.

right which best suit their legal, social, cultural and geophysical conditions, and that some of these (for example, rights of access over other people's land) would be common to most kinds of society whereas others (such as the right of thirst) would be found in some societies but not in others.

However, what is perhaps surprising is that most (but not all) legal systems strictly regulate the number and type of rights in things that they will recognise as property rights, keeping to a short and closed list (a '*numerus clausus*') of allowable types of property interest.

It is important to be clear that this restrictive approach applies only to *property* rights and interests in things, not to the legally enforceable personal rights and interests in things which may be created or arise out of a contractual or status relationship between two or more specific people. There are no restrictions at all on the types of right that specific people can give to each other by contract over things under their control. Equally, there is no *numerus clausus* restricting the number or kind of legally enforceable *personal* rights and interests that people may have over things belonging to their parents, or their spouses. When family law or employment law has to decide whether a party to a family or employment relationship has a particular legally enforceable right over a thing under the control of the other party, the only issue is whether it is appropriate to imply that particular right into that kind of relationship in those circumstances: there is no closed list of allowable rights.

The crucial difference is of course that property rights and interests in things are enforceable against the whole world, whereas personal rights in things arising out of a contractual or status relationship are enforceable only as between the parties to that relationship. We consider in Part II whether that difference is enough to explain why at least some societies tend to keep to a *numerus clausus* of property interests, and what other factors may be relevant.

We have a limited adherence to the *numerus clausus* principle in this jurisdiction, in that the courts feel constrained by it to some extent even though Parliament does not. We look at this in Part III where we go on to consider the factors the courts take into consideration when they have to decide for the first time whether a given right should be categorised as a property right. We end Part III with one particular criterion that the courts adopt in making this kind of decision. This is the requirement of certainty: the courts will not categorise a right in a thing as a property right unless the thing is sufficiently certain. We look at the way this works, in particular in relation to territorial certainty and to fluctuating bodies of assets, in para. 6.13 of Part III.

6.3 *Typenzwang* and *Typenfixierung*: Recognised Types of Property Interest and Required Characteristics of Recognised Property Interests

When thinking about the *numerus clausus* principle it is useful to note the distinction German law makes between *Typenzwang* (when parties wish to create a property right, they must choose from the types of property interest already on the list of available interests – no new types of property interest will be recognised) and *Typenfixierung* (the core characteristics of a recognised type of property interest are set by law, and may not be varied by the parties).

In this jurisdiction we often fail to make this distinction, which may be important. In particular, in a common law system where the law is developed case by case, it is relatively easy for the courts to modify common law characteristics of long-established property interests if they feel it appropriate to keep pace with changing patterns of land use.[2] It is a quite different task for the courts to create a wholly new category, for example when faced with status or statutory rights and having to decide whether they should be categorised as property rights.[3]

6.4 Why It Matters Whether a Right Is Categorised as a Property Right

Before we consider all these issues, however, we need to clarify why it matters whether a right is categorised as a property right and not just a personal right. If a right is categorised as a property right, a number of consequences follow.

(a) Enforceability and Attachment to Land

The most obvious consequence is that if it is not a property right, it is in principle enforceable only against the person who granted the right (if the right arose because it was granted to me by contract or by someone authorised to grant such rights over the thing in question) or, if the right arises because of my relationship with someone, enforceable against the person with the reciprocal duty towards me. If, however, it is a property right, it is enforceable not only against that person, but also against the whole world. The practical effect of this is that the right becomes 'attached' to the thing, or to put it in another way, my right 'burdens' the thing. As we have seen, this means that anyone who later acquires any other property interest in the thing will take subject to my right in it.[4]

However, it goes further than that. If my right in the thing is a property right, it also attaches to the thing in the sense that I can take direct action against any outsider who interferes with my right in the thing. For example, a neighbouring landowner will be liable to me in the tort of nuisance if he does anything on his land which amounts to an actionable interference with my property right. This was confirmed by the House of Lords in *Hunter* v. *Canary Wharf Ltd* [1997] AC 656, where the problem was that the erection of the Canary Wharf tower in London interfered with television reception in the surrounding area. The House of Lords actually held that interference with a neighbour's television reception did not constitute the tort of nuisance. However, the court went on to say that, even if it

---

[2] See, for example, the cases we look at below where the issue was enlargement of the category of easements or nuisance.

[3] See, for example, *National Provincial Bank Ltd* v. *Ainsworth* [1965] AC 1175 (refusal to recognise family home rights arising out of matrimonial status as property rights), para. 6.11 below, and the regulatory licence cases we look at in para. 6.12 below.

[4] Subject to the specific rules about enforceability which we look at in Chapter 15 *Enforceability and Priority of Property Interests: General Principles* and Chapter 16 *Registration*.

did, the interference would have been actionable only by neighbours who had a property interest in their neighbouring land because, so the court re-affirmed, the tort of nuisance is confined to unlawful interference with the use and enjoyment of a person's *property rights* in land. So, neighbours who are, for example, people occupying their homes under licences or as members of the home owner's family, or working in neighbouring businesses, or who are teachers or pupils at neighbouring schools, have no right to sue for an injunction to stop the nuisance or for damages for the harm caused.[5]

(b) Property Rights Impose Duties on Strangers

This last point leads to a consequence which may have more theoretical force than practical significance. If we accept Hohfeld's rights analysis, every right necessarily involves a reciprocal duty on someone else. This means that the consequence of categorising a right I have in relation to a thing as a property right, is that a duty not to interfere with my right is imposed upon every person in the world, not just on the person who granted me the right. This makes property rights dangerous things, so it is said. However, we might feel a bit sceptical about the importance of this apparent proliferation of duties.

First, non-property rights can sometimes be enforced against third parties too. In particular, contract and tort law may extend their range of enforceability, for example under the Contracts (Rights of Third Parties) Act 1999, or by imposing personal liability for the tort of unlawful interference with contractual relations.[6] Other jurisdictions go further in allowing non-property rights to be enforceable against subsequent purchasers etc. So, for example in civil law systems where leases are personal and not property interests, they do nevertheless have third party effect in that buyers of the land are bound by them.[7]

Secondly, as we noted in para. 1.25 (a) of Chapter 1 *What Property Is and Why It Matters*, the Hohfeldian duty imposed on complete strangers by a property right is largely illusory. A potential buyer of your land will be interested to know whether I am occupying your land because you granted me a lease of it or because you granted me a personal licence, but it is difficult to think of many other people who will care which it is.

Thirdly, we should be cautious about using this apparent proliferation of duties as justifying a *numerus clausus* of property interests. If we really thought that every time we create a property interest, we impose significant burdens on everyone in the world, this might justify limiting the *number* of property interests that can exist in

---

[5] In other words, they cannot enforce the limitations on property owners we look at in Part III of Chapter 10 *Limitations on Property* paras. 10.12–10.16.

[6] *Lictor Anstalt* v. *Mir Steel UK Ltd* [2014] EWHC 3316, noted in para. 16.29(c) below.

[7] Bram Akkermans, 'Standardization of property rights in European property law' in Bram Akkermans, Ernst Marais and Eveline Ramaekers (eds.), *Property Law Perspectives II* (Cambridge, Antwerp and Portland, OR: Intersentia, 2014) Ius Communae Europaeum, pp. 221–249 at p. 233: see further Chapter 17 *Leases*.

relation to any given thing. It is however difficult to see how it would justify a limitation on the different *kinds* of property right we allow.

(c) Property Rights in Things Continue into Mixtures and Substitute Assets

This is another aspect of the way property rights in things attach to the thing in a way that non-property rights relating to the thing do not. There are legal principles governing property interests in mixtures, and the circumstances in which a property interest holder may follow or trace her interest into a substitute asset, which put a property interest holder in a much stronger position than someone who has merely personal rights in relation to a thing. We are not covering these principles here, but broadly the position is as follows.

First, if I have a property right in a thing, and the thing is irreversibly mixed with someone else's thing, I may have a property right in the mixture, whoever now holds it, depending on the nature of the things which have been mixed together. So, for example, there are different rules governing the position where someone paints a mural on my wall,[8] or I lose my sheep in someone else's flock of 99 identical sheep, or my oil is inadvertently mixed in a tanker with someone else's oil.[9] If, however, I had had only a non-property right in relation to the thing in the first place, there would be no grounds on which I could claim to have any rights in the mixture.

In addition, if the thing in which I have a property interest comes into the hands of a third party, we already know that my interest may be enforceable against the third party, but it is also the case that I may be entitled to elect instead to have an equivalent property interest in a substitute asset. So, if you steal my BMW car, and then give it to a car dealer in exchange for a Rolls Royce, I may or may not be entitled to claim the BMW back from the car dealer (depending on the rules we look at in paras. 15.5 and 15.6(b) of Chapter 15 *Enforceability and Priority of Property Interests*). However, if I choose not to do that, I can instead claim the Rolls Royce you now have, or a proportion of its value if, for example, you had given the car dealer your mini as well as my BMW in exchange for the Rolls Royce. None of this would apply if I had had only a personal right in the BMW, for example an exclusive personal right to use it given to me by a generous employer.[10]

(d) Priority on Insolvency

The question of whether an interest is a property interest is important if the interest holder goes bankrupt. Insolvency has two significant consequences as far as property rights are concerned. The first is that if I go bankrupt, all property interests I hold will be taken away from me and sold, with the sale proceeds being distributed pro rata between my creditors (i.e. so that each creditor gets paid the same percentage of

---

[8] Governed by the law relating to fixtures we look at in Chapter 7 *Objects of Property Interests* para. 7.25.

[9] For the detailed rules see Michael Bridge, Louise Gullifer, Gerard McMeel and Kelvin F. K. Low, *The Law of Personal Property* (2nd edn, London: Sweet & Maxwell, 2018) paras. 16.016–16.035.

[10] For a helpful analysis of the principles see *Foskett* v. *McKeown* [2001] 1 AC 102.

the amount owed to them). These pro rata payments wipe out the debts I owed to them. None of this applies to any personal rights I have in relation to things: I keep those. This explains the circumstances considered by the Court of Appeal in *Dear v. Reeves* [2001] EWCA Civ 277 which we noted in para. 5.22(a) of Chapter 5 *Ownership and Other Property Interests*. The issue was whether a right of pre-emption that the bankrupt held over land with development potential which was owned by his ex-employee, was a property interest or just a personal right. As we saw in para. 5.22(a), it was held that it was a property interest, and therefore it passed to the official responsible for getting in all the bankrupt's property and selling it for the benefit of the bankrupt's creditors. If the right of pre-emption had been held to be not a property interest, the bankrupt would have been able to keep it. This would have meant that if his ex-employee then decided to sell the land after the bankrupt was discharged from bankruptcy, the then ex-bankrupt would have been entitled to buy it for himself.

The second effect focusses on the interests of my creditors rather than on any interest belonging to me, the bankrupt. We have already noted that, when all my property has been sold by the bankruptcy officials, the sale proceeds will be divided between my creditors so that each will get back just a proportion of the amount they are owed.[11] However, this does not apply to a creditor (usually a bank or building society) which has a security interest in one of my assets, such as a mortgage or charge over it.[12] The creditor – called a 'secured creditor' – is entitled to sell that asset itself and take the full amount of its debt out of the sale proceeds, so it gets repaid 100 per cent of what it is owed.[13] So, from the point of view of the secured creditor and of all my other creditors, it matters very much (although not to me) whether the security interest the secured creditor has over my asset is a property interest. If it is, the secured creditor will be repaid everything it is owed (provided the value of the asset is greater than the amount it is owed). If it is not a property interest, the asset it affects will be sold unburdened by it, along with all my other assets, and the creditor will get back the same proportion of what it is owed as all the other creditors.

(e) Human Rights Act protection – Limitation on State Action

The final consequence of categorising a right as a property right is that, as we saw in Part V of Chapter 4 *Property and Human Rights*, the right becomes protected against state interference by article 1 Protocol 1 of the European Convention of Human Rights. In practical terms, this means that the state may not take away or interfere with

---

[11] If there was enough for them all to be paid in full, I was not insolvent and so should not have been made bankrupt.

[12] See Chapter 5 *Ownership and Other Property Interests* para. 5.37 as to the nature of a security interest.

[13] If there is anything left over after paying off everything owed to it out of the sale of the mortgaged property, the secured creditor pays it to the bankruptcy official, who adds it to the pot to be divided up between all the other creditors; if the sale proceeds of the mortgaged property are not sufficient to pay off the secured creditor in full, it queues up with the other creditors to get the proportion of what it is still owed out of the general pot.

the exercise of the right except in the public interest and on payment of adequate compensation. As we saw in Chapter 4, protection under article 1 Protocol 1 extends to all 'possessions', which is arguably wider than 'property', but it certainly covers all interests recognised as property interests in England and Wales. This explains why there has been so much litigation over the question of whether regulatory licences are property interests. If they are, the licensing body – effectively, the government – faces the prospect of having to pay compensation to licence holders if it wants to make changes to the licensing regime, as we see in para. 6.12 below.

PART II *NUMERUS CLAUSUS* OF PROPERTY INTERESTS

6.5 Justifications for Prohibiting the Recognition of New Types of Property Interest and the Variation of Pre-existing Types

It would be interesting to trace the evolution of the *numerus clausus* principle in civil law and common law property systems to find out how most (but not all) of these systems have come to adhere to the principle at least to some extent, and also to consider why it is that the 'fixed list' is so similar in so many of these jurisdictions. However, we are not going to deal with these essentially historical questions here.[14] In common law systems at least it is tied up with the fundamental question, beyond the scope of this book, of how judges come to make law at all in a precedent system: a judicial refusal to recognise a new kind of property right or a variation of a pre-existing type can nearly always be explained on the basis of adherence to earlier authorities, without having to justify the decision by reference to a 'closed list' *numerus clausus* principle.

Instead, our starting point is that most civil law and common law systems *do* recognise the *numerus clausus* principle at least to some extent, and we need to consider how far it is justifiable in the modern law, and whether we might not be better off adhering to it less strictly (or more strictly), or abandoning it altogether.

6.6 Objections to the Limitations Imposed by the *Numerus Clausus* Principle

With that in mind, we need first to consider possible objections to the limitations imposed by the *numerus clausus* principle.

(a) Inflexibility

The obvious objection is the one we have already made in para. 6.1. There is a continuous process by which people's relationships with things change in response

---

[14] They are raised by Bernard Rudden in 'Economic theory v. property law: The numerus clausus problem' in John Eekelaar and John Bel (eds.), *Oxford Essays in Jurisprudence*, Third Series (Oxford: Oxford University Press, 1987) 239, which provides a good starting point for thinking about the answers.

to societal and technological changes. In a common law system property law can accommodate these evolutionary shifts if the courts have sufficient power to modify the scope of existing property rights and, where necessary, create new kinds of property right. Strict adherence to the *numerus clausus* principle prevents that. So, the argument is that if it becomes evident that people do now want to make a particular kind of bargain about their respective rights in relation to a particular thing, and it seems a reasonable kind of bargain for them to make but contract law rules cannot give the bargain sufficient durability, why should the courts not be able to solve the durability problem by giving the bargain property status? The Chancery Court concluded that it could and should in the classic case of *Tulk* v. *Moxhay*,[15] deciding for the first time that a contractual promise restricting the use of land for the benefit of neighbouring land could give rise to a property right (what became known as a restrictive covenant[16]). In that case the buyer of what is now Leicester Square in London had promised the seller, for the benefit of the land surrounding the Square which the seller retained, that he, the buyer would 'at all times thereafter' maintain the land he had bought as open land and not build on it.[17] The Square was then sold on several times, and the court held that the freehold owner of the surrounding land could enforce the promise against the present freehold owner of the Square, who had bought it knowing all about the covenant. In other words, the court decided that the benefit of the promise was attached to the surrounding land as a property right, enforceable against any subsequent purchaser of the Square who had notice of it. This was justifiable, the Lord Chancellor said, because 'nothing could be more inequitable than that the original purchaser should be able to sell the property the next day for a greater price, in consideration of the assignee being allowed to escape from the liability which he had himself undertaken'.

We can see the same kind of approach in *Regency Villas Title Ltd* v. *Diamond Resorts (Europe) ltd* [2018] UKSC 57, where the Supreme Court decided to modify a previous limitation on the scope of a pre-existing type of property right. Specifically, it abandoned the old rule that a private right to make recreational use of someone else's land cannot be an easement. The old rule had been justified on the basis that a 'mere right of recreation and amusement, possessing no quality of utility and benefit' should not be capable of being a property right, burdening neighbouring land. The Supreme Court disagreed, and extended the easement category to include a right granted to timeshare owners to use the sporting and recreational facilities in a leisure complex on neighbouring land, so as to make the right enforceable against the company which subsequently bought the neighbouring land. As Lord Briggs said:

> the advantages to be gained from recreational and sporting activities are now so universally regarded as being of real utility and benefit to human beings that the pejorative expression 'mere right of recreation and amusement, possessing no quality of utility and benefit' has become a contradiction in terms ... Recreation, including

---

[15] *Tulk* v. *Moxhay* (1848) 2 Ph 774, 41 ER 1143.   [16] A 'covenant' is a promise made in a deed.

[17] The covenant also imposed positive obligations on the buyer to maintain the land as an ornamental square, but for reasons we consider later, only the restrictive obligations were held to be enforceable as property rights.

sport, and the amusement which comes with it, does confer utility and benefit on those who undertake it.[18]

So, this objection to the *numerus clausus* principle is that it prevents the law moving with the times – in both these cases, the chances of Parliament making these changes in the law if the courts had been unable to do so, were probably not great.

(b) The Libertarian Objection

There is also an obvious libertarian objection to the *numerus clausus* principle, which is that it interferes with the freedom of a private owner to do whatever she wants with her thing, including her freedom to grant whatever property rights over the thing she wants. Richard Epstein is a strong proponent of this argument,[19] which Merrill and Smith summarise succinctly in the following way, before discounting it:

> The whole point of property law, [Epstein] argues, is to establish a sphere in which individuals' choices are respected (and facilitated through enforcement) rather than overruled by collective preferences. As long as actors do not infringe upon the rights of third parties, there is no principled basis for disrespecting choices ... any more than in property or contract law more generally.[20]

As we see in para. 6.7(b) below, the Merrill and Smith response is that the costs of abandoning the *numerus clausus* principle and giving property status to whatever rights in respect of things the parties choose to create, are not borne only by the parties. It is on this basis, they argue, that 'disrespecting choices' is justified.

(c) Private Resource-Sharing Arrangements

However, we can go further than Epstein and argue that there is a positive utility in allowing a property owner to craft her own resource-sharing arrangements with others, particularly when the resource is land or another kind of natural resource. Not only does it respect landowners' freedom of action, it also promotes better use of resources. The argument, echoing Ostrom's analysis of successful self-regulating communal resource use,[21] is that natural resources are scarce, and if my neighbour and I can work out a way of sharing them in a way that is mutually beneficial, the law ought to uphold the arrangement. This is so even if (or perhaps especially if) the arrangement is idiosyncratic, because the resource-sharing arrangements which are

---

[18] Lord Briggs in *Regency Villas Title Ltd* v. *Diamond Resorts (Europe) ltd* [2018] UKSC 57 para. 59. We come back to this case in Chapter 13 *Non-Possessory Land Use Rights* para. 13.9, where we look at this case in detail.

[19] Richard A. Epstein, 'Notice and freedom of contract in the law of servitudes' (1982) 55 *South California Law Review* 1353.

[20] Thomas W. Merrill and Henry E. Smith, 'Optimal standardization in the law of property: The numerus clausus principle' (2000) 110 *Yale Law Journal* 1 at p. 44.

[21] Chapter 2 *Conceptions and Justifications* paras. 2.14–2.17.

most likely to be successful are those devised by the resource-sharers themselves –
they know more about the capacities of the resource, and their own preferences, than
anyone else. It is true that the *numerus clausus* principle does not stop them making
that kind of agreement between themselves by contract. However, resource-sharing
arrangements which are enforceable only in contract are dangerously fragile. We can
see this from *Hill* v. *Tupper* (1863) 2 H & C 121, 159 ER, another classic English case
upholding the *numerus clausus* principle. In that case the owner of Basingstoke
Canal granted to a pleasure boat operator the exclusive right to put pleasure boats
for hire on the Canal for the next seven years. The owner of an inn on the bank of
the Canal just next to the pleasure boat operator started hiring out pleasure boats
himself, operating from the inn, allowing 'gentlemen [who] had come from time to
time to his inn [to use] these boats for fishing and bathing'. The pleasure boat
operator brought an action against the innkeeper, claiming that the innkeeper had
infringed his exclusive right to put pleasure boats for hire on the Canal. He lost. The
Court held that the rights granted by the Canal Company to the pleasure boat
operator were not capable of being property rights so had to take effect only as
contract rights, and as such were enforceable only against the Canal Company. So, if
the pleasure boat operator wanted to sue the innkeeper, he would have to sue in the
Canal Company's name. As Pollock CB said:

> A new species of incorporeal hereditament cannot be created at the will and pleasure
> of the owner of property; but he must be content to accept the estate and the right to
> dispose of it subject to the law as settled by decisions or controlled by act of
> parliament. A grantor may bind himself by covenant to allow any right he pleases
> over his property, but he cannot annex to it a new incident.

The problem with that analysis is that whilst the holder of the contractual right
might be able to protect it against third parties by suing in the name of the grantor,
he has no adequate remedy if the grantor sells his interest to a purchaser who does
not want to re-affirm the contract. So, if immediately after granting the pleasure boat
operator the exclusive right, the Canal Company had sold the Canal to someone else,
or gone into liquidation, the pleasure boat operator would have lost his right. He
might have been able to sue the Canal Company or the liquidator for damages for
breach of contract, but he would no longer be entitled to put pleasure boats for hire
on the Canal, and anyway would probably never recover the damages if the Canal
Company was in liquidation.

This makes contractual resource-sharing arrangements between neighbours very
unstable; to ensure durability of the arrangement it has to be enforceable as a
property relationship. It could of course be a problem if the arrangement is too
durable. If neighbours are able to attach their own idiosyncratic sharing arrangements permanently to the resource, it may cause problems for future generations:
they will be deprived of the opportunity to devise new arrangements for sharing (or
not sharing) the resource in a way that is more efficient, or more sustainable or just
more congenial. However, property rights do not necessarily have to last for ever. In
our present law, restrictive covenants are in principle perpetual, but the person
owning the land burdened by the covenant has the right to apply to a tribunal to

have the covenant modified or discharged.[22] The court has the jurisdiction to do this, if, for example, the covenant is obsolete because of changes in the character of the property or the neighbourhood, or if it is impeding a reasonable use of the land and is either not providing practical benefits of substantial value or advantage, or is contrary to the public interest. It can also order payment of compensation where appropriate. If, as the Law Commission has recommended,[23] this jurisdiction is extended to all non-possessory land burdens (what they call 'land obligations'), we can ensure that resource-sharing arrangements between neighbours which give rise to idiosyncratic property rights can be modified or ended when no longer promoting successful resource-sharing.

6.7 Justifications for the *Numerus Clausus*

So, the *numerus clausus* principle requires justification strong enough to override these objections.

(a) The Unitary Theory of Ownership

One argument is that the idea that the range of property interests has to be limited is inherent in the concept of ownership. As Henry Hansmann and Reinier Kraakman point out,[24] however, this rather depends on what one's concept of ownership is:

> [The rule that the] owner of an asset is not ... free ... to grant to other persons property rights in that asset ... is most conspicuous in the civil law countries of Europe, which since the nineteenth century have adhered self-consciously to a 'unitary theory of property rights' under which, as a general rule, all property rights in an asset must be concentrated in the hands of a single owner rather than divided into partial rights shared among two or more persons. Only a relatively small, closed number (numerus clausus) of specifically defined exceptions to this principle of unitary ownership are permitted. . .[25]

This sounds a plausible explanation of why civil law systems might adopt a *numerus clausus* principle, or why they might adhere to it more strictly than we do. But it is difficult to see a concept of unitary ownership as underlying a common law property rights system such as ours. In our system, after all, we are quite happy to accept a 'split' of ownership between a freeholder and a leaseholder with, say, a 21 year or even 999 year lease: we do not require ownership to be unitary. Also, if the objection is to fragmentation of ownership, the point we made in para. 6.4(b) arises: the *numerus clausus* principle does not limit the *extent* to which ownership can be

---

[22] S. 84 of the Law of Property Act 1925 as amended by the Law of Property Act 1969.

[23] Law Commission, *Making Land Work: Easements, Covenants and Profits a Prendre* (2011) Law Com No 327, Part 7: see further Chapter 13 *Non-Possessory Land Use Rights* para. 13.13(b).

[24] Henry Hansmann and Reinier Kraakman, 'Property, contract and verification: The numerus clausus problem and the divisibility of rights' (2002) 31 *Journal of Legal Studies* 373.

[25] Ibid. p. 375.

fragmented, because it restricts only the *kinds* of encumbrance which can attach to a thing, not the numbers of them.[26]

(b) Optimal Standardisation

For common law systems the justification that commentators take most seriously is that the *numerus clausus* principle promotes efficiency in land markets. It is said to do this by standardising the property burdens which can affect land, so that they have to take one of a strictly limited number of forms, the contents of which are also standardised. The argument, most strongly association with Thomas Merrill and Henry Smith,[27] is that this reduces the information-processing costs of potential purchasers of property rights and of potential tortfeasors (who need to know which rights in relation to things are property rights, because of their potential tort liability for interfering with property rights). It is necessary to have a trade-off between the advantages to individuals of allowing them to create whatever forms of property interest they want, so the argument goes, and the information processing costs this imposes on outsiders. These costs are incurred not only by the potential purchasers of that particular encumbered land, or of that particular novel property interest, but also by other market participants (all potential purchasers of all potential plots). As between the original parties to the transaction creating the novel property interest, these costs are internalised (if I grant a novel property interest over my land, I can expect to sell my land at a correspondingly lower price). However, they are external costs for other market participants, because a potential purchaser of any land has to search for an unlimited variety of property interests that may or may not affect the title, and cannot compensate by lowering the price if it turns out that none of them encumber the land he is buying. As Merrill and Smith say,

> Idiosyncratic rights create a common-pool problem, which does impose external costs on third parties... Third parties incur heavier measurement costs in processing 'notice' when the universe of property rights includes idiosyncratic servitudes or other 'fancies' than when these are prohibited. Moreover, these costs are true externalities of any given transaction. The costs to third parties who do not deal even indirectly with the creator of the unusual servitude are not capitalized into the price of the creator's property, and hence the creator cannot be expected to take these costs into account. In particular, the higher measurement costs for parties considering other parcels are not reflected in a lower price for the parcel of the creator of such rights.[28]

On this basis, Merrill and Smith argue, standardisation of property interests is in the interests of society as a whole:

> The existence of unusual property rights increases the cost of processing information about all property rights. Those creating or transferring idiosyncratic property rights

[26] Merrill and Smith, 'Optimal standardisation', fn. 20 above, make much the same point at pp. 51–53.
[27] Most famously in Merrill and Smith 'Optimal Standardisation', fn. 20 above, although together and separately they have refined and developed the argument elsewhere.
[28] Ibid. p. 44.

cannot always be expected to take these increases in measurement costs fully into account, making them a true externality. Standardization of property rights reduces these measurement costs.[29]

Bernard Rudden points out that these benefits of standardisation are usually thought to apply only to things that are marketed in bulk.[30] Bulk trading of property interests in land does exist, and it is certainly true that those engaged in it demand standardisation of the terms of the property interest involved. So, for example, landlords of multi-tenanted developments who want to trade their freehold interests (i.e. their reversionary interests in the land under the leases), will ensure that all leases granted to tenants contain identical terms, and the same applies to lenders who take mortgages over multiple properties and want to trade in their mortgages in bulk.[31] However, as far as land transactions are concerned, bulk trading is a fringe activity and those engaged in it can enforce standardisation by commercial pressure. It is not so clear why participants in one-off land transactions should have to have their range of options restricted by a *numerus clausus* principle.

As Merrill and Smith acknowledge, their standardisation argument depends heavily on the costs potential purchasers etc. have to incur to find out what property interests burden any given piece of land, and a principal difficulty with their argument is that these costs differ dramatically depending on the rules a jurisdiction adopts to govern the enforcement of property interests against purchasers. In most systems even if a right against a thing is a property interest, the question of whether it is enforceable against purchasers etc. will depend on whether it is registered in a public register and/or on whether the purchaser actually knew or should have known about it. So, the costs of discovering whether there is an idiosyncratic property interest *which would or would not affect the land if you bought it* are not nearly as high as you might think from what Merrill and Smith say.[32] We look at our enforceability rules in England and Wales in Chapter 15 *Enforceability and Priority of Property Interests: General Principles* and in Chapter 16 *Registration*, where we see how our land registration system works. Merrill and Smith are talking primarily about the system in the USA, where each state has different enforceability rules, and

---

[29] Ibid. p. 8. They go on to argue that *total* standardisation would bring equally unacceptable 'frustration costs' (frustrate bargains that self-interested parties want to make): a property rights system achieves *optimal* standardisation by finding the correct balance between absolute freedom to customise property interests and an absolute ban on customising altogether (ibid. p. 38). Their conclusion is that the US system achieves roughly the right balance by refusing to allow courts to create new forms of property interest but allowing the legislature to do so.

[30] Rudden, 'Economic theory v property law', fn. 14 above, pp. 253–254.

[31] The securitisation of mortgages which lead to the global financial crash in the 1980s involved bulk trading of residential mortgages (i.e. of the mortgage interests that banks and other lenders held in people's homes), and this was made possible only because there was a standardisation of mortgage terms imposed on homeowners if they wanted to borrow money secured by mortgages over their homes. This experience has not left many people feeling that bulk trading in interests in land is something that should be facilitated.

[32] As they acknowledge at p. 42, where they say that "the rise of land registers allow[s] some loosening of the numerus clausus". Epstein, 'Notice and freedom of contract in the law of servitudes' (fn. 19 above) takes the view that registration reduces the information processing costs to such an extent that it makes the numerus clausus principle unnecessary.

few, if any, have comprehensive and efficient land registration systems.[33] By contrast, most civil law systems which adhere strictly to the *numerus clausus* principle have extremely efficient land registration systems, as we see in Chapter 16. Whether those systems could accommodate a broader variety in property forms is a different matter.

PART III RECOGNITION OF NEW PROPERTY INTERESTS IN ENGLAND AND WALES

6.8 The *Numerus Clausus* in the Law of England and Wales

The first point to make is that in England and Wales Parliament does not regard itself as bound by a *numerus clausus* of property interests at all. When it creates a new statutory right relating to a thing, or modifies a pre-existing one, it does not take the *numerus clausus* principle into account, and it is other factors that dictate whether Parliament decides to give the right the status of a property right. If fact, the statute creating a new right relating to a thing or modifying a pre-existing one often does not expressly state whether or not it is a property right. In those cases it is then for the courts to decide on its status. This is very different from the situation in some codified civil law jurisdictions, where the code or even the constitution provides a *numerus clausus* and make it explicit that no other property interests will be recognised.[34]

However, as we have already seen, the courts in England and Wales do sometimes take note of the *numerus clausus* principle but it is increasingly rare for them to refuse to even consider a departure from it. In modern times they are more likely to approach an invitation to recognise a new kind of property interest or extend the boundaries of an existing type as a matter to be decided on a case by case basis. In other words, they will not regard a departure from the *numerus clausus* principle as objectionable in principle, but they will have to be satisfied that it is desirable and appropriate in that case. The fact that the parties to a grant wanted and intended the right granted to be a property right would not be regarded as conclusive, nor even necessarily relevant.

6.9 Strict *Numerus Clausus* Approach

The strict *numerus clausus* approach in England and Wales is usually traced back to the classic statement made by Lord Brougham in the Court of Chancery in 1834 in *Keppell* v. *Bailey*.[35] As we see, his justification for adopting that approach is much the same as that given by Merrill and Smith:

---

[33] See Chapter 16 *Registration* para. 16.4(b).

[34] Akkermans, 'Standardization of property rights in European property law', fn. 7 above, 221 at p. 233, and see also Sjef van Erp and Bram Akkermans, *Cases, Materials and Text on Property Law* (Oxford and Portland, OR: Hart Publishing, 2012) pp. 65–75.

[35] *Keppell* v. *Bailey* (1834) 2 My & K 517 at pp. 535–536, 39 ER 1042.

There are certain known incidents to property and its enjoyment; among others certain burthens wherewith it may be affected, or rights which may be created and enjoyed over it by parties other than the owner; all which incidents are recognized by the law ... But it must not, therefore, be supposed that incidents of a novel kind can be devised and attached to property at the fancy or caprice of any owner; It is clearly inconvenient both to the science of the law and to the public weal that such a latitude should be given. There can be no harm in allowing the fullest latitude to men in binding themselves and their representatives, that is, their assets real and personal, to answer in damages for breach of their obligations. This tends to no mischief, and is a reasonable liberty to bestow; but great detriment would arise, and much confusion of rights, if parties were allowed to invent new modes of holding and enjoying real property, and to impress upon their lands and tenements a peculiar character which should follow them into all hands, however remote. Every close ... might thus be held in a several fashion; and it would hardly be possible to know what rights the acquisition of any parcel conferred, or what obligations it imposed.

The court took the same view in *Hill* v. *Tupper*, as we saw in para. 6.6(c). In a variation on this approach, however, the courts have sometimes decided that it should not recognise a new property right because it would be inconsistent with earlier court decisions, even though the court now acknowledges compelling arguments for coming to a different conclusion. So, for example, in *Rhone* v. *Stephens* [1994] 2 AC 310 the House of Lords declined to overturn previous Court of Appeal authority that a positive (as opposed to a restrictive) covenant was not enforceable against third parties as a property interest. Lord Templeman explained why:

For over 100 years it has been clear and accepted law that equity will enforce negative covenants against freehold land but has no power to enforce positive covenants against successors in title of the land ...

Mr Munby, who argued the appeal persuasively on behalf of the plaintiffs, referred to an article by Professor Sir William Wade, 'Covenants – "a broad and reasonable view"'(1972) 31 CLJ 157, and other articles in which the present state of the law is subjected to severe criticism. In 1965 the *Report of the Committee on Positive Covenants Affecting Land* (Cmnd 2719), which was a report by a committee appointed by the Lord Chancellor and under the chairmanship of Lord Wilberforce, referred to difficulties caused by the decision in the *Austerberry* case and recommended legislation to provide that positive covenants which relate to the use of land and are intended to benefit specified other land should run with the land. In *Transfer of Land: Appurtenant Rights* (Law Commission Working Paper no 36, published on 5 July 1971) the present law on positive rights was described as being illogical, uncertain, incomplete and inflexible. The Law Commission Report *Transfer of Land: The Law of Positive and Restrictive Covenants* laid before Parliament in 1984 made recommendations for the reform of the law relating to positive and restrictive obligations and submitted a draft Bill for that purpose. Nothing has been done.

In these circumstances your Lordships were invited to overrule the decision of the Court of Appeal in the *Austerberry* case.[36] To do so would destroy the distinction between law and equity and to convert the rule of equity into a rule of notice. It is plain

---

[36] *Austerberry* v. *Oldham Corporation* (1885) 29 Ch D 750.

from the articles, reports and papers to which we were referred that judicial legislation to overrule the *Austerberry* case would create a number of difficulties, anomalies and uncertainties and affect the rights and liabilities of people who have for over 100 years bought and sold land in the knowledge, imparted at an elementary stage to every student of the law of real property, that positive covenants affecting freehold land are not directly enforceable except against the original covenantor. Parliamentary legislation to deal with the decision in the *Austerberry* case would require careful consideration of the consequences ...

So, the courts may well feel that, in such circumstances, the decision whether to propertise a right has to made by Parliament and not by the courts.[37]

6.10 Conscious Creationism

In other cases, however, where there are no precedent constraints the courts in England and Wales are more expansionist. In these cases the courts are willing to take each case on its own merits, and are prepared to recognise a new kind of property interest or modify the requirements for an existing one, or at least consider whether, as a matter of policy, it should do so in the particular situation it is considering. So, for example, as we saw in para. 6.6, in *Tulk* v. *Moxhay*,[38] the court created the restrictive covenant as a property interest, and in *Regency Villas Title Ltd* v. *Diamond Resorts (Europe) Ltd*[39] the Supreme Court extended the category of easements to cover the grant of a right to time-share owners to use sporting and recreational facilities in a leisure complex on neighbouring land. Similarly, in *Hunter* v. *Canary Wharf*,[40] as we saw in para. 6.4(a) above, although the House of Lords held that the right to receive uninterrupted terrestrial television signals over neighbouring land was not a property right, it did so only after considering the practical and policy implications. Specifically, it accepted that if the easement category was extended to cover such a right, it would unduly restrict a landowner's right to build on his own land, and therefore such a right should not, at least in present circumstances, be recognised as a property right. It did not say that a right to receive television signals over neighbouring land could not be an easement because it had never been accepted as an easement in the past.

6.11 'Essential Characteristics of a Property Right': The *Ainsworth* Test

In other cases in modern times the courts will base its decision not only on policy considerations but also on whether the proposed property interest has what the

---

[37] For a similar approach see the US decision of the Supreme Court of California in *Moore v. Regents of the University of California* (1990) 51 Cal 3d 120, where it was decided by a majority that it would not depart from the long-established rule that no-one can have property rights in a human body because of the complexity of the social, economic and moral arguments raised: see further Chapter 7 *Objects of Property Interests* para. 7.27.

[38] *Tulk* v. *Moxhay* (1848) 2 Ph 774, 41 ER 1143.

[39] *Regency Villas Title Ltd* v. *Diamond Resorts (Europe) Ltd* [2018] UKSC 57.

[40] *Hunter* v. *Canary Wharf Ltd* [1997] AC 656.

court regards as the essential characteristics of a property interest. Sometimes they do this by going through Honoré's incidents of ownership we looked at in Chapter 5 *Ownership and Other Property Interests*, apparently on the basis that, even if the interest held in the thing in question does not include *all* of Honoré's incidents and so cannot amount to 'ownership' of the thing, it does include enough of them for the interest to qualify as *some* kind of property interest of some sort.[41]

In other cases, the courts have adopted the test formulated by the House of Lords in *National Provincial Bank Ltd* v. *Ainsworth* [1965] AC 1175. In that case the House of Lords had to decide whether a wife had a property interest in her matrimonial home solely by virtue of being the wife of its freehold owner. The wife in that case had no other property interest in her home which (as was common in those days) was in her husband's sole name. He had deserted her and their four children, leaving them in the matrimonial home, and he had then transferred the freehold interest into the name of his company, which had mortgaged it to the Bank. At the time when the case was decided, there was a common law principle, founded on ecclesiastical law, that a wife had a right, enforceable against her husband, to occupy any house owned by her husband which was their matrimonial home. The immediate consequence of this principle was that a husband was not entitled to evict his wife from their family home: she had a personal right in the house (a right to occupy it) by virtue of her status as the owner's wife, which was enforceable against her husband. She argued that this right should be recognised as a property right in her matrimonial home, enforceable against the Bank so that it was not entitled to evict her. In earlier Court of Appeal decisions Lord Denning had recognised this right as a property right, giving it the label of the 'deserted wife's equity' and this had been followed in the lower courts. However, in *Ainsworth* the House of Lords refused to accept that it was a property right.[42] It took the view that the wife's right was *by its nature* a personal right enforceable against the husband only, not capable of being a property right. In Lord Wilberforce's view, the crucial factors were that the right the wife had by virtue of her status arose only out of her husband's duties to maintain her and cohabit with her. This meant it would arise only when he deserted her, and it would end whenever his duties ended (on divorce, or, under family law at that time, if she did something to forfeit her right to be maintained, such as refusing to allow him back or entering into a sexual relationship with someone else). Also, it did not entitle her to occupy any particular house – at any point the husband could change the matrimonial home for a suitable alternative. On this basis, Lord Wilberforce said:

> On any division . . . which is to be made between property rights on the one hand, and personal rights on the other hand, however broad or penumbral the separating band between these two kinds of rights may be, there can be little doubt where the wife's

[41] This was essentially the approach of the Court of Appeal in *Yearworth* v. *North Bristol NHS Trust* [2009] EWCA Civ 37, deciding for the first time that the law would recognise that men had a property interest in their sperm which had been stored for possible use in fertility treatment they might want after cancer treatment: see Chapter 7 *Objects of Property Interests* paras. 7.29–7.30.

[42] Or as Bridge J said in *Miles* v. *Bull (No. 2)* [1969] 3 All ER 1585, at p. 1587, the deserted wife's equity turned out to be 'the creature of the courts which the House of Lords had strangled'.

rights fall. *Before a right or an interest can be admitted into the category of property, or of a right affecting property, it must be definable, identifiable by third parties, capable in its nature of assumption by third parties, and have some degree of permanence or stability.* The wife's right has none of these qualities, it is characterised by the reverse of them.

It is instructive to note that Parliament almost immediately reversed the effect of the House of Lords decision by passing the Matrimonial Homes Act 1967. These provisions, now in Part IV of the Family Law Act 1996, and amended by the Civil Partnerships Act 2004 and the Marriage (Same Sex Couples) Act 2013, give all spouses and civil partners what are now called 'home rights' in the matrimonial or civil partnership home. Home rights are essentially rights not to be evicted or excluded from the home except with the leave of the court, and they are enforceable against third parties such as purchasers and lenders provided they are registered, and as from the date on which they are registered. So, all aspects of the judicially created 'deserted wife's equity' which, in Lord Wilberforce's view, made it inappropriate for property status have been eliminated. The right becomes enforceable against third parties as soon as it is registered and is ended by divorce or a court order (all of which are easily discoverable by a third party), and registration identifies the property which is subject to the rights. And, as a bonus, whereas only a wife could have had a deserted wife's equity (because wives have never had a duty to maintain husbands) all spouses and civil partners are entitled to the statutory right. So, Parliament has been able to create by legislation a much better property right than the House of Lords would have been able to create if it had recognised the deserted wife's equity as a property right.

However, the test laid down by Lord Wilberforce in *Ainsworth* (specifically, the words given in italics in the above quotation) has subsequently been relied on to as laying down the essential criteria for a property right in a wide variety of contexts. So for example, as we see in Chapter 9 *Multiple Property Rights Systems* para. 9.8, essentially the same formula was used in an early Australian indigenous land rights case *Milirrpum* v. *Nabalco Pty Ltd.*[43] In that case it was used as setting the criteria for deciding whether an indigenous group had rights in their land and resources which would have been categorisable as property rights in English law at the time when that area of Australia was colonised – hardly an appropriate test, given that the rights in question were collective nomadic use rights, whereas in *Ainsworth* Lord Wilberforce was talking about private property rights.

More appropriately and more recently, it was also applied by the court in *Armstrong DLW GmbH* v. *Winnington Networks Ltd* [2012] EWHC 10, where, as we note in Chapter 7 *Objects of Property Interests* para. 7.7(a), the court had to consider the precise nature of carbon emission allowances known as European Union Allowances (EUAs). EUAs are issued under the ETS EU carbon reduction scheme, and broadly what happens is that all carbon-emitting companies in the EU are given a quota of EUAs, each of which entitles it to emit a certain amount of CO_2

---

[43] *Milirrpum* v. *Nabalco Pty Ltd* (1971) 17 FLR 141; [1972–1973] ALR 65.

in a specified period. EUAs are tradeable, so any carbon-emitter (or anyone else) can buy or sell them at any time. If at the end of a period a carbon-emitter has emitted more CO_2 than represented by the EUAs it then holds, it is fined. If it has emitted less, it can sell or carry forward the surplus EUAs. The idea is that this creates a market in which rights to emit carbon are traded to those that value them most, and all emitters have the incentive to emit as little carbon as possible. EUAs are purely electronic and traded electronically, but each has a unique number and is easily identifiable. In *Armstrong* v. *Winnington,* Armstrong was seeking to get back from an innocent recipient 21,000 EUAs which had been fraudulently removed from Armstrong's account in a phishing attack, and it was necessary to establish the nature of an EUA in order to determine the remedies it could pursue. Applying the test in *Ainsworth,* the judge concluded that an EUA is property in the common law:

> 50 . . . It is definable, as being the sum total of rights and entitlements conferred on the holder pursuant to the ETS. It is identifiable by third parties; it has a unique reference number. It is capable of assumption by third parties, as under the ETS, an EUA is transferable. It has permanence and stability, since it continues to exist in a registry account until it is transferred out either for submission or sale and is capable of subsisting from year to year.

6.12 Alienability, Value and Regulatory Licences

In relation to regulatory licences, however, it is now accepted that the key criteria are whether the licence 'has a monetary value and can be marketed for consideration'. This is the test that has been established to decide whether a regulatory licence is a 'possession' for the purposes of article 1 Protocol 1 of the European Convention on Human Rights, and, although 'possessions' is a broader concept than the English and Welsh concept of 'property',[44] the test also appears apt for 'property'. As noted in Chapter 5 *Ownership and Other Property Interests*[45] a regulatory licence is a licence granted by a public body or regulatory authority which licences the grantee to use a specific resource in a specific way. Characteristically, it is granted as part of a regulatory scheme which makes it illegal for anyone to use that resource at all, or in that way, except in accordance with the terms of the licence which it has been granted by the regulatory authority. The idea is that the regulatory authority can ensure that the resource is used only by those in a position to exploit it efficiently (by imposing criteria to be met by those applying for a licence), and can control the use of the resource by imposing conditions in the licence, for example to ensure that the resource is extracted and used sustainably and in the public interest. Also, by paying fees for the licence, for example by reference to the quantity of the resource extracted, the licensee is made to 'buy' ownership of the extracted resource from the state, and cannot just acquire it for nothing by mixing labour with it or becoming

---

[44] See Chapter 4 *Property and Human Rights* paras. 4.27–4.28.   [45] para. 5.36.

the first taker.[46] So, for example, as we see in Chapter 7 *Objects of Property Interests* where we look at property rights in subsoil land,[47] the Oil and Gas Authority grants licences to an appropriate person for a specified period, granting them the exclusive right to explore for, extract and sell petroleum from a particular area in England and Wales for a specified period, on payment to the Crown of a royalty or other fee and subject to conditions imposed by the licence.[48] The objective of the licence regime is 'to maximise economic recovery of UK petroleum, with consequent benefits to security of energy supplies, employment, and to the Exchequer and the economy more generally, consistent with safety and environmental requirements'.[49] Critically for present purposes, many regulatory licenses are now alienable. This is in line with current economic thinking that allocation of licences to the most efficient user, and setting the value of the rights granted, should be done by the market rather than by the state, which, so it is argued, is ill-equipped for both tasks.[50]

In *UK Association of Fish Producer Organisations* v. *Secretary of State for Environment Food and Rural Affairs* [2013] EWHC 1959, as we noted in Chapter 4 *Property and Human Rights*,[51] it was held that fishing allocation quota units were 'possessions' for the purpose of article 1 Protocol 1 of the European Convention on Human Rights. Cranston J concluded from the authorities that the test for deciding whether regulatory licences were possessions looked to both monetary value and tradeability:

> In a well known passage in *R (Nicholds)* v. *Security Industry Authority* [2006] EWHC 1792 (Admin) Kenneth Parker J (as he now is) invoked as a test whether licences or permissions have a monetary value and can be marketed for consideration, either through outright sale, leasing, or sub-licensing. Thus milk quotas and certain spectrum licences fell within the concept of possessions in article 1 of protocol 1, but not licences or permissions which were neither marketable nor had been obtained at a market price, even though they had a value to the holder because, without them, it could not carry on the licensable activity: [74]–[75]. That approach has been approved in ... the Court of Appeal in *R (Malik)* v. *Waltham Forest NHS Primary Care Trust* [2007] EWCA Civ 265 [42]–[44] ... In Malik a medical practitioner was suspended from the performers' list entitling him to practice within the NHS. The Court invoked the distinction between goodwill, which is a possession, and an expectation of future income, which is not. In that case there was a legal prohibition on selling the goodwill in a doctor's practice. Thus it had no economic value, so that the personal right of the doctor to practice through inclusion on the performers' list was not a possession ...

---

[46] See further Chapter 3 *Allocation of Property Rights* para. 3.5.   [47] paras. 7.17 and 7.20.
[48] Ss. 3–4 of the Petroleum Act 1998.
[49] See *Dean* v. *Secretary of State for Business, Energy and Industrial Strategy* [2017] EWHC 1998 para. 44, confirming that such a licence (in that case to drill for and extract shale gas by fracking) is a property interest (paras. 128–132).
[50] See in relation to Water Abstraction Licences, Alison Clarke and Rosalind Malcolm, 'The role of property in water regulation: Locating communal and regulatory property rights on the property rights spectrum' in Christine Godt (ed.), *Regulatory Property Rights: The Transforming Notion of Property in Transnational Business Regulation* (Leiden and Boston: Brill Nijhoff, 2017) at pp. 129–132 and 137–138.
[51] para. 4.28.

He concluded that unused fishing allocation quota units were 'possessions' because they were in practice traded even though there was no official mechanism for doing so. On that basis they satisfied the test for possessions because they 'have a monetary value and can be marketed for consideration'.

Nevertheless, it will be appreciated that, like the *Ainsworth* test, this test does not take into account that under our law not all property interests are alienable. Inalienable property rights include communal and public property interests, and private property interests that are personal to the holder, such as the statutory right a tenant of business premises may have to renew the tenancy.[52] Also, private non-possessory land use rights like easements and restrictive covenants have to be appurtenant to the benefitted land and so cannot be alienated separately from it.[53] So, whilst the courts do now seem willing to take a policy view of when and whether a new right in relation to a thing should be recognised as a property interest, they have yet to come up with a satisfactory list of the essential characteristics a right must have to qualify as a property interest.

6.13 The Certainty Criterion

One characteristic that is undoubtedly essential is certainty: a right cannot be a property right unless the rights holder and the thing itself are certain. This is related to the principle that some civil law systems refer to as the principle of specificity.[54] The idea behind the certainty principle is that the law will not recognise an interest in a thing as a property interest unless it is possible for outsiders and all interested parties to be able to ascertain exactly what that thing is, who holds the interest and the precise scope of the interest holder's interest in the thing.

However, two qualifications of the certainty requirement are worth noting here.

(a) Territorial Certainty

The idea of territorial certainty needs to be treated with some caution. If we were to insist that land rights can only be property rights if it is possible to draw a line around the land affected, all pastoralists would be held to have no property rights in the land and resources they live on. This issue has caused problems in indigenous land rights cases. As we see in Chapter 9 *Multiple Property Rights Systems*, one of the reasons why early common law courts refused to accept that indigenous peoples had property rights in the land they inhabited and used, was that the courts were not

---

[52] Chapter 1 *What Property Is and Why It Matters* para 1.26(b).
[53] Chapter 13 *Non-Possessory Land Use Rights* para. 13.3.
[54] Van Erp and Akkermans *Property Law* pp. 75–76, and see p. 76 as to German law distinguishing the principle of specificity from the principle of certainty: we group both of these under our principle of certainty. As van Erp and Akkermans explain, civil lawyers view the principle of specificity and the principle of publicity (which we consider in Chapter 16 *Registration*) as components of an overarching principle of transparency. See also George L. Gretton and Andrew J. M. Steven *Property, Trusts and Succession* (3rd edn, Haywards Heath, UK: Bloomsbury Professional, 2017) paras. 4.14–4.16 and 4.19–4.21 for the scope and application of the principles of specificity and publicity in Scotland.

persuaded that the claimants could establish with sufficient certainty exactly what land they were claiming. This has now been convincingly rejected both in Australia and in Canada.[55]

In addition, it should be noted that in England and Wales it has always been accepted that boundaries between land and sea (and sometimes between land and inland waters) can fluctuate:[56] see further Chapter 7 *Objects of Property Interests* paras. 7.22-7.23.

(b) Fluctuating Assets, Funds and Floating Charges

In addition, the certainty principle does not prevent us from recognising property interests in something that we decide to conceptualise as an identifiable intangible thing, even though its contents fluctuate. We can think of this as everything which is, at a given moment in time, contained in an identifiable bucket, or covered by an identifiable umbrella, such as the stock held at any given moment in time by a shop, or the goodwill of a business, or its book debts (the debts at any given moment owed to it by all its customers, suppliers etc.).

The property interests of beneficiaries in the property held on trust for them provide a good example. If a person's interest in a thing cannot be categorised as a property interest unless the thing is certain, then at first sight this seems to prevent us from recognising a beneficiary's interests under a trust as a property interest, because it is a basic trust principle that trustees have the power to remove assets from the trust and acquire new assets without the consent or knowledge of the beneficiaries. However, equity solved this potential problem by inventing the concept of a trust fund, which can be described as an intangible thing comprising the assets which at any given time are subject to the trust. Since there is no uncertainty at any given moment in time over the assets that are then in the trust fund, the certainty principle is not a barrier to recognising a beneficiary's interest under the trust as a property interest.[57]

RECOMMENDED READING

Most readers will find it helpful to read fuller accounts of the arguments over the justifications for the *numerus clausus* principle and the way it operates. These can be found in the journal articles listed below. The cases listed should be read as illustrating how the courts approach the question of whether a 'new' property interest should be recognised. We come across other good examples in later chapters (for instance in Chapter 7 *Objects of Property Interest*, where we look at property in human bodies and human body parts). We come back to the cases listed below (especially the last three) in later chapters, where we look more closely at the nature of the property interest in question.

---

[55] See *Milirrpum* v. *Nabalco Pty Ltd* (1971) 17 FLR 141 (Australia) considered in Chapter 9 para. 9.8 and *Tsilhqot'in Nation* v. *British Columbia* [2014] 2 SCR 256 (Canada) in Chapter 9 paras. 9.15–9.16.

[56] *Lynn Shellfish Ltd* v. *Loose* [2016] UKSC 14.

[57] Nicola Jackson, 'Overreaching in registered land law' (2006) *Modern Law Review* 214 at pp. 223–224.

Thomas W. Merrill and Henry E. Smith, 'Optimal standardization in the law of property: The numerus clausus principle' (2000) 110 *Yale Law Journal* 1 at pp. 1–12, 25–38, 42–45 and 68–70 (note that Merrill and Smith are talking about the numerus clausus in US law, and that the illustrations and examples they give are all taken from US law; you should not assume the position is the same in England and Wales).

Bram Akkermans, 'Standardization of property rights in European property law' in Bram Akkermans, Ernst Marais and Eveline Ramaekers (eds.), *Property Law Perspectives II* (Cambridge, Antwerp and Portland, OR: Intersentia, 2014) Ius Communae Europaeum, p. 221, especially pp. 223–233 and 239–240 (the rest has interesting details on the way the numerus clausus principle works in some continental European countries).

Ezra Rosser, 'Destabilising property' (2015) 48 *Connecticut Law Review* 397 at pp. 408–411.

Bernard Rudden in 'Economic theory v. property law: The numerus clausus problem' in John Eekelaar and John Bell (eds.), *Oxford Essays in Jurisprudence, Third Series* (Oxford: Oxford University Press, 1987) p. 239.

Hill v. *Tupper* (1863) 2 H & C 121, 159 ER.

Tulk v. *Moxhay* (1848) 2 Ph 774, 41 ER 1143.

National Provincial Bank v. *Ainsworth* [1965] AC 1175.

Hunter v. *Canary Wharf* [1997] AC 656.

Rhone v. *Stephens* [1994] 2 AC 310.

Questions

(1)   Compare the reasons given in *Hill* v. *Tupper*, *Ainsworth* and *Hunter* v. *Canary Wharf* for refusing to recognise the right in question as a property right, and discuss whether the decisions were justified.

(2)   Compare the decisions in *Tulk* v. *Moxhay* and *Rhone* v. *Stephens*. If the court was able to treat the covenant as a property right in *Tulk* v. *Moxhay*, why was it unable to do so in *Rhone* v. *Stephens*?

(3)   How far does the *numerus clausus* principle apply in English law? How far should it apply?

(4)   Explain Merrill and Smith's optimal standardisation argument. How convincing is it?

(5)   After you have read Chapter 16, consider whether our land registration system would be capable of recording all 'fancies' on the land register.

7

Objects of Property Interests

PART I INTRODUCTION

7.1 Introduction

In Chapter 6 we noted that most legal systems allow some things but not others to be the objects of property interests. We also looked at how the courts approach the question of whether to recognise new property interests in things, whether new kinds of thing or previously unpropertised things. In this chapter we look more closely at the kinds of things that can be objects of property interests in this jurisdiction and at some of those where decisions about propertisation have proved controversial.

7.2 Categorising Objects of Property Interests

In Part II of the chapter we look at how objects of property interests are traditionally categorised in our legal system. This is important for several reasons. The first is that our traditional categorisation system, which is common to all common law jurisdictions, is derived from Roman law, on which civil law systems and mixed property systems such as the Scottish system are also based. So, a knowledge of our traditional categories helps us to 'read' other common law, civil law and mixed property systems more easily. Secondly, within our own system the property rules applicable to a thing may depend on its traditional categorisation. In particular, the rules about how a property interest can be created or transferred generally depend on the way the law categorises the object of the property interest, as we see in Chapter 14 *Acquiring Interests Informally*. Also, the remedies available to a property interest holder to enable her to enforce her property interest may depend on the categorisation of the object of her interest, as we see in Part II below.

7.3 Other Ways of Categorising Things

The third reason for looking at our traditional classification of things is to be aware that there are other ways in which our law does or could differentiate between things for property purposes. In Part III of this chapter we look at some ways of doing this. One of them, which we look at in para. 7.10 is to consider not just the objective differences between different kinds of thing, but also the different ways in which different people perceive, utilise or value the same kind of thing. An issue which crops up several times in the rest of the book is how far our property rules do and should take this into account. Should there be a difference between the rights and remedies of someone in respect of a thing which she values as part of her person-hood (the usual example given is someone's wedding ring, but it could also be a work of art that she created) and those of another holder of the same thing (a retail jeweller or art gallery, perhaps) who would happily exchange it for an objectively identical thing or for its market value? We consider these questions generally in para. 7.10, and then in para. 7.11 specifically in relation to land which is someone's home.

We then look at some kinds of object (common treasury resources and animals) which are so different from other kinds of object that arguably they ought to be in separate categories of their own, governed by sui generis property rights systems. We outline the issues in paras. 7.12 and 7.13.

7.4 Land and Human Bodies

In the rest of the chapter we take a detailed look at two very different kinds of thing: land in Part IV and human bodies and bodily material in Part V.

'Land' as an object of property interests is central to most property rights systems, including ours. However, exactly what, physically, is included in 'land' varies significantly between jurisdictions. In our legal system if you have the fee simple ownership of a plot of land, the traditional common law principle is that you 'own' the three dimensional space which stretches upwards and downwards from the surface of the ground within the boundaries of your plot, 'all the way up to heaven and all the way down to hell', together with the surface of the ground itself and everything built on or attached to or growing in it or found beneath it.[1] However, we have always made exceptions from the traditional principle for some things in, under or attached to the surface of the land (gold and silver for example, have always belonged to the Crown), and in more recent times we have had to adjust our rules about the upper and lower physical boundaries of land, to accommodate such developments as air travel, drones, overhead cranes and fracking. We consider these modifications of the traditional principle in Part IV of this chapter, where we also look at how 'land' can be disaggregated into separate physical elements for property purposes, and how this affects the property interests that might be held in them.

In Part V we consider a very different kind of object of property interests – human bodies and body parts and other bodily material separated from the body. These are things that have only recently come to be regarded as potential objects of property interests, and the main issue we are concerned with is the desirability and practicality of propertising them. We have always had rules about the treatment of live and dead human bodies but generally the common law has refused to recognise

---

[1] See further paras. 7.15–7.18 for the origins of the rule and its present scope.

them as objects of property rights (if we ignore the glaring exception of the periods in our history when we allowed one human being to own another as a slave). However, recently we have started to be able to make extensive use of body parts and other bodily material taken from live and dead bodies, converting them into objects of scarcity and value. We now do this on an industrial scale. Human bodily material of all kinds (blood, cells, skin, hearts, kidneys, corneas, sperm and other reproductive material, DNA, etc.) is now routinely taken from live and dead bodies, sometimes to be used for transplant back into the body of the donor or into the body of someone else, sometimes to be used in human reproductive medicine, sometimes to be put in a repository to be used for research or therapeutic or educational purposes, sometimes even to be used to create works of art or other artefacts for public display. Unsurprisingly, most of this activity is heavily regulated by the state. The question we are interested in here is whether state regulation ought to be supplemented by property law. In other words, to what extent do we and should we recognise property interests in these very different kinds of human body materials, and what kind of property interests should they be? We look at this question in Part V of this chapter.

PART II TRADITIONAL COMMON LAW CATEGORISATION OF THINGS

7.5 Real and Personal Property

Traditionally, we categorise property interests according to the nature of the thing to which the property interest relates. In common law systems such as ours, the primary distinction is between 'real property' (property interests in land) and 'personal property' (property interests in anything else).

(a) Distinction Between Real Property and Personal Property

In our jurisdiction 'real property' now consists of all property interests in land or in any of the constituent elements of land. For these purposes, 'land' is the three dimensional physical entity which includes the surface of the land, the airspace above it and everything below it,[2] including all things growing in or under it and all tangible things attached to or below the surface. Personal property consists of all property interests in all other kinds of thing, tangible or intangible.

The real/personal terminology is confusing. In civil law systems (and very often also in ours), the term 'real rights' (rights *in rem*) means *all* rights which are property rights (i.e. all rights in relation to a thing which are enforceable against the whole world), whereas 'personal rights' (rights *in personam*) means all rights which are not property rights (i.e. rights which are enforceable only against another person). So, whereas 'real rights/personal rights' is about the distinction between property and

---

[2] With upper and lower limits we look at in Part IV below.

non-property, 'real property/personal property' is all about the distinction between land and other things.

(b) What Comes Within the Real Property Category

For all practical purposes it is now no longer necessary to look beyond the general principle that all property interests in land are real property. At one time leasehold interests in land (which have always had an ambivalent status in English law, as we see in Chapter 17) used to be regarded as personal property,[3] but it is now accepted that they belong in the real property category with all the other property interests in land.

Similarly, at one time it was necessary to distinguish a sub-set of real property interests called *incorporeal hereditaments*. Although most of these are now rare or obsolete, two of them – easements and profits – are very common indeed, and we consider them in detail in Chapter 13 *Non-Possessory Land Use Rights*. However, nearly all the consequences of being categorised as an incorporeal hereditament have long been abolished, and as far as easements and profits are concerned, their status as incorporeal hereditaments does not distinguish them from other real property interests in any significant way.

(c) What Comes Within the Personal Property Category

In our system personal property is an open-ended residual category, comprising all tangible and intangible things which are the object of property interests, except things which fall within the description of 'land'. When the courts or Parliament recognise or create a new kind of property interest and it does not relate to land, then it must necessarily be a property interest in personal property. There are, however, significant distinctions between different sub-categories of personal property, and we look at these in paras. 7.6 and 7.7.

(d) Equivalent Distinctions in Other Legal Systems

The modern common law distinction between 'real' property and 'personal' property roughly approximates to similar distinctions drawn in civil law systems. So, for example French law distinguishes between 'immoveable' and 'moveable' things,[4] and Scottish law distinguishes between 'heritable' and 'moveable' property.[5] However, the comparisons between jurisdictions are rarely exact, and the importance of the distinction between what we call land and everything else also varies between jurisdictions. So, for example, in the common law the differences between the core rules and principles applicable to interests in land and those applicable to personal

---

[3] As a special sub-category of personal property, called 'chattels real'.

[4] See art. 516 of the French *Code Civil* Title I of Book II: 'Tous les biens sont meubles ou immeubles'.

[5] George L. Gretton and Andrew J. M. Steven, *Property, Trusts and Succession* (3rd edn, Haywards Heath, UK: Bloomsbury Professional, 2017) at paras. 1.21–1.23.

property are so different that law students nearly always study them as separate subjects, starting (and often ending) with land. In Germany, on the other hand, although a distinction is made between moveable things (*bewegliche Sache*) and land (*Grundstück*), the main body of property rules and principles in the Civil Code (the BGB) applies to both indiscriminately, and German law students study property as a single unified subject, *Sachenrecht*.

7.6 Tangible and Intangible Personal Property

(a) Distinction Between Tangible and Intangible Property

Within personal property, the primary distinction in common law systems is between property rights in tangible things and property rights in intangible things.[6] Tangible things, sometimes called 'goods' or 'chattels', are things (apart from land) that you can possess physically, in the sense of being able to take them under your physical control. This covers a great variety of things, including aircraft, computer hardware, clothes and jewellery, cut flowers and plants in pots, and living organisms such as humans and animals.

Intangible property is the label traditionally given to property rights and interests in intangible things. Intangible things cover a vast range, which increases as scientific and technological advances produce new conceptualisations of 'things'. A 5G radio spectrum frequency band, for example, is now a thing but once was not. The radio spectrum itself is a natural phenomenon which has always existed, but it only started to become conceptualised as a 'thing' when wireless communication was invented. At that point radio spectrum frequency bands became thought of as 'things' because specific frequency bands within the spectrum had to be allocated between different uses and users. Now that some of those 'things' are being assigned for 5G use, to be allocated to network operators, 5G radio spectrum frequency bands are becoming identifiable 'things' in their own right.[7]

We look at different kinds of intangible personal property in para. 7.7 and para. 7.8. However, we should appreciate that some property rights systems, such as the German system, do not recognise the category of intangible property at all.[8] In German law, property law is defined as the law of property rights in things (*Sache*), and para. 90 of the BGB states that 'Only corporeal objects are things as defined by

---

[6] Other jurisdictions, including Scotland, make the same kind of distinction by using the terms 'corporeal' (i.e. embodied) and 'incorporeal' (disembodied), but again, we should not assume that these terms are the exact equivalent of tangible and intangible: Lady Gloster in *Computer Associates UK Ltd* v. *The Software Incubator Ltd* [2018] EWCA Civ 518 at para. 29.

[7] See www.ofcom.org.uk/spectrum/spectrum-management for a (relatively) comprehensible account, and also Chapter 3 *Allocation of Property Rights* para. 3.5 on the system for allocating property rights in the radio spectrum.

[8] See Sabrina Praduroux, 'Objects of property rights: Old and new', in Michele Graziadei and Lionel Smith (eds.), *Comparative Property Law: Global Perspectives* (Cheltenham and Northampton, MA: Edward Elgar Publishing, 2017) p. 51 at pp. 53–56, and also Ugo Mattei, *Basic Principles of Property Law: A Comparative and Economic Introduction* (Westport, CT and London: Greenwood Press, 2000), Chapter 4 'The object of property rights' pp. 75–98.

law'.[9] This does not mean that rights in intangible things are not recognised in German law, or that they are necessarily less protected than they are in common law systems. For example, although intellectual property is not dealt with at all in the German Civil Code,[10] either in the property law part or anywhere else, it is governed by other legislation which provides sui generis rights, powers, liberties and obligations in relation to various types of intellectual property. These resemble German property rights under the BGB in some respects but not in others.[11]

(b) Significance of the Distinction

Historically the common law regarded the distinction between tangible and intangible things as important because it regarded possession as important, and the traditional dividing line between tangible things and intangibles is that tangible things are things that can be possessed, whereas intangible things are things that cannot. This affects the remedies available to the property interest holder, because the primary liability of someone who interferes with a personal property interest – liability in the tort of conversion – applies only to possessory interests, and therefore (on the face of it) only to tangible personal property, and not to intangible personal property. The tort of conversion is in other respects much broader in scope than other torts which give redress for interference with personal property, because, like trespass (interference with land) but unlike other relevant torts, conversion is a strict liability tort, so that you are liable in conversion even if your actions were wholly innocent (for example, you mistakenly thought you were entitled to do what you did). In other words, anyone who does an act inconsistent with my possessory rights in land or in a tangible thing, however innocently, is liable to me for any loss caused, either in the tort of trespass (if the tangible thing is land) or in conversion (if it is goods or chattels). If, on the other hand, someone interferes with my rights in an intangible thing (perhaps a piece of computer software I developed), thereby causing me loss, they will not be liable to me unless I can show that they acted wrongfully in some way.

The dramatic (and arguably unjustified) effect of this distinction is demonstrated by the decision in *OBG Ltd* v. *Allan*,[12] where the House of Lords nevertheless decided to reaffirm these long-established principles. OBG Ltd was a company which carried on business laying and maintaining underground pipes for commercial customers. One of its creditors wrongly appointed receivers over all the property of the company. The receivers, who had no reason to suspect that their appointment was invalid, took control over all the company's assets (its premises, all its plant and machinery and other goods, and all its contracts with customers and suppliers), as they would have been entitled to do if they had been validly appointed. The value of

---

[9] *'Sachen im Sinne des Gesetzes sind nur körperliche Gegenstände.'*
[10] The BGB (*Bürgerliches Gesetzbuch*).
[11] Thomas Drier, 'How much "property" is there in intellectual property? The German civil law perspective' in Helena H. Howe and Jonathan Griffiths (eds.), *Concepts of Property in Intellectual Property* (Cambridge: Cambridge University Press, 2013) p. 116.
[12] *OBG Ltd* v. *Allan* [2007] UKHL 21.

all these assets at this point was about £2 million, and about 90 per cent of that was attributable to OBG's interests under the contracts, that is, its intangible assets. OBG's business collapsed,[13] the company went into liquidation, and the liquidator brought this action on behalf of the company to recover the loss caused to it by the receivers' actions. It was accepted that the receivers were liable in trespass for the loss caused to OBG by the receivers' interference with OBG's property interest in its premises (its land), and in conversion for loss caused by their interference with OBG's property interests in its plant and machinery and other goods (its tangible goods) because both trespass and conversion are strict liability torts. However, the House of Lords held that the loss caused by interference with OBG's interests in its intangible assets was irrecoverable from the receivers, because, so the House of Lords re-affirmed, the tort of conversion involves an interference with possession and so cannot apply to intangible things because it is not possible to have possession of intangible things, and liability in any other property-related tort depended on fault.

(c) Arbitrary Distinctions

Such differences in available remedies might be justifiable if things you can possess are different in kind from things you cannot, but this is not universally true. For example, physical money (in the form of banknotes or coins) is tangible personal property, and so too are bank cards that enable you to extract cash from a cash machine or pay for things in a shop or restaurant. However, money in other forms, such as the money in your bank account, is intangible personal property. In legal terms, a credit balance in your bank account is a debt the bank owes you (so if your account shows a £100 credit it means the bank owes you £100), whereas an overdrawn account is a debt you owe the bank (if you are overdrawn by £100, you owe the bank £100). There seems no good reason why the remedies available to or against you in respect of a money claim should differ depending on whether the money you lost or gained was in tangible or intangible form.

In *Your Response Ltd* v. *Datateam Business Media Ltd*[14] the Court of Appeal drew a distinction between tangible and intangible which is even more difficult to defend by distinguishing between a database in paper form, an electronic database acquired by download from a website or email attachment and an electronic database held on a physical medium such as a disk or storage device. The case concerned an agreement between a magazine publisher and a database manager, which provided for the database manager to take charge of the magazine's electronic database, maintaining and updating it. After some time the magazine publisher became dissatisfied with the database manager's services and it demanded the database back and refused to pay the outstanding fees. The issue was whether the database manager was entitled to hang on to the database until it was paid what it was owed. The decision turned on whether the database manager was technically 'in possession' of

---

[13] Not necessarily caused by the appointment of the receivers or by what they did: Lord Hoffmann in
   OBG Ltd v. Allan (fn. 12 above) at para. 88.
[14] *Your Response Ltd* v. *Datateam Business Media Ltd* [2014] EWCA Civ 281.

the database. If it was, it was entitled to a 'possessory lien' over the database: it is settled law that a person who has been commissioned to carry out work on someone else's tangible property has a possessory lien over it, which gives her a right to retain the property until paid for the work done.[15] The Court of Appeal held that the database manager did not have a possessory lien over the database and therefore had no right to refuse to return it. It accepted that the database base manager would have acquired possession of the database if it had been sent to it in paper form, or in electronic form via a physical medium such as a storage device, in which case it would have been entitled to a possessory lien over that paper or over that physical medium, until paid what it was owed for the work it did on the database. If, however (as seems to have happened in *Your Response*), the database was sent to the database manager electronically (as an email attachment or a download), the database manager was holding no physical object belonging to the magazine publisher. There was, therefore, nothing over which the database manager could have a possessory lien, because (so the Court of Appeal held) a possessory lien is exercisable only over a tangible object and a database in itself is an intangible object. On this last point the Court of Appeal regarded itself as bound by the decision of the House of Lords in *OBG* v. *Allan*. In both cases the court declined to extend the meaning of possession so that it covered factual control over access to intangible things: as Moore-Bick said in *Your Response* at paras. 22 and 23, possession and control are different things. We come back to this point in Chapter 11 *Possession and Title*,[16] where we look more closely at the concept of possession.

The Court of Appeal has since applied the same principles to computer software, deciding that unless it is contained in a physical medium such as a disk, it is an intangible object and therefore cannot be considered to be 'goods' for the purposes of legislation which regulates dealings with goods.[17] On the other hand, gas and electricity have been held to be goods, and therefore tangible property.[18]

7.7 Traditional Categories of Intangible Personal Property

(a) Things in Action

There are conflicting views about whether intangible personal property consists of only a single category – 'things in action', traditionally called 'choses in action' – or whether 'things in action' is just one of several different categories of intangible personal property.

---

[15] A lien is a kind of security interest over tangible goods: see Chapter 5 *Ownership and Other Property Interests* para. 5.37(c).

[16] para. 11.11.

[17] *Computer Associates UK Ltd* v. *The Software Incubator Ltd* [2018] EWCA Civ 518. An appeal to the Supreme Court is, however, outstanding and so the Supreme Court will have the opportunity to consider whether to perpetuate or remove the anomaly.

[18] *Tamarind International Ltd* v. *Eastern Natural Gas (Retail) Ltd* [2000] Eu. LR. 708. In *Computer Associates UK Ltd* v. *The Software Incubator Ltd*, fn. 17 above, the Court of Appeal accepted that 'it is impossible coherently to explain why gas and electricity are any more tangible property than [the software supplied by email]' (para. 53).

A 'thing in action' is traditionally (and not very helpfully) defined as a property right in something other than land, which can only be claimed or enforced by court action and not by taking physical possession of the object of the property right.

If it is true that 'thing in action' is the only kind of intangible personal property recognised in the common law, and it is defined as a closed class, it follows that if a thing is not tangible, a right in that thing cannot be a property right unless it falls within the definition of 'thing in action'. A decision of the House of Lords in the nineteenth century, *Colonial Bank* v. *Whinney* is usually taken as authority in support of this view,[19] and in *Your Response Ltd* v. *Datateam Business Media Ltd*[20] Moore-Bick LJ said that *Colonial Bank* v. *Whinney* 'makes it very difficult to accept that the common law recognises the existence of intangible property other than choses in action'.[21]

However, this view is now disputed, and it is probably more accurate to say that a 'thing in action' is just one kind of intangible property. If you accept this view, the correct approach for the courts is to consider first whether an interest in an intangible thing *ought* to be recognised as a property interest; if the court decides it should, then the interest will come within the 'thing in action' category if it fits the definition, but if it does not, it will create a separate, sui generis, kind of intangible property right. This was the approach adopted by the Privy Council in *Attorney General of Hong Kong* v. *Nai-Keung* [1987] 1 WLR 1339, where it held that textile export quotas were not things in action but were intangible property, and later cases have adopted the same approach. So, for example, in *Armstrong DLW Gmbh* v. *Winnington Networks Ltd* [2012] EWHC 10,[22] which we looked at in Chapter 6 *New Property Interests and the Numerus Clausus* para. 6.11, the court held that a carbon emission unit was property, and that since it was not tangible property, it must be intangible property and therefore had to be either a thing in action or (more likely) intangible property of a sui generis kind.[23] The same analysis would seem to apply to all the other 'new' kinds of intangible property we look at in para. 7.8 below, that is, intellectual property, regulatory property and electronic resources.

(b) Documentary Intangibles

Whether we take things in action as the only category of intangible property or one of several, it is now generally accepted that there is a sub-set of things in action, namely 'documentary intangibles'.[24] Intangibles which are not 'documentary intangibles' are usually referred to as 'pure intangibles'.

---

[19] *Colonial Bank* v. *Whinney* (1886) 11 App. Cas. 426. The House of Lords approved Fry LJ's statement in the Court of Appeal that 'all personal things are either in possession or in action. The law knows no *tertium quid* between the two' and on that basis held that shares in a company are things in action.

[20] *Your Response Ltd* v. *Datateam Business Media Ltd* [2014] EWCA Civ 281.   [21] Ibid. para. 26.

[22] *Armstrong DLW Gmbh* v. *Winnington Networks Ltd* [2012] EWHC 10.

[23] Ibid. paras. 40–62. He did not have to decide which, because it made no difference to the remedies awarded.

[24] For a helpful account see *Armstrong DLW Gmbh* v. *Winnington Networks Ltd* [2012] EWHC 10 at para. 47.

Documentary intangibles are property rights in intangible things which are 'embodied' in a paper document, in the sense that the document is taken to represent the property right, with possession of the document treated as possession of the right itself, so that, for example, a physical transfer of the document is generally sufficient to transfer the property right. Because a tangible thing – the document – represents the intangible right, and you can have possession of a document, property law sometimes treats documentary intangibles as if they were tangibles. For example, it has been held that the tort of conversion applies to documentary intangibles, even though, as we saw in para. 7.6(b), it does not apply to other intangibles. So, we can view documentary credits as a hybrid form of personal property, part tangible and part intangible.

Documentary intangibles include cheques and other negotiable instruments, promissory notes, bearer bonds, bills of exchange and bills of lading. Leaving aside cheques, we now rarely come across documentary intangibles except in business transactions between commercial entities. In any event, they will become increasing less important as paper documents are replaced by electronic equivalents, unless the courts choose to extend the category to electronic documents or electronic entries recording dealings.[25]

7.8 New Kinds of Intangible Property

There are other kinds of intangible property which have little in common with each other or with other traditional categories of intangibles. These include the various things which are subject to intellectual property rights (patents, copyrights, trade-marks, registered designs rights and databases),[26] regulatory licences such as fishing quotas and water abstraction licences,[27] spectrum rights,[28] genetic information,[29] and electronic resources such as computer software, digital files, and bitcoins etc. Together, these assets represent a far greater proportion of the wealth of many commercial enterprises than their tangible assets or their traditional intangible assets. For this reason and others, there are arguments over whether some of them should be recognised as objects of property interests at all within our property rights system, and if they are, over the kinds of property rights structures that are appropriate.

7.9 Shortcomings of Traditional Common Law Categorisation of Things

It will be apparent from the preceding paragraphs that our traditional common law categorisation of things has some serious shortcomings. One criticism is that the boundary between tangible and intangible personal property can be arbitrary, as we

---

[25] Ibid. para. 51.   [26] See Chapter 3 *Allocation of Property Rights* para. 3.4.
[27] Chapter 6 *New Property Interests and the Numerus Clausus* para. 6.12.
[28] para. 7.6 above, and see also Chapter 3 *Allocation of Property Rights* para. 3.5 for the system of allocating property rights in the radio spectrum.
[29] para. 7.30 below.

saw in para. 7.6(c) above. Also, advances in our scientific knowledge cast doubt on our tangibles/intangibles distinction: are very small things such as neutrinos,[30] or genetic material such as DNA, for example, tangible or intangible?

Another criticism is that documentary intangibles – that is, rights in action which are embodied in documents – are put in the intangibles box, but treated as if they were in the tangibles box for the purposes of deciding what remedies are available for breach of the rights. Also, it is by no means clear how far intangibles 'embodied' in electronic documents will be treated in the same way, and whether they should be.

The most serious problem, however, is that the tangible personal property category and the intangible personal property category are both impossibly wide, failing to distinguish between things that ought to be (and often are) treated differently in property law terms. So, for example, we put in the tangible personal property box things as disparate as human body parts and bodily tissue (to the extent they are propertised),[31] animals and aeroplanes. No-one would suggest that the property rights, freedoms, duties, powers and remedies that a person might have in, say, a human kidney removed from her body to be transplanted into the body of a donee, should be the same as she has in her pet dog or in the fleet of aircraft she owns.

The intangible personal property box is unsatisfactory in the same kind of way. Until comparatively recently it was possible to conceive of a coherent category consisting of rights in action, but there is no coherence in a box that now has to contain all different kinds of financial instrument, all kinds of electronic resource and all the disparate kinds of thing we listed as intangible things in para. 7.8. Decisions about how property rights in such things should be protected, and how they should be created and transferred, really should not be dictated by the fact that they all fall into the same category box.

So, for all these reasons we have to question how useful our traditional common law classification system really is.

PART III OTHER WAYS OF CATEGORISING THINGS

7.10 Distinguishing Things by Reference to Subjective Value or Function

There are other ways of categorising things which might be more helpful. One way of doing it is to look at the value or function that something has *for its present holder*. The point is that the same kind of thing can have a *different kind of value or function* for some people than it has for others, and that the very same thing may have a subjective value for one person which is very different from the subjective value it has for others.

Many commentators have remarked on the fact that we value some things only for the wealth they represent (I would be unconcerned if, for example, a £20 note

---

[30] Neutrinos are sub-atomic particles which, apparently have mass, but they are impossible to see and very difficult to detect: www.britannica.com/science/neutrino.
[31] See Part V below.

I now have in my pocket was taken away and replaced with another £20 note), whereas there are other things which we value in themselves (the examples usually given are my wedding ring or my home). The crucial point is that just about *any* given thing can fall into either category depending on the circumstances: any given thing can mean different things to different people at different times. So, when I bought my wedding ring from a shop, it was valued as wealth by the shopkeeper but became valued for itself by me, and if I now pawn it in a pawnshop, it will represent wealth to the pawnshop owner but I will continue to value it for itself. Even a banknote, almost always valued only as wealth by whoever holds it, whatever the circumstances, might conceivably sometimes be valued for itself (if, for example, it is part of a particular series printed, very few of which are now in circulation, and I need it to complete my collection).

The issue we are concerned with here is how far, if at all, the law does and should take this wealth–thing distinction into account. This question most obviously arises when a court has to adjudicate between two people in dispute over the same thing: should it be relevant that for one of them the thing represents (only) wealth, whereas for the other it represents something more? However, it also arises in other contexts, as we see in later chapters.

In a much-cited article 'Property and personhood' published in 1982,[32] Margaret Jane Radin uses the idea of investing our will in an object as a basis for a theory of property and personhood, to account for the particularly strong psychological bond we develop with some of the things that we regard as our own (things like wedding rings and homes), and to raise questions about how far this special bond can and should be reflected by law. Radin's objective is to look more closely at what she describes as the 'personhood perspective' developed by Hegel,[33] which focusses on personal embodiment of ourselves in things, and the role this personal embodiment plays in our self-constitution, and to see how it can be applied in a modern legal setting. She takes the premise underlying the personhood perspective to be that, in order to achieve 'proper self-development – to be a person – an individual needs some control over resources in the external environment', in the form of property rights in external objects.[34] She suggests that this personhood perspective accounts for the empirically verifiable fact that we all tend to develop a special bond with some of the things we regard as our own: our intuitive feeling is that these things matter to us because we think of them as in some sense part of ourselves:

> These objects are closely bound up with personhood because they are part of the way we constitute ourselves as continuing personal entities in the world . . . one may gauge the strength or significance of someone's relationship with an object by the kind of pain that would be occasioned by its loss. On this view, an object is closely related to

---

[32] Margaret Jane Radin, 'Property and personhood' (1982) 34 *Stanford Law Review* 957.

[33] See Chapter 2 *Conceptions and Justifications* paras. 2.22 and 2.23.

[34] Whereas Hegel regards *property in general* as necessary for the development of the person, Radin sees it as necessary only for what she calls 'personal property', i.e. property that we feel is personally important to us, in the sense that we feel it is part of who we are: see further Jeffrey Douglas Jones, 'Property and personhood revisited' (2011) 1 *Wake Forest Journal of Law & Policy* 93.

one's personhood if its loss causes pain that cannot be relieved by the object's replacement . . .[35]

She calls these things 'personal property', to distinguish them from what she calls 'fungible things', which are the things we think of as important only for the wealth they represent, or things like a packet of cereal we bought and would happily exchange for an identical equivalent.

The question is, then, whether and when this intuitive feeling towards some of our things deserves moral recognition and legal protection. She argues that our relationship with these 'personal property' things deserves both recognition and protection because (or perhaps when[36]) these things are bound up with our feelings of personhood – our feelings of who we are – and so are necessary for our human flourishing.

More specifically, she argues that this personhood perspective provides 'a moral basis for protecting some rights more stringently than others in the context of a legal system'. One, often unnoticed, example she gives is of group rights. She points out that:

> in a given social context certain groups are likely to be constitutive of their members in the sense that the members find self-determination only within the groups. This might have political consequences for claims of the group on certain resources of the external world (i.e., property).[37]

In other words, this would support the proposition that when a community and its members regard certain resources they utilise as 'theirs' (in the sense that they see the resources as constitutive of their identity as a community), they should be regarded as having rights in those resources which prevail over the claims of others.

However, the main thrust of her argument is concerned with private property rights. She accepts that in the real world there is no sharp divide between the things we regard as 'personal' and those we regard as 'fungible' (i.e. the degree of our attachment to things varies along a continuum, and can change over time). Her argument is that

> those rights near one end of the continuum – fungible property rights – can be overridden in some cases in which those near the other – personal property rights – cannot be. This is to argue not that fungible property rights are unrelated to person-hood, but simply that distinctions are sometimes warranted depending upon the character or strength of the connection. Thus, the personhood perspective generates a hierarchy of entitlements: The more closely connected with personhood, the stronger the entitlement.

---

[35] Radin, 'Property and personhood', fn. 32 above, p. 959.

[36] She does suggest that sometimes our attachment to a thing is 'fetishistic' and so not worthy of respect or protection (ibid. p. 961 and p. 987), but if we accept that, it takes us into difficult questions of how far the outside world should have a say in what we value, and why and how. See also Margaret Davies, *Property: Meanings, Histories, Theories* (Abingdon: Routledge-Cavendish, 2007) p. 101, remarking on an 'unspoken politics of normality operating at this point of Radin's argument'.

[37] Radin, 'Property and personhood', fn. 32 above p. 978.

Radin sets out her conclusions as a series of propositions 'as a starting point for further thought...:

> (1) At least some conventional property interests in society ought to be recognized and preserved as personal.

> (2) Where we can ascertain that a given property right is personal, there is a prima facie case that that right should be protected to some extent against invasion by government and against cancellation by conflicting fungible property claims of other people. This case is strongest where without the claimed protection of property as personal, the claimants' opportunities to become fully developed persons in the context of our society would be destroyed or significantly lessened, and probably also where the personal property rights are claimed by individuals who are maintaining and expressing their group identity.

> (3) Where we can ascertain that a property right is fungible, there is a prima facie case that that right should yield to some extent in the face of conflicting recognized personhood interests, not embodied in property. This case is strongest where without the claimed personhood interest, the claimants' opportunities to become fully developed persons in the context of our society would be destroyed or significantly lessened.'[38]

The important point about these propositions is that they invite us to think about two fundamental questions. The first is whether, and if so in what circumstances, a 'personal' property interest should prevail over a 'fungible' one,[39] and, equally important, whether, and if so when, it can actually do so in our present law. The second is whether, and if so in what circumstances, a 'personhood' right which is not a property right should prevail over a property right,[40] and whether, and if so when, it can ever do so in our law. We have looked at some specific instances of these questions arising in relation to human rights in Chapter 4 *Property and Human Rights*, and they come up again in later chapters.[41]

7.11 'Home' as a Distinct Category

It is often argued that there should be a separate set of property rules and principles that apply to a place which is someone's home, different from those which would apply to the same place if it was not being used as someone's home. To a certain limited extent, our property rights system reflects this view. For example, it forms the basis of the human right to respect for one's private life and home which we looked at in Chapter 4 *Property and Human Rights*. As we saw there in para. 4.34(a), home in that context is regarded as especially deserving of protection for at least three reasons. To summarise Antoine Buyse's analysis already quoted in para. 4.34(a),[42] home provides us with a place of *shelter and security,* in the sense

---

[38] Ibid. pp. 1014–1015.   [39] Radin's proposition (2).   [40] Her proposition (3).
[41] For example, in relation to enforceability and priority of property interests (Chapter 15 *Enforceability and Priority of Property Interests* and Chapter 16 *Registration*).
[42] Antoine Buyse, 'Strings attached: The concept of "home" in the case law of the ECtHR' [2006] 3 EHRLR 294.

of protection against the physical elements and from physical intrusion by the state and by fellow citizens; it provides us with *privacy,* meaning a private sphere where we are free to do what we want,[43] and to live as we like free from outside interference, and within and from which we develop our social relationships; and we are likely to have a *bond of attachment* to it, which makes us regard it as part of our personhood in the way Margaret Radin described.[44]

Arising out of these and other factors, there are a number of arguments that can be made about treating 'home' as a distinctive kind of object of property rights.

(a) Implications of the Personhood Argument

If we accept the personhood argument made by Radin, the obvious implication is that the particular place which is now a person's home is likely to have become a part of their personhood to such an extent that each person who as a matter of fact occupies that place as her home should have an overriding property interest in it, giving her a proprietary right to continue to do so which prevails over any other proprietary right in the property. However, there are broader implications. We can argue that, because of the personhood attachment you have with the place where you live, you should be entitled to have a say in decisions about the way it is managed and whether and when it should be sold or mortgaged. In our system, you automatically will have that say if you are the legal owner of the house. However, many people have only an equitable interest in their home, usually a beneficial interest under a co-ownership trust.[45] It therefore becomes important to consider whether trust beneficiaries who live in a house held on trust for them, have adequate rights and powers as against each other and as against the trustees, so that their views and their interests are properly taken into account. As we see in Chapter 8 *Property Interest Holders*, beneficiaries under trusts who are (or are entitled to be) in occupation of the trust property do have special rights and powers under the Trusts of Land and Appointment of Trustees Act 1996.[46] We consider there whether these statutory provisions adequately protect the interests of beneficiaries in their home.

(b) Rights to *a* Home

A second argument focuses on the value to a person of *a* home. This is radically different from the personhood argument. It is that everyone needs *a* home to enable them to fulfil their human potential. We have already come across this argument in Chapter 3 *Allocation of Property Rights* paras. 3.13 and 3.16, and it surfaces again in relation to human rights.[47] As we saw in those chapters our human rights law does

---

[43] Cf. Jeremy Waldron's account of the plight of the homeless, deprived of a private sphere, which we looked at in Chapter 3 *Allocation of Property Rights* para. 3.13.
[44] para. 7.10 above.   [45] Chapter 8 *Property Interest Holders*, Part III.   [46] Ibid. para. 8.13.
[47] See Chapter 4 *Property and Human Rights* paras. 4.16 and 4.41–4.42, briefly comparing the radical housing and protection from eviction rights in s. 26 of the South African Constitution and in the Prevention of Illegal Eviction from and Unlawful Occupation of Land Act, 19 of 1998, with rights to housing in this jurisdiction under the Human Rights Act 1998.

not encompass a right to be housed. Instead, in this jurisdiction we see the issue largely as a matter of duties imposed on local authorities to provide housing under various statutory provisions, an area which is too big and too complex to be within the scope of this book.

(c) A Broader View of Home

A third argument takes a broader view of home, seeing it as extending beyond the space where we conduct our private life to the broader area where we conduct our social relationships. The argument is that we have a personhood kind of attachment to neighbourhood which is as important as our attachment to our private living space, and which the law ought to respect and protect. Lisa Austin gives a description of attachment to home which is equally apt for home in this wider sense:

> home is the 'scene' of one's life because it is the location of important projects and social relations. These projects and social relations are constitutive of identity, and can be constitutive in this sense quite independently of one's subjective relationship with the home. At the same time, many people remain in their home for a long time, and this stability of location can lead to the creation of memories in relation to the projects and social relations that have taken place over time in a particular location. People can become psychologically and emotionally attached to their home because of the important memories that they associate with it ... The point here is that on my account the normative underpinning for the special status that we ascribe to the home, and its connection to individual identity, is primarily its role as the location, sometimes over a long period, of important projects and direct social relationships.[48]

So, our neighbourhood may be the location of our cultural community, or of family and friends on whom we depend (or who depend on us) for socialising and support (babysitting, school runs, child care or care for dependents with disabilities or health problems), and of health care professionals, schools and social services who may know about any particular needs we and our families may have. It may also be the location of the places we socialise, whether going out with friends or family, or in casual encounters with neighbours in public access spaces such as roads, shops, etc. As Austin argues, locations such as these are not just places where social interaction happens, they positively 'foster direct social relations which are important to the very forming and sustaining of community'.[49]

So, one way or another, we do not just form an individual attachment to our private living space, we also form part of a community which has a collective emotional attachment to and investment in a place, and this collective attachment in itself builds and supports the community.

This has inevitable implications for property rights. It means that limitations on the property rights of others are justifiable not only to protect the individual attachment we have to our private living spaces, but also to protect the public access

---

[48] Lisa M. Austin, 'Person, place, or thing – property and the structuring of social relations' (2010) 60 *University of Toronto Law Journal* 445, at p. 453.
[49] Ibid. pp. 455–461.

rights we have to locations within our neighbourhood and the ties we have with them, not only because we regard our neighbourhood as part of what we are as a community, but also because these locations within our neighbourhood help build and sustain community.[50] It also suggests that loss of neighbourhood is something that ought to be taken into account by the law when assessing the effect of loss of home, and that interferences with our neighbourhood can have as great an effect on our welfare and flourishing (as individuals and as communities) as interferences with the private space where we live.

(d) Re-thinking the Idea of Home

Finally, however, we should note that whilst there is ample academic argument to justify our intuitions about the importance of home and the severity of the consequences of loss of home,[51] it is important to appreciate that they do not always depend on us having an emotional attachment to a particular home. Even if I do not regard my home as part of my personhood, losing it may still have an impact on my quality of life, status, personal relationships, and psychological and physical health and well-being,[52] if I left it unwillingly with nowhere else to go. Also, as Nestor Davidson points out,[53] the emotional attachment we may have with our home may not be all that it seems: empirical evidence certainly does not support the psychological claims about the importance of home which are made on the basis of Radin's personhood theory.[54] Davidson's assessment is as follows:

> Home ... may have less to do with a given physical property per se and more with the associations that come from interpersonal connections and experiences. As Ben Barros has argued, the intuitive view of the importance of home to the self 'tends to overstate an individual's personal connection to a home in a particular location because many of the important personal values associated with a home are movable.'[55] People need secure attachment and a base from which to foster positive relationships, but community and connection may matter more than any particular four walls and roof.
>
> The bottom line is that home matters, but perhaps for slightly different reasons than the law tends to acknowledge. Positive psychology reinforces the strain of doctrine that emphasises the relational and experiential aspects of home – home as a place of family, for example. That is not to minimise the Aristotelian insight that

---

[50] Ibid.

[51] See, for example, Lorna Fox, 'Re-assessing "home": A re-analysis of gender, homeownership and debtor default for feminist legal theory' (2008) 14 *William & Mary Journal of Women & Law* 423 and Lorna Fox Mahoney, 'The meaning of home: From theory to practice' (2013) 5 *International Journal of Law in the Built Environment* 156.

[52] Fox 'Re-Assessing "Home"', fn. 51, p. 434.

[53] Nestor Davidson, 'Property, well-being, and home: Positive psychology and property law's foundation' in Helen Carr, Brendan Edgeworth and Caroline Hunter (eds.), *Law and the Precarious Home: Socio Legal Perspectives on the Home in Insecure Times* (Oxford and London: Hart, 2018) p. 47, at pp. 49–50.

[54] Stephanie Stern, 'Residential protectionism and the legal myth of home' (2009) 107 *Michigan Law Review* 1094.

[55] Ben Barros, 'Home as a legal concept' (2006) 46 *Santa Clara Law Review* 255, at p. 280.

a minimum baseline of resources is critical – that without a home, questions about materialism, comparative consumption, and individual well-being are quite academic. But beyond the extreme, for the bulk of how the system of property approaches home, we need to understand that home is a means to a particular set of ends and perhaps temper the veneration that law has for home in that light.[56]

It is also worth noting the rather different reasons Margaret Davies has put forward for rejecting 'uncritical acceptance of the property for personhood paradigm' of home.[57] As she points out, 'The home is the barrier separating public from private – often to the detriment of women', and the neighbourhoods generated by clusters of homes often 'enforce racial and class divides'. Most importantly, the property for personhood idea, at least as presented by Radin, presupposes and emphasises a view of property as individualised and exclusionary. Davies suggests that, even if people do indeed construct themselves through this model of property, this is perhaps something that the law ought to challenge rather than acknowledge:

> Would it be preferable to think of our relationship with the external world not through the lens of property which connotes exclusion, power and control of external things, but through some other means?[58]

7.12 Common Treasury Resources

A category of resources which does not really find a place in our traditional categorisation of objects of property interests is what we can call 'common treasury resources'.[59] Broadly, these are resources which are seen by many as the common heritage of humankind, or of the natural world, because they are essential for the health and well-being of the environment and present and future generations of human life. On that basis, most people would agree that it is not appropriate for any one individual – or any one group or state – to have exclusive rights or unregulated control in or over them. This is a fairly common view of natural resources such as the Sun or the Moon, or Antarctica, or outer space, and also of resources which are essential to human existence and/or the health of the Earth, such as water, air, or land, or fisheries. However, many also take the same view of human constructs or discoveries, such as data, or the information commons, or the internet, or seed banks, or human tissue banks or genetic information.

On one view, all such natural things and human constructs on which human society and the environment depend, should be regulated by national or international agencies to ensure that they fulfil their role as common treasuries, but otherwise they should be free to all: no-one should have property rights in them.

---

[56] Davidson, 'Property and identity', fn. 53 above, p. 60.

[57] Davies, *Property: Meanings, Histories, Theories*, fn. 36 above, p. 103.   [58] Ibid.

[59] For reasons explained in Rosalind Malcolm and Alison Clarke, 'Water: A common treasury' in Ting Xu and Alison Clarke (eds.), *Legal Strategies for the Development and Protection of Communal Property* (published for The British Academy by Oxford University Press, 2018) p. 202 at pp. 204–205.

As we have seen in other contexts, there are arguments that this animosity towards property is misconceived. First, it ignores or underestimates the dangers of a property-free world. The absence of property rights of any kind in a thing does in theory leave everyone free to use the thing, but in practice it is difficult to devise a system (even one involving intensive state regulation and control) that effectively prevents de facto capture of control and benefit by elites.[60] Secondly, the animosity mistakenly assumes that property must mean exclusionary private ownership.

In modern societies a more appropriate property rights structure is likely to involve a mix of different types of property interest, to take into account the private, community, state and international interests in ensuring that the resource functions effectively as a common treasury. We see some examples of how this might work when we look at water and sub-surface minerals in para. 7.20. As we see there in relation to water, the property regime can consist of a mix of traditional private, communal and public use rights, underlying state ownership, privatised exploitation rights, and tight government regulatory control. To complete the picture we would also have to add in rights of local or stakeholder communities to make specific uses of local sections of the resource communally or co-operatively, and rights and duties they might also have to participate in the control and management of the resource at a local level.[61] In addition, it might be appropriate for private or state property interests to be responsibility-based rather than rights-based, and to be bound by property objectives which are not solely anthropomorphic.[62]

7.13 Humans and Animals

There have always been strongly expressed views about humans and animals as objects of property interests. We look at some of these in relation to property and human bodies in Part V of this chapter, but we can see echoes of the same arguments when we consider animals as objects of property interests.

There is an extensive academic literature arguing that animals have (or do not have) a moral status which precludes humans from having property rights in them,[63] but it has to be said that so far this has had no impact on our property rights system. In English law domesticated animals are chattels, and there are no common law or statutory provisions directly or indirectly curbing the property rights humans have in them as chattels, although there are criminal laws prohibiting cruelty and impos-ing duties on owners and other responsible persons to comply with statutory public health and animal welfare standards. This may be contrasted with the private

---

[60] Consider, for example, control of the internet, or the current trajectory of commercial exploitation of human bodily material and genetic information noted in para. 7.32 below.

[61] Malcolm and Clarke, 'Water: A common treasury', fn. 59 above, pp. 227–228.

[62] See Chapter 8 *Property Interest Holders* paras. 8.4, 8.31 and 8.34, and also the accounts of traditional indigenous property rights systems in natural resources we look at in Chapter 9 *Multiple Property Rights Systems.*

[63] *Stanford Encyclopedia of Philosophy*, 'The moral status of animals' https://plato.stanford.edu/entries/moral-animal.

property regime in Germany. By an amendment made to the BGB[64] in 1990, s. 90a was added, which provides:

> Animals are not things. They are protected by special statutes. They are governed by the provisions that apply to things, with the necessary modifications, except insofar as otherwise provided.

As Murray Raff explains, in a series of cases where separating couples each made rival claims to their family dog, courts in Germany have developed out of art. 90(a) a doctrine that the law relating to things has to be applied only by analogy to animals. In particular, in such cases they have to deal with the dog in the same way as other household objects, but at the same time:

> consider the principles of justice expressed in §90a, in which the legal order recognised animals as companions in creation. That means that they, unlike lifeless objects without feelings, cannot be dealt with without consideration of their nature and feelings.[65]

So, in the case Raff refers to in the passage just quoted, the *Poodle Access Case*,[66] the court acted on evidence from an animal psychologist 'that it would be better for the dog to remain in its familiar surroundings and that contact with the other party, measured in hours, would also promote its welfare' and made orders accordingly. Raff also refers to other cases where the pet animal has been awarded to the party better able to look after it.[67]

PART IV LAND

7.14 What is Land?

If we think of 'land' as meaning the three dimensional space we inhabit, then it seems implausible that there could ever be a legal system that did not recognise property interests in land. However, there is a very wide difference between jurisdictions in the way in which the physical elements of land are bundled. So, for example, some jurisdictions may regard trees as things that are separate from the land in which they are growing, and buildings as things that are separate from the land on which they are built.[68]

---

[64] Der Bürgerlichen Gesetzbuch (the German Civil Code).

[65] Murray Raff, *Private Property and Environmental Responsibility: A Comparative Study of German Real Property Law* (The Hague, London and New York: Kluwer Law International, 2003) p. 192.

[66] *Poodle Access Case* (1997) 50 NJW 3033, a decision of the Local Court at Bad Mergenheit. He gives examples from other court decisions on animal custody disputes in Germany.

[67] Raff, *Private Property and Environmental Responsibility*, fn. 65 above, p. 192.

[68] Quite common when land is state owned, as in Russia and urban China. For helpful historical and comparative accounts see Gerrit Pienaar, 'Legal aspects of private airspace development' (1987) 20 *Comparative and International Law Journal of South Africa* 94 at pp. 94–100, and Jill Morgan 'Subsurface ownership: The English or the American rule?' in Warren Barr (ed.) *Modern Studies in Property Law*, vol. 8 (Oxford and Portland, OR: Hart Publishing, 2015) pp. 234–236.

In England and Wales, however, as we noted in para. 7.4, 'land' is traditionally defined as the three dimensional space which stretches upwards and downwards from the surface of the ground, 'all the way up to heaven and all the way down to hell', together with the surface of the ground itself and everything built on or attached to it, or growing in it or found beneath it.[69]

However, this traditional definition has always been subject to exceptions and limitations, as we see below.

7.15 How Far Up and How Far Down?

The most important limitations are to the upper and lower limits of the three dimensional space. Unless you believe that the earth is flat, it makes no sense at all to say that landowners have property rights in the column of air that stretches from the surface of their plot of land 'all the way right up to heaven', and even flat-earthers would have to admit that it would make modern life very difficult if it was indeed true. The idea that landowners might also have property rights in the earth going all the way down to its core makes no more sense. On present scientific knowledge, technology cannot take us far below the surface of the earth. The average distance from the surface of the earth to its core is 3959 miles (6371 kilometres) and only about the top 10 miles is penetrable using present technology.[70] As Lord Hope noted in *Star Energy Weald Basin Ltd* v. *Bocardo SA* [2010] UKSC 35 'anything that is drilled below a depth of about 8.7 miles or 14 kilometers would be crushed by the earth's pressure of 50,000 pounds per square inch and vaporised by a temperature of 1,000 Fahrenheit'.[71] On our present knowledge, then, most of the earth that lies beneath the surface of the ground is so totally inaccessible that it is meaningless to talk of property interests in relation to it. That may change in the future, but even if it does, would we want to allocate private ownership of this vast space to the lucky individuals who happen to be the private owners of the surface of the ground which lies miles above it?

Legal commentators have always acknowledged that, for these and other reasons, there must be some limitations on the traditional principle,[72] and, as we see in the following paragraphs, modern courts agree. However, they have not been able to arrive at a principle which enables us to pinpoint exactly where the upper and lower boundaries of land lie.

---

[69] The basic principle dates back to the thirteenth century and is still sometimes given in Latin: *Cuius est solum, eius est usque ad coelum et ad inferos* ('whoever's is the soil, it is theirs all the way to heaven and all the way to hell'). Compare the unsatisfactory definition of land in s. 205(1)(ix) of the Law of Property Act 1925, which gives incomplete lists of the physical components of land and property interests capable of existing in land, not distinguishing between the two.

[70] See the statistics given by the BBC on the *Journey to the Centre of the Earth* website: www.bbc.com/future/bespoke/story/20150306-journey-to-the-centre-of-earth/.

[71] Lord Hope in *Star Energy Weald Basin Ltd* v. *Bocardo SA* [2010] UKSC 35 para. 19, referring to John Sprankling, 'Owning the center of the earth' (2008) 55 *UCLA Law Review* 979.

[72] See *Bernstein* v. *Skyviews & General Ltd* [1978] QB 479 at pp. 486–487 and *Star Energy Weald Basin Ltd* v. *Bocardo SA* [2010] UKSC 35 paras. 10–18 for useful summaries of judicial and textbook analyses.

7.16 The Upper Boundary of Land

As far as the upper boundary of land is concerned, the general principle is usually taken to be that stated by Griffiths J in *Bernstein* v. *Skyviews & General Ltd* [1978] QB 479. Skyviews was an aircraft business which flew planes over houses, taking aerial photographs of a house and then offering to sell the photographs to the houseowner. Lord Bernstein objected when they did this to his country estate without his consent or knowledge, and brought this action for damages for trespass to his airspace. Since trespass is a tort committed by physically invading land without authorisation,[73] Bernstein could only succeed if he could show that the airspace through which the aircraft flew was part of his land.[74] Griffiths J held that it was not, and therefore no trespass had been committed.[75] He reviewed the earlier cases and textbook analyses on the point and concluded that he was not obliged to accept 'the critical and literal application of the maxim' that a landowner's rights in the airspace above the surface of the ground extend to an unlimited height. Instead, he said, the rights of a landowner to enjoy the use of his land have to be balanced against 'the rights of the general public to take advantage of all that science now offers in the use of air space'.[76] He went on to say:

> This balance is in my judgment best struck in our present society by restricting the rights of an owner in the airspace above his land *to such height as is necessary for the ordinary use and enjoyment of his land and the structures upon it, and declaring that above that height he has no greater rights in the airspace than any other member of the public.*[77]

This principle has been criticised on the basis that it allows the upper boundary of land to fluctuate over time, as structures of different heights are erected and demolished on the land, and as changes are made to the way the land is used. However, the same applies to, for example, seaward boundaries of land at ground level, which can also shift over time through the doctrines of erosion and accretion, as we see in paras. 7.22 and 7.24. below. In practice, this kind of uncertainty over land boundaries is unlikely to cause problems in either case: the important point is that it will always be possible to ascertain the current position of the boundary at any given time.

---

[73] Either by entering it yourself or by allowing or causing something to cross the boundaries of the land (perhaps a bullet, or a cricket ball or a sign attached to your building which overhangs your neighbour's land): see further Chapter 10 *Limitations on Property* para. 10.12.

[74] If it was not part of his land, he might still have been able to rely on the tort of nuisance, which involves an indirect interference with someone's land: Chapter 10 *Limitations on Property* para. 10.12. Griffiths J explains at the end of his judgement in *Bernstein* (fn. 72 above, at p. 489) why he thought nuisance would not have been appropriate in this case.

[75] He went on to decide that even if Skyview's actions had amounted to trespass (or nuisance), it would have been exempt from liability because of s. 40(1) of the Civil Aviation Act 1949, now repealed and re-acted as s. 76(1) of the Civil Aviation Act 1982: 'No action shall lie in respect of trespass or in respect of nuisance, by reason only of the flight of an aircraft over any property at a height above the ground which, having regard to wind, weather and all circumstances of the case is reasonable, or the ordinary incidents of such flight, so long as [specified statutory regulations] have been duly complied with'.

[76] *Bernstein*, fn. 72 above, at p. 487.   [77] Ibid.

However, in later cases, courts which have had to deal directly with claims of trespass into airspace have expressed different reservations about the *Bernstein* principle. Most notably, in *Anchor Brewhouse Developments Ltd* v. *Berkley House (Docklands Developments) Ltd* [1987] 2 EGLR 173 Scott J said that the *Bernstein* principle was not relevant to the issue he had to decide in the case before him, which was whether the owner of a development site trespassed on neighbouring land when the booms of tower cranes erected on the development land 'oversailed' the neighbouring land. Scott J held that it was a trespass, and he granted the neighbour an injunction restraining the developer from allowing any part of his cranes to intrude into the air space above the surface of the neighbour's land. This is difficult to reconcile with the *Bernstein* principle, since the cranes swung over the neighbour's land at such a height that they could not conceivably have been said to invade airspace that was 'necessary for the ordinary use and enjoyment' of the neighbour's land or any structures on it. Scott agreed, but expressed the view that the *Bernstein* approach was appropriate only for intrusions into airspace by such things as 'overflying aircraft and missiles'. If, however, intrusion was by part of a structure erected on neighbouring land, Scott said, the intrusion would always be a trespass if unauthorised:

> The tort of trespass represents an interference with possession or with the right to possession. A landowner is entitled, as an attribute of his ownership of the land, to place structures on his land and thereby to reduce into actual possession the air space above his land. If an adjoining owner places a structure on his (the adjoining owner's) land that overhangs his neighbour's land, he thereby takes into his possession air space to which his neighbour is entitled. That, in my judgment, is trespass. It does not depend upon any balancing of rights.
>
> The difficulties posed by the overflying aircraft or balloons, bullets or missiles seems to me to be wholly separate from the problem which arises where there is invasion of air space by a structure placed or standing upon the land of a neighbour. One of the characteristics of the common law of trespass is, or ought to be, certainty. The extent of proprietary rights enjoyed by landowners ought to be clear. It may be that, where aircraft or overflying missiles are concerned, certainty cannot be achieved ... But certainty is capable of being achieved where invasion of air space by tower cranes, advertising signs and other structures are concerned.[78]

However, there are difficulties with Scott's analysis. It depends on his question-begging assumption, quoted above, that a landowner '*is entitled, as an attribute of his ownership of the land*, to place structures on his land and thereby to reduce into actual possession the air space above his land'. This assumes what Scott is seeking to establish, that is, it assumes a landowner has property rights that extend upwards indefinitely up into the sky.[79] Also, Scott fails to provide a good reason *why* we

---

[78] Ibid. at pp. 175–176.

[79] In other words, Scott's argument boils down to an assertion that, *because* a landowner owns the airspace above the surface of his land, he is entitled to build into it, and therefore he must own it ... Logically the true position must be that *if* he owns the airspace above his land, he is entitled to build into it and he can object to any invasion of airspace which might prevent him from doing so; if on the other hand he owns the airspace only up to a given level, he is *entitled* to build in it only up to that level:

should distinguish between overflying objects which are not attached to neighbouring land (e.g. aircraft, balloons, missiles, etc.) and those which are (cranes). And even if the distinction is justifiable, it is not satisfactory to apply one principle when we want to ascertain the upper boundary of land in order to decide whether independent flying objects are trespassing, but a different one when the issue is an alleged invasion by an overflying earthbound object or an object projecting from a building. We may have to live with land boundaries which fluctuate over time, but it is doubtful whether we can accommodate boundaries whose position at any one time varies depending on why we want to ascertain them.

The differences between Scott's analysis and the *Bernstein* principle were considered by Silber J in *Laiquat* v. *Majid* [2005] EWHC 1305. He preferred the Scott analysis and on that basis decided that an extractor fan erected in the wall of a hot-food take away shop which protruded over the neighbour's rear yard was a trespass into the neighbour's land. However, all three of these decisions are at High Court level, and so too are the other modern decisions on the point, so technically neither *Bernstein* nor *Anchor Brewhouse* is authoritative. Nevertheless, it is worth noting that in *Star Energy Weald Basin Ltd* v. *Bocardo SA* [2010] UKSC 35, which we look at in para. 7.17 below, the Supreme Court proceeded on the basis that *Bernstein* was correct. In other words, it took Griffith J's analysis in *Bernstein* as an accurate statement of the law, establishing that land does not extend upwards indefinitely, but only up to such a height as is necessary for the ordinary use and enjoyment of the land and the structures on it.[80] As we see below, it used that principle as a starting point for considering what principle should apply to what lies below the surface.

7.17 The Lower Boundary of Land

There are good reasons for treating the airspace above land differently from the ground beneath the surface, if we are looking at them as potential objects of property rights. Airspace above a certain level is easily accessible in practice without the authorisation of the surface owner, and scientific and technological developments have turned it into what has been described as 'a public highway ... to which only the public has a just claim'.[81] The ground beneath the surface, on the other hand, is more difficult and more expensive to reach. Outsiders must either have the surface owner's authorisation to dig down through the surface of his land, or must tunnel into the landowner's land from adjoining land. Also, the physical structure of the ground below the surface inevitably restricts anyone's passage through it and, as we saw in para. 7.15, no-one can penetrate very deeply below the surface anyway. So, the space between the surface of the earth and the core of the earth is never going to

above that level he is *free* to build whatever he wants (because neither he nor anyone else has any property rights in the airspace above his airspace) but, because this is a Hohfeldian liberty rather than a right, he has no right to object if a neighbour gets there first and erects a sign which gets in his way.

[80] *Star Energy Weald Basin Ltd* v. *Bocardo SA* [2010] UKSC 35 para. 26, and see also para. 20. However, the contrary does not seem to have been argued, and *Anchor Brewhouse* was apparently not cited.

[81] Douglas J in the decision of the US Supreme Court in *US* v. *Causby* (1946) 328 US 256 at p. 261.

resemble a public highway, even if technology develops to allow humans to exploit more of it than we can at present.

The different uses we make of airspace and sub-surface ground also suggest different kinds of property regime might be appropriate. Admittedly, if we are looking only at the airspace immediately above ground and the ground immediately below the surface, there is no great difference. Generally, anyone who owns the surface of land needs to use those immediate upper and lower strata to enable and enhance what he does on the surface – to move around the surface and build structures on it, and to grow things in the ground and use it to support the structures on it. So, it makes some sense to allocate private property in those narrow strata to whoever owns the surface. Once we get beyond those strata, however, the position changes. The value of upper airspace is indeed as a public highway, allowing uninterrupted passage of services benefitting the public, whether provided by the state or by commercial organisations. Few surface owners have ever been in a position to extract wealth from it for themselves, and probably few have ever developed proprietorial feelings towards it.

The value of the lower ground below the surface is different. Largely, it lies in what can be extracted from the ground – solid things (like gold and silver, coal and other minerals), liquid things (including water and petroleum), and natural gases. There is also value in using the spaces in between for storage,[82] and in using lower strata for carrying public infrastructure (water, drainage and sewerage pipes and channels; power and communications conduits; transport tunnels, underground railways, etc.). There are important public interests in all these subsurface activities. Most of them are or have been state monopolies at various times in our history, and nearly all of them are now heavily regulated by the state.[83] However, because the surface owner has always had some level of control over access, these resources are also traditional sources of private wealth. Historically, surface owners have expected to be compensated by anyone who wants to dig into or through the ground below the surface of their land in order to exploit the riches below, because generally it has been cheaper and more convenient for it to be done with the surface owner's co-operation rather than against their opposition. So, there is a traditional perception of ownership by surface owners, not only of the narrow subsurface strata which accommodates their own use of the surface, but also of strata below it.

All this may help to explain why the Supreme Court in *Star Energy Weald Basin Ltd* v. *Bocardo SA* [2010] UKSC 35 refused to extend the *Bernstein* principle to the ground beneath the surface of land. The case concerned pipelines that Star Energy's predecessor had drilled from land it controlled, diagonally down to the apex of an oilfield which lay under Bocardo's land, about 2800 feet below the surface.[84] The oilfield extended beyond the area beneath Bocardo's land, but the most effective way

---

[82] For example, landfill, nuclear waste, sequestrated carbon, etc.: see Jill Morgan, 'Digging deep: Property rights in subterranean space and the challenge of carbon capture and storage' (2013) *International & Comparative Law Quarterly* 813.

[83] para. 7.20 below.

[84] This is very deep: at its lowest point, the Channel Tunnel is 275 feet below the sea bed and 380 feet below sea level.

of extracting petroleum from it was to drill into the apex, which was under Bocardo's land. The pipelines had been drilled some years earlier and they had continued in operation ever since. In this country all petroleum (including mineral oil and natural gas) is owned by the Crown, together with the exclusive right to search and bore for it and extract it, which means that no-one may drill for or extract petroleum or natural gas from anywhere in the country without a statutory licence from the Crown.[85] Star Energy and its predecessor held such a licence for these pipelines, under which it paid royalties to the Crown of between 5 per cent and 12.5 per cent of the market value of the petroleum it extracted (the percentage rising as the amount of petroleum extracted increased). However, no permission had ever been sought from Bocardo, and for many years Bocardo did not even realise the pipelines were there or that petroleum was being abstracted from under its land. When it did find out what was happening, it brought this action in trespass against Star Energy.

If the Supreme Court had decided that the *Bernstein* principle applied to the ground below the surface of the land, it would have had to conclude that Star Energy was not liable in trespass. If *Bernstein* applied, neither Star Energy nor its predecessor had ever entered Bocardo's land because everything they had done beneath the surface of Bocardo's land was at a depth which was way below the level at which it could possibly have interfered with Bocardo's ordinary use and enjoyment of the surface of the land and the structures on it. However, the Supreme Court adopted a different test for the lower limit of land and held unanimously that Star Energy was liable.[86] Lord Hope accepted that 'the simple notion that each landowner is the proprietor of a column or cylinder of land that stretches down to the centre of the earth and upwards indefinitely into outer space [what he called the 'old brocard'] is plainly no longer tenable'.[87] However, he rejected Star Energy's argument that its application to subsurface land should be limited by the *Bernstein* principle.[88] In his view 'the reasons for holding that the old brocard has no place in the modern world as regards what goes on below the surface … are not by any means as compelling as they are in relation to the use of the airspace'.[89] He concluded that:

> The better view … is to hold that the owner of the surface is the owner of the strata beneath it, including the minerals that are to be found there, unless there has been an alienation of them by a conveyance, at common law or by statute to someone else… That was the view which the Court of Appeal took in *Mitchell* v. *Mosley* [1914] 1 Ch 438. Much has happened since then, as the use of technology has penetrated deeper

85 See further para. 7.20(a).
86 Lord Hope gave the only reasoned judgment on the liability point, with which all the other justices agreed, although they disagreed on the level of damages. By a majority of 3–2 the Court upheld an award of just £1,000 in damages, rejecting Bocardo's argument that it should be entitled to a share of the value of the petroleum Star Energy had extracted, and would in future abstract, from its land: see further Jill Morgan, 'Subsurface ownership and hydraulic fracturing in the UK: (Probably) under my backyard' (2015) *Journal of Business Law* 634.
87 *Star Energy* v. *Bocardo*, fn. 80 above, para. 19.   88 Ibid. para. 26 and see also paras. 20–25.
89 Ibid. para. 26.

and deeper into the earth's surface. But I see no reason why its view should not still be regarded as good law. There must obviously be some stopping point, as one reaches the point at which physical features such as pressure and temperature render the concept of the strata belonging to anybody so absurd as to be not worth arguing about. But the wells that are at issue in this case, extending from about 800 feet to 2,800 feet below the surface, are far from being so deep as to reach the point of absurdity. Indeed the fact that the strata can be worked upon at those depths points to the opposite conclusion.[90]

It would seem to follow from this that the lower boundary of land extends downwards so far as is necessary to include all strata which can be worked upon. This too, then, is a fluctuating boundary, which will move downwards over time as technological developments enable humans to reach further down into the earth: however far down into the earth technology takes us, the surface owner's title will always move downwards to keep pace with it.

7.18 The Government Response: s. 43 of the Infrastructure Act 2015

The problem with the Supreme Court decision in *Star Energy Weald Basin Ltd v. Bocardo SA* [2010] UKSC 35, as seen from the perspective of the oil and gas industry and the government, was not that landowners would have to be paid for access to their land. As already noted, the Supreme Court awarded Bocardo damages consisting only of a nominal one-off payment of £1,000. The real fear was that the decision would enable private landowners to disrupt deep level oil and gas production by withholding or delaying consent to enter 'their' land. The government responded by legislating to give the oil and gas industries statutory 'rights to use' any 'deep-level' land for exploration and exploitation, 'deep-level' land being defined as land at a depth of at least 33 metres below surface level (s. 43 of the Infrastructure Act 2015). The legislation went on to give the Secretary of State power to make regulations requiring anyone who wished to exercise these statutory 'rights to use' to make payments (of an amount specified in the regulations) to 'owners of relevant land or interests in land' and/or 'other persons for the benefit of areas in which relevant land is situated' (s. 45(1)–(4)). However, no regulations have yet been made. When the Bill was going through Parliament, the government announced that the power to make regulations ordering drillers to pay for access was a 'reserve power', only, because 'both industries have made voluntary commitments to make a one-off payment of £20,000 to affected communities for each unique lateral well that extends by more than 200 metres'.[91] So, for the present at least, whilst landowners still own the 'deep level' strata below ground, the oil and gas industries are entitled to gain access to and through it by paying 'affected communities', rather than by paying the landowner.

---

[90] Ibid. para. 27.

[91] Statement of the Secretary of State made in the House of Lords at the Committee Stage of the Infrastructure Bill 2015, quoted in the Westlaw annotations to s. 45 of the Infrastructure Act 2015. See further Morgan, 'Subsurface ownership and hydraulic fracturing', fn. 86 above.

7.19 The German Approach

The combined effect of the Supreme Court decision in *Star Energy Weald Basin Ltd v. Bocardo SA* [2010] UKSC 35 and ss. 43–50 of the Infrastructure Act 2015 is to bring our approach to subsurface land closer to the German approach. Whilst in the case of airspace above the ground we restrict how far upwards 'land' extends, in the case of what lies below the surface, 'land' extends downwards as far as its reachable depth, but we restrict the landowner's rights in it. This is the way German law approaches both the upper and lower boundaries of land, as established in s. 905 of the BGB:

> **905 Restriction of ownership**
> The right of the owner of a plot of land extends to the space above the surface and to the subsoil under the surface. However, the owner may not prohibit influences that are exercised at such a height or depth that he has no interest in excluding them.

The German courts considered the application of s. 905 in a case similar to the English overflying crane case, *Anchor Brewhouse Developments Ltd* v. *Berkley House (Docklands Developments) Ltd* [1987] 2 EGLR 173.[92] The German court concluded that the landowner was entitled to prohibit the crane owner from swinging the crane over his land, taking a broad view of what amounted to an 'interest' of the landowner: 'every interest worthy of protection is to be taken into consideration, even a mere future interest of the owner of the land, which can be recognised as such; the interest does not have to be of a proprietary nature but may also be an aesthetic interest. The interest merely has to be based upon a connection to the use of the land'.[93]

7.20 The Content of Subsurface Land

As appears from para. 7.17 above, land ownership does not extend to all the contents of subsurface land, and the same applies in most jurisdictions.[94] As far as the law in England and Wales is concerned, the position is broadly as follows:

(a) Crown Ownership

In this jurisdiction coal, gold and silver, petroleum and natural gases are all owned by the Crown, which grants private citizens or state monopolies licences to extract them. So, for example, we have already seen that s. 1 of the Petroleum (Production) Act 1934 (now s. 2 of the Petroleum Act 1998), vests all petroleum, oil and natural

---

[92] para. 7.16 above.

[93] The translation is taken from Sjef van Erp, and Bram Akkermans (eds.), *Cases, Materials and Text on Property Law* (Oxford and Portland, OR: Hart Publishing, 2012) p. 228, discussing restrictions on ownership in civil law jurisdictions at pp. 226–230.

[94] For a short comparative overview see Anita Rønne, 'Public and private rights to natural resources' in Aileen McHarg, Barry Barton, Adrian Bradbrook and Lee Godden (eds.), *Property and the Law in Energy and Natural Resources* (Oxford: Oxford University Press, 2009) at pp. 64–70. Later chapters in the book give detailed accounts of regimes operating in some other countries.

gas in the Crown and gives the Crown the exclusive right to exploit it. The Crown does not do so itself. Instead, it (in practice, the Oil and Gas Authority, the relevant government agency) grants a licence to an appropriate person for a specified period, granting them the exclusive right to explore for, extract and sell petroleum from a particular area for a specified period, on payment to the Crown of a royalty or other fee and subject to conditions imposed by the licence.[95] The objective of the licence regime is 'to maximise economic recovery of UK petroleum, with consequent benefits to security of energy supplies, employment, and to the Exchequer and the economy more generally, consistent with safety and environmental requirements'.[96] In addition, the licensee must obtain planning consent from the local planning authority, environmental authorisations from the Environment Agency, and satisfy regulatory requirements of the Health and Safety Executive.

(b) Private Ownership

As for subsurface minerals which are not owned by the Crown, the default position is that they are owned by the landowner. However, frequently in the past (and in the present) the landowner will have granted ownership or leasehold interests of them, and/or of the strata containing them to others, or will have granted others exclusive rights to extract them.[97] So, in practice ownership of the land is often separated off from ownership of some or all subsurface minerals and/or the strata containing them, and/or from the right to extract them. And whoever owns them, rights to exploit them will nearly always require planning permission and environmental licences.

(c) Unpropertised Water

Water is different because no-one owns the water itself which flows on or below the surface of the ground or which lies below the surface, unless and until it is 'captured', that is, extracted and/or enclosed (for example, in a bottle, or a closed tank or reservoir). Landowners do have common law rights to extract water which is flowing in defined channels on or below the surface of their land and to use the flow (for example, to run mills),[98] but these rights do not apply to subterranean water which percolates through the ground. This means that, at common law, anyone who can get access to percolating subterranean water is free to abstract it, regardless of the

---

[95] Ss. 3–4 of the 1998 Act.

[96] See *Dean* v. *Secretary of State for Business, Energy and Industrial Strategy* [2017] EWHC 1998 para. 44, confirming that such a licence (in that case to drill for and extract shale gas by fracking) is a property interest (paras. 128–132).

[97] See Morgan, 'Subsurface ownership and hydraulic fracturing', fn. 86 above, pp. 638–640 for analysis of the property rights possibilities.

[98] Common law water rights are complex and their precise nature and extent is contested: for a good historical account see William Howarth, 'The history of water law in the common law tradition', in T. Tvedt, O. McIntyre and T. K. Woldetsadik (eds.), *A History of Water Series III, Volume 2: Sovereignty and International Water Law* (London and New York, I. B. Taurus, 2015) pp. 66–104.

effect that may have on others.[99] However, the common law tells only part of the story. The reality is that no-one may abstract or impound uncaptured water from anywhere (except in small quantities), without a state Water Abstraction Licence,[100] and planning permission and various environmental licences may also be required.

7.21 Dividing Land into Horizontal or Vertical Segments

Similarly, freehold ownership of land can be split horizontally (as well as vertically) between different owners, both above and below ground level, and freehold owners can also grant leases of vertically and horizontally divided segments of their land, again whether above or below ground level.

(a) Airspace Which is Not Enclosed by a Physical Structure

It is important to appreciate that, if we are talking about land above ground level, it is the airspace itself which is being segmented, not the part of any building which happens to enclose that space. So, for example, if I build a block of flats on my land and grant you a lease of a flat on the top floor, what you acquire is a lease of the airspace the flat occupies. This means that if the building collapses before the end of your lease, your lease continues, but what you are left with is the right to exclusive possession of the airspace your flat occupied.[101] This is not as fanciful as it sounds. In *Eason* v. *Wong* [2017] EWHC 209 a number of prospective students (or perhaps their parents) had paid a 50 per cent deposit to be granted 999 year leases of 'student suites' in a privately owned students' accommodation block in Nottingham. However, the developer went into liquidation and the block was never built. The question was whether the claimants could claim any property interest in the development site, given that they had little chance of getting any money back from the liquidator.[102] It was held that, because each claimant had a contractual right to a lease of the airspace which would have been occupied by their suite, they were entitled to a property interest in that bit of airspace – specifically, a lien[103] over the developer's freehold interest in that bit of airspace. Technically that would have given them the right to have the developer's freehold interest in that bit of the airspace sold, and to have

---

[99] See *Bradford* v. *Pickles* [1895] AC 587, considered in Chapter 10 *Limitations on Property* para.10.7.

[100] See Alison Clarke and Rosalind Malcolm, 'The role of property in water regulation: Locating Communal and regulatory property rights on the property rights spectrum' in Christine Godt, (ed) *Regulatory Property Rights: The Transforming Notion of Property in Transnational Business Regulation* (Leiden and Boston: Brill Nijhoff, 2017) p. 121 at pp. 129–138 for an outline of the licensing regime and its effects on private property rights in water.

[101] In practice, the contractually agreed terms of the lease should deal with this by, for example, giving either party the right to end the lease early if this happens, or by requiring insurance, with the insurance proceeds paying for rebuilding and meanwhile covering the tenant's rent.

[102] See Chapter 6 *New Property Interests and the Numerus Clausus* para. 6.4(d) for the reasons why a claimant is better off if it can claim a property interest in a debtor's assets than it would be if it had just a claim to be repaid money.

[103] A form of security interest, like a charge: see Chapter 5, *Ownership and Other Property Interests* para. 5.37(c).

their deposit repaid out of the sale proceeds. However, since the liquidator had already sold the developer's freehold interest in the whole site, the court adopted the more practical solution of giving each claimant a proportionate share of those proceeds of sale.

(b) Flying Freeholds

Separate freehold ownership of horizontal slices above and below ground level is possible in English and Welsh law, and it does indeed occur occasionally, as for example when a landowner sells the freehold interest in a subsurface strata of land containing minerals,[104] or when a highway crosses privately owned land, as we see in (d) below. However, there are difficulties with freehold ownership of horizontal slices above ground level. When the freehold interest in an upper slice is held by someone other than the freehold owner of the slice below, and there is a physical horizontal boundary between the two which serves as floor of one and ceiling/roof of the other, both owners have problems. The difficulty is that both owners need to impose positive obligations on the other to maintain that physical boundary. English law, however, does not recognise positive obligations between neighbours as property interests. Suppose, for example, you and I are the freehold owners of adjoining terraced houses and there is a passageway between the two houses at ground floor level which you own, but my house extends over the passageway so that I have what is called a 'flying freehold' of everything above the passageway from first floor level upwards. You would want to impose a positive obligation on me to keep the floor of the structure above the passageway in repair so that the structure does not collapse into the passageway. You and I can enter into a contract in which I promise you to keep that structure in repair, and that will give you a legal right to enforce my promise. However, the law will treat that right as a contract right enforceable only against me personally: it will not treat it as a property right over my land, enforceable against all future owners of my land.[105] There are various ways we can try to get round the problem in a situation like this, but it is generally agreed that none of them is particularly satisfactory.

(c) Multi-Storey Blocks

In the example just given the problem is yours, but if my flying freehold rested on a structure you owned the problem would be mine as well: I would be equally reliant on a positive obligation by you to keep your ceiling in repair so that my floor did not collapse.[106] This of course is the situation that occurs in every building of two or more stories where the intention is that one of more of the storeys should be

---

[104] See above, para. 7.20(b).
[105] *Rhone v. Stephens* [1994] 2 AC 310. See further Chapter 13 *Non-Possessory Land Use Rights* para. 13.16, where the problem of positive covenants is considered more fully.
[106] The same problem arises between next-door neighbours but in practice it is not so serious because vertically divided units are less physically dependent on each other.

separately owned – in other words in all maisonettes, blocks of flats, blocks of mixed retail/office/residential use, etc. In all these very common situations the risk of being unable to enforce positive obligations between horizontally divided neighbours is so serious that, in practice, horizontal strata above the surface of the ground are almost never separately owned.[107] Instead, there will be a single freehold owner of the whole building and the land on which it is built. That freehold owner will then grant a long lease of each unit to whoever wants to buy it (a lease of anything up to 999 years is common for residential units, although commercial leases may be much shorter[108]). This works because all the terms of a lease, even those imposing positive obligations, are always enforceable by and against whoever happens at any given time to hold the landlord's interest and whoever happens to hold the tenant's interest. This is why, in England and Wales, all horizontal slices of land above the surface nearly always have a single freehold owner, who has granted a long lease of each separate unit to each intended buyer. If the lease is very long, the leaseholder (i.e. the tenant under the lease) has a property interest which is not much different from freehold ownership. The leaseholder has exclusive possession of the unit, and can sell the lease whenever it wants (usually at the same price that it would be able to get if it sold a freehold interest in equivalent space). In addition, in residential blocks it is now quite common for all the leaseholders to own the freehold interest in the block collectively (via a specially formed company which they own and control) so that they can manage the block and enforce all the terms of the leases in their collective self-interest. We look at this traditional property model for multi-storey blocks in Chapter 17 *Leases*, where we examine the problems and alternatives in more detail.[109]

(c) Highways

There is no fixed definition of a highway, but broadly it means a strip of land over which the public has rights of way, whether on foot, on horseback or in or on vehicles. For present purposes the important question is not the nature of the public rights held over the highway,[110] but the underlying ownership of the land above and below the highway. This is a contentious issue, recently reconsidered by the Supreme Court in *Southwark London Borough Council* v. *Transport for London*,[111] a case about the transfer of highways from one highways authority to another. In this case

---

[107] In Northern Ireland (which has the same problem as England and Wales) a solicitor was held liable in negligence for failing to make the risks sufficiently clear to her client: *Hickland* v. *Cormac McKeone* [2018] NIQB 81. The solicitor had acted for the client on the cash purchase of a freehold flat, and when the client died her executors were unable to find a buyer for the flat because of difficulties in persuading lenders to lend on the security of a freehold flat.

[108] See Chapter 17 *Leases* para. 17.2 and Part III.   [109] See Chapter 17 *Leases*, Part III.

[110] As to which see generally Nicholas Blomley, *Rights of Passage: Sidewalks and the Regulation of Public Flow* (Oxfordshire: Routledge, 2011), and, more specifically on public rights in England and Wales to occupy part of a highway as a protest camp or to use it for other forms of protest such as 'slow walking', *West Sussex County Council* v. *Persons Unknown* [2013] EWHC 4024 and *Boyd* v. *Ineos Upstream* [2019] EWCA Civ 515.

[111] *Southwark London Borough Council* v. *Transport for London* [2018] UKSC 63.

it occurred when the Greater London Authority (the GLA) took over the ownership and responsibility for roads in London which had been owned by local London Boroughs. This had happened in 2000, when the GLA was created as a new regional authority for the whole of London, taking a number of important powers and responsibilities away from the London Boroughs. The problem was that in the case of some of the roads concerned, the London Boroughs (like all other highway authorities in England and Wales) had owned only a horizontal strip of land consisting of the surface of the highway and a narrow strip of airspace above it and soil beneath it. This narrow strip is usually now called the 'zone of reasonable (or ordinary) use'.[112] It consists of 'the surface of the road over which the public has highway rights, the subsoil immediately beneath it, to a depth sufficient to provide for its support and drainage, and a modest slice of the airspace above it sufficient to enable the public to use and enjoy it, and the responsible authority to maintain and repair it, and to supervise its safe operation'.[113] In the case of other roads, however, the London Boroughs's ownership of the highway extended as far upwards and downwards as a private owner's ownership extends over privately owned land. The London Boroughs argued that when their highways were taken away from them, all that the GLA acquired was ownership of the surface of the highway and the zone of reasonable use. Everything above and below still belonged to them, they argued. The GLA disagreed. It argued that it had acquired all the airspace above and the soil beneath the highways. This mattered because, as Lord Briggs pointed out in the Supreme Court, the land below London roads and the airspace above them can be very valuable indeed,[114] and whoever owns it can expect to make quite a lot of money by selling or leasing it for development.

England and Wales has a long history, summarised by Lord Briggs,[115] of splitting the land bearing a highway into separately owned horizontal strips. Those responsible for the upkeep of public highways (usually the members of the parish through which the highway ran) did not have any property interest in them at all until 1835. This was remedied by a series of nineteenth century statutes which automatically vested a property interest in the land bearing the highway in the body legally responsible for maintaining, repairing and operating it. However, the courts viewed this as state confiscation of private property without compensation, and so decided that the property rights vested in a highway authority by these statutes[116] extended only so far as was necessary to enable it to perform its statutory duties – in other words, the highway authority acquired ownership of only what became known as the zone of reasonable use. Later, highways authorities were given additional powers to acquire ownership of land for highways. They could acquire ownership from a private owner by a voluntary sale or by compulsory purchase, either to use the land as a highway or to

---

[112] Once known as 'the top two spits' (a spit being a spade's depth), but that tells us only how far down below the surface the highway stretches, not how far above.

[113] *Southwark London Borough Council* v. *Transport for London* [2018] UKSC 63 para. 9.

[114] Ibid. para. 22. Lord Briggs (who gave the principal opinion in the Supreme Court, with all the other justices agreeing) gave the example of shooting galleries built under the approaches to the bridges across the Thames in the City of London (one of which is or was let to the Stock Exchange Rifle Club).

[115] Ibid. paras. 6–19.   [116] Which subsequently became freehold ownership interests.

use it for some other statutory purpose. In such cases the highway authority acquired ownership of the whole of the land bearing the highway, not just the zone of reasonable use. In other cases, a highway authority might have become, for one reason or another, the private owner of land adjoining what was or what became the highway. Private owners of land adjoining a highway own the land above and below it, up to the centre of the road, if the highways authority owns only the 'zone of reasonable use'. So, if the highways authority was also the private owner of the adjoining land, its ownership of the land bearing the highway extended upwards and downwards to the whole of the land, not just to the narrow 'zone of reasonable use' strip.

So, what happened when the roads belonging to the London Boroughs were automatically transferred to the GLA? Obviously, where the London Borough owned only the zone of reasonable user, that was all that the GLA could ever get – no-one can transfer more than they themselves have.[117] But what about the other roads, where the London Borough's ownership extended to the whole of the airspace above and the soil beneath the highway? Did the GLA get all of that, or only the zone of reasonable use?

The Supreme Court decided that it depended on the capacity in which the London Borough owned the land bearing the road, at the time of the transfer. If it held the land in its capacity as highways authority, GLA acquired everything that the London Borough had. If on the other hand the London Borough owned the land bearing the road in another capacity (as owner of the adjoining land, or for other statutory purposes), GLA acquired just the 'zone of reasonable use' and the London Borough kept the rest.

The Supreme Court's decision rested on its interpretation of the relevant statutory provisions, past and present. Lord Briggs did, however, express satisfaction that the end result did not result in irrational 'multi-layering':

> 40. . . . Where a local highway authority had acquired land by compulsory purchase (or private treaty) for the purpose of building a road, and thereby had the whole of the vertical plane conveyed or transferred to it, the effect of the [London Boroughs' argument, which he rejected] would be, for the first time, to split that vertical plane between two successive highway authorities, one owning the top slice and the bottom slice, and the other owning the middle slice constituted by the zone of ordinary use. As the arbitrator put it, at para. 104:

> With all due respect to the Councils, I cannot see what rational purpose is served by there being two public bodies owning different layers of what was formerly owned by one single public body.

> 41. I agree. The Court of Appeal acknowledged that this was a consequence of its interpretation but noted that multi-layering of the vertical plane was already endemic within Central London . . .

> 42. It is of course true that some layering of the vertical plane is inevitable in relation to highways, both in rural and urban areas . . . For example, it occurs whenever there is

---

[117] This is the general property principle known as the nemo dat principle, which we consider in Chapter 15 *Enforceability and Priority of Property Interests* paras. 15.5–15.6.

automatic vesting [under the historical statutory provisions]. But in such a case the layering arises between a public authority on the one hand and private owners on the other, for reasons which are not irrational. Equally, and particularly in the modern urban environment, there may be layering of the vertical plane between different public authorities, such as those responsible for highways, sewers and underground railways. Again, this is for reasons which have a rational purpose. By contrast, the irrationality identified by the arbitrator is that arising from two different highway authorities owning parts of the vertical plane in the same highway...

43. I acknowledge also that my interpretation ... which limits the rights transferred to those transferred by the former highway authority in its capacity as such, will also lead to layering of the vertical plane in some cases where it did not previously exist. This will occur, for example, where the former authority is an adjoining owner ... or where the former authority has rights in part of the vertical plane for other statutory purposes, such as sewerage or the operation of underground railways. But again, there is nothing irrational about layering of that kind.

One further point of relevance here is that the physical extent of the zone of reasonable use is both flexible and liable to fluctuate, in much the same way as the upper and lower boundaries of land[118] and the boundaries between land and water.[119] As in those cases, the courts do not seem to regard this as a problem. As Lord Briggs said at para. 10:

10. It is common ground that the zone of ordinary use is a flexible concept, the application of which may lead to different depths of subsoil and heights of airspace being vested in a highway authority, both as between different highways and even, over time, as affects a particular highway, according to differences or changes in the nature and intensity of its public use. A simple footpath or bridleway might only require shallow foundations, and airspace of up to about ten feet, to accommodate someone riding a horse. By contrast a busy London street might require deep foundations to support intensive use, and airspace sufficient to accommodate double-decker buses, and even the overhead electric power cables needed, in the past, by trolley buses and, now, by urban trams.

7.22 Shores, Beaches and Foreshore

There are two related physical features of land in Britain which affect the physical extent of land subject to property interests.[120]

The first is that the boundary between land and water is constantly shifting. It moves regularly twice a day between a low water mark and a high water mark by the operation of tides. In addition over most of our coastline the shoreline is gradually shifting either seawards by the process of *accretion* (i.e. over a period of years the sea line slowly recedes and new areas of 'land' are built up) or landwards by the process

---

[118] paras. 7.16–7.17.   [119] para. 7.22 and 7.24.
[120] To varying extents the following applies equally to land bordering estuaries, rivers and lakes, but here we focus on land bordering the sea.

of *erosion*, otherwise known as diluvion (the sea line slowly[121] moves forward, eroding the land).

The second special feature is that there is generally a strip of ground between the land and the sea bed, made up of loose particles such as sand, gravel, shingle, pebbles, etc. This is the beach.[122] At its seaward edge it may be permanently under water except in extreme weather conditions. The central part, however, is the *foreshore*, which is the intertidal area which lies between the high water mark and the low water mark, in other words the strip of beach which, in all but extreme weather conditions, is alternately exposed or submerged by the tide.[123] The foreshore may run right up to the shoreline or there may be an intervening dry bit of the beach not normally reached by the tide (sometimes called the nearshore or upper beach or, in the USA, the dry shore) running up to the shoreline (where the beach meets permanent vegetation or some permanent feature such as a cliff or a dune or built sea walls etc.). McGlashan et al. explain how the physical nature of the foreshore sets it apart from the rest of the land in Britain:

> the foreshore area ... is dynamic in form, being the area of physical interaction between land and sea. This coastal area is unusual in character, being neither land nor sea and constantly alternating between being covered and uncovered by the sea. The rates of change in this zone can be substantial due to erosion and/or accretion. Such changes can take place across the whole area directly influenced by the tides, often beyond the legally defined foreshore, which has led to the boundaries of the foreshore being the focus of some of the earliest coastal law arising from property disputes in the courts relating to the location and extent of the foreshore and its uses.[124]

In other words, the foreshore is not only dynamic in form, it also has fluctuating boundaries, location and extent. We consider the implications of these two factors in the following paragraphs.

7.23 Property Interests in the Foreshore

(a) Ownership of the Foreshore

The Crown owns the seabed (i.e. the land under the sea) up to 12 nautical miles out, around virtually the whole of England and Wales. It also owns all the foreshore, as demesne land,[125] except those stretches which have been granted away to someone

---

[121] The process is not always so slow: see www.dailymail.co.uk/news/article-4917024/Shocking-speed-erosion-England-s-south-coast.html (25 September 2017, Birling Gap in East Sussex).
[122] Derek J. McGlashan, Robert W. Duck and Colin T. Reid, 'Defining the foreshore: Coastal geomorphology and British laws' (2005) 62 *Estuarine, Coastal and Shelf Science* 183–192.
[123] See *Lynn Shellfish Ltd* v. *Loose* [2016] UKSC 14 paras. 62–67 for what amounts in law to the low and high water marks.
[124] McGlashan et al, 'Defining the foreshore', fn. 122 above, p. 183.
[125] That is, no-one has freehold ownership of it: see Chapter 5 *Ownership and Other Property Interests* para. 5.17.

else over the years since 1066.[126] Exactly which stretches of foreshore have been granted away is not at all clear, but it is estimated that about 50 per cent of the foreshore in England, Wales and Northern Ireland is now still owned by the Crown in demesne and managed by the Crown Estate.[127] Freehold ownership of other parts of the foreshore is held by local authorities, harbour authorities, the National Trust (which owns 778 miles of coast), the Ministry of Defence, a few other public authorities, and some private individuals (usually landowners of land adjoining the beach). In many cases, the identity of the freehold owner is unknown.

(b) Foreshore as a Public Resource?

Foreshore is distinctive in that historically it has generally been regarded as a public resource, to which everyone should have access by right. There have always been extensive public property rights exercisable over it including public fishing rights and public navigation rights. Also, although we do not (or perhaps not yet) recognise the doctrine of public trust in this jurisdiction,[128] the courts have accepted that the Crown holds its interest in the foreshore for the public good.[129] This may help to explain why the Crown has an unusually long limitation period during which it may bring an action removing trespassers on its land. As we see in Part III of Chapter 12 *Adverse Possession of Land*, under common law rules the title of a dispossessed freehold owner will be extinguished if she does not bring an action against the trespasser within 12 years. However, the equivalent period for the Crown is 60 years. In its 2002 Report[130] the Law Commission identified particular problems with adverse possession of foreshore by adjoining private landowners, which it is difficult for the Crown to prevent because of the difficulty of monitoring what are often quite remote areas of shoreline. The 60 year limitation period can therefore be seen as necessary to avoid creeping privatisation of the foreshore.

(c) Public right to use the beach?

Surprisingly, however, the question of whether the public has a right to make recreational use of the beach (i.e. the foreshore, the dryshore and the area of sea

---

[126] Until recently, the Crown also owned both the sea bed and the foreshore in Scotland, but on 1 April 2017 the Crown's powers over the revenue and management of all the Crown's resources in Scotland were transferred to the Scottish Government. At present they are administered by a newly created body called Crown Estate Scotland. On 24 January 2018 the Scottish Government published the Scottish Crown Estates Bill which would provide for a mix of national and local community management: www.parliament.scot/S5_Bills/Scottish%20Crown%20Estate%20Bill/SPBill24ENS052018.pdf.

[127] See www.thecrownestate.co.uk/en-gb/what-we-do/on-the-seabed/coastal/. The Crown Estate publishes a *Foreshore and Estuary Map*: https://crownestate.maps.arcgis.com/apps/Viewer/index.html?appid=0aac22685d2f4d78a2a3b0a5aa1660db.

[128] See Chapter 8 *Property Interest Holders* para. 8.31.

[129] *Lynn Shellfish Ltd* v. *Loose* [2016] UKSC 14 para. 52, and see also Lord Carnwath in *R (on the application of Newhaven Port and Properties Ltd* v. *East Sussex County Council)* [2015] UKSC 276 at para. 126.

[130] Law Commission, *Land Registration for the Twenty-first Century: A Conveyancing Revolution* (2002) Law Com No 271.

above the seabed where people swim from the shore) is unsettled. The Supreme Court missed an opportunity to settle the issue in *R (on the application of Newhaven Port and Properties Ltd)* v. *East Sussex County Council*.[131] In that case, as we see in Chapter 13 *Non-Possessory Land Use Rights*, Part VI, local inhabitants had applied to have West Beach in Newhaven Harbour in East Sussex registered as a town or village green under what is now the Commons Act 2006. The owner of the beach, a privately owned harbour authority, had closed off public access to it. If the local inhabitants had succeeded in having it registered as a town or village green, the harbour authority would have had to restore access because the effect of registration is that local inhabitants become entitled to use the land perpetually for 'lawful sports and pastimes'. In order to succeed, the local inhabitants had to prove that they had used the beach 'as of right' for more than 20 years. We look at this in more detail in Part VI of Chapter 13 but broadly long-term use of land can only be 'as of right' if it has been open and neither contested nor permitted by the landowner. The Supreme Court considered two ways in which it could be argued that, in this particular case, local inhabitants had been 'permitted' to use the beach, and therefore could not have it registered as a town or village green. The first was that public recreational use was, in this particular case, impliedly allowed by the harbour authority's statutory bye-laws. The Supreme Court decided that this was correct, and that therefore the beach could not be registered as a green. This meant, so the court decided, that it was unnecessary for them to come to a final decision on the second argument, which was that any use by the local inhabitants was not 'as of right' because it was permitted under a general revocable licence that the public has to make recreational use of any part of the foreshore. The problem with this argument, as the Supreme Court explained, was (and still is) that in old cases, largely decided long before people did actually use beaches recreationally very much, the courts had said that there was no such public right. The Supreme Court did not show much enthusiasm for this argument, but nor were they prepared to reject it and overrule the old cases, since it would have made no difference their decision that the beach could not be registered as a green. So, although the public does as a matter of observable fact use beaches in England and Wales recreationally on a mass scale, and no-one is prepared to say that they – we – are trespassing by doing so, we know very little about the legal basis on which it is done.

7.24 Shifting Boundaries of the Foreshore

(a) Accretion and Erosion

Where there are 'gradual and imperceptible' changes in the physical boundaries of land bordered by water, caused by accretion and erosion, the legal boundaries of the land follow the shifting physical boundaries. This is taken to have been established by the Privy Council decision in *Southern Centre of Theosophy Inc* v. *State of South*

---

[131] *R (on the application of Newhaven Port and Properties Ltd)* v. *East Sussex County Council* [2015] UKSC 7, which we come back to in Chapter 13 *Non-Possessory Land Use Rights* para. 13.24.

Australia [1982] AC 706 where Lord Wilberforce said the legal doctrines of accretion and erosion:

> [give] recognition to the fact that where land is bounded by water, the forces of nature are likely to cause changes in the boundary between the land and the water. Where these changes are gradual and imperceptible ... the law considers the title to the land as applicable to the land as it may be so changed from time to time. This may be said to be based on grounds of convenience and fairness. Except in cases where a substantial and recognisable change in boundary has suddenly taken place (to which the doctrine of accretion does not apply), it is manifestly convenient to continue to regard the boundary between land and water as being where it is from day to day or year to year. To do so is also fair. If part of an owner's land is taken from him by erosion, or diluvion (i.e. advance of the water) it would be most inconvenient to regard the boundary as extending into the water: the landowner is treated as losing a portion of his land. So, if an addition is made to the land from what was previously water, it is only fair that the landowner's title should extend to it. The doctrine of accretion, in other words, is one which arises from the nature of land ownership, from, in fact, the long-term ownership of property inherently subject to gradual processes of change.[132]

The doctrine of accretion has also been justified on Lockean grounds. In *The King* v. *Lord Yarborough*[133] in 1828 Best CJ made the point that the new land was of no use to anyone other the adjoining landowner whilst it was gradually emerging out of the sea because it was not yet it a usable state. However, if the landowner extended his own boundaries to take it in, he could put it to productive use from the outset:

> Much land, which would [otherwise] remain for years, perhaps for ever, barren, is, [thereby] rendered productive as soon as it is formed. The sea being gradually and imperceptibly forced back, the land formed by alluvion, will become of a size proper for cultivation and use, and in the mean time the owner of the adjoining lands will have acquired a title to it by improving it. The original deposit constitutes not a tenth part of its value, the other nine-tenths are created by the labour of the person who has occupied it, and, in the words of Locke, the fruits of his labour cannot, without injury, be taken from him.

(b) Substantial, Recognisable and Sudden Change in a Boundary

However, as Lord Wilberforce pointed out in the passage quoted above from *Southern Centre of Theosophy Inc* v. *State of South Australia* [1982] AC 706, the principle of accretion applies only to land that has emerged by the 'gradual and imperceptible' retreat of the sea. In *Lynn Shellfish Ltd* v. *Loose*[134] the disputed land consisted of sandbanks which at one time had been wholly or partially covered by the sea, separated from the foreshore by channels of water even at low tide. This

---

[132] *Southern Centre of Theosophy Inc* v. *State of South Australia* [1982] AC 706 at p. 716. The passage has been cited with approval by the Supreme Court in *Lynn Shellfish Ltd* v. *Loose* [2016] UKSC 14 at para. 77.

[133] *The King* v. *Lord Yarborough* 4 ER 1087; (1828) 2 Bli (NS) 147 at pp. 159–160.

[134] *Lynn Shellfish Ltd* v. *Loose* [2016] UKSC 14.

stretch of foreshore was not owned by the Crown, so the court found, but by the adjoining landowner. When the sandbanks were separated from the foreshore by the channels of water, they were clearly not part of the foreshore but part of the sea bed, and so were owned by the Crown.

However, what happened was that, as the shoreline moved landwards on that stretch of coast, these channels of water disappeared or re-routed themselves, leaving the sandbanks permanently attached to the foreshore. This was significant because the claimants were local fishing boat owners who had always exercised public rights to take shellfish (cockles and mussels) from the sea up to the seawards boundary of the foreshore, whereas the defendant, Mr Loose, had a lease of the local landowner's exclusive private right to take cockles and mussels from the foreshore. So, who now held the fishing rights over the sandbanks? If they had become part of the foreshore by accretion, the answer must have been Mr Loose. However, on the expert evidence heard by the Supreme Court, the sandbanks had become attached to the foreshore at a single moment in time, not gradually and imperceptibly.[135] The Supreme Court held that, because of this, the doctrine of accretion did not apply and so the sandbanks and the foreshore remained in separate ownership. This meant that Mr Loose's exclusive private fishing right did not extend to the former sandbanks: they were still part of the Crown's seabed area and therefore the local fishing community's public right of fishing continued to be exercisable over them. At one level, this may seem an irrational and inconvenient result. The point about the principle of accretion is that it tells us what to do when the physical extent of land is increased by natural forces: what is the rationale for having one rule for situations when this happens gradually and another for when it happens suddenly? And maintaining separate ownership of foreshore and foreshore-type material which has suddenly become added to it seems difficult to maintain in practice. How long will it be before people forget where one ends and the other begins, if there is no physical boundary between them?

The Supreme Court's reasoning in *Lynn Shellfish* was that there is a difference in kind between the gradual extension of one recognised area of land, and the joining up of two formerly distinct areas.[136] When two distinct areas are joined up, and one of them belongs to the Crown, 'the court should not be too easily persuaded that the Crown has been deprived of a property or a right, given that the property or right is held for the public good'.[137] This was particularly so in a case such as this, where Mr Loose had an exclusive private fishing right, acquired by the landowner by prescription, by long use going back over centuries. It is no longer possible for the Crown to grant this kind of exclusive private right over the foreshore (although it can be, and is, done by Parliament), as the Supreme Court noted: 'given the importance of the fishing industry both in ancient times and also today [exclusive private] fisheries were not popular'. So, the court went on to say, given that there was no clear rule that the exclusive private fishery should extend to the sandbanks, and the fact that if

---

[135] The sizes, shapes and routes of the channels of water between the sandbanks and foreshore changed gradually, but there came a point when they no longer separated one from the other.

[136] *Lynn Shellfish Ltd* v. *Loose*, fn. 134 above, paras. 76–81.   [137] Ibid. para. 52.

it did so, public fishing rights over them would be extinguished, it was entitled to conclude that when the sandbanks were joined up with the landowner's foreshore, the Crown's ownership of the sandbanks continued.[138]

7.25 Buildings and Fixtures

Buildings and other structures become part of the land when they are sufficiently attached to the ground, or to a structure which is already attached to the ground, to become 'fixtures'. The test for deciding whether or not something is sufficiently attached (or 'annexed') to the land to have become part of the land is not particularly contentious, but it can be difficult to apply in practice, which perhaps explains why the issue attracts so much litigation.

The traditional test for deciding whether an object has become part of the land is to look at two factors: the 'degree of annexation' (how firmly is it fixed) and the 'object of the annexation' (was it intended to become part of the land). In what is usually taken to be the classical statement of the law, Blackburn J said in *Holland* v. *Hodgson*:[139]

> ... articles not otherwise attached to the land than by their own weight are not to be considered as part of the land, unless the circumstances are such as to show that they were intended to be part of the land, the onus of showing that they were so intended lying on those who assert that they have ceased to be chattels, and ... on the contrary, an article which is affixed to the land even slightly is to be considered as part of the land, unless the circumstances are such as to shew that it was intended all along to continue a chattel, the onus lying on those who contend that it is a chattel.

More modern cases emphasise that the crucial point is whether the object was intended to become part of the land. However, we have to be clear about what we mean by 'intention' here. It has nothing to do with the subjective intention of the person who attached the object to the land, or the subjective intention of the landowner. Instead, it refers to the intended relationship between the object and the land. So, for example, in another classic case, *D'Eyncourt* v. *Gregory*,[140] it was held that statues, ornamental vases and stone garden seats, held in position only by their own weight, were essentially part of the architectural design of a house and its grounds, and so were fixtures. Similarly, in the leading modern case, *Elitestone Ltd* v. *Morris*[141] the House of Lords held that a wooden bungalow resting by its own weight on concrete pillars and not physically attached to the land was a fixture, because it was built in such a way that it could only be removed by being demolished, and therefore it must have been intended to be part of the land. As Lord Clyde said in that case,

> ... it may be that the use of the word intention is misleading. It is *the purpose which the object is serving* which has to be regarded, not the purpose of the person who put it there ...[142]

---

[138] Ibid. paras. 52–53.   [139] *Holland* v. *Hodgson* (1872) LR 7 CP 328 at p. 334.
[140] *D'Eyncourt* v. *Gregory* (1866) LR 3 Eq 382.   [141] *Elitestone Ltd* v. *Morris* [1997] 1 WLR 687, HL.
[142] Ibid. pp. 698–699, emphasis added.

Norris J found another way of saying essentially the same thing in *Tower Hamlets London Borough Council* v. *Bromley London Borough Council*,[143] a celebrated case about the ownership of a heavy bronze sculpture by Henry Moore, which a London Borough had bought in 1961 specifically to enhance a new tower-block housing development it was building on a site it owned in Stepney. This is where it was erected, mounted on a plinth. The question was whether it had become part of that land as a fixture. Norris J held that it had not:

> ... the following considerations are in my judgment material. The sculpture is an entire object in itself. It rested by its own weight upon the ground and could be (and was) removed without damage and without diminishing its inherent beauty. It might adorn or beautify a location, but it was not in any real sense dependent upon that location.[144]

This makes sense, but it means that each case is highly fact sensitive. As a result, the courts can come to different conclusions applying the same test in different cases involving superficially similar facts. So, for example, in *Spielplatz Ltd* v. *Pearson*[145] the Court of Appeal held that chalets built many years earlier on the landowner's naturist resort were fixtures, and were therefore owned by the landowner as part of his land. The chalets were originally built on the landowner's land by the chalet 'owners' at their own expense, and they subsequently paid the landowner an annual fee for the plot on which their chalet stood. Thereafter both the chalet 'owners' and the landowner always believed and intended that the chalets belonged to the chalet 'owner' (so, for example, when a chalet 'owner' moved out and was replaced by a new licensee of the plot, the outgoing chalet 'owner' would sell the chalet on to the incoming licensee). The Court of Appeal nevertheless held that the chalets were fixtures and belonged to the landowner, because they had been built in such a way that it could never have been envisaged that they could be removed in one piece rather than demolished.

But by way of contrast, again applying the same test, HHJ Paul Matthews held in *Gilpin* v. *Legg*[146] that people remained the owners of beach huts which a landowner had allowed them (for a fee) to build on part of his land. He decided that the huts had not become part of the landowner's land even though, over time, they had deteriorated so badly that they could not be removed without being damaged: as Matthews put it, they remained chattels because they were 'placed ... on the landowner's land so as the better to enjoy [them] from time to time for short periods'.[147]

So, whilst the test for ascertaining whether an object has become part of the land is uncontentious and rationally based, it does not always produce easily predictable results.

---

[143] *Tower Hamlets LBC* v. *Bromley LBC* [2015] EWHC 1954.   [144] Ibid. para. 17.
[145] *Spielplatz Ltd* v. *Pearson* [2015] EWCA Civ 804.   [146] *Gilpin* v. *Legg* [2017] EWHC 3220.
[147] Ibid. para. 58. He did, however, go on to decide that the beach hut owners had annual periodic tenancies of the land on which their hut rested: see further Chapter 17 *Leases* para. 17.12.

PART V HUMAN BODIES AND HUMAN BODY PARTS

7.26 Long-Standing Prohibitions Against Property Rights in Human Bodies

Whilst most societies in modern times probably recognise property rights in land, the same is certainly not true of property rights in human bodies. Our own society has long been reluctant to accept that human bodies or parts of human bodies can be objects of property interests, a reluctance that can be ascribed to three long-standing prohibitions.

(a) Prohibition Against Slavery

The first, which is perhaps not as long-standing as we like to think, is the prohibition against slavery. Until uncomfortably recent times, it was possible for a human person to have property rights in another living human (a slave, or a wife or daughter, or a child).[148] In our legal system now, however, it is a fundamental principle that no living human person can be the object of property rights held by someone else, whether that someone else is a human person, a private entity, the state or any other kind of public authority. Similarly, whilst you are alive, no-one may have any other kind of property interest in you or your body. The question that has troubled the law in more recent years is how far this should extend to property in body parts and bodily material once they have become separated from your body, as we see below.

(b) Prohibition Against Property in Dead Bodies

The legal prohibition against slavery is probably now near-universal throughout the world, although certainly not universally observed. Our second long-standing prohibition, however, is shared by some legal systems but not others, and it has a very different basis. This is the prohibition against property in dead bodies. Our courts have accepted this prohibition since at least the seventeenth century[149] and are still unwilling to abandon it altogether, although its historical pedigree has been doubted and the courts have shown some ingenuity in qualifying the principle, as we see below. There are several different reasons given for the prohibition: cultural or religious reverence for the dead, for example, or a more general feeling that allowing someone else to have property rights in a dead body is an affront to human dignity. There are also public interest arguments. Once someone has died and is no longer capable of being custodian of their own body and property, it is the duty of the state to step in and take over control. In particular, the state must ensure that all deaths are reported and investigated, and that there is a proper disposal of the body for public health reasons and for the preservation of the human dignity of the deceased,

---

[148] We come back to this point in Chapter 8 in Part VII *Fluidity in the Person–Object Distinction*.

[149] Shawn Harmon and Graeme Laurie, 'Yearworth v. *North Bristol NHS Trust*: Property, principles, precedents and paradigms' (2010) 69 *Cambridge Law Journal* 476 at pp. 480–481.

just as it must ensure that the deceased's property is collected in and distributed according to law. None of this is easily compatible with the notion that, on someone's death, another citizen acquires property rights in their body. Some of these arguments against propertisation of dead human bodies are equally applicable to body parts and other bodily material taken from a dead body, others less so.

(c) Prohibition Against Self-Ownership

The third legal prohibition is less often articulated, and less certain. This is that you cannot have property rights in your own body. Again, a mix of reasons can be put forward to justify this prohibition. One is that the notion of self-ownership is incoherent. Property deals with our relationships with the outside world – with objects which are external to ourselves and with other people (also necessarily external to ourselves): it is the mechanism society uses for deciding who gets privileged access to resources which are external to us all. On this view, it makes no sense to talk about having *property* rights in our own bodies, as if our body was in some way separate from our self. The reality is that our bodies are an inseparable part of what we are as persons. The most obviously appropriate legal mechanisms for giving us exclusive control over our bodies are therefore the mechanisms that protect our person against interference by the state or by other citizens, for example by giving us enforceable civic and human rights to bodily autonomy (the right to make your own choices and decisions about your body) and bodily integrity ('the right not to have your body touched or your body interfered with without your consent').[150] These are the rights that provide us with protection of our persons against, for example, torture, or unwanted medical treatment, or false imprisonment, or physical attacks or harassment by our neighbours. It seriously misunderstands our objection to these kinds of assault on our person if we equate them with interferences with our property, just as it fundamentally misunderstands the proper function of property.[151] These arguments bear some resemblance to Kant's explanation of property as an institution which we noted in Chapter 2 *Conceptions and Justifications*. Kant distinguishes between our innate right to bodily integrity (an integral part of our fundamental right to freedom), and our right to property, which becomes necessary only in order to extend the protection the law provides for our persons to external objects outside our physical control.[152] However, it is important to appreciate that all these conceptual argument against self-ownership, however they are put, can have no relevance to parts of our body which have been detached from it. As soon as a part of our body has become detached, it does indeed become an external object, and so, if we want to prohibit propertisation of it, we would have to find other reasons for doing so.

---

[150] Jonathan Herring and Jesse Wall, 'The nature and significance of the right to bodily integrity' (2017) 76 *Cambridge Law Journal* 566, also pointing out the difference between the right to bodily integrity and the right to bodily autonomy.

[151] Amongst the many who argue to the contrary, see e.g. Muireann Quigley, 'Property in human biomaterials – separating persons and things?' (2012) 32 *Oxford Journal of Legal Studies* 659.

[152] See further Chapter 2 *Conceptions and Justifications* para. 2.21 above.

The other major reason put forward for the prohibition against property rights in our own bodies is less convincing. This is that propertisation would lead to the commodification of human bodies, which, so it is argued, would be objectionable on two grounds. The first is that the buying and selling of human body parts and body products is in itself an affront to human dignity. The second, which raises interesting and important questions about the proper limits on our right to bodily autonomy, is that if we owned our own bodies, the law could not prevent us from selling parts of our bodies or our bodily products, which would put those in desperate need of money under intolerable pressures. However, these commodification arguments are difficult to sustain. If we want to prohibit the commodification of human bodies and parts of them, we need to prohibit *everyone* from buying or selling them, not just the originator (i.e. the person whose body it is or from whom the bodily part/material was taken). It would be odd to prohibit me from selling a part of my body, but allow others who had lawfully taken control of it (perhaps the doctor who had surgically removed it) to sell it for themselves.[153] The other problem with the commodification arguments, however, is that they mistakenly assume that any property rights that we might have in parts of or material from our own (or anyone else's) body must amount to absolute private ownership. If we want to prohibit commodification of human body organs and bodily materials we can do so by making property interests in them inalienable or alienable only in limited circumstances, as our legal system does with some property interests in other things.[154] We do not have to prohibit propertisation.

7.27 Reaffirmation of the No-Property Principle: *Moore* v. *Regents of the University of California*

Many of these arguments surfaced in the US decision *Moore* v. *Regents of the University of California*,[155] a decision of the Supreme Court of California in 1990. *Moore* was the first in a series of modern court decisions in the common law world in which the courts have had to re-assess the traditional prohibitions against property in human bodies in the light of the technological developments which have transformed the commercial and therapeutic value of human bodily material. So, although it has no binding authority in our jurisdiction,[156] it has set the terms of the modern debate in the western world.

---

[153] Odd, but precisely what was decided by the majority of the Supreme Court of California in *Moore* v. *Regents of the University of California* (1990) 51 Cal 3d 120, as we see below.

[154] Commercial dealings in human material for transplantation are anyway prohibited in our law by s. 32 of the Human Tissue Act 2004: see further para. 7.31 below.

[155] *Moore* v. *Regents of the University of California* (1990) 51 Cal 3d 120.

[156] Even in California, the law has moved on since *Moore*: see *Hecht* v. *Superior Court of Los Angeles County* (1993) 20 Cal Rptr 775, where it was held that a man had a property interest in sperm he had had stored for the future use of his partner, so that when he died his property interest in the sperm passed to his executor, to be passed on to the partner, the beneficiary entitled under the will. On this basis, the partner was held entitled in a preliminary hearing to an order restraining the sperm bank from destroying the sperm (as requested by the adult children of the man's previous marriage) pending the court's determination of her entitlement to it.

The case concerned actions brought by John Moore, who was undergoing treatment for hairy-cell leukaemia at the Medical Center of the University of California at Los Angeles in the 1970s. The doctor treating him, Dr Golde, realized that Moore's white blood cells had features which would make them useful for his own research, and he therefore took samples of them from Moore's body when Moore's spleen was being removed as part of his leukaemia treatment. Moore gave formal consent to the removal of his spleen but he knew nothing about the removal of his cells for Golde's research project. Golde and his research team used these cells of Moore's to develop a cell-line[157] which enabled them to identify and go on to produce for themselves a lymphokine of a particular kind, which had potential therapeutic value. Golde and the University, as his employer, patented the cell-line and the methods for producing the lymphokine,[158] and entered into a profit-sharing agreement with a drug company for the commercial exploitation of the patents. Moore claimed that Golde and the University were liable to him in damages (a) for breach of fiduciary duty and (b) for the tort of conversion. To establish the tort of conversion he had to prove that the defendants had unlawfully interfered with his property, and if he had succeeded he would have been entitled to claim a share in the profits Golde and the University had made by using his property. In other words, he could have demanded a share of the profits they were making out of the commercial exploitation of the patents.

This was a preliminary stage in Moore's litigation against Golde and the hospital: all the Court had to decide at this stage was whether, assuming Moore's account of the facts was true, Moore's claims should proceed to a full trial. The Court allowed his claim for breach of fiduciary duty to proceed, on the basis that Golde failed to disclose the extent of his research and economic interests in Moore's cells before obtaining his consent to the medical procedures by which the cells were extracted. However, by a majority of 5–2[159] the court rejected Moore's claim that Golde and the University were liable to him in conversion. According to the majority, there had been no interference (lawful or unlawful) at any stage with any property belonging to Moore. They said that, because of the complexity of the social, economic and moral arguments raised, it was not for the courts to change the long-standing prohibition against property in human bodies. It followed that Moore could not have had any property rights in the cells taken from his body, and therefore could have had no property in the cell-line developed from them, nor in the procedure for producing the crucial lymphokine. The minority disagreed on all these points, and accepted Moore's arguments that he had property in his body, and therefore in his body cells,

---

[157] 'Cells taken directly from the body (primary cells) are not very useful for [research] purposes. Primary cells typically reproduce a few times and then die. One can, however, sometimes continue to use cells for an extended period of time by developing them into a "cell line," a culture capable of reproducing indefinitely. This is not, however, always an easy task. "Longterm growth of human cells and tissues is difficult, often an art," and the probability of succeeding with any given cell sample is low': *Moore*, fn. 155 above, at p. 127, *per* Panelli J, in footnote 2 to his judgment.

[158] Lymphokines themselves are natural products and so cannot be patented.

[159] Panelli J gave the principal opinion, with Lucas J, Eagleson J and Kennard J concurring, and Arabian J also gave a separate opinion concurring with Panelli, adding what he saw as the moral case for Panelli's rejection of the notion that people can have property rights in their own bodies or body parts. Broussard J and Mosk J each gave separate dissenting opinions on the property issue.

and that consequently he was entitled to share in the profits of the defendants' commercial exploitation of the research they carried out using his cells.

The arguments made by both the majority and the dissenting minority were wide ranging and are worth detailed consideration. For present purposes, however, three of them are particularly interesting. The first is that the minority dismissed the majority's strongly argued objections about commodification, for much the same reasons as those noted in para. 7.26 above, and argued that allowing people property in their own body parts promotes rather than (as the majority argued) undermines human dignity and autonomy. The second concerned the social and economic benefits of research. Both the majority and the minority accepted that availability of human tissue and other bodily material was vitally important for socially beneficial biomedical research. However, whereas the majority argued that it would seriously inhibit biotechnology research and commercial investment in it if people had property rights in their bodily material, the minority dismissed these fears as groundless, arguing that the practical consequences the majority foresaw were not based on reality. Finally, there were interesting divergences on the morality of Moore's claim. As far as the majority was concerned, Moore deserved redress for the wrong that the defendants had done to him by removing cells and other tissue from his body without his informed consent, but this was a personal wrong which made them liable to pay him damages for breach of duty. He would have a fortuitous windfall, they argued, if he acquired a share in the profits they had made by happening to use his cells, rather than anyone else's, in research they were carrying out to enlighten science about 'the common workings of the human body'. The minority saw things differently. The supposed 'windfall' would be very small indeed, they pointed out, because only a tiny proportion of the value of the cell-line and resulting patents could be attributable to Moore's cell, as opposed to the skill and labour of the researchers and the contributions made by the drug company. But in any event, they said, if there are economic gains to be had by using human bodily material for research or therapeutic purposes it is illogical and unfair that the only person to be excluded from sharing in those gains should be the person from whose body the material was taken. On this basis, so they argued, it is morally unacceptable to deny people legally protectable property rights in their own bodies and body parts, leaving them exposed to 'the mining and harvesting' of their body parts by others for economic gain.

Nevertheless, the majority won, upholding the traditional prohibitions against property in human bodies and body parts.

7.28 The Work and Skill Exception

However, an exception to the traditional prohibitions had already been made by the High Court of Australia[160] in *Doodeward* v. *Spence* (1908) 6 CLR 406, although on very different facts which raised different moral, social and economic issues. More

---

[160] The highest court in Australia.

than 40 years before the hearing, a doctor had preserved the still-born body of a two-headed foetus and kept it on display in a jar in his surgery. When he died the jar and contents were sold with his other possessions and eventually inherited by Doodeward. He put it on public display, charging people to see it. The police confiscated it from him and charged him with outraging public decency by exhibiting it. Doodeward brought this action against the police demanding that they return the foetus to him (they had already returned the jar). The High Court of Australia decided by a majority that he was entitled to have it back. Their reasoning was that, although the general principle was that no-one could have property rights in a human body or part of a human body, this could not apply once someone had 'by the exercise of lawful work or skill ... so dealt with it that it has acquired some attributes differentiating it from' a body awaiting burial. Without such an exception, it was said, 'the many valuable collections of anatomical and pathological specimens or preparations formed and maintained by scientific bodies' would be at risk.

This exception to the general principle has been accepted by the English courts. In particular, in *R* v. *Kelly* [1999] QB 621 the Court of Appeal applied the 'work and skill' exception to support its finding that the Royal College of Surgeons had property in the anatomical specimens it kept and used for research and teaching purposes. Kelly, an artist, had been convicted of theft after taking away some of the specimens without authorisation, using them in his artworks which were subsequently displayed in public exhibitions. He appealed against his conviction on grounds that he could not have 'stolen' the specimens because no-one can have property in parts of human bodies.[161] The Court of Appeal rejected his argument, applying *Doodeward* v. *Spence,* and upheld his conviction. Rose LJ applied the *Doodeward* principle in the following terms:

> We accept that, however questionable the historical origins of the principle, it has now been the common law for 150 years at least that neither a corpse nor parts of a corpse are in themselves and without more capable of being property protected by rights ... If that principle is now to be changed, in our view, it must be by Parliament, because it has been express or implicit in all the subsequent authorities and writings to which we have been referred ... that a corpse or part of it cannot be stolen ... [However], in our judgment, parts of a corpse are capable of being property within section 4 of the Theft Act 1968 *if they have acquired different attributes by virtue of the application of skill, such as dissection or preservation techniques, for exhibition or teaching purposes.*[162]

7.29 Erosion of the General Principle

However, as Quigley[163] has pointed out, there are difficulties with the 'work and skill' exception. Although it has superficial Lockean attractions – apparently

161 Theft Act 1968 s. 1(1): 'A person is guilty of theft if he dishonestly appropriates *property belonging to another* with the intention of permanently depriving the other of it' and s. 4(1): '"Property" includes money and all other property, real or personal, including things in action and other intangible property.'
162 *R* v. *Kelly* [1999] QB 621 at p. 631.
163 Quigley, 'Property in human biomaterials', fn. 151 above, pp. 662–664.

awarding property in an unpropertised thing to the person who expends their labour on it – even Locke never intended his principle to apply to things like human bodies, regarded as not appropriate for propertisation at all for moral or public policy reasons. Also, whilst it might make sense to award ownership of land to the person who labours on it, it is not so clear that the 'labourer' on body parts is always the appropriate person to acquire ownership of them.[164] On a more practical level, it can produce arbitrary results.[165] And, of course, there are obvious difficulties in deciding how much 'work and skill' is enough (a lot in *R v. Kelly*, but very little in *Doodeward v. Spence*).

The Court of Appeal in *Kelly* acknowledged the difficulties, and suggested that, whilst the 'work and skill' exception adequately covered the case before them, in other cases it might become necessary for the courts to recognise property rights in *any* human bodily material which has 'a use or significance beyond [its] mere existence':

> ... the common law does not stand still. It may be that if, on some future occasion, the question arises, the courts will hold that human body parts are capable of being property for the purposes of section 4 [of the Theft Act 1968], even without the acquisition of different attributes, *if they have a use or significance beyond their mere existence. This may be so if, for example, they are intended for use in an organ transplant operation, for the extraction of DNA or, for that matter, as an exhibit in a trial.*[166]

The Court of Appeal took up the invitation in *Yearworth* v. *North Bristol NHS Trust* [2009] EWCA Civ 37, where it had to decide whether a group of men whose sperm had been frozen and stored by the North Bristol NHS Trust in advance of their cancer treatment, were entitled to damages to compensate them for the mental distress and/or psychiatric injury they suffered when the Trust negligently allowed the temperature in the storage facility to rise so that the sperm was irretrievably damaged. The difficulty with the men's claim was that negligence liability arises only in respect of personal injury (i.e. physical injury to their persons) or damage to property. The Trust argued that the men had suffered neither in this case, applying the traditional principle that no-one can have property in a part of their own (or anyone else's) body. The Court of Appeal disagreed, and held that the men did have property in their stored sperm and therefore the Trust was liable for the mental distress/psychiatric injury they suffered when they realised it had been destroyed. Most importantly for present purposes, the Court declined to rest its decision on the *Doodeward* v. *Spence* 'work and skill' exception to the traditional principle of no property in human bodies, even though, as it pointed out, the work and skill

---

[164] Consider, for example, the transplant surgeon.

[165] See e.g. *Yearworth* v. *North Bristol NHS Trust* [2009] EWCA Civ 37 at para. 45(d) on the differences in liability of a medical officer handling a severed limb awaiting re-attachment, depending on whether the limb was surgically removed (in which case the *Kelly* exception would apply) or accidentally severed (when it would not).

[166] *R v. Kelly* [1999] QB 621, CA, Rose LJ at p. 631 (emphasis added).

exception clearly would have applied here.[167] Instead, it said, the principle itself had to be re-assessed:

> 45 ... (a) In this jurisdiction developments in medical science now require a re-analysis of the common law's treatment of and approach to the issue of ownership of parts or products of a living human body, whether for present purposes (viz. an action in negligence) or otherwise....
>
> (d) ... as foreshadowed by Rose LJ in *Kelly*, we are not content to see the common law in this area founded upon the principle in *Doodeward*, which was devised as an exception to a principle, itself of exceptional character, relating to the ownership of a human corpse. Such ancestry does not commend it as a solid foundation....
>
> (e) So we prefer to rest our conclusions on a broader basis.[168]

However, the Court of Appeal did not arrive at its 'broader basis' by considering the moral, philosophical and economic arguments which were central to the reasoning of the Justices in the Supreme Court of California in *Moore*. Instead, the Court of Appeal examined the nature of the relationship that the men had with the Trust in respect of the stored sperm. The court took as its starting point the fact that the men had generated the sperm for their own future use, and the court then looked at the rights, duties and powers that they and the Trust had in relation to the sperm under the Human Fertilisation and Embryology Act 1990 as amended, which now regulates all activities involving human reproductive material.[169] In particular, the 1990 Act allows sperm storage facilities (and all other human reproductive treatment services) to be provided only by licensed bodies, and strictly regulates the storage, use and destruction of any sperm they hold. Under these regulations the licensed body must treat the welfare of any prospective child, or any other relevant child, as paramount. Subject to that, it may not do anything in relation to the stored sperm without the informed consent of the donor and it must use the sperm as directed by the donor, or destroy it at his request. From this, the Court of Appeal concluded that, although the men had only limited rights of control over the use of the sperm, it was sufficient to amount to 'ownership' of the sperm, particularly since it included an absolute right to have the sperm destroyed on demand. The Court added that, even if it was wrong to categorise the men's property interest in the stored sperm as ownership, it was still a property interest of some kind. At the very least, the Court of Appeal said, their property interest encompassed rights in the sperm which were extensive enough to make the Trust liable to them as bailees of the sperm. Bailees are people (like cloakroom attendants, car repair garages or the person who picks up the wallet you have dropped in the street) who have acquired possession of goods or chattels belonging to someone else, and for that reason owe a duty to the owner to take reasonable care of the property. The argument is that the Trust was undoubtedly in possession of the men's sperm, but they could not be said to own it (any use

---

[167] 'We would have no difficulty in concluding that the unit's storage of the sperm in liquid nitrogen at minus 196° was an application to the sperm of work and skill which conferred on it a substantially different attribute, namely the arrest of its swift perishability': Lord Judge, giving the judgment of the Court of Appeal in *Yearworth*, fn. 165 above, at para. 45(c.).

[168] Ibid. para. 45.   [169] See further para. 7.30 below.

they made of it required the men's consent, and they had none of Honoré's other incidents of ownership), so it makes some sense to say that they owed the duties of a bailee towards the only people who did have rights in the sperm, that is, the men who had generated it and entrusted it to their care.[170] On this basis the Court of Appeal held that the men were entitled to damages to compensate them for the mental distress and/or psychiatric injury they suffered, either because the Trust was liable to them in the tort of negligence for negligently damaging their property, or because the Trust was liable to them for failing to take reasonable care of their property (the sperm) which the Trust had taken into its possession.[171]

7.30 Effect of *Yearworth* on the No-Property Principle

(a) Scope of *Yearworth*

It seems clear from *Yearworth* that the English courts will no longer apply the traditional principle of no property in human body parts, even as a starting point, when considering the rights of living originators of body parts or products which have become detached from their bodies. However, it is not clear what principle the courts will apply instead, in cases going beyond the facts of *Yearworth*. It seems plausible that the same reasoning could apply to any other kind of human reproductive material covered by the Human Fertilisation and Embryology Act 1990, not just sperm, at least when it has been taken from a living originator, because the 1990 Act similarly requires informed consent from originators in relation to use of other human reproductive materials. It may also be possible to apply it to other kinds of bodily material. Most other bodily material is regulated by similar statutory regimes, so in theory at least the courts could adopt similar approaches. In other words, they could take as a starting point the rights and powers to control the use of the material which an originator has against others under the relevant statutory regulatory regime, and treat that person as 'owner' of the material if they have greater control over the use of the material than anyone else.

This looks more plausible when you look at the similarities between the relevant statutory regulatory regimes. They are mostly governed by the Human Tissue Act 2004, which regulates specified activities involving live and dead human bodies and nearly all kinds of human bodily material which are not covered by the Human Fertilisation and Embryology Act 1990.[172] The origins of the Human Tissue Act

---

[170] This argument can be accused of circularity, assuming what it seeks to prove (a bailee owes a duty of care only to the owner of the bailed object, or to the holder of another kind of property interest that gives the bailor the right to possession of the object). Kenneth Reid claims that the first half of the argument is also circular: Kenneth G. C. Reid, 'Body parts and property', University of Edinburgh School of Law Research Paper Series No 2015/25 at p. 7.

[171] In the same way that a cloakroom attendant would be liable to you if your coat was damaged whilst in the cloakroom because the cloakroom operators failed to take reasonable care of it.

[172] The 2004 Act applies to all material 'which consists of or includes human cells', excluding human reproductive material and embryos outside the human body (covered instead by the Human Fertilisation and Embryology Act 1990) and excluding also 'hair and nail from the body of a living person'. (s. 53 of the 2004 Act), although hair and nail *are* covered by the provisions of the 2004 Act

2004 are significant. It implements recommendations made by public inquires held in the 1990s, following public revulsion at revelations that, after carrying out post-mortem examinations, Bristol and Alder Hey hospitals and (as it turned out) most other hospitals and medical institutions in the UK, routinely removed, stored, used and disposed of organs and other tissue from the dead bodies of children (and adults) without the knowledge or consent of their families.[173] The activities regulated by the 2004 Act include organ and tissue transplants, and the removal, use, storage and disposal of human bodily material for anatomical examination, research, teaching, audit or public display. The regulatory system set up by the Human Tissue Act 2004 to deal with these activities is centred on informed consent, in much the same way as the system provided by the Human Fertilisation and Embryology Act 1990 for human reproductive material. Like the 1990 Act, the Human Tissue Act 2004 provides that these specified activities may be carried out only by bodies licensed by the relevant regulatory authority (the Human Tissue Authority), and that, when carrying out these activities, the licensed body must at all stages obtain the 'appropriate consent' of, generally, the originator of the material or nearest family members. In addition, the 2004 Act bans all 'commercial dealings' in any human organ or other human bodily material for transplantation.[174]

The end result is that just about all originators of human bodily material have some degree of control over the use of the material once it is separated from their body, because of the requirement under these statutory regulatory regimes that nothing may be done with the material without their informed consent. So, arguably *Yearworth* can be taken to establish a general principle that originators of human bodily material own, or have some other kind of property interest, in that material as soon as it is separated from their bodies. However, this leaves many unanswered questions. What kind of property interest is it? Is it a sui generis property interest, consisting of the rights of control and accountability that the originator has over it under the regulatory system and under any contract or bailment relationship she has with the current possessor of the material? Or is it full ownership, subject only to whatever restrictions the statutory regulatory regime imposes on activities involving it? And, in either case, is it a transmissible property interest, that is, an interest that can be passed on to successors of the originator, or is it by its nature capable of being

---

which regulate DNA testing (www.hta.gov.uk/faqs/analysis-dna-under-ht-act-faqs. For a good overview of the scope of the 2004 Act see www.hta.gov.uk/policies/human-tissue-act-2004. Blood and blood components also have their own regulatory regime, provided by the Blood Safety and Quality Regulations 2005/50).

[173] See J. K. Mason and G. T. Laurie, 'Consent or property? Dealing with the body and its parts in the shadow of Bristol and Alder Hey' (2001) 64 *Modern Law Review* 710.

[174] S. 32 of the Human Tissue Act 2004. Not all material covered by the 2004 Act is included in the ban. In particular, it does not cover cell-lines (i.e. the material that scientists can develop from cells taken directly from a human body, and which was part of the human bodily material claimed by John Moore in *Moore* v. *Regents of the University of California* (1990) 51 Cal. 3d 120: see fn. 155 above), nor material 'which is the subject of property because of an application of human skill': s. 54(7) and s. 32 (9) of the 2004 Act.

held only by the originator?[175] If it is transmissible, is it unlimited in duration (like ownership)[176] or is it limited to last only during the lifetime of the originator? These questions matter because, if an originator has a property interest in her separated bodily material which is transmissible and unlimited in duration, other people involved in activities relating to that material can acquire her property interest by succession[177] or transfer.[178] If, on the other hand, the originator's property interest is personal to her and/or ends on her death, we have to find some other basis for arguing that those who later acquire control over the originator's material have property interests in it.[179]

(b) Alternative Analyses of *Yearworth*

Others have argued for, or assumed, a broader or narrower interpretation of the *Yearworth* principle. One view is that it simply reverses the traditional common law prohibition against people having property rights in parts of their body, replacing it with a basic common law principle that originators of human bodily material acquire ownership of it as soon as it is separated from their body, subject to whatever restrictions may be imposed by statutory regulatory provisions, and that ownership can then be transferred to or acquired by others according to general property principles applicable to tangible personal property.[180] Another is that it only applies, or at least should only apply, to human bodily material taken from a living originator, and that *Doodeward* v. *Spence* continues to apply to bodily material

---

[175] Like, for example, the 'home rights' a spouse or civil partner has under s. 30 of the Family Law Act 1996 to occupy what is or was the matrimonial/civil partnership home (Chapter 6 *New Property Interests and the Numerus Clausus* para 6.11 and see also Chapter 1 *What Property Is and Why It Matters* para. 1.26(b)).

[176] That is, continues for so long as the bodily material continues to exist.

[177] This was assumed by the Californian court in *Hecht* v. *Superior Court of Los Angeles County*, fn. 156 above.

[178] See Reid, 'Body parts and property', fn. 170 above, at pp. 13–18, considering the ways in which the originator's property rights might be transmitted to successors, concluding that where patients consent to a medical procedure they will normally be taken to have donated their property interests in bodily material removed from their bodies to the person who removed it (generally, the medical authority employing the doctor who carried out the procedure), subject only to any conditions she imposed as to its future use. It seems plausible that the same applies in English law, despite the differences between English and Scottish concepts of ownership (Chapter 5 *Ownership and Other Property Interests* para. 5.12). An alternative analysis is that the originator abandons her property interest in the material when she consents to its removal from her body: see Imogen Goold, 'Abandonment and human tissue' in Imogen Goold, Kate Greasley, Jonathan Herring and Loane Skene (eds.), *Persons, Parts and Property: How Should We Regulate Human Tissue in the 21st Century* (Oxford and Portland, OR: Hart Publishing, 2016).

[179] An obvious possibility is that the person who next takes possession of the material acquires title to ownership of it by original acquisition, by the process we look at in Chapter 11 *Possession and Title* para. 11.3. This could also apply to confer ownership of bodily material removed during a medical procedure on the person who removed it, if the originator is taken to have abandoned her property interest by giving consent to the removal.

[180] The Supreme Court of Queensland in *Re Cresswell* [2018] QSC 184 took this to be the effect of *Yearworth* in English law, as pointed out by Samuel Walpole, 'Property in human bodily products' (2019) 135 *Law Quarterly Review* 31. See also Kenneth Reid's argument in 'Body parts as property', fn. 170 above, that this is in any event the position in Scots law.

taken from dead bodies.[181] Alternatively, since the Court of Appeal in *Yearworth* emphasised that the men had generated the sperm for their own future use, it could be argued that the decision applies only to bodily material separated from the originator's body *for the originator's future use*. However, it is difficult to see how this could be a relevant factor in deciding whether the originator has property rights in the separated material: what different considerations come into play if the material was separated accidentally, or intended for some other future use such as transplantation into the body of a stranger, or donation to a tissue bank, or for use in research or teaching, or public display?

7.31 Property or Regulation?

Leaving aside a brief reference in s. 32 of the Human Tissue Act (HTA) 2004,[182] neither the 2004 Act nor the Human Fertilisation and Embryology Act (HFEA) 1990 contains any reference to property rights or interests in human bodies or human bodily material. This raises the question of whether we need property at all, when relationships between people in respect of human bodily material are so extensively regulated by specific statutory provisions, monitored and enforced by public regulatory authorities. Why not rely only on the kind of comprehensive statutory regulatory regimes provided by the HFEA 1990 and the HTA 2004? Under these regimes the consent principle ensures that individuals fully participate in decisions made about their own bodies and those of their family members. The consent principle is monitored and policed by the specialist regulatory authorities set up under these regimes, and these regulatory authorities have effective control over all relevant activities involving human bodily material, because anyone who wants to be involved in such activities must be licensed by, and comply with all rules, regulations and practices imposed by, the relevant regulatory authority. The regulatory authorities supplement the statutory regulatory rules by issuing and enforcing detailed Codes of Practice and ethical guidelines, which can be regularly updated, allowing flexibility and ensuring best practice.[183] Because (unlike courts) they are specialists, the regulatory authorities build up experience and expertise in dealing with the kinds of issue likely to arise, enabling them to make informed and principled decisions about policy and practice, balancing the public interest with the moral rights of individuals to autonomy, human dignity and respect. They can also keep under review the moral, social and practical implications of impending technological developments, stimulating public debate and providing policy advice for the government.

---

[181] This is the position in Australia, following *Re Cresswell* (fn. 180 above), but see Mason and Laurie, 'Consent or property?', fn. 173 above, p. 741, and also Reid, 'Body parts and property', fn. 170 above, at p. 2 for persuasive arguments against distinguishing between human bodily material taken from live and from dead bodies.

[182] Excluding material 'which is the subject of property because of an application of human skill' from the ban on commercial dealings with human bodily materials for transplantation: see fn. 174 above.

[183] See HTA and HFEA websites.

Current academic debate broadly supports this kind of regulatory approach to activities involving human bodily material. The controversial question is whether it is sufficient in itself, or whether it ought to be supplemented by propertising human bodily material as well.[184] On one view property is inappropriate because property law's focus is on human bodies as objects in which people can have rights, rather than as the physical manifestation of personhood. In this sense, property law objectifies human bodies, and this may undermine the protection of people's rights to bodily autonomy and bodily integrity which are upheld by other branches of law. As Kate Greasley puts it, in an argument that goes beyond the commodification arguments noted in para. 7.26 above:

> we already do each own our own bodies, as much as anyone can own them, in the extra-legal realm. We control what happens to them, put them to use and move them from one place to another in ways that nobody else does. One immediate question arising, then, is what owning our own bodies as pieces of legal property would possibly mean, over and above all this. The law clearly has a role to play in protecting our liberty rights to control our own bodies, especially in protecting them from unwanted and harmful interference. These protections do not take the form of property rights, but of legal constraints on the actions ... of others – constraints found in criminal law, tort and public law ... Property rights, on the other hand, have never been the legal mechanism for protecting bodily integrity. Where legal property rights arise in anything, they are there chiefly to facilitate the possibility of transferring the possession, control or use of the object of property from one party to another – to make it possible that the object can be treated as a 'thing' in some fundamental ways.
>
> Consequently, one might think that the main interests we have in controlling our own bodies are protected by legal mechanisms outside of property law, and that property law itself – and indeed, the whole proprietary conception of the human body – might instead be seen to constitute the main threat of losing that control through the transfer of property rights ...[185]

A different argument against propertisation is that the property rules that are imported when we recognise that people can have property rights in human bodily material are those developed to deal with tangible personal property – that is, things like goods and chattels which the law regards as commodities.[186] These rules are simply 'too clumsy and inflexible' to be applied to human bodily materials. They are unable to take into account the 'unique nature' of different kinds of bodily material, and incapable of balancing their undoubted commercial value against their immense

---

[184] The arguments on both sides are usefully summarised in Reid, 'Body parts and property', fn. 170 above, at pp. 4–6. For fuller arguments from commentators taking a range of pro- and anti-property positions, see Goold et al. *Persons, Parts and Property*, fn. 178 above.

[185] Kate Greasley, 'Property rights in the human body: Commodification and objectification' in Goold et al., *Persons, Parts and Property*, fn. 178 above, at p. 73. She develops the point in the following pages, arguing that this does not necessarily rule out propertising human bodies, but does require us to scrutinise proposed property rights (such as those claimed in *Moore* or awarded in *Yearworth*) to see whether they might have the harmful effects associated with treating human bodies as objects which she summarises in pp. 86–87.

[186] Or, in the case of material like genetic information, perhaps on the uncertain borderline between tangible and intangible personal property we noted in para.7.9 above.

importance to the public for therapeutic and research purposes and for maintaining public health, as well as their 'emotional and relational value' to their originators and their families.[187] Jonathan Herring sees this as inevitably so, because the standard Western property model is 'largely based on individualistic values that protect rights of exclusion and control' and so cannot protect 'important social, communal and relational interests in bodies [or] ... capture important personal interests in body parts'.[188] He also claims that common law property rights will not be able to distinguish between different kinds of bodily material:

> the property approach claims that all our bodily material is property and in so doing imagines that we have similar interests in all parts of our bodies. We don't. We have utterly different attitudes towards different kinds of bodily material in different contexts.[189]

He acknowledges that 'statutory exceptions' to basic property principles could be created to take account of such special factors, but says that 'in doing so we would soon be departing so far from the standard property paradigm that it would barely resemble property as it is currently understood'.[190]

It is noticeable that the anti-property arguments mostly assume that the property model that must inevitably apply to human bodily material if we allow it to be propertised at all, is the traditional Western absolute private ownership model. There is no reason why that should be the case, and indeed *Yearworth* demonstrates that the courts will recognise people as holding property interests in human bodily material which have almost none of the incidents of private ownership described by Honoré. The private ownership model may be appropriate for some situations, for example in deciding whether strangers are at liberty to snatch away or damage human bodily material held by, for example, medical establishments or tissue banks or research institutions, but property law allows us to take a more nuanced approach in other situations, as we see in para. 7.29. Also, we have to remind ourselves not to underestimate the role that Parliament has, and has always had, in the formation of new kinds of property interest and in re-moulding pre-existing ones. Most of our major property interests have some constituent elements drawn from the common law and others from statute.[191] Others, especially those that have arisen recently in response to technological developments, derive almost wholly from statute and are tailored to the specific nature of the thing in question and the interest holder's interest in it.[192] So, Herring's fears that property law could only impose a one-size-fits all solution for very different kinds of human bodily material appear unfounded.

---

[187] Reid, 'Body parts and property', fn. 170 above, at p. 5.

[188] Jonathan Herring, 'Why we need a statute regime to regulate bodily material' in Goold et al., *Persons, Parts and Property*, fn. 178 above, at p. 215.

[189] Ibid. p. 216.   [190] Ibid. p. 214.

[191] See e.g. the diverse range of property interests we looked at in Chapter 5 *Ownership and Other Property Interests*, ranging from modern freehold ownership of land, the charge by way of legal mortgage, the respective interests of trustees and beneficiaries under a trust, and the communal interests of local inhabitants to use town and village greens.

[192] The best examples are the regulatory licences noted in Chapter 6 *New Property and the Numerus Clausus* para. 6.12.

In any event, whatever the origin and nature of any particular kind of property interest, there is nothing unusual about statute restricting the inherent rights or powers of the property interest holder (or imposing additional duties or prohibitions on him or on others). Property interests have always been subject to limitations and constraints imposed by the general law,[193] and there is no reason why the position should be different for property interests in human bodily material. So, for example, if English law was to recognise that an executor has a kind of property interest in a dead body until it is buried, there is no reason why this should override the many statutory duties already imposed on them and on others in relation to dead bodies. Similarly, there is no reason why statute should not prohibit or restrict the alienability of any property interest if alienability is thought to promote inappropriate commodification. As Reid says:

> Insofar as there is objectification or commodification [of human bodies and bodily material], this is much more due to the use made of body parts in practice than to the application of the label or the principles of property law . . . although all property can, in principle, be sold, there is nothing in the nature of ownership to prevent the imposition of restrictions on sale. Indeed this has already been done in respect of body parts supplied for transplantation [by the Scottish equivalent of s. 32 of the Human Tissue Act 2004[194]]. If further restrictions were thought necessary, property law would not stand in their way. The extent to which the market in biomaterials should be curbed is a policy question on which property law takes no sides.[195]

On the pro-property side, the basic argument is that public regulatory systems are by their nature incapable of providing adequate protection for the interests we, as individuals, have in our own bodies, or the interests of the many other private individuals and public or commercial bodies who are now engaged in activities involving human bodily material. These include all those institutions that now routinely hold, control, use and sometimes trade in vast quantities of human bodily material (hospitals, tissue banks, research institutions, Universities, museums, galleries, etc.), as well as the individuals and institutions who use the services of these repositories of human bodily material, and those who have provided them with material, data and/or financial or other support so that they can pursue general or specific altruistic ends. The focus of our statutory regulatory regimes is on setting up acceptable systems for monitoring and regulating all these activities and enterprises, and making sure the regulatory systems work. It is not primarily (or at all) concerned with providing redress for people when things nevertheless go wrong, or with the resolution of disputes between those with competing interests in the same material or competing interests in how it should be used. Property provides a

---

[193] As we see in relation to interests in land in Chapter 10 *Limitations on Property*.

[194] See fn. 174 above.

[195] Reid, 'Body parts and property', fn. 170 above, at p. 5. In his footnote 35 at the end of the quoted text, Reid notes the recent literature confirming that 'trading in bodily materials inside and outside the NHS is widespread, and there has been a proliferation of tissue banks in both the public and the private sectors'.

long-established and reasonably coherent set of rules for determining such questions, so the argument goes. As Reid says:

> The arguments in favour of a property model turn mainly on simplicity, certainty, and coherence. If body parts can be owned, then property law provides a ready-made set of rules for their use, preservation, defence, vindication, and transfer. Such rules are as necessary for biobanks and researchers as they are for the originators of the materials. And, crucially, the rights and remedies to which they give rise are enforceable against all challengers and not, as with contractual arrangements, against only a single person or group of persons. The alternative to property is endless improvisation against a background of disturbing legal uncertainty.[196]

Reid admits that it is not always clear how pre-existing property rules will apply to novel situations that are now arising out of the widespread use of bodily material, but his conclusion is that:

> property law will always be better than no-law. In its absence there is a vacuum which the rest of private law will struggle to fill. This would be private law operating at half-cock.[197]

These pro-property arguments are reinforced by our intuitive perceptions about property and human bodies and bodily materials. As Kate Greasley pointed out in the passage we have already quoted earlier on in this paragraph, when we are thinking outside the law, we think and act as if we own our own bodies and bodily material, and as if others own theirs. Reid makes a similar point at a more general level, and sees the virtue in making the law accord with 'prosaic reality':

> In practice, body parts are often treated as if they are owned. They are donated, preserved, worked on, and abandoned. The very language used to describe these activities is the language of property law. The law should be in alignment with the practice.[198]

7.32 Human Bodily Material as 'Commons'?

For many commentators, the unacceptable face of propertisation of human bodily material is the development of markets in various kinds of bodily material, made inevitable (so it is argued) because of the involvement of commercial profit-making organisations in the collection and banking of human bodily material and genetic information. The objection is that a commercial organisation is making money out of material unwittingly or altruistically donated by private individuals, and using it primarily for its own commercial ends rather than in the public interest. Donna Dickenson gives a number of examples, including 'public umbilical cord banks which receive their samples from women who have donated altruistically [and] are now engaging in a commodified international trade in cord blood units, resulting in

---

[196] Ibid. p. 6.   [197] Ibid.
[198] Reid 'Body parts and property', fn. 170 above, p. 5. For Kate Greaseley's comment see text to fn. 185 above.

what has been called "the economisation of life".[199] As Dickenson points out, a consent-based regulatory system cannot easily handle such cases.[200] Her argument is that property, however, can have a role to play if this kind of human bodily material is conceptualised as 'commons'.[201] In this context 'commons' can be taken to be resources like the internet, or the knowledge commons, or natural resources on which we all depend, such as water. The argument is that such resources are part of the common human heritage, and should be used for the common good of humanity, not for the sole use or benefit of a private individual or commercial enterprise. For this reason they are not appropriate objects of absolute private property interests. However, if they are capable of 'capture',[202] they should not be left unpropertised either, because that would leave them open to de facto appropriation by private interests. The obvious alternative is to subject them to some kind of state, public or communal property regime. As we see in Chapter 8 *Property Interest Holders*, there are various property models that might be appropriate for achieving this kind of objective. Ownership of the resource (or some other controlling property interest) can be vested directly in the state, or in a special purpose public body, or in a community of stakeholders (perhaps patients, campaigners and others interested in the cure of a particular disease, if we are thinking of human bodily material). However, it can also be done by developing a hybrid property model, and this may be more promising in the case of commons resources like human bodily material, because of the importance of protecting the private interests of the originators of the bodily material as well as the various community and public interests that may be relevant for that kind of bodily material. Dickenson describes two such models that have been developed recently to conceptualise and regulate holdings of various kinds of human bodily material and genetic material as 'commons'. One kind of model involves vesting ownership of the bodily material in a special purpose private institution, modelled on a charitable trust, which will operate as a private biobank. The biobank would have only a trustee-like property interest in the materials, holding them subject to limited private property interests of the originators of the material (perhaps resembling *Yearworth*-type property interests) but also bound by its constitution to use the materials only in specified ways and for specified purposes, and in accordance with the wishes of, and guidance provided by, not only the originators of the material but also other stakeholders[203] and community advisory boards.[204] Dickenson also describes an interesting alternative model developed by PXE International Foundation, a disease-specific advocacy group (a group whose goal is the elimination of or cure for a specific disease). The

---

[199] Donna Dickenson, 'Alternatives to a corporate commons: Biobanking, genetics and property in the body' in Goold et al., *Persons, Parts and Property*, fn. 178 above, at p. 179.

[200] Ibid. p. 194.   [201] Ibid. pp. 179 and 184–188.

[202] That is, it is factually possible for someone to take exclusive physical or de facto control over them (or strategic parts of them), excluding outsiders except on their own terms.

[203] For example, their families and friends, and those engaged in research and treatment of the disease.

[204] Dickenson, 'Alternatives to a corporate commons', fn. 199 above, at pp. 180–190, where she refers to the extensive academic literature examining the potential use of private charitable trusts in these contexts.

distinctive feature of this model is that it positively utilises commodification rather than seeking to eliminate it. Broadly, this model also involves setting up a special purpose private institution, this time directly controlled by the advocacy group. The institution sets up its own biobank from tissue and data provided by its members (patients suffering from the disease and their families), attracts public and charitable funding for research, and raises further money by commercial exploitation of the tissue and data, ploughing the profits back into the research. The objective of the group is 'to achieve positive health outcomes for their members – "to work until we turn the lights off and go home" – rather than focussing on the wealth and longevity of the organisation', which, in their view, is what traditional charitable institutions do. So, the biobank is set up by members of the advocacy group not only for the use of researchers acting in the public interest, but also so that they can commodify their own bodily material and data to fund research into their particular disease, in other words to further their own individual and collective interests.

7.33 Bodily Material as 'Person' Not 'Property'?

However, if we are thinking only of the individual's private interests in her own bodily material, there is another alternative to consider. This is that, even after it has become separated from her body, an individual's bodily material might in some circumstances be treated as still part of her person rather than as having become part of her property. This is a solution that was adopted in Germany by the Federal Court of Justice (the Bundesgerichtshof), Sixth Civil Senate, 9 November 1993, BGHZ, 124, 52, where, on facts almost identical to those in *Yearworth,* a man was held entitled to damages for personal injury from a clinic when it negligently damaged the sperm it was storing for him. This was on the basis that human reproductive material extracted from the body with a view to future reproductive use for the originator of the material retained a 'functional unity'[205] with the body, so that damage to it amounted to physical injury to the originator's person. The English Court of Appeal in *Yearworth* considered but rejected a similar 'functional unity' argument based on the German decision, concerned about the broader implications of importing into English law what it described as 'a fiction' that something outside the body was still part of it. However, in a later Scottish case, *Holdich* v. *Lothian Health Board,*[206] again on more or less identical facts, Lord Stewart in the Scottish Court of Session Outer House described the 'functional unity' theory as a plausible one, and thought that a similar argument might well succeed in a Scottish court.[207] The point did not arise for decision because Holdich, the man seeking redress for what he claimed was the negligent damage of his stored sperm by Lothian Health Board, relied instead on the argument that the Scottish courts should 'put a kilt on *Yearworth*'[208] and adopt it into Scots law, so entitling him to damages for injury to

---

[205] *Eine funktionale einheit.*   [206] *Holdich* v. *Lothian Health Board* [2013] CSOH 197.
[207] Ibid. paras 6–7.   [208] Ibid. para. 15.

his property.[209] Lord Stewart, however, was more attracted by the idea of adopting the German solution and extending the concept of injury to a person so that it covers 'damage to viable bio-matter produced or removed for the purposes of the living subject's own reproductive or medical treatment', and possibly also damage to other kinds of viable bio-matter to be used in out-of-body medical treatment (e.g. skin grafts and high-dose radiation of cancerous organs removed to protect surrounding tissue), or for transplant or transfusions:

> Would it be unreasonable to extend the concept of injury to damage to viable bio-matter produced or removed for the purpose of the living subject's own reproduction or medical treatment? ... would it be far-fetched to deal with [it] as part of the subject's person? Would it do violence to the law? Would it run counter to current norms of medical practice? Would it be inconsistent with the regulatory regimes? Would it offend morality?[210]

7.34 Human Bodily Material as Sui Generis?

A variation on this approach would be to treat some bodily material as a sui generis thing, neither person nor property, but somewhere in between. This would mean breaking away from our traditional classification of things for property purposes. In *Holdich* Lord Stewart considered whether this might provide a better solution in cases involving human reproductive tissue, pointing out that neither a property analysis nor a personal injury analysis would be of any help to an intended recipient of stored reproductive materials if they were damaged after the provider's death. He quoted what John Habgood, the Archbishop of York, had said in Parliamentary debate about what became the Scottish Human Fertilisation and Embryology Act 1990:

> One of the difficulties in the debate is that embryology, to coin a phrase, is sui generis. We are constantly trying to apply distinctions which pertain in ordinary life but which do not actually apply in a particular respect. For example, lawyers try to put everything in one of two baskets; it is either a person or a thing. However there are entities which are neither persons nor things ...[211]

Lord Stewart suggested that 'neither persons nor things' might be a more fruitful way of looking at all human reproductive material:

> Is there any need to disambiguate the idea of 'his' sperm, or 'her' ova or 'their' embryos? Accepting the ambiguity permits both personal-type remedies and

---

[209] This was a preliminary hearing, and the court had to decide only whether the *Yearworth* argument and Holdich's alternative contention that the Health Board owed him a duty of care in delict not to cause him mental injury, stood a sufficient chance of success to be allowed to proceed to a full trial. It decided that both should proceed, although Lord Stewart was much less impressed by the *Yearworth* argument: see further Reid, 'Body parts and property', fn. 170 above.

[210] *Holdich* v. *Lothian*, fn. 206 above, para. 6.

[211] Archbishop of York, the Most Revd Dr John Habgood, commenting on the embryo provisions during the passage of the bill which became the 1990 Act. (quoted in S. Andrews and others (eds.), *Scottish Current Law Statutes Annotated 1990* (Edinburgh, 1990), vol. 3, 37-7).

property-type remedies, as appropriate and depending on the situation, without distorting the doctrinal framework. Damage and disputes over control and use are only two of the potential issues. Mistakes happen: the wrong person can end up as the gamete-receiver and embryos can be implanted in the wrong womb. There are succession issues . . . [and also] family law issues . . .

He concluded by suggesting that we should perhaps now all agree to 'resist the almost overwhelming temptation to use established conventional models'.[212]

RECOMMENDED READING

This chapter covers a lot of different topics, and you may want to pick and choose between them, or at least spend longer on some than on others. The readings below offer good starting points for further research if you want to look further at any of the issues raised.

Margaret Jane Radin, 'Property and personhood' (1982) 34 *Stanford Law Review* 957 esp. p. 961 and pp. 965–968, 971–977 (if you are interested in following up Hegel's property analysis: Radin's interpretation is controversial), 986–1000 and 1013–1015. (Note that in most of the cases she discusses, US law is different from the law in England and Wales.)

Bernard Rudden, 'Things as thing and things as wealth' (1994) 14 *Oxford Journal of Legal Studies* 81, pp. 93–94 and 95–96 (the whole article is worth reading, but some of the rest requires quite detailed knowledge of land law in England and Wales).

Lisa M. Austin, 'Person, place, or thing – property and the structuring of social relations' (2010) 60 *University of Toronto Law Journal* 445 (on several ideas covered in this chapter, including a reassessment of personhood and home).

Nestor Davidson, 'Property, well-being, and home: Positive psychology and property law's foundation' in Helen Carr, Brendan Edgeworth and Caroline Hunter (eds.), *Law and the Precarious Home: Socio Legal Perspectives on the Home in Insecure Times* (Oxford and London: Hart, 2018) p. 47 (especially pp. 47–55 and 59–61: on personhood and home, drawing on the theoretical literature we outlined in Chapter 2 *Conceptions and Justifications* and Chapter 3 *Allocation of Property Rights*).

Muireann Quigley, 'Property in human biomaterials – separating persons and things?' (2012) 32 *Oxford Journal of Legal Studies* 659.

Kenneth G. C. Reid, 'Body parts and property', University of Edinburgh School of Law Research Paper Series No 2015/25 pp. 4–6.

Donna Dickenson, 'Alternatives to a corporate commons: Biobanking, genetics and property in the body' in Imogen Goold, Kate Greasley, Jonathan Herring and Loane Skene (eds.), *Persons, Parts and Property: How Should We Regulate Human Tissue in the 21st Century* (Oxford and Portland, Oregon: Hart Publishing, 2016) p. 51.

Sabrina Praduroux, 'Objects of property rights: Old and new', in Michele Graziadei and Lionel Smith (eds.), *Comparative Property Law: Global Perspectives* (Cheltenham and Northampton, MA: Edward Elgar Publishing, 2017) p. 51 (for a comparative European overview).

Star Energy Weald Basin Ltd v. *Bocardo SA* [2010] UKSC 35.

Bernstein v. *Skyviews & General Ltd* [1978] QB 479.

Laiquat v. *Majid* [2005] EWHC 1305.

---

[212] Lord Stewart in *Holdich*, fn. 206 above at para. 52.

Lynn Shellfish Ltd v. *Loose* [2016] UKSC 14 .

R (on the application of Newhaven Port and Properties Ltd) v. *East Sussex County Council* [2015]
    UKSC 7, paras 23–51 (Lord Neuberger) and paras 106–136 (Lord Carnwath) (we look at
    the other issues in the case in Chapter 13 *Non-possessory Land Use Rights*, part VI).

Moore v. *Regents of the University of California* (1990) 51 Cal. 3d 120.

Doodeward v. *Spence* (1908) 6 CLR 406.

R v. *Kelly* [1999] QB 621.

Yearworth v. *North Bristol NHS Trust* [2009] EWCA Civ 37.

Holdich v. *Lothian Health Board* [2013] CSOH 197.

Questions

(1)   Explain Margaret Radin's personal/fungible distinction, and her suggestions for how this distinction should be marked in the law. How useful do you find her distinction? When you have finished the course, consider how far our law observes her distinction.

(2)   In the materials listed above, Bernard Rudden draws a distinction between 'things as thing and things as wealth' which similarly identifies that some of our things matter to us for their own sake, whereas we are interested in the others only for the wealth they represent. Consider how this differs from Radin's personal/fungible distinction.

(3)   Should the law treat 'home' as a distinctive kind of object of property rights?

(4)   How far up into the sky does 'land' extend, and how far down? Why are the rules different?

(5)   Discuss how our law deals with shifting boundaries between land and water and the dynamic form of the foreshore.

(6)   Discuss, by reference to the arguments considered by Lord Neuberger and by Lord Carnwath in *R (on the application of Newhaven Port and Properties Ltd)* v. *East Sussex County Council*, whether the public has, or should have, either a right or a liberty to use beaches in England and Wales recreationally. Why does it make a difference whether it is a right or a liberty?

(7)   Examine the arguments of the majority and the minority in *Moore* and discuss how convincing they are.

(8)   How useful is the concept of property in regulating the use of human bodies, body parts and bodily materials?

(9)   Compare the decisions and the reasoning in *Yearworth* and in *Holdich*. Which do you think adopts the better approach?

8

Property Interest Holders

PART I INTRODUCTION

8.1 Who Can Hold Property Interests?

In Chapter 5 *Ownership and Other Property Interests* we saw that most jurisdictions recognise a spectrum of property interests ranging from absolute private ownership to (in our jurisdiction) very specific interests in things such as a government licence to use part of the radio spectrum for a specified purpose for a limited period and even indirect interests such as a right to have an unconscionable transaction relating to a property interest set aside.

Many of these property interests can be held by different kinds of property interest holder, and again it is helpful to think of these different kinds of property interest holder as ranging across a spectrum rather than as falling within discrete categories. In this chapter we look at this range.

A convenient broad categorisation of property interest holders is to group them into four classes – individuals, communities, the public and the state. In the rest of this chapter we look more closely at these classes and at the distinctions and overlaps they tend to obscure.

We start in Part II with individuals as holders of property interests. As we pointed out in Chapter 1 *What Property Is and Why It Matters* para. 1.16, 'individual' is an ambiguous term. Sometimes it is used to refer only to a human being, as opposed to an artificial legal entity (such as a company). However, it can also be used in the same way as 'person' is used, that is, as a composite term to cover both human beings and artificial private legal entities. This is how we use it in this chapter.

In Part II we start by considering the difference between humans and artificial private legal entities as property interest holders, and between artificial legal entities which are private individuals (e.g. privately owned corporate bodies) and those which we can classify as public authorities. We consider public authorities as property interest holders in Part VI.

When we are considering private individuals (human or artificial) as property interest holders, there is another distinction we need to keep in mind. We tend to think of private individual property interest holders as autonomous self-interested entities who are free to do whatever they like with their property interest, and who we can predict will act in their own selfish best interests. Indeed, the market economy depends on property being primarily in the hands of such actors. However, we should be aware that many private individual property interest holders (human and corporate) do not fit this model. They might hold their property interests for the benefit of other individuals, or for a group of people or for a community. Similarly (or additionally), they might hold their property interests for specified purposes. In other words, significant classes of private individuals (human and artificial) who hold property interests are subject to legally enforceable limitations on the rights and powers they have as against others in relation to the object of the property interest, and subject to duties and liabilities which the autonomous self-interested private property owner does not have. We look at these distinctions in the rest of Part II.

Another complication is that two or more private individuals (or other legal entity) can co-own any kind of property interest. Civil law recognises the same phenomenon, and as civil lawyers are keen to emphasise, co-ownership in both the common law and the civil law does not involve each co-owner holding different property interests in the same thing: it means that together they hold the same property interest. This is important for civil lawyers because otherwise co-ownership could be seen as splitting up ownership, contrary to the civil law principle of unitary ownership.[1] We do not share these concerns, but we do nevertheless have this same concept of co-ownership as being a situation where 'multiple people simultaneously hold the same right'.[2] In the common law of England and Wales, however, the co-ownership relationship is greatly complicated in the case of interests in land because of the rule introduced in 1925 that whenever an interest in land is co-owned, a trust is automatically imposed on the co-owners. We look at how this works, and at co-ownership generally, in Part III of this chapter.

We move on from there to look at property holdings by families in Part IV – a short section because the main point is that in this jurisdiction we do not recognise a concept of family property. We also consider the implications of that absence in Part IV.

We then look at property holdings by communities in Part V, and then property holdings by the public and by public authorities (including the state) in Part VI. Finally in Part VII we consider the fluidity between property interest holders and objects of property interests. As we see there, at various points in the history of many societies there are or have been some classes of human beings who are treated in law as the objects of property interests rather than as property interest holders – others have property interests in them – and there may also be some classes of animate and non-animate thing that are treated not just (or at all) as objects of property interests but also (or instead) as property interest holders in their own right. We look at this in Part VII.

---

[1] See Chapter 5 *Ownership and Other Property Interests* para. 5.12. The civil law concept of co-ownership is discussed in Sjef van Erp and Bram Akkermans, *Cases, Materials and Text on Property Law* (Oxford and Portland, OR: Hart Publishing, 2012) pp. 241–242.

[2] Yaëll Emerich, *Conceptualising Property Law: Integrating Common Law and Civil Law Traditions* (Cheltenham and Northampton, MA: Edward Elgar Publishing, 2018) p. 223.

PART II INDIVIDUALS

8.2 Individuals as Property Interest Holders

(a) Who or What Is an Individual?

As we said in para. 8.1, we use the term 'individual' to cover both human beings and artificial private persons, such as companies. So, we categorise all artificial legal entities as individuals, except public authorities. Here we can adopt the definition of public authorities which has been developed in human rights law and which we considered in Chapter 4 *Property and Human Rights* para. 4.21. Public authorities are bodies which are by their nature governmental (government departments, local authorities, the police, the armed forces, etc.) and also bodies which are not, but which carry out public functions. The question of whether a function is 'public' for these purposes is determined by reference to factors such as whether the function is publicly funded, or whether in carrying out that function the body is exercising statutory powers, or is taking the place of central government or local authorities, or is providing a public service.[3] Bodies which have some public and some private functions are sometimes called hybrid public authorities. For present purposes we can think of them as individual property interest holders when they are holding property interests in their private capacity, and public authorities when they hold a property interest in exercise of a public function.

(b) Which Individuals Can Hold Property Interests?

The first point to consider is whether all human individuals can hold property interests. The ability of a human individual to own property has often been regarded philosophically as an essential pre-requisite for personhood or for the proper development of a person. So, as for example, as we noted in para. 2.22 of Chapter 2 *Conceptions and Justifications*, Hegel can be read as taking property-holding as necessary for the ethical development of a human individual. This is on the basis that the development of the self cannot take place without some kind of transition from the inner subjective world of the individual to the external objective world: private property enables us to make this transition because property-holding involves us embodying our will in external objects. Radin's idea of property and personhood picks up this notion of property-holders embodying their will in external objects. As we saw in Chapter 7 *Objects of Property Interests* para. 7.10, she uses it to argue that it is the investment of our will in an object which explains the particularly strong psychological bond we develop with some of the things that we regard as our own (things like wedding rings or homes which we would not lightly exchange for a near identical object, or for their monetary value). This special bond, she says, is something that property law ought to respect and protect. Her argument is that this justifies the law giving greater protection for the property interests we

---

[3] See further para. 4.21.

have in these things with which we have this special bond, than it would give for the same property interest held by someone who does not have such a bond with the object. However, we can also say (although Radin might not agree) that the embodying of our will in an object *ought to require* the law to recognise that we have a property interest in it. In other words, all human individuals must have the capacity to hold property interests in the things in which they embody their will.

For other property theorists the argument might be that private property is essential for individual freedom and autonomy, and on that basis all human individuals must have the capacity to be property interest holders. So, for example, there is a strong association between property owning and freedom in Kant's view of property (freedom here meaning 'independence from being constrained by the choices of others)[4] and, in a very different way, in the liberal concept of private property as a means of promoting the ability to lead an autonomous life, free from interference by others and by the state. These are the views that underlie the international human right to hold property embodied in art. 17(1) of the Universal Declaration of Human Rights 1948, that 'Everyone has the right to own property alone as well as in association with others'.[5]

Consistently with these moral and philosophical justifications for the right to hold property, historically the ability to own property has generally been seen as an attribute of legal personality (human or artificial), and so denied to or restricted for human individuals whose legal personality was impaired. So, for example, in legal systems which recognised the institution of slavery (i.e. allowed some human individuals to have property rights in other human individuals) slaves were usually not capable of owning property.[6] Similarly, in legal systems (including ours, until relatively recently) which denied full legal personality to married women and children and foreigners, their capacity to hold property interests was correspondingly limited, as Margaret Davies explained:

> It is only in the twentieth century that the attributes of legal personality became formally (though still not practically) available to most human beings in most contexts, regardless of gender, race, religion, or class. Prior to that time, social hierarchies were often reflected in the law and many people were under severe legal disabilities on account of their religion, ethnicity, or sex ... In relation simply to the ability to own, for instance, in Britain in the early nineteenth century a Christian male citizen might have the right to own property, for instance, but unless he actually did, would not have been entitled to vote. A woman was able to own property if she was not married but, no matter how wealthy, was never entitled to vote. A married woman's legal personality was regarded as being subsumed by the legal being of her husband, meaning in simple terms that he had absolute rights to her personal property and possessed her real property for the duration of the marriage ... Foreigners and Jews could own personal but not real property ...[7]

---

[4] para. 2.21 above.   [5] See Chapter 4 *Property and Human Rights* para. 4.10.
[6] We come back to this point in Part VII below.
[7] Margaret Davies, *Property: Meanings, Histories, Theories* (Abingdon: Routledge-Cavendish, 2007) pp. 62–63.

In our present law these restrictions have disappeared, and as Davies says:

> Concepts of natural law and human rights have resulted in an expansion of the attribution of legal personality to human beings: human individuals are now formally, if not substantially, equal in rights, including the right to own.[8]

Consequently, in our property rights system now all private legal entities (including all adult humans) are capable of holding property interests.[9]

However, in other modern states, although not in ours, there are two exceptions to this principle of universality which are worth noting. First, in many modern states foreigners are not allowed to own land, out of national fears of foreign domination or in order to preserve scarce land or housing for citizens.[10] Secondly, problems of discriminatory laws about the holding of property interests are emerging in some states which have relatively recently made formal recognition of the traditional land rights of their indigenous populations. In principle, those indigenous property interests are available only to members of the indigenous community, and there are difficult questions of whether, and if so how, they should also be open to other citizens.[11]

8.3 Human and Artificial Individuals

In our property law we rarely make distinctions between human and artificial individuals. For example, as we saw in Chapter 4 *Property and Human Rights*, human rights relating to property under the European Convention on Human Rights are available indiscriminately to human and to artificial private legal entities (even the art. 8 right to respect for one's 'home'), and it is only fairly recently that serious arguments have been put forward challenging the justifications for this.[12]

However, there are some aspects of property holding by artificial individuals which we should note here.

(a) Large Commercial Companies: Defying the 'Traditional Logic of Property'

The first is that although the 'individual' – say, a company limited by shares – is legally an autonomous property interest holder in its own right, holding its property for its own benefit, in reality it is a network of human individuals, and the classic components of 'ownership' are split up between them. To take as an example a simplified model of a large company limited by shares, the company holds the legal

---

[8] Ibid. p. 63.

[9] This includes prisoners: *R. (on the application of Coleman)* v. *Governor of Wayland Prison* [2009] EWHC 1005.

[10] See, for example, the restrictions in Guernsey which were the subject of the proceedings in *Gillow* v. *United Kingdom* (1989) 11 EHRR 335 noted in Chapter 4 *Property and Human Rights* para. 4.34. There are similar bans or restrictions in Switzerland and proposed in New Zealand. Other countries surcharge foreign buyers instead.

[11] See, for example, the material on the Nordic Saami Convention noted in Chapter 9 *Multiple Property Rights Systems*.

[12] See para. 4.8.

title to the property interest, but the company itself is owned by the shareholders. A board of directors manages the property interest and is required to use the assets of the company as a whole (but not necessarily this particular asset) for carrying out the purposes of the company in order to provide a profit for the shareholders.[13] That profit is distributed to the shareholders by way of dividends on their shares, which the directors have a discretion to declare whenever they consider appropriate, and at a level they consider appropriate. For these and other reasons, in large companies control over the directors, which is technically vested in the shareholders (who exercise it by voting at company meetings) is diffuse. The opportunities and incentives for shareholders to control the actions of directors in large companies can be small. The shareholders are not liable for the debts of the company (the whole point of limited liability companies is to enable shareholders to invest a strictly limited portion of their wealth in the enterprise) and their only direct financial investment occurs when they buy shares issued by the company, either when the company is first formed or when the directors subsequently decide to issue new shares. Some shareholders, of course, have never directly invested in the company by buying shares from the company: if the company is publicly listed they will have bought their shares on the stock market from other shareholders, and may be primarily interested in making money by selling their shares on at a profit rather than by receiving profits from the company by way of dividend. These shareholders make no financial contribution to the company's assets. However, we have to remember that shareholders are not the only source of finance for a company. The directors can choose to obtain money to finance the operations of the company by borrowing it from professional providers of loan finance, who may in some cases and in some circumstances have much greater practical control over the directors' management decisions than the shareholders have. The directors themselves will have no stake in the company unless they are also shareholders, and whether or not they are also shareholders they have no liability for its debts: they are just salaried employees.

If you apply classic economic theory, this model of property holding should not work in a market economy, and indeed Adam Smith famously predicted that it would not:

> The trade of a joint stock company is always managed by a court of directors. The court, indeed, is frequently subject, in many respects, to the control of a general court of proprietors [shareholders]. But the greater part of those proprietors seldom pretend to understand anything of the business of the company; and ... give themselves no trouble about it, but receive contentedly such ... dividend ... as the directors think

---

[13] Since 2006 the duties of the directors have been more nuanced. The *Company Law Review* recommended that 'the basic goal for directors should be the success of the company in the collective best interests of shareholders, but that directors should also recognise, as circumstances require, the company's need to foster relationships with its employees, customers and suppliers, its need to maintain its business reputation, and its need to consider the company's impact on the community and the working environment'. This was, in effect, put into legislative form by the Companies Act 2006, which provides in s. 172 that directors are under a duty to 'promote the success of the company', for the benefit of shareholders as a whole, having regard to (amongst other things) the interests of specified stakeholders, including employees, customers and the environment.

proper to make them. This total exemption from trouble and risk . . . encourages many people to become adventurers in joint stock companies who would, upon no account, hazard their fortunes in any private copartnery . . . The directors of such companies . . . being the managers rather of other people's money than their own, it cannot well be expected that they should watch over it with the same anxious vigilance with which the partners in a private coparceny frequently watch over their own . . . Negligence and profusion . . . must always prevail, more or less, in the management of such a company.

. . . The joint stock companies . . . over and above managing their own affairs ill, to the diminution of the general stock of society, can in other respects scarce fail to do more harm than good [for their method of operation] necessarily breaks, more or less, that natural proportion which would otherwise establish.[14]

For basically similar reasons Berle and Means argued in an influential study published in the 1930s (about the time of the 1929 stock market crash and the Great Depression) that this traditional corporate model, especially as it evolved in relation to large corporate enterprise in the early twentieth century, was dysfunctional. The 'traditional logic of property', they argued, did not apply to the modern large corporation:

It has been assumed that, if the individual is protected in the right both to use his property as he sees fit and receive the full fruits of its use, his desire for personal gain, for profits, can be relied on as an effective incentive to his efficient use of any industrial property he may possess.

In the [modern large corporation], such an assumption no longer holds. [It] is no longer the individual himself who uses his wealth. Those in control of that wealth, and therefore in a position to secure industrial efficiency and produce profits, are no longer, as owners, entitled to the bulk of the profits . . . Those stockholders, on the other hand to whom the profits of the corporation go, cannot be motivated by those profits to a more efficient use of the property, since they have surrendered all disposition of it to those in control of the enterprise.[15]

The result of this separation of beneficial ownership from control, they argued, was that 'corporate control had been usurped by a new class of managers, the result of which included (1) shareholder loss of control . . . (2) questionable corporate objectives and behavior, and (3) the potential breakdown of the market mechanism'.[16] There is a vast modern literature debating these analyses, particularly in relation to the inadequacy of the classic limited liability model of corporation to promote corporate responsibility or to regulate such matters as managerial remuneration and management behaviour generally, and the narrow focus on 'shareholder value' (i.e. the idea that the overriding purpose of the organisation is to maximise

[14] Adam Smith, *An Enquiry in the Nature and Causes of the Wealth of Nations* (first published 1776, this edition London: Everyman's Library, 1991) Book V Ch. 1 Part III Art. 1 Joint stock companies were the precursors of the modern limited liability company.
[15] Adolf A. Berle and Gardiner C. Means, *The Modern Corporation and Private Property* (New York: Harcourt, Brace & World, 1932) pp. 299–301.
[16] Bernard C. Beaudreau, 'On the origins of the modern corporation and private property' (2019) 42 *Seattle University Law Review* 327.

value to shareholders).[17] However, for our purposes the important point is that property holding by large corporations is very different from property holding by human individuals. Property law rules treat human property interest holders and large corporate property interest holders as if they were identical, but in reality they are subject to quite different moral, social and economic incentives and constraints when exercising their property rights and powers.

(b) Small Companies Wholly Owned and Controlled by a Human Individual

Another side of corporate ownership which is relevant here is that small companies (where a single human individual, or a few people who are closely connected, own and control the company) are treated in law as legal entities wholly separate from the human individuals who own and control them, in just the same way as large companies. So, when a small company holds a property interest in a thing, the company is treated by the law as the full beneficial owner, even though management, control and benefit may well be all held by a single human controlling shareholder/director (or a small closely connected group of them), who undertakes no personal financial risks, liabilities or obligations. In practice, commercial outsiders who enter into property transactions with small companies like this (e.g. banks providing them with loan finance and landlords leasing business premises to them) are not willing to accept the consequences of this legal separation of the company from its human alter egos, and they will require the controlling shareholder/directors to give personal guarantees. However, this is obviously not feasible for all outsiders, and whatever economic advantages this corporate façade may bring, it also has significant disadvantages from a property perspective. The first is that it allows the human alter ego to escape the inherent obligations of ownership we talk about in Part II of Chapter 10 *Limitations on Property*. The second is that it allows human individuals to hide the nature and extent of their property holdings. As we see in Chapter 16 *Registration*,[18] this is seen as a particular problem in relation to land holdings. If humans are able to hide their property interests in land behind the façade of a company (or a trust) it makes money laundering and land fraud too easy, it infringes the public's legitimate interest in knowing who owns the land in the country and (a present concern of the government) it hinders public participation in land use decisions and land development because it makes it too difficult for outsiders to find out who really owns and controls the land.

(c) Incorporated Communities and Public Enterprises

The final point to note about artificial individuals is that although some of them are properly regarded as private persons – all the actors are human individuals acting in

---

[17] See, for example, Brian R. Cheffins, 'The rise and fall (?) of the Bearle-Means Corporation' (2019) 42 *Seattle University Law Review* 445; Paddy Ireland, 'Limited liability, shareholder rights and the problem of corporate irresponsibility' (2010) 34 *Cambridge Journal of Economics* 837; David Campbell, 'Marxism, the market and corporate responsibility: A comment on Paddy Ireland' (2010) 31 *Adelaide Law Review* 229.

[18] para. 16.31(b)–(d).

their private sphere – others are not. They are individual persons in form only, but in reality they are groups of human individuals who have taken the legal form of a corporation in order to carry out a public purpose or a community purpose. This blurs the distinction between private, communal and public property interest holders, as we see in the following paragraph.

8.4 Non-Beneficial and Limited Purpose Individual Property Holdings

In particular, it is important to appreciate that an individual property interest holder (human or artificial) does not necessarily hold the property interest for its own benefit as a legal entity (or for the benefit of its shareholder owners, if it is an artificial entity), nor is it necessarily free to use it for whatever purposes it chooses. An individual who is required to hold a property interest altruistically, and/or is required to use it only for a specific purpose, does not fit easily into the classic model of the private property owner. Even if she is a human individual, if she is required to hold her property interest altruistically it does not make sense to talk about her embodying her will in the object of her property interest, or about the property interest contributing to her freedom and autonomy. Also her motivation is different: her behaviour is determined not by self-interest but by duty towards some other person or some purpose. A property interest holder required to use it only for a limited purpose may or may not be in the same position, depending on whether she is entitled to pursue that purpose for her own benefit or required to do so for the benefit of others. Even if she is entitled to hold it for her own benefit, the limitation on use inevitably diminishes her freedom and autonomy, especially if a public authority is responsible for enforcing the limitation.

There are a number of different kinds of individual property interest holder which are not entitled to beneficial use of the property, and/or are required to use it only for a specified purpose.

(a) Trustees

Trustees are the archetypal private non-beneficial individual property interest holders. As we saw in Part V of Chapter 5 *Ownership and Other Property Interests*, trustees hold the legal title to the property interest,[19] but they hold it solely for the benefit of one or more specified beneficiaries rather than for their own benefit. As a matter of fundamental principle, a trustee may take no benefit from the property interest. The trustees have the full powers to manage and deal with the property interest that any other private property interest holder would have, but they are under a duty (enforceable by the beneficiaries) to do so solely in the interests of the beneficiary, who is consequently regarded in equity as the beneficial owner of the property interest. Nevertheless, even though trustees are not self-interested private property holders, they are not accountable to anyone other than other private individuals (the beneficiaries), and so trust holdings are wholly private property institutions.

---

[19] Assuming it is a legal property interest. Equitable property interests can also be held on trust: if they are, the title held by the trustee is an equitable title.

However, the picture changes when the trustees hold a property interest on trust for a purpose as opposed to for specified people. Generally, a trust for a purpose is only valid if the purpose is charitable, in which case the trust will be monitored, regulated and enforced by the Charity Commission, which is a public authority. There is a highly technical legal test for determining whether a purpose is 'charitable'.[20] A charitable trust has no human beneficiaries: there may be human individuals who receive direct benefits from the charitable trust, but the trustees have no duties or liabilities towards them. If these human recipients of charitable benefits want to complain about the actions of the trustees, there is nothing they can do apart from persuade the Charity Commission to take action. An additional factor is that charitable trusts (and charitable companies)[21] receive public funding in the form of extensive tax exemptions. So, for all these reasons, property interests held by charitable trustees are much closer to property holdings held by public authorities than they are to private property holdings.

The only significant exception to the general principle that trustees cannot hold property for non-charitable purposes is that the assets of unincorporated clubs and societies (e.g. members clubs such as amateur sports clubs, chess clubs, book clubs, etc., or groups of activists with a common social, political or environmental cause) are routinely held by trustees. The correct legal analysis of the property holdings in these cases is contentious, but they are probably best seen as examples of communal rather than individual property holdings, and we come back to them in Part V.

(b) Corporate Purposes

If we leave aside the companies which fall within the special categories noted in (c) below, most companies are no longer subject to restrictions limiting their purposes. Limited liability companies used to be required to state in their memorandum of association (i.e. the constitution of the company) the objects for which the company was established. The company's powers were limited to furthering those objects, and any action taken by a company which went outside those limits was ultra vires and void. However, this requirement was abolished by the Companies Act 2006, ceasing to apply to any company formed after 1 October 2009. All companies formed after that date (except those falling within the special categories noted in (c) below) therefore now have unrestricted objects:[22] they can act for any purpose whatsoever, in the same way as a human individual property interest owner.[23]

[20] Now set out in s. 2 of the Charities Act 2006, essentially consolidating the previous voluminous caselaw. For details, reference should be made to textbooks on trusts.

[21] An organisation which wants to carry out a charitable purpose can do so either by putting the assets into the hands of trustees to hold on trust for the purpose or by forming a company to carry out the purpose: see (c) below.

[22] S. 31(1) of the Companies Act 2006.

[23] They can still choose to include a provision restricting their objects, as we note in (c) below in relation to mission-led companies, but they have power to amend their memorandum of association to remove any such restrictions.

(c) Alternative Corporate Enterprises

Numerically, the vast majority of corporations (i.e. artificial legal entities formed by a group of people to carry on a particular activity and to hold and manage the assets they use in relation to that activity) are companies limited by shares of the kind we noted in para. 8.3 – that is, intended to carry on a business of some kind to make a profit for the shareholders, and shielding the shareholders from liability for any debts incurred in the business. Nina Boeger has characterised these corporations as corporations which are run to optimise shareholder value, and which:

> prioritize one type of value (financial value) for the benefit of one set of stakeholders (the shareholders), if necessary at the expense of other stakeholders who might contribute to the business (employees), or might be otherwise impacted by it, either directly (consumers, suppliers, local communities) or indirectly (citizens in the welfare state, tax payers, the environment, and so on).[24]

However, there are other kinds of corporation. A recent development is the emergence of business corporations which voluntarily adopt rules requiring them to take these wider stakeholder interests into account. Boeger describes these corporations, which may or may not also distribute profits to shareholders by paying dividends, as 'mission-driven' or 'mission-led'. As she points out, in law these rules can always be changed,[25] but nevertheless they involve the corporation making a long-term commitment 'to have a positive social impact as a central part of their business'.[26]

In addition, there are other kinds of private corporation which are legally bound to carry out alternative functions or pursue other purposes. These include the hybrid public authorities we noted in para. 8.2(a) above, which are private bodies given public functions, usually by statute, and usually regulated by a statutory Regulator. As we said in para. 8.2(a), when they hold property interests pursuant to their public functions, it is more realistic to regard them as public property interest holders.

Similarly, corporations carrying out charitable purposes are in the same position as trustees holding property on trust for charitable purposes, and like them they have to be registered as charities with, and are regulated by, the Charity Commission and have extensive tax exemptions. Two of the largest landowners in the country – the National Trust and the Royal Society for the Protection of Birds – come within this category. So, like charitable trustees, we should treat them as public property interest holders too, even though they might have been set up by private individuals.

Finally, again as already noted, there are other kinds of corporation which are essentially incorporations of communities (including communities of stakeholders in a shared resource or shared enterprise) or of groups formed for community purposes. They include a variety of different kinds of organisation, and under the present law of England and Wales, they can take a variety of different legal forms,

---

[24] Nina Boeger, 'Beyond the shareholder corporation: Alternative business forms and the contestation of markets' (2018) 45 *Journal of Law and Society* 10.

[25] Compare community interest companies and community benefit societies outlined in paras. 8.27 and 8.28 below.

[26] Boeger, 'Beyond the shareholder corporation', fn. 24 above, p. 18.

both corporate and non-corporate.[27] We look at these community entities (including the relatively new legal entities called community interest companies and community benefit societies) and at community organisations such as co-operatives, in Part V of this chapter.

PART III   CO-OWNERS

8.5   Co-Ownership

Co-ownership arises where two or more individuals share a property interest (for example, where a couple buy a house together and decide to hold the freehold interest in their joint names rather than in the name of just one of them). In this part of the chapter we look at the way the law regulates the relationship between people who share a property interest in this way.

Property interests are often co-owned for commercial purposes. So, for example, if you and I wanted to buy and develop land as a joint venture, we might decide to buy the freehold interest in our joint names, as co-owners, so that we each have a stake in the land. In most of the cases we come across, however, the co-owners are married or unmarried couples or other family members or friends, who have decided to co-own their property interest in their home. When common law co-ownership principles were simplified and modernised in 1925, cases like these were comparatively rare because most family property was held in the name of the (usually male) head of the household. Now, however, probably most couples and others planning to live together in a shared home expect to co-own the home (and other 'family' assets). So, like so many other areas of property law in England and Wales, our co-ownership law is the product of common law rules developed over centuries, which were then simplified and reorganised in 1925 to deal with situations which were very different from those in which they are now primarily used.

8.6   Forms of Co-Ownership

We used to have four different forms of co-ownership in England and Wales, but since 1925 we have been down to two:[28] joint ownership and ownership in common, more usually (and unfortunately) referred to by their feudal names of 'joint tenancy' and 'tenancy in common'. The word 'tenancy' here does not mean the same as it means when we use it as a synonym for 'lease'. It derives from the feudal 'tenure' by

---

[27] For a good comprehensive overview see Co-operatives UK, 'Simply Legal: All you need to know about legal forms and organisational types, for co-operatives and community owned enterprises', September 2015, available at www.uk.coop/resources/simply-legal, which includes at para. 2.2 a helpful explanation of the difference between legal forms of entity (e.g. limited liability company, or partnership) and organisational types (such as co-operatives) which generally have a choice of legal forms they can adopt.

[28] The other two were the tenancy by entireties (which applied as between married couples and which we mention briefly in Part IV below), and coparcenary, which applied as between female heirs of a person who died without having made a will (now obsolete).

which individuals used to hold land from the Crown or from some intermediate feudal lord.[29] So, *joint tenancy* means a joint holding of a property interest, and *tenancy in common* means a holding of a property interest in common.

The essence of these two forms of co-ownership is that in both, the property interest in the thing is shared between the co-owners, but the shares have not yet been separated off from each other. Yaëll Emerich describes it as a situation where 'multiple people simultaneously hold the same right'.[30] So, if you and I co-own the freehold interest in two adjoining fields, it does not mean (of course) that you hold the freehold in one field and I hold the freehold in the other: it means that we share the freehold interest in both fields, and in every part of them, so that if we were to take even the tiniest blade of grass growing in either of the two fields, we would still say that you and I co-own the freehold interest in that blade of grass.

8.7 Nature of Joint Tenancy and Tenancy in Common

The difference between co-ownership by joint tenancy and co-ownership by tenancy in common is this. If you and I co-own the freehold interest in the fields as *joint tenants* it means that we are each entitled to the whole of the freehold interest in the fields, subject only to the like interest held by the other. If, on the other hand, we co-own the freehold interest as *tenants in common*, we share the freehold interest in specified proportions (any proportions we may choose, equal or unequal). So, if we go back to the blade of grass growing in our fields, if we co-own the freehold interest in the fields as joint tenants, we are each entitled to the whole of the freehold interest in the blade of grass, subject only to the like interest in it which is held by the other, whereas if we co-own the fields as tenants in common, we each have a specified proportion of the freehold interest in the blade of grass (perhaps 50 per cent each, or 70 per cent yours and 30 per cent mine, or whatever). The significance of this difference becomes apparent when we look at the different characteristics of joint tenancies and tenancies in common in the next paragraph.

8.8 Different Characteristics of Joint Tenancy and Tenancy in Common

(a) Size of Shares

Given that, in a joint tenancy of a property interest, we each hold the whole of the interest subject only to the like interest held by the other, it follows that our respective interests are necessarily of equal value. If, on the other hand, we held the property interest as tenants in common our shares might be of equal value, but they do not have to be. So, if co-owners want to have unequal shares they have to use a tenancy in common.

---

[29] As in the full technical name for freehold ownership which we looked at in Chapter 5 *Ownership and Other Property Interests* para. 5.16, i.e. 'a holding of land by freehold tenure, for an estate which is in fee simple, absolute and in possession'.

[30] Emerich, *Conceptualising Property Law*, fn. 2 above, p. 223, and see generally pp. 223–228 for the difference between common law and civil law forms of co-ownership.

(b) Transmissibility of Shares

The interest of a joint tenant is not transmissible: she cannot sell, mortgage or otherwise dispose of her share to an outsider, either during her lifetime or by will when she dies. If she attempts to sell, mortgage or otherwise deal with her share, it is *automatically* converted into a share under a tenancy in common. This process of automatically converting a joint tenancy interest into a tenancy in common interest is called 'severance', and as we see in (c) below, a joint tenancy can also be severed unilaterally or by mutual agreement at any time. However, severance of the legal title (whether automatic or unilateral or by mutual agreement) can no longer take place if the jointly held property interest is a legal estate in land, for reasons we explain in paras. 8.11 and 8.12 below.[31]

The interest of a tenant in common is, however, fully transmissible. Unless the co-owners have agreed to the contrary, any tenant in common can always sell, give away, mortgage or do whatever he wants with his interest, and when he dies it will be inherited by whoever becomes entitled to his property on his death.

So, when a property interest is co-owned by a tenancy in common, the identity of the co-owners may change over time as one or more of them dispose of their shares to outsiders.[32] If, on the other hand, the co-owners are joint tenants, the original co-owners cannot be replaced, and indeed, as we see in (d) below when we look at survivorship, the interest of each joint tenant disappears when he or she dies. If joint tenants want to bring in an outsider as an additional joint tenant (perhaps to replace one who has died) they have to transfer the co-owned interest from themselves, as existing joint tenants, to the new group of joint tenants (i.e. themselves plus the new joint tenant).

(c) Nature and Effect of Severance

As we saw in (b) above, the share of a co-owner of a property interest who is a joint tenant will automatically be severed from the joint tenancy by an attempted sale etc. of the joint tenant's interest, and may also be severed at any time either unilaterally or by mutual agreement between the co-owners. A joint tenant cannot sever her interest by will – it must be done during her lifetime, using one of the methods we note in (e) below. We consider the significance of this in para. 8.9 below.

---

[31] Broadly, since 1925 a trust is always imposed whenever a legal estate in land is co-owned, so that the co-owners hold the legal estate on trust for themselves, and as trustees they can only hold the legal title as joint tenants. In principle, trustees of any property must *always* hold the legal title to trust assets as joint tenants, not as tenants in common. This rule was imposed in 1925 to ensure that individual trustees could never have transmissible shares in the trust assets, for reasons which become apparent in para. 8.12. The idea is that the original trustees must remain the sole trustees until they drop out of the picture by dying or are replaced by appointment of new trustees.

[32] Or to each other. This is straightforward if the co-owned asset is not an interest in land and so a trust is not automatically imposed on the co-owners. If it is an interest in land, the co-owning trustees are always joint tenants, as we saw in fn. 31 above, but the beneficial interest can be co-owned either by a tenancy in common or by a joint tenancy. In that case, everything we say here in (b) about transmissibility (and about severance in (c) below) still applies, but it applies only to the beneficial interest under the trust.

Severance operates only on the share which is being severed: it detaches the severed share from the shares of the other co-owners. So, if there are three or more joint tenants and one of them severs her interest, her share in the property interest becomes a one-third share under a tenancy in common, leaving the other two co-owners now holding the other two-thirds share as tenants in common as against the severer, but holding their two-thirds share as joint tenants as between themselves. Of course, if there are only two joint tenants, severance by one of them necessarily converts both shares into interests under a tenancy in common, with each former joint tenant now holding a 50 per cent share under a tenancy in common.

However, for present purposes the important point is that severance is *only* a process by which the share of a joint tenant is converted into a tenancy in common share. Severance does not end the co-ownership, it merely changes its nature. Nevertheless, the change is highly significant because it eliminates the possibility of survivorship, as we see below.

(d) Survivorship

The most important feature of joint tenancy which distinguishes it from a tenancy in common is that each joint tenant has *a right of survivorship*. This means that if one of the other joint tenants dies,[33] his share automatically ends, so that the shares held by the survivor(s) are correspondingly enlarged. So, if there are two joint tenants and one of them dies, the survivor is left holding the whole of the property interest freed from the interest of the dead joint tenant. In those circumstances, the co-ownership of course ends. If, on the other hand, there are three joint tenants and one of them dies, the other two are left as the sole surviving joint tenants, each now sharing the value of the property interest with just one other co-owner rather than with two (and, perhaps, hoping the other will die first so that they, as last survivor, get everything).

(e) Ways of Severing a Joint Tenancy

Because survivorship is an unavoidable consequence of a joint tenancy, it follows that a person who is proposing to co-own a property interest with someone else should never choose a joint tenancy in preference to a tenancy in common unless she wants her co-owner to have the whole of the interest when she dies. It also follows that, if she chooses to co-own a property interest with someone else by a joint tenancy, but then circumstances change and she no longer wants her co-owner to take everything by survivorship when she dies, she needs to sever the joint tenancy. This situation arises very frequently when married and unmarried couples separate. Unfortunately, the law as to what amounts to a valid severance of a joint tenancy is unclear and complex and has generated a lot of litigation. It is clear that a

---

[33] For these purposes, a corporate joint tenant 'dies' when it is wound up.

joint tenant cannot sever by will, that is to say, by declaring in her will that she severs the joint tenancy when she dies. It is also clear, because s. 36(2) of the Law of Property Act 1925 says so, that any joint tenant of an equitable interest in land[34] can at any time unilaterally sever her share by serving a notice in writing of his desire to sever the joint tenancy on all the other joint tenants. However, s. 36(2) makes this new form of severance by notice *additional to, and not instead of,* the other methods of severance which applied to property interests in personal property before 1926. These old methods of severance are extensively explored in modern cases and they can be summarised as (i) automatic severance by a joint tenant 'acting' on her own share (e.g. as we have already seen, by attempting to sell or mortgage it or do something else which purports to treat it as a separate share), (ii) severance by mutual agreement, (iii) severance by mutual conduct, and (iv) severance by court order.[35] There are two ways of viewing these various and imprecisely defined old methods of severance. One is to say that they are unnecessarily complex and ought to be abolished.[36] The other is to accept the contrary argument suggested by Gray and Gray that 'the classical non-statutory modes of severance provide a flexible recognition of the informality often present in the dealings of co-owners'.[37] In any event, we are not covering them here.

(f) The 'Four Unities'

It is often said (correctly, but not very helpfully) that a joint tenancy cannot exist unless the 'four unities' are present.[38] The four unities are unity of possession, unity of interest, unity of title and unity of time. The only 'unity' necessary for a tenancy in common is unity of possession.

Unity of Possession

Unity of possession is a crucial feature of all co-ownership in this jurisdiction. It means that each co-owner (whether joint tenant or tenant in common) is entitled, as against the others, to possession of the whole of the object of the co-owned property interest (whether it is land or goods) in common with every other co-owner. No co-owner is entitled to physically exclude another co-owner from any part of the property; correspondingly, each co-owner has a right not to be excluded from the co-owned property. So, even if the property consists of two physically separate units (perhaps a building divided into two flats), and the co-owners decide between

---

[34] As noted above, joint tenancies of legal estates in land cannot be severed at all, because from 1925 the joint tenants have to hold them as trustees: see further para. 8.11 below.

[35] The first three are the categories identified by Page Wood VC in *Williams* v. *Hensman* (1861) 70 ER 862 at p. 867, and usually referred to as such. For a full analysis of all the methods see Roger Smith, *Plural Ownership* (Oxford: Oxford University Press, 2005) pp. 48–82.

[36] See, for example, Louise Tee, 'Severance revisited' (1995) *Conveyancer and Property Lawyer* 105.

[37] Kevin Gray and Susan Francis Gray, *Elements of Land Law* (5th edn, Oxford: Oxford University Press, 2009) para. 7.4.68 n. 1.

[38] Unhelpful because the second, third and fourth all come down to essentially the same thing, as we see below.

themselves to occupy one unit each, that agreement can only be binding on them in contract: each retains a property right to share occupation of any part of the whole building with the other. For example, if you decide to take a one year lease of a four bedroom flat with three other students, so that you co-own the lease between you, each of you will be entitled to occupy all the bedrooms (and any other space in the flat) in common with all the others, unless you decide (as you probably will) to allocate one bedroom to each of you by mutual agreement.[39]

Unity of Interest, Title and Time

Co-owners can only be joint tenants if they each have the same property interest (unity of interest), granted by the same instrument (unity of title), and beginning and ending on the same date (unity of time). This does not apply to tenants in common. If we go back to the example of the four bedroom flat, this means that if the landlord granted each of you a one year lease of the flat (to share with the other three) and you each signed separate tenancy agreements, perhaps signing at different times and with each agreement starting on different dates, the courts could decide that together you co-own a single lease of the flat as tenants in common. However, it would be impossible for you to co-own the beneficial interest in the lease as joint tenants, because you each have separate interests, granted by different instruments at different times. In other words, you do not have unity of interest, title or time.[40]

8.9 Advantages and Disadvantages of Joint Tenancy and Tenancy in Common

The combined effect of the characteristics we looked at in the previous paragraph is that co-ownership by joint tenancy is essentially an insiders' club. If any joint tenant tries to bring in an outsider by selling or mortgaging her interest, she (and, necessarily also her buyer/mortgagee) becomes a tenant in common. So, as already noted above, the identity of the joint tenants does not change throughout the joint tenancy.[41]

It is also essentially a tontine club, because of the survivorship principle. Historically a 'tontine' was (and is) a fund contributed by members, which pays out a fixed sum each year to be divided equally between the members, where each member's right to an annual payout and his interest in the fund disappear when he dies. The

---

[39] It has to be said that this over-simplifies the picture, because unity of possession applies only as between the co-owners. If they are obliged to hold the co-owned property interest on trust (e.g. because it is a legal estate in land) the position becomes more complicated because the trustees have powers (now limited by the Trusts of Land and Appointment of Trustees Act 1995) to allocate rights of occupation etc.: see further para. 8.13(b) below.

[40] In fact, depending on the precise circumstances and the wording of the agreements, the courts may decide in the alternative that you do not have a lease of the flat at all on these particular facts, but only a license, or perhaps that you each have a separate lease of your own room in the flat: we look at these alternative constructions in Chapter 17 *Leases* para. 17.9 where we consider the difference between a lease and a licence.

[41] Ignoring for the moment joint tenancies of a legal estate in land, where, as already noted, the joint tenants hold the legal title as trustees.

effect of this is that annual payments to surviving members get bigger and bigger as their fellow members die off, and the last surviving member takes the whole fund.[42] So, investing in a tontine fund is a bit like buying a lottery ticket, and because of these overtones of gambling (and the fear that some members might want to increase their chances by murdering their fellow members), tontines are sometimes regarded with suspicion.[43] This and other factors have led some to question whether we would be better off by abolishing joint tenancies altogether, as providing no real advantage (tenants in common can always leave their shares to their co-owners by will, if that is what they want) but unfortunate consequences for estranged couples who fail to sever their interests in time.[44]

8.10 Identifying Joint Tenancies and Tenancies in Common

A more practical (and probably more important) issue is how to tell whether an acquisition of a property interest by two or more people creates a joint tenancy or a tenancy in common. If the property interest is acquired by a formal transfer to co-owners who are legally represented, this should be expressly stated in the transfer deed (although in practice it may not always be). Similarly, if the four unities noted in para. 8.8 above are not all present, or if it is clear that the co-owners are to have unequal shares, then it cannot be a joint tenancy and so must be a tenancy in common.

However, there are many cases which fall within neither of these categories, not least because co-ownership often arises informally through a resulting or construct-ive trust, as we see in Chapter 14 *Acquiring Interests Informally*, where we look at such cases in detail.

In these other cases, the question of whether the co-ownership is by joint tenancy or by tenancy in common depends on ascertaining the intentions of the co-owners, which may be difficult. Two presumptions may help where the property interest in question is a legal estate in land so that, as already noted, the legal title is held by the co-owners as trustees on an unseverable joint tenancy. First, it was said by the Privy Council in *Malayan Credit Ltd* v. *Jack Chia-MPH Ltd*[45] that in a commercial case, there is a presumption that they hold the beneficial interest under the trust as joint

---

[42] Tontines are said to have been invented by an Italian banker, Lorenzo Tonti in the seventeenth century, and to have been used by William III in England to raise money to fund wars against the French. They have been popular at various times in the USA and in some European countries, and occasionally in England (e.g. for raising state loans and funding insurance schemes, sometimes fraudulent), and they are currently the basis of a form of co-ownership in France (the *pacte tontinier*): Henry Dyson, 'The tontine in French law, with some English comparisons' (1993) *Conveyancer and Property Lawyer* 446; and David Pollard, 'King William's Tontine: Why the retirement annuity of the future should resemble the past' [2016] *Trust Law International* 196, reviewing a book of that title by Milevsky who, so Pollard notes, 'was unable to find any evidence of tontines increasing the murder rate'.

[43] They also figure quite frequently in the plots of novels (and in an episode of *The Simpsons*): Kent McKeever, 'A short history of tontines' (2009) 15 *Fordham Journal of Corporate & Financial Law* 491

[44] See Smith, *Plural Ownership*, fn. 35 above, Ch. 5, concluding, however, at p. 89 that 'the case for abolition is not made out'.

[45] *Malayan Credit Ltd* v. *Jack Chia-MPH Ltd* [1986] AC 549 at 559.

tenants *unless* they contributed to the purchase price in unequal shares, in which case the presumption is that they hold it as tenants in common in those shares. In that particular case the property interest was a lease of an office block taken in the joint names of two commercial organisations, and it was held that they were presumed to hold the beneficial interest in the lease as tenants in common because they paid the rent and other outgoings in unequal shares, proportionate to the areas of the separate parts of the building each occupied.

The second presumption, now authoritatively stated by Lady Hale in the House of Lords in *Stack* v. *Dowden*[46] and re-affirmed by Lady Hale and Lord Walker in the Supreme Court in *Jones* v. *Kernott*,[47] is that 'in the domestic consumer context' (primarily couples and others co-owning the home they share) there is a 'strong' presumption that the legal co-owners also hold the beneficial interest under the trust as joint tenants. It was said in these two cases that this is partly because of the principle that 'equity follows the law' (i.e. because the legal title is held by a joint tenancy the equitable interest is presumed to be held in the same way), but partly also because 'If a couple in an intimate relationship (whether married or unmarried) decide to buy a house or flat in which to live together . . . that is on the face of things a strong indication of emotional and economic commitment to a joint enterprise'.[48]

However, there are reasons to be cautious about the scope of these presumptions. The first is that, as we see in Chapter 14 *Acquiring Interests Informally* where we look at co-ownership arising out of resulting or constructive trusts, there is a competing long-established presumption that, where someone has contributed towards the acquisition cost of an asset, the asset is held on resulting trust for the contributor in proportion to his contribution. There is some authority that this continues to apply except in cases directly covered by *Stack* v. *Dowden* and *Jones* v. *Kernott* (i.e. except when considering co-ownership of the place where the co-owners live together). We look at this again in Chapter 14, where we also consider a further reason for being cautious about all these presumptions. This is that in *Marr* v. *Collie*[49] the Privy Council has down-played their significance by saying that in *all* cases the court's starting point must be to ascertain the intentions of the parties from looking at all the evidence; they may fall back on the presumptions *only* where there is no evidence from which the intentions of the parties can be identified.[50]

8.11 Co-ownership Trusts of Land in English Law

We have already noted that, although any property interest in any kind of thing can be co-owned, a trust is automatically imposed on the co-owners if the property interest is a legal estate in land. Specifically, if there are no more than four co-owners they hold the legal title on trust for themselves. If there are more than four, the legal

---

[46] *Stack* v. *Dowden* [2007] UKHL 17 at paras. 56–58.
[47] *Jones* v. *Kernott* [2011] UKSC 53 at paras. 19–22.   [48] Ibid. para. 19.
[49] *Marr* v. *Collie* [2017] UKPC 17.
[50] Ibid., Lord Kerr giving the judgment of the Privy Council at paras. 53–54, and see also *Gany Holdings (PTC) SA v Khan* [2018] UKPC 21, where much the same was said by the Privy Council at paras. 17–18 in relation to shares in a company.

title is vested in the first four named of them to hold on trust for all of them.[51] They hold the legal title on an unseverable joint tenancy: the legislation expressly states that it is not possible to co-own a legal estate in land by a tenancy in common.[52]

The rule that a trust is imposed whenever a legal estate in land is co-owned was introduced by the 1925 property legislation in order to make co-owned land more marketable. The point is that co-owners of any property interest can only exercise their powers unanimously. So, if there was no trust, co-owners who wanted to sell the property interest they co-own (or mortgage it, or grant a lease or enter into any other transaction affecting it) would all have to agree. This means that anyone who wanted to buy a co-owned property interest, or take a mortgage over it etc., would have to identify all the co-owners and check they have all authorised the transaction. And of course it also means that any co-owner, however small her share, could always block any proposed transaction for any (or no) reason, even if it would clearly be for the benefit of all the other co-owners. The imposition of a trust solves both of these problems. Potential purchasers etc. need deal only with the trustees,[53] and since the trustees necessarily hold the legal estate on an unseverable joint tenancy it will always be easy to check who they are: they will be the original trustees who are still alive, plus any additional trustee appointed through a formal process. The trustees must exercise their powers unanimously, but they are under a duty to act in the best interests of the beneficiaries as a whole, so cannot arbitrarily refuse to authorise a proposed transaction. And, unless there is a formal trust deed which says otherwise, beneficiaries who are not trustees cannot block any sale or other dealings either, because it is the trustees and not the beneficiaries who have the power to enter into such transactions.

From that perspective, the imposition of a trust on co-owners works well, and in practice co-owners of property interests in things other than land often elect to use a trust even though they are not obliged to do so. However, the trust undoubtedly makes co-ownership of interests in land more complicated. In particular, it adds to the complexity of the relationships arising where co-owners acquire shares (or their shares are modified) under the resulting or constructive trust principles we consider in Chapter 14 *Acquiring Interests Informally*. In those situations, and even in other routine cases where the terms of the co-ownership are known and agreed by the parties from the outset, the co-owners are unlikely to realise that they are trustees and/or beneficiaries under a trust, and the distribution of rights, powers and duties arising under the trust may not mirror those they want, and think they have, under the co-ownership.

---

[51] The co-owners can, if they want, have the legal title put in the names of fewer than four of them, or in the names of other people to hold as trustees for them. They might want to do this if the co-ownership is of commercial property.

[52] S. 1(6) and s. 36(2) of the Law of Property Act 1925.

[53] Because of the principle of overreaching (i.e. on any sale or other transaction entered into by at least two trustees of a trust of a property interest in land, the interests of all beneficiaries under the trust are overreached by being detached from the land and attached instead to the money received by the trustees under the transaction): see further Chapter 5 *Ownership and Other Property Interests* para. 5.30 (b) and (for more detail) Part III of Chapter 15 *Enforceability and Priority of Property Interests*.

8.12 The 'Trust of Land'

The trust imposed on co-owners of a legal estate in land is a 'trust of land' and its terms are governed by the Trusts of Land and Appointment of Trustees Act 1996. 'Trust of land' is a technical term, meaning all trusts of interests in land covered by the 1996 Act, not just co-ownership trusts.

Except where the 1996 Act provides otherwise, the position of beneficiaries and trustees under a trust of land is the same as in any other private trust for individuals, as described in para. 8.4(a) above. Outsiders dealing with trustees can usually assume that they have all the powers of an absolute private owner in relation to the trust property,[54] and if there are two of more of them, the trustees can overreach the equitable property interests of the beneficiaries in the co-owned property interest by a sale etc.[55] Before the 1996 Act, most trusts of land took a special form, the 'trust for sale', under which the trustees were under a duty, arising from the moment the trust arose, to sell the property, with only the power to postpone the sale. However, the trust for sale was abolished by the 1996 Act,[56] which converted all pre-existing trusts for sale into trusts of land under which the trustees have powers to sell the trust property which are just the same as in any other private trust.

There are nevertheless special provisions applicable only to trusts of land – and therefore to all co-ownership trusts of land – as we see in the next paragraph.

8.13 Special Provisions Applicable to Trusts of Land

(a) Duty to Consult Beneficiaries

The trustees have a qualified duty to consult the beneficiaries whenever they exercise any of their functions relating to the land, and to give effect to the wishes of the majority in value. The duty is set out in s. 11(1) of the 1996 Act, which provides that the trustees must:

(a) *so far as practicable*, consult the beneficiaries *of full age* and beneficially entitled to *an interest in possession* in the land, and

(b) *so far as consistent with the general interest of the trust*, give effect to the wishes of those beneficiaries, or (in case of dispute) of the majority (according to the value of their combined interests).

So, the qualifications to the duty are that the trustees only have to consult adult beneficiaries who have a *present* as opposed to a future interest[57] in the land, they need do so only 'so far as practicable', and they must do what the majority wants only 'so far as consistent with the general interest of the trust'.

This qualified duty to consult and act according to the wishes of the beneficiaries is a default duty only. In other words, it can be excluded by an express provision in

---

[54] S. 6 of the 1996 Act.   [55] See fn. 53 above.
[56] Although anyone expressly creating a trust can still, if they want, create one voluntarily.
[57] That is, their right to enjoyment of the land is immediate (as it would be for most co-owners) rather than in the future: see further Chapter 5 *Ownership and Other Property Interests* para. 5.16(c).

the deed under which the trust arises (usually the deed transferring the legal estate in the land to the co-owners).

Also, it does not apply to any decisions the trustees may want to make about occupation of the trust land. Occupation of the trust land is dealt with separately, by s. 12 and s. 13 of the 1996 Act.

(b) Beneficiaries' Right to Occupy the Trust Property

In a trust of land beneficiaries now have a statutory right to occupy the land. It applies only to beneficiaries with a present as opposed to a future right to enjoyment of the land (so will usually apply to all the beneficiaries under a co-ownership trust), and only where the purposes of the trust include making the land available for occupation by the beneficiaries, or the land is held by the trustees so as to be available for occupation by the beneficiaries.[58] Again, this condition will nearly always be satisfied in the case of co-ownership trusts.

If all the co-owning beneficiaries who want to occupy the land are able and willing to share occupation amicably, there is no problem. Difficulties arise where two or more qualifying beneficiaries each want to occupy the land but are unable or unwilling to occupy it together. The trustees are given extensive powers under s. 13 to resolve such conflicts, broadly by excluding one or more (but not all) of those entitled to occupy, and imposing conditions on the occupying beneficiary (for example, that the occupying beneficiary pays an occupational rent to those who are excluded).[59] However, the trustees cannot exclude a beneficiary who is already in occupation without the beneficiary's consent. If the trustees cannot obtain his consent, or they cannot agree how to exercise their powers to exclude a beneficiary, or any of the beneficiaries feel aggrieved by their decision, any of them can apply to the court for an order under ss. 14 and 15 of the 1996 Act. The court has wide powers under s. 14 to resolve the dispute (which we look at in (c) below) including power to order the sale of the property. If it orders sale, the co-ownership trusts ends and the proceeds of sale are divided up between the beneficiaries.

When deciding which of the beneficiaries should be excluded from occupation, and the conditions to be imposed on the others, the factors the trustees 'have regard to' must include:

(a) the intentions of the person or persons (if any) who created the trust,
(b) the purposes for which the land is held, and
(c) the circumstances and wishes of each of the beneficiaries [entitled to occupy].[60]

The conditions which the trustees may impose on the occupying beneficiary are stated to include conditions requiring him to pay any outgoings and expenses in respect of the land and comply with obligations relating to the land or the activities conducted there,[61] as well as conditions requiring him to make payments by way of compensation to the excluded beneficiary.[62] As already noted, this may mean ordering the occupying beneficiary to pay an occupational rent to the beneficiary

---

[58] S. 12(1) of the 1996 Act.   [59] S. 13(1)–(3).   [60] S. 13(4).   [61] S. 13(5).   [62] S. 13(6).

who is excluded. Alternatively, the trustees may be able to order the occupying beneficiary to buy out the share of the excluded beneficiary, although the circumstances in which the trustees could impose such a condition are controversial.[63]

(c) Court's Jurisdiction to Resolve Disputes Between Co-owners

The court has broad powers to resolve disputes between trustees, beneficiaries and other interested parties under ss. 14 and 15 of the 1996 Act, not just in relation to occupation of the trust property. Section 14 gives the court power to make any order it thinks fit 'relating to the exercise by the trustees of any of their functions (including an order relieving them of any obligation to obtain the consent of, or to consult, any person in connection with the exercise of any of their functions)'.[64] This includes power to make an order for the sale of the co-owned property.

Section 15 then provides that the matters 'to which the court is to have regard' in determining an application under s. 14 must include:

> (1) (a) the intentions of the person or persons (if any) who created the trust,
> (b) the purposes for which the property subject to the trust is held,
> (c) the welfare of any minor who occupies or might reasonably be expected to occupy any land subject to the trust as his home, and
> (d) the interests of any secured creditor of any beneficiary.[65]

In addition, the court must also have regard to 'the circumstances and wishes of each of the beneficiaries' who are entitled to occupy the property (if the application to the court relates to occupation of the property), or (if it does not) to 'the circumstances and wishes' of all adult beneficiaries with an interest in possession or (if they disagree) to those of the majority in value.[66] So, the court must look at a broader range of factors than those to be considered by the trustees: in particular, whilst the trustees must have regard only to the interests of the beneficiaries and the trust as a whole, the court must also have regard to the interests of interested non-beneficiaries (the minors and secured creditors referred to in s. 15(1)(c) and (d) above).

The scope and application of the court's powers under ss. 14 and 15 have been considered by the courts in many decided cases. In *White* v. *White* [2003] EWCA Civ 924, which we look at in more detail in para. 8.14(a) below, the Court of Appeal confirmed that in considering the 'intentions' of the persons who created the trust (i.e. the original co-owners in a co-ownership trust case) and the 'purposes' for

---

[63] Simon Gardner, 'Material relief between co-habitants 1: Liquidating beneficial interests other than by sale' [2014] 78 *Conveyancer and Property Lawyer* 93 has argued that, on the precise wording of s. 13, this cannot be done where (as often happens) one co-owner has left the co-owned property or been thrown out following a breakdown of her relationship with the other co-owner, and wants either to have the property sold or to have her interest bought out so that she can move on.

[64] S. 14(2)(a) of the 1996 Act. They may also make an order under s. 14(2)(b) 'declaring the nature or extent of a person's interest in property subject to the trust', which may be relevant where the co-ownership trust has arisen under a resulting or constructive trust in the circumstances we consider in Chapter 14 *Acquiring Interests Informally*, and there is disagreement as to the size of the co-ownership shares.

[65] S. 15(1).   [66] S. 15(2) and (3).

which the property is held on trust under s. 15(1)(a) and (b) above, the court may look only at the parties' intentions *at the time* the trust arose (in co-ownership cases, usually where the property was transferred into their joint names), and at the 'purposes' of the trust *at that time*. Later purposes, they said, are not relevant unless agreed by all the parties. In that case, where a married couple bought a house in their joint names and had their first child two years later, this meant that, for the purposes of s. 15(1)(a) and (b), their 'intentions' and the 'purposes' of the trust had to be taken to be to provide a home for themselves, not a home for themselves and their children.[67] The Court of Appeal also confirmed that the court must have regard to the 'circumstances and wishes' of *all* beneficiaries with an interest in possession (i.e. a present as opposed to a future interest) under s. 15(3), including the beneficiaries applying for and opposing the sale. So, in that case, where the wife was applying for an order for sale, the court had to have regard to the fact that the father (who remained living in the house with the two children after the wife left) could, if the house was sold, afford to buy a house big enough for the three of them in the same locality so that the children did not have to change schools, whereas the wife needed her share of the proceeds of sale in order to be able to provide herself with a home.

We come back to this case and other situations where the court has to decide whether to end the co-ownership by ordering a sale in para. 8.14. However, we should note that the court may also use its powers under s. 14 to impose conditions on the co-owners which enable them to continue the co-ownership. This was what happened in *Rodway* v. *Landy* [2001] EWCA Civ 471, where two doctors bought land in their joint names and constructed a purpose-built surgery on it. It was common ground that they held the legal title to the freehold interest in the land on trust for themselves as tenants in common in equal shares. They both practised from the surgery but before long they had fallen out. One of them wanted the property to be sold so that she could buy it for herself. The other wanted it to be partitioned (i.e. physically divided into two, with the freehold interest in one half being transferred to him and the freehold in the other half transferred to his co-owner).[68] Instead, the Court ordered them to exercise their powers as trustees to split the surgery into two self-contained units, and then, acting under the trustees' powers under s. 13, to exclude one of them from occupation of one unit and exclude the other from occupation of the other, conditional on each co-owner paying 50 per cent of the costs of the conversion works. There was also a further condition that, if either of them installed a lift for elderly or infirm patients, the lift could also be used by patients of the other.

---

[67] As we see in para. 18.14(a), it made no difference in that particular case because the court anyway had to take into account the interests of the children under s. 15(1)(c). In other cases, however, it might matter. Also, compare *First National Bank Plc* v. *Achampong* [2003] EWCA Civ 487 noted in para. 8.14 (b) below.

[68] Trustees have the power to partition the trust land under s. 7 of the 1996 Act with the consent of the beneficiaries: if one of them does not consent (as in *Rodway* v. *Landy*) the court can order the partition under s. 14.

8.14 Ending Co-Ownership Against the Will of One of the Co-Owners

Co-ownership of property interests can be ended amicably by one of the co-owners buying up the interests of all the others, or becoming the last surviving joint tenant by survivorship,[69] or by them all agreeing to have the co-owned interest sold and the proceeds of sale divided up between them.

Problems arise where one of the co-owners opposes sale. We can put these cases into three categories, each raising difficult questions and all made even more difficult if the co-owner who opposes sale is living in the co-owned property with the co-owners' children or other dependents. The first category (which includes cases like *White* v. *White*[70] which we noted in para. 8.13 above) is where the co-owners now have different and irreconcilable interests and there is no easy way of deciding which is to prevail. In many of these cases, the relationship between the co-owners has broken down and one of them wants to end the co-ownership and have the property sold so that she can get back the money she has invested in it and move on, whereas the other wants to continue occupying the property but cannot afford to buy out the share of the one who wants to leave. In the other two categories the relationship between the co-owners may or may not have broken down but the problem is that the person who wants the property sold is a creditor of one of the co-owners who has a mortgage or charge over his co-ownership interest (the second category) or the trustee in bankruptcy of one of the co-owners (the third category).

(a) Application for Sale by Co-owner

In these cases in our first category, where the person applying for sale is one of the co-owners, the matters the court must have regard to in deciding whether to order a sale are, as we saw in para. 8.13 above, those set out in s. 15 of the 1996 Act. It is worth noting that s. 15 broadly formalised the practice the courts had already developed in dealing with cases like these, but that the 1996 Act made one important change. Before the 1996 Act the trust imposed on the co-owners was, as we noted in para. 8.12 above, a 'trust for sale' under which the trustees *had to* sell the property unless it exercised its discretion to postpone sale. This meant that on an application to the court for sale, the onus was on the co-owner opposing sale to convince the court not to order sale. However, as we have seen, the trust for sale was abolished by the 1996 Act and replaced by the trust of land, under which there is no presumption for or against sale. In *White* v. *White*,[71] the Court of Appeal had to consider how to exercise its discretion under s. 15 in these circumstances. In that case, as we saw in para. 8.13, an estranged wife was applying for the sale of the house where she had lived with her husband and two daughters. After their marriage broke down both the wife and the husband continued to live separately in the house. As often happens in

---

[69] If the co-owned interest is a legal estate in land, this would be where the beneficial interest is held by the beneficiaries as joint tenants. When there is only one surviving beneficiary left, the trust of the legal estate does not end automatically but the beneficiary is entitled to call on the trustees to transfer the legal title to her, and so end the trust.

[70] *White* v. *White* [2003] EWCA Civ 924.   [71] Ibid.

these cases, the question of whether the house should be sold became tangled up with separate proceedings involving custody of the children and financial provision following the breakdown of the marriage. In this particular case there were parallel proceedings under the Children Act 1989 over who should be made primary carer of the children (which would have involved an order being made restricting the way the other parent could deal with her share in the house whilst the children were minors), as well as the proceedings under s. 14 of the 1986 Act. Eventually, the wife moved out of the house leaving the husband living there with the children, and sought sale of the house so that she would have the money to buy herself somewhere to live. Probably the most important part of the Court of Appeal's decision, which we are not concerned with here, was that in such cases all the parallel proceedings should be heard together.[72] However, the Court went on to consider the factors we noted in para. 8.13 and, taking those into account, concluded that the trial judge had been best placed to know how to strike a balance between 'the two most important competing considerations, namely the mother's need for realisation of her only capital in order to acquire a home, and the competing interests of the [children] who … have known no other home'.[73] Accordingly, The Court of Appeal approved his order that the house should be sold.

(b) Application by Mortgagee or Charge

Sections 14 and 15 of the 1996 Act also apply where the person applying for sale of the co-owned property is a creditor of a co-owner (not the co-owner who is objecting to the sale) and has a mortgage or charge over that co-owner's beneficial interest.[74] Some of these are cases where a creditor of one of the co-owners has obtained a charging order over that co-owner's beneficial interest to enable it to enforce a debt. In other cases, a mortgagee comes to have a mortgage over the beneficial interest of only one of two or more co-owners because that co-owner purported to grant the mortgagee a legal mortgage over the whole of the co-owned property interest, but for one reason or another the mortgage was unenforceable against the other co-owner. This might have been because the mortgaging co-owner forged the signature of the innocent co-owner, so the legal mortgage is void as against the legal title and against the innocent co-owner's beneficial interest, but

---

[72] Confirmed by the Court of Appeal in *Miller-Smith* v. *Miller-Smith* [2009] EWCA Civ 1297, where it was said that it would usually be better for a dispute between divorcing marital couples about sale of their co-owned marital home to be dealt with in the divorce proceedings rather than under s. 14 of the 1996 Act, because there 'the court will undertake a holistic examination of all aspects of the parties' finances, needs, contributions, etc.; will devise the fairest set of arrangements for the future housing and finances of each of them; and, to that end, will provide for the transfer of capital, as well perhaps as for payment of future income, from one to the other. By an order under TOLATA, on the other hand, the court lays down only one piece of the jigsaw …' (Wilson LJ at para. 18).
[73] Thorpe LJ at para. 18.
[74] See Martin Dixon, 'To sell or not to sell: That is the question – the irony of the Trusts of Land and Appointment of Trustees Act 1996' [2011] 70 *Cambridge Law Journal* 579 on the distinctive features of these cases.

takes effect as an equitable mortgage over the forger's beneficial interest.[75] Alternatively it might be that the innocent co-owner was induced to enter into the mortgage by undue influence or fraud or misrepresentation by the other co-owner, which again makes the mortgage unenforceable against her beneficial interest, but enforceable only against her co-owner. In those circumstances the innocent co-owner feels understandably aggrieved if the whole of the co-owned property has to be sold to pay off a debt for which she is not responsible, so that the mortgagee can have some of its debt repaid out of the other co-owner's share of the proceeds of sale. She will be even more aggrieved if she is living in the co-owned property with children or other dependents, and her half of the proceeds of sale will not be enough for her to buy somewhere else for them all to live. This is essentially what happened in *First National Bank Plc* v. *Achampong*,[76] where husband and wife had many years earlier bought in their joint names the house where the wife still lived with their grandchildren and one of their adult children who had a mental disability. The husband forged the wife's signature on a mortgage to the bank to secure his business debts, and when the bank mortgagee applied for an order for sale of the house under s. 14 of the 1996 Act it was held that the mortgage was not enforceable against the wife's beneficial interest in the house. Nevertheless, the Court of Appeal held that the house had to be sold. A number of factors influenced their decision, two of which are particularly interesting for our purposes. One was that husband and wife had been living apart for many years and it was accepted that their marriage was effectively over even though they were not formally divorced. On this basis, the Court of Appeal said it was irrelevant that their original intention in buying the house had been to provide a matrimonial home for themselves and that the purpose of the trust was to provide a matrimonial home because 'that consideration is now spent' given that their marriage was now over.[77] The other (and overwhelming) factor, however, was that:

> The effect of refusing a sale is to condemn the bank to wait — possibly for many years — until Mrs Achampong should choose to sell before the bank can recover anything. In the meantime its debt continues to increase. (It was £180,000 at the date of the trial as against a value of the property of £195,000.) Nor does it lie with Mrs Achampong to complain of delay since she has had the use of the whole property in the meantime.[78]

---

[75] Because of the equitable doctrine of 'partial performance' confirmed by the Court of Appeal in *Thames Guaranty Ltd* v. *Campbell* [1985] 1 QB 210 (if someone attempts to dispose of more than she has, the purported transaction will bite on whatever lesser interest she does have) and by operation of s. 63 of the Law of Property Act 1925 (*First National Bank Plc* v. *Achampong* [2003] EWCA Civ 487).

[76] *First National Bank Plc* v. *Achampong* [2003] EWCA Civ 487.

[77] The Court of Appeal said it was relevant insofar as the intention/purpose was to provide a home for their children, but that that was of little weight now that the children were all adult. The Court of Appeal accepted that the welfare of the grandchildren was relevant (under s. 15(1)(c)) and so too was the welfare of the mentally disabled daughter (as a matter which the court should take into account even though it did not come directly under any of the headings in s. 15), but it said they had to be given little weight because the wife had failed to produce adequate evidence as to the likely effect on them of a sale.

[78] Blackburne J at para. 65, Arden LJ agreeing.

Similar sentiments were expressed by the Court of Appeal in *Bank of Ireland Home Mortgages Ltd* v. *Bell* [2001] 2 All ER (Comm) 920 (another forgery case, where the house was also bought as a family home and the innocent wife was still living there, in failing health, with their son: sale was ordered) and later by the High Court in *Edwards* v. *Edwards* [2010] EWHC 652 (sale ordered on similar facts, except that the forging co-owner was the wife and the husband had ample funds to buy somewhere else to live), and in *C Putnam & Sons* v. *Taylor* [2009] EWHC 317 (sale ordered, rejecting the innocent wife's argument that this would infringe her rights to respect for family and private life under Article 8 of the European Convention on Human Rights and to peaceful enjoyment of her possessions under art. 1 Protocol 1).[79]

The effect of the current authorities in cases like these is summed up by Master Price in *Fred Perry (Holdings) Ltd* v. *Genis*:[80]

> The authorities demonstrate a recurring tension between these competing claims, but as I understand it the upshot has been to give precedence to commercial interests rather than to the residential security of the family. Whilst it may be argued that precedence to such commercial interest fails to take adequate account of the public interest in maintaining a stable family unit, bearing in mind the attendant social costs of eviction and family breakup, this does seem to be the current state of the authorities in relation to sections 14 and 15 of the 1996 Act.[81]

(c) Application by Trustee in Bankruptcy

In cases coming within the third category (one of the co-owners is bankrupt and her trustee in bankruptcy wants the property to be sold) the decision has to be made by the bankruptcy court under s. 335A of the Insolvency Act 1986. Under s. 335A(2) the court is required to make 'such order as it considers just and reasonable' having regard to three factors. The first and third of these (in s. 335A(2)(a) and (c)) are 'the interests of the bankrupt's creditors' and 'all the circumstances of the case *other than the needs of the bankrupt*'. The second, in s. 335A(b), applies only where the property includes the home or former home of the bankrupt or his/her spouse/civil partner/former spouse/civil partner. In such a case the court must also have regard to additional matters. These are the needs and financial resources of the spouse etc. and the needs of 'any children', but also, and more controversially, 'the conduct of the [spouse etc.] so far as contributing to the bankruptcy'. Even more controversially, s. 335A(3) then provides that, in all cases, if more than a year has elapsed since the start of the bankruptcy, the court must assume 'unless the circumstances of the case are exceptional' that the interests of the creditors 'outweigh all other considerations'. Unsurprisingly, the courts have consistently failed to find circumstances sufficiently exceptional to justify anything more than a short postponement of sale,

---

[79] Although see Dixon, 'To sell or not to sell', fn. 74 above, at pp. 599 and 604 for the argument that this conclusion might now require reconsideration.

[80] *Fred Perry (Holdings) Ltd* v. *Genis* [2014] 8 WLUK 40 at para. 8.

[81] Although in that case the court ordered sale to be deferred for a year to allow the husband and wife to make arrangements for new schools for their children and alternative accommodation.

and often have rejected even that concession. Broadly, they have taken the view that circumstances cannot be 'exceptional' unless they are highly unusual. As Nourse LJ said in the Court of Appeal in *Re Citro*[82] in a passage repeatedly cited with approval by the courts in later cases:

> What then are exceptional circumstances? As the cases show, it is not uncommon for a wife with young children to be faced with eviction in circumstances where the realisation of her beneficial interest will not produce enough to buy a comparable home in the same neighbourhood, or indeed elsewhere; and, if she has to move elsewhere, there may be problems over schooling and so forth. Such circumstances, while engendering a natural sympathy in all who hear of them, cannot be described as exceptional. *They are the melancholy consequences of debt and improvidence with which every civilised society has been familiar.*[83]

Commentators have argued that this approach is inappropriate. It does not require the courts to inquire into the likely effect *on these particular creditors* of refusing to order sale, and then weigh it against the level of hardship likely to be suffered by the innocent co-owner if a sale is ordered. A proportionality exercise of this kind would seem to be essential, given that in these cases the non-bankrupt spouse is being deprived of her home, and an unwanted sale is a serious interference with her possessions (her beneficial interest in the land is being sold against her will).[84] Nevertheless, the courts have so far not responded to these concerns.

8.15 Condominium Co-ownership

A particular co-ownership problem arises where a building or collection of buildings is split up into separate units, each designed for separate occupation and use, but physically interdependent and sharing common structures, facilities and access ways. The challenge is to develop a property rights structure which allows the individual unit holders to have private ownership-type rights over their own unit and also to have communal use rights over, and shared responsibility for, the common structures and facilities etc. Most jurisdictions in continental Europe, Australasia and North America have long had statutory special-purpose property structures for this, usually called condominiums or strata title schemes.[85] They can cover residential, commercial, industrial and holiday developments, as well as some with mixed uses. There are various different models. In one, individual unit-holders are co-owners of the whole development, and each also has exclusive rights in their own unit and membership of a management company. In another, the ownership of the common parts is held by a special purpose company which manages the

---

[82] *Re Citro* [1991] Ch. 132.   [83] Ibid. p. 157, emphasis added.
[84] See for example Dixon, 'To sell or not to sell', fn. 74 above; Adam Baker, 'The judicial approach to "exceptional circumstances" in bankruptcy: The impact of the Human Rights Act 1998' [2010] *Conveyancer and Property Lawyer* 352, and Alison Clarke, 'Children of bankrupts' (1991) 3 *Journal of Child Law* 116.
[85] Cornelius van der Merwe (ed.) *European Condominium Law* (Cambridge: Cambridge University Press, 2015).

development and is wholly owned and controlled by the unit holders, who each also own their own individual units.[86] And, of course, there are many variations on those two models.

We have our own condominium property rights structure, called commonhold, which we developed very late (it was introduced by the Commonhold and Leasehold Reform Act 2002), and which has been spectacularly unsuccessful. We adopted condominium law very late because our common law developed instead complex leasehold models to serve the same purposes. We explain how the leasehold models developed and how they now work in Chapter 17 *Leases*.

There was nothing obviously wrong with the condominium model we adopted. In a commonhold development, as provided under the Commonhold and Leasehold Reform Act 2002, each unit-holder is the legal freehold owner of its own unit. A company limited by guarantee,[87] is formed to hold the legal freehold estate in the common parts of the development. This company is called a 'commonhold association', and its sole members are the freehold owners of the units. The commonhold association is responsible for managing the whole of the commonhold development and collects the costs of doing so from the unit-owners by levying a 'commonhold assessment'. The rights and duties of the unit owners as between themselves and as between them and their commonhold association are set out in a prescribed form document, the 'commonhold community statement'. The only novelty of this arrangement is that, in a commonhold development, positive covenants entered into by unit-owners and by the commonhold association as owner of the common parts (i.e. positive obligations to carry out works, or pay money, or do anything else positive) are fully enforceable as property interests as between all parties. This is a novelty because, as we saw in Chapter 6 *New Property Interests and the Numerus Clausus* para. 6.9,[88] in our general law it is only restrictive, and not positive, covenants which are enforceable as property interests between successive freehold owners.

The only snag with commonhold, however, was that no-one was required to adopt it. Developers were given the right to use commonhold as the property rights structure for any new development, and landlords and tenants under pre-existing leasehold developments were entitled to convert to commonhold. However, no-one was made to do so, and as it happened, almost no-one did. Fewer than 20 commonhold developments have ever been created, and by 1 January 2014 there were only 16 in operation, many of them consisting of only a very small number of units. This has proved to be a disaster for the few who are now holding commonhold units: no-one wants to buy them or lend money on a mortgage of them, and it is impossible for them to be converted (back) into conventional leasehold units. Lu Xu, who has analysed the causes of the failure, has warned that, unless something can be done to revive commonhold or compensate those trapped in it:

---

[86] For a summary of UK and EU jurisdictions, see ibid. Ch. 1.   [87] As to which see para. 8.26 below.
[88] And see also, in more detail, Chapter 13 *Non-Possessory Land Use Rights* para. 13.16.

Commonhold will be a lesson of warning, if not a laughing stock, for decades to come as one of the worst examples of carefully considered legislation having done more harm than good, due to the lack of follow-up efforts and support from crucial stakeholders. That would of course not be of any comfort to those individual owners who happen to be stuck in a commonhold . . .[89]

The Law Commission has responded by publishing a Consultation Paper 'Reinvigorating commonhold: The alternative to leasehold ownership',[90] in which they consulted on proposals to change the law to persuade developers to build new commonhold condominiums, and also to persuade leaseholder associations who have bought, or are thinking of buying, the freehold to move over to the commonhold model. We come back to this issue in Chapter 17.

PART IV FAMILIES

8.16 Concepts of Family Property and Matrimonial Property

A striking feature of English law is that we do not recognise the institutions of family property or marital property in this country. We do not recognise 'the family' as an entity which is capable of holding property interests, and we treat spouses as separate individuals for property holding purposes: by s. 37 of the Law of Property Act 1925 'a husband and wife shall, for all purposes of acquisition of any interest in property . . . be treated as two persons'. Historically, this marked the end (or nearly the end) of a long campaign for the emancipation of women from the doctrine that married women had only restricted rights to hold property (and to sue and be sued in tort and for debts) because husband and wife were treated in law as one person 'it being the wife's personality that was merged into that of the husband'.[91]

The Law of Property Act 1925 also finally abolished the tenancy by entireties, which was a form of co-ownership whereby husband and wife held property interests by an unseverable joint tenancy, with the husband holding overall control of the property.[92]

So, on the one hand we can say that the law's present treatment of family members as autonomous individuals entitled to independence of their property holdings is a victory for gender equality. On the other hand, we can say that it

---

[89] Lu Xu, 'Commonhold developments in practice' in Warren Barr (ed.), *Modern Studies in Property Law*, vol. 8 (Oxford and Portland, OR: Hart Publishing, 2015) p. 331, and see also Lu Xu, 'Managing and maintaining flatted buildings: Some Anglo-Scottish comparisons' (2010) *Edinburgh Law Review* 236, where he contrasts commonhold (unfavourably) with Development Management Schemes introduced in Scotland in 2009 by the Tenements (Scotland) Act 2004.

[90] Law Commission Consultation Report CP No 241 (2018).

[91] W. R. Cornish and G. de N. Clark, *Law and Society in England 1750–1950* (London: Sweet & Maxwell, 1989) p. 367. For further details see their account at pp. 365–369 and 398–402.

[92] The tenancy by entireties was abolished prospectively by ss. 1 and 5 of the Married Women's Property Act 1882 in England and Wales, and the last surviving ones were automatically converted into joint tenancies by LPA 1925, Sch. 1 Pt VI. They survive in some states of the USA, but the US equivalents of Married Women's Property Acts have put husbands and wives on the same footing: Joseph Singer, *Property Law: Rules, Policies and Practices* (2nd edn, New York: Aspen Law and Business, 1997) pp. 728–733.

ignores the reality of financial interdependence of family members, and modern social attitudes towards family.[93] We might also point out that gendered power relationships are not an inevitable consequence of family property regimes: most modern civil law jurisdictions which recognise family property regimes now do so in a gender neutral way.

8.17 Recognition of De Facto Family Property

The reality is that many families do regard the assets they use as a family – their house, their household goods, their car, etc. – as 'theirs'. They may or may not know the precise property rights that they as individual family members have acquired in assets such as these as a matter of law, but family members often do regard themselves (and each other) as having legitimate claims on 'family' assets which are legally owned by another family member.

The law does recognise these claims to a limited extent, especially as between couples who are married or in a civil partnership. So, for example, as we saw in Chapter 6 *New Property Interests and the Numerus Clausus* para. 6.11, under Part IV of the Family Law Act 1996 spouses and civil partners have what are now called 'home rights' in the matrimonial or civil partnership home. These are rights not to be evicted or excluded from the home except with the leave of the court, which are enforceable not only against their spouse but also against third parties such as purchasers and lenders. In addition, the family courts have extensive powers to ascertain and redistribute the property interests of spouses and civil partners on divorce.

Also, but more indirectly, the courts have developed equitable principles of constructive and resulting trusts and proprietary estoppel which we look at in Chapter 14 *Acquiring Interests Informally.* These principles allow the courts to allocate or redistribute property interests in assets to which the claimant asserts an entitlement arising out of payments made or responsibilities undertaken, or because of legitimate expectations arising out of conduct. In most cases the asset will be the family home, but it may be any other asset which the claimant thinks of as his because of a family or dependence relationship he has with the legal title holder.

However, all of these provisions merely redistribute property interests between individual members of the family. They do not make the family as an entity into a property interest holder, nor do they require an individual family member to hold property interests for the benefit of the family as a whole.

PART V COMMUNITIES

8.18 Property Holdings by Communities

Communities – meaning here a group of people defined by reference to a common characteristic – are not legal entities and, as we saw in Chapter 5 *Ownership and*

---

[93] Adam J. MacLeod, *Property and Practical Reason* (Cambridge: Cambridge University Press, 2015) pp. 78–82.

Other Property Interests, this means that they cannot directly hold legal estates in land such as freehold and leasehold interests in land. However, as we noted in para. 5.33 of Chapter 5, they can (and do) hold them indirectly by having the legal title to the property interest put in the name of a legal entity owned and controlled by the community. Also, they can hold communal non-possessory land use rights directly. In this part of the chapter we look at the kinds of community that can hold these non-possessory land use rights, and at the corporate identities that communities can adopt to enable them to hold freehold and leasehold interests in land.

8.19 Communities

The communities we focus on here are groups of people who have shared characteristics which relate to locality, usually in the form of shared use of or interest in a particular area of land or land-related resource such as a watercourse. Membership of the community may be automatic for any person sharing the relevant characteristic (which might be, for example, being an inhabitant of the locality, or, in the cultures we look at in Chapter 9 *Multiple Property Rights Systems*, membership of a particular ethnic, kinship or cultural group). Alternatively, the community may be a voluntary association of individuals. They might perhaps be people who have pre-existing rights or liberties to use and/or control a particular resource in common with each other (for example, rights to graze animals on a particular pasture, or rights and liberties to use a particular watercourse in a particular way or in different ways), and who have decided to act collectively to avert a 'tragedy of the commons'.[94] These are the kinds of community that Elinor Ostrom had in mind when considering the viability of self-regulating resource-sharing communities.[95] Or the community may be a group of people who want to restore and maintain a particular stretch of river, or a local pub or community centre, or a local landmark, and have decided to act collectively to further those aims by acquiring communal use and/or control rights over the resource, whatever it is.

In any of these cases, membership of the community entitles the member to use and/or control the use of the land in common with other members (and possible also with outsiders), either generally or in a particular way, and usually in accordance with formal and/or informal rules made between themselves. So, for example, a group of neighbouring farmers who have rights to draw water from a particular source or to graze animals on a particular pasture, might agree rules to regulate their use as between themselves and negotiate with the landowner and with public regulatory authorities who themselves have use/control rights over the land.

In this part of the chapter, we are primarily interested in identifying the property rights that these kinds of community and their members have in the resource which they collectively use/control, either directly or indirectly through corporate entities they own and control.

---

[94] Chapter 2 *Conceptions and Justifications* para. 2.12.   [95] Ibid. paras. 2.14–2.19.

8.20 Difference Between Co-Owners and Communities

As a preliminary matter, however, it is worth considering how communal property differs from co-ownership. In co-owned property, the asset is administered for the benefit of the designated co-owners, each considered as an autonomous individual. If we ignore for the moment the complication that, in our law legal estates in land which are co-owned are held on trust, each co-owner of an interest in land is entitled to act it her own selfish best interests, subject only to the rules each has made with the other in order to achieve a workable (not necessarily 'fair') balance between their interests.

In communal property, on the other hand, the asset is administered for the benefit of the community, which means for the benefit of the members *for the time being, in their capacity as members* (making the community intergenerational), and to further their collective purposes or aims. These purposes or aims may or may not be wholly or partly altruistic, but the essential point is that in communal property the community is likely to regard itself as having a common stake or common interest in a resource. Co-ownership, on the other hand, generally mediates between the individual purposes or aims of the individual co-owners, who tend to regard themselves as co-operating in their individual self-interests, retaining an individual stake in the resource which can be separated off from the co-ownership and sold on to outsiders.

8.21 Property Interests Held Directly by Communities

Communal use rights over land used to be of great agricultural, economic and social importance, but they declined dramatically over the eighteenth and nineteenth centuries through the combined effects of approvement and enclosure, processes by which communally used land was converted to private ownership.[96] By the middle of the twentieth century they were thought to be facing extinction. A Royal Commission on Common Land was appointed in 1955, and it reported in its final report in 1958 (the 'Jennings Report')[97] that most remaining common land (land over which communal resource use rights had traditionally been exercised) was derelict, largely because of changes in agriculture and the disruption caused by government requisitions in the Second World War. The Report recommended that measures should be taken to preserve what were thought to be these last vestiges of our national heritage: there was no thought at that time that land which was communally used and/or regulated might provide an economically, socially or environmentally viable alternative to private property.

---

[96] Approvement was the process by which the lord of the manor could convert communal grazing land to his own private ownership, and enclosure the process, carried out initially by Private Acts of Parliament but subsequently by a series of statutory procedures, by which land was discharged from communal rights and parcelled out in private ownership between the landholder and the commoners: see further Alison Clarke, 'Property law: Re-establishing diversity' in Michael Freeman and Andrew Lewis (eds), *Current Legal Problems 1997: Law and Opinion at the end of the Twentieth Century* (Oxford: Oxford University Press, 1997) p. 119 at pp. 123–137.

[97] Report of the Royal Commission on Common Land 1958 Cmnd 462.

Accordingly, in partial implementation of the recommendations of the Jennings Report, Parliament passed the Commons Registration Act 1965 which set up local authority registers (Commons Registers and Town and Village Green Registers) on which all pre-existing communal land use rights, the land over which they were exercisable and the ownership of such land, had to be recorded. These registers had (and still have) nothing to do with our national land registration system which we look at in Chapter 16 *Registration* and which records private property interests in land. The intention was that the Commons and Town and Village Green registers would provide a permanent historical record of communally used land in England and Wales, and there was a cut-off date in 1970 after which all pre-existing communal use rights covered by the Act were extinguished if not recorded on the register.

However, as it happened, the Commons Registration Act 1965 did more than just preserve the remnants of traditional communal land use rights. It also resulted in, or at least marked, the resurgence of the communal land use rights it covered. There are a number of possible reasons for this. One is that the courts initially interpreted the 1965 Act broadly, confirming, amongst other things, that it allowed new communal use rights which arose or were created after the 1970 cut-off date to be registered. In particular, they confirmed that local inhabitants who could prove that they have made recreational use of land as of right for at least 20 years since 1970 could require the local authority to register the land as a town or village green, which would make it illegal for the landowner to carry out any development of the land. This provided a procedure by which local people who had customarily used derelict or undeveloped land for recreational purposes or who valued it in its present state could halt threatened development plans, and secure the permanent preservation of the land as a collective resource for local inhabitants. As we see in Part VI of Chapter 13 *Non-Possessory Land Use Rights* where we look at town and village green rights in more detail, these activities so alarmed government and planners that new legislation was brought in to give landowners greater powers to resist such applications by local inhabitants. At the same time, (and seemingly prompted by the same considerations) the Courts also took steps to limit the application of the relevant provisions of the 1965 Act in a series of high profile court decisions which we look at in Chapter 13. In the meantime, however, as we saw in Chapter 2 *Conceptions and Justifications* and elsewhere in the book, the traditional view of the economic efficiency of private property has been increasingly challenged, and there have been major and influential reassessments of the social, environmental and political value of communal property rights.

8.22 Communal Land Use Rights Under the Commons Registration Act 1965 and the Commons Act 2006

As noted in Chapter 5 *Ownership and Other Property Interests*, there are two types of communal land use rights which are subject to the statutory registration and regulation regime set up by the Commons Registration Act 1965, now in the process of replacement by the Commons Act 2006.[98] We look at them in detail in Chapter 13, but a brief outline may be useful here.

(a) Town and Village Green Rights

As noted above, under what is now s. 15 of the Commons Act 2006, when land is registered in the Town and Village Greens Register as a town or village green, local inhabitants have the right to use it for 'lawful sports and pastimes' in common with each other. The landowner is also entitled to go on using the land in whatever way she was using it immediately before the land was registered as a town or village green. Neither the 1965 Act nor the 2006 Act contains any provisions about the nature of the rights the inhabitants have over town or village greens, or about how the collective use is to be regulated once the land has been registered as a green.

The first of these omissions was remedied by the House of Lords in *Oxfordshire County Council* v. *Oxford City Council* [2006] UKHL 25, where it was authoritatively stated by Lord Hoffmann that the effect of registration was to confer on 'local inhabitants' the positive right to use the land for lawful sports and pastimes[99] As to who 'local inhabitants' are for these purposes, it should be appreciated that, after 1970, land can only be registered as a town or village green if 'a significant number of the inhabitants of any locality, or of any neighbourhood within a locality' have used it as of right for lawful sports and pastimes for at least 20 years.[100] This means that when local inhabitants apply for registration of the land they must specify the 'locality or neighbourhood' in question. If their application is successful, the people who acquire the rights to use it as a town or village green, Lord Hoffmann said, are *all* the inhabitants of that particular 'locality or neighbourhood'.

So far, neither Parliament nor the courts has remedied the second omission in the 1965 Act, so in practice the local inhabitants and the landowner have to devise, police and enforce their own rules for regulating their collective use of the land.

(b) Rights of Common Over Common Land

As noted in Chapter 5 *Ownership and Other Property Interests* para. 5.35 (b), a right of common is a right held by a private landowner to take a particular resource from adjoining land, in common with other neighbouring landowners. A right to graze animals on adjoining land is a right of common (on the basis that the adjoining owner takes the grass etc. from the grazed land via the mouths of her animals), but

---

[98] The 2006 Act is intended to remedy some of the glaring defects in the registration machinery set up by the 1965 Act, and also to make provision for the management and regulation of common land (originally recommended by the Jennings Report but not included in the 1965 Act). The 2006 Act is being brought into force by stages in different parts of England and Wales: it is not known when this process will be completed. See further Julian Farrand and Alison Clarke (eds.), *Emmet & Farrand on Title* (London: Sweet & Maxwell, looseleaf updated to 30 April 2019) para. 1.126 for details.

[99] *Oxfordshire County Council* v. *Oxford City Council* [2006] UKHL 25 at paras. 45–49 and 53; see also paras. 2–28 for historical background.

[100] Since 2006, land can also become a town or village green by application made by the landowner.

so too are rights to take other kinds of resource from the land. The holders of these rights of common are collectively known as 'commoners'. The land over which their rights are exercisable (which may be privately owned or owned by a public authority or a body such as the National Trust) has to be registered in the Commons Register as common land. The landowner may continue to use the land for other purposes provided they do not interfere with the rights of the commoners, and the common land also becomes access land open to the public under the Countryside and Rights of Way Act 2000.[101] This shared resource use is traditionally regulated by rules agreed between the commoners and the landowner, now supplemented by regulatory control by various public authorities (because of the agricultural and environmental importance of common land).

8.23 Tenants' Communal Use Rights in Multi-Unit Leasehold Developments

As noted in para. 5.35(b), communal non-possessory land use rights are also held directly by unincorporated groups of tenants who have communal rights and powers in the structure, infrastructure, common parts and communal accesses in multi-unit leasehold developments. Their communal use of these facilities is generally governed as between themselves by formal rules in their leases and/or regulations made by a management company (which may be controlled by the landlord or collectively by the tenants themselves), supplemented or modified by informal rules and conventions evolved by the tenants collectively).[102] We look at these in more detail in Chapter 17 *Leases*.

8.24 Co-Operatives

In England and Wales a co-operative is a particular kind of organisation which can choose to adopt any one of a number of different legal forms. Whichever form it takes, however, it has to satisfy the criterion required for a co-operative, which is that it must 'abide by the internationally recognised values and principles of co-operative identity as defined by the International Co-operative Alliance'.[103] The Alliance defines a co-operative as 'an autonomous association of persons united voluntarily to meet their common economic, social, and cultural needs and aspirations through a jointly-owned and democratically-controlled enterprise' and defines 'co-operative values' as 'based on the values of self-help, self-responsibility, democracy, equality, equity, and solidarity. In the tradition of their founders, cooperative members believe in the ethical values of honesty, openness, social responsibility and caring

---

[101] See further Chapter 13 *Non-Possessory Land Use Rights* paras. 13.17-13.20.

[102] On this aspect see further Sarah Blandy 'Collective property: Owning and sharing residential space' in Nicholas Hopkins (ed.), *Modern Studies in Property Law*, vol. 7 (Oxford and Portland, OR: Hart Publishing, 2013) p. 152.

[103] See www.uk.coop/resources/model-governing-documents.

for others'. Co-operative principles (stated to be guidelines by which co-operatives put their values into practice) include the following:

1. **Voluntary and Open Membership** Cooperatives are voluntary organisations, open to all persons able to use their services and willing to accept the responsibilities of membership, without gender, social, racial, political or religious discrimination.

2. **Democratic Member Control** Cooperatives are democratic organisations controlled by their members, who actively participate in setting their policies and making decisions. Men and women serving as elected representatives are accountable to the membership. In primary cooperatives members have equal voting rights (one member, one vote) and cooperatives at other levels are also organised in a democratic manner.

3. **Member Economic Participation** Members contribute equitably to, and democratically control, the capital of their cooperative. At least part of that capital is usually the common property of the cooperative. Members usually receive limited compensation, if any, on capital subscribed as a condition of membership. Members allocate surpluses for any or all of the following purposes: developing their cooperative, possibly by setting up reserves, part of which at least would be indivisible; benefiting members in proportion to their transactions with the cooperative; and supporting other activities approved by the membership.

4. **Autonomy and Independence** Cooperatives are autonomous, self-help organisations controlled by their members. If they enter into agreements with other organisations, including governments, or raise capital from external sources, they do so on terms that ensure democratic control by their members and maintain their cooperative autonomy . . .

7. **Concern for Community** Cooperatives work for the sustainable development of their communities through policies approved by their members.[104]

A co-operative does not have to form itself into a legal entity by forming a corporate body, but if it does so, it has to be registered in the Financial Conduct Authority (FCA) Mutuals Public Register and will come under the regulation of the FCA. It must also publish accounts and file them at the FCA's Mutuals Public Register. Whether registered as a corporate body or unregistered, co-operatives are governed by their rules, which must conform to UK Co-operatives Model Rules.[105]

8.25 Incorporating Communities

Whether a community holding property interests is a co-operative or not, incorporating the community has advantages and disadvantages. The disadvantages are mainly practical. It costs money to incorporate (although not huge amounts), and once incorporated the corporation becomes regulated by a regulatory authority, which will require accounts and other records to be prepared and filed, and the

---

[104] For the full text and Guidelines Notes on the 'principles', see www.ica.coop/en/cooperatives/cooperative-identity.

[105] See www.uk.coop/resources/model-governing-documents. Different model rules are provided for different kinds of co-operative, depending on the particular legal form they choose to adopt.

details of the corporation, usually including names of members, go on a public record. The advantages, however, are considerable. In practice, outsiders may prefer to interact with a legal entity rather than with a group of people. Communities are intergenerational in the sense we noted in para. 8.20 above, and they need mechanisms whereby human agents can make decisions/take actions in relation to the resources which are binding on all present and future members. This can be done internally by the rules of the association, but outsiders offering grants, loans, services or supplies, are likely to want to enter into a contract with a legal entity which they know is authorised to speak for, and take actions binding on, the group. The other advantage of incorporation is that most kinds of corporate group give the members limited liability: individual members are not liable for the group's debts. If an unincorporated group is proposing some kind of land development or business project, members have to appreciate that, if anything goes wrong, each member is liable jointly and severally for *all* the debts of the group. In other words, although under their rules the members may agree that debts are shared equally, outside creditors are entitled to recover the whole of the debt from any one or more of the members, who then have to rely on the other members to reimburse them for their share.

8.26 Legal Forms for Incorporating Communities

Communities which decide to incorporate can choose between a bewildering variety of legal forms.[106] They can become an ordinary limited liability company[107] under the Companies Act 2006, or a partnership. Alternatively (or as well) they can choose one of the new forms of legal entity recently introduced for community enterprises which we noted in para. 8.4 above. The most important are the community interest company and the community benefit society, and they are currently being used for a wide variety of social and community enterprises. These include where a community wants to acquire and run for itself a threatened community asset such as a pub or village shop or community centre, or an 'asset of community value' under the Localism Act 2011;[108] or to erect and run a wind turbine, paying a proportion of the turnover into a local community fund;[109] or to receive and administer the payments that the onshore oil and gas industry has undertaken to make to provide 'benefits to local communities . . . where hydraulic fracturing takes place';[110] or to

---

[106] For a good overview see Co-operatives UK, *Simply Legal: All You Need to Know About Legal Forms and Organisational Types, for Co-operatives and Community Owned Enterprises*, September 2015, available at www.uk.coop/resources/simply-legal.

[107] A company limited by shares, which is the classic shareholder company described in para. 8.3 above, or a company limited by guarantee, which is just like a company limited by shares except that it has no share capital: the original members of the company never put their own money into the company by paying to be allotted shares in it. Instead, they guarantee that, if the company is insolvent they will be personally liable for its debts, up to a specified amount (usually very small).

[108] As in *Banner Homes Limited* v. *St Albans City and District Council* [2018] EWCA Civ 1187.

[109] *R (on the application of Wright)* v. *Forest of Dean DC* [2017] EWCA Civ 2102.

[110] See Chapter 7 *Objects of Property Interests* para. 7.18, and also Adam Brown, David Cox and Roy Pinnock, 'United Kingdom: Community benefits incorporated: shale and other contentious infrastructure' (2013) *International Energy Law Review* 302.

carry out what Bronwen Morgan describes as 'community based sustainability initiatives and grass-roots innovations in response to climate change challenges' and also in response to 'the 2008 financial crash and subsequent austerity policies'.[111]

8.27 Community Interest Companies

A community interest company is intended for groups who want to carry out activities for the benefit of the community, encouraging private investment by paying limited dividends to members out of any profits, and by having an 'asset lock' which prevents its assets from being used for any purposes other than the benefit of the community. It owes its origins to a Cabinet Office Strategy Unit Report, 'Private Action, Public Benefit', published in 2002, reviewing charities and the not-for-profit sector, and recommending (among other things) the creation of 'a new legal form for social enterprise' which would not enjoy the tax advantages of charitable status but would enjoy 'light touch' regulation to ensure that its assets and profits are used 'for the community interest'. This recommendation was implemented by Part 2 of the Companies (Audit, Investigations and Community Enterprise) Act 2004. CICs have to be registered with the Office of the Regulator of Community Interest Companies, which regulates the way they operate. As at March 2018, there were about 14,250 CICs on the register.

More precisely, the community interest company has three distinctive features. First, in order to be registered as a community interest company, it must satisfy the 'community interest test'; secondly, its assets are subject to an 'asset lock' prohibiting transfer of its assets except for full consideration or to another asset-locked or equivalent body or purpose; and thirdly, members are entitled to take profits out of the company by way of dividend payments, but the payments are capped, and the members cannot dissolve the company and divide up its assets amongst themselves. We take a closer look at each of these.

(a) Community Interest Test

A company satisfies the community interest test if 'a reasonable person might consider that its activities are being carried on for the benefit of the community'.[112] 'Community' is defined as including a section of the community, and the legislation provides that 'any group of individuals may constitute a section of the community if (a) they share a common characteristic which distinguishes them from other members of the community; and (b) a reasonable person might consider that they constitute a section of the community'.

This test is less easy to satisfy than might appear at first sight. First, regulations set out some activities which are (conclusively) taken to be activities which a reasonable

[111] Bronwen Morgan, 'Telling stories beautifully: Hybrid legal forms in the new economy' (2018) 45 *Journal of Law and Society* 64 at pp. 64–65.
[112] S. 35(2) of the Companies (Audit, Investigations and Community Enterprise) Act 2004.

person would *not* consider as being activities carried on for the benefit of the community. So far, these cover two types of prohibited activity. The first is political activities,[113] defined very widely to cover promotion of or opposition to changes in UK law or in present or proposed government policy or policies of other public authorities, and also activities 'which can reasonably be regarded as intended or likely to' provide or affect support for a political party or political campaigning organisation; or influence voters in any election or referendum. The second is an activity that (or to the extent that) a reasonable person might consider it as benefitting only the members of a particular body or the employees of a particular employer.

The second factor which limits the flexibility of the community interest test is that the Regulator is made the arbiter of what a reasonable person might consider to be a activity carried on for the benefit of the community (subject to appeal).

(b) Asset Lock

The Asset Lock is designed to ensure that the assets of the CIC (including any profits or other surpluses generated by its activities) are used for the benefit of the community. Nevertheless, the CIC is allowed (and expected) to use its assets for normal trading, or for other business activities, and it may also mortgage them to raise loan finance. The combined effect of these two principles is that its assets must either be retained within the CIC to be used for the community purposes for which it was formed, or, if they are transferred out of the CIC, the transfer must satisfy one of the following requirements:

  (i) It is made for full market value so that the CIC retains the value of the assets transferred;
 (ii) It is made to another asset-locked body (a CIC or charity, a registered society or non-UK based equivalent) with the consent of the Regulator or which has already been identified in the CIC's Articles of Association; or
(iii) It is made for the benefit of the community.

CICs are also able to adopt asset lock rules that impose more stringent requirements (again, the idea is to help it to attract philanthropic investment), provided they also include these basic provisions.

(c) Limitations on Distributions to Members

As we saw above, a CIC does not have to be non-profit making, but limits are imposed on distributions it may make to its members. The first of these is that, although it may give itself the power to distribute profits to members by way of dividend, the level of dividends is capped at a level designed to ensure that at least 65 per cent of the CICs profits are reinvested back into the company or used for the

---

[113] Unless they can 'reasonably be regarded as' incidental to non-political activities. Charities are also prohibited from carrying out political activities (defined in essentially similar terms).

community it was set up to serve. The second is that the members are not allowed to dissolve the company and distribute its surplus assets between themselves, as the members in a limited liability company are allowed to do. If the company is dissolved and there are surplus assets left after paying off all creditors, the surplus must be transferred to another CIC (or other kind of asset-locked entity) with a similar purpose.

8.28 Community Benefit Societies

A community benefit society is a legal entity set up under the Co-operative and Community Benefit Societies Act 2014. It is a form of mutual body, run and managed by its members, which conducts its business for the benefit of the community, rather than for the benefit of members (as with co-operatives) or shareholders (as with companies).

Specifically, the 2014 Act requires a community benefit society to 'carry on a business, industry or trade' that is 'being, or intended to be, conducted for the benefit of the community', and also requires it to be registered with the Financial Conduct Authority (FCA). The FCA has issued detailed guidance on what it considers to be the four key characteristics of a community benefit society, and which it will require a proposed society to demonstrate before it can be registered. These are:

(a) Purpose

The conduct of a community benefit society's business must be entirely for the benefit of the community. There can be no alternative or secondary purposes, including any that may preferentially benefit the members.

(b) Membership

Community benefit societies should normally be run democratically on the basis of one member–one vote.

(c) Application of Profits

Any profit made by a community benefit society must be used for the benefit of the community. Unlike in a co-operative society,[114] or a community interest company, profits cannot be distributed to members.

(d) Use of Assets

Community benefit societies must only use their assets for the benefit of the community. If a community benefit society is sold, converted, or amalgamated with

---

[114] A co-operative can choose to take the legal form of a community benefit society: if it does, it must satisfy the requirements for registration as such.

another legal entity, its assets must continue to be used for the benefit of the community and must not be distributed to members. Subject to this, it does not have to have an asset lock, but it may adopt one if it wants (to encourage investors), and if it does, it is irrevocable.[115]

PART VI THE PUBLIC AND THE STATE

8.29 The Public as Property Interest Holder

We need to distinguish between *public* property interests, which are property interests vested in us all, as members of the public, and *state* property interests, which are property interests held by the state and by other public authorities. 'The public' is no more a legal entity than is a community, but nevertheless it holds property interests directly, without an intervening corporation or trustee or other kind of private or public body as formal title holder. Like communal property rights, public property rights necessarily involve shared resource use, and like a community (only to a lesser extent) 'the public' does sometimes evolve its own informal rules and conventions regulating how individual members of the public share use of the resource.[116] These informal rules and conventions may well supplement and/or modify formal regulations made by a public authority, such as local authority bye-laws regulating the use of a public park owned by the local authority.

A public property interest gives every member of the public a Hohfeldian *right* of access to a particular resource, as opposed to what Hohfeld would have called a mere liberty or freedom to use it. In other words, each member of the public has a right not to be excluded from the resource, although necessarily subject to regulation as to how and when the right can be exercised so that it can be exercised in common with the like right of every other member of the public. So, for example, if there is a public right to use the beach for recreation (a contentious issue in England and Wales, as we see in Chapter 7 *Objects of Property Interests* para. 7.23(c)), both you and I have a legally protected right (exercisable in common with each other and with every other member of the public) to use the beach for recreational purposes whenever we want. The owner of the beach may have statutory powers to regulate our use of it, and so too may the local authority or some other public authority. However, except when acting lawfully under those powers, they are not entitled to interfere with our exercise of our public right in any way.

Public property rights are generally non-possessory land use rights, exercisable over land which is privately owned or owned by the state or another public authority. They include rights to use land in a particular way – for example, rights to roam over public access land, rights of way over public footpaths and highways, or

---

[115] See the *Explanatory Memorandum* to the Community Benefit Societies (Restriction on Use of Assets) Regulations 2006.

[116] Consider how a collection of strangers share use of a public beach, or the conventions about when it is acceptable to sit on a public bench.

rights of navigation – and also rights to 'capture' a previously unowned resource (perhaps catching fish or abstracting water) from someone else's land.

8.30 The State and Other Public Authorities as Property Interest Holders

State property, on the other hand is property held by the state – which in England and Wales might mean the Crown, or a national or local government department, or any other public authority. The state (including for these purposes the Crown and other public authorities) may hold a property interest in land for a variety of different purposes and functions. These include property holdings of national monuments and other resources which are regarded as part of our national heritage or of national strategic importance (and here we could perhaps include the sea bed and foreshore and other areas of land held by the Crown or for military purposes), property holdings of land and other resources for administrative purposes and/or for carrying out the public functions of the specific state body holding the property interest, and property interests held to make the land available for direct use by citizens in some specified way (for example as a public park or library or leisure centre).

8.31 State Property Held on Public Trust?

There are interesting differences between our somewhat incoherent notions of state property and the highly systematised concepts of state (more usually referred to as public) property in most continental Europe systems, which we are not able to pursue here.[117] However, it is worth noting that in this jurisdiction the precise basis on which the state holds property has always been contentious. In *Blundell* v. *Catterall*,[118] in a decision concerning the public rights to use the foreshore which we look at in Chapter 7 *Objects of Property Interests* para. 7.23, Best J suggested that land held by the Crown was subject to a public trust for the benefit of all citizens:

> from the general nature of this property, it could never be used for exclusive occupation. It was holden by the King, like the sea and the highways, for all his subjects. The soil could only be transferred, subject to this public trust; and general usage shews that the public rights has been excepted out of the grant of the soil . . .[119]

This idea of land held by the state being held on public trust for the benefit of the public has been picked up and developed by the courts in the USA (particularly in relation to public rights of access to the beach) and elsewhere (on broader grounds),[120]

---

[117] For a very good account see Giorgio Resta, 'Systems of public ownership', in Michele Graziadei and Lionel Smith (eds.), *Comparative Property Law: Global Perspectives* (Cheltenham and Northampton MA: Edward Elgar Publishing, 2017) p. 216.

[118] *Blundell* v. *Catterall* 106 ER 1190 (1821).

[119] Best CJ in *Blundell* v. *Catterall* 106 ER 1190 (1821) at p. 287.

[120] For a good account see Christine Willmore, 'Constructing 'public land': The role of 'publicly' owned land in the delivery of public policy objectives' (2005) 16 *Stellenbosch Law Review* 378.

but has not gained much traction in England and Wales. In *R (on the application of Newhaven Port and Properties Ltd)* v. *East Sussex County Council* [2015] UKSC 276, however, after reviewing the US cases on the development of the public trust doctrine as it relates to rights in the beach, Lord Carnwath said:

> [This US] development of the law ... is of particular interest as an illustration of how the law in this country might have developed (and might yet develop) if the view of Best J had prevailed over that of the majority.[121]

This judicial comment and the modern expansion of the public trust doctrine in other jurisdictions as a mechanism for subjecting the state to a fiduciary duty of environmental protection, have prompted commentators in this jurisdiction to consider whether there is still scope of develop a public trust doctrine of a sort in English law.[122]

At present, however, it seems that we are a long way from that position except, perhaps, in relation to Crown land. The notion that Crown land may be held for the public benefit gets some support from comments made by Lord Neuberger in *Lynn Shellfish Ltd* v. *Loose* [2016] UKSC 14, a case we considered in Chapter 7 *Objects of Property Interests* para. 7.24. One of the issues in *Lynn Shellfish* was whether private fishing rights had been acquired by prescription (i.e. long use) over foreshore land owned by the Crown. Lord Neuberger accepted an argument that there was a presumption against the acquisition of private rights by prescription over Crown land, analogous to the established rule of construction that grants of private rights over Crown land should be construed narrowly. The justification of that rule of construction, he pointed out, is that 'the prerogatives ... of the Crown *being conferred upon it for great purposes, and for the public use*, it shall not be intended that such prerogatives ... are diminished by any grant, beyond what such grant by necessary and unavoidable construction shall take away'. And that justification of the rule of construction, he said:

> can ... properly be prayed in aid by the Crown in relation to a claim based on prescription, and therefore by the appellants in this case. It appears to us that that basic principle is that a court should not be too easily persuaded that the Crown has been deprived of a property or a right, *given that the property or right is held for the public good*.[123]

However, there are historical reasons why, even if Crown land is held for the public good, the same may not necessarily apply to property interests held by other state bodies.[124]

---

[121] *R (on the application of Newhaven Port and Properties Ltd)* v. *East Sussex County Council* [2015] UKSC 276 at para. 130.

[122] See, for example, Anne Richardson Oakes, 'Judicial resources and the public trust doctrine: A powerful tool of environmental protection' [2018] *Transnational Environmental Law* 469, concluding, however, that the answer is probably no.

[123] Lord Neuberger in *Lynn Shellfish Ltd* v. *Loose* [2016] UKSC 14, paras. 51 and 52.

[124] Oakes, 'Judicial resources and the public trust doctrine', fn. 122 above, at pp. 486–488.

PART VII FLUIDITY IN THE PERSON–OBJECT DISTINCTION: PEOPLE, ANIMALS, TREES, NATURE, THE ENVIRONMENT

8.32 Subjects or Objects of Property Interests?

As Margaret Davies points out, the dividing line between holders of property interests (the subjects of property) and things in which property rights are held (the objects of property rights) is not static.[125]

One aspect of this is that, if we accept something like Margaret Radin's personhood perspective,[126] there is no clear dividing line between 'me' and 'mine': as she argues, we can form a special bond with things which started out as being external objects of our property interests, so that we come to regard our personhood as invested in them. In a famous passage from his major work *The Principles of Psychology*,[127] much quoted by property theorists, William James emphasised this essential fluidity between 'me' and 'mine':

> *The Empirical Self or Me.*
> The Empirical Self of each of us is all that he is tempted to call by the name of me. But it is clear that between what a man calls me and what he simply calls mine the line is difficult to draw. We feel and act about certain things that are ours very much as we feel and act about ourselves. Our fame, our children, the work of our hands, may be as dear to us as our bodies are, and arouse the same feelings and the same acts of reprisal if attacked. And our bodies themselves, are they simply ours, or are they us? . . . We see then that we are dealing with a fluctuating material. The same object being sometimes treated as a part of me, at other times as simply mine, and then again as if I had nothing to do with it at all. In its widest possible sense, however, a man's Self is the sum total of all that he can call his, not only his body and his psychic powers, but his clothes and his house, his wife and children, his ancestors and friends, his reputation and works, his lands and horses, and yacht and bank-account . . .[128]

However, the fluidity of the person–object distinction becomes even more apparent when we remind ourselves that, at various times in human history some humans have, as Davies puts it, 'fallen on the wrong side of the subject/object divide',[129] whilst some non-human objects have been treated as property interest holders in themselves. We look at these phenomena in the following paragraphs.

8.33 People as Property: Slavery

Although women and children have often, at various times in various cultures, been treated as the property of their husbands and fathers to some extent, it is slaves who

---

[125] Davies, *Property: Meanings, Histories, Theories*, fn. 7 above, p. 76.

[126] Chapter 7 *Objects of Property Interests* para. 7.10.

[127] William James, *The Principles Of Psychology* (New York: Henry Holt & Co., 1890).

[128] Ibid. pp. 291–292, and see also Davies, *Property: Meanings, Histories, Theories*, fn. 7 above, pp. 75–82 and Margaret Radin, *Reinterpreting Property* (Chicago and London: University of Chicago Press, 1993) at pp. 8–10.

[129] Davies, *Property: Meanings, Histories, Theories*, fn. 7 above, p. 76.

are by definition people who are owned by other people. This ought to be of historic interest only, but it is not. Although slavery is thought to be now illegal in all states recognised in international law, there are estimated to be between 24 million and 40 million slaves in the world now, depending on the definition of slavery adopted.

The legal definition of slavery in international law has been contested throughout the twentieth and twenty-first centuries, but for present purposes the significant point is that at its core, slavery is defined in terms of ownership: it is 'the status or condition of a person over whom any or all of the powers attaching to the rights of ownership are exercised'.[130] In 1956 it was accepted that other forms of servitude – specifically, 'debt-bondage, serfdom, servile marriage and child trafficking' – should be treated as analogous to slavery in this core sense,[131] but it seems that this too was on the basis that these forms of exploitation involved elements of being treated as if owned by another person.[132] In what Jean Allain describes as 'the most authoritative pronouncement of what constitutes those powers attaching to a right of ownership',[133] the UN Secretary General described them in 1953 in the following way:

1. the individual of servile status may be made the object of a purchase;

2. the master may use the individual of servile status, and in particular his capacity to work, in an absolute manner, without any restriction other than that which might be expressly provided by law;

3. the products of labour of the individual of servile status become the property of the master without any compensation commensurate to the value of the labour;

4. the ownership of the individual of servile status can be transferred to another person;

5. the servile status is permanent, that is to say, it cannot be terminated by the will of the individual subject to it;

6. the servile status is transmitted *ipso facto* to descendants of the individual having such status.[134]

In other words, ownership of a slave falls neatly into Honoré's 'liberal conception of ownership', which we considered in Chapter 5 *Ownership and Other Property Interests*.

8.34 Objects of Property Reconceptualised as Entities Holding Rights in Themselves

There are long-standing debates about treating animals as legal entities in their own right, in the sense of holding rights in respect of themselves, which not only operate

---

[130] Article 1(1) of the 1926 Slavery Convention of the League of Nations.

[131] UN Supplementary Convention on the Abolition of Slavery, the Slave Trade, and Institutions and Practices Similar to Slavery (1956), and see Jean Allain, in Jean Allain (ed.), *The Legal Understanding of Slavery: From the Historical to the Contemporary* (Oxford: Oxford University Press, 2012) Ch. 11.

[132] United Nations Economic and Social Council, *Slavery, the Slave Trade, and Other Forms of Servitude* (Report of the Secretary-General), UN Doc. E/2357, 27 January 1953, p. 28.

[133] Allain, *Legal Understanding of Slavery*, fn. 131 above, p. 209.

[134] United Nations, *Slavery*, fn. 132 above, p. 28.

in an exclusionary way as against humans (i.e. humans have a Hohfeldian duty not to interfere with the right), but also impose positive obligations on humans to respect, protect and fulfil the right.[135] Such rights have been recognised in the past in respect of cultural objects,[136] and more recently arguments have been put that such rights ought to be recognised in respect of objects such as trees, rivers, and the environment as a whole.

These arguments have emerged because of dissatisfaction with pre-existing means by which private citizens (individuals, communities and non-state bodies) can prevent others from causing (or failing to avert) environmental harm. In most western legal systems, we as private citizens have no power to prevent actions or omissions which we fear will damage the environment unless we can show that we have legal standing to object. In this jurisdiction, as we see in Chapter 10 *Limitations on Property*, this means that we can only bring a private action against someone who we believe is causing (or failing to prevent) environmental harm if we can show either that the defendant owed us a duty of care, and in breach of that duty negligently caused damage to our property or injury to our person, or that the activities constitute a private nuisance (i.e. infringe the rights we have to the reasonable use and enjoyment of our own land) or that they constitute a public nuisance (a common injury to the community/public at large) and caused us special injury over and above that suffered by the public/community in general.

In other words, as private individuals we may be able to obtain redress from someone whose acts or omissions harm the environment, but only if, and to the extent that, they also damage our property or cause us physical or (exceptionally) mental or psychiatric injury.

It is argued that private individuals also have a human right 'to the environment', meaning something like a fundamental right to an environment adequate for their health and well-being.[137] Something like this right is recognised in some national constitutions, and also, arguably in international law.[138] However, even if it can be established that such a right is recognised in international law and/or in regional human rights instruments, and even if it can be seen as a right held by individuals on behalf of themselves and future generations, it is necessarily anthropocentric. In other words, it is concerned only with safeguarding the environment *for the benefit of humans*, not for its own sake. A better approach, so it is argued, is to recognise an environmentally threatened resource as an independent legal person, holding

---

[135] Out of a vast literature, see for example Christine M. Korsgaard, 'Kantian ethics, animals, and the law' (2013) 33 *Oxford Journal of Legal Studies* 529 and Alexia Slater, 'Should chimpanzees have standing? The case for pursuing legal personhood for non-human animals' (2017) 6 *Transnational Environmental Law* 485.

[136] The example usually given is the decision of the Privy Council in *Mullick* v. *Mullick* (1925) LR LII Indian Appeals 245, treating an idol as a legal entity, noted in P. W. Duff, 'The personality of an idol' (1927) 3 *Cambridge Law Journal* 42.

[137] For details see Susana Borràs, 'New transitions from human rights to the environment to the rights of nature' (2016) 5 *Transnational Environmental Law* 113.

[138] Ibid. pp. 124–126.

fundamental rights which human beings have the authority and responsibility to enforce on behalf of the resource.

As Catherine Magallanes points out,[139] this has already been accepted in a few countries in relation to specific rivers, including in New Zealand in relation to the Whanganui River. As she explains, control over the river had long been disputed between the Crown and the Whanganui Maori tribes, through whose ancient territories the river flows. As part of the NZ government's programme of settlement of Maori historical grievances (which the government has been pursuing since the 1980s) settlement was reached about the Whanganui River in 2014, and enacted in 2017 as the Te Awa Tupua (Whanganui River Claims Settlement) Act 2017. This Act gave the river a name (Te Awa Tupua) and made it a legal person, with 'all the rights, powers and liabilities of a legal person'. It also vested ownership of the river bed in the new legal person, recognised the Whanganui Maori tribes' 'inalienable connection' to and responsibility for the well-being of the river and provided for the appointment of legal guardians (one representative of the government and the other chosen by the Maori tribes) 'to promote and protect the health and well-being of the river' and speak and act in its name.[140]

Meanwhile, however, others have argued that nature itself should be recognised as a holder of rights. Susana Borràs explains why, in her view, this is necessary and desirable:[141]

> Firstly, the protection of the environment through a human right to an adequate environment, rather than through protective rules, has had no discernible positive impact on the conservation of natural resources. Secondly, protection of the environment is not really an individual right but an unenforceable programmatic norm. A new approach is emerging, however: the recognition of the rights of nature, which implies a holistic approach to all life and all ecosystems. In recent years, a series of normative precedents have surfaced, which recognize that nature has certain rights as a legal subject and holder of rights. These precedents potentially contribute not merely a greater sensitivity to the environment, but a thorough reorientation about how to protect the Earth as the centre of life. From this perspective, known as 'biocentrism', nature is not an object of protection but a subject with fundamental rights, such as the rights to exist, to survive, and to persist and regenerate vital cycles. The implication of this recognition is that human beings have the legal authority and responsibility to enforce these rights on behalf of nature in that rights of nature become an essential element for the sustainability and the survivability of human societies. This concept is based on the recognition that humans, as but one part of life on earth, must live within their ecological limits rather than see themselves as the purpose of environmental

---

[139] Catherine Magallanes, 'From rights to responsibilities using legal personhood and guardianship for rivers' in B. Martin, L. Te Aho and M. Humphries-Kil (eds.), *Responsibility: Law and Governance for Living Well with the Earth* (London: Routledge, 2019) at p. 216.

[140] See also Christopher Rodgers, 'A new approach to protecting ecosystems: The Te Awa Tupua (Whanganui River Claims Settlement) Act 2017' [2017] *Environmental Law Review* 266, and (more generally) Thijs Etty, Heyvaert Veerle, Cinnamon Carlarne, Dan Farber, Bruce Huber and Jolene Lin, 'The emergence of new rights and new modes of adjudication in transnational environmental law' (2016) 5 *Transnational Environmental Law* 1.

[141] Borràs, 'New transitions', fn. 137 above, at p. 114.

protection, as the 'anthropocentric' approach proposes. Humans are trustees of the Earth rather than being mere stewards. The idea is based on the proposition that ecosystems of air, water, land, and atmosphere are a public trust and should be preserved and protected as habitat for all natural beings and natural communities.

Leaving aside arguments as to whether it is conceptually coherent to regard non-humans as having 'rights' at all, it is worth considering why we might want to categorise these rights as property rights. A possible objection is that property is essentially a tripartite arrangement involving a rights holder, an object of the right, and a person against whom the right is exercisable. If the rights-holder (the subject of the property right) and the thing in which the rights are held (the object of the property right) are the same person, it may well make sense to describe that person as having a *right* as against a third party, but, so the argument goes, it subverts the notion of property to describe that right as a property right. There are two feasible responses to that kind of objection. The first is that similar objections have been dismissed in relation to the notion of people having property rights in their own bodies (as opposed to in parts of their bodies which have become detached), as we saw in Chapter 7 *Objects of Property Interests*. So, we can say that in our jurisdiction the notion that subject and object of a property right may be the same has already been accepted. The second response is that the tripartite notion of property is arguably confined to western property rights systems. As we see in Chapter 9 *Multiple Property Rights Systems*, some indigenous peoples regard the relationships that they have with the resources they utilise as one of obligation towards the resource itself. It has a tripartite aspect, in that a part of the obligation is to protect the resource against interventions by third persons, but its essential core is obligation by a person to a thing. The reasons why western systems nevertheless now categorise such relationships as property relations is apparent from the cases we look at in Chapter 9: in all legal systems that recognise the institution of property, property rights tend to trump any other kinds of rights that people have in respect of things. So, if rights of nature, or rights of personhood conferred on resources hitherto regarded as objects of property rights, are to be effective at all, they have to have the status of property rights if they are not to be subordinated to the private property rights of individuals in the same resources.

RECOMMENDED READING

Most of the topics in this chapter are covered here in outline only. As you can see from the text, some of them are followed up in more detail in other chapters, but others are not. If you are interested in finding out more about the topics which are not, such as those in Part VII of this chapter, a useful starting point would be the literature cited in the footnotes. The following readings should also help to fill out the details.

Margaret Davies, *Property: Meanings, Histories, Theories* (Abingdon: Routledge-Cavendish, 2007) pp. 51–55 and 61–66.

Roger Smith, *Plural Ownership* (Oxford: Oxford University Press, 2005) Ch. 5 (on abolition of joint tenancies).

Jones v. *Kernott* [2011] UKSC paras. 18–22 (on presumption of joint tenancy).

Rodway v. *Landy* [2001] Ch 703 (occupation of co-owned property – on s. 13).

Simon Gardner, 'Material relief between co-habitants 1: Liquidating beneficial interests other than by sale' [2014] 78 *Conveyancer and Property Lawyer* 93 (what happens when co-owners no longer want to live together – on s. 13 Trusts of Land and Appointment of Trustees Act 1996).

Martin Dixon, 'To sell or not to sell: that is the question – The irony of the Trusts of Land and Appointment of Trustees Act 1996' [2011] 70 *Cambridge Law Journal* 579.

Bronwen Morgan, 'Telling stories beautifully: Hybrid legal forms in the new economy' (2018) 45 *Journal of Law and Society* 64.

Alison Clarke, 'Property, human rights and communities' in Xu Ting and Jean Allein (eds.), *Property and Human Rights in a Global Context* (Oxford and Portland, OR: Hart Publishing, 2015) (on different kinds of locality community, and the difference between determinate and indeterminate communities).

Susana Borràs, 'New transitions from human rights to the environment to the rights of nature' (2016) 5 *Transnational Environmental Law* 113.

Questions

(1) Should we abolish the joint tenancy? Do the remarks made by Lady Hale and Lord Walker in *Jones* v. *Kernott* about the presumption of joint tenancy have any bearing on this?

(2) What happens when co-owners no longer want to share occupation of the co-owned property?

(3) In the cases noted in para. 8.14 of this chapter (ending co-ownership against the will of one of the co-owners), how far do the courts adopt the personhood approach advocated by Margaret Radin? Consider whether they should do so.

(4) Discuss the difference between co-owners and communities as property interest holders.

(5) Explain how far it is possible for an unincorporated community to hold property interests in land in England and Wales, and the circumstances in which a community might choose instead to incorporate itself in order to hold property interests.

(6) Explain the difference between a community interest company, a community benefit society and a co-operative, and the circumstances in which a community might choose to incorporate itself as a community interest company or community benefit society rather than as a limited liability company under the Companies Act 2006.

(7) Discuss whether it is feasible and desirable for a property rights system to recognise an environmentally threatened resource as a property interest holder.

9

Multiple Property Rights Systems: Recognition of Indigenous Land Rights

PART I INTRODUCTION

9.1 Multiple Property Rights Systems Under the Same State Authority

The issues we are considering in this chapter are those arising where two or more different property rights systems co-exist (formally or informally) under the same state authority. More specifically, our central concern is with the issues arising where a foreign property system has been superimposed on a pre-existing property system in a particular state or geographic area, and with what this tells us about the nature and significance of property.

(a) Federal States

There are a number of reasons why more than one property rights system might exist within a single sovereign state in modern times. It may simply be that 'the state' is a federated union of separate regions or states each of which has its own property rights system, or a property rights system that differs in some respects from those in the other regions. After a long history of foreign invasions and cross-invasions, this is what we now have in the United Kingdom.[1] As we saw in Chapter 5 *Ownership and Other Property Interests*,[2] Scotland has a mixed civil law and common law property system which has always been radically different from the common law property systems of the rest of the United Kingdom. These common law property systems – that is, those operating in England, Wales and Northern Ireland – now have much more in common with each other, but there are also significant differences, particularly between Northern Ireland[3] on the one hand and England and Wales on the other, and there are also emerging differences between England and

---

[1] Foreign invaders who brought their own property rights systems to the British Isles, imposing them on the indigenous populations, included the Romans and the Normans; cross-invasions consisted largely of England trying to impose its own property rights systems on Scotland, Ireland and Wales. See Hugh Kearney, *The British Isles: A History of Four Nations* (2nd edn, Cambridge: Cambridge University Press, 2006).

[2] para. 5.6.

[3] For an account of Northern Ireland's present system as a product of its history and its complex relationships with England and the Irish Republic see John Wylie, *Irish Land Law* (5th edn, London: Bloomsbury Professional, 2013) Ch. 1.

Wales.[4] This kind of confederation of countries with different property systems raises interesting questions in itself, particularly when law-making powers are split between federal and regional authorities, as they are in the UK and in many other federal states, including the USA, Canada and Australia. However, we are not primarily concerned with these questions here, if only because in federal states each regional authority operates its own property rights system within its own territorial area.[5]

(b) Culturally Distinct Groups Within the Same Territory

Our focus instead is on the situation that arises when one group of people within a sovereign state (often ethnically or culturally distinct) does not have sovereignty or devolved powers over its own territory, but nevertheless habitually observes and regulates its land use, and the land use of its members, by its own property rights system, rather than by the state's dominant property rights system which is applied throughout the state by national or regional government institutions. In other words, the distinctive feature of the kind of situation we consider in this chapter is that two or more ethnically or culturally distinct groups live by different property rights systems in the same territory.

(c) Post-colonial States

A variety of different circumstances may have led to this kind of situation. Peoples of different ethnic, racial or cultural heritages who have different property rights systems may have been brought together under the same state authority by migration, or by the re-drawing of national boundaries, or more directly by conquest or settlement. In this chapter we are particularly interested in cases where different cultures have been brought together by conquest or settlement by what becomes the dominant culture: what happens to pre-existing property rights when a foreign state assumes sovereignty over territory which is already occupied by others, particularly when the foreign state's primary objective is to colonise the new territory? In some colonised states, as a matter of history, the pre-existing inhabitants and their cultures

---

[4] English property law was extended to Wales by the Laws in Wales Acts 1535–1542, and the two countries shared the same legal system from then until the Government of Wales Act 2006, which devolved powers to the Welsh National Assembly to make legislation for Wales in what are now twenty general subject areas (Schedule 5 of the 2006 Act as amended). As a result of the exercise of these powers, the English and Welsh property law systems are beginning to diverge, particularly in relation to housing (see, for example, The Renting Homes (Wales) Act 2016, implementing the Law Commission's recommendations in its 2013 report *Renting Homes in Wales* (Law Com No 337) and introducing a new rented housing regime for Wales, and the Abolition of the Right to Buy and Associated Rights (Wales) Act 2018, which abolishes in Wales the rights of tenants of social landlords to buy their homes), but also in other areas such as the protection of communal recreational rights: see further Chapter 13 *Non-Possessory Land Use Rights*, Part VI.

[5] As it happens, many of the regional states within the confederations of the USA, Canada and Australia also have their own pre-colonial indigenous populations of the kind we note in (c) below. Recognition of the traditional property rights systems of these pre-colonial indigenous peoples then becomes a matter for both the regional and the federal state.

were completely wiped out or assimilated by the colonisers. We are concerned with the states where they survived: what rights do the descendants of these original inhabitants – the indigenous peoples – now have, as against the state and other citizens, in respect of the resources they have traditionally regarded as theirs?

9.2 Indigenous Property Rights Systems in Post-colonial States

This has been a vexed question of international law throughout its history. International law is primarily concerned with the moral and political questions of when it is justifiable for a foreign state to colonise territory outside its national boundaries, and how, if it does so, it *ought* to deal with pre-existing property rights of those who already live there. This second question is now addressed in international law by the United Nations Declaration on the Rights of Indigenous Peoples 2007,[6] which provides a benchmark for how nation states are expected to treat their indigenous peoples. We look at the 2007 UN Declaration in Part V of this chapter, where we consider which groups it protects and why, and what protection it expects states to provide for their indigenous peoples in respect of their traditional lands and resources.

However, it order to appreciate the significance of the UN Declaration we look first at how indigenous land rights have been treated in domestic law by post-colonial states. We do this in Parts II–IV of this chapter, focussing on the position in Australia (Part II) and in Canada (Part III) and then, in Part IV, drawing on these two examples, considering some of the characteristics of indigenous property rights systems which distinguish them from the property rights systems of their colonisers, and how these differences have made recognition difficult.

9.3 Do All Colonised Peoples Have a Property Rights System?

Assuming for the moment that a coloniser *does* accept in principle that it is morally and legally bound to respect the pre-existing patterns of resource usages and practices of any indigenous people, what exactly does that involve when the indigenous population does not appear (to the colonising state) to have a property rights system at all, or to have one which is very different from the coloniser's own property rights system?

This raises two successive issues which we need to consider. The first brings us back to the basic question we first introduced in Chapter 1 *What Property Is and Why It Matters*: What is a property rights system? Is it something that all social groups necessarily have if they inhabit a geographic area and live off its resources? Or can we categorise some peoples' way of life as a life without property, accepting the views of John Locke and some of the other property theorists we looked at in Chapter 2 *Conceptions and Justifications*?[7] As we see in this chapter, many British

---

[6] United Nations Declaration on the Rights of Indigenous Peoples, UN GA Resolution 61/295 of 13 September 2007, UN Doc A/RES/47/1 (2007).

[7] As we saw in Chapter 2 *Conceptions and Justifications* para. 2.5(b), John Locke certainly regarded the indigenous inhabitants of North America as having no property rights in their land. The same must

colonists were greatly attracted to the Lockean concept of property, generally with disastrous social and political consequences for the people they found inhabiting the land they wished to settle.

In the particular examples we look at in this chapter, the coloniser (the British Government), initially took this view of the indigenous inhabitants of Australia although not (except to a limited extent) those of Canada.[8] The unequivocal position of their post-colonial successors (the present governments of Australia and Canada) is that this Lockean view of property rights of indigenous peoples is simply wrong, and that the indigenous peoples of their countries did indeed have their own property rights systems, although they were very different from the English common law systems which Britain regarded as the norm. However, this brings us to our second issue. If these indigenous societies and their traditional property rights systems still survive, and the governing state acknowledges its obligation to 'recognise' them, what exactly does that involve?

9.4 Recognition of Indigenous Property Rights Systems

The difficulty in recognising traditional indigenous property rights systems in situations such as these is that they can be very different from the property rights systems of the dominant culture. In Australia and Canada, as in many other parts of the world, the indigenous people's traditional property rights systems are customary and collective, and access to and control over land and other natural resources is largely dictated by status within the community. The dominant state property rights systems, on the other hand, are predominately private property systems geared towards an individualistic society and a market economy. This makes it difficult for both the dominant and the indigenous societies to 'read' each other's property rights systems, in ways we explore in Part IV of this chapter.

A further complication we move on to in Part IV is that 'recognition' in this context is not straightforward. Those claiming recognition of their traditional property rights systems are the surviving members of traditional communities whose property rights and practices were disrupted by colonisers. Does 'recognition' mean that individual members should be given private 'ownership' of the resources they claim are 'theirs'? Or is it that they or their community should be entitled to go on using them in the way they have always done, free from interference by the state and by outsiders? Or that the community is entitled to take charge of the resources it has

---

necessarily be true of anyone else committed to the proposition that it is only private ownership of land that qualifies as 'property' in land.

[8] This gives an over-generalised impression of a complex and fluid situation, persuasively presented in Stuart Banner, *Possessing the Pacific: Land, Settlers and Indigenous People from Australia to Alaska* (Cambridge, MA and London: Harvard University Press, 2007). Chs. 1, 2 (Australia) and 6 (British Columbia, Canada) of *Possessing the Pacific* are particularly relevant to the areas we concentrate on in this chapter. Banner also notes in Ch. 3 the position in New Zealand, where the British recognised at the outset that the Maori people were 'owners of all the land in New Zealand', whose property interests had to be acquired by purchase or treaty. For reasons Banner explains, and which we touch on in para. 9.22 (c) below, this made the Maori people no less vulnerable to exploitation than the indigenous peoples of Australia and Canada.

customarily used, deciding for itself how it will continue to use them? And if the last of these, does this mean recognising that the community has title to the whole of the geographic area covered by its traditional uses and practices, or recognising that it has sovereignty over it? In either case, what is to happen where that geographic area is also inhabited by people who have property rights under the dominant property rights system, or where the traditional indigenous property rights system involves management of resources in ways that conflict with the rules or policies underlying national or international regulation of resources,[9] or with moral or political values of the dominant culture?[10] We look at these issues in Part IV of the chapter.

9.5 Indigenous Peoples in Australia and Canada

In this chapter we will be looking at two specific examples – Australia in Part II of the chapter and Canada in Part III – focussing on what are generally regarded as the breakthrough court decisions in these two countries, the decision of the High Court of Australia in *Mabo* v. *Queensland (No 2)* (1992) 175 CLR 1 and the decision of the Supreme Court of Canada in *Tsilhqot'in Nation* v. *British Columbia* [2014] 2 SCR 256. Before doing so, there are some preliminary points to make.

(a) Terminology

Both 'indigenous' and 'aboriginal' are politically highly charged terms, as we see in Part V of this chapter. Originally, when used in relation to inhabitants of a locality, 'indigenous' meant native to that locality in the sense of originating there rather than from elsewhere, whereas 'aboriginal' meant the original inhabitants of that area, in the sense of the first occupants. However, on our current knowledge about the origins of the human species and the movement of human peoples, most, if not all, groups with long established connections to territory would have severe difficulties in proving they came within either of those categories. Nowadays, therefore, both terms tend to be used to mean the same thing: broadly, people who were inhabiting territory before it was colonised or settled by an incoming society, which has since become the dominant society. In Australia and Canada the term 'aboriginal' is generally used to describe their minority groups which fall within this category (generally written with a capital A). In other parts of the world, and at the international level, 'indigenous' is preferred, and indeed this is the term Australians and Canadians use when referring to indigenous people in general and to the indigenous inhabitants of other parts of the world.

---

[9] For a good example, see the implications of the EU ban on seal products for Inuit seal hunting communities in Arctic Canada and Greenland analysed by Sanna Elfving in 'The European Union's animal welfare policy and indigenous peoples' rights: The case of Inuit and seal hunting in Arctic Canada and Greenland', PhD thesis, University of Surrey (2015).

[10] For example, on the position of women or minorities, or democratic decision making, within the indigenous culture: see further para. 9.25 below.

(b) Differences Between Indigenous Peoples

Although in Part IV of this chapter we discuss what we refer to as distinctive character-istics of indigenous property rights systems, it is important to keep in mind that indigenous property rights systems worldwide can also be very different from each other. Amongst the indigenous peoples of the world (and even amongst those inhabit-ing the same nation state) there are groups with different ethnic origins, different languages, different histories and distinctive geographic conditions, all of which form the basis of distinctive cultures and distinctive patterns of resource use. For example, the claimants in *Mabo* v. *Queensland (No 2)* (1992) 175 CLR 1, the High Court of Australia decision we focus on in Part II of this chapter, were the Meriam people, inhabitants of the Murray Islands, just one of many Australian and Torres Strait aboriginal groups who lived in Australia at the time when European settlers arrived. The Meriam people lived in groups of huts along the foreshore of the Murray Islands and cultivated gardens. Unsurprisingly, their traditional patterns of resource use and management, and hence their property rights systems, were very different from, for example, those of the nomadic Rirratjingu, Gumatj and Djapu clans in the Gove Peninsula of Northern Territory in Australia, whose claims were unsuccessful in the earlier indigenous land rights case we note in Part II, *Milirrpum* v. *Nabalco Pty Ltd* (1971) 17 FLR 141. The range of indigenous cultures in Canada is even broader. There are three distinct groups of peoples who are regarded as indigenous to Canada and are recognised as Aboriginal peoples in the Canadian Constitution. These are the First Nations, who are the descendants of Indian tribes who ranged across the whole of North America; the Inuit,[11] who are the indigenous inhabitants of the Arctic regions of Canada, Alaska, Greenland and Russia; and the Métis, the descendants of marriages between European fur traders (mainly French or Scottish) and First Nations or Inuit women. From the early eighteenth century the Métis established their own communities along the fur trade routes in western and north-western Canada, developing their own distinctive cultures separate from both the European and the First Nations or Inuit communities.

The Canadian case we look at in Part III of this chapter, *Tsilhqot'in Nation* v. *British Columbia* [2014] 2 SCR 256, concerns the claims brought on behalf of just one of the First Nations peoples, the Tsilhqot'in nation. As we see in Part III, their traditional way of life is different from that of other First Nations, and different again from the traditional cultures and ways of life of peoples categorised as Inuit or as Métis, and again unsurprisingly, there are corresponding differences in their respect-ive property rights systems.

PART II INDIGENOUS LAND RIGHTS IN AUSTRALIA

9.6 Recognition of Native Title in Australia

The British colonised different parts of Australia by annexation at different times. Broadly, the effect of annexation was that the British Crown acquired sovereignty

---

[11] Sometimes referred to as 'Eskimoes', which is now regarded as a derogatory term.

over the territory annexed. The question we are concerned with here is the effect this had on the property rights of the people who lived in that territory before annexation. This question was finally resolved for the whole of Australia in 1992 by the High Court of Australia in *Mabo* v. *Queensland (No 2)*,[12] which decided that when any land which had settled inhabitants was annexed, the rights of the inhabitants under their own law continued until they were ended by the new sovereign authority. This meant, so the High Court decided, that the present members of the traditional communities which inhabited Australia before annexation still had these rights, unless the rights had since been extinguished by the Crown, or the members of the community had abandoned them by ceasing to acknowledge their traditional laws and observe their traditional customs, or had surrendered them to the Crown.

We look more closely at the decision in *Mabo (No 2)* in paras. 9.9–9.10, but first we need to look at what led up to it.

9.7 The *Terra Nullius* Doctrine

At the beginning of the twentieth century, the generally accepted view in international law was that sovereignty over foreign land could be acquired in one of three ways: by conquest (defeating the foreign state by war), cession (the governing authority in the foreign land ceding sovereignty to the 'conqueror' by treaty), or by discovering and settling land that was *terra nullius*. In principle, *terra nullius* meant uninhabited land, but a controversial 'enlarged' doctrine of *terra nullius* developed in international law, by which land was treated as *terra nullius* if it was inhabited by 'backward' people.[13] The consequence of the enlarged doctrine of *terra nullius* was that, if a foreign country colonised land that was inhabited but deemed to be *terra nullius*, the inhabitants were treated as having no pre-existing property rights in the land they inhabited and the resources they used and controlled. This was notoriously explained by Lord Sumner in the Privy Council in *In re Southern Rhodesia* [1919] AC 211:

> The estimation of the rights of aboriginal tribes is always inherently difficult. Some tribes are so low in the scale of social organisation that their usages and conceptions of rights and duties are not to be reconciled with the institutions or the legal ideas of civilized society. Such a gulf cannot be bridged. It would be idle to impute to such people some shadow of the rights known to our law and then to transmute it into the substance of transferable rights of property as we know them.[14]

Adopting this analysis and the expanded doctrine of *terra nullius*, a colonising state regarded itself as legally entitled to treat the colonised land and its resources as unowned if occupied 'only' by what it considered to be 'backward' people. On this analysis it could regard itself as acquiring full beneficial owner of the land and its resources on asserting sovereignty over the territory, not bound by pre-existing rights or interests of the indigenous populations who were living there.

---

[12] *Mabo* v. *Queensland (No 2)* (1992) 175 CLR 1.   [13] Ibid. paras. 33 and 34.
[14] *In re Southern Rhodesia* [1919] AC 211 at pp. 233–234.

This unsavoury doctrine, condemned by the International Court of Justice in International Court of Justice in its *Advisory Opinion on Western Sahara*,[15] is no longer accepted in international law. It was eventually denounced by the High Court of Australia in *Mabo (No 2)* as we see in para. 9.10 below, but not before it had led the Supreme Court of Northern Territory in *Milirrpum v. Nabalco Property Ltd* (1971) 17 FLR 141 to reject the claims of the indigenous people of the Gove Peninsula to property rights in their land.

9.8 *Milirrpum v. Nabalco Property Ltd* (1971) 17 FLR 141

This was the first case to reach the courts in which indigenous people in Australia claimed to have title to the lands they traditionally inhabited. The claimants in *Milirrpum*, the Rirratjingu clan, were part of a group of indigenous peoples who had traditionally inhabited the Gove Peninsula. They claimed that they had property rights in their land arising out of their traditional customary use of it. They brought this action claiming that the Government's grant of a 42 year mineral lease to Nabalco Property Ltd to mine bauxite and set up a township in their land was an unlawful interference with those rights. Their argument was that there was a common law doctrine of native title, by which the rights that indigenous people had under their traditional law in territory acquired by the Crown, to use and enjoy the land in the way they had traditionally used it, were property rights binding the Crown when it acquired sovereignty of the territory. Applying that doctrine, they argued, they had property rights in their land pre-colonisation which survived annexation of the land by the Crown and continued to be enforceable against the Crown and its subjects unless and until they were validly terminated by the Crown. Blackburn J rejected the argument. He decided that the common law doctrine of native title could not apply to a settled colony, and that he had to accept that Australia was a settled colony because earlier cases had proceeded on the basis that it was *terra nullius.* This meant that the question of whether the claimants' relationship with their land at the time of settlement could be regarded as proprietary did not arise. Nevertheless, he went on to consider it.

He decided that although the claimants' ancestors did indeed have a system of law (contrary to the contentions of the government), the rights they had under their law in relation to their land and their other resources could not be categorised as property rights because they were not the kind of rights that the common law recognised as property rights. In other words, he took the view that he had to apply common law property principles in order to decide whether indigenous people in a common law colony had property rights in their resources pre-colonisation. As we see below and in Part III of this chapter, this is an approach which has now been decisively rejected in Australia and in the rest of the common law world.

It is instructive for our purposes, however, to consider what it was about the relationship between the Gove Peninsula indigenous people and their land that

---

[15] *Advisory Opinion on Western Sahara* (1975) ICJR 39.

Blackburn considered to be inconsistent with the common law idea of property. As we see when we look at the question in more detail in Part IV below,[16] the Gove Peninsula indigenous people were, so Blackburn accepted, a 'community ... which made ritual and economic use' of the land they claimed was theirs. They lived nomadically and collectively, organised in interlocking groups known as clans and bands. They regarded the land as given to them by their spirit ancestors, and themselves as having an ongoing spiritual relationship with it. They maintained sacred sites on the land which were associated with specific clans within the community, and they performed rites there with the object of 'fructification and renewal of the fertility of the land'. They were multilingual but had no written culture, and so had no maps, no written documents and no written evidence of who had what rights in which resources. It was argued on behalf of the government that this of itself meant that they had no property rights, because oral evidence produced no consensus on precise relationships between particular people and particular things. Blackburn rejected this particular argument:

> It seems to me to amount to saying that if there is property in land, there must be either a written or pictorial means of discovering who is the owner of any particular piece of land (the function carried out by title-deeds or registers of title) or, if that is not possible among primitive people, then there must be a sufficient number of witnesses who can produce a register of title out of their memories; that is that an oral register of title must be repeated in full detail by each witness. In my opinion, the fallacy in this argument is the assumption that there cannot be rights of property without records or registers of title.[17]

Nevertheless, he concluded that the claimant, which was one of the clans, had failed to demonstrate that it had had property rights in the land at the time of European settlement. Echoing the *Ainsworth* test sometimes used in English law to establish whether an interest relating to a thing is a private property interest in it,[18] Blackburn said:

> I think that property, in its many forms, generally implies the right to use or enjoy, the right to exclude others, and the right to alienate. I do not say that all these rights must co-exist before there can be a proprietary interest, or deny that each of them may be subject to qualifications. But by this standard I do not think that I can characterize the relationship of the clan to the land as proprietary.[19]

As far as the right to use and enjoy was concerned, his objection was that the claimant was one of the clans, which had a largely spiritual link to the land: the indigenous group's economic use of the land was carried on in 'bands', which were ad hoc groupings of the same people who made up the clans.[20] As Blackburn said,

> It makes little sense to say that the clan has the right to use or enjoy the land. Its members have a right, and so do members of other clans, to use and enjoy the land of

---

[16] See paras. 9.19(b), 9.20(a) and 9.22.   [17] *Milirrpum v. Nabalco Pty Ltd* (1971) 17 FLR 141, at p. 272.
[18] See Chapter 6 *New Property Interests and the Numerus Clausus* para. 6.11.
[19] *Milirrpum*, fn. 17 above, p. 272.   [20] See further para. 9.19(b) below.

their own clan and other land also. The greatest extent to which it is true that the clan as such has the right to use and enjoy the clan territory is that the clan may, in a sense in which other clans may not (save with permission or under special rules), perform ritual ceremonies on the land. That the clan has a duty to the land – to care for it – is another matter. This is not without parallels in our law, which sometimes imposes duties of such a kind on a proprietor. But this resemblance is not, or at any rate is only in a very slight degree, an indication of a proprietary interest.[21]

The right to exclude suffered the same problem: the clans were a part of an overarching group comprising interrelated clans and bands, and it was hardly surprising that Blackburn found little evidence of some clans excluding other from tracts of land, as opposed to from specific sacred sites. The question of whether the group *as a whole* excluded outsiders was put to one side, because the claimant was a clan, not the group as a whole.

Since, in addition, the claimants themselves expressly repudiated the right to alienate the land (also unsurprisingly, given that what they were claiming were intergenerational communal property rights rather than private individual property rights), Blackburn, equally unsurprisingly, concluded that their rights could not be property rights:

> In my opinion, therefore, there is so little resemblance between property, as our law, or what I know of any other law, understands that term, and the claims of the plaintiffs for their clans, that I must hold that these claims are not in the nature of proprietary interests.[22]

9.9 *Mabo* v. *Queensland (No 2)*

In *Mabo (No 2)* the High Court of Australia decided that Blackburn J was wrong on all points in *Milirrpum*. The High Court decided, in effect, that the common law doctrine of native title applied throughout Australia, and, properly understood, its effect was that on annexation, the Crown acquired only a radical title to the land, subject to the traditional rights of its indigenous inhabitants, which remained fully enforceable against the Crown and the rest of the world unless and until extinguished by the government, or surrendered or abandoned by the indigenous inhabitants.

As noted in para. 9.5(b) above, the indigenous people who were the claimants in *Mabo (No 2)* had a traditional way of life which was different from that of the claimants in *Milirrpum*. The claimants in *Mabo (No 2)* were the Meriam people who inhabited the Murray Islands. Like the Gove Peninsula indigenous peoples, they lived in highly organised communal groups, living off the resources of the land and the sea, and they regarded themselves as bound by a close spiritual relationship with

---

[21] *Milirrpum*, fn. 17 above, p. 272.

[22] Ibid. p. 273. See Sharon Mascher, 'The Australian approach to recognising the land rights of indigenous peoples: The Native Title Act 1993' in Nigel Bankes and Timo Koivurova, *The Proposed Nordic Saami Convention: National and International Dimensions of Indigenous Property Rights* (Oxford and Portland, OR: Hart Publishing, 2013) p. 323.

the land and its resources, and as collective owners and stewards of their territory. However, unlike the Gove Peninsula indigenous inhabitants, they lived in groups of huts along the foreshore of the Murray Islands and cultivated gardens, not just to produce food but also as part of traditional ritual and ceremonial practices.[23] So, in some ways it was easier for European settlers to see them as people with property rights in their land.

However, the High Court declined to make this distinction between different kinds of traditional indigenous land use practices. Instead, it laid down principles requiring recognition of the traditional land use practices of all indigenous peoples in Australia.

9.10 What the High Court Decided in *Mabo (No 2)*

(a) Terra Nullius

The High Court held that, as matter of law, no inhabited land can be *terra nullius*. Brennan J, giving the majority judgment, described the enlarged doctrine of *terra nullius* as having a basis which 'is false in fact and unacceptable in our society', and depending on 'a discriminatory denigration of indigenous inhabitants, their social organization and customs'.[24] He repudiated the idea accepted in *In re Southern Rhodesia* [1919] AC 211 that some indigenous people may be 'so low in the scale of social organization' that it is 'idle to impute to such people some shadow of the rights known to our law', and emphasised that 'it is imperative in today's world that the common law should neither be nor be seen to be frozen in an age of racial discrimination'.[25]

(b) Effect of Colonisation of Inhabited Land

If the enlarged doctrine of *terra nullius* was correct, it would have followed that when the Crown asserted sovereignty over Australia it would have acquired the absolute beneficial ownership of all the land, extinguishing all pre-existing rights, and thereafter all property rights in land in Australia could only be derived from the Crown. This was not only wrong, Brennan J said, it was also not in conformity with Australian history:

> The dispossession of the indigenous inhabitants of Australia was not worked by a transfer of beneficial ownership when sovereignty was acquired by the Crown, but by the recurrent exercise of a paramount power to exclude the indigenous inhabitants from their traditional lands as colonial settlement expanded and land was granted to the colonists. Dispossession is attributable not to a failure of native title to survive the acquisition of sovereignty, but to its subsequent extinction by a paramount power.[26]

---

[23] For further details see para. 9.20(a) below.   [24] Brenan J in *Mabo (No 2)*, fn. 12 above, at para. 39.
[25] Ibid. para. 41, rejecting the analysis of the Privy Council in *In re Southern Rhodesia* [1919] AC 211 at pp. 233–234.
[26] *Mabo (No 2)* , fn. 12 above, para. 63.

Rejecting the enlarged doctrine of *terra nullius*, the High Court accepted that the correct analysis was that on assertion of sovereignty, the Crown acquired only a 'radical title' to the land, resembling Crown ownership of land in the modern law of England and Wales,[27] encumbered by the 'native title' of its pre-existing indigenous populations.

(c) Content of Native Title

The High Court in *Mabo (No 2)* emphasised that the rights of the pre-existing indigenous peoples which continued following the Crown's acquisition of sovereignty were not to be ascertained by reference to common law notions of property. 'Native title' is not to be compared to any common law property interest, and its content is dictated by the traditional laws of the indigenous community in question – in other words, it will vary from community to community. As Brennan said in a crucial passage:

> Native title has its origin in and is given its content by the traditional laws acknowledged by and the traditional customs observed by the indigenous inhabitants of a territory. The nature and incidents of native title must be ascertained as a matter of fact by reference to those laws and customs.[28]

Subject to that, he said, it is not alienable but can be surrendered or sold to the Crown.[29] In addition, it can be abandoned by the indigenous group, and, according to Brennan J, this will happen if the group ceases to acknowledge and observe its traditional laws:

> Where a clan or group has continued to acknowledge the laws and (so far as practicable) to observe the customs based on the traditions of that clan or group, whereby their traditional connexion with the land has been substantially maintained, the traditional community title of that clan or group can be said to remain in existence. The common law can, by reference to the traditional laws and customs of an indigenous people, identify and protect the native rights and interests to which they give rise. However, when the tide of history has washed away any real acknowledgment of traditional law and any real observance of traditional customs, the foundation of native title has disappeared. A native title which has ceased with the abandoning of laws and customs based on tradition cannot be revived for contemporary recognition. Australian law can protect the interests of members of an indigenous clan or group, whether communally or individually, only in conformity with the traditional laws and customs of the people to whom the clan or group belongs and only where members of the clan or group acknowledge those laws and observe those customs (so far as it is practicable to do so). Once traditional native title expires, the Crown's radical title expands to a full beneficial title, for then there is no other proprietor than the Crown.[30]

---

[27] As to which see further Chapter 5 *Ownership and Other Property Interests* para. 5.17.
[28] *Mabo (No 2)*, fn. 12 above, para. 64.   [29] Ibid. paras. 65 and 67.   [30] Ibid. para. 66.

Brennan J also acknowledged that the traditional laws and customs of the community (and therefore the content of their native title interest) might change over time:

> It is immaterial that the laws and customs have undergone some change since the Crown acquired sovereignty provided the general nature of the connection between the indigenous people and the land remains. Membership of the indigenous people depends on biological descent from the indigenous people and on mutual recognition of a particular person's membership by that person and by the elders or other persons enjoying traditional authority among those people.[31]

(d) Extinguishment

It followed from all this that if present members of the community could show that they still acknowledged and observed the traditional laws and customs acknowledged and observed by their ancestors at the time when the Crown acquired sovereignty, they remain entitled to the same communal, group and individual interests and rights their ancestors enjoyed under their own law, unless something has happened since then to extinguish those rights and interests. We saw in (c) above that they might have been lost by abandonment (by the community ceasing to acknowledge and observe their traditional laws and customs) or by surrender or sale to the Crown. The High Court held, however, that in addition they will have been lost if expressly extinguished by the Crown, or by the Crown impliedly granting inconsistent property rights over the same land to someone else 'by a valid exercise of sovereign power'. It was accepted that any such implied extinguishment would have been unlawful once the Racial Discrimination Act came into force in 1975, entitling the community to compensation.[32]

9.11 Post-*Mabo* Developments

As a response to the *Mabo (No 2)* decision, the Australian government enacted the Native Title Act 1993, which essentially put Brennan J's analysis into legislative form. The 1993 Act has since been much amended, and a significant body of caselaw has built up interpreting its provisions (mainly restrictively).

(a) Native Title Act 1993

The basic scheme of the 1993 Act is set out in s. 3, which provides the following:

> The main objects of this Act are:
>
> (a) to provide for the recognition and protection of native title; and
> (b) to establish ways in which future dealings affecting native title may proceed and to set standards for those dealings; and

---

[31] Ibid. para. 83(6) and see also para. 68.
[32] This was decided by a bare majority of 4–3: the minority took the view that it was unlawful even before 1975, and therefore compensation was payable for all past implied extinguishments.

(c) to establish a mechanism for determining claims to native title; and

(d) to provide for, or permit, the validation of past acts, and intermediate period acts, invalidated because of the existence of native title.

'Native title' is defined in s. 223, essentially as formulated by Brennan J in *Mabo (No 2)*:

223 Native title

(1) The expression native title or native title rights and interests means the communal, group or individual rights and interests of Aboriginal peoples or Torres Strait Islanders in relation to land or waters, where:

   (a) the rights and interests are possessed under the traditional laws acknowledged, and the traditional customs observed, by the Aboriginal peoples or Torres Strait Islanders; and

   (b) the Aboriginal peoples or Torres Strait Islanders, by those laws and customs, have a connection with the land or waters; and

   (c) the rights and interests are recognised by the common law of Australia.

(2) Without limiting subsection (1), rights and interests in that subsection includes hunting, gathering, or fishing, rights and interests.

Section 10 of the Act then provides that 'Native title is recognised, and protected, in accordance with this Act', and s. 13 introduces a procedure whereby people claiming native title may apply to the Federal Court for a determination of native title in relation to a specified area. The legislation requires a determination of native title to be very detailed. By s. 225, it must determine the people or groups who hold the rights comprising the native title and also 'the nature and extent of the native title rights and interests in relation to the determination area' and also the nature and extent of 'any other interests' in the relevant land and their relationship to the native title rights and interests. In addition, it must determine whether the native title rights and interests 'confer possession, occupation, use and enjoyment of that land or waters on the native title holders to the exclusion of all others'.

Determination under these provisions is a slow process: when the Federal Court receives an application it refers it to the National Native Title Tribunal, where it is given a preliminary assessment. Notice is then given to people with an interest in the relevant area and the application goes back to the Tribunal for mediation. If that results in an agreement, the Federal Court can make a 'consent' determination of native title. If there is no agreement, the matter goes back to the Federal Court for a full trial.[33] Sharon Mascher records that between 1 January 1994 and 30 June 2011, 160 determinations went through the system, resulting in 119 determinations being made (covering, in total, about 20 per cent of the land in Australia) and 41 refused. The average time taken for a consent determination was found to have been 5 years 10 months, compared to 6 years 11 months for those that had to be determined by trial.[34] As at 31 December 2010 there were 458 native title applications still outstanding, of which 39 per cent had been filed before 1 January 2001.

---

[33] Mascher, 'Native Title Act 1993', fn. 22 above, pp. 332–333, and see also Australian Law Reform Committee, *Connection to Country: Review of the Native Title Act 1993* (2015).

[34] Mascher, 'Native Title Act 1993', fn. 22 above, p. 339.

These provisions, although long and detailed, take up only a relatively modest proportion of the Act. The rest deals with when and how native title can be extinguished or interfered with in the future, setting up 'future act' processes giving indigenous peoples the right to be informed about future activities which might infringe their rights, and the right to negotiate, and also making provision for indigenous groups to enter into negotiated Indigenous Land Use Agreements (ILUAs) with those proposing to carry out such activities. ILUAs have to be registered with the National Native Title Tribunal and when they are, their terms are binding on all parties.[35] Mascher also notes the huge cost of these 'future act' processes, and significant backlogs of applications.[36]

Finally, the 1993 Act as amended also contains detailed provisions about validation of past infringements and payment of compensation.

(b) Criticisms of the Legislation and its Interpretation by the Courts

The legislation, and the way it has been interpreted by the courts, has been heavily criticised as failing to provide for indigenous people the respect and protection for their rights intended by the High Court in *Mabo (No 2)*. These include criticisms that the legislation requires the Court and the Tribunal to particularise the rights that native title confers on the indigenous group in any particular case, often in common law terms (rights to hunt, fish, etc.), despite the insistence in *Mabo (No 2)* that the content of native title was to be determined by reference to the group's own idiosyncratic laws and customs. This, so it is argued, leads to a fragmented view of the overall relationship the people have with their land. For example, it does not take into account their relationship of responsibility and stewardship towards their land, or notions of overall control of the land and its resources.[37] As Gleeson CJ said in *Western Australia* v. *Ward*:[38]

> The difficulty of expressing a relationship between a community or group of Aboriginal people and the land in terms of rights and interests is evident. Yet that is required by the NTA. The spiritual or religious is translated into the legal. This requires a fragmentation of an integrated view of the ordering of affairs into rights and interests which are considered apart from the duties and obligation which go with them.

Another major criticism is that the courts have interpreted the legislation as imposing a heavy burden on claimants to prove 'continuity', that is, to prove a continuous connection between their community and the land dating back to pre-sovereignty

---

[35] Mascher records that during the same period 497 ILUAs were registered, covering another 1.28 million square kilometres of land and foreshore: ibid. p. 339.

[36] Ibid. p. 340.

[37] Ibid. at pp. 343–350, summarising this and other arguments, and see further Brendan Edgeworth, 'Extinguishment of native title: Recent High Court decisions' (2016) 8 *Indigenous Law Bulletin* 28 for other problems.

[38] *Western Australia* v. *Ward* (2002) 213 CLR 1 (HCA) at para. 14.

times and forward to the present day, without a break. In *Yorta Aboriginal Community* v. *Victoria*,[39] the High Court concluded that the legislation required native title claimants to prove:

(a) that traditional laws and customs existed pre-sovereignty;
(b) that the society asserting the right or interest continued to exist in the present; and
(c) that *each generation* of that society had continued to acknowledge and observe laws and customs substantially uninterrupted since sovereignty.[40]

This stringent test for continuity is particularly burdensome for indigenous claimants because of the cultural differences between indigenous and common law legal systems we note in paras. 9.21 and 9.22 below. It is also very different from the approach to continuity shown in the Canadian courts, as we see in para. 9.16 below.

The Australian Law Reform Committee has identified a number of defects in the 1993 Act and in a report published in 2015, *Connection to Country: Review of the Native Title Act 1993 (Cth)*, has made 30 recommendations for its reform, including the following on proving title:

> statutory construction of s 223 of the Native Title Act has expanded the requirements for proof of native title beyond the elements contained in the actual definition in the Act [It explains how in detail in Chs. 4–8]. The ALRC's recommendations retain the framework of native title derived from *Mabo [No 2]* but address entrenched difficulties in the proof of native title. The recommendations are directed to a specific range of connection requirements in order that the 'test' for proving native title better accords with the Preamble and guiding objectives of the Native Title Act.[41]

Finally, reference may be made to the extensive caselaw on extinguishment of native title and compensation, including decisions of the High Court of Australia in *Queensland* v. *Congoo* [2015] HCA 17 (extinguishment),[42] and *Northern Territory* v. *Griffiths and Jones on behalf of the Ngaliwurru and Nungali Peoples* [2019] HCA 7. This last decision concerned the basis on which compensation for infringement should be assessed. The High Court of Australia decided it had to be assessed on the basis that 'exclusive native title rights to and interests in land' had the same value as an unencumbered freehold interest in the land, and that the value of 'non-exclusive native title rights and interests' was 50 per cent of unencumbered freehold value. In addition to those payments, the HCA also awarded the claimants AU$1.3 million as compensation for 'loss or diminution of traditional attachment to the land or connection to country and for loss of rights to gain spiritual sustenance from the land'.

---

[39] *Yorta Yorta Aboriginal Community* v. *Victoria* (2002) 214 CLR 422.

[40] See Mascher, 'Native Title Act 1993', fn. 22 above, p. 345 (emphasis added) and the works she cites there.

[41] Australian Law Reform Committee, *Connection to Country: Review of the Native Title Act 1993* (2015) p. 16, and see also Margaret Stephenson and Maureen Tehan, 'The recording and management of indigenous lands and title: Is reform required?' (2015) 24 *Australian Property Law Journal* 235.

[42] Discussed, with the other recent cases and developments on extinguishment, in Edgeworth, 'Extinguishment of native title', fn. 37 above.

PART III ABORIGINAL RIGHTS AND ABORIGINAL TITLE IN CANADA

9.12 Aboriginal Rights and Aboriginal Title in Canada

The equivalent of the *Mabo (No 2)* decision in Canada was *Calder* v. *Attorney General of British Columbia* [1973] SCR 313, in which the Supreme Court of Canada first ruled that aboriginal land rights survived European settlement and remain valid to the present unless extinguished, by treaty or otherwise.[43] This led the Government of Canada to begin negotiations with aboriginal groups, particularly with those First Nations peoples who had not already settled their land claims by treaties.

9.13 Constitutional Recognition of 'Aboriginal and Treaty Rights' in Canada

The negotiation process culminated in the enactment of s. 35 of the Constitution Act 1982, which 'recognised and affirmed' existing aboriginal rights. Section 35 is short – startlingly so, when compared to Australia's Native Title Act 1993:

35 (1) Recognition of existing aboriginal and treaty rights
The existing aboriginal and treaty[44] rights of the aboriginal peoples of Canada are hereby recognized and affirmed.

(2) Definition of 'aboriginal peoples of Canada'
In this Act, 'aboriginal peoples of Canada' includes the Indian, Inuit and Métis peoples of Canada.

(3) Land claims agreements
For greater certainty, in subsection (1) 'treaty rights' includes rights that now exist by way of land claims agreements or may be so acquired.

(4) Aboriginal and treaty rights are guaranteed equally to both sexes
Notwithstanding any other provision of this Act, the aboriginal and treaty rights referred to in subsection (1) are guaranteed equally to male and female persons.

The immediate effect of s. 35 was to make aboriginal land rights constitutional rights. The status of constitutional right is important because it means that the Crown, and federal and state legislatures generally, have strictly limited powers to infringe the rights, as we see in para. 9.16(c) below. Otherwise, however, the scope of s. 35 was not immediately apparent, and as McLachlin CJ noted, giving the judgment of the Supreme Court of Canada in *Tsilhqot'in Nation* v. *British Columbia* [2014]

---

[43] For the most part, Canada never regarded any of its territories as *terra nullius*, although Stuart Banner points out that James Douglas, the first governor of British Columbia did belatedly introduce a policy of *terra nullius* there in the 1850s, in order to allocate reserves to the indigenous populations (intended to include their villages and cultivated areas) and sell the rest of the land off to settlers (Banner, *Possessing the Pacific*, fn. 8 above, pp. 204–222). Nevertheless, in *Tsilhqot'in Nation* v. *British Columbia* [2014] 2 SCR 256 considered below, the Supreme Court of Canada proceeded on the basis that British Columbia had never been treated as *terra nullius* (McLachlin CJ at para. 69).

[44] These are the rights that aboriginal peoples acquired under treaties made over the last two centuries settling their land claims and other traditional rights, sometimes in exchange for reservations of land.

2 SCR 256, it has taken some time for 'the meaning of the section to be fully fleshed out'.[45]

9.14 Aboriginal Title and Aboriginal Rights: *Delgamuukw* v. *British Columbia*

For our purposes the first significant step for the courts was to establish that 'aboriginal rights' in s. 35 encompasses a broad spectrum of rights, which includes, but is not confined to, aboriginal title, and to re-affirm that all of them – aboriginal title and aboriginal rights falling short of aboriginal title – are fully enforceable property interests.

(a) Distinction Between Aboriginal Title and Aboriginal Rights

This distinction between aboriginal title and the other kinds of aboriginal rights was first made by the Supreme Court of Canada in *Van der Peet* [1996] 2 SCR. 507 and confirmed by it in *Delgamuukw* v. *British Columbia* [1997] 3 SCR 1010. Aboriginal rights falling short of aboriginal title are not all directly related to land use. They may relate to traditional practices such as trading in furs or skins. However, they also include what are sometimes called site-specific rights, which are rights to engage in a specific activity in a specific place (perhaps to catch fish in a particular stretch of river, or hunt in, or take logs from, a particular forest, or use a particular location or particular resources for ceremonial purposes). *Aboriginal title*, on the other hand is more like – but crucially not the same as – ownership of the land as a whole. It was described by Lamer CJ in *Delmaguukw* as 'a right to the land itself'.[46] So, a particular aboriginal group might have aboriginal title over a particular area of land, as well as site-specific aboriginal rights over resources in other areas of land over which it does not have aboriginal title. This is a bit like the distinction we draw in English and Welsh law between freehold and leasehold ownership on the one hand and non-possessory land use rights (exercisable over land in someone's freehold ownership) on the other.

(b) Aboriginal Rights

However, the comparison should not be pushed too far. In particular, the range of aboriginal rights is unlimited, reflecting the activities that particular groups traditionally engaged in at a specific site or over a specific area. This means that aboriginal rights are by their nature idiosyncratic – they are rights to go on doing what you have traditionally done, in the way that you have traditionally done so. This is very different from non-possessory land use rights in the common law which, as we saw in Chapter 6 *New Property Interests and the Numerus Clausus*, are generally limited by a numerus clausus principle, in other words they have the status of property rights only if they fall within an accepted category of property interests

---

[45] *Tsilhqot'in Nation* v. *British Columbia* [2014] 2 SCR 256 para. 11.
[46] *Delgamuukw* v. *British Columbia* [1997] 3 SCR 1010 para. 140.

listed on a fixed list, and have the required characteristics of a right within that particular category.

(c) Aboriginal Title

Also, as the Supreme Court pointed out in *Delgamuukw*, there are distinctive features of aboriginal title which make it significantly different from common law or civil law ownership. Like common law and civil law private ownership, aboriginal title is a property interest; unlike them, however, it is inalienable and held by a community.

The most important difference, however, lies in its nature, that is, in its contents and incidents. In *Delgamuukw* the Supreme Court of Canada had resisted attempts to identify the nature of aboriginal title in Western property law terms, taking the view that it is sui generis, in the sense that:

> its characteristics cannot be completely explained by reference either to the common law rules of real property or to the rules of property found in aboriginal legal systems. As with other aboriginal rights, it must be understood by reference to both common law and aboriginal perspectives.

Accordingly, Lamer CJ declined to accept the claimants' argument in that case, which was that aboriginal title is 'tantamount to an inalienable fee simple [in the claimed land], which confers on aboriginal peoples the rights to use those lands as they choose'. Nor was he prepared to accept the definition proposed by British Columbia, which was either that aboriginal title consisted only of the aboriginal rights which the group had been able to establish over the claimed territory, or that it gave the right to exclusive use and occupation of that territory *in order* to engage in those activities.[47] In both of British Columbia's alternative formulations, aboriginal title would have given the claimants the rights to carry on in the future the activities which they could prove their ancestors carried on at the time of colonisation, and which they could prove they still engaged in now, but they could not do anything else. So, aboriginal title would not allow them to adapt their land use to meet changes in circumstances or needs or preferences of the community, or technological or climate changes, or anything else: the community could go on doing exactly what their ancestors had always done on their land, and in exactly the same way, or they could abandon or surrender the land.

Lamer CJ firmly rejected both of British Columbia's alternate formulations, but he was not willing to go as far as the claimants in saying that aboriginal title would give them rights to use their land as they choose. Instead, he said, the nature of aboriginal title:

> can be summarized by two propositions first, that aboriginal title encompasses the right to exclusive use and occupation of the land held pursuant to that title for a variety of purposes, which need not be aspects of those aboriginal practices, customs and

---

[47] Para. 110.

traditions which are integral to distinctive aboriginal cultures and second, that *those protected uses must not be irreconcilable with the nature of the group's attachment to that land.*[48]

In other words, they had exclusive use and occupation of the land, and the use they could make of it was not limited to carrying on the activities which they could prove were aboriginal rights, but it was limited to uses which were not 'irreconcilable with the nature of [their] attachment to that land'.

He justified this last limitation – which has since been modified by the Supreme Court of Canada in *Tsilhqot'in*, as we see below – by saying, in essence, that the function of aboriginal title is not just to preserve the traditional relationship between an aboriginal group and its resources which existed at the time of colonisation, but to ensure that it continues into the future. This explains why the way in which the group uses the land and its resources must not be 'irreconcilable with the nature of the attachment to the land which forms the basis of the particular group's aboriginal title', and why aboriginal title is inalienable:

> 126 ... aboriginal title arises from the prior occupation of Canada by aboriginal peoples. That prior occupation is relevant in two different ways: first, because of the physical fact of occupation, and second, because aboriginal title originates in part from preexisting systems of aboriginal law. However, the law of aboriginal title does not only seek to determine the historic rights of aboriginal peoples to land, it also seeks to afford legal protection to prior occupation in the present-day. *Implicit in the protection of historic patterns of occupation is a recognition of the importance of the continuity of the relationship of an aboriginal community to its land over time.*

> 127 ... The relevance of the continuity of the relationship of an aboriginal community with its land here is that it applies not only to the past, but to the future as well. That relationship should not be prevented from continuing into the future. *As a result, uses of the lands that would threaten that future relationship are, by their very nature, excluded from the content of aboriginal title.*

> 128 ... one of the critical elements in the determination of whether a particular aboriginal group has aboriginal title to certain lands is the matter of the occupancy of those lands. Occupancy is determined by reference to the activities that have taken place on the land and the uses to which the land has been put by the particular group. If lands are so occupied, there will exist a special bond between the group and the land in question such that the land will be part of the definition of the group's distinctive culture. It seems to me that these elements of aboriginal title create an inherent limitation on the uses to which the land, over which such title exists, may be put. For example, if occupation is established with reference to the use of the land as a hunting ground, then the group that successfully claims aboriginal title to that land may not use it in such a fashion as to destroy its value for such a use (e.g. by strip mining it). Similarly, if a group claims a special bond with the land because of its ceremonial or cultural significance, it may not use the land in such a way as to destroy

---

[48] Lamer CJ in *Delgamuukw*, fn. 46 above, at para. 117 (emphasis added in this and the following paras. 126 and 127 of his judgment).

that relationship (e.g. by developing it in such a way that the bond is destroyed, perhaps by turning it into a parking lot.)

129 It is for this reason also that lands held by virtue of aboriginal title may not be alienated. Alienation would bring to an end the entitlement of the aboriginal people to occupy the land and would terminate their relationship with it. . . What the inalienability of lands held pursuant to aboriginal title suggests is that those lands are more than just a fungible commodity. The relationship between an aboriginal community and the lands over which it has aboriginal title has an important non-economic component. The land has an inherent and unique value in itself, which is enjoyed by those with aboriginal title to it. The community cannot put the land to uses which would destroy that value.

It followed, he said, that if the community no longer wanted (or was no longer able) to keep within those limits, the proper course would be for it to surrender the land:

If aboriginal peoples wish to use their lands in a way that aboriginal title does not permit, then they must surrender those lands and convert them into non-title lands to do so.

9.15 *Tsilhqot'in Nation* v. *British Columbia*

This approach has, however, since been modified by the Supreme Court of Canada in *Tsilhqot'in Nation* v. *British Columbia.*[49] *Tsilhqot'in* was the first case in which an aboriginal group finally succeeded in proving that it had aboriginal title to its territory (as opposed to aboriginal rights in it), and for this and other reasons it marked a major breakthrough for Canadian aboriginal groups.

The Tsilhqot'in Nation is a grouping of six semi-nomadic bands of First Nation Indians sharing a common language, culture and history who have lived for centuries in a remote valley bounded by rivers and mountains in central British Columbia. They are traditionally based in villages in the winter and over the rest of the year they follow a traditional pattern of seasonal rounds of foraging for roots and herbs, fishing, hunting and trapping, and assemblies at various sites for spiritual celebrations. The evidence established that they have always been less hierarchical than neighbouring groups and had looser and more flexible organisational structures, but they have also always had a strong sense of identity as a Nation and regarded the resources of their lands as belonging to them all. The evidence also established that they have always regarded the land as exclusively theirs, repelling invaders and setting terms for the European traders who came onto their land before the assertion of European sovereignty. Like the Australian aboriginal groups we noted in Part II of this chapter, they regarded themselves as having a close spiritual relationship with the land and with the resources they lived on. Vickers J, the trial judge, quoted one witness as saying:

When we have to honour all the spirits, we acknowledge the spirits of water, all the elements, the fire, light, the earth, plants, animals. We all believe that they all have

---

[49] *Tsilhqot'in Nation* v. *British Columbia* [2014] 2 SCR 256.

spirits, the same spirit that we have, all humans. Spirits are no different. Say if we talk to any – to any spirits, like the tree spirit, I'll talk to the tree like he's another person.[50]

Vickers went on to conclude from the evidence he had heard that:

Respect for the earth, plants and animals meant that before an animal was killed, there would be a silent acknowledgment of its spirit; before the berries were picked, there would be a similar acknowledgment. There was a oneness of the earth, of animals and people . . .[51]

In this litigation the Tsilhqot'in were claiming aboriginal title to about 1,750 square kilometres of land, which was about 5 per cent of what they regarded as their traditional lands. The area claimed was inhabited by about 400 people at the time of the assertion of European sovereignty[52] and about 200 at the time of the litigation. This may sound like a small number, but it was found that, because of the nature of the land, it was capable of supporting only between 100 and 1,000 people.

The litigation arose because in 1983 the government of British Columbia granted a logging licence to a commercial logging company over land which the Tsilhqot'in regarded as theirs. They claimed that this was in breach of their title to their land.

The trial judge, Vickers J, found that the Tsilhqot'in had aboriginal rights including rights to hunt and trap at various sites and to trade in skins and pelts, and that British Columbia's grant of the logging licence infringed these rights. He also would have found that they had aboriginal title over the area they later claimed in the Supreme Court of Canada, but for procedural reasons was unable to make that finding. On appeal the British Columbia Court of Appeal affirmed his findings on aboriginal rights but, adopting a narrow view of what amounted to sufficient 'occupation' of an area, disagreed with him on the question of aboriginal title. The Tsilhqot'in were given permission to renew their aboriginal title claim before the Supreme Court of Canada, where they won, and the Supreme Court of Canada made a declaration of Aboriginal title over the area claimed.[53]

9.16 The Issues in *Tsilhqot'in*

The decision of the Supreme Court of Canada was wide-ranging, but for our purposes the most important issues it settled were as follows.

(a) The Test for Aboriginal Title

The first question the Supreme Court had to consider was what an aboriginal group had to prove in order to establish that it had aboriginal title to a given area of

---

[50] Vickers J in the first instance decision, *Tsilhqot'in Nation* v. *British Columbia* [2007] BCSC 1700 at para. 418. He gives a detailed account of the geographic nature of the land and the ways in which the claimants used it, and their traditional cultural and social practices, in paras. 29–33, 44–58 and 332–436.

[51] Ibid. para. 419.

[52] The date when this should be taken to have occurred was contested, but the Supreme Court of Canada accepted 1846 as the correct date.

[53] It also made a declaration that British Columbia breached the duty to consult that it owed to the Tsilhqot'in Nation: see further 9.16(c) below.

territory. The court confirmed that the claimants had to prove three things, all focussed on the group's relationship with its land at the time of assertion of European sovereignty (1846 in the case of British Columbia). These are (1) that at that time the group had '*sufficient occupation*' of the land it claims title over; (2) if the group is relying on its present occupation as evidence of its occupation at the time when European sovereignty was asserted, then it must prove *continuity of occupation* between those two periods; and (3) that at the time of assertion of European sovereignty, its occupation of the land was *exclusive*.[54]

Sufficient Occupation

In order to show that it had 'sufficient occupation' of land to support a claim of aboriginal title over it, a group must show that it used the land 'regularly'. However, the Supreme Court made it clear that what amounts to 'sufficient occupation' and 'regular' use depends entirely on the nature of the territory and the ways in which it was used. The British Columbia Court of Appeal in *Tsilhqot'in* had held that to prove 'sufficient occupation' a claimant had to show 'intensive use of a defined tract of land with reasonably defined boundaries'. On that basis the Court of Appeal had found that the claimants had title only to its village sites and the areas it cultivated for harvesting roots and berries. The Supreme Court said that that was too narrow a test. As McLachlin CJ pointed out in the Supreme Court:

> 29. For semi-nomadic Aboriginal groups like the Tsilhqot'in, the Court of Appeal's approach results in small islands of title surrounded by larger territories where the group possesses only Aboriginal rights to engage in activities like hunting and trapping.

This was wrong, she said, because it failed to take into account the nature of the terrain (in this case harsh conditions, capable of supporting only a small population who might be widely dispersed whilst engaging in some traditional activities) and it also failed to take into account the manner of life of the people using it (in this case, semi-nomadic). The correct test, she concluded, was that the group must show that historically it 'acted in a way that would communicate to outsiders that it held the land for its own purposes':

> This standard does not demand notorious or visible use akin to proving a claim for adverse possession,[55] but neither can the occupation be purely subjective or internal. There must be evidence of a strong presence on or over the land claimed, manifesting itself in acts of occupation that could reasonably be interpreted as demonstrating that the land in question belonged to, was controlled by, or was under the exclusive stewardship of the claimant group. As just discussed, the kind of acts necessary to indicate a permanent presence and intention to hold and use the land for the group's purposes are dependent on the manner of life of the people and the nature of the land.

---

[54] McLachlin CJ, giving the judgment of the Supreme Court of Canada in *Tsilhqot'in*, fn. 49 above, at para. 50.

[55] As to whether this is a requirement for adverse possession in the law of England and Wales, as opposed to Canadian law, see Chapter 12 *Adverse Possession of Land* para. 12.15.

Cultivated fields, constructed dwelling houses, invested labour, and a consistent presence on parts of the land may be sufficient, but they are not essential to establish occupation. The notion of occupation must also reflect the way of life of the Aboriginal people, including those who were nomadic or semi-nomadic.[56]

The important point, she emphasised, was that a 'culturally sensitive approach' to sufficiency of occupation had to be adopted, based on

the dual perspectives of the Aboriginal group in question – its laws, practices, size, technological ability and the character of the land claimed – and the common law notion of possession as a basis for title . . . The common law test for possession – which requires an intention to occupy or hold land for the purposes of the occupant – must be considered alongside the perspective of the Aboriginal group which, depending on its size and manner of living, might conceive of possession of land in a somewhat different manner than did the common law.[57]

So, in this case the Tsilhqot'in were found to be in sufficient occupation of the whole of the land claimed, including not only their 'fixed sites' (the villages and cultivated areas) but also the land over which they had established patterns of use for hunting, fishing, trapping, ceremonial and other traditional activities, and over which the group exercised effective control. This was so even though, for most of the year,[58] there may have been no physical signs on the ground of their presence or control.

Continuity of Occupation

We saw that in Australia, following the decision in *Yorta Yorta*, a group claiming native title has to prove continuity of traditional use, in the sense that they have to show that they continue to use the land in question in the same way as it was used by their ancestors at the time of assertion of European sovereignty, in accordance with the same practices, customs and traditions, and that so too have all generations up to theirs.[59] It is important to appreciate that nothing like this is required in Canadian law. The only relevance of present use and occupation in a claim for aboriginal title to land in Canada is that, in order to overcome some of the difficulties in proving past practices, customs and traditions in oral cultures to a common law audience,[60] claimants can rely on evidence of how they *now* use the land in order to prove how their ancestors used the land at the time of European assertion of sovereignty. In order to be able to do that, they must be able to show some continuity between present occupation and pre-sovereignty occupation, but they do not need do so for

---

[56] McLachlin CJ in *Tsilhqot'in*, fn. 49 above, at para. 38.

[57] Ibid. para. 41. See further Part III of Chapter 11 *Possession and Title* as to what amounts to possession of land sufficient to give the possessor title to the land in our law in England and Wales. It will be noted that in our law we try (not always successfully) to draw a distinction between occupation and possession, whereas in *Tsilhqot'in* McLachlin CJ often uses the terms interchangeably, as do the courts in passages from other aboriginal land decisions which McLachlin quotes with approval in *Tsilhqot'in*.

[58] Or occasionally for years at a time: the evidence was that, because the Tsilhqot'in regarded themselves as responsible for the sustainability of their resources, they would sometimes not visit sites every year.

[59] para. 9.11(b) above.   [60] See further para. 9.22 below.

any other purpose, and even when they do have to show continuity the requirement is easily satisfied.

This was confirmed by the Supreme Court in *Tsilhqot'in*, where McLachlin CJ explained that in Canadian law 'continuity' for these purposes means that:

> For evidence of present occupation to establish an inference of pre-sovereignty occupation, the present occupation must be rooted in pre-sovereignty times.

She did not go on to state more specifically how that could or should be proved.[61] She also confirmed that this is a question of fact, and on this basis accepted that the trial judge had been entitled to look at evidence of events that took place as recently as 1999:

> The trial judge considered this direct evidence of more recent occupation alongside archeological evidence, historical evidence, and oral evidence from Aboriginal elders, all of which indicated a continuous Tsilhqot'in presence in the claim area. The geographic proximity between sites for which evidence of recent occupation was tendered and those for which direct evidence of historic occupation existed also supported an inference of continuous occupation.[62]

For these reasons she saw no reason to disturb the trial judge's finding.

Exclusivity of Occupation

This is proved by showing that, at the time of European assertion of sovereignty, the group had 'the intention and capacity to retain exclusive control'.[63] As McLachlin CJ pointed out, regular use without exclusivity may give rise to aboriginal *rights* (which means that different aboriginal groups using the same resource at different times may each have proprietary rights to go on doing so), but for aboriginal *title* claimants must show exclusive occupation.[64] In *Tsilhqot'in* itself this was not a problem because there was evidence that others were excluded from the land and/or allowed access only with the permission of the group. In other cases it might be more difficult to prove that 400 people had the capacity to exert exclusive control over an isolated area of land of 1,750 square kilometres, although McLachlin did say that 'even the lack of challenges to occupancy may support an inference of an established group's intention and capacity to control'.[65]

(b) The Nature of Aboriginal Title

In *Tsilhqot'in* McLachlin CJ did not dissent from what Lamer CJ had said about the nature of aboriginal title in *Delgamuukw*, but she did reformulate the limitation on

---

[61] Presumably it was not intended to cast doubts on the remarks made by Lamer CJ in in *Delgamuukw* (fn. 46 above) at paras. 153–154 where he said (1) there is no need to establish 'an unbroken chain of continuity' between present and prior occupation, because occupation and use may have been disrupted for a time, 'perhaps as a result of the unwillingness of European colonizers to recognize aboriginal title' and so to require unbroken continuity 'would risk undermining the very purposes of s. 35(1) by perpetuating the historical injustice suffered by aboriginal peoples at the hands of colonizers who failed to respect their rights', and (2) that it did not matter that the precise nature of occupation may have changed 'as long as a substantial connection between the people and the land is maintained'.
[62] McLachlin CJ in the Supreme Court decision in *Tsilhqot'in*, fn. 49 above, at para. 57.
[63] Ibid para. 47.   [64] Ibid.   [65] Ibid. para. 48.

the group's inherent rights and powers in terms that seem significantly narrower and less specific. As we noted in para. 9.14(c) above, Lamer CJ had said in *Delgamuukw* that the group could not use the land in ways that were 'irreconcilable with the nature of the group's attachment to that land which forms the basis of the particular group's aboriginal title'.[66] He gave as examples using land for strip mining when its traditional use had been as a hunting ground, so that its value as a hunting ground was destroyed, or turning land which had traditionally had ceremonial or cultural significance into a parking lot. In *Tsilhqot'in*, on the other hand, McLachlin said:

> 88 ... Aboriginal title confers on the group that holds it the exclusive right to decide how the land is used and the right to benefit from those uses, subject to one carve-out – *that the uses must be consistent with the group nature of the interest and the enjoyment of the land by future generations.*

Her 'carve-out' is more generalised than the *Delgamuukw* limitation, and seems to give the group much more leeway in deciding whether radical changes of use are justified. She makes it clear that her carve-out means that the title must continue to be a collective title held for future generations as well as for the present generation, and that for this reason it cannot be alienated except to the Crown. She goes on to say that it also means that the land cannot be 'encumbered in ways that prevent future generations of the group from using and enjoying it', or 'developed or misused in a way that would substantially deprive future generations of the benefit of the land.'[67] However, beyond that she lays down no specific prohibitions:

> Some changes – even permanent changes – to the land may be possible. Whether a particular use is irreconcilable with the ability of succeeding generations to benefit from the land will be a matter to be determined when the issue arises ... Aboriginal title post-sovereignty reflects the fact of Aboriginal occupancy pre-sovereignty, with all the pre-sovereignty incidents of use and enjoyment enjoyed by the ancestors of the claimant group – *most notably the right to control how the land is used.* However, these uses are not confined to the uses and customs of pre-sovereignty times; like other landowners, Aboriginal title holders of modern times can use their land in modern ways, if that is their choice.[68]

(c) Infringement

The Canadian courts have interpreted s. 35 of the Constitution Act 1982 as meaning that, once aboriginal title[69] has been established, no-one else may use the land or interfere with the group's usages or practices without the group's consent. This applies to the government as it does to anyone else, except that, as McLachlin CJ explains in *Tsilhqot'in*, if the group refuses to give consent, the government may

---

[66] *Delgamuukw*, fn. 46 above, para. 117.

[67] McLachlin CJ in *Tsilhqot'in*, fn. 49 above, at para. 74. Presumably this would rule out granting long leases to outsiders.

[68] Ibid. paras. 74–75, emphasis added.   [69] Or aboriginal rights falling short of title.

override the wishes of the group on the basis of 'the broader public good'.[70] However, this public good justification is very precisely and strictly circumscribed. In order to be able to rely on it the government must show three things:

> (1) that it discharged its procedural duty to consult and accommodate; (2) that its actions were backed by a compelling and substantial objective; and (3) that the governmental action is consistent with the Crown's fiduciary obligation to the group.[71]

In many ways, these requirements are significantly stricter – or at least more specific – than those imposed on governments seeking to justify interference with 'possessions' under article 1 Protocol 1 European Convention on Human Rights. In particular:

Duty to Consult and Accommodate

The Canadian courts have made it clear that the duty to 'consult and accommodate' (meaning accommodate the group's interests which are threatened) arises as soon as a claim for aboriginal title has been asserted, with the level of consultation and accommodation required being 'proportionate to the strength of the claim and to the seriousness of the adverse impact' the proposed action would have on the claimed right'.[72] All this must, of course, be done before the government takes the proposed action.

'Compelling and Substantial Governmental Objective'

This must be considered from both the aboriginal perspective and the perspective of the broader public, which is said to mean that the broader public goal asserted by the government 'must further the goal of reconciliation' of aboriginal interests and the broader interests of society as a whole.[73] Perhaps more helpfully, it was said in *Delgamuukw* and quoted with approval in *Tsilhqot'in*, that consideration of whether the government's objective is sufficiently 'compelling and substantial' involves recognition that 'distinctive aboriginal societies exist within, and are a part of, a broader social, political and economic community'.[74] On this basis, Lamer CJ said in *Delgamuukw* in the passage approved in *Tsilhqot'in*, infringement of aboriginal title might in principle be justifiable (if consistent with the Crown's fiduciary obligation noted below) if pursuing a wide range of objectives: the examples he gave were 'the development of agriculture, forestry, mining and hydro-electric power, the general economic development of the interior of British Columbia, protection of the environment or endangered species, the building of infrastructure and the settlement of foreign populations to support those aims'.[75]

---

[70] McLachlin CJ in *Tsilhqot'in* , fn. 49 above, para. 77.   [71] Ibid.   [72] Ibid. paras. 78–79.
[73] Ibid. para. 82.
[74] Lamer CJ in *Delgamuukwu*, fn. 46 above, para. 73, quoted by McLachlin CJ in *Tsilhqot'in*, fn. 49 above, at para. 83.
[75] Lamer CJ in *Delgamuukw*, fn. 46 above, at para. 165, quoted by McLachlin CJ in *Tsilhqot'in*, fn. 49 above, at para. 83.

Crown's Fiduciary Obligation

This arises because the Crown's underlying title to the aboriginal group's land 'is held for the benefit of the Aboriginal group and constrained by the Crown's fiduciary or trust obligation to the group'.[76] In *Tsilhqot'in* McLachlin says this has two consequences. The first is that, because the Crown holds its title for the benefit of the collective title of the group, infringement by the government *cannot* be justified if it would 'substantially deprive future generations of the benefit of the land'.[77] The second is that it imports a principle of proportionality into the justification process.[78] This is not unlike the proportionality principle which applies in relation to interference with convention rights under the European Convention of Human Rights which we noted in Parts V and VI of Chapter 4 *Property and Human Rights*. In this context it means that infringement of aboriginal title must be necessary to achieve the government's aim, go no further than necessary to achieve it, and the benefits expected to flow from it must not be outweighed by the adverse effects on the aboriginal interest.[79]

9.17 Aftermath of *Tsilhqot'in*

The combined effect of these developments is that aboriginal groups in Canada who establish aboriginal title over their lands have significant autonomy over decision making and control over the use and enjoyment of their territory. This raises two important questions. One is the status of any land within an area over which aboriginal title is established, which is held as private property by an outsider under common law tenure. This issue did not arise in *Tsilhqot'in* because, although the claimed land did include some privately owned land, those involved supported the claim. However, it can be expected to arise in the future.

The second is the important political and constitutional question of the nature of the tripartite relationship which now arises between the aboriginal group and federal and provincial governments. This question was considered by the Supreme Court in *Tsilhqot'in* but is beyond the scope of this book.

PART IV PROBLEMS OF RECOGNITION

9.18 Characteristics of Indigenous Property Rights Systems

Developments in Australia and Canada suggest we can identify some common characteristics of the traditional property rights systems of at least some indigenous peoples in at least some countries, which are different from those we can identify as characteristic of most western European property rights systems (lumping together for these purposes English common law and continental European civil law systems). Nigel Bankes sees these as amounting to radically different concepts of property:

---

[76] *Tsilhqot'in*, fn. 49 above, at para. 85.   [77] Ibid. para. 86.   [78] Ibid. para. 87.   [79] Ibid. para. 87.

Not only is property a contested term within the legal and political systems of settler societies, it is also a term that may have radically different contents within indigenous cultures and legal systems. Modern western conceptions of property focus on the private and abstract aspects of property, and emphasise the economic rights (rather than obligations) associated with property, including the right to exclude and the right to sell. This western paradigm invokes an individual owner rather than a community owner, and routinely refers to property as a bundle of rights (good against the entire world) and therefore as a set of relationships with others rather than with the subject matter of the property itself. By contrast, indigenous communities are more likely to reflect on their relationship with land and territory, and to express their responsibility for that territory. That relationship may be of profound spiritual and religious significance, connected to both time past and time future. Individual entitlements may be tangled with family, clan and community entitlements and responsibilities.[80]

In the following paragraphs we look at three of these radical differences, the first two of which Bankes identifies in the above passage. The first is that indigenous property rights systems in Australia and Canada are essentially collectivist whereas western European systems are individualistic. We consider this distinction in para. 9.19. The second is that the indigenous property rights systems we look at tend to focus on the *responsibilities* that indigenous communities and their members regard themselves as having in respect of their resources (not only responsibilities *towards each other* in respect of their resources, but also, significantly, responsibilities *towards the resources themselves*). In western European systems, on the other hand, the central focus is on the economic rights of autonomous individuals (para. 9.20 below). The third is that indigenous property rights systems tend to be customary, whereas western European systems are primarily founded on formalised legislative pronouncements (constitutions, codes, statutes, regulations), on rulings of courts, and on formulations provided by jurists in treatises. We consider the implications of this distinction in paras. 9.21 and 9.22.

9.19 Collectivism and Individualism

Property holdings that we would recognise as private property do exist in indigenous property systems (probably in most if not all of them), and similarly, as we have seen in earlier chapters, western property systems (including our own) do recognise communal property to varying extents and in various forms. Nevertheless, in indigenous property systems the central organising principle is collective rights and responsibilities held by communities and their members in the resources they utilise, whereas in western systems it is absolute private ownership of demarcated space held by autonomous, self-interested individuals. In other words, in indigenous property systems private property rights exist within a collectivist framework,

---

[80] Nigel Bankes, 'Recognising the property interests of indigenous peoples within settler societies: Some different conceptual approaches' in Nigel Bankes and Timo Koivurova (eds.), *The Proposed Nordic Saami Convention: National and International Dimensions of Indigenous Property Rights* (Oxford and Portland, OR: Hart Publishing 2013) p. 21 at p. 23.

whereas in western European property rights systems collective rights exist within a private property framework.

Indigenous property systems of this kind are moulded by collectivism in a number of ways.[81]

(a) Collective Control and Responsibility for Territory

First, the core western European model is land split up into fenced parcels with a single private owner having absolute dominion over all resources within its own demarcated parcel. By contrast, the core model for indigenous peoples is a community which traditionally regards itself as collectively responsible for its territory as a whole and for all resources within it. The community utilises its territory collectively not by parcelling out ownership of specific geographic areas to individuals, but by allocating rights of access to specific resources and rights of control over them to individual members (perhaps by reference to their status in the community or relationship to other members), or to different groups within the community. So, instead of splitting the territory between a number of autonomous individuals, each having monolithic 'ownership' of her own plot of land, the community has collective control of and responsibility for the territory as a whole, and has its own complex rules regulating which of its members, and which groups of members, has rights of access, management and control over which of the resources within the territory and when.

(b) Organisational Structure of the Community

Secondly, whereas communities who hold communal property interests in western European property systems tend to be communities of otherwise autonomous individuals, indigenous land holding communities generally have a more complex structure in which collectivism is more deeply embedded. An indigenous land holding community characteristically consists of a structure of interlinked or 'nested' groups and individuals. At its simplest this structure might consist of a pyramid of resource utilising groups, with the family or household forming the bottom rung (each family or household might have its own house and cultivable land in a sedentary community, or its own cattle in a pastoral[82] community), with families or households grouped together as lineages or clans or in villages (each lineage, clan or village perhaps having rights to fish in a particular stretch of water, or pasture their animals on communal pasture land, or drive them over a particular route), and with elders or chiefs or other representatives of the community at the apex of the

---

[81] Compare the following with Du Plessis, arguing that there is a distinctive pan-African indigenous land tenure, in which '... firstly ... land is held as a transgenerational asset, secondly ... it is managed on different levels of the social organisational structure, and lastly ... it is used in function-specific ways. Access to and the control of land depends on an individual's place in the social order of the community ... ': W. J. Du Plessis, 'African indigenous land rights in a private ownership paradigm' (2011) 14 *Potchefstroom Electronic Law Journal* 44 at p. 57.

[82] In some parts of the world 'nomad' is regarded as derogatory, and 'pastoralist' is preferred.

hierarchy, in charge of allocating rights, powers and responsibilities as between the
various groups in the interests of the community as a whole. In many cases the
organisational structure may be more complex and/or more diffuse, and it may be
difficult for outsiders to locate the property rights holders amongst the different
interlocking groups. This was one of the reasons why the aboriginal claimants lost in
the early Australian case of *Milirrpum* v. *Nabalco Pty Ltd*[83] we noted in para. 9.8
above. After hearing evidence from aboriginal witnesses and anthropologists Blackburne J had no difficulty in concluding that the claimants had a sophisticated and
long established organisational structure and a system of law 'highly adapted to the
country in which the people led their lives, which provided a stable order of society
and was remarkably free from the vagaries of personal whim or influence'.[84]
However, he had much greater difficulty in resolving conflicting accounts of expert
and lay witnesses of exactly how the organisational structure worked and the ways in
which resource-utilising functions were split between the interlocking groups within
it. It was clear that every individual who belonged to the aboriginal groups which
inhabited the territory in question was a member of a 'moiety', a 'clan' and a 'band'.
What was less clear was the relationship between moiety, clan and band, and the
relevance of each to resource use within the territory. Blackburne J concluded.

> In the aboriginal belief, all things in the physical and spiritual universes (and the
> difference between them seems not to be important) belong to one or the other of two
> classes called 'moieties'. The names of the moieties are Dua and Yiritja. It is in the
> unchangeable natural order of things that every human being, every clan, every animal
> and plant species, and every inanimate thing, belongs to one or other of the moieties.
> ... Foremost in this system is the principle of the clan... The clan is essentially a
> patrilineal descent group. Every human being has his clan membership determined at
> the moment of his birth, and it is that of his father. Each clan, and therefore each
> member of it, belongs to either the Dua or Yiritja moiety. Each clan is strictly
> exogamous. This has two aspects: not only can a person marry only one of another
> clan, but also only one of a clan of the opposite moiety. This results in there often being
> a special relationship between some particular pairs of clans, brought about by the fact
> that so many marriages have taken place between persons from each clan of the pair.
> Polygamy is normal. Upon marriage, a woman does not cease to belong to her own
> clan, though of course her children belong to the clan of her husband.
> ... For the moment, I make no reference to the much disputed questions of the
> identity, extent and correct delineation of the land of each clan. It is not in dispute that
> each clan regards itself as a spiritual entity having a spiritual relationship to particular
> places or areas, and having a duty to care for and tend that land by means of ritual
> observances. Certain sacred objects, called rangga, are at once symbols of the continu-
> ity of the clan, and tangible indications of the relationship between the clan and certain
> land ...
> The clan, then, had a religious basis, it had a connexion with land, and the principle
> of its existence was patrilineal descent. But its relationships with other social phenom-
> ena were far from simple... The clan had no internal organization of its own, or any
> rate none relevant to this case. No chieftain ruled over it; rather, apparently, decisions

[83] *Milirrpum*, fn. 17 above.   [84] Ibid. at p. 267.

affecting the whole clan may have been made by a consensus of the older men. The clan had little significance in the economic sense; indeed, it was a matter of dispute whether it had any such significance. The economic relationship between the aboriginals and the land is not easy to describe. It seems that at any given time there would be various groups of aboriginals in various places about the land, each group living in a particular area, hunting animals, obtaining vegetable food, getting materials for clothing and ritual observances and moving about from area to area as the economic exigencies required. Each group consisted of a number of adult men, some with their wives and children and some unmarried. The composition of any given group at a given time could not be predicted, and did not, for any fixed or recognized time, remain constant; indeed, one group might not be recognizable as such over a period of one year or even less, or might persist for a longer period. Changes in the personnel of the group would occur not only by reason of births, deaths and marriages, but for purely economic reasons such as sufficiency of food supplies, and also because of ritual requirements at special sacred places at particular times. To refer to such a group, both the anthropologist witnesses used the technical word 'band'. The 'band' was the land-exploiting group . . .

I come therefore to the question of the relationship of the band to the clan . . . [U]pon consideration of all the evidence, my conclusion is . . . that neither the composition nor the territorial ambit of the bands was normally linked to any particular clan. My finding is that the clan system, with its principles of kinship and of spiritual linkage to territory, was one thing, and that the band system which was the principal feature of the daily life of the people and the modus of their social and economic activity, was quite another. . . [T]he evidence is that it was of great importance that a group of people performing a religious ceremony at a particular place should be either of the same clan, or of clans which traditionally celebrated the particular rite together. The people of each clan were deeply conscious of their clan kinship and of the spiritual significance of particular land to their clan. On the other hand, beyond the fact that a father and his children were necessarily members of the same clan, it was of no importance whether or not the members of a band, a food-gathering and communal living unit, had any clan relationships to each other, or conducted their food-gathering and communal living upon territory linked to any particular clan.[85]

So, it seems reasonably clear that the clans and the bands were essentially different groupings of the same individuals within a single organisational structure. It would probably now be accepted that the community as a whole had title to the whole of the territory they inhabited, grouping themselves as bands in order to utilise some resources in their territory for economic and social purposes, and as clans to carry out their religious obligations towards these and other resources. However, the case was brought on the basis that named *clans* had title to their own parcels of land within the Gove Peninsula. Blackburne decided that they did not. The main reason, as we saw in para. 9.8, was that he concluded that any property rights that aboriginal people did have would have been wiped out when Britain colonised that part of Australia. However, he went on to say that even if that was incorrect (as the High Court of

---

[85] Ibid. Blackburne J at pp. 166–172.

Australia subsequently said it was in *Mabo (No 2)*[86]) he did not believe that *the clans* would have had any property rights in the territory anyway, because he did not think that their purely custodial, spiritual relationship with the land could be characterised as proprietary. We looked at his reasons in para. 9.8 above, but for present purposes the important point is that he acknowledged that *the bands* did make economic use of the resources they utilised, but no-one suggested that they were property rights holders, and indeed it would have been difficult in that case to argue that they were, because they were informal ad hoc groupings who would not be regarded as capable of holding property rights in western European property systems.[87]

The result was that a community of interlocking groups which, it was accepted, had a stable legal system and a highly sophisticated system of rules for utilising the resources of the land they inhabited, nevertheless failed to establish that it recognised the institution of property. In western eyes, up until the 1970s, they could not be said to have property rights in the land or its resources because they split their resource utilisation between different interlocking groups within their overall collective framework in a way that was not familiar to western European property systems.

(c) Intergenerational Group Holdings

When any group of people gets together to act collectively to further their own interests, each individual member necessarily sacrifices a degree of personal autonomy: if the group is to function as a group at all, members must regard themselves as bound, to some extent at least, by decisions made collectively in accordance with the group's rules. However, when membership groups like these exist in indigenous property rights systems like the ones we look at here, the personal autonomy of individual members is characteristically eroded even further by the fact that membership is generally regarded as intergenerational, comprising not just present members but also future and past members. In other words, when making decisions about how it utilises its resources, the community as a whole, and each of the groups and individuals within it, must take into consideration not only the immediate interests of the present members of the group but also the interests of future generations, as well as perceived obligations to ancestors. Taking into account the interests of past members might amount to no more than a sense that, in an abstract kind of way, we 'owe it' to our ancestors to conserve the traditional resources and patterns of resource use we have inherited from them, and to pass them on to future generations. However, it might go as far as regarding ancestors as deities having resource-specific needs, desires and commands which must be respected and fulfilled by the present generation and which the next generation must be taught to respect, or as part of a life cycle in which the present generation participates.[88]

---

[86] *Mabo v. Queensland (No 2)* (1992) 175 CLR 1: see paras. 9.9–9.10 above.
[87] See Chapter 8 *Property Interest Holders*.
[88] See, for example, Kerry Prosper et al., 'Returning to Netukulimk: Mi'kmaq cultural and spiritual connections with resource stewardship and self-governance' (2011) 2 *International Indigenous Policy Journal* 1 at pp. 5–6.

(d) Individual Rights Determined by Status

In indigenous property systems any given individual's access to and control over any resource is typically determined by that person's status within the group (wife, husband, daughter, son, sister, brother, cousin, head of household or lineage, member of one lineage rather than another, or one clan rather than another). Status is nearly always gender specific: the resource rights and obligations of wives, sisters, daughters and mothers are typically different from those of husbands, brothers, sons and fathers. For present purposes these factors have two significant implications. One is that it limits the transferability of an individual's resource rights, especially if allied with strict inheritance laws. Status rights in general are determined by your gender, who you are born to and who you marry, and they continue only for so long as you hold that status. The community will typically have elaborate rules which will dictate who will take over your access and control rights if you no longer want them, or lose your status, or die: it will rarely be a matter for you to decide. Hence, a market in individual resource rights is unlikely to develop within the group. The other implication is that status brings responsibilities as well as rights: you may be required to exercise your rights in resources for the benefit of those for whom you are responsible. So, to take a very simple example, a male head of household allocated land may be required to set aside a plot to be cultivated by his wife, who may be required to use it to grow the crops which are required to feed the household. This leads to an interdependence of individual property rights which modern western systems might recognise as mirroring functional divisions of labour within families, but probably would not recognise as giving rise to property rights.[89]

9.20 Right, Duty, Obligation and Responsibility

Western European property rights systems typically see property as all about relationships between people. Specifically, we commonly characterise property as being a relationship of reciprocal rights and duties between individuals (or between the individual and the state) in respect of a thing, typically centring on one individual's right to exclude other individuals and the state from that thing (if only for some periods or some purposes). This must also be true of indigenous property rights systems at a certain level, given that rights of access and control of things is determined by your status in a community as against others. However, there are other important dimensions.

(a) Relationship Between Humans, Resources and Cultural Identity

One of them is that they regard property as also a direct relationship between themselves and their resources, a key component of which is a stewardship-type

---

[89] So, even when indigenous property rights systems are recognised within a private property rights framework, there is a danger of these kinds of rights being overlooked: Susana Lastarria-Cornhiel, 'Impact of privatization on gender and property rights in Africa' (1997) 25 *World Development* 1317.

obligation owed by them to their resources. As we have already seen, this was apparent in the way the clans regarded their territory in *Milirrpum,* and Blackburne J summed it up as the antithesis of a property relationship as understood in the common law:

> The spiritual relationship [of the clans to the land to which they claimed title] is well proved. One of the manifestations of this is the fact that sacred sites associated with a particular clan are to be found there (though sometimes other clans have spiritual links with these sites). Another manifestation is that the rites performed by the clans have as part of their object the fructification and renewal of the fertility of the land. The evidence seems to me to show that the aboriginals have a more cogent feeling of obligation to the land than of ownership of it. It is dangerous to attempt to express a matter so subtle and difficult by a mere aphorism, but it seems easier, on the evidence, to say that the clan belongs to the land than that the land belongs to the clan.[90]

This leads to (or perhaps results from) a particularly strong connection between the community's traditional way of life and its natural resources, to the extent that the community may come to regard its identity as being bound up with the land and with the pattern of resource use it has evolved to enable it to survive, given the resources available to it, and its dependence on those resources. This interrelation between community, resources and cultural identity is equally apparent in *Mabo v. Queensland (No 2),*[91] as we saw in paras. 9.9–9.10 above. In his first instance judgment in the *Mabo (No 2)* litigation, Moynihan J[92] described the way of life of the Meriam people, the claimants in *Mabo (No 2)*, who lived in family huts and cultivated gardens, in the following terms:

> Communal life based on group membership seems to have been the predominant feature of life [for the Meriam people]. Many of the activities of daily life were social activities which took place in the context of group activities of a ceremonial or ritualistic nature. Behaviour was regulated in the interest of the community by social pressures ... The people lived in groups of huts strung along the foreshore or strand immediately behind the sandy beach ... The cultivated garden land was and is in the higher central portion of the island ... The groups of houses were and are organized in named villages. It is far from obvious to the uninitiated, but is patent to an islander, that one is moving from one village to another ...
>
> Gardening was of the most profound importance to the inhabitants of Murray Island at and prior to European contact ... Gardening was important not only from the point of view of subsistence but to provide produce for consumption or exchange during the various rituals associated with different aspects of community life. Marriage and adoption involved the provision or exchange of considerable quantity of produce. Surplus produce was also required for the rituals associated with the various cults at least to sustain those who engaged in them and in connexion with the various activities associated with death. Prestige depended on gardening prowess both in terms of the production of a sufficient surplus for the social purposes such as those to which I have

---

[90] *Milirrpum*, fn. 17 above, at p. 271.   [91] *Mabo v. Queensland (No 2)* (1992) 175 CLR 1.

[92] In his determination of the facts in the early stages of the *Mabo (No. 2)* proceedings, quoted by Brennan J in the High Court in *Mabo v. Queensland (No 2)* at para. 3.

referred and to be manifest in the show gardens and the cultivation of yams to a huge size. Considerable ritual was associated with gardening and gardening techniques were passed on and preserved by these rituals. Boys in particular worked with their fathers and by observations and imitations reinforced by the rituals and other aspects of the social fabric gardening practices were passed on ... Children were inculcated from a very early age with knowledge of their relationships in terms of social groupings and what was expected of them by a constant pattern of example, imitation and repetition with reinforcing behaviour. It was part of their environment – the way in which they lived... [and] initiation and other group activities reinforced these patterns ...

As we saw in Part II of this chapter, a similar relationship between people, resources and cultural identity was described in *Tsilhqot'in* in relation to indigenous groups living collectively in very different geographic conditions, and within a quite different organisational structure.

(b) Exclusion and Sharing

An allied dimension is that whereas in the western European property rights system the paradigm is often seen as one individual *excluding* the rest of the world from a resource, in the indigenous system it may be closer to having *a right to participate in the sharing* of the resource. This can work at two levels. The first is identifiable in western European property systems as well as in indigenous systems. In both, collective use of resources necessarily involves evolving rules for resource sharing between the users. It is true that the sharers may well also regard themselves as having the right to exclude outsiders, and even to exclude each other from encroaching on to their allotted entitlements, but it would be perverse to regard the arrangement as being all about excluding others rather than primarily about sharing with others. The second is, however, characteristic of indigenous property systems but absent from traditional western European property theory. This is that 'sharing' may extend beyond sharing between humans to sharing in a cycle of resource use connecting humans to the animal and plant world and to the environment as a whole. This idea is captured by the Canadian Mi'kmaq[93] concept of *netukulimk* described by Prosper et al.:

... for most Indigenous peoples, relationship with the land, water, sea and life entails culturally and spiritually rooted sensibilities. Theirs is ordinarily a holistic and interdependent relationship wherein they are 'of' their environmental-ecological context and this context is every bit as much 'of' them.... [Netukulimk is a] culturally rooted concept [which] operates as a guide to responsible co-existence and interdependence with natural resources, each other and other than human entities. It is considered as a body of living knowledge, which underpins the moral and ethical relationships that explains their world in the past and provides for the present by sustaining the future ... 'avoid not having enough' [can be taken to be] a synonym of netukulimk. The constant need to supply sustenance was managed by the leadership of the

---

[93] The First Nations people whose claim to aboriginal title was rejected by the Supreme Court of Canada in *R v. Marshall, R v. Bernard* (2005) SCC 43.

Mi'kmaq. Netukulimk was mobilized as a management structure and guidelines for harvesting. This is evident in the decisions made respecting the distribution and regulation of hunting activities within the seasonal round. The expectation was that respectful resource procurement was to be carried out by taking only enough to satisfy while avoiding waste. The distribution of hunting territories regulated the impact of resource extraction in Mi'kmaq lands and allowed for the replenishment of resources in a sustainable manner. The manner in which hunting territories were allocated was a spiritual, economic and political process. The leaders assured the availability of game and other resources by altering gathering, fishing and hunting territorial allocations. Care was taken to assure that hunting territories were not exhausted. Thus, through netukulimk a human and animal relationship formed that allowed the survival of both in a sustainable manner. This was reinforced by a set of values that expressed Mi'kmaq consciousness and which helped Mi'kmaq peoples understand their place in the biosphere.[94]

9.21 Customary Rules and Institutions

The third main difference between indigenous property rights systems and western European property rights systems is that indigenous property rights systems are generally the product of custom rather than of formal pronouncements of legislatures, courts or jurists. It is this factor, as much as any other, which has made it so difficult for indigenous peoples to persuade western European settlers and their courts that they live under a system of property law rules. It is important to be clear about the nature of this difficulty. The fact that a set of property rules has evolved by custom rather than having been formally pronounced by a legislature or a court or a jurist is not of itself alien to western European property rights systems, which all recognise customary resource rules to some extent. It also tells us nothing about the content of the rules. It explains the source of the rules,[95] and generally it also signals that the rules have become embedded in the society's culture and way of life. As we know from Chapter 2 *Conceptions and Justifications*,[96] established customary property rules typically have been self-generated by a community of resource users, evolving to regulate the community's resource use in its own best interests to avert over-use. If these rules have survived over generations it is generally because they enforce sustainable and co-operative use of the available resources and because the members of the community have the will and means to abide by the rules themselves, police and enforce each other's compliance, adapt the rules to meet environmental and demographic changes, and fend off intruders.[97] None of this necessarily

---

[94] Prosper et al., 'Returning to Netukulimk', fn. 88 above, and see also Kirsten Anker, 'Law, culture and fact in indigenous claims: Legal pluralism as a problem of recognition' in René Provost (ed.), *Culture in the Domains of Law* (Cambridge: Cambridge University Press 2016) pp. 15–17.

[95] To outsiders, at least: what look to outsiders like rules evolved by a community by custom may be regarded by members of the community as rules laid down by deities or ancestors.

[96] Part III of Chapter 2, especially paras. 2.15–2.17.

[97] In other words, they conform to Elinor Ostrom's design principles for successful self-regulated common pool resources noted in para. 2.17 of Chapter 2 *Conceptions and Justifications*. There may of

makes the rules themselves unrecognisable or unreadable by western European legal systems, although modern western systems might find them uncomfortably at odds with principles of personal autonomy, gender equality and non-discrimination against disadvantaged minorities. We come back to this point in para. 9.25.

So, the fact that indigenous property rights systems are customary does not in principle make it more difficult for western European legal systems to recognise them. The problem lies in proof. For a variety of reasons we look at in the next paragraph, historically it has been difficult (almost insuperably difficult) for indigenous people with customary property rights systems to *prove* to western outsiders that they have a property rights system at all, and even more difficult to prove its content.

9.22 Proving Indigenous Land Rights

It is important to appreciate what it is that indigenous people have to prove in the post-colonial cases we are looking at. Their argument is that even if the colonisers never formally recognised their property interests in the land they inhabit, and there has been no formal recognition of them by the state since then, nevertheless their community has and has always had property interests in the land which pre-date colonisation and still subsist. As we saw in Parts II and III of the chapter, what precisely has to be proved varies from jurisdiction to jurisdiction. However, generally it involves proving that the claimants' ancestors had a pre-existing connection with the land *at the time when the colonisers first asserted sovereignty over their land*, and that the claimants are the current members of the community which has continued that traditional connection up until colonisation, and that they continue to use the land in those same traditional ways.[98] Each of these steps can present a formidable hurdle for the claimants, for a number of obvious and not so obvious reasons.

(a) Oral Culture

Absence of Written Evidence

A group which has an oral culture has the obvious difficulty they have no written laws or legal documents which set out the rules which governed their collective resource use at the time of colonisation, since the rules evolved by custom. However, they also have no other written evidence either, no maps, no written histories and no written records of who had what interests in which resources. For European settler societies, this could translate into 'no evidence'. Katner notes that in one US case on Native American rights in the 1970s, 'the bias towards written evidence was so

---

course be other explanations. Communities with despotic and repressive leaders who enforce resource use patterns that unnecessarily impoverish some members of the community may also be long-lived, as may destructive resource use patterns where resources are plentiful, or inflexible sub-efficient resource use patterns practised by communities who have yet to come up against dramatic environmental or demographic changes or intrusion by outsiders.

[98] Kent McNeil, 'Developments on aboriginal title' (2016) Osgoode Hall Digital Commons, http://digitalcommons.osgoode.yorku.ca/all_papers/321

strong that even the expert witness for the Mashpee Tribe had telling language creep into his testimony when he stated that he looked at *every piece of paper* surviving from that period'.[99]

The state, on the other hand, does have written evidence – a super-abundance of it – and it all tells the story from the western perspective. It includes historical written evidence from government officials, missionaries, explorers and traders who first encountered indigenous populations and often were blind to, or misunderstood, their cultures and their complex property rights systems. Some western records from the colonial era might also be self-serving, seeking to justify the taking over of what appeared to settlers and traders to be vacant or under-used land. In any event, they were likely to accept the Lockean view that only those who cultivated land had moral and economic claims to property in it, and not at all likely to identify any positive environmental or societal effects of local cultural and resource use rules and practices.[100] Ravna quotes the following from the Statement of the Lapp Commission which reported to the Norwegian Government in 1892:

> One must respect the rights of the Lapps. But when weighing the Lapp and the settled farmers' mutual rights and obligations towards each other, one cannot forget the different conditions of their way of life, and that farmers, undertaking the hard and laborious work of cultivation, often incur heavy burdens. The Lapp, for whom life alternates between hardships and laziness, usually lives free of such impositions. From the state's economic point of view the Lapp livelihood is of little significance. Although he, for his reindeer husbandry, makes free use of significant pastures and much wood, it is nevertheless rare for the Lapp to accumulate wealth for any length of time.[101]

Proving What Happened in the Past

Written and oral cultures have different rules and conventions about how you 'prove' what happened in the past. In Australia and Canada the forum of adjudication for indigenous land rights cases was historically a common law style court room. In early cases the courts took the view that claimants had to prove their case using common law rules of evidence, which, understandably, are geared towards a written culture. In *Milirrpum*, 15 pages of Blackburne J's judgment are taken up with his analysis of the arguments put by counsel as to the admissibility of various kinds of evidence. He concluded that 'proof of all the facts asserted by the plaintiffs must be by evidence admissible at common law', but he attempted to modify its effect by adding that:

> the rules of evidence are to be applied rationally, not mechanically. The application of a rule of evidence to the proof of novel facts, in the context of novel issues of

---

[99] Max Katner, 'Native American oral evidence: Finding a new hearsay exception' available at https://ssrn.com/abstract=3323923, p. 3: he quotes this from Gerald Torres and Kathryn Milun, 'Translating Yonnondio by precedent and evidence: The Mashpee Indian case' (1990) *Duke Law Journal* 625 at p. 649.

[100] This is evident from many of the historical sources quoted by Stuart Banner, *Possessing the Pacific: Land, Settlers, and Indigenous People from Australia to Alaska* (Cambridge, MA and London: Harvard University Press, 2007).

[101] Quoted by Øyvind Ravna, 'Assessment of evidence of Saami use of land' in Bankes and Koivurova (eds.), *The Proposed Nordic Saami Convention*, p. 177 at p. 195.

substantive law, must be in accordance with the true rationale of the rule, not merely in accordance with its past application to analogous facts.[102]

On this basis he was able to find that evidence from aboriginal witnesses as to what they had heard from their ancestors about their land and resource use patterns was admissible despite the common law hearsay rule,[103] because it could be brought within an established exception to the rule:

> I reject, therefore, the defendants' objections to the admission of statements by the aboriginal witnesses as to what their deceased ancestors had said about the rights of the various clans to particular pieces of land, and the system of which these rights form part. In my opinion, such evidence is admissible under the exception to the hearsay rule relating to the declarations of deceased persons as to matters of public and general rights (commonly known as reputation evidence).[104]

However, there has since been a greater relaxation and modification of rules of evidence in modern courts and tribunals hearing indigenous land rights claims in Australia and Canada, prompted by an acknowledgment of the cultural differences in 'proving' past events, as we see in Parts II and III above.

(b) Lack of Physical Evidence 'On the Ground' of Property Rights

A particular problem for traditionally nomadic or semi-nomadic indigenous claimants seeking to prove what use they made of their territory is that nomadic resource use tends to leave no physical traces on the ground. The same applies to control over resources used only seasonally. Seasonal use is not necessarily marked by buildings or other structures or by signs of cultivation, and nor are hunting and gathering trails. Similarly, boundaries and borders may be marked, if at all, only by natural physical features on the land which may be evident to or known by the community and its traditional neighbours but not necessarily recognisable by outsiders.

(c) Legitimacy of Purchases and Treaties

One immediate response of settlers who encountered indigenous populations was to buy their property rights from them, or enter into treaties with them which involved 'establishing' (at least in the eyes of the settlers) what their rights were, and perhaps designating geographic areas for their occupation. This was an obvious pragmatic response when the indigenous population had physical control of their resources, and was able and willing to defend them against incursion. Purchase might be by individual settlers, or by the Crown, and of course treaties were entered into by the Crown.

Leaving aside the very real question of whether, on any particular occasion the indigenous people were deliberately cheated out of their rights by any of these

---

[102] *Milirrpum*, fn. 17 above, pp. 153–154.
[103] See also Katner, 'Native American oral evidence: Finding a new hearsay exception', fn. 99 above.
[104] *Milirrpum*, fn. 17 above, at p. 159.

arrangements, in many other cases the legitimacy of these arrangements is undermined by mutual misunderstandings between the two sides over what exactly was being agreed and by whom. So, for example, there was often considerable uncertainty (on both sides) as to who amongst the indigenous people had the authority to negotiate on behalf of whom, and a mismatch between what each side thought was being offered and accepted by the other. Stuart Banner[105] gives the example of land purchases in New Zealand by British settlers, and later by the Crown, from the indigenous Maori people. In the early years of settlement there were scandalous instances of individual purchases at gross undervalues by entrepreneurial land dealers. Then, after some uncertainty, the British, who had established sovereignty over the whole of New Zealand in 1840, formally recognised the indigenous Maori people as owners of all the land in New Zealand and then set about the task of purchasing it from them. Banner details the many problems: the British did not understand the Maori property rights system; the British were familiar with the idea of buying and selling land and the procedures for doing so, which put them in a strong negotiating position, whereas sale was an alien concept for the Maori, and they had to make up the rules as they went along, often with differing results in different areas.[106] Also, the buyers assumed they are buying 'ownership' of a geographic space, whereas the sellers assumed they are selling their rights (i.e. permitting the buyers to do what they had been doing on the land, but not to do anything else with it – for which they came back and demanded further payment).[107]

(d) Length, Cost of Proceedings

Unsurprisingly, given all of this, the proceedings for proving that a claimant community once had, and still has, property interests in and/or title to its land are long and expensive. In *Mabo (No 2)* for example, the case was remitted to Justice Moynihan of the Supreme Court of Queensland to hear the evidence and determine the facts. It is recorded that the hearing took 67 court sitting days. There were 313 exhibits, including a detailed report by a Cambridge anthropological expedition of the 1890s, and many government records. A significant part of the evidence comprised oral accounts by the Murray Islanders, much of which recounted tradition and statements made by people long dead. A great deal of this evidence was challenged as 'hearsay', but was eventually accepted by Justice Moynihan. He released his finding of facts in 1990: it came in three volumes containing 500 pages in all. And as we noted in para. 9.11, the length and cost of proceedings have not lessened under the regime introduced by the Native Title Act 1993.[108]

Similarly, Vickers J gives the following description of the trial of the Canadian *Tsilhqot'in* case before the Supreme Court of British Columbia:

---

[105] Banner, *Possessing the Pacific*, fn. 100 above, Ch. 2 'New Zealand: Conquest by contract'.
[106] Ibid. pp. 54–56 and 58–59.   [107] Ibid. pp. 70–73.
[108] For further evidence, and discussion of possible remedies, see Australian Law Reform Committee, *Connection to Country*, fn. 41 above, paras. 3.61–3.79.

The trial commenced in Victoria on November 18, 2002. There were a total of 339 trial days. In the late fall and early winter of 2003, the Court sat for five weeks in the language resource room of the Naghataneqed Elementary School at Tl'ebayi in Xeni (Nemiah Valley). The balance of the trial took place in Victoria. In the course of this lengthy trial, the court heard oral history and oral tradition evidence and considered a vast number of historical documents. Evidence was tendered in the fields of archeology, anthropology, history, cartography, hydrology, wildlife ecology, ethnoecology, ethnobotany, biology, linguistics, forestry and forest ecology.[109]

His judgment covers 463 pages, excluding Appendices of evidence. The *Tsilhqot'in* people were said to have spent more than Can$10 million on legal and other fees relating to the protracted litigation.

(e) Burden of Proof

We have already noted the burden of proof this places on the claimant in Australia and Canada, and in particular the additional hurdles to be surmounted by claimants under the Native Title Act 1993 in Australia following the decision in *Yorta Yorta*.[110] It is worth noting that other jurisdictions have taken steps to ease the burden of proof. So, for example, Kirsten Anker notes that New Zealand recently enacted a rebuttable presumption in favour of the non-extinguishment of customary interests,[111] and Ravna explains that under Norwegian law, in Reindeer Husbandry districts there is a presumption that there are pastoral reindeer husbandry rights over the land, rebuttable by the landowner proving the contrary.[112] However, in 2015 the Australian Law Reform Committee considered but rejected the idea of introducing similar presumptions into Australian law, concluding that it would be more effective to provide guidance on inferences that can properly be drawn from, for example, recent or current practice or events.[113]

9.23 Coexistence of Multiple Property Rights Systems

Once the claimant community has established that it had, and still observes, its own idiosyncratic property rights system, there is then a further politically charged question to determine: what exactly is involved in 'recognition' of this property rights system by the state? There are at least three possibilities. One, now largely discredited, is that the state should provide procedures for the community itself, and/or the members of the community, to convert their customary property relationships into the nearest equivalent property interests recognised in the dominant property system. This has often been attempted but nearly always failed, for a variety of reasons. Leaving aside failures in political will and failure to provide sufficient

---

[109] *Tsilhqot'in Nation and British Columbia* (2007) BCSC 1700.
[110] *Yorta Yorta Aboriginal Community* v. *Victoria* (2002) 214 CLR 422: para. 9.11 above.
[111] Anker, 'Law, culture and fact in indigenous claims', fn. 94 above, p. 41, noting s. 106 of the Marine and Coastal Area (Takutai Moana) Act 2011.
[112] Ravna, 'Assessment of evidence of Saami use of land', fn. 101 above, at pp. 188–192.
[113] Australian Law Reform Committee, *Connection to Country*, fn. 41 above, Ch. 7.

resources, the most serious failure has tended to be in understanding the nature of the indigenous property interests in question, and precisely who held them, exacerbated by a tendency to be blind towards the idea that women and groups within the community might have their own kinds of property interests in the community's resources. An even more formidable problem has been that even when the state fully understands the property rights system customarily observed in the minority culture, it does not recognise equivalent property interests within its own system. The inevitable result is that some members of the community will be given too much and others too little or nothing at all. So, for example, the man who at the relevant time was taken to be the current head of a household would often be given an absolute private ownership interest in the house which was customarily treated as his family's home and in the land which his family customarily farmed, even though under the customary system his interest might have been a non-transferable interest which he held for the benefit of both present and future generations; it might have been held subject to enforceable obligations to the community and family members to use the land to feed, house and make other provision for current family members; and he might also be under an enforceable obligation to the community to care for the land and its resources in traditional ways that ensured its environmental sustainability and preservation for future generations. In any event, even if successful, this approach to 'recognition' would inevitably involve the elimination of the indigenous group's traditional property rights system and arguably also radical changes – for good or for bad – to its traditional culture.[114]

It is now generally agreed that proper recognition must, rather, involve the state accepting that it is bound to protect the rights and interests that people have in their land and other resources under their own property rights system, guaranteeing their enforcement against the state and against other citizens. However, as we saw in Parts II and III, this has its own difficulties. Does it mean that the indigenous community will be entitled only to go on using their resources in the way they have always done, free from interference by the state and by outsiders? Or does it go further than that, entailing recognition that the community is entitled to take charge of the resources it has customarily used, deciding for itself how it will continue to use them? The first commits the national state (and the community) to preserving that group's traditional ways of life, and this is difficult enough, because there are then difficult questions about, for example, forums for adjudicating disputes within the community, and whether and how the customary property rights system should be allowed or required to change to adapt to demographic, geographic, scientific and social and economic developments. The second involves the state allowing that group to have a degree of self-determination over its own territory, which may bring its own political and constitutional problems.

---

[114] See further Maureen Tehan, 'Customary land tenure, communal titles and sustainability: The allure of individual title and property rights in Australia' in Lee Godden and Maureen Tehan (eds.), *Comparative Perspectives on Communal lands and Individual Ownership: Sustainable Futures* (Abingdon and New York: Routledge, 2010) p. 353 and Penny Lee, 'Individual titling of aboriginal land in the Northern Territory: What Australia can learn from the international community' (2006) 29 *University of New South Wales Law Journal* 22.

9.24 Conformity With National and International Values

Whichever it is, there is a further question of how far the community should be required to adapt its traditional culture and way of life to conform with national and international rules and principles which, for example, require democratic decision-making, or prohibit discrimination against some sectors of the group, or require compliance with regulatory regimes for the protection of public health, or the environment, or child protection. We have already seen that s. 35(4) of the Constitution Act 1982 in Canada provides that aboriginal rights 'are guaranteed equally to male and female persons'. Hendry and Tatum argue that recognition of distinct legal cultures within a state does not mean that each legal culture must be impermeable to outside influences. Their argument is that the true position is that different legal cultures within the same state are inherently interactive, and they identify examples of indigenous groups in the USA adapting their traditional legal and procedural forms through this interactive process as a means of enriching and enhancing their traditional way of life. They note, however, that so far the necessary reciprocal adaptations on the part of the dominant US legal culture 'are far harder to identify'.[115]

9.25 Land Registration

Most post-colonial states have land registration systems which were designed to accommodate the dominant property rights systems, which in most cases means a property rights system where private ownership is the central focus and where one of the main objectives of the system is to promote the marketability of land. This is certainly true of land registration systems in Australia and in Canada. Land registration systems of these kinds have immense difficulties in accommodating the traditional land rights of their indigenous peoples. The traditional response in post-colonial jurisdictions like Australia and Canada has been to keep indigenous land rights off their land registers, but this approach is difficult to justify on anything other than practical grounds. It is difficult for a post-colonial jurisdiction to argue convincingly that multiple property rights systems operate on equal terms within their territory, if they maintain a register covering every piece of land in their territory which records the property interests arising under one of their land rights systems but not the property interests arising under the others. This is particularly unfortunate when (as in the land registration systems in Australia and Canada) the primary purpose of the land register is to protect property rights and to guarantee to purchasers that ownership of the land they are buying is free from any property interests not recorded on the register.

Stephenson and Tehan consider the current problems about land registration and indigenous land rights in Australia and discuss possible solutions,[116] and Stephenson

---

[115] Jennifer Hendry and Melissa Tatum, 'Justice for native nations: Insights from legal pluralism' (2018) *Arizona Legal Studies Discussion Paper No. 18-14* pp. 111–113.

[116] Margaret Stephenson and Maureen Tehan, 'The recording and management of indigenous lands and title: is reform required?' (2015) 24 *Australian Property Law Journal* 235.

also compares the positions in the USA, Canada and Australia in an earlier study in 2010.[117] In particular, she describes the Métis Settlement Land Registry in Alberta, which records both collective and individual titles in Métis settlement land, and lesser interests, and was set up by the Alberta Métis Settlement Act 2000, which provides for Métis self-governance of Métis settlement lands by (amongst other things) providing for the transfer and allocation of Métis settlement lands and resources to Métis.[118]

There is an added problem in other countries where governments selling land to foreign investors are tempted to pass off land subject to indigenous land rights as 'empty' land open for development.[119] It is too easy for them to do that if the land in question is registered in the country's land register as 'owned' by the government or by a private landowner, and there is nothing on the register to suggest that it is also subject to indigenous rights or indigenous title.

For both of these reasons it is now increasingly acknowledged that if there are multiple property rights systems in operation in a state, property rights in land under all systems must be brought within the state registration system in some way, even if there are significant differences in the form and nature of the property rights arising under the different systems. We come back to this point in Chapter 16 *Registration* para. 16.32, where we consider the implications this has for registration of communal and public property rights in our own land registration system.

PART V INTERNATIONAL LAW PROTECTION FOR INDIGENOUS AND MINORITY PEOPLES' RIGHTS

9.26 United Nations Declaration on the Rights of Indigenous Peoples 2007

The United Nations Declaration on the Rights of Indigenous Peoples[120] was adopted by the General Assembly of the United Nations on 13 September 2007, nearly 25 years after the United Nations Economic and Social Council set up the UN Working Group on Indigenous Populations.[121] The Declaration recognises the right of indigenous people, collectively and individually, to self-determination and to the preservation and flourishing of their cultures, and – most important for present

---

[117] Margaret Stephenson, 'You can't always get what you want: Economic development on indigenous individual and collective titles in North America: which land tenure models are relevant to Australia' in Lee Godden and Maureen Tehan (eds.), *Comparative Perspectives on Communal lands and Individual Ownership: Sustainable Futures* (Abingdon and New York Routledge 2010) p. 100.

[118] Ibid. pp. 122–124.

[119] This is just one aspect of the relatively recent 'land-grab' problem facing underdeveloped countries, whose richer neighbours are short of land for food production, or want to exploit resources which are not available in sufficient quantities in their own country: see further Olivier de Schutter, 'The green rush: The global race for farmland and the rights of land users' (2011) 52 *Harvard international Law Journal* 503.

[120] United Nations Declaration on the Rights of Indigenous Peoples, UN GA Resolution 61/295 of 13 September 2007, UN Doc A/RES/47/1 (2007) ('UNDRIP').

[121] For the procedural history see Stephen Allen and Alexandra Xanthaki (eds.) *Reflections on the UN Declaration on the Rights of Indigenous Peoples* (Oxford and Portland, OR: Hart Publishing, 2011).

purposes – it recognises their rights to the 'lands, territories and resources which they have traditionally owned, occupied or otherwise used or acquired',[122] and their rights to 'own, use, develop and control' them.[123] States are required by the Declaration to give 'legal recognition and protection' to these lands, territories and resources, 'with due respect to the customs, traditions and land tenure systems of the indigenous peoples concerned'.[124]

In addition, the Declaration prohibits the dispossession or forcible removal of indigenous peoples from their lands, territories or resources,[125] and gives them the right to restitution 'or, when this is not possible, just, fair and equitable compensation' as redress for past confiscations, takings, occupation, use or damage made 'without their free, prior and informed consent'.[126] States are also required to 'consult and co-operate in good faith' with indigenous peoples' representative institutions, in order to obtain 'their free and informed consent' prior to the approval of any project affecting their land, territories or other resources.[127]

The 2007 Declaration, like other UN declarations, did not become directly binding on the States who voted in favour of it.[128] However, because of its wide acceptance by States over the decade since it was adopted, it has probably become recognised by custom as laying down rules binding on States in international law.[129] Some states have already incorporated it into their domestic law whilst others have equivalent provisions in their constitutions, and the only four states who voted against it in 2009 – the USA, Canada, Australia and New Zealand – did so only because they already had as part of their domestic law what they considered to be more appropriate and more extensive protection for indigenous and other minorities.[130] In any event, even those four dissenting countries have now reversed their positions and expressed support for the Declaration.

However, over the world there is considerable disagreement over which oppressed ethnic minority groups qualify as 'indigenous peoples' and so attract the protection of the 2007 Declaration. There are also those who argue that the protection of the 2007 Declaration should be extended to all oppressed minorities, not just those who qualify as 'indigenous peoples'. Both problems become apparent when we look more closely at what we mean by 'indigenous' and why 'indigenous peoples' have been thought to deserve special protection.

---

[122] UNDRIP, fn. 120 above, art. 26.1.   [123] Ibid. art. 26.2.   [124] Ibid. art. 26.3.
[125] Ibid. art. 8.2(b) and art. 10.   [126] Ibid. art. 28.   [127] Ibid. art. 32.
[128] 143 States voted in favour, four against and there were 11 abstentions.
[129] Report of the Commission on Human Rights, E/3616/Rev. l, para. 105 (on the process by which UN Declarations can become, in effect, part of customary international law) and see also H Patrick Glenn, 'The three ironies of the UN Declaration on the rights of Indigenous Peoples' in Allen and Xanthaki, *Reflections on the UN Declaration on the Rights of Indigenous Peoples* (fn. 121 above) p. 171 at pp. 180–181, specifically on the status and importance of the 2007 Declaration.
[130] H Patrick Glenn pointed out the irony of these four countries, which had been 'in the vanguard of judicial affirmation of indigenous rights', being the only countries to reject the 2007 Declaration: Glenn, 'The three ironies of the UN Declaration on the Rights of Indigenous Peoples' pp. 172 and 179–180.

9.27 Who Are 'Indigenous Peoples?'

This has always been contested. The most-often quoted definition is that provided by the UN Special Rapporteur of the Sub-Commission on Prevention of Discrimination and Protection of Minorities José R Martinez Cobo:[131]

> Indigenous communities, peoples and nations are those which, having an historical continuity with preinvasion and pre-colonial societies that developed on their territories, consider themselves distinct from other sectors of the societies now prevailing on those territories, or parts of them. They form at present non-dominant sectors of society and are determined to preserve, develop and transmit to future generations their ancestral territories, and their ethnic identity, as the basis of their continued existence as peoples, in accordance with their own cultural patterns, social institutions and legal system.
>
> [Indigenous peoples are] composed of the existing descendants of the peoples who inhabited the present territory of a country wholly or partially at the time when persons of a different culture or ethnic origin arrived there from other parts of the world, overcame them and, by conquest, settlement or other means, reduced them to a non-dominant or colonial condition; who today live more in conformity with their particular social, economic and cultural customs and traditions than with the institutions of the country of which they now form part, under a State structure which incorporates mainly the national, social and cultural characteristics of other segments of the population which are predominant.

One of the many criticisms of this definition is that it does not cover other minority peoples who have traditionally suffered the same levels of discrimination. For example, there are immigrant peoples such as African Americans who have never had the opportunity to develop traditional attachments to land, and mixed race peoples such as the Métis in Canada whose existence was a product of settlement by outsiders.

9.28 Why Should Indigenous Peoples Have Special Claims?

A number of rationales have been put forward to justify special treatment for indigenous peoples (many of which are equally applicable to other minority groups such as those we noted in the previous paragraph)

(a) Past Oppression and Discrimination

The first is that they have special claims for protection because they have historically suffered racial discrimination, cultural disrespect and other kinds of oppression based on their cultural identity, and this has led to them being systematically disadvantaged, sometimes over generations. This is explicitly recognised in the preamble to UNDRIP.

---

[131] José R Martinez Cobo, 'Study of the problem of discrimination against indigenous populations', UN Doc. E/CN.4/Sub.2/1986/7/Add 4, para. 379, 1986.

(b) Prior Occupancy

A separate argument is that they have special claims because of what Waldron has described as prior occupancy (they were dispossessed by the current possessors). Waldron and others have argued that this should give rise to stronger claims to land rights than first occupancy (they were here first), for the reasons we considered in paras. 3.8 and 3.9 in Chapter 3 *Allocation of Property Rights*. As Waldron put it 'they are the descendants . . . of those who inhabited a country or a geographical region at the time when people of different cultures or ethnic origins arrived. The new arrivals later became dominant through conquest, occupation, settlement or other means'[132]. In other words, they were dispossessed by people of a different culture or ethnic origin, who went on to become the dominant culture.

(c) Environmentally Sensitive Resource Management

Another argument is that there is an inherent value in the relationship that traditional indigenous communities have with their environment. This operates at two levels. We can say that their continued occupation of their traditional lands is (objectively) an environmental good, because their way of living with their resources is a product of accumulated wisdom and environmental sensitivity (they regard themselves as stewards of their land, for its own sake and for future generations) and has evolved to suit their unique physical environment. And if we can take it that they have come to know best how to manage their environment in the interests of themselves, future generations and the sustainability of the resources, then it is in everyone's interests that the state allows them to remain in control. Sandberg makes this point in relation to state recognition of Saami rights of reindeer husbandry, hunting and salmon fishing. Recognition enables the state, he says:

> . . . to replace costly and unsustainable centralized governing of natural resources with more local, more legitimate, more efficient and more flexible self-governing institutions and thus decentralize some of the state's dilemmas connected with overuse of and exclusion from biological resources.[133]

(d) Personhood Claims on Resources

On another level, we can say that their intense sustained relationship with their environment merits special treatment by the law because their resources have become part of their personhood, in the ways recognised by Hegel and by Radin which we considered in Chapter 7 *Objects of Property Interests* para. 7.10. Because their natural environment has a spiritual and cultural significance for indigenous

---

[132] Jeremy Waldron, '"To bestow stability upon possession:" Hume's alternative to Locke' in James Penner and Henry E. Smith (eds.) *Philosophical Foundations of Property Law* (Oxford: Oxford University Press, 2013) p. 1.

[133] Audun Sandberg, 'Collective rights in a modernizing North – on institutionalizing Sami and local rights to land and water in northern Norway' (2008) 2 *International Journal of the Commons* 269 at pp. 271.

people, not just an economic one, they have become personally embodied in their land and its resources, and this interrelationship between themselves and their resources demands a higher respect. This view is echoed by the statement of the United Nations Permanent Forum on Indigenous Issues in its Factsheet, that for indigenous people 'Their ancestral land has a fundamental importance for their collective physical and cultural survival as peoples'.

(e) Protection of Minority Cultures as a Good in Itself

As Kirsten Anker has pointed out, the Canadian Courts' approach to s. 35 of the Constitution Act 1982 in *Van der Peet*[134] and in *Tsilhqot'in*[135] is linked to what she describes as 'the group-based rights or identity politics' promoted by Will Kymlicka and Charles Taylor'.[136] They argue for the recognition and protection of minority cultures[137] by the larger state on the basis that it is a basic good in itself. For Kymlicka, the good lies in the 'individuals' access to a cultural heritage in which their classic liberal choices between values can be meaningful to them', whereas for Taylor it is that respect for cultural identity is essential for 'human dignity and a healthy identity'.[138] For Taylor, our culture – our 'authentic way of being' provides 'both a 'horizon' or background criteria of value that enable us to make distinctions, judgments and decisions, and are the context in which individual identities are worked out through social interaction. Cultures can therefore lay claim to a right to survive for future generations, but they also require a presumption of equal worth'.[139]

One can add to these arguments the separate arguments that respect for and protection of minority cultures promotes cultural *diversity*, an added good in itself, and is an essential function of democracy.[140]

9.29 Redressing the Wrongs

If those are the rationales for singling out indigenous peoples for special treatment, it is worth considering what special treatment is appropriate. In particular, it is important to be clear whether the objective is to provide indigenous peoples with *reparation* (compensation for the disadvantage, oppression and lack of opportunity

---

[134] *R v. Van der Peet* [1996] 2 Supreme Court Reporter 507.
[135] *Tsilhqot'in Nation v. British Columbia* [2014] 2 SCR 256.
[136] Anker, 'Law, culture and fact in indigenous claims', fn. 94 above, at p. 11, drawing primarily on Will Kymlicka, *Liberalism, Community and Culture* (Oxford: Oxford University Press, 1989) at pp. 163–165 and Charles Taylor, 'The politics of recognition' in Amy Gutmann (ed.), *Multiculturalism: Examining the Politics of Recognition* (Princeton, NJ: Princeton University Press, 1994).
[137] Québécois as well as aboriginal.
[138] All this from Anker, 'Law, culture and fact in indigenous claims', fn. 94 above, at p. 11: she goes on to say more about what Taylor, drawing on Hegel, means by 'identity'.
[139] Ibid. pp. 11–12.
[140] For further justifications and arguments see the Introduction and Ch. 1 in Bankes and Koivurova (eds.),*The Proposed Nordic Saami Convention*, fn. 80 above.

they have suffered and now suffer as a consequence of their dispossession, in the form of, for example, extra provision for housing, health care, education or employment); or *recognition* of their surviving patterns of resource use as a property rights system requiring protection and enforcement on an equal footing with other property rights systems recognised by the state; or *restitution* of their traditional territories from which they have been dispossessed; or *self-determination*, in the form of either 'internal' self-determination providing a right to autonomy and self-government or 'external' self-determination involving secession, in other words independence from the dominant State.[141]

The Nordic Sami Convention[142] gives detailed consideration to what self-determination might involve in the context of the complex position of the Nordic Sami people, whose traditional territories span three different sovereign states,[143] and cover geographic areas where non-indigenous people also live, and whose resources may also be of importance to other local communities and to the nation as a whole. Moreover, whilst the Saami population still utilizes parts of its traditional territory more or less exclusively, and other areas have an overwhelming Saami majority, in substantial parts of its traditional territories they are in a minority position. Nevertheless, the drafters of the Convention concluded that the Saami people is entitled to a right of self-determination in respect of the whole of its territory, despite these factors, for reasons which may be of interest to indigenous groups in other jurisdictions who are not the sole occupiers of their territory, and who share their resources with other cultural groups.[144]

RECOMMENDED READING

This chapter covers a wide range of issues drawing on a lot of material. Some readers may want to concentrate on just one of the two jurisdictions covered – Australia or Canada – or on comparing the two, in which case they should focus on Part II and/or Part III of this chapter, drawing on the rest as appropriate. An alternative approach would be to concentrate on the general issue of the protection of minority property rights systems within a state where the dominant property rights system arises out of a different cultural relationship between people and their land and resources. If you prefer to do this, you could focus on Parts IV and V, dipping into Parts II and III for illustrations and examples.

---

[141] Joshua Castellino and Jérémie Gilbert, 'Self-determination, indigenous peoples and minorities' (2003) 3 *Macquarie Law Journal* 155; Anker, 'Law, culture and fact in indigenous claims', fn. 94 above, pp. 12–13 – though she doesn't put it this way – summarising the views of those who criticise the ways in which the dominant culture is given 'classificatory authority', i.e. defining the content of aboriginal rights in terms of European understandings of culture.

[142] The Nordic Saami Convention was negotiated between Norway, Sweden and Finland and an agreed text was signed by the official negotiators on 15 January 2017. It has now been submitted for approval by the governments of the three nations: Atle Staalesen, 'Historic Sámi agreement starts long way towards ratification', *Independent Barents Observer*, 17 January 2017, https://thebarentsobserver.com/en/2017/01/historic-sami-agreement-starts-long-way-towards-ratification.

[143] In fact four, but the fourth, Russia, has not participated in the Saami Convention.

[144] Mattias Åhrén, Martin Scheinin and John B. Henriksen, 'The Nordic Sami Convention: International human rights, self-determination and other central provisions' (2007) 3 *Journal of Indigenous Peoples Rights* 8.

Milirrpum v. *Nabalco Pty Ltd* (1971) 17 FLR 141.

Mabo v. *State of Queensland (No 2)* (1992) 175 CLR 1.

Tsilhqot'in Nation v. *British Columbia* [2014] 2 SCR 256.

Australian Law Reform Commission, *Connection to Country: Review of the Native Title Act 1993* (2015) (for reference: for a useful summary see Robyn Gilbert, 'Connection to country: The Australian Law Reform Commission recommends change to the Native Title Act' (2015) 8 *Indigenous Law Bulletin* 12).

Stuart Banner, *Possessing the Pacific: Land, Settlers, and Indigenous People from Australia to Alaska* (Cambridge, MA and London: Harvard University Press, 2007) (for those interested in a historical account of the attitudes of British settlers and the British government to the land rights of the indigenous peoples of Australia and British Columbia at the time of settlement and assertion of sovereignty: see Introduction and Chs. 1 and 6).

Kirsten Anker, *Declarations of Interdependence: A Legal Pluralist Approach to Indigenous Rights* (Farnham, Surrey: Ashgate, 2014) pp. 41–53 (a good summary of the progress of 'recognition' of indigenous land rights in Australia and Canada, through the cases covered in this chapter, although published before the SCC decision in *Tsilhqot'in*).

Yaëll Emerich, *Conceptualising Property Law: Integrating Common Law and Civil Law Traditions* (Cheltenham: Edward Elgar Publishing Ltd, 2018) pp. 12–15 (a good short summary of the issues in Canada).

L Godden and M Tehan, 'Translating native title to individual "title" in Australia: Are real property forms and indigenous interests reconcilable?' in E. Cooke (ed.), *Modern Studies in Property Law*, vol. 4 (Oxford and Portland, Hart Publishing, 2007) p. 262.

Brendan Edgeworth, 'Extinguishment of native title: recent High Court decisions (2016) 8 *Indigenous Law Bulletin* 28 (post-*Mabo* developments, especially on extinguishment).

Sharon Mascher, 'The Australian approach to recognising the land rights of indigenous peoples: the Native Title Act 1993' in Nigel Bankes and Timo Koivurova, *The Proposed Nordic Saami Convention: National and International Dimensions of Indigenous Property Rights*, (Oxford and Portland, OR: Hart Publishing, 2013) p. 323.

Maureen Tehan 'Customary land tenure, communal titles and sustainability: The allure of individual title and property rights in Australia' in Lee Godden and Maureen Tehan (eds.), *Comparative Perspectives on Communal lands and Individual Ownership: Sustainable Futures* (Abingdon and New York: Routledge, 2010) p. 353

Margaret Stephenson, 'You can't always get what you want: Economic development on indigenous individual and collective titles in North America: which land tenure models are relevant to Australia', also in Godden and Tehan (eds.), *Comparative Perspectives* at p. 100.

Gerrit Pienaar, 'The reality of fragmented property rights' in Bram Akkermans, Ernst Marais and Eveline Ramaekers (eds.), *Property Law Perspectives II* (Cambridge, Antwerp and Portland, OR: Intersentia, 2014) p. 341 (on the mix of indivisible Civil Law private ownership, urbanised fragmented tenure, and communal lands tenure, including discussion of land registration issues).

Daniel Fitzpatrick, '"Best practice" options for the legal recognition of customary tenure' (2005) 36 *Development and Change* 449 (classic theoretical analysis, with a useful resume of the literature).

W.J Du Plessis, 'African indigenous land rights in a private ownership paradigm' (2011) 14 *Potchefstroom Electronic Law Journal* 44 (on the need to see customary property rights systems through an indigenous law lens).

Stephen Allen and Alexandra Xanthaki (eds.), *Reflections on the UN Declaration on the Rights of Indigenous Peoples* (Oxford and Portland, OR: Hart Publishing, 2011) (a collection of essays on UNDRIP, for reference and for guidance on specialist literature).

Susanna Lastarria-Cornhiel, 'Impact of privatisation on gender and property rights in Africa' (1997) 25 *World Development* 1317 (this and the next two all focus on the position of women in indigenous societies).

Ann Whitehead and Dzodzi Tsikata, 'Policy Discourses on women's land rights in sub-Saharan Africa: The implications of the re-turn to the customary' (2003)3 *Journal of Agrarian Change* 67.

Jennifer Koshan, 'The Nordic Saami Convention and the rights of Saami Women: Lessons from Canada' in Nigel Bankes and Timo Koivurova, *The Proposed Nordic Saami Convention: National and International Dimensions of Indigenous Property Rights* (Oxford and Portland, OR: Hart Publishing, 2013) p. 379.

Questions

(1) Explain the difference between 'aboriginal title' and 'aboriginal rights' in Canada. What are the implications for an aboriginal group of acquiring aboriginal title over an area rather than aboriginal rights over it?

(2) What is 'native title' in Australia? What rights over an area does an indigenous group acquire if it is determined that it has native title over it?

(3) Discuss the differences between aboriginal title in Canada and native title in Australia. In relation to each of them consider (a) how the title can be lost and (b) how far an indigenous group can change its way of life and its use of its resources without forfeiting its title.

(4) Explain what indigenous people in Canada and in Australia have to prove in order to establish aboriginal title/native title. Why has it been so difficult for them to do so?

(5) What does 'continuity' mean (a) in Canada and (b) in Australia? Explain the criticisms of the requirement of continuity in Australia.

(6) Why does it take so long for courts in Australia to determine whether an indigenous group has native title? Why does it take the courts in Canada so long to decide whether an indigenous group has aboriginal title? If this is a problem, consider how it could be remedied.

(7) Explain and discuss the importance of the decision of the High Court of Australia in *Mabo (No 2)*. Has it led to adequate recognition and protection of indigenous land rights in Australia? If not, why not?

(8) Are the traditional land rights of indigenous people in Canada now adequately recognised and protected in Canadian law, following the decision of the Supreme Court of Canada in *Tsilhqot'in*? If not, what are the outstanding problems?

(9) Why has it taken so long for post-colonial states to recognise the traditional land rights of their indigenous peoples?

(10) How convincing are the arguments put forward for requiring states to give special recognition and protection for the land rights of their indigenous peoples? Examine the case for extending this recognition and protection to all minority groups.

10

Limitations on Property

PART I INTRODUCTION

10.1 Duties, Liabilities and Obligations of Property Interest Holders

We have already noted that even an absolute private owner of a thing – still less the holder of any other property interest in the thing – does not have unlimited rights or freedoms in respect of the thing she owns. One fundamental limitation, as we saw in Chapter 4 *Property and Human Rights*, is that most states have power to deprive citizens of their property in the public interest, if certain conditions are satisfied and compensation is paid, as well as powers to control or interfere with the exercise of a citizen's property rights in the public interest.[1] However, this is by no means the only limitation on the rights and freedoms of owners and other property interest holders. In this chapter we look more closely at some of the others.

   We are primarily interested in two categories of limitation. First, in Part II of the chapter we consider whether there are responsibilities and obligations inherent in the notion of property which limit the permissible exercise of the rights and freedoms of a property interest holder. As we see in Part II, this idea of property as a source of obligations – towards neighbours, or to society generally, or to the environment – as well as, or instead of, a source of rights or a source of personal wealth, is expressly adopted in the constitutions of many countries, including Germany and South Africa.[2] In addition, US progressive property theorists argue that it also does, or should, underlie US property law.[3] And, whilst there may be doubts about how far this view of property does indeed find expression in US property law, it is undoubtedly fundamental to many non-western legal systems, in particular to the indigenous property rights systems we looked at in Chapter 9 *Multiple Property Rights Systems*. We look at the nature of and effect of these kinds of limitations in Part II, and also at the more specific restraint on property owners represented by the civil law doctrine of abuse of rights, recognised in many jurisdictions but rejected by the English courts.

---

[1] See Part V of Chapter 4 *Property and Human Rights* where we look at the limits imposed by art. 1 Protocol 1 of the European Convention on Human Rights.

[2] Ibid. paras. 4.13–4.14 and para. 4.16.   [3] Ibid. para. 4.15.

In Part III we outline the extensive but piecemeal limitations on property which result from statutory regimes for regulation of land use by the state and other public authorities, and from mainly common law mechanisms by which land use can be restricted by neighbours. Our focus is on this private land use regulation, which in this jurisdiction means restrictions on land use enforceable by neighbouring landowners via restrictive covenants (which we cover in Part III of Chapter 13 *Non-Possessory Land Use Rights*) and by the torts of trespass and private nuisance. In particular, we consider the role private nuisance plays in limiting property interest holders' freedom to exercise their property rights. This is a common law limitation which has evolved primarily to reduce the externalities[4] of a landowner's use of her own land which are borne by her neighbours. This inevitably brings us back to the economic analysis of property rights we introduced in Part III of Chapter 2 *Conceptions and Justifications*.

PART II INHERENT OBLIGATIONS OF PROPERTY INTEREST HOLDERS

10.2 Constitutional Expression of Inherent Obligations of Property

As we saw in Chapter 4 *Property and Human Rights*, some human rights instruments and some national constitutions expressly state that property entails obligations and responsibilities as well as rights and powers. As we saw in para. 4.14, the outstanding example is Article 14(2) of the German *Grundgesetz* (the German Constitution), which provides that 'Property entails obligations. Its use shall also serve the public good.'

10.3 Progressive Property's Concept of Property Obligations

We saw in Chapter 2 *Conceptions and Justifications*,[5] that progressive property theorists argue that similar obligations and restrictions are inherent in property in US law as well, moulding and limiting the rights, powers and liberties of property interest holders.

(a) Gregory Alexander's Social Obligation Norm

Gregory Alexander compares Article 14(2) of the German constitution with the property provisions of the US constitution. The German Article 14(2), he says, is

> a powerful symbolic statement of two crucial propositions. First, there is an inherently social dimension to private property. Second, where conflicts between individual self-interest and the public good exist, the public good has priority. Neither of these propositions is self-evident, and both would be sharply contested by certain advocates

---

[4] For an explanation of 'externalities' and their significance see para. 2.11(f) of Chapter 2 *Conceptions and Justifications* and Daniel Cole and Peter Grossman, *Principles of Law & Economics* (2nd edn, New York: Wolters Kluwer, 2011) pp. 16–21.

[5] para. 2.26.

of absolute or near-absolute property rights in the United States. There is nothing really analogous to this provision in the US Constitution, and the absence of such an acknowledgment has encouraged the belief that property rights are absolute and exist solely to maintain boundaries between individuals.[6]

Nevertheless, he argues, a similar 'social obligation norm' does indeed operate in US property law:

> Property owners owe far more responsibilities to others, both owners and non-owners, than what the conventional imagery of property rights suggests. Property rights are inherently relational, and because of this characteristic, owners necessarily owe obligations to others. But the responsibility, or obligation, dimension of private ownership has been sorely under-theorised … [the] theory of property [I outline here] … emphasises the obligations that owners owe to others, specifically, to certain members of the various communities to which they belong. These obligations vary in different contexts and at different times. As society has grown more complex and more interdependent, the obligations have thickened. Capturing all of these obligations under one theoretical umbrella, one may speak of a social-obligation norm that the law does and should impose on owners. This norm, I want to stress, is inherent in the concept of ownership itself. This is an important point because it means that when the law, whether by way of statutes, administrative action or judicial decisions, announces some restriction on an owner's use of her land or building, insofar as that announcement restates what is already part of the social-obligation norm, it is simply a legal recognition of a restriction that is inherent in the concept of ownership rather than being externally imposed and engrafted upon the owner's bundle of right.[7]

He goes on to explain that his social obligation theory 'builds on the claim that the basic purpose of property is to enable an individual to achieve human flourishing', in other words to have 'the opportunity to live a life as fulfilling as possible for him or her.[8]

For present purposes, the important point is that Alexander sees the kinds of restriction we look at in Parts III and IV of this chapter as evidence that his 'social obligation norm' is inherent in US property law. It is beyond the scope of this book to examine whether or not he is right about US law: our concern is whether, because of the limitations on property we recognise in this jurisdiction, there is such a norm inherent in our own property system which 'does and should' impose similar social obligations on property interest holders in England and Wales.

(b) Joseph Singer's Duty of Attentiveness and Rules of Reason

Similarly, as we saw in para. 2.26, Joseph Singer sees his democratic model as imposing on property owners 'a duty of attentiveness' to the externalities of their

---

[6] Gregory Alexander, 'Civic property' (1997) 6 *Social & legal Studies* 217 at p. 225. He expands the argument in Gregory Alexander, 'Property as a fundamental constitutional right – The German example' (2003) 88 *Cornell Law Review* 733.

[7] Gregory S. Alexander, 'Ownership and obligations: The human flourishing theory of property' (2013) 43 *Hong Kong Law Journal* 451, at pp. 452–453. He develops the argument in more detail in Gregory S. Alexander, 'The social-obligation norm in American property law' (2009) 94 *Cornell Law Review* 745.

[8] Alexander, 'Ownership and obligations', fn. 7, at pp. 452–453.

actions. He has also argued that the law uses 'rules of reason' to limit how property owners may use their land, not just because of the immediate externalities of our acts borne by our neighbours, but also because of what he describes as the 'systemic effects' of the exercise of our property rights:

> Judgment is required to respond both to externalities and to the systemic effects of the recognition and exercise of individual property rights. Individual entitlements that appear innocent in themselves may both cause harm to others and result in systemic consequences that we cannot live with and which cause us to narrow the scope of those entitlements. It may not limit one's opportunities if one store refuses to serve you because of your religion because you can always shop elsewhere. But what if religious prejudice is widespread and you happen to belong to a minority religion that is the object of scorn and derision? The multiple effects of the exercise of the right to exclude by many individual owners could severely narrow your ability to engage in market transactions. Similarly, it might not matter if one person built a house on the coast but if the entire coast is built up, the cumulative effect of each small construction project may be massive, destroying the land on which the houses are built and undermining property further inland. Both nuisance and environmental law take into account the systemic effects of individual property use decisions, as antidiscrimination law takes into account the cumulative impact of individual acts of discrimination.
>
> Rules of reason provide an escape valve when the individual exercise of property rights has the cumulative effect of negatively affecting the system of property rights for everyone . . .[9]

10.4 Stewardship

Many commentators, including but not exclusively environmental law scholars, argue that property interests in land should be reconceived in terms of stewardship, which is, broadly, that those with property interests in land hold them as custodians for themselves and others who may have an interest in the land and for future generations. There is not much consensus over what this concept entails,[10] but William Lucy and Catherine Mitchell argue that stewardship ought to be seen as:

> a relationship between agents in respect of particular scarce and material resources, such as land. The concept requires that control over these resources be exercised with due regard to the interests that other persons, apart from the holder or steward, may have in the resource. The hallmark of stewardship is land holding subject to responsibilities of careful use, rather than the extensive rights to exclude, control and alienate that are characteristic of private property. The steward is, in essence, a duty-bearer, rather than a right-holder, but this should not be taken to suggest that the steward has no rights. An analogous concept that captures the relationship between duties and

---

[9] Joseph William Singer, 'The rule of reason in property law' (2013) 46 *University of California, Davis Law Review* 1369 at pp. 1424–1425.

[10] For a good overview of different conceptual approaches see Emily Barritt, 'Conceptualising stewardship in environmental law' (2014) 26 *Journal of Environmental Law* 1, and see also Helena Howe, 'Lockean natural rights and the stewardship model of property' (2013) 3 *Property Law Review* 36.

rights in something like the right way is that of the trust. This is a medium whereby the administrative and enjoyment functions of a resource are separated and vested in different persons. The trustee is the nominal owner of the trust property, and has control over it, but holds the trust property on behalf of the beneficiary, who is entitled to benefit from the property. In a similar way, an abstract account of stewardship maintains that the holder, or steward, has some control and rights over the resource, but that control must in the main be exercised for the benefit of specific others. Since the steward's control must in the main be exercised in favour of others, it is not the case that he must be completely selfless, an island of altruism in a sea of self-interest ...[11]

There are differences of opinion between advocates of stewardship on a number of critical issues, including two which are of particular interest here. The first is whether stewardship modifies our pre-existing notions of property, or whether it replaces the notion of private ownership. On this, Lucy and Mitchell rule out the possibility that stewardship can simply be grafted on to traditional notions of private ownership:

> If our characterisation of private property is correct, then the existence of a duty of stewardship cannot be compatible with a claim to have private property in land. It is not feasible to claim the most extensive rights of exclusion, control and alienation over a resource, and yet be subject to a vast range of duties in relation to that resource for the benefit of other persons. We are not suggesting that the steward enjoys none of the privileges associated with private property in land. However, on our analysis the very existence of these other duties renders nugatory the idea of private property in land: the steward simply does not enjoy the extensive trinity of rights characteristic of private property. It is a mistake to think private property and stewardship are compatible: the true significance of the latter is that it stands as a replacement for and not as an adjunct to private property in land.

However, this objection disappears if we take the more expansive, real-world, view of private property we outlined in paras. 8.2-8.4 of Chapter 8 *Property Interest Holders*. We saw there that there is a range of private (and communal) property interest holders who may have the rights of exclusion, control and alienation Lucy and Mitchell describe, but nevertheless are required to exercise them only for the benefit of other people or other purposes. Against the background of those kinds of private and communal property, it does not look so strange to conceptualise stewardship as an obligation of property interest holders generally.

The second difference of view amongst advocates of stewardship, however, is whether it is/should be essentially anthropocentric (i.e. the duties of custodianship imposed on stewards are exercisable primarily or exclusively in the interests of the present and future human population, as opposed to the interests of the environment in its own right), or whether it is/should be ecocentric. We considered this distinction in para. 8.34 in Chapter 8, where we looked at the notion of the environment, or a specific natural resource such as a river, being the holder of property

---

[11] William Lucy and Catherine Mitchell, 'Replacing private property: The case for stewardship' (1996) *Cambridge Law Journal* 566 at p. 584.

rights rather than an object of human property rights. We come back to it in para. 10.6 below where we look at 'Wild Law'.

10.5 Inherent Obligations and Responsibilities in Indigenous Land Rights Systems

The reconceptualising of landowners as stewards of their land moves us closer to the idea of property 'owning' which is characteristically held by indigenous communities who retain their traditional relationship with the land and other resources they utilise. As we saw in Chapter 9 *Multiple Property Rights Systems* para. 9.20, whereas rights to exclude others from resources is central to western European notions of private property, in indigenous property rights systems the emphasis is instead on *rights to participate in the sharing* of the resource, and 'sharing' here extends beyond sharing between humans to sharing in a cycle of resource use connecting humans to the animal and plant world and to the environment as a whole.[12] As McNeil points out, this introduces a 'sustainability' component into the notion of property:[13]

> In Canada, Aboriginal title is also a right to exclusive possession and use of the land, including surface and subsurface resources, for whatever purposes the titleholders choose. [He footnotes *Delgamuukw* v. *British Columbia* at paras. 116–124; *Tsilhqot'in Nation* v. *British Columbia* at paras. 67, 73.] Because Aboriginal title is a complete beneficial interest, the Crown's underlying title has no beneficial content whatsoever [*Tsilhqot'in* para. 70–71].
>
> However, unlike in the United States, there is an inherent limit on Aboriginal title in Canada – the lands can't be used in ways that will substantially deprive future generations of Indigenous titleholders of the benefit of the land [*Delgamuukw* paras. 125–132 and *Tsilhqot'in* paras. 74–75, 86]. There is thus a sustainability component to Aboriginal title that, in my opinion, would be well worth applying to all land in Canada.

He goes on to say (at p. 10) that this sustainability proviso also acts as a limitation on the legislature's power to infringe Aboriginal title:

> Moreover, in *Tsilhqot'in Nation*, the Supreme Court said that, even if justified, infringements can't substantially diminish the benefit of the land for future generations [*Tsilhqot'in* para. 86]. So the sustainability restriction on Aboriginal title applies to governments as well as to the titleholders themselves.

10.6 A 'Wild Law' of Property

A 'Wild Law' of property builds on this idea of interdependence of humans and their natural resources, which is inherent in the traditional property rights systems of indigenous peoples. A Wild Law of property, its proponents argue, would be based

---

[12] See further Murray Raff, *Private Property and Environmental Responsibility: A Comparative Study of German Real Property Law* (The Hague, London and New York: Kluwer Law International, 2003) p. 5.
[13] Kent McNeil, 'Developments on aboriginal title' (2016) Osgoode Hall Digital Commons, http://digitalcommons.osgoode.yorku.ca/all_papers/321 p. 5.

on the same view of the relationship between humans and nature, and here we come back to the idea of moving from an anthropocentric view of the relationship that humans have with nature to an ecocentric one, as Helena Howe points out:[14]

> The former places humans as separate from the rest of the natural world but at its 'imagined centre.' In essence, nature's value is seen in terms of its human benefit; its value lying in its role as a resource, useful for 'maintaining and enhancing the quality of life for humans'. From this perspective, benefits derived from nature are commensurable with other types of benefit and frequently ascribed monetary value. [By contrast], an ecocentric approach is based on the 'assumption that all life is interdependent and that human beings are part of a wider whole'; from the latter perspective, nature is not a commodity belonging to us to be valued instrumentally, rather it is a community to which we belong, with some degree of intrinsic value … . the anthropocentric approach to value is the dominant perspective on nature's value in the Western legal tradition. However, it is clear that this approach is problematic. It is in conflict with both modern scientific understandings in which humans are interdependent with the rest of the natural world and the more integrated relationship with nature which characterises many – typically indigenous – communities' perspective … . While we labour under our 'delusion of difference and separation' we create legal frameworks that foster ecologically unsound policies and decision-making and support environmentally myopic institutions, such as private property. The tendency to treat nature as just one of several competing (economic) interests 'results in a tendency to trump more qualitative public interest notions, such as ecosystem protection, intergenerational and intragenerational equity and even cultural values'. An anthropocentric approach to nature's value may not be the sole cause of the present environmental crisis but it is a significant factor.[15]

She argues that the idea of 'connection with nature' (which she defines as 'broadly [expressing] the idea of an emotional and empathic relationship with the rest of the natural world and a perception of interdependence') has a strategic role to play in reforming our property law so that it more closely resembles a Wild Law of property:

> There is a huge literature on the contribution made by a rights-based, liberal concept of private property to environmentally myopic land use decisions and the need for an alternative model of land 'ownership' if ecological sustainability is to be achieved. From an Earth Jurisprudence perspective, the fundamental problems with this dominant concept of private property flow from its anthropocentrism and the perception that property in land is solely concerned with power relationships between people. From this perspective, land is too often treated by law as a de-physicalised 'thing' – a commodity – divorced from its wider connections as part of the Earth community and with its ecological and social values under-represented and respected. In principle, according to this conceptualisation, human owners are granted extensive rights to despoil the land – to extract financial value from it regardless of the impact – to exclude others from it and to alienate it, unless prevented by a rule which restricts such actions. … . the starting point for conceptualising ownership in the rights-based

---

[14] Helena R. Howe, 'Making Wild Law work – The role of 'connection with nature' and education in developing an ecocentric property law' (2017) 29 *Journal of Environmental Law* 19.

[15] Ibid. pp. 22–23.

tradition is the freedom to treat the land as a source of individual wealth creation, regardless of wider community considerations. This, in turn, influences the shape of the rights and obligations in respect of land use, access and alienation and the practical effects of exercising these rights. Decisions about land ... are made on the basis of entitlement; good ecological or social reasons are rarely required.

She agrees that limitations on private owners of the kind we look at in the rest of this chapter 'mitigate some of the worst effects of these freedoms'. However, the problem with those kinds of limitation is that they are seen as 'external limits placed on the owner's inherent entitlements, for the public good', which have to be restricted in scope (and therefore reduced in efficacy) and require positive justification 'to avoid the perception of unjust interference in individual property rights'. This involves a misunderstanding of the true nature of the relationship between humans and the environment, she argues, which a Wild Law reconceptualisation of property would correct:

> ... the central aim of a Wild Law of property is the replacement of the rights-based liberal concept of private property, in which land is seen as a dephysicalised object or commodity, with a more ecocentric perspective that recognises the uniqueness and ecological integrity of land. Taking this approach, the legal and governance structures must reflect human interdependency with land and ensure that 'ownership' involves understanding and care of the land; for land is not a mere object of wealth or backdrop to rights-claims, but a community of which we are an integral part. In this way, land – and the ecosystems it supports – is an important entity in any legal decision being made which affects it. Thus, under a Wild Law of property, the land becomes the recipient of the responsibilities and obligations which ownership carries as well as, potentially, the subject of rights. On this basis, the owner is subject to legal obligations, intrinsic to the idea of property, to use the land in accordance with the fundamental principle of the common good of the Earth community and to know, care about and respect its ecological capacities. The attributes of the land itself operate to shape the extent of the rights and responsibilities that attach to ownership, as do the needs and interests of human society. It is fundamental to a Wild Law of property that property rights would continue to be limited by competing interests of other human beings as well as by 'integral responsibilities we have to the Earth Community'.

She goes on to consider what a Wild Law of property might look like. She sees it as involving:

> potentially radical changes to substantive and procedural property law rules ... The obligations might be framed in terms of giving priority to the interests of the Earth community or having regard to those interests, depending on the context. As such, a Wild Law of property is likely to involve a baseline obligation to respect the ecological integrity of all land. This might involve, for example, the extension of the requirement that land is kept in good agricultural and environmental condition from just those in receipt of subsidies under the EU Common Agricultural Policy to all those in possession of farmland. However, a Wild Law of property is also likely to involve additional responsibilities attaching to plots of land, on the basis of ecological or social value. Significantly, these responsibilities would arise even where land is not designated for conservation on the basis of a particular feature, or enrolled in an

agri-environment-climate scheme. If land supports (or may be capable of supporting) ecologically significant habitats and species – such as wetland, heathland and mixed woodland – or has an important role in promoting human well-being and relationship with nature – such as a park or urban school playing field – rights to develop or dispose of that land may be substantially restricted, where the exercise of such rights would conflict with these interests. . . .

A Wild Law of property . . . holds that humans understand that they play a part in a wider ecological whole and they must exercise rights over the land in ways which respect the ecological sustainability of that whole. This is not just a sense of interdependence with non-human nature, although this is vital. Property, on this view, is a social relationship which shapes human interaction. The significance of property to the development or protection of autonomy, identity and freedom is recognised but it is interpreted as socially situated and thus as involving obligations to others who may need to use or access the land . . . .

For proponents of Wild Law, the exemplars of property law are often indigenous or native communities, who are still very much living a physical relationship with the land, aware of the interactions between their own needs and those of the land . . . . The role of emotion and 'special ties' with place and nature have long been marginalised in favour of reason and an abstracted perception of the natural world. However, an ecocentric value system relies on both emotion and reason as well as on close relationships with special places through which empathy and the capacity to care flourish . . . The expectation that owners will care for the land under their control and take their responsibilities flows not only from a recognition of the ecological significance of this care at a biospheric, regional and local level but because the owner has an emotional or spiritual attachment to the land . . .[16]

10.7 Abuse of Rights

The distance between our present property law in this jurisdiction and a Wild Law of property is marked by the absence in our law of an 'abuse of rights' doctrine. An abuse of rights doctrine prohibits the exercise of rights – including property rights – so as to cause harm to others. In many jurisdictions such a doctrine is expressly acknowledged. So, for example, in Germany s. 226 of the BGB says:

Section 226 Prohibition of chicanery
  The exercise of a right is not permitted if its only possible purpose consists in causing damage to another.

Similar provisions appear in art. 933 of the Italian Civil Code (specific to property rights) and in art. 1295(2) of the Austrian Civil Code, and the doctrine is also acknowledged, although not codified, in France, where it is termed *abus de droits*.[17]

---

[16] Ibid. pp. 25–30.
[17] Ugo Mattei, *Basic Principles of Property Law: A Comparative Legal and Economic Introduction* (Westport, CT and London: Greenwood Press, 2000) p. 149, and see also Elspeth Reid, 'The doctrine of abuse of rights: Perspective from a mixed jurisdiction' (2004) 8 *Electronic Journal of Comparative Law* 3.

However, it has been expressly repudiated by the House of Lords in *Bradford* v. *Pickles*.[18] The central issue settled by the House of Lords in *Bradford* v. *Pickles* was the ownership of water: it was held that, unlike the position with surface water and water running in defined channels over or underground, no-one has any kind of property rights in or to percolating groundwater at common law. On this basis the House of Lords concluded that Pickles, a private landowner, was entitled to drain groundwater from his land even though the (predicted) result was to cut off the supply of water to a nearby spring which was used by the municipal water company to supply water to the rapidly expanding industrial city of Bradford. This was because, given that, as the House of Lords decided, no-one can have any property rights in groundwater, Pickles must have had a Hohfeldian liberty to do whatever he wanted with the groundwater under his land, including abstracting and diverting it so that it never reached the spring on Bradford Corporation's land which fed the City of Bradford's water supply (which is what Pickles did). It had been argued by the water company that, even if Pickles' actions would otherwise have been lawful (in the Hohfeldian sense that he under no duty to the water company *not* to abstract the water, since at that point the water company had no rights in or to it), nevertheless they were made unlawful by the fact that they were done 'maliciously', that is, deliberately to harm the water company. The House of Lords decisively rejected this argument. Lord Watson stated categorically:

> No use of property, which would be legal if due to a proper motive, can become illegal because it is prompted by a motive which is improper or even malicious.[19]

Lord Ashbourne agreed, equally unequivocally:

> Mr. Pickles has acted within his legal rights throughout; and is he to forfeit those legal rights and be punished for their legal exercise because certain motives are imputed to him? If his motives were the most generous and philanthropic in the world, they would not avail him when his actions were illegal. If his motives are selfish and mercenary, that is no reason why his rights should be confiscated when his actions are legal.[20]

Lord Macnaghten also agreed, and added that in any event it was wrong to suggest that Pickles had acted 'maliciously':

> they say that Mr. Pickles' action in the matter is malicious, and that because his motive is a bad one, he is not at liberty to do a thing which every landowner in the country may do with impunity if his motives are good. Mr. Pickles, it seems, was so alarmed at this view of the case that he tried to persuade the Court that all he wanted was to unwater some beds of stone which he thought he could work at a profit. In this innocent enterprise the Court found a sinister design. And it may be taken that his real object was to shew that he was master of the situation, and to force the corporation to buy him out at a price satisfactory to himself. Well, he has something to sell, or, at any rate, he has something which he can prevent other people enjoying unless he is paid for it. Why should he, he may think, without fee or reward, keep his land as a store-room for a commodity which the corporation dispense, probably not gratuitously, to the

---

[18] *The Mayor, Aldermen and Burgesses of the Borough of Bradford* v. *Pickles* [1895] AC 587.
[19] Ibid. p. 598.   [20] Ibid. p. 599.

inhabitants of Bradford? He prefers his own interests to the public good. He may be churlish, selfish, and grasping. His conduct may seem shocking to a moral philosopher. But where is the malice? Mr. Pickles has no spite against the people of Bradford. He bears no ill-will to the corporation. They are welcome to the water, and to his land too, if they will pay the price for it. So much perhaps might be said in defence or in palliation of Mr. Pickles' conduct. But the real answer to the claim of the corporation is that in such a case motives are immaterial . . .[21]

Elspeth Reid has argued that the lack of an abuse of right doctrine in England and Wales is not significant, because common law achieves the same ends by different means[22] (including by the law of nuisance, which we look at in Part III below). We see in Part III how far this is correct, but in any event it might seem of symbolic importance that we expressly denounce a doctrine that many other western states see as an inherent limitation on the exercise of property rights.

PART III REGULATION OF LAND USE

10.8 Public Regulation of Land Use

In England and Wales the exercise of property rights in land is highly restricted and regulated by a vast amount of state regulation, well beyond the scope of this book. It includes legislative schemes governing such matters as planning, environmental regulation, health and safety standards, pollution, protection of cultural heritage and much more. Some of these schemes are of general application, others are specific to particular resources such as water, canals and rivers, forests, oil and gas, mines and road, rail and telecommunications infrastructures, etc. Yet others are specific to particular areas of land regarded as in special need of protection such as national parks, coastal areas, green belt land, etc.[23]

10.9 Planning Regulation

The only aspect of all this that we need touch on here is planning regulation. A very brief outline of the way it works is useful because it provides background to the law of private nuisance which we deal with later in this part of the chapter, and also to restrictive covenants which we look at in Chapter 13.

A systematic national planning regime was first introduced into England and Wales[24] by the Town and Country Planning Act 1947, and as from 1 July 1948, the

---

[21] Ibid. at pp. 600–601, and see also Lord Halsbury saying much the same thing on p. 596. Michael Taggart, *Private Property and Abuse of Rights in Victorian England: The Story of Edward Pickles and the Bradford Water Supply* (Oxford: Oxford University Press, 2002) investigates the whole story behind the *Bradford* v. *Pickles* case, and there is no doubt that Lord Macnaghten was right about Pickles' motives.

[22] Reid, 'The doctrine of abuse of rights', fn. 17 above.

[23] There is also a certain amount of state control over private land use through the common law doctrine of statutory nuisance.

[24] Responsibility for planning has been devolved to Wales, and there are increasing divergences between planning policy and law in Wales and in England. For an overview of the present position in Wales see

date it came into force, it has been illegal to carry out any 'development' of land without planning permission granted by the local planning authority. 'Development' is defined very broadly to cover any building work or change of use, specifically 'the carrying out of building,[25] engineering, mining or other operations in, on, over or under land' or 'the making of any material change in the use of any buildings or other land',[26] although the legislation goes on to list significant exceptions.

So, anyone who wants to carry our building works or change the use of any land must first apply to the local planning authority for planning permission. The local planning authority has power to refuse to grant permission, or to grant it with or without conditions. In practice conditions are almost invariably imposed. In deciding whether to grant planning permission, and if so, the conditions to be imposed, the local planning authority must have regard to the 'development plan', which includes local authority and neighbourhood development policy for their areas (required to be determined in accordance with national planning policy), and to any other 'material considerations'. These include any factors relevant to the use of the land, including (and most significantly) national planning policy as presently set out in the National Planning Policy Framework 2019.[27] Appeals from the decisions of planning authorities can in some circumstances be made to the Secretary of State, and in addition in some circumstances the Secretary of State can 'call in' a planning application and decide for itself whether permission should be granted or refused. In other words, there is dual system of control and regulation by local planning authorities and central government. As Lord Clyde put it in *R (on the application of Alconbury Developments Limited)* v. *Secretary of State for the Environment, Transport and the Regions* [2001] UKHL 23:

> Planning and the development of land are matters which concern the community as a whole, not only the locality where the particular case arises. They involve wider social and economic interests, considerations which are properly to be subject to a central supervision. By means of a central authority some degree of coherence and consistency in the development of land can be secured. National planning guidance can be prepared and promulgated and that guidance will influence the local development plans and policies which the planning authorities will use in resolving their own local problems . . . the need to take account of economic, environmental, social and other factors requires a framework which provides consistent, predictable, and prompt decision making. At the heart of that system are development plans. The guidance sets out the objectives and policies comprised in the framework within which the local authorities are required to draw up their development plans and in accordance with which their planning decisions should be made . . . . The whole scheme of the planning

---

Welsh Government, *Planning Policy Wales*, Edition 10, December 2018, available at https://gov.wales/sites/default/files/publications/2018-12/planning-policy-wales-edition-10.pdf.

[25] Defined to include demolition or rebuilding of a building, making structural alterations or additions, or 'other operations normally undertaken by a person carrying on business as a builder'.

[26] S. 55(1) of the Town and Country Planning Act 1990, which now contains the basic provisions of the current law (although subsequently much amended).

[27] Amending and replacing the original NPPF 2012 (as amended in 2018) which in its turn consolidated a large mass of Ministerial Circulars setting out national planning policy.

legislation involves an allocation of various functions respectively between local authorities and the Secretary of State.[28]

So, the whole point of the planning system is to regulate the development and use of land, taking into account the interests of the immediate neighbourhood, the local authority region and the country as a whole, in line with government policies formulated at each of these levels.

10.10 Range of Private Limitations on Land Use Enforceable by Fellow Citizens

In addition to these state-enforced restrictions and limitations on landowners, there are further limitations which are enforceable against a landowner as property rights by other private or community owners. Some of them are imposed on a landowner (or leaseholder) by contract. This may be as part of a free-standing agreement between neighbours which is enforceable as a restrictive covenant, or as a term imposed on the landowner/leaseholder in a mortgage granted to a lender, or as a term of the lease granted to the leaseholder.

Here, however, we are primarily concerned with the way your neighbour can, by using the torts of trespass and private nuisance, prevent a use of your land when the external effects of what you are doing falls on him, restricting his rights and freedoms in respect of his own land. From this perspective, trespass and private nuisance are the mechanisms our law uses to balance the inherent freedom of every landowner to do whatever she wants on her land. Logically, my freedom to do whatever I want on my land must be subject to my neighbour having the like right in relation to his land. This means that neither of us can have an absolute freedom to do whatever we want, any more than co-owners of land or those holding communal or public property rights over a piece of land can each have absolute freedom to exercise their own rights whenever and however they want: the rights and freedoms of each resource sharer must necessarily be subject to the like rights and freedoms of every other sharer. In the case of co-owned, communal and public property rights, potential conflicts between the sharers are avoided or resolved by voluntary co-operation and/or internal or external regulation, as we saw in Parts III, V and VI of Chapter 8 *Property Interest Holders*. In the case of neighbouring landowners, it is done by tort law, but we should not allow this to blind ourselves to the essential point made by the economist Ronald Coase which we note in the following paragraph: problems of conflicting land uses between neighbours are nearly always bilateral (sometimes multilateral) problems rather than perpetrator-victim problems.

Broadly, the tort of trespass protects the physical integrity of my neighbour's land (including his airspace): I am liable to him in trespass if anything I do on my land involves a physical invasion of his land. The tort of private nuisance, on the other

---

[28] Lord Clyde at paras. 140–141 in *R (on the application of Alconbury Developments Limited)* v. *Secretary of State for the Environment, Transport and the Regions* [2001] UKHL 23.

hand, imposes a standard of reasonableness to decide when one landowner's free-dom to use her land as she wishes (perhaps by playing loud music in the garden) must be curtailed in order to prevent infringement of her neighbour's like freedom (to be able to use his land without being distracted by noise).[29]

10.11 The Economic Approach to Entitlements to Impose Externalities on Neighbours

Before looking at trespass and private nuisance in more detail, it is useful to be aware of Ronald Coase's classic economic analysis of nuisance as a means of allocating entitlements to impose negative externalities on neighbours, which we noted briefly in Chapter 2 *Conceptions and Justifications* para. 2.11. This analysis has had some influence on the development of nuisance law, although more so in the USA than in this country, and it provides a useful tool for clarifying what factors courts take into account (and perhaps ought to take into account) when deciding nuisance cases.

In his seminal article 'The problem of social cost',[30] Coase's starting point was Arthur Pigou's proposed solution to problems of pollution and similar external-ities,[31] which Coase disputed. Pigou argued that externalities should be solved by imposing centralised solutions: the polluter (or originator of the externality) must be made to pay for any harm caused, through taxation or through payment of penalties or fines imposed in criminal proceedings.[32] This, so the argument goes, provides an incentive for the polluter to internalise the externalities of its actions.

Coase rejected this assumption that nuisance cases should be categorised as disputes between perpetrator and victim. Taking the example of cattle straying from a rancher's land on to neighbouring farm land, where they destroy the neighbour's crops, Coase pointed out the bilateral nature of the problem. As Cole and Grossman explain it,[33] the problem is bilateral in two senses. The first is that, as they say (taking the example of air pollution emitted from the smokestack of a manufacturer's factory which harms a neighbour):

> it takes at least two to create an external cost: someone to produce it and someone else to bear it. If the neighbour were not there, there would be no externality just as surely as if no pollution ever went up the factory's smokestack. The neighbour's contribution to the joint or social cost problem is easiest to comprehend where the polluter is there first, and the neighbour moves in later . . .[34]

The second way in which the externality is bilateral is that whenever the preferences of neighbours conflict (the rancher wants to raise cattle, the crop farmer wants cattle

---

[29] Mattei, *Basic Principles of Property Law*, fn. 17 above, pp. 156–157.

[30] Ronald H. Coase, 'The problem of social cost' (1960) 3 *Journal of Law and Economics* 1.

[31] Arthur Pigou, *The Economics of Welfare* (first published 1920, new edn Abingdon: Routledge, 2017).

[32] That is, the polluter pays the state, rather than paying damages to the private victim of the externalities .

[33] Cole and Grossman, *Principles of Law & Economics*, fn. 4 above, Ch. 4.

[34] Ibid. p. 89, explaining Coase's analysis. It is salutary to remind ourselves that Coase was writing in 1960. Writing today, he might not want anyone to think that he was suggesting that the problem of air pollution (and similar kinds of externality) disappears if no-one's land is immediately affected by it.

kept off his crops; the manufacturer wants to be able to emit air pollution from her chimney, the neighbour wants to be free from pollution on her land) one of them will be harmed if the other is allowed to do what it wants. So, if the rancher is entitled to let his cattle stray, it harms the crop farmer; if the crop farmer is entitled to insist that the rancher prevents them straying, it harms the rancher. Similarly, if the factory is entitled to pollute, it harms the neighbour; if the factory is not entitled to pollute, the factory suffers harm.

As Cole and Grossman point out, the issue then becomes: 'Who gets to impose harm on whom?'[35] Coase's insight was that, in a world without transaction costs,[36] it would not matter. If the crop farmer has the entitlement to be free from crop damage, so the argument goes:

> [the rancher] will adopt the strategy that gives the highest level of cattle production at the lowest cost. This will include the possibility of paying the farmer not to plant on acres adjacent to the rancher's land. The farmer will accept payment over planting if as a net result her net benefit is greater .... [So, if] the damage to the farmer from the rancher's cattle amounts to $90, it would cost the rancher $110 for fencing, it would cost the farmer $100 in foregone net profits not to plant crops in the first place, and it would cost the rancher $200 not to raise the cattle ... the lowest-cost approach would be for the rancher to allow his cattle to roam and pay the farmer $90 in damages. If transacting is costless, that is what would happen.[37]

However, the point is that the *total overall costs* (what Coase calls the 'social costs') would be the same if the rancher was given the entitlement, that is, he was entitled to let his cattle stray without any liability for the damage it causes the crop farmer:

> the farmer has to consider the cost of fencing [$110, the same as it would cost the rancher] absorbing the crop damage costs [$90], or leaving the field unplanted [$100]. The costs are exactly the same as above, and so is the outcome. The farmer's lowest-cost solution is to plant and suffer the $90 in crop damages from the rancher's cattle. The only difference is that, instead of receiving compensation from the rancher for the damage, the farmer absorbs the damage cost herself.[38]

Cole and Grossman go on to explore the significance of this. As they explain, Coase's point is that in a world without transaction costs, it would not matter who gets the entitlement because the most efficient overall solution (the total social cost) is the same: in this case, 'the herd size remains the same, and the fields will be planted'. The only difference is distributional, that is, who gets to bear the $90 cost: does the rancher pay it to the farmer, or does the farmer bear the cost herself?

But of course in the real world there *always are* transaction costs, including imperfect information on both sides, costs of negotiating, etc.,[39] and in the real world it *does* matter which party gets the entitlement (who gets to bear the $90). This

---

[35] Ibid.   [36] As to which see Chapter 2 *Conceptions and Justifications* para. 2.11(d).
[37] Cole and Grossman, *Principles of Law & Economics*, fn. 4 above, pp. 90–91.
[38] Ibid. at p. 91, where Cole and Grossman also put it all in tabular form (very helpfully).
[39] Chapter 2 *Conceptions and Justifications* para. 2.11(d)–(e).

is why law matters, according to Coase. It is the courts who have to decide who in any given situation gets the entitlement, with fallible judges and incomplete and imperfect information. It is important that they recognise the social cost nature of externalities, that they appreciate that they are engaging in economic policy making (deciding which of two conflicting activities should be given preference, rather than seeing the parties as polluter and victim), and that their general goal is to maximise the social product (i.e. minimise total social costs). This means allocating property rights and duties so as to minimise social costs by

> imposing the burden (or duty) of cost avoidance or abatement on the party that can do so at the lowest cost. Thus, the entitlement or property right should be allocated to the party with the highest costs of avoidance or abatement.[40]

This of course does not deal with the issue of fairness: in the cattle straying example, why should it be the crop farmer rather than the rancher who, in effect, loses $90? Cole and Grossman suggest that it should be possible to 'combine a Coasean least-cost solution with a more equitable remedy'. So, they suggest that in this particular example the court might hold the rancher liable (i.e. give the entitlement to be free of straying cattle to the crop farmer) but limit the remedy it gives the crop farmer to damages rather an injunction, and limit the damages to either the crop farmer's actual loss or the costs of reasonable avoidance, whichever is lower.[41] This way, as they say, 'the court would merely redistribute the least-cost solution in order to achieve what it might consider a more just outcome'.[42]

10.12 The Common Law Solution: Trespass and Private Nuisance

We see how all this plays out in the real world in the rest of this chapter by looking primarily at private nuisance. However, we need to say a bit more about trespass as well because the boundary between the two is not always clear.[43]

---

[40] Cole and Grossman, *Principles of Law & Economics*, fn. 4 above, p. 106.

[41] Ibid. For the significance of the remedy in this context, see the classic analysis of Guido Calabresi and A. Douglas Melamed, 'Property rules, liability rules, and inalienability: One view of the cathedral' (1972) 85 *Harvard Law Review* 1089, pointing out the important distinctions between protecting an entitlement by a 'property' rule (awarding to the winner an entitlement which she is free to 'sell' to the loser – so winner and loser are allowed to negotiate the price, if any, that the winner is willing to accept to reverse the decision), protecting it by a liability rule (awarding the entitlement to the winner but giving her the remedy of damages only – essentially, the court insists the seller 'sells' to the loser, and fixes the price) and protecting the entitlement by an inalienability rule (the winner is not allowed to sell the entitlement to the loser, as for example if she has been awarded an injunction to restrain the loser from emitting toxic waste which harms her land but is also an environmental hazard).

[42] Cole and Grossman, *Principles of Law & Economics*, fn. 4 above, p. 106, and see also Aleksandar Slaeva and Marcus Collier, 'Managing natural resources: Coasean bargaining versus Ostromian rules of common governance' (2018) *Environmental Science and Policy* 47.

[43] The tort of negligence imposes additional limitations, but it is a broader tort, covering damage to any kind of property and personal injury and we are not concerned with it here. For the crossover between negligence and nuisance in land use conflicts between neighbours, see *Hunter* v. *Canary Wharf* [1997] AC 655.

(a) Trespass

As we have already seen, trespass is a tort committed by physically invading land in someone else's possession,[44] without authorisation or lawful excuse. You commit the tort of trespass either by entering the land yourself or by allowing or causing something to cross the boundaries of the land (perhaps a bullet or a cricket ball). If you consciously go on to someone else's land in either of these ways you will be liable to them in trespass even if you mistakenly thought it was your land or thought you were allowed on the land, and *even if the invasion caused no harm or damage to them or to their land*. So, for example, in *Star Energy Weald Basin Ltd v. Bocardo SA* [2010] UKSC 35, as we saw in Chapter 7 *Objects of Property Interests* para. 7.17, Star Energy was held liable in trespass to Bocardo for drilling petroleum wells from land controlled by Star Energy, by drilling diagonally down to an oilfield far beneath the surface of adjoining land owned by Bocardo, even though the wells were so deep that neither the drilling nor the later operation of the wells interfered 'one iota' with Bocardo's enjoyment of its land.[45]

(b) Private Nuisance

A private nuisance, on the other hand is an unlawful interference by something done by a landowner on her land, with property rights in neighbouring land held by the neighbour. It has sometimes been said that there can be no liability in nuisance unless the interference causes harm on the neighbouring land, but as we see in para. 10.16 below, this is probably no longer accurate (if it ever was). However, we can say that, whilst a trespass is automatically actionable once it has been proved that, as a matter of fact, there has been an unauthorised intrusion into someone else's land, a landowner is liable in nuisance only if the court considers that the landowner has *unreasonably* interfered with a neighbour's *reasonable* use and enjoyment of her land. We look more closely at this test of reasonableness in paras. 10.13 and 10.15 below.

(c) Boundary Between Trespass and Nuisance

So, the boundary between trespass and nuisance does matter. Unfortunately, it is not always clear. Whilst it has always been clear that buildings encroaching on neighbouring land give rise to an action in trespass, the position is less clear in relation to projections into airspace. In a series of cases we noted in Chapter 7 *Objects of Property Interests* it has been accepted that various structures projecting into airspace constituted a trespass (an advertising sign in *Kelsen v. Imperial Tobacco Company (of Great Britain and Ireland) Ltd* [1957] 2 QB 334, cranes oversailing

---

[44] Liability in trespass is owed to the person entitled to possession of the land. This means that if a landlord intrudes into the land she has let to a tenant, she is liable to the tenant in trespass: *Lavender v. Betts* [1942] 2 All ER 72.

[45] *Star Energy Weald Basin Ltd v. Bocardo SA* [2010] UKSC 35 at para. 54, quoting from the judgment of Peter Smith LJ in the Court of Appeal.

neighbouring land in *Anchor Brewhouse Developments Ltd* v. *Berkley House (Dock-lands Developments) Ltd* (1987) 284 EG 625 and an extractor fan in *Laiquat* v. *Majid* [2005] EWHC 1305). On the other hand, it has long been established that if branches from a tree in your garden overhang your neighbour's land, you are liable to them in nuisance rather than in trespass: *Lemmon* v. *Webb* [1895] AC 1. Similarly and more recently, in *Network Rail Infrastructure Ltd* v. *Williams* [2018] EWCA Civ 1514, which we look at in para. 10.16 below, the Court of Appeal proceeded on the basis that the encroachment of rhizomes of the noxious weed Japanese knotweed from the railway company's embankment into the soil under the ground of the claimants' land was actionable, if at all, in nuisance. The issue of whether it could not also (or instead) have been categorisable as trespass was not considered.

10.13 What is a Private Nuisance?

It is difficult to find a comprehensive definition of private nuisance, beyond the general statement made above that it is an unreasonable interference with someone's reasonable use and enjoyment of their land. This is echoed by Lord Neuberger's much quoted definition in *Coventry* v. *Lawrence* [2014] UKSC 13:[46]

> A nuisance can be defined, albeit in general terms, as an action (or sometimes a failure to act) on the part of a defendant, which is not otherwise authorised, and which causes an interference with the claimant's reasonable enjoyment of his land, or to use a slightly different formulation, which unduly interferes with the claimant's enjoyment of his land.[47]

However, this definition disguises the essential point that, as Sir Terence Etherton MR said in *Network Rail Infrastructure Ltd* v. *Williams* [2018] EWCA Civ 1514, private nuisance is an interference with someone's *property rights* in their land (or, as Etherton put it 'a violation of real property rights').[48]

So, when Lord Neuberger talks about an interference with 'reasonable enjoyment' of land, what he means is *either* an interference with a *specific property right* held by the claimant, *or* an interference with what Etherton called '*the amenity of the land, that is to say the right to use and enjoy it*'[49] which is, of course, one of the rights in land that a possessor has by virtue of being in possession. If, for example, as a matter of law the claimant has a right to light through one of her windows, or a right of way over the land, interference with the access of light through that window or interference with the right of way would be a nuisance. Equally, however, if the claimant's possession of her land is impaired because of noise, smoke or dust generated by a neighbour's land, this too is an actionable nuisance (assuming it is 'unreasonable' in the sense we look at in para. 10.15 below).

---

[46] Sometimes referred to as *Lawrence* v. *Fen Tigers*.

[47] *Coventry* v. *Lawrence* [2014] UKSC 13 para. 3. For a helpful analysis of the decision as a whole see Maria Lee, 'Private nuisance in the Supreme Court: Coventry v. Lawrence' (2014) *Journal of Planning and Environmental Law* 705.

[48] *Network Rail Infrastructure Ltd* v. *Williams* [2018] EWCA Civ 1514 para. 40.   [49] Ibid.

The House of Lords decision in *Hunter* v. *Canary Wharf Ltd* [1997] AC 656 shows the difference between the two – direct interference with a specific property right, and interference with the amenity of the land in the sense of the right to use and enjoy the land. In *Hunter* v. *Canary Wharf*, as we noted in para. 6.4 in Chapter 6 *New Property Interests and the Numerus Clausus*, the problem was that the erection of the Canary Wharf tower in London interfered with television reception (terrestrial only, in those days) in the surrounding area. The claimants, owners and lessees of the houses in the affected area brought an action in nuisance against the owners of the Canary Wharf tower. They failed, so the House of Lords decided, because (i) English law does not recognise a property right to receive television signals over neighbouring land, and (ii) watching television is not inherent in the amenity of the land or the right to use and enjoy it.[50]

Lord Lloyd in *Hunter* v. *Canary Wharf* suggested that a helpful way of looking at it would be to focus on the nature of the interference:

> Private nuisances are of three kinds. They are (1) nuisance by encroachment on a neighbour's land; (2) nuisance by direct physical injury to a neighbour's land; and (3) nuisance by interference with a neighbour's quiet enjoyment of his land.[51]

However, in *Network Rail Infrastructure Ltd* v. *Williams* Etherton MR expressed reservations about breaking nuisance cases down into rigid categories like this, first because what amounts to a nuisance in any given case is so fact-specific and context-specific but secondly because nuisance is a common law concept which has to adapt to changing social and economic conditions. He preferred to see Lord Lloyd's categories as

> merely examples of a violation of property rights as I have described them … The difficulty with any rigid categorisation is that it may not easily accommodate possible examples of nuisance in new social conditions or may undermine a proper analysis of factual situations which have aspects of more than one category but do not fall squarely within any one category, having regard to existing case law.[52]

Also, and for the same reasons, he pointed out that older authorities on nuisance have to be treated with caution:

> In recent times a number of decisions at the highest level have introduced greater coherence and consistency to the legal principles governing the cause of action for private nuisance. The consequence is that it is neither necessary nor profitable to focus on historic cases of nuisance …[53]

On that basis, the Court of Appeal in *Network Rail* was able to find that Network Rail was indeed liable in nuisance for the intrusion of the Japanese knotweed rhizomes into the subsoil of the claimants' gardens and under their bungalows.

---

[50] We come back to (i) in paras. 13.8–13.10 of Chapter 13 *Non-Possessory Land Use Rights*, where we consider the criteria the courts require to be satisfied before a right can be accepted as a valid easement.

[51] *Hunter* v. *Canary Wharf Ltd* [1997] AC 665 at p. 695C.

[52] Sir Terence Etherton in *Network Rail Infrastructure Ltd* v. *Williams* [2018] EWCA Civ 1514 at para. 41.

[53] Ibid. para. 38.

Network Rail had argued that it was not liable, relying on old authorities suggesting that physical damage was an essential prerequisite for liability in nuisance for a physical intrusion into neighbouring land, and arguing that the rhizomes had (not yet) caused any physical damage. The Court of Appeal rejected that argument, taking the view that damage had indeed been caused, but that even if it had not, the absence of damage would not necessarily have ruled out liability. We come back to this point in para. 10.16.

10.14 Extending the Boundaries of Nuisance

In *Fearn* v. *Tate Gallery* [2019] EWHC 246 Mann J agreed with Sir Terence Etherton that it was open to the courts to extend the boundaries of nuisance in appropriate cases. On that basis he accepted arguments by the claimants in that case that the boundaries could and should be extended so as to prevent neighbours overlooking your property, at least when the property was your home and the overlooking amounted to an invasion of privacy,[54] although he found that, on the facts, there was no actionable nuisance in this case.

The claimants in this case owned flats in a new block of glass-walled luxury flats which had been built next to a new extension of the Tate Modern Gallery in London (the Blavatnik Building). Their complaint was that their flats were overlooked by visitors to the Tate using a walkway the Tate had just constructed all the way around the 10th floor of the Blavatnik Building. The walkway was intended as a viewing gallery, giving visitors to the Tate a 360-degree panoramic view of London, and from it visitors could (and did) look straight into the claimants' flats through the floor-length glass walls. The claimants argued that this amounted to a nuisance, as an interference with a right to privacy which, so they argued, was an integral part of their right to the reasonable use and enjoyment of their flats, and that it was also an interference with their right to respect for private and family life and home under art. 8 of the European Convention on Human Rights.

Mann J held that the claimants could not rely directly on art. 8 because, so he held, the Tate was not a public authority. However, he went on to consider whether there was an actionable nuisance. He reviewed the authorities on nuisance by invasion of privacy, which were generally unfavourable to the idea that a right to privacy, in the form of a right not to be overlooked, might be a feature of the reasonable use and enjoyment of land. In particular, in *Victoria Park Racing* v. *Taylor* (1937) 58 CLR 497 the High Court of Australia had decided by a majority that it did not amount to a nuisance when a man built an elevated platform on his land from which he looked down into the adjoining racecourse owned by the claimants and broadcast radio commentaries on the races. Evatt J, in the minority, had disagreed. Noting the case of neighbours of a Balham dentist who had set up an arrangement of large mirrors so that they could see everything that went on in the dentist's surgery,[55] Evatt J said:

[54] *Fearn* v. *Tate Gallery* [2019] EWHC 246 para. 178.
[55] Referred to by Professor Winfield in 'Privacy' (1931) 47 LQR 23.

In my opinion, such conduct certainly amounted to a private nuisance and should have been restrained by injunction, although the sole object of the 'peeping Toms' of Balham was to satisfy their own degraded curiosity and not to interfere with the dentist's liberty of action. In truth, no normally sensitive human being could have pursued his profession or business under so intolerable an espionage, and the result would have been to render the business premises practically uninhabitable. The motive of the wrongdoers at Balham was to satisfy their curiously perverted instincts. But let us suppose that, by such devices as broadcasting and television, the operating theatre of a private hospital was made inspectable, so that a room outside the hospital could be hired in order that the public might view the operations on payment of a fee. It would not be any less a nuisance because in such a case the interference with the normal rights of using and enjoying property was accentuated and aggravated by the wrongdoers making a profit out of their exhibition.[56]

However, the majority in *Victoria Park Racing* took a different view and held there was no right not to be overlooked. As Dixon J said:

English law is, rightly or wrongly, clear that the natural rights of an occupier do not include freedom from the view and inspection of neighbouring occupiers or of other persons who enable themselves to overlook the premises. An occupier of land is at liberty to exclude his neighbour's view by any physical means he can adopt. But while it is no wrongful act on his part to block the prospect from adjacent land, it is no wrongful act on the part of any person on such land to avail himself of what prospect exists or can be obtained. Not only is it lawful on the part of those occupying premises in the vicinity to overlook the land from any natural vantage point, but artificial erections may be made which destroy the privacy existing under natural conditions.[57]

Latham CJ agreed, pointing out that the remedy for someone who did not want to be overlooked was to 'erect a higher fence'.[58]

In *Fearn* v. *Tate* Mann J's view of the authorities was that none of them, apart from *Victoria Park Racing*, established that nuisance could *never* protect privacy, and even in that case, he said, 'the dissents ... are in my view somewhat compelling'.[59] He also noted that it had been conceded on behalf of the Tate that 'deliberate overlooking, if accompanied by malice, could give rise to a nuisance', and he concluded that even on the existing authorities he would have been willing to conclude that 'given the right circumstances, a deliberate act of overlooking could amount to an actionable nuisance'.[60]

The important point for our purposes, however, is that he then went on to say that if there were any doubt about that 'then in my view that doubt has been removed by the Human Rights Act and Article 8'.[61] Although he had already decided that the claimants could not rely directly on art. 8 because the Tate was not a public authority, Mann J said that the court 'can, where appropriate, give effect to the Article by developing existing causes of action'.[62] He concluded that it not only

---

[56] Evatt J, dissenting, in *Victoria Park Racing* v. *Taylor* (1937) 58 CLR 497.
[57] Ibid. per Dixon J at p. 507.   [58] Ibid. per Latham CJ at p. 494.
[59] Mann J in *Fearn* v. *Tate Gallery* [2019] EWHC 246 at para. 164.   [60] Ibid. para. 169.
[61] Ibid. para. 170.   [62] Ibid. para. 172.

could but should do so by recognising a qualified right not to be overlooked, developing the law of nuisance so that it was 'capable, in an appropriate case, of operating so as to protect the privacy of a home as against another landowner'.[63]

He did nevertheless decide that there was no actionable nuisance in this particular case: the Tate, in operating the viewing gallery as it did, was not 'making an unreasonable use of its land, bearing in mind the nature of that use, the locality in which it takes place, and bearing in mind that the victim is expected to have to put up with some give and take appropriate to modern society and the locale'.[64] We consider the importance of these factors in the next following paragraph.

10.15 Reasonableness as the Underlying Principle

In *Coventry* v. *Lawrence* [2014] UKSC 13 it was indisputable that the interference which was the subject of complaint – noise from neighbouring land used as a motor-racing Stadium and race track – was capable of being an actionable nuisance. The issue was whether it was a nuisance in this case, given the circumstances. The circumstances were that the owners of the Stadium and track had been using them for motor racing for about 30 years before the claimants bought and moved into a neighbouring house, and that the Stadium and track owners had always had planning permission to use the land in that way. The Supreme Court held that nevertheless the Stadium and track owners were liable to the claimants in nuisance.

In coming to this conclusion the Supreme Court accepted that the principle underlying private nuisance is reasonableness. Lord Neuberger set out the position as follows:

3 . . . As Lord Wright said in *Sedleigh-Denfield* v. *O'Callaghan* [1940] AC 880, 903, 'a useful test is perhaps what is reasonable according to the ordinary usages of mankind living in society, or more correctly in a particular society'.

4. In *Sturges* v. *Bridgman* (1879) 11 ChD 852, 865, Thesiger LJ, giving the judgment of the Court of Appeal, famously observed that whether something is a nuisance 'is a question to be determined, not merely by an abstract consideration of the thing itself, but in reference to its circumstances', and 'what would be a nuisance in Belgrave Square would not necessarily be so in Bermondsey'. Accordingly, whether a particular activity causes a nuisance often depends on an assessment of the locality in which the activity concerned is carried out.

5. As Lord Goff said in *Cambridge Water Co* v. *Eastern Counties Leather plc* [1994] 2 AC 264, 299, liability for nuisance is:

'kept under control by the principle of reasonable user – the principle of give and take as between neighbouring occupiers of land, under which 'those acts necessary for the common and ordinary use and occupation of land and houses may be done, if conveniently done, without subjecting those who do them to an action' . . .[65]

---

[63] Ibid. para. 178.   [64] Ibid. paras. 180 and 224.

[65] And see also Lord Etherton MR in *Network Rail Infrastructure Ltd* v. *Williams* [2018] EWCA Civ 1514 at para. 45 as to 'the broad unifying principle in this area of the law' being reasonableness between neighbours (real or figurative)'.

Reasonableness in this context is an objective but not an absolute standard, as Lord Carnworth emphasised in *Coventry* v. *Lawrence,* quoting with approval a comment by Tony Weir:

> the question is neither what is reasonable in the eyes of the defendant or even the claimant (for one cannot by being unduly sensitive, constrain one's neighbour's freedoms), but what objectively a normal person would find it reasonable to have to put up with.[66]

So, it does not take us very far, except to suggest the factors the court takes into account in deciding whether a landowner's actions are an unreasonable interference with a neighbour's reasonable use and enjoyment of his land.

(a) Unusual Sensitivity

Since reasonableness is to be judged by reference to 'what a normal person can expect to have to put up with', it must follow that a neighbour will not be liable for an interference which would not trouble a 'normal' claimant, but does trouble this particular claimant because he is unusually sensitive to this particular kind of interference. This has been repeatedly confirmed by the courts, and in *Fearn* v. *Tate* Mann J pointed out that it was highly relevant to the case he was considering:

> The developers in building the flats, and the claimants as successors in title who chose to buy the flats, have created or submitted themselves to a sensitivity to privacy which is greater than would the case of a less-glassed design. It would be wrong to allow this self-induced incentive to gaze, and to infringe privacy, and self-induced exposure to the outside world, to create a liability in nuisance. Other architectural designs would have reduced the invasion of privacy to levels which should be tolerated; that is the appropriate measure in my view. If the claimants have a design which raises the privacy invasion then they have created their own sensitivity and will have to tolerate what the design has created
> ... [in addition] the owners and occupiers of the flat have created their own additional sensitivity to the inward gaze. They have moved more of their living activities into a quasi-balcony area and provided more to look at. Had they not done that, there would have been less worth looking at – less to attract the eye – and fewer living activities to be intruded upon. It is true that to a degree there would still have been a view through the winter gardens and through the double-glazed doors, and to that extent the privacy of the living accommodation would still have been compromised ... but the whole package would have been a less sensitive one.
> I therefore consider this to be a case in which the claimants are occupying a particularly sensitive property which they are operating in a way which has increased the sensitivity. A differently built, but perfectly acceptable, property would have had more privacy built in, or rather would not have had the same degree of exposure. These properties are impressive, and no doubt there are great advantages to be enjoyed in such extensive glassed views, but that in effect comes at a price in terms of privacy.[67]

---

[66] Lord Carnworth in *Coventry* v. *Lawrence* [2014] UKSC 13 para. 179, quoting Tony Weir, *An Introduction to Tort Law* (2nd edn, Oxford: Oxford University Press, 2006) p. 160.

[67] Mann J in *Fearn* v. *Tate Gallery* [2019] EWHC 246 at paras. 205 and 210–211.

(b) Give and Take

In addition, the courts have made it clear that reasonableness between neighbours also involves considering what 'give and take' can be expected from both of them so that they can both go on using their property as they wish. In noise cases such as *Coventry* v. *Lawrence,* for example, this may mean that any order made by the court will be conditional on the noise being kept below a specified decibel level, and confined to specified hours, or that other alleviating measure are taken on either or both sides. Similarly, in *Fearn* v. *Tate Gallery* where it was held that the Tate was not liable in nuisance, Mann J took into account that there were preventative (or ameliorative) measures that the claimants could take, like lowering their solar blinds, putting up net curtains or putting plants in the windows.[68] Similarly, he also took into account that, in response to the complaints, the Tate had imposed limits on the hours when the walkway was open to viewers and taken other measures ('not quite wholly useless') to limit the extent of the overlooking, and made it clear that he expected those measures to be kept in place.[69]

(c) Locality

As Lord Neuberger said in *Coventry* v. *Lawrence*, it has long been established that whether or not an activity amounts to a nuisance depends on the locality.[70] This obviously applies only to amenity harm such as noise, smells, dust, etc., rather than to direct interest with property rights.[71] However, it is not always easy to decide whether a particular activity is appropriate in a given locality. As Lord Carnwath pointed out in *Coventry* v. *Lawrence*, in many localities there is 'a varied pattern of uses all of which need to coexist in a modern society'[72] and they may well be long-established uses:

> After more than 60 years of modern planning and environmental controls, it is not unreasonable to start from the presumption that the established pattern of uses generally represents society's view of the appropriate balance of uses in a particular area, taking account both of the social needs of the area and of the maintenance of an acceptable environment for its occupants. The common law of nuisance is there to provide a residual control to ensure that new or intensified activities do not need lead to conditions which, within that pattern, go beyond what a normal person should be expected to put up with.[73]

This suggests that private landowners have to put up with a certain amount of interference with their land because it is in the public interest that the activity they are complaining about continues. This is made even clearer in the example that Carnwath then gives, which is 'a major football stadium':

---

[68] Ibid. paras. 212–215.   [69] Ibid. para. 221.

[70] For a good overview see Sandy Steel, 'The locality principle in nuisance' (2016) 76 *Cambridge Law Journal* 145.

[71] Lee, 'Private nuisance in the Supreme Court', fn. 47 above, p. 706.

[72] Lord Carnwath in *Coventry* v. *Lawrence* , fn. 66 above, para. 181.   [73] Ibid. para. 183.

Significant disturbance on match days may be regarded as a necessary price for an activity regarded as socially important, provided it is subject to proper controls by the public authorities, including the police, to ensure that the disturbance is contained as far as reasonably practicable. In those circumstances, if someone buys a house next to such a stadium, he should not be able to sue for nuisance, even though the noise may be highly disturbing to ordinary home life on those days. This is not because he came to the nuisance, nor (necessarily) because it has continued for 20 years. Rather it is because it is part of the established pattern of uses in the area, and society attaches importance to having places for professional football within urban areas. He can however sue if there is something about the organisation, or lack of it, which takes the disturbance beyond what is acceptable under the reasonableness test.[74]

This leads on to further difficult issues. The first is whether, in assessing the character of the locality, the court should take into account the use the defendant is making of the land and which the claimant argues is a nuisance. In *Coventry* v. *Lawrence* this question was particularly important because the defendant had been running the motor sports business on his land for such a long time that it had become an established part of the locality. Lord Neuberger pointed out that the character of the locality is a question of fact, and that therefore the defendant's activities on his land has to be taken into account – *but only to the extent that those activities do not constitute a nuisance*.[75] This makes a certain kind of sense, because, as Lord Neuberger says, if you ignore the defendant's established use of his land altogether you may give a false picture of the locality which may be unfair on the defendant, whereas if you take it fully into account without modification 'there could rarely be a successful claim for negligence'.[76] The difficulty, however, is that it requires the court to engage in a question-begging exercise – discounting the thing that they are supposed to be establishing – and it is not easy to see how they should go about that.[77]

(d) Planning

An equally, if not more, difficult issue is the significance that the court should attach to the fact that the defendant has planning permission for the activities which are the causes of the claimant's complaint. On one view, it should be totally irrelevant. As we saw in paras. 10.9 and 10.10, the planning system and the law of private nuisance fulfil wholly different functions. The planning system regulates the use of land in the public interest, balancing local, community and national interests in accordance with Government policy. The law of nuisance, on the other hand, is concerned with balancing the conflicting interests of neighbours so that they can each, as far as possible, do whatever they want with their land without causing undue harm to the other. In general terms, this is the approach taken by the courts, and in *Coventry* v. *Lawrence*, where the issue was discussed at length, Lord Neuberger said:

---

[74] Ibid. para. 185.   [75] Ibid. Lord Neuberger at para. 74, and see generally on this issue paras. 59–76.
[76] Ibid. para. 73.
[77] See further Lee, 'Private nuisance in the Supreme Court', fn. 47 above, pp. 712–713.

> I consider that the mere fact that the activity which is said to give rise to the nuisance has the benefit of a planning permission is normally of no assistance to the defendant in a claim brought by a neighbour who contends that the activity causes a nuisance to her land in the form of noise or other loss of amenity.[78]

However, in reality there is some significant overlap between the factors relevant to planning decisions and those relevant to assessing whether activities on one person's land constitute an actionable nuisance by his neighbour, and it is not always easy (or desirable) to keep the two separate. This means that the planning position is rarely irrelevant. To give just two examples, firstly the planning background is crucial to assessing the character of the locality, and secondly conditions attached to planning permissions are often designed to mitigate the effects of the permitted activities on neighbours. So, suppose a landowner obtains planning permission to carry out a noisy activity (such as operating a motor sports track) but subject to a planning condition that the noise is kept below a specified level and limited to specified hours. In those circumstances, should a neighbour be entitled to obtain an injunction prohibiting noise within those permitted levels on the basis that it is still an unreasonable interference with her reasonable use and enjoyment of her land?[79]

(e) Coming to the Nuisance

A related question is whether it is relevant that the claimant came to the nuisance. There is an intuitive view that it should be relevant, perhaps best articulated by Lord Denning in *Miller* v. *Jackson* [1977] QB 966, CA, where occupants of a house in a newly-built housing development complained about nuisance caused by cricket balls being hit into their gardens from the next door cricket pitch, where the local cricket club had played cricket for more than 70 years. In a dissenting judgment Lord Denning said:

> I recognise that the cricket club are under a duty to use all reasonable care consistently with the playing of the game of cricket, but I do not think the cricket club can be expected to give up the game of cricket altogether. After all they have their rights in their cricket ground. They have spent money, labour and love in the making of it: and they have the right to play upon it as they have done for 70 years. Is this all to be rendered useless to them by the thoughtless and selfish act of an estate developer in building right up to the edge of it? Can the developer or a purchaser of the house say to the cricket club: 'Stop playing. Clear out'. I do not think so.[80]

However, the majority disagreed, and pointed to long-established authority that it is not a defence to a claim of nuisance that the claimant came to the nuisance. No serious challenge to that authority has been made since, but following the decision in

---

[78] Lord Neuberger in *Coventry* v. *Lawrence*, fn. 66 above, para. 94.
[79] See further *Coventry* v. *Lawrence*, fn. 66 above, in particular Lord Sumption at para. 161 and generally at paras. 155–161, arguing that a claimant in nuisance should never be entitled to an injunction to restrain an activity which is authorised by planning permission, but should be limited to a remedy of damages only.
[80] Lord Denning in *Miller* v. *Jackson* [1977] QB 966, CA at p. 978.

Coventry v. *Lawrence*, the position appears more nuanced. Lord Neuberger re-affirmed the general proposition that it is irrelevant that the claimant acquired her interest in the neighbouring land after the activity alleged to be a nuisance began.[81] However, he went on to say that the position might be different in the case of a neighbour who built on or changed the use of her own land, so that activities of a neighbour which were not a nuisance before, become a nuisance to the land in its changed state.[82]

10.16 Is Damage an Essential Requirement for Nuisance?

Another general proposition about nuisance which now appears more nuanced than it once did is that, whereas liability in trespass arises whether or not the land encroached upon is damaged, damage is a prerequisite for liability in nuisance. The qualifications to this general proposition are now best summed up by Sir Terence Etherton MR in *Network Rail Infrastructure Ltd* v. *Williams* [2018] EWCA Civ 1514:

> . . . the frequently stated proposition that damage is always an essential requirement of the cause of action for nuisance because nuisance is derived from the old form of action on the case must be treated with considerable caution . . . . It is clear both that this proposition is not entirely correct and also that the concept of damage in this context is a highly elastic one. In particular, interference with an easement or a profit à prendre is actionable as a nuisance without the need to prove specific damage: *Harrop* v. *Hurst* (1868–1869) LR 4 Ex 43, 46–47, 48; *Nicholls* v. *Ely Beet Sugar Factory Ltd* [1936] Ch 343, 349–350. Furthermore, in the case of an artificial object protruding into a claimant's property from the neighbouring land [counsel for Network Rail] accepted that the claimant has a cause of action in nuisance without proof of damage. Although McNair J said in *Kelsen* v. *Imperial Tobacco Co* [1957] 2 QB 334 that an advertising sign erected by the defendant which projected into the airspace above the plaintiff's shop was a trespass and was not capable of constituting a nuisance, he so held without any reference to the previous authority to the contrary in *Baten's Case* (1610) 9 Co Rep 53b and *Fay* v. *Prentice* (1845) 1 CB 828 and so *Kelsen* must be considered *per incuriam* in relation to that issue. So far as concerns such nuisance from encroachment by an artificial object, the better view may actually be that damage is formally required but damage is always presumed: *Baten's Case*; *Fay* v. *Prentice* at 841. That, in itself, shows both the artificiality and elasticity of any requirement of damage for the purpose of establishing nuisance.

> 43. It is also well established that, in the case of nuisance through interference with the amenity of the claimant's land, physical damage is not necessary to complete the cause of action. To paraphrase Lord Lloyd's observations in *Hunter* at 696C,[83] in relation to his third category, loss of amenity, such as results from noise, smoke, smell or dust or other emanations, may not cause any diminution in the market value of the land, such

---

[81] Lord Neuberger in *Coventry* v. *Lawrence*, fn. 66 above, at paras. 47–55.

[82] See further ibid. Lord Neuberger at paras. 56–58, and Maria Lee's comments in Lee, 'Private nuisance in the Supreme Court', fn. 47 above, pp. 711–712.

[83] The reference is to *Hunter* v. *Canary Wharf* [1997] AC 665, noted in para. 10.13 above.

as may directly follow from, and reflect, loss caused by tangible physical damage to the land, but damages may nevertheless be awarded for loss of the land's intangible amenity value. Reflecting the fact that the cause of action is one for interference with property rights, loss of amenity value and the right to claim damages for it does not turn on any exceptional sensitivity or insensitivity of the person entitled to exclusive possession: *Barr* v. *Biffa Waste Services Ltd* [2012] EWCA Civ 312 at [36]. What is relevant is the objective effect on the amenity value of the land itself, and it is that effect which satisfies any requirement there may be to show damage. Provided, by reference to all the circumstances of the case and the character of the locality, and according to the objective standards of the average person, the interference with amenity is sufficiently serious, there will be an actionable private nuisance.

So, in this case, there was an actionable nuisance and would have been even if the Japanese knotweed had not yet caused any damage.

RECOMMENDED READING

The best way of finding out about private regulation of land use, and how it fits in with public regulation, is to read the nuisance cases. However, it is very much more rewarding to read them with an awareness of the issues raised in the theoretical literature outlined in Part II of this chapter. In particular, if you are interested in the economic analysis of law and/or progressive property theory, this is a good opportunity to go back over the material covered in the relevant parts of Chapter 2 *Conceptions and Justifications* and consider how they relate to the cases listed below.

The Mayor, Aldermen and Burgesses of the Borough of Bradford v. *Pickles* [1895] AC 587 (on abuse of rights, and also as an illustration of the difference between having a Hohfeldian *right* to use/abstract a resource and a Hohfeldian *liberty* to do so).
Coventry v. *Lawrence* [2014] UKSC 13.
Fearn v. *Tate Gallery* [2019] EWHC 246.
Network Rail Infrastructure Ltd v. *Williams* [2018] EWCA Civ 1514.
Daniel H. Cole, 'The law and economics approach to property' (2014) 3 *Property Law Review* 212 (extract pp. 215–219).
Maria Lee, 'Private nuisance in the Supreme Court: Coventry v Lawrence' (2014) *Journal of Planning and Environmental Law* 705.

Questions

(1) Identify the passages in *Bradford* v. *Pickles* where the judges in the House of Lords used the word 'right' in relation to Pickles when, if they had read Hohfeld, they would have used the word 'freedom' or 'liberty' or 'privilege'.

(2) How, if at all, would the decision of the House of Lords in *Bradford* v. *Pickles* have been different, if the House of Lords had accepted that property owners have obligations as described in paras. 10.2–10.4 of this chapter?

(3) Do you agree with Elspeth Reid that we do not need a doctrine of abuse of rights, because the common law achieves the same ends through the law of nuisance?

(4) Explain the difference between the tort of trespass and the tort of nuisance, taking into account what was said by Etherton MR in *Network Rail Infrastructure Ltd* v. *Williams.*

(5) To what extent did the Supreme Court in *Coventry* v. *Lawrence* and the High Court in *Fearn* v. *Tate* take into account (i) which party was the lowest cost avoider and (i) whether the entitlement should be protected by a property rule, a liability rule or an inalienability rule?

(6) Are we justified in saying that, on the basis of the limitations on property in the English law that we note in this chapter, there is a social obligation norm in English law?

11

Possession and Title

PART I INTRODUCTION

11.1 Possession and its Role in Property Rights Systems

In English and Welsh law, possession is the intentional exclusive physical control of land or tangible goods. In other words, it involves a combination of physical fact and intention: you are in possession of something if you are in physical control of it, on your own behalf and with the intention of excluding others. We look more closely at what this involves in English and Welsh law in Part III, but here we should notice that possession is a concept which is recognised in all civil law and common law property systems, and it is of fundamental importance in all of them. However, although there are similarities in the concept and function of possession in these jurisdictions, they disguise some quite significant differences, as we see in this chapter.[1]

Also, it is important to appreciate that possession, in the sense we understand it, is not a necessary concept in all kinds of property rights systems. The common law and civil concept of possession involves exclusion of all others from a physical space or physical object. As we noted in Chapter 3 *Allocation of Property Rights*, this may make it inappropriate for the patterns of resource use practiced by, for example, the indigenous peoples whose property rights systems we considered in Chapter 9 *Multiple Property Rights Systems*. As we saw there, although some of the relationships that a group and its members have with some of their resources may involve exclusive control over a physical space or object, they have other resource use patterns which are quite different. They may involve transient or intermittent use, for example, passing

---

[1] For good comparative accounts see Yaëll Emerich, 'Possession' in Michele Graziadei and Lionel Smith (eds.), *Comparative Property Law: Global Perspectives* (Cheltenham and Northampton, MA: Edward Elgar, 2017) pp. 171–190 (comparing France, Quebec, England, Canada, and Germany 'with additional forays into the laws of Switzerland and the United States', as Emerich puts it on p. 171); Andreas Rahmatian, 'A comparison of German moveable property law and English personal property law' (2008) 3 *Journal of Comparative Law* 197 at pp. 205–209 and 213–216; Sjef van Erp and Bram Akkermans (eds.) *Cases, Materials and Text on Property Law* (Oxford and Portland, OR: Hart Publishing, 2012) pp. 97–129 (protection of possession in France, Germany and Austria) and pp. 702–745 (acquiring ownership by possession in France, Germany, the Netherlands and England and Wales); and Ugo Mattei, *Basic Principles of Property Law: A Comparative and Economic Introduction* (Westport, CT and London: Greenwood Press, 2000) pp. 109–111.

through or across territory, as pastoralists[2] do, or attending specific sites at fixed intervals for various purposes. Equally, the group may share the use of, and responsibility for, certain areas or resources between all the inhabitants of an area so that different groups are entitled to make different specific uses of them, perhaps at different times and for different purposes, in accordance with rules agreed between themselves. Or the group may act as custodians of a site without feeling it necessary to exclude outsiders from it, for example if they regard it as a sacred site which it is their duty to venerate and protect. Some societies may insist on excluding outsiders from sacred sites, but others may tolerate or even welcome them so long as they behave respectfully.[3] None of these relationships between people and their resources characteristically involves one person or group taking physical control of a physical space or object with the intention of excluding everyone else from it. So, it is perfectly possible for a sophisticated property rights system to exist without our western concept of possession, as we saw in Chapter 9 *Multiple Property Rights Systems*.

11.2 Title in English Law

In common law property rights systems possession is closely linked to title, in the ways we go on to explain in para. 11.4. In our law, 'title' usually means entitlement to a property interest, and this is the way we use it in this book.[4] Most often when we use the term 'title' in this way we mean entitlement to ownership, but we do also use the term in relation to the holding of any kind of property interest. So, for example, if I grant you a 10 year lease of a studio and you sell the lease to a purchaser, and there is some dispute about the validity of the sale, we might describe this as a dispute over title to the lease: who has title to the lease now, is it you or the intended purchaser?

In English and Welsh law the concept of title applies to equitable as well as to legal property interests. As we saw in Part IV of Chapter 5 *Ownership and Other Property Interests*, it is possible (and quite common) for one person to have a legal title to a property interest whilst another has an equitable title to the same interest. Suppose, for example, that in the lease example above the problem was that the transfer of title from you to the purchaser was never registered at the Land Registry, so that you remain registered as the legal title holder of the lease but the purchaser paid you the purchase price and moved into the studio. You will hold the legal title to the lease until the transfer of title is completed at the Land Registry, but from the moment she paid you the purchase price, your purchaser has had an equitable title to the lease.

---

[2] As we saw in Chapter 3 *Allocation of Property Rights*, 'pastoralist' means the same as 'nomadic' (i.e. moving from place to place rather than settling in a fixed place) but does not have what some people see as the pejorative connotations of 'nomadic'. We look more closely at these patterns of land usage, and at others which do not approximate to possession in the common law or civil law senses, in Chapter 9 *Multiple Property Rights Systems*, Part IV.

[3] This is not a concept that is wholly alien to western property rights systems. Consider, for example, places of worship run by some religious communities in western societies.

[4] In relation to goods in particular, it is sometimes used differently. For a discussion of these other possible meanings see Luke Rostill, 'Relative title and deemed ownership in English personal property law' (2015) *Oxford Journal of Legal Studies* 31.

In the rest of this chapter we are concerned primarily with legal title, and specifically with legal title to ownership. Our main interest lies in the way in which title can be acquired by taking possession. We see how this works in the following paragraphs.

11.3 Three Fundamental Principles of Possession in English Law

In English and Welsh law three fundamental principles put possession at the core of our property rights system. They apply to both land and goods.

(a) Factual Possession Gives Rise to a Right to Possession

The first is that the law protects any possessor – even if she is a wrongful possessor – against dispossession or interference with her possession by strangers. In other words, if I take possession of land or an object without any right or justification whatsoever – for example, if I was to manage to get possession of Buckingham Palace, or of your house or your wallet – the law must protect my possession of it against everyone except a person who has a better right to possession of it.[5] So, if the Crown brings an action against me to recover possession of Buckingham Palace it will succeed, but if anyone else does so they will lose. The same applies to your house and your wallet: even though I took them from you unlawfully, I can bring a successful action against anyone who now attempts to take them away from me – anyone, that is, except you or someone else acting on your behalf. What this comes down to is that, simply by taking factual possession, I acquire a *right* to possession which is enforceable against the whole world except a person with a better right to possession. We look at this principle in more detail in Part II of this chapter.

(b) Relativity of Title: Possession Confers Title to Ownership

The second fundamental principle is that this right to possession of a thing which I acquire by taking factual possession of it, also gives me *a legal title to ownership* of the thing. This does not affect the legal title to ownership of the thing which the 'real' owner still holds. The real owner's title continues to be enforceable against the whole world, including me, whereas my title – sometimes referred to as a 'possessory title' to distinguish it from the 'real' owner's title – is enforceable against everyone *except* a person who has a better right to possession of the thing than I have. The 'real' owner[6] will have a better right to possession than me, but so too will a prior possessor if there has been a string of dispossessions. So, if X took possession of your wallet without your consent, and I then take possession of it, taking it away

---

[5] The position is complicated by criminal law if I commit a criminal offence when taking possession – but not so as to disturb the basic principle.

[6] Or his lessee, if he has granted a lease or bailment of the thing to a lessee (because leases and bailments involve the owner granting possession of the thing to the lessee/bailee for the period of the lease/bailment: see further Chapter 17 *Leases.*

from X, without the consent of you or X, you have a better right to possession than anyone else in the world (including X and me), but X has a better right to possession than I have. The effect of this is that all three of us, simultaneously, hold titles to ownership of the same thing, that is, your wallet. Your title is absolute, in the sense that there is no-one with a better title than you, whereas X's title is good against me but not against you, and my title is good against everyone in the whole world except you and X. This is the common law principle of *relativity of title*, which is fundamental to the whole of our property rights system.[7]

A consequence of all this is that, in disputes between rival title holders, the courts are interested only in which of the two rivals has the better title, that is, the better right to possession. So, in the wallet example, if X was to bring an action against me demanding that I return to him the wallet which he wrongly took from you, the court will order me to return it to him, even if I can prove that he wrongly took it from you. This was confirmed by the Court of Appeal in *Costello v. Chief Constable of Derbyshire*,[8] where the police had seized a car they had found in Costello's possession, believing him to have stolen it or to have received it from the thief, knowing it was stolen. The police had statutory powers to keep the car, but only for so long as they were investigating the crime. However, they could not find sufficient evidence against Costello so they had to drop the charges against him. The Court of Appeal ordered them to return the car to Costello, as the prior possessor, even though there was no evidence whatsoever that it was ever his:

> as a matter of principle and authority possession means the same thing and is entitled to the same legal protection whether or not it has been obtained lawfully or by theft or by other unlawful means. It vests in the possessor a possessory title which is good against the world save as against anyone setting up or claiming under a better title . . . . even a thief is entitled to the protection of the criminal law against the theft from him of that which he has himself stolen.[9]

(c) Adverse Possession: Extinguishing Titles of the Dispossessed

The third general principle is that the title of a dispossessed owner will be extinguished if she takes no steps to recover possession within a certain period of years after having been dispossessed. This will leave the person who dispossessed her (the 'adverse possessor') and who has remained in possession throughout, with the only title to ownership of the thing.[10] This is known as the doctrine of adverse possession. In this jurisdiction, the common law mechanism by which the law achieved this

---

[7] Anthony Honoré, 'Ownership' in A. G. Guest (ed.), *Oxford Essays in Jurisprudence (First Series)* (Oxford: Clarendon Press, 1961) p. 107 at pp. 136–141. See also Robin Hickey, *Property and the Law of Finders* (Oxford: Hart Publishing, 2010) pp. 96 and 107–109 and David Fox, 'Relativity of title in law and equity' (2006) 65 *Cambridge Law Journal* 330.

[8] *Costello v. Chief Constable of Derbyshire* [2001] 1 WLR 1437 CA.

[9] Lightman J giving the judgment of the Court of Appeal in ibid. para. 31.

[10] This is assuming the simplest case, i.e. where A, the 'real' owner is dispossessed by B, who remains in possession until A's time to sue has run out. If there has been a string of dispossessors, as in the example in (b) above, where B in his turn is dispossessed by C, the title of each dispossessed title-holder

result has traditionally been limitation of action rules.[11] In this and most other legal systems, there is a statutory time limit for bringing any legal action before the courts: for example, if I fail to repay a debt I owe to you on the date I promised to repay, in this jurisdiction you will lose the right to recover the debt from me unless you bring an action to recover it within the next six years.[12] In the case of actions to recover possession of land the time limit in this jurisdiction is 12 years, and for possession of goods it is generally 6 years.[13] So, when I take wrongful (i.e. adverse) possession of land, the person I dispossess becomes entitled to ask the court for an order restoring possession to him. If he fails to bring an action before the court within 12 years *of being dispossessed* he loses the right to do so, and his title is extinguished. The same basic rule applies in the case of adverse possession of goods.

As we see in the next chapter where we look at adverse possession in detail, most common law and civil law systems have mechanisms similar to adverse possession (generally called 'acquisitive prescription' in civil law systems), which allow wrongful possessors to acquire full ownership after a period of time in undisturbed possession. There are, however, significant differences between civil law acquisitive prescription and common law adverse possession, as we see in Chapter 12 *Adverse Possession of Land*.

11.4 Why and How the Law Protects Possession

In the rest of this chapter we consider the general question of why possession assumes such importance in property systems like ours (Part II). We then move on to more specific questions in Part III (what amounts to possession in our system, and its particular significance in our law) and Part IV (why and how the law discourages self-help evictions of wrongful possessors by those entitled to possession, and also the civil and now criminal liabilities of wrongful possessors). This paves the way for us to look in detail at the issue of adverse possession in Chapter 12.

PART II WHY DO PROPERTY SYSTEMS PROTECT POSSESSION?

11.5 Possession as the Origin of Property

All civil law and common law property systems provide at least some legal protection of possession against interference by strangers (i.e. against those with no right to possession at all), even when the possession was taken unlawfully. This is not so surprising. Many theoretical analyses of the nature and origins of the institution of property have assumed or argued that property rights emerged out of, or are the

---

(A then B) will be extinguished as and when he or she fails to take action within the requisite time *after the date he or she were themselves dispossessed.*

[11] These common law rules still apply to goods, and also to land where the true owner's title is not registered at the Land Registry. If it is registered, the common law procedure is modified, currently by the Land Registration Act 2002: see Chapter 12 *Adverse Possession of Land*.

[12] S. 5 of the Limitation Act 1980.

[13] Ibid. s. 15 for land and s. 2 for goods (although see ss. 3 and 4 for exceptions where taking goods amounts to the tort of conversion or to theft).

logical progression on from, factual possession, as we saw when we looked at Locke, Kant and Hegel in Chapter 2 *Conceptions and Justifications* and at Hume in Chapter 3 *Allocation of Property Rights*. Also, as we noted when we looked at queuing and claims based on prior possession in Chapter 3, many societies, including our own, observe social norms which give preference to prior possession (we do not approve of people who try to jump the queue) and intuitively feel that it is just that the first possessor should be protected against later comers.

11.6 Justifications for Legal Protection of Possession

So, the legal protection of wrongful possession against strangers is not at odds with societal views of possession, and it can also be justified on a variety of other grounds.

(a) Possession is Easily Recognisable

On the pragmatic side, we can say that we protect possession as a proxy for ownership. People in possession of land and goods have the outward appearance of owners (and indeed often *are* owners), and it is much easier and cheaper to recognise and prove possession than it is to recognise and prove ownership. Possession is a fact that we can recognise with our own eyes, whereas ownership is an abstract right which can be proved only by checking in a register or poring over deeds to establish provenance, in the way we describe in para. 3.7(a) of Chapter 3 *Allocation of Property Rights*. Police, courts and officials can protect property rights in land and goods much more quickly and efficiently if they need check only that the person seeking protection is in intentional physical control of the thing, than they could if they first had to check whether she had an abstract property right to be in possession. So, if we adopt a rule of protecting possessors we will mostly also be protecting owners, and we will be providing protection more quickly, more cheaply and more efficiently than if we withheld it until we had satisfied ourselves that the person seeking protection held the necessary property rights.

Thomas Merrill, whose arguments on information theory we noted in Chapter 2 *Conceptions and Justifications*, sees this as a question of information costs. He says that the considerably lower cost of proving possession helps to explain why a court, in resolving a dispute between two rival claimants to land or goods, does not ask each to try to prove ownership, but instead decides in favour of the one in possession, unless the other can prove she has a better right to possession.[14] However, he says it goes further than that. He points out that whereas the identification of property rights is a high-order activity requiring the assistance of lawyers, we can all identify possession for ourselves without any assistance:

> Possession is determined by observing the relationship between natural persons and tangible objects. In ascertaining whether some object is possessed, we rely on physical

---

[14] Thomas W. Merrill, 'Ownership and possession' in Yun-Chien Chang (ed.) *Law and Economics of Possession* (Cambridge: Cambridge University Press, 2015) p. 9 at p. 24.

cues that tell us whether some person has brought the object under control and intends to maintain control to the exclusion of others. These cues are often rooted in functional logic, such that sitting in a seat in a theatre, reeling in a fish on a line, or putting up a fence around a field is understood to signify being in control of the relevant object without any further form of communication. In terms of signalling an intention to remain in control, symbolic acts enter the picture, and decoding these acts requires some cultural knowledge. Thus, blazes on trees will signify an intention to remain in control of land in one culture, whereas cairns of rock will communicate such an intention in another. But these cultural signals appear to be ones that members of the community easily learn without any need for formal instruction. Information costs remain low because the relevant communication consists of visual observation of physical cues about objects, mediated by cultural knowledge that is easy for all members of the community to assimilate, typically simply by observing others.[15]

This is important, he says, because property has to speak to two different audiences, the 'audience of strangers' and the 'audience of potential transactors'. The audience of strangers consists of all those people who come across hundreds of objects every day (he invites us to think about luggage in an airport or cars in a car park) and who have no interest in any of them, other than to avoid interfering with those claimed by others. The concept of possession, he argues, provides a low-cost means of identifying which of these objects are claimed by others:

> If the audience of strangers had to rely on the concept of ownership in order to determine which things are 'claimed by other' in everyday life, the informational burden would be overwhelming. Suppose we go on a one-day airplane trip to another city, and in the process cross paths with 10,000 different strangers, each of whom is accompanied by ten objects, subject to six different types of status in law (e.g., owner, co-owner, lessee, agent, bailee, trust beneficiary). Knowing the ownership of each thing would entail the need to call upon 600,000 separate bits of information. Perhaps in some futuristic world persons could be equipped with a new generation of Google glasses that automatically scan bar codes on objects, convey this information to a computer with massive data processing capacity, which in turn would respond with information about the ownership status of every object encountered. Even in such a world, it would be necessary to process and comprehend the information generated. Some shorthand surely would be developed, such as beeping a message to us equivalent to 'claimed by other' so as to allow us to avoid interfering with the things to which we have no relationship or interest. We do not need to develop such a system, because we already have the concept of possession. The concept of possession allows us to navigate in a world filled with objects of value that belong to strangers without suffering from information overload.[16]

[15] Ibid. pp. 27–28.
[16] Ibid. p. 30. This is not a particularly persuasive example. In an environment like an airport we surely all rightly assume that we are not allowed to touch *anything* we come across unless specifically invited, apart from our own luggage, but this is not because all other things are in someone else's possession. In that kind of environment we can safely assume (and we do) that everything that is not ours is someone else's, whether or not it is in someone else's possession. We do not need, and do not use, possession as a signal to tell us that. Possible exceptions, such as rubbish in rubbish bins or free newspapers will be clearly labelled – we know everything else is out of bounds. A better example (and it is difficult to think of many others) might be fish in a stretch of water where there is a public right to fish: we know we may catch any fish we want apart from those already possessed by someone else.

The 'audience of potential transactors' on the other hand, so Merrill says, is very small and usually focussed on a single identifiable object, with a view to buying, leasing or taking a mortgage over it, or perhaps insuring it. If the object is of a sufficiently high value (Merrill suggests land or 'a late model BMW', as opposed to food, clothing or personal computers), these people want to know exactly what they are paying for, and are willing to pay the significantly higher information costs involved in investigating what property rights the other party holds.[17]

(b) Possession and the Publicity Principle

Carol Rose, in her classic journal article 'Possession as the origin of property',[18] also makes the point that possession is a useful signalling device, giving notice to the world at large that a particular area of land (or some other tangible object) is claimed:

> Society is worst off in a world of vague claims; if no one knows whether he can safely use the land, or from whom he should buy it if it is already claimed, the land may end up being used by too many people or by none at all.[19]

So, on this view possession is a communicating device and *for so long as it lasts* it works well to alert the outside world that this particular object is claimed by someone. This helps to explain why possession is grounded on physical (therefore visible) control. It also helps to explain why most property rights systems in which possession is a significant factor, have institutions functionally similar to the common law doctrine of adverse possession – to communicate claims successfully, possession must be continuous. As Rose says,

> Possession ... requires a kind of communication, and the original claim to the property looks like a kind of speech, with the audience composed of all others who might be interested in claiming the object in question. Moreover, some venerable statutory law obligates the acquiring party to *keep on* speaking, lest he lose his title by 'adverse possession' . . . . suppose I own a lot in the mountains, and some stranger to me, without my permission, builds a house on it, clears the woods, and farms the lot continuously for a given period, say twenty years. During that time, I am entitled to go to court to force him off the lot. But if I have not done so at the end of twenty years, or some other period fixed by statute, not only can I not sue him for recovery of what was my land, but the law recognizes him as the title owner. The doctrine of adverse possession thus operates to transfer property to one who is initially a trespasser if the trespasser's presence is open to everyone, lasts continuously for a given period of time, and if the title owner takes no action to get rid of him during that time ... it [is] designed to require the owner to assert her right publicly. It requires her to make it clear that she, and not the trespasser, is the person to deal with if anyone should wish to buy the property or use some portion of it.[20]

---

[17] Ibid. pp. 31–32.
[18] Carol Rose, 'Possession as the origin of property' (1985) 52 *University of Chicago Law Review* 73.
[19] Ibid. at p. 78.
[20] Ibid. at pp. 78–79. However, it should be noted that Rose's description of adverse possession as 'transferring' property in this passage is misconceived: adverse possession transfers nothing. As we saw

This explains why possession has traditionally been regarded in the civil law and in the common law as an 'act of publicity' satisfying the principle of publicity which, as we see in para. 16.6(b) of Chapter 16 *Registration*, is explicit in many civil law property rights systems and implicit in ours. The principle of publicity is that you are entitled to state protection of your property interests (protection against interference by the state and by fellow citizens) only if you take specified steps ('acts of publicity') to make your interests known to the outside world. An obvious act of publicity is registration of your interest in a public register. In both common law and civil law systems, possession is sometimes a permissible alternative, as we see in para. 16.6(b) in Chapter 16 *Registration*.[21] Emerich provides these examples of similar sentiments expressed by French and Swiss scholars:

> The French author Raymond Saleilles, for example, sees a possessor as 'a person who appears in the world of external facts as the person in actual control of the thing, and who desires to be so'. Therefore, possession is 'the conscious and intended actualization of the economic appropriation of things' ... and [in relation to Swiss legal doctrine] Steinauer notes that 'the owner of the mailbox is ... the possessor of the mail deposited in it even before having collected it, because by setting it out, he has already expressed, in a general sense, his will to have its contents in his custody.'[22]

(c) Maintaining Civil Order and Keeping the Peace

It has long been argued that the prime function of the state is to keep the peace, that is, to preserve public order by, amongst other things, preventing people from snatching things away from others. The obvious way of doing this is by protecting the status quo (the peaceful possession of those who have taken physical control of something) against everyone who threatens it, except a person who can prove that they have a *right* to challenge it.[23]

The law does not want to be obliged to challenge all possessors and physically remove all those who cannot prove they are lawfully in possession, and it is wary of allowing other citizens to physically dispossess even wrongful possessors because of the potential for violent confrontation and disruption – as Mattei says, the use of

---

in para. 11.3(b)–(c) above, adverse possession confers an immediate but relatively inferior entitlement to ownership as soon as possession is taken. This becomes 'full' ownership simply by the superior title (held by the dispossessed owner) being eliminated over time. Nothing is ever 'transferred' from the 'real' owner to the adverse possessor.

[21] Yaëll Emerich, *Conceptualising Property Law: Integrating Common Law and Civil Law Traditions* (Cheltenham, UK and Northampton, MA, USA: Edward Elgar Publishing, 2018) pp. 49 and 60–64, and see also Lisa Austin, 'Property and the rule of law' (2014) *Legal Theory* 79, at pp. 93–97.

[22] Emerich, 'Possession', fn. 1 above, at pp. 179–180, quoting from Raymond Saleilles, *Études sur les éléments constitutive de la possession* (Dijon: Imprimerie Darantière, 1984) at pp. 376 and 113 and Paul-Henri Steinauer, *Précis de droit Stämpfli*, vol. 1 (5th edn, Berne: Stämpfli, 2012).

[23] Sir Frederick Pollock and Frederick Maitland, *The History of English Law* (first published 1895, this edition Cambridge: Cambridge University Press, 1989) Book II Ch. IV 'Ownership and Possession' section 2, p. 41. Austin makes much the same point in Austin, 'Property and the rule of law', fn. 21 above, at p. 94 where she talks about the modern law's protection of possession as 'not about ownership so much as the maintenance of social order with respect to things'.

force should be the monopoly of the state.[24] As we see below, in our law even those entitled to possession are rarely permitted take it for themselves without having first obtained a court order. So, it makes for a more peaceful and settled society if the law is required to repulse all challenges to established possession unless and until someone can come forward and *prove* they have a better right to possession than the current possessor.

(d) Reinforcement of Social Norms

Merrill also suggests another societal justification. He points out that a social norm protects possession: people intuitively respect prior possession. Merrill argues that it is important for the law to reinforce this social norm, 'to underscore the importance of respecting possession' (which seems to bring us back to the civic order point) and not 'sap [the social norm] of . . . its strength'.[25] He sees an economic advantage as well in this reinforcement of social norms: if the law did not protect possession, he argues, possessors would be tempted to engage in costly behaviour, such as seeking more documentary proof of their property rights to satisfy strangers, or investing more heavily in self-help protection. As Merrill puts it, these costs would be deadweight losses, that is, losses in economic efficiency.[26]

(e) Personhood Arguments and the Endowment Effect

There are also strong moral arguments for protecting the possession of even wrongful possessors, which arises out of what is now generally accepted to be a close and deeply rooted link between property and personhood. As we noted in earlier chapters,[27] it has often been argued that in some circumstances things can seem to us to have become a part of ourselves, so that any assault or interference with them, and any attempt to remove them from us without our consent, feels like an assault on our own person. This investment of our will in our things (as Hegelians would put it) does not depend on how we acquired possession of them, or whether we had or have a legally recognised property interest in them. There are various explanations put forward for this effect, not mutually exclusive. For some, time is the central factor: a bond grows up over time between ourselves and our things. As Oliver Wendell Homes, the great nineteenth century American jurist, put it:

> [a] thing which you have enjoyed and used as your own for a long time, whether property or an opinion, takes root in your being and cannot be torn away without your resenting the act and trying to defend yourself, however you came by it.[28]

---

[24] Mattei, *Basic Principles of Property Law*, fn. 1 above, p. 110.
[25] Merrill, 'Ownership and possession', fn. 14 above, p. 33.   [26] Ibid. pp. 33–34.
[27] Chapter 2 *Conceptions and Justifications* paras. 2.22–2.23, Chapter 7 *Objects of Property Interests* para. 7.10 and Chapter 9 *Multiple Property Rights Systems* para. 9.29(d).
[28] Oliver Wendell Holmes, 'The path of the law' (1897) 10 *Harvard Law Review* 457 at p. 477.

Others such as Margaret Radin, see this bond between ourselves and our things as something that arises in relation to things which have a special significance for us (the thing is our home, or was given to us by someone we love, or is the last stamp we need to complete our collection).[29] For Hegelians and others, the institution of property is justified *because* of this bond we form with the things we regard as ours, a bond which Kevin Gray suggests is innate:

> The imperative to conserve and protect assets in our possession may simply be rooted in our evolutionary biology. Some have even spoken of a 'property recognition gene' as playing an important role in the natural selection of our species.[30]

As Gray points out, this bond also has a discernible economic effect, labelled by economists as the 'endowment effect' and its corollary, 'loss aversion'. People demonstrably value the thing they possess, both over and above its objective monetary value, and also over and above the value they would put on it if they did not possess it,[31] simply because it is in their possession:

> According to this widely accepted analysis of human behaviour [i.e. the endowment effect], the sheer fact of possession confers on one's holdings an additional, subjective, and economically irrational value. A thing, once acquired, seems to its possessor more precious than was thought immediately prior to its acquisition. This 'endowment effect', when coupled with the closely allied theory of loss aversion ([whereby] losses have a greater subjective impact than objectively commensurate gains) emphasizes the heightened salience of apprehended deprivation.[32]

There is some disagreement over whether the endowment effect is simply the economic manifestation of the idiosyncratic value that people put on the things in which they have invested their will, or whether it is an additional independent effect of owning or possessing things.[33] However, for our purposes the point is that, for whatever reason, things that people possess have a special value to them which is bound up with their feelings of self or personhood. It is this, so the argument goes,

---

[29] Margaret Radin, 'Property and personhood' (1982) 34 *Stanford Law Review* 957, considered in Chapter 7 *Objects of Property Interests* para. 7.10.

[30] Kevin Gray, 'Property in a queue', in Gregory S. Alexander and Eduardo M. Peñalver (eds.), *Property and Community* (Oxford: Oxford University Press, 2010) pp. 165–195, at p. 179, referring in the omitted footnotes to Jeffrey E. Stake, 'The uneasy case for adverse possession' (2001) 89 *Georgetown Law Journal* 2419 at p. 2425 and Owen D. Jones and Sarah F. Brosnan, 'Law, biology, and property: A new theory of the endowment effect' (2008) 49 *William and Mary Law Review* 1935.

[31] Specifically, there is experimental and empirical research which appears to confirm that the minimum amount people would be willing to accept before they would agree to sell something they already have, is significantly higher than the maximum amount they would be willing to pay to acquire it if they did not have it. See Gregory Klass and Kathryn Zeiler, 'Against endowment theory: Experimental economics and legal scholarship' (2013) 61 *UCLA Law Review* 2.

[32] Gray, 'Property in a queue', fn. 30 above, at p. 179. Footnotes omitted from this passage refer to Daniel Kahneman, Jack L. Knetsch, and Richard H. Thaler, 'The endowment effect, loss aversion, and status quo bias' (1991) 5 *Journal of Economic Perpsectives* 193 and Brian Knutson et al., 'Neural antecedents of the endowment effect' (2008) 58 *Neuron* 814. Gray is talking about the 'stake' that people in a queue feel that they have in their place in the queue, which we looked at in Chapter 3 *Allocation of Property Rights* paras 3.2–3.3.

[33] Klass and Zeiler, 'Against endowment theory', fn. 31 above, reject the latter view.

that gives possessors a moral claim to the things they possess which is independent of any moral claim they may have as owners.

11.7 Effect of Time on Possession

All of these reasons for protecting unlawful possession become more and more compelling the longer the possessor remains in possession, and the passage of time brings additional factors to bear, so that eventually the claims of the possessor can be taken to outweigh even those of the true owner. We look at these additional factors in the next chapter, where we examine the circumstances in which the true owner's title can eventually be eliminated, leaving the possessor with the sole and now undisputed title to ownership.

PART III POSSESSION IN ENGLAND AND WALES

11.8 What Amounts to Possession

In common law and in civil law jurisdictions, possession generally requires both factual physical control[34] and an element of intention. In some jurisdictions it is an intention to be owner, in others an intention to exclude the owner: in ours, it is an intention to occupy and use as one's own. We look more closely at what amounts to possession in our law in the next paragraph, but here we should note that the balance between fact and intention, and what is covered by each of the two elements, varies between jurisdictions. Also, it is important to note that, whilst in some civil law jurisdictions there is an additional requirement of publicity (i.e. possession must be apparent to the public),[35] there is no such requirement in the law of England and Wales.

11.9 Possession of Land in England and Wales

After a period of uncertainty, it was reaffirmed by the House of Lords in *J.A. Pye (Oxford) Ltd* v. *Graham*[36] that possession of land in England and Wales has just two requirements. As Lord Browne-Wilkinson put it:

> there are two elements necessary for legal possession:
>
> 1. a sufficient degree of physical custody and control ('factual possession');
> 2. an intention to exercise such custody and control *on one's own behalf and for one's own benefit* ('intention to possess').[37]

---

[34] France allows 'acts of enjoyment' of the thing as an alternative to control: Emerich, 'Possession', fn. 1 above, p. 175.

[35] Emerich, 'Possession', fn. 1 above, pp. 174–181, and see further Chapter 15 *Enforceability and Priority of Property Interests: General Principles* para. 15.1(a) and Chapter 16 *Registration* para. 16.6(b) for the principle of publicity and the significance of possession as an 'act of publicity'.

[36] *J.A. Pye (Oxford) Ltd* v. *Graham* [2002] UKHL 30.   [37] Ibid. at para. 40.

Lord Hope in the same case agreed, but he also warned that 'factual possession' and 'intention to possess' are interconnected:

> The acquisition of possession requires both an intention to take or occupy the land ('animus') and some act of the body ('corpus') which gives effect to that intention. Occupation of the land alone is not enough, nor is an intention to occupy which is not put into effect by action. Both aspects must be examined, and each is bound up with the other. But acts of the mind can be, and sometimes can only be, demonstrated by acts of the body. In practice, the best evidence of intention is frequently found in the acts which have taken place.[38]

In particular, as Lord Hope went on to explain, intention can be inferred from the acts of the occupier *because* the only intention required is an intention to be in possession on one's own behalf and for one's own benefit – the occupier does not have to go further and show that she intended to exclude the 'real' owner:

> it is reasonably clear that the animus which is required is the *intent to exercise exclusive control over the thing for oneself* . . . The important point for present purposes is that it is *not necessary to show that there was a deliberate intention to exclude the paper owner* . . . The only intention which has to be demonstrated is *an intention to occupy and use the land as one's own* . . . . So I would hold that, if the evidence shows that the person was *using the land in the way one would expect him to use it if he were the true owner*, that is enough.[39]

The significance of this becomes apparent when we look at the decision in *J.A. Pye (Oxford) Ltd* v. *Graham,* which is the leading case on adverse possession in England and Wales. We look at the adverse possession aspect of the decision in Part III of Chapter 12 *Adverse Possession of Land,* but the significant point here is whether the claimants in that case ever had the necessary intention to be in possession of the disputed land. The claimants, the Grahams, were farmers who had been using the disputed land – grazing land adjoining their farm – for many years. They argued that they had been in adverse possession of the grazing land for more than 12 years and so were entitled to be registered as owners of it in place of Pye, the company which was then registered as the landowner. Pye opposed the application, and its central argument was that, although the Grahams had been occupying the land for all those years they had never been in possession of it. The Grahams had first occupied the land under a grazing agreement Pye had granted them which entitled them to graze animals on the land for 11 months for a fee of £2,000. When the grazing agreement expired in 1983 the Grahams wanted to renew it but Pye refused: it had sold off the rest of its nearby land but had retained this part of it in the hope that it would be able to obtain planning permission to develop it, and it had been advised that any application it made would be more likely to succeed if the land was 'in hand' (i.e. not let out to anyone else). So, the Grahams were told to vacate the land. However, they kept on using it and over the next few years they asked for a new grazing agreement a couple of times, offering to pay licence fees, but gave up when

[38] Ibid. Lord Hope at para. 70   [39] Ibid. Lord Hope at para. 71.

they received no reply, and went on using the land. Eventually, more than 12 years later, they made this application for registration as owners of the land. Pye's argument was that the Grahams were never *in possession* of the land under the grazing agreement because the agreement granted them only a right to make a particular use of the land (to graze animals on it). When the grazing agreement ended, they argued, the Grahams went on using the land in the same way as they had used it before (except now without Pye's agreement), and so they never had possession of it. The Court of Appeal accepted that argument and held that the Grahams' claim failed, but the House of Lords disagreed. They doubted that the Court of Appeal had been right to find that the Grahams never had possession of the land under the grazing agreement: although the agreement appeared to grant only grazing rights it also required the Grahams to take care of the land (to keep it weed-free, keep the gates and boundary fences etc. in good repair and use the land in a 'good and husband-like manner') and not to permit any trespass in the land, nor to 'part with possession of it'. However, the House of Lords said, whether or not the Grahams were in possession whilst the grazing agreement continued, they clearly had the requisite physical control and intention to be in possession after the end of it. They had physical control of the land: it was enclosed by hedges in which there were gates, one giving public access over a pathway and the rest either inaccessible by the landowner or padlocked with the keys held by the Grahams, and on the rare occasions when Pye's agents went to inspect the land they made no attempt to do more than look at it from the road. And the Grahams' intentions could be inferred from what they did with the land: they did more than just graze their animals on it; they also fertilised it, over-wintered cattle there and generally 'made such use of the disputed land as they wished irrespective of whether it fell within the terms of any hypothetical grazing agreement', treating it and their adjoining farm as a single unit.[40] Lord Brown-Wilkinson said:

> If the view of the Court of Appeal were to be correct, the result would be anomalous. Although from 1984 to 1997 the Grahams were the only people who did anything on the disputed land and Pye had throughout that period been physically excluded from the land, nevertheless Pye was throughout to be treated as in possession. In my judgment, however favourably one approaches the claim of a paper owner to possession, such a conclusion would be so unrealistic as to be an impossible one. For all practical purposes the Grahams used the land as their own and in a way normal for an owner to use it throughout the period from August 1984 onwards. During that whole period Pye did nothing on the disputed land, from which they were wholly excluded save on foot.[41]

Similarly, in *Thorpe v. Frank* [2019] EWCA Civ 150 the issue was whether a house owner had acquired factual possession of her neighbour's half of a shared open forecourt at the front of her house and the neighbouring house. The house owner had paved over the whole area, and the Court of Appeal held that, given the

---

[40] Ibid. Lord Browne-Wilkinson at paras. 58–59.
[41] Ibid. para. 61, and see also Lord Hutton at paras. 75–76 to similar effect.

circumstances and the nature of the land, this did amount to taking possession of the neighbour's half, even though the neighbour continued to pass and repass over it as before. This was on the basis that the work done by the house owner involved ripping up the old paving, altering the surface level, and re-laying a permanent new surface using material chosen by the house owner: 'precisely the sort of action which an occupying owner would quite normally carry out on land of this character'. The houseowner was accordingly held to have acquired title to the forecourt by adverse possession (with her neighbour continuing to have rights over the forecourt to get to and from the neighbouring house).

11.10 Possession and Ownership

Owners and others who have a legal right to possess are presumed to be in possession unless they can be proved to have been dispossessed or to have granted the right to possession to someone else (for example, by granting a lease). This principle was reaffirmed by the Supreme Court in *Star Energy Weald Basin Ltd v. Bocardo SA*,[42] which we looked at in para. 7.17 of Chapter 7 *Objects of Property Interests*. In that case a company drilled diagonally down from land it controlled through the subsoil under the claimant's land to reach and extract oil from the apex of an oil field which lay 2,800 feet below the surface of the claimant's land. The claimant brought this action claiming that this was an invasion of their land, making the oil company liable to them in trespass. Trespass is a tort consisting of invasion of someone's possessory rights,[43] and one of the oil company's arguments was that its pipelines entered the claimant's land so far below the surface of the claimant's land that (a) it was beneath the lower boundary of the claimant's land and (b) whether it was or not, the claimant could not be said to have been in 'possession' of the subsoil at that depth (and therefore entitled to bring an action in trespass), because it could not conceivably have been said to have had physical control of it.[44] The Supreme Court held that the claimant's land did extend at least as far down as the oil field, and that therefore it owned the land through which the oil company had been drilling and where it was now operating.[45] It also confirmed that a claim in trespass could only be brought by someone in possession of land, but that it was conclusively presumed that an owner of land was in possession of it unless it could be proved that someone else was. Lord Hope said:

> As Aikens LJ said in the Court of Appeal [in *Star Energy Weald*], it is difficult to say that the appellant has actual possession of the strata below the Oxted Estate as it has done nothing to reduce those strata into its actual possession: [2010] Ch 100, para 66. But he held that the appellant, as the paper title owner to the strata and all within it . . . has the prima facie right to possession of those strata so as to be deemed to be in

---

[42] *Star Energy Weald Basin Ltd* v. *Bocardo SA* [2010] UKSC 35.
[43] Chapter 10 *Limitations on Property* para. 10.12(a).
[44] The evidence was that subsurface land at that depth was impenetrable by humans without highly sophisticated mining equipment.
[45] See further Chapter 7 *Objects of Property Interests* para. 7.17.

factual possession of them. I think that he was right to conclude that this was the effect of [previous authority]. As the paper title carries with it title to the strata below the surface, the appellant must be deemed to be in possession of the subsurface strata too. There is no one else who is claiming to be in possession of those strata through the appellant as the paper owner.[46]

11.11 Possession and Intangibles

It has long been established in English law that possession applies only to land and to other tangible things – it is not possible to be in possession of intangibles. As we saw in para. 7.6(b) of Chapter 7 *Objects of Property Interests* this was confirmed by the House of Lords in *OBG* v. *Allan* [2007] UKHL 21. The rationale is that possession requires physical control, and, so it is said, you cannot be in physical control of an intangible thing. Plausible grounds for challenging this view were put forward in *Your Response Limited* v. *Datateam Business Media Limited* [2018] EWCA Civ 281, where it was argued by a data management company that it was in possession of its publisher client's database of subscribers, which the data manager kept on its servers and managed on behalf of the publisher. When the publisher and the data manager fell out, the publisher unilaterally terminated the contract between them, and the data manager refused to give the database back or allow the publisher access to it until its fees were paid. It was accepted that the data manager was entitled to do that if it had a possessory lien[47] over the database, and it was also accepted that, if the database had been in paper form rather than in electronic form, the data manager would have had a possessory lien over the paper, and therefore over the information written on the paper. However, the publisher argued that you cannot have a possessory lien over something unless you are in possession of it, and it is not possible to be in possession of an intangible thing, like an electronic database. The judge at first instance disagreed. He said:

> It seems to me in the present case that a lien can apply to the electronic data which was in the possession of the [data manager]. It would not be appropriate for the law to ignore the development in the real world of record keeping moving from hard copy records into electronic media . . . for the purpose of the particular decision which I have to reach in this case, I do not accept the submissions . . . that a lien cannot exist over the electronic data which was in the [data manager's] possession in just the same way as it could exist over the hard copy records in the [data manager's] possession.[48]

---

[46] Lord Hope in *Star Energy Weald Basin Ltd* v. *Bocardo SA* [2010] UKSC 35 at para. 31. The authority referred to here is an observation made by Slade J in *Powell* v. *McFarlane* (1977) 38 P & CR 452, 470: 'In the absence of evidence to the contrary, the owner of land with the paper title is deemed to be in possession of the land, as being the person with the prima facie right to possession', approved by Lord Bowne Wilkinson in *J.A. Pye (Oxford) Ltd* v. *Graham* [2003] UKHL 30, para 40.

[47] A kind of charge you have over something in your possession, if the owner of the thing owes you money and the debt is in some way connected with your possession of her property: see further Chapter 5 *Ownership and Other Property Interests* para. 5.37(c).

[48] The judge at first instance in *Your Response Ltd* v. *Datateam Business Media Ltd* at para. 111 of his judgment, as quoted by Moore-Bick LJ in his judgment in the Court of Appeal [2018] EWCA Civ 281 at para. 9.

On appeal, counsel for the data manager unsuccessfully urged the Court of Appeal to accept the judge's conclusion. Two of the arguments put forward in support are particularly attractive. The first was, essentially, that an electronic database is not really intangible at all, in that it 'exists in a physical form on the data manager's servers'. Moore-Bick LJ accepted that 'entering information into an electronic data storage system results in an alteration to the physical characteristics of the equipment', but this, he said 'takes the case nowhere', because, essentially, it confuses the 'box' with its contents, pointing out that there was a distinction between 'a disk or other medium on which data is held (which is a tangible object) and the data itself (which is not)':

> the process is similar to making a manuscript entry in a ledger: there is a physical change in the condition of the ledger by the application of ink to a sheet of paper. However, that does not in my view render the information itself a physical object capable of possession independently of the medium in which it is held and in the electronic world the distinction is of some importance because of the ease of making and transmitting intangible copies.[49]

However, this rather misses the point of the argument. Generally (for obvious reasons) a person in possession of a box is taken to be in possession of its contents.[50] If you can put intangible things in a tangible box, and take possession of the tangible box so that you control all access to the intangible contents, there seems to be no reason why you should not be treated as being in possession of the intangible contents. This is essentially the second argument. Even if the database is to be regarded as intangible, so the argument goes, nevertheless it is possible to be in possession of it because 'the essence of possession is physical control coupled with an intention to exclude others' and someone who holds an electronic database can (and in this case did) exercise compete practical control over who has access to it, just as the holder of the only key to a warehouse can be said to be in possession of the goods in the warehouse because she has practical control over access to them. Moore-Bick described this argument as having 'greater attraction' but nevertheless refused to accept it:

> Although an analogy can be drawn between control of a database and possession of a chattel, I am unable to accept Mr. Cogley's argument. It is true that practical control goes hand in hand with possession, but in my view the two are not the same.
>
> Possession is concerned with the physical control of tangible objects; practical control is a broader concept, capable of extending to intangible assets and to things

---

[49] Moore-Bick LJ in *Your Response Ltd* v. *Datateam Business Media Ltd* [2018] EWCA Civ 281 at para. 19.

[50] *Warner* v. *Commissioner of Police of the Metropolis* [1969] 2 AC 256, accepting, however, that it would be different if the possessor of the box genuinely believed that the box contained a different kind of thing (perhaps thought it contained jars of honey when in fact it contained Class A drugs), and had had no reasonable opportunity of examining its contents. The decision is no longer good law as to what amounts to possession for the purposes of criminal liability for possession of prohibited drugs, but the comments of Lord Reid at pp. 280F–282F and Lord Pearce at pp. 307C–308A on when possessors of containers should generally be taken to also possess their contents, are still instructive.

which the law would not regard as property at all. The case of goods stored in a warehouse, the only key to which is held by the bailee, does not in my view undermine that distinction, because the holder of the key has physical control over physical objects. In the present case the data manager was entitled, subject to the terms of the contract, to exercise practical control over the information constituting the database, but it could not exercise physical control over that information, which was intangible in nature.

He concluded: 'Indeed, I do not think that the concept of possession in the hitherto accepted sense has any meaning in relation to intangible property.'[51]

11.12 Possession as a Proprietary Concept

Possession is a proprietary concept,[52] in that anyone in possession of land and goods has a right in relation to those specific objects which is enforceable against the whole world (except the person with a better right to possession). However, in English law there is deep confusion over whether it can ever be a free-standing property interest. It is undoubtedly true that in English law possession is most often found as an ingredient of either ownership or lease/bailment or a beneficial interest under a trust.[53] These are the only property interests we recognise which include the right to physically exclude all others from a physical space or a physical object. In the case of ownership and lease/bailment the holder of the property interest necessarily has a right to possession unless she has granted it to someone else by a lease/bailment. Beneficiaries under a trust of land or goods do not necessarily have a right to possession of them, but they might.[54] In principle, it should follow from this that *whenever* a person is in possession of land or goods they must also have a title to a legally recognised property interest in the land or goods. As we see in Chapter 17 *Leases*, there is some authority in support of the proposition that leases are a catch-all category for these purposes, so that any person in possession who does not have a title to any other kind of property interest in the land or goods must have a tenancy/bailment of them.[55] However, as we also see in Chapter 17, there are some anomalous cases.

---

[51] Moore-Bick LJ in *Your Response Limited* v. *Datateam Business Media Limited*, fn. 49 above, at para. 16.

[52] See Jonathan Hill, 'The proprietary character of possession', in Elizabeth Cooke (ed.), *Modern Studies in Property Law, Volume 1: Property 2000* (Oxford and Portland, OR: Hart Publishing, 2001) p. 21 at pp. 26–30.

[53] Mortgagees also have a right to possession as an incident of their mortgage, but that is only because in a mortgage of land, the mortgagee has all the rights of a lessee, and in a mortgage of goods the mortgagee takes a transfer of the ownership of the goods: see further Chapter 5 *Ownership and Other Property Interests* para. 5.34.

[54] For example, if the beneficiary is the sole beneficiary under the trust or is in occupation of trust land under s. 12 of the Trusts of Land and Appointment of Trustees Act 1996 (see Chapter 8 *Property Interest Holders* para. 8.13(b)), or if a co-owning couple hold the legal title on trust for themselves.

[55] In the case of land, a tenancy at will or tenancy at sufferance, as we see in Chapter 17 *Leases* para. 17.10 (c) and (d).

PART IV PROTECTING POSSESSION AND PENALISING WRONGFUL POSSESSORS

11.13 How the Law Protects Possession in England and Wales

As we saw in Chapter 10 *Limitations on Property*, those entitled to possession of land and goods are protected from unauthorised interference with their possession by the torts of trespass (or conversion in the case of goods), private nuisance (in the case of property interests in land) and negligence.

   In addition, if someone is wrongfully dispossessed from her land, or prevented from taking possession when she is entitled to it, she is entitled to bring an action in court for possession. She was traditionally also entitled to take the law into her own hands and repossess the land, evicting the wrongful possessor. However, the law is increasingly wary of self-help remedies, and self-help repossessions now give rise to civil and/or criminal liability in many (although not all) circumstances. We consider why in para. 11.14, and then in para. 11.15 we consider the relatively recent phenomenon of criminal liability for wrongful possession.

11.14 Restrictions on Self-Help Remedies

It is worth considering why it is that, if I am in possession of land, but as against you I have no right to be there (perhaps you own the land and I am a squatter, or perhaps I was your tenant but my tenancy has now ended and I refuse to leave), the criminal law might intervene to prevent you 'taking the law into your own hands' by throwing me out. The answer lies in the phrase 'taking the law into your own hands'. Self-help remedies usurp the functions of the state, which claims for itself a monopoly over the use of force,[56] and for all the reasons given in para. 11.6 above, self-help remedies are simply too dangerous. The law insists that dispossession, at least when it is from residential premises, should usually be done only by public officials, and only after a court has confirmed that the applicant is indeed entitled to take possession from the defendant, because the consequences of dispossession, particularly from land the wrongful possessor was using as her home, are so grave for the dispossessed, and the risks that it will lead to public disorder and violence are so high, and the temptations for someone who wants to dispossess someone else to resort to bullying and intimidation are so great.

   So, for example, section 3 of the Protection from Eviction Act 1977 makes it unlawful for an owner to enforce her right to take possession from a former tenant or licensee of a dwelling who has remained in occupation after the end of the tenancy or licence, otherwise than by proceedings in court. And by section 6 of the Criminal Law Act 1977 it is an offence for anyone to use or threaten violence towards a person or property for the purposes of securing entry into *any* premises if, to the knowledge of the entrant, there is someone present on the premises at the time who is opposed to the entry. However, s. 6 does not apply if the entrant is a 'displaced residential occupier' (defined in s. 12 as someone who was living there,

---

[56] Mattei, *Basic Principles of Property Law*, fn. 1 above, p. 110.

other than as a trespasser, and was displaced by the person now in possession) or an 'intending residential occupier' (by s. 12A, a person entitled to possession of the property who requires it for his own occupation as a residence).

11.15 Criminal Liability for Unauthorised Possession of Land

It has only recently become an offence to take possession of land away from a lawful possessor. The crime of theft has never applied to land,[57] and there is no criminal offence which is the equivalent of theft of land.

The first significant exception to this general principle that taking possession of land unlawfully is not a criminal offence came with s. 7 of the Criminal Law Act 1977. Section 7 made it an offence for any person who is on any premises as a trespasser, having entered as a trespasser, to fail to leave the premises having been required to do so by a displaced residential occupier or a protected intended occupier, unless she can show that the premises are used mainly for non-residential purposes and she is not on any part of the premises used for residential premises.

11.16 The Criminalisation of Squatting

However, it was not until s. 144 of the Legal Aid Sentencing and Punishment of Offenders Act 2012 came into force that it became a criminal offence simply to *be* a trespasser. Specifically, s. 144 creates the offence of 'squatting in a residential building', which is committed by any person who (a) is in a residential building[58] as a trespasser having entered it as a trespasser, and (b) knows or ought to know that he or she is a trespasser, and (c) is living in the building or intends to live there for any period.

Analytically this is a curious development, because it means that a person who takes possession of a residential building without the authorisation of the person entitled to possession simultaneously acquires a right to possession of the land enforceable in the civil law courts, and commits a criminal offence. We look more closely at this ambivalent position in the next chapter, Chapter 12 *Adverse Possession,* where we consider what (if any) effect it has had on our law of adverse possession.

RECOMMENDED READING

This chapter is closely related to the next chapter on adverse possession, and some of the material to be read here comes up again there. However, it is useful to do the reading and answer the questions for this chapter as a separate exercise before starting on adverse

---

[57] See now s. 4 of the Theft Act 1968, which does, however, make an exception for theft of land by fiduciaries.

[58] Defined by s. 144(3) to include the whole or part of any structure, including a temporary or moveable structure.

possession in Chapter 12, so as to be able to focus on basic principles of possession and relative titles.

Costello v. *Chief Constable of Derbyshire* [2001] 1 WLR 1437 (relativity of title).

J.A. Pye (Oxford) Ltd v. *Graham* [2002] UKHL 30 (on what amounts to possession).

Thorpe v. *Frank* [2019] EWCA Civ 150 (what amounts to possession).

Robin Hickey, *Property and the Law of Finders* (Oxford and Portland, OR: Hart Publishing, 2010) pp. 96–98 and 107–109 (acquiring title to land and goods by taking possession).

Robin Hickey, 'A property law critique of the criminalisation of squatting' in L. Fox-O'Mahony, D. O'Mahony and R. Hickey (eds.), *Moral Rhetoric and the Criminalisation of Squatting* (Abingdon, Oxfordshire and New York: Routledge, 2015) Ch. 7.

Questions

(1)   What does relativity of title mean? Why does it matter?

(2)   What does possession mean, and what role does it play in the law of England and Wales?

(3)   Consider why the law confers a right to possession of land on anyone who takes possession of land without the authorisation of the person entitled to possession of it. How convincing do you find the justifications put forward by commentators which are noted in Part II of the chapter?

(4)   Why should the law confer title to ownership of land on a person who takes possession of it without authorisation? Are the reasons the same as those you gave in response to Question (3)

(5)   Consider the factors the court took into account in *J.A. Pye (Oxford) Ltd* v. *Graham* [2002] UKHL 30 and in *Thorpe* v. *Frank* [2019] EWCA Civ 150 in determining whether or not 'possession' of the land in question had been taken. In what sense could the claimant in *Thorpe* v. *Frank* be said to have taken 'physical control' of the forecourt?

(6)   Examine the reasons given by the Supreme Court in *Star Energy Weald Basin Ltd* v. *Bocardo SA* for saying that Bocardo was in possession of the subsoil through which Star Energy drilled its pipelines. After Star Energy had installed the pipelines and its other oil drilling machinery, who was in possession?

12

Adverse Possession of Land

PART I INTRODUCTION

12.1 Adverse Possession and the Effect of Time on Titles

As we saw in Chapter 11 *Possession and Title*, in common law countries two immediate consequences follow if I take possession of your land without authorisation. The first is that I immediately acquire a title to ownership of your land which is enforceable against everyone else in the world apart from you (for the reasons we explained in Chapter 11). The second is that if you fail to take sufficient steps to regain your land from me within a given period of time, you will lose the right to do so, and your title will be extinguished. This is what we are looking at in this chapter.

The procedure for extinguishing your title was changed by the Land Registration Act 1925, and then again, and much more drastically, by the Land Registration Act 2002. As a result it is now very much more difficult for you to lose your title in this way if it is a registered title. However, the two basic principles continue to apply: even if you are registered as owner of your land under our land registration system, I will acquire a title to ownership of the land as soon as I take possession of it,[1] and ultimately if you take none of the steps available for you to reassert your title, I can have it extinguished and become registered owner in your place.

12.2 Adverse Possession in Civil Law and Common Law Worlds

It should be appreciated that most legal systems have a system equivalent to adverse possession.[2] Civil law systems reach the same end point as we do by a process sometimes referred to as *acquisitive prescription*. This differs from adverse

---

[1] See Chapter 16 *Registration* para. 16.34.

[2] For a survey of principles of adverse possession and equivalent doctrines across a range of ECHR and common law jurisdictions, see *Adverse Possession*, A Report by the British Institution of International and Comparative Law for Her Majesty's Court Service (September 2006); also Yaëll Emerich, 'Possession', in Michele Graziadei and Lionel Smith (eds.), *Comparative Property Law: Global Perspectives* (Cheltenham and Northampton MA: Edward Elgar Publishing, 2017) p. 171 at pp. 181–183: France and Quebec; Sjef van Erp and Bram Akkermans (eds.), *Cases, Materials and Text on Property Law* (Oxford and Portland, OR: Hart Publishing, 2012) pp. 702–745 (England and Wales, France, Germany and the Netherlands); Ugo Mattei, *Basic Principles of Property Law: A Comparative and Economic Introduction* (Westport, CT and London: Greenwood Press, 2000) pp. 114–116.

possession in that in the case of acquisitive prescription the squatter does not acquire a title to ownership until *after* a period of unauthorised possession. The common law recognises the doctrine of prescription as well as the doctrine of adverse possession, but in the common law prescription is used only for the acquisition of non-possessory land rights. In common law prescription, as in prescription in the civil law, a property interest is acquired only *at the end* of the period of long use, as we see in Chapter 13 *Non-Possessory Land Use Rights* paras. 13.14(b) and 13.24 (in relation to easements and town and village green rights) and in Chapter 14 *Acquiring Interests Informally* para. 14.1(b). So, in our jurisdiction you acquire a title to ownership of land as soon as you take adverse possession of it, and your title will ultimately become the undisputed (absolute) title to ownership when the dispossessed's title is extinguished; you acquire a non-possessory land use right in the common law, on the other hand, only after having used someone else's land for a sufficiently long period, as if you already had such a right, by the process of prescription. The common law process of prescription is broadly the same as the process by which, in the civil law, both ownership and non-possessory land use rights (servitudes in the civil law) are acquired by long use.[3]

So, adverse possession in the common law world is fundamentally different from acquisitive possession in the civil law (and common law prescription) in that the basic principle underlying adverse possession is the common law's concept of relativity of title, which is unknown to the civil law. In the civil law, titles are acquired by acquisitive prescription only after, and as a result of, having been in adverse possession for a long period, and it is the acquisition of the new title which extinguishes the dispossessed person's title. There is no point in time when the two co-exist.

Another significant difference between civil law and common law systems is that civil law systems generally allow acquisitive prescription only to 'good faith' possessors,[4] whereas in the common law (at least as it has developed in England and Wales) good faith has traditionally been irrelevant, and it is still largely irrelevant even in our registered land system.[5]

12.3 Evolution of Adverse Possession Law in England and Wales

In Part III of this chapter we first consider how the common law rules on adverse possession operate. We still need to know them because they continue to apply to goods, and because the registered land rules developed out of them. Also, some of the theoretical literature on adverse possession which we draw on in this chapter

---

[3] See further Emerich, 'Possession', fn. 2 above, pp. 181–186.
[4] van Erp and Akkermans, fn. 2 above, pp. 709–713 and 726 et seq.
[5] The only exception is in para. 5(4) of Sch. 6 of the Land Registration Act 2002, which allows for registration of an adverse possessor as the registered proprietor of land *even if* the registered proprietor objects, provided that the land in question is adjacent to the applicant's own land, and that he has been in adverse possession of it for at least 10 years, and that he 'reasonably believed that the land . . . belonged to him': see further para 12.13(b) below.

comes from scholars in the USA, where the common law rules continue to apply, basically unmodified (although with significant differences between states).

In Part III of this chapter we then see how (and why) the system was changed, first by the Land Registration Act 1925 and then by the Land Registration Act 2002.

First, however, in Part II we need to consider why we (and so many other jurisdictions) have a system whereby owners can lose their land to long-term dispossessors.

PART II WHY SHOULD TITLES BE EXTINGUISHED BY ADVERSE POSSESSION?

12.4 From Protecting Possessors Against Strangers to Protecting Adverse Possessors Against True Owners

In Part II of Chapter 11 we suggested at least five principal reasons why the law protects possessors, even wrongful possessors, against those who have no proprietary claims: possession can be used as a proxy for ownership by third parties and by law enforcement officers because it is easily recognisable, easily proved and usually held by owners; it acts as a signal to the outside world that the possessor asserts a proprietary claim, and so it serves a useful publicity function; protecting possession maintains the status quo, and so helps maintain civil order; people intuitively respect prior possession, and so protecting possession reinforces social norms; and possessors have a moral claim to protection because things possessed (rightfully or wrongly) become part of our personhood, and this claim ranks higher than the moral claim of anyone else to the thing possessed, other than a person with a better right to possess it.

However, as we know, the legal protection of possession goes even further than that. After a period of time we protect possessors (rightful and wrongful) even against the person who has a better legal right to possession, and in the process we eliminate for all time not only her legal right to possession but also her property interest in the resource. We need to consider why this is so.

12.5 Effect of Time on Psychological Attachment/Detachment

The first reason might be that our psychological and social attachment to our possessions tends to increase over time. After a period of time, the attachment of the possessor to a thing increases to such an extent that it outweighs the claim of the owner – the thing has become part of his personhood to such an extent that it would be disproportionate to remove it from him. Correspondingly, the attachment of the owner to the thing progressively decreases, until it is not part of her personhood at all, she has no emotional or psychological attachment to it, and it has no value to her other than its open market monetary value. Losing this will mean less to her than losing the thing itself will mean to the long-term possessor, and it may well represent no loss to her at all, for example if she did not realise or had forgotten that she had a proprietary claim to the thing. As John Stuart Mill says, there comes a point when possession has been established for such a long period that it would be unjust to interfere with it, even in favour of someone who can prove that it was wrongly taken from them or their predecessors in the first place:

> Possession which has not been legally questioned within a moderate number of years, ought to be, as by the laws of all nations it is, a complete title. Even when the acquisition was wrongful, the dispossession, after a generation has elapsed, of the probably bona fide possessors, by the revival of a claim which had been long dormant, would generally be a greater injustice, and almost always a greater private and public mischief, than leaving the original wrong without atonement. It may seem hard that a claim, originally just, should be defeated by mere lapse of time; but there is a time after which (even looking at the individual case, and without regard to the general effect on the security of possessors), the balance of hardship turns the other way. With the injustices of men, as with the convulsions and disasters of nature, the longer they remain unrepaired, the greater become the obstacles to repairing them, arising from the aftergrowths which would have to be torn up or broken through. In no human transactions, not even in the simplest and clearest, does it follow that a thing is fit to be done now, because it was fit to be done sixty years ago. It is scarcely needful to remark, that these reasons for not disturbing acts of injustice of old date, cannot apply to unjust systems or institutions; since a bad law or usage is not one bad act, in the remote past, but a perpetual repetition of bad acts, as long as the law or usage lasts.[6]

In addition to this intensification of the rationales for the protection of even wrongful possession against strangers, additional new factors emerge over time, providing additional reasons for concluding that the claims of the long-term possessor outweigh those even of the true owner, as we see in the following paragraphs.

12.6 Expiration of Moral Rights to Enforce Claims

The passing of time may also weaken the true owner's moral right to assert her claim. As Mill has also pointed out, there is something oppressive about delayed enforcement of civil claims. After a time people need to know where they stand. No-one is obliged to assert their civil claims (you need not sue someone who injures you, or who breaks a contractual promise to you, or who fails to return a book you lent them), and there comes a point where the injurer (and others) should be entitled to assume you have abandoned or foregone your rights by not exercising them. A threat of enforcement should not be allowed to hang over peoples' heads indefinitely.

12.7 Elimination of Stale Claims

Richard Epstein acknowledges the need to reconcile the rival claims of long-term possessor and true owner, but he sees it as a balancing exercise, with the scales tipping over in favour of the possessor largely because of the practical problems of proof in adjudicating stale claims. He makes the point that it is not just that stale

---

[6] John Stuart Mill, *Principles of Political Economy* Book II Ch. II section 2 (first published 1848, published London: Penguin, 1970).

claims are difficult to adjudicate: if adjudicated, they are likely to be decided wrongly because poor evidence creates a bias in favour of the party with the weaker case, in much the same way as the weaker tennis player is favoured by a poor quality tennis court.[7] John Stuart Mill points out another problem with stale claims: if long dispossessed rightful owners can bring them, so too can spurious claimants, and their chances of succeeding or at least putting the rightful possessor to considerable trouble increase as the evidence grows scantier with time:

> According to the fundamental idea of property, indeed, nothing ought to be treated as such, which has been acquired by force or fraud, or appropriated in ignorance of a prior title vested in some other person; but it is necessary to the security of rightful possessors, that they should not be molested by charges of wrongful acquisition, when by the lapse of time witnesses must have perished or been lost sight of, and the real character of the transaction can no longer be cleared up.[8]

All this makes obvious sense in a legal system where titles are not recorded on a public register: after all, we have limitation periods for asserting all other legal rights, so why should we not have them for asserting property rights? However, we need to consider whether the 'stale claims' justification still works when titles are publicly recorded, as they largely are in England and Wales under what is now the Land Registration Act 2002. As Carol Rose points out, registration of title takes over the signalling role that possession performs, and does so more clearly and unequivocally. It is certainly true that because of registration of title, the claim of a registered owner should not become more difficult to prove over time. She does not have to rely on paper documents (which might get lost over time) or people's recollections (which might become distorted): all she has to do to prove her title is to point to the register. However, there are problems with this. The first is that the register may not be correct. It may record as owner someone who is long dead so that the 'true owner' is now her next of kin, as happened in *R (on the application of Best)* v. *Chief Land Registrar* [2015] EWCA Civ 17, or it may fail to record a deed of transfer of title (as in *Palfrey* v. *Palfrey* (1974) 229 EG 1593, CA). The registered owner may be a defunct company, or someone who became registered owner by fraud or forgery or misrepresentation, and who therefore holds only the bare legal title (*Rashid* v. *Nasrullah* [2018] EWCA Civ 2685). More importantly, the dispute may not be about who the true owner is at all, but whether, for example she is estopped from asserting her claim against this particular possessor, or granted away her right to possession to someone else. Ironically, the registration if title system we now have under the Land Registration Act 2002 is likely to make the problem of stale claims worse, because, as we see in Part III of this chapter, there is now little incentive for an adverse possessor to apply for registration as owner. If he does so, the Land Registry will immediately have to try to find the true owner to ascertain whether she consents to the registration. If, however, it is reasonably clear that the person registered as

---

[7] Richard Epstein, 'Past and future: The temporal dimension in the law of property' (1986) 64 *Washington University Law Quarterly* 667. The tennis game analogy is on p. 676.

[8] Mill, *Principles of Political Economy* Book II Ch. II section 2 (see fn. 6 above).

owner cannot still be owner (because now dead, or a company no longer in existence, or for any of the other reasons noted above) and it is not obvious who is now entitled to be registered instead, it makes sense for the adverse possessor to keep quiet. So we are likely to see more cases of longstanding adverse possession, which do not reach the courts for decades or longer.

12.8 Lockean and Stewardship Justifications

Long-term adverse possessors can also draw on arguments that they have a moral claim to the land through having taken on the responsibility to care for it, whilst the true owner let it go to ruin. This could be put as a Lockean justification, based on having improved the land through mixing their labour with it, although put in that way it is not an argument that Locke himself would have accepted. More convincing, it can be put as a stewardship claim. Ownership carries with it responsibilities to care for the resource, so owners who have neglected their property are 'not adequately fulfilling the duty of stewardship over their land'.[9]

12.9 Efficiency

There are also allied efficiency arguments. Ugo Mattei sees these arguments as the main reason why 'all legal systems recognise adverse possession or similar doctrines', and even suggests that there would be advantages in shortening the period before which undefended titles can be extinguished:

> On theoretical grounds, it is not difficult to reconstruct the reason why all legal systems recognize adverse possession or similar doctrines as the most important involuntary transfer from the owner to the possessor. The law prefers to grant possession to the individual who is actually using the immovable property against the absent, uninterested owner. The former is actually economically exploiting the immovable, while the latter is keeping it idle. In economic terms, this justification is obvious as a way to avoid economic waste. The justification is also reinforced by the fact that the absence of the owner makes impossible the transfer of the piece of immovable property from whoever values it less to whoever values it more within a voluntary transaction. The prolonged absence, whatever its reason, shows that the owner appreciates his or her property very little, or at least less than the possessor. While the owner is doing nothing in terms of investments to improve the property, the possessor invests, at a minimum, in occupying the property by periodically policing to eject other possible claimants of it. Most probably, the possessor is actually economically exploiting the property by putting labor into the maintenance of the immovable in proper conditions. Once the problem of adverse possession is framed in such a way, it becomes clearly justifiable within a theory of just dessert. At this point, one could argue, on a normative ground, that by having such long terms, legal systems are possibly overprotective of the absent owner. The needs of stability of ownership that counterbalance the principle of adverse possession would possibly be served also by shorter terms, such as,

---

[9] David Cowan, Lorna Fox O'Mahony and Neil Cobb, *Great Debates in Property law* (Basingstoke: Palgrave Macmillan, 2012) pp. 117–122.

for example, five years. This is particularly true because a variety of devices (like suspension of the terms in given circumstances, or maintaining long terms for bad-faith possession) are available to protect the absent but 'deserving' owners, such as those whose emigration has been forced by dramatic events or similar occurrences.

A shorter term would give an incentive to put labor into abandoned immovable property, something very much needed in transitional economies. Moreover, the security and reliability of signals coming from property rights would not be impaired, but generally would be promoted by shorter terms that merge ownership and possession in the same person ...[10]

A similar argument about adverse possession encouraging investment in the development of land was suggested by Sales LJ in *R (on the application of Best)* v. *Chief Land Registrar* [2015] EWCA Civ 15, having noted the comments about the advantages of adverse possession made in Law Com 271, the joint Land Registry and Law Commission Report leading to the Land Registration Act 2002. Sales said:

The reference to adverse possession securing the marketability of land covers a range of considerations, such as encouraging investment in the development of land for better use of the land (rather than directly for the purposes of selling it). The public interest in the marketability of land promoted by the law of adverse possession can be said to be the public interest in securing its economic utility more widely, rather than allowing it to be sterilised through abandonment or non-use by an owner who has no interest in it or who may have disappeared: see paragraph 2.72 of the Law Commission report on the Land Registration Bill (Law Com No. 271, of July 2001) ('Land is a precious resource and should be kept in use and in commerce').[11]

However, Lee Ann Fennel notes these efficiency arguments but also points out that some environmentalists consider this an adverse rather than a positive effect of adverse possession:

Applying the reasoning of efficient trespass to settings involving wilderness areas is likely to elicit objections from environmentalists and others devoted to low-intensity uses of land. John Sprankling[12] faults adverse possession doctrine for hewing to a cultural vision of land that privileges development over nondevelopment ...[13]

12.10 Law and Lived Boundaries

However, probably the conclusive reason why we need a law of adverse possession is that property is what Kevin Gray describes as an organic phenomenon, and, for the

---

[10] Mattei, *Basic Principles of Property Law*, fn. 2 above, pp. 116–117.

[11] Sales LJ in *R (on the application of Best)* v. *Chief Land Registrar* [2015] EWCA Civ 15 para. 20; we come back to this decision in para. 12.16 below.

[12] John G. Sprankling, 'An environmental critique of adverse possession' (1994) 79 *Cornell Law Review* 816, at pp. 821, 874–875.

[13] Lee Anne Fennell, 'Efficient trespass: The case for 'bad faith' adverse possession' (2006) 100 *Northwestern University Law Review* 1037 at p. 1077.

reasons he explains, it must remain sufficiently flexible to subordinate formal land titles to lived boundaries. As Gray argues:

> For the most part . . . we rally together to preserve the systemic integrity of property as a normative order and, historically, one of the principal ways in which this order has been maintained lies in the conscious condonation of certain isolated misappropriations of entitlement . . . . Although – perhaps because – it allows the maturing of wrongs into rights, the law of adverse possession has served to promote the overall stability and integrity of the regime of property.
>
> In a variety of contexts – whether the arena of international law or a modern municipal legal order or even the humble microcosm of the queue – property is an organic phenomenon. It has a certain self-defining quality. It comprises, is founded upon, and is ultimately no more than, socially or politically constituted fact. It is for this reason that statutes of limitation regularize what are usually relatively minor deviations from existing property allocations. By incorporating a principle of efficient trespass, the law ensures that land titles conform to lived boundaries. In so doing, the law marks a controlled trade-off between moral right and social reality – an absorption of wrongdoing within the mainstream of proprietary entitlement – which, in the long perspective of legal history, has reinforced rather than weakened the institution of property.[14]

PART III EXTINGUISHING TITLE TO LAND BY ADVERSE POSSESSION IN ENGLAND AND WALES

12.11 How Adverse Possession of Land Works in the Common Law

As we have seen, someone who takes possession of land without the consent of the person who is entitled to possession of it, immediately acquires a title to ownership of the land which is enforceable against the whole world except the person with a better right to possession of it. In the law of England and Wales a person who takes possession without consent is commonly called an *adverse possessor* or *squatter*. Once dispossessed, the person with a better right to possession thereby acquires a right to take possession back. The person with a better right to possession is usually the freehold owner, but if the freehold owner had previously granted the right to possession to someone else by granting them a lease of the land, it will be the lessee. In the rest of this chapter, to keep things simple, we will assume there is no lease, and so the person entitled to re-take possession is the freeholder owner ('the paper owner'). The common law rule is that if the paper owner does not exercise that right for 12 years, he loses the right to do so and his title is automatically extinguished. This rule is now set out in s. 15 of the Limitation Act 1980.

---

[14] Kevin Gray, 'Property in a queue' in Gregory S. Alexander and Eduardo M. Peñalver (eds.), *Property and Community* (Oxford: Oxford University Press, 2010) p. 165 at p. 188.

12.12 Adverse Possession Under the Land Registration Act 1925

The common procedure for extinguishing the paper owner's title was modified by the Land Registration Act 1925 to make it work in a system where legal (as opposed to equitable) title to a freehold or leasehold estate in land could not be acquired except by registration. The idea behind the changes made by the 1925 Act was to make the adverse possession system work in registered land in the same way as it worked in unregistered land. The way this was done was to provide that, at the point in time when an adverse possessor had been in possession for more than 12 years, the paper owner automatically held her title on trust for the adverse possessor (even though neither of them might have been aware of that happening). Thereafter, the adverse possessor, as sole beneficiary under a bare trust, had an absolute right to have the legal title put into his name, and therefore was entitled to apply to the Land Registry at any time to have the registered title transferred from the name of the paper owner into his own name. In this way, the paper owner's beneficial interest was automatically extinguished as soon as the 12 years of adverse possession had run, and her legal title was extinguished when the Land Registry formally extinguished it by removing it from the register and replacing it with the adverse possessor's title.

12.13 Adverse Possession After the Land Registration Act 2002

The second modification of the common law principle, however, was much more substantial, and it was made by the Land Registration Act 2002. The 2002 Act was intended to decrease the likelihood that a registered title would ever be acquired by an adverse possessor. It has probably succeeded in doing that,[15] but whether it has also decreased the incidence of adverse possession is another matter.

(a) Rationale of the Land Registration Act 2002

The 2002 Act implements the recommendations of a joint Law Commission and Land Registry Report into the reform of land registration *Land Registration for the Twenty-first Century: A Conveyancing Revolution*[16] ('Law Com 271'). The Report expressed strong views that it was wrong in principle that an owner should ever lose title to an adverse possessor, and that this was a necessary evil in an unregistered land system because it facilitated unregistered conveyancing, but was no longer justifiable in registered land. In outline, the arguments put in Law Com 271 were that allowing the true owner's title to be extinguished as against an adverse possessor is 'at least in some cases, tantamount to theft' and has given rise to 'growing public disquiet'. The Report gives as principal support for both assertions a dictum of

---

[15] It is still difficult to predict exactly what effect it will have, because at the moment most adverse possessors applying for registration are still able to rely on periods of adverse possession which occurred before the new regime under the LRA 2002 took full effect.

[16] Law Commission, *Land Registration for the Twenty-first Century: A Conveyancing Revolution* (2001) Law Com No 271.

Neuberger J in the first instance hearing of *J A Pye (Oxford) Ltd* v. *Graham*,[17] where he said:

> A frequent justification for limitation periods generally is that people should not be able to sit on their rights indefinitely, and that is a proposition to which at least in general nobody could take exception. However, if as in the present case the owner of land has no immediate use for it and is content to let another person trespass on the land for the time being, it is hard to see what principle of justice entitles the trespasser to acquire the land for nothing from the owner simply because he has been permitted to remain there for 12 years. To say that in such circumstances the owner who has sat on his rights should therefore be deprived of his land appears to me to be illogical and disproportionate. Illogical because the only reason that the owner can be said to have sat on his rights is because of the existence of the 12-year limitation period in the first place; if no limitation period existed he would be entitled to claim possession whenever he actually wanted the land ... I believe that the result is disproportionate because, particularly in a climate of increasing awareness of human rights including the right to enjoy one's own property, it does seem draconian to the owner and a windfall for the squatter that, just because the owner has taken no steps to evict a squatter for 12 years, the owner should lose 25 hectares of land to the squatter with no compensation whatsoever.[18]

However, the Report made no reference to the arguments noted in Part II of this chapter, nor to the views expressed by the Court of Appeal in *Pye*, which were very different from those expressed by Neuberger J at first instance. In the Court of Appeal it had been argued on behalf of Pye, the paper owner, that the English law which allows the title of the paper owner to be extinguished in favour of an adverse possessor contravenes article 1 Protocol 1 of the European Convention on Human Rights, by depriving the paper owner of his possessions or interfering with his peaceful enjoyment of them. This was rejected decisively by the Court of Appeal.[19] Mummery LJ said:

> (2) [The provisions of the Limitation Act 1980 extinguishing the title of the paper owner] do not deprive a person of his possessions or interfere with his peaceful enjoyment of them. They deprive a person of his right of access to the courts for the purpose of recovering property if he has delayed the institution of his legal proceedings for 12 years or more after he has been dispossessed of his land by another person who has been in adverse possession of it for at least that period. The extinction of the title of the claimant in those circumstances is not a deprivation of possessions or a confiscatory measure for which the payment of compensation would be appropriate: it is simply a logical and pragmatic consequence of the barring of his right to bring an action after the expiration of the limitation period.

> (3) Even if, contrary to my view, that Convention right potentially impinges on the relevant provisions of the 1980 Act, those provisions are conditions provided for by law and are 'in the public interest' within the meaning of article 1. *Such conditions are reasonably required to avoid the real risk of injustice in the adjudication of stale claims,*

---

[17] *J A Pye (Oxford) Ltd* v. *Graham* [2002] Ch 676, 710.   [18] Ibid.
[19] *J A Pye (Oxford) Ltd* v. *Graham* [2001] EWCA Civ 117.

to ensure certainty of title and to promote social stability by the protection of the established and peaceable possession of property from the resurrection of old claims. The conditions provided in the [Limitation Act 1980] are not disproportionate; the period allowed for the bringing of proceedings is reasonable; the conditions are not discriminatory; and they are not impossible or so excessively difficult to comply with as to render ineffective the exercise of the legal right of a person who is entitled to the peaceful enjoyment of his possessions to recover them from another person who is alleged to have wrongfully deprived him of them.[20]

The joint Law Commission and Land Registry Report, however, adopted a fundamentally different approach. It categorises the typical adverse possessor as a 'landowner with an eye to the main chance who encroaches on his or her neighbour's land'. It expressed the view that the stale claims justification is not applicable in registered land, and that allowing adverse possessors to acquire registered title is incompatible with the principle of indefeasibility of title.[21] Otherwise, as already noted, the Report did not address the arguments considered in Part II of this chapter.[22]

(b) The New Scheme Under the Land Registration Act 2002

The 2002 Act does not change the first part of the common law rule: it remains the case that a person who takes possession of land without the consent of the paper owner (who we will assume is the registered freehold owner) immediately acquires a title to ownership of it which is enforceable against everyone else in the world owner except the paper owner. However, the procedure from then on is changed. If the adverse possessor does nothing, nothing will change: the paper owner's better title will never be extinguished and will continue to be the best title to the land, which can be freely sold or inherited, subject, however, to the adverse possessor's new statutory rights under the 2002 Act. Similarly, the adverse possession will continue to have a possessory title indefinitely (which is also sellable and inheritable) for so long as the adverse possession continues. The adverse possession can be ended by any of the ways it can end under the common law, that is, by the adverse possessor giving up possession, or by the paper owner taking possession back (either physically, or by bringing a court action). However, the 2002 Act now provides in Schedule 6 that at any time if an adverse possessor has been in adverse possession for 10 years or more, she may apply to the Land Registry to be registered as proprietor in place of the paper owner. If and when she does that, the Land Registry must inform the paper owner (and anyone else interested) of the application and ask them whether they object. If they make no objection within two years, the registry must register the adverse possessor as registered owner, extinguishing the registered owner's title,

---

[20] Ibid. para. 52.

[21] See further Chapter 16 *Registration* for consideration of the question of whether absolute indefeasibility of title is (a) achievable and (b) desirable. It is certainly not yet achieved, as we see in Chapter 16.

[22] See further Alison Clarke, 'Use, time and entitlement' (2004) 57 *Current Legal Problems* 239, pp. 246–263.

provided it is satisfied that she has indeed been in adverse possession for 10 years or more.[23] If, however, the registered owner objects and within two years either retakes possession or starts court proceeding to recover possession, the adverse possessor's application will be dismissed, except in a Sch. 6 para. 5 case, as we see below. If he objects but does not either re-take possession or start proceedings within the two year period, the result is the same as if he had not objected, that is, the registrar must register the adverse possessor as registered owner.[24]

However, if para 5 of Sch. 6 applies, the adverse possessor is entitled to be registered as proprietor, despite objections by or on behalf of the paper owner, if she can prove one of the three conditions set out in para. 5. These are, essentially, where the applicant has encroached beyond the boundary of her land and for at least the last 10 years has reasonably believed that the land belonged to her (para 5(4)) where it would be unconscionable because of an equity by estoppel for her to be dispossessed and she ought to be registered as proprietor (para. 5(2)); and where for some other reason she is entitled to be registered as proprietor (para. 5(3)). So, para. 5 is of less help to an adverse possessor than might at first appear. Para. 5(4) deals only with cases where neighbours genuinely have differing views, reasonably held, about the location of the boundary between their properties. Paras. 5(2) and 5(3), on the other hand, appear to add nothing to the general law: *anyone* who 'ought' to be, or 'is entitled' to be registered as proprietor (either because of an estoppel or for some other reason) is surely by definition someone with a right to be registered as proprietor without having to rely on adverse possession.

12.14 Meaning of Adverse Possession

The Land Registration Act 2002 makes no changes in the substance of adverse possession law. In particular it has no effect on the essential point, which is that 'possession' in this context means the same as it means in any other context, and it is 'adverse' if it is without the consent of the person legally entitled to possession – nothing more is required. In other words, an adverse possessor is someone who has a sufficient degree of physical control and an intention to exercise physical control 'on one's own behalf and for one's own benefit', and this is something that can be inferred from the behaviour of the possessor: he is in adverse possession if he is *'using the land in the way one would expect him to use it if he were the true owner'*.[25]

---

[23] The 2002 Act is unclear on this: the Land Registry's current practice is to register the adverse possessor with only a 'possessory' title, which gives it a discretion to re-open the question if the paper owner later emerges with a good explanation for why it failed to object or retake possession on time. The practice has not yet been challenged in court, but some commentators have argued convincingly that it is wrong, and that the registrar is required to register the adverse possessor with an absolute title. We come back to the question of how an adverse possessor's possessory title fits into the 2002 Act scheme in Chapter 16 *Registration* para. 16.34.

[24] Sch. 6 para. 7 of the LRA 2002.

[25] Lord Hope in *JA Pye (Oxford) Ltd* v. *Graham* [2003] 1 AC 419 at para. 71, as noted in Chapter 11 *Possession and Title* para. 11.9.

12.15 Rejection of Requirements Additional to Intentional Physical Control

It is now beyond dispute that the only condition necessary to make possession adverse is that it is without the consent of the person entitled to possession: there are no other requirements. In the past it has often be suggested that something more is needed to make the clock start ticking against the true owner. In many other common law and civil law jurisdictions, something else *is* required – in some, the possession must be 'open and notorious',[26] in others, in must be taken in good faith[27] (i.e. you genuinely believed you were entitled to take possession, perhaps because the land adjoined yours and you wrongly thought it was within your boundary). In England and Wales the courts have made several attempts over the years to introduce additional requirements, but these have all, eventually, been rejected, and in *JA Pye (Oxford) Ltd* v. *Graham* [2003] 1 AC 419 the House of Lords reiterated that nothing else was required. Lord Browne-Wilkinson (who delivered the leading speech) pointed out that at one time in the history of adverse possession law it had been necessary for the possessor to prove 'ouster' of the true owner but that this requirement had been abolished in 1833 and that since then 'should not have formed part of judicial decisions' because 'the only question was whether the squatter had been in possession in the ordinary sense of the word'.[28]

It should also be emphasised that, in determining whether someone has acquired possession of land which is 'adverse' to the possession of the 'true' owner, the intentions of the paper owner are almost wholly irrelevant. So, for example, the squatter's possession will be 'adverse' even if the paper owner is unaware of it.[29] This can happen, even in a crowded island like ours, for example where the paper owner dies and her title devolves to someone who does not realise that they have inherited it, as may have happened in *R (on the application of Best)* v. *Chief Land Registrar* [2015] EWCA Civ 17, which we look at in para. 12.16 below. It can also occur when someone is unaware of a gift made in their favour, as in *Palfrey* v. *Palfrey*.[30] In that case, which concerned an unregistered title, it was held that the paper owner's title was extinguished under the Limitation Act 1980 even though he did not realise until long after the expiry of the limitation period that he had any title (many years earlier, without telling him or anyone else, his grandfather had executed a deed transferring title to him).

---

[26] See e.g. Canada and France, according to Emerich, 'Possession', fn. 2 above, at p. 182,

[27] France allows acquisitive prescription after ten years for a good faith possessor in some circumstances, or after 30 years of bad faith possession: van Erp and Akkermans, *Property Law*, fn. 2 above, at pp. 705–724, and see also pp. 726–730 on what amounts to 'good faith' adverse possession in Dutch law.

[28] *JA Pye (Oxford) Ltd* v. *Graham* [2003] 1 AC 419, at para. 35.

[29] Unless, in unregistered land, fraud, concealment or mistake led to the paper owner being unaware of the adverse possession (s. 32 of the Limitation Act 1980). There is no equivalent provision where title is registered, because, as we saw in para. 12.13(b) above, the Land Registry is under a duty to notify the 'true' owner (whether or not the true owner is the person registered as proprietor) and ask whether she objects to the registration of the adverse possessor as registered proprietor: Sch. 6 para. 2 of the Land Registration Act 2002.

[30] *Palfrey* v. *Palfrey* (1974) 229 EG 1593, CA.

There have since been other attempts to persuade the courts to impose additional requirements. For example, as we see in para. 12.16 below, the Court of Appeal in *Best* v. *Chief Land Registrar* [2015] EWCA Civ 17 rejected an argument that (in effect) periods during which it was a criminal offence to be in possession could not 'count' as adverse possession.

Again, in *Rashid* v. *Nasrullah* [2018] EWCA Civ 2685 the Court of Appeal rejected arguments that your possession of land cannot be adverse as against the 'true' owner (i) if you are the registered proprietor (as had been suggested by the Court of Appeal in *Parshall* v. *Hackney* [2013] EWCA Civ 240) or (ii) if you became registered proprietor by fraud. In *Rashid* v. *Nasrullah* the adverse possessor's father had become registered proprietor of a house by forging a transfer from the 'true' owner (a fraud in which the son was complicit), and then transferred the house to the son by a deed of gift. Thirteen years later, the 'true' owner applied for rectification of the register to be reinstated as registered owner. His application failed. The Court of Appeal held that his title had been extinguished by the Limitation Act 1980 (before the changes made by the Land Registration Act 2002 came into force) because the registered proprietor had been in adverse possession for more than 12 years after the 'true' owner had found out about the fraud (by s. 32 of the Limitation Act 1980, time does not start running in cases of fraud unless and until the true owner has discovered the fraud 'or could with reasonable diligence have discovered it'). The Court of Appeal said that it was simply irreconcilable with the House of Lords decision in *J A Pye (Oxford) Ltd* v. *Graham* to impose a requirement that a registered proprietor could not be in adverse possession, and that it was 'entitled and indeed bound' to follow *Pye* in preference to the Court of Appeal decision in *Parshall*. The Court of Appeal also firmly rejected the argument that a true owner's title could not be defeated by adverse possession of a person who became registered proprietor by fraud. Lewison LJ said that when the lower court had said it would be 'manifestly unjust' for the 'true owner' to be deprived of his property by fraud:

> [the court] failed to appreciate the importance of limitation periods generally. They also failed to appreciate that the Limitation Act itself contains limitation periods specifically applicable to the recovery of property acquired as a result of crime.[31]

He referred to various other statutes that 'show quite clearly that Parliament intended' that even criminals should have the benefit of a limitation period'.[32] In any event, as he pointed out, what entitled the son to remain registered as proprietor, and wiped out the 'true owner's' title, was not the fraud but the fact that the son had been in adverse possession for more than 12 years.[33]

12.16 Adverse Possession and the Criminal Law

As we noted in para. 11.15 of Chapter 11 *Possession and Title*, 'theft' of land has never been a criminal offence in England and Wales.[34] This explains why we have

---

[31] Lewison LJ in *Rashid* v. *Nasrullah* [2018] EWCA Civ 2685 para. 76.   [32] Ibid. para. 74.
[33] Ibid. para. 78.   [34] Except by a fiduciary: see s. 4 of the Theft Act 1968.

never had a rule, equivalent to the rule that operates in relation to goods, that time cannot run against an owner of land in favour of an adverse possessor whose taking of possession amounted to theft of the land. In fact, in the law of England and Wales, it has never been a criminal offence either to *take* possession of land without authorisation, or to *be* in adverse possession of land (although, as we saw in Chapter 11 *Possession and Title* para. 11.15 it is an offence under s. 7 of the Criminal Law Act 1977 for anyone who entered residential premises as a trespasser *to fail to leave* having been required to do so by a 'displaced residential occupier'). It has of course always been a tort: both *taking* possession without authorisation and *being* in adverse possession have always constituted the tort of trespass, but this is actionable only by the person with a better right to possession of the land. And the whole point of the law of adverse possession is that it is this right – the right to bring an action in trespass to evict an adverse possessor – which is eventually lost if not exercised within a specified period.

However, as we saw in para. 11.16 of Chapter 11 *Possession and Title*, s. 144 of the Legal Aid Sentencing and Punishment of Offenders Act 2012 ('LASPOA') has now made it a criminal offence to *be* in adverse possession of a residential building if you are living there or intending to live there. Specifically, it is now a criminal offence to be living in a residential building as a trespasser or intending to live there for any period, having entered it as a trespasser, when you know or ought to know that you are a trespasser.[35]

The relevance of this provision to adverse possession was first raised in the courts in *R. (on the application of Best)* v. *Chief Land Registrar* [2015] EWCA Civ 17. The case concerned a builder, Mr Best, who was carrying out some work on a property when he noticed an empty and vandalised house nearby. He was told it had belonged to a Mrs Curtis, who had died, and that she had had a son who had not been seen for over a year. Best started to carry out repairs to the house with a view to moving in there himself. Over the years he repaired the roof, cleared the garden, replaced ceilings, woodwork and heating and electric fittings, and generally made the place wind and watertight. On his evidence, he had been treating the property as his own since 2001, and in 2010 he started to live there, a couple of years before s. 144 of LASPOA 2012 came into force. In 2012 he then applied to the Land Registry to register his title to the property on the basis that he had been in adverse possession 'for the period of ten years ending on the date of the application', as required by Sch. 6 para. 1 of the Land Registration Act 2002. The Land Registrar refused to accept the application, arguing that no-one applying for registration of title as an adverse possessor was entitled to rely on any period of adverse possession which involved a criminal offence under s. 144 of LASPOA. The reason for this, so the argument went, was that it would be contrary to the public interest for someone to be able to obtain rights through committing crimes. The Court of Appeal disagreed,

---

[35] S. 144(1) reads: '(1) A person commits an offence if (a) the person is in a residential building as a trespasser having entered it as a trespasser, (b) the person knows or ought to know that he or she is a trespasser, and (c) the person is living in the building or intends to live there for any period.' It does not apply to someone who became a trespasser by holding over after the end of a tenancy or licence (s. 144 (2) of the Legal Aid Sentencing and Punishment of Offenders Act 2012).

and confirmed the order at first instance that the Land Registrar's rejection of the application for registration should be struck out. In other words, Mr Best's application for registration of title must be allowed to proceed.[36]

It was accepted both at first instance and in Court of Appeal that s. 144 of LASPOA 2012 was not targeted at adverse possession. As Ouseley J noted in the first instance decision,[37] after explaining the consultation process leading up to the enactment of the 2012 Act:

> The 'Proposals for further action' in the Response Paper simply do not address adverse possession. The Explanatory Notes [to the 2012 Act] are striking for the absence of any consideration of any possible effect which the Act might have on the acquisition of title by adverse possession or on the adverse possessor's entitlement to registration of title to registered land. There is no Ministerial statement in Parliament to which reference can be made. But it is clear that the mischief behind s144 was not the difficulty of removing those who had squatted unchallenged in domestic property for sufficient years to raise a claim based on adverse possession. The mischief struck at was the difficulty faced by the householder, and particularly by the occupying householder, dispossessed by squatters, removing them without police assistance and with only unduly slow and cumbersome civil processes.[38]

In other words, the rationale of the new s. 144 criminal offence was that criminalising squatting in residential property would enable householders to call on the police to remove squatters who had moved in and dispossessed them, rather than having to rely on civil law procedures.

Equally, as pointed out both by Ouseley J at first instance and by Sales and Arden LLJ in the Court of Appeal,[39] the objective of the Land Registration Act 2002 was not to prevent adverse possessors ever becoming registered owners of land. Rather, it was to restrict the circumstances in which it could be done. As Sales LJ said, it had been provisionally recommended in the Consultation Paper leading up the joint Land Registry and Law Commission Report No 271 that:

> (1) the law of adverse possession as it applies to registered land should be recast to reflect the principles of title registration; and

> (2) its application should be restricted to those cases where it is essential to ensure the marketability of land or to prevent unfairness.[40]

---

[36] In the end, Mr Best succeeded. As a result of the publicity surrounding the case, the *Daily Mail* managed to track down Mrs Curtis's son, and he started the process of applying to be appointed to administer her estate so that he could challenge Mr Best's application to the Land Registry. However, it was all too late and his objection to Mr Best's registration failed. For the full story see Robin Hickey, 'The Best outcome: The application of Schedule 6 and the reinforcement of adverse possession policy under the Land Registration Act 2002' (2017) *The Conveyancer and Property Lawyer* 53, arguing that this was an illustration of exactly how the 2002 Act was intended to operate in cases of adverse possession of property which had been left abandoned for years after the registered owner had died.

[37] *Best* v. *Chief Land Registrar* [2014] EWHC 1370.   [38] Ibid. para. 27.

[39] *R. (on the application of Best)* v. *Chief Land Registrar* [2015] EWCA Civ 17. McCombe LJ agreed without adding any further comment.

[40] Law Commission Consultation Paper, *Land Registration for the 21st Century: A Consultative Document* (1998) Law Com No 254, para. 10.19.

He also pointed out the emphasis placed on the need to maintain the marketability of land:

> The reference to adverse possession securing the marketability of land covers a range of considerations, such as encouraging investment in the development of land for better use of the land (rather than directly for the purposes of selling it). The public interest in the marketability of land promoted by the law of adverse possession can be said to be the public interest in securing its economic utility more widely, rather than allowing it to be sterilised through abandonment or non-use by an owner who has no interest in it or who may have disappeared: see paragraph 2.72 of the Law Commission report on the Land Registration Bill (Law Com No. 271, of July 2001) ('Land is a precious resource and should be kept in use and in commerce').[41]

On this view, the Land Registration Act 2002 ('LRA') was, therefore, a carefully balanced scheme, designed to adjust the law of adverse possession so that it worked in a way that the Land Registry and the Law Commission considered appropriate for registered land. There was no indication that Parliament intended s. 144 of LASPOA 2012 to upset that balance, or to upset the balance previously drawn between the need for an adverse possession principle and the general principle that no-one should be entitled to benefit from their own wrong:

> [in the past] the wider idea that a person should not benefit from his own wrong has not prevented the law of adverse possession from operating. Adverse possession is, of course, founded on the tort of trespass to land. The public interest in having land put to good use and in having clear rules to govern acquisition of title to land which has been abandoned has been taken to override the general concern that a person should not benefit from their unlawful actions. Since 1833, that balance of public interest has been expressed in statutory form by the law of limitation in relation to unregistered land, which is now set out in sections 15 and 17 of the Limitation Act 1980. Since 1925, the same balance of public interest has been expressed by similar provision allowing for title to registered land to be acquired by adverse possession, as now set out in the relevant provisions of the LRA.

> 45. The question which arises on this appeal is whether the priority given to the public interest in active use and marketability of land, outweighing the general concern that a person should not be able to benefit from their own wrong, should continue to be recognised even where aspects of a person's adverse possession of land involve the commission of a criminal offence, and in particular an offence or series of offences under section 144 of LASPOA.[42]

The Court of Appeal concluded that it could and should, and that:

> the relevant balance of public policy considerations shows clearly that the fact that a relevant period of adverse possession for the purposes of the LRA included times during which the possessor's actions constituted a criminal offence under section 144 of LASPOA does not prevent his conduct throughout from qualifying as relevant adverse possession for the purposes of the LRA.[43]

---

[41] Sales LJ in *R. (on the application of Best)* v. *Chief Land Registrar* [2015] EWCA Civ 17, para. 20.
[42] Ibid. paras. 44–46.   [43] Ibid. para. 69.

Sales LJ also pointed to various other factors which reinforced this conclusion. The most important for our purposes brings us back to the stale claims arguments we noted in para. 12.7 above. If some periods of adverse possession could not be counted because during them the possessor was committing a criminal offence, but others could be counted because during them she was not (for example, because she was not living there), it would mean that the *whole* period of claimed 'adverse possession' would have to be scrutinised carefully in every case. This would become increasingly difficult as the years passed, and would introduce precisely the kind of uncertainty into adverse possession claims that registration of title was intended to avoid.

RECOMMENDED READING

J A Pye (Oxford) v. *Graham* [2003] 1 AC 419.
R. (on the application of Best) v. *Chief Land Registrar* [2015] EWCA Civ 17.
Alison Clarke, 'Use, time and entitlement' (2004) 57 *Current Legal Problems* 239 at pp. 243–275. (prescription, adverse possession and the LRA 2002).
Richard Epstein, 'Past and future: The temporal dimension in the law of property' (1986) 64 *Washington University Law Quarterly* 667.
John G. Sprankling, 'An environmental critique of adverse possession' (1994) 79 *Cornell Law Review* 816, at pp. 821 and 874–875.
David Cowan, Lorna Fox O'Mahony and Neil Cobb, *Great Debates in Property law* (Basingstoke: Palgrave Macmillan, 2012) Ch. 6 'Unlawful occupation of land: Squatting and adverse possession' (covers general issues on adverse possession and criticisms of the LRA 2002 and the Legal Aid, Sentencing and Punishment of Offenders Act 2012).
Neil Cobb and Lorna Fox, 'Living outside the system? The (im)morality of urban squatting after the Land Registration Act 2002' (2007) 27 *Legal Studies* 236.
Robert Brown and Clare Cullen, 'Trespassers will definitely be prosecuted – maybe' (2012) 15 *Journal of Housing Law* pp. 39–43 (Part 1) and pp. 52–57 (Part 2) (on the criminalisation of squatting).
Robin Hickey, 'The *Best* outcome: The application of Schedule 6 and the reinforcement of adverse possession policy under the Land Registration Act 2002' (2017) *The Conveyancer and Property Lawyer* 53.

Questions

(1) Can the decisions in *Pye, Thorpe* and *Best* be justified on Lockean grounds? Consider how far each is also (or nevertheless) justifiable on other grounds.

(2) Explain what Lord Bingham said in his short judgment in the House of Lords decision in *Pye* (at paras. 1 and 2). Do you agree with what he says?

(3) Explain the changes made to the law of adverse possession by the LRA 2002, and consider whether, and if so how far, they have made the law fairer and more efficient.

(4)   Discuss whether (a) the law of adverse possession and (b) the principle that a person who takes possession of land without authorisation acquires a good title to the land, are compatible with a system of registration of title. (You might want to come back to these questions after reading Chapter 16 *Registration*).

(5)   Explain the reasoning of the Court of Appeal in *R. (on the application of Best)* v. *Chief Land Registrar* [2015] EWCA Civ 17. Do you agree that s. 144 of the Legal Aid, Sentencing and Punishment of Offenders Act 2012 is compatible with a law that allows adverse possessors to be registered as proprietors of the land?

13

Non-Possessory Land Use Rights

PART I INTRODUCTION

13.1 Possessory and Non-Possessory Land Use Rights

In this chapter and the next we look at property rights and interests allowing the interest holder to make a particular use of someone else's land. In this respect these property interests are different from property interests in land like freehold ownership of land, or a lease of land, which give the interest holder a right to possession of land and therefore a freedom to do whatever they want on the land (subject to the limitations we looked at in Chapter 10 *Limitations on Property*, and, in the case of leases, subject also to any contractual restrictions imposed by the landlord in the lease.[1])

Property interests which give the interest holder non-possessory land use rights, on the other hand, allow the interest holder to do just one specified thing on or to someone else's land. Most of these rights are positive – for example, a right to pick fruit from trees growing on someone else's land (a 'profit'), or to use a path or driveway going across it (an easement), or to use the land for recreational purposes (an easement, a communal right to use a town or village green, or a public recreational right). However, a few of them are negative: the best example is a right to restrict the use of neighbouring land, as, for example, where I have a property right to prevent you building any additional buildings on the land you own which adjoins my land. We look at these negative use rights in para. 13.11 (negative easements) and in Part III of this chapter (restrictive covenants).

One particular characteristic of these rights is that generally they can be acquired by customary use, through doctrines such as prescription, presumed grant and dedication, as well as by being expressly granted by the owner of the land burdened by the right. We look at that aspect of non-possessory land use rights in Chapter 14 *Acquiring Interests Informally* para. 14.1 and also in this chapter in para. 13.14 (in relation to easements) and para. 13.24 (town and village green rights).

---

[1] So, for example, if you have a lease of a flat for 10 years, there will probably be a provision in the tenancy which forbids you to use it for any purpose other than as a single private residence, as we see in Chapter 17 *Leases*, para. 17.3.

13.2 Different Kinds of Non-Possessory Land Use Property Rights and Who Can Hold Them

In the rest of this chapter we look at various different kinds of non-possessory land use property interests we recognise in this jurisdiction. Some of them are private property interests which can be held only by legal entities. The most important of these are *easements* (private rights held by a landowner to do something on someone else's land), which we look at in Part II of this chapter, and *restrictive covenants* (private rights held by a landowner to restrict the use of someone else's land), which are covered in Part III.

Profits, on the other hand, which are rights to take a specific kind of natural produce from someone else's land, can be either private or communal property interests. Private property profits are more helpfully known as *exclusive profits*, in that they give the interest holder the exclusive right to take that kind of natural produce from that land: we look at them in Part IV of this chapter. In Part V we look at *communal property profits*, which are now more usually known as *rights of common*, where two or more individuals, or a community, have the right to take a particular natural product from a piece of land, exercisable in common with each other. A striking feature of rights of common is that the land over which they are exercisable automatically acquires a special status – it becomes 'common land'. We look at the implications of this in Part V.

The communal recreational rights we look at in Part VI of this chapter have a similar effect, in that once they become exercisable over a piece of land, the land acquires a special status: it becomes what is misleadingly called a 'town or village green'.[2] We look at these recreational property interests (which can only be held by communities), and at the implications of the town and village green designation of the land, in Part VI.

13.3 Anchoring the Benefit to Neighbouring Land or Locality

An important characteristic of private and communal non-possessory land use property interests is that generally (but with a few exceptions) the benefit of the use must be anchored to specific neighbouring land or to the immediate locality. This is important because it sets limits to the burden placed on the burdened land, and ensures that any burden placed on land by private or community neighbours produces a roughly equivalent benefit to their land or their locality.

In the case of easements, restrictive covenants and most profits (both exclusive profits and rights of common), this effect is achieved by the requirement of *appurtenance*: the property interest holder must be the freehold or leasehold owner of neighbouring land and the rights conferred by the property interest must benefit *that land*. We see how that works in Parts II–IV.

---

[2] Misleading because it need not be either green or in a town or a village.

In the case of communal non-possessory land use rights the equivalent effect is achieved by limiting the rights to, for example, inhabitants of a specified locality, as we see in Parts V and VI.

13.4 Non-Possessory Land Use Rights Cannot Impose Positive Obligations on the Burdened Land

The general rule (to which there are a few exceptions) is that a proprietary non-possessory land use right does not impose positive obligations on the owner of the burdened land. This applies to non-possessory land use rights whether they are held privately, or by communities or by the public. So, if I am the freehold owner of land, and you, my neighbour, have a right of way over part of it, and another part of it is registered as a town or village green so that inhabitants of the locality have a right to use it for lawful sports or pastimes, constraints are imposed on my rights and liberties over my land, but generally I am not put under an obligation to maintain it to facilitate the use you and the local community are entitled to make of it. So, if you have a right of way over my drive I have no inherent obligation to maintain the surface of the drive, although we may agree by contract that you or I will be responsible for maintenance if the other pays half the cost.

PART II EASEMENTS

13.5 Function of Easements

An easement is a private property interest, in that it is a property interest held by an individual and exercisable for the benefit of land she owns. Specifically, it is a property interest attached to one piece of land which allows the landowner[3] of that piece of land to use neighbouring land in a specific way which will enhance the utility of the benefitted land. It attaches a permanent burden to one piece of land and a corresponding permanent benefit to another piece of land.[4] Easements serve several public functions. One is to ensure that land is not physically isolated, cut off from nationally or locally provided utilities such as roads, water, drainage, sewers, gas, electricity, telecommunications, etc. Another is to ensure that land and buildings have access to light and air. A third function also relates to efficient land use, but from a different perspective. If the utility of one piece of land can be increased by having a right over

---

[3] That is, the freehold or leasehold owner.

[4] More precisely, easements acquired by the freehold owner of the dominant land are always perpetual, unless expressly stated to be either for a fixed period of years or for some other period. An easement for a perpetual period or a fixed period of years will be a legal easement, provided it was created by deed. An easement expressly granted for a different period (e.g. during someone's lifetime, or until a specified building is demolished) will still be an easement, but it will be an equitable easement only. All implied easements and easements acquired by long use are legal easements and are perpetual in duration (unless acquired by a lessee of the dominant land, in which case they will last only as long as the lease lasts, if the lessee acquired the easement for the benefit of the lease; if the lessee acquired the easement for the benefit of the freeholder's interest in the land, the easement will have a perpetual duration): see further para. 13.13(a) below.

neighbouring land which does not diminish the utility of the neighbouring land, or does not diminish it by more than the increased utility of the benefitted land, then the overall efficiency of land use will be increased. Property law therefore needs to provide a mechanism which enables the neighbours to agree between themselves the 'transfer' or sharing of that benefit of the land between one piece of land and a neighbouring piece of land. So, this is not just an agreement between two individuals for their respective personal benefits, but an agreement between present owners of neighbouring land which will result in one person's land being permanently burdened to provide a permanent benefit to the other person's land, to the mutual benefit of both.[5]

13.6 Nature of Easements

These functions of easements make it easier to account for some of the requirements the law imposes to enable a right over land to qualify as an easement.

In particular, we should note that a right to take something from someone else's land cannot be an easement: an easement must allow the dominant owner to *do* something on the servient land.[6] A right to take natural produce from someone else's land can be a property interest, but it will be a profit and not an easement, as we see in Part IV of this chapter.

Another notable feature of easements is that the appurtenance requirements we noted in para. 13.3 above are very strict, as we see in the next paragraph.

13.7 Requirements for a Valid Easement

Neighbours can come to whatever personal agreements they want about their uses of their respective pieces of land. So, I can grant to my neighbour any right I want over my land – a right for her to swim in my swimming pool whenever she wants, or to park her car on my drive, or to picnic in my garden or lay broadband cables under my land – and the right will remain enforceable between us personally in contract whatever the nature of the right. However, only limited classes of such rights will qualify as an easement (i.e. will 'stick' to both my land and my neighbour's land, so that the right continues to be enforceable by and between each of us and our respective successors in title).

13.8 The Classic Requirements: *Re Ellenborough Park*

The classic requirements for a valid easement are still taken to be those set out by Lord Evershed giving the judgment of the Court of Appeal in *Re Ellenborough Park* [1956] Ch 131, CA. The case concerned a large rectangle of land facing the sea in a

---

[5] See further Andre van der Walt, 'The continued relevance of servitude' (2013) 3 *Property Law Review* 3, and also Sonja von Staden, 'Ancillary rights in servitude law' (2015) unpublished Ph.D. thesis, University of Stellenbosch, and Andre van der Walt, 'Sharing servitudes' (2014), unpublished conference paper, available at www.iuscommune.eu/html/activities/2014/2014-11-27/plenair_vdWalt .pdf.

[6] Although see para. 13.11 below on 'negative' easements.

seaside resort which the owners developed as a residential estate in the middle of the nineteenth century. The development consisted of houses built on the three sides of the rectangle which were not bordering the sea and a large central area ('Ellenborough Park') which was laid out as a communal garden for the houses. The houses were sold off to purchasers and the developer retained ownership of the central area. When the houses were sold off, each purchaser was granted:

> the full enjoyment ... at all times hereafter in common with the other persons to whom such easements may be granted of the pleasure ground set out and made in front of the said plot of land ... in the centre of the square called Ellenborough Park ... subject to the payment of a fair and just proportion of the costs charges and expenses of keeping in good order and condition the said pleasure ground.

Each conveyance also included a covenant by the developers that, subject to each purchaser paying a proportion of the costs, they and subsequent owners of Ellenborough Park (the 'Trustees') would keep it 'as an ornamental pleasure ground ... and also that they would not at any time thereafter erect or permit to be erected any dwelling house or other building (except any grotto bower summerhouse flower stand fountain music stand or other ornamental erection) within or on any part of the said pleasure ground ... but that the same shall at all times remain as an ornamental garden or pleasure ground.'

During the Second World War, Ellenborough Park was requisitioned by the War Office and compensation was paid to the Trustees. After the war, when the property was handed back by the authorities, the Trustees applied to the court to determine whether the then owners of the houses bordering Ellenborough Park (i) had an enforceable right to use it and (ii) were entitled to a share of the compensation.

The Court of Appeal held that the house owners did have a valid easement over Ellenborough Park, and therefore were entitled to a share in the compensation.

Lord Evershed stated that there are four characteristics which are necessary for a right to be a valid easement:

> They are (1) there must be a dominant and a servient tenement; (2) an easement must 'accommodate' the dominant tenement; (3) dominant and servient owners must be different persons, and (4) a right over land cannot amount to an easement, unless it is capable of forming the subject-matter of a grant.[7]

Requirements (1) and (3) are straightforward: an easement is a property right held by one landowner (the 'dominant' owner) over land owned by someone else (the 'servient' land held by the 'servient' owner). The difficult ones are (2) – does the right 'accommodate the dominant tenement' – and (4) – is it 'capable of forming the subject matter of a grant'. We take these separately.

(a) Does the Right Accommodate the Dominant Tenement?

The second requirement is the appurtenance requirement we referred to in para. 13.3 above: a right over neighbouring land cannot be an easement unless it

---

[7] *Re Ellenborough Park* [1956] Ch 131, CA at p. 163.

'accommodates' the dominant land. According to Lord Evershed in *Re Ellenborough Park* this means that the right must 'serve' the dominant land and be 'reasonably necessary for the better enjoyment of that tenement, for if it has no necessary connection therewith, although it confers an advantage upon the owner and renders his ownership of the land more valuable, it is not an easement at all, but a mere contractual right personal to and only enforceable between the two contracting parties'.[8] In other words, as in the law of nuisance which we look at in Chapter 10 *Limitations on Property*, the right must enhance the owner's use and enjoyment of the land, not merely provide a personal benefit to him. So, it is not sufficient that it enhances the value of the property unless it is also shown that it is 'connected with the normal enjoyment of that property'.[9] The question of whether there is a sufficient connection with the dominant owner's 'normal enjoyment' of his land is, Lord Evershed said, a question of fact. He accepted that something like a right for the purchaser of a house to have free entry to Lords Cricket Ground or London Zoo would not pass the test:

> Such a right would undoubtedly increase the value of the property conveyed, but could not run with it at law as an easement, because there was no sufficient nexus between the enjoyment of the right and the use of the house ... it would be wholly extraneous to, and independent of, the use of a house as a house, i.e. as a place in which the householder and his family live and make their home.[10]

However, he thought a right for a house owner to use his neighbour's land as the garden to his house would 'accommodate' the dominant owner's use and enjoyment of his land:

> In such a case the test of connection or accommodation would be amply satisfied; for just as the use of a garden undoubtedly enhances, and is connected with, the normal enjoyment of the house to which it belongs, so also would the right granted, in the case supposed, be closely connected with the use and enjoyment of the part of the premises sold.[11]

He concluded that the same must apply to the right to use land adjoining a house as a communal garden:

> The park became a communal garden for the benefit and enjoyment of those whose houses adjoined it or were in its close proximity. Its flower beds, lawns and walks were calculated to afford all the amenities which it is the purpose of the garden of a house to provide; and apart from the fact that these amenities extended to a number of householders instead of being confined to one ... we can see no difference in principle between Ellenborough Park and a garden in the ordinary signification of that word. It is the collective garden of the neighbouring houses to whose use it was dedicated by the owners of the estate and as such amply satisfied, in our judgment, the requirement of connection with the dominant tenements to which it is appurtenant.[12]

---

[8] Ibid. at p. 170, quoting from *Cheshire's Modern Real Property* (7th edn, 1954), at p. 457. Lord Evershed adopted this passage from *Cheshire* as an accurate statement of the law.
[9] Ibid.   [10] Ibid. Lord Evershed at p. 174.   [11] Ibid.   [12] Ibid. pp. 174–175.

(b) Is the Right 'Capable of Forming the Subject Matter of a Grant'?

Lord Evershed explained what this means. He said that a right over someone else's land is not 'capable of forming the subject-matter of a grant' – and so not capable of being a valid easement – if:

   (i) it is 'expressed in terms too wide and vague a character'; or
   (ii) it 'amounts to rights of joint occupation or would substantially deprive [the servient owner] of proprietorship or legal possession; or
  (iii) it constitutes a 'mere right of recreation' 'possessing no quality of utility or benefit'.[13]

Applying these criteria to the case before him, Lord Evershed said:

> To the first of these questions the interpretation which we have given to the [1864 conveyances] provides, in our judgment, the answer; for we have construed the right conferred as being both well defined and commonly understood. In these essential respects the right may be said to be distinct from the indefinite and unregulated privilege which, we think, would ordinarily be understood by the Latin term 'jus spatiandi', a privilege of wandering at will over all and every part of another's field or park, and which, though easily intelligible as the subject matter of a personal licence, is something substantially different from the subject matter of the grant in question, viz., the provision for a limited number of houses in a uniform crescent of one single large but private garden. Our interpretation of the deed also provides, we think, the answer to the second question: the right conferred no more amounts to a joint occupation of the park with its owners, no more excludes the proprietorship or possession of the latter, than a right of way granted through a passage or than the use by the public of the gardens of Lincoln's Inn Fields (to take one of our former examples) amount to joint occupation of that garden with the London County Council, or involve an inconsistency with the possession or proprietorship of the council as lessees. It is conceded that in any event the owners of the park are entitled to cut the timber growing on the park and to retain its proceeds. We have said that in our judgment, under the deed, the flowers and shrubs grown in the garden are equally the property of the owners of the park. We see nothing repugnant to a man's proprietorship or possession of a piece of land that he should decide to make of it and maintain it as an ornamental garden, and should grant rights to a limited number of other persons to come into it for the enjoyment of its amenities."[14]

The third, however, was more difficult. Was a right to use a garden a 'mere right of recreation'? Perhaps counter-intuitively, Lord Evershed thought not:

> if the proposition [that there is a requirement of utility and benefit] is well founded, we do not think that the right to use a garden of the character with which we are concerned in this case can be called one of mere recreation and amusement ... No doubt a garden is a pleasure, and on high authority it is the purest of pleasures; but, in our judgment, it is not a right having no quality either of utility or benefit as those

---

[13] The quoted words are from Lord Evershed's judgment in *Ellenborough Park*, fn. 7 above, at pp. 175–176.
[14] Ibid. p. 176.

words should be understood. The right here in suit is, for reasons already given, one appurtenant to the surrounding houses as such, and constitutes a beneficial attribute of residence in a house as ordinarily understood. Its use for the purposes, not only of exercise and rest but also for such normal domestic purposes as were suggested in argument – for example, for taking out small children in perambulators or otherwise – is not fairly to be described as one of mere recreation or amusement, and is clearly beneficial to the premises to which it is attached.[15]

Overall, therefore, he was satisfied that the rights granted over Ellenborough Park were easements:

As appears from what has been stated earlier the right to the full enjoyment of Ellenborough Park which was granted by the [1864 conveyances] was in substance no more than a right to use the park as a garden in the way in which gardens are commonly used. In a sense, no doubt, such a right includes something of a jus spatiandi in as much as it involves the principle of wandering at will round each and every part of the garden except, of course, such parts as comprise flower beds, or are laid out for some other purpose, which renders walking impossible or unsuitable. We doubt, nevertheless, whether the right to use and enjoy a garden in this manner can with accuracy be said to constitute a mere jus spatiandi. Wandering at large is of the essence of such a right and constitutes the main purpose for which it exists. A private garden, on the other hand, is an attribute of the ordinary enjoyment of the residence to which it is attached, and the right of wandering in it is but one method of enjoying it."[16]

He went on to say that, even if it was categorisable as a jus spatiandi, he was satisfied that the authorities did not exclude such a right from being a private easement, provided that, as here, the right was clearly delineated.[17]

13.9 Relaxation of the *Ellenborough Park* Test for Recreational Easements

Nevertheless, it has always been difficult to reconcile the test as formulated in *Ellenborough Park* with the decision actually made in the case: the right in question was a right to use a garden, and, despite Lord Evershed's comments, it is not clear why that is not a right of 'mere recreation.' However, the Court of Appeal reached a similar conclusion in *Mulvaney* v. *Gough* [2002] 44 E.G. 175 (CA). In that case the Court of Appeal held that owners of cottages surrounding a back yard had acquired rights to use it as communal 'garden and amenity land' (to plant and maintain flower beds, hang washing, store dustbins, etc.), and that, applying *Ellenborough Park*, those rights were easements, even though they included rights to make use of the yard for recreational purposes.

In any event, the 'mere recreation' part of the *Ellenborough Park* test has now been modified by the Supreme Court in *Regency Villas Title Ltd* v. *Diamond Resorts (Europe) Ltd* [2018] UKSC 57, holding that a right to use servient land for recreational purposes can indeed be an easement. The case concerned the development of

---

[15] Ibid. p. 179.   [16] Ibid. pp. 179–180.   [17] Ibid. pp. 184–185.

a seventeenth century country estate and parkland near Canterbury as a leisure resort and timeshare complex. Part of the land and a house built on it (Elham House) were sold off and converted into timeshare units. A timeshare scheme involves the provision of holiday accommodation units in a development to 'time-share owners', each of whom buys the right to occupy one of the units for a fixed period of time (perhaps two weeks) each year, usually for a fixed number of years.[18] In the case of Elham House, the freehold of the land was held by Trustees on trust for the timeshare owners in the Elham House development. On the other part of the original estate there was a main Mansion House, which at about the same time was converted into 18 additional timeshare units on the upper floors,[19] and, on the ground floor and basement level, leisure facilities, gym, snooker room, etc. In the grounds of the Mansion House the developer built a heated outdoor swimming pool (later filled in and replaced by an indoor pool) and other sporting and leisure facilities including a golf course, squash and tennis courts and formal gardens. The Trustees and timeshare owners in the Elham House development (now known as Regency Villas) sought a declaration regarding the rights to use the sporting and leisure facilities in the Mansion House and grounds which had been granted to them when they bought their units in 1981. They argued that these rights were easements and were therefore enforceable against the present holders of the freehold interest in the Mansion House development. The relevant grant in 1981 was as follows:

> the right for the Transferee its successors in title its lessees and the occupiers from time to time of the property to use the swimming pool, golf course, squash courts, tennis courts, the ground and basement floor of Broome Park Mansion House, gardens and any other sporting or recreational facilities (hereafter called 'the facilities') on the Transferor's adjoining estate.

The freehold owners of the Mansion House development argued that these rights failed to qualify as easements because they amounted to no more than 'mere rights of recreation' The Supreme Court rejected this argument and held by a majority (Lord Carnwath dissenting) that the rights were easements, reversing in part the decision of the Court of Appeal. The Court of Appeal had gone through each of the facilities one by one and concluded, broadly, that the fact that the rights were to use

---

[18] In the early form of timeshare scheme introduced in England and Wales in the 1980s, each timeshare owner was granted a right to occupy her unit for a discontinuous term, for example for 2 weeks each year for 80 years, and the courts held that this gave her a property interest in the unit which amounted to a lease of the unit for a term of 2 × 80 weeks: *Cottage Holiday Associates Ltd* v. *Customs And Excise Commissioners* [1983] 1 QB 735. This was the kind of arrangement used in the *Regency Villas* case. Under more complex schemes developed later, timeshare owners were granted a variety of different kinds of rights, not all of which amounted to property interests: see, for example, *Fortyseven Park Street Limited* v. *The Commissioners For Her Majesty's Revenue And Customs* [2018] UKUT 41 (TCC), where each timeshare owner had only a right to apply to reserve any one of a group of apartments in a luxury Mayfair Development for specified dates, with the landowner allocating whichever apartment, if any, was free on those dates.

[19] The freehold owner of the Mansion House granted a lease of the upper floors to a separate company, which granted timeshare subleases of each timeshare unit to each unit holder. These timeshare subleases included rights for the unit holders to use all the sporting and recreational facilities on the estate.

sporting or recreational facilities did not prevent them from being easements, but that only the rights to use the outdoor facilities were easements: the rights to use the indoor facilities were simply rights to use chattels. Lord Briggs, giving the principal judgment of the majority in the Supreme Court, agreed on the first point (that rights to use sporting and recreational facilities could be easements) but disagreed on the second. He said that it was not appropriate to take each facility separately:

> ... although reference is made to a number of different specific facilities within the park, the facilities grant is in my view in substance the grant of a single comprehensive right to use a complex of facilities, and comprehends not only those constructed and in use at the time of the 1981 Transfer, but all those additional or replacement facilities thereafter constructed and put into operation within the park as part of the leisure complex during the expected useful life of the Regency Villas timeshare development for which the 1981 Transfer was intended to pave the way. It is, in short, a right to use such recreational and sporting facilities as exist within the leisure complex in the park from time to time.[20]

He was therefore able to interpret the grant as a single grant to use the recreational facilities as whole, and on that basis he said that, given the nature of the dominant land (the timeshare units) and its intended use for holiday purposes, there was no difficulty in seeing such a right as 'accommodating' the dominant land:

> In my view this court should affirm the lead given by the principled analysis of the Court of Appeal in *Re Ellenborough Park* [1956] Ch 131, by a clear statement that the grant of purely recreational (including sporting) rights over land which genuinely accommodate adjacent land may be the subject matter of an easement, provided always that they satisfy the four well-settled conditions which I have described. Where the actual or intended use of the dominant tenement is itself recreational, as will generally be the case for holiday timeshare developments, the accommodation condition will generally be satisfied. Whether the other conditions, and in particular the components of the fourth condition, will be satisfied will be a question of fact in each case. *Whatever may have been the attitude in the past to 'mere recreation or amusement', recreational and sporting activity of the type exemplified by the facilities at Broome Park is so clearly a beneficial part of modern life that the common law should support structures which promote and encourage it, rather than treat it as devoid of practical utility or benefit.*[21]

It was left to Lord Carnwath, dissenting, to point out the practical difficulties in having an easement consisting of a right to use a fluctuating set of sports facilities and equipment, and how far this extended the concept of an easement as a right to do something on someone else's land without imposing any positive obligations on the owner of the burdened land:

> An easement is a right to do something, or to prevent something, on another's land; not to have something done: see *Gale on Easements*, 20th edn (2017) para. 1–80. The intended enjoyment of the rights granted in this case, most obviously in the case of the

---

[20] Lord Briggs in *Regency Villas Title Ltd* v. *Diamond Resorts (Europe) Ltd* [2018] UKSC 57 at para. 26.
[21] Ibid. para. 81.

golf course and swimming pool, cannot be achieved without the active participation of the owner of those facilities in their provision, maintenance and management. The same may apply to a greater or lesser degree to other recreational facilities which have been or might be created, such as the skating-rink or the riding stables (who provides and keeps the horses?). Thus the doing of something by the servient owner is an intrinsic part of the right claimed.[22]

In effect, he said, 'what is claimed is not a simple property right, but permanent membership of a country club'.[23]

13.10 Recognised Categories of Easement

We can get a clearer idea of how these tests work in practice by looking at some new categories of easement that have emerged (or been rejected by the courts) over the last few years. It is clear from what the Supreme Court said in *Regency Villas* that the proper approach to the *Ellenborough* requirements is now to interpret them quite flexibly, preferring to give effect to the rights the parties clearly intended to create rather than invalidate them, and willing to accept that social changes might require the recognition of new classes of easement.

This is in line with the decision in *Fearn* v. *Tate Gallery*,[24] which we looked at in Chapter 10 *Limitations on Property* paras. 10.14–10.15. As we saw there, Mann J first reviewed the decision of the House of Lords in *Hunter* v. *Canary Wharf* [1997] AC 656 (which had held that a right to receive television signals was not an amenity right inherent in ownership) and the decision of the High Court of Australia in *Victoria Park Racing* v. *Taylor* (1937) 58 CLR 497 (that the common law does not recognise a right not to be overlooked). The conclusion Mann J nevertheless reached in *Fearn* v. *Tate* was that it was necessary for the courts to now recognise a proprietary right not to be overlooked, by 'developing' the common law so that it upheld Convention rights (here, article 8 of the European Convention on Human Rights on rights to respect for private life and home).

Similarly, in *Coventry* v. *Lawrence*,[25] which we also considered in Chapter 10 *Limitations on Property* paras. 10.13–10.15, the Supreme Court was prepared to accept that a right to cause a nuisance by noise is capable of being an easement. As Lord Neuberger said:

> 33. . . . I am of the view that the right to carry on an activity which results in noise, or the right to emit a noise, which would otherwise cause an actionable nuisance, is capable of being an easement. The fact that the noise from an activity may be heard in a large number of different properties can fairly be said to render it an unusual easement, but, as Mr McCracken QC for the respondents said, whether or not there is an easement is to be decided between the owner of the property from which the noise emanates and each neighbouring property-owner.

---

[22] Lord Carnwath, dissenting, in *Regency Villas Title Ltd*, fn. 20 above, at para. 95.   [23] Ibid. para. 96.
[24] *Fearn* v. *Tate Gallery* [2019] EWHC 246.
[25] *Coventry* v. *Lawrence* [2014] UKSC 13. per Lord Neuberger; the other justices all agreed with him on this point.

Equally, as Lewison LJ said at [2012] 1 WLR 2127, para. 88, the fact that a right is only exercisable at specified times does not prevent it from being an easement. As he also pointed out at para. 89, one can characterise a right to emit noise in relatively conventional terms in the context of easements, namely as 'the right to transmit sound waves over' the servient land. Lord Parker of Waddington clearly assumed that the right to emit noise could be an easement in *Pwllbach* [1915] AC 634, 646, referring to *Lyttleton Times Co Ltd* v. *Warners Ltd* [1907] AC 476. Furthermore, where there is an express grant, it should normally be reasonably easy to identify the level of permitted noise, the periods when it may be emitted, and the activities which may produce the noise.

34. Subject to questions of notice and registration, the benefit and burden of an easement run with the land, and, therefore, if a right to emit noise which would otherwise be a nuisance is an easement, it would bind successors of the grantor, whereas it is a little hard to see how that would be so if the right were not an easement. Given the property-based nature of nuisance, and given the undesirable practical consequences if the benefit and burden of the right to emit a noise would not run with the relevant land, it appears to me that both principle and policy favour the conclusion that that a right to create what would otherwise be a nuisance by noise to land can be an easement.[26]

The recognition of such a right as an easement is particularly significant because Lord Neuberger also concluded that it could be acquired by prescription as well as by direct grant.[27] This means that if I have been carrying on a noisy activity on my land for a sufficiently long period 'as of right' (in the sense we note in para. 13.24 below, in other words without opposition or licence or permission from a neighbour[28]) I will acquire, through the doctrine of prescription,[29] a property right enforceable against that neighbour to continue to make that of kind and level of noise on my land perpetually.

13.11 Negative Easements

Most easements allow the dominant owner to do something positive on the servient land, but there is an anomalous class of easements which give the dominant owner the right to preserve the enjoyment and amenities of her own land by restricting what the servient owner can do on his own land. These include a right to light through pre-existing apertures in buildings on the dominant land, a right to prevent the servient owner from doing anything on his land to obstruct the access of light and air to the dominant land, and a right of support for buildings on the dominant land from structures on the servient land.

---

[26] Ibid paras. 32–34. The other justices all agreed with Lord Neuberger on this point.

[27] Ibid. paras. 35–46 and 140–146.

[28] It is generally said that an additional requirement for an action to be 'as of right' is that it must not be secret, but that is hardly appropriate for noise: to the extent that noise is hidden, it does not travel on to someone else's land.

[29] See paras. 13.14 and 13.24 below and Chapter 14 *Acquiring Interests Informally* para. 14.1.

13.12 Fencing Easement

It is generally an essential requirement of an easement that it cannot impose on the servient owner an obligation to spend money or otherwise do something positive on his land. However, there are a few exceptions. These include an ancient common law easement known as a fencing easement, which requires the servient owner to erect and maintain fences along the boundaries of her land where they adjoin the dominant owner's land, for the benefit of the dominant owner's land. In all the old cases (and indeed in the few modern ones as well), the objective is to keep farm animals straying on to neighbouring land. However, counterintuitively, the dominant owner is usually the farmer, and it is the farmer's neighbour who is put under an obligation to fence her own land off from the farm, to prevent the farmer's cattle and sheep from straying into her land. So, for example, in the most important of the modern cases, *Egerton* v. *Harding* [1975] QB 62, where the Court of Appeal confirmed the continuing existence of this ancient easement, it was held that the owner of a cottage was not entitled to complain when cattle owned by a neighbouring farmer got into her garden from the common where they were grazed, devastating the garden. This was because, so it was decided, it had been established by custom that she and the owners of other houses adjoining the common, was under a duty (alternatively expressed as 'an obligation in the nature of an easement') to keep her land fenced off from the common.[30] One explanation put forward for why fencing easements usually require a neighbour to fence her land to keep a farmer's animals off her land, rather than requiring the farmer to fence his land to keep his animals in, is that grazing was traditionally done communally by farmers on common land, and adjoining freehold land had usually been carved out of the common land by enclosure without the commoners' consent, depriving the commoners of the grazing on that land.[31] However, the dominant land need not be, or ever have been, common land. In other words, a private landowner who grazes only his own animals on his land, may acquire an easement over neighbouring land which gives him a right to make the neighbour fence her land off from his, to keep his animals off her land. So, for example, in the most recent case, *Churston Golf Club* v. *Haddock* [2019] EWCA Civ 544, in a 1972 transfer of a golf course to the local authority, the local authority 'covenanted' with the owner of the adjoining farm that it would maintain and keep in repair the walls, fences and hedges which separated the farm from the golf course. The farmer argued that the effect of the term was to give him a fencing easement enforceable against the golf club, that is, a right attached to his land that the owner for the time being of the golf course would maintain and keep the fences etc. in repair. The Court of Appeal held that, on the proper construction of the 1972 transfer, the golf club did not grant the farmer a fencing easement (which would have been a property interest enforceable by and between

---

[30] An additional oddity is that the benefit of the easement in this case attaches to the grazing rights of the farmers rather than to their freehold or leasehold interest in their farms. In other words, every farmer who has the right to graze animals on the common (as to which see Parts IV and V below) is entitled to enforce the cottage owner's obligation to fence her garden off from the common.

[31] Lord Scarman in *Egerton* v. *Harding* [1975] QB 62 at p 69.

their successors), but merely made the farmer an enforceable *promise* (i.e. a covenant) to maintain and repair the fences etc. Such a covenant amounts in law to a positive covenant which, as we see in Part IV, creates a purely contractual relationship and, unlike a restrictive covenant, it is not a property right enforceable between successive owners of the benefitted and burdened land. However, the court accepted that, in principle, a fencing easement could have been implied into the 1972 conveyance had the wording been different.

13.13 Duration, Modification and Termination of Easements

One of the reasons why a court might hesitate to expand the range of rights categorised as easements is that generally they last for ever and there is no mechanism for modifying or terminating an easement, even if it has become obsolete or now unreasonably restricts the servient owner in his use of his land.

(a) Duration

For historical reasons, the doctrine of estates applies to easements, so that if they are legal easements they must last either perpetually (i.e. for a fee simple estate) or for a fixed period of years (i.e. for a leasehold estate). In practice, this means that easements expressly created for the benefit of the freehold owner of the dominant land are always perpetual, unless expressly stated to be for a fixed period only (which hardly ever happens in practice). Consistently with this, easements acquired by the freehold owner by implied grant or long use are always perpetual (and always legal rather than equitable).[32] An easement expressly granted for a different period (e.g. during someone's lifetime, or until a specified building is demolished) will still be an easement, but it will be an equitable easement only. All implied easements and easements acquired by long use are perpetual in duration (unless acquired by a lessee of the dominant land, in which case they will last only as long as the lease if acquired for the benefit of the lease, or perpetually if treated as acquired for the benefit of the freeholder's interest in the land).

(b) Modification

At present there is no mechanism to discharge or modify easements which have become obsolete or unduly restrictive of the servient land without bringing any real benefit to the dominant land. However, the Law Commission has proposed that the courts' existing jurisdiction to modify or discharge restrictive covenants under s. 84 of the LPA 1925, which we note in para. 13.15 below, should be extended to cover easements. This is part of the Law Commission's recommendations to adopt a

---

[32] All property interests acquired by implication of law and by prescription or adverse possession are always legal and not equitable because they arise out of old common law rules which were never affected by equity, and they were not re-classified by the LPA 1925: Chapter 5 *Ownership and Other Property Interests* para. 5.23(a).

unified system of land obligations, removing the distinctions between easements and freehold covenants.[33]

13.14 Express and Implied Grant or Reservation of Easements

(a) Express Grant or Reservation of Easements

An easement can be created by an express agreement between neighbours. Most often this happens when land is sub-divided. If I want to sell off part of my back garden to you so that you can build a house on it, I will need to grant you whatever rights are necessary over my retained land and reserve for myself whatever rights I want over the land I am selling you, to enable the two pieces of land to function independently. I might perhaps grant you a right of way over my driveway to give you access from your new house to the road, and rights for you to run pipes and cables under my retained land so that you can connect to the mains services running under the road. And, if the drainage on my land has always been to a septic tank which is under the land I am selling to you, I will have to reserve for the benefit of my land rights for my drainage to get across your land to the septic tank, and then rights for my drainage to be processed through what will now be your septic tank.

(b) Easements arising by prescription

Because the reciprocal rights and duties between neighbours of the kind we describe in (a) above are so essential in practice, they often evolve informally by custom. It is unsurprising, then, that the common law has recognised for centuries that easements can arise by prescription. Unfortunately, the modern law relating to prescription is notoriously complex and illogical, and the 2011 Law Commission Report, *Making Land Work: Easements, Covenants and Profits a Prendre Law*,[34] has recommended more or less total abolition and restatement of the rules. This is just one in a long series of calls for reform. We do not cover the various regimes currently governing the acquisition of easements by prescription, but we should mention here just two notable features.

The first is that four out of the five different routes by which an easement can be acquired by prescription in our present law are based on the fiction that the right was originally intentionally granted to the user. So, in these cases long use does not lead directly to the creation of the right, as it does in civil law prescription.[35] Instead, it leads to a presumption (in many cases irrebuttable) that the right was granted at some fictitious point in the past and has been a valid enforceable easement ever since that date.[36] Unsurprisingly, this causes a certain amount of conceptual confusion.

The other notable feature lies in the nature of the long use which gives rise to the presumption of an original lawful grant. In order for the presumption to arise, it is

---

[33] See Law Commission Report, *Making Land Work: Easements, Covenants and Profits a Prendre* (2011) Law Com No 327, Part 7.
[34] Ibid.   [35] See Chapter 12 *Adverse Possession of Land* para. 12.2.
[36] See Alison Clarke, 'Use, time and entitlement' (2004) 57 *Current Legal Problems* 239 at pp. 263–272.

necessary for the person claiming the benefit of the easement to demonstrate not just that she had used her neighbour's land for the relevant purposes for a sufficiently long period of time. She must also prove that throughout the period her use has been 'as of right'. This is usually expressed in Latin: the use must have been 'nec vi, nec clam and nec precario', meaning that it must have been without force, without secrecy and without the permission or licence of the freehold owner of the land over which the easement is claimed. We examine these requirements in more detail in para. 13.24, where we consider how they apply in relation to the statutory requirements for having land registered as a town or village green.

(c) Implied Grant or Reservation

The other method by which easements can come into existence, as well as by direct grant or reservation or by long use, in by implied grant or reservation. Because easements are often almost essential whenever land is sub-divided, English law will imply them into transfers sub-dividing land in a number of circumstances. The most important is where the land would otherwise be landlocked: an easement by necessity will be implied where necessary to prevent this happening. The rationale of easements of necessity is that every landowner must have essential means of access to the land for people and for essential services such as water and drainage, either by direct connection to a public network or by property rights over private networks and services. An easement by necessity is implied regardless of the parties' intention, and regardless of what is said in the transfer. Easements can also be implied under three other rules: under s. 62 of the LPA 1925, under the so-called rule in *Wheeldon* v. *Burroughs*, and on the basis of common intention. However, these last three are all default rules: they apply only if and so far as a contrary intention does not appear in the transfer or surrounding circumstances. In practice, standard form transfers routinely exclude the operation of all these rules, although of course they cannot exclude the implication of easement by necessity.[37]

PART III RESTRICTIVE COVENANTS

13.15 What a Restrictive Covenant Is, and Why They Are Imposed

Restrictive covenants allow a private landowner to restrict the way neighbouring landowners use their land. They are sometimes referred to as freehold covenants

---

[37] For further reference, see *Parker* v. *Roberts* [2019] EWCA Civ 121 for a modern reappraisal of implication in general, and also *Harris* v. *Flower* (1905) 74 LJ Ch 127 (right of way can be used to access additional dominant land, but only in so far as its use is ancillary to original dominant land), as restated in *Gore* v. *Naheed* [2017] EWCA Civ 369. Reference may also be made to the rule in *Halsall* v. *Brizzel* [1957] Ch 169 on reciprocal rights and burdens (if a right is granted simultaneously with a positive obligation to contribute towards maintenance, the continued exercise of the right is conditional on the performance of the obligation), and the Law Commission recommendations in Law Com No 327 (fn. 33 above), and also paras. 4.62–4.94 in the Law Commission Consultation Analysis (2011) to the Easements, Covenants and Profits a Prendre Consultation Paper No. 186, 2008.

(because usually made between freehold owners of adjoining land) to distinguish them from leasehold covenants, which are the covenants made between landlord and tenant which are contained in a lease.[38] A restrictive covenant is an equitable property interest which allows the owner of a plot of land ('the benefitted land') to impose restrictions on the use of neighbouring land, for the benefit of the benefitted land. Given that this is already restricted by the state through planning and environmental law, it may seem surprising that restrictive covenants (which were first recognised as property interests in 1849, when public regulation was much less extensive than it is now) are not now obsolete.

In fact, they are not even obsolescent. They are used very often indeed, probably more frequently now than they have ever been. It throws some light on why this might be the case if we look at the situations in which they are now commonly used.

(a) Use of Restrictive Covenants

Restrictive covenants are always initially created by a contract. Sometimes this happens when neighbouring landowners enter into an agreement whereby one of them promises (covenants) to restrict the use of his land in a specified way that will benefit the other person's land. Suppose, for example, you and I each own the freehold interest in adjoining decrepit houses with large semi-derelict gardens in a street which shows signs of gentrification. I have heard that you are thinking of knocking your house down and replacing it with a large block of flats. I could stop you (and your successors) from doing that if I could persuade you to enter into an agreement with me, for the benefit of my land, that you will not use your land for any purpose other than as a single private dwelling house for occupation by one family. If you agreed (and I guess you will not, unless I pay you a lot of money in exchange for this limitation on your freedom to use your land as you want) and we entered into the agreement, it would take effect as a grant by you to me of a property interest over your land (a restrictive covenant), which I would hold for the benefit of my land. The property interest would be appurtenant to my land, in the sense explained in para. 13.3 above, so that it would be enforceable by me only for so long as I remain freehold owner of my land, and thereafter by whoever succeeds me as freehold owner. Similarly, it would be enforceable against you for as long as you remained freehold owner of your land, and thereafter against whoever is the freehold owner at the relevant time. I could of course hope that planning law will stop you building the flats in this kind of situation, without me having to go to the trouble and expense of extracting a restrictive covenant from you. However, as we saw in Chapter 10 *Limitations on Property* para. 10.9, planning decisions take into account only the public interest. Building a block of flats on your land may well spoil my view and lower the value of my house, without it harming national, local or community interests.

[38] See further Chapter 17 *Leases* para. 17.3(d).

Much more often, restrictive covenants are created not by agreement between people who are already neighbouring landowners, but by an owner of a large plot of land who wants to sell off one or more parts of the land for development, and wants to restrict the way in which the sold-off parts of the land are developed. There are two typical situations. One would be where I own a house with a large garden, and I want to sell part of the garden to you so that you can build a house on it. Whether I am proposing to go on living in my old house, or to sell it and go and live elsewhere, I will almost certainly want to make it a condition of the sale that you will grant me, for the benefit of my retained land, restrictive covenants over the part of the garden you are buying from me, which will restrict what you and subsequent owners of that land can build on it and how it can be used.

The other typical situation is where I am a property developer owning a large development site, and I am proposing to build an estate of houses and/or offices or shops on the land and sell off the freehold interest in each unit to individual purchasers. Again, almost certainly I will make it a condition of each individual sale that the purchaser grants me restrictive covenants over the land they buy that will enable me to restrict what they and their successors can do on that land in the future, and how they can use it. I may then be able to pass on the benefit of those covenants to all the other purchasers of the units, so that eventually they can each enforce all their neighbours' covenants.[39]

(b) Discharge or Modification of Restrictive Covenants

One of the reasons why restrictive covenants are still so widely used, despite the many difficulties in ensuring that they remain enforceable between successors of the original parties, is that any person adversely affected by a restrictive covenant can apply to a tribunal to have it discharged or modified. The discharge and modification provisions are set out in s. 84(1) of the Law of Property Act 1925, as amended and expanded by s. 28 of the Law of Property Act 1969. In outline, they give the Tribunal power to discharge or modify a restrictive covenant on any one of four different grounds:

(i) if, because of changes in the character of the property or the neighbourhood or other material circumstances, the restriction is obsolete (s. 84(1)(a) of the LPA 1925 as amended);

(ii) if the continued existence of the covenant would impede some reasonable use of the land for public or private purposes, and is either contrary to the public interest or does not provide the person who is entitled to the benefit with any practical benefits of substantial value or advantage and (in either of those cases) money would be adequate compensation for the person entitled to the benefit of the covenant (s. 84(1)(aa) and s. 81(1A));

---

[39] The rules governing enforcement of restrictive covenants between neighbours are complex and not wholly satisfactory. We do not cover them here: a useful starting point for those who want to find out more would be the Law Commission Report, *Making Land Work: Easements, Covenants and Profits a Prendre*, fn. 33 above, Part V.

(iii) if the person entitled to the benefit has expressly or impliedly agreed to the covenant being discharged or modified[40] (s. 84(1)(b));

(iv) if the proposed discharge or modification will not injure the person entitled to the benefit of it, and the person applying to have the covenant discharged or modified pays 'just' compensation either for any loss or disadvantage suffered by the person entitled to the benefit, or to 'make up for' any sum the person entitled to the benefit 'paid' for the benefit of the covenant when it was first imposed (s. 84(1)(c)).

This wide-ranging jurisdiction is much used, often successfully, and this undoubtedly helps to explain why freehold covenants are so widely imposed and widely accepted by purchasers. As we saw in para. 13.13 above, the Law Commission's recommendation is that the jurisdiction should be extended to easements, as part of their overall recommendations that we should adopt a unified system of private land obligations, removing the distinctions between easements and freehold covenants.

13.16 Enforcement of Positive Obligations

(a) Unenforceability of Positive Covenants

However, the major defect in our present law of freehold covenants is that positive covenants are not property interests. This means that if neighbours enter into an agreement under which either or both undertake positive obligations towards the other (perhaps to repair common structures, etc.), those obligations are enforceable between them in contract law, but, since they do not give rise to property interests, they are not enforceable against the whole world. Specifically, they are not enforceable against successive owners of the neighbouring land, nor are they automatically enforceable by successive owners of the land intended to be benefitted by the obligation.[41] As Gray and Gray put it, 'One of the scarcely credible features of the modern law of freehold covenants is that it acknowledges no straightforward means by which the burden of a positive covenant can be transmitted to third parties.'[42] The rule has recently been reaffirmed by the House of Lords in *Rhone* v. *Stephens*, on the basis of being too long-established and deeply entrenched to be abolished or modified by the courts, rather than by Parliament.[43]

(b) Law Reform Proposals

In 2011 the Law Commission recommended in Law Com No 327[44] that positive covenants should be recognised as property interests. However, agreeing with what Lord Templeman had said in *Rhone* v. *Stephens* about the extent to which the ban on

---

[40] Perhaps by failing to protest or take action when that covenant, or similar covenants in the same neighbourhood, have been broken, or by agreeing to discharge or modify similar covenants imposed on neighbours.

[41] The detailed rules governing the passing of the burden and the benefit of freehold covenants by various contractual devices are also not covered here: for a full account see Kevin Gray and Susan Francis Gray, *Elements of Land Law* (5th edn, Oxford: Oxford University Press, 2009) paras. 3.3.1–3.4.1.

[42] Ibid. para. 3.3.24.   [43] Lord Templeman in *Rhone* v. *Stephens* [1994] 2 AC 310, at pp. 316–323.

[44] Law Com 327, fn. 33 above.

enforcement of positive covenants is now entrenched in our modern law,[45] they recommended that this should be done only as part of a package of reforms including the creation of a new kind of property interest, the Land Obligation. The new Land Obligation would replace easements and restrictive covenants and also be extended to cover positive obligations, and all of them would be reviewable under a jurisdiction similar to the present LPA s. 84 jurisdiction to discharge or modify restrictive covenants, which we noted in para. 13.15(b). The recommendations have, however, been quite strongly criticised,[46] and in any event it is difficult to envisage the enactment of any legislation covering such a broad area of technical land law reform in the immediate future.

PART IV PROFITS

13.17 Nature of Profits

Profits a prendre (we call them 'profits' in this book) are rights held by an individual[47] to take a naturally occurring product from land belonging to someone else.

Profits can be divided into two categories: exclusive profits and rights of common. An exclusive profit[48] gives the holder of the profit the exclusive right to take that particular product from the land. Exclusive profits are therefore simply private property rights, very like easements in many ways.

Most profits, however, are rights of common. The distinguishing feature of a right of common is that the holder's right to take the product from someone else's land is exercisable only in common with others having a like right. Typically, these others will be the owner of the land over which the profit is exercisable and/or neighbouring landowners who have acquired a like right over that land. A profit exercisable in common with one or more other people in this way is best seen as a hybrid private/communal property interest: although from one perspective each profit holder has a private property interest in the resource, it is exercisable only in common with others. This makes it look more like a private right to share in the communal use of the resource, and indeed it is the archetypal communal property rights system which Garrett Hardin described as leading to the tragedy of the commons,[49] and which Elinor Ostrom demonstrated need not necessarily do so.[50] We look at rights of common in Part V.

---

[45] Ibid.

[46] See, for example, Walsh and Morris, 'Enforcing positive covenants: a practical perspective' [2015] *Conv* 324; O'Connor, 'Careful what you wish for: positive freehold covenants' [2011] *Conv* 191; Andrew Cash, 'Freehold covenants and the potential flaws in the Law Commission's 2011 reform proposals' (2017) 81 *Conv* 212 (referring to Law Com No 327, 2011, *Making Land Work: Easements, Covenants and Profits a Prendre*, fn. 33 above).

[47] Profits can also be held directly by communities, although in modern times they are rare: see Part V below.

[48] The technical term is 'sole' or 'several' profit.

[49] Garrett Hardin, 'The tragedy of the commons' (1968) 162 *Science* 1243.

[50] See further Chapter 2 *Conception and Justifications* paras. 2.14–2.17 and also *Lynn Shellfish Ltd* v. *Loose* [2016] UKSC 14, *Robinson* v. *Duleep Singh* (1879) 11 Ch D 798, 814 (on the difference between a

PART V RIGHTS OF COMMON AND COMMON LAND

13.18 Profits as Rights of Common

Rights of common, which have always been important parts of the agricultural economy, were brought back into prominence by the Commons Registration Act 1965, which required all rights of common to be registered in newly created Commons Registers set up under the 1965 Act by local authorities as commons registration authorities. The 1965 Act also required all land over which rights of common were exercisable to be registered in the Commons Register as 'common land'.

The main consequences of land being registered as common land are that public rights of access are exercisable over it under s. 1 of the Countryside and Rights of Way Act 2000, and, under Part III of the Commons Act 2006, no 'restricted works' may be carried out without the consent of the Secretary of State. 'Restricted works' include fencing, building or earthworks which would prevent or impede access, and resurfacing other than by way of repair of existing surfaces. Common land therefore constitutes quite highly regulated public access space, over which communal land use rights are also exercised.

13.19 Regulation of Communal Grazing Rights

One of the objectives of the Commons Registration Act 1965 was to provide mechanisms to regulate the number of animals grazing on common land. The Act therefore provided that when a grazing right was registered in the commons register, the number of animals grazeable had to be specified, with provision for objections to be made and adjudicated by a Commons Commissioner. However, registration of a right of common under the 1965 Act does not result in the right holder having an unqualified *right* to graze the specified number of animals. In *Dance* v. *Savery* [2011] EWCA Civ 1250 the Court of Appeal held that it is implicit in the 1965 Act (and now made explicit in s. 18(5) of the 2006 Act which replaces it) that the numerical limit specified in the register under s. 15 represents an upper limit only, which will be subject to customary constraints. *Dance* v. *Savery* demonstrates how significantly registered rights might be curtailed by customary limitations not apparent on the register. In that case the claimant's right to graze '56 bullocks or ponies and 224 sheep' was exercisable over three separately registered areas of common land, and this total number of animals was entered as the specified number in each of the registration entries. However, although this was nowhere stated in any of the register entries, these rights were, so it was argued, 'split rights', in other words the specified number of livestock was the maximum that could be grazed on all the units between

common of fishery and a right to fish in common) and Christopher P. Rogers, Eleanor A. Staughton, Angus Winchester and Margherita Peraccini, *Contested Common Land: Environmental Governance Past and Present* (London: Earthscan, 2011).

which the rights were split, leaving it up to the rights holder to decide how to distribute them between the units. The Court of Appeal held that this was correct, at least as between two of the registered units, and that the registered rights were indeed limited in this way, even though the limitation could have been, but was not, recorded in the register.

A similar conclusion was reached in *Hall* v. *Moore* [2009] EWCA Civ 201 (decided on the 1965 Act provisions and applying *Dance* v. *Savery*), where it was accepted that registered grazing rights were exercisable only one year in three, in accordance with local custom, even though this limitation did not appear anywhere on the register. This was confirmed by a differently constituted Court of Appeal as a matter of decision in related litigation reported as *Hall* v. *Harris and Moore* [2012] EWCA Civ 671, accepting that, in the absence of a limitation on the register (temporal or otherwise), the burden of proving that a limitation nevertheless exists is on the party asserting it, but finding ample evidence to support the conclusion that the limitation did indeed exist in that case.

However, the register is conclusive in that it states the *maximum* extent of the registered right. In other words, it is not open to a claimant to contend that the rights are more extensive than appears from the register. In *Dance* v. *Savery* the Court of Appeal rejected the claimant's argument that if a right could be 'split' when it was not described as such on the register, it must follow that a right which is described on the register as 'split' may not necessarily be so, that is, it could be more extensive than appeared from the register.

It was also held in *Hall* v. *Moore* [2009] EWCA Civ 201 that registered rights of common are not lost by non-exercise. Consequently, it was held, the claimant had not lost his registered grazing rights by entering into annual personal grazing licenses with the servient owner. In that case there was an additional complication, in that the servient common land was subject to multiple grazing rights which, if all fully exercised, would have exhausted the grazing land. In order to avert this, there was a long established but informal Common Committee which, acting on behalf of the commoners, had for many years entered into agreements with the freehold owners of the common land waiving the commoners' grazing rights in consideration of a triennial payment. The claimant had never approved or expressly consented to the Committee's actions, and it was held that he was not bound by the waiver agreements: on the facts, they did not have the power to waive proprietary rights of the commoners.

13.20 Appurtenance

At common law some rights of common can exist in gross (i.e. the holders of the rights need not own any land benefiting from the right). Also, some types of right that were created as appurtenant to benefited land could, until recently, be severed by the rights holder either selling the rights separately from the benefited land, or by selling one and retaining the other. The pre-1965 Act position on this, as on the circumstances in which rights of common can exist in gross generally, was considered by the House of Lords in *Bettison* v. *Langton* [2001] 2 AC 27. The House of Lords held by a majority that the (unintended) effect of s. 15 of the 1965 Act (which, as noted above, provided for all grazing rights to be quantified by reference to specific numbers of animals) was to make all appurtenant grazing rights severable in this way. This would have made it possible for any grazing right to be converted into a right in gross, making grazing rights freely tradeable independently of benefited land. However, this has been reversed by s. 9 of the Commons Act 2006 (deemed by s. 9(7) of the Act to come into force on 28 June 2005, the day after the date on which the Commons Bill was introduced into Parliament). Section 9 now prohibits any further severance of any right of common (not just grazing rights) with retrospective effect from 28 June 2005, subject to very limited exceptions set out in Sch. 1 to the 2006 Act.

PART VI COMMUNAL RECREATIONAL RIGHTS – TOWN AND VILLAGE GREENS

13.21 Nature of Town and Village Greens

The history and present nature of town or village green are considered in a number of post-1965 court decisions, most notably by Lord Denning MR in *New Windsor Corporation* v. *Mellor* [1975] 1 Ch 380, CA and by Lord Hoffmann and Lord Scott in *Oxfordshire County Council* v. *Oxford City Council* [2006] UKHL 25.[51] The statutory framework for the law since 1965 is that any land may be registered as a town or village green. The courts have now accepted that 'any land' does indeed mean just that. Specifically, the majority of the House of Lords in *Oxfordshire County Council* v. *Oxford City Council* confirmed that any land can be a town or village green: it need not be in a town or village, it need not be green or grassy, nor need it resemble in any other respect what is traditionally thought of as a village green.[52]

13.22 Application for Registration of Land as a Town or Village Green

Under what is now s. 15 of the Commons Act 2006, land is registrable as a new green if 'a significant number of the inhabitants of any locality, or of any neighbourhood within a locality have indulged in lawful sports and pastimes as of right' on the land. After a great deal of uncertainty it is now accepted that whereas 'locality' is a technical term, 'neighbourhood' is not, and that any area can be a neighbourhood provided that it has a sufficient degree of 'cohesiveness'. It is for the applicants to specify what the locality/neighbourhood is, and the choice is quite significant, because if the application is successful, all the inhabitants of the specified areas will acquire the right to use the green for 'lawful sports and pastimes'.

13.23 Nature of the Use

The applicants have to prove that they have used the land 'as of right' for 'lawful sports and pastimes'. The courts have interpreted 'lawful sports and pastimes' very

---

[51] Lord Hoffmann and Lord Scott in *Oxfordshire County Council* v. *Oxford City Council* [2006] UKHL 25 at paras. 2–28 and 37–39, and paras. 71–83 respectively.
[52] Ibid. Lord Hoffmann at paras. 37–39.

broadly, so it covers any kind of 'informal recreation' such as dog-walking and playing with children. The land in question can be registered as a green even if only part of it is physically capable of being used for lawful sports and pastime. This was accepted by the House of Lords in *Oxfordshire County Council* v. *Oxford City Council* [2006] UKHL 674, where the land registered as a green was about nine acres of derelict land lying between a canal and railway line, about one third of which was permanently under water, and the rest largely impenetrable scrub, about one quarter of which was accessible to 'the hardy walker'. Similarly, land can be registered as a green if it is only physically usable for regular short periods. So, for example, in *Newhaven Port and Properties Ltd* v. *East Sussex County Council* [2013] EWCA Civ 276 it was held in the Court of Appeal that a tidal beach was capable of registration as a green even though, because of the tides, for 48 per cent of the time none of the land was available for lawful sports and pastimes (swimming, boating and fishing were prohibited by bye-laws), half or more of it was available for no more than 30 per cent of the time, and no more than one tenth was available for more than 50 per cent of the time. There was no appeal from the decision of the Court of Appeal on this point, although the Supreme Court reversed the Court of Appeal on other grounds and held that the beach was not registrable as a town or village green, as we see below.

The lawful recreational use by the inhabitants does not have to be the only, or even the dominant, use of the land. This was amply demonstrated by the decision in *R. (on the application of Lewis)* v. *Redcar and Cleveland BC* [2010] UKSC 11, where a golf course was registered as a green following user as of right by local walkers. Both golfers and walkers used the land regularly, but the walkers 'overwhelmingly deferred' to the golfers, keeping out of the way when a golfer was about to take a shot. In other words, use by the landowner of all or part of the land for its own commercial (or indeed personal) purposes does not of itself prevent the land from being registered as a green, provided the local inhabitants have also used it as of right at the same time for a sufficiently long period. The reasoning is that during that period, if the local inhabitants have indeed been using the land as of right (i.e. as we see below, peacefully, openly and without permission from the land owner), they and the land owner must have evolved a way of sharing the use of the land co-operatively, in a spirit of 'give and take'. On this basis, it follows that the landowner may continue to use the land in the same way after registration as a green, in common with the local inhabitants continuing to use it as they have done before registration, all continuing to co-operate in a spirit of 'give and take'.[53]

13.24 User 'As of Right'

Applicants for registration of land as a town or village green have to prove that their recreational use of the land over the last 20 years had been 'as of right'. It was established by the House of Lords in *R* v. *Oxfordshire County Council, Ex*

---

[53] *TW Logistics Ltd* v. *Essex County Council* [2018] EWCA Civ 2172 Lindblom LJ at para. 107 and Lewison LJ at paras. 32 and 80.

p. Sunningwell Parish Council [2000] 1 AC 335 that this means the use has been 'nec vi, nec clam and nec precario', which is an old legal Latin formulation for prescriptive use, that is, the kind of unauthorised use of land which, in English law, gives rise to legal use rights if it continues for a sufficiently long period of time. Literally translated, 'nec vi, nec clam and nec precario' means without force, without secrecy and without permission. A use cannot be 'nec vi' if it is contentious or contested. So, for example, local recreational use cannot be 'as of right' if the landowner has made its opposition known, for instance by putting up 'keep out' notices in sufficiently prominent positions. Beyond this point, the question of when use is 'nec vi' is in itself contentious, as is the question of what amounts to 'permission' ('precario') for these purposes. In particular, the courts have had considerable difficulty in deciding precisely what is meant by use which is neither contested nor permitted by the landowner. So, for example, in *R (on the application of Beresford)* v. *Sunderland City Council* [2003] UKHL 60 the House of Lords confirmed the registration of local authority land in the centre of a new town as a town or village green. The land had originally been earmarked by the new town development corporation as 'parkland/open space/playing field' but nothing was done to dedicate the land for any particular purpose. Local inhabitants had subsequently used it for more than 20 years for ball games and other recreational activities, however, and over the years the local authority had grassed the land over, installed seating around part of the perimeter and kept the grass mowed. The House of Lords confirmed that if the local recreational use had been by implied licence of the local authority, then it could not have been as of right, and so the land could not be registered as a green. However, it held that licence or permission by the local authority could not be inferred from the actions that had taken place over the years, and therefore the recreational use was as of right, and therefore the inhabitants were entitled to have the land registered as a green.Nevertheless, both the decision and the reasoning of the House of Lords in *Beresford* have subsequently been criticised by the Supreme Court, first in *Barkas* v. *North Yorkshire County Council*[54] and then again in *R (on the application of Newhaven Port and Properties Ltd* v. *East Sussex County Council.*[55] In each of these two decisions the Supreme Court made it clear that it would have held that the recreational use in *Beresford* was not 'as of right', although for different reasons.

In *Newhaven* the Supreme Court held that user by local inhabitants is not 'as of right' if it is incompatible with the statutory purpose for which the landowner holds the land. On that basis it held that an application to register a beach owned by a private port authority as a green failed, because registration as a green might in the future interfere with the statutory purposes of the port authority which it might, in the future, want to carry on at the beach. Meanwhile, in *Barkas*, the Supreme Court had also held that user '*by* right' could not be user '*as of* right'. This means that if a local community makes recreational use of local land it cannot be registered as a town or village green if there are already public recreational rights exercisable over

---

[54] *Barkas* v. *North Yorkshire County Council* [2014] UKSC 31.
[55] *R (on the application of Newhaven Port and Properties Ltd* v. *East Sussex County Council* [2015] UKSC 7.

that particular area of land – because, so the Supreme Court thought, the local inhabitants have to be taken to be using it 'by right' of the public right, and not therefore 'as of right'.

These two decisions have threatened to make it dramatically more difficult for land to be registered as a town or village green.[56] They are also difficult to reconcile with other earlier House of Lords and Supreme Court decisions insisting that, for the purposes of registration of land as a town or village green, use of the land for recreational purposes will be as of right if the three requirements of 'nec vi, nec clam and nec precario' are satisfied *and that there are no other requirements.*[57]

13.25 Statutory Restrictions

In addition to these judicial restrictions introduced by the Supreme Court in *Newhaven* and in *Barkas*, two new statutory restrictions have been introduced by the government, alarmed at the potential disruption and delay caused to land development by applications for registration of development sites as town or village greens. The first statutory restriction, introduced by s. 15 of the Growth and Infrastructure Act 2013, allows a landowner to stop a period of 'user as of right' from running (or prevent it starting in the first place) by lodging a statutory statement with the local authority, which is then put on a public register. Since a landowner can anyway prevent user being 'as of right' by putting up 'keep out' notices, as we noted in para. 13.24, this restriction merely provides a simpler method of achieving what a landowner can otherwise do by more cumbersome means.

The second new statutory restriction, however, is likely to have a much greater impact. It is introduced by s. 16 of the Growth and Infrastructure Act 2013, and prohibits applications for registration of land as a town or village green once the land has become 'identified for potential development within the planning system', even if the local inhabitants have been using the land as of right for more than 20 years before that happens. It does this by excluding the right to apply for registration once a 'trigger event' has occurred. The right to apply only becomes exercisable again in relation to that land if and when the appropriate 'terminating event' subsequently occurs. These new provisions have been interpreted very broadly by the Court of Appeal, even more drastically cutting back the circumstances in which local people who have habitually used land for recreational purposes can have the land registered as a town or village green, however long the recreational use has continued unopposed by the landowner. The problem is that local recreational users are

---

[56] In *R. (on the application of Lancashire CC)* v. *Secretary of State for Environment, Food and Rural Affairs and Bebbington; R. (on the application of NHS Property Services Ltd) and Surrey County Council* v. *Jones* [2018] EWCA Civ 721 ('*Bebbington*') the Court of Appeal has attempted to narrow the scope of the 'statutory incompatibility' restriction introduced by the Supreme Court in *Newhaven*. However, the Supreme Court's decision on an appeal from the Court of Appeal's decision in *Bebbington* is pending.

[57] Lord Hoffmann in *R.* v. *Oxfordshire CC, Ex p. Sunningwell Parish Council* [2000] 1 AC 335 at pp. 355H–356D, and see also pp. 349–355; and *R. (on the application of Kevin Lewis)* v. *Redcar and Cleveland BC* [2010] UKSC 11 (Lord Walker at para. 20, Lord Hope at paras. 63 and 67–69, Lord Brown at para. 107 and Lord Kerr at para. 116).

unlikely to get together to safeguard their long-established recreational use unless and until it comes under threat. Generally, it will only come under threat if the local planning authority designates the land as land with potential for development, and/ or if the owner of the land decides it wants to develop the land by building on it or changing its use. It is precisely those circumstances which are specified as 'trigger events' by s. 16 of the Growth and Infrastructure Act 2013, the happening of which prohibit applications for registration of the land as a green. In *Wiltshire Council v. Cooper Estates Strategic Land Ltd* [2019] EWCA Civ 840 the Court of Appeal took the view that this was Parliament's intention in enacting s. 16, and that therefore, in order to give effect to the policy endorsed by Parliament, the 'trigger events' listed in s. 16 had to be construed broadly:

> it [is] imperative, in my judgment, to interpret [them] in accordance with the policy underlying the change in the law. That policy, as I understand it, was that whether or not to protect a piece of recreational land with identified development potential should be achieved through the planning system and not by means of registration of a TVG ... To allow a registration of a TVG within the [area identified in general terms as available for new housing in the local planning authority's development plan, in that particular case] would, in my judgment, frustrate the broad objectives of the plan. That is precisely the reason why Parliament decided that, in circumstances like the present, a TVG should not be registered; but, instead, the question of development should be left to the planning system.[58]

At present, therefore, it seems likely that, as a result of s. 16 of the 2013 Act and the restrictive Supreme Court decisions in *Newhaven* and *Barkas*, successful applications for the registration of land as a town or village green will be increasingly rare.

RECOMMENDED READING

This chapter covers several major cases which are worth reading in detail, not just because of the legal arguments but also because of the general background they provide. This is especially true of the cases on easements, rights of common and town and village greens, which all include far more than this chapter has been able to cover.

Bettison v. *Langton* [2001] UKHL 24, especially Lord Nicholls (on appurtenance, speaking specifically about rights of common, but applicable generally to all appurtenant non-possessory land use rights).
Re Ellenborough Park [1956] Ch 131, CA (rights to use a communal garden).
Mulvaney v. *Gough* [2002] 44 EG 175 (CA) (rights to use communal back yard).
Regency Villas Title Ltd v. *Diamond Resorts (Europe) Ltd* [2018] UKSC 57 (rights to use sporting and time share facilities).
Coventry v. *Lawrence* [2014] UKSC 13 (on right to cause a nuisance by noise as an easement).
Dance v. *Savery* [2011] EWCA Civ 1250 (on effect of registration of rights of common).
Oxfordshire County Council v. *Oxford City Council* [2006] UKHL 25 (town and village green rights).

---

[58] Lewison LJ in *Wiltshire Council* v. *Cooper Estates Strategic Land Ltd* [2019] EWCA Civ 840, giving the principal judgment in the Court of Appeal, at paras. 47–48.

R (on the application of Newhaven Port and Properties Ltd v. *East Sussex CC* [2015] UKSC 7. (town and village green rights).

Barkas v. *North Yorkshire CC* [2014] UKSC 31. (town and village green rights).

Wiltshire Council v. *Cooper Estates Strategic Land Ltd* [2019] EWCA Civ 840. (statutory restrictions on registration of land as a town or village green).

Questions

(1)   Why should private non-possessory land use property interests be appurtenant to ownership of neighbouring land? What functions are performed by appurtenance? Are there other ways of achieving them as or more effectively?

(2)   Explain the reasons Lord Carnwath gave for dissenting from the majority in *Regency Villas Title Ltd* v. *Diamond Resorts (Europe) Ltd* [2018] UKSC 57. Do you find his reasons convincing?

(3)   Consider how far the decision in *Regency Villas Title Ltd* v. *Diamond Resorts (Europe) Ltd* [2018] UKSC 57 has changed the law on easements. Are the changes to be welcomed?

(4)   In *Regency Villas* it was common ground that the timeshare owners whose units were in the Mansion House (see fn. 19 above) would never have had any difficulty in enforcing their rights to use the sporting and leisure facilities on the estate. Why was their situation different from that of the timeshare owners in Elham House? (you might want to come back to this question after reading Chapter 17 *Leases*).

(5)   Discuss the similarities and differences between (1) the private easements claimed in *Ellenborough Park, Mulvaney* v. *Gough* and *Regency Villas* and (2) communal rights of common and town and village green rights claimed in *Newhaven* and *Barkas* (you might find it useful to refer back to Chapter 8 *Property Interest Holders* for the discussions on the difference between individual and communal property interest holders)

(6)   Discuss the function of the register of common land and rights of common (you might want to come back to this question after reading Chapter 16 *Registration* where we consider why we have registers of land rights).

(7)   Explain why the applications for registration as a town and village green failed (a) in *Newhaven* and (b) in *Barkas*. What criticisms can be made of the Supreme Court decisions in these two cases?

(8)   Is it true that the courts and Parliament have become increasingly hostile to registration of land as a town or village green? To the extent that they have, what are the reasons?

14

Acquiring Interests Informally

PART I INTRODUCTION

14.1 Justifications for Allowing Property Interests in Land to be Acquired Informally

(a) Acquisition of Property Interests in Land by Formal Transfer and Grant

Property interests in land are usually acquired by a formal transfer or grant made by the current holder of the property interest to be transferred, or by a person with power to transfer or grant the interest. In the case of property interests in land, these deliberate formal transfers and grants nearly always have to be made using specified formalities, for example some have to be made by writing, others by deed or by a special form of signed writing etc. We outline these formalities briefly in para. 14.2. The consequences of failing to use the appropriate formalities in any transaction are often quite severe. The transaction might be void altogether, or it might fail to have the intended effect, perhaps taking in effect in equity only and not transferring or creating a legal title.

So, the law takes formal requirements seriously. As Peter Birks pointed out:

> Formal requirements oblige people to do thing in particular ways, usually ways which put them to some slight extra trouble.[1]

He suggests some reasons why this should be so:

> What does formality facilitate? What ends does it serve? . . . it is convenient to answer by reference to the best-known formality of all. Everyone knows that a last will has to be made in writing and signed before witnesses. It is no use just scribbling it on the back of an envelope or whispering it to one's best friend. There are huge advantages in this formal requirement. It helps the person making the will think hard about the job to be done. Later, it goes a long way towards eliminating doubt and argument at a juncture in human affairs at which strife is all too near the surface. All hell would break

---

[1] Peter Birks, 'Five keys to land law' in Susan Bright and John Dewar eds, *Land Law: Themes and Perspectives* (Oxford: Oxford University Press, 1998) p. 457 at p. 482, and see also Frederick Pollock and Frederick W. Maitland, 'Ownership and possession' in *The History of English Law* (first published 1895, this edition Cambridge: Cambridge University Press, 1968) Book II Ch. IV section 3 p. 85, on ancient ceremonial formalities.

out if a deceased's last will were a matter of proving by general evidence, and in the absence of the only person who could really know, what the last wishes really were. The formal will settles the matter.

It is much the same in land law. There is an extra reason too. It derives from the invisibility of real rights. Just as one cannot see a fee simple, so one cannot see an easement or a restrictive covenant … Real rights have to be made apparent through documents. Acquiring land would otherwise be a nightmare … There is an inescapable tension. Formality breeds hard cases. What of the person who did not know or was badly advised? She did the job but not in the precise way in which the law required it to be done. In such cases there is a terrific clash between two simple principles. One is that you cannot have your cake and eat it. You cannot take the advantages of formality and at the same time let off all those who do things in their own informal way. The other is that pain should not be inflicted except in cases of pressing need. It is not so easy to send someone away empty-handed who would have taken a fortune if only the right piece of paper had been used.[2]

(b) Acquisition of Property Interests in Land by Long User

As we saw in Chapter 12 *Adverse Possession of Land* and Chapter 13 *Non-Possessory Land Use Rights* paras. 13.14(b) and 13.24, property interests in land can also be acquired without formalities by one person using someone else's land without their permission for a sufficiently long period. We considered the general justifications for allowing property interests in land to be acquired in this way when we looked at the idea of a right *to* property in Chapter 4 *Property and Human Rights* para. 4.5(d).

A title to freehold ownership of land can be acquired like this, by a trespasser taking possession of someone's land through the process of adverse possession, and the trespasser's title will become an absolute title to ownership of the land if the dispossessed owner neglects to take action after a specified period of time. We looked at this, and considered why this is a feature of most property rights systems, in Chapter 12. We also considered in Chapter 13 the equivalent process of prescription, by which some non-possessory land use rights can be acquired by individuals and communities habitually using other people's land in a particular way as if entitled to do so.

(c) Acquiring Property Interests in Land through Equity

In this chapter, however, we are interested in the devices equity uses to rescue the situation where the correct formalities have not been used, and equity considers it would be unjust to deprive someone of a property interest they thought they had or could reasonably expect to have acquired. The specific devices we focus on here are proprietary estoppel, resulting trust and constructive trust. We also come back to these equitable doctrines in Chapter 15 *Enforceability and Priority of Property Interests* and in Chapter 16 *Registration* where we see how they also sometimes

---

[2] Birks, 'Five keys to land law' pp. 483–484.

modify formal rules about enforceability and priority of property interests. First, however, we need to know more about the formalities rules which are being side-stepped by adverse possession and prescription and by these equitable devices.

14.2 Formalities Which Should be Used to Transfer or Grant Property Interests in Land

There are generally three occasions in the life of a property interest in land when formal requirements must be observed. The first is when the property interest is first created, if it is created by grant of a derivative interest. The second is when a contract is made to transfer or grant the property interest at a future date. The third is when the interest is subsequently transferred from one person to another. The formalities required at these three stages are not always the same. So, for example, s. 54(2) of the Law of Property Act 1925 provides that a lease of land for a term not exceeding three years can be created orally (subject to the limitations set out in s. 54(2)) but once it has come into existence it cannot be transferred except by deed.[3] Similarly, whatever the nature of the property interest, an agreement to dispose of any interest in land[4] at a future date (whether it is an agreement to transfer an existing interest or to grant a new one) must be made in signed writing incorporating all the expressly agreed terms of the agreement, as required by s. 2 of the Law of Property (Miscellaneous Provisions) Act 1989.[5] This is more significant than might appear at first sight. Sales of freehold interests in land and also grants and sales of long leases tend to be preceded by protracted negotiations, and it is usual practice for the buyer and seller to enter into a formal contract some weeks before the transaction itself takes place. This contract will be entered into as soon as the terms of the transaction are agreed, and once that is done and the parties know that they are now committed to the transaction, they can go ahead and make the necessary practical and legal arrangements for the transaction itself to be completed. So, the parties will first enter into a contract complying with s. 2 of the 1989 Act and then some time later the transfer or grant itself will be made by deed as required by s. 52 of the 1925 Act.

The other formal rules for interests in land are as follows. The grant of a legal interest in land, and outright gifts and sales of legal interests, must be made by deed (s. 52(1) of the Law of Property Act 1925: the relatively few exceptions are listed in s. 52(2), amplified by s. 54(2)). A deed is now just any piece of signed writing that satisfies the not very stringent requirements of subsections (2) and (3) of s. 1 of the Law of Property (Miscellaneous Provisions) Act 1989. The 1989 Act simplified and rationalised the old law about deeds, implementing the recommendations of the Law Commission Report, *Deeds and Escrows*.[6] The most significant change was the abolition of the need for individuals to seal deeds. Sealing originally involved the

---

[3] *Crago* v. *Julian* [1992] 1 WLR 372, CA.
[4] Except a short lease covered by s. 54(2) of the Law of Property Act 1925.
[5] Significantly for present purposes, it is expressly stated in s. 2(5) that 'nothing in this section affects the creation or operation of resulting, implied or constructive trusts'.
[6] Law Commission Report, *Deeds and Escrows* (1987) Law Com No 163.

imprint of a real metal seal on real wax, but as far as individuals were concerned this had long degenerated into fixing an anonymous mass-produced self-adhesive red sticker on to the document. The sealing requirement was therefore removed by s. 1 of the 1989 Act for individuals. Similar provisions were made for companies by the Companies Act 1989.

In addition, transfers and grants of registrable property interests in land (legal freehold and long leasehold interests and mortgages) do not transfer or create legal titles unless and until the transaction is completed by registration. Until then they take effect in equity only, even if having been made by deed. We come back to this point in Chapter 16 *Registration*.

Declarations of trust relating to land do not have to be made in writing, but there does have to be written and signed evidence of the declaration, as required by s. 53 (1)(b) of the 1925 Act. However, signed writing is required to create any other type of equitable interest in land and also to dispose of any equitable interest, but in some cases the writing must satisfy the requirements of s. 53(1)(a) or (c) of the 1925 Act, whilst in others it must satisfy the rather different requirements of s. 2 of the Law of Property (Miscellaneous Provisions) Act 1989.[7]

As we have already said, notwithstanding failure to comply with these formal rules, a person may still be able to acquire a property interest in land through the application of doctrines of adverse possession and prescription, and also through the equitable doctrines of proprietary estoppel or resulting or constructive trusts. We see how these equitable doctrines work in the rest of this chapter.

PART II PROPRIETARY ESTOPPEL

14.3 What is Proprietary Estoppel?

English and Welsh law recognises different kinds of estoppel. Here we are interested in one kind, proprietary estoppel. Like all other kinds of estoppel, proprietary estoppel is an equitable doctrine which the courts can use to prevent someone from relying on their strict legal rights when the court considers that it would be unconscionable to allow them to do so.

Broadly, proprietary estoppel can arise whenever an owner (or other property interest holder in land or in any other thing) has led someone else (the claimant) to believe that she, the claimant, has or will have a property interest in the thing the owner owns, and the claimant has acted to her detriment in reliance on that belief. If the claimant's belief turns out to have been mistaken (she did not have the property interest she thought she had, or the owner fails to provide the property interest the claimant expected to get from him) the claimant acquires a proprietary estoppel

---

[7] This is because of the anomalous decision of the Court of Appeal in *United Bank of Kuwait* v. *Sahib* [1997] Ch 107, that transfers or grants of property interests that should have been made by deed but were not (and so the transfer/grant cannot have any legal effect) will take effect in equity *but only if there has been sufficient signed writing satisfying s. 2 of the 1989 Act.*

interest if, in the circumstances, it would be unconscionable for the owner to deny her the interest.

We need to look more closely at this broad definition in para. 14.4 below, but for the present the important point is that this kind of estoppel is in itself an equitable property interest in the land or other thing owned,[8] which the claimant acquires as soon as all those requirements are satisfied. To be more precise, it is up to the court to decide whether, on the facts, the requirements necessary to establish an estoppel have been satisfied, so the equitable property interest is not established until declared by the court. However, it is now generally accepted that the property interest then takes effect retrospectively as at the date when the necessary requirements were satisfied.[9] If the court decides that the requirements have been satisfied, and that therefore the claimant has an estoppel interest in the land, the court then has a wide discretion to decide how that estoppel interest should be satisfied. In other words, it does not necessarily follow that a claimant found to have an estoppel interest will be granted the property interest she mistakenly thought she had or would have. The court may decide that that would be inappropriate (perhaps because disproportionate to the detriment that the claimant has suffered), and it can instead make whatever other order it thinks would be equitable in the circumstances (perhaps just award damages, or order that the claimant is entitled to a property interest less extensive or different from the one she thought she had or would have). This gives the court a quite remarkable flexibility, which we look at more closely in para. 14.5.

14.4 Requirements for Establishing Estoppel

As we noted above, the essential elements of proprietary estoppel are that an owner (or other property interest holder in land or in any other thing) must have made some kind of assurance which led someone else (the claimant) to believe that she, the claimant, has or will have a property interest in the thing the owner owns, and the claimant has acted to her detriment in reliance on that belief. If the claimant's belief turns out to have been mistaken (she did not have the property interest she thought she had, or she fails to get the property interest she expected) the claimant acquires a proprietary estoppel interest if, in the circumstances, it would be unconscionable for the owner to deny her the interest.

We look at each of these elements separately in this paragraph, but we should be aware of the warning frequently given by the courts, that the situation needs to be viewed in the round. As Walker LJ said in *Gillett* v. *Holt*:[10]

> . . . it is important to note at the outset that the doctrine of proprietary estoppel cannot be treated as subdivided into three or four watertight compartments . . . the quality of the relevant assurances may influence the issue of reliance, . . . reliance and detriment are often intertwined, and . . . whether there is a distinct need for a 'mutual understanding' may depend on how the other elements are formulated and understood.

---

[8] In the framework of property interests in land we outlined in Part VI of Chapter 5 *Ownership and Other Property Interests*, proprietary estoppel comes under the heading of 'equities' in para. 5.39.
[9] We come back to this point in para. 14.6 below.   [10] *Gillett* v. *Holt* [2001] Ch 210 at pp. 225C–E.

Moreover the fundamental principle that equity is concerned to prevent unconscionable conduct permeates all the elements of the doctrine. In the end the court must look at the matter in the round.

(a) Assurance

The person to be estopped must have given – or be reasonably understood to have given – an assurance that was sufficiently clear, and it must have been that the claimant has or would have a proprietary interest in specified property. However, the assurance need not have been expressly stated. In *Thorner* v. *Majors* [2009] UKHL 18, a farmer, David, had worked for more than 30 years without pay on the farm owned by Peter, his father's cousin, and for about the last 15 years Peter encouraged David to believe that he would inherit the farm. However, Peter then died without leaving a will and David brought this action claiming that Peter's estate was estopped from denying that he had acquired the beneficial interest in the farm. It was accepted that Peter never expressly said to David that he was leaving him the farm, but it was 'a matter of implication and inference from indirect statements and conduct'. The trial judge found as a fact that these words and acts were reasonably understood by David as an assurance that was intended to be taken seriously and that could be relied on. It was held that that was sufficient. It was irrelevant whether Peter intended them to be so understood, or knew or foresaw that David would rely on them: what mattered was how they were reasonably understood by David.[11]

(b) Detrimental Reliance

In *Gillett* v. *Holt*,[12] Walker LJ confirmed that the claimant must have suffered some detriment in reliance on the assurance:

> the overwhelming weight of authority shows that detriment is required. But the authorities also show that it is not a narrow or technical concept. The detriment need not consist of the expenditure of money or other quantifiable financial detriment, so long as it is something substantial. The requirement must be approached as part of a broad inquiry as to whether repudiation of an assurance is or is not unconscionable in all the circumstances.
>
> ... Whether the detriment is sufficiently substantial is to be tested by whether it would be unjust or inequitable to allow the assurance to be disregarded – that is, again, the essential test of unconscionability.

This does not mean that the claimant should have received no benefit from acting in reliance on the assurance: it can be enough that he has foregone the opportunity to pursue a different way of life, as was claimed in *Henry* v. *Henry*[13] or 'deprived himself of the opportunity to better himself in other ways'.[14] *Henry* v. *Henry* concerned a man, Calixtus Henry, who had lived and worked on a plot of land for

---

[11] Lord Hoffmann in *Thorner* v. *Majors* [2009] UKHL 18 at paras. 3–5.
[12] *Gillett* v. *Holt*, fn. 10 above, at pp. 232A–F.   [13] *Henry* v. *Henry* [2010] UKPC 3.
[14] Walker LJ in *Gillett* v. *Holt*, fn. 10 above, at pp. 235B.

many years, latterly with his partner and their now adult children. The plot was half owned by an elderly relative, Geraldine Pierre, and it was accepted that Henry stayed on the land and cultivated it in reliance on an assurance by her that she would leave her share in the land to him if he looked after her until she died and cultivated the plot. In fact she sold her share in the plot to someone else just before she died aged 95. The trial judge had held that Henry's proprietary estoppel claim failed because he had not established that he suffered detriment through his reliance on her promise, because of the benefits he had received from living there. However, the Privy Council said that any benefit that has accrued has to be balanced against any detriment:

> [the trial judge had said that] Calixtus Henry could not say that he had acted to his detriment and that, far from having suffered detriment because of his reliance on the deceased's promises, he positively benefited. But he did not attempt to weigh the disadvantages suffered by Calixtus Henry by reason of his reliance on Geraldine Pierre's promises against the countervailing advantages which he enjoyed as a consequence of that reliance ... Instead ... the judge merely listed three advantages which he considered that Calixtus Henry had enjoyed in consequence of his reliance on Geraldine Pierre's promises: viz. the fact that he had lived rent-free on the plot, the fact that the plot was the source of his livelihood in large measure, and the fact that he had reaped the produce of the plot and was able to sell any surplus and retain all the proceeds of such sales. The judge made no reference to the evidence [of the disadvantages Henry had suffered by relying on Pierre's assurance] ... he should have weighed any disadvantages which Calixtus Henry had suffered by reason of his reliance on Geraldine Pierre's promises against any countervailing advantages which he had enjoyed by reason of that reliance. Had he done so, he would have brought into account on, as it were, the debit side of the account the evidence [that Henry had kept Geraldine Pierre supplied with produce from the plot and that he had cared for her and] ... the fact that other members of the family had not responded to Geraldine's offer of 'an opportunity to possess land on the mountain ... if they would work the land and care for her in her own country' ... but instead had moved to St Croix where they were able to live more comfortably.[15]

The Privy Council reversed the judge's decision and held that Henry had an equity by estoppel as against Pierre, which was a property interest binding on the purchaser of her half share because Henry had been in actual occupation of the land.[16] The Privy Council also held that Henry's equity should be satisfied by awarding him one half of Pierre's half share in the beneficial ownership of the land.

(c) Unconscionability

There is some disagreement over whether there is a separate requirement of unconscionability, or whether it is simply that the court must find that overall it would be unconscionable for the claimant not to have a remedy. In *Henry* v. *Henry* [2010]

---

[15] *Henry* v. *Henry*, fn. 13 above, para. 53.

[16] Under the land registration system in operation in St Lucia, his actual occupation of the land made his estoppel interest in the land an 'overriding interest', enforceable against purchasers of the land, just as it would under our land registration system: see further Chapter 16 *Registration* paras. 16.25-16.27.

UKPC 3 Sir Jonathan Parker referred to *Cobbe v. Yeoman's Row Management Ltd* [2008] 1 WLR 1752 where Lord Walker said:[17]

> 92. [Counsel for the defendant argued] that even if the elements for an estoppel were in other respects present, it would not in any event be unconscionable for [the defendant] to insist on her legal rights. That argument raises the question whether 'unconscionability' is a separate element in making out a case of estoppel, or whether to regard it as a separate element would be what Professor Peter Birks once called 'a fifth wheel on the coach' . . . But Birks was there criticising the use of 'unconscionable' to describe a state of mind . . . Here it is being used (as in my opinion it should always be used) as an objective value judgment on behaviour (regardless of the state of mind of the individual in question). As such it does in my opinion play a very important part in the doctrine of equitable estoppel, in unifying and confirming, as it were, the other elements. If the other elements appear to be present but the result does not shock the conscience of the court, the analysis needs to be looked at again.

14.5 Satisfying the Estoppel Interest: The Scope of the Courts' Discretion

As already noted, the courts have a more or less unfettered discretion to make whatever award to the claimant that they consider appropriate to prevent unconscionability. As in all other areas of judicial discretion, it must be exercised in a principled way. Unfortunately, however, there is some disagreement as to what the relevant principles are here. Specifically, it is not clear whether the court's objective in deciding what remedy to award should be to fulfil the claimant's expectations or to compensate her for the detriment she has suffered. In *Davies v. Davies* [2016] EWCA Civ 463 Lewison LJ's commented as follows, giving a useful summary of the arguments ranged on either side:

> There is a lively controversy about the essential aim of the exercise of this broad judgmental discretion. One line of authority takes the view that the essential aim of the discretion is to give effect to the claimant's expectation unless it would be disproportionate to do so. The other takes the view that the essential aim of the discretion is to ensure that the claimant's reliance interest is protected, so that she is compensated for such detriment as she has suffered. The two approaches, in their starkest form, are fundamentally different: see *Cobbe* v. *Yeoman's Row Management Ltd* [2006] EWCA Civ 1139 at [120] . . . Much scholarly opinion favours the second approach: see Snell's Equity (33rd ed) para. 12-048; Wilken and Ghaly Waiver Variation and Estoppel (3rd ed) para. 11.94; McFarlane The Law of Proprietary Estoppel para. 7.37; McFarlane and Sales: 'Promises, detriment, and liability: lessons from proprietary estoppel' (2015) LQR 610. Others argue that the outcome will reflect both the expectation and the reliance interest and that it will normally be somewhere between the two: Gardner: 'The remedial discretion in proprietary estoppel – again' [2006] LQR 492. Logically, there is much to be said for the second approach. Since the essence of proprietary estoppel is the combination of expectation and detriment, if either is absent the claim must fail. If, therefore, the detriment can be fairly quantified and a claimant receives

---

[17] *Cobbe v. Yeoman's Row Management Ltd* [2008] 1 WLR 1752 at para. 92.

full compensation for that detriment, that compensation ought, in principle, to remove the foundation of the claim: Robertson: 'The reliance basis of proprietary estoppel remedies' [2008] Conv 295. Fortunately, I do not think that we are required to resolve this controversy on this appeal.[18]

This was quoted by Henderson LJ giving the principal judgment in *Moore* v. *Moore* [2018] EWCA Civ 2669, saying that he found the second approach – that the essential aim of the discretion is to ensure that the claimant's reliance interest is protected, so that she is compensated for such detriment as she has suffered – logically attractive. However, he did say that 'I would be wary of according it primacy in a field where cases are so fact sensitive and proportionality has such a prominent role to play.'[19]

14.6 Nature and Enforceability Against Third Parties

As already noted, a proprietary estoppel interest is a property interest and the property interest is necessarily equitable – specifically, it is categorisable as an 'equity'[20] – because it arises through the operation of an equitable doctrine, the doctrine of estoppel. As we saw in para. 14.5, the property interest arises automatic- ally out of the estoppel, but until it has been declared by a court it is an inchoate interest.[21] In other words, the property interest is not crystallised until a court has decided that all the requirements were satisfied (necessarily, satisfied at some point in the past), but the interest then takes effect retrospectively as from the date when all the necessary requirements were in fact satisfied. To make matters even more complicated, as soon as the property interest is crystallised by the court declaring that it has been established, the interest is then immediately extinguished by the court making whatever order it considers appropriate for satisfying the estoppel: the claimant will then get instead either the property interest she expected to get, or some other property interest, or a money award.

The issue is then whether this inchoate property interest is enforceable against third parties before it is crystallised by the court. The Privy Council held that it is, as a matter of general law, in *Henry* v. *Henry*,[22] and this was confirmed 'for the avoidance of doubt' by s. 116 of the Land Registration Act 2002, at least as far as registered land is concerned:

116 It is hereby declared for the avoidance of doubt that, in relation to registered land . . . an equity by estoppel . . . has effect from the time the equity arises as an

---

[18] Lewison LJ in *Davies* v. *Davies* [2016] EWCA Civ 463 at para 32.

[19] Henderson LJ in *Moore* v. *Moore* [2018] EWCA Civ 2669 at para. 26. He went on to adopt the guidance provided by Robert Walker LJ in *Jennings* v. *Rice* [2002] EWCA Civ 169, as to the distinction between 'near-contract' cases and cases where 'the claimant's expectations are uncertain, or where the high level of the claimant's expectations is incommensurate with the assurances which have been given. In such cases, the claimant's expectations may still be taken as a starting point, but no more.'

[20] See Chapter 5 *Ownership and Other Property Interests* para. 5.39.

[21] *Griffiths* v. *Williams* [1978] 2 EGLR 121 at p. 122.   [22] *Henry* v. *Henry*, fn. 13 above.

interest capable of binding successors in title (subject to [the enforceability and priority rules in the LRA 2002]).

However, this does not completely answer all our questions. It seems reasonably clear from the wording quoted, that once the equity by estoppel 'arises', it is a property interest and its enforceability and priority are governed only by the LRA 2002 rules which we look at in Chapter 16 *Registration*,[23] and this is confirmed by the decision in *Halifax plc* v. *Curry Popeck* [2008] EWHC 1692. However, it does not tell us when the equity arises. In its consultative paper which led to the recommendations which were ultimately enacted in the Land Registration Act 2002, the Law Commission and Land Registry said:[24]

> It has not been definitively settled when an equity arises. At the very latest it will be when the circumstances make it unconscionable for the land owner, A, to go back on the expectation which he has created by representation or conduct: *Lim* v. *Ang* [1992] 1 WLR 113, 118. In most cases that will be when the other party, B, has acted to his detriment in reliance upon the expectation. That moment will not always be easy to define.

Once the equity has arisen, again it is not clear whether it is automatically enforceable against third parties in the same way as any other equitable interest is enforceable against them. A possible alternative is that there are special enforceability rules which mean that third parties will not be bound by the estoppel interest unless it would be unconscionable for them to take free from it. This was argued persuasively by Gray and Gray:

> Of course, the mere fact that, in one or other way, an inchoate equity survives a registered disposition is not, in itself, determinative of its actual impact on the disponee of the registered title. The newly recognised status of the inchoate equity certainly marks an important acknowledgment that third parties are not immune from the requirements of conscionable dealing: the mandate of conscience is no respecter of persons. But the binding effect of the inchoate equity simply means that third parties must discharge the burden of showing that their proposed assertion of strict legal entitlement is not, in its own turn, unconscionable. The call of conscience requires to be measured de novo in the light of the circumstances in which each disponee takes title. The ultimate effect of the inchoate equity is tailored specifically, in the discretion of the court, to the particular disponee whom it is sought to affect. The mere fact that an equity of estoppel might command a particular remedial outcome as against one estate owner in no way precludes the possibility that another estate owner remains free, without injury to conscience, to enforce his strict legal rights or to proffer only some limited money compensation as the precondition for doing so. The question of

---

[23] Specifically, it will be enforceable, even against a purchaser for valuable consideration who becomes registered proprietor if the claimant either protected it by entering a notice on the register, or was in actual occupation of the land in question and the other conditions required by Sch. 3 para. 2 of the LRA 2002 are satisfied: see Chapter 16 *Registration*.

[24] Law Commission and HM Land Registry, *Land Registration For The Twenty-First Century: A Consultative Document* (1998) Law Com No 254, n. 98 to para. 3.36.

overriding conscientious obligation arises afresh on each occasion and may well admit of divergent responses on different occasions.[25]

This argument was put in *Henry* v. *Henry*, where it was argued on behalf of the purchaser that 'the test of unconscionability must be considered afresh in relation to the position of [the purchaser]'.[26] The argument was rejected in the Privy Council on technical grounds (it had not been pleaded or raised in the lower courts) but the Privy Council was not prepared to reject the substance of the argument. Sir Jonathan Parker left it that 'the Privy Council does not rule out the possibility that cases may arise in which the particular circumstances surrounding a third party purchase may, notwithstanding the claimant's overriding interest, require the court to reassess the extent of the claimant's equity in the property'.[27]

PART III RESULTING AND CONSTRUCTIVE TRUSTS

14.7 Resulting and Constructive Trusts

Sometimes the courts will decide that the holder of a legal property interest is not entitled also to the equivalent equitable interest, but must instead hold the legal interest on trust, either entirely for the benefit of others, or partly for the benefit of others and partly for her own benefit. There are two mechanisms it can use to achieve this result. One is to find that the holder of the legal interest holds it on a *resulting trust*. The other is to find that the legal interest holder holds it on a *constructive trust*.

(a) Resulting Trust

In the classic analysis, a resulting trust arises where the claimant has contributed towards the acquisition costs of property acquired in the name of someone else. When that happens, on the classic analysis, there is a presumption that the legal title holder holds the title on trust for the claimant, in shares proportionate to the claimant's contribution. That presumption is then rebuttable by evidence that that contribution was intended to be a gift or loan to the legal title holder.[28]

(b) Constructive Trust

By way of contrast, there are a number of different circumstances in which the courts might impose a constructive trust on a legal title holder: the broad principle is that they will impose a constructive trust whenever it appears to the court that it is

---

[25] Kevin Gray and Susan Francis Gray, *Elements of Land Law* (5th edn, London: Butterworths, 2009) para. 9.2.93.
[26] *Henry* v. *Henry*, fn. 13 above, para. 46.   [27] Ibid. para. 56.
[28] Although see now *Gany Holdings (PTC) SA* v. *Khan* [2018] UKPC 21 paras. 16–22: 'In reality the so-called presumption of resulting trust is no more than a long stop to provide the answer when the relevant facts and circumstances fail to yield a solution.'

fair to do so, but in practice they do so only in specific kinds of situation. The situation we are particularly interested in here is where the legal title holder and the claimant have a common intention that the claimant should have a share in the beneficial interest, and the claimant acts in reliance on that common intention. This may or may not include making a financial contribution towards the acquisition costs of the property. This kind of a constructive trust is commonly referred to as a *common intention constructive trust.*

(c) Why the Distinction Between Resulting Trust and Constructive Trust Matters

It matters whether the court treats the situation as one that gives rise to a resulting trust or one that gives rise to a common intention constructive trust because the size of share awarded to the claimant is likely to be different. As already noted, if the court decides to impose a resulting trust in favour of a claimant, the automatic consequence is that the claimant will have a share in the beneficial interest proportionate to her contribution. So, if the claimant provided the whole of the costs of the acquisition, the legal title holder will hold on trust wholly for the claimant – that is, the claimant gets the whole of the beneficial interest. If, on the other hand, the claimant provided two thirds of the acquisition costs, with the legal title holder providing the rest, the legal title holder holds on trust for the claimant and herself, with the claimant getting two-thirds of the beneficial interest and the legal title holder getting one-third.

However, if the court decides to impose a common intention constructive trust (or indeed any other kind of constructive trust) on the legal title holder, the court has a discretion as to the size of the share to be awarded to the claimant – broadly, the claimant will get the share that the court considers to be fair in the circumstances, although as we see later a more precise formulation is likely to be used in the case of a common intention constructive trust.[29] This requires the court to take into account all relevant factors, not just who paid what towards the acquisition of the property.

Unfortunately, there has, and continues to be, considerable uncertainty over the relationship between the common intention constructive trust and the resulting trust. At one point this was thought to have been settled by the Supreme Court in *Jones* v. *Kernott* [2011] UKSC 53. In *Jones* v. *Kernott* the Supreme Court confirmed that the common intention constructive trust principles we look at in paras. 14.8 and 14.9 below, which were established by the House of Lords in *Stack* v. *Dowden* [2007] UKHL 17 and clarified in *Jones* v. *Kernott* apply only in situations concerning married or unmarried couples (and others in domestic relationships: see further below) who acquire a house or flat for their joint occupation for domestic rather than business purposes.[30]

---

[29] Hilary Blehler, 'The scope of common intention constructive trusts: where to draw the line?' (2018) *Trusts Law International* 63.

[30] *Jones* v. *Kernott* [2011] UKSC 53 at paras. 10, 19, 25 and 51 in the joint judgment of Lord Walker and Lady Hale, all the other five Justices agreeing on this point, approving and clarifying what was said in *Stack* v. *Dowden* [2007] UKHL 17.

(d) The *Stack* v. *Dowden* and *Jones* v. *Kernott* analysis

In such domestic situations the position, as confirmed in *Jones* v. *Kernott*, was as follows. The basic presumption was that equity follows the law so that, if the legal title to the property was in the sole name of one of the parties, the initial presumption was that that party would also hold the entire beneficial interest, whereas if they held the legal title jointly, they would also be jointly entitled to the beneficial interest (unless in either case there was an express declaration of trust to the contrary). That presumption could, however, be rebutted by evidence that the parties had a common intention (relied on by the claimant) that the beneficial interests should be held differently. If that was established, the claimant's share was to be calculated in accordance with the principles considered in the following paragraphs. On the other hand, outside such domestic situations, so it was said, the basic presumption was one of resulting trust, i.e. a party contributing to the acquisition of property in the name of another was rebuttably presumed to be entitled to a share in the beneficial interest proportionate to her share. In these circumstances this initial presumption of resulting trust could then be rebutted by (amongst other things) evidence that the parties had a common intention that the shares in the beneficial interest would be different.

This reasoning was followed in *Agarwala* v. *Agarwala* [2013] EWCA Civ 1763, where a bed and breakfast hotel was bought in the name of one member of a family. It was claimed by her brother in law that she had bought it pursuant to an oral agreement between them that he would run the business there and she would hold the title to the land on bare trust for him. She agreed that there had been a prior oral agreement between them but asserted that the agreement was that she would be the absolute legal and beneficial owner of the property. The Court of Appeal said that the trial judge was right to approach it as a case where there was a presumption that the equitable interest followed the legal title, but that the brother in law could rebut that presumption by demonstrating that they shared a common intention that he should have the entire beneficial interest. The court went on to confirm that a constructive trust would be imposed on her to give effect to that common intention if he could demonstrate that he had acted to his detriment in reliance on it. The Court of Appeal dismissed the sister in law's appeal from the judge's finding that the brother in law had succeeded in doing all this and that therefore she held the property on bare trust for him.

The same approach was adopted in *Laskar* v. *Laskar* [2008] EWCA Civ 347, decided after *Stack* v. *Dowden* [2007] UKHL 17 but before *Jones* v. *Kernott* [2011] UKSC 53. The issue in *Laskar* v. *Laskar* was over the beneficial interests held by mother and daughter in the former council house where the family had lived for many years and which had been bought in the joint names of mother and daughter under the statutory 'right to buy' and then let out. Neuberger LJ (who had dissented in *Stack* v. *Dowden* but subsequently returned to sit in the Court of Appeal) said:[31]

---

[31] *Laskar* v. *Laskar* [2008] EWCA Civ 347 at paras. 17–18.

In this case, the primary purpose of the purchase of the property was as an investment, not as a home. In other words this was a purchase which, at least primarily, was not in 'the domestic consumer context' but in a commercial context. To my mind it would not be right to apply the reasoning in *Stack* v. *Dowden* to such a case as this, where the parties primarily purchased the property as an investment for rental income and capital appreciation, even where their relationship is a familial one.

Consequently, he applied a resulting trust analysis which meant that the parties' respective shares should reflect the size of their contributions to the price (Rimer and Tuckey LJJ agreed).[32]

(e) Collapse of the Distinction?

However, any appearance of certainty about when to apply resulting trust principles and when to apply the very different principles of common intention constructive trust, has been dispelled by the Privy Council decision in *Marr* v. *Collie* [2017] UKPC 17. In *Marr* v. *Collie* it was held that in all cases, whether domestic or not, the starting point is the common intention of the parties. In that case over the period of their 17 year relationship a gay couple had bought several properties in the Bahamas in their joint names for investment purposes, and one in the sole name of the appellant, Mr Marr, apparently to enhance his claim to be entitled to permanent residency. In all these cases most of the purchase money was provided by Mr Marr. The first instance judge in the Bahamas essentially adopted the approach thought to have been confirmed by *Jones* v. *Kernott*: he found that, since all of the properties had been bought for non-domestic purposes, resulting trust principles applied and Mr Marr was entitled to the entire beneficial interest in all the properties. The decision was reversed in relation to the jointly held properties by the Bahamas Court of Appeal but only on the basis that Mr Collie had produced sufficient evidence of a common intention to rebut the presumption of resulting trust. The Privy Council, however, adopted a different approach, and remitted the case for re-hearing in order to determine 'the intention of the parties at the time of the purchase ... and in the course of dealings with those properties'.[33] Lord Kerr, delivering the decision of the Privy Council, reviewed the authorities and concluded that there was no difference in the initial presumptions to be applied in domestic and non-domestic cases 'save perhaps where there is no evidence from which the parties' intentions can be identified'.[34] The starting point in all situations, he said, is the intentions of the parties:

A clash of presumptions?

53. If what Lady Hale described [in *Stack* v. *Dowden*] as a 'starting point' (that joint legal ownership should signify joint beneficial ownership) is to be regarded as a presumption, is it in conflict with the presumption of a resulting trust where the parties have contributed unequally to the purchase of property in their joint names?

---

[32] See also *Erlam* v. *Rahman* [2016] EWHC 111 (Ch) and *Kali* v. *Chawla* [2007] EWHC 2357 (Ch), adopting the same approach.
[33] *Marr* v. *Collie* [2017] UKPC 17 at para. 61.   [34] Ibid. para. 54.

A simplistic answer to that question might be that, if the property is purchased in joint names by parties in a domestic relationship the presumption of joint beneficial ownership applies but if bought in a wholly non-domestic situation it does not. In the latter case, it might be said that the resulting trust presumption obtains.

54. The Board considers that, *save perhaps where there is no evidence from which the parties' intentions can be identified, the answer is not to be provided by the triumph of one presumption over another. In this, as in so many areas of law, context counts for, if not everything, a lot. Context here is set by the parties' common intention – or by the lack of it.* If it is the unambiguous mutual wish of the parties, contributing in unequal shares to the purchase of property, that the joint beneficial ownership should reflect their joint legal ownership, then effect should be given to that wish. If, on the other hand, that is not their wish, or if they have not formed any intention as to beneficial ownership but had, for instance, accepted advice that the property be acquired in joint names, without considering or being aware of the possible consequences of that, the resulting trust solution may provide the answer.[35]

(f) Legal Title in Single or Joint Names?

Although Lord Kerr in *Marr* v. *Collie* was dealing with a case where the properties were held in the joint names of the claimant and the defendant, there seems no reason in principle or in practice why the same should not also apply to cases where the legal title is in the name of the defendant only. Certainly, Lord Kerr suggested no such distinction himself. Nevertheless, some academic commentators take the view that the analysis in *Stack* v. *Dowden* and *Jones* v. *Kennott* applies only where the legal title to the property is in the joint names of the claimant and the defendant. On this view, in 'single-name' cases (in other words, where the defendant is sole holder of the legal title) the claimant can rely only on the resulting trust principles taken to have been established by the House of Lords in *Lloyds Bank* v. *Rosset* [1991] 1 AC 107.[36] However, it was explicitly stated in *Jones* v. *Kernott* that common intention constructive trust principles apply equally whether the property is in the single name of one of the couple or in their joint names, in other words that the initial presumptions arising out of the way in which the legal title is held are always rebuttable by evidence of a common intention to the contrary.[37]

It is also worth noting that in *Stack* v. *Dowden* Lord Walker doubted whether the relevant remarks of Lord Bridge in *Lloyds Bank* v. *Rosset* 'took full account' of earlier judicial pronouncements in the House of Lords, adding that, in any event, even if

---

[35] See also Lord Briggs in *Gany Holdings (PTC) SA* v. *Khan* [2018] UKPC 21 at paras. 17–18, saying much the same thing in relation to a transfer of shares.

[36] See, for example, Ben McFarlane, Nicholas Hopkins and Sarah Nield *Land Law: Text, Cases and Materials* (4th edn, Oxford: Oxford University Press, 2015) pp. 460–461, and Martin George and Antonia Layard (eds) *Thompson's Modern Land Law* (7th edn, Oxford: Oxford University Press, 2019) p. 274.

[37] *Jones* v. *Kernott* [2011] UKSC 53 at para. 52, confirming the post-*Stack* v. *Dowden* Privy Council decision in *Abbott* v. *Abbott* [2007] UKPC 53 (Lady Hale delivering the judgment of the Privy Council, on appeal from the Eastern Caribbean Court of Appeal, restoring the trial judge's finding that a former husband held the matrimonial home on trust for himself and his wife in equal shares).

what Lord Bridge had said 'was justified in 1990 ... in my opinion, the law has moved on, and your Lordships should move it a little more in the same direction'.[38] Also, there is little if any evidence that the courts do now in fact make a distinction between joint name and single name cases when deciding whether a claimant is entitled to a beneficial interest in a residential or commercial property under a resulting or constructive trust. *Lloyds Bank* v. *Rosset* is rarely mentioned in any of the very many constructive/resulting trust cases decided since *Jones* v. *Kernott*. So, it is difficult to see any good reason for thinking that single name cases are treated in law differently from joint name cases, and even less reason why they should be.

(g) Other situations

In any event, it is clearly established that the *Stack* v. *Dowden*/*Jones* v.*Kernott* common intention constructive trust principles apply where the property is held in joint names, but the claimant is not one of the joint title-holders.[39] Also, there can be no doubt that they also apply to property which the couple did not originally acquire for joint domestic purposes, but which they later decided should be used for such purposes. However, in such cases it is for the claimant to prove that, at that later stage, they did in fact change their original intentions and instead formed an actual shared intention that the claimant was to have a share in the beneficial interest in the asset.[40]

It is similarly clear that in all the cases no distinction is to be drawn between married and unmarried couples and others living together in family or shared home relationships.[41]

14.8 The Common Intention Constructive Trust

Leaving aside for the present the overlap between common intention constructive trusts and resulting trusts, it is established that whether or not an interest will arise under a common intention constructive trust depends on the intentions of the parties. The difficulty lies in ascertaining those intentions. The difficulty arises in its most acute form in relation to family homes occupied by unmarried couples, or other family members or house sharers, and in these cases the modern principles can now be taken to be as laid down in the House of Lords decision in *Stack* v. *Dowden* [2007] UKHL 17 and the Supreme Court decision in *Jones* v. *Kernott* [2011] UKSC 53. It should be appreciated that these principles also have a wider application, and in particular they can arise in commercial contexts.[42] Here, however, we focus on the principles as they apply to family and quasi-family property.

---

[38] Lord Walker in the majority in *Stack* v. *Dowden* [2007] UKHL 17 at para. 26.

[39] *Amin* v. *Amin* [2009] EWHC 3356 (Ch).   [40] *Geary* v. *Rankine* [2012] EWCA Civ 555.

[41] See, for example, *Gallarotti* v. *Sebastianelli* [2012] EWCA Civ 865 (incidentally, also a 'single name' case) where it was held that the *Stack* v. *Dowden* common intention constructive trust principles were appropriate for assessing the beneficial interests of two close friends (described by Arden LJ at para. 26 as 'not in a family unit' and living together 'for convenience ... until they established their own homes') who had bought a flat in the name of one of them.

[42] *Crossco No.4 Unltd* v. *Jolan Ltd* [2011] EWCA Civ 1619, confirming that the so-called *Pallant* v. *Morgan* equity is properly analysed as a common intention constructive trust.

Ascertaining the parties intention is important because is dictates not only whether or not the common intention constructive trust arises at all, but if it arises, the size of the claimant's share in the beneficial interest.[43]

14.9 Establishing Intention in a Common Intention Constructive Trust

It had been established in earlier House of Lords decisions that the courts must ascertain the actual intentions of the parties, not an 'intention' to be imputed to them. However, the courts have subsequently had difficulty in drawing the line between inferring and imputing intention, and it is now confirmed by the majority in *Stack* v. *Dowden* [2007] UKHL 17 and unanimously by the Supreme Court in *Jones* v. *Kernott* [2011] UKSC 53 that in some circumstances common intention may be imputed.

The precise circumstances in which common intention can be imputed are considered below, but broadly the position is this. First, in determining whether the parties had a common intention that the claimant should have a share at all or, if the legal title is in their joint names, that the beneficial interest should not be shared jointly, the court must first seek 'to ascertain the parties' actual shared intention, whether express or to be inferred from their conduct'.[44]

(a) Ascertaining Actual Intentions

Ascertaining actual shared intention is not necessarily easy. In *Eves* v. *Eves* [1975] 1 WLR 1338 CA and *Grant* v. *Edwards* [1986] Ch 638 CA it had been accepted that an actual shared intention that the claimant should have a share in the beneficial interest might be inferred from an excuse made by the legal title holder as to why the property had not been vested wholly or jointly in the claimant's name. These decisions were confirmed but distinguished in *Curran* v. *Collins* [2015] EWCA Civ 404, where the excuse given was that it would be too expensive for the claimant to be put on the title. Lewison LJ said (Davis LJ agreeing):

> 69 . . . it cannot be right that the giving of a reason why someone is not on the title deeds inevitably leads to the inference that it must have been agreed that they would have an interest in the property. If one who is not versed in the difference between legal and beneficial ownership asks to be on the deeds and is told 'No', the more usual inference would be that they would have understood that they were not to become owners or part owners of the property. I cannot see that the result is very different if the reason given is that it is too expensive. There are, however, two cases in which a specious excuse has been held to give rise to the inference of a constructive trust. However, these cases are fact-sensitive and need to be carefully examined.

> 70 In *Eves* v. *Eves* [1975] 1 WLR 1338 Janet and Stuart Eves were already cohabiting and had a daughter together. They were looking for a family home. It was in that context that Stuart Eves made the representation:

[43] Confirmed by the Supreme Court in *Jones* v. *Kernott* [2011] UKSC 53.
[44] Ibid. at para. 31, and also paras. 47 and 51(3).

'He told her that it was to be their house and a home for themselves and their children. He said that, as she was under 21, it could not be in joint names and had to be in his name alone; and that, but for her age, it would have been purchased in joint names. She accepted his explanation: but he admitted in the witness-box that it was simply an "excuse". He all along was determined that it was to be in his name alone.'

71 There are two important parts to this representation, neither of which is present in our case. First, Stuart Eves told Janet Eves that the house was to be a home for both of them and their children. In our case Ms Curran had no intention of moving into the Feltham house at the time it was acquired. Second, Stuart Eves told Janet Eves that the house would have been bought in both names but for her age. It is that positive assertion that it would have been bought in joint names that was capable of giving rise to an expectation that Janet Eves would acquire an interest in the house. In our case nothing of the sort was said to Ms Curran. She was simply told that she could not be on the deeds because it was too expensive.

72 The second case is *Grant* v. *Edwards* [1986] Ch. 638. Once again the parties were living together at the time of the purchase, and had had a child together. The exact representation that was made to Mrs Grant is not set out verbatim, but Browne-Wilkinson V-C described it thus:
'... the representation made by the defendant to the plaintiff [was] that the house would have been in the joint names but for the plaintiff's matrimonial disputes ...'.

73 Again there are two factors present in that case which are absent from ours. First, in that case (but not in ours) the house being acquired was acquired as a family home. Second, in that case (but not in ours) there was a positive representation that Mrs Grant would have been a joint owner but for her matrimonial dispute.

74 These cases do not establish the proposition that the mere giving of a 'specious excuse' necessarily or even usually leads to an inference that the person to whom the excuse is given can reasonably regard herself as having an immediate entitlement to an interest in the property in question.

The Court of Appeal according held that the trial judge was not wrong to conclude that there was no evidence of actual common intention that the claimant should have an interest, and dismissed her appeal against the finding that she had no beneficial interest.

However, if the parties' actual intentions as to beneficial ownership can be discovered, whether by direct evidence or by inference, it is not open to the court to impose a solution on them which contradicts those intentions, even if their intentions lead to an unfair result.[45]

If the claimant fails to establish an actual shared intention, express or inferred from conduct, to displace the initial presumptions (of sole beneficial ownership in sole name cases, or joint beneficial ownership in joint name cases), then the presumptions stand. This approach was endorsed by the Court of Appeal in *Thompson* v. *Hurst* [2012] EWCA Civ 1752, which we come back to below. In this case a couple had intended to buy the freehold title in their house in their joint names, and had only had it put instead into the woman's sole name when their

---

[45] Ibid. at para. 46.

mortgage advisor pointed out that it would be difficult for them to obtain mortgage finance if they bought in joint names (the man was then out of work). When the man subsequently claimed a share in the beneficial interest, it was argued on his behalf that the proper inference to be drawn from these facts was that the couple had a common intention that the couple should be beneficial joint tenants. In principle, it was argued, if parties intend to purchase a property in joint names for their occupation as a couple, but fail to do so only as a result of a 'random intervening event', then the court ought to proceed on the basis of what would have occurred if the parties had done what they intended to do. In other words, there should be a presumption that the beneficial interest is held by them jointly, as there would have been if it had been put into their joint names.[46] The Court of Appeal rejected this argument as unsupported by either *Stack* v. *Dowden* or *Jones* v. *Kernott*, and as consistent with neither principle nor sound policy.[47] As in other sole name cases, the Court said, the starting point is that the title holder is the sole legal and beneficial owner, and it is for the claimant to rebut that presumption.

(b) Imputing Intentions as to Size of Share

If, however, the presumptions are rebutted by proof of actual (i.e. expressed or inferred) shared intention, but the court is unable to find out or infer exactly what it was that the parties actually intended (for example because there is no evidence they ever discussed the matter, or even if there is positive evidence that there never was any such discussion or agreement), the court must 'search . . . for the result which reflects what the parties must, in the light of their conduct be taken to have intended'.[48]

In other words, while the search is ostensibly for the parties' intentions, in these relatively narrow circumstances it is permissible for the court to impute to the parties intentions which the court knows they never had. In *Stack* v. *Dowden* Lady Hale was careful to distinguish this from the formulation provided by Chadwick LJ in the Court of Appeal in *Oxley* v. *Hiscock* [2004] EWCA Civ 546 at para. 69 ('each is entitled to the share which the court considers fair having regard to the whole course of dealing between them in relation to the property'). Finding the result 'which reflects what the parties must, in the light of their conduct be taken to have intended' is not the same, Lady Hale said in *Stack* v. *Dowden*, as imposing on the parties the result that the court considers to be fair.[49] Also, she emphasised that the court could only look at matters which related to the parties' intentions about the property in question. The trial judge in the instant case was wrong, she said, to look at the 'entire course of their conduct together', that is, to found his conclusion on the length and nature of their relationship. The fact that, in *Stack* v. *Dowden*, the cohabiting couple had a relationship of 27 years, had had four children together and 'both co-operated in looking after the home and bringing up their children' was not of primary importance in 'ascertaining' their intentions about ownership of the house:[50]

---

[46] *Thompson* v. *Hurst* [2012] EWCA Civ 1752 para. 16.   [47] Ibid. Etherton LJ at para. 21.
[48] *Stack* v. *Dowden*, fn. 30 above, per Lady Hale at para. 61, and see also Lord Walker at para. 36.
[49] Ibid. at para. 61.   [50] Ibid. per Lady Hale at para. 86.

Mr Stack was held entitled only to a 35 per cent share, since he had paid considerably less than half the acquisition costs and they had kept their finances separate to what the House of Lords considered to be an unusual extent.

The factors which were relevant, Lady Hale said, were likely to be as follows:

> Each case will turn on its own facts. Many more factors than financial contributions may be relevant to divining the parties' true intentions. These include: any advice or discussions at the time of the transfer which cast light upon their intentions then; the reasons why the home was acquired in their joint names; the reasons why (if it be the case) the survivor was authorised to give a receipt for the capital moneys; the purpose for which the home was acquired; the nature of the parties' relationship; whether they had children for whom they both had responsibility to provide a home; how the purchase was financed, both initially and subsequently; how the parties arranged their finances, whether separately or together or a bit of both; how they discharged the outgoings on the property and their other household expenses. When a couple are joint owners of the home and jointly liable for the mortgage, the inferences to be drawn from who pays for what may be very different from the inferences to be drawn when only one is owner of the home. The arithmetical calculation of how much was paid by each is also likely to be less important. It will be easier to draw the inference that they intended that each should contribute as much to the household as they reasonably could and that they would share the eventual benefit or burden equally. The parties' individual characters and personalities may also be a factor in deciding where their true intentions lay. In the cohabitation context, mercenary considerations may be more to the fore than they would be in marriage, but it should not be assumed that they always take pride of place over natural love and affection.[51]

So, it seems there is some scope for 'imputed intention': if it is clear that the beneficial interests are to be held other than as dictated by the relevant presumption (depending on whether the property is in one name or in joint names) but 'it is impossible to divine a common intention as to the proportions in which they are to be shared', then 'the court is driven to impute an intention to the parties which they may never have had'.[52] As to what intention is to be imputed to them, the formulation that now seems accepted by the courts is that the parties will be entitled to the shares 'the court considers fair having regard to the whole course of dealing between them in relation to the property'.

This was the formulation adopted in *Thompson* v. *Hurst*, where it was held that it was 'fair' that the claimant should have only a 10 per cent share. The house was in the sole name of the claimant's partner, who had bought the freehold as a former tenant under the right to buy legislation. He had lived with her in the house for 16 years before she bought the freehold. They continued to live together as a family in the house for another four years, their two children were born there and lived there with them, and the claimant contributed 'perfectly reasonable' amounts from his wages towards housekeeping and council tax. However, the title-holder paid all

---

[51] Ibid. para. 69.
[52] *Jones* v. *Kernott* at paras. 31 and 47 per Lord Walker and Lady Hale; the minority disagreed and would have given imputed intention a broader scope.

the rent and mortgage payments, holding down two jobs to be able to do so, and the whole of her £8,000 Equal Pay award was spent on the only substantial improvements they made to the house. As noted above, the first instance judge inferred that they had a common intention that the claimant should have a share in the beneficial interest. However, she found that '... there was no common intention about the beneficial aspect because neither of them thought about it',[53] and that consequently it must be imputed to them. There was no appeal from her finding that there was a common intention that the claimant should have a share (a conclusion Etherton LJ doubted in the Court of Appeal[54]) but the Court of Appeal upheld her decision that a 10 per cent share for the claimant would be 'fair'. The Court of Appeal emphasised that an appellate court would be slow to overturn the trial judge's conclusion on 'fairness', and should not do so unless the trial judge had made an error of principle or the overall decision 'was plainly wrong'.[55] So, a trial judge's assessment of a fair share is unlikely to be challengeable.

Similarly, in *Barnes* v. *Phillips* [2015] EWCA Civ 1056, the Court of Appeal imputed an intention that the beneficial shares in property held in the joint names of a couple should be 85 per cent for the woman, Ms Phillips, and 15 per cent for the man, Mr Barnes. Two factors taken into consideration by the court in arriving at this figure are worth noting here. First, although it was common ground that the couple initially held the beneficial interest jointly, their action in re-mortgaging to pay off Mr Barnes' business debts amounting to 25 per cent of the then value of the house was taken to be equivalent to him taking out for himself 25 per cent of the value of the property, so increasing Ms Phillips' share to 75 per cent. The second factor was Mr Barnes' failure to make some maintenance payments for their two children after the relationship ended and he left the house. The Court of Appeal rejected his argument that this was not relevant to the quantification of beneficial shares and could lead to double counting as he would remain liable to the Child Support Agency for any missed payments. Lloyd Jones LJ said (Hayden J and Longmore LJ agreeing):[56]

> 41. In view of the very wide terms in which the House of Lords in *Stack* v. *Dowden* and the Supreme Court in *Jones* v. *Kernott described* the relevant context [i.e. the whole course of dealing in relation to the property], I consider that, in principle, it should be open to the court to take account of financial contributions to the maintenance of children (or lack of them) as part of the financial history of the parties save in circumstances where it is clear that to do so would result in double liability.

In the present case, Lloyd Jones LJ said, the judge had been right to take the missed payments into account because Ms Phillips had delayed referring the matter to the CSA for some years, with the result that Mr Barnes' liability to the CSA was limited to payments for one year, and 'in the context of the case as a whole such liability is of very limited significance'.

---

[53] *Thompson* v. *Hurst*, fn. 47 above, at para. 9.   [54] Ibid. para. 23.   [55] Ibid. para. 25.
[56] *Barnes* v. *Phillips* [2015] EWCA Civ 1056, at para. 41.

(c) Changing Intentions

It is confirmed in *Jones* v. *Kernott* [2011] UKSC 53 and in *Geary* v. *Rankine* [2012] EWCA Civ 555 that a common intention constructive trust is in a sense ambulatory, in other words that the trust may arise after the property was acquired by the parties, and that the interests under the trust may change as and when the parties change their common intention (as indeed was found to have happened in *Jones* v. *Kernott* itself). So, for example, in *Gallarotti* v. *Sebastianelli* [2012] EWCA Civ 865 the Court of Appeal inferred a change in the parties' common intention, from an original intention that their shares would be equal, to an intention that the split should be 75/ 25. The Court of Appeal inferred this from the fact that the two were close but platonic friends, not a family unit, who had originally thought they would make roughly equal financial contributions, but then found that there was a substantial disparity between what each could afford. Similarly, in *Insol Funding Company Ltd* v. *Cowey* [2017] EWHC 1822, it was held that although the original intention was that the couple should hold the beneficial interest as joint tenants, their common intention changed and the claimant's share was increased to 80 per cent because, on the facts, her increased financial commitment to the property and the corresponding shortfall in her partner's contributions evidenced a change in their original common intention so that they were 'no longer … mutually and equally committed to the shared ownership of the Property, as a long term joint commitment, such as to reflect a continued common intention as to their equal joint ownership of the Property'.[57]

14.10 Detrimental Reliance

It has to be remembered that the court's decision as to whether or not there is a common intention constructive trust, and if so what are its terms, is still governed by equitable principles. It remains true following *Jones* v. *Kernott* [2011] UKSC 53 that in all types of constructive trust, before the court will impose a constructive trust in favour of a non-legal title holder or allow the *Stack* v. *Dowden* presumptions as to beneficial ownership to be rebutted on the basis of a common intention constructive trust, the claimant must satisfy the court that the intervention of equity is justifiable to remedy the failure to use an express trust or valid contract to confer an interest on the claimant. A common intention not accompanied by detrimental reliance on shared intentions as to ownership or some equivalent will not give rise to a constructive trust.[58]

In simpler cases direct financial contribution towards the purchase price usually amounts to sufficient detrimental reliance on, as well as evidence of, the common intention so as to justify equity's intervention. However, detrimental reliance may

---

[57] *Insol Funding Company Ltd* v. *Cowey* [2017] EWHC 1822 para. 91 and see also paras. 92–97 for the factors the judge took into account.

[58] Reaffirmed in *Insol Funding Company Ltd* v. *Cowey* [2017] EWHC 1822 and *Taylor* v. *Taylor* [2017] EWHC 1080.

take other forms. So, for example, where two men bought a house in joint names with the initial intention of sharing the beneficial interest equally, but one of them moved out and orally agreed to transfer his beneficial share to the other for £2,500 to be paid when he could afford it, it was held that the other was entitled to the whole of the beneficial interest under a constructive trust, having taken on full responsibility for repaying the mortgage and also subsequently paying for improvements: *Oates* v. *Stimson* [2006] EWCA Civ 548. It was held that this was sufficient detrimental reliance on their agreement that he should take the other's share to justify the imposition of a constructive trust, even though the agreement itself was void because not satisfying s. 2 of the Law of Property (Miscellaneous Provisions) Act 1989.

RECOMMENDED READING

As in Chapter 13, the most important reading for this chapter is in the cases listed below. However, if you want further clarification of some of the points made above, or you would like a different perspective, you should search out the many valuable journal articles on the cases published in the last two decades.

Thorner v. *Majors* [2009] UKHL 18.
Henry v. *Henry* [2010] UKPC 3.
Davies v. *Davies* [2016] EWCA Civ 463.
Matchmove Ltd v. *Dowding* [2016] EWCA Civ 1233.
Stack v. *Dowden* [2007] UKHL 17.
Jones v. *Kernott* [2011] UKSC 53.
Thompson v. *Hurst* [2012] EWCA Civ 1752.
Curran v. *Collins* [2015] EWCA Civ 404.
Gallarotti v. *Sebastianelli* [2012] EWCA Civ 865.
Marr v. *Collie* [2017] UKPC 17.
Martin Dixon, 'More moves in constructive trusts and estoppel' [2017] Conv 18.
Hilary Blehler, 'The scope of common intention constructive trusts: where to draw the line?'
   (2018) *Trusts Law International* 63.

Questions

(1)   What are the essential elements of proprietary estoppel? To what extent is 'unconscionability' a separate requirement? Why is detrimental reliance an essential element?

(2)   Discuss the difficulties in categorising an estoppel interest as a property interest. If it is a property interest, when does it arise?

(3)   What principles do and should the court apply in deciding what remedy to award a claimant who has established a proprietary estoppel interest?

(4)   Explain the differences between a resulting trust and a common intention constructive trust.

(5) Discuss the circumstances in which the courts will impose (a) a resulting trust and (b) a common intention constructive trust, when a person claims a beneficial interest in property held in someone else's name, or claims to be entitled to more than a half share in the beneficial interest in property held in the joint names of herself and someone else.

(6) Explain what the Privy Council meant in *Marr* v. *Collie* [2017] UKPC 17 when it referred to 'a clash of presumptions', and the reasons the court gave for rejecting the 'simplistic answer'. Is this consistent with what the majority and the minority said in *Stack* v. *Dowden?*

(7) Explain the difference between *inferring* an intention and *imputing* an intention. Do the courts ever impute intentions in the context of a common intention constructive trust? Should they?

(8) What inferences about intention may the court properly draw from the fact that a legal title holder gave the claimant a specious reason for having the legal title in her sole name rather than in their joint names?

(9) Discuss when a person can rely on proprietary estoppel if she claims a beneficial interest in property held in someone else's name, (or claims to be entitled to more than a half share in the beneficial interest in property held in the joint names of herself and someone else), and when she can rely on the principles of common intention constructive trust. Will the outcomes be the same, whatever equitable principles she chooses to rely on?

15

Enforceability and Priority of Property Interests: General Principles

PART I INTRODUCTION

15.1 GENERAL PRINCIPLES GOVERNING ENFORCEABILITY AND PRIORITY OF PROPERTY INTERESTS

In Chapter 1 *What Property Is and Why It Matters* we pointed out the fundamental property principle – shared by common law and civil law property systems – that property interests in things are different from other rights that people have in relation to things, in one important respect: property interests are enforceable against the whole world (or against a class of people generally), whereas other rights are personal, enforceable only between two or more specific people.[1]

When we say that a property interest in a thing is enforceable against others, we mean (amongst other things) that the property interest is in some sense 'attached' to the thing, so that everyone who later acquires an interest in the same thing is bound by the prior property interest. So, for example, if I have a property interest in a thing which is owned by my uncle (perhaps I have a lease of land he owns, or a beneficial interest in shares which he holds on trust for me), and he sells his ownership interest in the thing to you, then provided certain conditions are satisfied, you will be bound by my prior interest (your freehold ownership of the land will be subject to my lease, or you will hold the shares on trust for me). This chapter is mainly concerned with these conditions which have to be satisfied for a property interest to be enforceable against others in this way, but here we should note three underlying principles.

(a) The Principle of Publicity

The first is the *principle of publicity*, regarded as fundamental in most civil law property rights systems although not explicitly acknowledged in ours. The principle, as stated in Scotland, is that:

> acts that can affect third parties should be made public, so that third parties can know of them.[2]

---

[1] Sjef van Erp and Bram Akkermans (eds.), *Cases, Materials and Text on Property Law* (Oxford and Portland, OR: Hart Publishing, 2012) pp. 37–38 and 51–53.

[2] George Gretton and Andrew Steven, *Property, Trusts and Succession* (3rd edn, Haywards Heath: Bloomsbury Professional, 2017) paras. 4.19–4.20.

The idea here is that a property rights system needs to have rules which lay down publicity conditions which have to be satisfied before a property interest can be enforceable against others – for example, the interest has to be registered in a public register, or the property interest holder has to be in possession or occupation of the object in question (i.e. the land or shares in the previous example).[3] This publicity principle explains many of the restrictions we impose on enforceability in our system, as we see in the rest of this chapter, and it also underlies the formalities rules we noted in Chapter 14 *Acquiring Interests Informally* para. 14.2. We look at the principle again in Chapter 16 *Registration* to see how far it is observed in our land registration system.[4]

(b) The *Nemo Dat* and *First in Time* Principles

There are other principles relating to enforceability and priority of property interests in our jurisdiction which are common to civil law and common law systems, although applied in different ways in different systems. Two of the most important of these in our system are the *nemo dat* principle and the first in time principle. Van Erp and Akkermans explain the *nemo dat* and first in time principles as ground rules in civil and common law jurisdictions:

> The first ground rule is that one cannot transfer more than one has (the *nemo dat* or *nemo plus iuris* rule). The second is that older property rights have priority over younger property rights (the *prior tempore* rule), with the exception of a younger property right created with the consent of the older property right.[5]

We look at these principles, and at the many exceptions to them that we recognise in our system, in paras. 15.5 and 15.6 in this chapter.

(c) Good Faith, Value and Notice

We can add to these ground rules a third principle, which is that most jurisdictions give special protection to *good faith purchasers*. In other words, interests that would otherwise be enforceable against third parties are not always enforceable against a *good faith purchaser*. So, for example, if I have stolen a car from my brother and then sell it to you, the circumstances in which you will get a good title to the car (i.e. as an exception to the *nemo dat* principle) vary between jurisdictions, but in most jurisdictions, even if it is possible at all, it will only be if you can show that you were a good faith purchaser, that is, that you paid value for the car and bought it in good faith.[6] In English and Welsh law the good faith purchaser is especially important, because, as we see later, we have a general common law principle that

---

[3] See further para. 16.6(b) of Chapter 16 *Registration* for the idea that possession or occupation of can amount to an 'act of publicity' for these purposes.

[4] Ibid.

[5] Van Erp and Akkermans, *Property Law*, fn. 1 above, p. 53. For a fuller account see pp. 93–94.

[6] See, for example, Andreas Rahmatian, 'A comparison of German moveable property law and English personal property law' (2008) 3 *Journal of Comparative Law* 197 at pp. 220–226, and generally Van Erp and Akkermans, *Property Law*, fn. 1 above, pp. 916–948.

equitable property interests are enforceable against the whole world *except* a good faith purchaser of a legal property interest who has no notice of the equitable interest ('the doctrine of notice').

Our land registration system has formally abandoned the doctrine of notice (and the requirement of good faith) for most registered land transactions and replaced them with the statutory provisions we look at in Chapter 16 *Registration*.[7] However, good faith and the doctrine of notice remain fundamental to all other transactions involving equitable interests in this jurisdiction, as we see below.

15.2 DISTINCTIVE FEATURES OF ENGLISH ENFORCEABILITY AND PRIORITY RULES

Our enforceability and priority rules, which we look at more closely in Parts II and III of this chapter, are complicated by three special factors.

(a) Distinctions Between Legal and Equitable Interests and Mere Equities

The first is that, as we have already noted, different rules apply to legal property interests, equitable property interests and the 'mere equities' and other equitable rights we noted in Chapter 5 *Ownership and Other Property Interests* paras 5.22 and 5.39. Broadly, the main difference between legal property interests, equitable property interests and mere equities is that in principle (but with exceptions we look at in this chapter) legal property interests in a thing are enforceable against everyone, whereas, as we have just seen, equitable property interests are enforceable against everyone *except* a later good faith purchaser of a legal property interest in the same thing who has no notice of the prior interest. Mere equities, on the other hand, are enforceable against everyone except a good faith purchaser of *any* property interest (legal or equitable) in the same thing who has no notice of the equity.[8] In all these formulations, 'notice' has a special meaning, as we see in para. 15.9(b) and (c).

---

[7] Although, as we see in Chapter 16, both 'good faith' and 'notice' have re-emerged in some parts of the registration system.

[8] *Bainbrigge* v. *Browne* (1881) 18 Ch D 188. Everything said in this chapter about enforceability and priority of equitable interests should be taken as also applying to mere equities, except that a later holder of an equitable interest can take advantage of the doctrine of notice to defeat a prior equity. In registered land, as we see in Chapter 16 *Registration* para. 16.27(a) (equities as overriding interests) and 16.10(c) (equities are not on the list of interests which cannot be protected by a formal 'notice' on the register and so, like those equitable interests which are not on that list, they can be protected in that way), even this difference is removed, and for all practical purposes mere equities and equitable interests can be assumed to be identical in effect when the land registration rules apply.

[9] Other forms of overreaching apply in other circumstances, for example when a mortgagee sells mortgaged property (see Chapter 5 *Ownership and Other Property Interests* para. 5.37) but in this chapter we are concerned only with overreaching by trustees.

(b) Overreaching

The second special factor is the doctrine of overreaching, which applies when trustees transfer or mortgage property they hold on trust.[9] Overreaching is an antiquated doctrine which now operates in circumstances very different from those in which it was intended to apply, so, unsurprisingly, its precise scope and effect in the present law are uncertain. The basic principle is that when trustees sell or mortgage the trust property, the equitable interests of the beneficiaries under the trust are 'overreached', meaning that they automatically shift from the trust property to the proceeds of sale (or the mortgage loan, in the case of a mortgage) which the trustees now hold in the place of the trust property. We look at the many problems with the operation of overreaching in Part III of this chapter.

(c) Modifications for Registered Land

The third factor is that, in the case of land where title is registered at the Land Registry, not only is the doctrine of notice abolished, but all the other general enforceability and priority rules are extensively modified (although the doctrine of overreaching is not). We see how all this works out in Chapter 16 *Registration*.

15.3 WHY THE GENERAL ENFORCEMENT AND PRIORITY RULES MATTER

Despite the fact that different rules now apply in registered land, the general enforceability and priority rules we look at in this chapter continue to be fundamentally important. They apply in full force to all property interests in all tangible and intangible things in our jurisdiction, apart from property interests in land within our land registration system. And, even within the land registration system, as we see in Chapter 16 *Registration*, sometimes we have to fall back on our general enforceability and priority rules as default rules. Even more often, courts and commentators assess the fairness and workability of our land registration rules by reference to the general rules, so it is important to know what they are and how they work.

15.4 POLICY OBJECTIVES

Before we look at the detailed rules as they apply in our system, we need to say more about the policy objectives of enforceability and priority rules.

(a) Protection of Property or Protection of Purchasers: Static or Dynamic Security?

One way of looking at enforceability and priority rules is to see them as attempting to strike a balance between two opposing policy objectives. On the one hand, people who hold property interests in things expect their interests to be secure once they have been established. The whole point of a property law system is to protect property interests in things against interference by the state and by other citizens. On the other hand, a market economy can only work if purchasers of property interests can be assured that they will get what they are paying for, in other words that they will get a good title from the seller, free from unknown encumbrances. As Lord Denning put it in *Bishopsgate Motor Finance Corporation Ltd* v. *Transport Brakes Ltd*:

> In the development of our law, two principles have striven for mastery. The first is for the protection of property: no one can give a better title than he himself possesses. The second is for the protection of commercial transactions: the person who takes in good faith and for value without notice should get good title.[10]

The tension between these two objectives is sometimes referred to as a tension between static security and dynamic security, and it arises most acutely in two kinds of situation. The first is what has become known as an A-B-C situation.[11] In an A-B-C situation, A is a duped owner, B is a fraudster and C is a duped purchaser. Without the knowledge of A the owner, B the fraudster tricks C the duped purchaser into believing that she, B, is the owner and she purports to sell her title to C – who of course pays the purchase price to B the fraudster, who disappears with the money. The issue the law has to face in this situation, and in the many possible variations on it, is whether to protect A, the duped property owner or C, the duped purchaser. Does A keep his title, leaving C with nothing (the static security solution), or does C acquire a good title, leaving A with nothing (the dynamic security solution)?

The second situation, which we will call an O-T-C situation, does not involve rival claims to the same property interest. It arises where O the owner of land[12] is bound by a subsidiary interest in that land which is held by T, but O then transfers her ownership to an innocent purchaser C, who is unaware of T's interest. So, for example, O the landowner might have granted T a lease of the land, or declared she held the land on trust for T, but then sells her ownership interest to C the innocent purchaser, hiding the existence of T's interest from C. Does the innocent T's interest in the land remain attached to the land, which is now owned by C the innocent purchaser, so that C, who paid O for full ownership, ends up instead with a much less valuable interest (ownership subject to the lease or trust)? This is the static security solution, protecting the pre-existing property interest of the innocent T. Or do we adopt the dynamic security solution, which is that T's property interest is extinguished, protecting C the innocent purchaser at the expense of the innocent property interest holder T, who loses everything?[13]

---

[10] *Bishopsgate Motor Finance Corporation Ltd* v. *Transport Brakes Ltd* [1949] 1 KB 322, CA at pp. 336–337.

[11] Amy Goymour, 'Mistaken registrations of land: Exploding the myth of "title by registration"' (2013) *Cambridge Law Journal* 617 at p. 623.

[12] Or anything else – these policy conflicts can arise in relation to any kind of marketable asset.

[13] As we see when we come back to this point in Chapter 16 *Registration*, the policy considerations are in reality more complex than this suggests, and it can be misleading to see it as a stark choice between static and dynamic security: see further para. 16.7.

(b) 'The Mud' or 'the Money'?

A further complication is that in both situations, either or both of the rival innocent claimants may be able to obtain financial compensation if they lose, either through insurance or by suing their professional advisors, or by suing the fraudster (B in the first example, O in the second). If that is the case, then the law faces a different dilemma. Which of the two innocent claimants should end up with the property interest, and which should have to make do with monetary compensation? This can be seen as a choice between 'the mud' and 'the money',[14] and as we saw in Chapter 7 *Objects of Property Interests*, in many situations at least one and possibly both of the claimants will have a strong preference for the 'mud' rather than 'the money', especially when the conflict is over rights in land. This dilemma has an added dimension in registered land, where the operation of the registration system itself produces funds which could be used to compensate the innocent victim who does not end up with the 'mud'. The funds are there because all users of the registration system have to pay a small fee every time they have access to the register. This means we have a real choice as to which of the rival claimants gets the mud and which gets the money. We come back to this question in Chapter 16 *Registration*.

PART II GENERAL ENFORCEABILITY AND PRIORITY RULES AND PRINCIPLES

15.5 THE *NEMO DAT* PRINCIPLE

'*Nemo dat*' is short for the Latin maxim '*nemo dat quod non habet*'. The literal meaning is 'no-one can give what she does not have'. Specifically, the *nemo dat* principle in English law is all about titles to property interests,[15] and a better formulation of the principle might be that 'no-one can pass a better title than she herself has'. This seems a statement of the obvious, but if applied literally it tilts the balance significantly in favour of property holders, and makes markets hazardous for good faith purchasers if fraudulent transactions are common. We can see this if we go back to the A-B-C example we outlined in para. 15.4.

Suppose A is a farmer who owns three sheep in a field. B is a fraudster, and without A's consent or knowledge, B sells the sheep to you, C the innocent purchaser, telling you she owns them. If we applied the *nemo dat* rule, the result would be that A remains owner of the sheep, and you have no title to them whatsoever, because B the fraudster had no title to them. Similarly, if A owned the

---

[14] Goymour, 'Mistaken registrations of land', fn. 11 above, p. 622. She traces the use of the expression back to T. W. Mapp, 'Report of the Alberta Institute for Law Research and Reform and the University of Alberta Faculty of Law', *Torrens' Elusive Title: Basic Legal Principles of an Efficient Torrens' System* (Alberta: University of Alberta, Faculty of Law, 1978) at para. 4.20, and subsequently adopted by the Scottish Law Commission, *Report on Land Registration* (2010) Scottish Law Com No 222, at para. 1.1.

[15] 'Title' in the sense of an 'entitlement' to a property interest: Chapter 11 *Possession and Title* para. 11.2.

[16] B could do it either by forging A's signature on a transfer deed transferring the freehold interest from A to herself, and then executing a deed transferring the freehold simple from herself to you, or by impersonating A and forging A's signature on a deed purporting to transfer the freehold from A to you: see further Chapter 14 *Acquiring Interests Informally* para. 14.2.

freehold interest in the field, and B the fraudster purported to sell you the field as well as the sheep by forging the necessary deeds,[16] then again the *nemo dat* rule would ensure that you get no title to the freehold interest, because B never had a title to it. Finally, if on the way home celebrating her success, B the fraudster had bought a sandwich in a pub with a £10 note she had stolen from A, the *nemo dat* rule would result in the pub getting no title to the £10 (although B the fraudster would of course get a good title to the sandwich – assuming the pub had a good title – even though she bought it with stolen money).

In these three situations, blanket application of the *nemo dat* rule seems to make life very hard, and not only for people like you and the pub, who innocently bought property interests from thieves. If frauds like these are very common, it also seems to make life hard for *all* purchasers of *any* property interests from *anybody*, because every time they buy anything from anyone they will always have to go to great lengths to ensure that their seller has a good title.[17] This may seem only right if we are talking about people like you making one-off purchases of land or sheep: you should have checked more carefully that B really was the owner. But it is perhaps unrealistic to expect people like the pub – taking cash for mass sales of small items to multiple purchasers – to go to such lengths.

Unsurprisingly, then, in this country as in most market economies, whilst we recognise the *nemo dat* principle, we also recognise significant exceptions to it. In English law you *can* give more than you have in some circumstances or, rather, a good faith purchaser from you can end up with more than you were able to give him.

15.6 EXCEPTIONS TO THE *NEMO DAT* PRINCIPLE

The exceptions we recognise to the *nemo dat* principle represent a series of rather unsatisfactory and confused compromises, producing different results depending on the nature of the thing in question.

(a) Land

The *nemo dat* rule operates differently depending on whether the property interests are in land which is not yet in the registration system ('unregistered land') or in land which is already in the system (registered land).

---

[17] This is the point made in Thomas W. Merrill and Henry E. Smith, 'Optimal standardization in the law of property: The numerus clausus principle' (2000) 110 *Yale Law Journal* 1, which we discussed in Chapter 6 *New Property Interests and the Numerus Clausus* para 6.7(b): a problem or idiosyncracy in one particular transaction creates externalities for *all* market participants, not just the parties to that transaction, because everyone has to check that the same problem/idiosyncracy is not present in the transaction they are proposing to enter into.

[18] S. 52 of the Law of Property Act 1925. The only significant exception for our purposes is leases for three years or less, or for a periodic term (e.g. weekly, monthly, annually, etc.): see Chapter 17 *Leases*), which can be made orally: ss. 52(1)(d) and 54(2) of the LPA 1925.

[19] An alternative term is 'constitutive': see further Chapter 16 *Registration* para. 16.6(a).

Unregistered Land

In unregistered land there are no exceptions to the *nemo dat* rule. As we saw in Chapter 14 *Acquiring Interests Informally* para. 14.2, legal titles to interests in land can be granted or transferred only by deed.[18] A valid deed is dispositive, that is, it actually grants or transfers the legal title that it says it is granting or transferring, provided that the grantor/transferor holds the necessary legal title.[19] So, if the transferor or grantor does hold a legal title to the property interest in question, and executes a deed transferring it or granting a lesser interest out of it to a transferee, then provided the deed is valid, the transferee will automatically get the legal title transferred or granted. If the grantor or transferor does hold the necessary legal title but there is no deed or the deed is defective in some other way, then as we saw in Chapter 5 *Ownership and Other Property Interests* para. 5.23(b), the transferee may get an equitable interest in the property but the legal title will stay with the transferor/grantor. If, however, the transferor does not have the necessary legal title, the person who does have it, keeps it: it does not pass to the transferee.[20] We can see how this works if we go back to the A-B-C example in para. 15.4, where B the fraudster purported to sell you the freehold interest in the field owned by A. If A's title to the freehold was not yet registered at the Land Registry, the *nemo dat* rule would apply and you would get no title to the field, however carefully you had checked: forged deeds are invalid, so they could not have transferred A's title either to B the fraudster or to you. Note, however, that the opposite result would have been reached if B the fraudster had managed to trick A into executing the deeds, rather than forging A's signature: the deeds would then have been valid (although possibly voidable by A, depending on the nature of the trick), and so they would have transferred A's legal title to you.[21]

Registered Land

The position is radically different in registered land because, as we see in Chapter 16 *Registration*, legal titles can pass only by registration. So, if I am the registered title holder of a freehold interest, I hold the legal title to the freehold interest simply by virtue of that registration. If I then want to transfer the legal title to you, I must execute a transfer deed transferring it to you, but the legal title will not leave me and

---

[20] The transferee might get something: if the person who purported to sell to her happened to have a possessory title because he had been in possession without the consent of the true owner, the transferee will get the possessory title, but of course it would not be enforceable against the true owner. Also, if the person who purported to sell to the transferee does have a property interest in the land but it is a lesser interest than the interest he purported to sell or grant, the deed will grant/transfer whatever interest he does have. So, if the deed says the transferor is transferring the freehold interest but all he has is a 10 year lease, the deed will transfer his legal title to the lease. This is achieved by s. 63 of the Law of Property Act 1925, but if s. 63 is excluded by express or implied provision in the deed (as it can be, by s. 63(2)), the purchaser may be able to reach the same result by the equitable doctrine of partial performance: *Thames Guaranty Ltd.* v. *Campbell* [1985] QB 210, p. 235, although see *United Bank of Kuwait plc* v. *Sahib* [1997] 107 at pp. 121–122 for the limited application of this equitable doctrine.
[21] If they were voidable by O, and he succeeded in having them declared void retrospectively when he found out what had happened, the freehold interest would at that point automatically go back to O.
[22] S. 27(1) of the Land Registration Act 2002.

arrive with you unless and until you then send the transfer deed to the Land Registry and they act on it by replacing my name with yours on the register.[22] So, if we go back to the A-B-C example in para. 15.4, if A was the registered title holder of the freehold interest in the field, and the Land Registry had been taken in by the deeds forged by B and registered you as title holder instead of A, you would have acquired the legal title and A would have lost it, even though he had no idea what was happening. This is quite startling because what has happened in substance is that a fraudster has tricked the Land Registry into believing that the title is being passed on to you by the person who does have it (A), and so the land registration system has unilaterally extinguished A's title and conferred title on you. This reversal of the *nemo dat* rule would be of little practical importance if it was purely mechanistic, in other words if, once A finds out what has happened, he is entitled to have the register rectified to reinstate him as the registered title holder. However, the position is that the innocent A will be entitled to have the register rectified in some circumstances, but by no means in all, and may not even be entitled to compensation from the Land Registry if rectification is refused.[23]

All of this is perhaps consistent with the professed policy behind the Land Registration Act 2002, which is to achieve 'title by registration', in other words an enclosed enforceability and priority system in which titles are not transferred by one person to another but are *conferred* by registration. However, as we see in Chapter 16 *Registration*, it is doubtful whether this is actually achieved by the system, and even more doubtful whether there are sound policy reasons for making this fundamental reversal in the *nemo dat* rule. Significantly, other land registration systems have come up with different solutions, as we see in Chapter 16.[24]

(b) Goods

The status of the *nemo dat* rule is clearer in relation to goods, but the net effect of the exceptions to it is not at all clear. The basic rule appears in s. 21 of the Sale of Goods Act 1979, headed 'Sale by person not the owner'. Section 21(1) provides that:

> Subject to this Act, where goods are sold by a person who is not their owner, and who does not sell them under the authority or with the consent of the owner, the buyer acquires no better title to the goods than the seller had, unless the owner of the goods is by his conduct precluded from denying the seller's authority to sell.

However, s. 21(2) and ss. 23–25 then contain or refer to a patchwork of additional exceptions, most of which have been 'interpreted' by generations of court decisions. The overall result is generally regarded as incoherent and uncertain in effect. Michael Bridge et al. explain the problem:

> [The *nemo dat* rule, in so far as it relates to goods] stems from the general principle of protection of property which the common law held sacred, but which has over the last few centuries, increasingly been found to be an impediment to commercial

---

[23] Chapter 16 *Registration* para. 16.38 and 16.39.   [24] See further Chapter 16 *Registration* para. 16.16.

transactions. Thus, over the years, exceptions to the rule grew up, firstly at common law and then, when the common law did not move fast or radically enough for the mercantile community, by statute. The broad effect of the application of an exception is that a transferee obtains better title than the transferor had. Many of these exceptions originated in a response to a particular problem which beset commerce at a particular point, mainly in the nineteenth century, with the result that there is now a patchwork of provisions, each with a certain amount of common law modifications, unified by only the vaguest of principles . . . It is not surprising that the law is complex and hard to apply, or that is not necessarily appropriate for modern day commerce.[25]

As the authors go on to say, there have been repeated proposals for reform, the earliest in modern times dating back to 1966, but none has yet been implemented.[26]

The effect of all this is that it is not actually possible to give a clear answer to the very straightforward question about the sheep we posed in para. 15.4, where B the fraudster sold you sheep which belonged to A. The best we can do is to say that you probably would not have obtained a good title to them unless you had paid B for them in good faith, and the circumstances were such that B the fraudster had A's apparent authority to sell the sheep, or that A the owner had allowed B the fraudster to appear as owner of them or had 'entrusted' B with possession of them.[27] You might, however, have been better off if B the fraudster had tricked A the owner into transferring the title to the sheep to her before she 'sold' them to you. This is because of the (relatively straightforward) provision in s. 23 of the 1979 Act, which deals with sales under a voidable title. If B the fraudster had obtained title to the sheep from A the owner by a trick, then (depending on the nature of the trick) the transaction would have been voidable by A. If B had managed to then 'sell' the sheep to you before A had avoided the A to B transfer, you would have obtained a good title to the sheep (i.e. good against A the owner as well as against B the purchaser) if you were a good faith purchaser without notice of the circumstances that made B's title voidable.

---

[25] Michael Bridge, Louise Gullifer, Gerard McNeel and Sarah Worthington, *The Law of Personal Property* (London: Sweet & Maxwell, 2013) para. 13.001.

[26] They refer to Law Reform Committee, *Twelfth Report (Transfer of Title to Chattels)* (1966) Cmnd 2958; A. L. Diamond, *A Review of Security Interests in Property* (Department of Trade and Industry, 1989); Department of Trade and Industry, Consultation Document, *Transfer of Title: Sections 21 to 26 of the Sale of Goods Act 1979* (1994). They also note that the Law Commission included 'Transfer of title to goods by non-owners' in its Ninth Programme of Law Reform (March 2005), and deferred it in its Tenth Programme (2008) for consideration in its Eleventh Programme, but that the Law Commission then said in its Eleventh Programme (July 2011, para. 3.4) that it was not considering the topic and would not be deferring it for consideration in its Twelfth Programme.

[27] For a fuller – and necessarily more accurate – summary of the exceptions see Bridge et al., *Law of Personal Property*, fn. 25 above, paras. 13.009–13.012.

[28] S. 2(h) of The Foreign Exchange Management Act 1999 defines currency to include 'all currency notes, postal notes, postal orders, money orders, cheques, drafts, traveler's cheques, letters of credit, bills of exchange and promisory notes, credit cards or such other instruments as may be notified by the RBI'. It is not at all clear whether bitcoins and other virtual currencies are, or should be, treated as currency for the purposes of the questions we are considering here: see Tatiana Cutts, 'Bitcoin ownership and its impact on fungibility' (2015), www.coindesk.com/bitcoin-ownership-impact-fungibility/ and Samraat Basu and Sayan Basak, 'The dawn of the digital currency era: A global analysis of Bitcoin and its implications in India' (2017) *International Company and Commercial Law Review* 22.

(c) Money

As we saw in Chapter 7 *Objects of Property Interests*, 'money' can mean at least three different things. It can refer to banknotes, coins and other financial tokens when they are being treated as currency,[28] that is, as a medium of exchange. It can also refer to any particular banknote, coin, etc., or a collection of them, valued for their own intrinsic qualities (perhaps because they are rare, and so worth more than their face value, or have some other quality which makes them not fungible in the eyes of the owner or collector). The distinction between these two categories is the distinction Bernard Rudden draws between 'things as wealth' and 'things as thing' which we noted in Chapter 7.[29] There is also what we can call 'intangible money', best exemplified by money in a bank account, which is essentially a debt owed by the bank to the account holder, and so technically a chose in action.[30]

When banknotes, coins, etc. come within our second category – they are valued for their own intrinsic qualities rather than as currency – they are 'goods',[31] and the *nemo dat* rule applies to them in the same way as it applies to the other goods we considered in (b) above.

However, money which is treated as currency (whether in the form of tangible tokens such as coins and banknotes or intangible money) has had its own special rule since at least the eighteenth century. It was held in *Miller* v. *Race* (1758) 1 Burr 452 that the *nemo dat* rule does not apply to any form of property that circulates as currency. Instead, the rule is that a good faith purchaser always gets a good title, even if buying from a thief. There are obvious policy reasons for this, as David Fox points out:

> Bona fide purchase now underlies the currency of all forms of money – coins, banknotes and purely abstract sums represented as bank balances. It is a common law rule, historically distinct from the much wider equitable defence of bona fide purchase for value without notice. The common law rule only applies to money [and has nothing to do with the conscience of the purchaser being affected, which is the basis of the equitable defence] . . .
>
> Currency is a special legal attribute which allows a recipient of money to take a fresh legal title which is good against the whole world. Money passes into currency in this way when it is received by a bona fide purchaser for valuable consideration. At this point the title of any previous owner of the money from whom it may have been stolen is extinguished. It helps money to circulate readily in the economy in that it reduces the need for recipients to make detailed inquiries into the title of people who tender money in payment of debts or to buy goods.
>
> The rule of bona fide purchase originated in the practices of merchants and bankers in the late seventeenth and eighteenth centuries. The common law progressively absorbed these practices, refined them and gave them the status of legal rules. Lord

---

[29] Bernard Rudden, 'Things as thing and things as wealth' (1994) 14 *Oxford Journal of Legal Studies* 81; see also Chapter 7 *Objects of Property Interests* para. 7.10 and Question (2).

[30] See Chapter 7 *Objects of Property Interests* para. 7.7.

[31] S. 60 of the Sale of Goods Act 1979 defines goods as excluding 'money', but this appears to refer only to money as currency.

[32] David Fox, 'Bona fide purchase and the currency of money' (1996) 55 *Cambridge Law Journal* 547 at pp. 564–565.

Mansfield's decision in *Miller* v. *Race* was the final point in this process. It confirmed that bona fide purchase was the rationale for the currency of all kinds of money. The decision put an end to the old common law rule that coins had the attribute of currency because they had 'no earmark' by which their original owner could specifically identify them.[32]

So, in our example in para. 15.4, the pub does at least get a good title to the £10 note, assuming it took the note in good faith.

15.7 THE BASIC ENFORCEABILITY PROBLEM

When we look at enforceability rules our attention shifts to a different question. Assume I do have a good title to a legal or equitable property interest in a thing, but my interest is subject to lesser property interests in the same thing held by other people. If I then transfer my title to you,[33] are those lesser property interests enforceable against you, in the same way they were enforceable against me?

Suppose a situation where my interest is a legal freehold interest in land, and I granted a perpetual right of way over a path on the land to my neighbour N in 2010, then I granted a 10 year lease of the land to T in 2015, and then last year, because my brother B had put a lot of money into my business, I declared that I held the freehold interest in the land on trust for him, promising I would not sell it without his consent. I have now sold my freehold interest to you without telling you about any of these interests (and without telling B), and at a price agreed on the basis that there were no other property interests in the land which would affect your title. Should you be bound by these interests or not?

Here the law faces the same dilemma it faces with the *nemo dat* rule. On the one hand, property interests in a thing are secure only if they remain attached to the thing for the duration of the interest. In our example, N, T and B all have property interests in the land, and each of them is entitled to expect that their property interest will stay attached to the land for the promised duration of the interest (perpetually, in the case of N's easement, until 2025 in the case of T's lease, and until B consents to a sale, in the case of his trust interest). It is a major infringement of their property rights if at any time I can sell my freehold interest to a purchaser who will not be bound by their interests. On the other hand, if we look at it from the point of view of you the purchaser, and indeed from the point of view of everyone interested in maintaining a healthy market for buying and selling land, it is very important that purchasers should be able to get a good title to the seller's interest free from lesser property interests they knew nothing about (assuming they were acting in good faith).

The problem is not unique to land. I might have shares in a company which I have mortgaged to the bank: if I sell the shares to you without telling you about the mortgage, will the mortgage be enforceable against you? Or perhaps I hold my car on

---

[32] The same principles apply if I grant you a legal mortgage or lease instead of transferring my interest to you, but in this section we assume a transfer to keep it simple.

[34] See Chapter 14 *Acquiring Interests Informally*, Part III.

resulting trust for my sister because I used her money to buy it in my name.[34] If I sell you the car without telling you about this, is her equitable interest enforceable against you?

15.8 ENFORCEABILITY RULES

The basic rules governing these situations are very straightforward. Legal property interests are enforceable against everyone. Equitable property interests, on the other hand, are enforceable against everyone except a good faith purchaser for value of a legal interest in the thing in question, who is without notice of the interest. As already noted in para. 15.1, this second principle, applicable to equitable interests, is known as the doctrine of notice.

These two rules apply to the enforceability of all property interests in all kinds of thing except where they are displaced by registration rules. In this jurisdiction we have several different registration systems providing for registration of a variety of different things (land, carbon trading units, ships, company shares, etc.). In theory a registration system could provide that all property interests in the kind of thing governed by the registration system are registrable on the register, and that if they are registered, they are enforceable against everyone, and if not registered they are not enforceable against anyone. However, none of the registration systems we have in our legal system adopt that kind of simple, absolute enforceability rule. Instead, our general enforceability and priority rules apply except to the extent that they are modified by the specific legislation governing the relevant registration system. We see how this works out in relation to land registration under the Land Registration Act 2002 in Part III of Chapter 16 *Registration*.

If we apply these basic enforceability principles to our examples in para. 15.7 above the answers are reasonably clear and straightforward. In the land example, assuming my freehold interest was not registered at the Land Registry,[35] N's right of way is an easement and would probably be a legal rather than an equitable easement,[36] and so it will be enforceable against you (the purchaser of the freehold interest) whether you knew of it or not. Similarly T's 10 year lease will have been legal if made by deed and so will also be enforceable against you, whether you knew of it or not. B's interest under the trust I declared is an equitable interest, so it will be enforceable against you unless *you can prove* that you bought the legal freehold interest in good faith without notice of B's interest (i.e. that you were a good faith purchaser for value of a legal estate without notice).

---

[35] And ignoring for the moment the partial system of registration of property interests under the Land Charges Act 1972 (replacing the Land Charges Act 1925, which first introduced the land charges registration system), which still applies to land until the freehold interest is first registered at the Land Registry: see further Chapter 16 *Registration* para. 16.18 fn. 128. None of the interests in this example would have been registrable as land charges.

[36] See Chapter 13 *Non-Possessory Land Use Rights* para. 13.13.

[37] See Chapter 5 para. 5.22(d). In practice, goods and intangibles are usually made subject to a charge (which is an equitable security interest) rather than a mortgage: see further Chapter 5 paras. 5.22(e) and 5.37.

As for the company shares, if the mortgage was a legal mortgage (unlikely[37]) it would be enforceable against you whether or not you knew about it, whereas if it was an equitable charge or lien (much more likely) it will be enforceable against you unless you can prove that you were a good faith purchaser for value of a legal interest without notice. In the case of the car, my sister's interest under the resulting trust is an equitable interest, and so again it will be enforceable against you (the buyer of the car) unless you can show you are a good faith purchaser for value of a legal interest without notice.

15.9 THE DOCTRINE OF NOTICE

As far as the enforceability of equitable interests is concerned, then, the critical question is whether the 'purchaser' – that is, the person against whom the equitable interest holder seeks to enforce her interest – is a good faith purchaser for value of a legal property interest without notice of the prior equitable interest. As already noted, this is for the purchaser to prove.[38] There are three elements to consider here: Who is a purchaser for value? What constitutes notice? And what amounts to good faith?

(a) Purchaser for Value of a Legal Interest

As we saw when we looked at the exceptions to the *nemo dat* rule, the justification usually given for preferring dynamic to static security – that is, for allowing someone who innocently acquires a property interest in a thing to extinguish, or take priority over, the pre-existing property interests of equally innocent prior interest holders – is to facilitate commercial transactions. If that is correct,[39] it would seem to follow that the protection of the doctrine of notice should go only to market participants, which means essentially only to those who gave valuable consideration for their property interest: those lucky enough to receive gifts should not expect to be protected from the claims of pre-existing property interest holders. So it makes sense that, for these purposes, 'value' excludes a purely nominal consideration,[40] but the consideration does not have to be adequate.[41] It is irrelevant *how much* consideration is paid because it is being paid directly to the seller for his own benefit: it is not going to be used to compensate the prior interest holders for the loss of their interests.

---

[38] *Crédit Agricole Corporation and Investment Bank* v. *Papadimitriou* [2015] UKPC 13 para. 21.

[39] Arguably it over-simplifies the problem: see further Chapter 16 *Registration* para. 16.7.

[40] The definition of valuable consideration in s. 206(1)(xxi) of the Law of Property Act 1925 includes marriage and the formation of a civil partnership (so consideration need not take the form of money) but specifically excludes nominal consideration.

[41] Lord Wilberforce in *Midland Bank Ltd* v. *Green* [1981] AC 513 at p. 531 described 'valuable consideration' as 'a term of art which precludes any inquiry as to adequacy'.

(b) Notice

For the purposes of the doctrine of notice, you have notice of something not only if you actually know about it (*actual notice*), but also if you would have known about it if you had taken 'proper steps' (*constructive notice*) and also if your agent has actual or constructive notice of it (*imputed notice*). This is formulated for land transactions by s. 199(1) of the Law of Property Act 1925:

> A purchaser[42] shall not be prejudicially affected by notice of ... any ... instrument or matter or any fact or thing unless –
>
> (a) it is within his own knowledge, or *would have come to his knowledge if such inquiries and inspections had been made as ought reasonably to have been made by him* or
> (b) in the same transaction with respect to which a question of notice to the purchaser arises, it has come to the knowledge of his counsel, as such, or of his solicitor or other agent, as such, or would have come to the knowledge of his solicitor or other agent, as such, if such inquiries and inspections had been made as ought reasonably to have been made by the solicitor or other agent.

Although, as already noted, the doctrine of notice now applies to land transactions only in the comparatively rare cases where the seller's title has not yet been registered at the Land Registry, this definition still encapsulates the meaning of 'notice' in English law for the purposes of the doctrine of notice generally. The difficult question is what amounts to constructive notice in this context.[43]

(c) Constructive Notice

According to the statutory definition, the purchaser has constructive notice of any prior equitable interest that she would have found out about if she had made 'such inquiries and inspections' as she ought reasonably to have made. But the 'inquiries and inspections' she ought reasonably to have made depend entirely on the nature of the transaction. When a house buyer is buying a house for herself, it seems reasonable to expect that she (or her lawyer or surveyor) would, for example, make a physical inspection of the land and the house, demand and scrutinise the

---

[42] Which includes a legal mortgagee: s. 205(1) of the Law of Property Act 1925.
[43] And, indeed, in other contexts where the issue is whether a person has received a property interest with notice or knowledge of a prior interest or claim: see Lord Sumption in *Crédit Agricole Corporation and Investment Bank* v. *Papadimitriou* [2015] UKPC 13 para. 33. Where the issue is different, constructive notice may mean something different. In *Royal Bank of Scotland* v. *Etridge* (No 2) [2001] UKHL 44, for example, Lord Scott pointed out (paras. 143-145) that it did mean something different where (as in the case the House of Lords was considering) the issue was whether a bank had constructive notice that a spouse or cohabiting partner's agreement to mortgage property had been procured by the undue influence of the other spouse/cohabiting partner. The distinction is important because the steps that, so the House of Lords held, a bank has to take to avoid having constructive notice that agreement to a mortgage was procured by undue influence are very different from those it would have to take to avoid having constructive notice of a prior equitable interest affecting the mortgaged property.
[44] *Kingsnorth Finance Co Ltd* v. *Tizard* [1986] 1 WLR 783 (Ch D).

documentary evidence that the seller has the title he is purporting to sell, and check that in all other respects the seller has accurately represented the physical condition of the property and the legal rights, duties and liabilities affecting it. *Kingsnorth Finance Co Ltd* v. *Tizard*,[44] which we look at below, illustrates how this works in practice when the seller's title is not yet registered at the Land Registry.

However, this tells us little about the 'inquiries and inspections' that, for example, a car dealer ought reasonably to have made when buying a classic car, as we see from *Gray* v. *Smith*[45] below, or those that a bank ought reasonably to have made before agreeing to open an account for a stranger to receive a large amount of money (*Crédit Agricole Corporation and Investment Bank* v. *Papadimitriou*[46] below).

So, if there is no standard list of the checks all buyers of all kinds of thing ought to make in all circumstances, what is a purchaser to do? How does he know what he ought to do in order to make sure that, if there are any undisclosed prior equitable interests, he finds out about them in time to back out of the purchase or lower the purchase price to compensate?[47] Can he and his advisors rely on following standard practice, arguing that the inquiries and inspections he ought reasonably to have made are those that it is standard practice for professionals to make on that kind of purchase? As we see from the following cases, standard practice is certainly relevant, but the more difficult question is what a purchaser is supposed to deduce from the information that he does it fact acquire (or ought reasonably to have acquired) from making the standard inquiries and inspections. *Kingsnorth Finance Co Ltd* v. *Tizard*[48] demonstrates the difficulties.

Kingsnorth Finance Co Ltd v. *Tizard*

Mr Tizard held the freehold interest in the house where he lived with his wife and two children, but he held it on trust for himself and his wife. Mr Tizard's title was not registered at the Land Registry, and so land registration principles did not apply.[49] He and his wife separated and she moved out. After the separation he continued to live in the house with the children, but Mrs Tizard came in nearly every morning to get the children ready for school before she went off to work. She would then come back in the evening to prepare the children's evening meal and the three of them would eat together. She would also stay overnight if, as often happened, Mr Tizard was away. She kept most of her clothes there in the wardrobe in the main bedroom, and also kept her toiletries, dressing gown, etc. there. Without Mrs Tizard's knowledge, Mr Tizard then mortgaged the freehold interest to secure repayment of £60,000 he borrowed from a finance company. When he applied for the loan he stated on the application form that he was single. The mortgage brokers

---

[45] *Gray* v. *Smith* [2013] EWHC 4136.

[46] *Crédit Agricole Corporation and Investment Bank* v. *Papadimitriou* [2015] UKPC 13.

[47] In practice, if it is the kind of transaction where buyers use solicitors, the problem is the problem of his solicitor, who will want to avoid being liable in negligence to her client for failing to make the 'inquiries and inspections' she ought reasonably to have made on behalf of her client.

[48] *Kingsnorth Finance Co Ltd* v. *Tizard* [1986] 1 WLR 783 (Ch D).

[49] We consider in Chapter 16 *Registration* para. 16.27(g) what the outcome would have been if his title had been registered and if the case had been decided under the Land Registration Act 2002.

sent a surveyor to the house to make a survey report to the finance company. The surveyor's visit took place at a time pre-arranged with Mr Tizard, who made sure that it was a time when Mrs Tizard and the children would be absent and hid the evidence of Mrs Tizard's presence. The surveyor found evidence of the children's occupation of the house, and Mr Tizard told him he was married but separated and his wife lived elsewhere and he lived in the house with the two children. Without opening cupboards or drawers, the surveyor looked for indications that someone else was living there (whether a wife or a new partner), and found nothing. He made no reference to any of this in his report to the finance company, other than to state that the occupants of the house were 'Applicant, son and daughter'. Mr Tizard never repaid any of the money he borrowed from the finance company and soon after the mortgage was completed he emigrated with the son and never returned. The issue the court had to decide was whether the finance company took subject to Mrs Tizard's equitable interest in the house. The court held that it did (and therefore it could not sell the house to a third party free from her beneficial interest in it), because it was unable to demonstrate that it was a good faith purchaser without notice. Although it had acquired a legal interest (the mortgage) and had acted in good faith, it had constructive and imputed notice of Mrs Tizard's interest, the court decided. The reasoning behind the judge's finding that the finance company had constructive notice of her interest is quite convoluted. The crucial point for the judge was that Mrs Tizard was, so the judge decided, in occupation of the house.[50] If the finance company or its surveyor had known that someone other than the husband and children were in occupation, the finance company would have had constructive notice of her equitable interest, because it would then have been reasonable for them to have made further enquiries as to who that person was and whether she had an interest in the property.[51] Admittedly, neither the finance company nor its surveyor knew that Mrs Tizard was in occupation of the house (Mr Tizard saw to that), but, the judge said, *they would have found out that someone was in occupation* if they had made the inquiries and inspections they ought reasonably to have made. So, according to the judge, what should they have done? The answer seems to be that the surveyor should not have let Mr Tizard dictate the time of the physical inspection, and both the finance company and the surveyor should have been alerted to make further enquiries by the discrepancy between what Mr Tizard said on the application form and what the surveyor found out on his visit.

In the very different context of an international banking transaction in the twenty-first century, the Privy Council came to a remarkably similar conclusion in *Crédit Agricole Corporation and Investment Bank* v. *Papadimitriou*.[52]

---

[50] We come back to the question of what amounts to 'occupation' in these kinds of situation in Chapter 16 *Registration* para. 16.27.

[51] It has long been established that a purchaser has constructive notice of the property interests of a person in occupation of the property: *Hunt* v. *Luck* [1902] 1 Ch 428 and *City of London* v. *Flegg* [1988] AC 54 at pp. 80F–G.

[52] *Crédit Agricole Corporation and Investment Bank* v. *Papadimitriou* [2015] UKPC 13.

Crédit Agricole Corporation and Investment Bank v. *Papadimitriou*

Here, the issue was this: if a bank agrees to open a bank account for someone – not an established client, but a stranger – and accepts a payment into that bank account of a very large amount of money, what investigations and inquiries would it be reasonable for the bank to have made in order to avoid having constructive notice of any equitable property interest anyone else may have in the money? The money in question, US$10.3 million, was part of the proceeds of sale of a collection of art deco furniture. The collection was owned by Irene Michailidis but for some reason it had come into the possession of her son. The son died, and without Irene's consent or knowledge the collection was sold for US$15 million by the fraudster Symes, who had been the son's partner and had lived with him for many years. Symes then entered into an elaborate series of artificial transactions in order to disguise his connection with the money, which culminated in a Gibraltar bank, Crédit Agricole, opening an account for a company called Lombardi (a newly formed company wholly owned by Symes), into which another company paid US$10.3 million from the sale proceeds of the collection. All this was orchestrated by Symes. It was accepted that Irene's family (Irene had since died) had an equitable property interest in the US$10.3 million which would be enforceable against Crédit Agricole unless it (Crédit Agricole) could show that it was a good faith purchaser of the proceeds of sale without notice of the family's interest. It was also common ground that the bank did not have actual notice, so the issue was whether it had constructive notice. The Privy Council concluded that it did have constructive notice, and that therefore the family's claim to the money succeeded. It was accepted that 'there was ample evidence that at the relevant time a bank which was contemplating entering into a transaction of the type that took place should and would inquire as to the commercial purpose' of the transaction.[53] The bank had not done this. Although it made enquiries about Symes, and satisfied itself that he was a wealthy and apparently reputable art dealer in London, it did not enquire into the commercial purpose of the transaction. If it had made enquiries as to the source of the money to be paid into the account it would have discovered that the payment was part of a series of transactions between a 'web of legal entities' which had no obvious commercial purpose and which involved significant costs in banking and professional fees and charges. This would have given 'a reasonable banker in the position of the particular banker serious cause to question the propriety of the transaction'.[54] This was enough to give the bank constructive notice of the prior equitable interest (Irene's beneficial interest in the money) because it would have been reasonable for a bank which had such 'serious cause' to question the propriety of the payment-in to make further enquiries. The further enquiries it would have been reasonable for them to make would, so the Privity Council decided, have led them to find out that there was a serious possibility that the money was not the depositor's own money. This was enough to give the bank constructive notice of Irene's equitable interest.

---

[53] Lord Clarke, giving the judgment of the Privy Council: ibid. at para. 26.   [54] Ibid. at para. 20.
[55] *Gray* v. *Smith* [2013] EWHC 4136.

Gray v. Smith

However, what the courts thought could reasonably be expected from Mr Tizard's Finance Company and the Crédit Agricole bank can be contrasted with what the court thought it was reasonable to expect from the car dealer buying a classic (i.e. not mass-produced) car in *Gray* v. *Smith*. [55] The car was a McLaren Formula One racing car. The issue was whether Mr Smith, the innocent dealer who bought the car, took subject to an equitable interest that Mr Gray already had in the car. Gray had instructed a fraudulent dealer to buy the car for him in the United States and to ship it back to England for him. The fraudster did buy the car, using the £1 million Gray had already paid him for it, and shipped it to this country, but instead of delivering it to Gray he transferred the title to it to another (but this time reputable) dealer to settle a debt, and the reputable dealer in turn sold it to the equally reputable Smith. The court held that when the fraudulent dealer bought the car he bought it as Gray's agent, which meant he, the fraudster, acquired the legal title to the car but held it on trust for Gray. It was accepted that if the reputable dealer could show that it was a good faith purchaser from the fraudster without notice of Gray's interest, it would have acquired a good title to it free from Gray's equitable interest, and therefore it would have passed a good title free from Gray's interest on to Smith. It was argued for Gray that, although the reputable dealer was a good faith purchaser, it had constructive notice of Gray's interest because it did not require the fraudster to provide a documentary chain of title from the original owner to the fraudster. Any reasonably prudent purchaser of a car of this kind would have required this, it was argued, and if the reputable dealer had done so it would have been alerted to the possibility of Gray (or someone else) having an interest, and it would then have been reasonable to make further enquiries which would have resulted in the dealer discovering the truth. However, the judge rejected this argument and held that the reputable dealer had had no notice, actual or constructive, of Gray's equitable interest and that therefore Smith also took the car free from Gary's interest. After hearing expert evidence of international dealings in classic cars, the judge concluded that reasonable enquiries in this kind of case did not include investigating the chain of title or requiring documentary evidence of title:

> [the expert's evidence was that] as between dealers, it was normal to make an oral contract which was later recorded in writing in an invoice. It was not normal to investigate a chain of title. When he or any other reputable garage sold a car, all they ever did in the ordinary way was to produce an invoice or bill of sale to the purchaser. All dealers in the UK and Europe operated in the same way, making deals by handshake or on the telephone and confirming them in an invoice. The only document that changed hands on sale was ordinarily an invoice and that was all he ordinarily supplied to his purchasers. That happened every other day in his experience for the last few hundred cars he had sold. Other well-known and reputable garages did the same, giving their warranty of title to the purchaser.[56]

---

[56] Ibid. Cooke J. at para. 112.

So, since the reputable dealer had made only the cursory enquiries that any reasonable dealer would have made in his position in those circumstances (so it was found), he was not fixed with constructive notice of what would have been revealed by more searching enquiries.

(d) Good Faith

It is not clear what the requirement of 'good faith' adds to the requirement that the purchaser is without notice. It is noticeable that when a civil law system such as the German system provides protection for good faith third parties against unknown property interests affecting the land, there is no additional requirement that the third party should be without notice, but 'good faith' is itself then defined in terms of notice.[57] Lord Wilberforce in *Midland Bank* v. *Green*[58] expressed the view that 'good faith' is 'a separate test which may have to be passed even though absence of notice is proved'. However, it is difficult to envisage circumstances in which a purchaser without actual or constructive notice of a prior equitable interest could nevertheless be said to be acting in bad faith *in relation to the prior interest holder*.

It is doubtful whether purchasers are in bad faith in this jurisdiction if registration rules allow them to take free from a prior interest which they do know about, and they go ahead with the purchase with the intention of defeating the prior interest. This situation arises where a prior interest is registrable, and the registration statute provides that failure to register makes the interest unenforceable against a purchaser. If the title holder knows that the interest holder has not protected her interest by registration, and then sells his title (even at an undervalue) to a purchaser with the deliberate intention, shared by the purchaser, of defeating the unregistered interest, is the purchaser acting in bad faith? In a famous dictum in *In re Monolithic Building Co.* [1915] 1 Ch 643, p. 663, Lord Cozens Hardy said: 'it is not fraud to take advantage of legal rights'. Referring to this in *Midland Bank* v. *Green*, Lord Wilberforce pointed out that the Land Charges Act 1972, which he was considering and which had such a provision, did not expressly provide that 'purchasers' had to be in good faith, and the House of Lords refused to imply a good faith requirement into the statute because of the enquiry into motives that this might require. This was applied in *Coles* v. *Samuel Smith Old Brewery (Tadcaster)*,[59] and in both cases it was held that the purchase was not a sham, even though the sale was to a close associate of the seller (to the seller's wife, in *Midland Bank* v. *Green*, and to a subsidiary

---

[57] Lars van Vliet, 'Transfer of property *inter vivos*' in Michele Graziadei and Lionel Smith (eds.), *Comparative Property Law: Global Perspectives* (Cheltenham, UK and Northampton, MA: Edward Elgar Publishing, 2017) pp. 159–162, explaining §892 of the Civil Code (BGB).

[58] *Midland Bank* v. *Green* [1981] AC 513 at pp. 528D–H.

[59] *Coles* v. *Samuel Smith Old Brewery (Tadcaster)* [2007] EWCA Civ 1461.

[60] See Chapter 16 *Registration* for the equivalent position under the Land Registration Act 2002, which also contains no requirement that purchasers who become registered proprietors must have purchased in good faith in order to take free from prior unprotected interests (see s. 29(1) and s. 30(1) of the 2002 Act). For the possibility that the purchaser might, however, be liable in tort in such circumstances, see Chapter 16 para. 16.29(c).

company in *Coles*), at a significant undervalue, and the sole reason for the sale was to defeat the prior equitable interest. Accordingly, in both cases the purchaser took free from the prior unregistered equitable interest.[60]

15.10 THE DOCTRINE OF NOTICE AS A PRO-PURCHASER RULE?

Although the doctrine of notice originated as a means of protection for holders of equitable interests, it is important to appreciate the limitations of the protection. It is not much use to the holder of an equitable interest who wants to make sure that her interest will always be enforceable against all purchasers of the legal title, because there is no certain way of ensuring that a purchaser will always have actual or constructive notice of her interest. As we see from the cases we looked at in para. 15.9 (c), her interest will only be safeguarded if it would necessarily be discovered by the kind of inquiries and inspections which are currently market practice in commercial dealings of the kind the legal title holder is likely to enter into. If the legal title holder is a determined and accomplished fraudster, it is not be too difficult to ensure that a prior interest is not reasonably discoverable by standard enquiries. So, protection by the doctrine of notice is not obviously better than protection by registration, although it may be a good second best if registration is not feasible for that kind of interest. We return to this question in Chapter 16 *Registration*.

On the other hand, the doctrine of notice seems to operate very efficiently for the honest and well-advised purchaser. If he wants to ensure that he is not bound by prior equitable interests he knows nothing about, all he has to do is to ensure that he and his advisors follow current market practice, however ineffective it may be in unearthing prior interests hidden by fraud.

15.11 PRIORITY OF INTERESTS – THE FIRST IN TIME PRINCIPLE

The final rules we need to note here are those which govern the priority between two or more property interests in the same thing. Suppose, for example, I hold the freehold interest in some land. In 2015 I grant a lease for 10 years to T, and then in 2016 I mortgage the land to M to secure repayment of £50,000 I owe to M. If T's lease takes priority over M's mortgage, it means that, if M sells my freehold interest as mortgagee to recover the £50,000 I owe her, she can sell only my freehold interest subject to T's lease. If, on the other hand, M's mortgage takes priority over L's lease, it means that M can sell the freehold interest free from T's lease.

The basic priority rule here is the *prior tempore* (first in time) principle that van Erp and Akkermans identified as one of the ground rules of common law and civil law property systems.[61] However, in our system it is modified to accommodate our

---

[60] para. 15.1 above.

[62] If a legal interest is registrable under a registration scheme, the registration scheme usually provides that the priority date is the date of the registration of the interest (or even the date of application for registration) rather than the date of its creation: see van Erp and Akkermans, *Property Law*, fn. 1 above, pp. 861–862 and 870, and Chapter 16 *Registration* para. 16.24 for the position under the Land Registration Act 2002.

distinction between legal and equitable property interests. The way it works is as follows:

(a) Prior and Later Interests are Both Legal

If there are two or more legal property interests in the same thing, they take priority as between themselves in the order in which they were created.[62] This is, of course, just another way of saying that legal interests are enforceable against everyone. So, if T's lease was a legal lease and M's mortgage was a legal mortgage, the lease takes priority over the mortgage.

(b) Prior Interest Legal; Later Interest Equitable

If the first interest (T's lease) is legal and the second (M's mortgage) is equitable, then the first takes priority over the second. This is sometimes said to result from a special priority principle that legal interests take priority over equitable interests, but there is no need for a special priority rule to explain the result – it follows inevitably from the basic principle that legal interests are enforceable against everyone.

(c) Prior Interest Equitable; Later Interest Legal

If the first interest (T's lease) is equitable and the second (M's mortgage) is legal, then the first takes priority over the second *unless* M can prove she was a good faith purchaser of her mortgage interest without notice of T's lease. Again, this is sometimes said to result from a priority rule that 'where the equities are equal', legal interests take priority over equitable interest,[63] but it is just another way of saying that equitable interests are enforceable against everyone except a good faith purchaser of a legal interest without notice.

(d) Both Interests Equitable

As between two or more equitable interests, however, there *is* a special priority rule which cannot be deduced from the basic principle that legal interests are enforceable against everyone, whereas equitable interest are enforceable against everyone except a good faith purchaser of a legal interest without notice. This special priority rule is that 'where the equities are equal', the first in time rule applies, *but* a prior equitable interest (T's lease in our example) can be postponed to a later one (M's mortgage) if the later one can prove that there was something about the prior interest holder's conduct which would make it inequitable for him to take priority over the later interest.

---

[63] Astron Douglas, 'Equitable priorities under registered land' (2017) University of Cambridge Faculty of Law Legal Studies Research Paper Series Paper No. 5/2017, www.law.cam.ac.uk/ssrn/.
[64] *Freeguard* v. *Royal Bank of Scotland* (1990) 79 P & CR 81.

This is a long established equitable principle, and the kind of conduct that would lead to T forfeiting his priority over M – variously described in the old cases as 'fraud or gross negligence' – depends very much on the circumstances. It may involve T deliberately hiding his interest from M, or doing something that allows the legal title holder (me, in our example) to deceive M into believing that there is no prior interest.

Freeguard v. *The Royal Bank of Scotland plc*[64] provides a rare example of the kind of conduct that might postpone priority of an equitable interest in land in modern times.[65] Mr and Mrs Freeguard had owned development land in Devon, which included a strip of land adjoining neighbouring land owned by the Cloudesleigh Trustees. The Freeguards believed that the Cloudesleigh land also had development potential, but that the Cloudesleigh development would be impossible without access over their adjoining strip of land. So, when the Freeguards sold their development land to a local builder, Mr Edgar, they retained ownership of that strip of land (the ransom strip). Subsequently, they persuaded Edgar that he ought to buy the Cloudesleigh land and develop it with them, as owners of the ransom strip, in a joint venture. However, the Freeguards wanted to hide their involvement from the Cloudesleigh Trustees, so they arranged with Edgar that he would tell the Cloudesleigh Trustees, when he approached them offering to buy their land, that he owned the ransom strip. To make this plausible, they 'sold' the freehold interest in the ransom strip to Edgar (the transfer recorded a purchase price which Mr Edgar did not, and was not expected to, pay) and he became registered as owner in the Land Registry. However, he then granted Mrs Freeguard an option to buy the strip back from him, effectively for no consideration. Mrs Freeguard could have protected her option to purchase on the register but she did not do so: if she had, anyone checking Edgar's title to the ransom strip would have found out about it. Meanwhile, unbeknownst to the Freeguards, Edgar was having financial problems and he mortgaged the ransom strip to the bank to secure his debts, without telling the bank about Mrs Freeguard's option to purchase. For reasons not relevant here, the bank did not register its mortgage at the Land Registry and so it took effect as an equitable interest only.

When the Freeguards found out about the bank's mortgage Mrs Freeguard brought this action claiming that her option to purchase (also an equitable interest) took priority over the bank's equitable mortgage. Her action failed: the Court of Appeal held that although her interest was first in time it had to be postponed to the bank's mortgage because in the circumstances it would be inequitable for it to take priority over the bank's mortgage. In the Court of Appeal Robert Walker LJ, giving the principal judgment, emphasised the seriousness of upsetting the prima facie first

---

[65] The case was decided under the old system of registered land created by the Land Registration Act 1925, which was replaced by the present system introduced by the Land Registration Act 2002. In *Freeguard* the Court of Appeal held that the general law rules as to priority of equitable interests was imported into the LRA 1925. In Chapter 16 *Registration* para. 16.24 we consider whether the same is true of the LRA 2002.

[66] Quoted by Robert Walker LJ in *Freeguard*, fn. 64 above, at p. 87.

in time order of priority for property interests, pointing to what Turner LJ had said in *Cory* v. *Eyre* (1863) DGJ & S 149 at p. 167:

> [once an equitable interest is created] there is an estate or interest to be displaced. No doubt there may be cases so strong as to justify this being done, but there can be as little doubt that a strong case must be required to justify it. A vested estate or interest ought not to be disturbed upon any light grounds ...[66]

Robert Walker also referred in *Freeguard* (at p. 87) to Cairns LJ's comment in *Shropshire Union Railways and Canal Company* v. *R* (1875) 7 LR 496 at p. 507:

> I conceive it to be clear and undoubted law, and law the enforcement of which is required for the safety of mankind, that, in order to take away any pre-existing admitted equitable title, that which is relied upon for such a purpose must be shewn and proved by those upon whom the burden to shew and prove it lies, and that it must amount to something tangible and distinct, something which can have the grave and strong effect to accomplish the purpose for which it is said to have been produced.

It will be noted that this approach demonstrates a much greater concern for the inviolability of equitable property interests than we find in the cases we noted above in relation to enforceability of equitable interests against purchasers of a legal title.

However, consistently with this approach, Robert Walker LJ went on to say in *Freeguard* that the fact that Mrs Freeguard had not protected her interest on the register was not of itself sufficient to justify postponing her interest:

> ... the main purpose of an encumbrancer protecting his interest [on the register is] to ensure that it bound any later encumbrancer. If in this case Mrs Freeguard had taken that step she would have ensured priority. The fact that she did not do so did not automatically result in the loss of priority, but it opened the door for the loss of priority if there were further circumstances, as the judge held there were, making it inequitable for her interest, earlier though it was, to take priority over the bank.[67]

He confirmed that he agreed with the judge that in this case there *were* further circumstances, sufficient to justify postponing her interest even though she knew nothing about the bank's mortgage and was attempting to deceive someone else altogether:

> in addition to the omission to make any entry on the register, Mrs Freeguard, in co-operation with and, it seems, at the prompting of her husband, entered into what the judge called a 'thoroughly artificial transaction' designed, if not to deceive, at any rate to give to the world (and especially to the Cloudesleigh Trustees) the impression that Mr Edgar was the unincumbered owner of the ransom strip and could deal with it as he pleased. That was, in my judgment, much more than mere omission to register. It armed Mr Edgar with the appearance of absolute and unencumbered ownership ... It is perfectly true, as Mr Shah has urged on us, that his client's intention was to conceal facts from the Cloudesleigh Trustees and not from the bank. But, having set up this arrangement and having armed Mr Edgar as against the whole world, It seems to me that the appellant cannot now be heard to say, 'My intention was that the stratagem should be much more selective in its effect'.[68]

---

[67] *Freeguard*, fn. 64 above, at p. 87.   [68] Ibid. at p. 89.

So, an equitable property interest holder may lose priority to a later equitable interest, but it will be only be as a result of her own conduct, and that conduct must be something more than carelessness or negligence: it must be something that would make it unconscionable for her to assert her priority.

15.12 OTHER EQUITABLE PRINCIPLES MODIFYING ENFORCEABILITY AND PRIORITY RULES

It should be appreciated that other general equitable principles may modify the operation of the enforceability and priority rules we are considering here in this chapter. In particular, a prior interest holder may be able to persuade the court that, even if a purchaser would otherwise take free from his interest under general enforceability or priority rules, the purchaser should nevertheless be bound by his interest in these particular circumstances through estoppel or constructive trust, applying the principles outlined in Chapter 14 *Acquiring Interests Informally*.[69] Conversely, there may be cases where a prior equitable interest will lose its priority, or fail to be enforceable against a purchaser when it would otherwise have been, through estoppel or some other equitable principle such as apparent authority.[70]

We look at these cases in Chapter 16 *Registration*, since very similar principles apply in relation to enforceability and priority under the Land Registration Act 2002, and most of the modern law on the point has been developed in recent land registration cases.[71]

PART III OVERREACHING

15.13 WHAT OVERREACHING IS AND WHEN IT OPERATES

As we noted in para. 15.2, there is some uncertainty and disagreement over the nature and scope of overreaching. There is a species of overreaching which occurs when mortgagees sell the mortgaged property, as we noted in para. 15.2(b), and overreaching in that context is straightforward both in nature and in operation. Here, however, we are concerned with the overreaching of equitable interests under trusts, which can occur when the trustees sell or mortgage the trust property.

---

[69] Chapter 14 Part II (estoppel) and para 14.17(b) and Chapter 16 *Registration* para. 16.29(a) (constructive trust principles).

[70] See Douglas, 'Equitable priorities under registered land', fn. 63 above, criticising the decision in *Wishart* v. *Credit and Mercantile plc* [2015] EWCA Civ 655 where these principles were considered. We look at *Wishart* in detail in Chapter 16 *Registration* para. 16.28.

[71] See para. 16.29 for the circumstances in which an otherwise unenforceable prior equitable interest might become enforceable against a subsequent registered proprietor by constructive trust or estoppel, and also para. 16.28 for cases where the holder of a prior equitable interest is estopped from asserting her interest or is taken to have given the registered proprietor apparent authority to sell his title free from her interest.

[72] para. 5.3(b).

15.14 HOW OVERREACHING WAS ORIGINALLY INTENDED TO WORK

The idea behind overreaching by trustees of land was, originally at least, that the beneficial interests under a trust should not be enforceable against purchasers and mortgagees of the land held on trust for them. This is consistent with the classic notion of the trust we noted in Chapter 5 *Ownership and Other Property Interests*, that is, as a mechanism which enables the trust property to operate as a fund held for the benefit of the beneficiaries, with the trustees having the exclusive power to buy and sell the property which makes up the trust fund, so that it produces the best return for the beneficiaries.[72] Overreaching provides the mechanism by which this is done: if the correct procedures are followed, the equitable interests under the trust are detached from the land which the trustees hold on trust for them and attach instead to the proceeds of sale paid by the purchaser to the trustees.[73]

It is important to appreciate that, whether the transaction by the trustees is a sale or a mortgage, this overreaching process does not extinguish the beneficiaries' property interests: it shifts them from outgoing trust property (the land) to incoming trust property (the sale proceeds or mortgage loan). This is easier to see when we look more closely at what happens when trustees mortgage the trust land rather than selling it. The beneficiaries' interests are detached *only* from the mortgage interest which the mortgagee acquires, to be replaced by equivalent interests in the money lent to the trustees by the mortgagee. However, they remain attached to the property interest in the land still held by the trustees,[74] that is, the legal freehold interest[75] out of which the trustees granted the mortgage interest to the mortgagee. When the trustees pay off the mortgage debt, the mortgagee's mortgage interest is automatically extinguished, leaving the trustees holding on trust for the beneficiaries what is now once again an unencumbered title to the trust land.

It follows that overreaching by trustees was always intended to apply only to transactions which involved the purchaser or mortgagee paying money to the trustees, into which the beneficiaries' interests could transfer.[76] This of course still left beneficiaries vulnerable to being defrauded by their trustees: the beneficiaries' interests in the land would still be overreached even if the trustees dishonestly kept the money for themselves. If the trustees were found out, they would be personally liable to the beneficiaries for breach of trust, but this might not be of much practical use to the beneficiaries. When our modern overreaching mechanism was set up in 1925, it was decided not to limit overreaching so that it did not apply to this kind of

---

[73] For a clear modern statement see Matthews J in *Banwaitt* v. *Dewji* [2015] EWHC 3441 at para. 22.

[74] Sometimes referred to (rather inaccurately) as the 'equity of redemption': see further Chapter 5 *Ownership and Other Property Interests* para. 5.22(d).

[75] Or whatever other property interest the trustees hold on trust.

[76] Although see the contrary views noted in para. 15.18.

[77] A trust corporation is a body, usually formed by a bank or firm of solicitors to act as a professional trustee for clients: www.lawsociety.org.uk/support-services/advice/practice-notes/trust-corporations. They tend to be appointed only in commercial trusts or trusts of large family estates.

[78] Law Commission Report, *Transfer of Land – Overreaching: Beneficiaries in Occupation* (1989) Law Com No 188, para. 2.19.

fraudulent transaction, but instead to limit the risk of fraudulent transactions occurring at all, by insisting that overreaching could occur only when there were at least two trustees or a trust corporation[77] and the money was paid to no fewer than two of them. The thinking was that fraud by two people was less likely than fraud by a person acting on her own.[78]

15.15 THE MODERN REALITY

That was how the system was intended to work. The reality, however, is very different, in two main respects.

(a) The Principle Confused

The first is that this relatively simple principle has been confused by court decisions which have extended the scope of overreaching beyond its intended (and arguably proper) limits, influenced by academic disputes over what those intended limits were. This has led to some anomalous decisions which we look at in paras. 15.17–15.19.

(b) Transformation of the Social and Economic Purposes of Trusts of Land

However, the underlying and fundamental problem with overreaching is that it was designed to deal with trust situations which are very different from those in which it now operates in the vast majority of cases. As we have already noted, the premise of overreaching assumed by the legislators in 1925 who reformulated the principle was that sales by trustees of land held on trust should always be free from the interests of the beneficiaries. It was for the trustees to decide whether and when the land should be sold, and the market value of trust property could only be maintained if potential purchasers of trust land could be assured that they would buy the land free from the interests of the beneficiaries under the trust. In other words, in the interests of their beneficiaries, trustees had to be able to compete in land markets on equal terms with absolute owners. This approach would cause no hardship for the beneficiaries because the trustees are merely exchanging land for money (the sale proceeds) as the trust property. If any of the parties to the trust were unhappy with this, they could always provide for the contrary in the deed setting up the trust. Viewed from this perspective, overreaching benefits both beneficiaries and purchasers – it enables beneficiaries to realise the full value of their investment and allows trust land to be traded on equal terms with non-trust land.

However, whilst beneficiaries of most trusts probably shared that perspective in 1925, it seems likely that most would be more ambivalent about it now. In 1925 most trusts were expressly created and had professional trustees, or at least trustees who were aware that they were trustees and had some idea of their powers and responsibilities as trustee. Similarly, beneficiaries would have been aware that their property

---

[79] Rudden, 'Things as thing and things as wealth', fn. 29 above; see further Chapter 7 *Objects of Property Interests* Question (2).

was in the hands of trustees, and if they (or their settlor) wanted the beneficiaries to have some control over sales of any trust land, they could put appropriate controls in the trust deed. It also seems likely that a substantial proportion of beneficiaries regarded their interests in the trust property as 'wealth' rather than as 'thing', to adopt Bernard Rudden's terminology.[79] Trusts of land which are like this still exist, but they are now vastly outnumbered by inadvertent trusts, most of which are of residential property occupied by one or more of the beneficiaries as their home, and trusts which are automatically imposed, whether the parties want them or not, because the property is co-owned. A substantial proportion of people own their own homes, and whilst in 1925 most family homes which were owned rather than rented would have been owned by the male head of household, most are now formally or informally co-owned, whether by married or co-habiting couples, or relatives or house-sharers.[80] If the house is formally co-owned – in other words, if the legal title is in their joint names – then, as we saw in Chapter 8 *Property Interest Holders*, a trust is automatically imposed, so that the joint owners[81] hold the legal title on trust for themselves and any other co-owner who is not on the title. Depending on the nature of the legal advice the co-owners received when they bought the house, they may or may not realise that there is a trust and that they are trustees and/or beneficiaries, or what that entails, and there is unlikely to be a trust deed setting out their intentions as to sale. But even if the house is formally in the name of only one of them, there is a strong possibility that a common intention constructive trust will be imposed on the title holder entitling at least one of the others to a share in the beneficial interest. As we saw in Chapter 14 *Acquiring Interests Informally*,[82] this common intention to share the beneficial interest may not have been even discussed by the co-owners: it may be inferred from their conduct or even imputed to them because the court considers it would be fair to do so because of their conduct in relation to the property. So, in all these cases, even when the co-owners realise there is a trust, it is not something they positively chose or wanted, and most often they have no real knowledge or understanding that there is a trust: they simply regard themselves as co-owners.

It is not just that beneficiaries and trustees under these kinds of trusts are probably unaware of the existence of a trust. They are probably also keenly interested in whether or not the trust property is sold or mortgaged. In most cases the trust property is the home of most if not all of the people who are trustees and/or beneficiaries under the trust. Whilst they probably also regard their home as a financial investment (and to that extent want and benefit from a mechanism which allows it to be freely sold and mortgaged) they undoubtedly regard themselves as having a property interest in that particular property and expect to be involved in decisions as to whether and when it should be sold or mortgaged. For all these

---

[80] Nicola Jackson, 'Overreaching in registered land law' (2006) 69 *Modern Law Review* 214, pp. 216–221; see also Law Commission Report, *Transfer of Land – Overreaching*, fn. 78 above, paras. 3.1–3.3.

[81] Or, if there are more than four of them, the first four named.   [82] para. 14.9.

[83] Law Commission Report, *Transfer of Land – Overreaching*, fn. 78 above, para. 4.3. The problem cases we look at in paras. 15.16–15.19 were all decided after that Law Commission Report was published, and so the question of whether the effects of these cases should be reversed was not considered.

reasons, the Law Commission recommended in 1989 that a sale or mortgage of land by trustees should not overreach the interest of 'anyone of full age and capacity who is entitled to a beneficial interest in the property and who has a right to occupy it and is in actual occupation of it at the date of the conveyance, unless that person consents'.[83] However, that proposed reform was never implemented, and in the Law Commission Consultation Paper *Updating the Land Registration Act 2002* (2016) Law Com No 227, the Law Commission rejected calls to take on the reform of overreaching as part of their project of updating land registration, on grounds that it raised wider issues:

> 1.21 ... The treatment of beneficial interests [under a trust] ... reflects an ongoing debate about the correct balance to strike between the rights of purchasers and mortgagees on the one hand, and beneficiaries on the other, particularly in the context of beneficial interests that people may own in their home. That debate raises broad questions of social policy that ultimately touch on the appropriate balance the law strikes between property as a 'home' and as a financial investment for homeowners to realise. The treatment of beneficial interests in the LRA 2002 sits within a much wider matrix of considerations of how the law balances the desire of home owners to secure their interest in the home, with the interests of purchasers and of those (such as mortgage lenders) with a financial interest in the property. We did not consider that it would be appropriate to interfere with long-established assumptions by looking at how beneficial interests are dealt with by the LRA 2002 in isolation from the broader debates.

We return to these debates in Chapter 16 *Registration*, but here we must first look more closely at the technical difficulties with the current operation of overreaching, and at their practical implications.

15.16 THE STATUTORY FRAMEWORK FOR OVERREACHING

The principle of overreaching first emerged early on in the development of trusts,[84] but the modern system is largely governed by the Law of Property Act 1925. The 1925 Act provisions were amended by the Trusts of Land and Appointment of Trustees Act 1996 to accommodate the new form of trust of land introduced by the 1996 Act, which is the form we use now.[85]

---

[84] For a good historical overview of the nineteenth century developments in the doctrine of overreaching see Jackson, 'Overreaching in registered land law', fn. 80 above, at pp. 216–224. There is a more detailed but more partial account in Charles Harpum, 'Overreaching, trustees' powers and the reform of the 1925 legislation' (1990) 49 *Cambridge Law Journal* 277, centred around his argument as to 'the true nature of overreaching' (ibid. p. 282) noted in para. 15.18 below.

[85] The modern trust of land introduced by the 1996 Act replaced an anachronistic form of trust, the trust for sale, under which trustees were under a duty to sell the trust land with only a power to postpone sale. There were technical arguments that under a trust for sale, the interests of beneficiaries were 'really' only interests in the potential financial value of land held on trust, even before it was sold. These arguments are not tenable in relation to the modern trust of land. In this and other respects, the characteristics of the old style trust for sale complicated the analysis of overreaching, and this makes some of the older academic and judicial pronouncements about overreaching difficult to follow and often unreliable as to the present law.

The overreaching provisions of the 1925 Act as amended by the 1996 Act, are s. 2 and s. 27. Section 2(1) sets out the basic principle:

> (1) A conveyance to a purchaser of a legal estate in land shall overreach any equitable interest or power affecting that estate, whether or not he has notice thereof, if . . . (ii) the conveyance is made by trustees of land and the equitable interest or power is at the date of the conveyance capable of being overreached by such trustees under the provisions of subsection (2) of this section or independently of that subsection, and the statutory requirements of section 27 of this Act respecting the payment of capital money arising on such a conveyance are complied with . . .

Section 27 (also amended by the 1996 Act to fit the new trust of land introduced by the 1996 Act) then sets out the statutory requirements referred to which deal with payment of capital money:

> 27(1) A purchaser of a legal estate from trustees of land is not to be concerned with the trusts affecting the land, the net income of the land or the proceeds of sale of the land whether or not those trusts are declared by the same instrument as that by which the trust is created.
>
> (2) Notwithstanding anything to the contrary in the instrument (if any) creating a trust of land . . . the proceeds of sale or other capital money shall not be paid to or applied by the direction of fewer than two persons as trustees, except where the trustee is a trust corporation, but this subsection does not . . . , except where capital money arises on the transaction, render it necessary to have more than one trustee.

The combined effect of these provisions, and their interaction with other provisions of the LPA 1925, is hotly disputed, as we see in the following paragraphs. The broad effect, however, is that sales of (or other dealings with) trust property by trustees will not overreach the beneficiaries' interests under the trust unless the proceeds of sale of the transaction are paid to at least two trustees or a trust corporation. Since trust corporations are rare in the kind of transactions we will come across, the practical effect is that transactions by a single trustee cannot overreach the beneficiaries' equitable property interests: there must be at least two of them for overreaching to occur.

To complete the picture we should also note that 'conveyance to a purchaser of a legal estate in land' in s. 2(1) of the LPA 1925 includes not only a sale of the freehold interest in land but also the grant or sale of a legal lease or legal mortgage,[86]

---

[86] But not the grant of a legal easement: *Baker* v. *Craggs* [2018] EWCA Civ 1126, where the Court of Appeal held that, although s. 1(4) of the LPA 1925 suggests otherwise, 'legal estate in land' in s. 2(1) is confined to the two estates in land which, by s. 1(1), are the only legal estates capable of subsisting in land after 1925, i.e. the fee simple absolute in possession and the term of years absolute (see Chapter 5 *Ownership and Other Property Interests* para. 5.16(d) above). The Court of Appeal went on to say that, nevertheless, a legal mortgage does also come within s. 2(1) because, by s. 87(1) of the LPA 1925, a legal mortgagee has 'the same protection, powers and remedies . . . as if' it had been granted a three thousand year lease (Chapter 5 para. 5.37(b)), and therefore it is *deemed* to grant to the mortgagee a legal estate in land within s. 1(1), namely a term of years absolute: *Baker* v. *Craggs* at para. 29.

[87] Proponents of differing views include Harpum, 'Overreaching, trustees' powers and the reform of the 1925 legislation', fn. 84 above; Graham Ferris and Graham Battersby in a series of articles (agreeing on some but not all point with Harpum): 'The impact of the Trusts of Land and Appointment of Trustees

confirming that these overreaching provisions apply not only to sales by trustees of trust property, but also to mortgages and leases.

15.17 UNAUTHORISED TRANSACTIONS BY TRUSTEES

(a) Authorised Transactions or all Transactions?

There is long-running academic disagreement about whether trustees of land over-reach beneficial interests only by 'authorised' transactions (meaning those that trustees have power to make) or by *any* transaction, authorised or unauthorised.[87] However, it has to be said that the disagreement has not received the attention of the courts in the very many overreaching cases that have come before them since the point was first made in the academic literature in 1990. This is probably because, although very nearly all of these cases involve transactions by trustees which are made in breach of trust, a sale or mortgage in breach of trust is not necessarily 'unauthorised', in the sense of a transaction *of a kind* that a trustee has no power to make. In any event, in its 2016 Consultation Paper on reforms to the Land Registration Act 2002, the Law Commission has invited consultation on a proposal to amend the 2002 Act to make it clear that purchasers from trustees who are registered proprietors should be entitled to assume that the trustees have full powers of disposition (in other words, all sales and mortgages by them are capable of over-reaching the equitable interests under the trust) unless the contrary appears in an entry on the register.[88]

(b) Dishonest Transactions?

Meanwhile, however, it seems clear that trustees cannot overreach the equitable interests by a dishonest transaction consisting of a sale, in effect, to themselves. In *HSBC Bank plc* v. *Dyche* [2009] EWHC 2954 a daughter and her husband held the legal title to the house occupied by her father on constructive trust for him. In the course of their divorce proceedings, the daughter and her husband transferred the legal title into her sole name, and the daughter then dishonestly mortgaged the property to the bank, using the mortgage loan for her own purposes. The issue was whether the father's beneficial interest was enforceable against the bank. It was held that it was, and so the father was entitled to be registered as proprietor of the house

Act 1996 on purchasers of registered land' [1998] *Conveyancer* 168, 'The general principles of overreaching and the reforms of 1925' [2002] 118 *Law Quarterly Review* 270 and 'The general principles of overreaching and the modern legislative reforms 1996–2002' [2003] 119 *Law Quarterly Review* 94; Martin Dixon, 'Overreaching and the Trusts of Land and Appointment of Trustees Act 1996' [2000] *Conv.* 267 (disagreeing with Ferris and Battersby on registered land); Jackson, 'Overreaching in registered land law', fn. 80 above; and Nicola Jackson, "Overreaching in registered land law" (2006) 69 *Modern Law Review* 214 and 'Overreaching and the rationale of the Law of Property Act 1925' [2006] 15 *Nottingham Law Journal* 1 (disagreeing with Harpum).

[88] Law Commission, *Updating the Land Registration Act 2002* (2016) Consultation Paper No 227, paras. 5.54–5.62.

[89] *HSBC Bank plc* v. *Dyche* [2009] EWHC 2954 paras. 38–40.

free from the mortgage. It was accepted that the daughter's mortgage to the bank could not have overreached her father's interest because she was the only trustee. The more difficult question was whether his interest was overreached when the daughter and her husband transferred the house into her sole name. It was held that, although the transfer was for consideration, and it was by two trustees, it did not overreach the father's beneficial interest under the trust. The principle reason the judge gave for coming to this conclusion is difficult to support. He said that overreaching could not have occurred because s. 2(1) applies only to a conveyance to a 'purchaser', and the daughter was not a 'purchaser' because she was not in good faith.[89] This is unsatisfactory because 'good faith' is not required for overreaching under s. 2(1).[90] However, the decision itself is clearly right, and the judge's conclusion can be supported on much more convincing grounds. He himself referred to the observation by Millett J in *Ingram* v. *IRC*,[91] where Millett J pointed out that for overreaching purposes there must be not merely two parties to the transaction but two independent parties who are capable of dealing with each other at arm's length, which was not the case here. Alternatively, and equally convincingly, a purchaser who is one of the selling trustees and who fraudulently procures a sale of the trust property to herself, should be bound by the equitable interests of the beneficiaries under a constructive trust,[92] and in any event should have been de-barred from relying on the overreaching provisions of s. 2(1) by the principle that equity will not permit a statute to be an instrument of fraud.[93]

15.18 DO TRANSACTIONS UNDER WHICH NO CAPITAL MONEY IS PAYABLE OVERREACH BENEFICIAL INTERESTS?

A more serious problem is that in *State Bank of India* v. *Sood*[94] the Court of Appeal came to the surprising conclusion that a transaction by trustees of land overreaches the beneficial interests under the trust even if no capital money is payable to the trustees at the time of the transaction. *Sood* concerned a mortgage by two trustees, who held the legal title to a family house on trust for themselves and other family members who lived in the house. The mortgage was to secure the repayment of debts which had already been incurred by family businesses and also future indebtedness: no money was actually payable by the bank to the trustees when the mortgage was granted. It was argued for the beneficiaries that, although the mortgage was granted by two trustees, the beneficiaries' interests were not overreached by the mortgage because there was no capital money paid to the trustees. The Court of Appeal

---

[90] In s. 205(1)(xxi) of the 1925 Act 'purchaser' is defined as meaning a 'purchaser in good faith for valuable consideration' throughout the 1925 Act *except* for in Part I of the Act (which includes s. 2), where it means 'a person who acquires an interest in or charge on property for money or money's worth'.

[91] *Ingram* v. *IRC* [1997] STC 1234 at p. 1259.

[92] That is, under the principles considered in Chapter 16 *Registration* paras. 16.17(b) and 16.29. .

[93] *Rochefoucauld* v. *Boustead (No.1)* [1897] 1 Ch 196, CA and see Martin Dixon, Editorial Note (on *Dyche*) (2010) *Conveyancer* 1.

[94] *State Bank of India* v. *Sood* [1997] Ch 276.   [95] Harpum, 'Overreaching', fn. 84 above.

rejected the argument and held that the interests of the beneficiaries were over-reached. Misled by an argument put by Charles Harpum in a journal article in 1990 as to overreaching being, by its 'true nature',[95] any process by which 'existing interests are subordinated to a later interest or estate created pursuant to a trust or power', the Court of Appeal came to the doubtful conclusion that trustees always overreach the interests under the trust whenever they enter into any transaction which is within their powers, irrespective of s. 2(1) of the 1925 Act. On that view, the function of s. 2(1) is merely to provide that, if capital money is payable under the transaction, overreaching will not occur unless the capital money is paid to at least two trustees or a trust corporation. If, however, there is no capital money payable, the interests are overreached.

Leaving aside the fact that this is not at all what s. 2(1) and s. 27 of the LPA 1925 actually say, this novel reading of s. 2(1) seriously erodes the position of beneficiaries under a trust, as Peter Gibson LJ admitted in the Court of Appeal in *Sood*:

> Much though I value the principle of overreaching as having aided the simplification of conveyancing, I cannot pretend that I regard the resulting position in the present case as entirely satisfactory. The safeguard for beneficiaries under the existing legislation is largely limited to having two trustees or a trust corporation where capital money falls to be received. But that is no safeguard at all, as this case has shown, when no capital money is received on and contemporaneously with the conveyance.[96]

Although it is quite common for bank mortgages to secure only past and future indebtedness (i.e. with no capital sum payable to the borrower when the mortgage is granted) there have been no later cases either applying or casting doubt on the Court of Appeal's decision in *Sood* or the analysis of s. 2(1) on which it was based. However, it should be appreciated that it is incompatible with the still generally accepted principle that overreaching is by definition a process by which, on a disposition of trust property, beneficial interests under the trust are detached from the property and attach instead to its proceeds of sale.[97] If there are no proceeds of sale, it is difficult to see how the detachment of the beneficiaries' interests from the land can be justified.

15.19 WHAT EQUITABLE INTERESTS OUTSIDE THE TRUST CAN BE OVERREACHED?

On the face of it, s. 2(1) of the LPA 1925 allows overreaching only of beneficial interests under the trust. This makes sense, because the only purpose of overreaching

---

[96] *State Bank of India* v. *Sood,* fn. 94 above, at p. 290.
[97] See, for example, the definition adopted by the Law Commission, *Updating the Land Registration Act 2002,* fn. 88 above, para. 1.2; also Lewison LJ in *Mortgage Express* v. *Lambert* [2016] EWCA Civ 555 at para. 31; Matthews J in *Banwaitt* v. *Dewji* [2015] EWHC 3441 para. 5.151; and Julian Farrand and Alison Clarke (eds.), *Emmet & Farrand on Title* (London: Sweet & Maxwell, looseleaf updated to 30 April 2019) para. 5.141.
[98] *Birmingham Midshires Mortgage Services Ltd* v. *Sabherwal* [2000] 80 P & CR 256.
[99] *Mortgage Express* v. *Lambert,* fn. 97 above.

is to allow the trustees to deal with trust property as if they are absolute owners: it has never been the intention that it should allow them to sell or mortgage trust property free from prior interests which would have been enforceable against purchasers if the sale had been by an absolute owner. However, the courts have not always appreciated this and in *Birmingham Midshires Mortgage Services Ltd* v. *Sabherwal*[98] and again in *Mortgage Express* v. *Lambert*[99] the Court of Appeal has held that a disposition by trustees is also capable of overreaching equitable interests and equities which have nothing to do with the trust. This misconception seems to have arisen partly out of a misunderstanding of s. 2(2) of the LPA 1925, which *does* allow trustees under a trust of land to overreach 'prior' equitable interests – that is, interests which arise before and independently of the trust – but s. 2(2) applies only to dispositions made by trustees who are specially approved or appointed by the court.[100] Very few trusts (and none of those in the reported court decisions on overreaching) fall within this category. Neither s. 2(2) nor s. 2(3), which lists exceptions to s. 2(2) (i.e. prior interests which even 'approved' trustees cannot overreach), has anything to do with dispositions by ordinary trustees.

In *Birmingham Midshires Mortgage Services Ltd* v. *Sabherwal* two brothers jointly held the legal title to a house where they lived with their mother and other members of the family. The sons mortgaged the house to a bank and the issue was whether any beneficial interest that the mother had in the house had been overreached by the mortgage. The Court of Appeal held that it had. The difficulty in the case is that it was accepted that the mother had made substantial financial contributions to the purchase price of the house which would have entitled her to a share in the beneficial interest under resulting trust principles,[101] and it was also accepted that if she had made her claim on that basis, her beneficial interest would have been an interest under the trust and so would have been overreached by the mortgage. However, the argument made on her behalf was that her interest arose by estoppel, and that an equity of estoppel was not capable of being overreached because it did not arise under the trust. As already noted, this argument should have succeeded. However, the Court of Appeal rejected it. Robert Walker LJ, giving the principal judgment, drew a distinction between 'commercial' equitable interests outside the trust and 'family' equitable interests which were outside the trust. Commercial equitable interests (e.g. an equitable easement over the trust land), could not be overreached by a disposition of the trust land, he said, because they could not be transferred to the proceeds of sale of the disposition. But family equitable interests like the mother's equity of estoppel could, so he said:

> 27. Equitable interests [such as equitable easements] ought not to be overreached, since they are rights which an adjoining owner enjoys over the land itself, regardless of its ownership from time to time. The principle is in my view correctly stated in Megarry and Wade, *The Law of Real Property* (5th ed) p. 409:
>
>> 'In fact the only examples of such equities likely to occur are commercial (as opposed to family) interests, which it is absurd to speak of overreaching. Two instances

---

[100] Or a trust corporation: s. 2(2)(a) and (b).
[101] See Chapter 14 *Acquiring Interests Informally* para. 14.7.
[102] Robert Walker LJ in *Birmingham Midshires* v. *Sabherwal,* fn 98 above, at paras. 27–28.

are an equitable right of way which is yet not an equitable easement, and an equitable right of entry to secure performance of a covenant, and there are probably others. To overreach such interests is to destroy them . . .'

28. . . . The essential distinction is, as the authors of Megarry and Wade note, between commercial and family interests. An equitable easement or an equitable right of entry cannot sensibly shift from the land affected by it to the proceeds of sale. An equitable interest as a tenant in common can do so . . .'[102]

If this was intended to lay down a principle that all 'family' equitable interests are overreached by transactions made by trustees even if the equitable interests do not arise under the trust, it is simply wrong. If that was the case it would not have been necessary to give approved trustees special powers under s. 2(2) to overreach prior equitable interests. However, it seems that Robert Walker LJ was strongly influenced by the fact already noted, which was that the mother's interest could properly have been categorised either as an interest under a resulting trust or as an interest arising by estoppel. In 2000, when *Sabherwal* was before the Court of Appeal, there was considerable confusion over the difference between resulting trusts, constructive trusts and estoppel,[103] to the extent that Robert Walker described them as 'almost interchangeable'. If one accepted that analysis, it would be arguable that if an interest is overreachable when it is categorised as an interest under a resulting or constructive trust, it should also be overreachable when categorised as an interest arising by estoppel.

However, in *Mortgage Express* v. *Lambert*[104] the Court of Appeal took the principle much further. Mrs Lambert was persuaded by two fraudsters to sell them her leasehold interest in her flat at a gross undervalue, for just enough money to pay off her pressing mortgage debts and a promise that she could live there for the rest of her life. This was a common kind of sale and leaseback fraud at that time, conning desperate homeowners fearing eviction for mortgage arrears into parting with the legal ownership of their homes.[105] Armed with the legal title and concealing the existence of the arrangement with the homeowner, the fraudsters would then be able to mortgage the house to a bank to secure a loan for the full value of the house, and disappear, taking the money with them. This is what the two fraudsters did in this case. Mrs Lambert first discovered what had happened when the bank brought possession proceedings to evict her from her home after the fraudsters failed to make any payments under the mortgage which the fraudsters had granted to them. The issue was whether Mrs Lambert had any property interest in the lease which was enforceable against the bank. The Court of Appeal held that she did have a property interest consisting of a right, enforceable against the fraudsters, to have the whole

---

[103] Arguably still not fully resolved: in many of the cases discussed in Chapter 14 *Acquiring Interests Informally* estoppel and constructive trust were pleaded in the alternative.

[104] *Mortgage Express* v. *Lambert*, fn. 97 above.

[105] Caroline Hunter, 'Certainty rules in uncertain times!' (2016) *Journal of Housing Law* 85.

[106] The trial judge had also held that she had a long sub-lease, but Mrs Lambert was forced to relinquish this claim in order to pursue her alternative claim in the Court of Appeal that she could have the whole arrangement set aside as an unconscionable bargain.

[107] See Chapter 5 *Ownership and Other Property Interests* para. 5.39.

bargain set aside as an unconscionable bargain.[106] The Court of Appeal accepted that this right to have the bargain set aside as an unconscionable bargain was a 'mere equity'[107] in the lease, which by its nature was capable of being enforceable against the bank. The issue was whether it had been overreached by the mortgage, given that the mortgage had been granted to the bank by the two fraudsters, to whom the bank had paid the mortgage advance. Relying on *Sabherwal*, the Court of Appeal held that Mrs Lambert's equity in the lease had been overreached by the mortgage. Lewison LJ, giving the principal judgment, followed the line taken by the Court of Appeal in both *Sood* and *Sabherwal*, and refused to accept that s. 2(1) of the LPA 1925 was limited to equitable interests under the trust.[108] This allowed him to accept the Court of Appeal's proposition in *Sabherwal* that dispositions by trustees of land overreach all 'family' interests in the land, even if they are outside the trust, and that this included not only equities such as the equity by estoppel held by Mrs Sabherwal but also the equity to set aside the unconscionable bargain held by Mrs Lambert in this case. This goes further than the Court of Appeal in *Sabherwal*: Mrs Lambert's property interest in the lease had nothing at all to do with the trust under which the fraudsters held the lease. They held the lease on trust only because a trust was automatically imposed by statute when they acquired the lease from Mrs Lambert in their joint names, and of course under that trust they simply held the lease on trust for themselves. If the lease had been acquired in the name of only one of them, he would have acquired an absolute title to the lease subject only to Mrs Lambert's equity to have the transaction set aside as an unconscionable bargain. There would have been no trust, and no question of overreaching. The fact that the lease was put in the name of the two of them did introduce a trust, but it had nothing to do Mrs Lambert's interest. Section 2 makes it clear that dispositions by ordinary trustees cannot overreach this kind of prior equitable interests: it can only be done by trustees specially approved by the court under s. 2(2), and for obvious reasons of fairness towards the prior interest holder.[109]

15.20 OVERREACHING AND REGISTERED LAND

Overreaching remains essentially an exception to the general rule about the enforceability of equitable interests in land. As the court decisions noted in this part of the chapter demonstrate, we are now in a state of confusion over the rationale of the overreaching mechanism and there are real problems with the way it operates in modern trusts of land. Unfortunately, these problems are exacerbated in registered land. One of the reasons is that our registration of title system, which we go on to consider in Chapter 16 *Registration*, was devised to deal with a similarly outdated model of trusts (i.e. one where the beneficiaries regarded their interests essentially as investments). Another reason is that the registration of title system modifies all our other general rules about enforceability of equitable interests in land, but then also

[108] Lewison LJ in *Mortgage Express* v. *Lambert*, fn. 97 above, at para. 37.
[109] For further criticism of the decision in *Lambert* see further Chapter 16 *Registration* para. 16.27.

imports overreaching with virtually no changes. We see how all this works out in Chapter 16.

RECOMMENDED READING

Freeguard v. *Royal Bank of Scotland* (1990) 79 P & CR 81 (priority of equitable interests in land).

Kingsnorth v. *Tizard* [1986] 1 WLR 783 (constructive notice).

Crédit Agricole Corporation and Investment Bank v. *Papadimitriou* [2015] PC 13 (constructive notice).

Gray v. *Smith* [2013] EWHC 4136 (constructive notice).

Banwaitt v. *Dewji* [2015] EWHC 3441 (what overreaching is).

Baker v. *Craggs* [2018] EWCA Civ 1126 (overreaching).

State Bank of India v. *Sood* [1997] Ch 276 (extension of overreaching).

Law Commission, *Trusts of Land: Overreaching* (1988) Law Com WP No 106, paras. 6.3 and 6.14 (reform of overreaching).

Law Commission Report, *Transfer of Land – Overreaching: Beneficiaries in Occupation* (1989) Law Com No 188 (reform of overreaching).

QUESTIONS

(1)   Is a principle of publicity apparent in our general enforcement and priority rules? (Think about this question again after reading Chapter 16 *Registration*.)

(2)   In our enforceability rules, are we right in treating innocent mortgagees in the same way as we treat innocent purchasers?

(3)   What is the relationship between good faith and notice?

(4)   Discuss whether the doctrine of notice provides a fair and effective enforceability principle. (Think about this again after reading Chapter 16.)

(5)   Should we change our law so that overreaching could not take place except where (a) at least one of the trustees was a solicitor, or (b) the trustees could prove they acted in good faith or (c) the purchaser could prove she acted in good faith, or (d) all beneficiaries in occupation of the trust property consented?

16

Registration

PART I INTRODUCTION

16.1 Land Registration Systems

Land registration systems can take many different forms. We look at our principal system in England and Wales, currently governed by the Land Registration Act 2002, in Parts II–V of this chapter.

Our system is more recently established, less complete and in some ways less satisfactory than many of those operating in other parts of the world. Some of the shortcomings of our system are probably inevitable given the complexity and fluidity of property interests in land in this jurisdiction. Comparisons with registration systems in other jurisdictions suggest that others are not.

In this part of the chapter we outline the main differences between the different models of land registration system which are currently operating in other jurisdictions whose economies and patterns of land use are broadly similar to ours. We focus on the German system and the Scottish system, for reasons we explain in para. 16.8, and we consider how our land registration system fits into that picture. Later, in Parts II–V when we look at our system in more detail, we refer back to some of these comparisons.

We end this part by considering in general terms what land registration is for: what exactly is it that we are seeking to achieve when we set up a procedure for the public registration of property interests in land?

16.2 Land Rights Registers and Cadastres

We start our consideration of the different kinds of land registration system with the distinction between land rights registers and cadastres. Traditionally, land rights registers and cadastres were different things, performing different functions. The distinction is more blurred now, but it is important to appreciate that our current land register in England and Wales – the heart of the registration of title system maintained by HM Land Registry – began life as, and essentially still is, a land rights register and not a cadastre. We do not have a cadastre. Many European systems, on the other hand, have both registers of land rights and cadastres, as we see below.

(a) Land Rights Registers

Land rights registers are local or centralised records *either* of transactions by which property interests in land change hands (in which case the register is a *register of deeds*), *or* of current holdings of property interests in land (which makes the register a *register of titles*). We look at the difference between registers of deeds and registers of titles in para. 16.4, but the point here is that both are designed to provide up-to-date evidence of who holds what property interests in which land. All legal systems which allow land rights to be bought and sold generally develop land rights registers of some kind. The register itself will usually be run by the state or some other public body,[1] but in most systems the state registry does not take the initiative in acquiring or up-dating the information which is put on the register. This comes from private individuals involved in land transactions: whenever a relevant land transaction takes place, the parties are required to notify the Land Registry and submit the required documents to it.[2] We see later how this actually works in our system, but for present purposes the point is that the registry is reactive, not proactive.

(b) Cadastres

A cadastre, on the other hand, is a comprehensive record of all land in a territory and its physical characteristics and uses. Cadastres are usually drawn up by the state, traditionally for public purposes, often to provide information for taxation of land holdings and information about the patterns of land use within the state. In other words, the state itself takes the initiative to acquire and update the information in the cadastre, and indeed historically cadastres were often the product of, or provided the basis for, a national survey and mapping of all land in the territory.[3] The one and only cadastre we have ever had in this country is said to have been the Domesday Book.[4]

---

[1] Recently some national land registries have been privatised (e.g. Ontario and Manitoba in Canada and New South Wales and South Australia in Australia); other national governments (including our own, and the governments of other Canadian and Australian states) have considered but rejected privatisation: see para. 16.9 below, fn. 54.

[2] 'Transaction' for these purposes includes voluntary transfers, mortgages, etc. and also transmission of property interests on death or bankruptcy, in which case a public official responsible for administering the estate of the person who has died or gone bankrupt is responsible for transmitting the relevant information.

[3] Histories of cadastres in some European countries can be found at www.eurocadastre.org/documents .html, and see also Antonella Alimento, 'Eighteenth century cadastres, between tradition and modernity' (2002) (Italy, Spain and France), available at www.catastro.minhap.gob.es/documentos/publicaciones/ ct/ct46/09.2%20Antonella%20Alimento.pdf.

[4] Peter Mayer and Alan Pemberton, *A Short History of Land Registration in England and Wales* (HM Land Registry, 2000), available at www.academia.edu/35055170/A_Short_History_of_Land_ Registration_in_England_and_Wales. We nearly had another one: a detailed land valuation of the whole of the UK – sometimes called the Lloyd George Domesday – was carried out between 1910 and 1915 to provide baseline valuations for the levying of a new tax on incremental land values introduced by the Finance (1909–1910) Act 1910, at a time when nationalisation of land was a key political issue. However, the tax was abolished in 1920 and so the records (anyway not made public until the late 1970s) were not maintained (Brian Short, *Land and Society in Edwardian Britain*, Cambridge Studies in

Many European countries have had both land rights registers and cadastres (often first established centuries ago) and still retain both. In most of these countries the land rights register and the cadastre are now combined, or operate in conjunction with each other, so as to provide a complete record of the geophysical features, the use of, and the property interests in, every parcel of land in the country.[5]

16.3 Function of Modern Cadastres

In modern land administration, surveyors and other professionals often use the term 'cadastre' to refer to these modern combined land rights and land survey systems, or as a generic term to cover all land information systems. FIG (the International Federation of Surveyors) provides the following definition of cadastre when used in this modern general sense:

> A Cadastre is normally a parcel based, and up-to-date land information system containing a record of interests in land (e.g. rights, restrictions and responsibilities). It usually includes a geometric description of land parcels linked to other records describing the nature of the interests, the ownership or control of those interests, and often the value of the parcel and its improvements. It may be established for fiscal purposes (e.g. valuation and equitable taxation), legal purposes (conveyancing), to assist in the management of land and land use (e.g. for planning and other administrative purposes), and enables sustainable development and environmental protection.[6]

International development agencies regard the provision of cadastres (in the modern general sense) as essential for the development of a properly functioning state, basically for two reasons. The first is that they are thought by some to have an important role in the eradication of poverty in developing countries. The argument is that this kind of cadastre is more likely to 'catch' informal land rights of the poor,[7]

Historical Geography (Cambridge: Cambridge University Press, 1997) and also www.nationalarchives .gov.uk/help-with-your-research/research-guides/valuation-office-survey-land-value-ownership-1910- 1915).

[5] So, for example, in Austria the 'Land Book' was established for the public registration of property transfers and mortgages in the twelfth century, whilst a cadastre for taxation purposes was set up by Emperor Franz I in 1817. Based on the cadastre, the whole of the territory of the then Austrian monarchy was surveyed in the period from 1817 to 1861. Both the Land Book (now a register of ownership and other property rights in each numbered parcel of land, with a separate electronic Collection of Deeds containing copies of all the deeds which form the basis of a registration) and the Cadastre (which covers survey and land use data) are still maintained, and together they form a unified National Joint Information System: See Centre of Legal Competence, *Land Registration and Cadastre in Selected European Countries*, vol. 29 (Antwerp: Intersentia, 2009) pp. 27–61, and compare the combined system in the Netherlands outlined at pp. 165–189. For the relationship between the land title registers and cadastres in Germany and in Australia (under the Torrens system) see Murray Raff, 'Characteristics of the international model of land title registration illuminated by comparative study of the German and Torrens systems' (2012) 1 *European Property Law Journal* 54, pp. 59–62.

[6] International Federation of Surveyors, *The FIG Statement on the Cadastre* (1995) Fig Publication No. 11, available at www.fig.net/resources/publications/figpub/pub11/figpub11.asp. This definition appears in the Introduction.

[7] For reasons which will become clear when we look at registration of title in England and Wales, traditional registers of transactions and of land titles have difficulties in accommodating informal land rights.

giving official recognition to their landholdings, so making it less easy for the state and others to dispossess them. It is also argued that it makes it easier for the poor to use their landholdings as security to raise capital, but this is more contentious.[8]

The second reason is that, as FIG pointed out in the quotation above, a cadastre is useful for managing and measuring economic development and environmental sustainability. Land and land-related resources (ranging from minerals, forests, waterways and agriculturally productive land to buildings, transport infrastructures and communications and utilities networks) are central to our physical environment and to national and local economies. A cadastre can provide governments and other policy makers with the comprehensive information they need about all these resources within their territory, including their state and condition, how they relate to each other, what they are used for, and who has what rights, responsibilities and interests in them.[9]

16.4 Two Ways to Register Land Rights: Registration of Titles and Registration of Deeds

As already noted, land rights registers consist primarily of data about property interests in land. There are essentially two ways of organising data about property interests in land.

(a) Registration of Title

One is to have a *register of titles to land*, which is the system we have. In a registration of title system, each parcel of land is given a unique identifying number and file, which records the address and/or physical description of the land, details of the ownership of the land (who holds it and on what terms) and details of other

---

[8] Paul Van Der Molen, 'Future cadastres' in Jan Michiel Otto and André Hoekema (eds.), *Fair Land Governance: How to Legalise Land Rights for Rural Development* (Leiden: Leiden University Press, 2012) p. 111 at pp. 111–113 and 122–126, and see also Alison Clarke, 'Land titling and communal property' in Warren Barr (ed.), *Modern Studies in Property Law*, vol. 8 (Oxford and Portland, OR: Hart Publishing, 2015) p. 215 at pp. 215–221.

[9] HM Land Registry has recently been involved in two government initiatives to increase the 'interoperability' of public bodies who manage geographic ('spatial') data and services, with the intention of generating, publishing and increasing access to co-ordinated spatial data-sets. The first is the INSPIRE programme, the UK implementation of the EU INSPIRE Directive 2007 (Directive 2007/2/EC of the European Parliament and the Council establishing an Infrastructure for Spatial Information in the European Community (INSPIRE), intended to be an EU-wide environmental management tool (see UK INSPIRE Regulations 2009 No. 3157, amended by SI 2012/1672). The second is the Geospatial Commission set up by the government in 2018, intended to bring together the activities of HM Land Registry and five other 'core partners' (including the British Geological Survey, Ordnance Survey and the UK Hydrographic Office) to '[generate and facilitate the use of] domestic geospatial data, products and services across the private and public sectors … bring[ing] together data producers, particularly those in the public sector, to make the production and access to data more coordinated, useful and seamless' with the overarching objective of '[increasing] economic growth and [improving] social and environmental outcomes': Geospatial Commission Charter, Annex A to HM Government, *National Geospatial Strategy – call for evidence* (August 2018). It is not yet clear how far these initiatives will end up by providing us with the equivalent of a cadastre.

property rights and interests in it. Registration of someone as owner is proof of their ownership (conclusive in some systems, rebuttable in others), and the same may apply to other property interests recorded on the register.[10]

(b) Deeds Registration

The other basic type is a *deeds registration* system, which is the system once used in parts of this country[11] and still used in many other countries including the Netherlands and (up until recently) Scotland,[12] and in most states of the United States.[13] A deeds registry records the details of all deeds relating to transactions or other dispositions of ownership and the creation or disposition of other property interests in land. The deeds registry does not investigate the legal validity of the deeds, or of the transactions or other dispositions recorded by the deeds. In other words, as Anderson puts it, if you think of a titles register as 'a register of conclusions' (it tells the world who owns a particular piece of land, and what other property interest affect it), then a deeds register is 'a register of data from which conclusions still [remain] to be drawn' (a lawyer can work out who owns the land and what other property interests affect it by examining the deeds on the register).[14]

So, in its simplest form, as Van Der Molen explains, a deeds register can consist of no more than 'a shoebox containing simple transfer documents approved by the buyer and seller and endorsed by witnesses, together with a reference to a description of the object'.[15] However, at the opposite extreme is a highly sophisticated digitalised system such as the one currently operating in the Netherlands, in which a deeds register is combined with a cadastre and reinforced by a notarial system. As we see later, in some countries (but not ours) notaries play a significant role in land

---

[10] The extent to which the state guarantees the correctness of the register, and to which the public may rely on the correctness of the register, varies widely between systems. For a comparison between the German system and the Torrens system see Raff, 'Characteristics of the international model of land title registration', fn. 5 above, at pp. 68–114, and compare the position in our system as described later in this chapter, in particular in paras. 16.6–16.7 and paras. 16.16–16.17.

[11] Jean Howell, 'Deeds registration in England: A complete failure?' (1999) *Cambridge Law Journal* 366. The Real Property Commission set up in the 1820s to investigate land law reform in England and Wales (including the introduction of a national land registration system) recommended deeds registration rather than land title registration. The recommendation was rejected by Parliament in 1834, but the idea re-surfaced periodically until our first system of (voluntary) title registration was introduced in 1862: J. Stuart Anderson, 'Property rights in land: Reforming the heritage' in William Cornish et al. (eds.), *The Oxford History of the Laws of England: Volume XII: 1820–1914 Private Law* (Oxford: Oxford University Press, 2010) at pp. 64–71 and 73–78.

[12] See para. 16.8 below.

[13] There is no Federal register in the USA. Deeds registration ('recordation') takes place at county level and there is no uniform system for recording or indexing data. In practice the system is supported by title insurance provided by private companies, which generally carry out the searches of the registers, and often maintain their own versions of the title records: Thomas W. Merrill and Henry E. Smith, *Oxford Introductions to US Law: Property* (Oxford: Oxford University Press, 2010) pp. 166–171.

[14] J. Stuart Anderson, 'Changing the nature of real property law' in William Cornish et al. (eds.), *The Oxford History of the Laws of England: Volume XII: 1820–1914 Private Law* (Oxford: Oxford University Press, 2010) at p. 192.

[15] Van der Molen, 'Future cadastres', fn. 8 above, pp. 129–130.

transactions, and in the Netherlands this is closely tied in to the deeds registry system.[16] In the Netherlands deeds transferring titles to land and mortgaging land have to be made by a 'notarial act', which is the equivalent of a deed in our system, except that it must be drawn up and completed by a notary, an independent legal official who advises the parties but also has public functions, which include the recording of all notarial acts in the appropriate public register. By this process the information contained in land transfers and mortgages is automatically recorded in the public land deeds register, which in turn automatically feeds the information into the cadastre register. This combined system allows immediate public access to up-to-date and comprehensive information about every parcel of land in the country, including its geographic features, its usage and who holds what property rights in it.[17]

16.5 Two Ways of Introducing Land Titles Registration: Systematic and Sporadic Registration

There are two ways of introducing a registration of titles system. One is by systematic registration, where the state systematically registers all land titles in a given area at the same time. This usually involves surveying the land to settle boundaries between the land included in each title. The other – which we decided to opt for when we set up our modern system in 1925 – is sporadic registration. Under the sporadic system titles are not registered unless and until they are transferred, or some other trigger event occurs. The International Federation of Surveyors' *FIG Statement on the Cadastre* explains the choice we faced in 1925, and which is still faced by any country setting up a land registration system now:

> When introducing new systems of land registration . . . and surveying in a jurisdiction, the work can be undertaken area by area in a systematic manner or sporadically, for instance, whenever there is a new land transaction . . . A major disadvantage of the sporadic approach is that it will generally take a much longer time to obtain complete coverage within the jurisdiction. A major advantage is that it requires fewer new resources and is therefore less expensive in the short term.
>
> If the objective is to extend the Cadastre to a more comprehensive land information system within a reasonable time frame, the systematic approach is generally more effective . . . . In general, the systematic approach will reduce the time required to begin reaping direct benefits from the new systems.[18]

Most countries which established cadastres before or at the same time as establishing land registration systems adopted the systematic approach – the systematic geographic survey of the country was, after all, often the main objective of the exercise. Consequently, they have long had land registration systems covering all land in the

---

[16] See para. 16.6(c) below, where we consider the possible effects this has on fraudulent transactions.

[17] Centre of Legal Competence, *Land Registration and Cadastre in Selected European Countries*, fn. 5 above, p. 165. For a fuller account of the differences between title registration systems and deeds registration systems see *FIG Statement on the Cadastre*, fn. 6 above, para. 6.2.

[18] *FIG Statement on the Cadastre*, fn. 6 above, para. 6.3.

country. We are certainly not the only country to have opted for the sporadic approach instead, but by any standard our progress towards comprehensive registration of title has been extraordinarily slow, and it is still not yet completed. By 2018, 14.6 per cent of all land in England and Wales was still not yet within the system, and it is not certain when the process will be completed.[19] We come back to this point in para. 16.15. The other consequence of adopting the sporadic approach in England and Wales is that, since we did not start out with a systematic geographical survey, our registration of title system does not show definitive boundaries between landholdings: boundaries are shown on the register, but they may or may not be correct. As we see in para. 16.15, this has advantages and disadvantages.

16.6 Policy Objectives: What is Land Registration For?

The obvious function of any registration of title or deeds registry system is to provide a record of property interests in land, in other words a record of who holds what property interests in relation to which physical spaces. What is less obvious is what that record is for.

(a) Ownership of Land as a Matter of Public Interest

For some, the overriding objective of land registration is to provide a public record of who owns the land in our country. However, not everyone agrees: there are conflicting views on whether the public has a legitimate interest in knowing who owns and controls land. On the one hand, there are those who argue that private citizens have a right to privacy which is infringed by any requirement to make public disclosure of their financial affairs and their wealth, particularly the land they own or control. Others, however, regard land as a national resource in which all citizens have a legitimate interest. This might be because the land is regarded as part of the nation's patrimony, or because of political concerns about concentrating in private hands (or in the state) the wealth and political power generated by land ownership and control, or because of the environmental, social and economic importance of decisions made about national land use and distribution. For all or any of these reasons, it is argued, the public has a right to know who owns and controls land, and the obvious way of fulfilling this right is by having a comprehensive land register which makes all this information known to, and readily accessible by, the public. As we see in the rest of the chapter, our land register is more public than most but less comprehensive, and less helpful than you might expect in telling us who really owns and controls land in England and Wales.[20] We come back to this point in para. 16.13 below.

---

[19] Compare the position in Scotland, where the current land title registration system was first established in 1981 by the Land Registration (Scotland) Act 1979, heavily revised by the Land Registration etc. (Scotland) Act 2012, and it is expected that all titles will be registered by 2024: paras. 16.8 and 16.15 below.

[20] See, for example, www.theguardian.com/books/2019/apr/28/who-owns-england-guy-shrubsole-review-land-ownership, reviewing Guy Shrubsole, *Who Owns England? How We Lost Our Green and Pleasant Land and How to Take It Back* (London: William Collins, 2019) for the political arguments.

(b) The Publicity Principle

An alternative perspective is provided by looking at the essential nature of property interests. If the essence of a property right is that it binds the whole world, then the core function of a land rights register might be seen as making the existence of the property right known to those who could be affected by it. Registration is an obvious way of satisfying what many civil law systems call the *publicity principle*, regarded as a fundamental principle underlying state protection of property. The general principle is that respect for property is owed by the state and other citizens only if property rights have *transparency*, taken to mean that they must have *specificity* and *publicity*.[21] The specificity principle is the equivalent of the general common law principle that property interests must be certain, which we looked at in Chapter 6 *New Property Interests and the Numerus Clausus*.[22] The publicity principle is that 'acts which can affect third parties should be made public, so that third parties can know of them'.[23] We do not expressly acknowledge the publicity principle in our property rights system, but it is implicit in, and helps to explain, many of our land law rules, particularly those relating to possession and registration, as we see later on in this chapter.

However, there are different ways of looking at the publicity principle. On one view, publicity is seen as the responsibility of the property rights holder. The argument is that if you are, say, the freehold owner of land, so that everyone else in the world is put under a duty not to interfere with your rights, you cannot expect the law to penalise anyone who *does* interfere with your rights (perhaps by picnicking in your garden, thinking it is part of the park next door) unless you have taken reasonable steps to make your ownership known to the public. Murray Raff suggests that this view underlies the French and Belgian approach to land registration:

> A valid proprietary interest is a source of social protection against dealings with the object undertaken by third parties who have no connection with the proprietor. The theoretical question of why within the structures of the civil law the proprietor is able to call for social protection of his or her interests in the object has many different answers. In Belgian and French property systems a proprietor's interest is owed respect by other members of society, who have no other legal relationship with the proprietor, when the proprietor makes the existence of his or her interest widely known through a legitimate act of publicity.[24]

Current government policy is influenced by similar concerns, although (unsurprisingly) from a different perspective: see para. 16.13 below. The issue is equally emotive in Scotland: see Scottish Land Commission, *Review of Scale and Concentration of Land Ownership: Report to Scottish Ministers*, 20 March 2019.

[21] Sjef van Erp and Bram Akkermans (eds.), *Cases, Materials and Text on Property Law* (Oxford and Portland, OR: Hart Publishing, 2012) pp. 75–77 and 87.

[22] See Chapter 6 para. 6.13.

[23] George Gretton and Andrew Steven, *Property, Trusts and Succession* (3rd edn, Haywards Heath: Bloomsbury Professional, 2017) paras. 4.19–4.20, explaining the principle as it applies in Scotland.

[24] Murray Raff, *Private Property and Environmental Responsibility: A Comparative Study of German Real Property Law* (The Hague, London and New York: Kluwer Law International, 2003) p. 5, citing in support E. Beysen, 'Belgien' and 'Frankreich' in C. von Bar (ed.), *Sachenrecht in Europa*, vol. 4 (Osnabrück: Universitätsverlag Rasch, 2000) at p. 34 and p. 201.

Land registration systems based on this rationale may accept other 'acts of publicity' as alternatives to registration, but usually only in very limited circumstances. The most obvious alternative 'act of publicity' is possession: as we saw in Chapter 11 *Possession and Title*, in common law and civil law jurisdictions physical control of land has traditionally been regarded as signalling to the world that you claim legal entitlement to the land.[25] As we see later on in this chapter, in this jurisdiction we have carried this notion through into our land registration system to a limited extent, in that in some circumstances we treat possession or occupation of land as a sufficient act of publicity, justifying protection of a property interest held by a possessor even if the interest has not been publicly recorded on the register.[26]

The converse of the publicity principle, seen through the eyes of the property interest holder, is that if you hold a property interest and you perform the relevant act of publicity required under the system – you register your interest in the public register or, when this is an allowable alternative under the system, you give public notice of you property interest by being in possession – you should be entitled to expect that you will get an unchallengeable title[27] in return.

If we view the publicity principle from the perspective of outsiders, however, we might want to say instead that the function of the publicity principle is to protect members of the public who might come into contact with a property interest holder and the land affected by her interests. From this perspective, the central objective of a land registration system is to give any member of the public who needs to know, the means of finding out who has what interests in any given piece of land. In the German system this is articulated as a principle of 'public faith' in the land register.[28] This is taken to mean that the public should be able to rely on the correctness and completeness of the register: if I buy land from someone who is registered as owner of it, I should be guaranteed a good title (even if the owner was not entitled to be registered), free from any property interest affecting the land which is not revealed by the register.[29]

(c) Preventing Fraud

If we look at it on a practical rather than a principled level, the central policy objective of many long established registration systems was, initially at least, to prevent

---

[25] See Luz M. Martínez Velencoso and Saki Bailey (eds.), *Transfer of immoveables in European Private Law* (Cambridge: Cambridge University Press, 2017) at p. 153 on possession as 'an instrument of publicity for property right' in Spanish law, and at p. 154: 'Given the deficiencies of the publicity mechanism based on possession, land registry systems have developed as the principal alternative to them'.

[26] For example, the overriding interests of persons in actual occupation of land (para. 16.27).

[27] Or 'indefeasible' title, using conventional land registration terminology.

[28] *Das materielle Publizitätsprinzip*. There is also a 'formal' publicity principle – *das formelle Publizitätsprinzip* – which requires legitimate public access to the register: Raff, Private Property and Environmental Responsibility, fn. 24 above, p. 13.

[29] Raff, Private Property and Environmental Responsibility, fn. 24 above, pp. 13, pp. 147–153 and 277, and see also BGB s. 891 and s. 892. The German system, like many others, limits the guarantee to certain classes of purchaser: see para. 16.16 below.

fraudulent practices by landowners and by outsiders. Many land titles registers and deeds registers were reportedly set up specifically to prevent landowners selling the same land twice or hiding mortgages or other burdens they had created over the land.[30] These are the typical land frauds we noted in para. 15.4 of Chapter 15 *Enforceability and Priority of Property Interests*. Registration can make this kind of fraud more difficult by, for example, making a public official like a notary responsible for completing and registering transactions,[31] or (as in our system) giving the responsibility to the purchaser or mortgagee or other person acquiring property rights under the transaction. Registration of titles to land (and deeds registration) should also make it more difficult for outsiders to get away with the other kinds of fraud we looked at in at para. 15.4, for example where a fraudster manages to pass herself off as an owner, and 'sells' or 'mortgages' to an innocent purchaser/mortgagee.

(d) Facilitating Land Transactions

If you were to ask any UK lawyer in England and Wales what the point of land registration is, most would probably say that it is to make it quicker, easier and cheaper to buy, sell or mortgage land or carry out other land transactions. The legislation which set up our registration of title system, the Land Registration Act 1925, was an integral part of the 1925 property legislation we outlined in Chapter 5 *Ownership and Other Property Interests* para. 5.5(b). As we noted there, the 1925 property legislation was a compromise (and in some places a fudge) between competing objectives, so we have to be cautious about attributing any clear intentions to the legislators who brought in our land registration system. However, we can say that for at least some of them a central objective was to simplify land holdings to make them more easily marketable: as J. Stuart Anderson pointed out, at one stage in the debate a favoured model for land ownership was the kind of simple ownership then used for investment stock and bonds issued by the government.[32] The underlying idea was to make land a more attractive investment, which could be bought and sold easily and which banks would be happy to accept as security for loans. Registration of titles to land in a central register was a key element in this strategy, because it would mean that it was no longer necessary for the provenance of a title to be investigated and reinvestigated every time a title changed hands.[33] Instead,

---

[30] Prevention of this kind of fraud appears to have been a primary motivation behind the Scottish Registration Act of 1617 which set up the Register of Sasines (see para. 16.8 below), and also land registration legislation in France and Denmark at about the same time: Kenneth G. Reid and George Gretton, *Land Registration* (Edinburgh: Avizandum Publishing Ltd, 2017) pp. 2–4.

[31] For the role of notaries in land transactions in civil law countries see Centre of Legal Competence, *Land Registration and Cadastre in Selected European Countries*, fn. 5 above, p. 17 and (in the Netherlands) pp. 167–174. Notaries in the Netherlands are required to exercise their function 'independently and represent impartially and with the greatest possible care the interests of all parties involved' in the transaction. Notaries do not have any role in land transactions or land registration in England and Wales (see www.thenotariessociety.org.uk).

[32] Anderson, 'Changing the nature of real property law', fn. 14 above, at pp. 197–198.

[33] That is, going through the deeds by which the legal title had been transferred from one person to another, up to the deed transferring it to the person currently claiming to hold it and going back in

prospective buyers and mortgagees could find out everything they needed to know simply by checking a public register, and they could rely on what the register said because of the state's guarantee of titles that were registered there.

This link between land registration and land markets – that is, the assumption that the whole point of land registration is to make it easier to carry out commercial transactions in land – is even more evident in the Land Registration Act 2002, which modified the system we set up in 1925,[34] and this mirrors international developments. So, from the late twentieth century it became accepted wisdom internationally that land registration is necessary for the development of a market economy in which land is a marketable commodity. This helps to explain why, for many years, development agencies funded land titling programmes in countries which were moving towards (or were being urged to move towards) a market economy.[35]

16.7 Balancing Conflicting Objectives

It will be apparent from the previous paragraph that land registration objectives may sometimes conflict. In particular, it may not always be possible for the state to honour its commitment to protect property interests publicised on the register without betraying the faith of those who have acted in reliance on the correctness of the register (and vice versa). This brings us back to the distinction we noted in para. 15.4 of Chapter 15 *Enforceability and Priority of Property Interests*, when we looked at general principles of enforceability and priority of property interests. This is the distinction some scholars make when talking about protection of property rights, between static security (which focuses on protection of pre-existing property rights) and dynamic or transactional security (which focuses on protection of purchasers).

(a) Why Conflicts Arise

The problem of potential conflict between the two arises in an acute form in relation to land registration systems because sometimes the register will be wrong. This may be because someone – perhaps someone at the Land Registry, or the person responsible for preparing title documents or presenting them to the registry – has made a clerical or careless mistake. Misled by this kind of mistake, the Land Registry may

---

theory to the first taking of the land into private ownership, but in practice (in modern times) to a transfer or grant at least 15 years ago: see Julian Farrand and Alison Clarke (eds.), *Emmet & Farrand on Title* (London: Sweet & Maxwell, looseleaf updated to 30 April 2019) para 5.018.

[34] The joint Law Commission and Land Registry Report and draft Bill later enacted as the Land Registration Act 2002 was entitled *Land Registration for the Twenty-first Century: A Conveyancing Revolution* (2001) Law Com No 271, and its opening paragraph puts its proposed 'transformation' of the way conveyancing (i.e. carrying out land transactions) is conducted ahead of the 'other profound changes to the substantive law' it proposed (most of which were also geared towards making it easier to buy, sell and mortgage land). We consider later in the chapter how far these claims have been realised.

[35] Including former socialist states and developing countries in Asia, Africa and South America: see further Clarke, 'Land titling and communal property', fn. 8 above, pp. 215–217 and the works cited there.

perhaps (taking examples from three recent English court decisions), have registered me as registered leaseholder of the flat on the third floor of a building when in fact the lease I have just bought is of the flat on the second floor,[36] or wrongly registered a purchaser of land next door to me as registered owner of a strip of land adjoining the land he has bought, when that strip of land is already registered in my name as part of my land,[37] or wrongly de-registered the bank's mortgage over my registered title to my home when I have not yet repaid the mortgage loan.[38] And of course, as already noted in the previous paragraph, a wrong entry on the register, or a wrongful omission from it, can also be the result of a fraud.

(b) Rival Claims

It is not always easy for a registration system to deal with the consequences of these mistakes, and, as already noted, it often comes down to deciding between the rival claims of a person whose pre-existing property rights were extinguished or prejudiced by the mistake, and another person (perhaps a transferee or mortgagee) who has innocently acted on the assumption that the mistaken entry on (or omission from) the register was correct.

It is worth reminding ourselves that the protection of pre-existing property rights is not just an objective of a land registration system. It is also a basic function of the state, and a state authority which extinguishes or interferes with our pre-existing property rights is acting in breach of our human rights under article 1 protocol 1 of the European Convention on Human Rights (unlawful interference with possessions) and in some situations also article 8 (right to respect for our home). So, a registration system has to have a very good reason indeed for preferring the interests of an innocent transferee/mortgagee over those of a pre-existing property interest holder. It is not free to adopt rules that, for example, always and automatically prefer protection of innocent transferees/mortgagees (dynamic security) over protection of pre-existing property interest holders (static security). The human rights arguments will not always be as straightforward as that, or as one-sided. In some circumstances the innocent transferee/mortgagee may also be able to rely on human rights arguments under article 1 Protocol 1 and/ or article 8 (consider, for example, my position if a fraudster 'sells' your house to me whilst you are away and tricks the Land Registry into wrongly registering me as owner, and I then move in and start living there). However, the important point here is that in resolving conflicts of these kinds, human rights arguments have to be taken into consideration, as well as arguments based on the realisation of land registration objectives such as promoting efficient market exchanges of land or maintaining public faith in the register.

---

[36] *Isaaks (by Bank of Scotland Plc Acting as Attorney) v. Charlton Triangle Homes Ltd* [2015] EWHC 2611.

[37] *Parshall v. Hackney* [2013] EWCA Civ 240.   [38] *NRAM Ltd v. Evans* [2017] EWCA Civ 1013.

(c) Static and Dynamic Security: A False Dichotomy?

The human rights angle is one of several reasons why we should be wary of representing registered land conflicts as stark choices between static security and dynamic security. It is tempting to think of static security as something that registered property owners want, and dynamic security as something that potential purchasers and mortgagees want, but that would be wrong. The truth is that everyone wants both. The person who has registered her property interest does want to be assured that her interest cannot accidently or mistakenly be extinguished or prejudiced by the Land Registry, but she also wants to be assured that, as and when she wants to sell or mortgage her interest, she will be able to do so easily, quickly and cheaply. That is, after all, the only way she can realise the capital value of her property interest. Similarly, the prospective purchaser or mortgagee certainly wants a guarantee that if he enters into a transaction with the registered holder of a property interest, he will get the title he is paying for free from any unknown interests adversely affecting it. But he also wants a guarantee that, once he has got that title, it will be unchallengeable. This is probably an inescapable problem inherent in any land titles registration system: as J. Stuart Anderson points out, English critics opposing the introduction of a land title registration system in England and Wales were arguing in the 1850s that 'it suffered from the inescapable logical problem that the very concept of indefeasibility used to lure a proprietor on to the register also threatened his removal by forgery'.[39]

(d) Alternatives to Full Guarantees

So, if a registration system fully guarantees either static security at the expense of dynamic security, or dynamic security at the expense of static security, it pleases nobody. One alternative is to limit the scope of the guarantees, and there are various ways of doing this. In our land registration system we do it by giving a more limited guarantee of security of title to registered owners who are not in possession of the land, and by guaranteeing the correctness of the register only to 'purchasers', that is, transferees and mortgagees who gave value. Other systems guarantee the correctness of the register to any kind of arms-length transferee, whether or not they gave value, but only to transferees who acted in good faith and had no notice of the mistake on the register. These are limitations that we impose in our unregistered land system, as we saw in Chapter 15 *Enforceability and Priority of Property Interests* when we looked at the doctrine of notice,[40] but we have not carried them over into our registered land system. We see how all this works in our jurisdiction in Part III below, where we look at the rules about enforcement and priority of property interests under the Land Registration Act 2002, and in paras. 16.38 and 16.39 in Part V below, where we outline the circumstances in which the register can be altered to correct mistaken entries and omissions.

---

[39] Anderson, 'Changing the nature of real property law', fn. 14 above, at p. 195.
[40] paras. 15.9 and 15.10.

(e) Compensating the Losers

Another thing a registration system can do is provide compensation for the loser in a conflict between an innocent property interest holder and an innocent purchaser. As we noted in para. 15.4(b) of Chapter 15 *Enforcement and Priority of Property Interests*, land registration systems can generate funds to pay for this by charging small fees for searching the register, inspecting entries and registering interests. Most registration systems do charge small fees for processing applications of this kind and the total amounts received each year are usually substantial because the number of applications processed is so high.[41] Most of these funds are used to pay for the operating costs of the registration system itself, but there is no obvious reason why operating costs should not include an insurance fund which can be used to compensate innocent victims of the system. We could count innocent losers in property conflicts as victims of the system for these purposes. In other words, if someone will suffer loss through no fault of their own because the register is wrong in some respect, and for one reason or another it is decided that the register cannot be corrected to reverse their loss, then they can be compensated out of the insurance fund. Our land registration system does provide for compensation of this kind to be paid by the Land Registry out of its funds (called *indemnity*), but other jurisdictions do not,[42] and even in our system the circumstances in which it is payable are very limited, as we see in para. 16.39 below.

(f) Who Gets the Mud and Who Gets the Money?

So, in our land registration system we could, in principle at least, resolve all property conflicts between innocent parties arising out of mistakes in the register by awarding the disputed property interest to one of them and giving the other one compensation for the financial loss caused by losing the property interest. However, that would still leave the subsidiary question we noted in para. 15.4(b) of Chapter 15 *Enforceability and Priority of Property Interests*: who gets 'the money' and who gets the 'the mud'? As Amy Goymour points out, where the dispute concerns land, some classes of property interest holder have a strong and justifiable preference for 'the mud' – the land itself – over the 'money'.[43] After reading the rest of this chapter we will need to consider how far our land registration system does and should reflect those preferences, particularly where 'the mud' is the home of one of the rival claimants.

16.8 Other Land Registration Models: Germany, the Torrens System and Scotland

In this chapter we make occasional references to land registration systems in other jurisdictions. These include the German land title registration system which was

---

[41] See para. 16.39(a) below for the figures in England and Wales.

[42] See, for example, Germany: Raff, 'Characteristics of the international model of land title registration', fn. 5 above, pp. 114–115.

[43] Amy Goymour, 'Mistaken registrations of land: Exploding the myth of 'title by registration' (2013) *Cambridge Law Journal* 617 at p. 622, and see further para. 15.4(b) above.

established in the 1900s, and which is interesting not only as an example of land title registration in a civil law system,[44] but also because it has been used as a model for the development of land title registration systems in some other European jurisdictions, and in Taiwan, South Korea, Japan and China.[45]

The second model to note here, which is often referred to in the cases and literature cited in this chapter, is the Torrens system. This system originated in South Australia in the 1850s and is said to have been modelled on the system then operating in the Hanseatic City of Hamburg (now part of Germany), which also influenced the current German system.[46] The Torrens system itself has been widely copied, with variations, throughout Australasia and other jurisdictions, including several countries in Africa and states in Canada and in the USA.[47] In some ways our system is very like a Torrens system (not least because the property rights systems in Australia and in England and Wales share the same roots). However, this chapter does not make specific comparisons between our system and Australian Torrens systems, because each state in Australia has its own registration system and there are significant variations between them.

Our third model is Scotland, a mixed civil law and common law jurisdiction, which has had its own unique system for registration of land transactions, the Register of Sasines, since 1617. The Register of Sasines is a deeds register and it is claimed to be the oldest, still running, national public property register in the world.[48] However, it is now being phased out, to be replaced by a system of registration of title. This process has not been straightforward. A system of registration of title, closely modelled on the land registration system in England and Wales, was first introduced in Scotland by the Land Registration (Scotland) Act 1979 and the intention was that it would gradually supersede the Register of Sasines. However, long before that process could be completed, the 1979 system was itself remodelled by the Land Registration etc. (Scotland) Act 2012, which came into force in December 2014, and which brought the 1979 Act system closer to the German model.[49] The plan (perhaps optimistic) is that all land in Scotland will be put into

---

[44] We have to bear in mind that there are significant differences between European civil law countries. For a good overview, see Raff, Private Property and Environmental Responsibility, fn. 24 above, pp. 8–17. For useful surveys see Centre of Legal Competence, *Land Registration and Cadastre in Selected European Countries*, fn. 5 above. Other technical (mainly non-legal) surveys and historical accounts of cadastres in EU countries, some country-specific and others comparative, can be downloaded from the website of the Permanent Committee on Cadastre in the European Union at www.eurocadastre.org/documents.html.

[45] See further Raff, 'Characteristics of the international model of land title registration', fn. 5 above, pp. 55–56.

[46] Raff, Private Property and Environmental Responsibility, fn. 24 above, pp. 25–60.

[47] Raff, 'Characteristics of the international model of land title registration', fn. 5 above, at pp. 55–58.

[48] John King, 'Completion of the land register: The Scottish approach' in Frankie McCarthy, James Chalmers and Stephen Bogle (eds.), *Essays in Conveyancing and Property Law in Honour of Professor Robert Rennie* (Cambridge: Open Book Publishers, 2015) p. 317.

[49] For a good overview of the origins of the Register of Sasines and its subsequent development, and the origins and rationales of the 1979 Act and the 2012 Act changes, see Reid and Gretton, Land Registration, fn. 30 above, Chs. 1–2 and pp. 44–46.

this new registration system by 2024, and when this happens the Register of Sasines will be closed.[50]

PART II REGISTRATION OF TITLE IN ENGLAND AND WALES: LAND REGISTRATION ACT 2002

16.9 How Registration of Title Works in England and Wales

The principal land registration system in England and Wales[51] is a title registration system, now governed by the Land Registration Act 2002 (the 'LRA 2002'),[52] which modified the title registration system first established by the Land Registration Act 1925 (the 'LRA 1925').[53]

Broadly, the scheme is that there is a central land register covering the whole of England and Wales, administered by HM Land Registry, which is a government department.[54] This central register is a register of titles to freehold and long leasehold interests in land. The way it works is that anyone who holds a freehold interest in land or a long lease (i.e. a lease for more than seven years[55]) must register their title to that interest in the register.[56] The registrar will then record the name of the current holder of the title, and the land covered by the title. The land covered by each registered title is described on the register by reference to an address (or some

---

[50] Ibid. pp. 106–107, and see also Kenneth G. Reid, 'De-throning King Midas: The new law of land registration in Scotland' in Amy Goymour, Stephen Watterson and Martin Dixon (eds), *New Perspectives on Land Registration: Contemporary Problems and Solutions* (Oxford: Hart Publishing, 2018) p. 157 and King, 'Completion of the land register', fn. 48 above.

[51] We have separate registration systems for some communal and public property interests in land (see further para.16.32) and, under the Land Charges Act 1972, for some 'commercial' private property interests in land (including restrictive covenants, some mortgages and estate contracts, options, etc.) which affect titles to land which have not yet been brought into the system now governed by the LRA 2002 (see fn. 35 to para. 15.8 in Chapter 15 *Enforceability and Priority of Property Interests*). We look at why some land is not yet covered by the system in para. 16.15.

[52] The LRA 2002 resulted from a joint Report and Bill published by the Law Commission and HM Land Registry, *Land Registration for the Twenty-first Century: A Conveyancing Revolution* (2001) Law Com No 271.

[53] There had been earlier attempts to introduce national land registration, following a Royal Commission on Registration of Title 1857 and starting with the Land Registry Act 1862, but they were largely unsuccessful. The (relatively) few registrations made under the old Acts were transferred on to the new register set up by the LRA 1925. For a short history see Mayer and Pemberton, *A Short History of Land Registration in England and Wales*, fn. 4 above. For a full history up to 1925 see J. Stuart Anderson *Lawyers and the Making of English land law 1832–1940* (Oxford: Clarendon Press, 1992) and see also Nicola Jackson, 'Overreaching in registered land law' (2006) 69 *Modern Law Review* 214 at pp. 224–229.

[54] Technically, a non-ministerial government department which is an executive agency: HM Land Registry, *Land Registry Annual Report 2017–2018* (HC 1118, published 19 July 2018) p. 4. Privatisation of HM Land Registry was proposed in 2016 (not for the first time), but in the Treasury's Autumn Statement 21 November 2016 it was announced that 'Following consultation the Government has decided that HM Land Registry should focus on becoming a more digital data-driven registration business, and to do this will remain in the public sector'.

[55] Including any sublease or sub-underlease etc., provided it is for more than seven years.

[56] See para. 16.19 for the circumstances in which this obligation to register arises and the consequences of failing to register.

other geographic description) and by reference to its location on the Land Registry's official map.[57] Other property interests which affect the registered freehold or leasehold title are then also recorded on the register, as against the relevant title. The idea is that anyone who searches for a piece of land on the register (for example, by its postal address) will find out:

- who is the present holder of the freehold title to that land;
- who, if anyone, holds a leasehold title to all or part of the same land under a lease or sublease of more than seven years, and the terms of the relevant lease/sublease;
- what other property interests (for example, a mortgage or charge held by a bank, or a right of way over the land held by a neighbour) adversely affect the registered title(s); and
- what property interests over any other land (for example, a right of way over neighbouring land) are attached to the registered title-holder's title.

As we see later in para. 16.13, anyone can search the register, but it is organised in such a way that you can search only against a piece of land (by giving its address or physical description or a map reference). You cannot search against the name of a person. So, you can find out who has what interests in any given piece of land,[58] but you cannot find out what property interests in land are held by any given person.

16.10 Information Recorded on the Land Register

To be more precise, the information that can be found on the register, and the way it is organised, is as follows.

(a) Registered Titles

Each registered freehold title and each registered leasehold title has a separate digitised file in the land register and is given a unique title number. 'The land register' consists of all these separate title files and the Land Registry's official map, on which each registered title is recorded. Every time a registered title is transferred, the transfer is recorded on the register in the title's file, with the transferee recorded as the new title holder (the technical term is 'registered proprietor') in place of the transferor.

If there are leasehold registered titles affecting a registered freehold title, the leasehold and freehold titles are cross-referenced. This is done by recording details of every registered lease in the relevant landlord's title file. Similarly, details of the landlord's registered title will be recorded in the file of the lessee's registered leasehold title.

---

[57] A map of England and Wales derived from Ordnance Survey maps, currently the OS MasterMap: see HM Land Registry, *HM Land Registry Plans: The Basis of Land Registry Plans* (practice guide 40, supplement 1), updated 30 January 2016.

[58] The list may, however, not be comprehensive: as we see in Part IV below, many property interests are not recorded on the register at all. This means that, to get a complete picture of the property interests affecting any given piece of land, a Land Registry search may not be sufficient.

Registrable titles become legal titles once they are registered.[59] Until then they are valid, but equitable only. We look more closely at the effect of registration of registrable titles in Part III below.

(b) Registrable Interests

Titles to legal mortgages and to expressly granted legal easements[60] are also said to be 'registrable',[61] but here 'registration' takes a different form. A registered mortgage does not have a separate file or a title number. Instead, information about the mortgage is 'registered' in the file of the freehold or leasehold title which is mortgaged by the mortgage. The same applies to a registered easement: it does not have a separate file or a title number, but information about it is 'registered' in the file of the registered freehold and leasehold titles which relate to the land over which the easement is exercisable. In other words, the burden of an easement is 'registered' as a property interest against the registered freehold title to the servient land (i.e. the land over which the easement is exercisable); meanwhile the benefit of the easement will be recorded against the registered freehold title to the land benefitted by the easement.

Like registrable freehold and leasehold titles, registrable mortgages and registrable easements do not become legal property interests unless and until they are registered against the title of the land they affect adversely. Until that happens, they are still property interests, but equitable only. We look at the effect this has on their enforcement and priority in Part III below.

(c) Interests Protected by Notice

There is only one other mechanism – the 'notice' – for entering details of property interests in land on the land register, and this is available for only a limited class of property interests.[62] A property interest which is within that class can be 'protected' by 'entering' a notice of the property interest[63] on the register of the title that it affects adversely. For example, if I have a restrictive covenant over your registered freehold title to your land, or an option to purchase it, I may protect it by entering a notice of it in the register of your title to the land.

---

[59] S. 6 and s. 7 of the LRA 2002.

[60] Easements which arise by implication or by long use/prescription are not registrable, and nor are some equitable easements. Instead, they are governed by quite different rules. For this and other reasons, the treatment of easements in our registration system is often criticised: see para. 16.35 below.

[61] There are other legal interests (e.g. franchises and profits a prendre in gross) which come within the same 'registrable interest' category (all listed in s. 27(2) of the LRA 2002). They are not often encountered and we do not deal with them here.

[62] Ss. 32–39 of the LRA 2002.

[63] The terminology – 'protection' of interests by a 'notice' which is 'entered' on the register – is significantly different from the equivalent terminology used in relation to registrable interests, signalling the much weaker position of an interest 'protected by notice' compared to that of an interest which is 'registered'.

A notice does not guarantee the validity of the property interest which it protects, nor does it affect its legal/equitable status, or its priority over other unregistered property interests affecting the registered title. However, it does make the property interest enforceable against subsequent purchasers of the title it affects (so if I protect my restrictive covenant or option to purchase by entering a notice against your title, it will be enforceable against anyone you sell or mortgage your land to). We look at the way this works in para. 16.24(a).

The most important point is that, as we have already noted, not all property interests can be protected on the register by notice. The LRA 2002 does not list the property interests which *can* be protected by notice: instead, by s. 33, it lists those which cannot. The list includes some major categories of property interest, the most significant of which are the interests of beneficiaries under a trust, and leases for three years or less. Since, as we saw in (b) above, these interests are not registrable either, it means that the property interests listed in s. 33 *never* appear on our land register. We look at the way our land registration system is supposed to deal with these interests in paras. 16.25–16.27 when we consider the overriding interest category, and in paras. 16.33 and 16.36 we take a closer look at the implications of keeping short leases and beneficial interests under trusts off the register.

Meanwhile, however, we should note that there is some overlap between, on the one hand, registrable long leasehold titles and registrable interests, and, on the other hand, interests which can be protected by notice. Specifically, long leases (but not freeholds) and mortgages and easements which could have been registered but were not, can instead be protected by notice. When that happens, they will be equitable property interests and not legal property interests, but they will still be enforceable against subsequent purchasers and mortgagees of the registered freehold title to the land, and against subsequent purchasers and mortgagees of any registered leasehold titles.

(d) Indirect Protection of an Interest by Entry of a Restriction

The only other entry that may be made on the land register is a 'restriction'.[64] Restrictions are entered against the registered freehold or leasehold titles they affect. A restriction prohibits the registration of any further dealings with that title unless certain specified conditions are met. The restriction does not disclose any specific property interest affecting the title, nor does it give it direct protection. Instead, the idea is that, if a registered proprietor has no power to enter into a specified kind of transaction, either at all or without complying with specified conditions, this will be recorded in the restriction, warning prospective purchasers that the registry will not register any dealings which contravene those limitations. The most common conditions imposed by a restriction are that consent for the dealing from some other person is required (for example, if the registered proprietor is a charity, that no disposition will be registered without the authorisation of

---

[64] Ss. 40–47 of the LRA 2002.

the Charity Commission) or that payment of any capital payable under the transaction must be made to at least two trustees. This last restriction is probably the most commonly used, and the least satisfactory.[65] It is used to warn prospective purchasers that a title is held on trust for beneficiaries, but it does not identify or directly protect the interests of the trust beneficiaries. All it does is to tell prospective purchasers how to overreach any beneficial interests there may be (i.e. by paying any purchase price to at least two trustees). We come back to this important point in para. 16.36(b) below.

16.11 How the Information is Organised on the Land Register

So, in more precise terms, the land register records registered freehold titles and registered titles to leases of more than seven years, and against each of these registered titles it records:

- legal mortgages and easements which have been registered against those titles;
- appurtenant property rights such as easements and covenants which the registered proprietor of a registered freehold or leasehold title has over neighbouring land and which have been registered (or protected by notice) against the registered titles to the burdened neighbouring land;[66]
- in the case of a freehold title, details of any registered lease which affects it; in the case of a registered lease, details of the landlord's registered title and of the titles of any registered sub-leases';
- any 'notices' of other property interests which adversely affect the title; and
- any 'restrictions' on dealings with the registered title.

This information is organised in three sections. The first section, the *Property Register*, gives the title number, it states whether the title is freehold or leasehold, and it identifies the land covered by the title. Identification is by reference to a physical description or postal address, and also by reference to the official Land Registry plan. If it is a leasehold title the Property Register will also give brief details of the lease. The Property Register then goes on to record all the property rights over other land which are appurtenant to this title (for example, the benefit of any easements or covenants over other land which have been protected by registration or entry of a notice against the titles of the other land).

---

[65] Not least because of the obscure wording of the relevant standard form: 'No disposition by a sole proprietor of the registered estate (except a trust corporation) under which capital money arises is to be registered unless authorised by an order of the court' (Form A, set out in HM Land Registry, *Practice Guide 19: Notices, Restrictions and the Protection of Third Party Interests in the Register*, updated March 2019).

[66] The registrar will automatically have made these entries against the titles to the neighbouring land when it was provided with evidence of the existence of these appurtenant rights, either when the title claiming the appurtenant rights was first registered, or when the registered title was subsequently transferred (because restrictive covenants and expressly created easements are usually granted or reserved in transfers of title).

The next section is the *Proprietorship Register*. It gives the name and address of the current registered proprietor, the date they were registered as proprietor and the price they paid for the title, and it also sets out any 'restrictions' on their power to sell, mortgage or otherwise deal with the title.

The Proprietorship Register also states the 'class' of the proprietor's title. Nearly all freehold and leasehold titles come within the 'absolute' class, but provision is made for the Land Registry to issue 'qualified', 'possessory' or 'good' titles instead on first registration of the title, if at that time there were defects in the title.[67] We will not be considering these lesser titles in the rest of this chapter. They are rarely issued, and in any event they may be up-graded if the defect is removed or (in the case of possessory title) the title has remained unchallenged for a sufficient period.

Finally, the *Charges Register*, which is the third part of the register, identifies the property interests in the land which are held by others and which are enforceable against the registered proprietor. This is where we find the mortgages, charges, leases and easements which have been 'registered' against the title, and the burden of any other interest, such as a restrictive covenant or unregistered easement, which has been protected by a 'notice'.

16.12 Changes in the Form of the Register

The form the register takes has changed over the last few decades, driven by digitalisation. At one time each registered title had its own (paper) index card, and the registered title's file consisted of that index card. All the information on the register for each title was entered manually on its index card, and the land register consisted of the filing cabinets containing those index cards.[68] Now, however, it is all electronic: the register itself is in electronic form and all entries on it and searches of it are done electronically. These changes have had some significant and not necessarily intended consequences:

(a) Historical Information

First, under the old paper system the register used to provide a historical record of the title (details of previous owners and mortgagees, and details of interests that had expired or been discharged, were shown crossed out on the index card). The present electronic system does not provide this historic information: the land register of any given title shows only a snapshot of the current entries,[69] or what the Scottish Law Commission has described as 'a sort of memory-less continuous present'. Scotland had the same problem under its 1979 Act, but on the recommendation of the

---

[67] Ss. 9–10 of the LRA 2002.

[68] Apparently the index cards were filed on spikes (to keep track of the order in which successive transactions took place) rather than in cabinets.

[69] S. 69 of the LRA 2002 provides that the registrar 'may on application' provide information about the history of a registered title. Under the current procedure, applications can be made requesting the Land Registry to search their records for former entries which no longer appear on the register: www.gov.uk/get-information-about-property-and-land/search-the-register.

Scottish Law Commission[70] the 2012 Act now requires the Keeper to maintain an Archive Record,[71] which forms the third part of their land register.[72]

(b) Paper Evidence of Title

Second, under the old system, the Land Registry used to issue to the title holder (the 'registered proprietor' of the title) an official paper copy of the entries on its index card at the register. This official paper copy, issued in an elaborately decorated cover, was called a Land Certificate and it guaranteed the accuracy of its contents as at the date it was issued.[73] The relevant Land Certificate had to accompany all applications to the Land Registry to deal with the registered title. So, if there was a sale of the title the seller had to send her Land Certificate in to the Land Registry, and when the transfer of title was registered, the Land Registry issued a new Land Certificate to the purchaser. Similarly, if the registered proprietor granted a lease of more than seven years, she would have to send her Land Certificate in to the Land Registry with the lease so that the lease could be registered. Her Land Certificate would be sent back to her, now recording the grant of the lease, and a new Land Certificate for the leasehold title would be sent to the tenant (now the registered proprietor of the leasehold title). If, on the other hand, there was a mortgage of the title, the registered proprietor did not get her Land Certificate back until the mortgage was discharged. Instead, the Land Registry issued the lender with a re-packaged duplicate copy of the entries on the registered proprietor's index card. This was called a Charge Certificate. So, whilst the mortgage lasted, the registered proprietor had no Land Certificate but the mortgagee had a Charge Certificate, which provided the mortgagee with evidence of the registered proprietor's title and proof of its own mortgage over it. This system had a number of practical advantages. It effectively prevented the registered proprietor of the mortgaged title from doing anything with the title without the mortgagee's consent for so long as the mortgage lasted, which suited the mortgagee. Also, it enabled the mortgagee to sell the mortgagor's title if the registered proprietor defaulted on the mortgage repayments: all the mortgagee had to do was send the Charge Certificate in to the Land Registry with the deed of transfer to a purchaser, and the Land Registry would then issue a new Land Certificate to the purchaser. An uncooperative title holder could not impede the process, which again was an advantage for the mortgagee's point of view. However, the most important point was that Land Certificates and Charge Certificates were evidence of title, and provided some protection against fraud: if a fraudster wanted to trick the Land Registry into altering the register in her favour,

---

[70] paras. 3.15–3.16 SLC 222 and see now s. 14 of the Land Registration etc. (Scotland) Act 2012.

[71] It appears that this imposes on the Keeper a requirement to do what she had already been doing in practice: Gretton and Steven, *Property, Trusts and Succession*, fn. 23 above, para. 7.26.

[72] Ibid. paras. 7.26–7.45.

[73] For a facsimile of a cover issued in the early days of land registration, see Mayer and Pemberton, *A Short History of Land Registration in England and Wales*, fn. 4 above. By the time Land and Charge Certificates were abolished in 2003, the covers looked a bit more modern but were not much less elaborate (so still difficult to forge).

she would have to not only forge the necessary deeds but also somehow get hold of (or forge) the relevant Land Certificate or Charge Certificate.

Land and Charge Certificates were abolished in 2003. The Land Registry still issues 'official copies' of the entries on the register in paper form (as well as electronic copies) but their function is different. The official paper or electronic copy still provides evidence of what is on the register, and the Land Registry guarantees that the official copy accurately reflects what is on the register as at a given date. However, anyone who is willing to pay the appropriate (small) fee is entitled to obtain an official copy of the entries for any title – in paper or electronic form – so possession of an official copy implies no entitlement to deal with the title.

16.13 Public Access to the Register

Another significant change is that formerly there was no public access to the land register. Given what we said about the public interest function of land registration in para. 16.6, it now seems extraordinary that, until the position was changed in 1990, the contents of the register were secret: no-one was entitled to search or inspect any part of the register except a registered proprietor of a title (who had access only to the entries on her title) and anyone formally authorised by her. It was thought that we were the only country in the world to have a wholly secret land register.[74]

This anomalous position was changed by the Land Registration Act 1988, which came into force in 1990, implementing a recommendation by the Law Commission[75] that the land register should be fully open to the public. It is worth noting that whilst this has brought us into line with Scotland, which has always had a fully public register,[76] some other countries do not go so far. In Germany, for example, where the Land Title Register is now integrated with the electronic cadastre, access to the Land Title Register is restricted to those with a 'legitimate interest'.[77] As Murray Raff explains, this restriction was imposed on privacy grounds and 'legitimate interest' is construed accordingly, covering, for example, media investigations legitimately exercising constitutional freedom of the press.[78] Raff also suggests that a justification for limiting public access to the register in Germany may be that the German Land Title Register records fuller financial information than that provided in, say, Torrens title registration systems (which are generally fully open to the

---

[74] Law Commission Working Paper on Land Registration No 32 (1971) para. 43 and see also Law Commission, *Property Law: Second Report on Land Registration: Inspection of the Register* (1985) Law Com No 148, para. 9 and the works cited there.

[75] Law Commission, *Second Report on Land Registration: Inspection of the Register* (1985) Law Com No 148.

[76] The deeds registry, the Register of Sasines set up in 1617, which records all details of transactions and is only now being phased out, has always been open to the public, and the same applies to the land titles register established by the Land Registration (Scotland) Act 1979 (as originally enacted and as now modified by the Land Registration etc. (Scotland) Act 2012): see further Reid and Gretton, *Land Registration*, fn. 30 above, paras. 1.2–1.3 and para. 3.2.

[77] *Das berechtigte Interesse.*

[78] Raff, 'Characteristics of the international model of land title registration', fn. 5 above, pp. 60–61.

public).[79] However, that does not explain why access is more limited under the German system than it is under our system and the Scottish system, both of which record the price a purchaser paid for a registered title and (in theory at least) the amount of money secured by a registered charge.[80]

Nevertheless, the principle of public access to the register is now under fire in England and Wales, not because of privacy concerns, but because it is thought to give fraudsters too easy access to the information they need to impersonate registered proprietors and 'sell' or 'mortgage' their land to innocent purchasers.[81]

A final point to make here is the obvious one that public access to the land register guarantees access only to the information that is recorded on the register. The most important information currently omitted from our land register and from those in most other countries is the beneficial ownership of land.[82] This means that if the registered proprietor of a freehold or long leasehold title holds the title on trust for, or as a nominee for, someone else, the register will not tell us who that 'someone else' is. Similarly, if the registered proprietor is a company, the register will not tell us who owns and controls the company. This makes it impossible to find out from the land register who 'really' owns the land. There are strong feelings in many countries, not least in England and Wales and in Scotland, that the 'real' ownership of land in our country ought to be a matter of public knowledge, and that elites and/or foreign nationals should not be able to hide their landownership by registering in the names of trustees or shell companies.[83] In the UK, recent government responses to these concerns have centred on establishing separate registers showing the beneficial ownership of UK and overseas companies and trusts which own land in the UK, but so far it has no plans to establish a public record of beneficial interests in land held by trustees based in England and Wales.[84]

16.14 How the System Operates

The previous paragraphs give a snapshot picture of what the land register now looks like at any given moment in time. However, it is only a snapshot. To understand how the system operates dynamically, we need to look at three other matters.

---

[79] Ibid. p. 62.

[80] In practice, the statement of the amount secured by a mortgage in England and Wales may not be very informative, because the general practice is to state it only in general terms in the mortgage deed (e.g. as 'all money owed by the borrower to the lender') rather than to give specific figures.

[81] Steven Evans, 'Was privacy in land ownership such a bad thing?' (2017) 81 *Conveyancer and Property Lawyer* 351.

[82] In this jurisdiction, because beneficial interests under a trust are not recorded on the register: para. 16.36 below.

[83] Department for Business, Energy and Industrial Strategy, *A Register of Beneficial Owners of Overseas Companies and Other Legal Entities: The Government Response to Call for Evidence* (March 2018), https://assets.publishing.service.gov.uk/government/uploads/system/uploads/attachment_data/file/681844/ROEBO_Gov_Response_to_Call_for_Evidence.pdf.

[84] The current developments in England and Wales and in Scotland are summarised by Federico Mor in House of Commons Briefing Paper Number 8259, 15 March 2019, *Registers of Beneficial Ownership*, available at https://researchbriefings.files.parliament.uk/documents/CBP-8259/CBP-8259.pdf.

The first is how land comes within the land registration system for the first time. This is still relevant today because, as we noted in para. 16.5, land in England and Wales has been brought into the registration system gradually over the period since 1925 by a sporadic process which is not yet complete. We outline the procedure, and the knock-on effects of sporadic registration, in the next paragraph.

The second is what happens when the person who is registered as the holder of a registered title ('the registered proprietor') transfers her interest, or grants a new registrable interest (such as a lease or mortgage) to someone else, and the effect these transactions have on other property interests affecting the land. This involves looking at the rules governing the enforcement and priority of property interests, which we do in Part III of this chapter.

The final matter to bring into the picture is that some kinds of property interest which affect registered titles do not appear anywhere on the register, and others are only partly within the system. We look at these 'off register' interests, and at how they affect registered titles, in Part IV.

16.15 Sporadic Registration and Its Consequences

As we saw in para. 16.5, 14.6 per cent of the land in England and Wales is still not yet in the land registration system.[85] This is because historically we opted to introduce land titles registration by registering titles sporadically. Essentially, neither freehold nor long leasehold titles to land had to be registered immediately when the land registration system came into operation in 1925. Instead, as we see in (a) below, compulsory registration was phased in region by region, and even then a title did not have to be registered until it was first transferred (or granted, in the case of a new long lease) after the compulsory registration date for that region. As a result, both the land register and the Land Registry map resemble unfinished patchwork quilts (except that the patches are irregularly shaped rather than square), with each patch having been stitched on to a backing cloth in random order, and with some patches still missing.

(a) How Land Comes into the Registration System

Voluntary registration of titles to land in England and Wales became possible in 1862,[86] and a system of compulsory registration was later introduced by the Land Transfer Act 1879, but for various reasons it was not very successful. When our present land registration system was introduced in 1925, the Land Registry therefore started with a more or less blank Ordnance Survey map of the whole of England and Wales, on which the few titles registered under the old Acts were plotted.[87] It then

---

[85] *Land Registry Annual Report 2017–2018*, fn. 54 above, at p. 60.   [86] Land Registry Act 1862.

[87] The Ordnance Survey was founded in 1791 but the Ordnance Survey map did not become the official basis for all description of registered land until 1879: see C. J. Sweeney and J. A. Simson, 'The Ordnance Survey and land registration' (1967) 133 *Geographical Journal* 10 at pp. 12–13, and R. Oliver, *A Short History of the Ordnance Survey of Great Britain*, available at www.charlesclosesociety.org/files/ HistoryOSGB.pdf. For the present relationship between the Land Registry and the Ordnance Survey see

divided the land into registration areas, introducing compulsory registration area by area. Once an area had become a compulsory registration area, unregistered freehold and long leasehold titles became registrable as soon as a trigger event occurred. For freehold titles the trigger event was a transfer[88] of the title. For long leasehold titles, the trigger events were the grant by a freeholder or leaseholder of a new lease or sublease of more than 21 years, or the transfer of an unregistered lease which had more than 21 years left to run. Once a trigger event had occurred, the transferee/lessee had to apply to the registry to have their title investigated and then registered. The land covered by the new registered title was then plotted on to the Land Registry's master map, by reference to a plan and description of the relevant land supplied by the transferee/lessee applying for registration.

Essentially the same system operates today, except that a 'long lease' now means a lease of more than seven years rather than 21 years (or, in the case of a transfer of an unregistered lease, the transfer of a lease with more than seven years to run) and the trigger events now also include the grant of a first legal mortgage over an unregistered freehold or long leasehold title.[89] All areas in England and Wales had become compulsory areas by 1990, but it remains the case that an as yet unregistered freehold or long leasehold title does not *have* to be registered unless and until a trigger event occurs.[90] If the trigger event is the grant or transfer of a lease, the landlord does not have to apply for first registration of its freehold or leasehold interest at the same time, although it may do so if it wants. If the trigger event is the grant of a mortgage, however, the freehold or leasehold interest that is being mortgaged must also be registered.[91]

So, the present position is that the land register is still not complete because some unregistered freehold and leasehold titles have not yet been affected by a trigger event, and the holders of the unregistered titles have not been persuaded to register voluntarily. It seems that this state of affairs will continue indefinitely unless the rules are changed to allow or require the Land Registry to take the initiative and register the outstanding titles without the titleholder's consent and co-operation.

In fact, the Land Registry does not seem to have ever seriously contemplated coercion. In Law Com No 271, the Joint Report and Bill published by the Law Commission and HM Land Registry which led to the enactment of the Land Registration Act 2002,[92] it was said that 'unregistered conveyancing must be given its quietus as soon as possible'[93] and it was recommended that 'ways in which all remaining land with unregistered title in England and Wales might be brought on to the register should be re-examined' 5 years after the LRA 2002 came into force.[94] In

---

Joint Statement of the Ordnance Survey and Land Registry (2014), www.gov.uk/government/publications/joint-statement-ordnance-survey-and-land-registry.

[88] Which included (as it does now) a sale or a gift, but not a transfer by operation of law: s. 4 of the LRA 2002.

[89] See Land Registry, *Practice Guide 1: First Registrations* (updated 8 October 2018).

[90] Voluntary registration at any earlier time is and has always been possible: see now s. 3 of the LRA 2002.

[91] S. 6(2) of the LRA 2002.

[92] Law Commission and HM Land Registry, *Land Registration for the Twenty-first Century*, fn. 52 above.

[93] Ibid. para. 2.6.   [94] Ibid. para. 2.13, and see also paras. 2.9–2.12.

2002, HM Land Registry accordingly launched a marketing campaign to promote and encourage voluntary registration, providing help to organisations who volunteered to register their portfolios of unregistered titles. The campaign ran until 2012 and it seems to have been remarkably successful: at its peak in 2008–2009 more than 55 per cent of all first registrations were voluntary registrations.[95] Nevertheless, the campaign was ended in 2012 because it was thought to be no longer cost-effective, and for the next few years completion of the register was no longer stated to be a 'strategic objective' of the Land Registry. It has come back on to the political agenda, however, and in 2017 the Government announced that the Land Registry 'will aim to achieve' a complete register by 2030.[96]

This can be contrasted with the position in Scotland, where, as noted in para. 16.5 above, the government's aim is to complete the process, started in 1981, by 2024.[97]

(b) Gaps and Overlaps Between Registered Titles

A predictable consequence of this process of sporadic registration just described is that there are gaps and overlaps between registered titles. Applicants for first registration of title or for dealings with part of a title have always been required to provide a plan and verbal description of the relevant land, but they are not, and have never been, required to agree them with their neighbours before submitting them to the Land Registry. Similarly, the Land Registry is not required to check that plans and verbal descriptions in applications for first registration of title tally with the information already recorded in the files of neighbouring registered titles, or with the boundaries of neighbouring titles shown on the Land Registry map. Inevitably, therefore, there are discrepancies which eventually have to be resolved by agreement or litigation between the neighbouring title holders.

(c) Mapping and Boundaries

It is important to appreciate that these disputes between neighbours as to the precise physical extent of their respective lands have to be settled solely by reference to common law rules about boundaries and construction of deeds. This is because the LRA 1925 opted for a 'general boundaries' rule,[98] which means that the correctness of the boundaries of the land shown on the Land Registry map is not guaranteed.[99] The same applies to other features on the filed plan which are relevant to property interests: ownership of boundary walls and fences may be indicated on the Land Registry map, but is not guaranteed to be correct and cannot be relied on in any

---

[95] See the Tables at p. 327 in King, 'Completion of the land register, fn. 48 above.

[96] *Fixing our Broken Housing Market* (2017) Cm 9352, para. 1.18 and see also *HM Land Registry Annual Report and Accounts 2017–2018* available at www.gov.uk/government/publications/hm-land-registry-annual-report-and-accounts-2017-to-2018 p. 21 for current progress as at July 2016.

[97] For a useful comparison between the Scottish approach and the approach adopted for England and Wales see King, 'Completion of the land register', fn. 48 above.

[98] Now set out in s. 60 of the LRA 2002.   [99] See now s. 60 of the LRA 2002.

dispute between neighbours. Similarly, routes of easements such as rights of way, pipelines, etc. may be shown on the map, but they may or may not be correct.

The decision to make the map indicative but not decisive as to legal boundaries was inevitable once it was decided not to carry out a wholesale survey of the land in England and Wales preparatory to establishing the land register. The historic reasons for not supporting land registration by a national survey are instructive. The obvious reason was time and short-term costs, but there were other reasons. Equally important was a desire not to stir up boundary disputes between neighbours, and this is a real fear for any government introducing a land titles registration system even today.[100] Another connected reason is that there is something to be said for respecting the 'lived' boundaries that neighbours accept in practice, rather than those originally imposed by developers dividing land up into sellable plots, or those described by lawyers drafting transfer deeds, which may not accurately reflect what their clients have agreed or assumed to be correct. This is particularly important because 'lived' boundaries tend to evolve over time to reflect changes in usage and custom as well as changes in physical features on the ground. Most neighbours tacitly rely on physical features on the ground and on custom (what they were told by their sellers, what they and their neighbours and their predecessors and their neighbours' predecessors have worked out between themselves over the years, common practice in the locality, etc.) to tell them where their boundaries lie, and the same applies to the routes of easements. The common law acknowledges these fluid 'lived' boundaries to some extent by allowing neighbours involved in boundary disputes to rely on doctrines such as adverse possession, prescription and estoppel. All these doctrines continue to operate in relation to other aspects of our land registration system[101] and it is difficult to see how they could be excluded from applying to modify a guaranteed boundaries rule as well, even if we decided to move away from the general boundaries rule. So, whilst boundary disputes are notoriously bitter, protracted and disproportionately expensive, and everyone agrees that if outcomes were less uncertain, many of them could be resolved earlier, more cheaply and possibly even more amicably, it is not obvious that a guaranteed boundaries rule would have that effect.

PART III EFFECT OF REGISTRATION OF TITLE TO LAND ON VALIDITY, ENFORCEABILITY AND PRIORITY OF PROPERTY INTERESTS

16.16 'Title by Registration' or 'Registration of Title'?

It may seem surprising that, after nearly a century, the effect of registration of title under our registration system is controversial. In this paragraph and the next we

---

[100] Hence the development of 'participatory mapping' techniques: see Greg Brown and Marketta Kyttä, 'Key issues and research priorities for public participation GIS (PPGIS)' (2014) 46 *Applied Geography* 122, and also Tor A. Benjaminsen and Espen Sjaastad, 'Where to draw the line: Mapping of land rights in a South African commons' (2008) 27 *Political Geography* 263 on the sometimes unintended effects of mapping and registering titles to individual plots.

[101] See e.g. paras. 16.28–16.29 and 16.34.

outline the nature of the controversy before looking more specifically at the detailed rules in the rest of this part of the chapter.

(a) Is Registration of Title Constitutive or Probative?

In some registration of title systems the effect of registration of a title to land (broadly, title to ownership in a civil law system, and title to a freehold or long leasehold interest in common law systems) is *constitutive*. This means that no-one can acquire ownership (in civil law systems) or a freehold/long leasehold interest (in common law systems) except by being registered as holder of the interest. In other words, the title is *constituted* by registration, in the sense that, if a title (or a registrable interest such as a charge) is registrable, it does not come into existence until someone is registered as the title holder, and registration has the effect of vesting the interest in him so that it remains vested in him until someone else is registered in his place.[102] The effect of this is that whoever is registered as title holder of a particular interest (a freehold or long leasehold interest, or a long lease or mortgage granted out of it) *is* the lawful title holder and, conversely, anyone who is *not* registered as the title holder is not. This kind of system is sometimes referred to as a system of 'title *by* registration' (i.e. lawful titles to registrable interests are acquired *by* registration, and only by registration). The implication is that land registration of this kind provides a self-contained system of rules for determining who has what property interests in any given piece of land: general law provisions about the creation, enforceability and disposition of property interests are irrelevant.

An alternative model is a system of 'registration *of* title', in which titles are acquired under general property law rules (e.g. by transfer, grant, inheritance or operation of law) and then recorded on the register. In this model registration does not *confer* title. Instead it provides evidence (which can be challenged) that the registered title holder is the lawful title holder. In the German system, for example, registration of someone as owner of a right creates only a rebuttable presumption that she is the true owner.[103] The implication is that in this kind of system, general law property rules and principles continue to apply except in so far as they are modified by land registration rules.

(b) Defects in the Models

Few title registration systems, if any, would ever adopt either model without qualification. This is because each, if applied without qualification, would produce unacceptable results in some situations where the 'wrong' person becomes registered as title holder. Suppose you were the registered freehold owner of your house, but the Land Registry has just mistakenly registered me as owner instead of you. It might have been an administrative mistake (I had just bought the house next door, and the

---

[102] Or, in the case of derivative registered interests such as leases and mortgages, unless and until the register closes the title because it believes the interest itself has ended.

[103] S. 891 of the BGB, but see further fn. 105.

Land Registry registered me as owner of the wrong house). Alternatively it might have been as a result of my fraud: perhaps I sent the Land Registry a purported transfer from you to me, on to which I had forged your signature. In an unqualified 'title by registration' model I acquire your freehold interest and you lose it, whether I was registered by mistake or by fraud, and even if the fraud was mine. In an unqualified registration *of* title model, on the other hand, you keep your freehold interest and the fact that the register wrongly names me as holding the freehold title means that the register is wrong: there is a mistake which has to be corrected. Presumably, most people would agree that, in that simple situation, where no third parties are involved, the registration of title model gets it right, whereas the title *by* registration model produces the wrong outcome and would need to be modified so that you can get your title back from me. However, if we take the example further, and now assume that I then sell your house to an innocent purchaser, both models are unsatisfactory unless qualified in some way. In an unqualified registration of title model, even though the register says that the innocent purchaser is the title holder of your freehold title, the register is wrong: you still hold the title and the register must be corrected, and this will continue to be the case even if the innocent purchaser subsequently sells to another innocent purchaser, who later sells on to another, and so on. This would make it risky for any outsider to rely on the register: to be absolutely certain of getting an unchallengeable title, prospective purchasers and mortgagees would always have to make the same kind of investigations and enquiries they would have had to have made if the seller's title had not been registered. Whatever one's views of the objectives of land registration,[104] this does not seem like a good idea. On the other hand, an unqualified 'title by registration' model is at least as bad: any innocent purchaser will always, no matter what the circumstances, acquire a good title to your house and you will lose everything.

The reality is that, whether they opt for title *by* registration or registration *of* title, each registration system has to modify the basic model so as to strike the right balance between protection of pre-existing property rights and protection of purchasers, as we saw in para. 16.7. This can be done by adopting specific registration rules limiting or extending the protection title registration brings to property interest holders and limiting or extending guarantees given to purchasers and others who rely on the register. So, for example, going back to the German rule we mentioned above, although the basic rule is that registration of someone as owner of a right creates only a rebuttable presumption that she is the true owner, the rule is explicitly modified to make the presumption conclusive in favour of a good faith purchaser with no knowledge of the incorrectness of the register.[105] However, it can also be done by allowing general law principles (for example, about limitation of actions, or unconscionable behaviour, fraud, etc.) to modify land registration rules. In addition

---

[104] See para. 16.6 above.

[105] Raff, 'Characteristics of the international model of land title registration', fn. 5 above, pp. 70–76 and pp. 80–96; the presumption is laid down in s. 891 BGB, and by s. 892 it is (irrebuttably) deemed to be correct in favour of a good faith purchaser who acquires a right in the land without knowledge of the incorrectness.

or instead of either or both of these, the registration system might simply list the circumstances in which the register may or must be changed, with or without provision for payment of compensation for anyone suffering loss. As we see in the rest of this part of the chapter, our system adopts a mix of all of these.

16.17 Effect of Registration of Title Under LRA 2002

(a) The Title by Registration Issue

Despite what was said in para. 16.16(b) above, contemporary commentators have attached considerable importance to the question of whether our title registration system in England and Wales should be categorised as a title by registration system.

We are not alone in these concerns. In Scotland the land registration system introduced by the Land Registration (Scotland) Act 1997, modelled on the England and Wales LRA 1925, was strongly criticised as introducing into Scottish law, for the first time, a provision that registration of a person as entitled to a registrable interest 'shall have the effect of vesting' that interest in that person.[106] This was seen by many as importing an alien model of 'title by registration' into Scottish law, inconsistent with the *nemo dat* principle (no-one can give a better title than they themselves have)[107] which up until then had always been the dominant principle in Scottish law. According to the Scottish Law Commission, the introduction of this alien concept was one of the root causes of the difficulties caused by the 1997 Act.[108] As Reid and Gretton tell us, the Scottish Law Commission:

> Unkindly if not unfairly . . . likened [the principle of title by registration] to the 'touch' of King Midas: just as everything that the mythical King touched was changed into gold, even his food or his daughter, so everything that the Keeper [the registrar] registered was changed into 'valid', even where that result was undesirable, and indeed undesired by the Keeper . . .[109]

It therefore recommended that the principle of title by registration should be abandoned, and on its recommendation there is no provision in the Land Registration etc. (Scotland) Act 2012 stating that title to a registrable interest vests the interest in the person stated in the register to hold it. Instead, the question of who is the 'true' owner of any given registrable interest depends on the general law, with purchaser protection provided for good faith purchasers, roughly as in the German system.[110]

In England and Wales, on the other hand, our Law Commission currently holds the view that our land registration system has taken the reverse journey, and is now firmly (and, in the Law Commission's view, rightly) committed to title by

---

[106] s. 3(1) of the Land Registration (Scotland) Act 1997.

[107] See further Chapter 15 *Enforcement and Priority of Property Interests* paras. 15.5–15.6.

[108] Reid and Gretton, *Land Registration*, fn. 30 above, pp. 30–34 and 36–40.   [109] Ibid. p. 39.

[110] For the Scottish Law Commission's detailed discussion of the title by registration issue and its recommendations see Scottish Law Commission Discussion Paper 125 (2004) Part 5 and SLC Report 222, paras. 13.11–13.28.

registration, apparently in its strictest form. In its Consultation Paper *Updating the Land Registration Act 2002*,[111] the Law Commission described title by registration as 'a relatively new idea' (introduced, or perhaps reinforced by, the LRA 2002), which is 'now an entrenched and fundamental part of the regime of land registration in England and Wales'.[112]

However, this view, that the LRA 2002 has revolutionised our registration system by introducing a strict title by registration principle, is energetically disputed. It perhaps accords with what the architects of the LRA 2002 thought would be achieved by the changes made by the Act,[113] but it is at least doubtful that this is what has actually been achieved, although some contemporary commentators would disagree.

The first point to make is that the LRA 2002 has not really made significant changes to the system put in place by the LRA 1925. It is true that s. 27 of the LRA 2002 provides that a registrable 'disposition' of a registered estate or registered charge 'does not operate at law until the relevant registration requirements are met', and that s. 58, headed 'Conclusiveness', provides in subsection (1) that 'If on the entry of a person in the register as the proprietor of a legal estate, the legal estate would not otherwise be vested in him, it shall be deemed to be vested in him as a result of the registration'. It is also true that these provisions are indicative of a title by registration system. However, these provisions of the LRA 2002 are not new: similar (although not identical) provisions appeared in the LRA 1925,[114] and it is generally accepted that the 2002 Act provisions have the same effect, whatever it is.[115]

(b) Effect of the 'Title by Registration' Provisions of the LRA 2002

The important disagreement lies in what the effect of these 'title by registration' provisions is. On the one hand there are those who argue that a forged or fraudulent transfer is not a 'disposition' within what is now s. 27 of the LRA 2002,[116] and that s. 58 deals only with the legal title, leaving general law principles to determine whether the legal title also carries the beneficial interest with it in any particular case.[117] This is what was decided by the Court of Appeal in *Malory Enterprises Ltd v. Cheshire Homes Ltd* [2002] EWCA Civ 151, where a fraudster set up a new company with the same name as the registered proprietor of the freehold interest in derelict development land, tricked the Land Registry into sending it a land certificate for the title[118] and then 'sold' the registered freehold to an innocent purchaser, who

---

[111] Law Commission Consultation Paper, *Updating the Land Registration Act 2002* (2016) Law Com CP No 227.
[112] para. 5.79.   [113] Simon Gardner, 'Alteration of the register: An alternative view' [2013] Conv 530.
[114] S. 20 and s. 69(1) of the LRA 1925.
[115] *Fitzwilliam v. Richall Holdings Services Ltd* [2013] EWHC 86 and Patten LJ in *Swift 1st Ltd v. Chief Land Registrar* [2015] EWCA Civ 330 at para. 40. Compare Goymour, 'Myth of title by registration', fn. 43 above, at p. 643, arguing that s. 69 of the LRA 1925 is 'materially different in function to s. 58 LRA 2002'.
[116] See para. 16.24(a) below.   [117] Gardner, 'Alteration of the register', fn. 113 above, at pp. 533–534.
[118] As to which see para. 16.12(b) above.

became registered proprietor. It was held that the transfer of the title from the fraudulent company to the innocent purchaser was ineffective,[119] but that the registration of the innocent purchaser as registered proprietor vested the *legal* title in the innocent purchaser (because of s. 69(1) of the LRA 1925, the predecessor of s. 58 of the LRA 2002), *but not* the beneficial interest, which remained with the original company. The reasoning was approved by the Court of Appeal in *John Lyon School* v. *Helman* [2014] EWCA Civ 17 and in *Rashid* v. *Nasrullah* [2018] EWCA Civ 2685, where a father had forged a transfer of the registered freehold interest in a house into his own name and became registered as proprietor. He then transferred the title to his son (who was complicit in the fraud) by a deed of gift, and the son then became registered proprietor in his turn. It was held that the effect of s. 69(1) of the LRA 1925 (and hence s. 58 of the LRA 2002) was to vest the legal title but not the beneficial interest in the father, and that the son, as a donee rather than a purchaser from his father, was in the same position. This view of s. 69 of the LRA 1925 and the equivalent s. 58 of the LRA 2002 receives strong support from, amongst others, Simon Gardner, and from *Emmet & Farrand on Title*,[120] as consistent with the overall land registration scheme and achieving the right balance between innocent property interest holders and innocent purchasers.

Others, on the other hand, argue that *Malory* was wrongly decided and that the effect of the statutory provisions in both the 1925 Act and the 2002 Act is that the entire legal and beneficial interest is automatically and invariably vested in the registered proprietor, subject only to the 'protected' interests identified in s. 29 of the LRA 2002, which we look at in para. 16.24 below (i.e. overriding interests and interests which are registered or noted on the register). On this view, the LRA 2002 creates a self-contained statutory system in which general law principles are irrelevant.[121] This second view – that we have a strict title by registration system – was endorsed by the Court of Appeal in *Swift 1st Ltd* v. *Chief Land Registrar* [2015] EWCA Civ 330, where Patten LJ reviewed the academic arguments and concluded that *Malory* was wrongly decided on the beneficial interest point.[122]

(c) The Present State of the Argument

Taking an overall view, Amy Goymour makes a compelling case for the argument that we neither have, nor want, a strict system of title by registration.[123] Her main

---

[119] And so not covered by what would now be s. 27 of the LRA 2002.

[120] Gardner, 'Alteration of the register', fn. 113 above, and *Emmet & Farrand on Title,* fn.33 above, at para. 9.009.1.

[121] For the arguments in support of this view see the literature cited by Gardner in 'Alteration of the register', fn. 113 above, in particular Elizabeth Cooke, 'The register's guarantee of title' [2013] 77 Conv 344, and also Stuart Bridge, Elizabeth Cooke and Martin Dixon, *Megarry & Wade: The Law of Real Property* (9th edn, London: Sweet & Maxwell, 2019) paras. 6.116 and 6.117 (briefly noting the Court of Appeal decision in *Rashid* v. *Nasrullah* but not taking account of the criticisms made there of Patten LJ's analysis in *Swift 1st*).

[122] He also said it was not binding because decided *per incuriam,* but on demonstrably untenable grounds, as pointed out by Lewison LJ in *Rashid* v. *Nasrullah* [2018] EWCA Civ 2685.

[123] Amy Goymour in 'The myth of title by registration', fn. 43 above.

argument is that the courts have not been willing to accept the bias towards outcomes favouring purchasers which is inherent in a strict system of title by registration. This judicial response, she argues,

> reflects both a deep-rooted judicial commitment to the fundamental values that inhere in the general law, and a corresponding scepticism for the socio-economic choices underpinning the orthodox view of the LRA 2002. These observations, in turn, raise serious doubts about the viability of self-contained formalist legal codes, not only with respect to registered land, but also across the law more generally.[124]

It is worth adding that there are other factors which make a strict title by registration model a poor fit for a registration system such as ours. To view s. 27 and s. 58 of the LRA 2002 as 'statutory magic', uniquely conferring legal titles to registrable interests, ignores at least two features of our system: (a) an adverse possessor acquires a legal title to the freehold interest in the land she possesses (albeit not enforceable against the registrable proprietor) just by taking possession,[125] and (b) legal titles pass automatically by operation of law (e.g. on death, bankruptcy or dissolution of a company) and there is nothing in the LRA 2002 to displace the statutory provisions which automatically vest the legal title in statutory successors, regardless of registration.[126] Also, and perhaps more fundamentally, title by registration does not mean much in a system such as ours which recognises unregistered registrable interests as valid equitable property interests pending registration. So, whilst it is true that, leaving aside the exceptions just mentioned, *legal* title to registrable interests cannot be acquired or transmitted except by registration, the grantee/transferee gets an equitable property interest (an estate contract) as soon as it has a contractual right to have the interest granted/transferred, and then gets another equitable property interest (the equitable equivalent of the interest she has contracted to acquire) as soon as all other formalities required to complete the transaction have been completed. Both of these equitable interests are capable of being enforced against subsequent registered proprietors, as we see in paras. 16.22–16.27 below. In other words, in the vast majority of cases it seems more accurate to describe registration of title under our system as the final formality required to vest a legal title in a grantee/transferee (the functional equivalent of a deed in unregistered land) rather than all-or-nothing statutory magic.

Overall, then, the better view is that s. 58 of the LRA 2002 refers only to legal title to the registered estate. In order to determine whether the legal title holder does indeed also hold the beneficial interest, we need to apply general property principles, that is, there is a presumption that the legal title holder also holds the beneficial interest, rebuttable by evidence that it is held by someone else under general property principles.[127]

---

[124] Ibid. p. 616.   [125] para. 16.34 below.   [126] para. 16.30 below.

[127] *Stack* v. *Dowden* [2007] UKHL 17: see further Chapter 14 *Acquiring Interests Informally* para. 14.7(d). It was accepted that this was the correct approach to registered titles by King J in *Liscott* v. *Crown Prosecution Service* [2013] EWHC 501 (application for the appointment of a receiver to enforce a confiscation order against the beneficial interest a convicted drug dealer was alleged to have in property registered in someone else's name).

16.18 LRA 2002 Rules on Enforceability and Priority of Property Interests

With this in mind, in this and the following paragraphs we look at the detailed rules in the LRA 2002 on the effect of registration of title on enforceability and priority of property interests.

It is worth reminding ourselves first of the equivalent rules governing enforceability and priority in unregistered land which we outlined in Chapter 15 . Under those basic common law rules, the general principle is that if you sell me your unregistered freehold or leasehold interest in a piece of land, I will acquire it subject to all legal property interests affecting your title (such as legal mortgages, or leases or legal easements) whether or not I knew about them.[128] The question of whether I also take subject to any equitable interests affecting your unregistered title depends on the nature of the interest. If it is an interest which is registrable as a land charge[129] I will take subject to it if it is registered in the land charges register, otherwise not. If it is not registrable as a land charge, its enforceability against me will depend on whether I was a purchaser, and whether I was acting in good faith and had notice of the interest,[130] and (if the equitable interest is a beneficial interest under a trust) whether it was overreached by the sale.[131]

Once a freehold or long leasehold title has been registered at the land register, enforcement and priority of it and of any property interest affecting it are governed instead by the provisions of the LRA 2002. As we see in the following paragraphs, however, the statutory provisions are not completely comprehensive, and sometimes the courts fall back on the common law rules to fill the gaps.

16.19 Effect of First Registration of Title on Priority and Enforceability

We are not going to look in any detail at the provisions of the LRA 2002 governing first registration of title. However, a general idea of the procedure makes it easier to understand how enforcement and priority work once the land has been brought within the land registration system, which is our main concern.

Broadly, when a freeholder or long leaseholder applies for first registration of title, she has to provide the Land Registry with the same evidence of her title and of the property interests affecting it as she would have to provide if she was selling it to a purchaser. The Land Registry then registers her title and makes appropriate entries in her title file about the other property interests affecting it which she revealed when

---

[128] Except for the relatively small group of legal mortgages (mortgages where the mortgagee was not given custody of the title deeds of the mortgaged property) which are registrable as 'land charges' under the interim land charges system set up in 1925 and now governed by the Land Charges Act 1972. The 1972 Act requires registration of these legal mortgages and some commercial equitable property interests (restrictive covenants, some charges estate contracts, options, etc.) in a separate register (the land charges register) if the title to the freehold/leasehold interest they affect has not yet been registered at the Land Registry: see fn. 51 above. Interests registrable as land charges are enforceable against purchasers if registered in the land charges register, but void as against them if not.

[129] See fn. 128.   [130] That is, the doctrine of notice we looked at in paras. 15.9–15.10 applies.

[131] As to which see Part III of Chapter 15. The way overreaching works within the land registration system is considered in para. 16.36 below.

she proved her title and which are capable of being protected on the register. These would include interests such as easements over her land, or restrictive covenants restricting its use, or perhaps an option to purchase it.[132] If her title also has the benefit of property rights affecting other registered titles (e.g. an easement over neighbouring land), the Land Registry will also make the necessary entries in the files of those neighbouring titles (assuming, of course, that those titles have already been registered).

The effect of registering the applicant as 'proprietor' of the freehold/long leasehold interest (or 'estate', as it is called in the LRA 2002) is governed by s. 11 of the 2002 Act (registration as first proprietor of a freehold estate) and s. 12 (registration as first proprietor of a leasehold estate).

By s. 11, registration gives the first proprietor the legal title to her estate and to all property interests which benefit it.[133] Her title is, however, stated to be *subject to* the following interests:[134]

- the property interests which the Land Registry has just entered on the register against her title;[135]
- a special class of overriding interests (i.e. interests which are not on the register but are nevertheless enforceable against registered proprietors).[136] The interests within this special class are listed in Sch. 1 of the 2002 Act and they are broadly the same as, but not identical to, the overriding interests which affect purchasers of registered titles once they are within the registered system, which we look at in paras. 16.25–16.27 below;
- rights of some adverse possessors of land (most adverse possessors come within the overriding interest class noted above);[137]
- if the first registered proprietor holds the title for the benefit of anyone else, the rights of those beneficiaries, provided she has notice of them.[138]

There are similar provisions in s. 12 applicable to first registration of leasehold titles.

---

[132] para. 16.10 above.

[133] S. 11(3). She already had a legal title as a result of it having being transferred to her by deed when she bought the land (because at that stage unregistered land rules still applied), but it will have reverted back to the person who transferred it to her if she failed to apply for first registration of her title within two months after the transfer deed (s. 7). So, s. 11(3) merely confirms that once her title is registered, she has the legal title even if she had temporarily lost it by failing to register in time.

[134] The 'subject to' list set out here applies only when the applicant is registered as proprietor with *absolute title*. As noted in para. 16.11, the vast majority of titles are absolute, but the Land Registry does have power to grant lesser titles if the applicant for first registration is unable to provide satisfactory evidence of her title and of the interests which might affect it. We are not concerned with these lesser titles, but broadly they are made subject to not only the interests on this list, but also to any which *may* affect them, even though the Land Registry has been unable to establish whether or not they do so.

[135] S. 11(4)(a).   [136] S. 11(4)(b).

[137] S. 11(4)(c). This is an oversimplification of complex rules about how far a person applying for first registration of title is affected by the claims of someone who is in adverse possession of the land. For a full account see Kevin Gray and Susan Francis Gray, *Elements of Land Law* (5th edn, Oxford: Oxford University Press, 2009) para. 9.1.34.

[138] S. 11(5).

16.20 Dealings by a Registered Proprietor

Once someone has become registered proprietor of a freehold or long leasehold title, she has the same powers to transfer her title and grant new property interests as she would have if her title was outside the land registration system.[139] Similarly, property rights affecting her registered title can be acquired by others by long use, prescription and implied grant, and adverse possessors acquire a rival common law legal title by taking adverse possession,[140] all just as if her title was outside the registration system. Also, equitable doctrines such as estoppel and constructive trust operate in relation to registered titles in much the same way as they do in unregistered land.[141] However, there are some significant differences in effect between dealings by registered proprietors and dealings by holders of unregistered titles.

16.21 Registrable Dispositions and Passing of the Legal Title

The first is that, as already noted in para. 16.17, when a registered proprietor makes a 'registrable disposition' of her registered title (defined in s. 27 as a transfer of it to someone else, or the grant of a long (registrable) lease or a registrable interest such as a mortgage or an easement) the transferee/grantee does not get a *legal* title to the interest he has acquired unless and until it is registered.[142] This is consistent with (and, as we saw in para. 16.17, best seen as an extension of) the general formalities rule that applies to transactions involving property interests outside the land registration system, that is, that legal title to an interest does not pass until all relevant formalities have been completed.[143] However (again consistently with, and an extension of the formalities rules which operate outside the land registration system), the transferee/grantee *does* acquire the equivalent equitable interest (an equitable freehold or leasehold interest, or an equitable mortgage etc.) as soon as the other formalities have been completed: we come back to this point in para. 16.22 below.

It will be appreciated that under the LRA 2002 some legal property interests which affect registered freehold and leasehold titles are not registrable. The most important for present purposes are leases for seven years or less, the freehold interest an adverse possessor acquires as soon as he takes adverse possession,[144] and easements acquired by implication or prescription. Nothing in the LRA 2002 tells us how they must be created/granted or transferred, so the general law formalities rules we looked at in Chapter 14 para. 14.2 continue to apply to them. Their *enforceability* against registered proprietors of the freehold and leasehold titles they affect is, however, governed by the LRA 2002, as we see in para. 16.24.

---

[139] Ss. 23–24. There are a number of difficulties with these provisions, discussed at length in the Law Commission Report *Updating the Land Registration Act 2002*, fn. 111 above, Ch. 5, and see also Amy Goymour and Stephen Watterson, 'A tale of three promises: (3) The empowerment promise' in A. Goymour, S. Watterson and M. Dixon (eds.), *New Perspectives on Land Registration: Contemporary Problems and Solutions* (Oxford: Hart Publishing, 2018) pp. 379–409. We do not deal with them here.
[140] See further para. 16.34 below.   [141] See paras. 16.28–16.29.   [142] S. 27(1).
[143] Chapter 14 *Acquiring Interests Informally* para. 14.2.   [144] See para. 16.34 below.

16.22 Equitable Interests Arising in Default of Registration of Registrable Dispositions

Before looking into the enforceability rules under the LRA 2002, however, we should note the complexity we have introduced into our registration system by incorporating this general law rule that dispositions take effect in equity prior to, and in default of, registration. It makes our registration of title system much more complicated than civil law systems, which do not property interests equivalent to these 'default' equitable property interests. We could of course change our land registration system to bring it in line with civil law systems and the Scottish system, so that no-one acquired any kind of a property interest in land by a transaction which is registrable unless and until the transaction is completed by registration. However, that would be to make a fundamental structural change in our property rights system, and before taking such a major step we would need to evaluate the advantages (if any) of making the change, and the implications it would have for the continued existence of other kinds of equitable interests within our system.

16.23 Impact of Electronic Conveyancing

Without carrying out the kind of evaluation referred to in the previous paragraph, the architects of the LRA 2002 proceeded on the basis that the problem of these 'default' equitable interests (if it is indeed a problem) would simply disappear with the introduction of 'electronic conveyancing', which was then seen as imminent.[145] This was, however, based on two questionable assumptions. The first assumption (perhaps questionable only with the benefit of hindsight) was that, very soon, all deeds making dispositions of registrable property interests could be completed electronically (by completing online forms which would be executed using digital signatures) with the disposition being simultaneously recorded on the register. In other words, there would be no gap between completion and registration of the disposition. The drafters of the LRA 2002 were so certain that this would happen that they included in the Act detailed provisions for how it would work.[146] The second assumption, however (questionable even without the benefit of hindsight), was that, once it became *possible* for such deeds to be completed in this way, it was necessary and/or desirable to make it *mandatory* for them to be completed in this way.[147] It is not clear why this was thought necessary or desirable, other than as a means towards a stricter 'title by registration' system.[148] All that was said in the Explanatory Notes to the LRA 2002 (at para. 12) was:

---

[145] Law Commission and HM Land Registry, *Land Registration for the Twenty-first Century*, fn. 52 above, para. 1.12 and paras. 2.41–2.68, and see Part 8 of the LRA 2002, which sets out the legislative framework for the electronic conveyancing system which the Law Commission and the Land Registry thought was just about to be introduced.

[146] In Part 8 of the 2002 Act, entitled 'Electronic conveyancing'.   [147] See s. 93 in Part 8.

[148] As discussed in para. 16.16 above.

Some of the benefits of electronic conveyancing can only be maximised if it is used universally. The Act, therefore gives the Lord Chancellor power to make the use of electronic means for conveyancing compulsory, subject to appropriate consultation.

However, as things have turned out, none of this has happened.[149] Digitalisation of land registration processes has developed in a different direction, and it now seems unlikely that 'computerised' simultaneous completion and registration of registered land transactions will ever be widespread.[150] This is partly because of the way the technology has developed, but also because of difficulties in making it fit in with our current processes for buying, selling and mortgaging land. Accordingly, the Law Commission has now recommended amendments to Part 8 of the LRA 2002 which would allow 'computerised' conveyancing to proceed without it necessarily involving simultaneous completion and registration of registrable dispositions.[151] So, for the foreseeable future, registrable dispositions will continue to take effect in equity (i.e. to confer an equitable property interest on the transferee/grantee) prior to, and in default of, registration.

16.24 Enforceability and Priority of Property Interests: Sections 28–30 of the LRA 2002

This brings us to the other major difference between the disposition of a registered title and the disposition of an unregistered freehold or leasehold title. This is that different enforceability and priority rules apply. When a registered proprietor of a freehold or long leaseholder makes a 'registered disposition'[152] *and it is made for valuable consideration*, the effects on other property interests affecting the title are governed by ss. 28–30 of the LRA 2002.

These sections are not a model of clarity. It is first stated in s. 28 that the basic rule is that 'the priority' of an interest (presumably *any* property interest) affecting a registered title is *not* affected by any disposition of that title *except* as provided by s. 29 or s. 30. This appears to mean, first, that *all* property interests affecting registered titles will be enforceable against successors of the registered proprietor *unless* s. 29 or s. 30 say otherwise, and secondly that priority between these interests will remain the same as it was before the disposition. From this we can work out the following rules.

(a) Enforceability Against Later Registered Proprietors: Sections 28–30

The first rule is that if there is a registrable disposition (as defined in s. 27) of a registered freehold or leasehold title and it is *not* made for valuable consideration, all property interests which were enforceable against the transferor/grantor will be

---

[149] For a detailed account, see *Emmet & Farrand on Title*, fn. 33 above, para. 9.003.
[150] For the current position see HM Land Registry, *Annual Report 2017–2018*, fn. 54 above, Appendix A, pp. 119–120.
[151] Law Commission Report, *Updating the Land Registration Act 2002* (2018) Law Com No 380, Ch. 20.
[152] As defined in s. 27 of the LRA 2002: para. 16.21 above.

enforceable against the transferee/grantee. This is because s. 28 says that dispositions of registered titles do not affect the enforceability of other property interests affecting them, unless s. 29 or s. 30 applies, and ss. 29 and 30 apply only to dispositions for valuable consideration. This replicates the general law principle that all legal and equitable property interests affecting a legal freehold or leasehold interest in land are enforceable against donees: you cannot expect to be able to release your land from burdens affecting it just by giving it away.

If, however, the registrable disposition is for valuable consideration, s. 29 or s. 30 apply. We are interested primarily in s. 29, which deals with dispositions of registered freehold and leasehold titles. Section 30 contains similar provisions applicable to registrable dispositions of a mortgage (i.e. the mortgagee's interest is sold on to another mortgagee), which do not concern us here.

As already noted 'registrable disposition' is defined in s. 27, and the most important transactions it covers are a transfer of the title,[153] the grant of a lease (or sublease if the registered title is leasehold) for more than seven years and the grant of a legal mortgage or charge. There is some uncertainty over the precise scope of 'valuable consideration',[154] and also as to whether a fraudulent transfer or grant qualifies as a 'disposition' for these purposes.[155]

Section 29 provides that if a registered disposition is made for valuable consideration, and is then completed by registration, the person who becomes registered proprietor takes free from all property interests which affected the registered title immediately before the disposition, except interests which were 'protected' at the time he was registered as proprietor. 'Protected' has a special meaning here: by s. 29(2), interests are 'protected' for these purposes if registered (as to which see para. 16.10(b) above), or if protected on the register by notice (para. 16.10(c) above), or if they are overriding interests. We look at overriding interests in paras. 16.25–16.27 below.

(b) Relevance of Good Faith and Notice

There is no suggestion in s. 29, or elsewhere in the LRA 2002, that a person who becomes registered proprietor has to have purchased in good faith in order to take advantage of s. 29, or that he will be disqualified from relying on s. 29 if he had notice of an 'unprotected' interest (i.e. an interest which was not registered, protected by notice or overriding). This marks a significant difference in principle between the registered land enforceability rules and those that apply to property interests outside the land registration system. It also makes our land registration

---

[153] Except when the transfer takes place on death or bankruptcy by operation of law.

[154] 'Valuable consideration' is not comprehensively defined in the LRA 2002 and it is not clear how far it extends: see Law Com No 380, *Updating the Land Registration Act 2002*, fn. 151 above, Ch. 7, where, however, the Law Commission recommended only one minor change to the 2002 Act, despite the lack of clarity.

[155] It was held that it does not in *Malory Enterprises Ltd* v. *Cheshire Homes Ltd* [2002] EWCA Civ 151, but this is disputed, as we saw in para. 16.17 above.

system notably different from other systems operating in other jurisdictions.[156] However, notice is reintroduced into our land registration system to some extent by the LRA 2002 provisions about overriding interests of those in actual occupation, as we see in paras. 16.25–16.27 below, and in relation to easements.[157] Also, as we see in para. 16.29 below, the courts have accepted that, in strictly limited circumstances, a prior 'unprotected' interest may become enforceable against a purchaser for valuable consideration through estoppel or constructive trust, in effect bringing in requirements of good faith by the back door.

(c) Priority Between Unregistered Interests

The LRA 2002 makes it clear that, whilst *registration* of an interest gives it priority over all later property interests affecting the land it affects, *protection on the register by notice* has a more limited effect. Although, as we saw in (b) above, *protection by notice* makes the interest enforceable against all later *registered proprietors*, it has no effect on its priority as against any other unregistered property interest affecting the same land.[158]

However, the LRA 2002 does not seem to tell us anything about the priority of unregistered property interests as against each other (other than that it is not affected by registered dispositions except as provided by ss 29–30). We know that ss. 28–30 were *intended* to mean that for all priority purposes, unregistered property interests (whether unprotected, protected by notice or overriding) take their priority between themselves strictly according to their date of creation, except where s. 29 and s. 30 say otherwise.[159] It is sometimes assumed that s. 28 achieves this,[160] but it is doubtful whether this is correct. The wording of s. 28 ('the priority of an interest affecting a [registered title] *is not affected by*' a disposition except as provided by ss. 29 and 30) suggests that there is a rule to be found elsewhere, telling us what priority an unregistered interest *does* have as against other property interests affecting that title. No such rule appears anywhere in the LRA 2002 except in relation to registered interests,[161] and to rights of pre-emption, equities by estoppel and mere equities.[162] So, for all other interests, including interests protected by

---

[156] Including, as we saw in para. 16.17, Germany and Scotland.   [157] Sch. 3 para. 3 of the LRA 2002.

[158] There are some circumstances in which this could have unfair consequences, but the Law Commission has concluded that they are not sufficiently common to justify changing the law to give notices priority effect, given the expense and increased complexity in the law which would result from the change: Law Com No 380 fn. 151 above, Ch. 6.

[159] Law Commission and HM Land Registry, *Land Registration for the Twenty-first Century*, fn. 52 above, paras. 2.17 and 5.5.

[160] Darren Cavill et al., *Ruoff & Roper: Registered Conveyancing* (London: Thomson Reuters, looseleaf updated to May 2019), para. 15.025 and *Megarry & Wade*, fn. 121 above, para. 7.060. It was also assumed to be correct, but without argument, by Norris J in *Halifax plc* v. *Curry Popeck* [2008] EWHC 1692 at paras. 24–25.

[161] S. 27(1) provides that they do not take effect as legal interests *until* registered, which suggests that their priority as between themselves depends on date of registration even when ss. 29 does not apply (e.g. when a registered proprietor acquired her title by gift).

[162] S. 115 provides that a right of pre-emption 'has effect from the date of creation as an interest capable of binding successors in title', and s. 116 provides that an equity by estoppel and a mere equity 'has

notice and overriding interests, we must turn to the general law to find the basic rule governing the priority of these property interests as between themselves, in other words to the rules we looked at in Chapter 15 *Enforceability and Priority of Property Interests*. Under those rules, legal interests rank according to date of creation, but equitable interests do so *only* where 'the equities are equal'.[163] As we saw in para. 15.11 in Chapter 15, in *Freeguard* v. *Royal Bank of Scotland* (1990) 79 P & CR 81 the Court of Appeal held that this qualification of the first in time rule had to be imported into the LRA 1925, with the result that Mrs Freeguard's option to purchase was postponed to a later unregistered mortgage because she had deliberately tried to hide her interest from subsequent purchasers. There is nothing in the LRA 2002 to suggest that the position would be different under the 2002 Act.[164]

16.25 Overriding Interests

As we noted in the previous paragraph, interests categorised as 'overriding interests' are not mentioned on the land register, but under the statutory scheme set up by the LRA 1925 they are nevertheless enforceable against everyone who takes any kind of interest in the land they affect, even someone who becomes a registered proprietor of a freehold or long leasehold title or a mortgage following a registrable disposition for valuable consideration. The current categories of overriding interests are set out in Sch. 3 of the LRA 2002.[165] These are fewer and narrower than those made overriding by the LRA 1925. The intention of the LRA 2002 was to minimise the number of interests which might be overriding because of their potential adverse effects on purchasers, and, more broadly, in line with the 'fundamental objective' that 'the register should be a complete and accurate reflection of the state of the title to the land'.[166]

It is worth noting here, however, that earlier Law Commission considerations of overriding interests adopted a more nuanced approach. In its Third Report on Land Registration in 1987,[167] the Law Commission quoted and adopted a comment from a much earlier consultation paper about balancing the competing interests of property interest holders and purchasers:

effect from' the 'time the equity arises' (without telling us when they do, as a matter of law, arise: a separate issue we can leave aside here).

[163] See Chapter 15 *Enforceability and Priority of Property Interests* para. 15.11.

[164] See Astron Douglas, 'Equitable priorities under registered land' (2017) University of Cambridge Faculty of Law Legal Studies Research Paper Series Paper No. 5/2017, www.law.cam.ac.uk/ssrn/, who comes to a similar conclusion although by a different route.

[165] Schedule 3 replaces s. 70(1) of the LRA 1925, with some significant changes. The term 'overriding interest' comes from the LRA 1925, but the LRA 2002 changed the terminology, referring instead to 'interests which override'. The new terminology has never really caught on, and most people still call them overriding interests (even the Law Commission: see the heading to Ch. 11 of its Report, *Updating the Land Registration Act 2002* (2018) Law Com No 380).

[166] Law Commission and HM Land Registry, *Land Registration for the Twenty-first Century*, fn. 52 above, para. 1.5. We come back to this point in Part IV, where we look at property interests which are outside the land registration system.

[167] Law Commission, *Third Report on Land Registration: Overriding Interests, Rectification and Indemnity and Minor Interests* (1987) Law Com No 158.

Those who advocate eliminating or drastically reducing the number of overriding interests sometimes, we think, tend to look at the matter solely from the point of view of purchasers of land without paying sufficient regard to the interests of others.[168]

Their policy conclusion in the 1987 Third Report was this:

The ideal of a complete register of title is certainly compatible with the policy of the law for over one hundred and fifty years of both simplifying conveyancing and maintaining the security of property interests on the one hand and the marketability of land on the other. But the longevity of a policy hardly guarantees its acceptability to-day in the light of modern developments affecting land ownership. Plainly no policy should be followed blindly which works against rather than for 'rights conferred by Parliament, or recognised by judicial decision, as being necessary for the achievement of social justice' (per Lord Scarman in *Williams & Glyn's Bank Ltd.* v. *Boland* [1981] AC 487 at p. 510). Put simply, it may be unjust to require that a particular interest be protected by registration on pain of deprivation ... These considerations persuade us to adopt *two principles, with the first being subject to the second: (1) in the interests of certainty and of simplifying conveyancing, the class of right which may bind a purchaser otherwise than as a result of an entry on the register should be as narrow as possible but (2) interests should be overriding where protection against purchasers is needed, yet it is either not reasonable to expect nor sensible to require any entry on the register.*[169]

However, focussing instead primarily on the effect on purchasers, the LRA 2002 cut back the overriding interest list and sought to reduce the impact of two of the classes – easements and the interests of persons in actual occupation – by introducing notice-type requirements.[170]

16.26 Categories of Overriding Interests under LRA 2002

The current list of overriding interests is set out in Sch. 3 paras. 1–9 of the LRA 2002.[171] It no longer includes adverse possessors, whose interests were expressly stated to be overriding in the LRA 1925, but the precise effect of the omission is unclear, as we see in para. 16.34 below.

As to what is now included in the list of overriding interests, we have already noted short leases, that is, leases of seven years or less (paras. 1 and 1A) and some easements and profits in some circumstances (para. 3), and we should add 'customary and public rights' (paras. 4 and 5). We look at all of these in Part IV, where we look at off-register property interests. There are also, listed in paras. 4–9, some specialised rights we are not concerned with here, including interests in mines and minerals. That leaves the most important class for our purposes, which is provided by para. 2, 'interests of persons in actual occupation'. We look at this class in the

---

[168] Law Com Working Paper No 37 (1971), para. 7.
[169] Law Commission, *Third Report on Land Registration*, fn. 167 above, para. 2.6 (italics added). For fuller discussion of the policy issues see *Emmet & Farrand on Title*, fn. 33 above, paras. 9.002 and 9.005.
[170] See para. 16.35 below (easements) and para. 16.27 below (interests of persons in actual occupation).
[171] Paras. 10–16 contain transitional provisions governing interests that were overriding under the LRA 1925 but were removed by the LRA 2002. There is a separate and broader list in Sch. 1 of interests which are overriding on first registration of a title.

following paragraph. Meanwhile, however, we should note that the overriding interest category includes some property interests (most notably beneficial interests under a trust and leases for three years or less) which *cannot be protected on the land register, or on any other public register*. We come back to this point in Part IV when we look at off-register property interests, but it is also worth bearing in mind here when considering arguments about restricting the range of overriding interests.

16.27 'Interests of Persons in Actual Occupation'

Although the policy behind the LRA 2002 was to keep the number of overriding interests to a minimum, it was acknowledged that this 'actual occupation' category (originally provided by s. 70(1)(g) of the LRA 1925) was still justified in principle:

> it is unreasonable to expect all encumbrancers to register their rights, particularly where those rights arise informally, under (say) a constructive trust or by estoppel. The law pragmatically recognises that some rights can be created informally, and to require their registration would defeat the sound policy that underlies their recognition. Furthermore, when people occupy land they are often unlikely to appreciate the need to take the formal step of registering any rights that they have in it. They will probably regard their occupation as the only necessary protection. The retention of this category of overriding interest is justified ... because this is a very clear case where protection against purchasers is needed but where it is 'not reasonable to expect or not sensible to require any entry on the register'.[172]

Nevertheless, the LRA 2002 imposed more stringent conditions on the circumstances in which interests can be overriding through the 'actual occupation' gateway. The position is now as stated in Sch. 3 para. 2 of the LRA 2002:

> 2. An interest belonging at the time of the disposition to a person in actual occupation, *so far as relating to land of which he is in actual occupation*, except for –
>
> ...
>
> (b) an interest of a person of whom inquiry was made before the disposition and who failed to disclose the right when he could reasonably have been expected to do so;
> (c) an interest –
>   (i) which belongs to a person whose occupation would not have been obvious on a reasonably careful inspection of the land at the time of the disposition, and
>   (ii) of which the person to whom the disposition is made does not have actual knowledge at that time ...[173]

This means that there are two preliminary conditions which must be satisfied before an interest can come within this category, and then two grounds for exclusion of

---

[172] para. 5.61 of the joint consultation paper published by the Law Commission and Land Registry in 1998, Law Com No 254, which preceded the Law Commission Report and Draft Bill, *Land Registration for the Twenty-first Century: A Conveyancing Revolution* (2001) Law Com No 271, echoing the words of the Law Commission Third Report 1987 noted in para. 16.10 above. The principle was endorsed in para. 8.53 of Law Com No 271.

[173] There are two other exceptions in (a) (interests under Settled land Act settlements) and (d) (leases taking effect at a future date) which are rarely encountered and do not concern us here.

even those people who satisfy those two conditions. The two preliminary conditions are that:

- the interest is an '*interest*'; and
- the interest holder is '*in actual occupation*' of *the relevant land* and *at the relevant time*.

The two grounds for exclusion are, that even if the interest holder has an interest and she is in actual occupation at the right time, her interest will still not be overriding if either:

- she 'failed to disclose' her interest on enquiry when she 'could reasonably have been expected' to disclose it (Sch. 3 para. 2(b)); or
- the purchaser or mortgagee had no 'actual knowledge' of her interest, *and* her occupation 'would not have been obvious on a reasonably careful inspection of the land at the time of the disposition' (para. 2(c)).

Some of these elements require a closer look.

(a) 'Interest'

It had long been established that under the LRA 1925 this meant any kind of property interest,[174] and in *Mortgage Express* v. *Lambert* [2016] EWCA Civ 555 the Court of Appeal confirmed that the same applies under the LRA 2002. There does not have to be a connection between the property rights of an occupier of registered land and the fact of her occupation: para. 2 is not confined to property rights *by virtue of which* the occupier is in occupation.

So, 'interest' includes any legal or equitable interest in the land, including beneficial interests under a trust,[175] and also rights of pre-emption, mere equities and equities arising by proprietary estoppel.[176] In the *Lambert* case itself, which we looked at in Chapter 15 *Enforceability and Priority of Property Interests* para. 15.19, it was held to include Ms Lambert's right to have her sale and leaseback arrangement with the fraudsters set aside as an unconscionable bargain. It has to be said that, as we saw in para. 15.19, this was no help to Ms Lambert herself, because she was unlucky enough to be conned by fraudsters who put her freehold title in the names of two of them rather than one, and the innocent mortgagee persuaded the Court of Appeal that this meant that her interest was overreached.[177]

So, even if an occupying claimant can show she had an 'interest' under para. 2, the general law principle of overreaching may bar it from being enforceable against a

---

[174] Except a few expressly stated to be excluded by various provisions of what is now LRA 2002 (e.g. ss. 87 (3), 29(3) and 30(3)), which we are not concerned with, and some property interests created by statutes which state that the interests they create are not overriding interests within the LRA 1925 or 2002: see e.g. family home rights under the Family Law Act 1996.

[175] *Williams & Glyns Bank* v. *Boland* [1981] AC 487.

[176] Expressly stated in the LRA 2002 to be capable of binding successors in title (ss. 115 and 116).

[177] She also failed to get past the other hurdles imposed by Sch. 3 para. 2, as we see in (f) below.

later registrable proprietor,[178] as may equitable doctrines such the *Brocklesby* principle of apparent authority, estoppel and imputed intention.[179]

However, other victims of fraud may not even get this far. The much criticised Supreme Court decision in *Scott* v. *Southern Pacific Mortgages Ltd* [2014] UKSC 52 concerned a similar sale and leaseback fraud, and in that case the unfortunate victim, also desperate to repay mortgage arrears, agreed with a fraudster that she would sell her registered freehold interest in her home to the fraudster in exchange for the right that she and her son could go on living there as tenants at a reduced rent for the rest of their lives, plus the right to receive a lump sum pay of £15,000 in 10 years' time. The formal agreement between her and the fraudster was completed at the same time as the sale of her freehold interest to the fraudster. Also at the same time but unknown to Ms Scott, the fraudster mortgaged the freehold interest to an innocent lender and kept the mortgage money for itself, after paying off Ms Scott's old mortgage debts. She then remained in possession for the next four years, paying the new rent to the fraudster's representative, when by chance she found out about the mortgage, and also found out that the mortgage payments were in arrears and the mortgage lender had already obtained a court order for possession and was about to sell the house. The mortgage lender claimed that it was not bound by any interest she might have, or have had, in her home. The Supreme Court, hearing this appeal together with appeals in nine other test cases,[180] agreed. It held that although Ms Scott would have been entitled to an estoppel interest as against the fraudster which was capable of being an overriding interest enforceable against the mortgage lender under Sch. 3 para. 2 of the LRA 2002, she acquired it too late. The Supreme Court accepted the mortgagee's ingenious argument that her estoppel interest arose only when the fraudster acquired the legal title to the freehold interest,[181] and that that happened as part of an indivisible composite transaction by which the fraudster simultaneously acquired the freehold title and mortgaged it to the lender. So, on the basis of these highly technical, and arguably unsound, arguments, the Supreme Court was able to find that, at the time when the mortgagee acquired its property interest, Ms Scott's property interest (the equitable estoppel interest) did not yet exist, so could not have been an overriding interest within Sch. 3 para. 2.[182]

[178] As confirmed by the House of Lords in *City of London Building Society* v. *Flegg* [1988] AC 54, and see further para. 16.36 below.
[179] para. 16.28 below.
[180] Apparently chosen from hundreds of similar cases arising out of serial frauds.
[181] Not at the fractionally earlier point when the fraudster acquired an estate contract in the house under the sale agreement made between Ms Scott and the fraudster. The Supreme Court decided that her estoppel interest could not arise until the person estopped – the fraudster – had acquired a property interest in the house, and, much to everyone's surprise, went on to say that an estate contract did not count as a property interest for these purposes (see para. 5.22(a) of Chapter 5 *Ownership and Other Property Interests*).
[182] Lady Hale did express unease at the result at para. 122, suggesting that the system may not be striking the right balance between victims of fraud and mortgagees.

(b) Actual Occupation

'Actual occupation' also appeared in s. 70(1)(g) of the Land Registration Act 1925, the predecessor of para. 2, and, again, it has long been established that it is a question of fact whether or not someone is in actual occupation of land. As Lord Wilberforce said in the seminal House of Lords decision in *Williams* v. *Glyn's Bank* v. *Boland*:[183]

> These words are ordinary words of plain English, and should, in my opinion, be interpreted as such ... Given occupation, i.e., presence on the land, I do not think that the word 'actual' was intended to introduce any additional qualification ... it merely emphasises that what is required is physical presence, not some entitlement in law.

However, this makes the 'plain English' meaning of 'actual occupation' seem more straightforward than it is. *Boland* concerned the home of a married couple where the registered freehold title was held by the husband on trust for himself and his wife. The husband mortgaged the title to the mortgagee bank to secure repayment of his business debts and the bank registered its charge at the Land Registry. The bank called in the loan and sought to enforce the mortgage, and the wife argued that her beneficial interest was enforceable against the bank as an overriding interest because she was in actual occupation of the home at the time when the mortgage was granted.[184] Lord Wilberforce's remarks were made in the context of the bank's argument that a wife who lived with her husband in their home was not in 'actual occupation' of it because 'the wife's occupation was nothing but the shadow of the husband's'. Lord Wilberforce described this argument as 'heavily obsolete'[185] and it was decisively rejected by the House of Lords.[186] They also rejected the broader argument that a person could only be in 'actual occupation' if their occupation would seem to the outside world to be inconsistent with the registered owner's title. As Lord Scarman said, this latter argument would limit 'actual' occupation to 'occupation, which by its nature necessarily puts a would-be purchaser (or mortgagee) upon notice of a claim adverse to the registered owner'. To limit it in this way, he said, was not justified by the wording of the statutory provision and would be inconsistent with the objective of the legislation as a whole, which was to replace the 'wearisome and intricate task of examining title, and with it the doctrine of notice' with a statutory scheme in which the determinant of an overriding interest was to be 'a plain factual situation' in place of 'the uncertainties of notice, actual or constructive'.[187] We come back to this issue of notice in (f) below.

Meanwhile, however, there are other situations where the 'plain English' meaning of 'actual occupation' is not so clear. Are you in actual occupation of my house when you come to visit me for, say, an afternoon, a week or a month? Am I in actual

---

[183] *Williams* v. *Glyn's Bank* v. *Boland* [1981] AC 487 at pp. 504–505.

[184] Relying on s. 70(1)(g) of the LRA 1925, the predecessor of Sch. 3 para. 2 of the LRA 2002.

[185] *Boland* at p. 505.

[186] Surprisingly, the argument was later accepted by the Court of Appeal in relation to occupying children in *Hypo-Mortgage Services ltd* v. *Robinson* [1997] 2 FLR 71, in relation to another aspect of s. 70(1)(g) of the LRA 1925.

[187] *Boland* at p. 511.

occupation of my house whilst I am out shopping, or away on holiday or working abroad? Lord Oliver of Aylmerton considered some of these more difficult cases in *Abbey National Building Society* v. *Cann* [1991] 1 AC 56.[188] In that case, Mrs Cann was just completing her purchase of her house and the question arose whether she was in actual occupation of it at the critical time, which was when the purchase was completed. At that point she herself was away on holiday but her furniture and possessions had been moved into the house half an hour earlier. It was held that, on those particular facts, she was not in actual occupation. Lord Oliver said at pp. 93–94:

> It is, perhaps, dangerous to suggest any test for what is essentially a question of fact, for 'occupation' is a concept which may have different connotations according to the nature and purpose of the property which is claimed to be occupied. It does not necessarily, I think, involve the personal presence of the person claiming to occupy. A caretaker or the representative of a company can occupy, I should have thought, on behalf of his employer. On the other hand, it does, in my judgment, involve some degree of permanence and continuity which would rule out mere fleeting presence. A prospective tenant or purchaser who is allowed, as a matter of indulgence, to go into property in order to plan decorations or measure for furnishings would not, in ordinary parlance, be said to be occupying it, even though he might be there for hours at a time. Of course, in the instant case, there was, no doubt, on the part of the persons involved in moving Mrs Cann's belongings, an intention that they would remain there and would render the premises suitable for her ultimate use as a residential occupier. Like the trial judge, however, I am unable to accept that acts of this preparatory character carried out by courtesy of the vendor prior to completion can constitute 'actual occupation' for the purposes of s. 70(1)(g).

Similarly, in *Thompson* v. *Foy* [2009] EWHC 1076 Lewison J concluded that, even if Mrs Thompson did retain a property interest in the cottage where she had lived, and which she had transferred to her daughter, she was not in actual occupation of it at the relevant time (10 April, the date when a mortgage granted by the daughter was registered[189]). The background was that mother and daughter had agreed that the property would be transferred to the daughter as a gift so that the daughter could raise £400,000 by mortgaging and then letting it, giving the mother £200,000 out of the mortgage loan. On 5 April when the transfer and mortgage were completed, it had not finally been decided where the mother would move to, or when. On 6 April Mrs Thompson went to house-sit for another daughter who was going away on holiday for the weekend, planning to return home on 9 April. However, between 6 and 9 April she changed her mind: the daughter who now owned the property and had received the mortgage loan, told her that she was not going to give her the £200,000, and Mrs Thompson decided she was never going to go back to the cottage. She never did, except to collect her belongings. So, when she left her home, Mrs Thompson intended to be away just for the weekend, to house-sit for her other daughter, but by the 10 April, the critical date for deciding whether the right she

---

[188] *Abbey National Building Society* v. *Cann* [1991] 1 AC 56.
[189] See further (e) as to why this was held to be the relevant date.

claimed in the property[190] was an overriding interest as against the mortgagee, she had decided never to go back. In deciding that she was not in actual occupation, Lewison J relied on five factors: as at 10 April (i) she had packed some of her pictures and ornaments some months earlier, anticipating that she would be leaving at some stage; (ii) she had been away from the cottage for four days; (iii) she had (on 9 April) collected personal possessions from her bedroom, taken anything of value away from the cottage and emptied her safe; (iv) she had decided that she would not go back to the cottage to live there; but (v) most of her furniture, bedding, etc. remained at the cottage and would not be collected for another few days.[191] Lewison J said at para. 131:

> But for the fourth of these features I would have concluded that Mrs Thompson remained in actual occupation of the cottage at Valley View on 10 April. However, since Mrs Thompson was neither physically present at Valley View on 10 April, nor had any intention of returning to occupy the cottage, I do not consider that she can be said to have been in actual occupation of it on 10 April.

This analysis of the law by Lewison J was approved by the Court of Appeal in *Link Lending Ltd* v. *Bustard* [2010] EWCA Civ 424. That case concerned a woman, Ms Bustard, who had been duped into transferring her registered title of her home to a fraudster, who had then mortgaged the title to an innocent bank mortgagee. It was held that she had an equity entitling her to have the fraudulent transfer set aside, and that it was enforceable against the bank as an overriding interest under Sch. 3 para. 2. This was because, so it was held, she was in actual occupation of her home at the relevant time, even though living elsewhere by necessity but making regular short visits: she had been sectioned under the Mental Health Act 1983 and for the past year she had been living in a care unit in a psychiatric hospital, under medical orders not to return to live in her house, although the household bills continued to be paid on her behalf and she visited the house once a week under supervision to collect her post. Lord Justice Mummery concluded that it would not be right to interfere with the judge's finding that she was in actual occupation:

> ... Ms Bustard's is not a case of a 'mere fleeting presence', or a case, like *Cann*, of acts preparatory to the assumption of actual occupation. It is also distinguishable from *Stockholm*,[192] which involved the domestic living arrangements of a Saudi princess living with her mother in Saudi Arabia and owning a house in London, where there was furniture and clothing and caretaking arrangements in place, but where she had not lived for more than a year. In this case the new and special feature is in the psychiatric problems of the person claiming actual occupation. The judge was, in my view, justified in ruling, at the conclusion of a careful and detailed judgment, that Ms Bustard was a person in actual occupation of the Property. His conclusion was supported by evidence of a sufficient degree of continuity and permanence of occupation, of involuntary residence elsewhere, which was satisfactorily explained by

[190] A right to set aside the transfer on the basis of undue influence by the daughter.
[191] *Thompson* v. *Foy* [2009] EWHC 1076 at para. 130.
[192] An unreported decision, *Stockholm Finance Ltd* v. *Garden Holdings Inc* [1995] LTL (26 October 1995).

objective reasons, and of a persistent intention to return home when possible, as manifested by her regular visits to the Property.

These last two decisions have been criticised for introducing a subjective element into what should, so it is said, be a purely factual question. Christopher Bevan has argued that the introduction of subjective elements such as the applicant's intentions and wishes and their personal circumstances unjustifiably broadens the scope of the 'actual occupation' category of overriding interests, beyond the 'traditional, objective 'question of fact' analysis of Lord Wilberforce ... *in Boland*.[193] However, this underestimates the difficulties in deciding whether physical presence is sufficiently prolonged or continuous to amount to occupation. How else can the courts deal with long-term occupiers who are physically absent for a short time up to and including the critical date (or, indeed, a physical presence which has lasted for only a short time up to and including the critical date, or periods of intermittent physical presence) except by interpreting 'facts' such as physical absence or presence of claimants and their belongings on a particular day, in the light of their 'intentions and wishes'?

(c) Additional Factors Relevant to Actual Occupation

It had already been established by the House of Lords in *Boland* that someone can be in actual occupation of a place even though someone else is also in actual occupation. Less obviously, it seems that someone might be in actual occupation of two places at the same time, for example if having a second home and living part of the time there and part of the time in their main home (*AIB Group (UK) Ltd* v. *Turner* [2016] EWHC 3994, where, however, it was held that Ms Turner had effectively moved to her second home in Barbados and was no longer occupying her cottage in England – another case where, surely, intentions were rightly held to be relevant).

A further difficulty is that there are some kinds of spaces that we use in a way that we would not normally describe as 'occupation'. So, for example, in *Chaudhary* v. *Yavuz* [2011] EWCA Civ 1314 it was held that Mr Chaudhary was not in actual occupation of a metal stairway and landing built in an alleyway on his neighbour's land, and forming part of his neighbour's title. The metal structure linked Mr Chaudhary's premises to his neighbour's premises and was used by each of them to get to and from the upper floors of their respective premises to the street. Mr Chaudhary had an equitable easement over the structure which, he argued, was an overriding interest under para. 2 because he was in actual occupation of the structure. The Court of Appeal disagreed, taking the view that passing and re-passing over an area was not the same as occupying it:

---

[193] Christopher Bevan, 'Overriding and over-extended? Actual occupation: A call to orthodoxy' (2016) 80 *Conveyancer and Property Lawyer* 104 at p. 111, and see also Barbara Bogusz, 'The relevance of "intentions and wishes" to determine actual occupation: A sea change in judicial thinking?' (2014) 78 *Conveyancer and Property Lawyer* 27.

I dare say that no-one else was in occupation of the metal structure either, but not every piece of land is occupied by someone, let alone in someone's actual occupation (as distinct from possession).[194]

(d) Occupation of the Relevant Land

Even if a person with an interest in land can show that she was in actual occupation of it, her interest will be overriding *only* so far as it relates to the land she is occupying, because of the opening words of para. 2. This means that if her interest is in large area of land (perhaps a house with a large garden including a shed is held on trust for her) but she occupies only part of it (perhaps just the shed), her interest will be enforceable against a purchaser only in so far as it relates to the small part she occupies. This reverses the law as established by the Court of Appeal decision in *Ferrishurst Ltd* v. *Wallcite Ltd*,[195] decided under the LRA 1925, which had come to the opposite conclusion in relation to an option to purchase a block of offices and an adjoining garage held by the occupier of the offices. This decision had aroused criticism because of the additional burden of enquiry it was said to place upon potential purchasers of large developments: the example was given of a potential purchaser of the freehold interest in a large residential development comprising hundreds of separate units who (so it was argued) would have to enquire of every occupier of every unit whether they happened to have a property interest covering the whole of the freehold estate, such as an option to purchase it. This potential hazard for purchasers has now been removed by para. 2, but perhaps at the cost of increasing the risk of unfairness to occupiers in some circumstances. This is apparent from the Court of Appeal decision in *Ashburn Anstalt* v. *Arnold* [1989] Ch 1, which we look at in more detail in para. 16.29, which was decided under the LRA 1925 before *Ferrishurst* v. *Wallcite*. At that time it was thought that the law was as it now is, that is, that an interest overriding because of actual occupation is overriding only in respect of the land the interest holder occupies. In *Ashburn Anstalt* a lessee with a long lease of a shop agreed with his landlord, who was proposing to redevelop a large area of land which included the shop, that he would surrender his lease in exchange for a licence to continue to trade in the shop until the redevelopment started, and the grant of a new lease of a shop 'in a prime position' in the redevelopment. The landlord sold its interest to a purchaser at a time when the lessee was still occupying his old shop under the licence. The Court of Appeal held that the lessee had a property right affecting the landlord's title to the whole of the redevelopment site, but that it was enforceable against the purchaser only so far as it related to the part of the site he occupied. That meant, so the Court of Appeal held, that the lessee was entitled to a new lease of any shop which the purchaser might happen to build on the site of the old shop, but not of any shop the purchaser built elsewhere in the

---

[194] Lord Lloyd at para. 140. For other problematic aspects of the case see paras. 16.29 and 16.35 below.
[195] *Ferrishurst Ltd* v. *Wallcite Ltd* [1999] Ch 355.

redevelopment. When the redevelopment was subsequently completed, the site of the lessee's old shop had become a pedestrian forecourt to the new shops.

(e) Occupation at the Relevant Time

An additional requirement is that an interest will only be overriding under Sch. 3 para. 2, that is, enforceable against a subsequent transferee/grantee, if the interest holder was in occupation at 'the time of the disposition' to the transferee/grantee. It had been held under the equivalent provisions in the LRA 1925 that this meant the time when the disposition was completed rather than the later date when the transferee/grantee applies for registration.[196] It is not at all obvious from the wording of the LRA 2002 that the same applies under the present law, and in *Thompson* v. *Foy*,[197] Lewison J took the view that, reading s. 27(2), s. 29 and Sch. 3 para. 2 of the 2002 Act together, the interest holder has to be in actual occupation both at the date when the disposition was completed and at the later date when the transferee/grantee applied for registration.[198] In that particular case it would have mattered, because Mrs Thompson was in occupation when a charge was granted by her daughter, but not, so the court found, on the later date when it was registered.[199] However, since Mrs Thomson failed to convince the court that she had the interest in the land she claimed, Lewison J's analysis was obiter, though none the less convincing.[200]

This is one of the many problems that those responsible for the LRA 2002 thought would soon disappear, because, so it was thought, 'e-conveyancing' would make completion and registration of dispositions happen simultaneously. As already noted, however, this is not what has happened.[201]

(f) 'Failure to Disclose' the Interest on Enquiry

The provision in para. 2 that an interest holder's interest will not be overriding if he failed to disclose it on enquiry 'when he could reasonably have been expected to do so' originated in the LRA 1925. It is not clear what it adds to the general law, since in such circumstances the interest holder would usually be estopped from asserting her interest as against the enquirer.[202]

The way it works in practice is that standardised forms of enquiries are routinely sent out by potential purchasers and mortgagees to sellers in conveyancing transactions, usually via solicitors and surveyors, and these include standard questions enquiring about overriding interests, including enquiries about whether there is anyone else in occupation and if so whether they have any interests in the property. It is only if these enquiries are made by or on behalf of the potential purchaser and

---

[196] *Abbey National Building Society* v. *Cann* [1991] 1 AC 56.
[197] *Thompson* v. *Foy* [2009] EWHC 1076, noted in (b) above.   [198] Paras. 121–125.
[199] See (b) above.
[200] Barbara Bogusz, 'Defining the scope of actual occupation under the LRA 2002: Some recent judicial clarification' [2011] *Conveyancer and Property Lawyer* 268.
[201] para. 16.23 above.   [202] para. 16.28 below.

addressed to the interest holder that they are relevant here, and in more complex cases it is not always easy to ascertain whether this is what has happened. In *Mortgage Express* v. *Lambert*,[203] as we saw in (a) above, Mrs Lambert's equitable interest was an equity to set aside an unconscionable bargain she had been persuaded to enter into with two fraudsters. Under this arrangement she sold the fraudsters her leasehold interest in her flat at a gross undervalue in exchange for a promise that they would grant a lease back to her which would enable her to live there for the rest of her life. The fraudsters then mortgaged the lease to the bank to secure a loan for the full value of the lease, telling the bank that they had just bought it with vacant possession. The issue was whether Mrs Lambert's equitable interest was enforceable against the bank as an overriding interest under Sch. 3 para. 2, given that she was indisputably in actual occupation of the flat when the mortgage was granted. As we saw in Chapter 15 *Enforceability and Priority of Property Interests* para. 15.19 her claim failed because, so it was held, her interest was overreached. However, the Court of Appeal went on to say that even if it had not been overreached, it would still not have qualified as an overriding interest under para. 2, because she failed to disclose it on enquiry. This is difficult to follow on the facts. Before the sale to the fraudsters and in anticipation of it, Mrs Lambert's solicitors had sent her their own standard form questionnaire which asked her whether there were any overriding interests affecting her title and whether vacant possession of her flat would be given when she sold. In answer to those enquiries she did not mention the leaseback arrangement, although she did mention it to her solicitors orally and her solicitors knew the sale was at a gross undervalue. Her solicitors then received standard form enquiries from solicitors acting for both the fraudsters and the bank. Ms Lambert's solicitors replied to those questions on her behalf, relying on the information she had supplied to them in their questionnaire, not revealing the leaseback arrangement, or that she would be continuing to live in the house after completion of the sale. In addition, in the contract for sale to the fraudsters which Ms Lambert had signed, she was expressed to sell with vacant possession and to sell 'with full title guarantee'. This is a technical term, meaning that she was contracting to dispose of the whole of her interest in the flat. The Court of Appeal said all of this amounted to a failure to reveal her interest when she could reasonably be expected to have done so, in response to an enquiry made by the mortgagee. Fox LJ said:

> While I would accept that Ms Lambert could not reasonably have been expected to have attached the label 'unconscionable bargain' to the right she now claims, I agree ... that it would have been reasonable for her to have disclosed that she was not in fact giving vacant possession; and that the lease [of her flat] would be encumbered in the hands of the purchasers by the tenancy she had agreed to take.[204]

It was not mentioned that she might quite reasonably have presumed that the enquiries were coming from her fraudster purchasers (or even from her own solicitors), who she knew to be fully aware of all these facts. The outcome for Ms Lambert is made even more disturbing by the fact that the bank mortgagee had

---

[203] *Mortgage Express* v. *Lambert* [2016] EWCA Civ 555.   [204] Ibid. Para. 41.

actual notice that the sale from Ms Lambert to the fraudsters was at an undervalue: they had all the figures before them. Fox LJ dismissed this as irrelevant:

> Schedule 3 para. 2 does not mention notice, and the philosophy underlying the LRA 2002 is that notice is irrelevant.[205]

(g) Occupation Which is Not Obvious on a Reasonably Careful Inspection, Unless the Purchaser has Actual Knowledge of the Occupier's Interest

This comment about notice made by Fox LJ in *Mortgage Express* v. *Lambert* is particularly surprising, given that Sch. 3 para. 2 of the LRA 2002 in effect brings notice back into the registration scheme. This is by providing (in para. 2(c)) that an interest is not made overriding by actual occupation if the *occupation* 'would not have been obvious on a reasonably careful inspection of the land at the time of the disposition', unless the transferee/grantee has 'actual knowledge' of *the interest* at the time of the disposition.[206] The first limb is objective: it is irrelevant whether or not an inspection did in fact take place. The only issue is whether, if a reasonably careful inspection had been made, the occupation would have been 'obvious'. The second, however, is wholly subjective, in that it appears to be concerned only with what the transferee/grantee actually knew – that is, with actual notice. It is odd that 'knowledge' here does not extend to include imputed as well as actual knowledge, given the basic principle that as against the rest of the world, people are deemed to know what is known by those acting on their behalf in that particular matter. However, a more difficult question is whether the combined effect of the two limbs of para. 2(c) is to bring in something approaching constructive notice. If the circumstances are such that the transferee/grantee should have suspected that something was being hidden from him, does that colour what a 'reasonably careful inspection' would involve? It is instructive in this context to look back at *Kingsnorth* v. *Tizard*, the unregistered land case we looked at in Chapter 15 para. 15.9(c), where the estranged husband hid signs of his wife's occupation but there were discrepancies in what he told the mortgagee and the mortgagee's surveyor, which should have alerted them to the possibility that his wife might have an interest and might still be living there. In those circumstances, might a reasonably careful inspection involve more opening of cupboards and looking under beds (from which her occupation would certainly have been obvious) than might be required of someone without those causes for suspicion?

16.28 Equitable Principles Barring Enforceability

Even if the holder of a property interest is in actual occupation of the land, and all other conditions in Sch. 3 para. 2 are satisfied, his interest may nevertheless be defeated by overreaching (primarily a problem for beneficial interests under trusts,

---

[205] Ibid.

[206] 'Date of the disposition' meaning in both cases date of registration, according to Lewison J in *Thompson* v. *Foy*: see (e) above.

as we see in para. 16.36 below) or by the application of equitable principles of apparent authority, estoppel or imputed intention. If any of these doctrines apply, his interest will not be enforceable against a registered transferee/grantee. The same applies to an interest which would otherwise amount to an overriding interest under any of the other paragraphs of Sch. 3 para. 2.

This was confirmed by the Court of Appeal in *Wishart* v. *Credit and Mercantile plc* [2015] EWCA Civ 655, where they applied the equitable principle of apparent authority to hold that the interest of a beneficiary under a trust was not enforceable against a bank mortgagee as an overriding interest. The beneficiary was Wishart, who was involved in property development deals with his business partner, Sami. They agreed that Wishart's share of the proceeds of one of these deals should be used to buy a house to be lived in by Wishart and his family. Wishart left the purchase of the house to Sami, and without Wishart's knowledge Sami arranged for the house to be bought in the name of a company he, Sami, controlled. He then arranged for the house to be mortgaged to the bank, telling the bank that the company was the unencumbered freehold owner. Sami spent the mortgage loan gambling and disappeared. It was held that the company held the freehold on trust for Wishart. However, the Court of Appeal went on to decide that, even though Wishart and his family were clearly occupying the house, he was barred from relying on Sch. 3 para. 2 as against the bank because of the *Brocklesby* principle.[207] This principle is that an owner who has provided an agent with the means of holding himself out as the owner, must bear the risk of fraud on the agent's part. The principle applied here, the Court of Appeal said, because Wishart had left the acquisition of the property completely in Sami's hands, and although Sami had acted outside the limits of his authority by arranging the mortgage over the property, the bank was not put on notice of any restriction on his authority. Wishart had exercised no supervisory function over what Sami might do to acquire the house, and in practical terms Wishart had provided Sami with the means to hold himself out (in the persona of the company) as the beneficial owner. The Court of Appeal was careful to emphasise that the effect of this was to extinguish Wishart's beneficial interest, so that he had no property interest which could be overriding within Sch. 3 para. 2.

Principles of estoppel and imputed intention were used to achieve a similar result in a particularly hard case, *Bank of Scotland* v. *Hussain & Qutb* [2010] EWHC 2812. Mrs Qutb, who had Alzheimer's disease, sold her house at an undervalue to Mr Hussain, who mortgaged it to the bank. This was not a trust case, although Mrs Qutb would have had little difficult in persuading the court that Hussain held the title on constructive trust for her. Instead the court held that she had a right to have the sale set aside as having been procured by Mr Hussain's undue influence and as an unconscionable bargain. It was accepted that this right was a property right, and the issue was whether it was overriding under Sch. 3 para. 2, given that Mrs Qutb was in actual occupation when the charge was granted. It was held that she was estopped from relying on para. 2 because, on the facts, there had to be imputed to

---

[207] *Brocklesby* v. *Temperance Permanent Building Society* [1895] AC 173. For critical comment see Douglas, 'Equitable priorities under registered land', fn. 164 above.

her an intention to authorise the mortgage. She had known that Mr Hussain would be obtaining a mortgage over the property and had not objected to it, her convey-ancing solicitors had represented that the property would be sold with vacant possession and that she would not retain any rights in it, and the bank had relied on those representations by proceeding with the loan. A submission that this sort of estoppel could not arise because of her Alzheimer's disease was rejected: any lack of capacity was immaterial as the bank had had no notice of it.[208]

16.29 Enforceability on the Basis of Constructive Trust or Estoppel

Conversely, there are some circumstances in which a transferee/grantee who becomes registered proprietor will be required to take subject to a prior interest affecting the transferor/grantor's title on the basis that it would be unconscionable for him to take advantage of s. 29 to defeat the prior interest. We have seen how this can happen following a forged or fraudulent transfer under the principles established in *Malory Enterprises Ltd* v. *Cheshire Homes Ltd* [2002] EWCA Civ 151 we looked at in para. 16.17(b) and (c) above. In addition, there are other circumstances in which equitable principles of constructive trust and estoppel may override the statutory enforceability rules.

(a) Constructive Trust and the *Lyus* v. *Prowsa* Principle

The foundational case is the decision of Dillon J in *Lyus* v. *Prowsa Developments Ltd* [1982] 1 WLR 1044, which concerned a sale by a mortgagee of an unfinished residential development. The mortgagor developer had already entered into con-tracts to sell individual units to prospective purchasers but then became insolvent, and the mortgagee called in the loan and put the developer's freehold interest up for sale. The individual purchase contracts were not enforceable against the mortgagee because they had been entered into after the mortgage was granted. Nevertheless, the mortgagee wanted to ensure that any buyer of the freehold would give effect to them, and it therefore sold the freehold to a purchaser 'subject to and with the benefit of' those specific contracts. Dillon J held that, given the circumstances, this was suffi-cient to impose a constructive trust on the purchaser, making the contracts enforce-able against the purchaser. He pointed out that the fact that the title was sold to the purchaser expressly subject to and with the benefit of a prior interest would not necessarily make the prior interest enforceable under a constructive trust:

> . . . there are many cases in which land is expressly conveyed subject to possible incumbrances when there is no thought at all of conferring any fresh rights on third parties who may be entitled to the benefit of the incumbrances. The land is expressed to be sold subject to incumbrances to satisfy the vendor's duty to disclose all possible

---

[208] *Bank of Scotland* v. *Hussain & Qutb* [2010] EWHC 2812, at paras. 103 and 107. See also *Thompson* v. *Foy* [2009] EWHC 1076 (Ch) above, at paras. 139–144, where Lewison J came to the same conclusion on different facts. For similar cases predating the LRA 2002 see *Emmet & Farrand on Title*, fn. 33 above, para. 5.119.

incumbrances known to him, and to protect the vendor against any possible claim by the purchaser if a third party establishes an overriding right to the benefit of the incumbrance against the purchaser.

However, this case was different, he said, because here the words were used to impose a positive obligation on the purchaser in favour of the prior interest holder, and it would therefore be unconscionable for the purchaser not to honour it:

> It seems to me that the fraud on the part of [the purchaser] in the present case lies not just in relying on the legal rights conferred by an Act of Parliament, but in … reneging on a positive stipulation in favour of the [contract holder] in the bargain under which [the purchaser]. That makes, as it seems to me, all the difference. It has long since been held, for instance in *Rochefoucauld* v. *Boustead* [1897] 1 Ch 196, that the provisions of the Statute of Frauds 1677, now incorporated in certain sections of the Law of Property Act 1925, cannot be used as an instrument of fraud, and that it is fraud for a person to whom land is agreed to be conveyed as trustee for another to deny the trust and relying on the terms of the statute to claim the land for himself.[209]

This statement of principle was approved by the Court of Appeal in *Ashburn Anstalt* v. *Arnold* [1989] Ch 1, the decision we noted in para. 16.27(d) above. As we saw there, the case concerned an agreement made in 1973 between Arnold, who had a long lease of a shop, and his landlord, who was proposing to redevelop a large area of land which included Arnold's shop. Under the agreement Arnold surrendered his lease and in exchange the landlord (a) agreed to grant him a new lease of alternative premises in the new development when it was completed and (b) granted him a licence to continue trading at the shop rent free until the redevelopment work started. Before it started the landlord sold its freehold interest to a purchaser, 'subject to, and with the benefit of, [the 1973 Agreement] so far as [it was] enforceable against the vendor'. Several years later, when the redevelopment work had still not started and Arnold was still occupying the shop under the licence, the purchaser tried to evict Arnold, claiming that it was not bound by the 1973 agreement. Arnold argued that the 1973 agreement granted him an immediate lease of the old shop pending redevelopment of the site, and an estate contract over the whole development (in the form of a contractual right to be granted a lease of a new shop in the development when it was completed). Both of these interests were enforceable against the purchaser as overriding interests, he argued, because of his actual occupation of the shop. The Court of Appeal agreed with Arnold that the rent free 'licence' granted by the 1973 agreement took effect as a lease, for reasons we consider in Chapter 17 *Leases*, and that therefore it was enforceable against the purchaser as an overriding interest under what was then s. 70(1)(g) of the LRA 1925.[210] On this particular point the Court of Appeal decision was later overruled by the House of Lords in *Prudential Assurance* v. *London Residuary Body* [1992] 2 AC 386, on the basis that a lease is invalid if the duration is uncertain.[211] However, the Court of

---

[209] Dillon J in *Lyus* v. *Prowsa Developments Ltd* [1982] 1 WLR 1044, at pp. 1054–1055.
[210] Although see para. 16.27(d) above as to the practical implications of the finding.
[211] Chapter 17 *Leases* para. 17.11.

Appeal in *Ashburn Anstalt* went on to consider whether, even if it was only a contractual licence (and so not a property interest at all) it could have been enforceable against the purchaser under a constructive trust. The Court of Appeal held that in principle it could, approving *Lyus* v. *Prowsa*, but that on the facts there was no constructive trust because there was insufficient evidence that the 'subject to and with the benefit of' wording in this particular case was intended to impose a positive obligation on the purchaser to be bound by Arnold's licence. Fry LJ said that a constructive trust could only be imposed if the purchaser 'has so conducted himself that it would be inequitable to allow him to deny the claimant an interest in the property'[212] (what the Court of Appeal described as 'a beneficial adaptation of old rules to new situations'[213]), and in this kind of case that could only arise if the purchaser was seeking to evade a positive obligation to give effect to a prior interest which he had undertaken:[214]

> In matters relating to the title to land, certainty is of prime importance. We do not think it desirable that constructive trusts of land should be imposed in reliance on inferences from slender materials. In our opinion the available evidence in the present case is insufficient . . . In general, we should emphasise that it is important not to lose sight of the question: 'Whose conscience are we considering?' It is the [purchaser's], and the issue is whether the [purchaser] has acted in such a way that, as a matter of justice, a trust must be imposed on it . . .[215]

Since *Ashburn Anstalt* the *Lyus* v. *Prowsa* principle has been repeatedly reaffirmed by the courts but held not to apply on the facts, because of no or insufficient evidence that the intention was to impose a new obligation on the purchaser. In particular, in *Lloyd* v. *Dugdale* [2001] EWCA Civ 1754, Sir Christopher Slade declined to accept that a purchaser of commercial premises from the registered freeholder was bound by constructive trust to take subject to an equity arising by estoppel entitling the occupier of premises to a long lease of the premises, even though the purchaser was well aware of the claimant's occupation and of the circumstances giving rise to the estoppel. Slade's view was that the operation of the *Lyus* v. *Prowsa* principle was necessarily limited in registered land:

> There is no general principle which renders it unconscionable for a purchaser of land to rely on a want of registration of a claim against registered land, even though he took with express notice of it. A decision to the contrary would defeat the purpose of the legislature in introducing the system of registration embodied in the 1925 Act.[216]

This is echoed in even stronger terms by Lloyd LJ in *Chaudhary* v. *Yavuz* [2011] EWCA Civ 1314, again acknowledging the *Lyus* v. *Prowsa* principle but refusing to apply it, in a case where the purchaser's conduct might be thought to have been particularly unmeritorious. The facts were that Mr Chaudhary, owner of a building consisting of a ground floor shop with residential flats above, built a metal stairway and landing in an alleyway owned by his neighbour which lay between his building

---

[212] Fry LJ in *Ashburn Anstalt* v. *Arnold* [1989] Ch 1 at p. 22F.   [213] Ibid. at p. 22D.
[214] Ibid. pp. 22–23.   [215] Ibid. p. 27C.   [216] *Lloyd* v. *Dugdale* [2001] EWCA Civ 1754 at para. 50.

and his neighbour's building. The structure was built by informal oral agreement between the neighbours for the benefit of both of them: the stairway led up from the street to the upper floors of the neighbour's building and also gave access, via the metal landing, to the flats on the upper floors of Chaudhary's building. The legal effect, so it was found, was to vest ownership of the metal structure (all built in the neighbour's airspace) in the neighbour, but to give Chaudhary a right of way over it by proprietary estoppel, that is, an equitable easement. Chaudhary could have protected his easement on the register by entering a notice but (unsurprisingly in the circumstances) he did not. The neighbour later sold his title to Yavuz, by a transfer which did not refer to the staircase but did include a standard form term stating that the transfer was subject to (amongst other things) 'incumbrances discoverable by inspection of the property'. When he bought the neighbouring land, Yavuz did not realise that the alleyway (and therefore also the metal structure) was included in the land he was buying, but it was common ground that it would have been obvious at a glance, never mind an inspection, that the structure provided access (as it happened, the only access) to the flats in Chaudhary's building. The issue was whether Chaudhary's rights over the metal structure were enforceable against Yavuz. It was decided that they were not. The Court of Appeal held that they were not enforceable as overriding interests, for the reasons noted in paras. 16.27 and 16.29 above and para. 16.35 below, nor was Yavuz bound by them by constructive trust. Lloyd LJ said that there was nothing in the sale contract to suggest that a positive obligation to respect Chaudhary's rights was being imposed on Yazuv. As far as the constructive trust point was concerned, Lloyd LJ described *Lyus* v. *Prowsa* as 'an exceptional case, and it is right that it should be', in that the prior interest was expressly identified in the sale contract, and the holder of the interest could not have made it enforceable against a purchaser by 'taking the proper steps' to protect it on the register.[217]

So, in the present state of the law, the scope of the *Lyus* v. *Prowsa* principle appears strictly limited.

(b) Proprietary Estoppel

In principle, if a prior interest would otherwise by unenforceable against a registered proprietor because it does not come within s. 29(2) (i.e. at the date of the disposition to the registered proprietor the prior interest was not registered or protected on the register and was not overriding), it can nevertheless become enforceable against her by estoppel. For this to be the case, the prior interest holder has to be able to establish that the purchaser/mortgagee who has become registered proprietor is estopped *by her own conduct* from denying the enforceability of the prior interest. So, for example, in *Chaudhary* v. *Yavuz* Chaudhary could have succeeded on this basis only if he had been able to establish that *Yavuz* had assured him that he, Chaudhary, would be able to go on using the stairway, and he, Chaudhary, had acted

---

[217] *Chaudhary* v. *Yavuz* [2011] EWCA Civ 1314 at paras. 64–65.

to his detriment in reliance on that assurance (perhaps by carrying out improvements to the upper floor which would be useless without the stairway access) so that it would be unconscionable to deny that the easement was binding on him. This was assumed to be the position in an unregistered land decision, *E.R. Ives Investments Ltd* v. *High*.[218] In that case, Mr High had been granted a right of way over his neighbour's land informally, in exchange for allowing the neighbour's foundations to encroach into Mr High's land. The majority in the Court of Appeal took the view that the agreement was enforceable against the neighbour's immediate purchaser (P1) on the basis of estoppel arising out of P1's conduct: P1, knowing about the informal agreement, had stood by watching whilst Mr High built a garage on his own land but accessible only from the passageway on the neighbour's land over which he had the right of way, and complimented him on the garage. P1 was therefore estopped from denying that the right of way was enforceable against them.[219] There is no reason why the position should be different in registered land, that is, where the title to the neighbouring land is registered at the Land Registry.

(c) Personal Liability in Tort

Another possibility is that a purchaser who knows about a prior property interest which is not 'protected' on the register within the meaning of s. 29 of the LRA 2002 may be personally liable in tort for wrongful interference with a contract if he refuses to give effect to the prior interest. This was confirmed in *Lictor Steel* v. *Mir*,[220] where it was held that, where the supplier of steel used to construct a steel mill on land had a right to enter the land and remove the steel if it was not paid for, it was held that this was 'an equitable proprietary right in relation to the land' (because the mill had become part of the land). The registered proprietor went into administration before the supplier had been paid, and the administrators sold the land to a purchaser. The administrators and the purchaser knew that the supplier was claiming an interest in the land and that it had not taken any steps to protect the interest in the register, and the sale price was discounted on the basis that the purchaser would bear the risk of the supplier's claim succeeding. It was held that although any property interest the supplier had in the land was unenforceable against the purchaser because of s. 29 of the LRA 2002, the purchaser was liable in tort to the supplier for unlawfully inducing a breach of contract. The judge explained the limits of this personal liability:

> a person who acquires land with actual notice of an unregistered property right does not, without more, commit a tort . . . [but] a person who acquires land with knowledge of a contractual right the breach of which he intentionally procures does commit a tort.

---

[218] *E.R. Ives Investments Ltd* v. *High* [1967] 2 QB 379.

[219] The issue in the case was whether it was also enforceable against the person who subsequently purchased the land from P1. The Court of Appeal held unanimously that it was, but for different reasons not relevant here.

[220] *Lictor Anstalt* v. *Mir Steel UK Ltd* [2014] EWHC 3316.

It had been argued that it was 'offensive to the entire scheme of land registration'[221] to make a purchaser of a registered title personally liable in relation to contractual rights affecting the purchased land, given that those contractual rights did not appear on the register. The argument was that the risk of incurring such liability would oblige potential purchasers to engage in the kind of enquiries and investigations that the LRA 2002 was designed to avoid. The judge dismissed this argument. As she pointed out, s. 29 is concerned only with property rights affecting land and not with personal liability of purchasers, and in any event the tort liability depends on actual knowledge of the contractual rights having been broken, so potential purchasers without such knowledge have no need to make further enquiries and investigations.[222]

PART IV OFF-REGISTER PROPERTY INTERESTS

16.30 The Existence of Off-Register Property Interests

In the joint report of the Law Commission and HM Land Registry, *Land Registration in the Twenty-First Century: A Conveyancing Revolution*, which led to the LRA 2002, it was said that:

> The fundamental objective of the [Act] is that, under the system of electronic dealing with land that it seeks to create, the register should be a complete and accurate reflection of the state of the title to the land at any given time, so that it is possible to investigate title to the land on line, with the absolute minimum of additional enquiries and inspections.[223]

This is a puzzling statement, if we take it to mean that the objective of our land registration system is that the register should provide a 'complete and accurate' record of all registered freehold and leasehold titles, and of all property interests affecting them. As we have seen, the LRA 2002 did nothing to alter the basic design of the scheme introduced by the LRA 1925, which is that only a limited class of property interests affecting registered titles are registrable. It is worth noting that this makes our system unusual. For example, Germany recognises a smaller range of private property interests in land than we do in England and Wales, but broadly, all of them are registrable.[224]

It is true that in our system some other property interests can be noted on the register, but the only effect of that is to make the noted interest enforceable against subsequent registered proprietors *if it is found to be a valid property interest*. In addition, it is an integral part of the design that other property interests are overriding, that is, enforceable against a purchaser/grantee of a registered title even though not apparent from the register, and yet others either need not, or may not, be

---

[221] Ibid. Mrs Justice Asplin recounted the argument at para. 283.   [222] Ibid. para. 294.

[223] Law Commission and HM Land Registry, *Land Registration for the Twenty-first Century*, fn. 52 above, para. 1.5.

[224] See Raff, 'Characteristics of the international model of land title registration', fn. 5 above, pp. 62–65.

mentioned on the register but are enforceable against registered proprietors and their purchasers/grantees under the general law. So, the register is certainly not, and was never intended to be, a *complete* record of all property interests affecting registered owners and lessees.

In addition, there are other factors inherent in the system which make it inevitable that the register is sometimes inaccurate and sometimes incomplete, as we have already seen in Part III of this chapter. So, we know that the person registered as proprietor of a freehold or leasehold title or mortgage is presumed also to hold the beneficial interest, but that the presumption may be rebutted by applying general law principles to show that it is held by someone else, whose interest will not appear on the register.[225] We also know that registrable property interests that are not regis-tered take effect as equitable property interests, which will not appear on the register,[226] and that legal titles acquired by adverse possession also do not appear on the register, nor do interests acquired by prescription or implication (e.g. easements). Also, property interests may be omitted from the register through fraud or mistake, giving the property interest holder a right to apply for rectification.[227]

Another factor is that in our legal system property interests can pass from one person to another by operation of law as well as by deliberate transfer. When that happens – for example, an individual registered proprietor dies, or goes bankrupt, or a corporate registered proprietor is dissolved – the registered proprietor automatic-ally loses their property interest[228] but continues to be registered as proprietor unless and until someone takes the necessary steps to inform the Land Registry. In cases of death, in particular, this may never happen.[229] It will be appreciated that this is one of the consequences of having a reactive rather than a proactive land register: the Land Registry makes or alters entries on the register only in response to an applica-tion made by an outsider, and since it is not embedded in a computerised cadastral-type system, it is not automatically notified of events recorded elsewhere which may affect registered titles. So, there is an inevitable time-lag between the automatic passing of a title by operation of law from one person to another, and the necessary change being recorded on the register. And, of course, there is a risk of some transfers by operation of law slipping through the net altogether.[230]

---

[225] para. 16.17 above.   [226] para. 16.22 above.

[227] See Part V below for an outline of the way this works.

[228] Confirmed by Rimer LJ (Arden and Keene LLJ agreeing) in *John Lyon School* v. *Helman* [2014] EWCA Civ 17 at para. 29.

[229] If the transfer by operation of law takes place as a result of an official procedure such as bankruptcy or dissolution of a company, appointed officials are responsible for finding out about and disposing of all property interests, and there are statutory procedures designed to ensure that appropriate applications are made to the Land Registry to make consequential changes to the register. There are also procedures to be followed by personal representatives appointed to administer the estates of people who have died, but occasionally when a person dies holding a property interest in land no personal representatives are appointed, and the estate is never administered. The dead person could then remain the registered proprietor indefinitely.

[230] The freehold title to land adjoining the author's flat was registered in the names of two (human) individuals in 1913 (under the previous system: see fn. 53 above). At the time of writing, they are still the registered freehold proprietors. It seems safe to assume that both are now long dead.

16.31 Property Interests Deliberately Kept Off the Register

In the previous paragraph we focussed on features of our property rights system which make it inevitable that the land register will at times be incomplete and/or inaccurate. We also noted, however, that the land registration system deliberately excludes some property interests from the land register. In this paragraph, before going on to look at some of these excluded categories, we consider in general terms whether it matters that some parts of the spectrum of property interests in land recognised in England and Wales are deliberately kept off the land register.

(a) Links with Other Public Registers of Land Rights/Burdens

Many off-register property interests are registrable elsewhere, and so there is no great problem if they are not ascertainable from the land register, provided the registers where they are recorded are open to the public and easily accessible, and provided also that the information recorded on them can be easily correlated with the information on the land register (not always the case with, for example, land registered as common land or town or village greens in local registers: para. 16.32 below). In this respect modern cadastral systems have a great advantage over ours because a land register embedded within a cadastral system can be (and usually is) linked administratively, and probably also now electronically, to other public registers. This makes it feasible for the land registry to provide details of all property (and other) interests affecting any given piece of land which are registered elsewhere, as well as those registered or mentioned on the land register. In England and Wales it is government policy to develop links to replicate those that exist in a cadastral system. Two current developments in this direction are worth noting here:

Land Registry Links with Other Sources of Land Information

We saw earlier that the Land Registry has started to develop links with other sources of information about land use which may affect landowners,[231] and the government has also announced proposals to link the Land Register with the public registers of beneficial ownership of companies which it is setting up.[232] In addition, it is involved in the promotion of commercial searching services which will now (for a fee) search all public registers to reveal property interests affecting any specified interest in land.

Local Land Charges

The Land Registry has also just started to take over responsibility for registration of 'local land charges'.[233] Up until now each local government authority has been responsible for maintaining its own public register of local land charges under the Local Land Charges Act 1975. Local land charges are mostly financial charges or restrictions on the use of land imposed by public authorities under statutory powers. They include restrictions imposed on listed buildings or land within a conservation

---

[231] See fn. 9 above.   [232] See (d) below.
[233] Authorised by s. 34 and Sch. 5 of the Infrastructure Act 2015.

area or by tree preservation orders, and planning and enforcement notices as well as conditions imposed in a planning permission. The distinctive feature of these 'public' local land charges is that the consequences of registering them in the local land charges register is different from (and much simpler than) the consequences of registering or protecting a property interest in the Land Registry. The principle is that once the relevant public authority has made a local land charge order, the charge attaches to the land and is enforceable against all present and future holders of property interests in the land affected, whether or not it is registered as a local land charge. However, a purchaser of a freehold or leasehold interest in, or a mortgage over, the land will be entitled to compensation if he searched the local land charges register at the time of the purchase and the charge was not then registered. A few 'private' restrictions are also registrable as local land charges, most notably Light Obstruction Notices which any landowner can register and which have the effect of preventing a neighbouring owner from acquiring a right to light by prescription. However, these 'private' restrictions are not effective as against the neighbouring owner unless registered in the local land charges register.

The data currently held in the 316 local authority local land charges registers will be transferred over to the Land Registry in phases, starting in summer 2018 and expected to be completed 'up to 7 years' later.[234]

(b) Public Right to Know Who Owns and Controls Land

However, despite these developments we are still nowhere near the position we would be in if we had a proper cadastre, and it is argued that it is still unacceptably difficult for the public to ascertain who owns and controls land in England and Wales.[235] This is a major defect in our land registration system if we accept that a key objective of the system is to give the public access to this information, for all the reasons we noted in para. 16.6(a) and para. 16.13 above.

(c) Public Participation in Land Use Decisions and Land Development

In addition there is an argument, presently accepted by the government, that the existence of off-register interests hinders land development, and that the Land Registry ought to be providing a public record of a much wider range of property interests in land in furtherance of the Government project of 'fixing the broken housing market':

---

[234] HM Land Registry, *Guidance: Local Land Charges Programme*, updated April 2019, available at www
.gov.uk/government/publications/hm-land-registry-local-land-charges-programme/local-land-
charges-programme.

[235] See fn. 20 above. The difficulties are outlined in Shrubsole, *Who Owns England?* (fn. 20 above), Ch. 10,
where the problems in obtaining information from the Land Registry are contrasted with the relative
ease in obtaining information from local cadastres in other countries (ibid. at p. 273, and see also
pp. 273–275 for the changes that, Shrubsole argues, should be made to the Land Registry to give the
public full access to information about the ownership and control of land).

A.33 Alongside the improved registration of land, the Government proposes to improve the availability of data about wider interests in land. There are numerous ways of exercising control over land, short of ownership, such as through an option to purchase land or as a beneficiary of a restrictive covenant. There is a risk that because these agreements are not recorded in a way that is transparent to the public, local communities are unable to know who stands to fully benefit from a planning permission. They could also inhibit competition because SMEs and other new entrants find it harder to acquire land. There is the additional risk that this land may sit in a 'land bank' once an option has been acquired without the prospect of development.

A.34 Therefore, the Government will consult on improving the transparency of contractual arrangements used to control land. Following consultation, any necessary legislation will be introduced at the earliest opportunity. We will also consult on how the Land Register can better reflect wider interests in land with the intention of providing a 'clear line of sight' across a piece of land setting out who owns, controls or has an interest in it.

In addition, the Government has expressed concern that keeping beneficial interests under trusts off the register makes it more difficult 'for communities and authorities to engage in and make informed decisions about planning, development and investment'.[236]

(d) Hidden Dealings in Land

The Government is also concerned that keeping beneficial interests under trusts off the register is a serious hindrance to combatting fraud. Because the land register does not record beneficial interests in land, it also does not record dealings in beneficial interests, and this makes money laundering, tax evasion and fraudulent land transactions too easy, and too difficult to detect. However, the Government is not (for the present at least) advocating direct recording on the land register of equitable interests under trusts of land. Instead it is setting up public registers of beneficial ownership of companies and of beneficial ownership under overseas trusts, and also private government registers of some private trust interests. There are also proposals to link some but not all of these registers to the land register.[237]

(e) Vulnerability

If we are looking at the issue of off-register property interests from the perspective of the property interest holders, however, the obvious risk is that, if they are not allowed to protect their interest on the register, the enforceability and priority of their interest as against the rest of the world will be prejudiced. This risk can be removed by ensuring that all off-register interests are either made overriding interests or have their priority and enforceability governed by clear general law protection

---

[236] *Fixing the Broken Housing Market* para. A.32.
[237] Ibid. para. A.35. There is a useful summary of the present position in House of Commons Briefing Paper No. 8259, *Registers of Beneficial Ownership,* 15 March 2019.

rules which cannot be overridden by land registration rules. This is done for some off-register property interests but not for others, most notably some easements (see para. 16.35 below) and beneficial interests under trusts (para. 16.36).

(f) Marginalisation

Whether or not off-registered interests are properly protected as overriding interests or by other means, they face the additional risk of marginalisation. There is a danger that interests in the land which are not recorded on the land register will be discounted by those making and implementing policy decisions, and that the voice of interest holders will not be heard in discussions about resource allocation. Marginalisation may also be a matter of perception: the danger is that property interests not recorded on the register will be perceived as not recorded because not important, in a class different from and inferior to 'proper' property interests like ownership or mortgage. This is particularly important in relation to the interests that people have in their homes. As we see in paras. 16.33 and 16.36, the combined effect of keeping both short leases and beneficial interests under a trust off the register, is that the register does not record the property interests that most people have in their home. This is because most renters have non-registrable leases, and most owner-occupiers co-own the legal and/or beneficial interest, and therefore a trust is imposed. Leaving aside the question of vulnerability, this means that the most important property interest in land that most people have is, as a matter of policy, excluded from the land register.[238] It would be easy to take from this the impression that the land register is the register for land interests of elites (large corporate enterprises, landlords, trustees of family trusts, public bodies, etc.) and not for the land interests of ordinary people.[239]

16.32 Communal and Public Property Rights

Marginalisation is also a problem for communal and public property interests. The land register is a register of private property interests only. It does not reveal communal or public property interests, even though many of them are exercisable over privately owned land and so directly affect titles registered at the Land Registry.

In England and Wales most communal and public property interests are registrable or recorded in other public registers or maps, some locally rather than nationally organised, but there is no formal co-ordination between the Land Registry and the public bodies responsible for these other registers and records. For example, common land and town or village greens are registered in local authority Commons Registers and Town or Village Green Registers, together with the rights of commons

---

[238] If an owner-occupier occupying under a trust happens to be a trustee as well, this is not a problem because her interest as trustee is registrable, giving her the appearance of ownership, even though her valuable property interest – her beneficial interest – is not allowed on the register. If she is not a trustee, the message put across by the land register is that she has no property interest in her home.

[239] Similar unease has been expressed about the absence of indigenous land rights from the land registers of private land rights in Australia and Canada: para. 16.32 below.

registered over them,[240] but none of this information will appear on the land register in the registry entries for the underlying freehold title to the land which these rights affect. Similarly, public rights of way (including rights over public highways, public footpaths, bridleways, byways, etc.) over private land are required to be registered or recorded by local government authorities (as Highways Authorities and Surveying Authorities, who maintain Definitive Maps of them),[241] and public rights to roam over private land which is Open Access Land under the Countryside and Rights of Way (CROW) Act 2000 are recorded on the CROW Map, but again none of these rights appear on the register of title to the underlying freehold interest in the land they affect, which is kept at the Land Registry.

We are not alone in keeping communal and public property interests in land off the register. As we noted in Chapter 9 *Multiple Property Rights Systems* para. 9.26, most post-colonial states have centralised land registration systems which were designed exclusively for the land rights systems of the dominant culture, that is, for systems based on private ownership and free markets in land rights. Because of the complex and heterogeneous mix of non-marketable private and communal land use rights in many indigenous property rights systems, and the fact that many of them are non-exclusive and arise and are transmitted by customary rules, colonial-based land registration systems have immense difficulties in accommodating the land rights of their indigenous peoples. The traditional response in most post-colonial states has been to keep these indigenous land rights off their registers. However, as we saw in para. 9.26 this can make indigenous land rights both vulnerable and marginalised, and in any event it is difficult to reconcile with a commitment by the state to recognise indigenous land rights systems and put them on an equal footing with the dominant land rights system.[242] For these reasons it is now being acknowledged that they must be brought within the system, as the author noted in 'Land titling and communal property':[243]

> There is now a growing recognition amongst those advocating land titling ... [that] problems in registering communal property rights have to be tackled, as part of an overall project of registration of all property rights within complex land tenure systems, not just private property rights. The World Bank and the International Federation of Surveyors (FIG), once foremost amongst those who advocated 'formalisation' of land rights in developing countries by moving towards private ownership titles, are now adopting a more nuanced approach. In their joint report, *Fit-For-Purpose Land Administration* published in 2014 [FIG/World Bank, Fig Publication No 60, *Fit-For Purpose Land Administration* (2014)] they say, in the context of discussing what makes land administration systems 'fit for purpose:'

---

[240] Under the Commons Registration Act 1965 and the Commons Act 2006.

[241] For an overview see www.nationalarchives.gov.uk/help-with-your-research/research-guides/public-rights-of-way/.

[242] See J. M. Pienaar, *Land Reform* (Cape Town: Juta, 2014) p. 7 and pp. 842–844, and works cited there, especially in fn. 52.

[243] Alison Clarke, 'Land titling and communal property' in Warren Barr (ed.), *Modern Studies in Property Law*, vol. 8 (Oxford and Portland, OR: Hart Publishing, 2015) p. 215 at pp. 229–230.

The fit-for-purpose concept directly supports what is called 'Continuum of Continuums' ... This term occurred in response to the view that the traditional cadastral systems, as known in most developed countries and which often operate with fixed (high level) technical standards and a legal perspective, predominantly support freehold as the sought after form of tenure. The concept 'Continuum of Continuums' ... recognizes that a continuum of tenure exists in terms of social tenure relationships, such as occupancy, usufruct, informal rights, customary rights, indigenous rights and nomadic rights. In the same way, parties holding the rights may not only be natural or legal persons, but could be a family, tribe, community, village, or a farmers' cooperative.

Meanwhile FIG has put forward a Land Administration Domain Model as a design standard for land administration systems ... [which] recognises that rights holders may be groups as well as individuals, that land rights to be represented on a register may not be confined to traditional real rights, and that representing rights on a register does not always require or involve drawing a line on the ground enclosing an area from which the owner is entitled to exclude all others.

This confirms that putting communal and public property rights on our central land register is by no means impossible or impractical, and may bring significant advantages.[244]

16.33 Short Leases

Another notable deliberate omission from the land register is short leases. A lease of seven years or less cannot be registered[245] but by Sch. 3 para. 1 of the LRA 2002 it is an overriding interest.[246] The sheer number of leases which fall within this category makes their omission from the register remarkable. Nearly all homes which are not owner-occupied are likely to be the home of tenants with leases of seven years or less, whether they are renting from a social landlord or a private sector landlord. Many of these tenants will have periodic tenancies which in practice will run on for many years,[247] or short fixed-term tenancies which are regularly renewed. In other words, the reality is that many are long-term tenants of their homes, even though their property interest is technically a short-term one.

Similarly, many business premises are occupied by tenants who have leases of seven years or less but who continue to occupy the same premises for many years, with each short tenancy being renewed as it expires. In 2015 the average leasehold term for all

---

[244] For developments in that direction in Canada and Australia see further Nigel Bankes, Sharon Mascher and Jonnette Watson Hamilton, 'The Recognition of Aboriginal Title and Its Relationship with Settler State Land Titles System, (2014) 47 *University of British Columbia Law Review* 829 and Margaret Stephenson and Maureen Tehan, 'The recording and management of indigenous lands and title: is reform required?' (2015) 24 *Australian Property Law Journal* 235.

[245] It can also be protected by notice if it is longer than three years in length: s. 33.

[246] Whether or not the tenant is in actual occupation.

[247] Leases not exceeding seven years include periodic tenancies which continue indefinitely unless and until terminated by notice to quit, including standard assured shorthold tenancies granted in the private sector for a short fixed period which roll on from week to week or month to month until terminated by notice to quit.

commercial premises in the UK was 7.2 years, but that average is misleading: 73 per cent were for a term of five years or less, and for SMEs ('small and medium sized enterprises') the average periods were even lower: for offices, it was 4.2 years, for retail premises 4.6 years, and for industrial premises 4.1 years. Overall rates of renewal at the end of the term were 43 per cent,[248] so again many of these 'short-term' lessees actually occupy their premises long-term under successive leases.

So, as noted in para. 16.31 above, the long-term property interests under which many people occupy their homes, and most small businesses occupy their business premises, are completely outside the land registration system. Since non-registrable leases are overriding interests, they are adequately protected as against purchasers and mortgagees of their landlords, but they are not regarded as of sufficient public interest to be recorded on the public record of property interests. With that in mind it is interesting to note that in its 2016 Consultation Paper, *Updating the Land Registration Act 2002*, the Law Commission provisionally proposed no change.[249] It acknowledged that 'short leases constitute common and important estates in land which cannot necessarily be discovered by searching the register; their omission from registration appears to be against the policy of having a complete and accurate register' (para. 3.80) and that their omission is also 'detrimental to the transparency of the property market' (para. 3.83). However, it also noted that reducing the level to more than three years[250] could be expensive for the Land Registry because of the large increase in the number of registrations which might put extra pressure on the indemnity fund (para. 3.89), and would be 'burdensome' for both tenants and landlords, and, without corresponding benefits, would 'run counter to the trend in favour of reducing regulation on businesses' (para. 3.88). It concluded:

> We are not convinced . . . that the practical advantages to a tenant of registering a short lease outweigh the disadvantage of additional regulation and cost to businesses. Registration could also be burdensome for landlords who would need to be vigilant to ensure that leases were cleared from the register at their termination.[251]

No reference was made to residential tenancies.

16.34 Relative Titles Acquired by Adverse Possession

There is nothing in the Land Registration Act 2002 to oust the basic common law principle we noted in Chapter 11 *Possession and Title*, that someone who takes

---

[248] The figures are taken from British Property Federation, *UK Lease Events Review*, November 2015, www.bpf.org.uk/sites/default/files/resources/A4-LeaseEventsReport2015-cbr-en.pdf.

[249] Law Commission Consultation Paper, *Updating the Land Registration Act 2002* (2016) Law Com No 227.

[250] It did not contemplate reducing it further: the attraction of more than three years, for the Law Commission, was that under the general law leases of more than three years have to be made by deed, and it was originally envisaged that under e.conveyancing all interests created by deed would be registrable. However, in Law Com No 227 the Law Commission acknowledged that now that the prospect of e.conveyancing is receding (para. 16.23 above) this is not a persuasive argument (para. 3.85 of Law Com No 227).

[251] Law Com CP No 227, Summary para. 1.21.

possession of land without the consent of the person then entitled to possession, acquires a legal title to freehold ownership which is enforceable against everyone else in the world apart from those with a better right to possession. Although some commentators have argued or assumed that this principle of acquiring a relative title by taking possession is incompatible with a system of acquiring title by registration, Amy Goymour and Robin Hickey argue convincingly that not only does the doctrine of relativity of title continue to apply in registered land, but that there are good reasons why it should continue to do so.[252] Amongst other arguments, they point out that some provisions of the LRA 2002 assume that an adverse possessor has a title to the legal freehold estate,[253] although others are more ambiguous,[254] and that the principle of relativity of title is the most straightforward explanation for what happens to a registered title on a transfer by operation of law (i.e. the registered title holder retains her title under the LRA 2002 even after it has been vested in a statutory successor under other statutory provisions providing for transfers of title by operation of law, for example on death or bankruptcy).[255] Most importantly, as they point out:

> there are important reasons of doctrine and policy why adverse possession should continue to be regarded as generating an independent title, even if that title is unlikely ever to become indefeasible . . . As has long been recognised in the chattels context, it is in the interests of preserving a peaceful society that possession – however obtained and even where the possessor is not the true owner – is safeguarded against the unauthorised incursions of strangers. Were this not the case, strangers could lawfully take property from any non-owning possessor, potentially leading to a 'free-for-all' between non-owners – a situation which should be neither encouraged nor permitted. If the legislation was intended to remove a squatter's ability to protect his possession of the land against strangers, one would expect substantial discussion of the point, and sound reasons offered for any such change. A squatter's rights should not be regarded as being swept aside, in a side-wind, by the title-stabilising provisions of the LRA 2002.
>
> It follows from these arguments that, in appraising the continued relevance of title relativity, care should be taken not to conflate 'title' with 'indefeasible title'. The fact that under the LRA 2002, the only way that a squatter might rely on his adverse possession to acquire an indefeasible title is via schedule 6, does not inevitably commit English law to the proposition that this is the only way to acquire a title to that land. Indeed, there are sound reasons of substantive law and policy for recognising the continued existence of the squatter's independent relative title, notwithstanding the decreasing likelihood that he will successfully oust the registered proprietor of the estate.[256]

[252] Amy Goymour and Robin Hickey, 'The continuing relevance of relativity of title under the Land Registration Act 2002' in Amy Goymour, Stephen Watterson and Martin Dixon (eds.), *New Perspectives on Land Registration: Contemporary Problems and Solutions* (Oxford: Hart Publishing, 2018) p. 65.

[253] Including paras. 9(1) and 11(2)(a) of Sch. 6.

[254] Goymour and Hickey, 'The continuing relevance of relativity of title', fn. 252 above, pp. 74–75.

[255] Ibid. pp. 72–73.   [256] Ibid. pp. 66–67.

However, the property interests of adverse possessors fit awkwardly into the LRA 2002. Under the LRA 1925, the interests of adverse possessors were expressly stated to be overriding interests, but this category of overriding interest does not appear in the LRA 2002. This means that any property interest that an adverse possessor now has under LRA 2002 will be enforceable against the registered title holder only if the adverse possessor is in actual occupation and so has an overriding interest under Sch. 3 para. 2 of the LRA 2002. In cases where at least 10 years of the adverse possession accrued after the registered title was first registered and after the date when the 2002 Act came fully into force,[257] whichever is later, this does not matter. Under the LRA 2002 the only right that an adverse possessor has is the right, after 10 years of adverse possession, to apply to the Land Registry to be registered as proprietor in the place of the dispossessed registered proprietor. This triggers the procedure laid down in Sch. 6 of the Act, which we consider in Part III of Chapter 12 *Adverse Possession of Land*. This is the only way an adverse possessor can become registered proprietor in place of the dispossessed registered proprietor. However, it is a statutory right, conferred by Sch. 6 para. 1 on any person 'who has been in adverse possession of the estate' for ten years. It cannot be read as making the right exercisable only if enforceable against the registered proprietor as an overriding interest. So, for adverse possessors whose situation is covered wholly by para. 1, it is unnecessary and irrelevant to talk about enforceability of their rights as against registered proprietors. The picture becomes more confused, however, in transitional cases, that is, when the adverse possession started before the 2002 Act regime came into operation and/or before the paper title was first registered. There are differing views on how the statutory provisions apply to the complex difficulties that then arise, which the courts have yet to resolve, and which we are not covering here.[258]

16.35 Easements and Profits

The treatment of easements and profits in the land registration system is anomalous and inexcusably complex. Under the Land Registration Act 1925 all profits and most easements were overriding interests under s. 70(1)(a) of the 1925 Act. However, when the LRA 2002 drastically reduced the categories of overriding interests, easements and profits were among the worst casualties. Broadly, the present position is that easements and profits which were in existence before the LRA 2002 came into force continue to be overriding interests. However, legal easements and profits which were expressly granted after 2002 are registrable, and if not registered they take effect as equitable interests only. But no equitable easement or profit arising after 2002, whether expressly granted or not, can now be an overriding interest.[259] This means that, unless protected by entry of a notice on the register,[260] equitable easements and

---

[257] That is, after the date transitional periods are fully phased out.

[258] For a full discussion see *Emmet & Farrand on Title*, fn. 33 above, paras. 5.097–5.100.

[259] Unless the holder of the benefit of the easement or profit happens to be in actual occupation of the burdened land, which is unlikely: *Chaudhary* v. *Yavuz* [2011] EWCA Civ 1314.

[260] Unlikely if the interest is equitable because it was registrable but not registered.

profits (whether created as equitable or created as legal but not yet registered) are not enforceable against subsequent purchasers of registered titles, even those who are aware of the existence of the easement or profit. So, in *Chaudhary* v. *Yavuz* [2011] EWCA Civ 1314, which we looked at in paras. 16.27 and 16.29 above, Mr Chaudhary's equitable easement by estoppel over a metal staircase, which would have been an overriding interest within the easement category before the LRA 2002, was held to be unenforceable against his neighbour's successor in title.

The position of implied easements[261] and easements acquired by long use (i.e. prescription) is less precarious but also more complex, in theory at least. A large proportion of easements and profits in this country arise by implication or by long use. They are not registrable, because not expressly granted. However, in the general law they are legal, not equitable, and they continue to be so when affecting titles which are registered. In theory they can be protected by notice, but since they arise by implication or long use, they are not the kind of property interest which we would usually expect people to protect on the register. In other words, we should expect to find them in the overriding interest category. We do find them there, but only if the one of the 3 conditions specified in Sch. 3 para. 3 of the LRA 2002 is satisfied. The effect of para. 3 is that an implied or prescriptive easement will be an overriding interest enforceable against a subsequent registered proprietor only if it was 'within the actual knowledge of' the registered proprietor at the time of the disposition of the title to him, *or* if it would have been 'obvious on a reasonably careful inspection' of the land at that time, *or* if the holder of the easement or profit can prove that she exercised it within the year ending with the date of the disposition. It has been suggested that in practice most implied and prescriptive easements and profits will get through one or other of those gateways and be enforceable as overriding interests,[262] but if that is so, it is questionable whether it was worth constructing such an elaborate hurdle to exclude the few that would not.

So, for no obvious reason, some easements and profits appear on the register but others do not; and some, but not all, of those which are not on the register will nevertheless be enforceable against purchasers for value from a registered proprietor of the land affected.

16.36 Beneficial Interests Under a Trust of Land

However, by far the most troublesome omission from our land register is beneficial interests under a trust. As we saw in Part III of Chapter 15 *Enforceability and Priority of Property Interests*, they were deliberately excluded in 1925 as a matter of policy, and that policy has been reaffirmed as recently as 2018.[263] However, there are serious doubts as to whether this policy is now appropriate, given the transformation

---

[261] That is, arising by necessity, common intention, the rule in *Wheeldon* v. *Burrows* (1879) 12 Ch D 31 or s. 62 of the Law of Property Act 1925.

[262] Ruoff and Roper, fn,. 160 above, para. 17.022

[263] By the Law Commission, in its Report, *Updating the Land Registration Act 2002* (2018) Law Com No 380, paras. 2.1 and 2.2.

of the social and economic purposes of trusts of land which we noted in Chapter 15 para. 15.15. Trusts now arise in nearly all cases of home ownership, since co-ownership of homes now far exceeds sole ownership. Also, they are routinely used to hide wealth and conceal the identity of those who really own and control land. We have already noted in para. 16.31 above that the government is concerned that the omission of beneficial interests from the register aids fraud and money-laundering, hinders public participation in land use decisions, and prevents the public from finding out who owns and controls land, and that others share those concerns. We also noted that keeping beneficial interests under trusts off the register marginalises the property interests people have in their homes. Here we focus on the other problem we noted in para. 16.31(e), which is that keeping them off the register also makes them dangerously vulnerable.

(a) Non-Occupying Beneficiaries

As we have seen, equitable interests under a trust are not registrable at the Land Registry, nor can they be protected by notice, and nor are they overriding interests in their own right. They can only come into the overriding interest category if they can qualify under Sch. 3 para. 2 of the LRA 2002, in other words if the beneficiary happens to be is in actual occupation of the relevant land and her occupation is reasonably discoverable. For a beneficiary not in occupation this is a disaster. Her beneficial interest can *never* be enforceable against a purchaser or mortgagee of a registered title who provided valuable consideration, even if there is only one trustee (and so there is no question of overreaching) and whatever the circumstances,[264] unless she can persuade the court that equitable principles such as those we considered in para. 16.29 should be imported to modify the effect of the land registration rules.

(b) Occupying Beneficiaries

A beneficiary who is in occupation is not much better off. In *City of London* v. *Flegg*,[265] the House of Lords held, in effect, that overreaching trumps an overriding interest. In other words, so the House of Lords confirmed, if there are two or more registered proprietors of a title, the interest in the land of a beneficiary under the trust is automatically extinguished by overreaching, which means that even if she is in actual occupation, she has no 'interest' within Sch. 3 para. 2, and so nothing that could override a registered disposition. It is not obvious why overreaching, which is essentially a general law enforceability rule should have been imported into the statutory land registration system in this way. If the policy behind Sch. 3 para. 2 is

---

[264] The only exception would be if it was provided under the trust that there could be no sale or mortgage without that beneficiary's consent, and the beneficiary had entered a restriction on the trustee's title to that effect. The sale/mortgage could not then have been registered without her consent. But this could occur only in an expressly created trust.

[265] *City of London Building Society* v. *Flegg* [1988] AC 54.

that property interests which are otherwise not enforceable against purchasers and mortgagees should become so if the holder of the interest is in actual occupation of the land, it is difficult to see why the courts had to imply an exception excluding beneficial interests under a trust, given that there is nothing in the wording of the land registration legislation to require it.[266]

If there is only one trustee registered as registered proprietor, then overreaching cannot take place,[267] and so the interests of beneficiaries in actual occupation should be enforceable as overriding interests against purchasers and mortgagees, However, the conditions for overriding set out in para. 2 must be satisfied, and as we saw in para. 16.27, the occupying beneficiary can fail to satisfy them without any fault on her part.

(c) Increasing Beneficiary Protection

Arguably, the real problem here is overreaching, which, as we noted in Part III of Chapter 15, needs to be reconsidered in the light of the fundamental changes in function and use of trusts that have occurred since 1925. However, if the overreaching principle has to be imported into the land registration system as a means of determining the enforceability of trust interests against third parties, it is difficult to justify the addition of land registration rules which narrow still further the circumstances in which a beneficial interest under a trust can be enforced against outsiders.

Overreaching is not the only problem. Under the general law beneficiaries have statutory rights under the Trusts of Land and Appointment of Trustees Act 1996 to be consulted about such matters as sale, with the trustees under a duty to give effect to the wishes of the majority in value, as we saw in Part III of Chapter 8 *Property Interest Holders.* Under the present law, purchasers have no obligation to check that a sale or mortgage by trustees does not infringe these rights. It would be a major inroad into the principle that trust interests should be kept off the register if we were to require transferees/grantees under a registrable disposition to make that kind of check in order to be able to take free from the beneficial interests. However, it may be thought justifiable in order to provide adequate protection for beneficiaries.

PART V RECTIFICATION, INDEMNITY AND FRAUD

16.37 What Happens When the Register is Wrong

As we saw in of this chapter, the register will sometimes be 'wrong', judged by reference to general property principles. The LRA 2002 contains complex provisions

---

[266] *Flegg* was decided under the Land Registration Act 1925, but the position is the same under the LRA 2002. For an argument that overreaching should not have been imported into the statutory land registration scheme by the courts, see Nicola Jackson, 'Overreaching in registered land law' (2006) 69 *Modern Law Review* 214. Her conclusion would remove all possibility of beneficial interests being enforceable against purchasers in registered land as the registered land scheme stands at the moment, but it clarifies the issues to be taken into account in considering how the scheme might be changed.

[267] Leaving aside the anomalous and doubtful decision in *State Bank of India* v. *Sood* [1997] Ch 276 we noted in Chapter 15 *Enforceability and Priority of Property Interests* para. 15.18.

giving the court and the land registrar powers to alter the register to put it 'right', with additional powers to order indemnity to be paid out of Land Registry funds to anyone suffering loss by reason of the register being corrected in this way, or the court/registrar deciding that, in the circumstances, no change should be made.

The meaning and effect of these provisions, set out in Schs. 4 and 8 of the LRA 2002, is contested, both by academic commentators and by the courts, and we are not going to deal with them in any detail here.[268] Instead, we note the basic principles underlying them.

16.38 Alteration and Rectification of the Register

The powers that the court and the registrar have to alter the register are set out in Sch. 4, and they are intended to be significantly different from the equivalent powers in the LRA 1925.[269] An initial difficulty is that new terminology is introduced by the 2002 Act. Under the LRA 1925 any change made to the register by the court or by the registrar under the equivalent statutory powers was referred to as 'rectification'. Under the LRA 2002 some changes are classified as 'alterations' and others (as we see in (a) below) as 'rectifications'.

Provision for the register to be changed by the court is made in Sch. 4 paras. 2–3, and by the registrar in paras. 4–5. There are differences between the two, but none material here, so we will concentrate on the court powers.

(a) Court's Powers to Order Changes to the Register

The Court may order a change to be made in the register for any one of three purposes, set out in para. 2(1):

(a) correcting a mistake
(b) bringing the register up to date, or
(c) giving effect to any estate, right or interest excepted from the effect of registration ...

There are two significant differences between these three purposes. The first is that, as we see in para. 16.39, compensation ('indemnity') is available only under (a), and not under (b) or (c). The second is that the register can be altered to 'correct a mistake' (i.e. under (a)) only if certain conditions are satisfied. For these two reasons, it matters which (if any) of the three headings is appropriate in any given case. Unfortunately this is not at all clear, largely because the meaning of 'mistake' in this context is contested.[270]

---

[268] For a full and reasonably up-to-date account see Law Com CP No 227, fn. 249 above, Chs. 13 and 14.
[269] See Law Commission and HM Land Registry, *Land Registration for the Twenty-first Century*, fn. 52 above, Part X.
[270] See *NRAM Ltd* v. *Evans* [2017] EWCA Civ 1013 and *Antoine* v. *Barclays Bank UK plc* [2018] EWCA Civ 2846, and *Emmet & Farrand on Title*, fn. 33 above, para. 9.028 for the contrary view.

(b) Registered Proprietors in Possession

The point about the 'correcting a mistake' ground for rectification is that it singles out for special treatment changes to the register which 'prejudicially affect the title of a registered proprietor'. Such changes are referred to in LRA 2002 as 'rectifications' and they are given special treatment in that they are the only changes for which indemnity is payable. This is consistent with the idea that a change in the register which prejudicially affects a registered proprietor can be seen as both an infringe-ment of the state guarantee of registered titles, and an infringement of the registered proprietor's human right to peaceful enjoyment of possessions under article 1 Proto-col 1 of the European Convention on Human Rights.[271]

However, the LRA 2002 goes further than this and gives special protection against rectification to a registered proprietor *who is in possession of the relevant land.* So, it provides that the court may not order *rectification* (i.e. an alteration which involves the correction of a mistake and which prejudicially affects the title of a registered proprietor) in respect of land in the registered proprietor's possession unless the conditions in para. 3(2) are satisfied. These are:

> 3(2)(a) the proprietor has by fraud or lack of proper care caused or substantially contributed to the mistake, or
> (b) it would for any other reason be unjust for the alteration not to be made ...

The court's power to rectify against a registered proprietor in possession is then restricted still further by para. 3(3), which provides that even if one of the conditions set out in 3(2) is satisfied, the court still has a discretion to refuse to order the rectification if there are 'exceptional circumstances which justify it in not doing so'.

The obvious reason for limiting the possibilities of changing the register to the prejudice of registered proprietors *in possession* is to give preference to innocent property interest holders in possession over innocent purchasers. Because they are in possession of the land, it can be argued, they ought to be allowed to keep 'the mud', leaving innocent purchasers with 'the money'.[272] However, it is interesting to see that Scotland has recently abandoned similar provisions about rectification in the Land Registration (Scotland) Act 1979 which were modelled on the England and Wales provisions, favouring registered proprietors in possession. The problem with such provisions, as Reid and Gretton point out,[273] is that they look only at who has possession *now*, rather than at long-standing possession, leading to unfortunate cases of competing claimants trying to oust each other from physical possession in order to acquire the status of 'proprietor in possession'. For the same reason, they argue, the Scottish experience was that, contrary to what might have been expected, such provisions tended to favour innocent acquirers at the expense of pre-existing property holders:

> for in practice acquirers usually took possession and did so at once (that being the reason for buying the property in the first place); and with that single act of possession,

---

[271] See Chapter 4 *Property and Human Rights*, Part V.   [272] See para. 16.7(f) above.
[273] Reid and Gretton, *Land Registration*, fn. 30 above, p 37.

they destroyed any advantage which might have derived from the previous possession of the 'true' owner or, it may be, of past generations of his family.[274]

For these (and other) reasons, Scotland has adopted a more nuanced 'deferred indefeasibility' approach in the Land Registration etc. (Scotland) Act 2012.[275]

16.39 Indemnity

(a) The Indemnity Fund

We noted in para. 16.7(e) that one of the advantages of having a land registration system is that it generates funds which can be used to compensate the loser when, through no fault of either, two or more people end up with conflicting claims to a property interest.

Whether or not sufficient funds are always and necessarily available in all registration systems, they certainly are in ours, because of the high volume of applications made to the Land Registry to search the register and enquire about or deal in registered titles. A small fee is charged for each of these applications and for the registration of transactions,[276] and this generates a lot of money. In the year ending 31 March 2018 there were 24.5 million titles registered at the Land Registry, and the Land Registry received over 30 million applications for searches, enquiries and registration of titles and dealings with titles. Their total fee income in that year was £317 million and their operating costs were £257.4 million, allowing them to keep an 'operating surplus' of £59.8 million and pay a 'Treasury dividend' of £28.7 million.[277]

In England and Wales, the potential cost of compensating all losers in property conflicts between innocent property interest-holders and innocent purchasers in registered land is unknown. In 2017/2018 the Land Registry received just 852 claims for compensation and paid out a total of £5.4 million. So, they certainly could afford to pay out more by way of compensation even on the present level of fee income, and it would not require a large increase in fees to produce a much larger compensation pot, if that was what we wanted.

---

[274] Ibid.

[275] Ibid. pp. 37–39. Roughly, a good faith purchaser acquires an unchallengeable title from a seller who was a registered proprietor in possession, even though the seller became registered proprietor as a result of a mistake (perhaps because she forged the transfer of the title to herself), *but only if the seller had been registered proprietor in possession for at least a year* when she sold the title to the good faith purchaser.

[276] Currently, a maximum of £7 for an application for an official copy of the register of a title or an official search of the register, and a maximum of £40 to register the sale of a title if the sale price is up to £80,000, rising to a maximum of £910 if the sale price is over £1 million: see Land Registration Fee Order 2013 and www.gov.uk/guidance/hm-land-registry-information-services-fees.

[277] The Land Registry, which, as noted earlier, is state owned, is required to pay an annual 'dividend' to the government, currently at a rate of 3.5 per cent of the 'average capital employed' in that year: HM Land Registry, *Land Registry Annual Report 2017–2018*, fn. 54 above, p. 49. The other figures in this paragraph are also taken from the *Annual Report 2017–2018*.

(b) When Indemnity is Payable

As it is, however, entitlement to indemnity is limited to the cases listed in Sch. 8 of the LRA 2002. These are cases where a person suffers loss by reason of rectification of the register (in the special sense of rectification noted in the previous paragraph, that is, an alteration of the register which involves the correction of a 'mistake' and which prejudicially affects the title of a registered proprietor) or, broadly, by reason of a mistake made by the Land Registry.

As *Emmet & Farrand* point out, this is a very restricted model of insurance:

> ... possible claims are essentially against the Land Registry in the sense of seeking compensation for [the Land Registry's] own mistakes with documents. The [LRA 2002] does not purport to provide any general insurance protection for proprietors of land or charges against the acts, defaults or neglects of others 'off the register' but adversely effecting ownership. Comparing a contemporary statute illustrates the limitation: the compensation scheme set up under the Financial Services and Markets Act 2000 (ss. 212–224) is not directed at mistakes by the Financial Services Authority but at losses suffered by investors despite the regulatory and registration requirements it imposes ... . In substance, the indemnity fund kept by the Land Registry exists to insure itself against liability for causing losses ... .[278]

Generally, the provisions of the Act have been interpreted in the spirit of that limitation. For example, they have taken a restrictive view of whether a claimant has suffered 'loss *by reason of*' the mistake and on this basis established the rule that no indemnity is payable where the register is rectified to give effect to an overriding interest.[279] Similarly, because of the restrictive interpretation of 'correction of a mistake' we noted above, no indemnity is payable to anyone suffering loss by reason of the correction of an entry made on the basis of a *voidable* transaction (e.g. entered into under undue influence, or fraud, or misrepresentation) even though it would have been available if the transaction had been void (e.g. made by a forged document).[280]

---

[278] *Emmet & Farrand on Title*, fn. 33 above, para. 9.030.

[279] *Re Chowood* [1933] Ch 574. The reasoning is that the registered title has always been subject to the overriding interest, even though the registered proprietor was unaware of it. On this basis, all that happens when the register is changed to give effect to the overriding interest is that the registered proprietor becomes aware of an interest which has always burdened her title. Compare, however, *Swift 1st Ltd* v. *Chief Land Registrar* [2015] EWCA Civ 330, where a person who acquired her interest under a forged document (and therefore acquired nothing) was held entitled to an indemnity when the register was rectified to remove the interest from the register (because of a special provision relating to forgery in para. 1(2)(a)). Applying the *Re Chowood* reasoning, this can be seen as compensating her for losing something that she never had but thought she had.

[280] The reasoning is that the original entry was not a mistake if, at the time it was made, the voidable transaction had not yet been avoided, and therefore removing it did not involve 'correcting a mistake'. The position is different, so it is argued, if the original entry was made on the basis of a forged document because a forgery is a nullity from the outset, so it was a 'mistake' to make an entry on the register in reliance on it: see *NRAM Ltd* v. *Evans* [2017] EWCA Civ 1013, *Antoine* v. *Barclays Bank UK plc* [2018] EWCA Civ 2846, and *Emmet & Farrand on Title*, fn. 33 above, para. 9.028.

RECOMMENDED READING

Land registration is now a very large topic. The many recent cases have stirred controversy amongst commentators, and the controversial issues nearly all involve complex technical law as well as serious questions about social policy. They also reveal some quite fundamental differences of opinion amongst academic property lawyers about the nature of our property rights system. For all these reasons, most people studying the topic for the first time will have to be selective in their reading (and in the issues they want to focus on). The best advice is to concentrate on reading the recent controversial cases, listed below, which draw together several of the detailed issues covered in this chapter. We also list a few of the very many excellent commentaries on these cases and the current issues they raise. There are many more out there, for those who want to take any of the issues further.

Finally, for a summary of what the Law Commission currently sees as problems with land registration, it is worth looking at the Law Commission's Consultation Paper, *Updating the Land Registration Act 2002* (2016) Law Com CP No 227 (the 2018 Report is less comprehensive and more narrowly focussed). And, for easier reading and a different perspective, Guy Shrubsole, *Who Owns England? How We Lost Our Green and Pleasant Land and How to Take It Back* (London: William Collins, 2019) has some unlawyerly things to say about what is wrong with land registration today.

Cases

Scott v. *Southern Pacific Mortgages Ltd* [2014] UKSC 52 ('interests' which can override; balancing the interests of innocent title holders and innocent purchasers).

Mortgage Express v. *Lambert* [2016] EWCA Civ 555 (overriding interests; failure to disclose interest; overreaching).

Chaudhary v. *Yavuz* [2011] EWCA Civ 1314 (actual occupation; enforceability of prior interests under constructive trust; enforcement of informally created property interests in registered land).

Swift 1st Ltd v. *Chief Land Registrar* [2015] EWCA Civ 330 (effect of registration of title).

Rashid v. *Nasrullah* [2018] EWCA Civ 2685 (effect of registration of title, and adverse possession).

Link Lending Ltd v. *Bustard* [2010] EWCA Civ 424 (actual occupation).

Bank of Scotland v. *Hussain & Qutb* [2010] EWHC 2812 (overriding interests, imputed authorisation of mortgage, estoppel).

Other material

Amy Goymour, 'Mistaken registrations of land: exploding the myth of "title by registration"' (2013) *Cambridge Law Journal* 617.

Graham Ferris, 'How should a system of registered title to property respond to fraud and sharp practice?' in Heather Conway and Robin Hickey (eds.), *Modern Studies in Property Law*, vol. 9 (Oxford: Hart Publishing, 2017).

Caroline Hunter, 'Certainty rules in uncertain times!' (2016) *Journal of Housing Law* 85.

Amy Goymour and Robin Hickey, 'The continuing relevance of relativity of title under the Land Registration Act 2002' in Amy Goymour, Stephen Watterson and Martin Dixon (eds.), *New Perspectives on Land Registration: Contemporary Problems and Solutions* (Oxford: Hart Publishing, 2018) 65.

Alison Clarke, 'Land titling and communal property' in Warren Barr (ed.), *Modern Studies in Property Law,* vol. 8 (Oxford and Portland, OR: Hart Publishing, 2015) p. 215 (on communal property and indigenous land rights under title registration systems).

Questions

(1)   In the cases you have read for this chapter which involve competing claims of a person in possession of property and an innocent purchaser, to what extent do the courts take into account the question of whether the property is the home of one of the claimants? Are there any cases where, in your view, it was unjust for the claimant to lose his home? If so, can you suggest any changes in the law which might have enabled/required the court to allow the claimant to stay in his home?

(2)   In the cases you have read for this chapter, would the result have been the same if protection for purchasers/mortgagees against prior property interests under LRA 2002 had been restricted to good faith purchasers without notice? Should a purchaser/mortgagee who is *not* in good faith, or has notice of prior property interests affecting the land, be allowed to take advantage of registration systems which are designed to strike a fair balance between innocent prior property interest holders and innocent purchasers?

(3)   Should the LRA 2002 distinguish between mortgagees and other purchasers? If so, how?

(4)   What factors, if any, limit public access to the land register in this country? How convincing are the arguments for (a) increasing and (b) decreasing public access?

(5)   What changes would have to be made to land registration in England and Wales to enable the public to find out, easily and cheaply, who owns and controls land in England and Wales?

(6)   Consider whether the policy of keeping (a) beneficial interests under a trust and (b) short leases off the register should be changed. If so, what changes in the law do you suggest?

(7)   Advise the Law Commission what changes, if any, should be made to the law relating to overriding interests under LRA 2002.

(8)   In *Scott* at para. 96, Baroness Hale drew a distinction between the 'conveyancing machinery' of land registration and general property law principles, and warned of the dangers of 'letting the land registration tail wag the land ownership dog'. Commenting on this, Nicholas Hopkins (now the Law Commissioner responsible for property law) said:

> The extent to which the LRA 2002 should be treated as a distinct 'code' or body of property law is unclear ... However, with the greatest of respect, the description of land registration as 'machinery' appears inappropriate ... The description jars with the ethos of the LRA 2002 of providing 'not a system of registration of title but a system of

title by registration'. That ethos reflects the idea that registration is no longer 'bolted on to transactions taking place under the general law, but is dispositive'.[281]

Explain the difference between the views expressed here by Baroness Hale and by Professor Hopkins. Which do you think more accurately describes the land registration system in England and Wales?

---

[281] Nicholas Hopkins, 'Priorities and sale and lease back: A wrong question, much ado about nothing and a story of tails and dogs' [2015] *Conveyancer and Property Lawyer* 245 at p. 252.

17

Leases

PART I INTRODUCTION

17.1 What is a Lease?

The law relating to leases is a vast subject, and in this chapter we are giving only the barest outline of the basic principles and some idea of the contexts in which they operate.

Our starting point is that a lease is a property interest which is created when a freehold or leasehold owner of land grants *possession*[1] of the land (or a horizontal or vertical section of it) to someone else for a limited period. If granted by a freehold owner, we call the property interest created by the grant of possession a 'lease' or 'tenancy'; if it is granted by a lessee, we called it a 'sublease' or 'subtenancy'. 'Lease' and 'tenancy' can now be taken to mean the same thing. In practice we tend to use the terms 'lease', 'lessor' and 'lessee' when talking about longer leases and 'tenancy', 'landlord' and 'tenant' when talking about shorter ones, but either set of terms will do, and in practice they are often mixed together (as sometimes they are in this chapter).

(a) Sub-letting

As will be apparent from what we have just said, a lessee can always sub-let to a third person by sub-granting possession to the third person. Both lessee and sub-lessee each then have separate property interests in the land. A lease (or a sublease) may contain a term restricting or prohibiting sub-letting: if it does, any sub-letting will be a breach of the terms of the lease, but it will still be effective to create the sublease.

A sub-letting can be of the whole or part of the land covered in the lease, but it must be for a period which ends before the lease ends (because it is carved out of the lease). The subtenant then has similar rights to sub-underlet to someone else for a period shorter than her own sub-lease, and that sub-underlessee may in his turn sub-sub-underlease all or part of the area comprised in his sub-underlease to someone else, and so on indefinitely. In practice, it is quite common to have two or three

---

[1] Used here in the technical sense considered in Chapter 11 *Possession and Title*, i.e. intentional physical control for one's own benefit.

rungs of leases and subleases. So, for example, the freehold owner of a development site might grant a developer a 99 year lease of the site requiring the developer to build a shopping centre on the land, and when the development is completed the developer might then sub-let each shop unit to a retailer for 10 years, and one of the retailers might decide after a year or so that the shop is too big for her business, and so she might sub-underlet one floor of her shop to another business for a period lasting until two or three days before the end of her own sub-tenancy.

Generally, the term 'lease' can be used to refer both to the original lease granted by the freehold owner, and to any sublease or sub-underlease etc. granted out of the original lease. If there are two or more rungs of leases and subleases, the one at the top is often called the 'head lease' and those in the middle are called 'intermediate leases'.

The important point is that when a lessee sub-lets, her lease is not extinguished: it continues to exist as a property interest until the term ends, and she continues to be liable to her landlord under her lease (she must continue to pay the rent to the landlord, and to do everything else required of the tenant under the lease). Also, as against her landlord, she remains entitled to possession. However, as between herself and her sub-lessee, she is now her sub-lessee's landlord, and the sub-lessee is now her tenant: her subtenant must now pay her the rent payable under the sublease and do everything required of the tenant under the sub-lease. And, of course, for so long as the sub-tenancy lasts, the sub-tenant is now entitled to possession as against the tenant. Exactly the same applies as between sub-tenant and sub-undertenant if the sub-tenant sub-lets in his turn, and as between sub-undertenant and sub-sub-undertenant if the sub-undertenant then sub-lets.

So, the original lease (the head lease) is a bit like a traditional Russian Matryoshka wooden doll: when you open up the doll, you find another – slightly smaller – doll inside, and inside that doll is another yet smaller doll, which in its turn opens up to reveal a still smaller doll etc.

(b) Rent and Other Payments Payable Under a Lease

The grant of a lease is usually a commercial transaction, granted in exchange for consideration paid to the landlord by the tenant. The consideration nearly always consists of a payment of a periodic rent throughout the term of the lease and/or payment of a lump sum at the beginning of it.

If it is a very long lease the consideration payable is usually primarily a lump sum payable when the lease is first granted, together with a very small periodic payment (called a 'ground rent') which may be a token amount (perhaps £1 a year) or even a notional payment (traditionally a peppercorn a year).[2]

In shorter leases and nearly all periodic leases (e.g. weekly, monthly or annual leases which continue indefinitely until ended by landlord or tenant serving a notice

---

[2] Recently, some developers granting very long leases of houses and flats have started to charge much higher ground rents, and to include provisions in the lease allowing the landlord to increase the level of the ground rent periodically throughout the lease: see further Part III para. 17.16 below.

to quit) the main or only element of the consideration paid by the tenant to a landlord is a periodic rent (sometimes called a 'rack rent' to distinguish it from a 'ground rent'). It is quite common to have a provision in the lease allowing the landlord to increase the amount of the rack rent to keep up with inflation or rises in market rents.

Many leases, particularly residential and commercial leases, require the landlord to provide services to the tenant (perhaps to maintain the structure of the building, insure it and provide services such as heating etc.) at the tenants' expense. The tenant is then required to pay for these services by paying the landlord a periodic service charge.

At one time it was thought that rent was an essential feature of a lease, but it is now settled that it is not.[3]

(c) Assignment

Lease and subleases are transmissible property interests, so in principle they can always be sold or transferred by gift or pass to a successor on the death of the tenant. However, in practice it is usual in all but the longest leases for the lease to contain restrictions on the lessee's right to transfer the lease, either at all, or without the landlord's consent. These restrictions are heavily controlled by statute, and we do not deal with them here. Long leases are, of course, frequently bought and sold in practice.

Like sub-letting in breach of restrictions and prohibitions in the lease against sub-letting, an assignment of a lease in breach of restrictions in the lease on assignments will be a breach of covenant under the lease. This will entitle the landlord to bring an action against the tenant for damages or to threaten to forfeit the lease,[4] but the assignment itself will nevertheless not be invalidated.

17.2 How Leases Are Used in England and Wales

Leases are used very extensively in England and Wales, much more so than in other countries. The vast majority of commercial premises (shops, offices, factories, etc.) are occupied by lessees,[5] and the same is true (although not to the same extent) of

---

[3] *Ashburn Anstalt* v. *Arnold* [1989] Ch 1, CA and *Canadian Imperial Bank of Commerce* v. *Bello* [1992] 24 HLR 155, CA.

[4] We do not deal with forfeiture and the other remedies that landlord and tenant have against each other if there is a breach of the terms of the lease. Forfeiture is a remedy available only to landlords, not to tenants, and it has the effect of terminating the lease. Essentially, any breach of a term of a lease by the tenant entitles the landlord to start proceedings to terminate the lease by forfeiture, but tenants have extensive rights to stop the process by remedying the breach or (if the court is willing to order relief on these terms) by paying appropriate damages. The procedures for forfeiting a lease, and for the tenant to apply for relief from the forfeiture, are complex and highly regulated by statute (and by general equitable principles).

[5] For statistics on commercial and residential leases see British Property Federation, *UK Lease Events Review*, November 2015, www.bpf.org.uk/sites/default/files/resources/A4-LeaseEventsReport2015-cbr-en.pdf and para. 16.33 in Chapter 16 *Registration*.

agricultural land – many if not most farmers are tenants rather than freehold owners of the land they farm. As far as residential property is concerned, there are two separate and distinct leasehold sectors. On the one hand, many houses and flats are occupied by short-term or periodic tenants. On the other, some houses and all flats are usually subject to very long leases (the length is commonly 99 or 999 years). As far as flats are concerned leases are almost universally used because flats are (necessarily) units in multi-unit structures where the units are physically inter-dependent. In this jurisdiction anyone who wants to 'own' a flat in a multi-unit building will almost invariably want a long leasehold interest in the unit rather than a freehold interest, because the 'owner' of each unit needs to be able to enforce positive obligations by the neighbouring units (e.g. to repair and maintain shared structural parts of the building). As we saw in Chapter 13 *Non-Possessory Land Use Rights*, this cannot be done between successive freehold owners of neighbouring units in this jurisdiction (because positive land obligations entered into by neigh-bouring freehold owners – that is, restrictive covenants – are not property interests in the law of England and Wales). However, it can be done between successive lessees who have a common landlord. In other words, in these circumstances we use long leases as substitutes for ownership. We come back to this point in Part III of this chapter.

The legal nature of a lease is the same in each of the four major sectors – commercial leases, agricultural leases, long residential leases and short/periodic residential leases – but leases in each sector have their own distinctive provisions and there are significant differences in the social and economic functions of each sector.

To add to the complexity, whilst some statutory provisions apply to all leases, each sector also has its own additional and unique statutory regulatory systems which provide statutory protection for that kind of tenant (by, for example regulating rents, or giving the tenant some security of tenure, for instance by giving the tenant a statutory right to stay on after the contractual end of the tenancy and/or removing or restricting the landlord's right to evict the tenant except on specified and restricted grounds and after obtaining a court order). It is beyond the scope of this book to look at the detailed statutory regimes governing each of these categories of lease, but we should note that, apart from in the long residential leasehold sector,[6] they are all much less extensive and less effective than they once were.

In this chapter we concentrate on the fundamental principles applicable to all leases in Parts I and II of this chapter, and then in Part III we look more closely at the long residential leasehold sector, concentrating on the role played by such leases as substitutes for ownership. We see how this works, and the possible alternatives, in Part III.

---

[6] Statutory protection for holders of long leases of residential premises is of a different kind from that provided for tenants in other sectors. Instead of rent restrictions and security of tenure, the statutory regimes give e.g. rights for tenants to extend the term of their lease, collective rights for tenants in a building or an estate with a common landlord to buy out the landlord's freehold interest, or to take over the management of the estate, and statutory regulation of service charges.

17.3 Sources of the Terms of a Lease

The terms of any given lease are derived from four sources.

(a) Rights, Duties, Liberties, Powers, etc. Inherent in the Leasehold Property Relationship

The first source of the terms of a lease is the property relationship itself. Some of the terms of a lease are inherent in the leasehold relationship that exists between landlord and tenant. So, for example, it is inherent in the leasehold relationship that the tenant and not the landlord is entitled to possession of the three dimensional space covered by the lease. Because the tenant has possession of the part of the landlord's land which is covered by the lease, she has an inherent liberty to use it for whatever purposes she wants. However, in practice she can expect to have that liberty cut back by express terms of the lease (i.e. under (d) below). Similarly, as we have already noted, both landlord and tenant have an inherent right to transfer their interests[7] under the lease to a third party without asking or even telling the other, and to carve subsidiary interests to third parties out of their respective interest. Again, in practice a tenant can expect to have these inherent rights to transfer and sub-let cut back by express terms in a lease. It is, however, rare to find the landlord's inherent rights to transfer his interest (or grant subsidiary interests out of it) restricted by express terms in the lease. More usually, the landlord remains fully entitled to do whatever he wants with his interest without obtaining the consent of, or even informing, the tenant.

It is worth noting here two important gaps not covered by inherent terms. The first, which we have already noted, is that there is no inherent obligation on a tenant to pay rent. Rent is payable under the lease only if there is an express term in the lease stating that it is, and then only to the extent that the amounts are specified with sufficient certainty in the lease. The other gap, much more significant in practice, is that neither party has an inherent duty to maintain or repair the premises let by the lease. The only exception is that tenants with short-term tenancies probably have a minimal obligation to the landlord to use the premises 'in a tenant-like manner', which means to avoid or repair wilful or negligent damage, and to do minor acts necessary to keep the premises in a reasonable state, but this does not extend to making good deterioration due to fair wear and tear or, for example, damage caused by failure to paint and decorate the premises.[8]

(b) Common Law Obligations

Each party does however have potential liabilities to the other in tort, most notably negligence. Also, as far as the landlord is concerned, he will be liable in nuisance or

---

[7] The technical term for the landlord's interest is the 'reversion' on the lease, which consists of the present right to have possession back at the end of the lease. The lessee's interest is, of course, the lease itself.

[8] *Warren* v. *Keen* [1954] 1 QB 15.

trespass for any interference with the tenant's possession and in nuisance for any interference with the tenant's reasonable use and enjoyment of the premises.[9] In addition, at common law there are implied terms in a lease whereby the landlord covenants to give the tenant 'quiet enjoyment' of the premises (not to do anything to interrupt the tenant's peaceful enjoyment of the premises) and not to 'derogate' from its grant of the lease to the tenant (essentially, not to do anything which interferes with or prevents the tenant using the premises for the purposes for which the they were let to her, for example by erecting scaffolding outside the windows of a building let as an artist's studio, so obstructing the light). There is quite a lot of overlap between these tortious liabilities of a landlord and its potential liabilities for breach of the covenants for quiet enjoyment and non-derogation from grant,[10] and in practice tenants complaining about interferences with their use of the premises often state their claim as breaches by the landlord of its obligations under the law of nuisance and under the implied covenants.

(c) Statute

The third source is statute. Historically landlords and tenants have rarely had equality of bargaining power in any of the sectors we are considering here, and statutes have regulated the terms of leases for centuries. There are now extensive statutory regimes governing just about every aspect of the landlord and tenant relationship, including maintenance and repair (putting minimal obligations on landlords in some sectors), restrictions on the inherent rights and liberties of the tenant to assign and sub-let, and regulating the exercise of the landlord's remedies for breach of covenant by the tenant. Some of these are 'default' provisions, that is, they apply only except and in so far as they are not excluded or varied by the express terms of the lease. Most, however, are overriding provisions, that is, they apply notwithstanding anything to the contrary in the express terms of the lease.

These statutory provisions are separate from, and additional to, the special statutory tenant protection regimes particular to each sector which we briefly noted in para. 17.2 above.

(d) Express Contractual Terms

Finally, there are the contractual terms agreed between the parties to the lease. Most leases set out detailed written terms, often covering several pages, and in some commercial leases running on for dozens of pages. Again, it is important to appreciate that landlords and tenants are rarely of equal bargaining power, so almost invariably the lease terms are drafted by the landlord and have to be accepted by the tenant. This is true even of most commercial leases.

---

[9] See Chapter 10 *Limitations on Property*.
[10] See *Southwark BC* v. *Mills* [1999] 1 AC 1 where the House of Lords considered the relationship between them.

The express (and implied) contractual terms of a lease are generally referred to as 'covenants'.[11] Technically, a 'covenant' (whether used in relation to leases or in relation to anything else) is just a promise made by one party to a deed to another party to the same deed. So, a landlord's covenant is a promise made in the lease by the landlord to the tenant (for example to provide specified services, or to maintain the structure of the building of which the leased premises form part), and a tenant's covenant is a promise made in the lease by the tenant to the landlord (for example, to pay the rent, or not to assign the lease or sub-let without first obtaining the consent of the landlord).

17.4 Enforcement of Landlord's and Tenant's Covenants by and Against Successors

Because a lease is a property interest, *all* the terms of the lease remain enforceable throughout the term of the lease, between whoever is for the time being the present holder of the landlord's and the tenant's respective property interests. This includes the contractual terms, unless (as sometimes happens) they are expressed to be personal to the original landlord and tenant.[12] This means that, in effect, the contractual terms of the lease are propertised, in the sense that they are automatically attached to the property interest held by the tenant (the lease) and the property interest held by the landlord (the reversion on the lease) rather than being personal to the original contracting parties. Another way of looking at it is to see each lease as creating a unique property relationship between the original contracting parties, which is not personal to them but is transmitted to successors.

The technical way of expressing this is to say that the terms of any lease are always enforceable by and between the present landlord and the present tenant, provided there is *privity of contract* between them (i.e. they are the original contracting parties, or the contractual rights/liabilities of the original parties have been contractually assigned to them), or *privity of estate* (i.e. they are the present holders of the property interests that the original landlord and the original tenant had under the lease).

It follows from all this that if a lessee sub-lets, there are now two separate and unconnected leasehold relationships affecting the same land at the same time: the original one between the original landlord and lessee, and the newly created one between the lessee and the sub-lessee. There is privity of contract and privity of estate as between the original landlord and original lessee, and also as between original lessee and sub-lessee, but there is neither privity of contract nor privity of estate between the original landlord and the sublessee. In other words, *neither the original landlord (the head landlord) nor the sublessee has any rights, liberties,*

---

[11] There is a technical difference between a 'covenant' and a 'condition' in a lease, which need not concern us here.

[12] At one time it was necessary to distinguish between those terms that 'touched and concerned' the lease and those that did not: only the former survived after the landlord or tenant transferred their respective interests. However, this distinction was abolished by the Landlord and Tenant (Covenants) Act 1995 and now all contractual terms are propertised – i.e. fully enforceable by and between successors – except and to the extent that the lease provides otherwise.

liabilities, powers, etc. as against each other in respect of the land. So, if the lessee wrongly evicts the sublessee, the sublessee cannot bring an action against the head landlord, because the head landlord has no responsibility to the sub-lessee for the actions of the lessee, and no power to put the sublessee back into possession because she has granted her right to possession of the land to her lessee. Similarly, if the lessee fails to pay the rent due under the head lease, or the premises are in disrepair, the landlord can sue the lessee but not the sub-lessee: the sublessee may have liabilities under his sublease to pay the rent under his lease and to keep the premises in repair, but they are owed only to the lessee, not to the head landlord.

Suppose, for example, I grant you a lease of my house for 10 years at a rent of £20,000 a year, and it is a term of that lease that you will keep the house in repair, and you sub-let the house to 5 students at a rent of £5,000 a year each, and they never pay their rent and they trash the house. Your liability to pay me the £20,000 a year rent payable under the lease between you and me continues unaffected by the fact that you have, in effect, subcontracted your right to possession of the premises to your subtenants, and irrespective of the fact that you are receiving no rent from them. By the same token you are liable to me for breach of your covenant to keep the premises in repair, even though the damage was not caused by you but by your subtenants, and even though you may well have no right to enter the house to carry out the repairs for yourself. The only thing you can do is bring an action against your sub-tenants for breach of any repairing obligation they undertook to you in their subleases.

17.5 Leases as Property Interests and Contracts

Leases in common law jurisdictions were originally personal relationships, and it was not until the seventeenth century that they started to develop the characteristics of property interests.[13] Eventually, as we saw in para. 5.16(d) of Chapter 5 *Ownership and Other Property Interests*, s. 1 of the Law of Property Act 1925 made a legal lease of land into a legal estate in land. So, in the law of England and Wales (and in most if not all common law jurisdictions) leases are fully fledged property interests in land, capable of being either legal or equitable, and if legal, being enforceable against the whole world and transmissible. In most civil law systems, on the other hand, leases are not regarded as property interests and they are not transmissible, although they are enforceable against successors of the landlord.[14] This means that

---

[13] A. W. B. Simpson, *A History of the Land Law* (2nd edn, Oxford: Oxford University Press, 1986) pp. 247–256 and see also Brendan Edgeworth, 'The contractualization of leases in common law jurisdictions: Recent developments' in Bram Akkermans, Ernst Marais and Eveline Ramaekers (eds.), *Property Law Perpectives II* (Cambridge, Antwerp and Portland. OR: Intersentia, 2014) Ius Communae Europaeum, pp. 205–218.

[14] For a good comparative overview, see Bram Akkermans, 'Standardization of property rights in European Property Law' in Akkermans et al. (eds.), *Property Law Perpectives II* 221 at p. 233, and see also George Gretton and Andrew Steven, *Property, Trusts and Succession* (3rd edn, London: Bloomsbury Publishing Plc, 2017) Ch. 20 for the position in Scotland.

in the civil law a lease lies somewhere between a property right and a personal right, as Sjef van Erp explains:[15]

> According to the civilian tradition, lease is a contract from which mutual obligations arise. The lessor has to provide the lessee with the use of an object, and the lessee has to pay the price that has been agreed upon. However, the lessee is granted special protection in a situation where a lessor, who also owns the object of the lease, sells and transfers that object to a third party. According to general principle, the lessor would still be bound by the lease agreement, even though he is no longer able to perform. Only the new owner can provide the lessee with the use of the object. But then, he is not a party to the contract of lease and thus not bound by it. If the new owner were to use his right of ownership as the basis for a *res vindication* [i.e. an action for the recovery of the thing owned] to evict the lessee, the latter would only have a personal claim for non-performance against his lessor. Civilian systems have, however, protected the lessee against eviction by allowing him to assert his right even against the new owner. The legal maxim that has been coined in that respect is that 'sale does not break lease'. Effectively, therefore the lease has been turned into a legal status. The moment someone other than the original owner/lessor acquires ownership of the object of the lease, the legal status of lessor also passes to the new owner. The latter will not only be bound by the contract of lease, but will also have the corresponding rights. That the contract of lease has effectively turned into a status is, however, only true from the perspective of the lessor, not from that of the lessee. From the lessee's point of view his right to the object of the lease is still personal, and hence not freely transferable or otherwise marketable. English law has gone further and also given the lessee a legal status, resulting in a right that the lessee can transfer. The consequence is that under English law (as well as under other common law systems) lease has developed into an 'estate', a right that is not strictly personal, but valid 'against the world'. [16]

So, although in civil law systems a lease is not technically a full property interest, it still has effective protection against third parties because of the 'sale does not break lease' principle.

It is also as well to remember that in the law of England and Wales a lease is a common law relationship which has never been defined by statute, other than by the assertion in s. 1 of the Law of Property Act 1925 that it is an interest which is capable of being a legal estate in land. So, the courts are still quite regularly called upon to question the fundamental nature of a lease in this jurisdiction, as we see for example in *Bruton* v. *London and Quadrant Housing Trust* [2000] 1 AC 406, where the House of Lords reached the novel (and still very much disputed) conclusion that it is possible to have a lease which is not a property interest at all. We come back to this in para. 17.9(c) below.

---

[15] Sjef van Erp, 'Comparative property law' in Mathias Reimann and Reinhard Zimmermann (eds.), *The Oxford Handbook of Comparative Law* (Oxford: Oxford University Press, 2006) p. 1043.

[16] Ibid. In a footnote to the passage quoted here, Van Erp refers to, amongst other provisions, s. 566 of the German BGB (leases of residential space). and to Reinhard Zimmermann, *The Law of Obligations: Roman Foundations of the Civilian Tradition* (Oxford: Clarendon, 1996) on the historical background.

PART II REQUIREMENTS FOR A VALID LEASE

17.6 Lease as a Grant of Possession for a Term Certain

The only necessary requirements for a valid lease of land is that it must involve the grant of *possession* of the land, for a 'term certain', which means a period of time which has a *certain duration*. This was reaffirmed by the House of Lords in *Street v. Mountford* [1985] 1 AC 809, as we see below. Both elements – possession and certain duration – cause difficulties, although for different reasons, as we see in the following paragraphs. We consider what amounts to possession in this context in paras. 17.7–17.9, and then look at certainty of duration in paras. 17.10–17.13.

17.7 Possession and the Lease-Licence Distinction

'Possession' in this context is often referred to as 'exclusive possession'. However, the 'exclusive' is redundant, because 'possession' here bears the technical meaning we looked at in Chapter 11 *Possession and Title,* that is, exclusive physical control of the premises for one's own benefit. It was established by the House of Lords in *Street v. Mountford* that any occupier who is in possession of land for a fixed or periodic term is a tenant (subject to a few exceptions we look at in para. 17.9 below). So, on the face of it there should be no difficulty in identifying a tenancy when we see one.

However, the problem is that, since at least the beginning of the twentieth century when different categories of tenant were given statutory protection against their landlords, landlords have sought to disguise leases as contractual licences (i.e. as personal rights to occupy the property), so as to avoid giving occupiers of their land statutory protection. We saw an example of this in *J.A. Pye (Oxford) Ltd v Graham* [2002] UKHL 30, the adverse possession case we looked at in para. 11.9 of Chapter 11 *Possession and Title* and in para. 12.15 of Chapter 12 *Adverse Possession of Land*. In that case the adverse possessors were originally granted an 11 month 'licence' to 'graze and mow' the disputed land (to which they had the only usable means of access) because there was a danger that a licence for 12 months or more would have been construed as an agricultural tenancy protected under what was then the Agricultural Holdings Act 1948.

Most of these cases concern short-term or periodic tenancies of residential premises. From the perspective of the landowner, the essential problem is how to grant occupiers the right to pay to live in their property without giving them the statutory protection which Parliament has decided should be conferred on short-term/periodic residential tenants. The answer is to not grant the 'tenant' a property interest – a lease – at all, but to grant them instead only a personal right to occupy the property on payment of a fee. Personal rights to occupy land are usually referred to as licences: 'licence' is a non-technical term meaning a personal permission to do something on someone else's land which would otherwise be a trespass. Here we are concerned primarily with 'tenants' of residential premises, but, as we have seen, the same kind of situation can arise in relation to a business or agricultural occupier.

So, the fundamental problem here is this: if a landowner grants someone a right to live in his property for a fixed or periodic term, has he granted a lease of the land or just a personal licence? The first and obvious point to make is that we are seeking to establish the *legal nature of the rights which have been granted* – does someone who has those rights in respect of land have a property interest in the land, or just a personal permission to be there? So, it is irrelevant how the agreement is labelled, and whether it purports to be a licence – it can be a lease even if it is called a licence, and even if it carefully uses the language of licences rather than of leases. So, an agreement may in law create a tenancy even if it calls the parties 'licensor' and 'licensee' rather than 'landlord/lessor' and 'tenant/lessee', and calls the money payable a 'licence fee' rather than 'rent', and includes a declaration that the agreement gives rise to a licence only and not a lease. This was confirmed by the House of Lords in *Street* v. *Mountford* [1985] 1 AC 809. Lord Templeman, giving the principal opinion in the House of Lords, rejected the landowner's argument that, given the parties were free to create whatever interest they wanted, the use of such language proved conclusively that what the parties intended to create, and thought they had created, was a licence and not a lease. He said:

> Mr. Street (the owner of the house) enjoyed freedom to offer Mrs. Mountford (the occupier) the right to occupy the rooms comprised in the agreement on such lawful terms as Mr. Street pleased. Mrs. Mountford enjoyed freedom to negotiate with Mr. Street to obtain different terms. Both parties enjoyed freedom to contract or not to contract and both parties exercised that freedom by contracting on the terms set forth in the written agreement and on no other terms. But the consequences in law of the agreement, once concluded, can only be determined by consideration of the effect of the agreement. If the agreement satisfied all the requirements of a tenancy, then the agreement produced a tenancy and the parties cannot alter the effect of the agreement by insisting that they only created a licence. *The manufacture of a five-pronged implement for manual digging results in a fork even if the manufacturer, unfamiliar with the English language, insists that he intended to make and has made a spade.*[17]

In that case the agreement signed by Mr Street and Mrs Mountford granted Mrs Mountford the right to occupy two rooms in Mr Street's house for £37 a week, subject only to a right for Mr Street to enter the rooms 'to inspect its condition, read and collect money from meters, carry out maintenance works, install or replace furniture or for any other reasonable purposes'. So, the issue was: did those rights granted to Mrs Mountford give rise to a lease or only a personal right to occupy?

In an earlier Court of Appeal decision, *Marchant* v. *Charters* [1977] 1 WLR 1181, CA, Lord Denning had said that it depended on 'the nature and quality' of the occupation:

> was it intended that the occupier should have a stake in the room or did he have only permission for himself personally to occupy the room?[18]

---

[17] *Street* v. *Mountford* [1985] 1 AC 809 at pp. 819E–F. Lord Templeman was perhaps not a gardener: the standard digging fork has four prongs.

[18] *Marchant* v. *Charters* [1977] 1 WLR 1181, CA, at p. 1185.

Applying this test, the Court of Appeal had held that Mr Charters, who occupied a single furnished bed-sitting room with cooking facilities on payment of a fixed sum a week, with the landowner providing a housekeeper who cleaned the room and supplied clean bed linen, had only a personal licence, and so was not entitled to the protection of the Rent Acts.

However, in *Street* v. *Mountford* the House of Lords rejected this approach, and said that the only test was whether the agreement gave the occupier 'possession' of the premises, that is, exclusive physical control over them for the occupier's own benefit. Lord Templeman cited with approval the classic formulation of this principle provided by Windeyer J in the High Court of Australia in the Australian case *Radaich* v. *Smith* (1959) 101 CLR 209, which is still worth quoting:

> What then is the fundamental right which a tenant has that distinguishes his position from that of a licensee? It is an interest in land as distinct from a personal permission to enter the land and use it for some stipulated purpose or purposes. And how is it to be ascertained whether such an interest in land has been given? By seeing whether the grantee was given a legal right of exclusive possession of the land for a term or from year to year or for a life or lives. If he was, he is a tenant. And he cannot be other than a tenant, because a legal right of exclusive possession is a tenancy and the creation of such a right is a demise. To say that a man who has, by agreement with a landlord, a right of exclusive possession of land for a term is not a tenant is simply to contradict the first proposition by the second. A right of exclusive possession is secured by the right of a lessee to maintain ejectment [the traditional common law action for the recovery of land] and, after his entry, trespass. A reservation to the landlord, either by contract or statute, of a limited right of entry, as for example to view or repair, is, of course, not inconsistent with the grant of exclusive possession. Subject to such reservations, a tenant for a term or from year to year or ... can exclude his landlord as well as strangers from the demised premises.[19]

Lord Templeman accepted this unreservedly and concluded that:

> There can be no tenancy unless the occupier enjoys exclusive possession ... To constitute a tenancy the occupier must be granted exclusive possession for a fixed or periodic term certain in consideration of a premium or periodic payments.[20]

On this basis the House of Lords held that Mrs Mountford was a tenant.

Lord Templeman added two comments which are significant here. The first was to point out that a person may be in possession of land because of holding some other kind of property interest in the land – perhaps as freehold owner, or adverse possessor, or mortgagee in possession, or as a beneficiary under a trust. Clearly, if the occupier is in possession in any of those capacities, she is not a tenant. Secondly, he said there were some exceptional cases where a person was in possession of land (and here it is not clear whether he meant possession or exclusive occupation, as we see in para. 17.8 below) for a fixed or periodic term and yet was not a tenant. He gave

---

[19] *Radaich* v. *Smith* (1959) 101 CLR 209, at p. 222.;quoted by Lord Templeman in *Street* v. *Mountford*, fn. 17 above, at pp. 827C–E.

[20] Lord Templeman in *Street* v. *Mountford*, fn. 17 above, at p. 818.

as examples 'service occupants',[21] cases where the occupier was an 'object of charity', cases where the landowner and occupier had no intention to create legal relations, and cases where a contractual purchaser was let into possession before the purchase was complete. However, leaving aside those exceptional cases, which we come back to in para. 17.8, he stated the following proposition:

> where as in the present case the only circumstances are that residential accommodation is offered and accepted with exclusive possession for a term at a rent, the result is a tenancy.[22]

It is important to appreciate that Lord Templeman is *not* saying here that it cannot be a tenancy *unless* rent is payable: as we have already noted, this is not correct.[23] What he is saying is that a requirement that rent is paid is an additional indication that a tenancy is intended, to the extent that the presence of all three elements – exclusive possession, a fixed or periodic term and rent – is enough to establish that an agreement is a tenancy.

17.8 The Exceptional Cases

There is some inconsistency in the terminology used by Lord Templeman in *Street* v. *Mountford* in that occasionally when he says 'exclusive possession' it seems that he means 'exclusive occupation'. In particular, it seems that in at least some of the examples of exceptional cases he gave, what he meant was that these are cases where, although the occupier has exclusive occupation, she does not have possession of the property. This must be true of, for example, cases where there is no intention to create legal relations: to grant someone possession of land is by definition to enter into a legal relationship with them. It also seems to be true of the 'objects of charity' category, and this is confirmed by the Court of Appeal decision in *Watts* v. *Stewart* [2016] EWCA Civ 1247. In that case it was held that an occupant of an almshouse run by a charity had a licence only, even though she had exclusive occupation of the apartment allocated to her by the charity, where she had lived for 11 years. The Court of Appeal put forward two reasons. The first was that the terms of the agreement were not consistent with her having *possession* of the apartment, as opposed to a personal right of exclusive occupation: under the agreement she could be required to vacate her apartment and move, either temporarily or permanently, to another one; visitors were not permitted to stay in her apartment except with the consent of the trustees; she was not allowed to vacate her apartment for more than 28 days in any one year without the prior consent of the trustees; she had to inform the trustees/warden if she would be away for more than a week at a time; and the trustees could terminate her rights and require her to leave for good cause. The second reason, which reinforced the first, was that the trustees could only properly discharge the trusts of the charity (which were limited to providing accommodation

---

[21] That is, employees such as caretakers required to live in premises provided for them, to enable them to carry out their job more effectively.

[22] Lord Templeman in *Street* v. *Mountford*, fn. 17 above, at p. 827.   [23] para. 17.1(b) above.

for those in need, hardship or distress) if a personal revocable licence was granted, so the rights they intended to grant her were by their nature personal, not proprietary.

By way of contrast, in Lord Templeman's 'exceptional case' of a prospective purchaser of land being allowed to move in before completion of the purchase, a more convincing analysis is that if the terms of the proposed purchase are not yet agreed and the prospective purchaser is allowed in pending negotiations, he is likely to be treated as a tenant at will (as to which see para. 17.10 below) unless the circumstances are such that the courts consider there is no intention to create legal relations. The same would seem to apply if a prospective lessee is let into possession without paying a rent before the lease is granted. These were described by Lord Millett in *Ramnarace* v. *Lutchman* [2001] 1 WLR 1651, PC as situations in which a tenancy at will 'commonly arises', and he added:

> a person allowed into possession while the parties negotiate the terms of a lease or purchase ... has no interest in the land to which his possession can be referred, and if in exclusive and rent-free possession is a tenant at will. In *Hagee (London) Ltd* v. *Erikson and Larson* [1976] QB 209, 217 Scarman LJ described this as one of the 'classic circumstances' in which a tenancy at will arose.[24]

On that basis, in *Ramnarace* a niece who was allowed to take possession of land and built a house on it, on the understanding that she could live there rent free until she could afford to buy it from her uncle and aunt on terms to be agreed, was held to be in possession of the land as a tenant at will.

17.9 Does the Agreement Grant Possession to the Occupiers?

There are other cases, which we look at here, where it might be difficult to determine whether an agreement grants *possession* to an occupier, so that the occupier has a tenancy rather than a licence.

(a) Agreement Requiring Occupier to Share With the Grantor or Others

If the grantee is required to share occupation of the property with someone else, then clearly she cannot be in possession of it, because possession requires exclusive control over the property. In the past it was common practice for owners granting an occupier the right to occupy their residential premises to include in the agreement, as a device to exclude Rent Act protection, a provision that the grantor reserved the right to stay at the premises himself whenever he wanted, or granted the occupier the right to occupy the premises together with some other person to be nominated by the grantor. If such a provision is taken at its face value the occupier has no right to possession and therefore can only be a licensee. However, in *Street* v. *Mountford* Lord Templeman warned that 'the court should, in my opinion, be astute to detect and frustrate sham devices and artificial transactions whose only object is to disguise the grant of a tenancy and to evade

---

[24] *Ramnarace* v. *Lutchman* [2001] 1 WLR 1651, PC at para. 18.

the Rent Acts'.[25] And in a subsequent House of Lords decision on conjoined appeals in *AG Securities* v. *Vaughan and Antoniades* v. *Villiers* [1990] 1 AC 417, which we look at in (b) below, Lord Templeman said first that 'parties to an agreement cannot contract out of the Rent Acts' and secondly that 'where the language of licence contradicts the reality of lease, the facts must prevail. The facts must prevail over the language in order that the parties may not contract out of the Rent Acts'.[26] On this basis, in *Antoniades* v. *Villiers* a couple occupying a flat consisting of a bedroom, living room, kitchen and bathroom were held to be tenants and not licensees even though their agreement provided that their use of the rooms was 'in common with the licensor and such other licensees or invitees as [he] may permit from time to time to use'. The House of Lords said that the purported right of the landlord to share occupation and introduce further occupiers into the flat was a pretence to avoid the provisions of the Rent Acts: the reality was that he never intended to exercise those rights but intended that the couple should have exclusive possession of the flat. Accordingly, since it was in reality a grant of exclusive possession for a term in consideration of periodical payments, the agreement created a tenancy.

(b) Separate Agreements for Sharers

Another complication in *Antoniades* v. *Villiers* was that the couple were not given a single agreement made between the landlord and the two of them jointly. Instead, each was required to sign separate agreements. This meant that each of them was required, in effect, to share occupation with the other so that neither of them could be said to be in possession. However, the House of Lords refused to accept that conclusion and held that they jointly had possession of the flat, and therefore jointly held a tenancy of it, on the basis that the two agreements were 'interdependent and fell to be read together so as to constitute a single agreement'. The House of Lords was, however, unable to reach the same conclusion in the conjoined appeal in *AG Securities* v. *Vaughan*, which concerned four sharers, each of whom was required to sign a separate agreement. The House of Lords held that in *AG Securities* each of the sharers held a separate licence. Their licences could not be read together to constitute a single agreement, so the House of Lords decided, because their agreements were made on different dates and required different payments. These differences made it impossible to find the four unities (of possession, interest, time and title) necessary for the creation of a joint tenancy.[27]

(c) Grantor has no Property Interest in the Land

A different device to avoid the creation of tenancies had to be considered by the House of Lords in *Bruton* v. *London & Quadrant Housing Trust* [2000] 1 AC 406. The London Borough of Lambeth entered into an agreement with the Housing Trust

---

[25] *Street* v. *Mountford* [1985] 1 AC 809 at 825.
[26] *AG Securities* v. *Vaughan and Antoniades* v. *Villiers* [1990] 1 AC 417 at p. 463.
[27] See Chapter 8 *Property Interest Holders* para. 8.8(f).

whereby Lambeth granted the Housing Trust a licence of a block of flats for the Housing Trust to use to provide temporary housing for the homeless, discharging the statutory duty Lambeth had to provide such accommodation. Under the licence the Housing Trust was required to manage the building and the flats, and it was responsible for organising the allocation of the accommodation and granting each occupant a weekly licence of the flat allocated to them. Lambeth granted the Housing Trust a licence of the building rather than a lease because, so it was hoped, this would ensure that the licences of individual flats granted by the Housing Trust to occupiers could not take effect as tenancies. Both Lambeth and the Housing Trust were anxious to avoid granting tenancies to occupants because they feared it would make it more difficult for them to manage their limited supply of housing stock so as to meet the needs of the homeless. They argued that, if the Housing Trust had no property interest in the building and the flats but only personal contractual rights, powers and duties granted to them by Lambeth under the licence, it could have neither the capacity nor the power to grant a property interest in a flat to anyone else. This, so it was argued, was because of the *nemo dat* principle – the basic property principle which we looked at in Chapter 15 *Enforceability and Priority of Property Interests*, that no-one can give anyone else a greater or more extensive interest in a thing than she herself has. So, if the Housing Trust had only a personal licence to use and manage the flats, it could not grant an occupier anything more than a person right to occupy a flat. This argument was challenged by Mr Bruton, an occupier of one of the flats, who wanted to bring an action against the Housing Trust under s. 11 of the Landlord and Tenant Act 1985 requiring them to carry out repairs to the flat. Section 11 of the 1985 Act imposes repairing obligations on landlords under leases of dwelling houses for a term of less than 7 years. So, if Mr Bruton had a lease of his flat, he could rely on s. 11 to make the Housing Trust carry out repairs to his flat. If he had only a licence, he could not.

The House of Lords held that he did have a lease for the purposes of s. 11. They regarded themselves as bound by the decision in *Street* v. *Mountford* to come to this conclusion. As Lord Hoffmann said, all the elements that, according to Lord Templeman in *Street* v. *Mountford,* were required to create a lease were present:

> The decision of this House in *Street v. Mountford* [1985] AC 809 is authority for the proposition that a 'lease' or 'tenancy' is a contractually binding agreement, not referable to any other relationship between the parties, by which one person gives another the right to exclusive occupation of land for a fixed or renewable period or periods of time, usually in return for a periodic payment in money. An agreement having these characteristics creates a relationship of landlord and tenant to which the common law or statute may then attach various incidents. The fact that the parties use language more appropriate to a different kind of agreement, such as a licence, is irrelevant if upon its true construction it has the identifying characteristics of a lease.
>
> The meaning of the agreement, for example, as to the extent of the possession which it grants, depends upon the intention of the parties, objectively ascertained by refer-ence to the language and relevant background … . But the classification of the agreement as a lease does not depend upon any intention additional to that expressed in the choice of terms. It is simply a question of characterising the terms which the parties have agreed. This is a question of law.

In this case, it seems to me that the agreement, construed against the relevant background, plainly gave Mr. Bruton a right to exclusive possession. There is nothing to suggest that he was to share possession with the Trust, the council or anyone else.[28]

It was argued on behalf of the Housing Trust that there were special circumstances in this case which required the House of Lords to construe the agreement as a licence despite the presence of all the characteristics identified in *Street* v. *Mountford*. Their argument was that the Trust was a responsible landlord performing socially valuable functions, it had agreed with the council not to grant tenancies, Mr. Bruton had agreed that he was not to have a tenancy and the Trust had no estate out of which it could grant one. Lord Hoffmann rejected the argument:

In my opinion none of these circumstances can make an agreement to grant exclusive possession something other than a tenancy. The character of the landlord is irrelevant because although [there are statutes which] make distinctions between different kinds of landlords, it is not by saying that what would be a tenancy if granted by one landlord will be something else if granted by another. The alleged breach of the Trust's licence is irrelevant because there is no suggestion that the grant of a tenancy would have been ultra vires either the Trust or the council ...

Mr. Bruton's agreement is irrelevant because one cannot contract out of the statute ...[29]

This, however, still left the difficult question of how the Housing Trust could have granted Mr Bruton a property interest in the flat when it had no property interest in it itself.

One possibility would be to say that he had a tenancy by estoppel, which would have been fully enforceable between himself and the Housing Trust but not enforceable against Lambeth or anyone else.[30] A tenancy by estoppel is well established in English law: if I purport to grant you a tenancy of Buckingham Palace when I have no interest in it, of course you do not acquire a tenancy in it which is enforceable against whoever owns it. However, I am estopped from denying to you that you have such a tenancy, so you do have a kind of relative title to a tenancy which is enforceable against me even though not enforceable against anyone who 'really' has an interest in Buckingham Palace. However, if I then later acquire a freehold or leasehold interest in Buckingham Palace, your tenancy by estoppel (so far enforceable only against me) will automatically become a 'real' tenancy enforceable against the whole world, by a process called 'feeding the estoppel'. This is in fact what happened to Mr Bruton's tenancy. After the House of Lords' decision in *Bruton* v. *London & Quadrant* Lambeth did in fact grant the Housing Trust a lease of the building in question, and of other buildings it had licensed to the Housing Trust on similar terms. In *Kay* v. *London Borough of Lambeth* [2006] UKHL 10 (which concerned tenants occupying another of those buildings) Lord Scott said that the

---

[28] Lord Hoffmann in *Bruton* v. *London & Quadrant Housing Trust* [2000] 1 AC 406 at pp. 413E–414A.

[29] Ibid. at p. 414.

[30] And it would not have been difficult for the House of Lords to have construed 'lease' in s. 11 of the Landlord and Tenant Act 1985 as extending to cover a tenancy by estoppel.

effect of this was that all occupiers of properties held by the Housing Trust who had acquired 'non-estate' leases as a result of the decision in *Bruton*, automatically then acquired 'full leases' of their flats 'so to speak, fed by the estate that' the Housing Trust had acquired when it was granted a lease of the building.[31]

The difficulty with this analysis is, however, that it was expressly rejected in *Bruton*, by both Lord Hoffmann and Lord Hobhouse, for reasons which are not wholly clear.[32] They described what Mr Bruton acquired as a 'non-estate lease', which seems to mean a non-proprietary lease,[33] but that seems a contradiction in terms. In any event the idea of there being a wholly different kind of lease which is non-proprietary has not been picked up in later cases.

17.10 Duration of Leases

One of the defining characteristics of a leasehold, as opposed to a freehold, interest is that it is of a limited duration – not perpetual – and it has long been accepted that the limit of the duration must be certain. Unfortunately, however, the rules about what amounts to a 'certain' duration (i.e. a 'term certain') are arcane and inconveniently complex. In one of the leading modern cases, *Berrisford* v. *Mexfield Housing Co-operative Ltd* [2011] UKSC 52, Lady Hale described the law in this area as having 'an Alice in Wonderland quality'.[34]

There are two basic rules about duration of leases. The first is that there are four different types of duration which count as a 'term certain': a fixed period of time (e.g. five years); a periodic duration (such as weekly, monthly or annually); a duration which lasts 'at will'; and a duration which lasts 'at sufferance'. The second basic rule is an overarching one which applies to all four categories. This is that the *maximum* duration of a lease must be ascertainable from the date the lease commences.

(a) Tenancy for a Fixed Period

A tenancy may be granted for any fixed period, however short or however long. The period may even be intermittent. So, for example, a time-share arrangement which gave the time-share owner a right to possession of a holiday cottage in Cornwall for one week a year for 80 years has been held to be a valid lease for a single period comprised of 80 discontinuous weeks.[35]

---

[31] Lord Scott in *Kay* v. *London Borough of Lambeth* [2006] UKHL 10 at para. 146. See also Lord Neuberger in *Berrisford* v. *Mexfield Housing Co-operative Ltd* [2011] UKSC 52 (which we look at in paras. 17.11–17.13 below), who described *Bruton* as 'about relativity of title, which is the bedrock of English land law' at para. 65, and Patrick Routley, 'Tenancies and estoppels – after Bruton v. London & Quadrant Housing Trust' (2000) *Modern Law Review* 424.

[32] *Bruton*, fn. 28 above, at pp. 416E–F and pp. 418A–B. Lord Slynn and Lord Hope both expressed agreement with Lord Hoffmann's opinion.

[33] Susan Bright, 'Leases, exclusive possession and estates' (2000) 116 *LQR* 7.

[34] *Berrisford* v. *Mexfield Housing Co-operative Ltd* [2011] UKSC 52 at para. 88.

[35] *Cottage Holiday Associates Ltd* v. *Customs and Excise* [1983] QB 735, QBD.

However, the period must end on a date which is ascertainable at the start of the lease. That usually means that the period must be stated to be for a specified number of years (e.g. 'for 10 years from the date of the commencement of the lease') or to end on a specified date ('until 31 December 2030'). It is doubtful whether it can instead be stated to last until the happening of a specified event: we come back to this point in para. 17.11.

It is permissible (and fairly common practice in commercial leases) for there to be an express term in a fixed-term lease for either or both parties to have a right to terminate the lease early on a specified date or on the happening of a specified event. This right is usually exercisable by serving notice of the desire to terminate on the other party. We come back to the question of how this fits into the certainty of duration rule in para. 17.11.

(b) Periodic Tenancy

A periodic term is one that continues from period to period (for example, week to week, month to month, or year to year) until terminated by either party giving notice to quit to the other. So, a periodic tenancy can last indefinitely, and in practice a significant proportion of them do indeed end up as long-term property relationships. As Simpson explains, the periodic tenancy was a comparatively late development, not fully recognised by the courts until 1702. By then, as he notes, it was being used as a means of giving tenants an interest in the land they occupied which was marginally less precarious interest than the tenancy at will.[36] They have become more secure through statutory security of tenure, which applies primarily to periodic tenancies of agricultural and residential property

Periodic tenancies are probably now the most significant form of tenure for occupiers of social housing and for short-term (and sometimes long-term) private rented accommodation. With this in mind, it is important to note that they take effect as legal leases if granted by deed or if they arise by operation of law, and that (as we saw in para. 16.33 of Chapter 16 *Registration*) they are not registrable at the Land Registry but are automatically enforceable against third parties as overriding interests.

The nature of a periodic tenancy was considered by the House of Lords in *Hammersmith and Fulham LBC* v. *Monk* [1992] 1 AC 478, where it was held that in the very common situation where a periodic tenancy is held jointly by two (or more) people,[37] it can be terminated by just one of them serving notice to quit on the landlord, without the consent or even knowledge of the other. This, so the House of Lords decided, is because a periodic tenancy is by its nature a tenancy which will not continue after the end of the current period *unless* the tenant positively decides to extend it for a further period (the decision being signified by an omission to give notice to quit). It follows that if the tenancy is held jointly, it cannot continue beyond

---

[36] Simpson, *A History of the Land Law*, fn. 13 above, pp. 253–254.
[37] Most tenancies of social housing are periodic tenancies, and they are very likely to be held jointly by couples or other family members.

the current period unless *all* the joint lessees positively agree *not to serve a notice to quit.* In other words, it continues beyond the initial period 'only if and so long as all parties to the agreement are willing that it should do so'.[38] So, although a notice to quit is in form a positive dealing with joint property (and therefore prima facie requiring the concurrence of all joint tenants) in substance it is not.

At first sight this analysis might seem counter-intuitive, and the decision in *Monk* might also be thought to operate unfairly on the joint holder of a periodic tenancy who wants the tenancy to continue. As Lord Bridge pointed out:

> For a large part of this century there have been many categories of tenancy of property occupied for agricultural, residential and commercial purposes where the legislature has intervened to confer upon tenants extra-contractual rights entitling them to continue in occupation without the consent of the landlord, either after the expiry of a contractual lease for a fixed term or after notice to quit given by the landlord to determine a contractual periodic tenancy. It is primarily in relation to joint tenancies in these categories that the question whether or not notice to quit given by one of the joint tenants can determine the tenancy is of practical importance, particularly where, as in the instant case, the effect of the determination will be to deprive the other joint tenant of statutory protection. This may appear an untoward result and may conse-quently provoke a certain reluctance to hold that the law can permit one of two joint tenants unilaterally to deprive his co-tenant of 'rights' which both are equally entitled to enjoy.[39]

However, the problem is that the reverse rule could be equally unfair, as Lord Browne-Wilkinson pointed out:

> there are two instinctive reactions to this case which lead to diametrically opposite conclusions. The first is that the flat in question was the joint home of the appellant and Mrs. Powell: it therefore cannot be right that one of them unilaterally can join the landlords to put an end to the other's rights in the home. The second is that the appellant and Mrs. Powell undertook joint liabilities as tenants for the purpose of providing themselves with a joint home and that, once the desire to live together has ended, it is impossible to require that the one who quits the home should continue indefinitely to be liable for the discharge of the obligations to the landlord under the tenancy agreement.[40]

A termination of the periodic tenancy by just one joint lessee serving notice to quit on the landlord without consulting the other has also been challenged on the basis that it amounts to a breach of trust. This issue was raised but not decided in *Hammersmith* v. *Monk* and it seems doubtful that such a challenge would succeed.[41] Similarly, challenge under the Human Rights Act also seems unlikely to succeed. In *Sims* v. *Dacorum Borough Council* [2014] UKSC 63 the Supreme Court was invited to revisit the decision in *Monk*, on the basis that the effect of *Monk* was, so it was argued, an infringement of the remaining joint tenant's rights under article 8 and

---

[38] Lord Bridge in *Hammersmith and Fulham LBC* v. *Monk* [1992] 1 AC 478 at p.483.
[39] Ibid. at pp. 482–483.   [40] Ibid. Lord Browne-Wilkinson at p. 492.
[41] Ibid. Lord Browne-Wilkinson at p. 493, and see also *Notting Hill Housing Trust* v. *Brackley* [2001] 35 EG 106, CA.

under article 1 Protocol 1 of the European Convention on Human Rights. The Supreme Court decisively rejected these arguments and upheld the immediate order for possession made by the District Judge against the remaining joint tenant. It was accepted that both article 8 and article 1 Protocol 1 were engaged, but the Supreme Court nevertheless held that in the circumstances the remaining joint tenant's Convention rights were not infringed.

(c) Tenancy at Will

A tenancy at will lasts indefinitely until terminated by either party.[42] In other words, it is a tenancy which continues only so long as it is the will of both parties that it should continue, and either party can at any time signify her unwillingness that it should continue by serving notice to quit on the other party.[43] Traditionally, tenants at will have been excluded from statutory protection, so in reality they are as precarious as they sound.

They are most often used as a temporary measure which can safely be accepted by a landlord on an interim basis because rent can be charged but the tenancy does not attract security of tenure. So, a tenancy at will may arise (or be inferred by the court) when a proposed lessee or purchaser is let into possession whilst negotiations are pending or prior to completion of the transaction, or where a tenant holds over after the end of the tenancy temporarily and the landlord is willing to allow her to remain, paying rent, for a limited time.[44] Also, in some circumstances a tenancy at will may arise by implication of law, as we see in para. 17.12 below.

(d) Tenancy at Sufferance

It is also possible, although rare in practice, to have a tenancy at sufferance. This arises where a former tenant remains in occupation after the tenancy has ended without either the consent or dissent of the landlord.[45] In other words, the tenant is (not yet) a trespasser. However, the longer the situation lasts, the more likely it is that the court will decide that the tenant at sufferance has become an adverse possessor.[46]

17.11 The Certainty of Duration Rule

The certainty of duration rule has recently been re-considered and re-formulated first by the House of Lords in *Prudential Assurance Co Ltd* v. *London Residuary Body* [1992] 2 AC 386 and then by the Supreme Court in *Berrisford* v. *Mexfield Housing Co-operative Ltd* [2011] UKSC 52. The Supreme Court in *Berrisford* confirmed the

---

[42] *Wheeler* v. *Mercer* [1957] AC 426.
[43] Lord Bridge in *Hammersmith* v. *Monk* [1992] 1 AC 478 at p. 483.
[44] See *Javid* v. *Aquil* [1991] 1 WLR 1007.
[45] *Remon* v. *City of London Real Property Co Ltd* [1921] 1 KB 49 at p. 58.
[46] See Chapter 12 *Adverse Possession of Land*.

basic rule re-affirmed by the House of Lords in *Prudential*, but modified what was said in *Prudential* about the consequences of a lease being void because of uncertain duration.

In *Prudential* the House of Lords held that the basic certainty of duration rule is that both parties to the lease must know from the outset the earliest date on which their commitment under the lease can be brought to an end – or, as the House of Lords put it, *the maximum duration of their liability under the lease*. As we noted in para. 17.10 above, this is clearly satisfied if the lease is for a specific period of time, with a known end date. However, it was held not to be satisfied by the lease the House of Lords was considering, which was granted for a duration stated to be 'until the landlord requires the land for road-widening'. In coming to this conclusion the House of Lords re-affirmed what it took to be the orthodox position as formulated by the Court of Appeal in *Lace* v. *Chantler* [1944] KB 368, where a lease granted during the second world war 'for the duration of the war' was held to be of uncertain duration and therefore void.

There are two additional points made by the House of Lords in *Prudential* which it is important to note here. The first is that this basic rule does *not* apply to provisions in a fixed-term lease which entitle either party to terminate the lease early. As we noted earlier, a fixed-term lease may legitimately be made terminable earlier on the happening of any event (provided the event is objectively ascertainable at the time it occurs) either at the option of one or other of the parties, or automatically. So, for example, as the House of Lords confirmed in *Prudential*, a lease stated to be for 99 years but terminable earlier by the landlord 'if the landlord requires the land for road-widening' would be valid, as would be a lease for, say, 50 years but terminable earlier by either party 'if the war ends before then'.

The second important point is that the basic rule applies to periodic tenancies as well as to fixed-term tenancies.[47] The way it operates in relation to periodic tenancies is as a rule that neither parties' right to terminate the periodic tenancy may be subject to a fetter which makes it impossible for that party to know at the outset the earliest date on which she can bring the tenancy to an end. In other words, either there must be no fetter on the right of either party to end the periodic tenancy by notice to quit, or, if there is a fetter, it must satisfy the certainty rule. This means that the fetter must either postpone the right to end the tenancy by notice to quit until a specified date, or (if the parties want to postpone it to the happening of a specified event) until *either* a specified date *or* the happening of that event, whichever happens first. So, as the Houses of Lords confirmed in *Prudential*, an annual periodic tenancy in which the landlord's right to terminate by notice to quit is postponed 'until the landlord requires the land for road-widening' is not allowed.[48] However, an annual periodic tenancy in which the landlord's right to terminate by notice to quit is

---

[47] It also applies to, and is automatically satisfied in, a tenancy at will and a tenancy at sufferance, because both parties can bring either of these to an end at any time.

[48] According to the House of Lords, the precise effect would be that the lease would be valid but the *fetter* would be void, so that either party could terminate by serving at any time the appropriate length of notice to quit.

postponed until *either* 1 January 2099 *or* the landlord 'requires the road for road-widening (whichever occurs first) is perfectly valid.[49]

So, the highly unsatisfactory result is that, if the parties adopt the appropriate artificial device, they can draft a lease which achieves what they want (i.e. the tenant can keep the land until the landlord needs it for road-widening), but if they (or their lawyers) are foolish enough to simply say what they mean, their intentions will be frustrated.

17.12 Consequences of Lease Being Void for Uncertainty of Duration

In *Berrisford* the Supreme Court confirmed everything the House of Lords had said in *Prudential* about the basic rule, but differed over the consequences of failing to comply with the rule.

In *Prudential* the House of Lords said that if a fixed-term lease is void because of uncertain duration but the tenant has already taken possession under the void lease (as usually happens), the tenant will acquire by operation of law either a legal periodic tenancy (if rent was paid) or a tenancy at will (if no rent had been paid). Consequently the landlord (and the tenant) will be entitled to bring the relationship to an end immediately, by serving the appropriate notice to quit if it is a periodic tenancy, or by merely notifying the other party if it is a tenancy at will.[50]

If, on the other hand the lease was a periodic tenancy to start with, but there is a fetter on the right to terminate by notice to quit which postpones the right for an uncertain duration, the fetter will be void but the lease itself will be valid, according to the House of Lords in *Prudential*. Again, the effect will be that either party can take immediate steps to terminate by giving the appropriate notice to quit.

Following the Supreme Court decision in *Berrisford* these effects of the basic rule remain true but, bizarrely, only if the tenant under the void lease is an artificial legal entity rather than a human individual. This is because in *Berrisford* it was held that where a lease is granted to a human individual and the term violates the uncertainty of duration rule (whether because a fixed term of uncertain duration or a periodic term with a fetter of uncertain duration), a provision of the Law of Property Act 1925 (which no-one before had considered relevant) comes into operation. This is s. 149(6), which, so the Supreme Court decided, has the effect of automatically turning such leases into leases for a fixed term of 90 years, terminable either by the landlord giving one month's notice if the tenant dies before then *or* on the event which was intended to mark the end of the term or the end of the fetter on the right to serve a notice to quit.[51] So, a lease 'until the landlord requires the land for road-widening' takes effect (if it is granted to a human individual) as a lease for 90 years terminable earlier by the landlord on the tenant's death or if and when it requires the

---

[49] Lord Templeman in *Prudential Assurance Co Ltd* v. *London Residuary Body* [1992] 2 AC 386 at pp. 394–395.

[50] Ibid. at p. 391.

[51] We need not trouble ourselves at this point with the convoluted argument supporting the conclusion that s. 149(6) of the Law of Property Act 1925 has this effect: it is certainly not what s. 149(6) appears to say.

land for road-widening. Similarly, a periodic lease subject to a provision that the landlord may not serve notice to quit unless and until it requires the land for road-widening, takes effect as a periodic lease subject to a provision that the landlord may not serve notice to quit for 90 years or (if earlier) until either the tenant's death or until it requires the land for road-widening.

In the *Berrisford* case itself this meant that the tenancy was allowed to take effect essentially as the parties intended, even though the tenancy agreement as drafted violated the basic certainty of duration rule. The case concerned a tenancy of residential premises granted by a fully mutual co-operative housing association and stated to be terminable by the tenant on one month's notice, but by the landlord only on the happening of specified 'default' events (default by the tenant, the tenant ceasing to be a member of the housing association or the housing association winding up). The Supreme Court accepted the tenant's concession that the tenancy was prevented from taking effect as it stood as a valid tenancy by the *Prudential* uncertain duration rule. However, it held that instead, because of s. 149(6) of the LPA 1925, it took effect as a tenancy for 90 years determinable by the tenant on one month's notice, and by the landlord on the tenant's death by one month's notice, or on the earlier happening of any of the 'default' events. The landlord's argument that it was entitled to evict the tenant on one month's notice therefore failed.

The Supreme Court in *Berrisford* acknowledged that this escape from the consequences of the *Prudential* uncertain duration rule is not available where the tenant is a company (because s. 149(6) is concerned with tenancies for life, now abolished, but which could only be held by humans).[52] However, it was left open whether in these cases the tenancy made void by the uncertain duration rule is replaced by a periodic tenancy implied by law, as held by the House of Lords in *Prudential*, or whether alternatively the correct (and incompatible) analysis is that the offending tenancy is void only as a property interest, but valid in contract and so fully enforceable as between the original parties.

So, following *Berrisford* the basic certainty of duration rule reaffirmed by the House of Lords in *Prudential* remains intact, but the consequences of falling foul of the rule differ depending on whether the original tenant was a human individual or a company, an illogical distinction that none of the justices in *Berrisford* attempted to justify. Lord Clarke, in particular, commented:

> It is a mystery to me why in 2011 the position of a tenant who is a human being and a tenant which is a company should in this respect be different.[53]

There are a few points to be made about the *Berrisford* analysis, which has been much criticised. First, it was made clear in *Berrisford* (and amply supported by the authorities) that it applies regardless of the intentions of the parties.[54] As Lady Hale pointed out in *Berrisford*, while a determinable 99 year lease happened to coincide with the parties' intentions in that particular case it would not be difficult 'to imagine

---

[52] *Berrisford v. Mexfield Housing Co-operative Ltd* [2011] UKSC 52 per Lord Dyson at para. 119, and see also Lady Hale at para. 93 and Lord Clarke at para. 105.
[53] Ibid. para. 105.   [54] Ibid. Lord Neuberger at para. 44 and Lord Dyson at para. 117.

circumstances in which the same analysis would apply but be very far from the intentions of the parties'.[55] In *Southward Housing Co-operative Ltd* v. *Walker* [2015] EWHC 1615, Hildyard J concluded that he had such a case before him and came to the surprising conclusion that, while the Supreme Court in *Berrisford* established that the 'rule' applies regardless of the intentions of the parties, nevertheless 'the judgments of the Supreme Court ... leave open the possibility that it may be disapplied where those intentions and fundamental aspects of their agreement would be confounded by it'.[56] On this rather doubtful basis he decided that *Berrisford* did not apply to the facts before him (only marginally different from those in *Berrisford*) and held that, although the weekly tenancy was void for uncertainty under the *Prudential* rule, it was replaced by a contractual licence (a possibility which had been canvassed but rejected in *Berrisford*), which had been validly terminated by the landlord.[57]

17.13 Justifications for the Certainty of Duration Rules

The undesirable effects of the *Prudential* rule are amply demonstrated by the facts of the case itself. The purported tenancy was entered into as part of a sale and leaseback arrangement made in 1930 between the freehold owner of a shop in the Walworth Road in London and London County Council, which had plans to widen Walworth Road. The land in question was a wide strip of land which lay between the front of the shop and the road. The County Council bought the strip from the shop owner so that it could use it to widen the road, but because the works were not going to be carried out immediately, it leased the land back to the shop-owner 'until it needed the land for road-widening'. So, the intention of the parties was that the County Council would *never* get the land back unless and until it needed it to widen the road, and that the shop owner would be allowed to remain in occupation indefinitely paying little or no rent, unless and until the road was actually widened. As it happened, the road was never widened. The result of the House of Lords decision was that the County Council's successor was given the right to 'take back' this strip of land (which lay between the lessee's shop and the road and functioned as the frontage of the shop leading up to the side of the road) *without widening the road*. If it did that, the lessee would be deprived of the road frontage for its shop, and the County Council's successor would be given what was in effect a ransom strip, unusable except in conjunction with the lessee's shop. As Lord Browne-Wilkinson remarked:

---

[55] Ibid. Lady Hale at para. 94.
[56] *Southward Housing Co-operative Ltd* v. *Walker* [2015] EWHC 1615 at para. 91.
[57] Ibid. at paras. 94–95, and see also *Gilpin* v. *Legg* [2017] EWHC 3220 (the case about beach huts resting on land which, so the court decided, was let to the beach hut owners on annual periodic tenancies: see para. 7.25 of Chapter 7 *Objects of Property Interests*) where HHJ Paul Matthews was equally unenthusiastic about the reasoning in *Berrisford*, doubting (at paras. 84–86) that the authorities relied on supported the Supreme Court's argument; he too found it possible to avoid applying *Berrisford* by distinguishing it.

It is difficult to think of a more unsatisfactory outcome or one further away from what the parties to the 1930 agreement can ever have contemplated. ...

This bizarre outcome results from the application of an ancient and technical rule of law which requires the maximum duration of a term of years to be ascertainable from the outset. No-one has produced any satisfactory rationale for the genesis of this rule. No-one has been able to point to any useful purpose that it serves at the present day. If, by overruling the existing authorities, this House were able to change the law for the future only I would have urged your Lordships to do so. But for this House to depart from a rule relating to land law which has been established for many centuries might upset long established titles. I must therefore confine myself to expressing the hope that the Law Commission might look at the subject to see whether there is in fact any good reason now for maintaining a rule which operates to defeat contractually agreed arrangements between the parties (of which all successors in title are aware) and which is capable of producing such an extraordinary result as that in the present case ...[58]

In *Berrisford* a strict application of the *Prudential* rule would have been even more unfortunate. This was a test case concerning a standard form non-assignable residential tenancy granted by a fully mutual housing co-operative association. The function of the association was to operate a mortgage rescue scheme by buying properties from home owners having difficulty with mortgage payments and then letting the properties back to them, and this is what had happened in Ms Berrisford's case. All lessees were, and were required to be, members of the association, and because the association was a mutual housing association the lessees fell outside the statutory tenancy protection scheme that then applied to other tenants of social landlords. Instead, as noted in para. 17.12 above, the tenancy contained a standard form provision that the landlord could not terminate the tenancy except in specified circumstances (default by the tenant, the tenant ceasing to be a member of the association or the association being wound up). Given this context, the Supreme Court found that the clear intention of the parties was that Ms Berrisford would be entitled to remain as tenant indefinitely as long as she wished (she had an express right to terminate at any time on one month's notice), terminable by the landlord *only in the specified circumstances.*[59] The Supreme Court accepted the convoluted s. 149(6) argument as a means of achieving this objective.

It is worth emphasising again that the *Prudential* certainty of duration rule has been heavily criticised judicially, not least by three of the five judges sitting in the House of Lords in the *Prudential* case itself, and unanimously by the panel of seven Justices convened to hear the appeal in *Berrisford*. We have already noted that Lady Hale in *Berrisford* described the present law as having 'an Alice in Wonderland quality'[60] and in the same case Lord Neuberger (with whose judgment all the Justices expressed agreement) said:[61]

As the judgment of Lady Hale demonstrates (and as indeed the disquiet expressed by Lord Browne-Wilkinson and others in *Prudential* [1992] 2 AC 386 itself shows), the

[58] Lord Browne-Wilkinson in *Prudential Assurance Co Ltd* v. *London Residuary Body* [1992] 2 AC 386 at pp. 396–397; Lord Griffiths and Lord Mustill expressed agreement at pp. 396 and 397.
[59] Lord Neuberger in *Berrisford*, fn. 52 above, at para. 22.   [60] Ibid. at para. 88.   [61] Ibid. at para. 34.

law is not in a satisfactory state. There is no apparent practical justification for holding that an agreement for a term of uncertain duration cannot give rise to a tenancy, or that a fetter of uncertain duration on the right to serve a notice to quit is invalid. There is therefore much to be said for changing the law, and overruling what may be called the certainty requirement, which was affirmed in *Prudential* [1992] 2 AC 386, on the ground that, in so far as it had any practical justification, that justification has long since gone, and, in so far as it is based on principle, the principle is not fundamental enough for the Supreme Court to be bound by it. It may be added that Lady Hale's Carrollian characterisation of the law on this topic is reinforced by the fact that the common law accepted perpetually renewable leases as valid: they have been converted into 2000-year terms by section 145 of the Law of Property Act 1922.

What has dissuaded the Courts so far from abolishing or changing the rule is primarily its longevity, reinforced in *Berrisford* by the fact that the correctness of the rule was conceded and its worst effects avoided in the case before them.[62] Nevertheless in *Berrisford* Lord Neuberger and Lord Hope seemed to leave open the possibility of the Supreme Court reconsidering the rule at a later date,[63] whilst Lord Dyson took the view that this would best be done by Parliament after consideration by the Law Commission.[64] In any event, it was made clear that change is needed, as Lady Hale said:

> . . . it seems to me obvious that the consequence of our having reached the conclusions which we have on the first issue [that the tenancy in the case before them, as drafted, violated the *Prudential* uncertain duration rule] is to make the reconsideration of the decision in *Prudential*, whether by this Court or by Parliament, a matter of some urgency.[65]

PART III LEASES AS OWNERSHIP SUBSTITUTES

17.14 The Problem of Interdependent Living and Working Spaces

Most jurisdictions provide a property institution to be used where there are physically interdependent units, each intended for independent private use, but where the units have shared fabric (they form part of a larger building or group of buildings), and/or shared infrastructure (the structure of the building itself, installations for supplying electricity, gas, water, heating, telecommunications, etc. to each unit and to common parts), and/or common access ways (private roads, paths, common staircases, etc.) and common parking, storage and recreational areas. In a residential context the units are usually flats, apartments or maisonettes forming part of a building, but they can also be physically separate or semi-detached houses in a private estate. The same kind of arrangement can be used for commercial premises in, for example, office blocks, industrial estates and shopping centres.

---

[62] Ibid. at paras. 35–37.   [63] Ibid. at paras. 35 and 80 respectively.   [64] Ibid. para. 115.
[65] Ibid. at para. 96.

The legal problem is that each unit holder wants private ownership of its own unit, but there must also be a web of reciprocal rights, liberties, powers and duties between the unit holders in respect to the common parts and common facilities.

As we saw in para. 8.15 of Chapter 8 *Property Interest Holders*, most western jurisdictions have created by legislation bespoke special purpose property institutions to be used in these situations, usually referred to as condominiums, or strata titles. These institutions, which we outlined in Chapter 8, constitute the commonest forms of mixed private and communal property in western jurisdictions.

As we also saw in Chapter 8, we did introduce a condominium model called commonhold into the law of England and Wales by the Commonhold and Leasehold Reform Act 2002, but so far hardly anyone has adopted it, choosing to use instead the long leasehold models we describe in the following paragraphs.

17.15 The Traditional English Long Leasehold Model

England and Wales is unusual in using general leasehold law to regulate holdings in physically interdependent units with shared and common parts and facilities, although it has to be said that general leasehold principles and rules have now been heavily modified by statute in so far as they apply to these kinds of development.

The traditional model is to have a private owner of the freehold interest in the whole of the site, including the units and the common parts etc. The freeholder then grants long leases (typically 99 years or 999 years) of each unit to individual lessees, each lease granting the lessee exclusive possession of her own unit plus a right to use the common parts and facilities in common with all the other leaseholders, and a right to enforce the landlord's obligations. Typically the relationship between the landlord and the leaseholders is an arms-length commercial relationship and the landlord treats its freehold interest as an investment from which it intends to make a profit. The landlord does this by taking responsibility for providing common facilities and common services, which it does on a commercial basis (either for itself or via a management company it employs or controls) by charging the costs to the leaseholders of the units by way of a service charge, with those costs including fees charged by the landlord and/or management company for their services.

The usual pattern is for the lease to require the leaseholder to pay the developer a substantial capital sum when the lease is first granted (usually equal to the amount a buyer would have to pay for a freehold interest in residential premises of an equivalent standard in the same locality) and thereafter an annual ground rent during the term of the lease.[66] The landlord will retain ownership of the structure of the building and the common parts and common facilities in the development and will covenant with the leaseholder to maintain, repair, operate and insure the structure of the buildings and the common and shared parts and facilities. In return, the leaseholder will covenant with the landlord to repair, maintain, etc. its own unit, and to pay to the landlord a service charge consisting of a fixed proportion of the

---

[66] As to which see further para. 17.16(b) below.

landlord's costs of performing its covenants under the lease, including its management and insurance costs. The landlord will also covenant with the leaseholder to grant leases of the other units in the development on the same terms, and to enforce the covenants of the other leaseholders under their leases. In this way, each leaseholder has the power to enforce the positive and negative obligations of its neighbouring leaseholders indirectly via their common landlord. They may also be able to do so if the leaseholder covenants are expressed to be for the benefit of the other lessees of the common landlord and directly enforceable between them.[67]

17.16 Advantages and Disadvantages of the Traditional Leasehold Model

(a) Leasehold as Ownership

In many ways long leasehold in the traditional model is the equivalent of freehold ownership. Long leaseholders usually think of themselves as owners of their own flat or house (i.e. of the premises they lease for their own exclusive use), even though they share use of and responsibility for the areas and structures owned by the landlord and used in common with the other leaseholders. As already noted in para. 17.15, the original leaseholder typically will have paid a premium to the freeholder at the start of the lease, usually the same amount she would have paid if she was buying the freehold interest in a property of the equivalent size and standard in a similar locality. Provided the lease is long enough, mortgage lenders will have been as willing to lend her mortgage finance as they would be if she was buying the freehold interest in an equivalent property. If and when the leaseholder then wants to move house, she can usually expect to sell the unexpired residue of her lease for the same amount as she could expect if she was selling an equivalent freehold interest, again assuming there are sufficient years left to run on her lease.

Similarly, a long leaseholder is in at least as good a position as a freehold owner when it comes to enforcing mutual rights, obligations and responsibilities of neighbours. Both freehold owners and leaseholders can bring actions in negligence, nuisance and trespass (because leaseholders, like freeholders, are entitled to possession of the areas they occupy). In the case of neighbours who are freeholders, rights and duties in respect of shared facilities can be regulated by easements and restrictive covenants, whereas in the case of neighbouring leaseholders they will be governed by the terms of their leases, which, as we noted in para. 17.15 above, are enforceable between leaseholders, either directly or indirectly via the common landlord. The only significant difference is that positive covenants are enforceable by and between leaseholders, whereas they are not enforceable by and between neighbouring freeholders. As already noted, this difference is very significant indeed when the units of occupation are interdependent.

---

[67] For the way enforceability between leaseholders works, see further *Duval* v. *11–13 Randolph Crescent Ltd* [2018] EWCA Civ 2298 and Julian Farrand and Alison Clarke (eds.), *Emmet & Farrand on Title* (London: Sweet & Maxwell, looseleaf updated to 30 April 2019) ss. 17.039 and 26.264.01.

(b) Drawbacks of Leasehold Ownership in the Traditional Model

However, there are three drawbacks of leasehold ownership in the traditional model which are worth noting here.

Leasehold as a Depreciating Asset

The first and obvious one is that the property interest – the lease – is a depreciating asset whose capital value falls as the years pass. This is much less of a problem for residential leases now that conventional lease lengths are commonly 999 years, but it used to be customary for them to be shorter – often 99 years – and it been long been necessary for governments to intervene by passing legislation giving leaseholders statutory rights to extend their leases on fair terms.[68]

Vulnerability to Exploitation

The second disadvantage – also obvious – is that in the traditional model the leaseholder is vulnerable to exploitation by the landlord. Theirs is a commercial relationship, landlord and leaseholder are not in an equal bargaining position and the landlord has no obligation to act other than its own selfish best interests (if we put aside for the moment the arguments we considered in Part II of Chapter 10 *Limitations on Property* where we considered the inherent obligations of ownership). This inherent vulnerability to exploitation explains the many statutory rights which have been conferred on residential leaseholders over the last century, currently including rights to challenge service charges, individual and collective enfranchisement rights (i.e. rights to buy out the landlord at a statutorily regulated price) and collective rights to take over the landlord's management functions via a Right to Manage company.[69] However, statutory protection is necessarily reactive, and new opportunities for exploitation continue to open up, most recently in relation to ground rents.

The ground rent payable by a long leaseholder is traditionally a small or nominal amount (perhaps £1 a year) or even a token which is never demanded or handed over – typically a peppercorn a year. Recently, however, some commercial developers have woken up to the fact that limiting the ground rent payable under a long residential lease to a nominal or notional sum is traditional rather than obligatory,

[68] See now the Leasehold Reform Act 1967 (as extensively amended, most notably by the Housing Act 1996 and the Commonhold and Leasehold Reform Act 2002) for rights to an extended lease for leaseholders with a long lease of a house, and the Leasehold Reform, Housing and Urban Development Act 1993, also as amended by the Commonhold and Leasehold Reform Act 2002, giving leaseholders with long leases of flats in a building individual rights to an extension of their lease of a house, and giving tenants with a long lease of a house rights to an extended lease or to compulsorily purchase the landlord's freehold interest at below market value; the Landlord and Tenant Act 1987 giving long leaseholders of flats a right of first refusal if their landlord wishes to dispose of its interest; and collective rights to buy compulsorily their landlord's freehold interest in the building.

[69] See the statutes noted in fn. 68, which also give rights of enfranchisement individually to long leaseholders of houses and collectively to long leaseholders of flats, and in addition the Landlord and Tenant Act 1987 giving long leaseholders of flats collective rights of first refusal if their landlord wants to dispose of its interest, and rights to appoint a Right to Manage Company, and the Landlord and Tenant 1985 (extended by the 1987 Act) regulating service charges payable by lessees of a dwelling.

and have started to grant leases for ground rents which may initially be small but which rapidly escalate so that within a few years leaseholders are required to pay over substantial sums every year. This is proving to be so lucrative for developers that some of them will now not sell freehold ownership to buyers of new-build houses, but only long leases with escalating ground rent charges. There has been a (comparatively) swift response by the Government, as evidenced by this Ministerial statement:

> Leasehold has been a part of the UK's housing landscape for generations, usually put to sensible use in buildings with shared fabric and infrastructure, such as blocks of flats.
>
> Leasehold should be just that, a tool for making multiple ownership more straight-forward. It should not be a means of extracting ever-more cash from the pockets of already over-stretched housebuyers. Yet, in the hands of unscrupulous freeholders, that is exactly what it has become.
>
> Over the past 20 years, the proportion of new-build houses sold as leasehold has more than doubled. Huge numbers of properties – including standalone houses with no shared facilities or fabric – are being sold as leasehold simply to create a reliable revenue stream for whoever owns the freehold. In some parts of the country, it's now almost impossible for a first-time buyer to purchase a new-build home on any other basis.
>
> As if that wasn't bad enough, some of these leases contain exceptionally onerous terms, creating future liabilities that can leave homeowners stranded and unable to find a buyer.
>
> These practices are practically feudal and entirely unjustifiable – which is why, earlier this year, I set out plans to end them once and for all.[70]

These plans have in fact materialised to the extent that in June 2019 the Government announced proposals to introduce legislation to stop what it regarded as an abuse of the system, by prohibiting the grant of new residential long leases of houses (i.e. as opposed to flats, maisonettes, etc.) other than in exceptional circumstances, and restricting ground rents in newly established leases of houses and flats to a nominal amount.[71]

Complexity

Legal institutions for regulating interdependent multi-unit developments are inevit-ably complex because of the mix of individual, reciprocal and collective rights, obligations and responsibilities involved. However, the complexity of the traditional leasehold model is undoubtedly increased by the fact that the basic building block – the lease – is an ancient common law institution which has evolved incrementally in

---

[70] Ministerial Forward to the Department of Communities and Local Government, *Tackling Unfair Practices in the Leasehold Market: Summary of Consultation Responses and Government Response*, December 2017, https://assets.publishing.service.gov.uk/government/uploads/system/uploads/attachment_data/file/670204/Tackling_Unfair_Practices_-_gov_response.pdf.

[71] Press Release, 'Leasehold axed for all new houses in move to place fairness at heart of housing market', published by the Ministry of Housing, Communities and Local Government, June 2019 (available at www.gov.uk/government/news/leasehold-axed-for-all-new-houses-in-move-to-place-fairness-at-heart-of-housing-market.

social and economic conditions which are very different from those we now live in, and (as we saw in Part II of this chapter) it is encumbered by rules which are often inappropriate or disproportionately complicated, and difficult for the courts to change. The attraction of a condominium model is that it can jettison the leasehold model and adopt instead a mix of private and communal property interests, which are arguably more appropriate for regulating the mix of private and communal space.

17.17 Evolution of the Collective Landlord Model

However, the traditional long leasehold model is in practice not being replaced by a condominium model but by a collective landlord leasehold model, where the leaseholders collectively own the landlord, but they all remain separate legal entities. This is probably now the most commonly used legal structure for managing interdependent residential units where the unit holders expect to have ownership-type interests in their units. This model has emerged partly as a result of leaseholders buying out their landlords by exercising their statutory rights of enfranchisement noted in para. 17.16 above, and partly also because the other statutory leaseholder protection measures we noted in para. 17.16 have made freehold reversions on long residential leases less financially attractive. Private landlords are therefore more willing to sell voluntarily to their leaseholders.

In the collective landlord model the landlord's interest is vested in the leaseholders themselves communally. Because leaseholders as a community do not have legal personality, this has to be done either by the leaseholders incorporating themselves as a private company and vesting the landlord's interest in their company, or (less often) by using a trust. In the trust model the landlord's interest will be vested in up to four of the leaseholders as trustees to hold on trust for all of them. The trust model is rarely used except perhaps for maisonettes, where there are only two leaseholders in all, so they can hold the landlord's interest jointly on trust for themselves, which gives each of them equal rights, powers and obligations. In the corporate model the company holding the landlord's interest will be wholly owned and controlled by the leaseholders, with the company being under a duty to act solely in the interests of the leaseholders as a whole. The dynamic in this model is very different from the dynamic in long leasehold relationships where there is a commercial or charitable landlord. Whereas a commercial landlord holds its property interest for its own commercial purposes and runs the development as a business, and a charitable landlord holds its property interest for public charitable purposes, running the development as a charitable organisation, the collective leaseholder company holds its property interest for the private benefit of the leaseholders as a collective entity (not necessarily solely for the benefit of the present leaseholders).

Typically, the collective landlord steps into the shoes of the private landlord, carrying out the landlord's functions and obligations under the leases of the units, responsible for whatever works are necessary or wanted, running the development, levying and collecting service charges, and managing disputes with and between the leaseholders.

17.18 Emerging Problems with the Collective Landlord Model

The obvious problem with the collective landlord model is that the legal relationships which exist between collective managers and unit holders, and as between unit holders, are imported wholesale from the traditional long leasehold model, and they are fundamentally inappropriate for what is essentially a self-regulating resource-sharing community.[72]

(a) Vertical Relationships

As far as vertical relationships are concerned, the collective landlord model is saddled with a landlord–tenant relationship between the managers and the unit holders, developed over centuries to regulate an arms-length commercial relationship between self-interested individuals. This runs awkwardly alongside the relationship between the incorporated community (the company formed by the unit holders to hold the landlord's freehold reversion) and its members (the unit holders). The problems this can cause are particularly apparent when collective landlords are engaged in disputes with individual unit-holders, where a collective landlord has a duty to act in the interests of the other unit holders and of the community as a whole, which a commercial landlord would not have. The reality of the relationship where there is a collective, as opposed to a commercial, landlord is occasionally acknowledged by the courts, but not often. A rare example is *Victory Place Management Co Ltd* v. *Kuehn* [2018] EWHC 132 (Ch), where it was a term of the leases of the units that leaseholders could not keep pets on the premises without the consent of the management company, which was wholly owned by all the leaseholders. Acting in accordance with the views of the majority of the leaseholders, the management company operated a policy that no pets were allowed except in exceptional circumstances, and so refused consent to an application by new leaseholders to keep their pet dog in their flat. The trial judge held that, in exercising its powers and discretions under the leases (including its power to refuse consent to an application to keep a pet) the management company was under an implied duty to act reasonably, in a *Wednesbury* sense (i.e. its decision was challengeable on the grounds that it failed to take the right matters into account, or was so outrageous that no reasonable management company/landlord could have reached it).[73] This, so the judge said, was because otherwise 'there would be a risk of tyranny by majority'. The judge then found that both the decision reached and the procedure followed by the management company in reaching it, were reasonable, and that it had been entitled to take

---

[72] In other words, the kind of resource sharing institution described by Elinor Ostrom in *Governing the Commons: The Evolution of Institutions for Collective Action* (Cambridge: Cambridge University Press, 1990) which we considered in Chapter 2 *Conceptions and Justifications* paras. 2.14–2.17.

[73] Relying on the decision in *Braganza* v. *BP Shipping Ltd* [2015] UKSC 17 that public law standards of reasonableness could be applicable to private individuals exercising discretions e.g. in employment relationships: see further *Emmet & Farrand on Title*, fn. 67 above, para. 26.356 for the possible implications for leases.

into account the majority view of the leaseholders. An appeal against his decision was dismissed.

So, the courts do have the capacity to recognise the real nature of the relationship between the collective landlord and an individual leaseholder, but it remains to be seen how far they will do so.

Meanwhile, however, leaseholder protection legislation does not distinguish between commercial arms-length landlords and collective landlords owned by their tenants. This means that collective landlords remain bound by statutory duties which were designed to curb commercial exploitation of leaseholders, not to ensure that the collective landlord acts in the best interests of the leaseholders and in accordance with their wishes.

(b) Horizontal Relationships

As far as horizontal relationships between unit holders is concerned, the problem is that the leasehold model leaves a vacuum. Under leasehold law there is no relationship between lessees of a common landlord, and certainly no duty on them to act co-operatively in exercising their rights and liberties in relation to common parts and common facilities, or to share responsibilities for them, as one might perhaps expect in a self-regulating resource sharing community. This may not matter if we assume that in many cases the leaseholders, already brought together as collective owners of the freehold, will evolve their own informal idiosyncratic rules. However, as Elinor Ostrom points out, there is no guarantee that this will always happen in a self-regulating resource-sharing community.[74]

(c) Complexity

The final problem is complexity. The collective landlord model consists of an impossibly complex (and sometimes incoherent) mix of corporate and leasehold relationships. In many cases these will be augmented by trust relationships if, as often happens with residential premises, the leases are co-owned by couples or family members (because of the trust relationship imposed by co-ownership law on co-owners). So, any given leaseholder may have simultaneous roles as trustee and as beneficiary of her leasehold interest in her unit, joint lessee of the lease vis a vis the landlord, holder of communal use rights in common parts and common facilities, and shareholder and possibly director of the corporate owner of the freehold interest in the land. The dangers of confusion of roles and heavy-handed procedures are obvious, particularly in smaller developments.

---

[74] See Chapter 2 *Conceptions and Justifications* paras. 2.14–2.18, and also Sarah Blandy, 'Collective property: Owning and sharing residential space', in Nicholas Hopkins (ed.), *Modern Studies in Property Law*, vol 7 (Oxford and Portland, OR: Hart Publishing, 2013) p. 152.

RECOMMENDED READING

Part II of this chapter covers some long and sometimes quite difficult cases which are worth reading. Depending on the amount of time you have to spend on this chapter, you might prefer to concentrate on just one of the two main topics in Part II, that is, either the lease/licence distinction, or the nature of periodic tenancies and the rules about certainty of duration of leases. Part II of this chapter – leases as ownership substitutes – provides an opportunity to go back to the material on condominiums and commonhold which we covered in Chapter 8, and the material on self-regulated resource-sharing communities in Chapter 2.

Street v. *Mountford* [1985] 1 AC 809 (lease/licence distinction).
AG Securities v. *Vaughan and Antoniades* v. *Villiers* [1990] 1 AC 417 (lease/licence distinction).
Watts v. *Stewart* [2016] EWCA Civ 1247 (lease/licence distinction).
Bruton v. *London & Quadrant Housing Trust* [2000] 1 AC 406 (non-proprietary lease).
Bermondsey Exchange Freeholders Ltd v. *Koumetto* [2018] 4 WLUK 619 (on Airbnb-type lettings).
Derek Whayman, 'Old issues, new approaches? Property guardians and the lease/licence distinction' (2019) *The Conveyancer and Property Lawyer* 47 (on 'property guardians').
Hammersmith and Fulham LBC v. *Monk* [1992] 1 AC 478 (periodic tenancies).
Notting Hill Housing Trust v. *Brackley* [2001] 35 EG 106, CA (periodic tenancies).
Prudential Assurance Company v. *London Residuary Body* [1992] 2 AC 386 (certainty of duration of leases).
Berrisford v Mexfield Housing Co-operative Ltd [2011] UKSC 52 (certainty of duration).
Victory Place Management Co Ltd v. *Kuehn* [2018] EWHC 132 (collective landlords).

Questions

(1) If you have a lease of your flat which contains a covenant by you not to sub-let the whole or part of the premises without the consent of the landlord, do you commit a breach of that covenant if you provide short-term accommodation via internet sites such as Airbnb without asking the landlord? Might you be in breach of other terms of your lease?

(2) What are 'property guardians'? What factors are relevant in deciding whether they are tenants or licensees?

(3) If you live in student accommodation or in a shared flat or house, what is the nature of your interest – do you have just a personal right to occupy the premises, or a tenancy of all or part of it?

(4) What is a periodic tenancy? Why, when it is held jointly by two or more lessees, can it be ended by just one of them serving notice to quit on the landlord? Should this rule be reversed, so that the periodic tenancy can never be ended by joint lessees unless they all agree to serve a notice to quit on the landlord?

(5) Why do we need certainty of duration rules for leases? Is the basic certainty of duration rule established (or re-established) by the House of Lords in *Prudential* satisfactory? Consider what rule (in any) would be better.

(6) Explain what the Supreme Court decided in *Berrisford*. What did Lady Hale mean when she said that the law relating to certainty of duration of leases has 'an Alice in Wonderland quality'? Was she right when she said that it was in urgent need of reform? What reform would you suggest? (This covers much the same ground as the previous question.)

(7) Discuss the differences between a commercial landlord of a long lease, and a landlord which is wholly owned and controlled by its common leaseholders.

Index